State Profiles
The Population and Economy of Each U.S. State

Third Edition, 2006

Editors
Diane Werneke
Katherine A. DeBrandt

Lanham, MD
BERNAN

ISBN: 1-59888-011-X

ISSN: 1524-3958

Printed by United Book Press, Inc., Baltimore, MD, on acid-free paper that meets the American National Standards Institute Z39-48 standard.

2007 2006   4 3 2 1

BERNAN PRESS
4611-F Assembly Drive
Lanham, MD 20706
800-274-4447
email: info@bernan.com
www.bernanpress.com

CONTENTS

LIST OF TABLES

STATE SECTIONS
The following tables are included for each state. Select tables are included for the District of Columbia.

PREFACE

BERNAN PRESS IS PLEASED TO PRESENT THE THIRD EDITION of *State Profiles*, a publication that provides a state-by-state view of the United States, including population composition by age, sex, race, and ethnicity; educational attainment levels; employment; earnings data; and other important aspects of the economy.

While giving an overall description of these characteristics for the nation as a whole, the publication's primary focus is on the 50 states and the District of Columbia, each of which possesses considerable differences in economic structure and demographics and has experienced various changes over time. Changes at the national level, including the diminished importance of agriculture and manufacturing and the growing influence of global trade, have resulted in today's information-based, service-providing economy. While national trends have laid the broad framework for change, each state has been affected differently. Cyclical fluctuations also affected states in various ways during the nationwide recessions in 1990–1991 and 2001 and the subsequent recovery periods. Both the recessions and the recoveries spread unevenly among regions and states. Migration patterns have also reflected these changes, as states have experienced different influxes of workers from within the country and new residents from abroad.

Beyond the market forces, economic circumstances have been influenced by local and national government policies and expenditures on items such as education, health care, energy production and conservation, national defense, and homeland security.

The information provided in *State Profiles* aims to illuminate these trends. As such, the analysis and statistics are of interest not only to researchers and policy analysts but also to businesses seeking a broad basis for investments and expansion or relocation plans. The volume also profiles recent voting patterns, which will be of interest to political scientists.

DATA SELECTION

THE THIRD EDITION OF *State Profiles* GENERALLY CONTINUES the broad selection of information from the two previous editions, which reported developments through 2000. Most of the data have been updated through 2004, as demographic estimates from the U.S. Census Bureau became available. Information has also been updated on employment, unemployment, earnings, income, and other economic data from various government sources.

As in the past, space constraints have influenced the amount of data presented for each state. The editors have focused on selecting and highlighting the most meaningful and relevant data. Nonetheless, this third edition expands upon the available information to include more detailed data on the demographics of each state, including population changes due to migration and housing and home prices—major factors in the location decisions of businesses and individuals. Due to the build-up in government defense and homeland security activities, estimates of expenditures by state are included in the rankings section. For most of the subjects addressed in this edition, further data are generally available from the source government agencies. Locations of related information are listed in the notes and definitions at the end of this volume.

Although the editors have taken care to present accurate data, all statistical data are subject to a degree of error, resulting from sampling variability, erroneous reporting, and other causes. Many of the data are subject to subsequent revision.

The data in this book meet the publication standards of the federal agencies from which they were obtained. The responsibilities of the editors and publisher of this volume are limited to reasonable care in the reproduction and presentation of the data from the established sources.

ACKNOWLEDGMENTS

THIS EDITION HAS BEEN EDITED BY DIANE WERNEKE, IN association with Katherine A. DeBrandt.

Diane Werneke was formerly an economist and senior congressional liaison at the Federal Reserve Board. She has also served on the House Budget Committee, the President's Commission on Employment and Unemployment Statistics, and in the International Labor Office in Geneva, Switzerland, specializing in macroeconomic and labor market policy and analysis. She holds a B.A. from the University of California at Berkeley and an M.A. from The George Washington University, both in economics.

Katherine A. DeBrandt is the data analyst team leader with Bernan Press. She received her B.A. in political science from Colgate University. She is also the co-editor of *The Who, What, and Where of America: Understanding the Census Results; The Almanac of American Education*; and *Social Change in America: The Historical Handbook,* all published by Bernan Press.

Bernan Press's editorial and production departments, under the direction of Tamera L. Wells-Lee, did the copyediting, layout, and graphics preparation. Jo A. Wilson, the production team leader, capably managed the production aspects of this volume and prepared the graphics and cover design, with the assistance of Rebecca Zayas. Jo and Rebecca assisted the editor tremendously with finalizing this publication. Thanks also to Shana Hertz, who copyedited this edition. Finally, special thanks are due to the many federal agency personnel who assisted us in obtaining the data, provided excellent resources on their Web sites, and patiently answered our questions.

USING THIS BOOK

STATE PROFILES 2006 PROVIDES:

- An overview of the United States
- Rankings of states for key demographic and economic indicators
- A 10-page chapter on each state with tables and figures to summarize and illustrate demographic and economic characteristics
- Notes and definitions to guide users through the sources for the information used in this volume

THE U.S. OVERVIEW. The chapter on the United States provides commentary and data analysis of overall trends, against which the data for each state can be compared and contrasted. It also gives some of the primary data definitions necessary for understanding the interpretation of the information presented for each state. The national overview includes the latest available population and demographic estimates, as well as data on health, households, income, employment, earnings, exports, agriculture, energy, government finance, education, and voter participation.

THE STATE RANKINGS. The ranking tables shown in the pages following the U.S. overview give state rankings by some 24 characteristics, including population, demographic and age composition, immigration, homeland security spending, employment, income, gross state product, housing prices, poverty, health indicators, education, and voter participation. These rankings provide the user with a quick analysis of the performance of each state in relation to the other states.

THE STATE CHAPTERS. The state chapters are the focus of this book. Each chapter follows a standard format and contains text highlighting the key features shown in the tables and figures. Many of these tables and figures contain references to the U.S. averages for the same characteristics. The emphasis of the text varies from state to state, reflecting their diversity.

Each of the state chapters is organized as follows:

Population: This section provides data on the state's total population and average annual population growth in comparison with the national average. It also shows the major population groups by sex, age, race, and ethnicity.

Health: This section provides information on leading health indicators, including the birth rate, infant mortality rate, age-adjusted death rates, and rate of health insurance coverage.

Households, income, and poverty: Data on household types, size, units (whether owner- or renter-occupied), median gross rent, and median value of owner-occupied housing are included. Median household income and poverty rates are also contained in this section.

Labor market: This section presents various data that illustrate each state's particular economic configuration. Employment status by detailed demographic groups, employment by industry using the new North American Industry Classification System (NAICS), average wages and salaries, and personal income by major source are included in this section.

Economic activity: Data on gross state product and government transfer payments to individuals, such as social security benefits, are detailed in this section.

Exports: This section provides detailed information on each state's leading exports and leading export markets.

Agriculture: In this section, data are provided on the number of farms, acreage, and value of sales, as reported on the Department of Agriculture's 2002 Census of Farms.

Energy: Information on energy consumption by sector, energy sources, total energy expenditures, and expenditures on a per capita basis are included in this section. The latest state-level data are from 2001.

Government finance: This section provides data on revenues and expenditures by source. In addition, state taxes, as compared to the national average, are included.

Education: Education indicators give information about a state's current and future workforce. This section provides the user with details on educational attainment, elementary and secondary school enrollment, student/teacher ratios, per student expenditures, and higher education enrollments.

Voter participation: New to this edition of *State Profiles* are voter participation data. Information is given on voter registration and voter participation in the 2000 and 2004 presidential elections, categorized by various demographic categories characteristics.

NOTES AND DEFINITIONS. Each chapter relies on the same standard set of federal data sources. Since the basic data sources are common to all chapters, the main body of the volume contains few footnotes. All the basic data and their definitions and sources are identified in the notes and definition section at the end of the volume. It provides brief descriptions of methodologies, and data availabity, information on calculations made by the editors, and references to additional sources of information. The notes are organized by topic, paralleling the structure of the state chapters.

THE PERIOD 2000–2004, WHICH IS THE PRIMARY FOCUS OF this book, was characterized by the 2001 recession and the subsequent uneven recovery of employment and income. The economy reached a peak in early 2001, growing at a sustained rate of over 3 percent per year throughout the 1990s. This reflected a strong recovery from the 1990–1991 recession; however, the recovery from the 2001 recession did not move ahead on all fronts. Consumer expenditures and residential housing investment propelled gross domestic product (GDP) forward, accounting for nearly 90 percent of real (GDP) growth, while business investment—a major source of future job creation—was more subdued, as companies waited for evidence that the economic recovery was firmly underway. Imports increased dramatically as consumer spending was largely directed to purchases of goods from abroad. The federal government's increased spending on homeland security, defense, and other policies and programs associated with the September 11 terrorist attacks, together with large tax cuts, resulted in large budget deficits that supported economic activity and employment in affected sectors. As a result of these patterns in overall activity, employment growth in the private sector was largely concentrated in areas connected with housing, such as construction, real estate, and mortgage financing and related financial services. According to *The Economist*, over 40 percent of job growth from 2001 to 2004 was in these housing-related sectors and in defense-related industries. Manufacturing and other service industries have not reported such stellar results.

As some parts of the national economy have fared better than others, differentials have also characterized states and regions, as defined by the Bureau of Economic Analysis (BEA). The differing definitions of regions by the Census Bureau and the BEA can be found in the notes and definitions at the end of this volume. In general, the Far West region (comprising Alaska, California, Hawaii, Nevada, Oregon, and Washington) exhibited the strongest growth during the 2000–2004 period, with Nevada showing the greatest growth rate (adjusted for inflation). The Rocky Mountain region (Colorado, Idaho, Montana, Utah, and Wyoming) and the Southwest region (Arizona, New Mexico, Oklahoma, and Texas) had the next-strongest economic growth. Real economic growth in the Great Lakes region (Illinois, Indiana, Michigan, Ohio, and Wisconsin) was the slowest, as it has been for some years; Michigan experienced the most sluggish pace of growth in the group.

State Profiles presents a look at each state that expands beyond economic characteristics. It provides a picture of each state's demographic and social characteristics, as well as an overview of the general state of the economy in terms of state output (real gross state product), employment, unemployment, and income. Each state's chapter also focuses on the changes in the population and its characteristics, housing and house prices, income and poverty status, agriculture (where appropriate), energy usage, government finance (including defense and homeland security expenditures), education, health, and citizen participation in the 2000 and 2004 presidential elections.

The U.S. summary provides national totals and averages, against which the individual states' data can be compared and summarized. In most cases, the chapters compare state data to national averages, and state-specific supplemental information is provided when relevant. The standard data tables for each state pertain to the 2000–2004 period, with some information from 1990 included to enable comparisons between decades. In cases where data for 2004 were incomplete or not available, the most recent information is reported.

POPULATION

The U.S. population grew 4.3 percent between 2000 and 2004, at an average annual rate of about 1.1 percent. This rate was nearly identical to the growth rate from 1990 to 2000. Net international immigration accounted for over 40 percent of the growth from 2000 to 2004. Among the immigrants who arrived from 2000 to 2004, the largest number were born in Mexico, followed by India, the Philippines, and China. Within the major age groups, the 45- to 64-year-old age group grew faster than the population as a whole, and its proportion of the total population increased to just over 24 percent. Utah, Alaska, and Texas had the highest proportions of population under 18 years old; Florida had the largest share of residents 65 years old and over. However, Florida was an exception to the pattern of states with high proportions of older people having slow-growing or declining populations and higher rates of out-migration of young people. Such states include West Virginia, Pennsylvania, North Dakota, and Iowa, all of which had more than 14.5 percent of their populations age 65 years and over. A more

Table US-1. Immigrants Admitted by Region and Country of Birth, 2004

(Number, percent.)

Region and country	Number of legal immigrants	Percent distribution
ALL COUNTRIES	946 142	100.0
Region		
Europe	127 669	13.5
North America	341 242	36.1
Caribbean	88 921	9.4
Central America	61 333	6.5
Asia	330 004	34.9
South America	71 785	7.6
Africa	66 309	7.0
Oceania	5 960	0.6
Unknown	3 173	0.3
Leading Countries		
Mexico	175 364	18.5
India	70 116	7.4
Philippines	57 827	6.1
China	51 156	5.4
Vietnam	31 514	3.3
Dominican Republic	30 492	3.2
El Salvador	29 795	3.1
Cuba	20 488	2.2
South Korea	19 766	2.1
Colombia	18 678	2.0

Table US-2. Population by Sex and Age, 1990, 2000, and 2004

(Number, percent.)

Sex and age	1990	2000	2004	Percent distribution, 2004	Average annual percent change, 2000–2004
Total Population	248 709 873	281 421 906	293 655 404	X	1.1
Sex					
Male	121 239 418	138 053 563	144 537 408	49.2	1.2
Female	127 470 455	143 368 343	149 117 996	50.8	1.0
Age					
Under 5 years	18 354 443	19 175 798	20 071 268	6.8	0.5
5 to 17 years	45 249 989	53 118 014	53 206 730	18.1	1.2
18 years and over	46 371 009	209 128 094	220 377 406	75.0	1.3
18 to 24 years	185 105 441	27 143 454	29 245 102	10.0	0.6
25 to 44 years	26 737 766	85 040 251	84 140 590	28.7	0.3
45 to 64 years	80 754 835	61 952 636	70 697 729	24.1	3.1
65 years and over	31 241 831	34 991 753	36 293 985	12.4	1.1
85 years and over	3 080 165	4 239 587	4 859 631	1.7	3.5
Median age (years)	32.8	35.3	36.0	X	X

X = Not applicable.

detailed breakdown of population age groupings reveals a decline in the proportion of children between the ages of 5 and 9 years, as well as a decline in the 25- to 44-year-old age group. The latter drop reflects the relatively low birth rates that occurred before the baby boomers began having families. At the other end of the age spectrum, those age 70 to 79 years declined slightly, reflecting the low birth rates of the 1930s. In future years, as the post-World-War-II generation reaches the age of 65, the proportion of the population age 65 years and over is expected to increase rapidly, reaching nearly 20 percent by 2030, compared with 12 percent in 2004.

States varied widely in their rates of population growth, but states with the highest growth rates from 2000 to 2004 were generally those that had the largest population expansions over the previous decade: the Southwest and Rocky Mountain states, followed by the Southeastern states of Florida, Georgia, and North Carolina. Slow population growth continued to characterize states in the Midwest, the Plains, and the Gulf regions. Immigration, both international and internal, played a significant role in state population changes. California, the most populous state, was the largest recipient of immigrants from abroad, followed by New York, Texas, and Florida. The largest influxes of residents from other states went to Florida, Arizona, and Nevada—states known as destinations for retirees.

Fastest-Growing States, Percent Population Change, 2000–2004

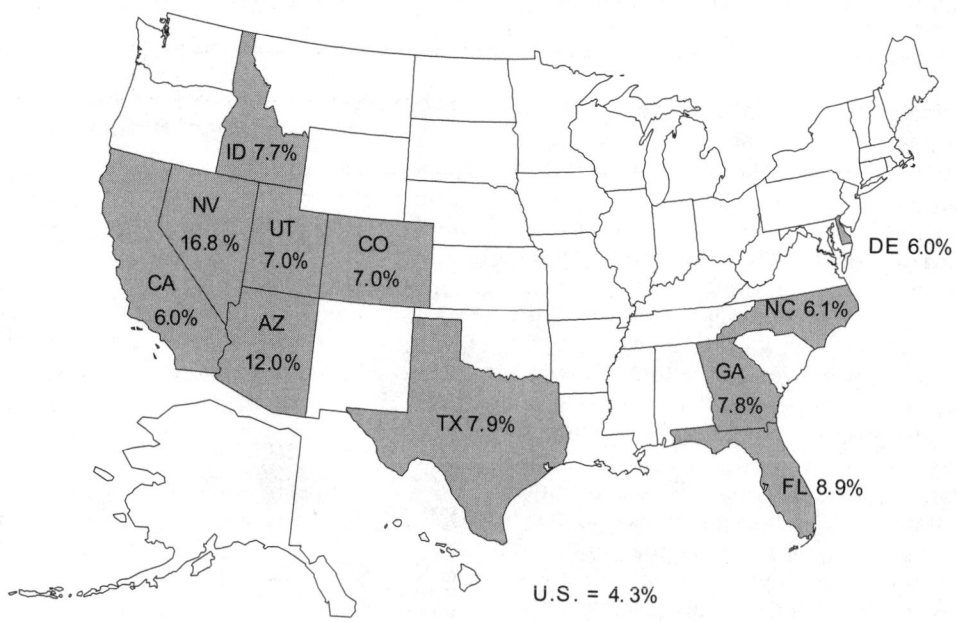

ID 7.7%
NV 16.8%
UT 7.0%
CO 7.0%
CA 6.0%
AZ 12.0%
TX 7.9%
DE 6.0%
NC 6.1%
GA 7.8%
FL 8.9%

U.S. = 4.3%

Table US-3. Population and Components of Population Change, 2000–2004

(Number.)

State	Population, 2000	Population, 2004	Components of population change, 2000–2004			
			Births	Deaths	Net international migration	Net internal migration
United States	281 421 906	293 655 404	17 198 187	10 297 024	5 329 639	X
Alabama	4 447 100	4 530 182	258 878	196 032	21 712	-703
Alaska	626 932	655 435	42 755	13 986	4 512	-4 481
Arizona	5 130 632	5 743 834	371 351	178 046	141 175	281 625
Arkansas	2 673 400	2 752 629	159 897	118 535	18 427	20 949
California	33 871 648	35 893 799	2 244 263	983 736	1 192 430	-415 313
Colorado	4 301 261	4 601 403	285 656	121 297	94 620	42 100
Connecticut	3 405 565	3 503 604	181 064	127 067	63 771	-18 255
Delaware	783 600	830 364	47 020	29 651	9 621	20 184
District of Columbia	572 059	553 523	33 197	25 203	17 156	-43 304
Florida	15 982 378	17 397 161	893 447	708 259	444 726	791 904
Georgia	8 186 453	8 829 383	577 914	279 352	161 522	181 296
Hawaii	1 211 537	1 262 840	78 349	38 712	24 204	-11 986
Idaho	1 293 953	1 393 262	88 369	42 609	12 208	40 761
Illinois	12 419 293	12 713 634	774 574	453 342	276 890	-304 775
Indiana	6 080 485	6 237 569	365 221	236 937	47 067	-18 818
Iowa	2 926 324	2 954 451	159 235	118 027	24 975	-37 315
Kansas	2 688 418	2 735 502	165 737	104 107	32 289	-48 141
Kentucky	4 041 769	4 145 922	230 345	170 046	22 745	22 512
Louisiana	4 468 976	4 515 770	284 740	177 971	16 680	-74 776
Maine	1 274 923	1 317 253	57 576	53 238	4 182	34 356
Maryland	5 296 486	5 558 058	318 169	188 517	91 278	21 969
Massachusetts	6 349 097	6 416 505	347 124	241 265	137 394	-173 062
Michigan	9 938 444	10 112 620	560 624	370 460	103 785	-116 477
Minnesota	4 919 479	5 100 958	287 611	160 686	60 274	-7 728
Mississippi	2 844 658	2 902 966	183 404	121 865	8 717	-10 423
Missouri	5 595 211	5 754 618	322 858	234 051	35 880	20 077
Montana	902 195	926 865	46 230	35 951	1 741	13 014
Nebraska	1 711 263	1 747 214	106 706	65 074	18 789	-23 672
Nevada	1 998 257	2 334 771	135 588	71 296	55 710	216 322
New Hampshire	1 235 786	1 299 500	60 933	40 203	9 624	33 774
New Jersey	8 414 350	8 698 879	491 048	311 614	244 994	-135 483
New Mexico	1 819 046	1 903 289	115 818	58 010	23 267	3 985
New York	18 976 457	19 227 088	1 093 899	662 269	562 265	-771 944
North Carolina	8 049 313	8 541 221	505 789	310 001	131 807	166 864
North Dakota	642 200	634 366	32 391	25 209	3 023	-17 742
Ohio	11 353 140	11 459 011	637 404	465 064	63 691	-133 416
Oklahoma	3 450 654	3 523 553	213 108	150 892	30 484	-18 211
Oregon	3 421 399	3 594 586	191 214	130 648	61 482	52 944
Pennsylvania	12 281 054	12 406 292	613 270	552 078	86 811	-19 365
Rhode Island	1 048 319	1 080 632	52 551	41 587	15 990	5 826
South Carolina	4 012 012	4 198 068	239 064	160 520	30 218	79 476
South Dakota	754 844	770 883	45 137	29 911	3 259	-1 973
Tennessee	5 689 283	5 900 962	334 641	238 191	42 226	71 204
Texas	20 851 820	22 490 022	1 570 403	639 884	558 004	157 893
Utah	2 233 169	2 389 039	204 213	55 349	42 176	-39 856
Vermont	608 827	621 394	26 841	21 842	3 722	4 118
Virginia	7 078 515	7 459 827	423 268	241 784	115 538	87 546
Washington	5 894 121	6 203 788	333 188	191 793	112 580	52 965
West Virginia	1 808 344	1 815 354	87 308	89 352	3 114	6 794
Wisconsin	5 363 675	5 509 026	291 703	198 158	39 044	15 381
Wyoming	493 782	506 529	27 094	17 347	1 840	1 380

X = Not applicable.

RACE AND ETHNICITY. For those reporting only one race to Census enumerators in 2004 (98.5 percent of respondents), 67.4 percent reported themselves as non-Hispanic White alone; 12.2 percent reported Black alone; 4.2 percent reported Asian and Pacific Islander alone; and 0.8 percent reported American Indian or Alaska Native alone. Another 1.3 percent of the population reported being two or more races. The non-Hispanic White alone population grew the most slowly from 2000 to 2004, increasing at an annual rate of only about 0.3 percent. However, as a proportion of the U.S. population, this group remained largest by far. The Black alone and American Indian or Alaska Native alone populations grew at above average annual rates of 1.2 and 1.3 per-

cent, respectively. Asian and Pacific Islanders alone had the highest rate of growth, with an increase of about 3.8 percent per year during this period.

The Hispanic or Latino population, which is an ethnic designation rather than a racial one (and therefore includes members of different races), grew rapidly from 2000 to 2004, rising at more than three times the rate of total population growth. In 2004, Hispanics accounted for 14.1 percent of the population, compared with 12.5 percent in 2000. During the 1990s, this ethnic group increased at an annual rate of 4.7 percent. The increasing number of Hispanics reflects immigration, the younger average age of the group, the group's subsequently higher birth rates, and a larger average family size.

States varied widely in the racial and ethnic composition of their populations and in the growth rates of different population groups. Non-Hispanic Whites alone made up more than 94 percent of the population in the New England states of Maine, Vermont, and New Hampshire; a similar proportion was also found in West Virginia. This group made up less than 50 percent of the populations of Hawaii, the District of Columbia, New Mexico, California, and Texas. Non-Hispanic Blacks alone repre-

sented the majority of the District of Columbia's population (56.7 percent) and about one-third of Mississippi's and Louisiana's populations. New Mexico, California, Texas, and Arizona had the highest proportions of Hispanics or Latinos. Neighboring states presented sharp contrasts: Texas's population of Hispanics totaled nearly 35 percent, which differed dramatically from Oklahoma, Arkansas, and Louisiana, as each of these states had Hispanic populations of 7 percent or less.

Table US-4. Population by Race and Hispanic Origin, 1990, 2000, and 2004

(Number, percent.)

Race and Hispanic origin	1990	2000	2004
Total Population	248 709 873	281 421 906	293 655 404
Non-Hispanic (Percent)			
One race[1]			
White	75.6	69.5	67.4
Black	11.7	12.2	12.2
American Indian, Alaska Native[2]	0.8	0.7	0.8
Asian and Pacific Islander[2]	2.9	3.8	4.2
Other race[2]	3.9	. . .	. . .
Two or more races	. . .	1.2	1.3
Hispanic or Latino[3] (Percent)	9.0	12.5	14.1

[1]Individuals could report only one race in the 1990 census and could report one or more races on the 2000 census. Data on race in 2000 and 2004 are not comparable to 1990.
[2]Data for 1990 include people of Hispanic or Latino origin.
[3]May be of any race.
. . . = Not available.

HOUSEHOLDS

HOUSEHOLDS. There were nearly 110 million households in the nation in 2004, defined as one or more persons occupying a single housing unit, such as a house, apartment, or room. Since 2000, the number of households has grown at a slower annual rate than during the 1990–2000 period. In 2004, the average household size was 2.6 persons. About 67 percent of households were family households, which contained two or more individuals related by blood or marriage. The remaining 33 percent consisted of individuals living alone or with a nonrelative. Of these nonfamily households, over 80 percent lived alone, with about one-third of householders over the age of 65 years.

Utah had the largest household size, with an average of about 3 persons per household. It was followed by California (2.93), Hawaii (2.87), and Texas (2.81). This reflected the relatively high proportions of young people in these states' populations, as well as increases in immigrant populations, in which shared living quarters may had been more prevalent. Because California and Texas had the largest populations, they heavily influenced the national average household size. Most states' household sizes were well below the U.S. average of 2.6. Washington, DC, had the smallest household size, with about 2 persons per household, reflecting a pattern of

Table US-5. Households and Housing Characteristics, 1990, 2000, and 2004

(Number, percent, and dollars.)

Characteristic	1990	2000	2004	Average annual percent change, 2000–2004
Total Households	91 947 410	105 480 101	109 902 090	1.0
Family households	64 517 947	71 787 347	73 885 953	0.7
Married-couple family	50 708 322	54 493 232	55 223 574	0.3
Other family	13 809 625	17 294 115	18 662 379	1.9
Male householder, no wife present	3 143 582	4 394 012	4 811 462	2.3
Female householder, no husband present	10 666 043	12 900 103	13 850 917	1.8
Nonfamily households	27 429 463	33 692 754	36 016 137	1.7
Householder living alone	22 580 420	27 230 075	29 572 372	2.1
Householder not living alone	4 849 043	6 462 679	6 443 765	-0.1
Housing Characteristics				
Average size	2.63	2.59	2.60	X
Housing units	102 263 678	115 904 641	122 671 734	1.4
Occupied housing units	91 947 410	105 480 101	109 902 090	1.0
Owner-occupied	59 024 811	69 815 753	73 754 173	1.4
Renter-occupied	32 922 599	35 664 348	36 147 917	0.3
Median gross rent of renter-occupied housing units (dollars) ...	447	602	694	3.6
Median value of owner-occupied housing units (dollars)	78 500	119 600	151 366	6.1

X = Not applicable.

childless couples and single individuals as city dwellers and couples with children choosing to live in the surrounding suburbs.

HOUSING OCCUPANCY. There were more than 122 million housing units in 2004; about 110 million were occupied, and of these, about 67 percent were owner-occupied. The remainder were rental units. The vacancy rate for rental units has edged up to about 10 percent in recent years, while the homeowner housing vacancy rate, which is the proportion of homes for sale, has remained stable at about 1.8 percent.

Nationally, homeownership rates increased as the age of the householder rose: more than 80 percent of those age 55 years and over owned homes, but this rate fell to about 40 percent for 25- to 29-year-olds and 57.4 percent for 30- to 34-years-olds. Non-Hispanic Whites were much more likely to be homeowners than members of other racial or ethnic groups: their rate was over 75 percent in 2004, compared with rates of about 50 percent for Blacks; 48 percent for Hispanics or Latinos (of any race); and about 60 percent for Asian and Pacific Islanders.

Regionally, homeownership rates were the highest in the Midwest, followed by the South, and lowest inside central cities. West Virginia had the highest rate of home-ownership—just over 80 percent in 2004—followed by Alabama, Delaware, Michigan, and Minnesota. The District of Columbia had the lowest rate at less than 46 percent, followed by New York and California, both of which had large urban concentrations and above average prices that had increased significantly in recent years.

HEALTH

Several health indicators, available for all states on a reasonably current basis, are presented in this book. Together, they give a general, though incomplete, picture of the health problems that may exist within a state, and the degree of progress being made in providing state residents with adequate health care.

BIRTH RATES. The number of births in the United States reached its most recent peak in 1990, when there were more than 4.1 million babies born and the number of births per 1,000 population reached 16.7. (This measure is commonly referred to as the birth rate.) This rate was at its highest since 1971, but far below the peak rates of the 1950s. In 2003, the birth rate fell to 14.1.

INFANT MORTALITY. The United States has made notable progress in reducing infant mortality. The infant mortality rate—the number of deaths of infants under 1 year old per 1,000 live births—fell from 9.2 in 1990 to 6.9 in 2003, the latest year for which data are available. All of the states have seen improvements in this area in the past two decades. During the 2000–2002 period, the lowest infant mortality rates were found in Massachusetts, New Hampshire, Maine, and Utah. The District of Columbia had the highest rate of infant mortality, followed by Mississippi, Louisiana, and Delaware.

HEALTH INSURANCE COVERAGE. Obviously, a major factor in the health of the population is access to health insurance to obtain affordable services for illnesses and preventive care. In 2004, 15.7 percent of the U.S. population did not have health insurance, a percentage that had risen since 1990, despite the coverage of the elderly and the poor under Medicare and Medicaid. Groups especially likely to lack insurance were the working poor and the foreign-born population, although many business owners eliminated or significantly scaled back plans due to the escalating costs of such insurance. Among the states, the proportion of population lacking coverage ranged from 8.9 percent in Minnesota to 25 percent in Texas. The status of each state is shown in the ranking tables.

Table US-6. Health Characteristics, 2000–2004

(Number, rate, percent.)

Item	U.S.
Births, 2003–2004	
Number of births	4 089 950
Birth rate (per 1,000 population)	14.1
Teenage birth rate (per 1,000 women age 15–19 years)	41.6
Mortality Rates, Average 2000–2002	
Infant mortality rate (per 1,000 live births)	6.9
Age-adjusted mortality rate (per 100,000 population)	
All races	853.3
Non-Hispanic White	843.1
Black	1 097.7
American Indian, Alaska Native	687.0
Asian and Pacific Islander	486.0
Hispanic or Latino[1]	642.7
Health Insurance, 2004	
Percent of all persons without health insurance	15.7
Percent of children without health insurance	11.2
Percent of low-income children without health insurance	7.1

[1]May be of any race.

AGE-ADJUSTED DEATH RATES AND LEADING CAUSES OF DEATH. The death rates are presented on an age-adjusted basis so that the same age distribution percentages— those of the United States in 2002—are applied to the actual death rates for each age group in the state. As a result, a state with a large elderly population, such as Florida, will not be tabulated to have a high death rate. The age-adjusted death rate makes comparisons among states, and over time, more meaningful in understanding the health of the population. Overall, death rates and the leading causes of death vary greatly by age. Children between the ages of 5 and 14 years and young people age 15 to 24 years had the lowest death rates in 2002; for both groups, the leading cause was accidents. After age 24 years, death rates rose rapidly for each 10-year cohort as the effects of disease increased. For persons age 45 to 64 years, the leading cause of death was cancer; for those over 65 years old, it was heart disease. For the United States average of 2000–2002, the age-adjusted death rate was 853 deaths per 100,000 persons. Heart disease and

Table US-7. Leading Causes of Death, Average 2000–2002

(Number, rate per 100,000 population.)

Cause	Number of deaths	Age-adjusted death rates					
		Total	Non-Hispanic White	Non-Hispanic Black	American Indian, Alaska Native	Asian and Pacific Islander	Hispanic or Latino[1]
ALL CAUSES	2 421 054	853.3	843.1	1 113.3	687.0	486.0	642.7
Leading Causes							
Major cardiovascular diseases	925 962	326.5	322.2	431.1	218.7	200.8	245.0
Heart disease	702 616	247.7	245.9	319.2	163.2	137.9	186.7
Coronary heart disease (CHD)	528 925	186.5	185.0	236.2	121.8	108.7	152.5
Essential (primary) hypertension and hypertensive renal disease	19 195	6.8	5.7	16.8	5.0	5.7	6.2
Stroke	164 624	58.0	56.3	79.8	40.7	50.0	43.5
All cancer	554 710	196.0	197.6	246.4	127.1	117.3	130.6
Oropharyngeal cancer	7 644	2.7	2.6	3.9	2.3	2.4	1.7
Colorectal cancer	57 035	20.1	19.9	27.9	13.2	12.7	13.8
Lung cancer	156 431	55.4	57.7	63.6	33.0	27.0	23.9
Melanoma cancer	7 492	2.6	3.2	0.5	0.7	0.4	0.8
Breast cancer	41 997	14.8	14.7	20.7	7.2	7.0	9.0
Cervical cancer	4 081	1.4	1.2	3.0	1.5	1.4	1.9
Uterine cancer	6 741	2.4	2.2	4.4	1.6	1.3	1.8
Ovarian cancer	14 385	5.1	5.3	4.5	2.9	2.7	3.5
Prostate cancer	30 748	10.9	10.0	23.1	6.9	4.6	8.5
Non-Hodgkin's lymphoma	22 315	7.9	8.3	5.4	4.6	4.8	5.9
Leukemia	21 429	7.6	7.9	6.7	4.0	4.0	5.1
Diabetes-related (multiple cause)	218 423	77.2	69.9	137.5	104.5	59.2	96.9
Chronic lower respiratory diseases	123 279	43.7	46.9	31.5	30.7	17.1	20.5
Unintentional injuries	102 060	35.7	36.4	38.0	52.1	17.6	30.3
Diabetes (underlying cause)	71 307	25.2	22.0	50.0	41.5	16.8	36.0
Influenza and pneumonia	64 343	22.7	22.5	24.7	21.6	18.5	19.8
Alzheimer's disease	54 092	19.0	20.2	14.4	8.9	5.4	10.7
Motor vehicle crashes	42 856	15.0	15.1	15.4	26.4	8.1	14.6
Nephritis, nephrotic syndrome, and nephrosis	39 235	13.8	12.3	29.6	14.2	8.6	11.8
Septicemia	32 442	11.4	10.4	24.4	10.2	5.2	8.5
Suicides	30 541	10.7	12.4	5.5	10.2	5.4	5.7
Firearm-related deaths	29 493	10.3	9.0	19.2	8.2	3.2	7.7
Cirrhosis	26 948	9.5	9.0	9.2	23.1	3.4	15.8
Drug-induced	22 466	7.9	8.4	9.5	6.6	1.3	5.6
Alcohol-induced	19 701	6.9	6.4	8.4	23.0	1.6	9.8
Homicides	17 263	6.0	2.8	21.2	7.3	2.9	7.4
Falls	14 866	5.2	5.5	3.1	5.1	3.7	4.1
HIV	14 249	5.0	2.1	23.2	2.3	0.7	6.2
Viral hepatitis	5 578	2.0	1.7	2.8	2.4	2.8	3.5
Anemias	4 578	1.6	1.4	3.6	1.4	0.9	1.1
Peptic ulcer	4 376	1.5	1.5	1.6	1.3	1.5	1.2
Nutritional deficiencies	3 908	1.4	1.3	2.2	2.3	0.7	1.1
Drownings	3 834	1.3	1.3	1.7	2.3	1.2	1.1
Fire deaths	3 282	1.2	1.0	2.7	1.8	0.4	0.7
Complications of medical and surgical care	2 974	1.0	1.0	1.8	1.1	0.5	0.7

[1]May be of any race.

INCOME AND POVERTY

cancer were the biggest killers.

The U.S. median household income (adjusted for inflation) declined significantly over the 2000–2004 period, although the decrease slowed in 2004. After reaching a peak of $46,129 in 1999, median household income fell to $44,389 in 2004, a decline of 3.8 percent. This trend reflected the 2001 recession and the subsequent slow recovery in employment and earnings. It contrasted with the steady rise in household income during the 1990s. The number of households in poverty moved inversely to income developments. The poverty rate had declined steadily since the mid-1990s, as the recovery from the 1990–1991 recession gained momentum. However, after dropping to a low of 11.3 percent in 2000, the rate moved steadily upward, reaching 12.7 percent in 2004. The number of people in poverty increased by 5.4 million from 2000 to 2004, an increase of 17 percent.

As in earlier years, the highest levels of median household income were generally found in the mid-Atlantic states, particularly Maryland, New Jersey, and Virginia. High median household incomes were also found in the New England states, notably New Hampshire, Connecticut, and Massachusetts. The Far West states of Hawaii, Alaska, Washington, and California also ranked among the top 15 median household incomes. The lowest median household incomes were found in the Southeast states, including West Virginia, Mississippi, Arkansas, and Kentucky. These four states ranked among the lowest five median household incomes in 2004. Poverty rates were generally inversely related to median income. When looking at income data by region or state, it is important to note that they are adjusted to constant dollars on the basis of a national price index—the Consumer Price Index—that does not reflect regional differences in cost of living. Consequently, real median income in states with a higher cost of living than the national average may be overstated in income rank relative to those with lower costs.

Table US-8. Household Income and Poverty Status, 1980–2004

(2004 CPI-U-RS adjusted dollars, rate.)

Year	Median household income (2004 dollars)	Poverty rate
2004	44 389	12.7
2003	44 482	12.5
2002	44 546	12.1
2001	45 062	11.7
2000	46 058	11.3
1999	46 129	11.9
1998	45 003	12.7
1997	43 430	13.3
1996	42 544	13.7
1995	41 943	13.8
1994	40 677	14.5
1993	40 217	15.1
1992	40 422	14.8
1991	40 746	14.2
1990	41 963	13.5
1989	42 524	12.8
1988	41 771	13.0
1987	41 322	13.4
1986	40 939	13.6
1985	39 545	14.0
1984	38 782	14.4
1983	. . .	15.2
1982	. . .	15.0
1981	. . .	14.0
1980	. . .	13.0

. . . = Not available.

INCOME MEASUREMENT AND ECONOMIC WELL-BEING. The two most commonly used measures of annual income, median household income and per capita personal income, address different aspects of economic well-being. The median household income concept is a mid-point—half of all households have incomes above that point and half have incomes below it. Per capita income is the average derived by dividing total personal income by the total population. Trends in per capita income reflect changes in the both the numerator and the denominator, while median household income captures the income of a household unit. This is why the government uses median household income in discussions of household income and poverty. These data are based solely on money income and do not include the value of noncash benefits such as food stamps, Medicare, Medicaid, or other in-kind benefits. Neither measure of income directly addresses the issue of income inequality, which is beyond the scope of this book. However, it does appear that overall inequality in income has risen in recent years, as the share of top income recipients (the highest quintile) has increased relative to the rest of the income distribution.

DEMOGRAPHICS OF INCOME AND POVERTY. Although not available on a state-by-state basis, it is worthwhile to briefly examine some of the broad patterns in income and poverty at the national level. Between 2000 and 2004, general trends in median household income and poverty did not show significant changes within demographic groups or between one demographic group and another. Median income was highest for married-couple family households at $63,813 and lowest for female non-family householders at $21,797. Among persons reporting one race, Asian and Pacific Islander households had the most substantial incomes at $57,518, compared with $48,977 for non-Hispanic White households and $30,134 for Black households. Hispanics (of any race) had an income of $34,241—about 70 percent of the median

income of non-Hispanic Whites. Median income rose sharply with the age of the householder, peaking with those age 45–54 years, but dropping to $24,509 for seniors 65 years and over.

Poverty rates in 2004 were lowest among non-Hispanic Whites (8.6 percent) and highest among Blacks (24.7 percent). Asian and Pacific Islanders had a poverty rate of 9.8 percent and Hispanics (of any race) had a rate of 21.9 percent. Disparities in poverty were also evident among families of female and male householders with no spouse present. For women, the rate was 28.4 percent, compared with 13.5 percent for men. Married couples had the lowest incidence of poverty at 5.5 percent. By age, only the poverty rates among those age 65 years and over showed a decline over the 2000–2004 period, dropping slightly to 9.8 percent in 2004.

COMPONENTS OF PERSONAL INCOME. Personal income is measured more broadly than median household income, as it includes in-kind benefits from sources such as food stamps and medical benefits. As noted above, household income excludes noncash income. This difference has become quite significant in recent years, as noncash income has been among the fastest-growing components of personal income.

Net earnings were by far the largest source of personal income, accounting for about 70 percent of income nationwide in 2004. Earnings include wages, salaries, most fringe benefits, and the net income of proprietors. Data on earnings are based on where an individual works. An "adjustment for residence" is then made to shift earnings to where a worker resides, thereby adjusting for cases in which the worker lives another state (or country). A positive adjustment indicates that, on balance, earnings are flowing into the state because residents cross state borders to work. A negative adjustment indicates the reverse: workers were taking earnings out of the state to their residences elsewhere. At the national level, the negative adjustment is an estimate of the amount by which earnings in the United States by workers living in another country exceed the earnings of U.S. residents working abroad.

The other major components of personal income are dividends, interest, and rent, which accounted for about 16 percent of the U.S. total, and transfer payments, which made up the remaining 15 percent of personal income. The vast majority of these transfer payments were from government sources; the largest of these came from Social Security and Medicare/Medicaid. Also included were needs-based transfers, including earned income credit, unemployment insurance, and veterans' benefits. Not surprisingly, states with higher rates of poverty and those with relatively large proportions of elderly individuals received an above average share of transfer benefits.

Government transfer payments to individuals increased by over 80 percent from 1990 to 2000, at an average rate of 6.1 percent per year. This trend accelerated from 2000 and 2004, as transfers grew at an annual rate of 7.5 percent. Medical payments, largely made by Medicare and Medicaid, rose the most during the 2000–2004 period, largely due to the continuous rise of medical care costs. In 2000, medical payments nearly equaled Social Security

Table US-9. Personal Income by Major Source, Selected Years 1980–2004

(Millions of dollars, except where noted.)

Item	1980	1990	2000	2001	2002	2003	2004	Average annual percent change, 2000–2004
Earnings by Place of Work	1 815 550	3 702 139	6 504 679	6 707 999	6 850 968	7 118 533	7 566 609	3.9
Wage and salary disbursements	1 370 432	2 743 016	4 825 906	4 939 944	4 976 552	5 105 689	5 383 759	2.8
Supplements to wages and salaries	271 152	577 074	948 315	993 918	1 104 311	1 202 968	1 290 402	8.0
Proprietors' income[1]	173 966	382 049	730 458	774 137	770 105	809 876	892 448	5.1
Farm proprietors' income	11 198	33 329	24 763	21 935	12 288	27 441	38 641	11.8
Nonfarm proprietors' income	162 768	348 720	705 695	752 202	757 817	782 435	853 807	4.9
(-) Contributions for government social insurance[2]	165 669	408 654	701 650	730 005	748 787	775 196	820 790	4.0
(+) Adjustment for residence[3]	-454	-737	-1 060	-1 093	-1 162	-1 198	-1 233	X
(=) Net Earnings by Place of Residence	1 649 427	3 292 748	5 801 969	5 976 901	6 101 019	6 342 139	6 744 586	3.8
(+) Dividends, interest, and rent[4]	368 611	973 575	1 536 284	1 546 360	1 485 161	1 469 423	1 529 780	-0.1
(+) Personal current transfer receipts	280 217	595 613	1 083 821	1 193 731	1 286 341	1 344 546	1 428 159	7.1
Personal income	2 298 255	4 861 936	8 422 074	8 716 992	8 872 521	9 156 108	9 702 525	3.6
Farm income	2 278 355	4 816 059	8 378 971	8 675 657	8 840 864	9 110 192	9 642 757	3.6
Nonfarm income	19 900	45 877	43 103	41 335	31 657	45 916	59 768	8.5
Per Capita Personal Income (Dollars)[5]	10 114	19 477	29 845	30 575	30 814	31 487	33 041	2.6

Note: Data may not add to total or may appear as zero due to rounding.

[1]Proprietors' income includes the inventory valuation adjustment and the capital consumption adjustment.
[2]Contributions for government social insurance are included in earnings by type and industry, but they are excluded from personal income.
[3]The adjustment for residence is the net inflow of the earnings of interarea commuters.
[4]Rental income of persons includes the capital consumption adjustment.
[5]Per capita personal income is total personal income divided by total midyear population.
X = Not applicable.

benefits, and by 2004, they exceeded Social Security benefits by nearly $92 billion.

There were divergent trends among income maintenance transfers. The largest component of this category was the Earned Income Tax Credit, which were payments to low-income families and to some individuals who reported income on their income tax returns. These payments have grown substantially, reflecting changes in government policies in the mid-1990s, as well as the increasing numbers of low-income individuals who have found work. These payments were reported under the category "Other income maintenance." Supplemental Security Income (SSI) was the second largest of the income maintenance transfers and has been growing steadily in virtually all states. Administered by the Social

Security Administration, the program supports needy elders and the blind and disabled. Disability payments have come to be dominated by children and by adults under 65 years of age. Notable is the sharp decline in Family Assistance, which historically consisted of Aid for Families with Dependent Children. This program was radically restructured in 1997 to impose strong work requirements upon beneficiaries and to give states, which largely administer the programs, broader authority over their requirements for family assistance. Food stamps, another large income maintenance program, grew rapidly over the 2000–2004 period, in part reflecting the declines in the inflation-adjusted median household income and increases in poverty.

Table US-10. Government Transfer Payments, Selected Years 1980–2004

(Millions of dollars, percent.)

Item	1980	1990	2000	2001	2002	2003	2004	Average annual percent change, 2000–2004
CURRENT TRANSFER PAYMENTS TO INDIVIDUALS	263 351	561 484	1 018 106	1 117 218	1 219 954	1 282 540	1 361 666	7.5
Retirement and Disability Insurance Benefits	128 802	264 230	424 810	450 415	474 863	493 894	517 840	5.1
Old-age, survivors, and disability insurance (OASDI) benefits	118 586	244 135	401 218	425 081	446 690	463 406	485 932	4.9
Railroad retirement and disability benefits	4 812	7 221	8 265	8 411	8 700	8 855	9 009	2.2
Workers' compensation	2 848	8 618	10 845	11 673	13 318	14 189	14 801	8.1
Other government retirement and disability insurance benefits	2 556	4 256	4 482	5 250	6 155	7 444	8 098	15.9
Medical Benefits	62 624	188 808	427 689	482 527	525 387	555 259	609 035	9.2
Medicare benefits	36 201	107 638	219 612	243 462	260 777	275 875	303 322	8.4
Public assistance medical care benefits	25 659	78 176	205 021	234 644	258 560	274 272	299 667	10.0
Military medical insurance benefits	764	2 994	3 056	4 421	6 050	5 112	6 046	18.6
Income Maintenance Benefits	34 276	63 481	106 616	109 403	119 718	131 225	141 490	7.3
Supplemental Security Income (SSI) benefits	7 941	16 670	31 675	33 162	34 664	35 703	37 299	4.2
Family assistance	12 516	19 187	18 440	18 106	17 684	18 367	18 492	0.1
Food stamps	8 214	14 741	14 896	16 000	18 612	22 127	25 779	14.7
Other income maintenance benefits	5 605	12 883	41 605	42 135	48 758	55 028	59 920	9.5
Unemployment Insurance Compensation	18 662	18 208	20 680	32 155	53 742	53 583	37 119	15.7
Veterans' Benefits	14 660	17 687	24 935	26 500	29 333	31 607	33 806	7.9
Federal Education and Training Assistance	4 106	7 300	10 985	13 129	14 523	13 947	14 833	7.8
Other Payments to Individuals	221	1 770	2 391	3 089	2 388	3 025	7 543	33.3

Note: See notes and definitions for more details. Data may not add to total or may appear as zero due to rounding.

LABOR MARKET

UNEMPLOYMENT. The decline in economic activity in 2001 caused unemployment to increase significantly as the overall jobless rate rose from its decades-low rate of 4.0 percent in 2000 to 6.0 percent in 2003. As market conditions improved in 2004, the rate dropped to 5.5 percent. However, this partly reflected the fact that many Americans remained outside the labor force, neither employed nor seeking work. This was reflected by the lower civilian labor force participation rate of 66.0 percent in 2004, down from 67.1 percent in 2000, before the recession began. The rise in unemployment was common to all regions of the country; it was most intense in the Midwest region (as defined by the Census Bureau), where manufacturing employment fell, and in the West region—particularly in the Pacific states. The recovery from the recession was as uneven as its impact. The Middle Atlantic, New England, and Pacific areas (Census divisions) had the largest reductions in unemployment, particularly in the states of Washington, New Jersey, and North Carolina. Only Iowa, Missouri, South Carolina, Delaware, and the District of Columbia continued to experience increasing unemployment rates. The ranking tables following this section show each state's unemployment rate in 2004. The lowest rates were found in Hawaii, where tourism rebounded, and in North Dakota and South Dakota. The highest rates were in the District of Columbia, Alaska, Oregon, and Michigan.

EMPLOYMENT. As measured by the Bureau of Labor Statistics's Survey of Establishments, which is part of the Current Employment Statistics program, employment was slow to regain its momentum following the 2001 recession. Indeed, payroll employment in 2004 remained below its previous peak in February 2001—the longest lag in employment recovery in the post-World-War-II period. Hence, until sustained overall job growth was observed in 2004, many commentators termed the expansion "the jobless recovery." Moreover, the pattern of recovery was uneven across industries and regions. While employment somewhat recuperated in some of the more cyclically-sensitive industries, such as machinery, transportation, trade, business and professional services, and leisure and tourism, other industries remained depressed. The evidence of employer caution in hiring as the major contributor to job growth was in the "temporary help services" industry, which supplied workers to all industries. Employers sought to keep pace with increased demand for their products and services without committing to providing permanent employment until assured that demand would be long-lasting. The demand for temporary workers was widespread across the country—in some areas, temporary workers filled positions in light manufacturing (relatively low-skilled work), while other employers hired temporary workers to fill clerical, freight transportation, information technology, and health care jobs.

Mortgage-sensitive industries also spurred job growth. Mortgage interest rates remained historically low over the 2001–2004 period, which sustained job growth in financial activities related to home financing (and building financing in general), real estate, and construction, particularly residential construction. The strong demand for housing also increased manufacturing employment in the fabricated metal, nonmetallic mineral, and wood products industries, all of which provided home-building products. These three industries combined accounted for much of the growth in manufacturing employment. State and local budgets were also favorably impacted, as rising home value assessments generated revenues from prop-

Table US-11. Employment Status, 1980–2004

(Numbers in thousands, rate.)

Year	Civilian noninstitutional population	Civilian labor force	Participation rate	Employed	Unemployed	Unemployment rate
2004	223 357 000	147 401 000	66.0	139 252 000	8 149 000	5.5
2003	221 168 000	146 510 000	66.2	137 736 000	8 774 000	6.0
2002	217 570 000	144 863 000	66.6	136 485 000	8 378 000	5.8
2001	215 092 000	143 734 000	66.8	136 933 000	6 801 000	4.7
2000	212 577 000	142 583 000	67.1	136 891 000	5 692 000	4.0
1999	207 753 000	139 368 000	67.1	133 488 000	5 880 000	4.2
1998	205 220 000	137 673 000	67.1	131 463 000	6 210 000	4.5
1997	203 133 000	136 297 000	67.1	129 558 000	6 739 000	4.9
1996	200 591 000	133 943 000	66.8	126 708 000	7 236 000	5.4
1995	198 584 000	132 304 000	66.6	124 900 000	7 404 000	5.6
1994	196 814 000	131 056 000	66.6	123 060 000	7 996 000	6.1
1993	194 838 000	129 200 000	66.3	120 259 000	8 940 000	6.9
1992	192 805 000	128 105 000	66.4	118 492 000	9 613 000	7.5
1991	190 925 000	126 346 000	66.2	117 718 000	8 628 000	6.8
1990	189 164 000	125 840 000	66.5	118 793 000	7 047 000	5.6
1989	186 393 000	123 869 000	66.5	117 342 000	6 528 000	5.3
1988	184 613 000	121 669 000	65.9	114 968 000	6 701 000	5.5
1987	182 753 000	119 865 000	65.6	112 440 000	7 425 000	6.2
1986	180 587 000	117 834 000	65.3	109 597 000	8 237 000	7.0
1985	178 206 000	115 461 000	64.8	107 150 000	8 312 000	7.2
1984	176 383 000	113 544 000	64.4	105 005 000	8 539 000	7.5
1983	174 215 000	111 550 000	64.0	100 834 000	10 717 000	9.6
1982	172 271 000	110 204 000	64.0	99 526 000	10 678 000	9.7
1981	170 130 000	108 670 000	63.9	100 397 000	8 273 000	7.6
1980	167 745 000	106 940 000	63.8	99 303 000	7 637 000	7.1

Note: Population age 16 years and over.

erty taxes, which some states used to increase spending on local public education. However, employment in some sectors suffered from consolidation, such as the telecommunications industry, or from the loss of competitiveness, such as the textiles and apparel industries.

Among the states, Nevada had the strongest recent rate of payroll employment growth, with the number of jobs growing 5.6 percent between 2003 and 2004. This was followed by Arizona (3.6 percent) and Florida (3.2 percent). Larger states, such as Texas, California, and New York, experienced gains closer to the national average of 1.6 percent.

A broader measure of employment by industry is contained in Table 13, which includes managers and professional employees in addition to production and non-supervisory workers. These employment data show similar trends. Notable employment growth did not occur until 2004, and much of the strength was in construction, real estate and related activities, health care and educational services, and tourism-related industries (such as accommodation and food services). Employment in manufacturing was well below its 2001 level.

Table US-12. Employment Status by Demographic Group, 2004

(Numbers in thousands, rate.)

Characteristic	Civilian noninstitutional population	Civilian labor force		Employed	Unemployment rate
		Number	Percent		
SEX AND AGE					
Total	223 357	147 401	66.0	139 252	5.5
16 to 19 years	16 222	7 114	43.9	5 907	17.0
20 to 24 years	20 197	15 154	75.0	13 723	9.4
25 years and over	186 937	125 133	66.9	119 622	4.4
25 to 34 years	38 939	32 207	82.7	30 423	5.5
35 to 44 years	43 226	36 158	83.6	34 580	4.4
45 to 54 years	41 245	33 758	81.8	32 469	3.8
55 to 64 years	28 919	18 013	62.3	17 331	3.8
65 to 69 years	9 800	2 710	27.7	2 614	3.5
70 to 74 years	8 381	1 280	15.3	1 234	3.6
75 years and over	16 429	1 007	6.1	971	3.6
Men	107 710	78 980	73.3	74 524	5.6
16 to 19 years	8 234	3 616	43.9	2 952	18.4
20 to 24 years	10 125	8 057	79.6	7 246	10.1
25 years and over	89 351	67 306	75.3	64 326	4.4
25 to 34 years	19 358	17 798	91.9	16 818	5.5
35 to 44 years	21 255	19 539	91.9	18 700	4.3
45 to 54 years	20 160	17 635	87.5	16 951	3.9
55 to 64 years	13 894	9 547	68.7	9 174	3.9
65 to 69 years	4 573	1 490	32.6	1 436	3.6
70 to 74 years	3 721	721	19.4	693	3.8
75 years and over	6 391	576	9.0	554	3.8
Women	115 647	68 421	59.2	64 728	5.4
16 to 19 years	7 989	3 498	43.8	2 955	15.5
20 to 24 years	10 072	7 097	70.5	6 477	8.7
25 years and over	97 586	57 826	59.3	55 296	4.4
25 to 34 years	19 581	14 409	73.6	13 605	5.6
35 to 44 years	21 970	16 619	75.6	15 880	4.4
45 to 54 years	21 085	16 123	76.5	15 518	3.7
55 to 64 years	15 025	8 466	56.3	8 157	3.6
65 to 69 years	5 227	1 220	23.3	1 178	3.5
70 to 74 years	4 660	560	12.0	541	3.3
75 years and over	10 038	431	4.3	416	3.4
RACE, HISPANIC ORGIN, SEX, AND AGE					
White	182 643	121 086	66.3	115 239	4.8
Both sexes, 16 to 19 years	12 599	5 929	47.1	5 039	15.0
Men, 16 years and over	89 044	65 994	74.1	62 712	5.0
Men, 20 years and over	82 615	62 944	76.2	60 159	4.4
Women, 16 years and over	93 599	55 092	58.9	52 527	4.7
Women, 20 years and over	87 430	52 212	59.7	50 040	4.2
Black	26 065	16 638	63.8	14 909	10.4
Both sexes, 16 to 19 years	2 423	762	31.4	520	31.7
Men, 16 years and over	11 656	7 773	66.7	6 912	11.1
Men, 20 years and over	10 461	7 414	70.9	6 681	9.9
Women, 16 years and over	14 409	8 865	61.5	7 997	9.8
Women, 20 years and over	13 182	8 462	64.2	7 707	8.9
Asian	9 519	6 271	65.9	5 994	4.4
Both sexes, 16 to 19 years	606	172	28.4	152	11.5
Men, 16 years and over	4 529	3 396	75.0	3 243	4.5
Men, 20 years and over	4 216	3 305	78.4	3 165	4.2
Women, 16 years and over	4 990	2 876	57.6	2 751	4.3
Women, 20 years and over	4 697	2 795	59.5	2 678	4.2
Hispanic or Latino[1]	28 109	19 272	68.6	17 930	7.0
Both sexes, 16 to 19 years	2 608	995	38.2	792	20.4
Men, 16 years and over	14 417	11 587	80.4	10 832	6.5
Men, 20 years and over	13 082	11 020	84.2	10 385	5.8
Women, 16 years and over	13 692	7 685	56.1	7 098	7.6
Women, 20 years and over	12 420	7 257	58.4	6 752	7.0

Note: Data in Table 12 are from the Current Population Survey (CPS) and do not match Bureau of Labor Statistics estimates in Table 11. See notes and definitions for more details.

[1] May be of any race.

EARNINGS. Wages for blue-collar industrial workers and for nonsupervisory workers in service-providing industries have been stagnant since economic recovery began in November 2001. Part of the reason lay in the rising cost of non-wage benefits, particularly health insurance. Inflation-adjusted compensation, or wages plus benefits as measured by the Bureau of Labor Statistics' Employment Cost Index, rose less than in past recoveries. Moreover, these pay gains were distributed unevenly, with educated workers experiencing the highest increases. Following employment patterns, the major gainers in weekly earnings, adjusted for inflation, were financial activities, educational services, health care services, and business and professional services. Real wages declined in natural resources and mining industries, as well as in transportation and manufacturing.

Average wage and salary disbursements encompassed all wage and salary workers and included earnings of payroll workers, salaries of managerial and professional employees, compensation of corporate officers, commissions, tips, and bonuses. Although these data were not adjusted for inflation, they showed little in the way of strong gains by workers across most industries.

High wage and salary jobs were generally found in the goods-producing sectors of mining and utilities and in the finance and insurance, company and enterprise management, professional and technical services, and information services sectors. The lowest earnings were in accommodation and food services, retail trade, and agriculture sectors, where hourly earnings were low and part-time and part-year employment were more prevalent. Average annual wages and salaries were the highest in the District of Columbia; the northeastern states of Connecticut, New York, Massachusetts, and New Jersey; and California. The lowest were in Montana, South Dakota, and Mississippi.

Table US-13. Employment and Average Wages by Industry, 2001–2004

(Estimates are based on the 2002 North American Industry Classification System [NAICS].)

Industry	2001	2002	2003	2004	Annual average percent change, 2001–2004
	Number of jobs				
TOTAL EMPLOYMENT BY PLACE OF WORK	167 014 700	166 634 100	167 487 500	170 103 500	0.6
Farm Employment	3 056 000	3 077 000	3 032 000	2 969 000	-1.0
Nonfarm Employment	163 958 700	163 557 100	164 455 500	167 134 500	0.6
Private employment	140 778 700	140 043 100	140 829 500	143 466 500	0.6
Forestry, fishing, hunting, and other[1]	1 022 500	1 053 700	992 300	979 300	-1.4
Mining	811 400	751 000	803 200	842 000	1.2
Utilities	618 800	603 600	590 200	582 300	-2.0
Construction	9 846 700	9 664 800	9 879 300	10 193 800	1.2
Manufacturing	16 994 600	15 822 700	15 060 000	14 878 100	-4.3
Durable goods manufacturing	10 675 900	9 817 100	9 290 200	9 255 000	-4.6
Nondurable goods manufacturing	6 318 700	6 005 600	5 769 800	5 623 100	-3.8
Wholesale trade	6 273 400	6 141 800	6 111 500	6 191 600	-0.4
Retail trade	18 528 800	18 470 100	18 506 100	18 774 900	0.4
Transportation and warehousing	5 474 000	5 342 300	5 287 300	5 361 600	-0.7
Information	4 053 800	3 724 200	3 601 400	3 537 600	-4.4
Finance and insurance	7 839 600	7 909 300	7 992 500	8 054 900	0.9
Real estate and rental and leasing	5 551 400	5 677 000	6 008 700	6 289 900	4.3
Professional and technical services	10 575 800	10 460 200	10 557 300	10 801 100	0.7
Management of companies and enterprises	1 779 300	1 806 000	1 753 500	1 764 100	-0.3
Administrative and waste services	9 621 000	9 640 300	9 805 400	10 295 900	2.3
Educational services	3 058 300	3 202 600	3 313 800	3 436 900	4.0
Health care and social assistance	15 611 400	16 079 000	16 530 100	16 885 400	2.6
Arts, entertainment, and recreation	3 243 100	3 343 200	3 368 800	3 457 600	2.2
Accommodation and food services	10 825 200	10 935 200	11 156 700	11 480 100	2.0
Other services, except public administration	9 049 600	9 416 100	9 511 400	9 659 400	2.2
Government and government enterprises	23 180 000	23 514 000	23 626 000	23 668 000	0.7
	Dollars				
AVERAGE WAGES AND SALARIES BY PLACE OF WORK	35 582	36 150	37 176	38 793	2.9
Farm Earnings	20 598	20 591	19 238	23 596	4.6
Nonfarm Earnings	35 677	36 249	37 292	38 885	2.9
Private earnings	35 868	36 234	37 212	38 834	2.7
Forestry, fishing, hunting, and other[1]	21 934	22 841	23 390	24 418	3.6
Mining	59 394	60 104	62 002	66 356	3.8
Utilities	65 491	66 988	68 303	72 354	3.4
Construction	38 416	39 052	39 515	40 540	1.8
Manufacturing	42 886	44 002	45 810	47 780	3.7
Durable goods manufacturing	45 293	46 288	48 239	50 271	3.5
Nondurable goods manufacturing	38 813	40 259	41 898	43 675	4.0
Wholesale trade	48 717	49 168	50 810	53 287	3.0
Retail trade	22 658	23 234	23 818	24 443	2.6
Transportation and warehousing	37 380	38 017	38 726	40 137	2.4
Information	57 208	56 070	57 903	61 108	2.2
Finance and insurance	63 775	62 878	65 064	70 171	3.2
Real estate and rental and leasing	32 946	33 991	35 123	37 359	4.3
Professional and technical services	58 544	58 542	59 766	62 333	2.1
Management of companies and enterprises	69 119	69 705	72 370	80 087	5.0
Administrative and waste services	24 467	25 326	26 065	27 229	3.6
Educational services	26 681	27 681	28 840	29 855	3.8
Health care and social assistance	32 440	33 634	34 748	36 262	3.8
Arts, entertainment, and recreation	26 099	26 961	27 999	28 660	3.2
Accommodation and food services	14 595	14 879	15 181	15 713	2.5
Other services, except public administration	22 167	22 758	23 561	24 452	3.3
Government and government enterprises	34 733	36 320	37 674	39 132	4.1

Note: Average wages and salaries are a calculation by the editors of wage and salary disbursements divided by full- and part-time wage and salary employment. Data may not add to total or may appear as zero due to rounding.

ECONOMIC ACTIVITY

Real gross domestic product (GDP) for the nation grew at an average annual rate of 2.8 percent between 2001 and 2004. In the recession year of 2001, growth was slight—only 0.8 percent—but the subsequent recovery gradually gained momentum. In 2004, real GDP increased at a healthy annual rate of 4.2 percent. Personal consumption expenditures, particularly for services (especially housing-related services) and residential construction, were the main contributing forces for growth over the period.

Gross state product (GSP) is the state counterpart to the nation's GDP. It is equal to a state's industries gross output (sales or receipts and other operating income, commodity taxes, and inventory change) minus its intermediate inputs (consumption of products imported or purchased from other industries). Thus, GSP accounts provide data by industry and state that are consistent with the national GDP accounts. However, the total GSP (the sum of all the states' GSPs) differs from the national GDP in the following way: GSP excludes compensation of federal military and civilian personnel stationed abroad, as well as their expenditures on buildings and other facilities and equipment. In 2004, GDP (adjusted for inflation) totaled $10,756 billion while total constant-dollar GSP was $10,720 billion.

As measured by GSP, the 2001 recession and subsequent recovery affected regions and states differently. Generally, the Southeast and Southwest regions (using Bureau of Economic Analysis regions, which differ from the Census regions and divisions; see the notes and definitions at the end of the book) fared the best over the recovery period. Florida, North Carolina, and Virginia in the Southeast and Arizona and Texas in the Southwest were the least affected by the slow growth from 2002 to 2003 that followed the 2001 recession. The Great Lakes region, particularly Illinois and Ohio, showed the weakest growth during this recovery period, reflecting the impact of the slowdown in manufacturing.

With the increase in momentum in 2004, real GSP grew in all states and the District of Columbia between 2003 and 2004. The Far West region grew the most quickly (5.5 percent), with growth in service-providing industries outpacing that of the goods-producing sector. Within the Far West region, Nevada had the strongest growth rate (9.3 percent) and was the fastest-growing state in the country. The GSPs of Arizona, Virginia, and the District of Columbia expanded briskly during this one-year period. The economies of the Great Lakes region recovered more slowly, with service-providing industries outpacing the growth of the goods-producing sector (the traditional base of economic activity in this region). Within this region, Michigan grew the least and was the slowest-growing state in the nation.

By size, California, New York, and Texas had the largest GSPs in 2004; North Dakota, Vermont, and Wyoming, the smallest—rankings that have not changed significantly in recent years.

Table US-14. Real Gross State Product, 1997–2004

(Millions of chained 2000 dollars, percent.)

Industry	1997	1998	1999	2000	2001	2002	2003	2004	Average annual percent change, 2001–2004
GROSS STATE PRODUCT	8 620 955	9 004 669	9 404 249	9 749 104	9 836 571	10 009 433	10 289 220	10 734 763	3.0
Private Industries	7 525 575	7 896 070	8 285 466	8 614 288	8 692 539	8 851 579	9 123 043	9 543 513	3.2
Agriculture, forestry, fishing, and hunting	86 566	84 578	87 396	98 020	91 806	98 068	103 507	96 902	1.8
Mining	124 322	123 375	126 551	121 335	114 922	112 446	104 600	106 945	-2.4
Utilities	172 560	171 272	179 204	189 291	179 980	190 736	202 043	212 953	5.8
Construction	406 564	423 216	433 346	435 914	436 624	425 141	424 053	433 358	-0.2
Manufacturing	1 205 414	1 286 184	1 342 121	1 426 218	1 346 866	1 378 211	1 439 998	1 501 315	3.7
As a percent of gross state product	14.0	14.3	14.3	14.6	13.7	13.8	14.0	14.0	X
Wholesale trade	506 767	564 655	594 132	591 687	633 123	643 042	630 977	651 562	1.0
Retail trade	569 950	598 829	633 853	662 430	708 602	746 447	788 387	829 726	5.4
Transportation and warehousing	266 552	275 845	287 449	301 622	293 641	299 142	314 238	324 749	3.4
Information	341 706	376 962	437 528	458 304	476 793	475 471	502 439	551 721	5.0
Finance and insurance	593 437	634 611	678 143	740 488	772 833	793 771	856 322	923 143	6.1
Real estate and rental and leasing	1 085 381	1 108 621	1 156 980	1 190 464	1 232 575	1 239 712	1 244 084	1 295 662	1.7
Services	2 188 443	2 260 096	2 335 228	2 398 513	2 406 410	2 451 965	2 520 454	2 630 474	3.0
As a percent of gross state product	25.4	25.1	24.8	24.6	24.5	24.5	24.5	24.5	X
Professional and technical services	542 520	585 863	623 894	675 122	679 057	681 197	701 845	730 527	2.5
Management of companies and enterprises	188 959	184 040	185 587	183 354	179 923	179 845	186 469	197 198	3.1
Administrative and waste services	270 029	281 005	296 887	282 373	274 423	286 699	299 636	317 683	5.0
Educational services	73 107	75 627	77 139	79 239	79 108	79 198	77 819	77 339	-0.8
Health care and social assistance	570 023	572 975	583 006	599 197	620 972	647 572	669 330	690 023	3.6
Arts, entertainment, and recreation	84 201	84 691	87 884	88 676	91 464	94 658	95 619	97 511	2.2
Accommodation and food services	232 117	242 495	251 175	261 443	256 161	259 375	265 216	279 798	3.0
Other services, except public administration	227 487	233 400	229 656	229 109	225 302	223 441	224 520	240 395	2.2
Government	1 085 200	1 100 168	1 113 472	1 134 817	1 146 452	1 161 567	1 175 255	1 201 753	1.6
As a percent of gross state product	12.6	12.2	11.8	11.6	11.7	11.6	11.4	11.2	X
GROSS DOMESTIC PRODUCT[1]	8 703 500	9 066 900	9 470 300	9 817 000	9 890 700	10 048 800	10 320 600	10 755 700	2.8

[1]GDP does not equal the sum of the states' GSP because the latter excludes the wages and salaries and wage and salary supplements of federal civilian and military personnel stationed abroad. GSP also excludes the capital consumption allowances associated with federal government equipment and structures located abroad and all military weaponry.
X = Not applicable.

HOUSING ACTIVITY. The housing market boom was a key factor in the recovery of the nation's economy from the recession. Historically low mortgage rates during the period, in combination with other factors, stimulated the demand for housing. In addition to primary residences, demand was also boosted by an increase in the purchases of second homes—either as vacation units or as investments—as well as by the greater availability of less conventional financing instruments (including interest-only mortgages and adjustable rate mortgages that allow borrowers a degree of flexibility in the size of their monthly payments). These instruments have enabled households to buy homes that would have been otherwise unaffordable. The strong housing demand pushed up housing prices quite substantially over the 2001–2004 period.

Although housing prices have risen steadily over the past 13 years, the extraordinary price increase of 24 percent for existing single-family homes and the over 12 percent price increase for new homes since 2001 led analysts to fear a housing "bubble," akin to the stock market's, which burst in 2000. Housing booms such as these must be defined in terms of areas rather than states, because these markets are localized. Indeed, in 2004, almost half of the metropolitan areas in the United States had housing prices that were not in line with historical median income/house price trends—making it necessary to measure prices with a house affordability index. These high-price markets included most of Southern California, New York City and surrounding areas, parts of Nevada, and the large metropolitan areas of southern Florida—combined, these areas were home to almost 25 percent of the nation's population. In these locations, buyers struggled to keep up with escalating home costs, despite low mortgage rates. However, in other areas of the country, housing prices and income were more fully in line: of the 110 largest metropolitan areas, 77 had price-to-income ratios of less than four to one, and were thus relatively affordable.

It is not yet known whether the "boom" housing markets are headed for a sharp correction. A slow rise in mortgage rates may cool, rather than freeze, rising home prices. Sustained economic recovery that stimulates job growth and rising household incomes could offset the gradual increase in interest rates. Household growth is likely to continue over the long term due to immigration and the subsequent demand for housing.

The importance of the prices and demand for housing for states lies in two dimensions. A robust housing market in a particular area tends to enrich the state. With rising property values causing the "wealth effect"(when the increase in personal asset values makes people feel richer), households increase their expenditures on goods and services. This generates income for housing-related goods and services, as well as income related to refinancing and new construction. Also, real estate tax revenues are generated for state and local budgets, which has led to windfalls for many states and localities. As a result, these governments are able to increase expenditures on public services, including education and infrastructure projects. The downside of booming demand and high housing prices is that businesses are more likely to bypass these high-priced localities as they seek to attract workers, who, in turn, seek affordable housing. Businesses may also prefer to construct facilities where building costs are relatively lower. Included in the rankings section are median values of owner-occupied housing units in 2004 by state. While the dynamics of local housing markets are not depicted, the more expensive states for owner-occupied housing are shown. California, Hawaii, and the District of Columbia ranked the highest for median value of owner-occupied housing, while North Dakota, West Virginia, Mississippi, and Arkansas had the lowest median values.

EXPORTS

TRADE. Nationally, the trade balance in goods and services has deteriorated sharply since the late 1990s, largely due to rising imports; by 2004, the trade deficit had reached $617.7 billion. The deficit in goods also increased substantially. Although U.S. goods exports have continued to grow steadily, led by advanced technology products, their expansion has been overwhelmed by imports from abroad. Exports of services, which accounted for about 30 percent of all U.S. exports in 2004, have outpaced services imports, creating a small offset to the overall trade deficit. The chief American goods exported in 2004 were capital goods (excluding automotive goods) and industrial supplies, which together represented about 65 percent of all goods exports. Agricultural products exports contributed positively to the trade balance, although their share of total exports has diminished steadily over the years. In 2004, agricultural products accounted for about 4 percent of total U.S. exports. Canada and Mexico were the principal trading partners for manufactured and agricultural goods, with relations governed by the North American Free Trade Agreement (NAFTA). These two countries accounted for over one-third of all U.S. goods exports in 2004. China became an increasingly important export market: the amount of U.S. goods exported to that country increased by about 80 percent from 2001 to 2004.

States varied greatly in their participation in global markets, in terms of the products they export and the destinations of these products. The data in this book provide a general indication of the importance of exports to a state, but must be interpreted with caution for several reasons. First, they pertain only to goods exports; comparable data for services are not available. Second, there are no data on foreign imports by state, and thus the totality of a state's role in international trade cannot be assessed. Third, state export data are reported by the exporter or agent and denote the state from which the merchandise actually starts its journey to the port of export. This method of calculation is called the "origin of movement," and reflects the state of transportation origin, which may not be the state in which the merchandise was grown or manufactured. When shipments are consolidated, the state of origin will reflect the consolidation point. This effect is particularly noticeable for nonmanufactured goods, which are generally exported by intermediaries. For example, intermediaries located in inland states ship agricultural products down the Mississippi River for export from the port of New Orleans, Louisiana. In this case, Louisiana would be reported as the state of origin. The most visible result is an understatement of agricultural exports from some states and an overstatement of these exports from Louisiana.

In 2004, the largest exporting states were Texas, California, New York, Michigan, Washington, Ohio, Illinois, Florida, Massachusetts, and Louisiana. By far, the largest share of exported goods went to Canada and Mexico. California, and to a lesser extent Washington and Texas, reported substantial exports to the East Asian countries of China, Japan, South Korea, and Taiwan. New York and California had large exports to the European

Union countries. In 2004, computers and electronic products were the nation's leading export, followed by transportation equipment, chemicals, machinery manufactures, and agricultural products. California was the leading exporter of computers and electronic products, followed by Texas. Michigan, Washington, and Texas led the nation in the export of transportation equipment. The chief exporter of chemicals and machinery manufactures was Texas. Louisiana was the top exporter of agricultural products (although this probably reflected the use of the port of New Orleans for the shipment of many products grown in other states).

Table US-15. Exports of Goods by Leading Products and Destinations, 2001–2004

(Millions of dollars, percent, rank based on 2004 dollar values.)

Product and market	2001	2002	2003	2004	Percent share of total, 2004	Average annual percent change, 2001–2004
Total Goods						
Total	731 026	693 257	723 743	817 936	100.0	3.8
Manufactures	656 453	622 000	644 906	727 857	89.0	3.5
Agriculture and livestock	26 186	26 829	31 553	34 192	4.2	9.3
Other commodities	48 387	44 428	47 284	55 887	6.8	4.9
Five Leading Exports (NAICS Code)						
Computers and electronic products (334)	165 345	145 848	149 993	164 200	20.1	-0.2
Transportation equipment (336)	130 233	130 897	128 854	140 439	17.2	2.5
Chemical manufactures (325)	79 034	80 504	91 017	108 484	13.3	11.1
Machinery manufactures (333)	81 513	74 945	74 925	92 674	11.3	4.4
Miscellaneous manufactures (339)	25 779	26 661	29 401	34 247	4.2	9.9
Five Leading Markets	637 917	605 954	633 258	710 005	86.8	3.6
Canada	163 724	160 799	169 481	189 101	23.1	4.9
Mexico	101 509	97 531	97 457	110 775	13.5	3.0
Japan	57 639	51 440	52 064	54 400	6.7	-1.9
United Kingdom	40 798	33 253	33 895	35 960	4.4	-4.1
China	19 235	22 053	28 418	34 721	4.2	21.8

AGRICULTURE

For many years, the United States has produced an abundance of farm products with progressively fewer farms and farm workers and less acreage devoted to agriculture. These trends continued from 1997 to 2002, as reported in the most recent Census of Agriculture (taken by the Department of Agriculture every five years). The number of farms declined by 3.9 percent from 1997 to 2002. U.S. farmland acreage decreased by 1.8 percent from 1997 to 2002, which was similar to the drop from 1992 to 1997. While the market value of agricultural products sold has declined slightly since 1997, the market value per acre has increased, offsetting the decline in total acreage.

Farm employment (owners and employees), as measured by the Bureau of Economic Analysis, declined by 2.8 percent over the 2001–2004 period. Employment had remained steady during the previous decade, before dropping below 3 million in 2004. However, farm employment had been decreasing as a proportion of overall employment for many years. In no state did farm employment reach 10 percent of that state's total employment. States with the largest share of farm employment were North Dakota, South Dakota, Iowa, Montana, and Nebraska. In each of these states, farm employment accounted for 5 percent or more of total employment. In states that led the nation in agricultural activity, such as California and Florida, farm employment constituted a relatively low share of overall employment. Farm employment statistics do not measure the total

importance of agriculture to a state's economy, as additional employment and income are generated by the provision of agricultural services, the processing of agricultural products in the manufacturing sector, and the sales of farm supplies and equipment.

In federal statistics, a farm is defined as any place from which $1,000 or more of agricultural products were pro-

Table US-16. Agriculture, 1997 and 2002

(Number, acres, and dollars.)

Item	1997	2002
Number of farms	2 215 876	2 128 982
Land in farms (acres)	954 752 502	938 279 056
Farm Size		
Average size of farm (acres)	431	441
Farms by size (percent distribution)		
Fewer than 50 acres	33.2	34.9
50 to 499 acres	50.7	49.2
500 acres or more	16.1	15.9
Market Value of Land and Equipment (Dollars)		
Land and buildings average value per farm	416 007	537 833
Average value per acre	967	1 213
Machinery and equipment average value per farm	53 861	66 570
Value of Sales (Thousands of Dollars)		
Agricultural products sold	201 379 812	200 646 355
Crops	100 668 794	95 151 954
Livestock, poultry, and their products	100 711 018	105 494 401
Average per farm (dollars)	90 880	94 245
Value of sales (percent distribution)		
Less than $10,000	55.3	59.3
$10,000 to $99,999	28.7	26.0
$100,000 or more	15.9	14.6
Government Payments		
Payments (thousands of dollars)	5 294 384	6 545 678
Percent of farms receiving government payments	38.7	33.2
Farm operators whose principal occupation is farming (percent)	47.1	57.5

duced or sold. Thus, the total number of farms included many for which farming generated only a minor fraction of household income. In 2002, almost 60 percent of all farms had sales of less than $10,000, and about 43 percent of all farm owners reported a principal occupation other than farming. Nebraska, South Dakota, and North Dakota had the highest proportions of farm operators reporting farming as their principal occupation. All three states had proportions exceeding 70 percent, compared with 57.5 percent nationally. California had the largest overall number of individuals reporting farming as their principal occupation. In terms of sales, the 15 percent of farms that had cash receipts above $100,000 accounted for more than 85 percent of sales. For the first time, the Census of Agriculture collected data on certified organically produced commodities, which were valued at $392.8 billion. This represented only 0.2 percent of the total value of agricultural products in 2002, but this proportion is likely to increase in future years.

Other highlights from the 2002 Census of Agriculture included: the top five states in terms of the value of agriculture products sold were California, Texas, Iowa, Nebraska, and Kansas; nearly 90 percent of farms were operated by an individual or family—the number of corporate farms declined by 18.4 percent from 1997 to 2002, reversing a trend that had continued without interruption since 1974; the average market value of land and buildings rose 29 percent from 1997 to 2002, as the average value increased by over $100,000 during the period; and the average age of the principal farmer or rancher increased to 55.3 years in 2002, up from 54.0 years in 1997. For the first time, the census collected information about multiple operators on the same farm and found that second and third operators were much younger (49.4 years and 41.9 years, respectively). Half of the nation's farms and ranches had access to the Internet; nearly 39 percent reported using a computer for their farm business.

ENERGY

In 2004, total energy consumption in the United States was 100.4 quadrillion Btu (British thermal unit). Total consumption rose rapidly during the economic expansion in the 1990s, but leveled off as the 2001 recession slowed the economy. During the recent economic recovery, consumption resumed its upward trend. In 2004, total consumption was 4.1 percent above the 2001 level and 18.5 percent above the 1990 level. Petroleum supplied about 40 percent of the energy used, followed by natural gas (23.0 percent) and coal (22.4 percent). Electrical power was obtained from several energy sources (70 percent from fossil fuel, 20 percent from nuclear power, and 10 percent from renewable energy sources), and from international imports, mainly from Canada. Each state was likely to have an interstate flow of electricity, or net imports or exports that added to or subtracted from the state's energy consumption.

In 2001, Texas was the largest consumer of energy, ranking first in the nation for its use of natural gas, petroleum,

and electricity. Its high ranking was largely due to the substantial consumption by Texas's industrial sector. (California ranked second.) In terms of per capita energy consumption, Alaska ranked first, due to its mining operations and heating requirements, followed by Wyoming (mining), Louisiana, North Dakota, and Texas. Rhode Island, New York, and California ranked the lowest in this category.

The District of Columbia, Hawaii, and Massachusetts paid the highest prices per Btu, while Louisiana, Alaska, and North Dakota had the lowest energy prices. In terms of per capita expenditures, which included direct purchases of energy by households as well as indirect costs related to items that use energy as an intermediate input, Wyoming paid the most (an average of $4,702 per person in 2001), compared with the U.S. average of $2,433 per person. Florida and Utah had the lowest per capita costs at less than $2,000 per person.

Table US-17. Energy Production and Consumption, Selected Years 1975–2004

(Btu [British Thermal Unit], percent distribution, and dollars.)

Item	1975	1980	1985	1990	1995	2000	2001	2002	2003	2004
Energy Overview (Quadrillion Btu)										
Total energy production	61.4	67.2	67.6	70.8	71.2	71.3	71.9	70.8	70.0	70.2
Total energy imports	14.0	15.8	11.8	18.8	22.3	29.0	30.2	29.4	31.1	33.5
Total energy exports	2.3	3.7	4.2	4.8	4.5	4.0	3.8	3.7	4.1	4.4
Total energy adjustments	-1.1	-1.1	1.2	-0.1	2.3	2.7	-1.8	1.4	1.3	1.1
Consumption by Sector (Percent Distribution)										
Residential	20.6	20.2	20.8	20.0	20.5	20.7	21.0	21.3	21.5	21.1
Commercial	13.1	13.5	15.0	15.7	16.1	17.3	17.9	17.8	17.7	17.5
Industrial	40.9	41.1	37.9	37.7	37.2	35.0	33.9	33.4	33.2	33.4
Transportation	25.3	25.2	26.3	26.7	26.3	27.0	27.2	27.4	27.6	27.9
Consumption by Source (Quadrillion Btu)										
Total	72.0	78.3	76.5	84.7	91.2	99.0	96.5	97.9	98.3	100.4
Coal	12.7	15.4	17.5	19.2	20.1	22.6	21.9	21.9	22.3	22.5
Natural gas	19.9	20.4	17.8	19.7	22.8	23.9	22.9	23.6	23.1	23.1
Petroleum products	32.7	34.2	30.9	33.6	34.6	38.4	38.3	38.4	39.0	40.6
Nuclear electric power	1.9	2.7	4.1	6.1	7.1	7.9	8.0	8.1	8.0	8.2
Hydroelectric power	3.2	2.9	3.0	3.0	3.2	2.8	2.2	2.7	2.8	2.7
Biomass	1.5	2.5	2.9	2.7	3.1	2.9	2.6	2.6	2.7	2.9
Geothermal	0.1	0.1	0.2	0.3	0.3	0.3	0.3	0.3	0.3	0.3
Solar	. . .	. . .	0.0	0.1	0.1	0.1	0.1	0.1	0.1	0.1
Wind	. . .	. . .	0.0	0.0	0.0	0.1	0.1	0.1	0.1	0.1
Other	19.3	23.7	27.7	31.4	34.0	36.8	35.4	36.0	36.4	37.0
Consumption Per Dollar of Gross Domestic Product (GDP)										
GDP (billions of chained 2000 dollars)	4 311.2	5 161.7	6 053.7	7 112.5	8 031.7	9 817.0	9 890.7	10 048.8	10 320.6	10 755.7
Total consumption per dollar of GDP	16.7	15.2	12.6	11.9	11.4	10.1	9.8	9.7	9.5	9.3
Petroleum and natural gas consumption per dollar of GDP	12.2	10.6	8.1	7.5	7.1	6.4	6.2	6.2	6.0	5.9
Other energy consumption per dollar of GDP	4.5	4.6	4.6	4.4	4.2	3.8	3.6	3.6	3.5	3.4

. . . = Not available.

GOVERNMENT FINANCE

Since the 2001 recession and the subsequent recovery, state and local government budgets have used their rising revenues to increase expenditures on services. In many states, these had been put on hold by budget shortfalls that occured during the recession. The brighter state budget picture, together with increased funds from the federal government, provided states with stronger job growth and increased economic activity.

Table US-18. State Government Finances, 2003
(Dollars, percent distribution.)

Item	Millions of dollars	Percent distribution	Dollars per capita
TOTAL REVENUE	1 295 658 820	100.0	4 464.2
General Revenue	1 112 349 024	85.9	3 832.6
Intergovernmental revenue	361 617 049	27.9	1 246.0
Taxes	548 990 867	42.4	1 891.6
General sales	184 596 707	14.2	636.0
Selective sales	89 214 514	6.9	307.4
License taxes	35 863 173	2.8	123.6
Individual income tax	181 932 513	14.0	626.8
Corporate income tax	28 384 474	2.2	97.8
Other taxes	28 999 486	2.2	99.9
Current charges	106 356 917	8.2	366.5
Miscellaneous general revenue	95 384 191	7.4	328.6
Utility revenue	12 517 945	1.0	43.1
Liquor store revenue	4 517 992	0.3	15.6
Insurance trust revenue	166 273 859	12.8	572.9
TOTAL EXPENDITURE	1 359 048 379	100.0	4 682.6
Intergovernmental Expenditure	382 196 570	28.1	1 316.9
Direct expenditure	976 851 809	71.9	3 365.8
Current operation	656 989 385	48.3	2 263.7
Capital outlay	91 942 748	6.8	316.8
Insurance benefits and repayments	168 978 731	12.4	582.2
Assistance and subsidies	25 900 969	1.9	89.2
Interest on debt	33 039 976	2.4	113.8
General Expenditure	1 163 968 202	85.6	4 010.5
Intergovernmental expenditure	382 196 570	28.1	1 316.9
Direct expenditure	781 771 632	57.5	2 693.6
Expenditure by Function			
Education	411 093 625	30.2	1 416.4
Public welfare	314 406 504	23.1	1 083.3
Hospitals	38 394 884	2.8	132.3
Health	50 220 638	3.7	173.0
Highways	85 726 099	2.1	295.4
Police protection	11 144 395	7.8	38.4
Correction	39 187 839	7.0	135.0
Natural resources	18 576 793	100.0	64.0
Parks and recreation	5 843 656	28.1	20.1
Government administration	43 908 538	57.5	151.3
Interest on general debt	31 294 763	30.2	107.8
Other and unallocable	114 170 468	23.1	393.4
DEBT AT END OF FISCAL YEAR	697 929 028	X	2 404.7
CASH AND SECURITY HOLDINGS	2 594 215 994	X	8 938.4

X = Not applicable.

FEDERAL ROLE. State and local budgets are substantially augmented by federal government expenditures or obligations. Data from the Census Bureau's *Consolidated Federal Funds Report for Fiscal Year 2004, State and County Areas* (described in the notes and definitions), provide some salient features on grants and expenditures, wages and salaries (discussed in the labor market section), procurement contracts, direct payments to individuals largely transfer payments (discussed in the personal income section), other direct payments, and insurance payments (the latter two categories include disaster relief). The federal government's largest expenditures to states were transfer payments for Social Security retirement and disability, Medicare, and Medicaid. However, expenditures by the Department of Defense (DoD) and the Department of Homeland Security have risen sharply

since 2001. In fiscal year 2004, federal government grants by these two departments totaled over $8 billion. The DoD's purchases represented more than two-thirds of procurement expenditures. By far, the largest grant recipient from DoD was California, followed by Maryland, Pennsylvania, Florida, and Texas. For homeland security, the largest grant recipients were New York, Texas, Louisiana, Oklahoma, and Alabama. For procurement from the DoD, California, Texas, Virginia, Florida, and Maryland were the top states.

STATE EXPENDITURES AND REVENUES. In fiscal year 2003, total state spending amounted to over $1,359 billion. Total state revenue was nearly $1,296 billion, causing states in aggregate to run budget deficits. The largest expenditure item was education, which accounted for about 30 percent of spending. About one-third of state spending was transferred to localities, a significant revenue-sharing process developed that strengthened local government budgets. Localities, in turn, spent a large proportion of their funds on elementary and secondary education, public safety, and health care. State general revenues were generated by taxes and federal transfers. Of the taxes, sales and individual income taxes were the most important. Total taxes per capita in fiscal year 2004 were the highest in Hawaii, Wyoming, Connecticut, Minnesota, and Delaware, and the lowest in Texas, South Dakota, Colorado, New Hampshire, and Alabama. However, these total tax per capita data conceal a wide variety of revenue sources among states. Some states, such as Connecticut, relied on the collection of individual income taxes, while others, including Hawaii, raised more revenue from sales taxes, a substantial portion of which were paid by nonresident visiting tourists. Wyoming increased its revenue per person through severance taxes, which were imposed on the removal of natural resources such as gas, coal, other minerals, and timber.

Table US-19. State Taxes, Fiscal 2004
(Dollars, percent distribution.)

Item	Thousands of dollars	Percent distribution	Dollars per capita
TOTAL TAXES	593 488 853	100.0	2 024.8
Property Taxes	11 410 018	1.9	38.9
Sales and Gross Receipts	294 104 344	49.6	1 003.4
General sales and gross receipts	198 431 303	33.4	677.0
Selective sales taxes	95 673 041	16.1	326.4
Alcoholic beverages	4 614 804	0.8	15.7
Amusements	4 990 713	0.8	17.0
Insurance premiums	13 775 340	2.3	47.0
Motor fuels	33 605 402	5.7	114.6
Public utilities	11 482 059	1.9	39.2
Tobacco products	12 300 310	2.1	42.0
Other selective sales	14 602 534	2.5	49.8
Licenses	39 541 021	6.7	134.9
Corporation	6 339 370	1.1	21.6
Motor vehicle	17 412 024	2.9	59.4
Occupation and business, not elsewhere classified	10 881 425	1.8	37.1
Other Taxes	248 433 470	41.9	847.6
Individual income	197 421 360	33.3	673.6
Corporation net income	30 801 302	5.2	105.1
Death and gift	5 734 958	1.0	19.6
Documentary and stock transfer	7 943 598	1.3	27.1
Severance	6 304 829	1.1	21.5

EDUCATION

Data on the proportion of the population age 25 years and over who have received high school diplomas or bachelor's degrees provide general education indicators. However, these data do not measure the quality of the education received. There are many quality measures, but few can be agreed upon by the whole of the educational community. However, information on per student expenditures and teachers' salaries provides some, albeit incomplete, measures of the educational efforts being undertaken. Missing from these data are information on the quantity and quality of school construction and the condition of school facilities, including libraries. It is beyond the scope of this publication to present information on the type of studies undertaken to determine the quality of education in the United States. In light of trends that are expected to influence the skills of the future workforce and international competitiveness, it is important to note that recent data show that degrees related to technology, mathematics, and sciences, as a proportion of all degrees, seem to be lagging behind earlier groups of students and behind major competitors elsewhere in the world. On the positive side, the latest information from the U.S. National Center for Education Statistics (NCES) shows that, in 2003, 93 percent of all public elementary and secondary school classrooms had access to the Internet, with most utilizing high-speed access.

EDUCATIONAL ATTAINMENT. The percentage of the population that completed high school and college refers to the entire population age 25 years and over and includes older persons who, on average, had less education than younger generations. In 2004, 85.2 percent of the population had completed high school and 27.7 percent were college graduates. Not surprisingly, the younger members of this age spectrum (age 25–29 years) were more highly educated than their elders. As a result, the educational attainment level of the U.S. population has increased steadily in recent years. As recently as 1995, only 81 percent of the population had graduated from high school and 23 percent had graduated from college. Blacks narrowed the achievement gap with their White counterparts over this period, although a large disparity still remains; Hispanics made smaller gains in educational attainment.

All states saw large gains in their high school graduation rates. In 2004, Minnesota led the nation in this category, followed closely by Montana, Wyoming, Nebraska, and Utah. Texas, Louisiana, Arkansas, and West Virginia had the lowest rates of high school attainment. In the case of West Virginia, this may be partly due to its large proportion of residents age 65 years and over. Educational attainment levels in Texas reflected its large immigrant population, much of which came from countries with fewer educational opportunities. States with high rates of high school graduates did not necessarily have high rates of college graduates. The District of Columbia had the highest rate of college graduates, reflecting its urbanized population and its high level of professional employment opportunities in government and in the private sector. The city was followed by Massachusetts, Colorado, and New Hampshire. The lowest college attainment rates were found in West Virginia, Arkansas, and Mississippi.

ELEMENTARY AND SECONDARY EDUCATION. Reflecting the fact that all states require children to attend school from age 6 to 16 years, enrollment rates were over 90 percent for those age 5–17 years (grades K–12). Most were enrolled in public schools—only 10 percent attended private (fee-paying) schools. Only Delaware, the District of Columbia, Pennsylvania, and Louisiana had private school enrollment rates of more than 15 percent. According to the NCES, the average number of students per teacher was 15.9 in public K–12 schools, a figure that has edged up in recent years. Utah, Arizona, California, and Oregon had the highest ratios; Vermont, Maine, Alabama, and New Jersey had the lowest. It should be noted, however, that the student/teacher ratio does not measure average class size, which is the number of students assigned to a classroom for instructional purposes. The student/teacher ratio reflects other factors, such as changes in enrollments, teacher remuneration, and public policies and program priorities. The average public school teacher salary for 2003–2004 was $46,752. Average salaries ranged from $57,337 in Connecticut and $57,009 in the District of Columbia to $33,236 in South Dakota and $35,061 in Oklahoma. In general, relatively low salaries were found in the Plains, Southeast, and Southwest regions, perhaps reflecting lower costs of living in these areas. Total expenditures per student tended to parallel the salary rankings. However, when looking at the proportion of the school operating budget spent on classroom teaching, as opposed to expenditures on administration and support services, Maine and New York ranked highest, with states such as Utah, Nebraska, Minnesota, Georgia, Tennessee, and North Carolina coming in at well above the national average of 61.3 percent. New Mexico, Colorado, South Dakota, Oklahoma, Michigan, and Ohio were well below the national average, according to statistics from the NCES.

HIGHER EDUCATION. Information on higher education enrollments includes 2- and 4-year institutions, as well as technical and professional schools. Total enrollment in 2002, the latest year for which data are available, was 16.6 million. Just under 40 percent of those enrolled attended 2-year schools, and 60 percent of these 2-year institutions were public schools. For all higher education institutions, about 60 percent of students attended full-time. The number of part-time enrollees has risen significantly in recent years, perhaps reflecting the sharp increase in tuition costs and the subsequent need to work while attending college.

Table US-20. Education Indicators, 2000–2004

(Percent, number.)

Item	U.S.
Total Population 25 Years and Over (Thousands), 2004	186 877
Educational Attainment, 2004	
Percent high school graduate or more	85.2
Percent college graduate or more	27.7
Elementary and Secondary Schools, 2002–2003	
Total students	48 202 324
Percent of students eligible for free or reduced-price lunch	40.6
Percent of students who were English language learners	7.8
Total schools	92 330
Student/teacher ratio	15.9
Per student expenditures	8 041
Higher Education, 2002–2003	
Total enrollment	17 035 027
Bachelor's degrees awarded	1 348 503
Percent women	57.5

VOTER PARTICIPATION

The percentage of eligible voters who participated in nationwide elections in the United States was relatively low compared to other industrialized democracies. In the presidential election years of 2000 and 2004, 54.7 percent and 58.3 percent of eligible voters, respectively, reported voting, as compared with over 61 percent in 1992. The highest rates of voter participation were among those age 65 years and over in both elections, with 67.6 percent and 68.9 percent of this age group casting votes in 2000 and 2004, respectively. Despite an increase in the proportion of voters from the 2000 to the 2004 election, young people age 18 to 24 years had substantially lower voter turnout. In non-presidential election years, voter partici-pation fell off significantly among all age groups, although less so among elderly voters age 65 years and over. Voter participation rates rose with educational attainment levels, with those holding college degrees having the highest rates. More women than men tended to vote, as did higher proportions of Whites than Blacks. Hispanics had very low participation rates. Regionally, the Midwest led the country in turnout in both 2000 and 2004, as well as for the mid-term elections, followed by the Northeast and South. Perhaps because of the time zone difference, the West lagged behind the rest of country. State comparisons appear in the ranking tables.

Table US-21. Reported Voting and Registration, November 2000 and November 2004

(Numbers in thousands, percent.)

Characteristic	Total population 18 years and over	Total citizen		Total registered		Total voted	
		Number	Percent	Number	Percent	Number	Percent
NOVEMBER 2000							
Total	202 609	186 366	92.0	129 549	63.9	110 826	54.7
Male	97 087	88 758	91.4	60 356	62.2	51 542	53.1
Female	105 523	97 608	92.5	69 193	65.6	59 284	56.2
NOVEMBER 2004							
Total	215 694	197 005	91.3	142 070	65.9	125 736	58.3
Male	103 812	94 147	90.7	66 406	64.0	58 455	56.3
Female	111 882	102 858	91.9	75 663	67.6	67 281	60.1
Race and Hispanic Origin							
White alone	176 618	162 958	92.3	119 929	67.9	106 588	60.3
Non-Hispanic White alone	151 410	148 159	97.9	111 318	73.5	99 567	65.8
Black alone	24 910	23 346	93.7	16 035	64.4	14 016	56.3
Asian alone	9 291	6 270	67.5	3 247	35.0	2 768	29.8
Hispanic or Latino[1]	27 129	16 088	59.3	9 308	34.3	7 587	28.0
White alone or in combination	179 050	165 244	92.3	121 527	67.9	107 930	60.3
Non-Hispanic White alone or in combination	153 399	150 128	97.9	112 703	73.5	100 726	65.7
Black alone or in combination	25 510	23 908	93.7	16 408	64.3	14 324	56.1
Asian alone or in combination	9 721	6 686	68.8	3 508	36.1	2 980	30.7
Age							
18 to 24 years	27 808	24 899	89.5	14 334	51.5	11 639	41.9
25 to 44 years	82 133	71 231	86.7	49 371	60.1	42 845	52.2
45 to 64 years	71 014	67 184	94.6	51 659	72.7	47 327	66.6
65 to 74 years	18 363	17 759	96.7	14 125	76.9	13 010	70.8
75 years and over	16 375	15 933	97.3	12 581	76.8	10 915	66.7

[1]May be of any race.

DEVELOPMENTS IN 2005—THE IMPACT OF THE HURRICANES

All of the data published in this book were compiled before Hurricanes Katrina and Rita hit the Gulf Coast areas of Louisiana, Mississippi, and Alabama, and before Hurricane Wilma struck Florida. While there are no definitive estimates of the number of evacuees from these states, or of the number that have since returned, the population that has left is clearly significant. According to government estimates, job losses have been widespread, unemployment is about three times the national average in the most adversely affected regions, and personal income growth has been sluggish in the states most severely impacted by the storms. Broader effects on the nation's economy have been felt in terms of rising energy prices. According to the Federal Reserve Bank of Atlanta, nearly 40 percent of normal natural gas and 50 percent of oil production remained off-line through mid-November 2005. While gasoline prices eased following the late summer spike, as more refineries went back on-line, natural gas prices remained high and were adversely impacting home heating bills across the country. Tourism, an important economic sector in these states, will likely be subdued in current months (which are customarily the height of their tourist season). On the other side of the coin, demand for new construction and for skilled workers and basic materials in the Gulf region has been considerable, and shortages have been reported as efforts turn from demolition and clean-up to rebuilding.

POPULATION ESTIMATES 2005

In late December 2005, the Census Bureau released its population estimates as of July 2005. The demographic details will not be available until later in 2006, after the release of this publication, but it is worth noting that only four of the state rankings for population size have changed. Arizona became the 17th largest state, after ranking 18th in 2004; Indiana became 15th in size, after being 14th in 2004; Washington replaced Indiana as the 14th largest state; and Missouri became the 18th largest state after ranking 17th in 2004.

In general, these data show that for the last 19 years, Nevada was the fastest-growing state in the country. In 2005, the state's rate of growth was followed by those of Arizona, Idaho, and Florida.

The South and the West (Census regions) again monopolized the list of the fastest-growing states in percentage terms: Idaho, Florida, Utah, Georgia, Texas, North Carolina, Delaware, and Oregon rounded out the top 10 fastest-growing states.

The South now accounts for 36.3 percent of the nation's population, with the West making up 23.0 percent, the Midwest 22.3 percent, and the Northeast 18.4 percent.

Florida experienced the largest numerical population growth between 2004 and 2005, followed by Texas, California, Arizona, and Georgia. These states accounted for more than half the nation's population growth between 2004–2005.

Other highlights:
- The South recorded both the largest numerical increase and the fastest growth rates among the Census regions between 2004–2005.
- The nation's most populous ten states, California, Texas, New York, Florida, Illinois, Pennsylvania, Ohio, Michigan, Georgia, and New Jersey, accounted for 54 percent of the population in 2005.

RANKINGS: POPULATION, LAND, AND POPULATION DENSITY

Population, 2004		Total Land Area, 2000		Population Density, 2004	
State and rank	Population	State and rank	Land area (square kilometers)	State and rank	Density (per square kilometer)
United States	293 655 404	**United States**	9 161 924	**United States**	32.1
1. California	35 893 799	1. Alaska	1 481 347	1. District of Columbia	3 481.3
2. Texas	22 490 022	2. Texas	678 051	2. New Jersey	452.8
3. New York	19 227 088	3. California	403 933	3. Rhode Island	399.3
4. Florida	17 397 161	4. Montana	376 979	4. Massachusetts	316.0
5. Illinois	12 713 634	5. New Mexico	314 309	5. Connecticut	279.2
6. Pennsylvania	12 406 292	6. Arizona	294 312	6. Maryland	219.6
7. Ohio	11 459 011	7. Nevada	284 448	7. Delaware	164.1
8. Michigan	10 112 620	8. Colorado	268 627	8. New York	157.2
9. New Jersey	8 829 383	9. Wyoming	251 489	9. Florida	124.6
10. Georgia	8 698 879	10. Oregon	248 631	10. Ohio	108.0
11. North Carolina	8 541 221	11. Idaho	214 314	11. Pennsylvania	106.9
12. Virginia	7 459 827	12. Utah	212 751	12. California	88.9
13. Massachusetts	6 416 505	13. Kansas	211 900	13. Illinois	88.3
14. Indiana	6 237 569	14. Minnesota	206 189	14. Hawaii	75.9
15. Washington	6 203 788	15. Nebraska	199 099	15. Virginia	72.7
16. Tennessee	5 900 962	16. South Dakota	196 540	16. Michigan	68.7
17. Missouri	5 754 618	17. North Dakota	178 647	17. North Carolina	67.7
18. Wisconsin	5 743 834	18. Missouri	178 414	18. Indiana	67.1
19. Maryland	5 558 058	19. Oklahoma	177 847	19. Georgia	58.9
20. Arizona	5 509 026	20. Washington	172 348	20. New Hampshire	55.9
21. Minnesota	5 100 958	21. Georgia	149 976	21. Tennessee	55.3
22. Louisiana	4 601 403	22. Michigan	147 121	22. South Carolina	53.8
23. Alabama	4 530 182	23. Iowa	144 701	23. Kentucky	40.3
24. Colorado	4 515 770	24. Illinois	143 961	24. Louisiana	40.0
25. Kentucky	4 198 068	25. Wisconsin	140 663	25. Wisconsin	39.2
26. South Carolina	4 145 922	26. Florida	139 670	26. Washington	36.0
27. Oklahoma	3 594 586	27. Arkansas	134 856	27. Alabama	34.5
28. Oregon	3 523 553	28. Alabama	131 426	28. Texas	33.2
29. Connecticut	3 503 604	29. North Carolina	126 161	29. Missouri	32.3
30. Iowa	2 954 451	30. New York	122 283	30. West Virginia	29.1
31. Mississippi	2 902 966	31. Mississippi	121 488	31. Vermont	25.9
32. Kansas	2 752 629	32. Pennsylvania	116 074	32. Minnesota	24.7
33. Arkansas	2 735 502	33. Louisiana	112 825	33. Mississippi	23.9
34. Utah	2 389 039	34. Tennessee	106 752	34. Arkansas	20.4
35. Nevada	2 334 771	35. Ohio	106 056	34. Iowa	20.4
36. New Mexico	1 903 289	36. Kentucky	102 896	36. Oklahoma	19.8
37. West Virginia	1 815 354	37. Virginia	102 548	37. Arizona	19.5
38. Nebraska	1 747 214	38. Indiana	92 895	38. Colorado	17.1
39. Idaho	1 393 262	39. Maine	79 931	39. Maine	16.5
40. Maine	1 317 253	40. South Carolina	77 983	40. Oregon	14.5
41. New Hampshire	1 299 500	41. West Virginia	62 361	41. Kansas	12.9
42. Hawaii	1 262 840	42. Maryland	25 314	42. Utah	11.2
43. Rhode Island	1 080 632	43. Vermont	23 956	43. Nebraska	8.8
44. Montana	926 865	44. New Hampshire	23 227	44. Nevada	8.2
45. Delaware	830 364	45. Massachusetts	20 306	45. Idaho	6.5
46. South Dakota	770 883	46. New Jersey	19 211	46. New Mexico	6.1
47. North Dakota	655 435	47. Hawaii	16 635	47. South Dakota	3.9
48. Alaska	634 366	48. Connecticut	12 548	48. North Dakota	3.6
49. Vermont	621 394	49. Delaware	5 060	49. Montana	2.5
50. District of Columbia	553 523	50. Rhode Island	2 706	50. Wyoming	2.0
51. Wyoming	506 529	51. District of Columbia	159	51. Alaska	0.4

RANKINGS: POPULATION CHANGE AND AGE

Percent Population Change, 2000–2004		Percent Under 18 Years Old, 2004		Percent Over 65 Years Old, 2004	
State and rank	Percent change	State and rank	Percent under 18 years old	State and rank	Percent over 65 years old
United States	4.3	**United States**	25.0	**United States**	12.4
1. Nevada	16.8	1. Utah	31.0	1. Florida	16.8
2. Arizona	12.0	2. Alaska	28.7	2. Pennsylvania	15.3
3. Florida	8.9	3. Texas	27.9	2. West Virginia	15.3
4. Texas	7.9	4. Arizona	26.9	4. Iowa	14.7
4. Georgia	7.9	5. California	26.7	4. North Dakota	14.7
6. Idaho	7.7	5. Idaho	26.7	6. Maine	14.4
7. Utah	7.0	7. Georgia	26.4	7. South Dakota	14.2
7. Colorado	7.0	8. Nevada	25.9	8. Rhode Island	13.9
9. North Carolina	6.1	8. New Mexico	25.9	9. Arkansas	13.8
10. California	6.0	10. Louisiana	25.8	10. Montana	13.7
10. Delaware	6.0	10. Mississippi	25.8	11. Hawaii	13.6
12. Virginia	5.4	12. Indiana	25.7	12. Connecticut	13.5
13. Washington	5.3	13. Colorado	25.6	13. Massachusetts	13.3
14. New Hampshire	5.2	14. Illinois	25.5	13. Missouri	13.3
15. Oregon	5.1	15. Maryland	25.1	13. Nebraska	13.3
16. Maryland	4.9	15. Michigan	25.1	13. Ohio	13.3
17. South Carolina	4.6	17. Kansas	25.0	17. Alabama	13.2
17. New Mexico	4.6	18. Nebraska	24.9	17. Oklahoma	13.2
19. Alaska	4.5	19. New Jersey	24.8	19. Delaware	13.1
20. Hawaii	4.2	19. North Carolina	24.8	20. Kansas	13.0
21. Tennessee	3.7	19. South Dakota	24.8	20. New York	13.0
21. Minnesota	3.7	22. Arkansas	24.6	20. Vermont	13.0
23. New Jersey	3.4	23. Oklahoma	24.4	20. Wisconsin	13.0
24. Maine	3.3	23. South Carolina	24.4	24. New Jersey	12.9
25. Rhode Island	3.1	25. Minnesota	24.3	25. Oregon	12.8
26. Arkansas	3.0	25. Ohio	24.3	26. Arizona	12.7
27. Connecticut	2.9	27. Alabama	24.2	27. Kentucky	12.5
28. Missouri	2.8	27. Virginia	24.2	27. Tennessee	12.5
29. Montana	2.7	29. Missouri	24.1	29. Indiana	12.4
29. Wisconsin	2.7	30. Washington	24.0	29. South Carolina	12.4
31. Indiana	2.6	31. Connecticut	23.9	31. Michigan	12.3
31. Wyoming	2.6	32. New York	23.8	32. Mississippi	12.2
31. Kentucky	2.6	33. Hawaii	23.7	33. District of Columbia	12.1
34. Illinois	2.4	33. Oregon	23.7	33. Minnesota	12.1
35. South Dakota	2.1	33. Wisconsin	23.7	33. New Hampshire	12.1
35. Oklahoma	2.1	36. Kentucky	23.6	33. New Mexico	12.1
35. Nebraska	2.1	36. Tennessee	23.6	33. North Carolina	12.1
35. Vermont	2.1	38. New Hampshire	23.5	33. Wyoming	12.1
39. Mississippi	2.0	39. Delaware	23.3	39. Illinois	12.0
40. Alabama	1.9	40. Wyoming	23.1	40. Louisiana	11.7
41. Michigan	1.8	41. Florida	23.0	41. Idaho	11.4
41. Kansas	1.8	41. Iowa	23.0	41. Maryland	11.4
43. New York	1.3	43. Pennsylvania	22.9	41. Virginia	11.4
44. Massachusetts	1.1	44. Massachusetts	22.8	44. Washington	11.3
45. Louisiana	1.0	45. Rhode Island	22.6	45. Nevada	11.2
45. Pennsylvania	1.0	46. Montana	22.5	46. California	10.7
45. Iowa	1.0	47. North Dakota	21.9	47. Texas	9.9
48. Ohio	0.9	48. Vermont	21.7	48. Colorado	9.8
49. West Virginia	0.4	49. Maine	21.4	49. Georgia	9.6
50. North Dakota	-1.2	50. West Virginia	21.2	50. Utah	8.7
51. District of Columbia	-3.2	51. District of Columbia	19.8	51. Alaska	6.4

RANKINGS: RACE AND ETHNICITY

Percent Non-Hispanic White Alone, 2004		Percent Non-Hispanic Black Alone, 2004		Percent American Indian, Alaska Native Alone, 2004	
State and rank	Percent non-Hispanic White alone	State and rank	Percent non-Hispanic Black alone	State and rank	Percent American Indian, Alaska Native alone
United States	67.4	**United States**	12.2	**United States**	0.8
1. Maine	96.1	1. District of Columbia	56.7	1. Alaska	15.5
2. Vermont	96.0	2. Mississippi	36.6	2. New Mexico	9.2
3. West Virginia	94.4	3. Louisiana	32.8	3. South Dakota	8.5
4. New Hampshire	94.3	4. Georgia	29.2	4. Oklahoma	7.8
5. Iowa	91.7	5. South Carolina	29.1	5. Montana	6.2
6. North Dakota	91.1	6. Maryland	28.6	6. North Dakota	5.1
7. Montana	89.1	7. Alabama	26.2	7. Arizona	4.5
8. Kentucky	88.7	8. North Carolina	21.5	8. Wyoming	2.2
9. Wyoming	88.6	9. Delaware	19.9	9. Washington	1.5
10. Idaho	87.2	10. Virginia	19.5	10. Idaho	1.2
11. South Dakota	87.1	11. Tennessee	16.7	10. North Carolina	1.2
12. Minnesota	86.7	12. Arkansas	15.6	10. Utah	1.2
13. Wisconsin	86.2	13. New York	15.1	13. Minnesota	1.1
14. Nebraska	85.7	14. Florida	14.9	13. Oregon	1.1
15. Indiana	84.6	15. Illinois	14.8	15. Nevada	1.0
16. Utah	83.8	16. Michigan	14.2	16. Wisconsin	0.9
17. Ohio	83.3	17. New Jersey	13.3	17. Kansas	0.8
18. Missouri	83.1	18. Ohio	11.7	17. Nebraska	0.8
19. Pennsylvania	82.9	19. Missouri	11.4	19. Colorado	0.7
20. Oregon	82.0	20. Texas	11.3	20. Arkansas	0.6
21. Kansas	81.9	21. Pennsylvania	10.1	20. Louisiana	0.6
22. Massachusetts	80.8	22. Connecticut	9.1	20. Maine	0.6
23. Rhode Island	80.5	23. Indiana	8.6	23. Alabama	0.5
24. Michigan	78.1	24. Oklahoma	7.5	23. California	0.5
24. Tennessee	78.1	25. Kentucky	7.4	23. Michigan	0.5
26. Washington	77.5	26. Nevada	7.0	26. Mississippi	0.4
27. Arkansas	77.2	27. California	6.3	26. Missouri	0.4
28. Connecticut	75.9	28. Wisconsin	5.8	26. Rhode Island	0.4
29. Oklahoma	72.9	29. Kansas	5.7	26. Vermont	0.4
30. Colorado	72.5	29. Massachusetts	5.7	30. Delaware	0.3
31. Delaware	70.2	31. Rhode Island	4.8	30. Florida	0.3
32. Alabama	69.5	32. Nebraska	4.1	30. Iowa	0.3
33. Virginia	68.7	33. Minnesota	4.0	30. Maryland	0.3
34. North Carolina	68.6	34. Colorado	3.7	30. New York	0.3
35. Alaska	66.9	35. Alaska	3.4	30. South Carolina	0.3
36. Illinois	66.2	36. Washington	3.3	30. Texas	0.3
37. South Carolina	65.6	37. West Virginia	3.2	30. Virginia	0.3
38. New Jersey	63.8	38. Arizona	3.1	38. Connecticut	0.2
39. Florida	62.8	39. Iowa	2.2	38. District of Columbia	0.2
40. Louisiana	61.8	40. Hawaii	2.0	38. Georgia	0.2
41. Nevada	61.2	41. New Mexico	1.8	38. Hawaii	0.2
42. Arizona	61.1	42. Oregon	1.6	38. Illinois	0.2
42. New York	61.1	43. New Hampshire	0.8	38. Indiana	0.2
44. Georgia	60.2	43. Utah	0.8	38. Kentucky	0.2
45. Mississippi	59.9	43. Wyoming	0.8	38. Massachusetts	0.2
46. Maryland	59.8	46. Maine	0.7	38. New Hampshire	0.2
47. Texas	49.8	46. North Dakota	0.7	38. Ohio	0.2
48. California	44.5	46. South Dakota	0.7	38. Tennessee	0.2
49. New Mexico	43.5	49. Vermont	0.6	38. West Virginia	0.2
50. District of Columbia	30.3	50. Idaho	0.4	50. New Jersey	0.1
51. Hawaii	23.3	51. Montana	0.3	50. Pennsylvania	0.1

RANKINGS: RACE ETHNICITY, AND INCOME

Percent Asian and Pacific Islander Alone, 2004		Percent Hispanic or Latino,[1] 2004		Median Household Income, 2004	
State and rank	Percent Asian and Pacific Islander alone	State and rank	Percent Hispanic or Latino[1]	State and rank	Dollars
United States	4.2	**United States**	14.1	**United States**	44 684
1. Hawaii	49.4	1. New Mexico	43.3	1. New Jersey	61 359
2. California	12.1	2. California	34.7	2. Connecticut	60 528
3. New Jersey	6.9	3. Texas	34.6	3. Maryland	57 424
4. Washington	6.6	4. Arizona	28.0	4. Alaska	57 027
5. New York	6.4	5. Nevada	22.8	5. Massachusetts	55 658
6. Nevada	5.8	6. Colorado	19.1	6. New Hampshire	55 580
7. Alaska	5.0	7. Florida	19.0	7. Hawaii	53 554
8. Maryland	4.6	8. New York	16.0	8. Virginia	51 689
8. Massachusetts	4.6	9. New Jersey	14.9	9. California	51 185
10. Virginia	4.4	10. Illinois	14.0	10. Minnesota	50 860
11. Illinois	3.9	11. Connecticut	10.6	11. Delaware	50 315
12. Oregon	3.6	11. Utah	10.6	12. Illinois	48 953
13. Minnesota	3.4	13. Rhode Island	10.3	13. Rhode Island	48 722
14. Texas	3.2	14. Oregon	9.5	14. Colorado	48 198
15. Connecticut	3.1	15. Idaho	8.9	15. Washington	47 659
16. District of Columbia	3.0	16. District of Columbia	8.5	16. New York	47 349
17. Rhode Island	2.7	16. Washington	8.5	17. Utah	47 074
18. Delaware	2.6	18. Kansas	8.1	18. District of Columbia	46 574
18. Georgia	2.6	19. Hawaii	7.9	19. Vermont	46 543
20. Colorado	2.5	20. Massachusetts	7.7	20. Wisconsin	45 315
20. Utah	2.5	21. Nebraska	6.9	21. Michigan	44 905
22. Michigan	2.2	22. Georgia	6.8	22. Nevada	44 646
22. Pennsylvania	2.2	23. Wyoming	6.7	23. Wyoming	44 275
24. Arizona	2.1	24. Oklahoma	6.3	24. Georgia	43 037
24. Kansas	2.1	25. North Carolina	6.1	25. Pennsylvania	42 941
26. Florida	2.0	26. Delaware	5.8	26. Ohio	42 240
27. Wisconsin	1.9	27. Virginia	5.7	27. Indiana	42 195
28. New Hampshire	1.7	28. Maryland	5.4	28. Maine	42 163
28. North Carolina	1.7	29. Alaska	4.9	29. Arizona	41 995
30. Oklahoma	1.6	30. Arkansas	4.4	30. Oregon	41 794
31. Nebraska	1.5	31. Indiana	4.3	31. Texas	41 759
32. Iowa	1.4	31. Wisconsin	4.3	32. Nebraska	41 657
32. Louisiana	1.4	33. Pennsylvania	3.8	33. Kansas	41 638
32. Ohio	1.4	34. Michigan	3.7	34. Missouri	41 473
35. Missouri	1.3	35. Iowa	3.5	35. Iowa	41 350
36. Indiana	1.2	35. Minnesota	3.5	36. Florida	41 236
36. New Mexico	1.2	37. South Carolina	3.1	37. Idaho	39 934
36. Tennessee	1.2	38. Louisiana	2.8	38. South Carolina	39 837
39. Idaho	1.1	38. Tennessee	2.8	39. North Dakota	39 447
39. South Carolina	1.1	40. Missouri	2.6	40. North Carolina	39 428
41. Arkansas	1.0	41. Montana	2.4	41. Tennessee	38 794
41. Vermont	1.0	42. Alabama	2.2	42. South Dakota	38 472
43. Kentucky	0.9	42. Ohio	2.2	43. Alabama	36 709
44. Alabama	0.8	44. New Hampshire	2.1	44. New Mexico	36 043
44. Maine	0.8	45. South Dakota	2.0	45. Oklahoma	35 357
46. Mississippi	0.7	46. Kentucky	1.9	46. Kentucky	35 269
46. North Dakota	0.7	47. Mississippi	1.7	47. Montana	35 239
46. South Dakota	0.7	48. North Dakota	1.5	48. Louisiana	35 110
46. Wyoming	0.7	49. Vermont	1.0	49. Arkansas	32 983
50. Montana	0.6	50. Maine	0.9	50. Mississippi	31 642
50. West Virginia	0.6	51. West Virginia	0.8	51. West Virginia	31 504

[1]May be of any race.

RANKINGS: HEALTH

Birth Rate, 2003		Infant Mortality Rates, Average 2000–2002		Population Lacking Health Insurance, 2004	
State and rank	Birth rate (per 1,000 population)	State and rank	Infant deaths (per 1,000 live births)	State and rank	Percent of population
United States	14.1	**United States**	6.9	**United States**	15.7
1. Utah	21.2	1. District of Columbia	11.4	1. Texas	25.0
2. Texas	17.1	2. Mississippi	10.5	2. New Mexico	21.0
3. Arizona	16.3	3. Louisiana	9.8	3. Florida	19.9
4. Idaho	16.0	4. Delaware	9.6	3. Oklahoma	19.9
5. Georgia	15.7	5. Alabama	9.3	5. Montana	19.1
6. Alaska	15.5	6. South Carolina	9.0	6. California	18.7
7. California	15.2	6. Tennessee	9.0	7. Nevada	18.5
7. Colorado	15.2	8. Georgia	8.7	8. Georgia	17.4
9. Nevada	15.0	9. North Carolina	8.4	9. Louisiana	17.2
10. Nebraska	14.9	10. Arkansas	8.3	10. Arizona	17.1
11. New Mexico	14.8	11. Michigan	8.1	10. Mississippi	17.1
12. Mississippi	14.7	12. Oklahoma	8.0	12. Alaska	17.0
13. Kansas	14.5	13. West Virginia	7.9	12. Colorado	17.0
13. Louisiana	14.5	14. Illinois	7.8	14. Oregon	16.5
13. Oklahoma	14.5	14. North Dakota	7.8	15. Arkansas	16.4
16. Hawaii	14.4	16. Indiana	7.7	15. West Virginia	16.4
16. Illinois	14.4	16. Maryland	7.7	17. North Carolina	15.7
16. South Dakota	14.4	16. Missouri	7.7	18. Idaho	15.4
19. North Carolina	14.1	16. Ohio	7.7	19. New Jersey	15.3
20. Indiana	14.0	20. Pennsylvania	7.3	20. South Carolina	14.7
21. Arkansas	13.9	21. Florida	7.2	21. Maryland	14.6
21. Delaware	13.9	21. Hawaii	7.2	22. Delaware	14.5
23. Minnesota	13.8	21. Virginia	7.2	23. Virginia	14.4
24. Virginia	13.7	24. Kansas	7.0	24. Kentucky	14.3
25. Maryland	13.6	24. Nebraska	7.0	25. Indiana	14.2
26. District of Columbia	13.5	26. Montana	6.9	25. New York	14.2
26. Missouri	13.5	26. Wisconsin	6.9	27. Tennessee	14.1
26. New Jersey	13.5	28. Alaska	6.8	27. Utah	14.1
26. Tennessee	13.5	29. Arizona	6.7	29. Illinois	14.0
30. Kentucky	13.4	29. Kentucky	6.7	29. Wyoming	14.0
30. South Carolina	13.4	29. Rhode Island	6.7	31. Alabama	13.5
30. Wyoming	13.4	32. Idaho	6.6	32. District of Columbia	13.3
33. Alabama	13.2	33. Wyoming	6.5	33. Washington	13.0
33. New York	13.2	34. Connecticut	6.4	34. Missouri	12.6
35. Ohio	13.1	34. New Mexico	6.4	35. South Dakota	12.0
35. Washington	13.1	34. South Dakota	6.4	36. Pennsylvania	11.9
37. Iowa	13.0	37. New Jersey	6.1	37. Massachusetts	11.7
37. Michigan	13.0	37. New York	6.1	37. New Hampshire	11.7
39. Oregon	12.9	39. Colorado	6.0	39. Connecticut	11.6
40. Wisconsin	12.8	39. Nevada	6.0	39. Michigan	11.6
41. North Dakota	12.6	41. Texas	5.9	41. Nebraska	11.4
42. Florida	12.5	42. Iowa	5.8	41. Ohio	11.4
42. Massachusetts	12.5	43. Minnesota	5.5	41. Rhode Island	11.4
44. Montana	12.4	43. Oregon	5.5	44. North Dakota	11.2
45. Connecticut	12.3	43. Vermont	5.5	44. Vermont	11.2
45. Rhode Island	12.3	43. Washington	5.5	46. Kansas	11.1
47. Pennsylvania	11.8	47. California	5.4	47. Wisconsin	10.4
48. West Virginia	11.6	48. Utah	5.3	48. Maine	10.0
49. New Hampshire	11.2	49. Maine	5.1	49. Hawaii	9.6
50. Maine	10.6	50. New Hampshire	4.9	50. Iowa	9.5
50. Vermont	10.6	51. Massachusetts	4.8	51. Minnesota	8.9

RANKINGS: EMPLOYMENT AND POVERTY

Employment Growth, 2001–2004		Unemployment Rate, 2004		Poverty Rate, 2004	
State and rank	Percent change	State and rank	Percent unemployed	State and rank	Percent below the poverty level
United States	1.8	**United States**	5.5	**United States**	13.1
1. Nevada	11.0	1. District of Columbia	8.2	1. Mississippi	21.6
2. Alaska	6.6	2. Alaska	7.5	2. Louisiana	19.4
2. Arizona	6.6	3. Oregon	7.4	3. New Mexico	19.3
4. Florida	6.4	4. Michigan	7.1	4. District of Columbia	18.9
5. New Mexico	6.2	5. South Carolina	6.8	5. Arkansas	17.9
6. Hawaii	5.4	6. California	6.2	5. West Virginia	17.9
6. Montana	5.4	6. Illinois	6.2	7. Kentucky	17.4
8. Wyoming	5.0	6. Mississippi	6.2	8. Texas	16.6
9. Idaho	4.9	6. Washington	6.2	9. Alabama	16.1
10. Maryland	3.7	10. Ohio	6.1	10. South Carolina	15.7
10. Utah	3.7	10. Texas	6.1	11. Oklahoma	15.3
12. Virginia	3.5	12. New York	5.8	12. North Carolina	15.2
13. North Dakota	3.3	13. Arkansas	5.7	13. Georgia	14.8
14. District of Columbia	3.0	13. Louisiana	5.7	14. Idaho	14.5
14. New Hampshire	3.0	13. Missouri	5.7	14. Tennessee	14.5
16. Delaware	2.9	13. New Mexico	5.7	16. Arizona	14.2
16. Rhode Island	2.9	17. Alabama	5.6	16. Montana	14.2
18. South Dakota	2.7	18. Colorado	5.5	16. New York	14.2
19. Vermont	2.6	18. Kansas	5.5	19. Oregon	14.1
20. Tennessee	2.4	18. North Carolina	5.5	20. California	13.3
20. Texas	2.4	18. Pennsylvania	5.5	21. Washington	13.1
22. Alabama	2.2	22. Tennessee	5.4	22. Rhode Island	12.8
22. Georgia	2.2	23. Kentucky	5.3	23. Nevada	12.6
22. Louisiana	2.2	23. West Virginia	5.3	24. Ohio	12.5
22. Maine	2.2	25. Indiana	5.2	25. Maine	12.3
22. New Jersey	2.2	25. Rhode Island	5.2	25. Michigan	12.3
27. South Carolina	2.1	25. Utah	5.2	27. Florida	12.2
28. California	1.8	28. Massachusetts	5.1	28. North Dakota	12.1
28. Minnesota	1.8	29. Arizona	5.0	29. Illinois	11.9
28. North Carolina	1.8	30. Connecticut	4.9	30. Missouri	11.8
28. Washington	1.8	30. Wisconsin	4.9	31. Pennsylvania	11.7
28. Wisconsin	1.8	32. Florida	4.8	32. Colorado	11.1
33. Arkansas	1.7	32. Iowa	4.8	33. Nebraska	11.0
33. West Virginia	1.7	32. New Jersey	4.8	33. South Dakota	11.0
35. Nebraska	1.6	32. Oklahoma	4.8	35. Utah	10.9
35. Oregon	1.6	36. Idaho	4.7	36. Indiana	10.8
37. Mississippi	1.4	36. Minnesota	4.7	37. Wisconsin	10.7
38. Kentucky	1.2	38. Georgia	4.6	38. Hawaii	10.6
39. Iowa	1.0	38. Maine	4.6	39. Kansas	10.5
40. Missouri	0.9	40. Montana	4.4	40. Wyoming	10.3
41. Indiana	0.8	41. Nevada	4.3	41. Delaware	9.9
42. Colorado	0.7	42. Maryland	4.2	41. Iowa	9.9
42. New York	0.7	43. Delaware	4.1	43. Virginia	9.5
42. Pennsylvania	0.7	44. Wyoming	3.9	44. Massachusetts	9.2
45. Connecticut	0.5	45. Nebraska	3.8	45. Vermont	9.0
45. Kansas	0.5	45. New Hampshire	3.8	46. Maryland	8.8
47. Oklahoma	0.1	47. Vermont	3.7	47. New Jersey	8.5
48. Ohio	-0.4	47. Virginia	3.7	48. Minnesota	8.3
49. Illinois	-1.0	49. South Dakota	3.5	49. Alaska	8.2
50. Michigan	-1.3	50. North Dakota	3.4	50. Connecticut	7.6
51. Massachusetts	-2.0	51. Hawaii	3.3	50. New Hampshire	7.6

RANKINGS: HOMELAND SECURITY, AGRICULTURE, AND EXPORTS

Homeland Security Grants Procurement Contracts, Fiscal Year 2004		Value of Agricultural Products Sold, 2002		Value of Exports, 2004	
State and rank	Thousands of dollars	State and rank	Millions of dollars	State and rank	Millions of dollars
United States	9 718 564	**United States**	200 646	**United States**	817 936
1. Virginia	2 237 730	1. California	25 737	1. Texas	117 245
2. Florida	1 087 617	2. Texas	14 135	2. California	109 968
3. Texas	909 803	3. Iowa	12 274	3. New York	44 401
4. District of Columbia	750 360	4. Nebraska	9 704	4. Michigan	35 625
5. California	592 960	5. Kansas	8 746	5. Washington	33 793
6. Maryland	528 569	6. Minnesota	8 576	6. Ohio	31 208
7. Alabama	225 703	7. Illinois	7 676	7. Illinois	30 214
8. New York	200 387	8. North Carolina	6 962	8. Florida	28 982
9. Georgia	174 758	9. Florida	6 242	9. Massachusetts	21 837
10. New Jersey	174 736	10. Wisconsin	5 623	10. Louisiana	19 922
11. North Carolina	173 785	11. Washington	5 331	11. Georgia	19 633
12. Washington	156 682	12. Missouri	4 983	12. New Jersey	19 192
13. Michigan	147 044	13. Arkansas	4 950	13. Indiana	19 109
14. Pennsylvania	137 432	14. Georgia	4 912	14. Pennsylvania	18 487
15. Ohio	130 616	15. Indiana	4 783	15. North Carolina	18 115
16. Arizona	122 253	16. Colorado	4 525	16. Tennessee	16 123
17. West Virginia	119 529	17. Oklahoma	4 456	17. Arizona	13 423
18. Tennessee	90 609	18. Ohio	4 264	18. South Carolina	13 376
19. Louisiana	89 228	19. Pennsylvania	4 257	19. Kentucky	12 992
20. Massachusetts	86 881	20. Idaho	3 908	20. Wisconsin	12 706
21. Kentucky	76 764	21. South Dakota	3 835	21. Minnesota	12 678
22. Indiana	60 205	22. Michigan	3 772	22. Virginia	11 631
23. Hawaii	55 928	23. Alabama	3 265	23. Oregon	11 172
24. Oregon	55 793	24. North Dakota	3 233	24. Alabama	9 037
25. Iowa	52 767	25. Oregon	3 195	25. Missouri	8 997
26. Arkansas	52 241	26. New York	3 118	26. Connecticut	8 559
27. South Carolina	51 526	27. Mississippi	3 116	27. Colorado	6 651
28. Illinois	47 999	28. Kentucky	3 080	28. Iowa	6 394
29. Connecticut	47 883	29. Arizona	2 395	29. Maryland	5 746
30. Alaska	47 183	30. Virginia	2 361	30. Kansas	4 931
31. Wisconsin	43 989	31. Tennessee	2 200	31. Utah	4 718
32. Kansas	43 775	32. Montana	1 882	32. Arkansas	3 493
33. Oklahoma	38 615	33. Louisiana	1 816	33. Vermont	3 283
34. Mississippi	38 317	34. New Mexico	1 700	34. West Virginia	3 262
35. New Mexico	36 977	35. South Carolina	1 490	35. Mississippi	3 179
36. Colorado	35 784	36. Maryland	1 293	36. Oklahoma	3 178
37. Missouri	32 968	37. Utah	1 116	37. Alaska	3 157
38. Minnesota	31 700	38. Wyoming	864	38. Idaho	2 915
39. Maine	22 512	39. New Jersey	750	39. Nevada	2 907
40. Nebraska	22 361	40. Delaware	619	40. Maine	2 432
41. North Dakota	17 281	41. Hawaii	533	41. Nebraska	2 316
42. Idaho	15 873	42. West Virginia	483	42. New Hampshire	2 286
43. Utah	14 181	43. Vermont	473	43. Delaware	2 053
44. Delaware	9 757	44. Connecticut	471	44. New Mexico	2 046
45. Nevada	9 709	45. Maine	464	45. Rhode Island	1 286
46. Montana	9 626	46. Nevada	447	46. District of Columbia	1 164
47. New Hampshire	8 925	47. Massachusetts	384	47. North Dakota	1 008
48. Vermont	8 184	48. New Hampshire	145	48. South Dakota	826
49. Wyoming	8 006	49. Rhode Island	56	49. Wyoming	680
50. South Dakota	5 889	50. Alaska	46	50. Montana	565
51. Rhode Island	5 340			51. Hawaii	405

RANKINGS: HOUSING AND EDUCATION

Median Value of Owner-Occupied Housing Units, 2004		Percent High School Graduate or More, 2004		Percent College Graduate or More, 2004	
State and rank	Dollars	State and rank	Percent of population 25 years and over	State and rank	Percent of population 25 years and over
United States	151 366	**United States**	85.2	**United States**	27.7
1. California	391 102	1. Minnesota	92.3	1. District of Columbia	45.7
2. Hawaii	364 840	2. Montana	91.9	2. Massachusetts	36.7
3. District of Columbia	334 702	2. Wyoming	91.9	3. Colorado	35.5
4. Massachusetts	331 200	4. Nebraska	91.3	4. New Hampshire	35.4
5. New Jersey	291 294	5. Utah	91.0	5. Maryland	35.2
6. Rhode Island	240 150	6. New Hampshire	90.8	6. New Jersey	34.6
7. Connecticut	236 559	6. Vermont	90.8	7. Connecticut	34.5
8. New York	220 981	8. Alaska	90.2	8. Vermont	34.2
9. New Hampshire	216 639	9. Iowa	89.8	9. Virginia	33.1
10. Maryland	216 529	10. Washington	89.7	10. Minnesota	32.5
11. Colorado	211 740	11. Kansas	89.6	11. California	31.7
12. Washington	204 719	12. North Dakota	89.5	12. Utah	30.8
13. Nevada	202 937	13. Connecticut	88.8	13. New York	30.6
14. Oregon	181 544	13. Wisconsin	88.8	14. Kansas	30.0
15. Minnesota	181 135	15. Virginia	88.4	15. Washington	29.9
16. Alaska	179 304	16. Colorado	88.3	16. Missouri	28.1
17. Virginia	179 191	17. Ohio	88.1	17. Arizona	28.0
18. Delaware	171 589	18. Hawaii	88.0	18. Georgia	27.6
19. Illinois	167 711	19. Idaho	87.9	19. Illinois	27.4
20. Utah	157 275	19. Michigan	87.9	20. Rhode Island	27.2
21. Vermont	154 318	19. Missouri	87.9	21. Delaware	26.9
22. Florida	149 291	22. New Jersey	87.6	22. Hawaii	26.6
23. Arizona	145 741	23. South Dakota	87.5	23. Florida	26.0
24. Michigan	145 177	24. Maryland	87.4	24. Oregon	25.9
25. Maine	143 182	24. Oregon	87.4	25. Wisconsin	25.6
26. Wisconsin	137 727	26. Indiana	87.2	26. Alaska	25.5
27. Georgia	136 912	27. Maine	87.1	26. Montana	25.5
28. Ohio	122 384	28. Massachusetts	86.9	26. South Dakota	25.5
29. Idaho	120 825	29. Illinois	86.8	29. Pennsylvania	25.3
30. Wyoming	119 654	30. Delaware	86.5	30. North Dakota	25.2
31. Montana	119 319	30. Pennsylvania	86.5	31. New Mexico	25.1
32. North Carolina	117 771	32. District of Columbia	86.4	32. South Carolina	24.9
33. Missouri	117 033	33. Nevada	86.3	33. Nebraska	24.8
34. Pennsylvania	116 520	34. Florida	85.9	34. Ohio	24.6
35. South Carolina	113 910	35. New York	85.4	35. Nevada	24.5
36. New Mexico	110 788	36. Georgia	85.2	35. Texas	24.5
37. Tennessee	110 198	36. Oklahoma	85.2	37. Michigan	24.4
38. Indiana	110 020	38. Arizona	84.4	38. Iowa	24.3
39. Nebraska	106 656	39. South Carolina	83.6	38. Tennessee	24.3
40. Kansas	102 458	40. Mississippi	83.0	40. Maine	24.2
41. Texas	99 858	41. New Mexico	82.9	41. Idaho	23.8
42. Kentucky	98 438	41. Tennessee	82.9	42. North Carolina	23.4
43. Louisiana	95 910	43. Alabama	82.4	43. Oklahoma	22.9
44. Iowa	95 901	44. Kentucky	81.8	44. Wyoming	22.5
45. South Dakota	95 523	45. California	81.3	45. Louisiana	22.4
46. Alabama	94 671	46. Rhode Island	81.1	46. Alabama	22.3
47. Oklahoma	85 060	47. North Carolina	80.9	47. Indiana	21.1
48. North Dakota	84 354	47. West Virginia	80.9	48. Kentucky	21.0
49. West Virginia	81 826	49. Arkansas	79.2	49. Mississippi	20.1
50. Mississippi	79 023	50. Louisiana	78.7	50. Arkansas	18.8
51. Arkansas	79 006	51. Texas	78.3	51. West Virginia	15.3

At a Glance:

- Alabama's population was over 4.5 million in 2004, making it the 23rd most populous state in the country.

- The population was nearly 70 percent non-Hispanic White and over 26 percent Black. Alabama had the seventh highest proportion of Black residents in the nation. Hispanics (of any race) constituted only a small part of the population, giving the state the eighth lowest proportion of this ethnic group in the country.

- Median household income in Alabama ranked 45th in the nation. The state's poverty rate of 16.9 percent was the third highest in the United States.

- Alabama's real gross state product showed steady growth after the 2001 recession. In 2004, it ranked 25th among the states.

- In 2004, the median value of owner-occupied housing rose to $94,671, which ranked 46th in nation.

- Alabama ranked 47th in the nation with more than 82 percent of its population age 25 years and over completing high school. The state ranked 44th for college attainment, with 22.2 percent of the population in this age group holding bachelor's degrees or more.

Table AL-1. Population by Sex and Age, 1990, 2000, and 2004

(Number, percent.)

Sex and age	1990	2000	2004	Percent distribution, 2004	Average annual percent change, 2000–2004
Total Population	4 040 587	4 447 100	4 530 182	X	0.5
Percent of total U.S. population	1.6	1.6	1.5	X	X
Sex					
Male	1 936 162	2 146 504	2 196 208	48.5	0.6
Female	2 104 425	2 300 596	2 333 974	51.5	0.4
Age					
Under 5 years	283 295	295 992	296 100	6.5	0.2
5 to 17 years	775 493	827 430	798 433	17.6	0.2
18 years and over	783 408	3 323 678	3 435 649	75.8	1.0
18 to 24 years	2 981 799	439 612	455 878	10.1	0.2
25 to 44 years	443 335	1 288 527	1 253 740	27.7	0.1
45 to 64 years	1 232 067	1 015 741	1 128 072	24.9	2.7
65 years and over	522 989	579 798	597 959	13.2	1.0
85 years and over	48 507	67 301	66 170	1.5	2.4
Median age (years)	32.9	35.8	36.9	X	X

X = Not applicable.

Average Annual Rate of Population Growth, 1980–2004

POPULATION

From 2000 to 2004, Alabama's population grew by 1.9 percent, which was well below the U.S. average. Although the state's growth rate approximated that of its western neighbor, Mississippi, it was well below those of its other neighbors, Tennessee, Georgia, and Florida. Alabama's largest metropolitan areas were Birmingham-Hoover, Mobile, Huntsville, and Montgomery, which together accounted for about half of the state's population. From 2000 to 2004, international immigration added to the population, substantially offsetting a small out-migration of residents. Compared with the nation as a whole, Alabama's population composition was older, with more than one-third of its residents over 45 years old.

Table AL-2. Population by Race and Hispanic Origin, 1990, 2000, and 2004

(Number, percent.)

Race and Hispanic origin	1990	2000	2004
Total Population	4 040 587	4 447 100	4 530 182
Non-Hispanic (Percent)			
One race[1]			
White	73.3	70.4	69.5
Black	25.2	25.9	26.2
American Indian, Alaska Native[2]	0.4	0.5	0.5
Asian and Pacific Islander[2]	0.5	0.7	0.8
Other race[2]	0.1	. . .	. . .
Two or more races	. . .	0.8	0.8
Hispanic or Latino[3] (Percent)	0.6	1.7	2.2

[1]Individuals could report only one race in the 1990 census and could report more one or more races on the 2000 census. Data on race in 2000 and 2004 are not comparable to 1990.
[2]Data for 1990 include people of Hispanic or Latino origin.
[3]May be of any race.
. . . = Not available.

Minority Population as a Percent of Total Population, 2004

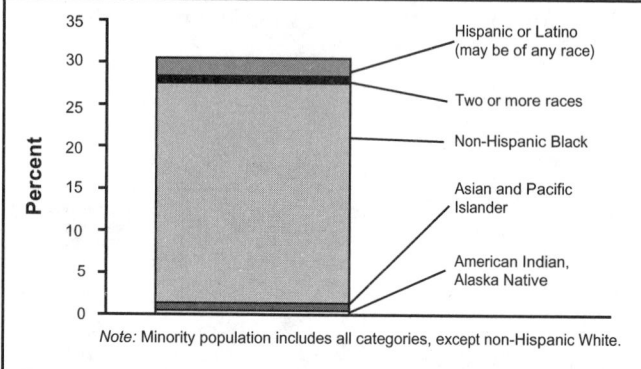

Note: Minority population includes all categories, except non-Hispanic White.

Age-Adjusted Death Rates, Average 2000–2002

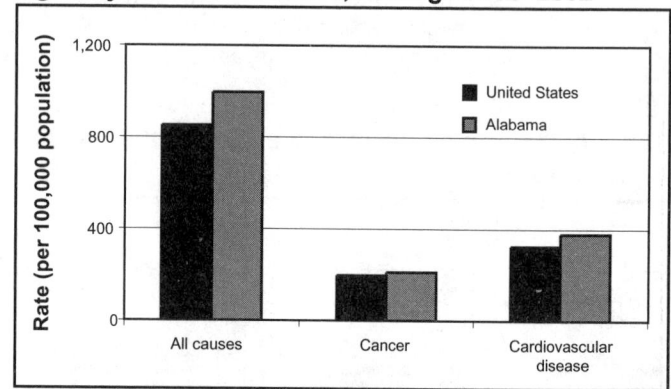

HEALTH

A below average proportion of Alabama's population lacked health insurance. The state had a low birth rate, but its birth rate for teenage mothers was the 13th highest in the nation. Alabama's infant mortality rate and age-adjusted death rates were relatively high.

Table AL-3. Health Characteristics, 2000–2004

(Number, rate, percent.)

Item	State	U.S.
Births, 2003–2004		
Number of births	59 552	4 089 950
Birth rate (per 1,000 population)	13.2	14.1
Teenage birth rate (per 1,000 women age 15–19 years)	52.4	41.6
Mortality Rates, Average 2000–2002		
Infant mortality rate (per 1,000 live births)	9.3	6.9
Age-adjusted mortality rate (per 100,000 population)		
All races	996.7	853.3
Non-Hispanic White	961.0	843.1
Black	1 161.5	1 097.7
American Indian, Alaska Native	. . .	687.0
Asian and Pacific Islander	332.0	486.0
Hispanic or Latino[1]	315.2	642.7
Health Insurance, 2004		
Percent of all persons without health insurance	13.5	15.7
Percent of children without health insurance	7.4	11.2
Percent of low-income children without health insurance	3.7	7.1

[1]May be of any race.
. . . = Not available.

Table AL-4. Leading Causes of Death, Average 2000–2002

(Number, rate per 100,000 population.)

Cause	Number of deaths	Age-adjusted death rates	
		State	U.S.
ALL CAUSES	45 482	996.7	853.3
Leading Causes			
Major cardiovascular diseases	17 358	380.8	326.5
Cancer	9 769	211.4	196.0
Chronic lower respiratory diseases	2 196	47.9	43.7
Unintentional injuries	2 177	48.4	35.7
Diabetes (underlying cause)	1 384	30.2	25.2
Influenza and pneumonia	1 154	25.5	22.7
Alzheimer's disease	1 062	23.6	19.0
Motor vehicle accidents	1 048	23.3	15.0
Nephritis, nephrotic syndrome, and nephrosis ..	982	21.6	13.8
Septicemia	770	16.9	11.4
Suicides	536	11.9	10.7
Firearm-related	742	16.5	10.3
Cirrhosis	426	9.2	9.5
Drug-induced	244	5.5	7.9
Alcohol-induced	222	4.8	6.9
Homicides	428	9.6	6.0
Falls	136	3.0	5.2
HIV	202	4.6	5.0
Viral hepatitis	76	1.7	2.0
Anemias	115	2.5	1.6
Drownings	80	1.8	1.3
Fire deaths	102	2.3	1.2

Note: The rates are age-adjusted to the U.S. 2000 standard population.

Table AL-5. Households and Housing Characteristics, 1990, 2000, and 2004

(Number, percent, and dollars.)

Characteristic	1990	2000	2004	Average annual percent change, 2000–2004
Total Households	1 506 790	1 737 080	1 755 332	0.3
Family households	1 103 835	1 215 968	1 220 290	0.1
Married-couple family	858 327	906 916	894 152	-0.4
Other family	245 508	309 052	326 138	1.4
Male householder, no wife present	44 288	62 586	59 870	-1.1
Female householder, no husband present	201 220	246 466	266 268	2.0
Nonfamily households	402 955	521 112	535 042	0.7
Householder living alone	358 078	453 898	467 559	0.7
Householder not living alone	44 877	67 214	67 483	0.1
Housing Characteristics				
Average size	2.62	2.49	2.51	X
Housing units	1 670 379	1 963 711	2 058 951	1.2
Occupied housing units	1 506 790	1 737 080	1 755 332	0.3
Owner-occupied	1 061 897	1 258 705	1 262 670	0.1
Renter-occupied	444 893	478 375	492 662	0.7
Median gross rent of renter-occupied housing units (dollars) ...	325	447	519	3.8
Median value of owner-occupied housing units (dollars)	53 200	85 100	94 671	2.7

X = Not applicable.

Median Housing Value and Median Rent, 2004

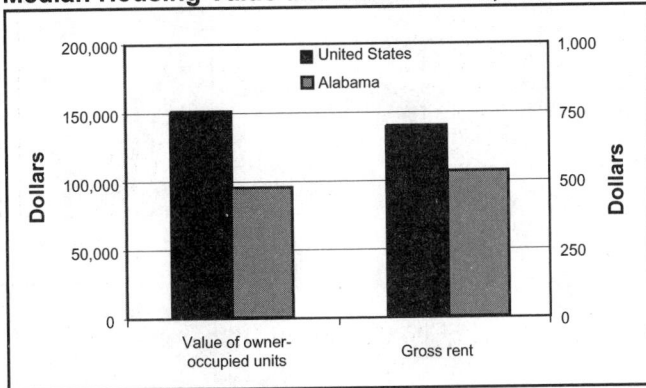

Median Household Income, 1984–2004 (2004 Dollars)

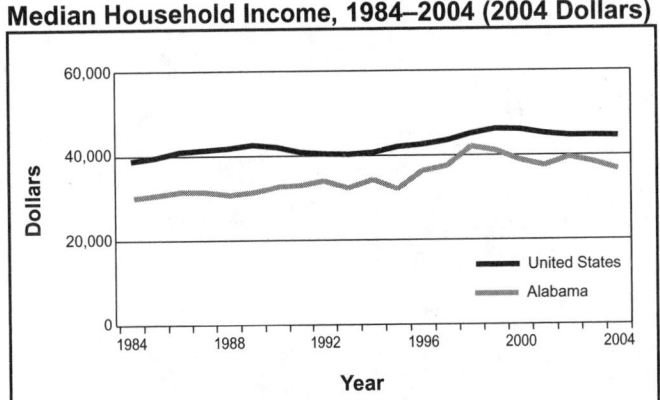

Table AL-6. Household Income and Poverty Status, 1980–2004

(2004 CPI-U-RS adjusted dollars, numbers in thousands, rate.)

Year	State		U.S.	
	Median household income (2004 dollars)	Poverty rate	Median household income (2004 dollars)	Poverty rate
2004	36 579	16.9	44 389	12.7
2003	38 256	15.0	44 482	12.5
2002	39 498	14.5	44 546	12.1
2001	37 519	15.9	45 062	11.7
2000	38 856	13.3	46 058	11.3
1999	41 090	15.2	46 129	11.9
1998	41 972	14.5	45 003	12.7
1997	37 485	15.7	43 430	13.3
1996	36 323	14.0	42 544	13.7
1995	31 992	20.1	41 943	13.8
1994	34 288	16.4	40 677	14.5
1993	32 289	17.4	40 217	15.1
1992	34 052	17.3	40 422	14.8
1991	32 928	18.8	40 746	14.2
1990	32 733	19.2	41 963	13.5
1989	31 311	18.9	42 524	12.8
1988	30 606	19.3	41 771	13.0
1987	31 380	21.3	41 322	13.4
1986	31 460	23.8	40 939	13.6
1985	30 696	20.6	39 545	14.0
1984	29 950	19.1	38 782	14.4
1983	. . .	23.0	. . .	15.2
1982	. . .	21.6	. . .	15.0
1981	. . .	24.1	. . .	14.0
1980	. . .	21.2	. . .	13.0

. . . = Not available.

Table AL-7. Employment Status by Demographic Group, 2004

(Numbers in thousands, rate.)

Characteristic	Civilian noninstitutional population	Civilian labor force		Employed	Unemployment rate
		Number	Participation rate		
SEX AND AGE					
Total	3 484	2 179	62.5	2 053	5.8
16 to 19 years	266	106	39.8	89	15.7
20 to 24 years	307	224	73.2	196	12.6
25 to 34 years	582	481	82.7	453	5.9
35 to 44 years	642	522	81.2	492	5.6
45 to 54 years	685	529	77.1	513	2.9
55 to 64 years	463	254	54.9	247	2.6
65 years and over	539	64	11.8	62	2.8
Men	1 651	1 156	70.0	1 096	5.3
16 to 19 years	137	57	41.2	48	16.0
20 to 24 years	166	124	75.0	109	12.3
25 to 34 years	278	252	90.5	239	5.1
35 to 44 years	296	265	89.4	254	4.2
45 to 54 years	330	280	84.8	272	2.9
55 to 64 years	224	143	63.6	139	2.7
Women	1 833	1 023	55.8	957	6.4
16 to 19 years	128	49	38.2	41	15.5
20 to 24 years	141	100	71.0	87	13.0
25 to 34 years	303	229	75.5	214	6.8
35 to 44 years	346	256	74.1	238	7.1
45 to 54 years	355	248	70.0	241	2.9
55 to 64 years	239	111	46.7	109	2.5
MARITAL STATUS					
Married men, spouse present	972	735	75.6	716	2.6
Married women, spouse present	969	571	59.0	552	3.4
Women who maintain families	234	150	64.0	132	11.8
RACE, HISPANIC ORIGIN, AND SEX					
White	2 518	1 595	63.4	1 535	3.8
Men	1 220	883	72.4	850	3.7
Women	1 298	713	54.9	685	3.9
Black	851	511	60.0	449	12.2
Men	374	233	62.1	207	11.2
Women	477	278	58.4	242	13.1
Hispanic or Latino[1]	57	50	87.1	48	3.7
RACE, HISPANIC ORIGIN, AND AGE					
White					
16 to 19 years	169	74	44.1	67	10.5
20 to 24 years	198	155	78.1	146	5.9
25 to 34 years	391	331	84.7	319	3.7
35 to 44 years	467	386	82.5	369	4.2
45 to 54 years	499	396	79.4	385	2.9
55 to 64 years	365	204	55.7	201	1.4
65 years and over	429	50	11.6	49	1.8
Black					
20 to 24 years	99	64	64.0	46	28.3
25 to 34 years	157	128	81.2	112	11.9
35 to 44 years	155	120	77.7	108	9.9
45 to 54 years	164	116	70.8	112	3.2
55 to 64 years	87	45	51.8	42	8.3

Note: Data in Table 7 are from the Current Population Survey (CPS) and do not match Bureau of Labor Statistics estimates in Table 8. See notes and definitions for more details.

[1]May be of any race.

Table AL-8. Employment Status, 1990–2004

(Numbers in thousands, rate.)

Year	Civilian labor force	Employed	Unemployed	Unemployment rate
2004	2 148 766	2 029 314	119 452	5.6
2003	2 133 206	2 009 039	124 167	5.8
2002	2 115 125	1 996 920	118 205	5.6
2001	2 136 633	2 033 230	103 403	4.8
2000	2 161 499	2 072 853	88 646	4.1
1999	2 162 603	2 070 210	92 393	4.3
1998	2 142 512	2 059 310	83 202	3.9
1997	2 129 797	2 035 156	94 641	4.4
1996	2 086 493	1 992 652	93 841	4.5
1995	2 063 870	1 955 846	108 024	5.2
1994	2 018 524	1 909 881	108 643	5.4
1993	1 981 641	1 850 610	131 031	6.6
1992	1 943 033	1 809 337	133 696	6.9
1991	1 915 087	1 783 434	131 653	6.9
1990	1 903 248	1 782 700	120 548	6.3

Note: Population 16 years old and over.

Unemployment Rate, 1980–2004

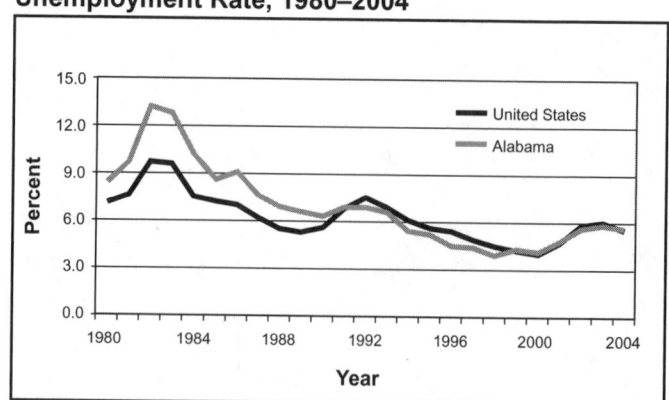

Table AL-9. Employment and Average Wages by Industry, 2001–2004

(Estimates are based on the 2002 North American Industry Classification System [NAICS].)

Industry	2001	2002	2003	2004	Annual average percent change, 2001–2004
	Number of jobs				
TOTAL EMPLOYMENT BY PLACE OF WORK	2 392 552	2 387 118	2 397 067	2 444 279	0.7
Farm Employment	54 914	55 360	53 591	53 582	-0.8
Nonfarm Employment	2 337 638	2 331 758	2 343 476	2 390 697	0.8
Private employment	1 952 516	1 942 661	1 950 637	1 992 804	0.7
Forestry, fishing, hunting, and other[1]	D	19 867	18 322	18 146	. . .
Mining	9 551	9 259	9 103	9 245	-1.1
Utilities	14 685	14 264	14 216	14 130	-1.3
Construction	160 742	154 100	156 639	160 640	0.0
Manufacturing	337 240	316 883	302 636	301 149	-3.7
Durable goods manufacturing	183 339	177 329	169 993	173 514	-1.8
Nondurable goods manufacturing	153 901	139 554	132 643	127 635	-6.0
Wholesale trade	87 348	85 069	83 835	85 110	-0.9
Retail trade	282 644	283 397	285 471	290 795	1.0
Transportation and warehousing	71 802	69 016	67 920	69 131	-1.3
Information	40 426	38 085	36 133	35 666	-4.1
Finance and insurance	89 455	89 833	92 003	92 746	1.2
Real estate and rental and leasing	63 036	64 331	67 951	71 034	4.1
Professional and technical services	119 091	121 721	126 472	130 643	3.1
Management of companies and enterprises	9 555	10 348	10 114	11 088	5.1
Administrative and waste services	121 270	124 872	126 398	136 122	3.9
Educational services	26 674	27 566	28 620	29 735	3.7
Health care and social assistance	183 738	190 912	196 388	200 257	2.9
Arts, entertainment, and recreation	27 255	27 700	27 889	29 218	2.3
Accommodation and food services	D	145 488	149 529	154 166	. . .
Other services, except public administration	144 252	149 950	150 998	153 783	2.2
Government and government enterprises	385 122	389 097	392 839	397 893	1.1
	Dollars				
AVERAGE WAGES AND SALARIES BY PLACE OF WORK	29 436	30 482	31 567	32 721	3.6
Farm Earnings	18 154	17 724	14 672	17 780	-0.7
Nonfarm Earnings	29 480	30 538	31 635	32 787	3.6
Private earnings	29 155	30 108	31 132	32 368	3.5
Forestry, fishing, hunting, and other[1]	D	25 043	26 082	26 930	. . .
Mining	51 092	52 461	53 470	54 529	2.2
Utilities	67 094	67 512	73 604	76 596	4.5
Construction	30 816	31 472	32 172	33 013	2.3
Manufacturing	34 695	36 193	37 612	39 491	4.4
Durable goods manufacturing	36 565	38 177	39 936	41 998	4.7
Nondurable goods manufacturing	32 478	33 677	34 641	36 084	3.6
Wholesale trade	39 928	40 955	42 636	45 321	4.3
Retail trade	19 887	20 593	21 122	21 745	3.0
Transportation and warehousing	31 883	33 304	34 378	36 184	4.3
Information	42 099	43 327	42 908	44 901	2.2
Finance and insurance	41 073	43 729	46 284	48 910	6.0
Real estate and rental and leasing	24 367	26 099	27 537	29 025	6.0
Professional and technical services	47 528	48 345	50 966	52 284	3.2
Management of companies and enterprises	51 257	51 303	56 474	61 784	6.4
Administrative and waste services	18 105	19 387	20 936	21 258	5.5
Educational services	19 976	21 063	21 913	23 439	5.5
Health care and social assistance	31 888	32 931	33 018	34 742	2.9
Arts, entertainment, and recreation	15 449	16 122	16 660	16 820	2.9
Accommodation and food services	D	11 711	11 942	12 108	. . .
Other services, except public administration	19 243	20 062	20 794	21 421	3.6
Government and government enterprises	30 844	32 297	33 664	34 486	3.8

Note: Average wages and salaries are a calculation by the editors of wage and salary disbursements divided by full- and part-time wage and salary employment. Data may not add to total or may appear as zero due to rounding.

1 "Other" consists of the number of jobs held by U.S. residents employed by international organizations and foreign embassies and consulates in the United States.
D = Suppressed to avoid disclosure of data of individual companies.
. . . = Not available.

LABOR MARKET

Alabama had one the nation's lowest employment/population ratios (the proportion of the civilian population age 16 years and over currently employed), reflecting similar rates in Mississippi and Tennessee. Unemployment was higher than the national average, but showed some improvement in 2004, as the recovery in economic activity gained strength. Total nonfarm employment has grown 2.6 percent since 2002. Employment in durable goods manufacturing continued its decline, while jobs in the nondurable goods sector rose slightly. Jobs in the largest industries in the service-providing sector showed improvement over the period, particularly those in administrative services, professional and technical services, and health care.

Employment by Industry, 2004

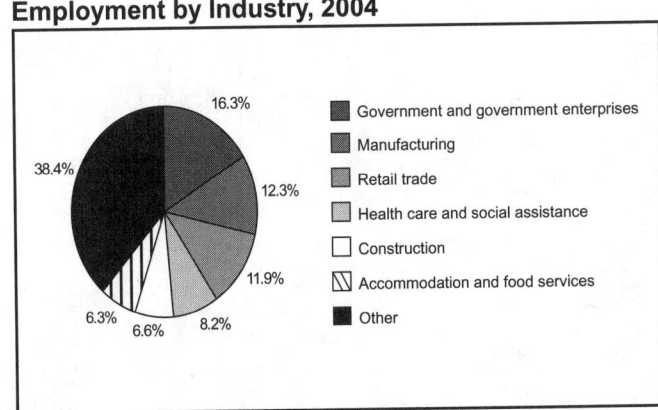

- Government and government enterprises — 16.3%
- Manufacturing — 12.3%
- Retail trade — 11.9%
- Health care and social assistance — 8.2%
- Construction — 6.6%
- Accommodation and food services — 6.3%
- Other — 38.4%

Table AL-10. Personal Income by Major Source, Selected Years 1980–2004

(Millions of dollars, except where noted.)

Item	1980	1990	2000	2001	2002	2003	2004	Average annual percent change, 2000–2004
Earnings by Place of Work	24 149	47 716	76 977	80 448	83 355	87 575	92 943	4.8
Wage and salary disbursements	18 377	35 478	57 643	59 088	60 658	62 688	66 049	3.5
Supplements to wages and salaries	3 753	7 807	12 017	12 730	14 282	15 546	16 748	8.7
Proprietors' income[1]	2 019	4 432	7 317	8 630	8 415	9 341	10 145	8.5
Farm proprietors' income	103	682	816	1 075	675	1 148	1 301	12.4
Nonfarm proprietors' income	1 916	3 749	6 501	7 555	7 740	8 192	8 844	8.0
(-) Contributions for government social insurance[2]	2 281	5 317	8 783	9 146	9 483	9 874	10 396	4.3
(+) Adjustment for residence[3]	328	525	1 238	1 252	1 264	1 310	1 380	2.7
(=) Net Earnings by Place of Residence	22 196	42 924	69 433	72 554	75 136	79 011	83 926	4.9
(+) Dividends, interest, and rent[4]	3 908	11 528	18 725	18 739	18 073	17 778	18 130	-0.8
(+) Personal current transfer receipts	4 460	9 227	17 648	19 129	20 576	21 692	23 111	7.0
Personal income	30 564	63 679	105 807	110 421	113 784	118 481	125 167	4.3
Farm income	30 366	62 867	104 859	109 188	112 941	117 204	123 692	4.2
Nonfarm income	198	812	947	1 233	843	1 277	1 474	11.7
Per Capita Personal Income (Dollars)[5]	7 836	15 723	23 764	24 714	25 392	26 307	27 630	3.8

Note: Data may not add to total or may appear as zero due to rounding.

[1]Proprietors' income includes the inventory valuation adjustment and the capital consumption adjustment.
[2]Contributions for government social insurance are included in earnings by type and industry, but they are excluded from personal income.
[3]The adjustment for residence is the net inflow of the earnings of interarea commuters.
[4]Rental income of persons includes the capital consumption adjustment.
[5]Per capita personal income is total personal income divided by total midyear population.

Per Capita Personal Income, 1980–2004 (Current Dollars)

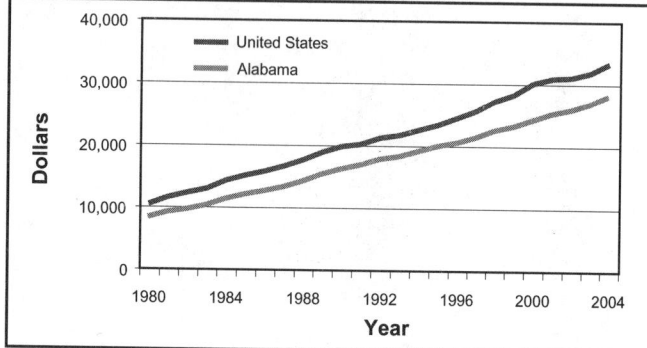

ECONOMIC ACTIVITY

Real gross state product showed vigor after the 2001 recession, growing by 4.3 percent in real terms over the 2003–2004 period. Manufacturing, retail trade, government, and finance and insurance made the largest contributions to the state's economic growth. Housing activity continued to increase, both in terms of jobs and income. However, Alabama's real estate market did not see the strong appreciation in housing prices experienced elsewhere in the nation. In 2004, the median value of owner-occupied housing in the state ranked 46th in the nation. From 2001 to 2004, average wages and salaries rose at an average annual rate of 3.6 percent, which was above the U.S. average rate.

Table AL-11. Real Gross State Product, 1997–2004

(Millions of chained 2000 dollars, percent.)

Industry	1997	1998	1999	2000	2001	2002	2003	2004	Average annual percent change, 2001–2004
GROSS STATE PRODUCT	107 563	110 069	114 168	114 204	115 235	118 205	122 675	127 947	3.5
As a percent of U.S. gross product	1.2	1.2	1.2	1.2	1.2	1.2	1.2	1.2	X
Private Industries	89 947	92 220	96 344	96 446	97 795	100 136	103 701	108 437	3.5
Agriculture, forestry, fishing, and hunting	1 589	1 781	2 037	2 027	2 003	1 789	2 072	2 041	0.6
Mining	1 273	1 377	1 307	1 191	1 160	1 047	1 061	1 001	-4.8
Utilities	2 769	2 778	3 044	3 094	3 193	3 212	3 569	3 729	5.3
Construction	5 485	5 506	5 547	5 349	5 234	4 930	4 931	5 002	-1.5
Manufacturing	20 061	20 096	21 190	21 267	20 194	20 857	21 614	22 843	4.2
As a percent of gross state product	18.7	18.3	18.6	18.6	17.5	17.6	17.6	17.9	X
Wholesale trade	6 025	6 580	6 920	6 879	7 290	7 351	7 201	7 538	1.1
Retail trade	8 738	9 024	9 378	9 477	10 091	10 675	11 341	11 992	5.9
Transportation and warehousing	3 260	3 296	3 391	3 394	3 155	3 221	3 405	3 563	4.1
Information	3 205	3 328	3 538	3 639	3 890	4 005	3 988	4 329	3.6
Finance and insurance	4 941	5 089	5 455	5 404	5 914	6 244	6 593	7 032	5.9
Real estate and rental and leasing	10 243	10 447	11 130	11 422	12 099	12 328	12 469	12 840	2.0
Services	22 532	23 013	23 425	23 303	23 594	24 544	25 552	26 720	4.2
As a percent of gross state product	20.9	20.9	20.5	20.4	20.5	20.8	20.8	20.9	X
Professional and technical services	5 238	5 631	5 922	5 971	6 325	6 572	7 178	7 468	5.6
Management of companies and enterprises	853	750	792	675	701	763	831	943	10.4
Administrative and waste services	2 379	2 437	2 552	2 417	2 373	2 602	2 782	2 949	7.5
Educational services	458	463	482	502	496	498	488	500	0.3
Health care and social assistance	7 564	7 443	7 345	7 479	7 607	7 981	8 074	8 373	3.2
Arts, entertainment, and recreation	452	481	490	465	482	509	510	525	2.9
Accommodation and food services	2 488	2 620	2 724	2 733	2 680	2 680	2 754	2 845	2.0
Other services, except public administration	3 100	3 188	3 118	3 061	2 930	2 930	2 935	3 127	2.2
Government	17 645	17 870	17 825	17 757	17 442	18 067	18 961	19 503	3.8
As a percent of gross state product	16.4	16.2	15.6	15.5	15.1	15.3	15.5	15.2	X

X = Not applicable.

Table AL-12. Government Transfer Payments, Selected Years 1980–2004

(Millions of dollars, percent.)

Item	1980	1990	2000	2001	2002	2003	2004	Average annual percent change, 2000–2004
CURRENT TRANSFER PAYMENTS TO INDIVIDUALS	4 189	8 701	16 643	18 018	19 563	20 758	21 950	7.2
Retirement and Disability Insurance Benefits	2 082	4 244	7 176	7 668	8 150	8 523	8 891	5.5
Old-age, survivors, and disability insurance (OASDI) benefits	1 917	4 020	6 944	7 432	7 892	8 246	8 609	5.5
Railroad retirement and disability benefits	72	113	134	137	143	147	149	2.7
Workers' compensation	15	48	57	60	72	72	74	6.7
Other government retirement and disability insurance benefits	78	63	41	38	43	59	59	10.0
Medical Benefits	847	2 767	6 576	7 195	7 793	8 395	9 094	8.4
Medicare benefits	533	1 744	3 683	4 096	4 400	4 672	5 132	8.7
Public assistance medical care benefits	292	958	2 813	2 987	3 239	3 590	3 799	7.8
Military medical insurance benefits	22	64	80	112	154	133	163	19.6
Income Maintenance Benefits	620	938	1 850	1 930	2 217	2 412	2 584	8.7
Supplemental Security Income (SSI) benefits	208	359	659	699	730	738	772	4.0
Family assistance	84	62	59	61	100	106	70	4.4
Food stamps	257	339	348	375	425	476	556	12.4
Other income maintenance benefits	71	178	783	796	962	1 092	1 186	10.9
Unemployment Insurance Compensation	247	202	235	327	419	411	285	5.0
Veterans' Benefits	314	402	570	608	678	733	792	8.6
Federal Education and Training Assistance	78	145	224	265	294	273	289	6.6
Other Payments to Individuals	1	4	13	24	13	11	15	4.4

Note: See notes and definitions for more details. Data may not add to total or may appear as zero due to rounding.

EXPORTS

Alabama ranked 24th in the nation in 2004 for total exports of goods (accounting for about 1.1 percent of total exports in the United States). The state's exports grew by about 19 percent during the 2001–2004 period. Transportation equipment, chemical manufactures, and computers and electronic products were the largest exports. Exports to Germany increased by over 150 percent from 2001 to 2004, making Alabama one of the leading states in exports to that country. In 2004, Germany was Alabama's second largest export market, behind only Canada. Mining exports increased by over 148 percent from 2001 to 2004, and are now among the state's top 10 exports.

Leading Exports, 2004

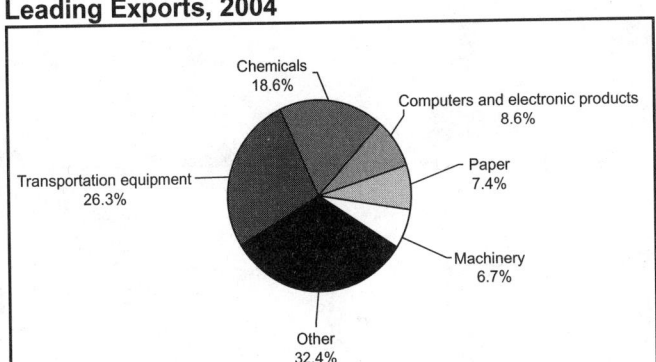

Table AL-13. Exports of Goods by Leading Products and Destinations, 2001–2004

(Millions of dollars, percent, rank based on 2004 dollar values.)

Product and market	2001	2002	2003	2004	Percent share of total, 2004	Average annual percent change, 2001–2004
Total Goods						
Total	7 570	8 267	8 340	9 037	100.0	6.1
Manufactures	6 858	7 477	7 531	8 138	90.1	5.9
Agriculture and livestock	548	558	646	719	8.0	9.4
Other commodities	163	232	162	181	2.0	3.4
Five Leading Exports (NAICS Code)						
Transportation equipment (336)	1 905	2 463	2 532	2 373	26.3	7.6
Chemical manufactures (325)	1 200	1 318	1 264	1 684	18.6	11.9
Computers and electronic products (334)	862	919	757	773	8.6	-3.6
Paper products (322)	613	634	658	673	7.4	3.1
Machinery manufactures (333)	352	361	463	605	6.7	19.8
Five Leading Markets	6 262	7 243	7 470	8 149	90.2	9.2
Canada	1 596	1 688	1 547	1 808	20.0	4.2
Germany	593	1 381	1 618	1 491	16.5	36.0
Mexico	657	662	751	731	8.1	3.6
Japan	620	514	481	637	7.1	0.9
United Kingdom	442	505	443	412	4.6	-2.3

Table AL-14. Agriculture, 1997 and 2002
(Number, acres, and dollars.)

Item	1997	2002
Number of farms	49 872	45 126
Land in farms (acres)	9 517 377	8 904 387
Farm Size		
Average size of farm (acres)	191	197
Farms by size (percent distribution)		
Fewer than 50 acres	37.1	37.1
50 to 499 acres	54.8	54.6
500 acres or more	8.1	8.3
Market Value of Land and Equipment (Dollars)		
Land and buildings average value per farm	282 304	335 217
Average value per acre	1 471	1 698
Machinery and equipment average value per farm	34 420	42 705
Value of Sales (Thousands of Dollars)		
Agricultural products sold	3 198 630	3 264 949
Crops	656 185	590 268
Livestock, poultry, and their products	2 542 444	2 674 681
Average per farm (dollars)	64 137	72 352
Value of sales (percent distribution)		
Less than $10,000	72.4	71.1
$10,000 to $99,999	17.9	18.6
$100,000 or more	9.6	10.4
Government Payments		
Payments (thousands of dollars)	46 022	77 930
Percent of farms receiving government payments	25.6	28.5
Farm operators whose principal occupation is farming (percent)	35.3	53.1

AGRICUTURE

Total cash receipts from farming in Alabama totaled nearly $3.3 billion on the 2002 Census of Agriculture, slightly more than those in the previous census year, 1997. The principal products were chicken broilers, corn, cotton, and soybeans. The state ranked fourth in the nation for value of sales of poultry and eggs. Government payments to farmers totaled nearly $78 million.

ENERGY

Energy prices were relatively low compared with other states: Alabama ranked 42nd in the nation in this category. Expenditures on energy per person in the state totaled $2,953 in 2001, the latest year for which data are available from the U.S. Department of Energy; these expenditures ranked 16th in the country. Alabama was the 8th largest consumer of coal, which accounted for over 43 percent of the state's energy consumption. The state's industrial sector was the largest user, followed by the transportation, residential, and commercial sectors.

Energy Consumption by Source, 2001

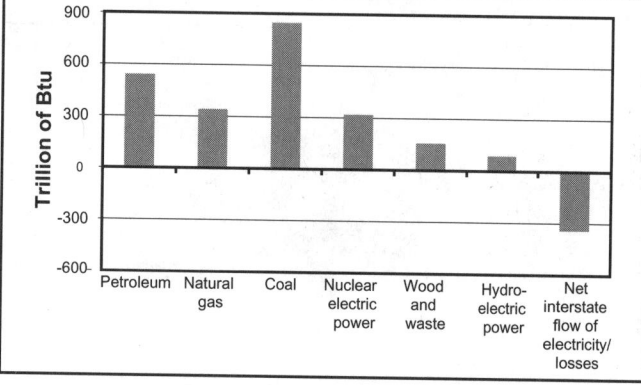

Energy Consumption by Sector, 2001

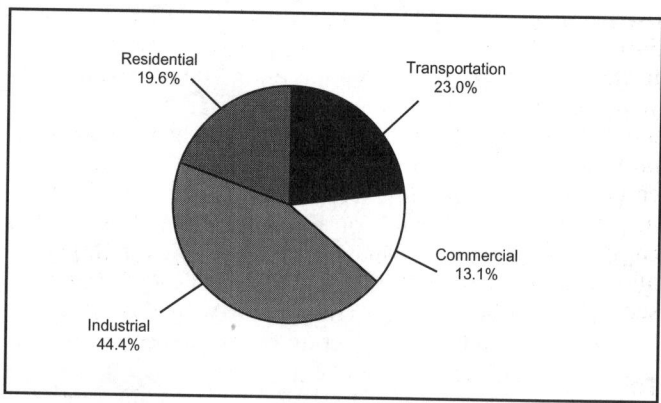

Table AL-15. Energy Consumption, Expenditures, and Prices, Selected Years 1960–2001
(Dollars, Btu [British Thermal Unit], percent distribution.)

Item	1960	1965	1970	1975	1980	1985	1990	1995	2000	2001
Total Consumption (Billion Btu)	867 190	1 047 212	1 396 865	1 518 737	1 647 924	1 534 742	1 693 092	2 011 001	2 128 840	1 942 650
Consumption per capita (million Btu)	265.4	304.2	405.6	412.8	423.2	386.3	419.0	471.8	478.7	434.9
Consumption by Sector (Percent Distribution)										
Residential	14.6	14.3	16.0	15.5	16.3	17.8	18.1	17.2	18.6	19.6
Commercial	6.5	7.7	7.7	7.9	7.6	9.1	10.0	8.8	12.1	13.1
Industrial	58.7	58.9	57.0	52.6	54.9	51.3	48.4	51.3	47.1	44.4
Transportation	20.3	19.2	19.2	23.9	21.2	21.7	23.4	22.6	22.2	23.0
Consumption by Source (Billion Btu)										
Coal	395 400	533 142	675 603	640 063	661 023	662 890	682 490	828 273	904 185	845 649
Natural gas	190 706	236 949	307 750	271 747	278 394	227 795	252 457	332 399	368 473	342 283
Petroleum	236 597	264 449	355 272	490 557	457 916	427 160	507 418	560 492	567 780	539 585
Nuclear electric power	0	0	0	29 978	256 310	152 028	127 533	218 045	327 143	317 171
Hydroelectric power[1]	67 128	74 247	80 092	127 086	97 733	71 935	107 832	97 980	59 346	85 018
Wood and waste	45 681	47 641	52 378	57 615	134 961	172 350	142 992	223 494	191 780	154 145
Other	0	0	0	0	0	0	154	171	183	170
Net interstate flow of electricity/losses[2]	-68 321	-109 216	-74 232	-98 309	-238 413	-179 417	-127 784	-249 852	-290 048	-341 371
Total Expenditures (Thousands of Dollars)	...	...	1 410 800	3 096 500	6 688 500	7 268 700	8 256 800	9 282 400	12 097 000	11 579 800
Expenditures per capita (dollars)	...	...	410	842	1 718	1 830	2 044	2 178	2 720	2 593
Prices by Sector (Dollars Per Million Btu)										
Total	...	...	1.37	2.83	6.30	7.67	7.49	6.92	8.78	9.31
Residential	...	...	2.42	4.43	9.02	12.53	13.42	14.02	16.34	17.19
Commercial	...	...	2.00	3.97	8.35	11.51	12.41	13.66	15.23	15.88
Industrial	...	...	0.64	1.85	3.89	5.24	4.51	3.79	4.48	5.11
Transportation	...	...	2.45	3.67	8.78	8.35	8.38	8.16	10.73	10.17

[1]A negative number in this row results from pumped storage for which, overall, more electricity is expended than created to provide electricity during peak demand periods.
[2]Net interstate flow of electricity is the difference between the amount of energy in the electricity sold within a state (including associated losses) and the energy input at the electric utilities within the state. A positive number indicates that more electricity (including associated losses) came into the state than went out of the state during the year; conversely, a negative number indicates that more electricity (including associated losses) went out of the state than came into the state.
... = Not available.

Table AL-16. State Taxes, Fiscal 2004

(Dollars, percent distribution.)

Item	Thousands of dollars	Percent distribution	Dollars per capita	
			State	U.S.
TOTAL TAXES	7 018 242	100.0	1 549.3	2 024.8
Property Taxes	221 470	3.2	48.9	38.9
Sales and Gross Receipts	3 675 562	52.4	811.4	1 003.4
General sales and gross receipts	1 892 560	27.0	417.8	677.0
Selective sales taxes	1 783 002	25.4	393.6	326.4
Alcoholic beverages	137 222	2.0	30.3	15.7
Insurance premiums	245 577	3.5	54.2	47.0
Motor fuels	535 493	7.6	118.2	114.6
Public utilities	600 558	8.6	132.6	39.2
Tobacco products	93 270	1.3	20.6	42.0
Other selective sales	167 559	2.4	37.0	49.8
Licenses	397 429	5.7	87.7	134.9
Corporation	73 183	1.0	16.2	21.6
Motor vehicle	172 815	2.5	38.2	59.4
Occupation and business, not elsewhere classified	107 177	1.5	23.7	37.1
Other Taxes	2 723 781	38.8	601.3	847.6
Individual income	2 243 537	32.0	495.3	673.6
Corporation net income	292 051	4.2	64.5	105.1
Documentary and stock transfer	45 080	0.6	10.0	27.1
Severance	113 646	1.6	25.1	21.5

GOVERNMENT FINANCE

State revenues amounted to nearly $16.6 billion and expenditures totaled $17 billion in 2003, ranking the state 34th and 32nd in the nation, respectively, in per capita terms. State taxes per person amounted to $1,549 in fiscal year 2004; about 32 percent, or $495, came from individual income taxes. Sales taxes proved to be the second largest category of tax collections, with about $418 per capita in fiscal year 2004. Alabama ranked ninth in the nation in terms of federal government expenditures per capita in 2004. The largest spending was for retirement and disability, followed by procurement. Alabama ranked second and seventh, respectively, in these categories.

Per Capita State Taxes, Fiscal 2004

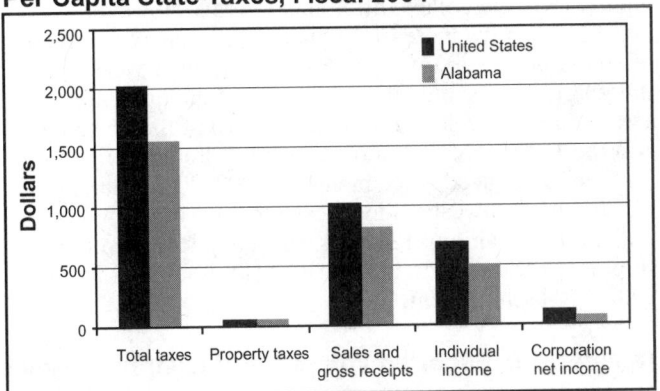

Table AL-17. State Government Finances, 2003

(Dollars, percent distribution.)

Item	Millions of dollars	Percent distribution	Dollars per capita	
			State	U.S.
GENERAL REVENUE	16 574 756	100.0	3 680.0	3 832.6
Intergovernmental revenue	6 668 784	40.2	1 480.6	1 246.0
Taxes	6 416 351	38.7	1 424.6	1 891.6
General sales	1 764 557	10.6	391.8	636.0
Selective sales	1 585 666	9.6	352.1	307.4
License taxes	399 871	2.4	88.8	123.6
Individual income tax	2 035 538	12.3	451.9	626.8
Corporate income tax	242 411	1.5	53.8	97.8
Other taxes	388 308	2.3	86.2	99.9
Current charges	2 471 414	14.9	548.7	366.5
Miscellaneous general revenue	1 018 207	6.1	226.1	328.6
GENERAL EXPENDITURE	17 009 944	100.0	3 776.6	4 010.5
Intergovernmental expenditure	4 074 005	24.0	904.5	1 316.9
Direct expenditure	12 935 939	76.0	2 872.1	2 693.6
Expenditure by Function				
Education	7 053 792	41.5	1 566.1	1 416.4
Public welfare	4 531 802	26.6	1 006.2	1 083.3
Hospitals	1 211 084	7.1	268.9	132.3
Health	762 009	4.5	169.2	173.0
Highways	1 163 904	6.8	258.4	295.4
Police protection	129 591	0.8	28.8	38.4
Correction	356 928	2.1	79.2	135.0
Natural resources	225 308	1.3	50.0	64.0
Parks and recreation	25 422	0.1	5.6	20.1
Government administration	439 143	2.6	97.5	151.3
Interest on general debt	252 401	1.5	56.0	107.8
Other and unallocable	858 560	5.0	190.6	393.4
DEBT AT END OF FISCAL YEAR	6 284 640	X	1 395.4	2 404.7
CASH AND SECURITY HOLDINGS	28 661 435	X	6 363.6	8 938.4

X = Not applicable.

Table AL-18. Education Indicators, 2000–2004

(Percent, number.)

Item	State	U.S.
Total Population 25 Years and Over (Thousands), 2004	2 891	186 877
Educational Attainment, 2004		
Percent high school graduate or more	82.4	85.2
Percent college graduate or more	22.3	27.7
Elementary and Secondary Schools, 2002–2003		
Total students	739 678	48 202 324
Percent of students eligible for free or reduced-price lunch ..	50.5	40.6
Percent of students who were English language learners	1.5	7.8
Total schools	1 391	92 330
Student/teacher ratio	12.6	15.9
Per student expenditures	6 300	8 041
Dropouts, Grades 9–12, 2000–2001 (Percent)	3.7	. . .
Higher Education, 2002–2003		
Total enrollment	247 805	17 035 027
Bachelor's degrees awarded	20 479	1 348 503
Percent women	59.2	57.5

. . . = Not available.

Educational Attainment, 2004

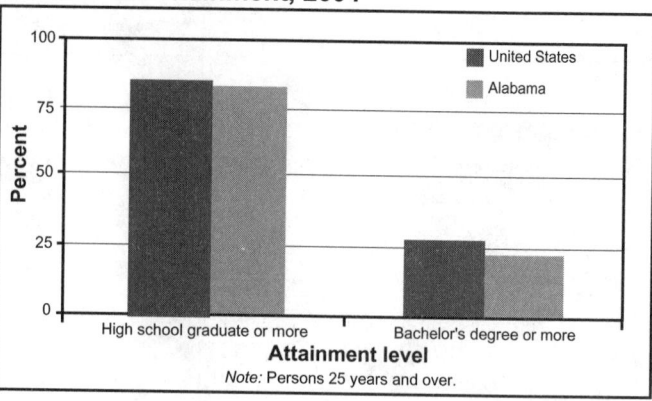

Note: Persons 25 years and over.

EDUCATION

Alabama ranked among the lowest 10 states for both high school and college attainment levels. However, these levels have increased since 2000, when 77.5 percent of Alabama's residents age 25 years and over were high school graduates and 20.4 percent were college graduates. Alabama ranked among the top 10 of the 46 states and the District of Columbia reporting student eligibility for free or reduced-price meals. In 2002–2003, Alabama had the third lowest student/teacher ratio in the nation. Alabama was among 12 states where student membership declined between the 1993–1994 school year and the 2003–2004 school year.

VOTER PARTICIPATION

Alabama's voter turnout was higher than the national average for both the 2000 and 2004 presidential elections. In 2000, 56.6 percent of eligible voters turned out on Election Day. According to official records from the Clerk of the House of Representatives, which provided the official tally of the vote, 41.6 percent of Alabamans voted Democrat while 47.8 percent voted Republican. In the 2004 election, voter participation rose slightly, with the proportion of votes for the Democratic candidate dropping to 38.8 percent and the proportion of votes for the Republican candidate rising to 62.5 percent.

Table AL-19. Reported Voting and Registration, November 2000 and November 2004

(Numbers in thousands, percent.)

Characteristic	Total population 18 years and over	Total citizen		Total registered		Total voted	
		Number	Percent	Number	Percent	Number	Percent
NOVEMBER 2000							
Total	3 278	3 233	98.6	2 411	73.6	1 953	59.6
Male	1 507	1 481	98.3	1 084	72.0	886	58.8
Female	1 771	1 752	98.9	1 326	74.9	1 067	60.2
NOVEMBER 2004							
Total	3 332	3 257	97.8	2 418	72.6	2 060	61.8
Male	1 568	1 521	97.0	1 109	70.7	935	59.6
Female	1 764	1 736	98.4	1 309	74.2	1 125	63.8
Race and Hispanic Origin							
White alone	2 450	2 400	97.9	1 808	73.8	1 523	62.2
Non-Hispanic White alone	2 412	2 392	99.2	1 806	74.9	1 522	63.1
Black alone	799	799	100.0	583	72.9	511	63.9
Asian alone	40	15	B	4	B	4	B
Hispanic or Latino[1]	39	8	B	2	B	2	B
White alone or in combination	2 474	2 424	98.0	1 823	73.7	1 539	62.2
Non-Hispanic White alone or in combination	2 435	2 415	99.2	1 822	74.8	1 537	63.1
Black alone or in combination	806	806	100.0	590	73.2	517	64.2
Asian alone or in combination	40	15	B	4	B	4	B
Age							
18 to 24 years	413	387	93.7	211	51.1	173	42.0
25 to 44 years	1 223	1 185	96.9	832	68.1	685	56.0
45 to 64 years	1 131	1 121	99.1	888	78.5	797	70.5
65 to 74 years	311	311	100.0	284	91.3	247	79.2
75 years and over	254	254	100.0	203	79.9	158	62.2

[1]May be of any race.
B = Base is too small to show derived measure.

At a Glance:

- Alaska's population was 655,435 in 2004, ranking 47th in the nation. Alaska had the largest total land area of any state; it was also the most sparsely populated state.

- Non-Hispanic Whites made up nearly 67 percent of the population, while Blacks accounted for only 3.4 percent. Over 15 percent of the population was American Indian or Alaska Native, which was the highest concentration of this racial group in the nation. Hispanics (of any race) made up 4.9 percent of residents, giving Alaska the 29th largest proportion of this ethnic group in the country.

- Alaska's median household income of $55,218 was relatively high, placing well above the national average of $44,389. The state's poverty rate of 9.2 percent was the eighth lowest in the country. High wages in the oil extraction industry and in government contributed to the above average median income and low rate of poverty. Alaska also distributed oil dividends to residents, which boosted government transfer payments.

- Alaska's unemployment rate of 7.5 percent was the second highest in the nation. Its gross state product ranked 46th in the nation.

Table AK-1. Population by Sex and Age, 1990, 2000, and 2004

(Number, percent.)

Sex and age	1990	2000	2004	Percent distribution, 2004	Average annual percent change, 2000–2004
Total Population	550 043	626 932	655 435	X	1.1
Percent of total U.S. population	0.2	0.2	0.2	X	X
Sex					
Male	289 867	324 112	338 910	51.7	1.1
Female	260 176	302 820	316 525	48.3	1.1
Age					
Under 5 years	54 897	47 591	49 758	7.6	-0.8
5 to 17 years	117 447	143 126	138 471	21.1	1.2
18 years and over	83 421	436 215	467 206	71.3	1.5
18 to 24 years	377 699	57 292	73 960	11.3	1.9
25 to 44 years	55 847	203 522	182 955	27.9	-1.2
45 to 64 years	216 062	139 702	168 404	25.7	5.2
65 years and over	22 369	35 699	41 887	6.4	4.7
85 years and over	1 251	2 634	3 502	0.5	8.0
Median age (years)	29.3	32.4	33.3	X	X

X = Not applicable.

Average Annual Rate of Population Growth, 1980–2004

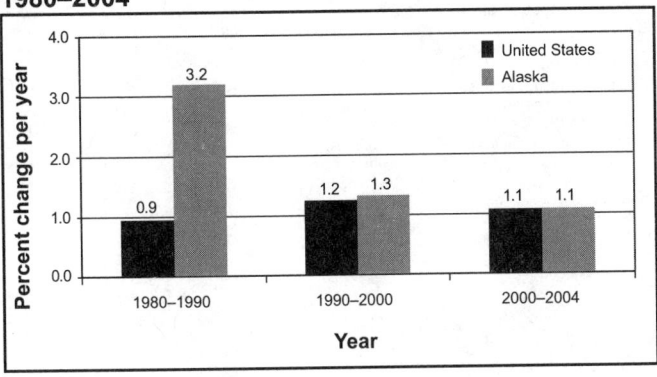

POPULATION

Although small, Alaska's population has increased steadily over the years. From 2000 to 2004, the state's population grew by 4.5 percent, a rate slightly above the national average. This population increase was mostly due to a high number of births relative to the total number of deaths. International immigration also helped offset out-migration from the state. Anchorage was the largest metropolitan area in the state. The age of the population was relatively young—nearly 29 percent of residents were under 18 years old. Only 6.4 percent of Alaska's residents were 65 years old or over, compared with 12.4 percent nationally.

Table AK-2. Population by Race and Hispanic Origin, 1990, 2000, and 2004

(Number, percent.)

Race and Hispanic origin	1990	2000	2004
Total Population	550 043	626 932	655 435
Non-Hispanic (Percent)			
One race[1]			
White	73.9	68.0	66.9
Black	4.0	3.4	3.4
American Indian, Alaska Native[2]	15.6	15.5	15.5
Asian and Pacific Islander[2]	3.6	4.5	5.0
Other race[2]	1.2	. . .	. . .
Two or more races	. . .	4.5	4.4
Hispanic or Latino[3] (Percent)	3.2	4.1	4.9

[1]Individuals could report only one race in the 1990 census and could report one or more races on the 2000 census. Data on race in 2000 and 2004 are not comparable to 1990.
[2]Data for 1990 include people of Hispanic or Latino origin.
[3]May be of any race.
. . . = Not available.

Minority Population as a Percent of Total Population, 2004

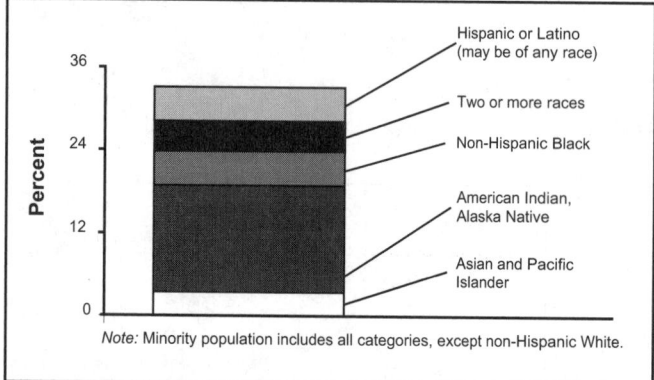

Note: Minority population includes all categories, except non-Hispanic White.

Age-Adjusted Death Rates, Average 2000–2002

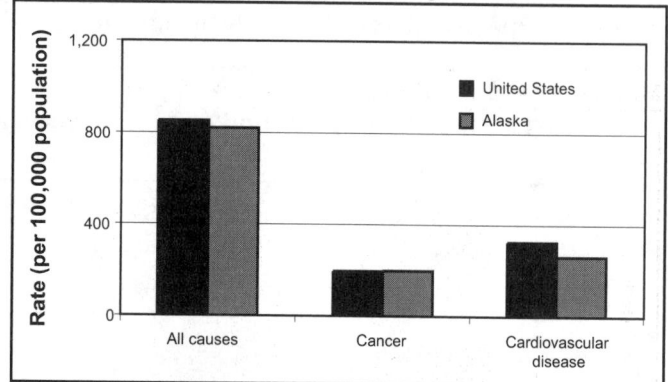

HEALTH

Alaska had an above average birth rate, but its rate of teenage births was below the U.S. average. The state's infant mortality rate just about matched the U.S. rate of 6.9 deaths per 1,000 live births. In 2004, 17 percent of Alaska's residents lacked health insurance, compared with the national average rate of 15.7 percent.

Table AK-3. Health Characteristics, 2000–2004

(Number, rate, percent.)

Item	State	U.S.
Births, 2003–2004		
Number of births	10 086	4 089 950
Birth rate (per 1,000 population)	15.5	14.1
Teenage birth rate (per 1,000 women age 15–19 years)	38.6	41.6
Mortality Rates, Average 2000–2002		
Infant mortality rate (per 1,000 live births)	6.8	6.9
Age-adjusted mortality rate (per 100,000 population)		
All races	825.4	853.3
Non-Hispanic White	781.2	843.1
Black	841.8	1 097.7
American Indian, Alaska Native	1 143.8	687.0
Asian and Pacific Islander	551.6	486.0
Hispanic or Latino[1]	702.8	642.7
Health Insurance, 2004		
Percent of all persons without health insurance	17.0	15.7
Percent of children without health insurance	10.9	11.2
Percent of low-income children without health insurance	7.5	7.1

[1]May be of any race.

Table AK-4. Leading Causes of Death, Average 2000–2002

(Number, rate per 100,000 population.)

Cause	Number of deaths	Age-adjusted death rates	
		State	U.S.
ALL CAUSES	2 973	825.4	853.3
Leading Causes			
Major cardiovascular diseases	822	267.3	326.5
Cancer	703	195.5	196.0
Chronic lower respiratory diseases	140	47.9	43.7
Unintentional injuries	345	61.0	35.7
Diabetes (underlying cause)	84	23.7	25.2
Influenza and pneumonia	44	16.1	22.7
Alzheimer's disease	51	21.8	19.0
Motor vehicle accidents	98	17.2	15.0
Nephritis, nephrotic syndrome, and nephrosis ..	25	8.4	13.8
Septicemia	22	6.9	11.4
Suicides	124	19.4	10.7
Firearm-related	113	17.6	10.3
Cirrhosis	52	9.9	9.5
Drug-induced	70	10.7	7.9
Alcohol-induced	114	19.5	6.9
Homicides	38	5.7	6.0
Falls	17	3.9	5.2
HIV	11	1.7	5.0
Viral hepatitis	10	1.9	2.0
Anemias	*	*	1.6
Drownings	38	5.9	1.3
Fire deaths	13	2.4	1.2

Note: The rates are age-adjusted to the U.S. 2000 standard population.

* = Unreliable data.

Table AK-5. Households and Housing Characteristics, 1990, 2000, and 2004

(Number, percent, and dollars.)

Characteristic	1990	2000	2004	Average annual percent change, 2000–2004
Total Households	188 915	221 600	228 358	0.8
Family households	132 837	152 337	156 309	0.6
Married-couple family	106 079	116 318	119 212	0.6
Other family	26 758	36 019	37 097	0.7
Male householder, no wife present	8 529	12 082	13 428	2.7
Female householder, no husband present	18 229	23 937	23 669	-0.3
Nonfamily households	56 078	69 263	72 049	1.0
Householder living alone	41 826	52 060	52 699	0.3
Householder not living alone	14 252	17 203	19 350	3.0
Housing Characteristics				
Average size	2.80	2.74	2.78	X
Housing units	232 608	260 978	271 533	1.0
Occupied housing units	188 915	221 600	228 358	0.8
Owner-occupied	105 989	138 509	149 669	2.0
Renter-occupied	82 926	83 091	78 689	-1.4
Median gross rent of renter-occupied housing units (dollars)	559	720	808	2.9
Median value of owner-occupied housing units (dollars)	94 400	144 200	179 304	5.6

X = Not applicable.

Median Housing Value and Median Rent, 2004

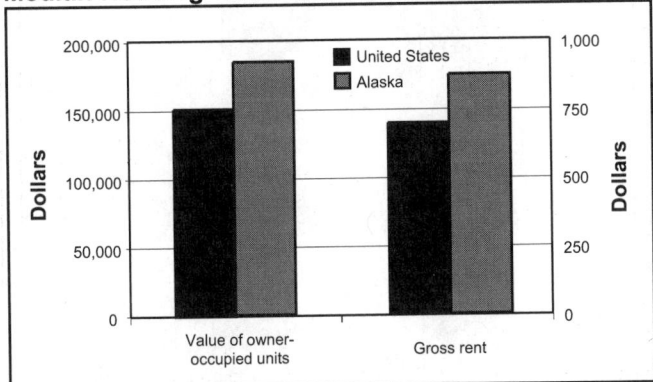

Median Household Income, 1984–2004 (2004 Dollars)

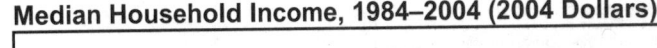
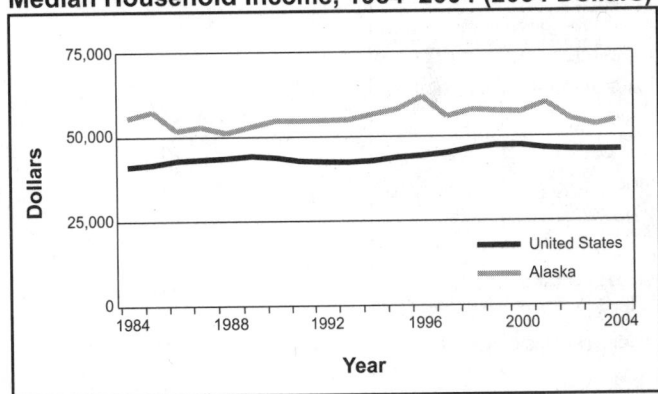

Table AK-6. Household Income and Poverty Status, 1980–2004

(2004 CPI-U-RS adjusted dollars, rate.)

Year	State — Median household income (2004 dollars)	State — Poverty rate	U.S. — Median household income (2004 dollars)	U.S. — Poverty rate
2004	55 218	9.2	44 389	12.7
2003	53 230	9.6	44 482	12.5
2002	55 434	8.8	44 546	12.1
2001	61 212	8.5	45 062	11.7
2000	57 967	7.6	46 058	11.3
1999	58 257	7.6	46 129	11.9
1998	58 668	9.4	45 003	12.7
1997	56 327	8.8	43 430	13.3
1996	63 266	8.2	42 544	13.7
1995	59 025	7.1	41 943	13.8
1994	57 197	10.2	40 677	14.5
1993	55 266	9.1	40 217	15.1
1992	55 155	10.2	40 422	14.8
1991	54 928	11.8	40 746	14.2
1990	55 073	11.4	41 963	13.5
1989	52 969	10.5	42 524	12.8
1988	50 790	11.0	41 771	13.0
1987	52 846	12.0	41 322	13.4
1986	51 560	11.4	40 939	13.6
1985	58 238	8.7	39 545	14.0
1984	55 982	9.6	38 782	14.4
1983	. . .	12.6	. . .	15.2
1982	. . .	10.6	. . .	15.0
1981	. . .	9.0	. . .	14.0
1980	. . .	9.6	. . .	13.0

. . . = Not available.

Table AK-7. Employment Status by Demographic Group, 2004
(Numbers in thousands, rate.)

Characteristic	Civilian noninstitutional population	Civilian labor force		Employed	Unemployment rate
		Number	Participation rate		
SEX AND AGE					
Total	465	331	71.1	306	7.5
16 to 19 years	38	18	47.7	14	22.5
20 to 24 years	44	33	74.3	29	12.6
25 to 34 years	83	68	81.4	63	7.3
35 to 44 years	90	77	85.4	73	5.9
45 to 54 years	105	88	83.5	82	6.1
55 to 64 years	57	37	65.7	36	3.6
65 years and over	46	9	20.1	9	4.7
Men	233	179	76.6	165	7.9
16 to 19 years	20	9	44.6	7	22.4
20 to 24 years	21	17	79.5	14	13.4
25 to 34 years	40	36	91.3	34	6.7
35 to 44 years	47	43	91.7	40	6.8
45 to 54 years	54	48	88.3	44	7.4
55 to 64 years	31	21	69.4	21	3.4
65 years and over	22	5	25.0	5	5.3
Women	232	152	65.6	141	7.2
16 to 19 years	19	9	51.0	7	22.6
20 to 24 years	23	16	69.7	14	11.9
25 to 34 years	44	32	72.5	29	8.0
35 to 44 years	44	35	78.8	33	4.8
45 to 54 years	51	40	78.3	38	4.6
55 to 64 years	26	16	61.3	16	3.8
65 years and over	25	4	15.9	4	3.8
MARITAL STATUS					
Married men, spouse present	125	102	81.4	97	4.8
Married women, spouse present	127	85	66.7	81	5.0
Women who maintain families	25	18	73.4	17	8.0
RACE, HISPANIC ORIGIN, AND SEX					
White	341	247	72.4	233	5.7
Men	175	136	77.5	128	5.8
Women	166	111	67.0	105	5.4
Black	14	10	72.5	9	8.5
Asian	30	22	73.1	20	5.2
Men	13	10	81.1	10	4.5
Women	17	11	67.0	11	5.9
Hispanic or Latino[1]	22	16	75.4	15	7.3
Men	11	9	81.6	8	7.1
Women	11	7	68.9	7	7.6
RACE, HISPANIC ORIGIN, AND AGE					
White					
16 to 19 years	24	12	49.7	10	19.7
20 to 24 years	29	22	75.9	20	8.9
25 to 34 years	60	50	83.0	47	5.3
35 to 44 years	66	57	86.8	55	4.3
45 to 54 years	82	70	85.1	66	5.1
55 to 64 years	45	30	66.6	29	3.0
65 years and over	36	7	18.5	6	2.0

Note: Data in Table 7 are from the Current Population Survey (CPS) and do not match Bureau of Labor Statistics estimates in Table 8. See notes and definitions for more details.

Table AK-8. Employment Status, 1990–2004
(Numbers in thousands, rate.)

Year	Civilian labor force	Employed	Unemployed	Unemployment rate
2004	332 689	307 704	24 985	7.5
2003	330 616	305 063	25 553	7.7
2002	325 842	302 622	23 220	7.1
2001	320 670	300 917	19 753	6.2
2000	318 835	299 099	19 736	6.2
1999	316 507	297 019	19 488	6.2
1998	313 079	293 939	19 140	6.1
1997	311 961	289 963	21 998	7.1
1996	308 573	285 552	23 021	7.5
1995	303 666	282 098	21 568	7.1
1994	300 742	278 198	22 544	7.5
1993	293 758	271 258	22 500	7.7
1992	288 777	262 980	25 797	8.9
1991	278 799	255 799	23 000	8.2
1990	270 040	251 026	19 014	7.0

Note: Population age 16 years and over.

Unemployment Rate, 1980–2004

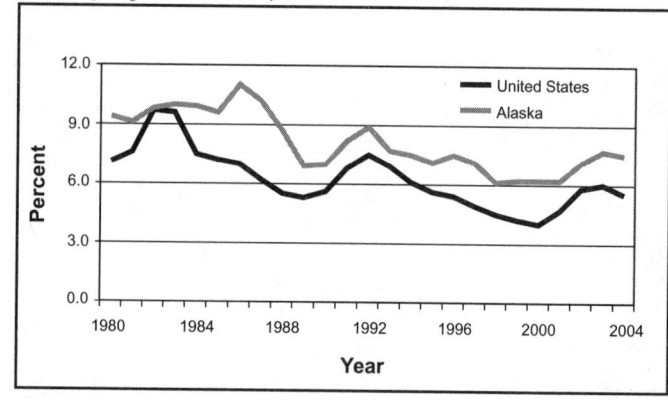

Table AK-9. Employment and Average Wages by Industry, 2001–2004

(Estimates are based on the 2002 North American Industry Classification System [NAICS].)

Industry	2001	2002	2003	2004	Annual average percent change, 2001–2004
	Number of jobs				
TOTAL EMPLOYMENT BY PLACE OF WORK	401 639	411 267	418 625	428 021	2.1
Farm Employment	874	964	949	963	3.3
Nonfarm Employment	400 765	410 303	417 676	427 058	2.1
Private employment	302 850	310 069	317 188	326 172	2.5
Forestry, fishing, hunting, and other[1]	D	14 182	10 827	10 285	...
Mining	D	11 520	11 008	11 260	...
Utilities	1 695	1 847	1 899	1 908	4.0
Construction	22 561	23 498	24 999	25 993	4.8
Manufacturing	14 361	13 107	13 531	14 358	0.0
Durable goods manufacturing	D	D	2 971	3 135	...
Nondurable goods manufacturing	D	D	10 560	11 223	...
Wholesale trade	7 292	7 263	7 190	7 415	0.6
Retail trade	43 021	43 819	44 134	45 470	1.9
Transportation and warehousing	22 707	22 581	22 180	22 331	-0.6
Information	8 354	7 949	7 999	7 871	-2.0
Finance and insurance	11 194	11 036	11 329	11 451	0.8
Real estate and rental and leasing	13 211	15 377	19 853	20 852	16.4
Professional and technical services	20 110	20 253	20 712	21 189	1.8
Management of companies and enterprises	1 983	2 153	1 245	1 308	-13.0
Administrative and waste services	15 401	15 536	16 087	16 596	2.5
Educational services	4 454	4 652	4 771	4 852	2.9
Health care and social assistance	34 462	36 397	39 458	42 221	7.0
Arts, entertainment, and recreation	9 144	9 526	9 540	9 725	2.1
Accommodation and food services	28 204	29 269	30 282	31 161	3.4
Other services, except public administration	D	20 104	20 144	19 926	...
Government and government enterprises	97 915	100 234	100 488	100 886	1.0
	Dollars				
AVERAGE WAGES AND SALARIES BY PLACE OF WORK	35 744	37 001	37 878	39 103	3.0
Farm Earnings	24 346	24 161	23 201	26 321	2.6
Nonfarm Earnings	35 755	37 015	37 894	39 117	3.0
Private earnings	34 853	35 774	36 349	37 511	2.5
Forestry, fishing, hunting, and other[1]	D	50 640	49 340	49 605	...
Mining	D	90 871	87 229	91 885	...
Utilities	57 119	58 168	58 973	60 310	1.8
Construction	49 038	50 684	52 480	52 825	2.5
Manufacturing	30 103	32 721	34 468	33 519	3.6
Durable goods manufacturing	D	D	38 969	38 799	...
Nondurable goods manufacturing	D	D	33 658	32 566	...
Wholesale trade	39 625	40 564	41 527	43 096	2.8
Retail trade	23 679	24 516	25 435	25 761	2.8
Transportation and warehousing	42 733	43 975	45 230	47 673	3.7
Information	42 910	44 408	44 860	47 962	3.8
Finance and insurance	41 134	43 027	45 380	46 306	4.0
Real estate and rental and leasing	26 277	27 503	27 866	29 328	3.7
Professional and technical services	44 556	45 627	46 215	48 515	2.9
Management of companies and enterprises	49 609	46 793	59 917	61 902	7.7
Administrative and waste services	28 364	29 861	29 868	31 584	3.6
Educational services	22 644	25 276	25 770	27 061	6.1
Health care and social assistance	32 552	33 530	34 256	35 187	2.6
Arts, entertainment, and recreation	14 451	15 136	16 252	16 897	5.4
Accommodation and food services	16 823	17 345	17 942	18 686	3.6
Other services, except public administration	D	25 990	26 787	27 731	...
Government and government enterprises	37 768	39 758	41 364	42 803	4.3

Note: Average wages and salaries are a calculation by the editors of wage and salary disbursements divided by full- and part-time wage and salary employment. Data may not add to total or may appear as zero due to rounding.

[1] "Other" consists of the number of jobs held by U.S. residents employed by international organizations and foreign embassies and consulates in the United States.
D = Suppressed to avoid disclosure of data of individual companies.
. . . = Not available.

LABOR MARKET

Alaska had one of the highest employment/population ratios in the country, reflecting its larger proportion of working-age residents. The state has long experienced a high unemployment rate; it reached 7.5 percent in 2004 and was among the highest in the country. Employment by place of work grew by 6.6 percent from 2000 to 2004. Particular growth occurred in real estate, rental, and leasing; health care and social assistance; and construction. Total earnings grew at a strong pace over the period, at a rate well above the national average. Wages and salaries in management of companies and enterprises and in educational services showed the greatest increases.

Employment by Industry, 2004

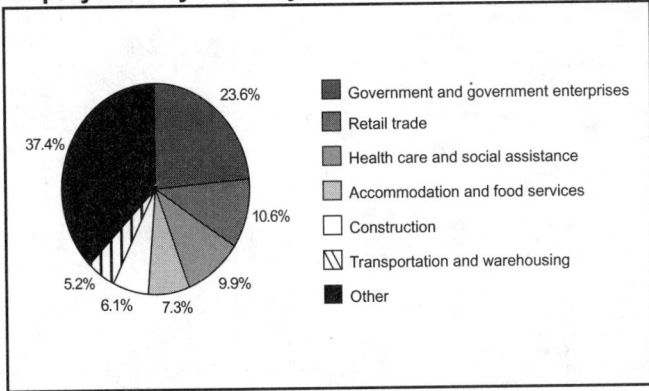

23.6% 37.4% 10.6% 5.2% 6.1% 7.3% 9.9%

- Government and government enterprises
- Retail trade
- Health care and social assistance
- Accommodation and food services
- Construction
- Transportation and warehousing
- Other

Table AK-10. Personal Income by Major Source, Selected Years 1980–2004

(Millions of dollars, except where noted.)

Item	1980	1990	2000	2001	2002	2003	2004	Average annual percent change, 2000–2004
Earnings by Place of Work	5 965	11 050	14 874	16 218	17 053	17 901	19 098	6.4
Wage and salary disbursements	4 403	7 809	10 725	11 322	11 915	12 370	13 017	5.0
Supplements to wages and salaries	1 035	2 021	2 598	2 812	3 186	3 450	3 825	10.2
Proprietors' income[1]	527	1 220	1 552	2 085	1 953	2 082	2 256	9.8
Farm proprietors' income	1	4	8	8	5	5	5	-10.6
Nonfarm proprietors' income	526	1 216	1 544	2 077	1 947	2 077	2 251	9.9
(-) Contributions for government social insurance[2]	527	1 097	1 527	1 629	1 718	1 781	1 893	5.5
(+) Adjustment for residence[3]	-329	-654	-887	-937	-998	-1 015	-1 081	X
(=) Net Earnings by Place of Residence	5 109	9 299	12 461	13 652	14 337	15 105	16 124	6.7
(+) Dividends, interest, and rent[4]	573	1 950	3 191	3 148	3 022	3 023	2 993	-1.6
(+) Personal current transfer receipts	343	1 369	3 090	3 249	3 351	3 275	3 223	1.1
Personal income	6 025	12 617	18 741	20 050	20 709	21 403	22 340	4.5
Farm income	6 022	12 610	18 727	20 034	20 694	21 389	22 325	4.5
Nonfarm income	3	7	14	16	15	14	16	2.0
Per Capita Personal Income (Dollars)[5]	14 866	22 804	29 867	31 704	32 316	33 015	34 085	3.4

Note: Data may not add to total or may appear as zero due to rounding.

[1]Proprietors' income includes the inventory valuation adjustment and the capital consumption adjustment.
[2]Contributions for government social insurance are included in earnings by type and industry, but they are excluded from personal income.
[3]The adjustment for residence is the net inflow of the earnings of interarea commuters.
[4]Rental income of persons includes the capital consumption adjustment.
[5]Per capita personal income is total personal income divided by total midyear population.
X = Not applicable.

Per Capita Personal Income, 1980–2004 (Current Dollars)

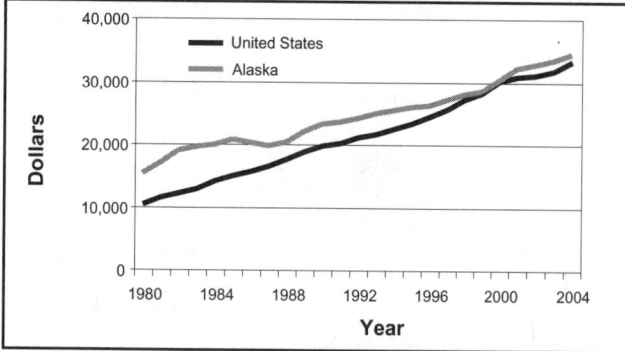

ECONOMIC ACTIVITY

Real gross state product (GSP) rebounded substantially from its decline during the 2001 recession, growing by 8.6 percent in 2002. Growth fell off in 2003 before increasing again in 2004. Government, transportation and warehousing, and real estate and rental and leasing made the largest contributions to GSP during the 2003–2004 period. Mining remains the state's leading private industry; however, it has declined in recent years. Housing prices rose steadily from 2000–2004, although at rates slightly below the national average. In 2004, the state ranked 16th in the country with a median value of owner-occupied housing of $179,304. This was up considerably from the 2000 median value of $144,200.

Table AK-11. Real Gross State Product, 1997–2004

(Millions of chained 2000 dollars, percent.)

Industry	1997	1998	1999	2000	2001	2002	2003	2004	Average annual percent change, 2001–2004
GROSS STATE PRODUCT	28 121	26 852	27 392	27 590	26 432	28 703	28 103	29 047	3.2
As a percent of U.S. gross product	0.3	0.3	0.3	0.3	0.3	0.3	0.3	0.3	X
Private Industries	22 669	21 466	22 189	22 381	21 183	23 332	22 612	23 279	3.2
Agriculture, forestry, fishing, and hunting	651	454	479	533	315	321	368	368	5.3
Mining	7 921	6 105	6 606	6 249	4 921	6 515	5 067	5 024	0.7
Utilities	266	280	287	308	272	313	353	360	9.8
Construction	1 312	1 257	1 218	1 171	1 216	1 279	1 360	1 381	4.3
Manufacturing	727	790	664	571	577	569	610	615	2.1
As a percent of gross state product	2.6	2.9	2.4	2.1	2.2	2.0	2.2	2.1	X
Wholesale trade	610	684	657	623	666	682	655	681	0.7
Retail trade	1 358	1 379	1 429	1 394	1 481	1 639	1 758	1 856	7.8
Transportation and warehousing	2 529	2 406	2 668	3 072	2 993	2 961	2 982	3 123	1.4
Information	630	672	735	784	813	824	859	941	5.0
Finance and insurance	868	941	866	795	776	870	1 005	1 036	10.1
Real estate and rental and leasing	2 272	2 295	2 439	2 510	2 617	2 653	2 724	2 859	3.0
Services	4 077	4 231	4 236	4 369	4 529	4 787	5 000	5 236	5.0
As a percent of gross state product	14.5	15.8	15.5	15.8	17.1	16.7	17.8	18.0	X
Professional and technical services	883	922	898	912	975	995	1 045	1 079	3.4
Management of companies and enterprises	158	152	160	161	198	212	174	181	-2.9
Administrative and waste services	498	552	513	473	459	497	531	551	6.3
Educational services	88	90	94	91	82	89	82	79	-1.2
Health care and social assistance	1 100	1 109	1 149	1 284	1 380	1 489	1 626	1 737	8.0
Arts, entertainment, and recreation	192	238	231	202	212	238	244	247	5.2
Accommodation and food services	653	657	685	736	707	750	786	834	5.7
Other services, except public administration	505	511	506	510	516	517	512	528	0.8
Government	5 434	5 358	5 200	5 209	5 249	5 379	5 494	5 769	3.2
As a percent of gross state product	19.3	20.0	19.0	18.9	19.9	18.7	19.5	19.9	X

X = Not applicable.

Table AK-12. Government Transfer Payments, Selected Years 1980–2004

(Millions of dollars, percent.)

Item	1980	1990	2000	2001	2002	2003	2004	Average annual percent change, 2000–2004
CURRENT TRANSFER PAYMENTS TO INDIVIDUALS	317	1 305	2 966	3 111	3 228	3 164	3 113	1.2
Retirement and Disability Insurance Benefits	75	217	482	523	566	595	637	7.2
Old-age, survivors, and disability insurance (OASDI) benefits	69	203	465	506	545	576	616	7.3
Railroad retirement and disability benefits	1	1	2	2	3	2	2	1.3
Workers' compensation	5	13	14	14	17	16	17	5.4
Other government retirement and disability insurance benefits	*	*	*	1	1	1	1	28.0
Medical Benefits	69	270	794	938	1 105	1 255	1 317	13.5
Medicare benefits	18	82	243	277	304	328	371	11.2
Public assistance medical care benefits	48	170	531	634	762	900	913	14.5
Military medical insurance benefits	2	18	20	27	39	27	33	13.7
Income Maintenance Benefits	67	139	276	286	311	325	342	5.5
Supplemental Security Income (SSI) benefits	7	27	89	94	101	103	107	4.7
Family assistance	27	62	70	67	69	65	59	-4.2
Food stamps	25	27	46	48	60	61	71	11.6
Other income maintenance benefits	8	24	71	77	81	95	105	10.1
Unemployment Insurance Compensation	52	79	109	110	159	167	124	3.1
Veterans' Benefits	15	31	86	96	108	116	124	9.5
Federal Education and Training Assistance	4	14	13	15	16	15	16	4.6
Other Payments to Individuals	35	554	1 206	1 143	965	692	554	-17.7

Note: See notes and definitions for more details. Data may not add to total or may appear as zero due to rounding.

* = Less than $500,000.

EXPORTS

In 2004, Alaska ranked 37th in the country for value of exports, which have increased 30 percent since 2000. The fishing, hunting, and trapping industry accounted for more than 50 percent of the state's exports. Most of these exports were related to fishing. The mining industry ranked second, with exports valued at over $500 million. The state's top commodity export was zinc ores and concentrates. Japan was Alaska's number one market for exports, followed by South Korea, Canada, and China. Exports to Switzerland have increased substantially, rising from $2 million in 2001 to over $92 million in 2004. Most of these exports were from the primary metal industry.

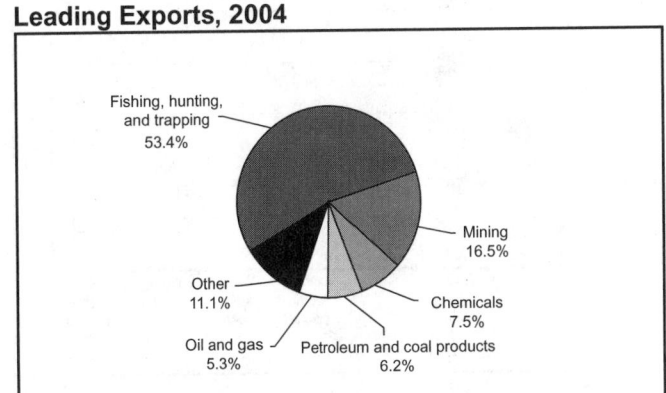

Leading Exports, 2004

Table AK-13. Exports of Goods by Leading Products and Destinations, 2001–2004

(Millions of dollars, percent, rank based on 2004 dollar values.)

Product and market	2001	2002	2003	2004	Percent share of total, 2004	Average annual percent change, 2001–2004
Total Goods						
Total	2 418	2 516	2 739	3 157	100.0	9.3
Manufactures	587	508	621	679	21.5	5.0
Agriculture and livestock	1 821	2 002	2 110	2 472	78.3	10.7
Other commodities	10	7	8	6	0.2	-17.1
Five Leading Exports (NAICS Code)						
Fishing, hunting, and trapping (114)	1 184	1 351	1 401	1 686	53.4	12.5
Mining (212)	346	389	418	520	16.5	14.6
Chemical manufactures (325)	202	166	202	238	7.5	5.5
Petroleum and coal products (324)	134	130	153	196	6.2	13.5
Oil and gas extraction (211)	145	141	148	166	5.3	4.6
Five Leading Markets	2 339	2 454	2 664	3 116	98.7	10.0
Japan	1 039	1 105	1 032	1 190	37.7	4.6
South Korea	463	417	567	580	18.4	7.8
Canada	188	155	231	247	7.8	9.5
China	102	148	154	242	7.6	33.1
Germany	115	118	113	147	4.6	8.4

Table AK-14. Agriculture, 1997 and 2002

(Number, acres, and dollars.)

Item	1997	2002
Number of farms	548	609
Land in farms (acres)	881 045	900 715
Farm Size		
Average size of farm (acres)	1 608	1 479
Farms by size (percent distribution)		
Fewer than 50 acres	35.4	42.0
50 to 499 acres	48.2	41.9
500 acres or more	16.4	16.1
Market Value of Land and Equipment (Dollars)		
Land and buildings average value per farm	486 827	543 213
Average value per acre	303	367
Machinery and equipment average value per farm	53 003	71 790
Value of Sales (Thousands of Dollars)		
Agricultural products sold	24 650	46 143
Crops	15 968	20 543
Livestock, poultry, and their products	8 682	25 600
Average per farm (dollars)	44 982	75 768
Value of sales (percent distribution)		
Less than $10,000	59.9	59.4
$10,000 to $99,999	31.6	28.9
$100,000 or more	8.6	11.7
Government Payments		
Payments (thousands of dollars)	1 195	1 765
Percent of farms receiving government payments	21.2	11.8
Farm operators whose principal occupation is farming (percent)	55.8	60.8

AGRICULTURE

The total value of sales from farming in Alaska reached $46 million in 2002 (the latest year for which data are available from the Department of Agriculture's Census of Agriculture), which was the smallest amount of any state. Greenhouse and nursery products were the most prominent products, followed by dairy items. Over 59 percent of the state's 609 farms sold total products valued at less than $10,000.

ENERGY

Energy prices in Alaska were very low in 2001. The state had the second lowest prices in the country, behind only North Dakota. However, energy expenditures per person totaled $4,394, which was the second highest in the nation. In terms of total energy consumption, Alaska ranked among the 20 lowest states, but on a per capita basis, the state ranked first with expenditures of $1,164. The industrial sector was the largest consumer, followed by the transportation, commercial, and residential sectors.

Energy Consumption by Source, 2001

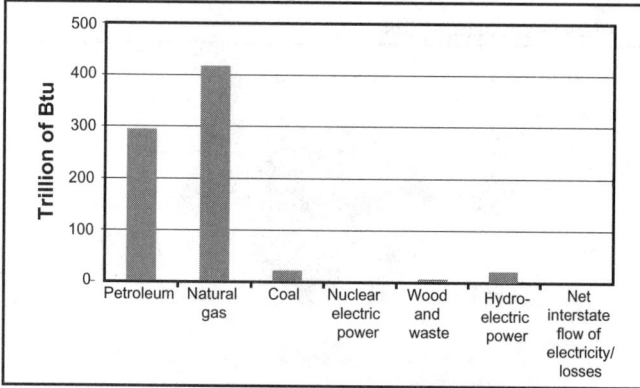

Energy Consumption by Sector, 2001

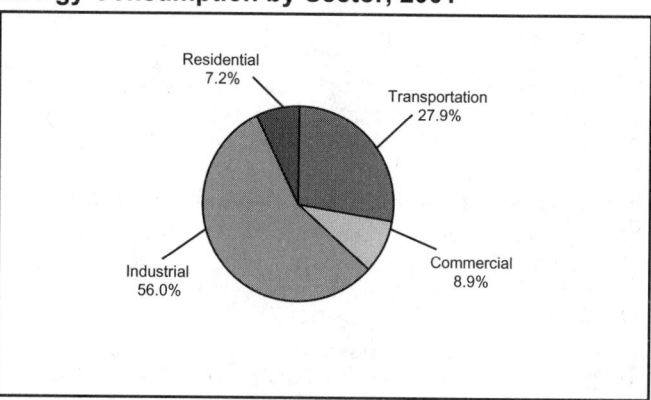

Table AK-15. Energy Consumption, Expenditures, and Prices, Selected Years 1960–2001

(Dollars, Btu [British Thermal Unit], percent distribution.)

Item	1960	1965	1970	1975	1980	1985	1990	1995	2000	2001
Total Consumption (Billion Btu)	61 441	87 797	182 041	232 185	296 080	474 187	584 633	704 355	637 920	736 647
Consumption per capita (million Btu)	271.9	324.0	601.6	617.2	736.8	890.5	1 062.9	1 171.3	1 017.5	1 164.3
Consumption by Sector (Percent Distribution)										
Residential	16.7	17.2	13.7	15.6	11.8	9.9	8.3	7.2	7.3	7.2
Commercial	11.8	17.3	16.3	14.5	11.4	12.2	10.3	9.4	9.8	8.9
Industrial	27.3	26.3	28.0	35.6	46.4	45.5	52.5	58.7	48.7	56.0
Transportation	44.2	39.2	42.0	34.3	30.3	32.5	28.9	24.7	34.2	27.9
Consumption by Source (Billion Btu)										
Coal	7 189	9 888	13 159	15 271	4 310	11 587	12 387	12 882	16 455	15 897
Natural gas	2 034	7 670	64 045	85 175	153 805	214 042	326 826	432 813	333 713	413 051
Petroleum	45 418	61 720	96 001	123 132	129 314	236 977	226 436	235 973	275 493	292 237
Nuclear electric power	0	0	0	0	0	0	0	0	0	0
Hydroelectric power[1]	3 120	3 655	3 806	3 713	5 599	7 816	10 137	14 149	10 220	13 691
Wood and waste	3 681	4 863	5 029	4 894	3 052	3 765	8 792	8 482	1 949	1 671
Other	0	0	0	0	0	0	0	55	91	100
Net interstate flow of electricity/losses[2]	0	0	0	0	0	0	0	0	0	0
Total Expenditures (Thousands of Dollars)	...	...	188 100	472 000	1 010 600	1 869 200	2 077 900	2 062 200	2 834 000	2 780 000
Expenditures per capita (dollars)	...	...	622	1 255	2 515	3 510	3 778	3 429	4 520	4 394
Prices by Sector (Dollars Per Million Btu)										
Total	...	...	1.39	2.70	5.05	5.93	6.87	6.40	8.52	8.12
Residential	...	...	2.30	3.24	6.62	9.16	10.36	9.37	12.49	11.79
Commercial	...	...	1.67	2.60	4.16	6.93	7.97	7.33	8.78	10.17
Industrial	...	...	0.78	1.83	1.91	2.54	2.62	3.17	5.26	5.09
Transportation	...	...	1.39	3.06	7.31	7.27	7.54	6.83	8.60	7.93

[1]A negative number in this row results from pumped storage for which, overall, more electricity is expended than created to provide electricity during peak demand periods.
[2]Net interstate flow of electricity is the difference between the amount of energy in the electricity sold within a state (including associated losses) and the energy input at the electric utilities within the state. A positive number indicates that more electricity (including associated losses) came into the state than went out of the state during the year; conversely, a negative number indicates that more electricity (including associated losses) went out of the state than came into the state.
... = Not available.

Table AK-16. State Taxes, Fiscal 2004

(Dollars, percent distribution.)

Item	Thousands of dollars	Percent distribution	Dollars per capita	
			State	U.S.
TOTAL TAXES	1 288 164	100.0	1 966.7	2 024.8
Property Taxes	47 368	3.7	72.3	38.9
Sales and Gross Receipts	168 392	13.1	257.1	1 003.4
Selective sales taxes	168 392	13.1	257.1	326.4
Alcoholic beverages	28 262	2.2	43.2	15.7
Insurance premiums	49 873	3.9	76.1	47.0
Motor fuels	40 660	3.2	62.1	114.6
Tobacco products	43 222	3.4	66.0	42.0
Licenses	83 738	6.5	127.8	134.9
Hunting and fishing	23 713	1.8	36.2	4.2
Motor vehicle	43 782	3.4	66.8	59.4
Occupation and business, not elsewhere classified	9 090	0.7	13.9	37.1
Other Taxes	988 666	76.8	1 509.4	847.6
Corporation net income	339 564	26.4	518.4	105.1
Severance	646 851	50.2	987.6	21.5

GOVERNMENT FINANCE

Total state per capita revenues and expenditures were quite high in Alaska. The state ranked first in the nation for its per capita expenditures of about $10,975, far exceeding Vermont, which ranked second with per capita expenditures of $5,806. However, the state's per capita taxes remained low, partly reflecting the large federal government expenditures directed to the state. Alaska was the only state with neither an individual income tax nor a sales tax. The state's permanent fund, which is derived from oil revenues, provides income dividends to Alaska residents. These distributions are shown in the "other taxes" revenue category in Table 17 and included in the severance totals in Table 16.

Per Capita State Taxes, Fiscal 2004

Table AK-17. State Government Finances, 2003

(Dollars, percent distribution.)

Item	Millions of dollars	Percent distribution	Dollars per capita	
			State	U.S.
GENERAL REVENUE	6 098 669	100.0	9 411.5	3 832.6
Intergovernmental revenue	1 997 175	32.7	3 082.1	1 246.0
Taxes	1 120 133	18.4	1 728.6	1 891.6
General sales	0	0.0	0.0	636.0
Selective sales	152 132	2.5	234.8	307.4
License taxes	70 107	1.1	108.2	123.6
Individual income tax	0	0.0	0.0	626.8
Corporate income tax	207 075	3.4	319.6	97.8
Other taxes	690 819	11.3	1 066.1	99.9
Current charges	349 567	5.7	539.5	366.5
Miscellaneous general revenue	2 631 794	43.2	4 061.4	328.6
GENERAL EXPENDITURE	7 111 497	100.0	10 974.5	4 010.5
Intergovernmental expenditure	1 091 391	15.3	1 684.2	1 316.9
Direct expenditure	6 020 106	84.7	9 290.3	2 693.6
Expenditure by Function				
Education	1 693 672	23.8	2 613.7	1 416.4
Public welfare	1 312 794	18.5	2 025.9	1 083.3
Hospitals	35 437	0.5	54.7	132.3
Health	168 955	2.4	260.7	173.0
Highways	810 807	11.4	1 251.2	295.4
Police protection	83 961	1.2	129.6	38.4
Correction	182 046	2.6	280.9	135.0
Natural resources	256 006	3.6	395.1	64.0
Parks and recreation	9 657	0.1	14.9	20.1
Government administration	377 700	5.3	582.9	151.3
Interest on general debt	256 233	3.6	395.4	107.8
Other and unallocable	1 924 229	27.1	2 969.5	393.4
DEBT AT END OF FISCAL YEAR	5 829 798	X	8 996.6	2 404.7
CASH AND SECURITY HOLDINGS	42 721 407	X	65 928.1	8 938.4

X = Not applicable.

Table AK-18. Education Indicators, 2000–2004

(Percent, number.)

Item	State	U.S.
Total Population 25 Years and Over (Thousands), 2004	387	186 877
Educational Attainment, 2004		
Percent high school graduate or more	90.2	85.2
Percent college graduate or more	25.5	27.7
Elementary and Secondary Schools, 2002–2003		
Total students	134 364	48 202 324
Percent of students eligible for free or reduced-price lunch ..	. . .	40.6
Percent of students who were English language learners	14.8	7.8
Total schools	500	92 330
Student/teacher ratio	17.2	15.9
Per student expenditures	9 870	8 041
Dropouts, Grades 9–12, 2000–2001 (Percent)	8.1	. . .
Higher Education, 2002–2003		
Total enrollment	30 066	17 035 027
Bachelor's degrees awarded	1 363	1 348 503
Percent women	64.1	57.5

. . . = Not available.

Educational Attainment, 2004

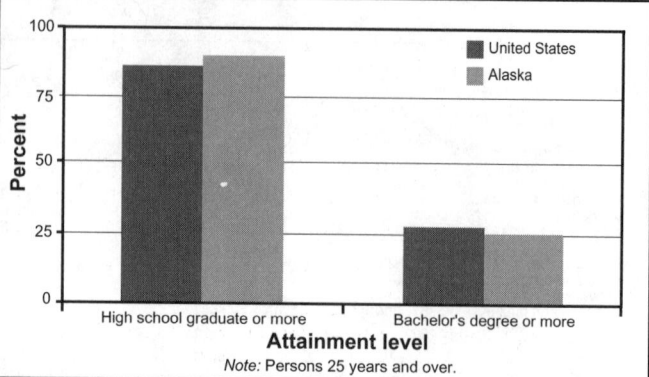

Note: Persons 25 years and over.

EDUCATION

Alaska had an above average proportion of student-age population. More than 21 percent of Alaska's population fell between the ages of 5 and 17 years, which ranked second in the nation (behind only Utah). In 2004, the state's student/teacher ratio was among the 10 highest in the nation. Alaska was one of 8 states with a proportion of high school graduates exceeding 90 percent. However, the state's college attainment level of 25.5 percent was below the U.S. average. Alaska's per student expenditures exceeded the national average and ranked eighth among the states. Alaska's dropout rate of 8.1 percent was the second highest among the 46 states reporting data.

VOTER PARTICIPATION

Alaska had relatively high voter turnout in both the 2000 and 2004 elections. Almost two-thirds of eligible voters went to the polls in both 2000 and 2004, ranking the state 6th and 10th in the nation, respectively, in terms of participation rates. Voting rates were about even for men and women in Alaska, while women had higher rates of voting in most other states. The state tended to vote for Republican candidates. In 2000, 58.6 percent of Alaskans voted for the Republican presidential candidate; in 2004, this proportion was 61.1 percent, according to the official tally by the Clerk of the U.S. House of Representatives.

Table AK-19. Reported Voting and Registration, November 2000 and November 2004

(Numbers in thousands, percent.)

Characteristic	Total population 18 years and over	Total citizen		Total registered		Total voted	
		Number	Percent	Number	Percent	Number	Percent
NOVEMBER 2000							
Total	412	399	96.8	299	72.5	270	65.5
Male	202	197	97.4	148	73.4	133	65.7
Female	210	202	96.3	150	71.6	137	65.4
NOVEMBER 2004							
Total	451	434	96.2	334	74.0	293	65.0
Male	224	219	97.8	168	74.8	146	65.1
Female	227	215	94.5	167	73.3	148	64.9
Race and Hispanic Origin							
White alone	359	350	97.3	278	77.3	249	69.3
Non-Hispanic White alone	343	336	98.1	269	78.4	241	70.4
Black alone	13	13	B	9	B	8	B
Asian alone	24	17	B	9	B	7	B
Hispanic or Latino[1]	22	18	B	13	B	10	B
White alone or in combination	376	367	97.4	290	77.0	259	68.9
Non-Hispanic White alone or in combination	359	352	98.1	280	78.0	251	69.9
Black alone or in combination	15	14	B	11	B	9	B
Asian alone or in combination	25	18	B	10	B	8	B
Age							
18 to 24 years	60	58	B	37	B	31	B
25 to 44 years	178	167	93.5	125	70.5	107	60.2
45 to 64 years	166	163	98.2	135	81.4	122	73.8
65 to 74 years	30	30	B	23	B	22	B
75 years and over	18	17	B	13	B	11	B

[1]May be of any race.
B = Base is too small to show derived measure.

At a Glance:

- Arizona's population was just over 5.7 million in 2004, ranking the state as the 18th largest in the nation.
- Non-Hispanic Whites composed 61.1 percent of the population, and 3.1 percent of the state's residents were Black. Nearly 5 percent of residents were American Indian or Alaska Native, giving Arizona the 7th highest proportion of this racial group in the nation. Hispanics (of any race) made up 28 percent of the population, which was among the 5 highest proportions of this racial group in the country.
- Median household income in Arizona was just below the national average, ranking 24th in the country.
- The state's poverty rate of 14.4 percent was above the national average of 12.7 percent. Arizona's rate was the 13th highest rate in the nation.
- The unemployment rate, at 5 percent, was below the national average in 2004.
- Real gross state product (GSP) grew strongly during the 2000–2004 period, seemingly unaffected by the recessionary forces felt elsewhere. In 2004, Arizona had the 22nd largest GSP in the country.

Table AZ-1. Population by Sex and Age, 1990, 2000, and 2004

(Number, percent.)

Sex and age	1990	2000	2004	Percent distribution, 2004	Average annual percent change, 2000–2004
Total Population	3 665 228	5 130 632	5 743 834	X	2.9
Percent of total U.S. population	1.5	1.8	2.0	X	X
Sex					
Male	1 810 691	2 561 057	2 873 663	50.0	2.9
Female	1 854 537	2 569 575	2 870 171	50.0	2.8
Age					
Under 5 years	292 859	382 386	449 904	7.8	2.9
5 to 17 years	688 260	984 561	1 097 356	19.1	3.4
18 years and over	649 048	3 763 685	4 196 574	73.1	3.3
18 to 24 years	2 684 109	514 101	570 795	9.9	2.6
25 to 44 years	392 680	1 511 469	1 630 429	28.4	2.5
45 to 64 years	1 163 607	1 070 276	1 263 279	22.0	4.9
65 years and over	478 774	667 839	732 071	12.7	3.1
85 years and over	37 717	68 525	85 886	1.5	6.2
Median age (years)	32.0	34.2	34.1	X	X

X = Not applicable.

Average Annual Rate of Population Growth, 1980–2004

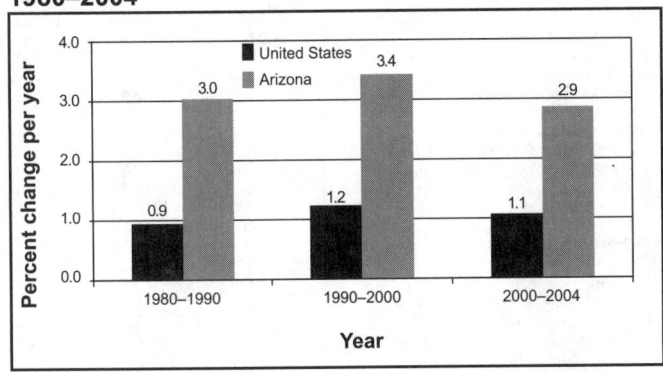

POPULATION

Arizona's population grew quite substantially over the 2000–2004 period. Its growth rate of 12 percent was the second highest in the nation, exceeded only by Nevada. Over two-thirds of this population increase was due to net immigration, with about 60 percent of these new residents migrating from other states and about 40 percent immigrating from abroad. Arizona was the second most popular destination for people moving from other states, behind only Florida. The two largest metropolitan areas in Arizona were Phoenix-Mesa-Scottsdale and Tucson. Nearly 256,000 of Arizona's residents were American Indian, giving the state the second highest number of residents of this racial group in the country.

Table AZ-2. Population by Race and Hispanic Origin, 1990, 2000, and 2004

(Number, percent.)

Race and Hispanic origin	1990	2000	2004
Total Population	3 665 228	5 130 632	5 743 834
Non-Hispanic (Percent)			
One race[1]			
White	71.7	64.2	61.1
Black	2.9	3.0	3.1
American Indian, Alaska Native[2]	5.6	4.6	4.5
Asian and Pacific Islander[2]	1.5	1.9	2.1
Other race[2]	9.1	. . .	. . .
Two or more races	. . .	1.1	1.2
Hispanic or Latino[3] (Percent)	18.8	25.3	28.0

[1]Individuals could report only one race in the 1990 census and could report one or more races on the 2000 census. Data on race in 2000 and 2004 are not comparable to 1990.
[2]Data for 1990 include people of Hispanic or Latino origin.
[3]May be of any race.
. . . = Not available.

Minority Population as a Percent of Total Population, 2004

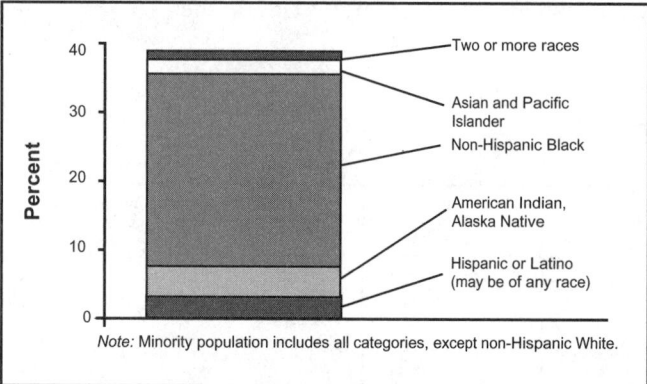

Note: Minority population includes all categories, except non-Hispanic White.

Age-Adjusted Death Rates, Average 2000–2002

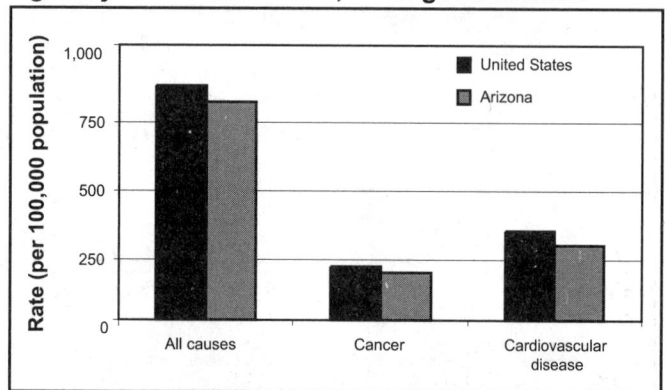

HEALTH

Arizona had the third highest birth rate in the nation. The state's teenage birth rate was the fourth highest in the United States. The infant mortality rate was below the U.S. average. More than 17 percent of the state's residents lacked health insurance.

Table AZ-3. Health Characteristics, 2000–2004

(Number, rate, percent.)

Item	State	U.S.
Births, 2003–2004		
Number of births	90 967	4 089 950
Birth rate (per 1,000 population)	16.3	14.1
Teenage birth rate (per 1,000 women age 15–19 years)	61.1	41.6
Mortality Rates, Average 2000–2002		
Infant mortality rate (per 1,000 live births)	6.7	6.9
Age-adjusted mortality rate (per 100,000 population)		
All races	795.3	853.3
Non-Hispanic White	782.5	843.1
Black	974.8	1 097.7
American Indian, Alaska Native	979.9	687.0
Asian and Pacific Islander	462.7	486.0
Hispanic or Latino[1]	758.3	642.7
Health Insurance, 2004		
Percent of all persons without health insurance	17.1	15.7
Percent of children without health insurance	14.7	11.2
Percent of low-income children without health insurance	9.9	7.1

[1]May be of any race.

Table AZ-4. Leading Causes of Death, Average 2000–2002

(Number, rate per 100,000 population.)

Cause	Number of deaths	Age-adjusted death rates	
		State	U.S.
ALL CAUSES	41 458	795.3	853.3
Leading Causes			
Major cardiovascular diseases	14 171	274.3	326.5
Cancer	9 192	173.8	196.0
Chronic lower respiratory diseases	2 527	47.9	43.7
Unintentional injuries	2 459	47.2	35.7
Diabetes (underlying cause)	1 100	20.9	25.2
Influenza and pneumonia	1 225	23.9	22.7
Alzheimer's disease	1 195	23.8	19.0
Motor vehicle accidents	1 018	19.4	15.0
Nephritis, nephrotic syndrome, and nephrosis ..	627	12.0	13.8
Septicemia	396	7.6	11.4
Suicides	812	15.6	10.7
Firearm-related	869	16.5	10.3
Cirrhosis	663	12.8	9.5
Drug-induced	608	12.0	7.9
Alcohol-induced	474	9.3	6.9
Homicides	469	8.8	6.0
Falls	436	8.5	5.2
HIV	160	3.2	5.0
Viral hepatitis	110	2.2	2.0
Anemias	66	1.3	1.6
Drownings	91	1.6	1.3
Fire deaths	45	0.9	1.2

Note: The rates are age-adjusted to the U.S. 2000 standard population.

Table AZ-5. Households and Housing Characteristics, 1990, 2000, and 2004

(Number, percent, and dollars.)

Characteristic	1990	2000	2004	Average annual percent change, 2000–2004
Total Households	1 368 843	1 901 327	2 131 534	2.9
Family households	940 106	1 287 367	1 434 980	2.8
Married-couple family	747 806	986 303	1 089 028	2.5
Other family	192 300	301 064	345 952	3.5
Male householder, no wife present	49 980	90 283	87 904	-0.7
Female householder, no husband present	142 320	210 781	258 048	5.2
Nonfamily households	428 737	613 960	696 554	3.2
Householder living alone	337 681	472 006	562 106	4.5
Householder not living alone	91 056	141 954	134 448	-1.3
Housing Characteristics				
Average size	2.62	2.64	2.64	X
Housing units	1 659 430	2 189 189	2 458 231	2.9
Occupied housing units	1 368 843	1 901 327	2 131 534	2.9
Owner-occupied	878 561	1 293 556	1 463 860	3.1
Renter-occupied	490 282	607 771	667 674	2.4
Median gross rent of renter-occupied housing units (dollars) ...	438	619	691	2.8
Median value of owner-occupied housing units (dollars)	79 700	121 300	145 741	4.7

X = Not applicable.

Median Housing Value and Median Rent, 2004

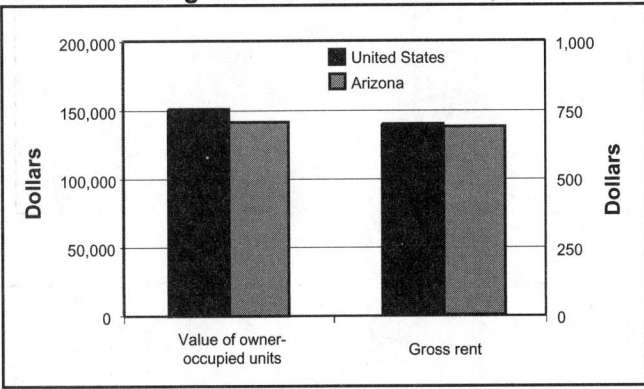

Median Household Income, 1984–2004 (2004 Dollars)

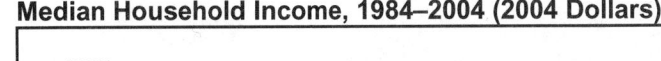
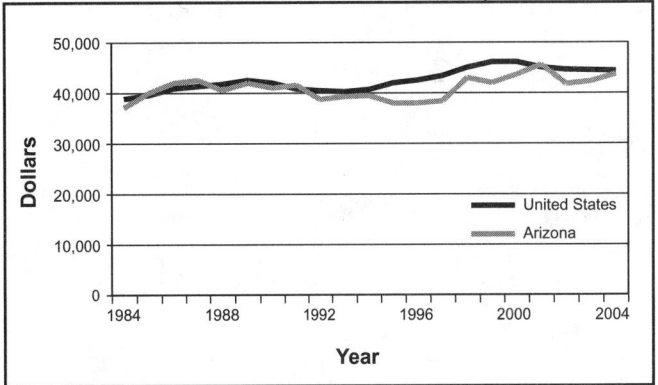

Table AZ-6. Household Income and Poverty Status, 1980–2004

(2004 CPI-U-RS adjusted dollars, rate.)

Year	State		U.S.	
	Median household income (2004 dollars)	Poverty rate	Median household income (2004 dollars)	Poverty rate
2004	43 761	14.4	44 389	12.7
2003	42 272	13.5	44 482	12.5
2002	41 737	13.5	44 546	12.1
2001	45 570	14.6	45 062	11.7
2000	43 638	11.7	46 058	11.3
1999	41 934	12.2	46 129	11.9
1998	42 926	16.6	45 003	12.7
1997	38 425	17.2	43 430	13.3
1996	37 923	20.5	42 544	13.7
1995	37 988	16.1	41 943	13.8
1994	39 453	15.9	40 677	14.5
1993	39 276	15.4	40 217	15.1
1992	38 736	15.8	40 422	14.8
1991	41 572	14.8	40 746	14.2
1990	40 955	13.7	41 963	13.5
1989	42 004	14.1	42 524	12.8
1988	40 559	14.1	41 771	13.0
1987	42 536	12.8	41 322	13.4
1986	41 931	14.3	40 939	13.6
1985	39 979	10.7	39 545	14.0
1984	37 069	18.2	38 782	14.4
1983	. . .	16.3	. . .	15.2
1982	. . .	14.8	. . .	15.0
1981	. . .	11.7	. . .	14.0
1980	. . .	12.8	. . .	13.0

. . . = Not available.

Table AZ-7. Employment Status by Demographic Group, 2004

(Numbers in thousands, rate.)

Characteristic	Civilian noninstitutional population	Civilian labor force		Employed	Unemployment rate
		Number	Participation rate		
SEX AND AGE					
Total	4 266	2 778	65.1	2 637	5.1
16 to 19 years	277	131	47.2	103	21.1
20 to 24 years	393	298	75.9	272	8.8
25 to 34 years	884	707	80.0	673	4.8
35 to 44 years	746	620	83.1	598	3.6
45 to 54 years	779	613	78.7	596	2.8
55 to 64 years	553	329	59.4	319	2.8
65 years and over	634	80	12.7	76	5.7
Men	2 101	1 536	73.1	1 458	5.0
16 to 19 years	140	62	44.3	45	27.2
20 to 24 years	195	166	85.1	153	8.2
25 to 34 years	458	421	92.0	400	4.9
35 to 44 years	380	346	91.2	335	3.4
45 to 54 years	372	325	87.3	318	2.3
55 to 64 years	272	181	66.3	176	2.8
Women	2 166	1 242	57.4	1 179	5.1
16 to 19 years	137	69	50.3	58	15.5
20 to 24 years	197	132	66.9	119	9.5
25 to 34 years	426	286	67.1	273	4.6
35 to 44 years	367	274	74.8	263	4.0
45 to 54 years	406	288	70.8	278	3.3
55 to 64 years	281	148	52.7	144	2.8
MARITAL STATUS					
Married men, spouse present	1 192	893	74.9	874	2.1
Married women, spouse present	1 142	635	55.6	615	3.1
Women who maintain families	241	167	69.4	157	6.4
RACE, HISPANIC ORIGIN, AND SEX					
White	3 880	2 526	65.1	2 405	4.8
Men	1 924	1 410	73.3	1 344	4.7
Women	1 956	1 116	57.1	1 061	4.9
Black	136	92	67.6	83	10.0
Men	67	49	73.7	44	10.7
Asian	94	59	62.8	56	4.5
Hispanic or Latino[1]	1 171	803	68.6	752	6.4
Men	600	500	83.2	469	6.0
Women	570	304	53.3	282	7.1
RACE, HISPANIC ORIGIN, AND AGE					
White					
16 to 19 years	246	117	47.8	93	20.6
20 to 24 years	343	267	77.9	246	7.7
25 to 34 years	797	642	80.5	613	4.6
35 to 44 years	670	557	83.0	537	3.4
45 to 54 years	704	558	79.3	544	2.6
55 to 64 years	520	309	59.5	301	2.8
65 years and over	600	76	12.7	72	5.8
Hispanic or Latino[1]					
20 to 24 years	159	126	79.0	115	8.3
25 to 34 years	345	258	74.8	244	5.2
35 to 44 years	227	183	80.5	172	5.5

Note: Data in Table 7 are from the Current Population Survey (CPS) and do not match Bureau of Labor Statistics estimates in Table 8. See notes and definitions for more details.

[1] May be of any race.

Table AZ-8. Employment Status, 1990–2004

(Numbers in thousands, rate.)

Year	Civilian labor force	Employed	Unemployed	Unemployment rate
2004	2 774 244	2 636 773	137 471	5.0
2003	2 706 934	2 553 169	153 765	5.7
2002	2 653 195	2 494 153	159 042	6.0
2001	2 573 817	2 453 066	120 751	4.7
2000	2 506 638	2 405 821	100 817	4.0
1999	2 466 281	2 355 357	110 924	4.5
1998	2 382 361	2 278 864	103 497	4.3
1997	2 302 734	2 196 901	105 833	4.6
1996	2 271 474	2 145 573	125 901	5.5
1995	2 214 148	2 095 749	118 399	5.3
1994	2 105 869	1 976 722	129 147	6.1
1993	1 961 825	1 836 869	124 956	6.4
1992	1 893 991	1 753 764	140 227	7.4
1991	1 819 740	1 715 227	104 513	5.7
1990	1 788 243	1 694 080	94 163	5.3

Note: Population age 16 years and over.

Unemployment Rate, 1980–2004

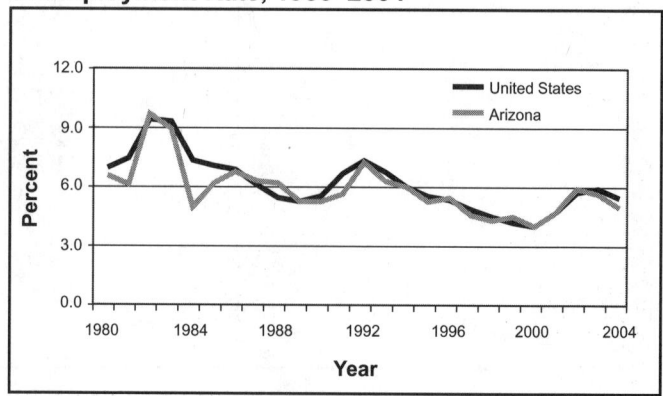

Table AZ-9. Employment and Average Wages by Industry, 2001–2004

(Estimates are based on the 2002 North American Industry Classification System [NAICS].)

Industry	2001	2002	2003	2004	Annual average percent change, 2001–2004
	Number of jobs				
TOTAL EMPLOYMENT BY PLACE OF WORK	2 856 941	2 877 247	2 941 541	3 046 430	2.2
Farm Employment	22 552	22 334	22 994	23 315	1.1
Nonfarm Employment	2 834 389	2 854 913	2 918 547	3 023 115	2.2
Private employment	2 435 948	2 444 952	2 499 757	2 600 477	2.2
Forestry, fishing, hunting, and other¹	23 918	23 938	21 896	21 696	-3.2
Mining	12 960	11 689	11 715	12 355	-1.6
Utilities	11 289	11 372	11 691	11 742	1.3
Construction	214 599	212 943	220 192	236 758	3.3
Manufacturing	211 289	194 021	186 415	186 967	-4.0
Durable goods manufacturing	170 482	154 534	147 686	148 945	-4.4
Nondurable goods manufacturing	40 807	39 487	38 729	38 022	-2.3
Wholesale trade	105 811	103 999	102 925	105 888	0.0
Retail trade	328 290	333 382	341 677	357 266	2.9
Transportation and warehousing	81 212	81 123	81 642	83 687	1.0
Information	61 481	58 758	57 494	55 926	-3.1
Finance and insurance	150 491	153 495	158 363	162 376	2.6
Real estate and rental and leasing	134 332	139 532	148 583	157 776	5.5
Professional and technical services	170 065	169 400	173 638	181 497	2.2
Management of companies and enterprises	22 628	22 872	22 346	23 950	1.9
Administrative and waste services	232 810	230 338	238 163	250 842	2.5
Educational services	32 328	37 093	40 493	44 140	10.9
Health care and social assistance	233 941	243 407	258 794	270 260	4.9
Arts, entertainment, and recreation	54 848	56 650	56 906	58 981	2.5
Accommodation and food services	213 670	214 229	217 938	226 142	1.9
Other services, except public administration	139 986	146 711	148 886	152 228	2.8
Government and government enterprises	398 441	409 961	418 790	422 638	2.0
	Dollars				
AVERAGE WAGES AND SALARIES BY PLACE OF WORK ...	33 023	33 709	34 710	36 298	3.2
Farm Earnings	26 582	31 843	25 892	24 290	-3.0
Nonfarm Earnings	33 056	33 718	34 757	36 362	3.2
Private earnings	33 037	33 504	34 484	36 089	3.0
Forestry, fishing, hunting, and other¹	15 000	15 549	16 650	17 719	5.7
Mining	47 327	46 891	50 147	53 467	4.1
Utilities	64 513	66 964	66 665	67 101	1.3
Construction	34 024	34 447	34 942	36 068	2.0
Manufacturing	47 966	48 859	50 495	52 657	3.2
Durable goods manufacturing	51 398	52 749	54 472	56 740	3.4
Nondurable goods manufacturing	33 080	33 011	34 742	36 005	2.9
Wholesale trade	48 679	48 729	50 031	53 772	3.4
Retail trade	24 426	24 799	25 604	26 434	2.7
Transportation and warehousing	37 053	37 474	38 666	40 985	3.4
Information	43 469	42 740	43 653	45 747	1.7
Finance and insurance	46 449	47 379	50 452	52 238	4.0
Real estate and rental and leasing	30 662	31 989	33 436	35 930	5.4
Professional and technical services	49 127	49 726	49 952	52 500	2.2
Management of companies and enterprises	53 305	54 003	59 260	68 761	8.9
Administrative and waste services	23 489	24 274	24 993	26 388	4.0
Educational services	27 301	28 843	30 444	32 870	6.4
Health care and social assistance	34 204	35 776	37 045	38 948	4.4
Arts, entertainment, and recreation	29 143	30 034	29 649	29 597	0.5
Accommodation and food services	14 474	14 856	15 319	16 004	3.4
Other services, except public administration	21 371	21 594	22 163	22 945	2.4
Government and government enterprises	33 154	34 742	36 049	37 694	4.4

Note: Average wages and salaries are a calculation by the editors of wage and salary disbursements divided by full- and part-time wage and salary employment. Data may not add to total or may appear as zero due to rounding.

¹ "Other" consists of the number of jobs held by U.S. residents employed by international organizations and foreign embassies and consulates in the United States.

LABOR MARKET

In 2004, Arizona's unemployment rate of 5 percent was below the national average, indicating a strong recovery from the 2001 recession. Employment growth was well above the national average during the 2000–2004 period and showed no overall declines, unlike most other states. Total nonfarm employment increased by 6.7 percent, with the strongest growth in educational services, real estate and rental and leasing, and health care and social assistance. Manufacturing employment declined over the period but represented only a small proportion of total jobs. Arizona's average wages of $36,298 ranked 22nd in the nation.

Employment by Industry, 2004

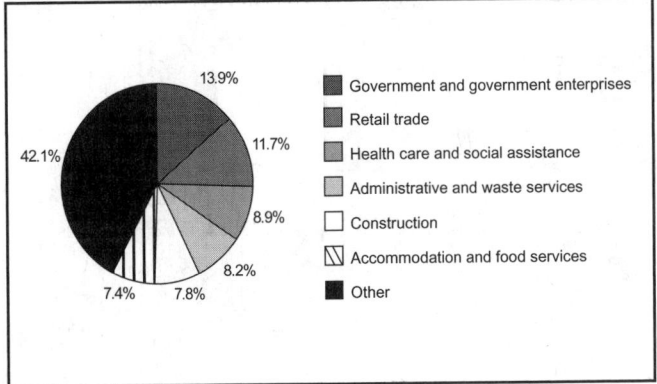

- 42.1% Government and government enterprises
- 13.9% Retail trade
- 11.7% Health care and social assistance
- 8.9% Administrative and waste services
- 8.2% Construction
- 7.8% Accommodation and food services
- 7.4% Other

Table AZ-10. Personal Income by Major Source, Selected Years 1980–2004

(Millions of dollars, except where noted.)

Item	1980	1990	2000	2001	2002	2003	2004	Average annual percent change, 2000–2004
Earnings by Place of Work	19 939	44 718	100 633	105 085	108 852	114 714	125 187	5.6
Wage and salary disbursements	15 105	34 174	75 990	78 512	80 154	83 864	90 670	4.5
Supplements to wages and salaries	2 875	6 746	14 092	14 987	16 490	17 955	20 056	9.2
Proprietors' income[1]	1 958	3 798	10 551	11 586	12 207	12 895	14 462	8.2
Farm proprietors' income	304	453	316	467	642	453	601	17.5
Nonfarm proprietors' income	1 654	3 345	10 235	11 119	11 566	12 442	13 860	7.9
(-) Contributions for government social insurance[2]	1 810	5 151	11 159	11 709	12 141	12 763	13 790	5.4
(+) Adjustment for residence[3]	-80	228	522	564	549	573	620	4.4
(=) **Net Earnings by Place of Residence**	18 049	39 795	89 997	93 940	97 260	102 523	112 018	5.6
(+) Dividends, interest, and rent[4]	5 055	14 485	25 454	25 454	25 188	25 730	26 887	1.4
(+) Personal current transfer receipts	2 969	8 369	17 107	19 460	21 652	23 463	25 419	10.4
Personal income	26 073	62 649	132 558	138 854	144 101	151 716	164 324	5.5
Farm income	25 606	62 009	131 898	138 045	143 063	150 914	163 384	5.5
Nonfarm income	467	639	659	809	1 038	802	940	9.3
Per Capita Personal Income (Dollars)[5]	9 524	17 005	25 660	26 214	26 494	27 193	28 609	2.8

Note: Data may not add to total or may appear as zero due to rounding.

[1]Proprietors' income includes the inventory valuation adjustment and the capital consumption adjustment.
[2]Contributions for government social insurance are included in earnings by type and industry, but they are excluded from personal income.
[3]The adjustment for residence is the net inflow of the earnings of interarea commuters.
[4]Rental income of persons includes the capital consumption adjustment.
[5]Per capita personal income is total personal income divided by total midyear population.

Per Capita Personal Income, 1980–2004 (Current Dollars)

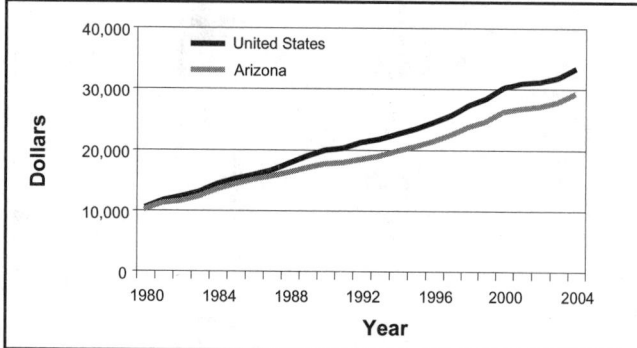

ECONOMIC ACTIVITY

Real gross state product showed substantial growth between 2001 and 2004, with particular increases over the 2003–2004 period, when the economy posted a gain of 7.1 percent (second only to its neighbor, Nevada). Manufacturing, real estate, and retail trade made the largest contributions to Arizona's growth over the period. Housing activity also provided a major stimulus. Housing prices were up sharply over the 2000–2004 period, according to the Office of Federal Housing Enterprise Oversight. However, the median value of owner-occupied housing remained below the U.S. average.

Table AZ-11. Real Gross State Product, 1997–2004

(Millions of chained 2000 dollars, percent.)

Industry	1997	1998	1999	2000	2001	2002	2003	2004	Average annual percent change, 2001–2004
GROSS STATE PRODUCT	127 439	138 173	149 036	157 639	162 407	167 980	175 536	187 953	5.0
As a percent of U.S. gross product	1.5	1.5	1.6	1.6	1.7	1.7	1.7	1.8	X
Private Industries	109 751	119 929	130 417	138 624	142 884	148 135	155 235	166 929	5.3
Agriculture, forestry, fishing, and hunting	1 224	1 389	1 499	1 609	1 619	2 246	1 741	1 628	0.2
Mining	1 417	1 232	1 277	1 374	1 078	976	1 081	1 067	-0.3
Utilities	2 269	2 373	2 513	2 770	2 606	2 747	3 093	3 164	6.7
Construction	8 001	8 548	8 921	9 154	9 204	9 103	9 238	9 824	2.2
Manufacturing	13 296	16 649	19 484	20 677	23 128	23 625	25 954	28 259	6.9
As a percent of gross state product	10.4	12.0	13.1	13.1	14.2	14.1	14.8	15.0	X
Wholesale trade	7 430	8 462	9 053	9 289	10 104	10 341	10 047	10 774	2.2
Retail trade	10 440	11 134	11 920	12 978	13 996	14 846	16 013	17 471	7.7
Transportation and warehousing	3 730	3 988	4 288	4 576	4 329	4 761	5 134	5 534	8.5
Information	3 595	4 039	4 753	5 583	5 618	5 674	5 945	6 427	4.6
Finance and insurance	9 825	10 278	11 183	11 403	12 060	13 181	14 471	15 525	8.8
Real estate and rental and leasing	17 875	18 572	19 855	20 552	21 104	21 520	21 742	23 547	3.7
Services	31 906	33 660	35 736	38 660	38 220	39 304	41 225	44 349	5.1
As a percent of gross state product	25.0	24.4	24.0	24.5	23.5	23.4	23.5	23.6	X
Professional and technical services	6 993	7 567	8 188	10 451	9 189	9 284	9 629	10 324	4.0
Management of companies and enterprises	1 471	1 460	1 536	1 480	2 063	2 113	2 352	2 778	10.4
Administrative and waste services	5 789	6 199	6 806	6 720	6 490	6 714	7 178	7 732	6.0
Educational services	525	621	660	714	765	792	842	922	6.4
Health care and social assistance	8 067	8 290	8 643	9 080	9 524	10 149	10 887	11 578	6.7
Arts, entertainment, and recreation	1 230	1 318	1 466	1 580	1 678	1 728	1 675	1 711	0.7
Accommodation and food services	4 737	4 917	5 144	5 423	5 246	5 302	5 445	5 843	3.7
Other services, except public administration	3 094	3 288	3 293	3 212	3 265	3 222	3 217	3 461	2.0
Government	17 828	18 307	18 631	19 015	19 524	19 860	20 346	21 122	2.7
As a percent of gross state product	14.0	13.2	12.5	12.1	12.0	11.8	11.6	11.2	X

X = Not applicable.

Table AZ-12. Government Transfer Payments, Selected Years 1980–2004

(Millions of dollars, percent.)

Item	1980	1990	2000	2001	2002	2003	2004	Average annual percent change, 2000–2004
CURRENT TRANSFER PAYMENTS TO INDIVIDUALS	2 773	7 886	15 959	18 170	20 497	22 383	24 320	11.1
Retirement and Disability Insurance Benefits	1 586	4 084	7 543	8 133	8 704	9 179	9 752	6.6
Old-age, survivors, and disability insurance (OASDI) benefits	1 456	3 703	7 166	7 716	8 246	8 689	9 245	6.6
Railroad retirement and disability benefits	64	112	145	148	153	155	158	2.2
Workers' compensation	61	260	220	253	285	310	323	10.1
Other government retirement and disability insurance benefits	5	9	12	15	20	24	26	20.8
Medical Benefits	534	2 414	5 899	7 168	8 288	9 329	10 625	15.9
Medicare benefits	391	1 602	3 443	3 853	4 171	4 463	4 974	9.6
Public assistance medical care benefits	125	739	2 366	3 182	3 928	4 706	5 466	23.3
Military medical insurance benefits	18	74	90	134	189	159	185	19.8
Income Maintenance Benefits	241	681	1 448	1 533	1 821	2 115	2 288	12.1
Supplemental Security Income (SSI) benefits	55	142	355	383	407	430	449	6.0
Family assistance	40	145	172	185	220	239	220	6.2
Food stamps	105	258	246	299	404	524	596	24.8
Other income maintenance benefits	42	136	674	665	790	923	1 023	11.0
Unemployment Insurance Compensation	95	164	186	297	504	512	359	17.9
Veterans' Benefits	236	317	557	605	678	734	797	9.4
Federal Education and Training Assistance	55	140	240	292	336	347	369	11.3
Other Payments to Individuals	26	87	87	143	166	168	130	10.5

Note: See notes and definitions for more details. Data may not add to total or may appear as zero due to rounding.

EXPORTS

Arizona ranked 17th in the nation in terms of the value of its exports. Computers and electronic products accounted for 42 percent of total exports, followed by transportation equipment. Mexico, which shares a border with Arizona, was the top recipient of the state's exports, followed by Canada. Exports to Malaysia fell sharply from 2003 to 2004, primarily as a result of a 60 percent drop in computers and electronic exports. However, Malaysia remains among the state's top five markets. Exports to China increased from $142 million in 2001 to $629 million in 2004, when the country became the sixth largest market for Arizona's goods.

Leading Exports, 2004

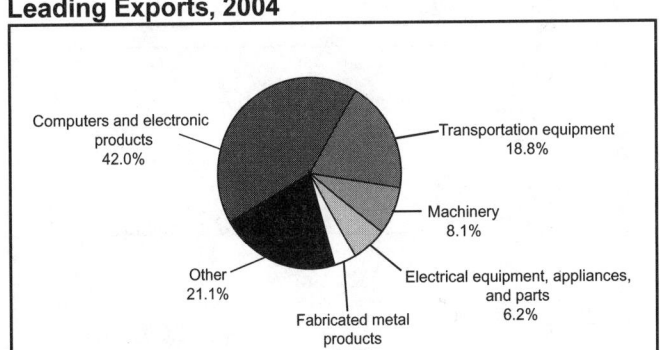

Table AZ-13. Exports of Goods by Leading Products and Destinations, 2001–2004

(Millions of dollars, percent, rank based on 2004 dollar values.)

Product and market	2001	2002	2003	2004	Percent share of total, 2004	Average annual percent change, 2001–2004
Total Goods						
Total	12 514	11 871	13 323	13 423	100.0	2.4
Manufactures	11 747	11 251	12 544	12 628	94.1	2.4
Agriculture and livestock	455	385	496	476	3.5	1.5
Other commodities	311	235	283	319	2.4	0.8
Five Leading Exports (NAICS Code)						
Computers and electronic products (334)	5 507	5 540	6 731	5 635	42.0	0.8
Transportation equipment (336)	2 513	2 262	2 135	2 518	18.8	0.1
Machinery manufactures (333)	801	684	808	1 087	8.1	10.7
Electrical equipment, appliances, and parts (335)	502	547	526	826	6.2	18.1
Fabricated metal products (332)	595	526	531	521	3.9	-4.3
Five Leading Markets	11 679	11 206	12 368	12 446	92.7	2.1
Mexico	3 581	3 044	3 230	3 794	28.3	1.9
Canada	1 336	1 167	1 131	1 387	10.3	1.3
Malaysia	915	1 211	1 629	744	5.5	-6.7
Germany	595	525	607	688	5.1	5.0
United Kingdom	984	928	742	657	4.9	-12.6

Table AZ-14. Agriculture, 1997 and 2002

(Number, acres, and dollars.)

Item	1997	2002
Number of farms	8 507	7 294
Land in farms (acres)	27 169 627	26 586 577
Farm Size		
Average size of farm (acres)	3 194	3 645
Farms by size (percent distribution)		
Fewer than 50 acres	51.4	58.0
50 to 499 acres	26.7	24.4
500 acres or more	22.0	17.6
Market Value of Land and Equipment (Dollars)		
Land and buildings average value per farm	1 293 804	1 456 759
Average value per acre	407	398
Machinery and equipment average value per farm	59 057	88 651
Value of Sales (Thousands of Dollars)		
Agricultural products sold	1 970 801	2 395 447
Crops	1 275 987	1 587 775
Livestock, poultry, and their products	694 814	807 672
Average per farm (dollars)	231 668	328 413
Value of sales (percent distribution)		
Less than $10,000	60.5	64.3
$10,000 to $99,999	22.6	19.4
$100,000 or more	16.9	16.3
Government Payments		
Payments (thousands of dollars)	25 134	31 760
Percent of farms receiving government payments	18.6	11.4
Farm operators whose principal occupation is farming (percent)	48.2	58.9

AGRICULTURE

Cash receipts from farming were a relatively small share of Arizona's gross state product (GSP), totaling only about $1.6 billion of the state's $188 billion GSP. The top commodities were cattle, dairy, lettuce, cotton, and greenhouse/nursery products. Arizona ranked second in the nation for lettuce acreage. The value of agricultural products sold was nearly $2.4 billion, which ranked 29th among all the states. Farms with sales of less than $10,000 accounted for the largest proportion of sales.

ENERGY

Energy prices were relatively high—the state ranked 11th in the nation in this category. However, given its favorable climate and relatively low industrial and commercial consumption, the state's per capita consumption ranked 44th in the nation. Expenditures per person ($2,014) were the third lowest in the country in 2001; only Florida and Utah had lower expenditures. The transportation sector was the largest user of energy, followed by the residential and commercial sectors.

Energy Consumption by Source, 2001

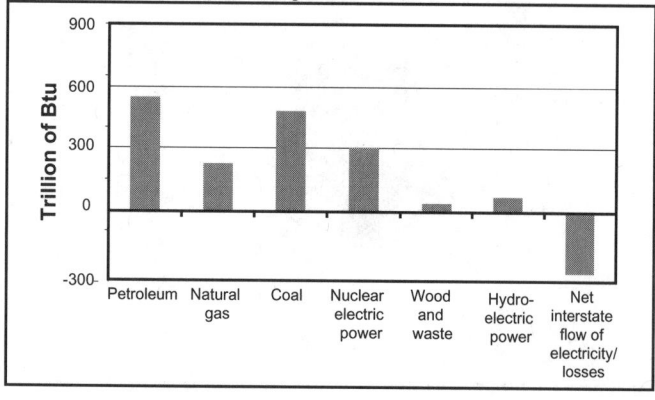

Energy Consumption by Sector, 2001

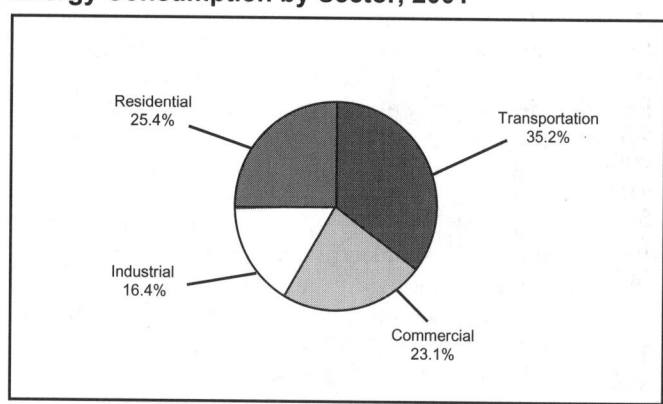

Table AZ-15. Energy Consumption, Expenditures, and Prices, Selected Years 1960–2001

(Dollars, Btu [British Thermal Unit], percent distribution.)

Item	1960	1965	1970	1975	1980	1985	1990	1995	2000	2001
Total Consumption (Billion Btu)	283 132	375 408	520 426	660 437	755 280	842 825	950 450	1 089 523	1 335 051	1 352 978
Consumption per capita (million Btu)	217.5	237.0	293.1	289.1	277.9	264.7	259.3	253.0	260.2	255.4
Consumption by Sector (Percent Distribution)										
Residential	17.3	15.6	17.1	19.7	20.4	21.9	23.1	22.6	24.7	25.4
Commercial	23.7	15.5	15.7	18.5	18.3	20.1	22.7	22.0	23.3	23.1
Industrial	17.8	31.7	29.9	27.0	26.1	23.2	19.9	21.1	17.5	16.4
Transportation	41.2	37.2	37.3	34.8	35.2	34.8	34.2	34.3	34.5	35.2
Consumption by Source (Billion Btu)										
Coal	210	7 030	8 623	92 449	244 994	342 013	343 407	342 895	432 810	424 072
Natural gas	140 275	166 063	204 383	164 346	173 977	137 315	130 781	127 944	208 137	245 236
Petroleum	121 480	145 913	213 266	306 742	301 248	316 909	347 128	410 324	512 888	524 155
Nuclear electric power	0	0	0	0	0	12 005	217 965	283 526	316 839	300 109
Hydroelectric power[1]	32 169	46 400	64 580	75 484	102 171	146 123	79 756	87 430	88 169	80 373
Wood and waste	4 013	3 695	4 339	5 414	17 846	23 981	13 365	15 246	11 885	10 513
Other	-51	-97	-175	-47	-138	0	3 931	5 359	4 019	3 835
Net interstate flow of electricity/losses[2]	-14 962	6 404	25 411	16 051	-84 818	-135 520	-185 882	-183 201	-239 695	-235 316
Total Expenditures (Thousands of Dollars)	...	...	743 700	1 795 000	4 169 000	5 454 700	6 502 000	7 692 300	10 594 200	10 671 800
Expenditures per capita (dollars)	...	...	419	786	1 534	1 713	1 774	1 786	2 065	2 014
Prices by Sector (Dollars Per Million Btu)										
Total	...	...	1.97	3.87	8.38	10.03	11.19	11.27	12.79	12.68
Residential	...	...	2.95	5.27	11.09	16.31	18.35	19.69	19.61	19.80
Commercial	...	...	2.51	4.68	9.99	15.25	16.14	16.67	16.18	16.85
Industrial	...	...	1.00	2.54	5.27	6.56	7.92	7.66	8.33	8.61
Transportation	...	...	2.20	3.93	8.79	8.40	8.69	8.88	11.26	10.64

[1]A negative number in this row results from pumped storage for which, overall, more electricity is expended than created to provide electricity during peak demand periods.
[2]Net interstate flow of electricity is the difference between the amount of energy in the electricity sold within a state (including associated losses) and the energy input at the electric utilities within the state. A positive number indicates that more electricity (including associated losses) came into the state than went out of the state during the year; conversely, a negative number indicates that more electricity (including associated losses) went out of the state than came into the state.
... = Not available.

Table AZ-16. State Taxes, Fiscal 2004

(Dollars, percent distribution.)

Item	Thousands of dollars	Percent distribution	Dollars per capita	
			State	U.S.
TOTAL TAXES	9 606 318	100.0	1 672.4	2 024.8
Property Taxes	346 427	3.6	60.3	38.9
Sales and Gross Receipts	6 070 737	63.2	1 056.9	1 003.4
General sales and gross receipts	4 719 642	49.1	821.7	677.0
Selective sales taxes	1 351 095	14.1	235.2	326.4
Alcoholic beverages	55 954	0.6	9.7	15.7
Insurance premiums	312 852	3.3	54.5	47.0
Motor fuels	671 765	7.0	117.0	114.6
Tobacco products	274 716	2.9	47.8	42.0
Licenses	289 803	3.0	50.4	134.9
Motor vehicle	161 398	1.7	28.1	59.4
Occupation and business, not elsewhere classified	63 308	0.7	11.0	37.1
Other Taxes	2 899 351	30.2	504.8	847.6
Individual income	2 315 865	24.1	403.2	673.6
Corporation net income	525 650	5.5	91.5	105.1

GOVERNMENT FINANCE

State revenue amounted to $16.9 billion in 2003, the fourth lowest in the country in per capita terms. Arizona's per capita expenditures of $3,137 were among the five lowest in the United States. Per capita spending on education and public assistance was particularly below those of other states. Only per capita highway expenditures were above the U.S. average. State taxes collected in 2004 amounted to $1,672 per person, ranking 41st in the country. Individual state income taxes were $403 per capita. The largest share of taxes collected came from sales taxes. Among the 37 states with property taxes, Arizona ranked 12th.

Per Capita State Taxes, Fiscal, 2004

Table AZ-17. State Government Finances, 2003

(Dollars, percent distribution.)

Item	Millions of dollars	Percent distribution	Dollars per capita	
			State	U.S.
GENERAL REVENUE	16 890 346	100.0	3 027.5	3 832.6
Intergovernmental revenue	6 092 557	36.1	1 092.0	1 246.0
Taxes	8 691 761	51.5	1 557.9	1 891.6
General sales	4 332 982	25.7	776.7	636.0
Selective sales	1 178 497	7.0	211.2	307.4
License taxes	271 023	1.6	48.6	123.6
Individual income tax	2 102 361	12.4	376.8	626.8
Corporate income tax	389 406	2.3	69.8	97.8
Other taxes	417 492	2.5	74.8	99.9
Current charges	988 573	5.9	177.2	366.5
Miscellaneous general revenue	1 117 455	6.6	200.3	328.6
GENERAL EXPENDITURE	17 503 052	100.0	3 137.3	4 010.5
Intergovernmental expenditure	6 936 753	39.6	1 243.4	1 316.9
Direct expenditure	10 566 299	60.4	1 893.9	2 693.6
Expenditure by Function				
Education	6 419 012	36.7	1 150.6	1 416.4
Public welfare	4 482 224	25.6	803.4	1 083.3
Hospitals	53 792	0.3	9.6	132.3
Health	845 027	4.8	151.5	173.0
Highways	1 839 644	10.5	329.7	295.4
Police protection	172 512	1.0	30.9	38.4
Correction	731 041	4.2	131.0	135.0
Natural resources	231 187	1.3	41.4	64.0
Parks and recreation	108 807	0.6	19.5	20.1
Government administration	464 598	2.7	83.3	151.3
Interest on general debt	192 416	1.1	34.5	107.8
Other and unallocable	1 962 792	11.2	351.8	393.4
DEBT AT END OF FISCAL YEAR	5 554 020	X	995.5	2 404.7
CASH AND SECURITY HOLDINGS	34 307 037	X	6 149.3	8 938.4

X = Not applicable.

Table AZ-18. Education Indicators, 2000–2004

(Percent, number.)

Item	State	U.S.
Total Population 25 Years and Over (Thousands), 2004	3 510	186 877
Educational Attainment, 2004		
Percent high school graduate or more	84.4	85.2
Percent college graduate or more	28.0	27.7
Elementary and Secondary Schools, 2002–2003		
Total students	937 755	48 202 324
Percent of students eligible for free or reduced-price lunch ..	50.9	40.6
Percent of students who were English language learners	15.4	7.8
Total schools	1 801	92 330
Student/teacher ratio	21.3	15.9
Per student expenditures	6 282	8 041
Dropouts, Grades 9–12, 2000–2001 (Percent)	10.5	. . .
Higher Education, 2002–2003		
Total enrollment	409 157	17 035 027
Bachelor's degrees awarded	23 372	1 348 503
Percent women	54.9	57.5

. . . = Not available.

Educational Attainment, 2004

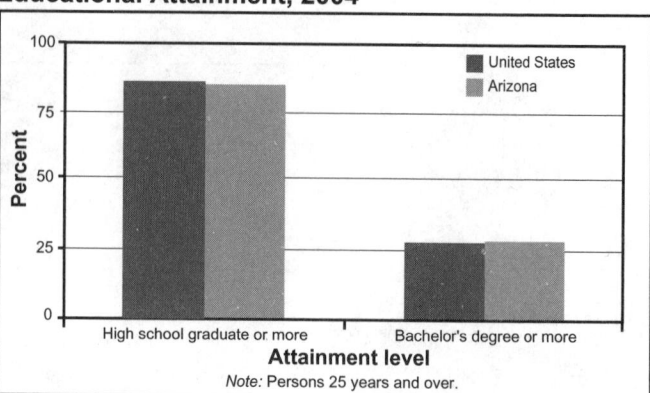

Note: Persons 25 years and over.

EDUCATION

Arizona's population, age 25 years and over, ranked slightly below the national average for high school attainment and above average for college attainment. The student/teacher ratio was the second highest in the nation, topped only by Utah's ratio. Expenditures per student in grades K–12 were among the 10 lowest in the country. These figures reflected the state's large population growth in recent years and its high proportion of student-age population. Arizona had the highest dropout rate out of the 46 states reporting data. Nearly 51 percent of the state's students were eligible for free or reduced-price lunch.

VOTER PARTICIPATION

Arizona did not have strong voter turnout in the 2000 and 2004 elections. Only 46.7 percent of those eligible voted in 2000, giving the state the third lowest turnout in the country. Although the participation rate rose to 54.3 percent in 2004, this rate was still well below the national average. The vote for president favored the Republican candidate, who received 51 percent of the vote in 2000 and 54.9 percent in 2004, according to the official tally by the Clerk of the U.S. House of Representatives.

Table AZ-19. Reported Voting and Registration, November 2000 and November 2004

(Numbers in thousands, percent.)

Characteristic	Total population 18 years and over	Total citizen		Total registered		Total voted	
		Number	Percent	Number	Percent	Number	Percent
NOVEMBER 2000							
Total	3 524	3 129	88.8	1 879	53.3	1 644	46.7
Male	1 734	1 528	88.1	885	51.0	773	44.6
Female	1 789	1 601	89.5	994	55.5	871	48.7
NOVEMBER 2004							
Total	4 122	3 508	85.1	2 485	60.3	2 239	54.3
Male	2 008	1 687	84.0	1 166	58.0	1 034	51.5
Female	2 114	1 822	86.2	1 319	62.4	1 205	57.0
Race and Hispanic Origin							
White alone	3 747	3 168	84.5	2 305	61.5	2 094	55.9
Non-Hispanic White	3 747	3 168	84.5	2 305	61.5	2 094	55.9
Non-Hispanic White alone	2 622	2 564	97.8	1 962	74.8	1 803	68.8
Black alone	142	136	95.7	81	57.0	66	46.6
Asian alone	57	38	B	20	B	17	B
Hispanic or Latino[1]	1 160	629	54.2	354	30.5	296	25.5
White alone or in combination	3 779	3 196	84.6	2 320	61.4	2 109	55.8
Non-Hispanic White alone or in combination	2 650	2 592	97.8	1 977	74.6	1 818	68.6
Black alone or in combination	152	146	96.0	84	55.3	70	45.6
Asian alone or in combination	63	44	B	23	B	20	B
Age							
18 to 24 years	522	436	83.4	249	47.8	184	35.2
25 to 44 years	1 616	1 256	77.8	819	50.7	708	43.8
45 to 64 years	1 339	1 189	88.8	960	71.7	914	68.3
65 to 74 years	363	344	94.9	248	68.2	239	65.8
75 years and over	283	283	100.0	209	74.0	194	68.7

[1]May be of any race.
B = Base is too small to show derived measure.

At a Glance:

- Arkansas's population was just under 2.8 million in 2004, making it the 32nd most populous state in the nation.
- Over 77 percent of the population was non-Hispanic White, and 15.6 percent was Black (the 12th largest concentration of this racial group in the nation). Hispanic residents (of any race) made up only 4.4 percent of the population, ranking Arkansas relatively low in terms of representation of this ethnic group.
- About half the state's population growth between 2000 and 2004 was due to immigration, both from other states and from abroad.
- Median household income in Arkansas was low, ranking 48th in the country. Arkansas's poverty rate of 15.1 percent was the 9th highest in the nation.
- The state's unemployment rate, 5.7 percent in 2004, was only slightly higher than the national average.
- Arkansas was among three states in which less than 80 percent of residents age 25 years and over had completed high school. Arkansas also had the second lowest proportion of population with a bachelor's degree or more.

Table AR-1. Population by Sex and Age, 1990, 2000, and 2004

(Number, percent.)

Sex and age	1990	2000	2004	Percent distribution, 2004	Average annual percent change, 2000–2004
Total Population	2 350 725	2 673 400	2 752 629	X	0.7
Percent of total U.S. population	0.9	0.9	0.9	X	X
Sex					
Male	1 133 076	1 304 693	1 348 719	49.0	0.8
Female	1 217 649	1 368 707	1 403 910	51.0	0.6
Age					
Under 5 years	164 667	181 585	185 555	6.7	0.7
5 to 17 years	456 464	498 784	490 995	17.8	0.5
18 years and over	456 732	1 993 031	2 076 079	75.4	1.3
18 to 24 years	1 729 594	261 738	279 818	10.2	1.2
25 to 44 years	237 056	750 972	745 046	27.1	0.6
45 to 64 years	685 748	606 302	670 109	24.3	2.8
65 years and over	350 058	374 019	381 106	13.8	0.6
85 years and over	35 216	46 492	47 842	1.7	2.4
Median age (years)	33.7	36.0	36.7	X	X

X = Not applicable.

Average Annual Rate of Population Growth, 1980–2004

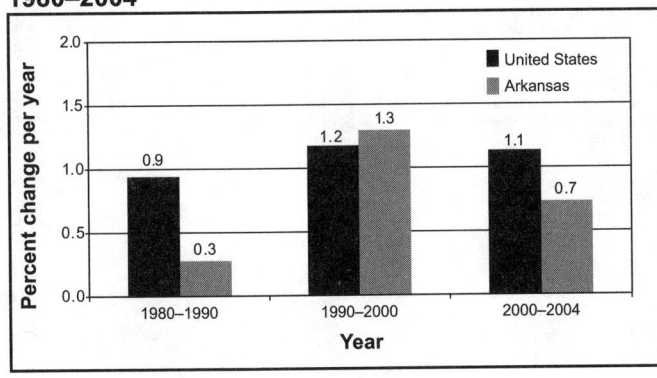

POPULATION

Arkansas's population increased by 3 percent between 2000 and 2004, a growth rate well below the U.S. average but slightly above those of its immediate neighbors, Missouri and Louisiana. The number of births from 2000 to 2004 was low relative to the number of deaths. As a result, about half of the state's growth was due to in-migration. Arkansas's largest metropolitan areas were Little Rock-North Little Rock and Fayetteville-Springdale-Rogers (shared with Missouri), both located in the northwest area of the state. In 2004, 13.8 percent of the state's population was 65 years old and over. This was the ninth highest proportion in the nation.

Table AR-2. Population by Race and Hispanic Origin, 1990, 2000, and 2004

(Number, percent.)

Race and Hispanic origin	1990	2000	2004
Total Population	2 350 725	2 673 400	2 752 629
Non-Hispanic (Percent)			
One race[1]			
White	82.2	78.7	77.2
Black	15.9	15.6	15.6
American Indian, Alaska Native[2]	0.5	0.6	0.6
Asian and Pacific Islander[2]	0.5	0.8	1.0
Other race[2]	0.3	. . .	. . .
Two or more races	. . .	1.0	1.1
Hispanic or Latino[3] (Percent)	0.8	3.2	4.4

[1]Individuals could report only one race in the 1990 census and could report one or more races on the 2000 census. Data on race in 2000 and 2004 are not comparable to 1990.
[2]Data for 1990 include people of Hispanic or Latino origin.
[3]May be of any race.
. . . = Not available.

Minority Population as a Percent of Total Population, 2004

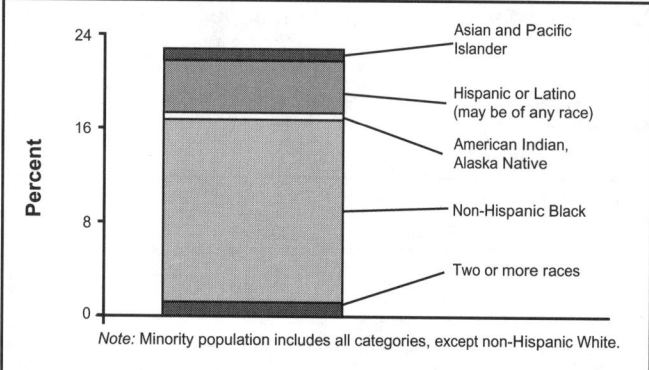

Note: Minority population includes all categories, except non-Hispanic White.

Age-Adjusted Death Rates, Average 2000–2002

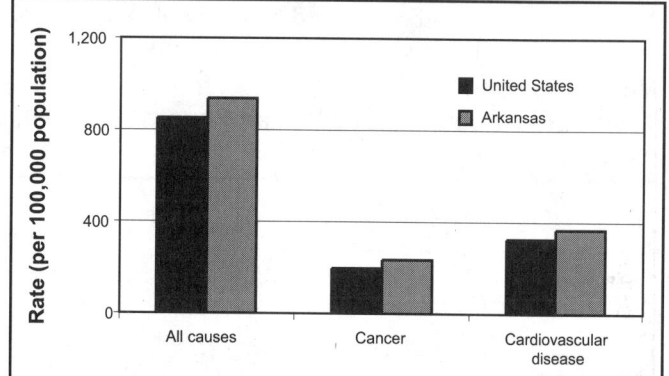

HEALTH

Arkansas's birth rate was slightly below the U.S. average, but the teenage birth rate was the sixth highest in the nation. The state's infant mortality rate was above the national average in 2004, despite having declined substantially since 1995. Age-adjusted mortality rates were higher than average in major categories.

Table AR-3. Health Characteristics, 2000–2004

(Number, rate, percent.)

Item	State	U.S.
Births, 2003–2004		
Number of births	37 784	4 089 950
Birth rate (per 1,000 population)	13.9	14.1
Teenage birth rate (per 1,000 women age 15–19 years)	59.0	41.6
Mortality Rates, Average 2000–2002		
Infant mortality rate (per 1,000 live births)	8.3	6.9
Age-adjusted mortality rate (per 100,000 population)		
All races	961.8	853.3
Non-Hispanic White	943.5	843.1
Black	1 191.2	1 097.7
American Indian, Alaska Native	. . .	687.0
Asian and Pacific Islander	609.0	486.0
Hispanic or Latino[1]	244.2	642.7
Health Insurance, 2004		
Percent of all persons without health insurance	16.4	15.7
Percent of children without health insurance	6.8	11.2
Percent of low-income children without health insurance	3.8	7.1

[1]May be of any race.
. . . = Not available.

Table AR-4. Leading Causes of Death, Average 2000–2002

(Number, rate per 100,000 population.)

Cause	Number of deaths	Age-adjusted death rates	
		State	U.S.
ALL CAUSES	28 163	961.8	853.3
Leading Causes			
Major cardiovascular diseases	11 133	375.8	326.5
Cancer	6 155	210.1	196.0
Chronic lower respiratory diseases	1 405	47.4	43.7
Unintentional injuries	1 285	46.7	35.7
Diabetes (underlying cause)	754	25.8	25.2
Influenza and pneumonia	770	25.8	22.7
Alzheimer's disease	478	15.9	19.0
Motor vehicle accidents	659	24.3	15.0
Nephritis, nephrotic syndrome, and nephrosis ..	541	18.3	13.8
Septicemia	478	16.2	11.4
Suicides	369	13.7	10.7
Firearm-related	423	15.7	10.3
Cirrhosis	228	8.0	9.5
Drug-induced	157	6.0	7.9
Alcohol-induced	133	4.8	6.9
Homicides	194	7.2	6.0
Falls	137	4.7	5.2
HIV	73	2.8	5.0
Viral hepatitis	57	2.1	2.0
Anemias	57	1.9	1.6
Drownings	63	2.3	1.3
Fire deaths	76	2.8	1.2

Note: The rates are age-adjusted to the U.S. 2000 standard population.

Table AR-5. Households and Housing Characteristics, 1990, 2000, and 2004

(Number, percent, and dollars.)

Characteristic	1990	2000	2004	Average annual percent change, 2000–2004
Total Households	891 179	1 042 696	1 099 086	1.3
Family households	651 555	732 261	745 795	0.5
Married-couple family	527 358	566 401	546 309	-0.9
Other family	124 197	165 860	199 486	4.7
Male householder, no wife present	25 273	39 299	45 421	3.7
Female householder, no husband present	98 924	126 561	154 065	5.0
Nonfamily households	239 624	310 435	353 291	3.3
Householder living alone	213 778	266 585	302 441	3.2
Householder not living alone	25 846	43 850	50 850	3.8
Housing Characteristics				
Average size	2.57	2.49	2.43	X
Housing units	1 000 667	1 173 043	1 233 203	1.3
Occupied housing units	891 179	1 042 696	1 099 086	1.3
Owner-occupied	619 938	723 535	720 053	-0.1
Renter-occupied	271 241	319 161	379 033	4.4
Median gross rent of renter-occupied housing units (dollars) ...	328	453	517	3.4
Median value of owner-occupied housing units (dollars)	46 000	72 800	79 006	2.1

X = Not applicable.

Median Housing Value and Median Rent, 2004

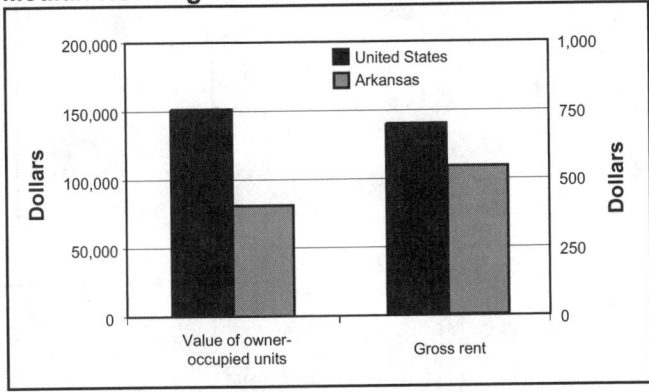

Median Household Income, 1984–2004 (2004 Dollars)

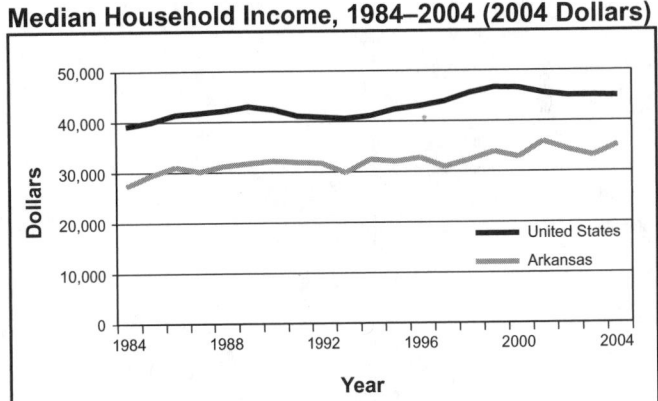

Table AR-6. Household Income and Poverty Status, 1980–2004

(2004 CPI-U-RS adjusted dollars, rate.)

Year	State		U.S.	
	Median household income (2004 dollars)	Poverty rate	Median household income (2004 dollars)	Poverty rate
2004	34 963	15.1	44 389	12.7
2003	32 862	17.8	44 482	12.5
2002	34 019	19.8	44 546	12.1
2001	35 576	17.8	45 062	11.7
2000	32 574	16.5	46 058	11.3
1999	33 644	14.7	46 129	11.9
1998	32 018	14.7	45 003	12.7
1997	30 705	19.7	43 430	13.3
1996	32 512	17.2	42 544	13.7
1995	31 774	14.9	41 943	13.8
1994	32 232	15.3	40 677	14.5
1993	29 659	20.0	40 217	15.1
1992	31 510	17.5	40 422	14.8
1991	31 696	17.3	40 746	14.2
1990	31 933	19.6	41 963	13.5
1989	31 531	18.3	42 524	12.8
1988	30 950	21.6	41 771	13.0
1987	29 938	21.8	41 322	13.4
1986	30 799	21.3	40 939	13.6
1985	29 220	22.9	39 545	14.0
1984	27 119	23.9	38 782	14.4
1983	. . .	21.5	. . .	15.2
1982	. . .	23.8	. . .	15.0
1981	. . .	24.1	. . .	14.0
1980	. . .	21.5	. . .	13.0

. . . = Not available.

Table AR-7. Employment Status by Demographic Group, 2004

(Numbers in thousands, rate.)

Characteristic	Civilian noninstitutional population	Civilian labor force		Employed	Unemployment rate
		Number	Participation rate		
SEX AND AGE					
Total	2 102	1 308	62.2	1 231	5.9
16 to 19 years	145	65	45.0	50	24.1
20 to 24 years	189	136	72.1	123	9.6
25 to 34 years	369	313	84.9	295	5.9
35 to 44 years	372	293	78.8	280	4.5
45 to 54 years	371	290	78.2	280	3.4
55 to 64 years	291	161	55.3	156	3.2
65 years and over	365	48	13.3	47	3.2
Men	1 008	707	70.1	668	5.5
16 to 19 years	70	34	48.4	26	23.2
20 to 24 years	87	68	78.7	63	7.2
25 to 34 years	186	173	92.6	164	5.1
35 to 44 years	189	167	88.3	160	4.3
45 to 54 years	186	155	83.5	150	3.4
55 to 64 years	142	85	60.1	82	4.2
Women	1 094	601	54.9	562	6.4
16 to 19 years	75	31	41.7	23	25.1
20 to 24 years	103	68	66.4	60	12.0
25 to 34 years	182	140	77.0	131	6.8
35 to 44 years	183	126	69.0	120	4.8
45 to 54 years	186	135	73.0	131	3.5
55 to 64 years	149	76	50.8	74	2.1
MARITAL STATUS					
Married men, spouse present	613	455	74.3	444	2.4
Married women, spouse present	581	343	59.1	335	2.5
Women who maintain families	138	93	67.3	81	12.6
RACE, HISPANIC ORIGIN, AND SEX					
White	1 718	1 066	62.1	1 016	4.7
Men	833	591	71.0	564	4.5
Women	885	475	53.6	451	5.0
Black	307	192	62.4	167	12.8
Men	137	86	62.7	75	13.1
Women	170	106	62.2	93	12.5
Hispanic or Latino[1]	70	51	73.9	49	5.3
Men	40	35	87.0	34	3.9
RACE, HISPANIC ORIGIN, AND AGE					
White					
16 to 19 years	110	52	47.3	41	21.3
20 to 24 years	141	105	74.3	98	5.9
25 to 34 years	288	246	85.5	235	4.6
35 to 44 years	306	241	78.9	232	3.8
45 to 54 years	302	238	78.8	231	2.9
55 to 64 years	245	141	57.5	136	3.1
65 years and over	327	43	13.3	42	3.4
Black					
25 to 34 years	66	55	83.7	49	11.8
35 to 44 years	53	43	81.5	40	8.5
45 to 54 years	55	40	72.2	36	8.2

Note: Data in Table 7 are from the Current Population Survey (CPS) and do not match Bureau of Labor Statistics estimates in Table 8. See notes and definitions for more details.

[1]May be of any race.

Table AR-8. Employment Status, 1990–2004

(Numbers in thousands, rate.)

Year	Civilian labor force	Employed	Unemployed	Unemployment rate
2004	1 306 227	1 232 126	74 101	5.7
2003	1 279 451	1 204 539	74 912	5.9
2002	1 273 675	1 205 232	68 443	5.4
2001	1 252 300	1 193 249	59 051	4.7
2000	1 256 147	1 203 421	52 726	4.2
1999	1 253 739	1 198 016	55 723	4.4
1998	1 241 706	1 179 338	62 368	5.0
1997	1 240 404	1 177 143	63 261	5.1
1996	1 242 883	1 179 020	63 863	5.1
1995	1 229 608	1 170 593	59 015	4.8
1994	1 213 191	1 148 393	64 798	5.3
1993	1 178 435	1 106 257	72 178	6.1
1992	1 155 737	1 073 382	82 355	7.1
1991	1 127 094	1 045 941	81 153	7.2
1990	1 125 962	1 049 819	76 143	6.8

Note: Population age 16 years and over.

Unemployment Rate, 1980–2004

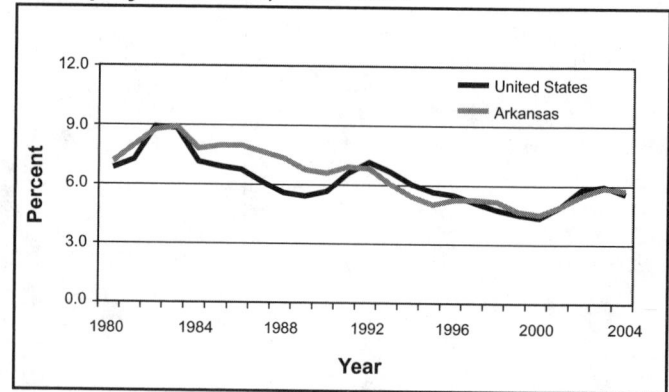

Table AR-9. Employment and Average Wages by Industry, 2001–2004

(Estimates are based on the 2002 North American Industry Classification System [NAICS].)

Industry	2001	2002	2003	2004	Annual average percent change, 2001–2004
	Number of jobs				
TOTAL EMPLOYMENT BY PLACE OF WORK	1 498 575	1 496 886	1 501 287	1 524 242	0.6
Farm Employment	62 395	62 221	61 503	60 657	-0.9
Nonfarm Employment	1 436 180	1 434 665	1 439 784	1 463 585	0.6
Private employment	1 226 562	1 224 112	1 225 615	1 247 831	0.6
Forestry, fishing, hunting, and other[1]	19 577	20 148	18 418	18 448	-2.0
Mining	7 015	6 407	7 136	7 592	2.7
Utilities	7 042	6 981	6 891	6 711	-1.6
Construction	91 700	91 330	90 431	91 719	0.0
Manufacturing	232 852	219 812	211 707	209 741	-3.4
Durable goods manufacturing	127 987	118 778	113 176	111 837	-4.4
Nondurable goods manufacturing	104 865	101 034	98 531	97 904	-2.3
Wholesale trade	50 263	49 306	48 880	50 435	0.1
Retail trade	165 672	165 215	164 695	167 667	0.4
Transportation and warehousing	70 947	72 858	72 197	71 609	0.3
Information	23 473	22 471	22 723	22 560	-1.3
Finance and insurance	47 770	49 015	49 456	49 922	1.5
Real estate and rental and leasing	37 667	37 761	38 948	41 063	2.9
Professional and technical services	49 847	50 278	51 822	55 436	3.6
Management of companies and enterprises	22 493	23 123	23 964	23 096	0.9
Administrative and waste services	68 340	69 022	71 702	76 026	3.6
Educational services	13 557	14 971	15 576	16 171	6.1
Health care and social assistance	137 891	142 085	146 848	150 310	2.9
Arts, entertainment, and recreation	15 991	16 253	16 418	16 687	1.4
Accommodation and food services	83 844	84 643	85 845	89 076	2.0
Other services, except public administration	80 621	82 433	81 958	83 562	1.2
Government and government enterprises	209 618	210 553	214 169	215 754	1.0
	Dollars				
AVERAGE WAGES AND SALARIES BY PLACE OF WORK	26 632	27 461	28 270	29 632	3.6
Farm Earnings	19 434	19 617	18 213	22 880	5.6
Nonfarm Earnings	26 713	27 547	28 384	29 703	3.6
Private earnings	26 684	27 419	28 193	29 465	3.4
Forestry, fishing, hunting, and other[1]	21 667	22 123	22 987	23 850	3.3
Mining	37 878	38 135	39 512	41 710	3.3
Utilities	53 091	54 336	56 447	60 963	4.7
Construction	28 987	30 162	29 664	30 614	1.8
Manufacturing	29 815	30 721	31 833	33 207	3.7
Durable goods manufacturing	30 104	31 229	32 435	33 836	4.0
Nondurable goods manufacturing	29 467	30 131	31 150	32 499	3.3
Wholesale trade	37 207	38 898	40 408	43 486	5.3
Retail trade	17 676	18 284	19 003	19 519	3.4
Transportation and warehousing	32 963	33 803	33 910	35 588	2.6
Information	35 042	35 490	36 516	38 731	3.4
Finance and insurance	37 218	37 842	39 866	41 703	3.9
Real estate and rental and leasing	21 676	22 764	22 919	24 611	4.3
Professional and technical services	39 724	39 165	40 171	43 491	3.1
Management of companies and enterprises	58 864	60 165	61 458	65 316	3.5
Administrative and waste services	16 399	17 205	17 871	18 857	4.8
Educational services	17 909	18 657	19 807	20 609	4.8
Health care and social assistance	28 158	28 936	29 656	31 025	3.3
Arts, entertainment, and recreation	14 016	14 287	14 531	15 023	2.3
Accommodation and food services	10 555	10 857	11 090	11 369	2.5
Other services, except public administration	18 661	19 340	19 889	20 620	3.4
Government and government enterprises	26 853	28 147	29 263	30 806	4.7

Note: Average wages and salaries are a calculation by the editors of wage and salary disbursements divided by full- and part-time wage and salary employment. Data may not add to total or may appear as zero due to rounding.

1 "Other" consists of the number of jobs held by U.S. residents employed by international organizations and foreign embassies and consulates in the United States.

LABOR MARKET

Arkansas's unemployment rate in 2004 was 5.7 percent, only slightly above the national average. Government and manufacturing were the largest employment sectors in Arkansas—each accounted for about 14 percent of total employment in 2004—followed by retail trade. Total nonfarm employment grew 1.7 percent over the 2001–2004 period, which nearly equaled the national growth rate. Most of the economic growth occurred in the service-providing sector (particularly in health care, educational, real estate, and managerial services). The number of jobs in construction was static, while most states saw growth in this industry. Earnings growth in Arkansas slightly outpaced the nation's average.

Employment by Industry, 2004

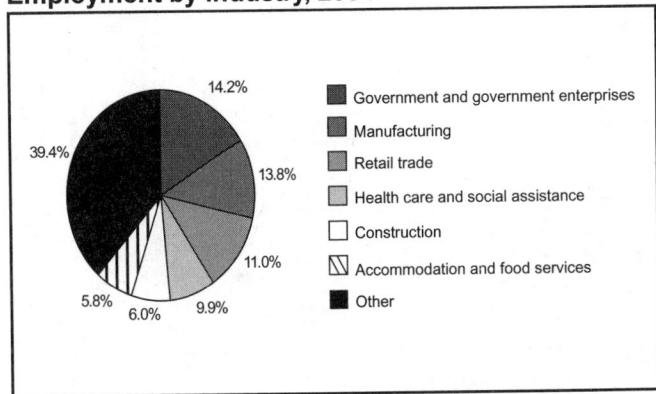

- 14.2% Government and government enterprises
- 13.8% Manufacturing
- 11.0% Retail trade
- 9.9% Health care and social assistance
- 6.0% Construction
- 5.8% Accommodation and food services
- 39.4% Other

Table AR-10. Personal Income by Major Source, Selected Years 1980–2004

(Millions of dollars, except where noted.)

Item	1980	1990	2000	2001	2002	2003	2004	Average annual percent change, 2000–2004
Earnings by Place of Work	12 837	24 776	43 070	45 249	46 239	48 998	52 812	5.2
Wage and salary disbursements	9 338	17 698	31 504	32 559	33 412	34 369	36 417	3.7
Supplements to wages and salaries	1 879	3 916	6 661	7 099	7 955	8 596	9 334	8.8
Proprietors' income[1]	1 620	3 162	4 905	5 591	4 871	6 034	7 061	9.5
Farm proprietors' income	179	750	943	1 017	355	1 566	2 165	23.1
Nonfarm proprietors' income	1 441	2 412	3 961	4 574	4 516	4 468	4 896	5.4
(-) Contributions for government social insurance[2]	1 227	2 875	5 065	5 296	5 476	5 702	6 015	4.4
(+) Adjustment for residence[3]	-3	-210	-346	-350	-380	-374	-396	X
(=) Net Earnings by Place of Residence	11 607	21 692	37 659	39 604	40 382	42 922	46 401	5.4
(+) Dividends, interest, and rent[4]	2 726	6 572	10 411	10 558	10 184	9 876	10 173	-0.6
(+) Personal current transfer receipts	2 888	5 813	10 656	11 805	12 758	13 285	14 236	7.5
Personal income	17 221	34 076	58 726	61 967	63 324	66 082	70 810	4.8
Farm income	16 869	33 078	57 524	60 670	62 696	64 252	68 337	4.4
Nonfarm income	353	998	1 202	1 297	628	1 830	2 473	19.8
Per Capita Personal Income (Dollars)[5]	7 524	14 460	21 925	23 018	23 388	24 226	25 724	4.1

Note: Data may not add to total or may appear as zero due to rounding.

[1]Proprietors' income includes the inventory valuation adjustment and the capital consumption adjustment.
[2]Contributions for government social insurance are included in earnings by type and industry, but they are excluded from personal income.
[3]The adjustment for residence is the net inflow of the earnings of interarea commuters.
[4]Rental income of persons includes the capital consumption adjustment.
[5]Per capita personal income is total personal income divided by total midyear population.
X = Not applicable.

Per Capita Personal Income, 1980–2004 (Current Dollars)

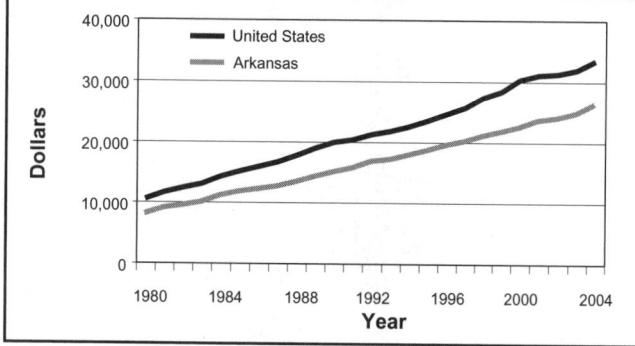

ECONOMIC ACTIVITY

Real gross state product (GSP) grew at about the national average rate following the 2001 recession. The GSP of Arkansas increased at an average annual rate of 3.3 percent during the 2001–2004 period, with a substantial growth rate of 5.3 percent from 2003 to 2004. The chief contributors to growth were agriculture, real estate, wholesale and retail trade, and business services. Housing activity provided some ongoing growth for the state, but housing price appreciation was below the national average. The $79,000 median value of owner-occupied housing in Arkansas was the lowest in the nation.

Table AR-11. Real Gross State Product, 1997–2004

(Millions of chained 2000 dollars, percent.)

Industry	1997	1998	1999	2000	2001	2002	2003	2004	Average annual percent change, 2001–2004
GROSS STATE PRODUCT	62 474	63 751	66 628	66 176	66 656	68 060	69 734	73 411	3.3
As a percent of U.S. gross product	0.7	0.7	0.7	0.7	0.7	0.7	0.7	0.7	X
Private Industries	54 493	55 617	58 379	57 763	58 167	59 541	61 119	64 427	3.5
Agriculture, forestry, fishing, and hunting	2 248	2 040	2 191	1 956	2 147	1 944	2 165	2 613	6.8
Mining	325	343	336	294	276	280	250	255	-2.6
Utilities	1 588	1 594	1 608	1 616	1 370	1 332	1 497	1 573	4.7
Construction	3 075	3 051	3 075	3 111	3 093	3 123	2 891	2 919	-1.9
Manufacturing	13 718	13 773	14 401	13 949	12 852	13 048	13 386	13 786	2.4
As a percent of gross state product	22.0	21.6	21.6	21.1	19.3	19.2	19.2	18.8	X
Wholesale trade	3 625	3 984	4 191	4 164	4 563	4 760	4 697	5 050	3.4
Retail trade	4 191	4 311	4 702	4 845	5 264	5 563	5 910	6 247	5.9
Transportation and warehousing	2 844	3 003	3 138	3 257	3 275	3 491	3 532	3 577	3.0
Information	1 914	2 084	2 304	2 305	2 647	2 832	3 105	3 440	9.1
Finance and insurance	2 654	2 769	2 826	2 951	3 012	3 087	3 165	3 336	3.5
Real estate and rental and leasing	5 307	5 470	6 025	5 866	6 163	6 207	6 229	6 625	2.4
Services	12 990	13 226	13 588	13 447	13 540	13 939	14 418	15 156	3.8
As a percent of gross state product	20.8	20.7	20.4	20.3	20.3	20.5	20.7	20.6	X
Professional and technical services	1 788	1 859	1 935	2 103	2 226	2 256	2 388	2 705	6.7
Management of companies and enterprises	2 019	2 038	2 084	1 785	1 678	1 781	1 868	1 799	2.3
Administrative and waste services	1 218	1 255	1 336	1 296	1 237	1 298	1 387	1 493	6.5
Educational services	220	223	236	239	244	246	248	248	0.5
Health care and social assistance	4 373	4 395	4 453	4 601	4 771	4 939	5 091	5 276	3.4
Arts, entertainment, and recreation	326	340	326	318	327	351	347	350	2.3
Accommodation and food services	1 369	1 413	1 467	1 476	1 483	1 502	1 524	1 607	2.7
Other services, except public administration	1 677	1 703	1 751	1 629	1 574	1 566	1 565	1 678	2.2
Government	7 986	8 138	8 247	8 413	8 489	8 522	8 624	8 993	1.9
As a percent of gross state product	12.8	12.8	12.4	12.7	12.7	12.5	12.4	12.3	X

X = Not applicable.

Table AR-12. Government Transfer Payments, Selected Years 1980–2004

(Millions of dollars, percent.)

Item	1980	1990	2000	2001	2002	2003	2004	Average annual percent change, 2000–2004
CURRENT TRANSFER PAYMENTS TO INDIVIDUALS	2 727	5 508	10 006	11 055	12 097	12 652	13 593	8.0
Retirement and Disability Insurance Benefits	1 374	2 712	4 422	4 674	4 943	5 152	5 374	5.0
Old-age, survivors, and disability insurance (OASDI) benefits	1 284	2 583	4 252	4 498	4 753	4 954	5 172	5.0
Railroad retirement and disability benefits	66	98	128	133	141	146	148	3.9
Workers' compensation	12	19	33	34	39	40	41	5.8
Other government retirement and disability insurance benefits	12	11	9	10	11	12	12	7.8
Medical Benefits	597	1 744	3 764	4 380	4 867	5 048	5 719	11.0
Medicare benefits	340	1 062	2 098	2 319	2 481	2 625	2 880	8.2
Public assistance medical care benefits	245	640	1 612	1 984	2 286	2 341	2 741	14.2
Military medical insurance benefits	12	42	54	77	101	82	98	16.0
Income Maintenance Benefits	325	514	1 077	1 088	1 223	1 347	1 469	8.1
Supplemental Security Income (SSI) benefits	108	187	333	341	354	361	378	3.2
Family assistance	51	57	65	45	38	33	28	-19.4
Food stamps	125	162	209	232	270	312	364	14.9
Other income maintenance benefits	41	108	470	470	560	641	699	10.4
Unemployment Insurance Compensation	149	154	206	311	404	406	296	9.5
Veterans' Benefits	244	299	420	439	484	519	547	6.8
Federal Education and Training Assistance	38	82	110	148	168	172	181	13.3
Other Payments to Individuals	*	2	8	15	8	7	6	-4.3

Note: See notes and definitions for more details. Data may not add to total or may appear as zero due to rounding.

EXPORTS

Arkansas ranked 32nd in the nation for the value of its exported goods, as the volume of exports in the state rose by 60 percent between 1999 and 2004 (the 8th highest rate of growth in exports in the nation). Transportation equipment exports were Arkansas's most valuable commodity in 2004, accounting about 20 percent of exports. Processed foods ranked second, accounting for over 16 percent of the state's exports. Canada was the top recipient of these goods and was the overall leading market for Arkansas's exports. The state's other major export destinations were Mexico, Russia, Japan, and the United Kingdom. Exports to Mexico increased over 72 percent from 2001 to 2004.

Leading Exports, 2004

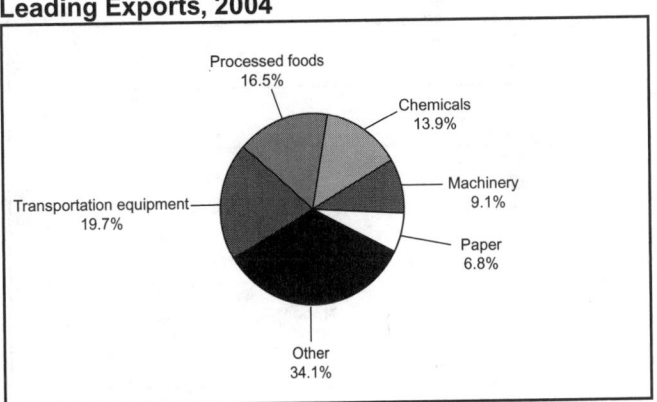

Table AR-13. Exports of Goods by Leading Products and Destinations, 2001–2004

(Millions of dollars, percent, rank based on 2004 dollar values.)

Product and market	2001	2002	2003	2004	Percent share of total, 2004	Average annual percent change, 2001–2004
Total Goods						
Total	2 911	2 804	2 962	3 493	100.0	6.3
Manufactures	2 790	2 659	2 817	3 306	94.6	5.8
Agriculture and livestock	103	131	122	157	4.5	15.2
Other commodities	19	13	23	31	0.9	17.9
Five Leading Exports (NAICS Code)						
Transportation equipment (336)	376	614	532	688	19.7	22.3
Processed foods (311)	641	469	575	575	16.5	-3.5
Chemical manufactures (325)	390	355	431	486	13.9	7.6
Machinery manufactures (333)	254	247	251	317	9.1	7.6
Paper products (322)	216	195	195	237	6.8	3.1
Five Leading Markets	2 461	2 253	2 607	3 123	89.4	8.3
Canada	917	811	807	975	27.9	2.1
Mexico	200	249	245	344	9.8	19.9
Russia	297	168	173	190	5.4	-13.9
Japan	224	181	178	185	5.3	-6.2
United Kingdom	105	100	147	164	4.7	16.1

Table AR-14. Agriculture, 1997 and 2002

(Number, acres, and dollars.)

Item	1997	2002
Number of farms	49 493	47 483
Land in farms (acres)	14 823 865	14 502 793
Farm Size		
Average size of farm (acres)	300	305
Farms by size (percent distribution)		
Fewer than 50 acres	25.9	27.3
50 to 499 acres	59.0	58.3
500 acres or more	15.1	14.5
Market Value of Land and Equipment (Dollars)		
Land and buildings average value per farm	354 095	447 104
Average value per acre	1 157	1 469
Machinery and equipment average value per farm	55 572	65 299
Value of Sales (Thousands of Dollars)		
Agricultural products sold	5 613 156	4 950 397
Crops	2 232 440	1 620 384
Livestock, poultry, and their products	3 380 717	3 330 014
Average per farm (dollars)	113 413	104 256
Value of sales (percent distribution)		
Less than $10,000	57.0	60.3
$10,000 to $99,999	22.2	21.8
$100,000 or more	20.8	17.9
Government Payments		
Payments (thousands of dollars)	148 316	238 577
Percent of farms receiving government payments	22.4	16.5
Farm operators whose principal occupation is farming (percent) ...	47.8	57.7

AGRICULTURE

Agriculture was important to Arkansas's economy, accounting for about 4 percent of the state's total employment. Farming was the second largest contributor to the growth in gross state product during the 2001–2004 period, lagging only behind the information sector. Total cash receipts totaled nearly $5 billion in 2002, with most farms having total sales of under $10,000. This was a decline from 1997, as the value of crop sales fell from $2.2 billion to $1.6 billion. Wheat, corn, chicken, and beef accounted for the majority of the state's agricultural output.

ENERGY

Arkansas's energy prices were relatively low compared with the rest of the nation, ranking 37th in 2001. However, per capita expenditures were over $2,700, which was the 11th highest amount in the country. (The U.S. average was $2,433.) The state's per capita consumption also ranked 11th in the nation in 2001, despite being below 2000 levels.

Energy Consumption by Source, 2001

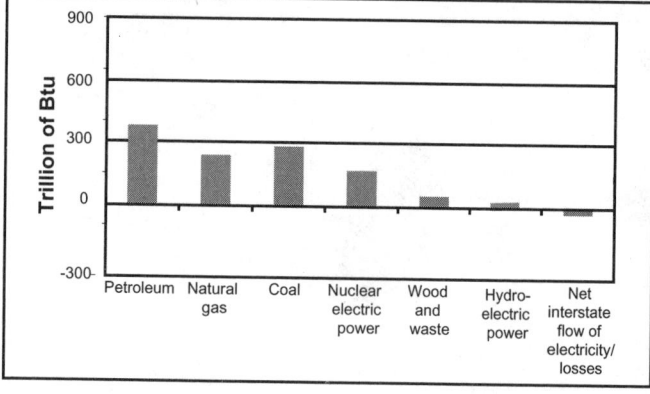

Energy Consumption by Sector, 2001

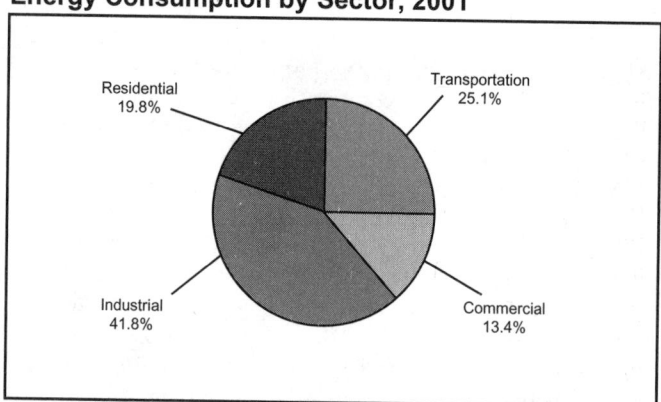

Table AR-15. Energy Consumption, Expenditures, and Prices, Selected Years 1960–2001

(Dollars, Btu [British Thermal Unit], percent distribution.)

Item	1960	1965	1970	1975	1980	1985	1990	1995	2000	2001
Total Consumption (Billion Btu)	426 866	529 777	708 675	790 227	876 073	796 976	857 331	1 027 683	1 154 080	1 106 349
Consumption per capita (million Btu)	239.0	279.7	368.5	365.9	383.2	342.5	364.7	414.4	431.7	411.0
Consumption by Sector (Percent Distribution)										
Residential	19.1	17.2	20.4	21.2	20.6	19.2	20.0	19.0	19.3	19.8
Commercial	8.4	10.1	11.1	12.2	11.3	12.6	12.2	11.7	12.5	13.4
Industrial	48.0	48.2	45.0	40.1	44.7	42.7	41.2	44.0	42.8	41.8
Transportation	24.5	24.5	23.5	26.5	23.3	25.5	26.6	25.4	25.5	25.1
Consumption by Source (Billion Btu)										
Coal	356	163	0	862	36 648	219 791	212 712	237 339	267 576	273 979
Natural gas	222 202	277 661	383 478	257 445	273 994	199 350	234 465	271 955	256 114	231 589
Petroleum	148 944	180 013	246 345	345 425	311 343	270 555	267 880	310 062	388 113	378 575
Nuclear electric power	0	0	0	53 676	85 438	105 042	119 387	122 486	121 516	154 430
Hydroelectric power[1]	10 671	11 291	22 668	35 719	35 719	46 323	38 463	33 181	24 181	25 926
Wood and waste	37 433	35 134	34 264	35 870	56 804	62 483	72 312	83 794	72 413	57 321
Other	0	0	0	0	0	0	1 420	1 404	1 042	914
Net interstate flow of electricity/losses[2]	7 260	25 514	21 919	61 230	94 241	-106 567	-89 307	-32 538	23 124	-16 384
Total Expenditures (Thousands of Dollars)	...	...	801 800	1 741 300	3 884 100	4 165 300	4 656 600	5 250 700	7 304 500	7 339 500
Expenditures per capita (dollars)	...	...	417	806	1 699	1 790	1 981	2 117	2 732	2 726
Prices by Sector (Dollars Per Million Btu)										
Total	...	...	1.51	2.96	6.58	8.02	8.14	7.58	9.33	9.94
Residential	...	...	1.88	3.82	8.02	11.40	13.43	13.53	15.01	16.95
Commercial	...	...	1.58	3.08	6.73	9.95	11.65	11.11	11.13	12.73
Industrial	...	...	0.72	1.63	4.07	5.81	4.83	4.27	6.06	6.62
Transportation	...	...	2.38	4.06	9.11	8.24	8.55	8.35	10.50	10.24

[1]A negative number in this row results from pumped storage for which, overall, more electricity is expended than created to provide electricity during peak demand periods.
[2]Net interstate flow of electricity is the difference between the amount of energy in the electricity sold within a state (including associated losses) and the energy input at the electric utilities within the state. A positive number indicates that more electricity (including associated losses) came into the state than went out of the state during the year; conversely, a negative number indicates that more electricity (including associated losses) went out of the state than came into the state.
... = Not available.

Table AR-16. State Taxes, Fiscal 2004

(Dollars, percent distribution.)

Item	Thousands of dollars	Percent distribution	Dollars per capita	
			State	U.S.
TOTAL TAXES	5 580 678	100.0	2 027.1	2 024.8
Property Taxes	520 324	9.3	189.0	38.9
Sales and Gross Receipts	2 934 030	52.6	1 065.8	1 003.4
General sales and gross receipts	2 149 527	38.5	780.8	677.0
Selective sales taxes	784 503	14.1	285.0	326.4
Alcoholic beverages	41 240	0.7	15.0	15.7
Insurance premiums	91 330	1.6	33.2	47.0
Motor fuels	453 148	8.1	164.6	114.6
Tobacco products	146 485	2.6	53.2	42.0
Other selective sales	47 726	0.9	17.3	49.8
Licenses	187 876	3.4	68.2	134.9
Motor vehicle	109 831	2.0	39.9	59.4
Other Taxes	1 938 448	34.7	704.1	847.6
Individual income	1 685 585	30.2	612.3	673.6
Corporation net income	181 830	3.3	66.0	105.1

GOVERMENT FINANCE

In 2003, Arkansas's general revenues amounted to $10.7 billion and its expenditures reached just over $11 billion. The state ranked 24th in the nation for per capita revenues and 23rd for per capita expenditures. Per capita taxes amounted to $2,027, which was close to the U.S. average. The leading sources of revenue were general sales and gross receipts ($781) and individual income taxes ($612). Arkansas ranked 7th for per capita property taxes among the 37 states with such taxes. The state's per capita debt was $1,200, which was half of the U.S. average and among the five lowest amounts in the nation.

Per Capita State Taxes, Fiscal, 2004

Table AR-17. State Government Finances, 2003

(Dollars, percent distribution.)

Item	Millions of dollars	Percent distribution	Dollars per capita	
			State	U.S.
GENERAL REVENUE	10 730 541	100.0	3 933.5	3 832.6
Intergovernmental revenue	3 685 249	34.3	1 350.9	1 246.0
Taxes	5 145 554	48.0	1 886.2	1 891.6
General sales	1 951 630	18.2	715.4	636.0
Selective sales	706 237	6.6	258.9	307.4
License taxes	206 286	1.9	75.6	123.6
Individual income tax	1 528 231	14.2	560.2	626.8
Corporate income tax	176 875	1.6	64.8	97.8
Other taxes	576 295	5.4	211.2	99.9
Current charges	1 396 967	13.0	512.1	366.5
Miscellaneous general revenue	502 771	4.7	184.3	328.6
GENERAL EXPENDITURE	11 081 356	100.0	4 062.1	4 010.5
Intergovernmental expenditure	3 210 582	29.0	1 176.9	1 316.9
Direct expenditure	7 870 774	71.0	2 885.2	2 693.6
Expenditure by Function				
Education	4 529 282	40.9	1 660.3	1 416.4
Public welfare	2 705 341	24.4	991.7	1 083.3
Hospitals	543 347	4.9	199.2	132.3
Health	292 724	2.6	107.3	173.0
Highways	1 098 172	9.9	402.6	295.4
Police protection	69 422	0.6	25.4	38.4
Correction	305 803	2.8	112.1	135.0
Natural resources	190 638	1.7	69.9	64.0
Parks and recreation	71 910	0.6	26.4	20.1
Government administration	443 224	4.0	162.5	151.3
Interest on general debt	115 076	1.0	42.2	107.8
Other and unallocable	716 417	6.5	262.6	393.4
DEBT AT END OF FISCAL YEAR	3 295 143	X	1 207.9	2 404.7
CASH AND SECURITY HOLDINGS	16 999 518	X	6 231.5	8 938.4

X = Not applicable.

Table AR-18. Education Indicators, 2000–2004

(Percent, number.)

Item	State	U.S.
Total Population 25 Years and Over (Thousands), 2004	1 763	186 877
Educational Attainment, 2004		
Percent high school graduate or more	79.2	85.2
Percent college graduate or more	18.8	27.7
Elementary and Secondary Schools, 2002–2003		
Total students	450 985	48 202 324
Percent of students eligible for free or reduced-price lunch ..	49.8	40.6
Percent of students who were English language learners	3.8	7.8
Total schools	1 129	92 330
Student/teacher ratio	14.7	15.9
Per student expenditures	6 482	8 041
Dropouts, Grades 9–12, 2000–2001 (Percent)	5.3	. . .
Higher Education, 2002–2003		
Total enrollment	132 194	17 035 027
Bachelor's degrees awarded	10 591	1 348 503
Percent women	58.4	57.5

. . . = Not available.

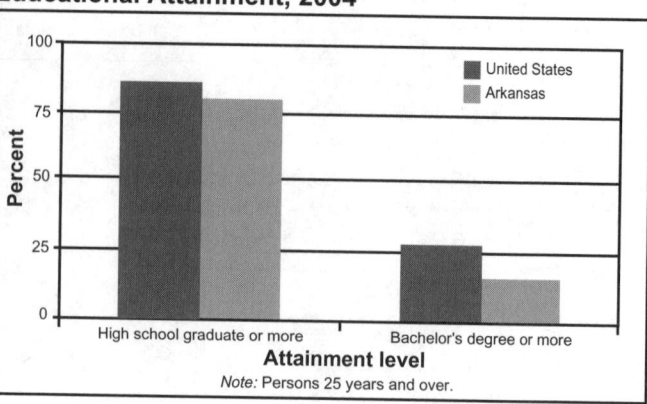

Educational Attainment, 2004

Note: Persons 25 years and over.

EDUCATION

In recent years, Arkansas has shown improvement in the educational attainment levels of its population age 25 years and over. However, the state was among just three states in which less than 80 percent of the population held a high school diploma. Arkansas ranked 50th in the nation, behind only West Virginia, for proportion of college graduates (18.8 percent). Arkansas's per student expenditures of $6,482 were among the 10 lowest in the nation. The state's student/teacher ratio of 14.9 was below the U.S. average. Arkansas ranked 12th among the 46 states reporting dropout data for the 2000–2001 school year.

VOTER PARTICIPATION

Despite having an Arkansan elected president in 1992 and 1996, Arkansas was not a state with high voter turnout. In the 2000 election, less than half of the state's eligible voters cast votes, which was one of the smallest proportions in the nation. In 2004, over 56 percent voted—a rate still below the U.S. average and among the 10 lowest in the nation. In 2000, 51.3 percent voted for the Republican presidential candidate; in 2004, this proportion rose to 54.3 percent, according to the official tally by the Clerk of the U.S. House of Representatives.

Table AR-19. Reported Voting and Registration, November 2000 and November 2004

(Numbers in thousands, percent.)

Characteristic	Total population 18 years and over	Total citizen		Total registered		Total voted	
		Number	Percent	Number	Percent	Number	Percent
NOVEMBER 2000							
Total	1 893	1 851	97.8	1 125	59.4	936	49.4
Male	897	869	96.9	513	57.2	423	47.2
Female	996	982	98.5	612	61.4	512	51.4
NOVEMBER 2004							
Total	2 010	1 942	96.6	1 328	66.1	1 140	56.7
Male	962	926	96.3	606	63.0	524	54.4
Female	1 048	1 015	96.9	723	69.0	617	58.9
Race and Hispanic Origin							
White alone	1 649	1 593	96.6	1 106	67.1	966	58.6
Non-Hispanic White alone	1 578	1 570	99.5	1 096	69.4	959	60.8
Black alone	295	295	100.0	188	63.7	145	49.4
Asian alone	24	13	B	-	B	-	B
Hispanic or Latino[1]	73	25	B	10	B	7	B
White alone or in combination	1 684	1 628	96.7	1 135	67.4	990	58.8
Non-Hispanic White alone or in combination	1 613	1 605	99.5	1 125	69.7	983	61.0
Black alone or in combination	297	297	100.0	190	63.9	147	49.7
Asian alone or in combination	25	14	B	-	B	-	B
Age							
18 to 24 years	258	236	91.7	117	45.5	85	32.9
25 to 44 years	726	689	95.0	442	60.9	366	50.4
45 to 64 years	688	680	98.7	504	73.3	442	64.3
65 to 74 years	178	178	100.0	134	75.2	126	70.9
75 years and over	160	159	99.1	131	82.0	121	75.7

[1]May be of any race.
- = Represents zero or rounds to zero.
B = Base is too small to show derived measure.

At a Glance:

- In 2004, California was the largest state in the nation in terms of population. The state's population was 35.9 million, giving it over 13 million more residents than Texas, the second most populous state.

- California's population was among four states and the District of Columbia with "majority-minority" populations. Non-Hispanic Whites composed only 44.5 percent of the state's population. California had the second highest proportions of Asian and Pacific Islanders and of Hispanics (of any race) in the country.

- Median household income in California was the 13th highest in the nation, and the state's poverty rate of 13.3 percent ranked 17th. California's unemployment rate of 6.2 percent was the 6th highest in the nation.

- Gross state product grew steadily after its decline during the 2001 recession. In 2004, economic activity was up 5.6 percent from the previous year, giving California the eighth fastest growth rate in the country.

- California ranked well below the national average in terms of the high school attainment level of its population age 25 years and over. However, the state's college attainment level was above the national average.

Table CA-1. Population by Sex and Age, 1990, 2000, and 2004

(Number, percent.)

Sex and age	1990	2000	2004	Percent distribution, 2004	Average annual percent change, 2000–2004
Total Population	29 760 021	33 871 648	35 893 799	X	1.5
Percent of total U.S. population	12.0	12.0	12.2	X	X
Sex					
Male	14 897 627	16 874 892	17 913 717	49.9	1.5
Female	14 862 394	16 996 756	17 980 082	50.1	1.4
Age					
Under 5 years	2 397 715	2 486 981	2 633 972	7.3	0.4
5 to 17 years	5 353 010	6 762 848	6 962 491	19.4	1.9
18 years and over	22 009 296	24 621 819	26 297 336	73.3	1.3
18 to 24 years	3 412 257	3 366 030	3 596 126	10.0	0.3
25 to 44 years	10 325 692	10 714 403	10 793 157	30.1	0.3
45 to 64 years	5 135 795	6 945 728	8 085 096	22.5	3.3
65 years and over	3 135 552	3 595 658	3 822 957	10.7	1.5
85 years and over	299 107	425 657	514 013	1.4	4.1
Median age (years)	31.3	33.3	34.2	X	X

X = Not applicable.

Average Annual Rate of Population Growth, 1980–2004

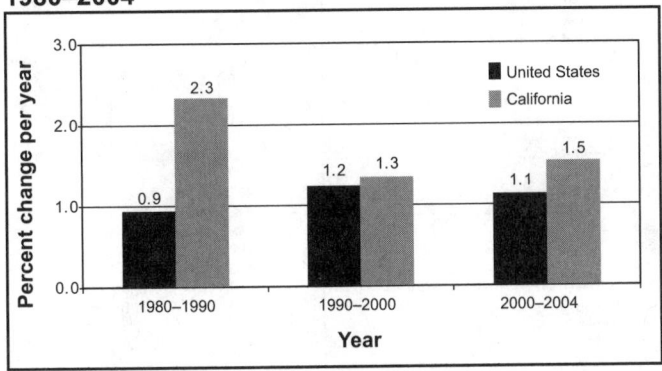

POPULATION

California's population grew at a rapid 6 percent from 2000–2004, which was among the 10 highest rates in the nation, but behind those of its fast-growing neighbors, Nevada and Arizona. California had the largest numerical increase in residents in the country over the 2000–2004 period. More than 60 percent of that growth was due to international immigration. From 2000 to 2004, the state received twice as many immigrants as New York, the second most popular state for new residents from abroad. However, California lost more than 400,000 residents to other states during the same period. Of the state's two largest cities, Los Angeles was the second largest in the United States; San Francisco was the 14th largest.

Table CA-2. Population by Race and Hispanic Origin, 1990, 2000, and 2004

(Number, percent.)

Race and Hispanic origin	1990	2000	2004
Total Population	29 760 021	33 871 648	35 893 799
Non-Hispanic (Percent)			
One race[1]			
White	57.2	47.4	44.5
Black	7.0	6.5	6.3
American Indian, Alaska Native[2]	0.8	0.5	0.5
Asian and Pacific Islander[2]	9.6	11.3	12.1
Other race[2]	13.2	. . .	. . .
Two or more races	. . .	1.9	1.9
Hispanic or Latino[3] (Percent)	25.8	32.4	34.7

[1]Individuals could report only one race in the 1990 census and could report one or more races on the 2000 census. Data on race in 2000 and 2004 are not comparable to 1990.
[2]Data for 1990 include people of Hispanic or Latino origin.
[3]May be of any race.
. . . = Not available.

Minority Population as a Percent of Total Population, 2004

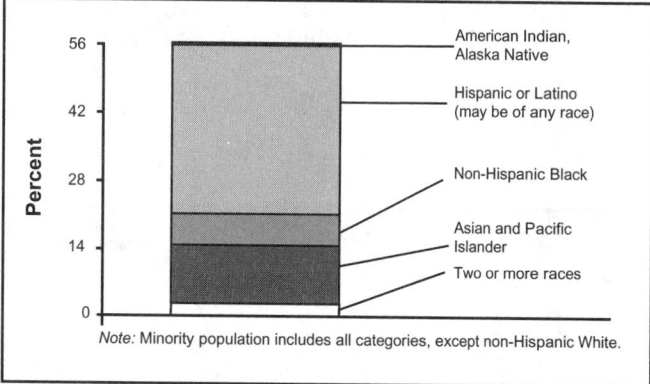

Note: Minority population includes all categories, except non-Hispanic White.

Age-Adjusted Death Rates, Average 2000–2002

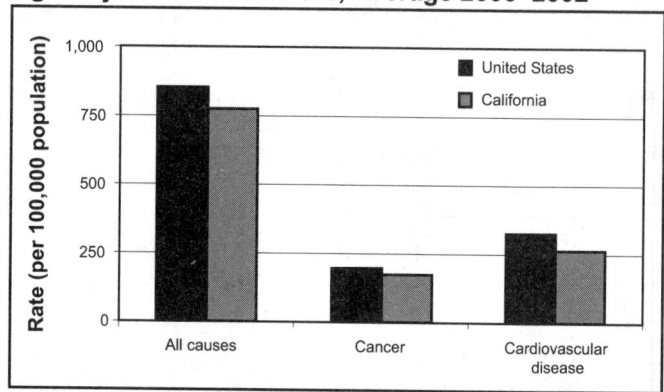

HEALTH

Over 18 percent of California's residents lacked health insurance in 2004, giving the state one of the lowest rates of coverage in the country. However, the state's infant mortality rate and teenage birth rate were below the national averages. California's age-adjusted death rates were among the lowest in the country.

Table CA-3. Health Characteristics, 2000–2004

(Number, rate, percent.)

Item	State	U.S.
Births, 2003–2004		
Number of births	540 997	4 089 950
Birth rate (per 1,000 population)	15.2	14.1
Teenage birth rate (per 1,000 women age 15–19 years)	40.1	41.6
Mortality Rates, Average 2000–2002		
Infant mortality rate (per 1,000 live births)	5.4	6.9
Age-adjusted mortality rate (per 100,000 population)		
All races	770.9	853.3
Non-Hispanic White	815.1	843.1
Black	1 053.6	1 097.7
American Indian, Alaska Native	. . .	687.0
Asian and Pacific Islander	506.1	486.0
Hispanic or Latino[1]	611.8	642.7
Health Insurance, 2004		
Percent of all persons without health insurance	18.7	15.7
Percent of children without health insurance	12.4	11.2
Percent of low-income children without health insurance	8.2	7.1

[1]May be of any race.
. . . = Not available.

Table CA-4. Leading Causes of Death, Average 2000–2002

(Number, rate per 100,000 population.)

Cause	Number of deaths	Age-adjusted death rates	
		State	U.S.
ALL CAUSES	232 720	770.9	853.3
Leading Causes			
Major cardiovascular diseases	92 455	312.2	326.5
Cancer	53 742	178.7	196.0
Chronic lower respiratory diseases	12 802	43.4	43.7
Unintentional injuries	8 939	26.9	35.7
Diabetes (underlying cause)	6 464	21.6	25.2
Influenza and pneumonia	8 194	27.8	22.7
Alzheimer's disease	4 925	16.8	19.0
Motor vehicle accidents	3 860	11.3	15.0
Nephritis, nephrotic syndrome, and nephrosis ..	1 981	6.6	13.8
Septicemia	867	2.9	11.4
Suicides	3 009	9.0	10.7
Firearm-related	3 239	9.4	10.3
Cirrhosis	3 702	11.7	9.5
Drug-induced	2 407	7.1	7.9
Alcohol-induced	3 412	10.7	6.9
Homicides	2 242	6.3	6.0
Falls	1 292	4.3	5.2
HIV	1 469	4.3	5.0
Viral hepatitis	910	2.9	2.0
Anemias	233	0.8	1.6
Drownings	411	1.2	1.3
Fire deaths	196	0.6	1.2

Note: The rates are age-adjusted to the U.S. 2000 standard population.

Table CA-5. Households and Housing Characteristics, 1990, 2000, and 2004

(Number, percent, and dollars.)

Characteristic	1990	2000	2004	Average annual percent change, 2000–2004
Total Households	10 381 206	11 502 870	11 972 158	1.0
Family households	7 139 394	7 920 049	8 193 359	0.9
Married-couple family	5 469 522	5 877 084	5 988 615	0.5
Other family	1 669 872	2 042 965	2 204 744	1.9
Male householder, no wife present	477 692	594 455	671 028	3.1
Female householder, no husband present	1 192 180	1 448 510	1 533 716	1.4
Nonfamily households	3 241 812	3 582 821	3 778 799	1.3
Householder living alone	2 429 867	2 708 308	2 941 536	2.1
Householder not living alone	811 945	874 513	837 263	-1.1
Housing Characteristics				
Average size	2.79	2.87	2.93	X
Housing units	11 182 882	12 214 549	12 804 702	1.2
Occupied housing units	10 381 206	11 502 870	11 972 158	1.0
Owner-occupied	5 773 943	6 546 334	7 012 185	1.7
Renter-occupied	4 607 263	4 956 536	4 959 973	0.0
Median gross rent of renter-occupied housing units (dollars)	620	747	914	5.2
Median value of owner-occupied housing units (dollars)	194 300	211 500	391 102	16.6

X = Not applicable.

Median Housing Value and Median Rent, 2004

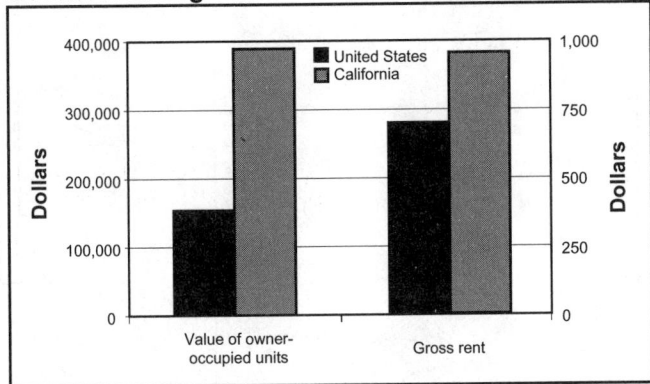

Median Household Income, 1984–2004 (2004 Dollars)

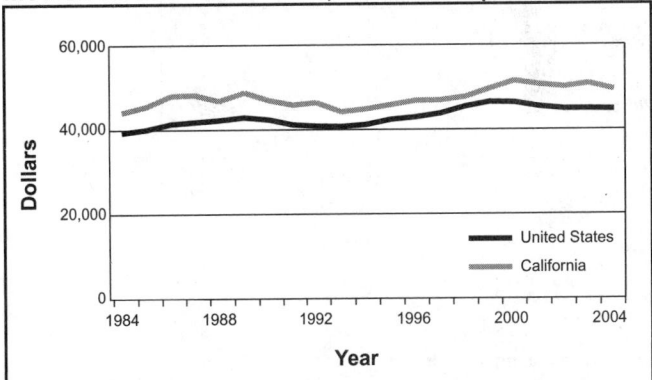

Table CA-6. Household Income and Poverty Status, 1980–2004

(2004 CPI-U-RS adjusted dollars, rate.)

Year	State Median household income (2004 dollars)	State Poverty rate	U.S. Median household income (2004 dollars)	U.S. Poverty rate
2004	49 230	13.3	44 389	12.7
2003	50 625	13.1	44 482	12.5
2002	49 828	13.1	44 546	12.1
2001	50 434	12.6	45 062	11.7
2000	51 352	12.7	46 058	11.3
1999	49 453	14.0	46 129	11.9
1998	47 375	15.4	45 003	12.7
1997	46 586	16.6	43 430	13.3
1996	46 524	16.9	42 544	13.7
1995	45 553	16.7	41 943	13.8
1994	44 544	17.9	40 677	14.5
1993	43 863	18.2	40 217	15.1
1992	46 052	16.4	40 422	14.8
1991	45 531	15.7	40 746	14.2
1990	46 653	13.9	41 963	13.5
1989	48 560	12.9	42 524	12.8
1988	46 469	13.2	41 771	13.0
1987	47 937	12.3	41 322	13.4
1986	47 703	12.7	40 939	13.6
1985	45 176	13.6	39 545	14.0
1984	43 751	13.2	38 782	14.4
1983	. . .	14.9	. . .	15.2
1982	. . .	14.1	. . .	15.0
1981	. . .	13.3	. . .	14.0
1980	. . .	11.0	. . .	13.0

. . . = Not available.

Table CA-7. Employment Status by Demographic Group, 2004

(Numbers in thousands, rate.)

Characteristic	Civilian noninstitutional population	Civilian labor force		Employed	Unemployment rate
		Number	Participation rate		
SEX AND AGE					
Total	26 768	17 551	65.6	16 466	6.2
16 to 19 years	2 020	751	37.2	595	20.8
20 to 24 years	2 591	1 895	73.1	1 710	9.8
25 to 34 years	5 029	4 068	80.9	3 819	6.1
35 to 44 years	5 411	4 394	81.2	4 185	4.8
45 to 54 years	4 831	3 896	80.6	3 726	4.4
55 to 64 years	3 214	2 002	62.3	1 912	4.5
65 years and over	3 671	544	14.8	520	4.5
Men	13 117	9 690	73.9	9 076	6.3
16 to 19 years	1 049	408	38.9	317	22.4
20 to 24 years	1 344	1 026	76.3	909	11.3
25 to 34 years	2 567	2 341	91.2	2 205	5.8
35 to 44 years	2 656	2 455	92.4	2 344	4.5
45 to 54 years	2 394	2 084	87.0	1 990	4.5
55 to 64 years	1 547	1 066	68.9	1 019	4.5
65 years and over	1 560	310	19.9	293	5.4
Women	13 650	7 860	57.6	7 390	6.0
16 to 19 years	971	343	35.3	279	18.9
20 to 24 years	1 247	870	69.7	800	8.0
25 to 34 years	2 463	1 727	70.1	1 614	6.5
35 to 44 years	2 755	1 939	70.4	1 841	5.0
45 to 54 years	2 436	1 811	74.3	1 736	4.2
55 to 64 years	1 667	936	56.1	894	4.5
65 years and over	2 111	234	11.1	226	3.3
MARITAL STATUS					
Married men, spouse present	6 989	5 507	78.8	5 299	3.8
Married women, spouse present	6 865	3 928	57.2	3 746	4.6
Women who maintain families	1 555	1 084	69.8	1 004	7.4
RACE, HISPANIC ORIGIN, AND SEX					
White	20 671	13 660	66.1	12 850	5.9
Men	10 226	7 663	74.9	7 200	6.0
Women	10 444	5 997	57.4	5 650	5.8
Black	1 719	1 065	61.9	953	10.6
Men	796	516	64.8	456	11.6
Women	923	549	59.5	497	9.6
Asian	3 412	2 182	64.0	2 071	5.1
Men	1 618	1 155	71.4	1 094	5.3
Women	1 794	1 028	57.3	977	4.9
Hispanic or Latino[1]	8 036	5 456	67.9	5 012	8.1
Men	4 086	3 267	80.0	3 021	7.5
Women	3 950	2 190	55.4	1 991	9.1
RACE, HISPANIC ORIGIN, AND AGE					
White					
25 to 34 years	3 751	3 060	81.6	2 878	5.9
35 to 44 years	4 139	3 362	81.2	3 213	4.4
45 to 54 years	3 759	3 061	81.4	2 940	4.0
55 to 64 years	2 531	1 592	62.9	1 524	4.3
65 years and over	2 939	454	15.4	435	4.1

Note: Data in Table 7 are from the Current Population Survey (CPS) and do not match Bureau of Labor Statistics estimates in Table 8. See notes and definitions for more details.

[1]May be of any race.

Table CA-8. Employment Status, 1990–2004

(Numbers in thousands, rate.)

Year	Civilian labor force	Employed	Unemployed	Unemployment rate
2004	17 552 240	16 459 862	1 092 378	6.2
2003	17 413 920	16 223 451	1 190 469	6.8
2002	17 326 895	16 165 052	1 161 843	6.7
2001	17 150 101	16 217 495	932 606	5.4
2000	16 869 744	16 034 095	835 649	5.0
1999	16 430 580	15 566 900	863 680	5.3
1998	16 166 912	15 203 693	963 219	6.0
1997	15 792 536	14 780 791	1 011 745	6.4
1996	15 435 896	14 303 507	1 132 389	7.3
1995	15 263 582	14 062 361	1 201 221	7.9
1994	15 271 041	13 953 855	1 317 186	8.6
1993	15 264 537	13 808 306	1 456 231	9.5
1992	15 309 846	13 874 246	1 435 600	9.4
1991	15 105 386	13 931 679	1 173 707	7.8
1990	15 168 531	14 294 115	874 416	5.8

Note: Population age 16 years and over.

Unemployment Rate, 1980–2004

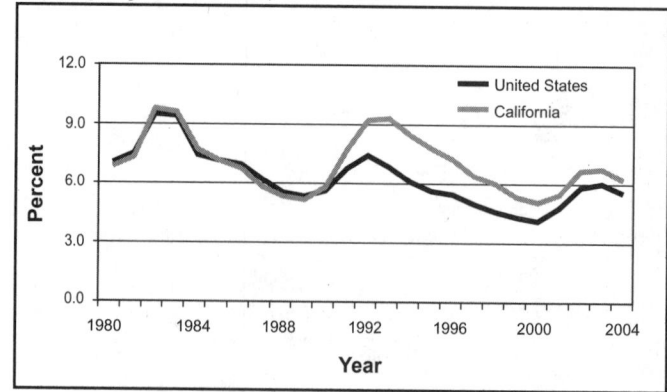

Table CA-9. Employment and Average Wages by Industry, 2001–2004

(Estimates are based on the 2002 North American Industry Classification System [NAICS].)

Industry	2001	2002	2003	2004	Annual average percent change, 2001–2004
	Number of jobs				
TOTAL EMPLOYMENT BY PLACE OF WORK	19 715 866	19 659 989	19 778 889	20 064 351	0.6
Farm Employment	292 496	324 482	322 351	292 986	0.1
Nonfarm Employment	19 423 370	19 335 507	19 456 538	19 771 365	0.6
Private employment	16 804 795	16 653 976	16 784 818	17 115 697	0.6
Forestry, fishing, hunting, and other[1]	237 202	234 296	232 920	231 085	-0.9
Mining	38 702	33 659	35 936	37 599	-1.0
Utilities	56 761	56 810	57 222	58 016	0.7
Construction	1 075 592	1 057 265	1 091 320	1 160 110	2.6
Manufacturing	1 881 924	1 733 346	1 629 232	1 618 050	-4.9
Durable goods manufacturing	1 220 168	1 105 507	1 027 089	1 019 051	-5.8
Nondurable goods manufacturing	661 756	627 839	602 143	598 999	-3.3
Wholesale trade	742 193	731 047	731 123	738 998	-0.1
Retail trade	1 999 197	2 009 411	2 030 588	2 072 593	1.2
Transportation and warehousing	576 214	557 566	548 351	552 470	-1.4
Information	638 272	570 365	556 321	566 403	-3.9
Finance and insurance	870 761	882 247	905 877	919 662	1.8
Real estate and rental and leasing	828 162	848 307	908 102	951 252	4.7
Professional and technical services	1 581 771	1 548 503	1 563 287	1 589 094	0.2
Management of companies and enterprises	297 246	284 142	264 435	242 441	-6.6
Administrative and waste services	1 237 729	1 231 980	1 251 570	1 290 165	1.4
Educational services	328 969	349 614	362 447	377 158	4.7
Health care and social assistance	1 550 005	1 599 933	1 649 838	1 675 578	2.6
Arts, entertainment, and recreation	475 048	485 671	490 185	500 545	1.8
Accommodation and food services	1 257 314	1 265 224	1 291 155	1 332 292	1.9
Other services, except public administration	1 131 733	1 174 590	1 184 909	1 202 186	2.0
Government and government enterprises	2 618 575	2 681 531	2 671 720	2 655 668	0.5
	Dollars				
AVERAGE WAGES AND SALARIES BY PLACE OF WORK	40 619	40 611	41 825	44 010	2.7
Farm Earnings	21 420	17 138	16 558	23 026	2.4
Nonfarm Earnings	40 874	40 973	42 218	44 296	2.7
Private earnings	40 875	40 692	41 848	44 042	2.5
Forestry, fishing, hunting, and other[1]	18 415	19 463	19 832	20 964	4.4
Mining	70 141	73 070	76 924	88 189	7.9
Utilities	68 744	69 229	73 654	82 061	6.1
Construction	41 892	42 424	42 500	43 760	1.5
Manufacturing	51 058	50 756	53 540	56 281	3.3
Durable goods manufacturing	58 315	57 539	60 581	63 631	3.0
Nondurable goods manufacturing	37 432	38 592	41 332	43 573	5.2
Wholesale trade	50 194	50 436	51 991	54 196	2.6
Retail trade	27 634	27 844	28 259	28 914	1.5
Transportation and warehousing	38 297	39 460	40 160	41 851	3.0
Information	70 993	70 428	73 291	80 114	4.1
Finance and insurance	72 398	71 959	73 887	80 190	3.5
Real estate and rental and leasing	36 967	37 939	40 043	42 803	5.0
Professional and technical services	67 856	66 333	67 539	70 383	1.2
Management of companies and enterprises	65 534	62 290	64 995	75 414	4.8
Administrative and waste services	26 909	27 253	27 864	29 537	3.2
Educational services	27 244	28 341	29 478	30 553	3.9
Health care and social assistance	35 544	37 547	39 105	41 162	5.0
Arts, entertainment, and recreation	37 079	38 868	42 163	44 022	5.9
Accommodation and food services	15 946	16 467	16 811	17 573	3.3
Other services, except public administration	22 117	22 359	23 263	24 241	3.1
Government and government enterprises	40 868	42 324	43 996	45 542	3.7

Note: Average wages and salaries are a calculation by the editors of wage and salary disbursements divided by full- and part-time wage and salary employment. Data may not add to total or may appear as zero due to rounding.

[1] "Other" consists of the number of jobs held by U.S. residents employed by international organizations and foreign embassies and consulates in the United States.

LABOR MARKET

From 2001 to 2004, total employment in California increased by 1.8 percent, which matched the U.S. average growth rate. However, the state's unemployment rate of 6.2 percent in 2004 was among the highest in the nation. Employment was spread over a large number of industries enterprises accounted for 13 percent of total employment, the largest share in the state. Retail trade was the next largest employer, followed by health care and social assistance services, manufacturing (largely durable goods industries), and accommodation and food services. Real estate and educational services showed the most growth from 2001 to 2004. California had the sixth highest average wages and salaries in the country in 2004.

Employment by Industry, 2004

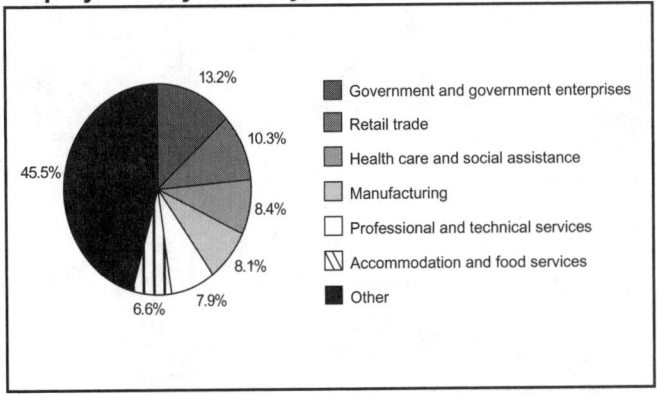

- 13.2% — Government and government enterprises
- 10.3% — Retail trade
- 8.4% — Health care and social assistance
- 8.1% — Manufacturing
- 7.9% — Professional and technical services
- 6.6% — Accommodation and food services
- 45.5% — Other

Table CA-10. Personal Income by Major Source, Selected Years 1980–2004

(Millions of dollars, except where noted.)

Item	1980	1990	2000	2001	2002	2003	2004	Average annual percent change, 2000–2004
Earnings by Place of Work	223 999	504 780	874 122	890 523	904 455	939 247	1 007 667	3.6
Wage and salary disbursements	164 267	368 315	637 401	645 607	641 984	659 509	699 035	2.3
Supplements to wages and salaries	32 912	78 105	119 427	125 236	139 571	152 708	167 850	8.9
Proprietors' income[1]	26 820	58 360	117 294	119 680	122 901	127 030	140 783	4.7
Farm proprietors' income	3 806	4 220	2 784	1 793	2 646	4 097	5 884	20.6
Nonfarm proprietors' income	23 014	54 140	114 510	117 887	120 254	122 933	134 899	4.2
(-) Contributions for government social insurance[2]	19 245	55 042	91 271	95 774	98 439	102 384	110 393	4.9
(+) Adjustment for residence[3]	-90	-79	-351	-354	-311	-315	-298	X
(=) **Net Earnings by Place of Residence**	204 664	449 660	782 500	794 395	805 705	836 547	896 976	3.5
(+) Dividends, interest, and rent[4]	49 064	129 702	199 052	204 379	195 208	192 536	200 978	0.2
(+) Personal current transfer receipts	30 727	68 901	122 290	136 531	146 955	154 975	164 500	7.7
Personal income	284 455	648 263	1 103 842	1 135 304	1 147 868	1 184 058	1 262 454	3.4
Farm income	278 967	641 270	1 096 195	1 128 615	1 140 658	1 175 515	1 251 230	3.4
Nonfarm income	5 488	6 992	7 646	6 689	7 210	8 543	11 224	10.1
Per Capita Personal Income (Dollars)[5]	11 951	21 638	32 464	32 877	32 807	33 389	35 172	2.0

Note: Data may not add to total or may appear as zero due to rounding.

[1]Proprietors' income includes the inventory valuation adjustment and the capital consumption adjustment.
[2]Contributions for government social insurance are included in earnings by type and industry, but they are excluded from personal income.
[3]The adjustment for residence is the net inflow of the earnings of interarea commuters.
[4]Rental income of persons includes the capital consumption adjustment.
[5]Per capita personal income is total personal income divided by total midyear population.
X = Not applicable.

Per Capita Personal Income, 1980–2004 (Current Dollars)

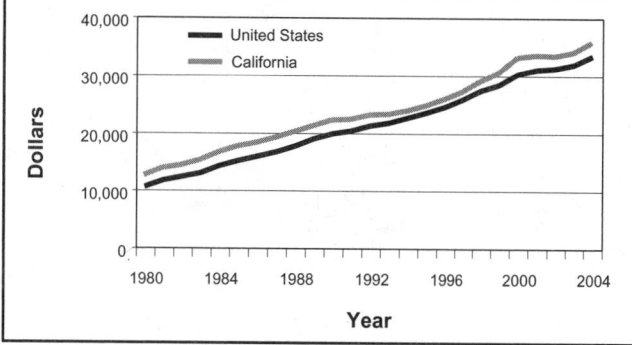

ECONOMIC ACTIVITY

California's real gross state product (GSP) showed a steady rebound from the 2001 recession, increasing by 12.2 percent from 2001–2004, one of the highest growth rates in the nation. Real estate and manufacturing made the largest contributions to GSP in 2004, followed by retail trade and professional and technical services. Utilities and finance and insurance showed the most growth from 2001 to 2004. The housing boom, a crucial strength of the Californian economy, continued to provide growth in jobs and income. The median value of owner-occupied housing in the state was the highest in the country, increasing by 85 percent from 2000 to 2004.

Table CA-11. Real Gross State Product, 1997–2004

(Millions of chained 2000 dollars, percent.)

Industry	1997	1998	1999	2000	2001	2002	2003	2004	Average annual percent change, 2001–2004
GROSS STATE PRODUCT	1 043 477	1 110 545	1 200 638	1 291 113	1 288 775	1 324 277	1 369 235	1 445 519	3.9
As a percent of U.S. gross product	12.1	12.3	12.8	13.2	13.1	13.2	13.3	13.5	X
Private Industries	919 410	982 578	1 070 863	1 154 900	1 148 183	1 181 341	1 226 651	1 301 155	4.3
Agriculture, forestry, fishing, and hunting	14 932	14 852	17 110	19 011	16 598	19 085	19 193	18 303	3.3
Mining	10 169	8 852	10 361	10 104	8 988	10 259	9 074	9 074	0.3
Utilities	16 613	16 446	18 409	18 849	13 811	20 607	21 922	24 338	20.8
Construction	43 751	47 387	50 267	52 670	54 486	53 102	53 848	57 043	1.5
Manufacturing	105 233	126 738	148 630	183 163	163 976	166 710	181 488	196 223	6.2
As a percent of gross state product	10.1	11.4	12.4	14.2	12.7	12.6	13.3	13.6	X
Wholesale trade	62 645	70 112	73 860	74 449	80 472	81 860	80 081	82 213	0.7
Retail trade	72 636	76 645	82 823	89 151	95 347	101 653	106 886	113 181	5.9
Transportation and warehousing	29 137	29 645	30 762	32 418	31 037	31 805	33 201	34 104	3.2
Information	52 735	57 271	76 044	81 449	81 542	80 426	85 449	97 991	6.3
Finance and insurance	56 521	61 724	66 469	72 249	80 917	87 774	96 304	105 795	9.3
Real estate and rental and leasing	170 924	176 408	186 425	191 434	196 603	198 761	203 549	214 309	2.9
Services	293 220	300 641	311 550	329 953	324 065	328 550	337 398	350 549	2.7
As a percent of gross state product	28.1	27.1	25.9	25.6	25.1	24.8	24.6	24.3	X
Professional and technical services	84 572	88 324	95 006	109 373	107 045	105 796	109 048	112 419	1.6
Management of companies and enterprises	30 985	31 085	31 713	33 177	25 356	23 376	22 996	23 037	-3.1
Administrative and waste services	39 292	39 306	40 804	38 462	38 103	39 276	40 804	42 928	4.1
Educational services	7 575	7 787	8 092	8 387	8 391	8 604	8 428	8 411	0.1
Health care and social assistance	60 490	60 948	62 348	64 023	67 644	72 334	75 336	77 831	4.8
Arts, entertainment, and recreation	13 941	13 596	13 705	14 422	15 086	15 914	16 675	17 187	4.4
Accommodation and food services	27 539	29 665	30 697	32 204	32 160	33 109	33 804	36 186	4.0
Other services, except public administration	28 826	29 930	29 185	29 905	30 280	30 141	30 307	32 550	2.4
Government	124 676	128 334	129 826	136 214	140 535	142 936	142 909	145 099	1.1
As a percent of gross state product	11.9	11.6	10.8	10.6	10.9	10.8	10.4	10.0	X

X = Not applicable.

Table CA-12. Government Transfer Payments, Selected Years 1980–2004

(Millions of dollars, percent.)

Item	1980	1990	2000	2001	2002	2003	2004	Average annual percent change, 2000–2004
CURRENT TRANSFER PAYMENTS TO INDIVIDUALS	29 027	64 895	114 559	127 885	138 755	147 326	156 745	8.2
Retirement and Disability Insurance Benefits	12 567	26 938	42 214	45 254	48 017	50 184	53 003	5.9
Old-age, survivors, and disability insurance (OASDI) benefits	11 235	23 305	38 154	40 376	42 363	43 894	46 290	5.0
Railroad retirement and disability benefits	337	456	469	473	485	487	495	1.4
Workers' compensation	368	1 273	1 406	1 670	2 253	2 661	2 778	18.6
Other government retirement and disability insurance benefits	627	1 904	2 186	2 735	2 916	3 142	3 440	12.0
Medical Benefits	7 786	20 943	47 231	56 150	59 259	64 199	71 071	10.8
Medicare benefits	4 314	11 865	24 660	27 419	29 427	31 198	34 496	8.8
Public assistance medical care benefits	3 343	8 638	22 254	28 289	29 260	32 541	36 064	12.8
Military medical insurance benefits	129	440	317	441	572	459	511	12.7
Income Maintenance Benefits	5 243	11 970	18 854	18 753	19 770	21 185	22 582	4.6
Supplemental Security Income (SSI) benefits	1 943	4 300	6 448	6 742	7 290	7 614	7 941	5.3
Family assistance	2 328	5 101	5 315	4 923	4 407	4 726	5 016	-1.4
Food stamps	537	1 027	1 612	1 606	1 707	1 832	2 093	6.7
Other income maintenance benefits	434	1 543	5 479	5 481	6 366	7 012	7 533	8.3
Unemployment Insurance Compensation	1 633	2 198	2 470	3 466	7 196	7 291	5 221	20.6
Veterans' Benefits	1 380	1 526	2 114	2 240	2 461	2 664	2 890	8.1
Federal Education and Training Assistance	403	793	1 510	1 741	1 879	1 673	1 788	4.3
Other Payments to Individuals	16	526	166	282	172	130	190	3.4

Note: See notes and definitions for more details. Data may not add to total or may appear as zero due to rounding.

EXPORTS

California was second only to Texas in terms of the value of its exports. Computers and electronic products were the state's leading export in 2004, accounting for over 38 percent of all its exports, although exports from this category declined by 16.0 percent from 2001 to 2004. The state's other leading exports were machinery, transportation equipment, and chemicals. Agricultural products accounted for 5.3 percent of exports and were up over 32 percent from 2001. Mexico, Japan, Canada, and China were California's largest trading partners. Exports to China increased over 46 percent from 2001 to 2004.

Leading Exports, 2004

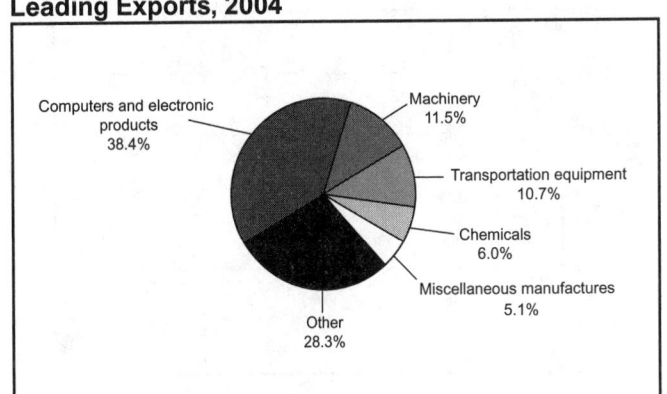

Table CA-13. Exports of Goods by Leading Products and Destinations, 2001–2004

(Millions of dollars, percent, rank based on 2004 dollar values.)

Product and market	2001	2002	2003	2004	Percent share of total, 2004	Average annual percent change, 2001–2004
Total Goods						
Total	106 777	92 214	93 995	109 968	100.0	1.0
Manufactures	98 431	84 053	84 343	99 243	90.2	0.3
Agriculture and livestock	4 382	4 441	5 575	5 794	5.3	9.8
Other commodities	3 964	3 720	4 078	4 931	4.5	7.5
Five Leading Exports (NAICS Code)						
Computers and electronic products (334)	50 311	39 672	36 715	42 247	38.4	-5.7
Machinery manufactures (333)	10 695	9 518	9 434	12 593	11.5	5.6
Transportation equipment (336)	8 445	7 100	8 644	11 759	10.7	11.7
Chemical manufactures (325)	5 190	5 418	5 964	6 644	6.0	8.6
Miscellaneous manufactures (339)	4 370	4 498	4 884	5 641	5.1	8.9
Five Leading Markets	99 944	85 755	87 482	101 914	92.7	0.7
Mexico	16 343	16 076	14 872	17 239	15.7	1.8
Japan	14 635	11 106	11 755	13 323	12.1	-3.1
Canada	11 816	10 075	11 232	12 111	11.0	0.8
China	4 676	4 482	5 465	6 842	6.2	13.5
South Korea	5 035	4 712	4 833	5 912	5.4	5.5

Table CA-14. Agriculture, 1997 and 2002
(Number, acres, and dollars.)

Item	1997	2002
Number of farms	87 991	79 631
Land in farms (acres)	28 795 834	27 589 027
Farm Size		
Average size of farm (acres)	327	346
Farms by size (percent distribution)		
Fewer than 50 acres	63.4	61.7
50 to 499 acres	26.1	27.7
500 acres or more	10.6	10.5
Market Value of Land and Equipment (Dollars)		
Land and buildings average value per farm	839 126	1 206 822
Average value per acre	2 643	3 526
Machinery and equipment average value per farm	62 129	81 933
Value of Sales (Thousands of Dollars)		
Agricultural products sold	23 280 110	25 737 173
Crops	17 201 736	19 152 722
Livestock, poultry, and their products	6 078 374	6 584 451
Average per farm (dollars)	264 574	323 205
Value of sales (percent distribution)		
Less than $10,000	49.9	46.0
$10,000 to $99,999	27.2	29.4
$100,000 or more	22.9	24.6
Government Payments		
Payments (thousands of dollars)	125 440	168 698
Percent of farms receiving government payments	9.4	9.1
Farm operators whose principal occupation is farming (percent)	49.8	61.7

AGRICULTURE

The market value of agricultural products sold in California was the highest of any state, totaling $25.7 billion in 2002, according to the Department of Agriculture's Census of Agriculture. Crop value far exceeded the value of livestock products, with corn and wheat as the state's chief products. The average price per acre of farmland appreciated significantly from 1997, reflecting the overall increase in land prices in the state. More than 60 percent of farms were small, with fewer than 50 acres of total land.

ENERGY

Energy expenditures in California were the highest in the nation, reflecting the size of the state's population. The state's energy price per Btu was the ninth highest in the nation. However, due to the state's temperate climate and low per capita consumption, California's energy expenditures per capita ranked only 46th in the country. The state was a large user of natural, petroleum, and electric energy.

Energy Consumption by Source, 2001

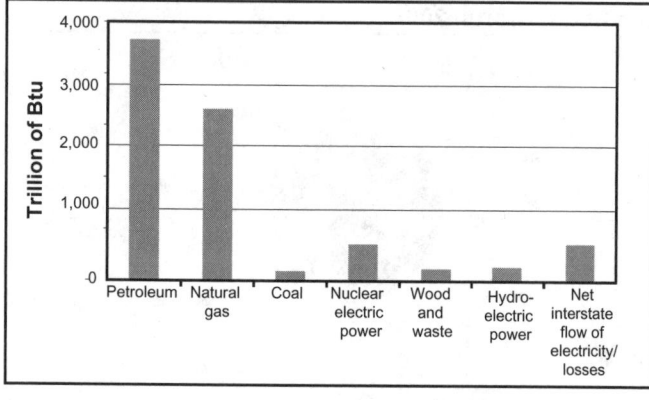

Energy Consumption by Sector, 2001

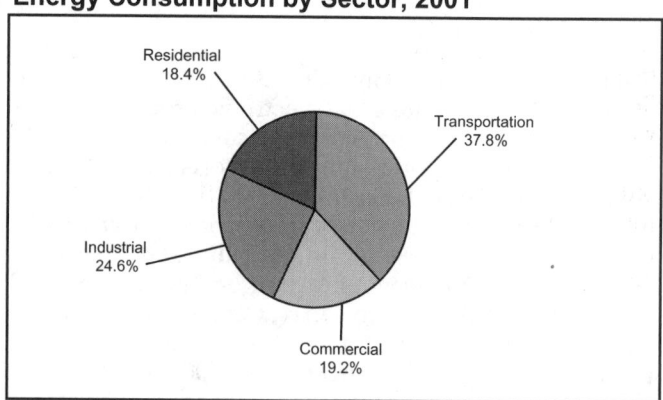

Table CA-15. Energy Consumption, Expenditures, and Prices, Selected Years 1960–2001
(Dollars, Btu [British Thermal Unit], percent distribution.)

Item	1960	1965	1970	1975	1980	1985	1990	1995	2000	2001
Total Consumption (Billion Btu)	3 451 709	4 394 324	5 515 345	6 056 710	6 596 207	6 621 416	7 541 112	7 387 656	7 994 653	7 853 442
Consumption per capita (million Btu)	219.6	236.4	276.2	281.2	278.7	250.4	253.4	234.6	236.0	227.4
Consumption by Sector (Percent Distribution)										
Residential	17.3	19.2	19.0	20.2	18.9	19.6	18.4	18.3	18.2	18.4
Commercial	12.6	13.1	14.0	16.0	16.4	16.3	17.8	17.3	17.3	19.2
Industrial	34.6	33.7	33.8	31.5	28.8	28.4	26.3	26.2	26.7	24.6
Transportation	35.5	33.9	33.2	32.3	35.8	35.7	37.5	38.2	37.8	37.8
Consumption by Source (Billion Btu)										
Coal	35 903	63 693	61 812	56 405	66 170	45 264	84 159	84 323	70 011	67 858
Natural gas	1 301 826	1 813 213	2 241 295	1 937 322	1 890 887	1 925 459	2 101 602	2 109 956	2 456 437	2 513 857
Petroleum	1 838 667	2 098 228	2 518 242	2 997 279	3 509 566	3 148 548	3 538 334	3 348 180	3 593 941	3 604 354
Nuclear electric power	1	3 193	34 375	66 855	53 665	209 565	345 955	317 794	366 845	347 078
Hydroelectric power[1]	187 705	319 052	399 628	417 309	423 618	331 348	257 749	521 166	400 611	256 304
Wood and waste	82 098	97 488	116 839	127 489	134 012	155 471	204 782	178 154	159 018	150 460
Other	-589	4 187	11 310	70 153	110 079	209 526	374 089	304 806	331 562	327 563
Net interstate flow of electricity/losses[2]	6 099	-4 729	131 843	383 897	408 210	596 235	634 441	523 278	616 227	585 969
Total Expenditures (Thousands of Dollars)	...	...	7 015 900	14 972 600	36 129 800	41 657 500	48 413 400	50 941 600	68 407 400	72 923 700
Expenditures per capita (dollars)	...	...	351	695	1 526	1 576	1 627	1 618	2 020	2 112
Prices by Sector (Dollars Per Million Btu)										
Total	...	...	1.74	3.46	7.70	8.89	9.00	9.64	12.04	13.04
Residential	...	...	1.91	3.19	6.69	9.85	12.41	14.90	16.58	19.02
Commercial	...	...	2.09	4.36	9.57	15.08	15.09	17.73	19.77	24.27
Industrial	...	...	0.90	2.25	6.24	7.93	6.98	6.97	8.15	9.13
Transportation	...	...	2.07	4.02	8.22	7.68	7.43	7.52	10.92	10.46

[1]A negative number in this row results from pumped storage for which, overall, more electricity is expended than created to provide electricity during peak demand periods.
[2]Net interstate flow of electricity is the difference between the amount of energy in the electricity sold within a state (including associated losses) and the energy input at the electric utilities within the state. A positive number indicates that more electricity (including associated losses) came into the state than went out of the state during the year; conversely, a negative number indicates that more electricity (including associated losses) went out of the state than came into the state.
... = Not available.

Table CA-16. State Taxes, Fiscal 2004

(Dollars, percent distribution.)

Item	Thousands of dollars	Percent distribution	Dollars per capita	
			State	U.S.
TOTAL TAXES	85 721 483	100.0	2 388.2	2 024.8
Property Taxes	2 079 326	2.4	57.9	38.9
Sales and Gross Receipts	33 984 188	39.6	946.8	1 003.4
General sales and gross receipts	26 506 911	30.9	738.5	677.0
Selective sales taxes	7 477 277	8.7	208.3	326.4
Insurance premiums	2 114 980	2.5	58.9	47.0
Motor fuels	3 324 883	3.9	92.6	114.6
Public utilities	520 589	0.6	14.5	39.2
Tobacco products	1 081 588	1.3	30.1	42.0
Licenses	5 744 089	6.7	160.0	134.9
Motor vehicle	2 155 042	2.5	60.0	59.4
Occupation and business, not elsewhere classified	3 062 827	3.6	85.3	37.1
Other Taxes	43 913 880	51.2	1 223.4	847.6
Individual income	36 398 983	42.5	1 014.1	673.6
Corporation net income	6 925 916	8.1	193.0	105.1
Death and gift	574 510	0.7	16.0	19.6

GOVERNMENT FINANCE

State revenues amounted to $148 billion, the highest amount in the nation. However, revenues per capita ranked 16th in the nation in 2003. Expenditures per capita, at $4,883, were among the 10 highest in the United States. In fiscal year 2004, taxes per capita were $2,388, which were also among the highest in the nation. California's per capita individual income taxes ranked 6th in the country and accounted for over 40 percent of total taxes. The other major source of revenue was sales receipts. California's per capita property taxes and its debt per capita were above the U.S. averages.

Per Capita State Taxes, Fiscal 2004

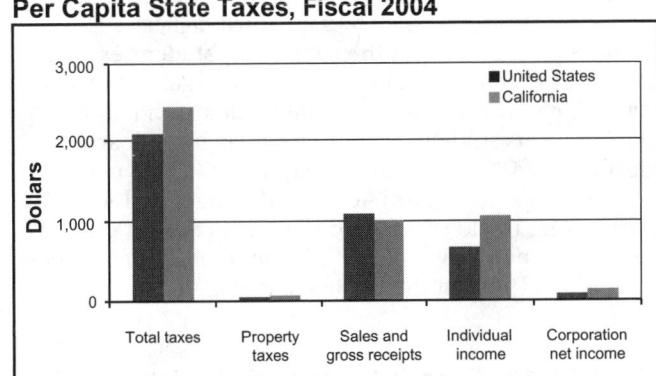

Table CA-17. State Government Finances, 2003

(Dollars, percent distribution.)

Item	Millions of dollars	Percent distribution	Dollars per capita	
			State	U.S.
GENERAL REVENUE	147 998 249	100.0	4 173.3	3 832.6
Intergovernmental revenue	48 245 951	32.6	1 360.5	1 246.0
Taxes	79 198 255	53.5	2 233.3	1 891.6
General sales	24 899 025	16.8	702.1	636.0
Selective sales	7 015 010	4.7	197.8	307.4
License taxes	4 916 856	3.3	138.6	123.6
Individual income tax	32 709 761	22.1	922.4	626.8
Corporate income tax	6 803 559	4.6	191.8	97.8
Other taxes	2 854 044	1.9	80.5	99.9
Current charges	11 980 766	8.1	337.8	366.5
Miscellaneous general revenue	8 573 277	5.8	241.8	328.6
GENERAL EXPENDITURE	173 158 060	100.0	4 882.8	4 010.5
Intergovernmental expenditure	84 468 847	48.8	2 381.9	1 316.9
Direct expenditure	88 689 213	51.2	2 500.9	2 693.6
Expenditure by Function				
Education	61 457 162	35.5	1 733.0	1 416.4
Public welfare	48 472 281	28.0	1 366.8	1 083.3
Hospitals	5 025 205	2.9	141.7	132.3
Health	9 291 005	5.4	262.0	173.0
Highways	7 158 608	4.1	201.9	295.4
Police protection	1 443 127	0.8	40.7	38.4
Correction	5 690 346	3.3	160.5	135.0
Natural resources	3 487 188	2.0	98.3	64.0
Parks and recreation	721 229	0.4	20.3	20.1
Government administration	8 102 816	4.7	228.5	151.3
Interest on general debt	3 557 753	2.1	100.3	107.8
Other and unallocable	18 751 340	10.8	528.8	393.4
DEBT AT END OF FISCAL YEAR	95 209 988	X	2 684.8	2 404.7
CASH AND SECURITY HOLDINGS	382 874 025	X	10 796.4	8 938.4

X = Not applicable.

Table CA-18. Education Indicators, 2000–2004

(Percent, number.)

Item	State	U.S.
Total Population 25 Years and Over (Thousands), 2004	22 096	186 877
Educational Attainment, 2004		
Percent high school graduate or more	81.3	85.2
Percent college graduate or more	31.7	27.7
Elementary and Secondary Schools, 2002–2003		
Total students	6 356 348	48 202 324
Percent of students eligible for free or reduced-price lunch ..	48.7	40.6
Percent of students who were English language learners	24.9	7.8
Total schools	9 087	92 330
Student/teacher ratio	21.1	15.9
Per student expenditures	7 552	8 041
Higher Education, 2002–2003		
Total enrollment	2 538 700	17 035 027
Bachelor's degrees awarded	135 844	1 348 503
Percent women	57.7	57.5

Educational Attainment, 2004

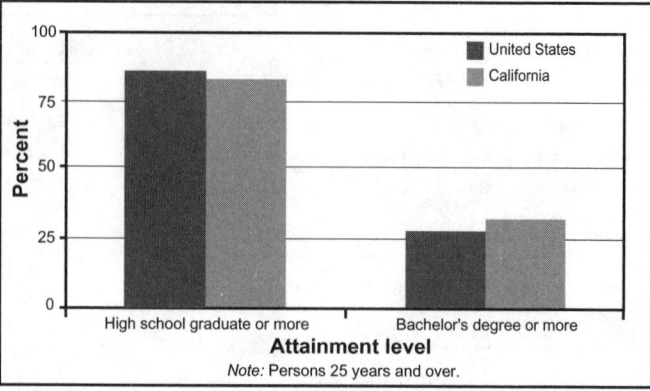

Note: Persons 25 years and over.

EDUCATION

California had an above average proportion of student-age population. The state had the third highest student/teacher ratio in the nation. Per student expenditures of $7,552 were below the U.S. average. California had a high proportion of migrant students, and about 25 percent of its students were English language learners during the 2002–2003 school year. In 2004, 81.3 percent of the state's population held a high school diploma. This was among the lowest 10 proportions in the nation. However, the state's college attainment level of 31.7 percent ranked 11th in the United States.

VOTER PARTICIPATION

California had the second lowest voter turnout rate in the country for both the 2000 and 2004 elections, behind only Hawaii in both elections. In 2000 and 2004, 53.4 percent Californian voters voted for the Democratic candidate, according to the official tally by the Clerk of the U.S. House of Representatives. Asians and Hispanics had the lowest proportions of voters, as reported in the Current Population Survey. Like most states, voting rates increased in relation to the age of the voter. Women and non-Hispanic Whites had the highest voter participation rates.

Table CA-19. Reported Voting and Registration, November 2000 and November 2004

(Numbers in thousands, percent.)

Characteristic	Total population 18 years and over	Total citizen		Total registered		Total voted	
		Number	Percent	Number	Percent	Number	Percent
NOVEMBER 2000							
Total	24 749	19 837	80.2	13 061	52.8	11 489	46.4
Male	11 932	9 554	80.1	6 170	51.7	5 463	45.8
Female	12 817	10 283	80.2	6 891	53.8	6 027	47.0
NOVEMBER 2004							
Total	26 085	20 693	79.3	14 193	54.4	12 807	49.1
Male	12 783	10 042	78.6	6 695	52.4	6 022	47.1
Female	13 302	10 651	80.1	7 498	56.4	6 785	51.0
Race and Hispanic Origin							
White alone	20 083	15 913	79.2	11 286	56.2	10 273	51.2
Non-Hispanic White alone	12 350	11 777	95.4	8 976	72.7	8 311	67.3
Black alone	1 678	1 564	93.2	1 141	68.0	1 035	61.7
Asian alone	3 524	2 511	71.3	1 318	37.4	1 113	31.6
Hispanic or Latino[1]	8 127	4 433	54.5	2 455	30.2	2 081	25.6
White alone or in combination	20 410	16 234	79.5	11 515	56.4	10 468	51.3
Non-Hispanic White alone or in combination	12 590	12 015	95.4	9 147	72.7	8 453	67.1
Black alone or in combination	1 757	1 642	93.5	1 193	67.9	1 077	61.3
Asian alone or in combination	3 636	2 620	72.1	1 379	37.9	1 162	31.9
Age							
18 to 24 years	3 366	2 659	79.0	1 447	43.0	1 194	35.5
25 to 44 years	10 785	7 596	70.4	4 912	45.5	4 327	40.1
45 to 64 years	8 234	7 047	85.6	5 224	63.4	4 818	58.5
65 to 74 years	2 007	1 829	91.1	1 400	69.8	1 343	66.9
75 years and over	1 692	1 561	92.3	1 209	71.5	1 125	66.5

[1]May be of any race.

At a Glance:

- Colorado's population was 4.6 million in 2004, making it the 22nd most populous state in the nation.

- The state was a large recipient of immigration, both from other states and other countries, during the 2000–2004 period. A total of 137,000 people relocated to Colorado during that 4-year period.

- Colorado's non-Hispanic White population comprised 72.5 percent of residents in 2004. Hispanics (of any race) made up 19.1 percent of the population, reflecting a sizable increase in the representation of this ethnic group over the 2000–2004 period. Colorado ranked sixth in the nation for proportion of Hispanic residents.

- Median household income in Colorado was well above the national average, ranking 10th in the country. Colorado's poverty rate was a relatively low 10 percent.

- Colorado's population, age 25 years and over, had high levels of both high school and college attainment. The state ranked 3rd in the nation for college attainment, with 35.5 percent of its population holding a bachelor's degree or more.

- Colorado had the 12th highest median value of owner-occupied housing in the nation.

Table CO-1. Population by Sex and Age, 1990, 2000, and 2004

(Number, percent.)

Sex and age	1990	2000	2004	Percent distribution, 2004	Average annual percent change, 2000–2004
Total Population	3 294 394	4 301 261	4 601 403	X	1.7
Percent of total U.S. population	1.3	1.5	1.6	X	X
Sex					
Male	1 631 295	2 165 983	2 321 504	50.5	1.7
Female	1 663 099	2 135 278	2 279 899	49.5	1.7
Age					
Under 5 years	252 893	297 505	339 079	7.4	2.0
5 to 17 years	608 373	803 290	839 810	18.3	2.3
18 years and over	588 224	3 200 466	3 422 514	74.4	2.5
18 to 24 years	2 433 128	430 111	456 691	9.9	2.2
25 to 44 years	335 525	1 400 850	1 425 841	31.0	1.4
45 to 64 years	1 179 936	953 432	1 089 011	23.7	4.5
65 years and over	329 443	416 073	450 971	9.8	2.3
85 years and over	32 953	48 216	55 636	1.2	3.9
Median age (years)	32.4	34.3	34.3	X	X

X = Not applicable.

Average Annual Rate of Population Growth, 1980–2004

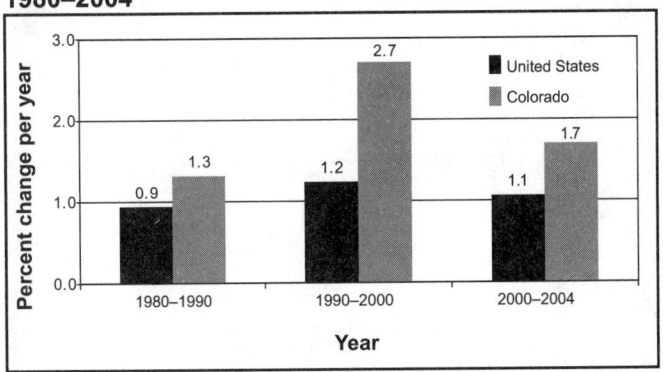

POPULATION

Colorado's population grew by 7 percent between 2000 and 2004, or about 1.7 percent per year. This was among the fastest growth rates in the country, as many new residents were attracted to the state's recreational and economic opportunities. Colorado was a large recipient of immigration—both international and from other U.S. states—during the 2000–2004 period. Nearly 137,000 people moved into the—state during that time, which represented one-third of its population increase. The largest metropolitan areas were Denver-Boulder-Greeley and Colorado Springs. Compared with the nation as a whole, Colorado's population was relatively young, with less than 10 percent age 65 years and over.

Table CO-2. Population by Race and Hispanic Origin, 1990, 2000, and 2004

(Number, percent.)

Race and Hispanic origin	1990	2000	2004
Total Population	3 294 394	4 301 261	4 601 403
Non-Hispanic (Percent)			
One race[1]			
White	80.7	74.8	72.5
Black	3.9	3.7	3.7
American Indian, Alaska Native[2]	0.8	0.7	0.7
Asian and Pacific Islander[2]	1.8	2.3	2.5
Other race[2]	5.1	. . .	. . .
Two or more races	. . .	1.4	1.5
Hispanic or Latino[3] (Percent)	12.9	17.1	19.1

[1]Individuals could report only one race in the 1990 census and could report one or more races on the 2000 census. Data on race in 2000 and 2004 are not comparable to 1990.
[2]Data for 1990 include people of Hispanic or Latino origin.
[3]May be of any race.
. . . = Not available.

Minority Population as a Percent of Total Population, 2004

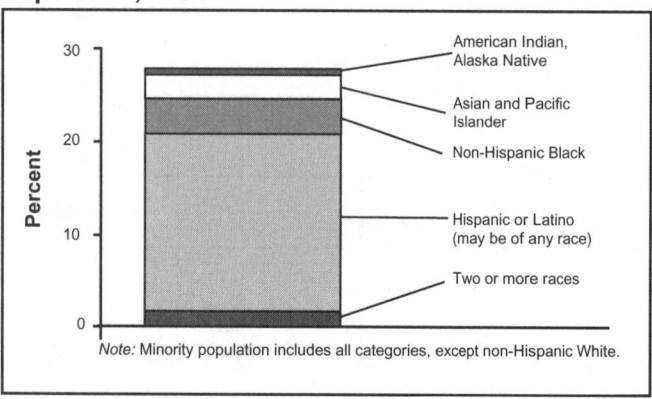

Note: Minority population includes all categories, except non-Hispanic White.

Age-Adjusted Death Rates, Average 2000–2002

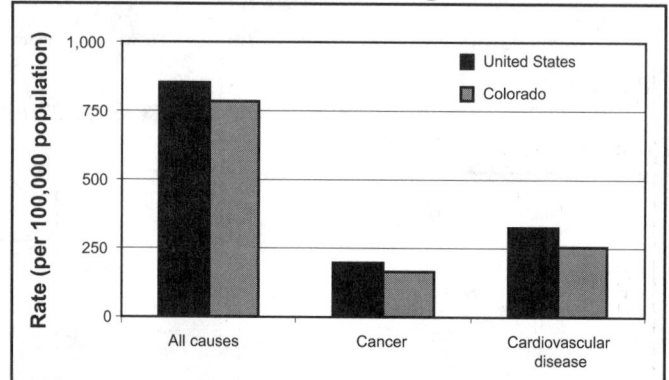

HEALTH

In 2004, 17 percent of Colorado residents lacked health insurance. This was the 12th highest proportion in the nation. Colorado's infant mortality rate was among the 15 lowest in the nation. The state's total age-adjusted death rate was also well below the U.S. average.

Table CO-3. Health Characteristics, 2000–2004

(Number, rate, percent.)

Item	State	U.S.
Births, 2003–2004		
Number of births	69 339	4 089 950
Birth rate (per 1,000 population)	15.2	14.1
Teenage birth rate (per 1,000 women age 15–19 years)	43.9	41.6
Mortality Rates, Average 2000–2002		
Infant mortality rate (per 1,000 live births)	6.0	6.9
Age-adjusted mortality rate (per 100,000 population)		
All races	787.0	853.3
Non-Hispanic White	782.9	843.1
Black	957.8	1 097.7
American Indian, Alaska Native	520.2	687.0
Asian and Pacific Islander	499.3	486.0
Hispanic or Latino[1]	763.7	642.7
Health Insurance, 2004		
Percent of all persons without health insurance	17.0	15.7
Percent of children without health insurance	15.0	11.2
Percent of low-income children without health insurance	10.3	7.1

[1]May be of any race.

Table CO-4. Leading Causes of Death, Average 2000–2002

(Number, rate per 100,000 population.)

Cause	Number of deaths	Age-adjusted death rates	
		State	U.S.
ALL CAUSES	28 264	787.0	853.3
Leading Causes			
Major cardiovascular diseases	9 184	266.0	326.5
Cancer	6 150	169.9	196.0
Chronic lower respiratory diseases	1 824	53.1	43.7
Unintentional injuries	1 745	42.1	35.7
Diabetes (underlying cause)	654	18.3	25.2
Influenza and pneumonia	670	19.6	22.7
Alzheimer's disease	839	25.5	19.0
Motor vehicle accidents	741	16.9	15.0
Nephritis, nephrotic syndrome, and nephrosis ..	388	11.2	13.8
Septicemia	287	8.1	11.4
Suicides	687	15.6	10.7
Firearm-related	490	11.2	10.3
Cirrhosis	419	10.2	9.5
Drug-induced	430	9.5	7.9
Alcohol-induced	487	11.3	6.9
Homicides	167	3.7	6.0
Falls	285	8.0	5.2
HIV	96	2.1	5.0
Viral hepatitis	81	1.9	2.0
Anemias	49	1.4	1.6
Drownings	47	1.0	1.3
Fire deaths	18	0.5	1.2

Note: The rates are age-adjusted to the U.S. 2000 standard population.

Table CO-5. Households and Housing Characteristics, 1990, 2000, and 2004

(Number, percent, and dollars.)

Characteristic	1990	2000	2004	Average annual percent change, 2000–2004
Total Households	1 282 489	1 658 238	1 850 238	2.8
Family households	854 214	1 084 461	1 187 252	2.3
Married-couple family	690 292	858 671	921 475	1.8
Other family	163 922	225 790	265 777	4.2
Male householder, no wife present	39 353	66 811	79 173	4.3
Female householder, no husband present	124 569	158 979	186 604	4.1
Nonfamily households	428 275	573 777	662 986	3.7
Householder living alone	340 962	435 778	517 274	4.4
Householder not living alone	87 313	137 999	145 712	1.4
Housing Characteristics				
Average size	2.51	2.53	2.43	X
Housing units	1 477 349	1 808 037	2 010 806	2.7
Occupied housing units	1 282 489	1 658 238	1 850 238	2.8
Owner-occupied	798 277	1 116 137	1 268 619	3.3
Renter-occupied	484 212	542 101	581 619	1.8
Median gross rent of renter-occupied housing units (dollars) ...	418	671	724	1.9
Median value of owner-occupied housing units (dollars)	82 400	166 600	211 740	6.2

X = Not applicable.

Median Housing Value and Median Rent, 2004

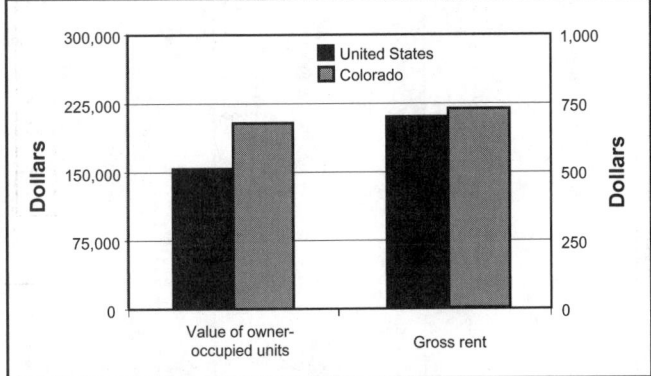

Median Household Income, 1984–2004 (2004 Dollars)

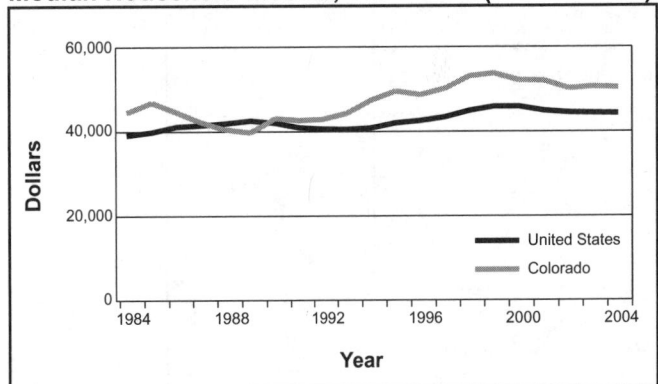

Table CO-6. Household Income and Poverty Status, 1980–2004

(2004 CPI-U-RS adjusted dollars, rate.)

Year	State		U.S.	
	Median household income (2004 dollars)	Poverty rate	Median household income (2004 dollars)	Poverty rate
2004	51 057	10.0	44 389	12.7
2003	51 282	9.7	44 482	12.5
2002	50 728	9.8	44 546	12.1
2001	52 712	8.7	45 062	11.7
2000	52 914	9.8	46 058	11.3
1999	54 609	8.5	46 129	11.9
1998	53 931	9.2	45 003	12.7
1997	50 740	8.2	43 430	13.3
1996	49 086	10.6	42 544	13.7
1995	50 104	8.8	41 943	13.8
1994	47 699	9.0	40 677	14.5
1993	44 397	9.9	40 217	15.1
1992	42 860	10.8	40 422	14.8
1991	42 603	10.4	40 746	14.2
1990	43 070	13.7	41 963	13.5
1989	39 435	12.1	42 524	12.8
1988	40 220	12.5	41 771	13.0
1987	42 101	12.5	41 322	13.4
1986	44 713	13.5	40 939	13.6
1985	47 187	10.2	39 545	14.0
1984	44 641	8.9	38 782	14.4
1983	. . .	12.6	. . .	15.2
1982	. . .	12.6	. . .	15.0
1981	. . .	9.6	. . .	14.0
1980	. . .	8.6	. . .	13.0

. . . = Not available.

Table CO-7. Employment Status by Demographic Group, 2004

(Numbers in thousands, rate.)

Characteristic	Civilian noninstitutional population	Civilian labor force		Employed	Unemployment rate
		Number	Participation rate		
SEX AND AGE					
Total	3 468	2 525	72.8	2 389	5.4
16 to 19 years	224	116	52.0	92	20.6
20 to 24 years	349	277	79.3	251	9.2
25 to 34 years	686	579	84.3	553	4.4
35 to 44 years	692	605	87.4	584	3.5
45 to 54 years	667	573	85.9	551	3.8
55 to 64 years	454	304	66.8	288	5.3
65 years and over	396	72	18.2	70	2.9
Men	1 718	1 383	80.5	1 305	5.7
16 to 19 years	109	56	51.1	43	22.4
20 to 24 years	178	149	84.0	131	12.4
25 to 34 years	353	333	94.5	319	4.3
35 to 44 years	354	334	94.4	323	3.2
45 to 54 years	330	305	92.3	294	3.7
55 to 64 years	212	164	77.2	155	5.6
65 years and over	182	42	23.1	40	4.1
Women	1 750	1 142	65.3	1 084	5.1
16 to 19 years	115	61	53.0	49	19.0
20 to 24 years	171	127	74.3	120	5.5
25 to 34 years	333	245	73.6	234	4.6
35 to 44 years	339	271	80.2	261	4.0
45 to 54 years	336	268	79.6	257	3.9
55 to 64 years	242	140	57.7	133	4.9
65 years and over	214	30	14.1	30	1.3
MARITAL STATUS					
Married men, spouse present	977	811	82.9	784	3.3
Married women, spouse present	938	600	63.9	580	3.3
Women who maintain families	169	125	73.8	116	7.6
RACE, HISPANIC ORIGIN, AND SEX					
White	3 168	2 319	73.2	2 202	5.1
Men	1 575	1 271	80.7	1 202	5.4
Women	1 593	1 048	65.8	1 000	4.6
Black	127	89	69.8	77	12.5
Men	63	50	79.3	43	13.1
Women	64	39	60.5	34	11.8
Asian	77	52	67.9	51	2.3
Men	36	28	77.2	27	1.9
Hispanic or Latino[1]	622	449	72.1	415	7.5
Men	329	275	83.7	258	6.3
Women	294	174	59.2	157	9.4
RACE, HISPANIC ORIGIN, AND AGE					
White					
20 to 24 years	319	255	80.1	233	8.9
25 to 34 years	613	522	85.2	500	4.2
35 to 44 years	620	543	87.6	526	3.2
45 to 54 years	620	533	86.1	515	3.4
55 to 64 years	428	291	67.9	276	5.1
65 years and over	370	66	17.8	64	2.5

Note: Data in Table 7 are from the Current Population Survey (CPS) and do not match Bureau of Labor Statistics estimates in Table 8. See notes and definitions for more details.

[1]May be of any race.

Table CO-8. Employment Status, 1990–2004

(Numbers in thousands, rate.)

Year	Civilian labor force	Employed	Unemployed	Unemployment rate
2004	2 522 225	2 382 873	139 352	5.5
2003	2 479 753	2 325 210	154 543	6.2
2002	2 443 321	2 300 065	143 256	5.9
2001	2 394 885	2 301 155	93 730	3.9
2000	2 359 323	2 296 805	62 518	2.6
1999	2 340 938	2 269 668	71 270	3.0
1998	2 307 907	2 226 296	81 611	3.5
1997	2 229 798	2 154 294	75 504	3.4
1996	2 175 704	2 083 740	91 964	4.2
1995	2 127 117	2 041 652	85 465	4.0
1994	2 040 382	1 953 111	87 271	4.3
1993	1 933 718	1 831 489	102 229	5.3
1992	1 855 871	1 744 235	111 636	6.0
1991	1 802 652	1 704 522	98 130	5.4
1990	1 768 954	1 678 229	90 725	5.1

Note: Population age 16 years and over.

Unemployment Rate, 1980–2004

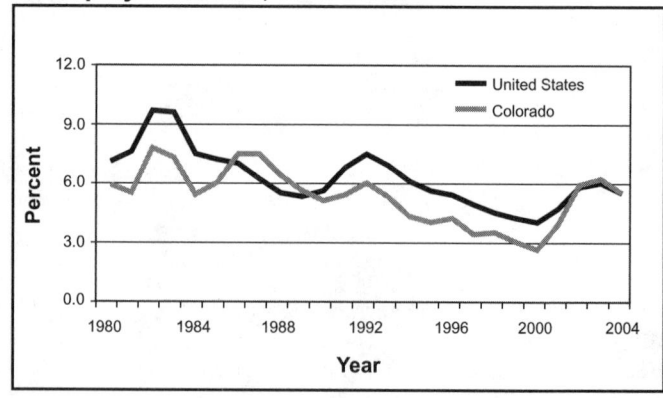

Table CO-9. Employment and Average Wages by Industry, 2001–2004

(Estimates are based on the 2002 North American Industry Classification System [NAICS].)

Industry	2001	2002	2003	2004	Annual average percent change, 2001–2004
	Number of jobs				
TOTAL EMPLOYMENT BY PLACE OF WORK	2 968 862	2 941 417	2 938 664	2 989 091	0.2
Farm Employment	46 588	44 894	46 794	45 408	-0.9
Nonfarm Employment	2 922 274	2 896 523	2 891 870	2 943 683	0.2
Private employment	2 530 743	2 493 719	2 487 137	2 538 441	0.1
Forestry, fishing, hunting, and other[1]	10 550	11 599	11 027	10 970	1.3
Mining	23 115	22 006	24 448	26 463	4.6
Utilities	8 401	8 437	8 231	8 292	-0.4
Construction	237 064	228 406	222 256	225 229	-1.7
Manufacturing	192 619	177 557	166 794	165 529	-4.9
Durable goods manufacturing	131 565	119 413	110 685	110 744	-5.6
Nondurable goods manufacturing	61 054	58 144	56 109	54 785	-3.5
Wholesale trade	109 697	104 817	102 024	102 160	-2.3
Retail trade	311 461	310 060	309 903	314 429	0.3
Transportation and warehousing	84 797	81 607	80 359	80 904	-1.6
Information	118 289	102 665	95 403	91 859	-8.1
Finance and insurance	154 865	156 447	158 894	160 936	1.3
Real estate and rental and leasing	136 629	140 109	148 884	155 612	4.4
Professional and technical services	237 692	229 767	229 781	238 104	0.1
Management of companies and enterprises	19 674	21 332	21 700	23 862	6.6
Administrative and waste services	175 394	169 866	170 719	179 085	0.7
Educational services	39 619	42 243	43 678	46 159	5.2
Health care and social assistance	226 459	232 863	238 346	243 941	2.5
Arts, entertainment, and recreation	74 235	76 988	76 082	78 158	1.7
Accommodation and food services	217 703	218 321	218 685	224 043	1.0
Other services, except public administration	152 480	158 629	159 923	162 706	2.2
Government and government enterprises	391 531	402 804	404 733	405 242	1.2
	Dollars				
AVERAGE WAGES AND SALARIES BY PLACE OF WORK ...	37 252	37 384	38 290	39 632	2.1
Farm Earnings	21 521	30 832	22 360	22 972	2.2
Nonfarm Earnings	37 357	37 420	38 398	39 738	2.1
Private earnings	37 918	37 657	38 553	39 870	1.7
Forestry, fishing, hunting, and other[1]	17 034	17 329	17 837	17 787	1.5
Mining	74 907	64 507	66 351	83 496	3.7
Utilities	65 121	64 246	64 294	71 622	3.2
Construction	38 947	39 232	39 323	40 274	1.1
Manufacturing	47 446	48 579	50 793	52 552	3.5
Durable goods manufacturing	51 257	52 685	55 323	57 068	3.6
Nondurable goods manufacturing	39 131	40 056	41 808	43 364	3.5
Wholesale trade	52 415	52 182	53 771	56 084	2.3
Retail trade	23 848	24 163	24 540	25 079	1.7
Transportation and warehousing	38 901	39 764	39 280	40 196	1.1
Information	65 784	63 154	66 528	65 746	0.0
Finance and insurance	55 683	55 090	58 294	59 343	2.1
Real estate and rental and leasing	33 443	34 137	35 634	37 046	3.5
Professional and technical services	60 982	60 497	61 221	64 208	1.7
Management of companies and enterprises	76 804	70 532	74 429	87 720	4.5
Administrative and waste services	26 624	27 641	28 451	29 191	3.1
Educational services	25 620	25 243	26 212	26 954	1.7
Health care and social assistance	33 566	35 061	36 054	37 433	3.7
Arts, entertainment, and recreation	28 252	28 037	29 125	28 044	-0.2
Accommodation and food services	14 668	14 871	15 198	15 741	2.4
Other services, except public administration	24 152	24 834	25 421	26 392	3.0
Government and government enterprises	34 540	36 297	37 682	39 121	4.2

Note: Average wages and salaries are a calculation by the editors of wage and salary disbursements divided by full- and part-time wage and salary employment. Data may not add to total or may appear as zero due to rounding.

[1] "Other" consists of the number of jobs held by U.S. residents employed by international organizations and foreign embassies and consulates in the United States.

LABOR MARKET

Colorado has had a very high civilian participation rate in the labor force in recent years, an indication of an active labor market. In 2004, the unemployment rate was equal to the U.S. average. Total employment growth was sluggish during the 2001–2004 period, as recovery from the 2001 recession was slow. In 2004, employment was only 0.7 percent above the total in 2001, and nearly all of the state's goods-producing industries had levels below those of 2001. Among the service-providing industries, information services experienced an especially sharp decline; only management, educational services, and real estate had above average increases in jobs. Average earnings in Colorado were slightly above the national average.

Employment by Industry, 2004

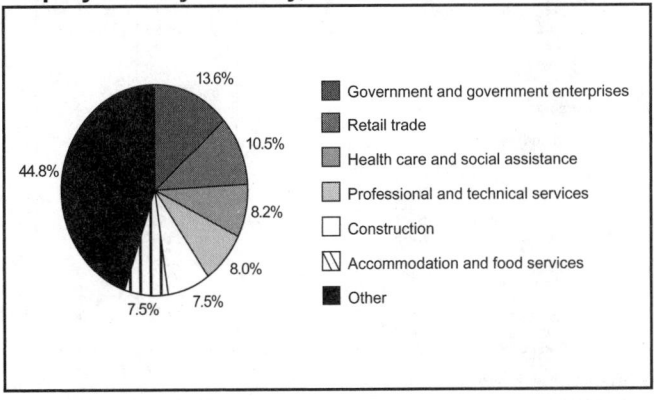

Table CO-10. Personal Income by Major Source, Selected Years 1980–2004

(Millions of dollars, except where noted.)

Item	1980	1990	2000	2001	2002	2003	2004	Average annual percent change, 2000–2004
Earnings by Place of Work	25 679	50 719	117 605	124 224	124 741	127 275	135 119	3.5
Wage and salary disbursements	19 451	37 119	85 909	88 297	86 936	87 832	91 863	1.7
Supplements to wages and salaries	3 481	7 808	16 382	17 308	18 599	19 490	21 420	6.9
Proprietors' income[1]	2 747	5 792	15 315	18 619	19 206	19 953	21 835	9.3
Farm proprietors' income	122	712	178	377	143	265	325	16.2
Nonfarm proprietors' income	2 625	5 080	15 137	18 242	19 062	19 687	21 510	9.2
(-) Contributions for government social insurance[2]	2 101	5 235	11 567	12 146	12 593	12 828	13 628	4.2
(+) Adjustment for residence[3]	28	91	290	336	346	361	389	7.6
(=) **Net Earnings by Place of Residence**	23 606	45 576	106 328	112 414	112 493	114 808	121 879	3.5
(+) Dividends, interest, and rent[4]	5 007	12 915	25 955	26 990	25 626	26 686	27 971	1.9
(+) Personal current transfer receipts	2 646	6 256	12 111	13 296	14 959	15 590	16 303	7.7
Personal income	31 259	64 748	144 394	152 700	153 078	157 083	166 153	3.6
Farm income	30 981	63 849	143 849	151 954	152 511	156 444	165 468	3.6
Nonfarm income	278	899	545	745	566	639	685	5.9
Per Capita Personal Income (Dollars)[5]	10 746	19 575	33 370	34 491	34 032	34 542	36 109	2.0

Note: Data may not add to total or may appear as zero due to rounding.

[1]Proprietors' income includes the inventory valuation adjustment and the capital consumption adjustment.
[2]Contributions for government social insurance are included in earnings by type and industry, but they are excluded from personal income.
[3]The adjustment for residence is the net inflow of the earnings of interarea commuters.
[4]Rental income of persons includes the capital consumption adjustment.
[5]Per capita personal income is total personal income divided by total midyear population.

Per Capita Personal Income, 1980–2004 (Current Dollars)

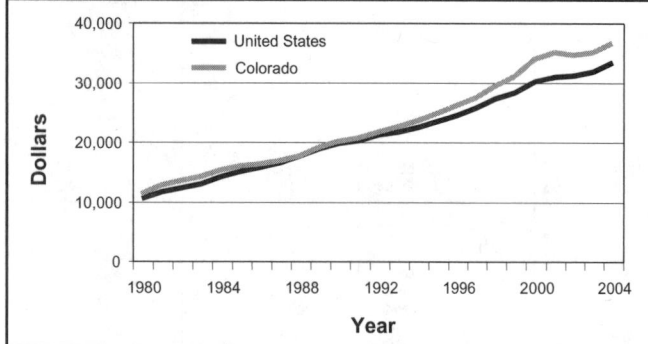

ECONOMIC ACTIVITY

Gross state product (GSP) did not decline during the 2001 recession, but the economy's growth rate was very slow. Even after recovery took hold in 2002, the state was not among the top performers. From 2003 to 2004, Colorado's economy expanded 3.9 percent, which was below the national average rate and the rates of its neighbors, Utah and New Mexico. Real estate, manufacturing, government, and retail trade made the largest contributions to the state's GSP. The value of owner-occupied housing appreciated at an above average rate over the 2000–2004 period, and ranked 11th in the nation in 2004.

Table CO-11. Real Gross State Product, 1997–2004

(Millions of chained 2000 dollars, percent.)

Industry	1997	1998	1999	2000	2001	2002	2003	2004	Average annual percent change, 2001–2004
GROSS STATE PRODUCT	137 900	148 032	159 509	171 363	174 187	174 682	178 327	185 352	2.1
As a percent of U.S. gross product	1.6	1.6	1.7	1.8	1.8	1.7	1.7	1.7	X
Private Industries	119 388	129 695	140 770	152 455	154 758	154 649	157 939	164 359	2.0
Agriculture, forestry, fishing, and hunting	1 176	1 261	1 400	1 381	1 540	1 515	1 589	1 301	-5.5
Mining	1 886	2 067	2 102	2 077	1 974	2 195	2 582	2 884	13.5
Utilities	1 766	1 739	1 881	1 874	2 050	2 186	2 254	2 507	6.9
Construction	8 127	9 106	9 645	10 552	10 657	10 208	9 657	9 760	-2.9
Manufacturing	11 758	12 272	12 837	15 164	13 835	13 863	14 781	15 622	4.1
As a percent of gross state product	8.5	8.3	8.0	8.8	7.9	7.9	8.3	8.4	X
Wholesale trade	7 753	8 623	9 257	10 083	10 607	10 438	9 939	10 072	-1.7
Retail trade	9 150	9 707	10 574	11 230	12 263	12 745	13 158	13 783	4.0
Transportation and warehousing	4 234	4 395	4 701	4 972	5 098	5 173	5 465	5 616	3.3
Information	9 806	12 524	15 463	17 857	17 283	16 584	17 231	17 887	1.2
Finance and insurance	7 569	8 727	9 743	10 708	11 495	11 651	12 396	12 777	3.6
Real estate and rental and leasing	19 560	20 516	22 003	23 062	24 022	23 804	24 067	24 868	1.2
Services	36 911	38 993	41 274	43 493	43 892	44 241	44 944	47 489	2.7
As a percent of gross state product	26.8	26.3	25.9	25.4	25.2	25.3	25.2	25.6	X
Professional and technical services	10 666	11 951	13 233	14 761	15 113	14 853	15 053	16 050	2.0
Management of companies and enterprises	1 858	2 017	2 127	2 328	2 001	2 008	2 228	2 750	11.2
Administrative and waste services	5 751	5 935	6 196	5 801	5 552	5 629	5 781	6 004	2.6
Educational services	724	759	831	903	900	870	833	835	-2.5
Health care and social assistance	7 738	7 831	7 978	8 427	8 982	9 507	9 753	10 047	3.8
Arts, entertainment, and recreation	1 974	1 966	2 125	2 185	2 277	2 279	2 214	2 153	-1.8
Accommodation and food services	4 508	4 674	4 894	5 174	5 139	5 147	5 182	5 470	2.1
Other services, except public administration	3 692	3 860	3 890	3 914	3 928	3 948	3 900	4 180	2.1
Government	18 630	18 381	18 753	18 908	19 427	20 012	20 370	20 979	2.6
As a percent of gross state product	13.5	12.4	11.8	11.0	11.2	11.5	11.4	11.3	X

X = Not applicable.

Table CO-12. Government Transfer Payments, Selected Years 1980–2004

(Millions of dollars, percent.)

Item	1980	1990	2000	2001	2002	2003	2004	Average annual percent change, 2000–2004
CURRENT TRANSFER PAYMENTS TO INDIVIDUALS	2 432	5 827	11 169	12 235	13 992	14 680	15 387	8.3
Retirement and Disability Insurance Benefits	1 259	2 985	4 881	5 190	5 864	6 118	6 465	7.3
Old-age, survivors, and disability insurance (OASDI) benefits	1 112	2 551	4 699	5 006	5 285	5 512	5 835	5.6
Railroad retirement and disability benefits	67	92	110	113	117	120	122	2.6
Workers' compensation	66	309	39	40	429	452	472	86.9
Other government retirement and disability insurance benefits	15	32	32	30	32	34	36	2.6
Medical Benefits	529	1 700	4 522	5 019	5 536	5 810	6 294	8.6
Medicare benefits	321	1 046	2 400	2 675	2 878	3 058	3 398	9.1
Public assistance medical care benefits	189	593	2 039	2 220	2 488	2 605	2 730	7.6
Military medical insurance benefits	18	61	83	124	170	147	166	18.9
Income Maintenance Benefits	278	587	1 017	1 031	1 146	1 273	1 368	7.7
Supplemental Security Income (SSI) benefits	78	153	305	317	333	335	350	3.5
Family assistance	81	137	144	143	171	163	157	2.2
Food stamps	75	163	125	137	171	215	268	21.0
Other income maintenance benefits	44	134	443	434	471	560	593	7.6
Unemployment Insurance Compensation	106	163	150	311	698	711	419	29.2
Veterans' Benefits	203	256	435	466	512	556	604	8.5
Federal Education and Training Assistance	49	122	146	179	197	183	196	7.7
Other Payments to Individuals	7	14	18	38	38	30	40	21.8

Note: See notes and definitions for more details. Data may not add to total or may appear as zero due to rounding.

EXPORTS

The growth of the state's exports was only moderate over the 2001–2004 period, as exports of manufactured goods fell sharply in 2002 and only showed renewed vigor in 2004. Computers and electronics comprised the largest share (nearly 60 percent of the total), followed by machinery manufactures and processed food. Canada received 25 percent of Colorado's exports, more than half of which were computers and electronic products. Mexico was also a major recipient of Colorado's goods, and exports to this country doubled from 2001 to 2004. Exports to Japan, the third largest purchaser, declined sharply over the 2001–2004 period.

Leading Exports, 2004

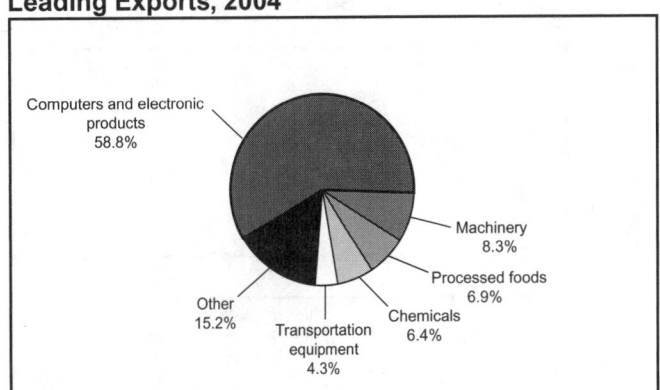

- Computers and electronic products 58.8%
- Machinery 8.3%
- Processed foods 6.9%
- Chemicals 6.4%
- Transportation equipment 4.3%
- Other 15.2%

Table CO-13. Exports of Goods by Leading Products and Destinations, 2001–2004

(Millions of dollars, percent, rank based on 2004 dollar values.)

Product and market	2001	2002	2003	2004	Percent share of total, 2004	Average annual percent change, 2001–2004
Total Goods						
Total	6 125	5 522	6 109	6 651	100.0	2.8
Manufactures	5 902	5 307	5 923	6 429	96.7	2.9
Agriculture and livestock	65	75	67	105	1.6	17.5
Other commodities	159	140	119	116	1.7	-9.8
Five Leading Exports (NAICS Code)						
Computers and electronic products (334)	3 405	3 034	3 460	3 913	58.8	4.7
Machinery manufactures (333)	543	459	457	552	8.3	0.6
Processed foods (311)	632	592	661	461	6.9	-10.0
Chemical manufactures (325)	364	343	398	429	6.4	5.7
Transportation equipment (336)	287	265	286	286	4.3	0.0
Five Leading Markets	5 817	5 275	5 833	6 306	94.8	2.7
Canada	1 146	1 426	1 432	1 660	25.0	13.2
Mexico	335	370	570	689	10.4	27.1
Japan	765	437	443	411	6.2	-18.7
China	169	153	213	356	5.4	28.3
South Korea	248	320	425	342	5.1	11.3

Table CO-14. Agriculture, 1997 and 2002

(Number, acres, and dollars.)

Item	1997	2002
Number of farms	30 197	31 369
Land in farms (acres)	32 349 832	31 093 336
Farm Size		
Average size of farm (acres)	1 071	991
Farms by size (percent distribution)		
Fewer than 50 acres	30.8	32.8
50 to 499 acres	37.5	38.2
500 acres or more	31.7	29.0
Market Value of Land and Equipment (Dollars)		
Land and buildings average value per farm	671 446	757 613
Average value per acre	629	756
Machinery and equipment average value per farm	68 937	87 871
Value of Sales (Thousands of Dollars)		
Agricultural products sold	4 553 732	4 525 196
Crops	1 350 817	1 216 278
Livestock, poultry, and their products	3 202 915	3 308 918
Average per farm (dollars)	150 801	144 257
Value of sales (percent distribution)		
Less than $10,000	50.7	60.4
$10,000 to $99,999	33.6	27.0
$100,000 or more	15.7	12.5
Government Payments		
Payments (thousands of dollars)	120 100	125 774
Percent of farms receiving government payments	32.7	32.4
Farm operators whose principal occupation is farming (percent)	52.3	58.4

AGRICULTURE

Total cash receipts from farming in Colorado were about $4.5 million as reported on the 2002 Census of Agriculture, down slightly the previous census in 1997. The principal products were cattle and grains. The size of the farms was relatively large, with 29 percent spanning 500 acres or more. Government payments to farmers totaled close to $126 million. About 58 percent of all farm operators reported that farming was their principal occupation, a rate slightly below the national average.

ENERGY

Energy prices were close to the national average, but energy expenditures per capita were low—they ranked 47th in the country. Total expenditures reached $9.3 billion in 2001, the latest year for which data are available from the Department of Energy. Energy consumption per capita, at 286.8 million Btu, was well below the national average of 337.7 in 2001. The transportation sector was the largest energy consumer. Major energy sources were petroleum, coal, and natural gas.

Energy Consumption by Source, 2001

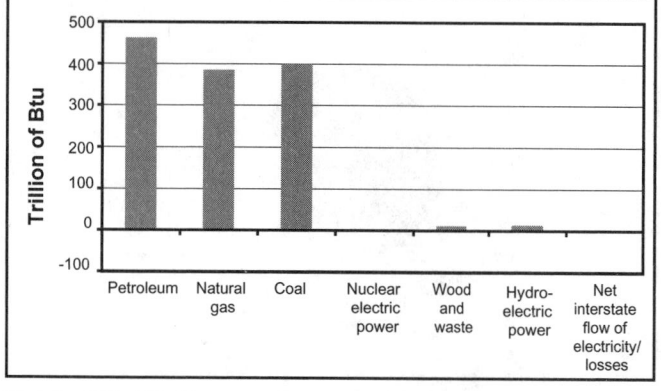

Energy Consumption by Sector, 2001

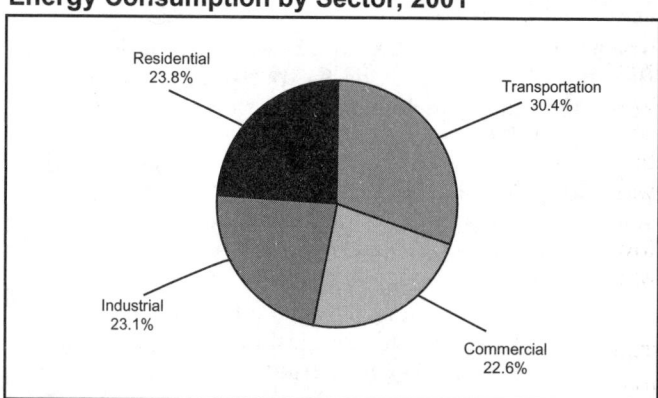

Table CO-15. Energy Consumption, Expenditures, and Prices, Selected Years 1960–2001

(Dollars, Btu [British Thermal Unit], percent distribution.)

Item	1960	1965	1970	1975	1980	1985	1990	1995	2000	2001
Total Consumption (Billion Btu)	425 129	509 548	678 492	785 046	850 490	877 203	935 559	1 074 606	1 250 823	1 270 023
Consumption per capita (million Btu)	242.4	256.7	307.1	303.6	294.3	273.4	284.0	287.5	290.8	286.8
Consumption by Sector (Percent Distribution)										
Residential	21.7	21.1	21.4	21.2	21.6	23.9	23.2	23.1	23.4	23.8
Commercial	13.3	15.2	17.4	18.6	18.6	24.7	25.3	21.8	22.6	22.6
Industrial	40.4	36.5	32.4	29.9	30.3	19.9	22.6	25.3	24.8	23.1
Transportation	24.6	27.2	28.8	30.2	29.5	31.5	28.9	29.8	29.3	30.4
Consumption by Source (Billion Btu)										
Coal	68 206	98 117	115 688	159 333	247 615	299 070	337 382	344 193	387 876	400 326
Natural gas	194 963	204 483	274 987	280 996	254 569	218 723	247 756	295 686	370 912	384 963
Petroleum	162 271	199 346	274 204	326 788	331 025	327 690	326 195	381 114	444 820	461 761
Nuclear electric power	0	0	0	0	7 273	-337	0	0	0	0
Hydroelectric power[1]	10 436	9 800	12 965	15 678	17 834	24 629	14 424	22 925	15 297	12 658
Wood and waste	6 479	6 569	8 364	9 050	10 760	15 347	10 572	11 424	11 411	10 538
Other	0	0	0	0	0	0	560	628	844	1 417
Net interstate flow of electricity/losses[2]	-17 226	-8 767	-7 716	-6 799	-18 585	-7 920	-1 331	18 636	19 664	-1 639
Total Expenditures (Thousands of Dollars)	...	...	865 800	1 833 700	4 183 300	5 154 100	5 241 400	6 221 100	8 653 900	9 279 400
Expenditures per capita (dollars)	...	...	392	709	1 448	1 606	1 591	1 664	2 012	2 095
Prices by Sector (Dollars Per Million Btu)										
Total	...	...	1.52	2.92	6.48	8.22	8.11	8.39	10.23	10.85
Residential	...	...	1.70	2.76	5.71	8.72	8.62	9.13	10.61	12.12
Commercial	...	...	1.67	2.73	6.07	9.48	9.28	9.77	10.96	11.68
Industrial	...	...	0.67	1.74	4.19	5.77	5.09	5.58	6.82	7.70
Transportation	...	...	2.17	3.99	8.75	8.43	8.77	8.87	11.45	11.16

[1]A negative number in this row results from pumped storage for which, overall, more electricity is expended than created to provide electricity during peak demand periods.
[2]Net interstate flow of electricity is the difference between the amount of energy in the electricity sold within a state (including associated losses) and the energy input at the electric utilities within the state. A positive number indicates that more electricity (including associated losses) came into the state than went out of the state during the year; conversely, a negative number indicates that more electricity (including associated losses) went out of the state than came into the state.
... = Not available.

Table CO-16. State Taxes, Fiscal 2004

(Dollars, percent distribution.)

Item	Thousands of dollars	Percent distribution	Dollars per capita	
			State	U.S.
TOTAL TAXES	7 051 457	100.0	1 532.6	2 024.8
Property Taxes	X	X	X	38.9
Sales and Gross Receipts	2 894 035	41.0	629.0	1 003.4
General sales and gross receipts	1 909 246	27.1	415.0	677.0
Selective sales taxes	984 789	14.0	214.0	326.4
Amusements	99 145	1.4	21.6	17.0
Insurance premiums	177 782	2.5	38.6	47.0
Motor fuels	597 558	8.5	129.9	114.6
Tobacco products	65 144	0.9	14.2	42.0
Licenses	337 911	4.8	73.4	134.9
Hunting and fishing	66 073	0.9	14.4	4.2
Motor vehicle	192 923	2.7	41.9	59.4
Occupation and business, not elsewhere classified	50 297	0.7	10.9	37.1
Other Taxes	3 819 511	54.2	830.2	847.6
Individual income	3 413 891	48.4	742.0	673.6
Corporation net income	239 591	3.4	52.1	105.1
Death and gift	50 145	0.7	10.9	19.6
Severance	115 884	1.6	25.2	21.5

X = Not applicable.

GOVERNMENT FINANCE

State revenues amounted to almost $14 billion in 2003. Per capita revenues were well below the national average, ranking 45th in the nation, largely as a result of relatively low taxes per person. They amounted to $1,533 in 2004, which ranked 48th in the United States. Just over $740 per capita was derived from individual income tax collections, ranking 18th in the country. General sales taxes were also a significant source of revenue. Colorado was among 13 states without state property taxes. The state's expenditures per person were commensurately low, ranking 46th in the nation. Per capita debt at the end of the fiscal year was below average.

Per Capita State Taxes, Fiscal 2004

Table CO-17. State Government Finances, 2003

(Dollars, percent distribution.)

Item	Millions of dollars	Percent distribution	Dollars per capita	
			State	U.S.
GENERAL REVENUE	13 998 588	100.0	3 078.0	3 832.6
Intergovernmental revenue	4 178 537	29.8	918.8	1 246.0
Taxes	6 636 190	47.4	1 459.1	1 891.6
General sales	1 833 200	13.1	403.1	636.0
Selective sales	960 701	6.9	211.2	307.4
License taxes	315 096	2.3	69.3	123.6
Individual income tax	3 235 796	23.1	711.5	626.8
Corporate income tax	199 853	1.4	43.9	97.8
Other taxes	91 544	0.7	20.1	99.9
Current charges	1 736 445	12.4	381.8	366.5
Miscellaneous general revenue	1 447 416	10.3	318.2	328.6
GENERAL EXPENDITURE	14 792 539	100.0	3 252.5	4 010.5
Intergovernmental expenditure	4 666 350	31.5	1 026.0	1 316.9
Direct expenditure	10 126 189	68.5	2 226.5	2 693.6
Expenditure by Function				
Education	6 133 704	41.5	1 348.7	1 416.4
Public welfare	3 442 625	23.3	757.0	1 083.3
Hospitals	297 784	2.0	65.5	132.3
Health	708 767	4.8	155.8	173.0
Highways	1 378 238	9.3	303.0	295.4
Police protection	105 653	0.7	23.2	38.4
Correction	723 572	4.9	159.1	135.0
Natural resources	198 642	1.3	43.7	64.0
Parks and recreation	72 418	0.5	15.9	20.1
Government administration	457 652	3.1	100.6	151.3
Interest on general debt	418 356	2.8	92.0	107.8
Other and unallocable	855 128	5.8	188.0	393.4
DEBT AT END OF FISCAL YEAR	8 921 416	X	1 961.6	2 404.7
CASH AND SECURITY HOLDINGS	39 820 285	X	8 755.6	8 938.4

X = Not applicable.

Table CO-18. Education Indicators, 2000–2004

(Percent, number.)

Item	State	U.S.
Total Population 25 Years and Over (Thousands), 2004	2 856	186 877
Educational Attainment, 2004		
Percent high school graduate or more	88.3	85.2
Percent college graduate or more	35.5	27.7
Elementary and Secondary Schools, 2002–2003		
Total students	751 862	48 202 324
Percent of students eligible for free or reduced-price lunch ..	30.2	40.6
Percent of students who were English language learners	12.8	7.8
Total schools	1 662	92 330
Student/teacher ratio	16.9	15.9
Per student expenditures	7 384	8 041
Higher Education, 2002–2003		
Total enrollment	305 795	17 035 027
Bachelor's degrees awarded	24 260	1 348 503
Percent women	53.3	57.5

Educational Attainment, 2004

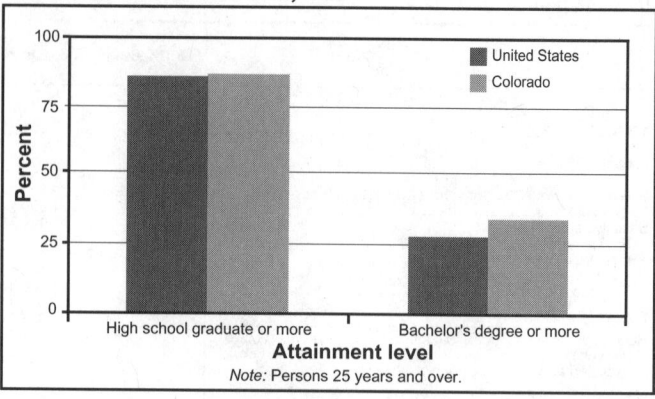

Note: Persons 25 years and over.

EDUCATION

Colorado was well above the national average educational attainment levels. In 2004, 88.3 percent of the state's population age 25 years and over had received a high school degree, ranking 16th in the country. Over 35.5 percent of the population had graduated from college, the third highest proportion in the nation. During the 2002–2003 school year, just 30.2 percent of students were eligible for free or reduced-price lunch, among the lowest proportion of reporting states. Colorado's student/teacher ratio was the 11th highest in the nation. Expenditures per student of $7,384 were below the U.S. average. Both of these measures reflected the rapid population growth in recent years.

VOTER PARTICIPATION

Colorado had a below average voter turnout rate in the 2000, but was slightly above the national average in 2004. According to the official tally by the Clerk of the U.S. House of Representatives, 50.8 percent of voters cast ballots for the Republican presidential candidate in 2000; this proportion increased to 51.7 percent in 2004. The respective percentages for the Democratic candidate were 42.5 percent and 47.0 percent. In 2004, less than 30 percent of eligible Hispanics voted. More than 75 percent of the population age 65 to 74 years reported voting in the 2004 election, compared with just 44 percent of persons age 18 to 24 years.

Table CO-19. Reported Voting and Registration, November 2000 and November 2004

(Numbers in thousands, percent.)

Characteristic	Total population 18 years and over	Total citizen		Total registered		Total voted	
		Number	Percent	Number	Percent	Number	Percent
NOVEMBER 2000							
Total	3 049	2 854	93.6	1 954	64.1	1 633	53.6
Male	1 514	1 383	91.3	959	63.4	805	53.1
Female	1 535	1 471	95.9	995	64.8	829	54.0
NOVEMBER 2004							
Total	3 398	3 109	91.5	2 307	67.9	2 097	61.7
Male	1 691	1 546	91.4	1 134	67.1	1 016	60.1
Female	1 708	1 563	91.5	1 173	68.7	1 081	63.3
Race and Hispanic Origin							
White alone	3 098	2 843	91.8	2 162	69.8	1 972	63.7
Non-Hispanic White alone	2 561	2 516	98.2	1 978	77.2	1 827	71.3
Black alone	123	114	92.7	67	54.3	56	45.6
Asian alone	87	63	B	23	B	18	B
Hispanic or Latino[1]	574	361	62.9	204	35.6	165	28.8
White alone or in combination ...	3 153	2 899	91.9	2 199	69.7	2 008	63.7
Non-Hispanic White alone or in combination	2 602	2 557	98.3	2 004	77.0	1 851	71.2
Black alone or in combination	130	121	93.1	72	55.2	57	43.9
Asian alone or in combination ...	94	70	B	28	B	23	B
Age							
18 to 24 years	479	429	89.5	266	55.6	212	44.2
25 to 44 years	1 384	1 198	86.5	837	60.5	758	54.8
45 to 64 years	1 131	1 085	95.9	872	77.1	825	73.0
65 to 74 years	234	229	97.9	187	80.0	177	75.7
75 years and over	170	169	99.1	144	84.4	125	73.2

[1]May be of any race.
B = Base is too small to show derived measure.

At a Glance:

- Connecticut's population was 3.5 million in 2004, ranking 29th in the nation.

- Non-Hispanic Whites made up more than three-quarters of the state's population in 2004, followed by Blacks at 9.1 percent. Hispanics (of any race) constituted over 10 percent of the state's population, giving it the 11th largest proportion of this ethnic group in the nation.

- The state's overall birth rate and its birth rate for teenage mothers were among the lowest in the country.

- Connecticut had the sixth highest median household income, which totaled $11,000 more than the national average. The state also had a relatively low poverty rate of about 10 percent.

- The unemployment rate in 2004 was 4.9 percent, the 22nd lowest in the country.

- Gross state product showed steady growth after 2002. In 2004, Connecticut had the 23rd largest economy in the country.

- Connecticut ranked quite high for its educational attainment levels, with 88.8 percent of its population holding a high school diploma and 34.5 percent holding a bachelor's degree or more.

Table CT-1. Population by Sex and Age, 1990, 2000, and 2004

(Number, percent.)

Sex and age	1990	2000	2004	Percent distribution, 2004	Average annual percent change, 2000–2004
Total Population	3 287 116	3 405 565	3 503 604	X	0.7
Percent of total U.S. population	1.3	1.2	1.2	X	X
Sex					
Male	1 592 873	1 649 319	1 700 186	48.5	0.8
Female	1 694 243	1 756 246	1 803 418	51.5	0.7
Age					
Under 5 years	228 356	223 344	213 048	6.1	-0.7
5 to 17 years	521 225	618 344	625 740	17.9	1.3
18 years and over	651 317	2 563 877	2 664 816	76.1	0.4
18 to 24 years	2 537 535	271 585	310 612	8.9	-0.8
25 to 44 years	345 433	1 032 689	973 944	27.8	-0.8
45 to 64 years	1 094 878	789 420	906 567	25.9	2.4
65 years and over	445 907	470 183	473 693	13.5	0.5
85 years and over	46 993	64 273	82 075	2.3	4.2
Median age (years)	34.3	37.4	38.8	X	X

X = Not applicable.

Average Annual Rate of Population Growth, 1980–2004

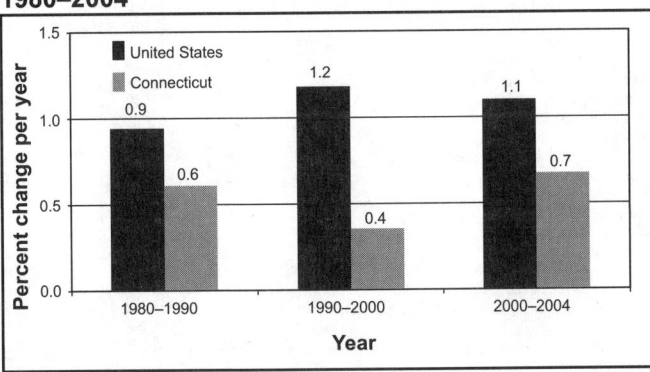

POPULATION

Connecticut's population increased by nearly 3 percent from 2000 to 2004, and growth was faster than in neighboring New York and Massachusetts. The state benefited from wealthy suburban areas located near New York City and Boston, as well as the financial services located throughout the state, which attracted new residents. Other parts of the state, however, suffered from the decline in manufacturing industries. Connecticut experienced steady international immigration during the 2000–2004 period, but lost more than 18,000 residents to other states. Compared with the nation as a whole, Connecticut had an older population with a median age of 38.8 years, the 8th highest median age in the nation.

Table CT-2. Population by Race and Hispanic Origin, 1990, 2000, and 2004

(Number, percent.)

Race and Hispanic origin	1990	2000	2004
Total Population	3 287 116	3 405 565	3 503 604
Non-Hispanic (Percent)			
One race[1]			
White	83.8	78.0	75.9
Black	7.9	8.9	9.1
American Indian, Alaska Native[2]	0.2	0.2	0.2
Asian and Pacific Islander[2]	1.5	2.5	3.1
Other race[2]	2.9	. . .	. . .
Two or more races	. . .	1.0	1.1
Hispanic or Latino[3] (Percent)	6.5	9.4	10.6

[1]Individuals could report only one race in the 1990 census and could report one or more races on the 2000 census. Data on race in 2000 and 2004 are not comparable to 1990.
[2]Data for 1990 include people of Hispanic or Latino origin.
[3]May be of any race.
. . . = Not available.

Minority Population as a Percent of Total Population, 2004

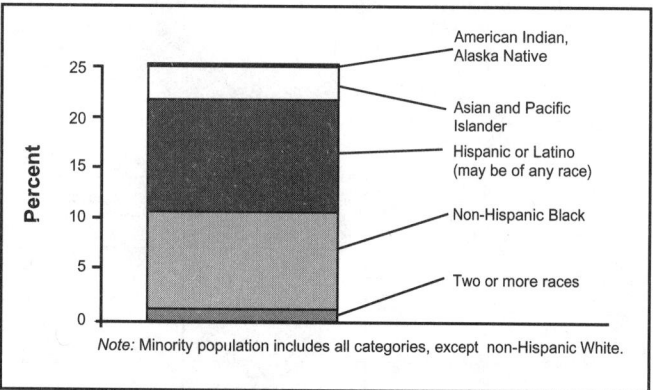

Note: Minority population includes all categories, except non-Hispanic White.

Age-Adjusted Death Rates, Average 2000–2002

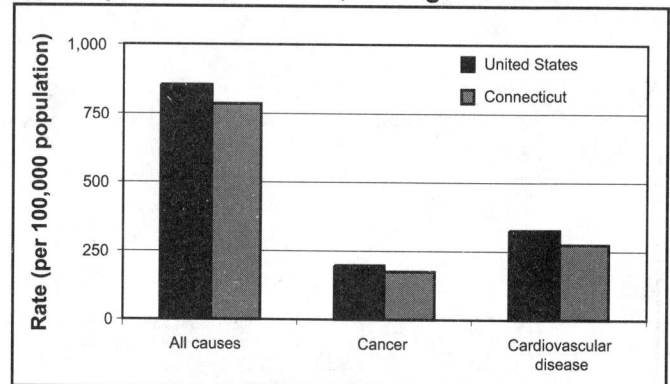

HEALTH

Less than 12 percent of Connecticut's residents had no health insurance, which was one of the lowest proportions of uninsured population in the country. The state's infant mortality rate was below average. Connecticut's age-adjusted death rate for all causes was among the five lowest in the nation.

Table CT-3. Health Characteristics, 2000–2004

(Number, rate, percent.)

Item	State	U.S.
Births, 2003–2004		
Number of births	42 873	4 089 950
Birth rate (per 1,000 population)	12.3	14.1
Teenage birth rate (per 1,000 women age 15–19 years)	24.8	41.6
Mortality Rates, Average 2000–2002		
Infant mortality rate (per 1,000 live births)	6.4	6.9
Age-adjusted mortality rate (per 100,000 population)		
All races	773.0	853.3
Non-Hispanic White	756.5	843.1
Black	918.5	1 097.7
American Indian, Alaska Native	. . .	687.0
Asian and Pacific Islander	321.0	486.0
Hispanic or Latino[1]	580.4	642.7
Health Insurance, 2004		
Percent of all persons without health insurance	11.6	15.7
Percent of children without health insurance	8.5	11.2
Percent of low-income children without health insurance	2.4	7.1

[1]May be of any race.
. . . = Not available.

Table CT-4. Leading Causes of Death, Average 2000–2002

(Number, rate per 100,000 population.)

Cause	Number of deaths	Age-adjusted death rates	
		State	U.S.
ALL CAUSES	30 026	773.0	853.3
Leading Causes			
Major cardiovascular diseases	11 492	288.9	326.5
Cancer	7 107	187.6	196.0
Chronic lower respiratory diseases	1 491	38.2	43.7
Unintentional injuries	1 138	31.6	35.7
Diabetes (underlying cause)	706	18.3	25.2
Influenza and pneumonia	877	21.4	22.7
Alzheimer's disease	556	13.4	19.0
Motor vehicle accidents	328	9.7	15.0
Nephritis, nephrotic syndrome, and nephrosis ..	554	14.1	13.8
Septicemia	539	13.7	11.4
Suicides	282	8.1	10.7
Firearm-related	172	5.1	10.3
Cirrhosis	315	8.6	9.5
Drug-induced	346	10.0	7.9
Alcohol-induced	180	5.0	6.9
Homicides	101	3.1	6.0
Falls	173	4.4	5.2
HIV	193	5.4	5.0
Viral hepatitis	45	1.2	2.0
Anemias	59	1.5	1.6
Drownings	30	0.9	1.3
Fire deaths	27	0.7	1.2

Note: The rates are age-adjusted to the U.S. 2000 standard population.

Table CT-5. Households and Housing Characteristics, 1990, 2000, and 2004

(Number, percent, and dollars.)

Characteristic	1990	2000	2004	Average annual percent change, 2000–2004
Total Households	1 230 479	1 301 670	1 329 950	0.5
Family households	864 493	881 170	899 496	0.5
Married-couple family	684 660	676 467	687 566	0.4
Other family	179 833	204 703	211 930	0.9
Male householder, no wife present	39 448	47 292	45 957	-0.7
Female householder, no husband present	140 385	157 411	165 973	1.3
Nonfamily households	365 986	420 500	430 454	0.6
Householder living alone	297 161	344 224	356 479	0.9
Householder not living alone	68 825	76 276	73 975	-0.8
Housing Characteristics				
Average size	2.59	2.53	2.55	X
Housing units	1 320 850	1 385 975	1 414 433	0.5
Occupied housing units	1 230 479	1 301 670	1 329 950	0.5
Owner-occupied	807 481	869 729	927 575	1.6
Renter-occupied	422 998	431 941	402 375	-1.8
Median gross rent of renter-occupied housing units (dollars) ...	598	681	811	4.5
Median value of owner-occupied housing units (dollars)	176 700	166 900	236 559	9.1

X = Not applicable.

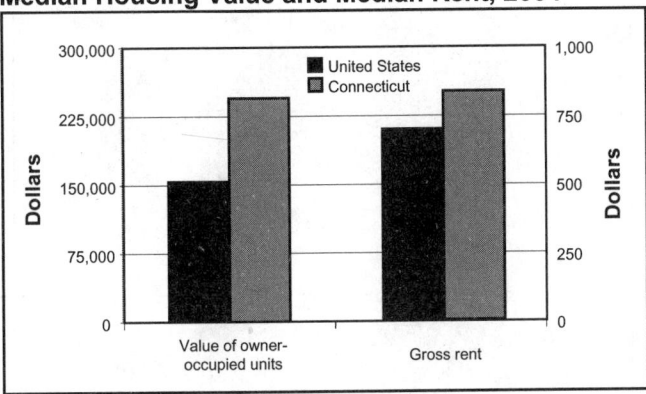

Median Housing Value and Median Rent, 2004

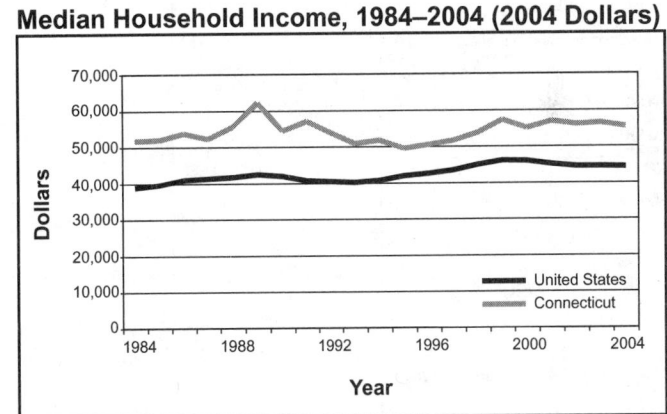

Median Household Income, 1984–2004 (2004 Dollars)

Table CT-6. Household Income and Poverty Status, 1980–2004

(2004 CPI-U-RS adjusted dollars, rate.)

Year	State		U.S.	
	Median household income (2004 dollars)	Poverty rate	Median household income (2004 dollars)	Poverty rate
2004	55 390	10.0	44 389	12.7
2003	56 442	8.1	44 482	12.5
2002	56 078	8.3	44 546	12.1
2001	56 927	7.3	45 062	11.7
2000	55 033	7.7	46 058	11.3
1999	57 347	7.2	46 129	11.9
1998	53 826	9.5	45 003	12.7
1997	51 622	8.6	43 430	13.3
1996	50 488	11.7	42 544	13.7
1995	49 534	9.7	41 943	13.8
1994	51 814	10.8	40 677	14.5
1993	50 870	8.5	40 217	15.1
1992	53 887	9.8	40 422	14.8
1991	57 014	8.6	40 746	14.2
1990	54 473	6.0	41 963	13.5
1989	62 259	2.9	42 524	12.8
1988	55 562	4.0	41 771	13.0
1987	52 256	6.6	41 322	13.4
1986	53 805	6.0	40 939	13.6
1985	52 056	7.6	39 545	14.0
1984	51 821	6.9	38 782	14.4
1983	. . .	8.8	. . .	15.2
1982	. . .	8.1	. . .	15.0
1981	. . .	8.2	. . .	14.0
1980	. . .	8.3	. . .	13.0

. . . = Not available.

Table CT-7. Employment Status by Demographic Group, 2004

(Numbers in thousands, rate.)

Characteristic	Civilian noninstitutional population	Civilian labor force		Employed	Unemployment rate
		Number	Participation rate		
SEX AND AGE					
Total	2 700	1 790	66.3	1 702	4.9
16 to 19 years	208	89	42.9	75	16.4
20 to 24 years	206	147	71.3	132	9.9
25 to 34 years	389	327	84.0	310	5.1
35 to 44 years	551	461	83.7	446	3.3
45 to 54 years	516	436	84.5	421	3.5
55 to 64 years	376	250	66.6	240	4.0
65 years and over	455	80	17.6	78	3.1
Men	1 287	943	73.3	895	5.1
16 to 19 years	105	50	47.5	41	17.6
20 to 24 years	106	78	73.4	69	11.1
25 to 34 years	189	173	91.6	164	4.9
35 to 44 years	266	245	92.1	238	3.0
45 to 54 years	248	221	89.4	213	3.9
55 to 64 years	177	131	73.7	126	3.8
65 years and over	196	46	23.2	44	3.4
Women	1 413	848	60.0	807	4.7
16 to 19 years	103	40	38.3	34	14.8
20 to 24 years	100	69	69.1	63	8.5
25 to 34 years	200	154	76.8	146	5.3
35 to 44 years	285	216	75.9	208	3.6
45 to 54 years	268	215	80.0	208	3.1
55 to 64 years	199	120	60.3	115	4.2
65 years and over	258	35	13.4	34	2.8
MARITAL STATUS					
Married men, spouse present	738	573	77.6	557	2.8
Married women, spouse present	719	455	63.4	445	2.2
Women who maintain families	161	117	73.0	108	7.5
RACE, HISPANIC ORIGIN, AND SEX					
White	2 353	1 562	66.4	1 490	4.6
Men	1 133	832	73.4	791	4.9
Women	1 220	731	59.9	700	4.2
Black	244	162	66.2	149	7.8
Men	109	77	70.5	71	7.3
Women	136	85	62.8	78	8.3
Asian	63	43	68.8	42	3.4
Men	30	24	80.3	24	2.0
Hispanic or Latino[1]	242	160	66.2	146	9.3
Men	120	85	70.3	76	9.6
Women	122	76	62.2	69	8.9
RACE, HISPANIC ORIGIN, AND AGE					
White					
20 to 24 years	173	122	70.6	111	9.1
25 to 34 years	324	276	85.3	263	5.0
35 to 44 years	470	393	83.8	382	2.9
45 to 54 years	458	389	85.0	375	3.5
55 to 64 years	337	230	68.4	222	3.6
65 years and over	418	72	17.2	70	2.9

Note: Data in Table 7 are from the Current Population Survey (CPS) and do not match Bureau of Labor Statistics estimates in Table 8. See notes and definitions for more details.

[1]May be of any race.

Table CT-8. Employment Status, 1990–2004

(Numbers in thousands, rate.)

Year	Civilian labor force	Employed	Unemployed	Unemployment rate
2004	1 797 344	1 709 836	87 508	4.9
2003	1 804 921	1 706 170	98 751	5.5
2002	1 784 555	1 706 066	78 489	4.4
2001	1 753 065	1 698 274	54 791	3.1
2000	1 738 831	1 697 662	41 169	2.4
1999	1 742 145	1 695 174	46 971	2.7
1998	1 741 640	1 684 831	56 809	3.3
1997	1 759 854	1 674 937	84 917	4.8
1996	1 752 773	1 659 643	93 130	5.3
1995	1 750 060	1 657 732	92 328	5.3
1994	1 767 042	1 670 083	96 959	5.5
1993	1 796 640	1 682 262	114 378	6.4
1992	1 826 769	1 693 563	133 206	7.3
1991	1 828 146	1 708 655	119 491	6.5
1990	1 814 924	1 725 381	89 543	4.9

Note: Population age 16 years and over.

Unemployment Rate, 1980–2004

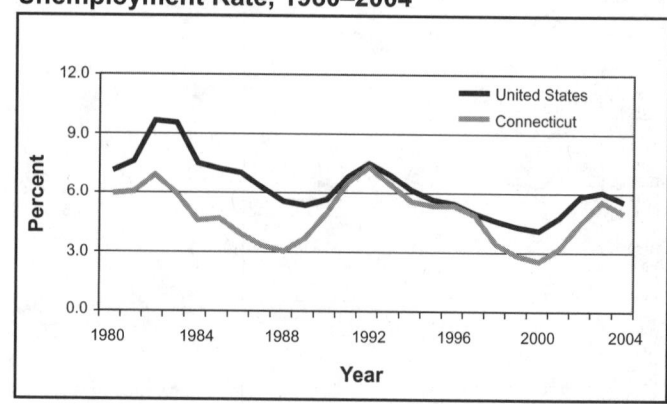

Table CT-9. Employment and Average Wages by Industry, 2001–2004

(Estimates are based on the 2002 North American Industry Classification System [NAICS].)

Industry	2001	2002	2003	2004	Annual average percent change, 2001–2004
	Number of jobs				
TOTAL EMPLOYMENT BY PLACE OF WORK	2 123 594	2 118 412	2 113 351	2 133 671	0.2
Farm Employment	10 349	10 449	10 575	9 560	-2.6
Nonfarm Employment	2 113 245	2 107 963	2 102 776	2 124 111	0.2
Private employment	1 852 881	1 843 777	1 842 248	1 866 411	0.2
Forestry, fishing, hunting, and other[1]	2 731	3 029	2 698	2 606	-1.5
Mining	1 972	1 757	2 034	2 120	2.4
Utilities	9 486	9 210	9 020	8 863	-2.2
Construction	110 409	107 029	109 337	114 492	1.2
Manufacturing	233 738	218 958	206 862	204 606	-4.3
Durable goods manufacturing	173 468	161 702	152 305	151 550	-4.4
Nondurable goods manufacturing	60 270	57 256	54 557	53 056	-4.2
Wholesale trade	74 018	72 174	71 670	72 257	-0.8
Retail trade	232 296	233 534	231 434	233 978	0.2
Transportation and warehousing	49 760	48 648	48 649	49 570	-0.1
Information	50 487	46 137	45 411	44 790	-3.9
Finance and insurance	161 148	162 351	162 583	160 691	-0.1
Real estate and rental and leasing	69 779	70 923	74 746	78 204	3.9
Professional and technical services	155 381	153 419	151 663	152 859	-0.5
Management of companies and enterprises	29 630	28 799	28 516	26 809	-3.3
Administrative and waste services	110 673	109 229	109 811	115 293	1.4
Educational services	59 880	62 511	64 683	66 948	3.8
Health care and social assistance	246 586	253 020	255 706	259 466	1.7
Arts, entertainment, and recreation	43 061	44 781	45 353	46 684	2.7
Accommodation and food services	105 863	108 446	111 490	113 911	2.5
Other services, except public administration	105 983	109 822	110 582	112 264	1.9
Government and government enterprises	260 364	264 186	260 528	257 700	-0.3
	Dollars				
AVERAGE WAGES AND SALARIES BY PLACE OF WORK	45 947	45 862	47 311	49 926	2.8
Farm Earnings	18 571	24 391	20 187	26 129	12.1
Nonfarm Earnings	46 044	45 939	47 413	50 001	2.8
Private earnings	47 026	46 651	48 190	50 805	2.6
Forestry, fishing, hunting, and other[1]	18 652	19 133	18 891	19 322	1.2
Mining	50 853	52 958	55 985	55 082	2.7
Utilities	77 999	73 838	80 060	97 296	7.6
Construction	48 191	48 371	48 057	49 613	1.0
Manufacturing	55 710	55 905	57 993	61 042	3.1
Durable goods manufacturing	53 693	54 294	56 377	59 672	3.6
Nondurable goods manufacturing	61 578	60 503	62 546	64 995	1.8
Wholesale trade	65 570	64 556	66 439	68 845	1.6
Retail trade	27 023	27 151	27 894	28 547	1.8
Transportation and warehousing	35 234	36 252	37 221	39 172	3.6
Information	57 670	56 159	57 519	60 922	1.8
Finance and insurance	98 219	98 353	104 416	118 471	6.4
Real estate and rental and leasing	42 487	42 903	43 044	44 530	1.6
Professional and technical services	72 323	69 312	70 398	72 627	0.1
Management of companies and enterprises	104 817	97 218	106 165	121 185	5.0
Administrative and waste services	28 640	29 399	30 219	31 357	3.1
Educational services	33 919	35 347	37 019	37 839	3.7
Health care and social assistance	36 119	37 305	38 433	39 834	3.3
Arts, entertainment, and recreation	25 725	24 640	25 139	25 714	0.0
Accommodation and food services	16 493	16 855	17 049	17 657	2.3
Other services, except public administration	24 111	24 707	25 500	26 053	2.6
Government and government enterprises	40 389	41 950	43 050	45 416	4.0

Note: Average wages and salaries are a calculation by the editors of wage and salary disbursements divided by full- and part-time wage and salary employment. Data may not add to total or may appear as zero due to rounding.

[1] "Other" consists of the number of jobs held by U.S. residents employed by international organizations and foreign embassies and consulates in the United States.

LABOR MARKET

Connecticut's unemployment rate rose following the 2001 recession, but remained below the U.S. average. Employment was concentrated in the private service-providing industries, particularly in health care, finance and insurance, and professional and technical services. Manufacturing remained a major sector, making up 9.6 percent of total employment in 2004; however, the number of manufacturing jobs fell over 12 percent from 2001 to 2004. Government and government enterprises represented the second largest number of jobs. The strongest job growth occurred in real estate and educational services. Average wages and salaries were well above the national average in most industries, particularly in management, finance and insurance, and utilities.

Employment by Industry, 2004

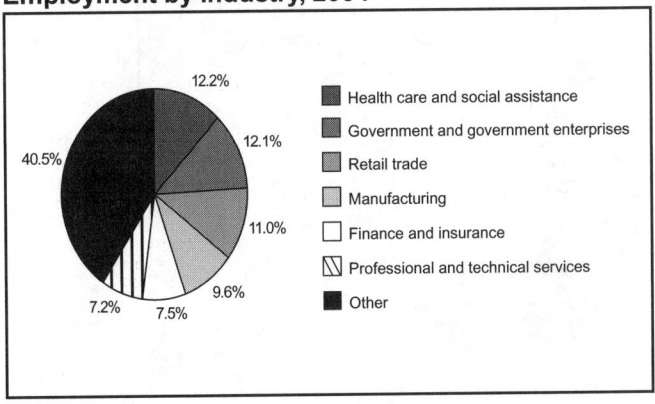

Table CT-10. Personal Income by Major Source, Selected Years 1980–2004

(Millions of dollars, except where noted.)

Item	1980	1990	2000	2001	2002	2003	2004	Average annual percent change, 2000–2004
Earnings by Place of Work	28 837	64 689	106 655	111 686	112 528	115 243	123 115	3.7
Wage and salary disbursements	22 199	49 077	78 950	81 133	80 311	81 824	86 577	2.3
Supplements to wages and salaries	4 346	9 949	14 449	15 292	17 193	18 169	19 770	8.2
Proprietors' income[1]	2 293	5 663	13 256	15 261	15 024	15 251	16 768	6.1
Farm proprietors' income	30	97	58	47	-15	5	12	-32.1
Nonfarm proprietors' income	2 263	5 566	13 198	15 214	15 040	15 246	16 756	6.1
(-) Contributions for government social insurance[2]	2 682	6 927	10 785	11 106	11 571	11 802	12 301	3.3
(+) Adjustment for residence[3]	1 695	2 780	5 678	5 035	4 485	4 314	4 752	-4.4
(=) Net Earnings by Place of Residence	27 850	60 542	101 549	105 615	105 442	107 755	115 566	3.3
(+) Dividends, interest, and rent[4]	6 884	18 214	25 164	25 979	24 790	24 247	25 456	0.3
(+) Personal current transfer receipts	3 737	8 495	14 858	15 762	16 931	17 274	18 412	5.5
Personal income	38 470	87 251	141 570	147 356	147 163	149 276	159 435	3.0
Farm income	38 391	87 075	141 387	147 182	147 013	149 129	159 269	3.0
Nonfarm income	79	176	183	174	150	147	166	-2.4
Per Capita Personal Income (Dollars)[5]	12 357	26 504	41 489	42 920	42 545	42 810	45 506	2.3

Note: Data may not add to total or may appear as zero due to rounding.

[1]Proprietors' income includes the inventory valuation adjustment and the capital consumption adjustment.
[2]Contributions for government social insurance are included in earnings by type and industry, but they are excluded from personal income.
[3]The adjustment for residence is the net inflow of the earnings of interarea commuters.
[4]Rental income of persons includes the capital consumption adjustment.
[5]Per capita personal income is total personal income divided by total midyear population.

Per Capita Personal Income, 1980–2004 (Current Dollars)

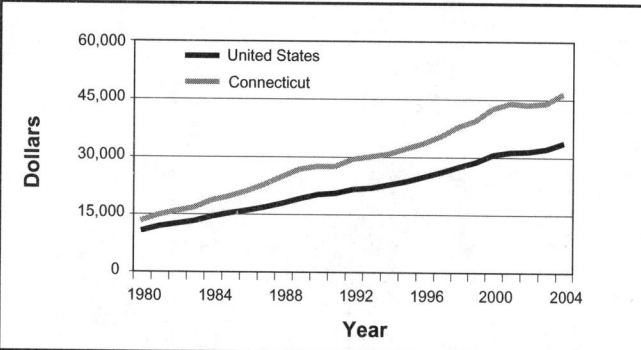

ECONOMIC ACTIVITY

Real gross state product growth was below the national average after the 2001 recession, but rebounded strongly with a growth rate of 4.5 percent between 2003 and 2004, which was in the top 20 rates of growth in the country. Finance and insurance, manufacturing, and real estate and related activities were the state's leading sectors. Utilities, finance and insurance, and information had the strongest rates of growth from 2001 to 2004. Statewide housing prices showed above average appreciation and were well above the national average. In 2004, the median value of owner-occupied housing ranked 7th in the nation at $236,559, an increase of nearly 42 percent from 2000.

Table CT-11. Real Gross State Product, 1997–2004

(Millions of chained 2000 dollars, percent.)

Industry	1997	1998	1999	2000	2001	2002	2003	2004	Average annual percent change, 2001–2004
GROSS STATE PRODUCT	144 921	150 752	153 699	160 685	161 595	160 115	164 137	171 479	2.0
As a percent of U.S. gross product	1.7	1.7	1.6	1.6	1.6	1.6	1.6	1.6	X
Private Industries	131 860	137 484	140 434	146 985	147 598	145 971	150 319	157 372	2.2
Agriculture, forestry, fishing, and hunting	221	257	299	358	304	291	297	250	-6.3
Mining	24	33	38	44	44	43	47	44	0.0
Utilities	2 385	2 368	2 412	2 691	2 497	2 552	2 700	3 152	8.1
Construction	4 927	5 014	5 039	5 069	5 047	4 925	4 876	5 170	0.8
Manufacturing	19 942	21 102	20 120	20 782	21 057	20 738	21 082	21 963	1.4
As a percent of gross state product	13.8	14.0	13.1	12.9	13.0	13.0	12.8	12.8	X
Wholesale trade	8 359	8 892	8 977	8 716	9 441	9 461	9 198	9 319	-0.4
Retail trade	8 491	8 890	9 425	10 379	10 429	10 943	11 437	11 970	4.7
Transportation and warehousing	2 386	2 482	2 508	2 581	2 533	2 518	2 632	2 736	2.6
Information	4 943	5 588	6 279	6 293	6 495	6 340	6 770	7 499	4.9
Finance and insurance	19 915	21 942	22 867	26 669	25 186	24 396	27 122	29 650	5.6
Real estate and rental and leasing	19 612	19 782	20 690	21 174	22 295	21 611	21 101	21 710	-0.9
Services	41 003	41 223	41 859	42 229	42 305	42 178	43 217	44 176	1.5
As a percent of gross state product	28.3	27.3	27.2	26.3	26.2	26.3	26.3	25.8	X
Professional and technical services	11 061	11 657	12 135	12 753	12 737	12 576	12 729	12 922	0.5
Management of companies and enterprises	4 734	4 568	4 679	4 803	5 013	4 568	5 055	5 088	0.5
Administrative and waste services	4 550	4 722	4 617	4 175	4 020	4 151	4 294	4 520	4.0
Educational services	2 081	2 104	2 106	2 058	2 013	2 038	2 023	1 985	-0.5
Health care and social assistance	10 935	10 645	10 763	10 947	11 124	11 429	11 622	11 831	2.1
Arts, entertainment, and recreation	1 324	1 366	1 382	1 384	1 432	1 442	1 468	1 493	1.4
Accommodation and food services	2 474	2 606	2 730	2 815	2 758	2 815	2 867	2 995	2.8
Other services, except public administration	3 844	3 555	3 447	3 294	3 208	3 159	3 159	3 342	1.4
Government	13 081	13 277	13 267	13 700	13 996	14 135	13 840	14 144	0.4
As a percent of gross state product	9.0	8.8	8.6	8.5	8.7	8.8	8.4	8.2	X

X = Not applicable.

Table CT-12. Government Transfer Payments, Selected Years 1980–2004

(Millions of dollars, percent.)

Item	1980	1990	2000	2001	2002	2003	2004	Average annual percent change, 2000–2004
CURRENT TRANSFER PAYMENTS TO INDIVIDUALS	3 514	8 063	14 086	14 904	16 176	16 599	17 738	5.9
Retirement and Disability Insurance Benefits	1 871	3 765	5 895	6 204	6 408	6 569	6 864	3.9
Old-age, survivors, and disability insurance (OASDI) benefits	1 819	3 650	5 714	6 017	6 253	6 423	6 710	4.1
Railroad retirement and disability benefits	30	40	43	43	45	45	46	2.0
Workers' compensation	18	57	119	121	86	58	60	-15.7
Other government retirement and disability insurance benefits	5	18	20	22	25	43	47	24.6
Medical Benefits	854	2 908	6 423	6 768	7 447	7 506	8 483	7.2
Medicare benefits	515	1 503	3 102	3 420	3 642	3 835	4 193	7.8
Public assistance medical care benefits	335	1 388	3 304	3 326	3 776	3 647	4 259	6.6
Military medical insurance benefits	5	18	17	22	29	25	31	16.4
Income Maintenance Benefits	414	733	1 141	1 117	1 125	1 215	1 293	3.2
Supplemental Security Income (SSI) benefits	58	184	306	314	321	333	348	3.3
Family assistance	209	307	334	306	292	268	251	-6.9
Food stamps	60	79	136	137	148	172	205	10.9
Other income maintenance benefits	87	163	365	361	363	442	488	7.5
Unemployment Insurance Compensation	185	425	334	494	847	927	598	15.7
Veterans' Benefits	146	166	200	212	240	254	259	6.7
Federal Education and Training Assistance	43	61	85	94	100	97	105	5.6
Other Payments to Individuals	*	5	8	15	8	30	137	101.8

Note: See notes and definitions for more details. Data may not add to total or may appear as zero due to rounding.

* = Less than $500,000.

EXPORTS

Connecticut ranked 27th in the nation for value of its exports, which totaled more than $8.5 million in 2004. Nearly 95 percent of its exports were manufactured goods, primarily transportation equipment, machinery, computers and electronic products, and chemical manufactures. Canada was the top market for Connecticut's exports, and these largely consisted of transportation equipment, machinery, and chemicals. France, Germany, and Mexico were the next largest importers of the state's products. Exports to Mexico increased by nearly 80 percent from 2001 to 2004, as the country overtook the United Kingdom to become Connecticut's fourth leading market. The majority of exports to Mexico were machinery and electronic equipment and parts.

Leading Exports, 2004

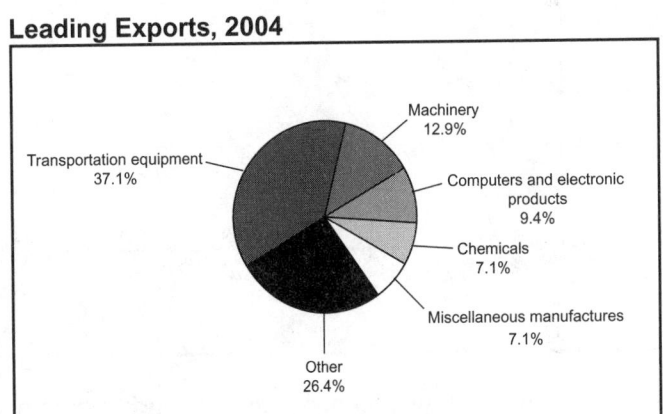

Table CT-13. Exports of Goods by Leading Products and Destinations, 2001–2004

(Millions of dollars, percent, rank based on 2004 dollar values.)

Product and market	2001	2002	2003	2004	Percent share of total, 2004	Average annual percent change, 2001–2004
Total Goods						
Total	8 610	8 313	8 136	8 559	100.0	-0.2
Manufactures	8 183	7 929	7 751	8 104	94.7	-0.3
Agriculture and livestock	140	107	84	143	1.7	0.7
Other commodities	288	277	302	312	3.6	2.8
Five Leading Exports (NAICS Code)						
Transportation equipment (336)	3 988	4 099	3 298	3 178	37.1	-7.3
Machinery manufactures (333)	898	670	784	1 107	12.9	7.2
Computers and electronic products (334)	804	760	790	804	9.4	0.0
Chemical manufactures (325)	567	500	749	608	7.1	2.3
Miscellaneous manufactures (339)	430	394	486	606	7.1	12.1
Five Leading Markets	7 866	7 421	7 390	7 819	91.3	-0.2
Canada	1 729	1 492	1 352	1 473	17.2	-5.2
France	1 416	1 178	1 096	1 182	13.8	-5.9
Germany	675	654	760	762	8.9	4.1
Mexico	327	402	478	586	6.8	21.5
United Kingdom	462	500	513	548	6.4	5.8

Table CT-14. Agriculture, 1997 and 2002

(Number, acres, and dollars.)

Item	1997	2002
Number of farms	4 905	4 191
Land in farms (acres)	406 222	357 154
Farm Size		
Average size of farm (acres)	83	85
Farms by size (percent distribution)		
Fewer than 50 acres	59.1	62.3
50 to 499 acres	38.7	34.9
500 acres or more	2.1	2.8
Market Value of Land and Equipment (Dollars)		
Land and buildings average value per farm	516 347	840 302
Average value per acre	6 270	9 491
Machinery and equipment average value per farm	37 167	51 214
Value of Sales (Thousands of Dollars)		
Agricultural products sold	434 970	470 637
Crops	274 048	327 527
Livestock, poultry, and their products	160 922	143 110
Average per farm (dollars)	88 679	112 297
Value of sales (percent distribution)		
Less than $10,000	66.7	67.3
$10,000 to $99,999	23.1	22.2
$100,000 or more	10.1	10.5
Government Payments		
Payments (thousands of dollars)	1 519	3 681
Percent of farms receiving government payments	12.7	6.1
Farm operators whose principal occupation is farming (percent) ...	45.4	49.6

AGRICULTURE

Total cash receipts amounted to over $470 million in 2002, an increase of 8 percent from the previous farm census in 1997. All of the gain was attributable to the sale of crops, particularly greenhouse items. From 1997 to 2002, the value of livestock exports fell by nearly $18 million. More than 67 percent of farms had sales of less than $10,000 and just under half of all farm operators reported farming as their principal occupation.

ENERGY

Energy prices in the state were high relative to the nation as a whole, ranking seventh overall. In terms of expenditures per person, Connecticut ranked only 35th in the country, according to the Department of Energy's 2001 report. The state's per capita consumption was among the lowest in the nation. The transportation sector was the largest consumer of energy, followed by the commercial sector. Petroleum was by far the leading energy source.

Energy Consumption by Source, 2001

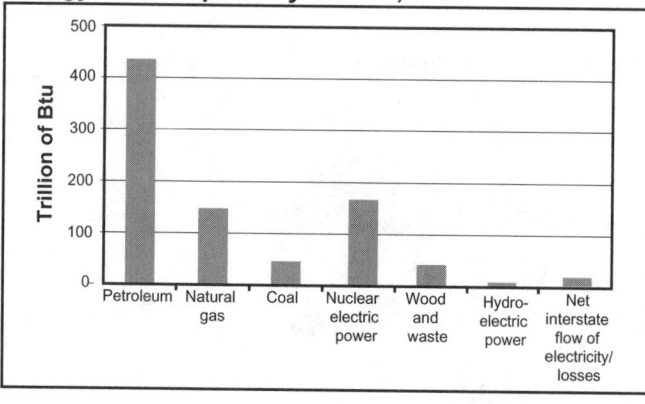

Energy Consumption by Sector, 2001

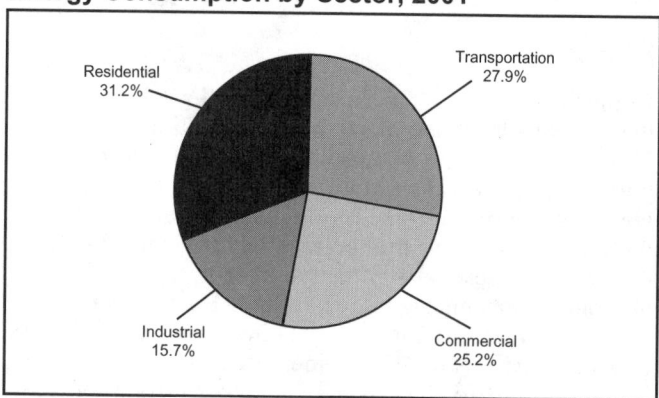

Table CT-15. Energy Consumption, Expenditures, and Prices, Selected Years 1960–2001

(Dollars, Btu [British Thermal Unit], percent distribution.)

Item	1960	1965	1970	1975	1980	1985	1990	1995	2000	2001
Total Consumption (Billion Btu)	508 210	572 032	722 393	692 306	731 805	730 397	771 316	778 902	854 645	853 081
Consumption per capita (million Btu)	200.5	200.2	238.2	224.6	235.5	228.2	234.6	238.5	251.0	248.5
Consumption by Sector (Percent Distribution)										
Residential	31.1	28.2	28.0	29.7	31.0	29.4	32.3	32.2	31.5	31.2
Commercial	12.4	12.8	14.4	16.8	17.7	21.9	23.4	24.2	25.1	25.2
Industrial	33.5	34.5	32.4	25.1	26.0	21.8	17.6	17.6	16.7	15.7
Transportation	23.0	24.6	25.3	28.4	25.3	26.9	26.6	26.0	26.7	27.9
Consumption by Source (Billion Btu)										
Coal	101 694	128 613	48 577	1 272	364	21 316	38 511	40 787	36 246	39 998
Natural gas	29 449	41 720	61 543	64 331	74 180	80 561	108 957	144 938	163 716	149 350
Petroleum	362 437	389 415	587 378	535 661	510 864	457 177	444 887	371 060	450 058	438 666
Nuclear electric power	0	0	39 567	89 590	129 094	135 127	209 272	196 995	170 674	161 189
Hydroelectric power[1]	4 564	1 959	3 456	5 135	2 659	2 760	6 003	3 624	5 324	2 914
Wood and waste	12 842	13 541	15 837	17 102	35 268	35 959	28 269	43 243	43 422	38 697
Other	0	0	0	0	0	145	192	4 510	5 622	1 729
Net interstate flow of electricity/losses[2]	-2 776	-3 215	-33 964	-20 784	-20 623	-2 649	-64 776	-26 254	-20 417	20 538
Total Expenditures (Thousands of Dollars)	. . .	. . .	1 199 800	2 377 100	4 747 400	5 667 100	6 254 200	6 702 000	8 151 700	8 062 100
Expenditures per capita (dollars)	. . .	. . .	396	771	1 528	1 770	1 903	2 052	2 394	2 349
Prices by Sector (Dollars Per Million Btu)										
Total	. . .	. . .	2.08	4.51	8.95	10.97	11.38	12.14	13.39	13.30
Residential	. . .	. . .	2.44	5.06	9.10	12.75	12.87	13.77	15.21	15.57
Commercial	. . .	. . .	2.59	5.92	10.28	13.28	14.08	15.73	14.46	15.17
Industrial	. . .	. . .	1.06	3.43	6.92	9.58	9.35	9.06	10.07	10.45
Transportation	. . .	. . .	2.63	4.30	9.69	9.29	9.76	10.35	12.74	11.75

[1]A negative number in this row results from pumped storage for which, overall, more electricity is expended than created to provide electricity during peak demand periods.
[2]Net interstate flow of electricity is the difference between the amount of energy in the electricity sold within a state (including associated losses) and the energy input at the electric utilities within the state. A positive number indicates that more electricity (including associated losses) came into the state than went out of the state during the year; conversely, a negative number indicates that more electricity (including associated losses) went out of the state than came into the state.
. . . = Not available.

Table CT-16. State Taxes, Fiscal 2004

(Dollars, percent distribution.)

Item	Thousands of dollars	Percent distribution	Dollars per capita	
			State	U.S.
TOTAL TAXES	10 291 289	100.0	2 937.0	2 024.8
Property Taxes	X	X	X	38.9
Sales and Gross Receipts	4 900 376	47.6	1 398.5	1 003.4
General sales and gross receipts	3 127 221	30.4	892.5	677.0
Selective sales taxes	1 773 155	17.2	506.0	326.4
Amusements	435 061	4.2	124.2	17.0
Insurance premiums	218 202	2.1	62.3	47.0
Motor fuels	456 805	4.4	130.4	114.6
Public utilities	195 646	1.9	55.8	39.2
Tobacco products	277 333	2.7	79.2	42.0
Other selective sales	135 422	1.3	38.6	49.8
Licenses	385 265	3.7	110.0	134.9
Motor vehicle	197 418	1.9	56.3	59.4
Occupation and business, not elsewhere classified	118 424	1.2	33.8	37.1
Other Taxes	5 005 648	48.6	1 428.6	847.6
Individual income	4 319 546	42.0	1 232.8	673.6
Corporation net income	379 822	3.7	108.4	105.1
Death and gift	130 464	1.3	37.2	19.6
Documentary and stock transfer	175 816	1.7	50.2	27.1

X = Not applicable.

GOVERNMENT FINANCE

In 2003, state revenues amounted to $16.2 million, or $4,651 per capita, which was the 11th highest per capita total in the nation. Per capita expenditures, at over $5,129, were also high relative to the rest of the country. Connecticut's per capita taxes were well above the national average in 2004, when they totaled $2,937. More than $1,232 of the total were individual income taxes, nearly double the U.S. average. A substantial portion of taxes were also raised from sales taxes. Connecticut had no property tax. The state's debt per capita in 2004 amounted to nearly $6,450, which was the third highest in the nation.

Per Capita State Taxes, Fiscal, 2004

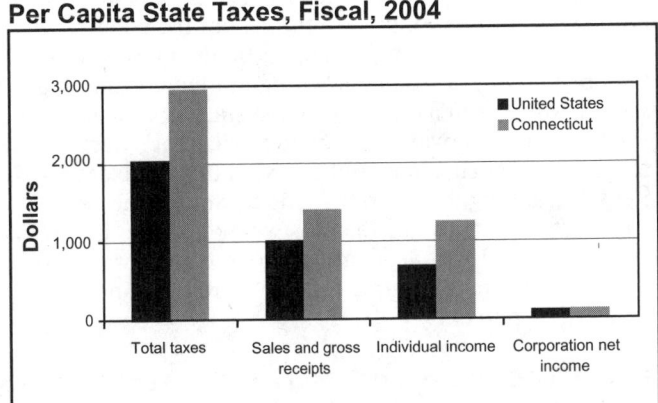

Table CT-17. State Government Finances, 2003

(Dollars, percent distribution.)

Item	Millions of dollars	Percent distribution	Dollars per capita	
			State	U.S.
GENERAL REVENUE	16 216 542	100.0	4 650.6	3 832.6
Intergovernmental revenue	4 020 036	24.8	1 152.9	1 246.0
Taxes	9 508 645	58.6	2 726.9	1 891.6
General sales	3 065 486	18.9	879.1	636.0
Selective sales	1 725 384	10.6	494.8	307.4
License taxes	387 546	2.4	111.1	123.6
Individual income tax	3 639 362	22.4	1 043.7	626.8
Corporate income tax	344 684	2.1	98.8	97.8
Other taxes	346 183	2.1	99.3	99.9
Current charges	1 148 029	7.1	329.2	366.5
Miscellaneous general revenue	1 539 832	9.5	441.6	328.6
GENERAL EXPENDITURE	17 885 021	100.0	5 129.1	4 010.5
Intergovernmental expenditure	3 030 485	16.9	869.1	1 316.9
Direct expenditure	14 854 536	83.1	4 260.0	2 693.6
Expenditure by Function				
Education	4 794 156	26.8	1 374.9	1 416.4
Public welfare	3 785 383	21.2	1 085.6	1 083.3
Hospitals	1 431 533	8.0	410.5	132.3
Health	585 249	3.3	167.8	173.0
Highways	693 891	3.9	199.0	295.4
Police protection	169 501	0.9	48.6	38.4
Correction	615 670	3.4	176.6	135.0
Natural resources	138 336	0.8	39.7	64.0
Parks and recreation	105 931	0.6	30.4	20.1
Government administration	1 011 312	5.7	290.0	151.3
Interest on general debt	1 240 680	6.9	355.8	107.8
Other and unallocable	3 313 379	18.5	950.2	393.4
DEBT AT END OF FISCAL YEAR	22 490 115	X	6 449.7	2 404.7
CASH AND SECURITY HOLDINGS	31 424 546	X	9 011.9	8 938.4

X = Not applicable.

Table CT-18. Education Indicators, 2000–2004

(Percent, number.)

Item	State	U.S.
Total Population 25 Years and Over (Thousands), 2004	2 254	186 877
Educational Attainment, 2004		
Percent high school graduate or more	88.8	85.2
Percent college graduate or more	34.5	27.7
Elementary and Secondary Schools, 2002–2003		
Total students	570 023	48 202 324
Percent of students eligible for free or reduced-price lunch ..	25.4	40.6
Percent of students who were English language learners	4.5	7.8
Total schools	1 087	92 330
Student/teacher ratio	13.6	15.9
Per student expenditures	11 057	8 041
Dropouts, Grades 9–12, 2000–2001 (Percent)	2.6	. . .
Higher Education, 2002–2003		
Total enrollment	178 117	17 035 027
Bachelor's degrees awarded	16 034	1 348 503
Percent women	58.3	57.5

. . . = Not available.

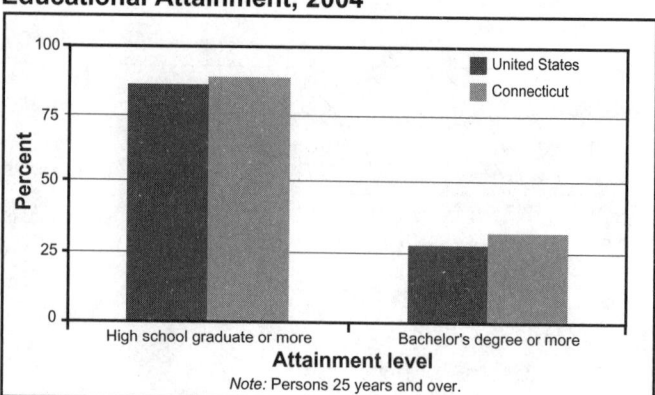

Educational Attainment, 2004

Note: Persons 25 years and over.

EDUCATION

The educational attainment levels of Connecticut's population were high compared to the rest of the country. The state ranked 13th for high school attainment, with more than 88 percent of residents having graduated from high school. More than 34 percent of the state's population age 25 years and over had earned a bachelor's degree or more. Connecticut's per student expenditures exceeded $11,000, ranking fourth in the United States. The state's student/teacher ratio of 13.6 was well below the U.S. average of 15.9. Connecticut had the second lowest proportion of students eligible for free or reduced-price lunch (25.4 percent).

VOTER PARTICIPATION

Voter participation rates were only slightly above the national average—55.2 percent of eligible voters voted in 2000 and 58.5 percent in 2004. According to the official tally by the Clerk of the U.S. House of Representatives, 55.9 percent voted for the Democratic presidential candidate in 2000; this percentage dropped to 54.3 percent in 2004. Less than 38 percent of eligible voters between the ages of 18 and 24 years voted in the 2004 election. Voting rates for people age 45 and over were close to 70 percent. Hispanics had low voter turnout, with just 33 percent of those eligible voting.

Table CT-19. Reported Voting and Registration, November 2000 and November 2004

(Numbers in thousands, percent.)

Characteristic	Total population 18 years and over	Total citizen		Total registered		Total voted	
		Number	Percent	Number	Percent	Number	Percent
NOVEMBER 2000							
Total	2 415	2 239	92.7	1 510	62.5	1 332	55.2
Male	1 146	1 054	92.0	682	59.5	605	52.8
Female	1 268	1 184	93.4	828	65.3	727	57.3
NOVEMBER 2004							
Total	2 606	2 409	92.5	1 695	65.0	1 524	58.5
Male	1 246	1 147	92.1	775	62.2	704	56.5
Female	1 359	1 262	92.8	919	67.6	820	60.3
Race and Hispanic Origin							
White alone	2 278	2 143	94.1	1 519	66.7	1 369	60.1
Non-Hispanic White alone	2 113	2 018	95.5	1 460	69.1	1 319	62.4
Black alone	233	207	88.8	135	57.9	117	50.2
Asian alone	75	39	B	28	B	26	B
Hispanic or Latino[1]	170	130	76.6	64	37.6	56	32.9
White alone or in combination	2 291	2 156	94.1	1 527	66.6	1 376	60.1
Non-Hispanic White alone or in combination	2 125	2 030	95.5	1 467	69.0	1 324	62.3
Black alone or in combination	237	211	89.0	138	58.2	120	50.7
Asian alone or in combination	75	39	B	28	B	26	B
Age							
18 to 24 years	301	278	92.1	135	44.6	114	37.9
25 to 44 years	944	819	86.8	525	55.6	460	48.7
45 to 64 years	892	855	95.9	673	75.4	623	69.8
65 to 74 years	196	189	96.3	149	75.9	138	70.4
75 years and over	273	269	98.7	214	78.5	189	69.4

[1]May be of any race.
B = Base is too small to show derived measure.

At a Glance:

- Delaware's population of 830,000 was among the smallest in the country.

- A high concentration of financial services and large chemical companies are headquartered in Delaware. Employment in 2004 was concentrated in private sector service-providing industries, primarily health care, finance and insurance, and professional and technical services.

- Immigration was the largest source of population gain, with the state experiencing an influx of over 9,600 new residents from other countries and 20,000 from other states between 2000 and 2004.

- Non-Hispanic Whites made up the largest proportion of residents, representing over 70 percent of the population in 2004; Blacks accounted for 26 percent of the population, which was the 9th highest proportion of this racial group in the country.

- Delaware had an above average median household income, ranking 15th in the nation. The state's poverty rate was correspondingly low, at 9.1 percent, compared with the U.S. rate of 12.7 percent.

- From 2001 to 2004, Delaware's gross state product increased by 12.5 percent, which was the 7th highest growth rate in the nation.

Table DE-1. Population by Sex and Age, 1990, 2000, and 2004

(Number, percent.)

Sex and age	1990	2000	2004	Percent distribution, 2004	Average annual percent change, 2000–2004
Total Population	666 168	783 600	830 364	X	1.5
Percent of total U.S. population	0.3	0.3	0.3	X	X
Sex					
Male	322 968	380 541	404 676	48.7	1.5
Female	343 200	403 059	425 688	51.3	1.4
Age					
Under 5 years	48 824	51 531	53 781	6.5	0.5
5 to 17 years	114 517	143 056	139 725	16.8	1.4
18 years and over	127 878	589 013	636 858	76.7	1.7
18 to 24 years	502 827	75 328	83 684	10.1	0.6
25 to 44 years	76 233	236 441	238 132	28.7	0.7
45 to 64 years	217 981	175 518	206 081	24.8	3.5
65 years and over	80 735	101 726	108 961	13.1	2.2
85 years and over	7 142	10 549	13 259	1.6	4.7
Median age (years)	32.7	36.0	37.4	X	X

X = Not applicable.

Average Annual Rate of Population Growth, 1980–2004

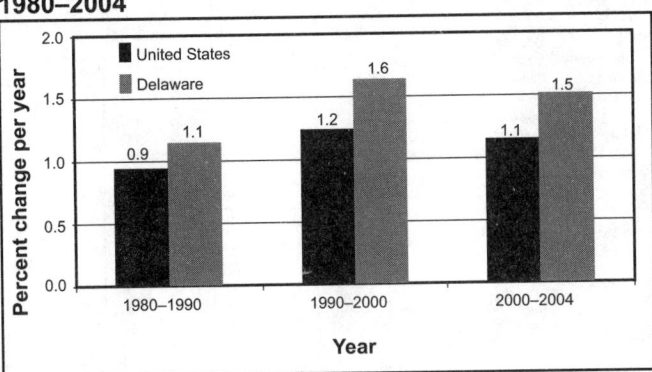

POPULATION

Delaware's population has increased steadily since 2000. Its growth rate of 6.0 percent from 2000 to 2004 was the 11th fastest in the nation. About 80 percent of Delaware's residents lived in Wilmington and Dover. The median age of the state's population was above average, as more than 13 percent of the state's residents were age 65 years and over. In 2004, 23.3 percent of the state's population was under 18 years old, compared with 25 percent nationally. Delaware had below average proportions of Hispanics (of any race), Asian and Pacific Islanders, and American Indians.

Table DE-2. Population by Race and Hispanic Origin, 1990, 2000, and 2004

(Number, percent.)

Race and Hispanic origin	1990	2000	2004
Total Population	666 168	783 600	830 364
Non-Hispanic (Percent)			
One race[1]			
White	79.3	72.7	70.2
Black	16.7	19.1	19.9
American Indian, Alaska Native[2]	0.3	0.3	0.3
Asian and Pacific Islander[2]	1.4	2.1	2.6
Other race[2]	1.1	. . .	. . .
Two or more races	. . .	1.0	1.2
Hispanic or Latino[3] (Percent)	2.4	4.8	5.8

[1]Individuals could report only one race in the 1990 census and could report one or more races on the 2000 census. Data on race in 2000 and 2004 are not comparable to 1990.
[2]Data for 1990 include people of Hispanic or Latino origin.
[3]May be of any race.
. . . = Not available.

Minority Population as a Percent of Total Population, 2004

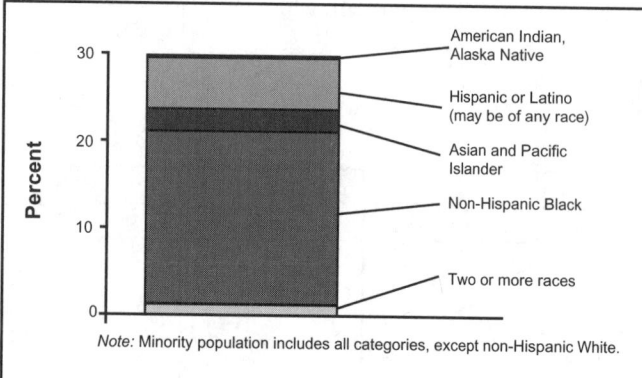

Note: Minority population includes all categories, except non-Hispanic White.

Age-Adjusted Death Rates, Average 2000–2002

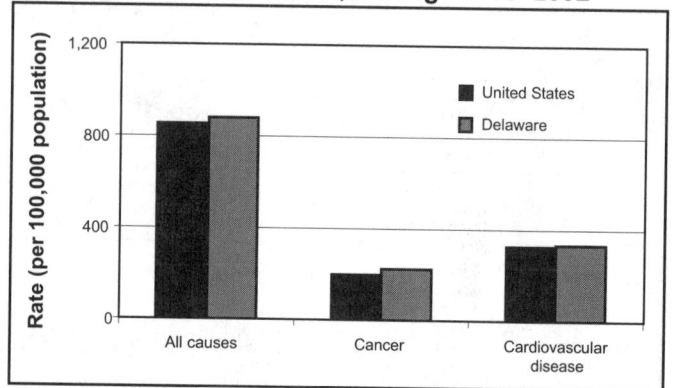

HEALTH

Delaware's health insurance coverage rate was above the national average in 2004. The state's infant mortality rate was the fourth highest in the nation. Delaware's birth rate was below average, but the birth rate for teenage mothers was higher than the U.S. average.

Table DE-3. Health Characteristics, 2000–2004

(Number, rate, percent.)

Item	State	U.S.
Births, 2003–2004		
Number of births	11 329	4 089 950
Birth rate (per 1,000 population)	13.9	14.1
Teenage birth rate (per 1,000 women age 15–19 years)	44.9	41.6
Mortality Rates, Average 2000–2002		
Infant mortality rate (per 1,000 live births)	9.6	6.9
Age-adjusted mortality rate (per 100,000 population)		
All races	872.2	853.3
Non-Hispanic White	843.7	843.1
Black	1 061.5	1 097.7
American Indian, Alaska Native	. . .	687.0
Asian and Pacific Islander	388.1	486.0
Hispanic or Latino[1]	707.1	642.7
Health Insurance, 2004		
Percent of all persons without health insurance	14.5	15.7
Percent of children without health insurance	12.6	11.2
Percent of low-income children without health insurance	7.4	7.1

[1]May be of any race.
. . . = Not available.

Table DE-4. Leading Causes of Death, Average 2000–2002

(Number, rate per 100,000 population.)

Cause	Number of deaths	Age-adjusted death rates	
		State	U.S.
ALL CAUSES	6 949	872.2	853.3
Leading Causes			
Major cardiovascular diseases	2 524	320.4	326.5
Cancer	1 672	204.9	196.0
Chronic lower respiratory diseases	332	41.5	43.7
Unintentional injuries	291	36.5	35.7
Diabetes (underlying cause)	209	25.8	25.2
Influenza and pneumonia	193	24.9	22.7
Alzheimer's disease	124	16.3	19.0
Motor vehicle accidents	121	15.0	15.0
Nephritis, nephrotic syndrome, and nephrosis ..	112	14.1	13.8
Septicemia	134	16.9	11.4
Suicides	88	10.9	10.7
Firearm-related	67	8.3	10.3
Cirrhosis	78	9.5	9.5
Drug-induced	71	8.8	7.9
Alcohol-induced	65	7.9	6.9
Homicides	31	3.9	6.0
Falls	35	4.5	5.2
HIV	68	8.4	5.0
Viral hepatitis	18	2.2	2.0
Anemias	10	1.2	1.6
Drownings	9	1.1	1.3
Fire deaths	12	1.5	1.2

Note: The rates are age-adjusted to the U.S. 2000 standard population.

Table DE-5. Households and Housing Characteristics, 1990, 2000, and 2004

(Number, percent, and dollars.)

Characteristic	1990	2000	2004	Average annual percent change, 2000–2004
Total Households	247 497	298 736	310 676	1.0
Family households	175 867	204 590	207 817	0.4
Married-couple family	137 983	153 136	151 402	-0.3
Other family	37 884	51 454	56 415	2.3
Male householder, no wife present	8 565	12 468	15 684	5.9
Female householder, no husband present	29 319	38 986	40 731	1.1
Nonfamily households	71 630	94 146	102 859	2.2
Householder living alone	57 451	74 639	80 694	2.0
Householder not living alone	14 179	19 507	22 165	3.2
Housing Characteristics				
Average size	2.61	2.54	2.59	X
Housing units	289 919	343 072	367 448	1.7
Occupied housing units	247 497	298 736	310 676	1.0
Owner-occupied	173 813	216 038	226 328	1.2
Renter-occupied	73 684	82 698	84 348	0.5
Median gross rent of renter-occupied housing units (dollars)	495	639	743	3.8
Median value of owner-occupied housing units (dollars)	99 700	130 400	171 589	7.1

X = Not applicable.

Median Housing Value and Median Rent, 2004

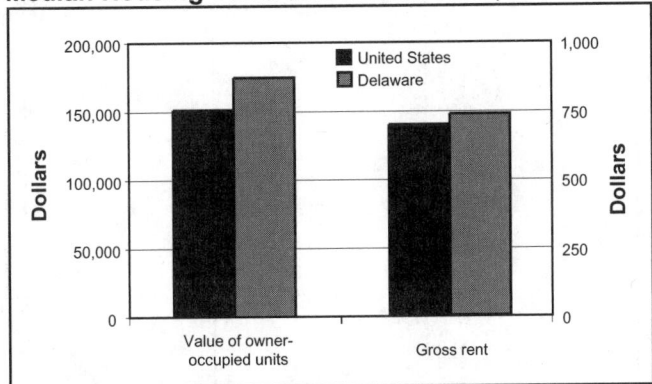

Median Household Income, 1984–2004 (2004 Dollars)

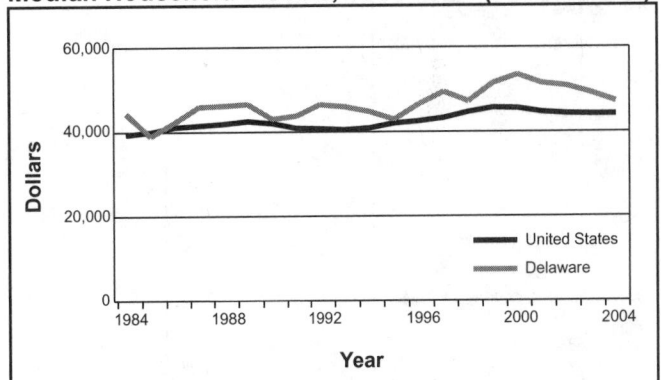

Table DE-6. Household Income and Poverty Status, 1980–2004

(2004 CPI-U-RS adjusted dollars, rate.)

Year	State		U.S.	
	Median household income (2004 dollars)	Poverty rate	Median household income (2004 dollars)	Poverty rate
2004	47 968	9.1	44 389	12.7
2003	50 336	7.3	44 482	12.5
2002	52 152	9.1	44 546	12.1
2001	52 931	6.7	45 062	11.7
2000	55 245	8.4	46 058	11.3
1999	52 853	10.4	46 129	11.9
1998	47 981	10.3	45 003	12.7
1997	50 505	9.6	43 430	13.3
1996	47 119	8.6	42 544	13.7
1995	42 992	10.3	41 943	13.8
1994	45 228	8.3	40 677	14.5
1993	46 426	10.2	40 217	15.1
1992	47 074	7.8	40 422	14.8
1991	44 071	7.5	40 746	14.2
1990	43 170	6.9	41 963	13.5
1989	47 176	10.0	42 524	12.8
1988	46 804	8.6	41 771	13.0
1987	46 503	6.6	41 322	13.4
1986	42 138	12.4	40 939	13.6
1985	38 477	11.4	39 545	14.0
1984	44 672	10.3	38 782	14.4
1983	. . .	8.6	. . .	15.2
1982	. . .	11.5	. . .	15.0
1981	. . .	12.3	. . .	14.0
1980	. . .	11.8	. . .	13.0

. . . = Not available.

Table DE-7. Employment Status by Demographic Group, 2004

(Numbers in thousands, rate.)

Characteristic	Civilian noninstitutional population	Civilian labor force		Employed	Unemployment rate
		Number	Participation rate		
SEX AND AGE					
Total	643	426	66.3	409	3.9
16 to 19 years	45	22	48.0	20	9.9
20 to 24 years	55	44	80.7	41	6.3
25 to 34 years	106	91	85.2	88	3.1
35 to 44 years	127	107	84.1	103	3.8
45 to 54 years	119	97	81.0	94	3.1
55 to 64 years	86	52	60.4	50	2.9
65 years and over	105	15	13.9	14	3.9
Men	306	220	72.0	212	3.9
16 to 19 years	21	10	47.0	9	10.9
20 to 24 years	28	24	84.1	22	6.1
25 to 34 years	53	49	92.2	47	4.0
35 to 44 years	60	54	89.5	52	3.3
45 to 54 years	57	51	88.0	49	2.8
55 to 64 years	40	26	65.8	26	2.0
Women	337	206	61.1	198	4.0
16 to 19 years	24	12	49.0	11	9.0
20 to 24 years	27	21	77.2	19	6.6
25 to 34 years	54	42	78.2	41	2.0
35 to 44 years	67	53	79.2	51	4.3
45 to 54 years	62	46	74.6	44	3.4
55 to 64 years	46	25	55.7	25	3.8
MARITAL STATUS					
Married men, spouse present	172	124	72.3	121	2.3
Married women, spouse present	168	102	60.4	99	2.4
Women who maintain families	41	29	71.4	28	6.4
RACE, HISPANIC ORIGIN, AND SEX					
White	506	333	65.9	322	3.5
Men	243	175	71.9	169	3.5
Women	262	158	60.4	153	3.5
Black	114	76	66.8	71	6.1
Men	51	36	70.2	34	5.8
Women	63	40	64.0	38	6.5
Asian	15	11	73.7	11	1.0
Hispanic or Latino[1]	36	26	73.7	25	5.5
Men	21	17	83.4	16	4.4
Women	15	9	60.6	8	7.5
RACE, HISPANIC ORIGIN, AND AGE					
White					
16 to 19 years	34	17	51.0	16	6.4
20 to 24 years	40	33	82.0	31	5.5
25 to 34 years	76	65	85.5	63	3.1
35 to 44 years	97	82	84.3	79	3.5
45 to 54 years	96	79	83.1	77	3.1
55 to 64 years	72	44	61.5	43	2.8
65 years and over	91	13	13.8	12	2.6
Black					
35 to 44 years	24	20	84.8	19	5.2
45 to 54 years	22	15	71.4	15	2.7

Note: Data in Table 7 are from the Current Population Survey (CPS) and do not match Bureau of Labor Statistics estimates in Table 8. See notes and definitions for more details.

[1]May be of any race.

Table DE-8. Employment Status, 1990–2004

(Numbers in thousands, rate.)

Year	Civilian labor force	Employed	Unemployed	Unemployment rate
2004	422 956	405 669	17 287	4.1
2003	420 415	403 759	16 656	4.0
2002	418 803	403 017	15 786	3.8
2001	419 773	405 111	14 662	3.5
2000	416 878	403 034	13 844	3.3
1999	401 139	387 808	13 331	3.3
1998	397 319	383 360	13 959	3.5
1997	393 493	378 117	15 376	3.9
1996	388 504	371 975	16 529	4.3
1995	383 034	366 200	16 834	4.4
1994	378 165	360 866	17 299	4.6
1993	371 718	353 156	18 562	5.0
1992	366 979	347 194	19 785	5.4
1991	363 321	342 525	20 796	5.7
1990	362 098	347 038	15 060	4.2

Note: Population age 16 years and over.

Unemployment Rate, 1980–2004

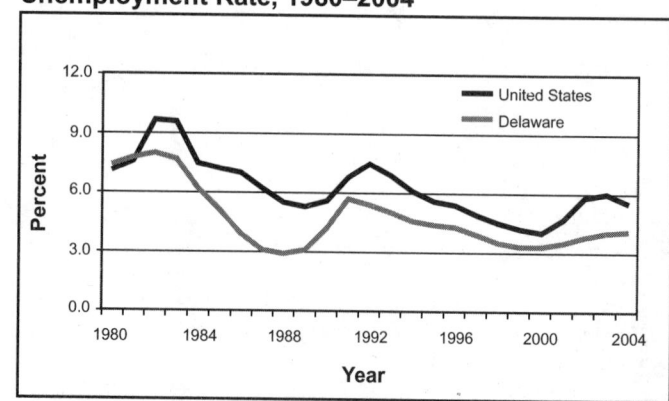

Table DE-9. Employment and Average Wages by Industry, 2001–2004

(Estimates are based on the 2002 North American Industry Classification System [NAICS].)

Industry	2001	2002	2003	2004	Annual average percent change, 2001–2004
	Number of jobs				
TOTAL EMPLOYMENT BY PLACE OF WORK	504 904	503 441	507 335	519 336	0.9
Farm Employment	4 282	4 146	3 770	3 744	-4.4
Nonfarm Employment	500 622	499 295	503 565	515 592	1.0
Private employment	433 619	431 964	436 018	447 905	1.1
Forestry, fishing, hunting, and other[1]	D	1 337	1 162	1 134	. . .
Mining	D	367	483	507	. . .
Utilities	2 283	2 213	2 202	2 199	-1.2
Construction	32 222	31 973	32 929	35 274	3.1
Manufacturing	40 245	37 845	36 448	35 566	-4.0
Durable goods manufacturing	17 732	16 661	14 917	14 861	-5.7
Nondurable goods manufacturing	22 513	21 184	21 531	20 705	-2.8
Wholesale trade	14 412	14 666	15 172	15 864	3.3
Retail trade	59 150	59 977	61 115	62 208	1.7
Transportation and warehousing	12 283	12 192	12 242	13 243	2.5
Information	8 954	8 463	8 135	7 822	-4.4
Finance and insurance	48 294	47 978	46 094	45 191	-2.2
Real estate and rental and leasing	15 217	15 429	16 397	17 344	4.5
Professional and technical services	36 073	34 296	35 076	36 491	0.4
Management of companies and enterprises	12 461	12 749	11 992	13 089	1.7
Administrative and waste services	29 565	26 669	26 443	27 591	-2.3
Educational services	7 345	7 804	8 133	8 466	4.8
Health care and social assistance	48 056	49 314	51 189	52 726	3.1
Arts, entertainment, and recreation	11 187	12 363	12 743	13 125	5.5
Accommodation and food services	30 467	30 895	31 458	32 995	2.7
Other services, except public administration	23 691	25 434	26 605	27 070	4.5
Government and government enterprises	67 003	67 331	67 547	67 687	0.3
	Dollars				
AVERAGE WAGES AND SALARIES BY PLACE OF WORK ...	37 502	38 720	40 037	41 597	3.5
Farm Earnings	18 544	23 714	23 594	26 035	12.0
Nonfarm Earnings	37 583	38 782	40 097	41 651	3.5
Private earnings	38 371	39 109	40 473	41 949	3.0
Forestry, fishing, hunting, and other[1]	D	15 688	16 877	17 436	. . .
Mining	D	38 588	43 301	43 808	. . .
Utilities	77 824	86 696	78 743	78 157	0.1
Construction	37 460	38 507	38 902	40 416	2.6
Manufacturing	43 864	44 547	50 030	50 409	4.7
Durable goods manufacturing	47 268	49 791	56 881	56 146	5.9
Nondurable goods manufacturing	41 209	40 453	45 332	46 331	4.0
Wholesale trade	52 302	53 180	58 348	62 081	5.9
Retail trade	21 694	22 394	23 066	23 962	3.4
Transportation and warehousing	34 217	33 533	33 844	36 026	1.7
Information	50 083	50 845	51 316	53 333	2.1
Finance and insurance	62 133	63 072	67 056	71 432	4.8
Real estate and rental and leasing	32 808	32 639	33 712	36 861	4.0
Professional and technical services	67 065	68 490	67 446	69 598	1.2
Management of companies and enterprises	64 471	67 130	68 247	66 138	0.9
Administrative and waste services	21 108	22 446	23 725	25 056	5.9
Educational services	25 790	26 618	27 825	29 933	5.1
Health care and social assistance	35 821	37 112	38 516	40 594	4.3
Arts, entertainment, and recreation	20 968	21 245	21 563	22 425	2.3
Accommodation and food services	14 803	15 181	15 305	15 908	2.4
Other services, except public administration	23 118	23 760	24 558	25 089	2.8
Government and government enterprises	33 218	37 004	38 051	39 997	6.4

Note: Average wages and salaries are a calculation by the editors of wage and salary disbursements divided by full- and part-time wage and salary employment. Data may not add to total or may appear as zero due to rounding.

[1] "Other" consists of the number of jobs held by U.S. residents employed by international organizations and foreign embassies and consulates in the United States.
D = Suppressed to avoid disclosure of data of individual companies.
. . . = Not available.

LABOR MARKET

Delaware's unemployment rate has declined since the 2001 recession, although both the civilian labor force participation rate and the employment/population ratio have decreased, suggesting a somewhat sluggish labor market. Employment in 2004 was concentrated in government, retail trade, health care, and finance and insurance. Manufacturing made up almost 7 percent of the state's employment; however, jobs in this sector experienced a significant decline during the 2001–2004 period. These losses were offset by gains in several service-providing sectors. Average wages and salaries were generally above the national average in 2004 and also increased more rapidly than average, particularly in wholesale trade, durable goods, manufacturing, administrative and waste services, and government.

Employment by Industry, 2004

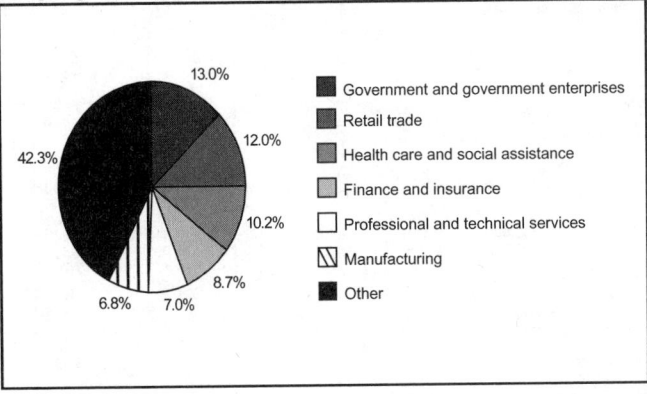

■	Government and government enterprises
▨	Retail trade
▨	Health care and social assistance
▨	Finance and insurance
□	Professional and technical services
▨	Manufacturing
■	Other

Table DE-10. Personal Income by Major Source, Selected Years 1980–2004

(Millions of dollars, except where noted.)

Item	1980	1990	2000	2001	2002	2003	2004	Average annual percent change, 2000–2004
Earnings by Place of Work	5 424	11 966	20 480	21 804	22 561	23 813	25 354	5.5
Wage and salary disbursements	4 177	9 077	15 779	16 508	16 870	17 456	18 519	4.1
Supplements to wages and salaries	890	1 917	3 134	3 240	3 708	4 048	4 267	8.0
Proprietors' income[1]	357	972	1 567	2 055	1 984	2 308	2 568	13.1
Farm proprietors' income	-8	113	82	144	67	149	195	24.2
Nonfarm proprietors' income[2]	365	859	1 485	1 911	1 917	2 160	2 373	12.4
(-) Contributions for government social insurance[2]	512	1 333	2 233	2 370	2 443	2 543	2 692	4.8
(+) Adjustment for residence[3]	-230	-678	-1 733	-1 833	-1 882	-1 977	-2 083	X
(=) Net Earnings by Place of Residence	4 682	9 954	16 514	17 601	18 237	19 293	20 579	5.7
(+) Dividends, interest, and rent[4]	1 018	2 948	4 705	4 600	4 659	4 531	4 842	0.7
(+) Personal current transfer receipts	694	1 442	3 058	3 337	3 613	3 849	4 106	7.6
Personal income	6 394	14 343	24 277	25 537	26 509	27 672	29 527	5.0
Farm income	6 383	14 206	24 157	25 356	26 398	27 484	29 289	4.9
Nonfarm income	11	138	120	181	112	188	238	18.7
Per Capita Personal Income (Dollars)[5]	10 748	21 422	30 869	32 097	32 886	33 822	35 559	3.6

Note: Data may not add to total or may appear as zero due to rounding.

[1]Proprietors' income includes the inventory valuation adjustment and the capital consumption adjustment.
[2]Contributions for government social insurance are included in earnings by type and industry, but they are excluded from personal income.
[3]The adjustment for residence is the net inflow of the earnings of interarea commuters.
[4]Rental income of persons includes the capital consumption adjustment.
[5]Per capita personal income is total personal income divided by total midyear population.
X = Not applicable.

Per Capita Personal Income, 1980–2004 (Current Dollars)

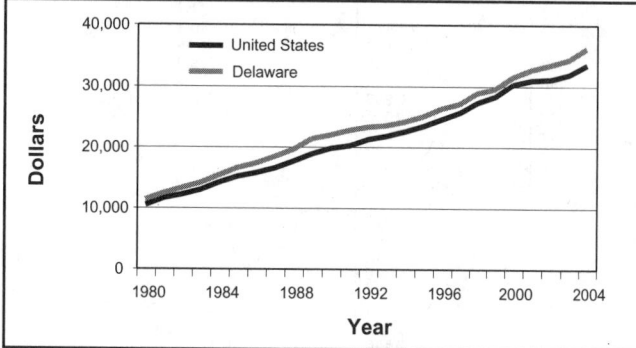

ECONOMIC ACTIVITY

Economic growth in Delaware seemed relatively immune to national trends over the 2001–2004 period, increasing at above average rates during that time. From 2003 to 2004, the gross state product (GSP) increased 5.0 percent. Much of this growth occurred in the finance and insurance, real estate, and retail trade sectors. The state's GSP ranked 39th in the nation in 2004. Housing prices played a lesser role than in other states in stimulating economic activity, as the growth was primarily along Delaware's coastline. In 2004, the median value of owner-occupied housing at $171,589 ranked 18th in the nation. This value increased by over 31 percent from 2000 to 2004.

Table DE-11. Real Gross State Product, 1997–2004

(Millions of chained 2000 dollars, percent.)

Industry	1997	1998	1999	2000	2001	2002	2003	2004	Average annual percent change, 2001–2004
GROSS STATE PRODUCT	38 274	38 945	41 104	42 359	43 802	44 545	46 952	49 288	4.0
As a percent of U.S. gross product	0.4	0.4	0.4	0.4	0.4	0.4	0.5	0.5	X
Private Industries	34 974	35 545	37 630	38 804	40 231	40 767	43 193	45 393	4.1
Agriculture, forestry, fishing, and hunting	163	198	212	230	242	155	193	271	3.8
Mining	6	6	7	7	9	8	8	8	-3.9
Utilities	599	599	648	661	735	816	837	839	4.5
Construction	1 481	1 460	1 540	1 417	1 406	1 403	1 400	1 497	2.1
Manufacturing	3 434	3 290	3 822	3 762	4 114	4 051	4 841	4 736	4.8
As a percent of gross state product	9.0	8.4	9.3	8.9	9.4	9.1	10.3	9.6	X
Wholesale trade	1 101	1 227	1 339	1 359	1 562	1 646	1 756	1 894	6.6
Retail trade	1 661	1 749	1 885	1 938	2 076	2 225	2 368	2 530	6.8
Transportation and warehousing	478	511	524	568	551	532	537	599	2.8
Information	591	668	782	794	822	869	923	1 007	7.0
Finance and insurance	12 424	12 195	12 727	13 376	13 276	14 150	15 232	15 937	6.3
Real estate and rental and leasing	5 148	5 430	5 767	5 855	6 006	5 347	5 302	5 828	-1.0
Services	7 954	8 240	8 374	8 839	9 455	9 574	9 847	10 277	2.8
As a percent of gross state product	20.8	21.2	20.4	20.9	21.6	21.5	21.0	20.9	X
Professional and technical services	2 343	2 543	2 607	2 737	2 829	2 846	2 849	2 989	1.9
Management of companies and enterprises	1 333	1 305	1 251	1 451	2 048	2 079	2 192	2 211	2.6
Administrative and waste services	777	799	875	831	748	722	756	806	2.5
Educational services	179	173	177	175	176	180	177	182	1.1
Health care and social assistance	1 816	1 871	1 875	1 982	2 036	2 108	2 207	2 312	4.3
Arts, entertainment, and recreation	229	223	236	247	260	290	292	307	5.7
Accommodation and food services	595	628	661	696	680	685	693	748	3.2
Other services, except public administration	682	698	692	720	678	664	681	722	2.1
Government	3 301	3 401	3 474	3 555	3 571	3 775	3 765	3 902	3.0
As a percent of gross state product	8.6	8.7	8.5	8.4	8.2	8.5	8.0	7.9	X

X = Not applicable.

Table DE-12. Government Transfer Payments, Selected Years 1980–2004

(Millions of dollars, percent.)

Item	1980	1990	2000	2001	2002	2003	2004	Average annual percent change, 2000–2004
CURRENT TRANSFER PAYMENTS TO INDIVIDUALS	650	1 341	2 857	3 116	3 406	3 661	3 915	8.2
Retirement and Disability Insurance Benefits	333	727	1 308	1 399	1 490	1 565	1 653	6.0
Old-age, survivors, and disability insurance (OASDI) benefits	314	691	1 269	1 358	1 447	1 519	1 606	6.1
Railroad retirement and disability benefits	15	23	26	26	27	28	28	2.3
Workers' compensation	2	9	10	10	11	11	12	4.1
Other government retirement and disability insurance benefits	2	5	4	5	5	7	7	16.1
Medical Benefits	135	412	1 170	1 302	1 416	1 544	1 721	10.1
Medicare benefits	88	268	612	681	736	784	869	9.2
Public assistance medical care benefits	45	136	547	606	661	743	831	11.0
Military medical insurance benefits	1	7	11	15	20	17	20	17.4
Income Maintenance Benefits	79	103	216	223	250	279	299	8.5
Supplemental Security Income (SSI) benefits	11	22	50	53	56	59	62	5.2
Family assistance	32	30	47	49	51	52	50	1.5
Food stamps	23	26	31	33	41	50	59	17.5
Other income maintenance benefits	13	24	88	88	102	118	129	10.1
Unemployment Insurance Compensation	59	41	70	90	142	160	116	13.6
Veterans' Benefits	34	40	67	71	76	82	88	7.0
Federal Education and Training Assistance	10	16	25	26	28	28	30	5.0
Other Payments to Individuals	*	2	2	4	3	4	8	35.6

Note: See notes and definitions for more details. Data may not add to total or may appear as zero due to rounding.

EXPORTS

Delaware was a relatively small exporter, ranking 43rd in the nation in 2004. The state's total exports climbed back over $2 billion in 2004, after a drop to less than $1.9 billion in 2003. By far, Delaware's largest export was chemical manufactures, which made up nearly 34 percent of total exports. Transportation equipment and computers and electronic products were also among the state's leading exports. Canada was Delaware's chief export market, followed by Germany (which increased its demand substantially in 2004) and Mexico (where the state's exports have continued to decline). Exports to Taiwan increased significantly from 2001 to 2004, making the country the fifth largest market for Delaware goods.

Leading Exports, 2004

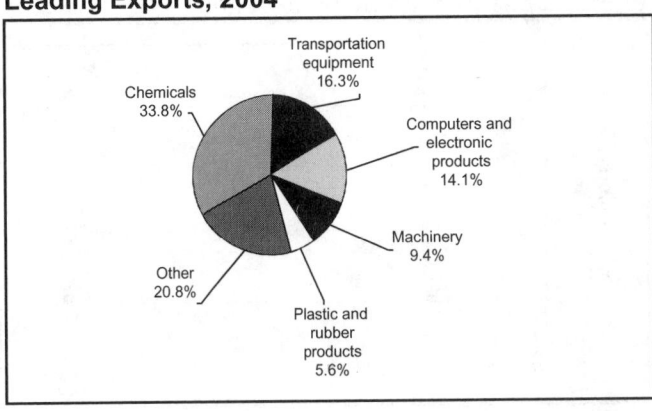

Table DE-13. Exports of Goods by Leading Products and Destinations, 2001–2004

(Millions of dollars, percent, rank based on 2004 dollar values.)

Product and market	2001	2002	2003	2004	Percent share of total, 2004	Average annual percent change, 2001–2004
Total Goods						
Total	1 985	2 004	1 886	2 053	100.0	1.1
Manufactures	1 893	1 897	1 742	1 928	93.9	0.6
Agriculture and livestock	76	79	85	112	5.4	13.8
Other commodities	16	27	59	14	0.7	-4.1
Five Leading Exports (NAICS Code)						
Chemical manufactures (325)	916	926	804	693	33.8	-8.9
Transportation equipment (336)	243	227	186	335	16.3	11.2
Computers and electronic products (334)	253	280	266	290	14.1	4.7
Machinery manufactures (333)	124	135	153	192	9.4	15.6
Plastic and rubber products (326)	99	83	94	116	5.6	5.3
Five Leading Markets	1 826	1 860	1 725	1 933	94.1	1.9
Canada	642	595	533	616	30.0	-1.4
Germany	138	122	149	263	12.8	24.0
Mexico	318	320	254	222	10.8	-11.2
Japan	105	103	104	128	6.2	6.7
Taiwan	59	70	78	96	4.7	17.6

Table DE-14. Agriculture, 1997 and 2002

(Number, acres, and dollars.)

Item	1997	2002
Number of farms	2 671	2 391
Land in farms (acres)	589 107	540 080
Farm Size		
Average size of farm (acres)	221	226
Farms by size (percent distribution)		
Fewer than 50 acres	50.2	52.3
50 to 499 acres	38.8	36.7
500 acres or more	11.0	11.0
Market Value of Land and Equipment (Dollars)		
Land and buildings average value per farm	576 420	980 323
Average value per acre	2 687	4 054
Machinery and equipment average value per farm	73 162	113 755
Value of Sales (Thousands of Dollars)		
Agricultural products sold	767 254	618 853
Crops	176 356	150 404
Livestock, poultry, and their products	590 898	468 449
Average per farm (dollars)	287 253	258 826
Value of sales (percent distribution)		
Less than $10,000	32.3	36.8
$10,000 to $99,999	24.5	20.3
$100,000 or more	43.2	42.8
Government Payments		
Payments (thousands of dollars)	3 845	8 643
Percent of farms receiving government payments	29.3	25.8
Farm operators whose principal occupation is farming (percent)	59.9	69.4

AGRICULTURE

Delaware's cash receipts were obtained largely from its sale of poultry and poultry products. In 2002, sales totaled $468 million—a considerable decline from the previous farm census in 1997. Over 42 percent of the state's farm operations were large, with cash receipts totaling $100,000 or more. Nearly 70 percent of farm operators reported farming as their principal occupation. This was considerably higher than the national average of 57.5 percent. More than half of farms in Delaware spanned fewer than 50 acres.

ENERGY

Energy prices in Delaware were slightly above the national average; the state ranked 18th overall. Delaware's per capita energy expenditures in 2001 were $2,495, which was also above average. Its per capita energy consumption of nearly 368 Btu ranked 21st in the nation. Industry, followed by transportation, were the largest consumers of energy. Delaware's primary source of energy was petroleum, which accounted for about half of the energy used in 2001.

Energy Consumption by Source, 2001

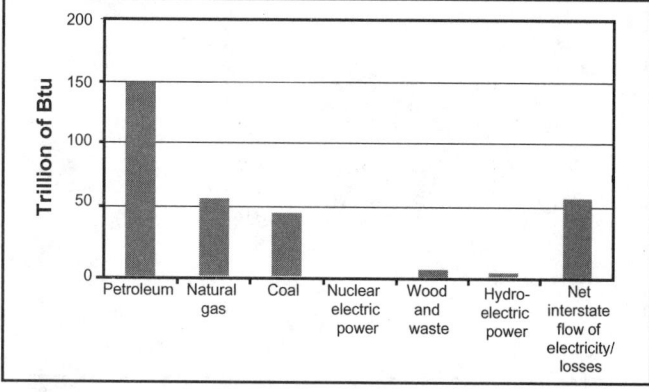

Energy Consumption by Sector, 2001

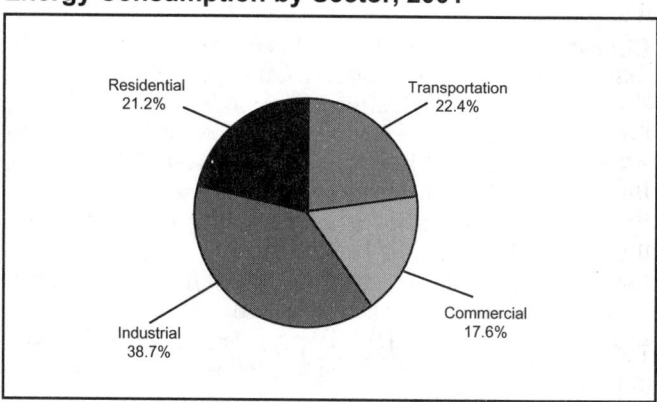

Table DE-15. Energy Consumption, Expenditures, and Prices, Selected Years 1960–2001

(Dollars, Btu [British Thermal Unit], percent distribution.)

Item	1960	1965	1970	1975	1980	1985	1990	1995	2000	2001
Total Consumption (Billion Btu)	156 624	184 596	219 939	220 628	250 198	218 717	252 127	272 882	306 634	292 494
Consumption per capita (million Btu)	351.2	364.1	401.3	376.1	421.0	353.8	378.5	379.9	391.3	367.6
Consumption by Sector (Percent Distribution)										
Residential	16.3	16.2	17.4	18.6	16.5	20.6	19.3	20.7	20.0	21.2
Commercial	13.2	13.7	13.4	14.0	20.8	12.0	14.0	15.2	18.1	17.6
Industrial	42.6	46.6	46.3	42.5	41.1	41.3	41.7	42.0	38.9	38.7
Transportation	27.9	23.5	22.9	25.0	21.6	26.0	25.0	22.0	23.0	22.4
Consumption by Source (Billion Btu)										
Coal	20 496	29 030	37 238	22 938	28 063	71 436	59 491	52 447	50 147	38 344
Natural gas	9 351	18 742	26 949	18 975	30 840	39 456	40 145	62 740	50 181	51 816
Petroleum	124 157	134 031	154 180	176 059	193 176	126 790	143 717	132 924	139 354	146 525
Nuclear electric power	0	0	0	0	0	0	0	0	0	0
Hydroelectric power[1]	0	0	0	0	0	0	0	0	0	0
Wood and waste	4 982	5 577	7 021	7 901	1 736	2 685	1 924	2 567	2 201	1 756
Other	0	0	0	0	0	0	83	95	107	115
Net interstate flow of electricity/losses[2]	-2 362	-2 785	-5 449	-5 245	-3 617	-21 650	6 766	22 109	64 643	53 937
Total Expenditures (Thousands of Dollars)	...	...	263 400	588 500	1 330 200	1 380 300	1 428 600	1 536 300	1 994 400	1 985 000
Expenditures per capita (dollars)	...	...	481	1 003	2 238	2 232	2 144	2 139	2 545	2 495
Prices by Sector (Dollars Per Million Btu)										
Total	...	...	1.70	3.90	7.37	9.10	8.65	8.90	10.36	11.11
Residential	...	...	2.37	5.10	10.07	12.21	13.30	13.98	15.23	16.01
Commercial	...	...	1.55	4.53	6.59	13.90	12.53	13.35	13.08	15.22
Industrial	...	...	1.02	3.16	5.89	6.65	5.14	4.96	6.11	7.39
Transportation	...	...	2.13	3.74	8.41	8.78	8.94	9.02	11.15	10.48

[1] A negative number in this row results from pumped storage for which, overall, more electricity is expended than created to provide electricity during peak demand periods.
[2] Net interstate flow of electricity is the difference between the amount of energy in the electricity sold within a state (including associated losses) and the energy input at the electric utilities within the state. A positive number indicates that more electricity (including associated losses) came into the state than went out of the state during the year; conversely, a negative number indicates that more electricity (including associated losses) went out of the state than came into the state.
... = Not available.

Table DE-16. State Taxes, Fiscal 2004

(Dollars, percent distribution.)

Item	Thousands of dollars	Percent distribution	Dollars per capita	
			State	U.S.
TOTAL TAXES	2 375 482	100.0	X	2 024.8
Property Taxes	X	X	X	38.9
Sales and Gross Receipts	383 383	16.1	461.9	1 003.4
Selective sales taxes	383 383	16.1	461.9	326.4
Alcoholic beverages	13 385	0.6	16.1	15.7
Insurance premiums	68 009	2.9	81.9	47.0
Motor fuels	112 435	4.7	135.5	114.6
Public utilities	35 536	1.5	42.8	39.2
Tobacco products	75 479	3.2	90.9	42.0
Other selective sales	78 351	3.3	94.4	49.8
Licenses	882 389	37.1	1 063.1	134.9
Corporation	568 190	23.9	684.6	21.6
Motor vehicle	33 592	1.4	40.5	59.4
Occupation and business, not elsewhere classified	220 992	9.3	266.3	37.1
Other licenses	53 334	2.2	64.3	2.6
Other Taxes	1 109 710	46.7	1 337.0	847.6
Individual income	781 212	32.9	941.2	673.6
Corporation net income	217 768	9.2	262.4	105.1
Documentary and stock transfer	98 556	4.1	118.7	27.1

GOVERNMENT FINANCE

Delaware's state revenues were just over $4.7 billion in 2004. This amounted to over $5,770 per person, the 3rd highest amount in the nation. The state's per capita expenditures of $5,350 were the 5th highest in the nation. The state's total taxes in fiscal year 2004 amounted to $2,862 per capita, which ranked 5th in the country. Taxes from licenses accounted for about 37 percent, or $1,063, which was nearly 8 times greater than the U.S. average. Individual income taxes and selective sales taxes were the other leading sources of tax revenue. Delaware had no sales or property taxes.

Per Capita State Taxes, Fiscal, 2004

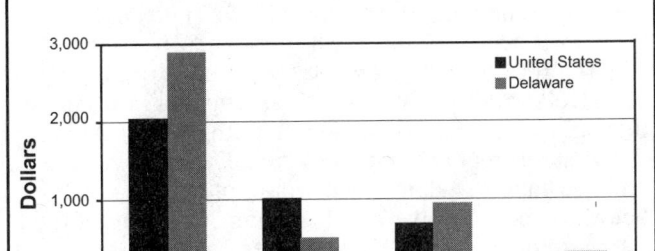

Table DE-17. State Government Finances, 2003

(Dollars, percent distribution.)

Item	Millions of dollars	Percent distribution	Dollars per capita	
			State	U.S.
GENERAL REVENUE	4 721 118	100.0	5 771.5	3 832.6
Intergovernmental revenue	994 952	21.1	1 216.3	1 246.0
Taxes	2 116 458	44.8	2 587.4	1 891.6
General sales	0	0.0	0.0	636.0
Selective sales	326 552	6.9	399.2	307.4
License taxes	755 354	16.0	923.4	123.6
Individual income tax	710 304	15.0	868.3	626.8
Corporate income tax	208 283	4.4	254.6	97.8
Other taxes	115 965	2.5	141.8	99.9
Current charges	684 528	14.5	836.8	366.5
Miscellaneous general revenue	925 180	19.6	1 131.0	328.6
GENERAL EXPENDITURE	4 376 306	100.0	5 350.0	4 010.5
Intergovernmental expenditure	903 476	20.6	1 104.5	1 316.9
Direct expenditure	3 472 830	79.4	4 245.5	2 693.6
Expenditure by Function				
Education	1 594 007	36.4	1 948.7	1 416.4
Public welfare	748 059	17.1	914.5	1 083.3
Hospitals	56 325	1.3	68.9	132.3
Health	282 530	6.5	345.4	173.0
Highways	345 859	7.9	422.8	295.4
Police protection	78 549	1.8	96.0	38.4
Correction	206 085	4.7	251.9	135.0
Natural resources	63 032	1.4	77.1	64.0
Parks and recreation	49 434	1.1	60.4	20.1
Government administration	308 943	7.1	377.7	151.3
Interest on general debt	253 383	5.8	309.8	107.8
Other and unallocable	390 100	8.9	476.9	393.4
DEBT AT END OF FISCAL YEAR	4 358 281	X	5 328.0	2 404.7
CASH AND SECURITY HOLDINGS	10 614 983	X	12 976.8	8 938.4

X = Not applicable.

Table DE-18. Education Indicators, 2000–2004

(Percent, number.)

Item	State	U.S.
Total Population 25 Years and Over (Thousands), 2004	536	186 877
Educational Attainment, 2004		
Percent high school graduate or more	86.5	85.2
Percent college graduate or more	26.9	27.7
Elementary and Secondary Schools, 2002–2003		
Total students	116 342	48 202 324
Percent of students eligible for free or reduced-price lunch ..	33.8	40.6
Percent of students who were English language learners	3.4	7.8
Total schools	201	92 330
Student/teacher ratio	15.2	15.9
Per student expenditures	9 693	8 041
Dropouts, Grades 9–12, 2000–2001 (Percent)	6.2	. . .
Higher Education, 2002–2003		
Total enrollment	49 927	17 035 027
Bachelor's degrees awarded	5 164	1 348 503
Percent women	62.3	57.5

. . . = Not available.

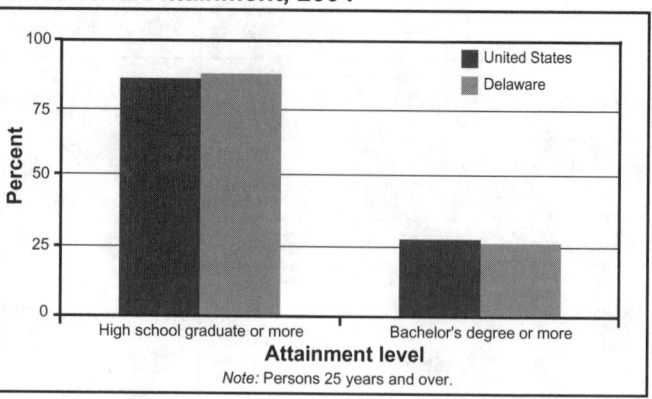

Educational Attainment, 2004

Note: Persons 25 years and over.

EDUCATION

Delaware had average educational attainment levels. In 2004, 86.5 percent of the population 25 years and over held high school diplomas. Just under 27 percent held a bachelor's degree or more, which ranked 21st in the country but was still below the U.S. average of 27.7 percent. Delaware's per student expenditures far exceeded the U.S. average and ranked ninth in the nation. Among the 46 states reporting dropout data, Delaware ranked 9th. The state's student/teacher ratio of 15.2 was slightly below the national average. Less than 34 percent of the state's students were eligible for free or reduced-price lunches, which was lower than the national average.

VOTER PARTICIPATION

Delaware had above average turnout rates in both the 2000 and 2004 elections. In 2004, nearly 63 percent of the state's eligible voters voted, which was the 19th highest proportion in the United States. However, the state ranked 31st for its proportion of registered voters, which was just 66.2 percent. According to the Clerk of the U.S. House of Representatives, 55.9 percent of those eligible voted for the Democratic presidential candidate in 2000 and 54.3 percent voted Democrat in 2004. More than 70 percent of eligible persons age 45 to 64 years voted in the 2004 election. Non-Hispanic Whites approached a 70 percent voter turnout rate.

Table DE-19. Reported Voting and Registration, November 2000 and November 2004

(Numbers in thousands, percent.)

Characteristic	Total population 18 years and over	Total citizen		Total registered		Total voted	
		Number	Percent	Number	Percent	Number	Percent
NOVEMBER 2000							
Total	567	543	95.9	385	67.9	352	62.2
Male	267	253	94.7	173	64.8	155	57.9
Female	299	290	96.9	211	70.6	197	66.0
NOVEMBER 2004							
Total	612	579	94.6	415	67.7	385	62.8
Male	292	272	93.4	189	64.9	174	59.6
Female	320	307	95.8	225	70.3	211	65.7
Race and Hispanic Origin							
White alone	485	462	95.3	344	70.9	322	66.4
Non-Hispanic White alone	445	441	99.0	333	74.8	311	69.9
Black alone	108	105	97.3	63	58.4	57	52.4
Asian alone	12	5	B	3	B	3	B
Hispanic or Latino[1]	44	24	B	13	B	12	B
White alone or in combination	488	464	95.1	346	70.9	323	66.2
Non-Hispanic White alone or in combination	447	443	99.0	335	74.9	312	69.9
Black alone or in combination	111	107	97.0	65	58.8	58	52.3
Asian alone or in combination	12	6	B	3	B	3	B
Age							
18 to 24 years	74	67	B	37	B	29	B
25 to 44 years	230	207	90.2	139	60.6	130	56.5
45 to 64 years	195	192	98.4	148	75.7	139	71.3
65 to 74 years	61	61	B	48	B	46	B
75 years and over	52	52	B	44	B	41	B

[1]May be of any race.
B = Base is too small to show derived measure.

At a Glance:

- The District of Columbia's population was over 553,000 in 2004. Only Wyoming had fewer residents. However, as the District of Columbia is a city, it is misleading to compare its population to the populations of the 50 states.

- Blacks made up 56.7 percent of the city's population, which was the highest proportion of this racial group in the nation. This proportion was also quite high when compared to the other large cities.

- The proportion of residents lacking health insurance was below the national average, partly reflecting the high number of federal government workers (almost all of whom had health insurance) residing in the city.

- Although surrounded by the wealthy suburbs of Maryland and Virginia, the District of Columbia's median household income was slightly below the national average. The city's poverty rate of 16.7 percent ranked fourth in the nation.

- The District of Columbia's unemployment rate of 8.2 percent was higher than those of all 50 states, as well as those of most major cities.

- The city had the highest proportion of college graduates in the nation, with 45.7 percent of its residents holding bachelor's degrees or more.

Table DC-1. Population by Sex and Age, 1990, 2000, and 2004

(Number, percent.)

Sex and age	1990	2000	2004	Percent distribution, 2004	Average annual percent change, 2000–2004
Total Population	606 900	572 059	553 523	X	-0.8
Percent of total U.S. population	0.2	0.2	0.2	X	X
Sex					
Male	282 970	269 366	261 730	47.3	-0.7
Female	323 930	302 693	291 793	52.7	-0.9
Age					
Under 5 years	37 351	32 536	35 029	6.3	-0.7
5 to 17 years	79 741	82 456	74 518	13.5	-0.5
18 years and over	112 931	457 067	443 976	80.2	-0.7
18 to 24 years	489 808	72 637	57 899	10.5	-2.6
25 to 44 years	82 558	189 439	190 838	34.5	-0.9
45 to 64 years	216 472	125 093	128 068	23.1	0.9
65 years and over	77 847	69 898	67 171	12.1	-1.0
85 years and over	7 847	8 975	9 288	1.7	1.5
Median age (years)	33.2	34.6	35.1	X	X

X = Not applicable.

Average Annual Rate of Population Growth, 1980–2004

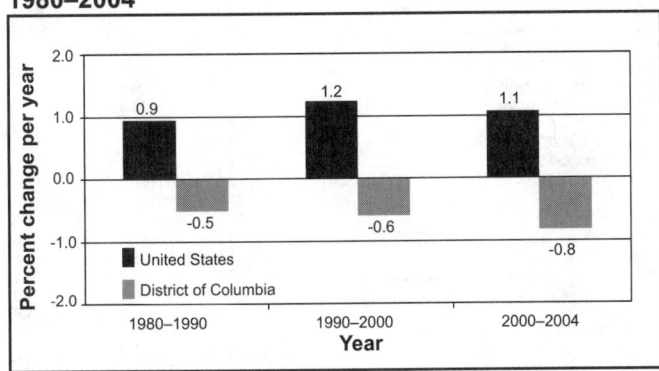

POPULATION

The District of Columbia is unique when compared to the 50 states. It is not a state, it does not have congressional representation, and its budget is largely determined by the U.S. Congress. The city's population, income, employment and earnings were largely influenced by trends in neighboring Maryland and Virginia. Between 2000 and 2004, the District of Columbia experienced a net decline in population of over 18,000 people, reflecting the migration of its residents to neighboring suburbs in Maryland and Virginia. Just 19.8 percent of the city's residents were 18 years old and under, a lower proportion than in any of the 50 states and among the lowest of the nation's major cities.

Table DC-2. Population by Race and Hispanic Origin, 1990, 2000, and 2004

(Number, percent.)

Race and Hispanic origin	1990	2000	2004
Total Population	606 900	572 059	553 523
Non-Hispanic (Percent)			
One race[1]			
White	27.4	28.2	30.3
Black	65.1	59.9	56.7
American Indian, Alaska Native[2]	0.2	0.2	0.2
Asian and Pacific Islander[2]	1.8	2.7	3.0
Other race[2]	2.5	. . .	. . .
Two or more races	. . .	1.1	1.3
Hispanic or Latino[3] (Percent)	5.4	7.9	8.5

[1]Individuals could report only one race in the 1990 census and could report one or more races on the 2000 census. Data on race in 2000 and 2004 are not comparable to 1990.
[2]Data for 1990 include people of Hispanic or Latino origin.
[3]May be of any race.
. . . = Not available.

Minority Population as a Percent of Total Population, 2004

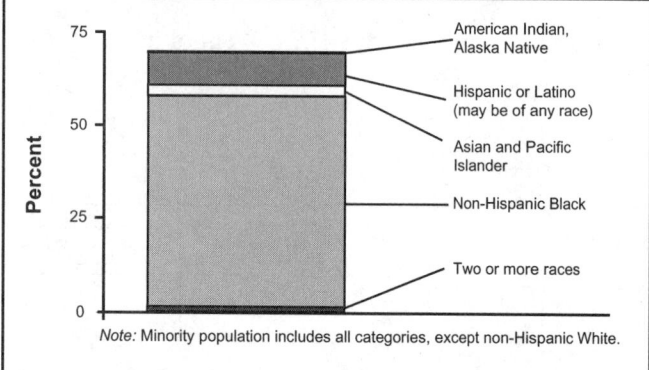

Note: Minority population includes all categories, except non-Hispanic White.

Age-Adjusted Death Rates, Average 2000–2002

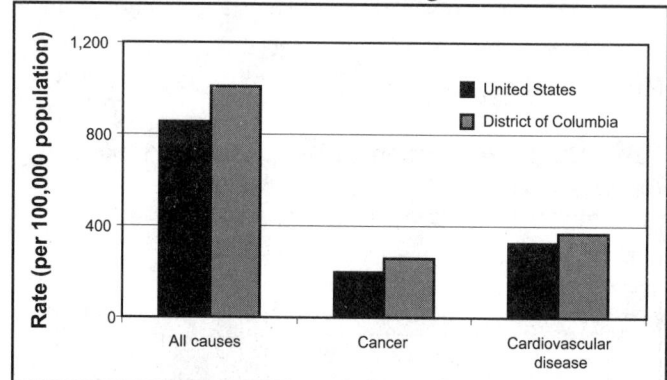

HEALTH

Although the proportion of the District of Columbia's population without health insurance was relatively low, coverage was not spread evenly across population groups. The city's infant mortality rate and age-adjusted death rates were the highest in the country. Its death rates due to homicide and HIV were particularly higher than the national averages.

Table DC-3. Health Characteristics, 2000–2004

(Number, rate, percent.)

Item	City	U.S.
Births, 2003–2004		
Number of births	7 619	4 089 950
Birth rate (per 1,000 population)	13.5	14.1
Teenage birth rate (per 1,000 women age 15–19 years)	60.3	41.6
Mortality Rates, Average 2000–2002		
Infant mortality rate (per 1,000 live births)	11.4	6.9
Age-adjusted mortality rate (per 100,000 population)		
All races	1 035.5	853.3
Non-Hispanic White	697.4	843.1
Black	1 258.3	1 097.7
American Indian, Alaska Native	. . .	687.0
Asian and Pacific Islander	520.4	486.0
Hispanic or Latino[1]	176.9	642.7
Health Insurance, 2004		
Percent of all persons without health insurance	13.3	15.7
Percent of children without health insurance	7.6	11.2
Percent of low-income children without health insurance	5.2	7.1

[1]May be of any race.
. . . = Not available.

Table DC-4. Leading Causes of Death, Average 2000–2002

(Number, rate per 100,000 population.)

Cause	Number of deaths	Age-adjusted death rates	
		City	U.S.
ALL CAUSES	5 934	1 035.5	853.3
Leading Causes			
Major cardiovascular diseases	2 106	368.8	326.5
Cancer	1 320	233.8	196.0
Chronic lower respiratory diseases	153	27.1	43.7
Unintentional injuries	209	36.0	35.7
Diabetes (underlying cause)	207	36.6	25.2
Influenza and pneumonia	93	16.2	22.7
Alzheimer's disease	94	16.1	19.0
Motor vehicle accidents	56	9.3	15.0
Nephritis, nephrotic syndrome, and nephrosis ..	78	13.6	13.8
Septicemia	117	20.6	11.4
Suicides	31	5.2	10.7
Firearm-related	171	26.8	10.3
Cirrhosis	69	12.2	9.5
Drug-induced	88	15.3	7.9
Alcohol-induced	112	19.3	6.9
Homicides	198	31.5	6.0
Falls	38	6.6	5.2
HIV	237	40.8	5.0
Viral hepatitis .:....................................	23	4.1	2.0
Anemias	13	2.2	1.6
Drownings	*	*	1.3
Fire deaths	8	1.4	1.2

Note: The rates are age-adjusted to the U.S. 2000 standard population.

* = Unreliable data.

Table DC-5. Households and Housing Characteristics, 1990, 2000, and 2004

(Number, percent, and dollars.)

Characteristic	1990	2000	2004	Average annual percent change, 2000–2004
Total Households	249 634	248 338	248 563	0.0
Family households	122 087	114 166	109 819	-1.0
Married-couple family	63 110	56 631	54 218	-1.1
Other family	58 977	57 535	55 601	-0.9
Male householder, no wife present	10 402	10 503	10 687	0.4
Female householder, no husband present	48 575	47 032	44 914	-1.1
Nonfamily households	127 547	134 172	138 744	0.8
Householder living alone	103 626	108 744	115 514	1.5
Householder not living alone	23 921	25 428	23 230	-2.2
Housing Characteristics				
Average size	2.26	2.16	2.08	X
Housing units	278 489	274 845	276 600	0.2
Occupied housing units	249 634	248 338	248 563	0.0
Owner-occupied	97 108	101 214	108 437	1.7
Renter-occupied	152 526	147 124	140 126	-1.2
Median gross rent of renter-occupied housing units (dollars)	479	618	799	6.6
Median value of owner-occupied housing units (dollars)	121 700	157 200	334 702	20.8

X = Not applicable.

Median Housing Value and Median Rent, 2004

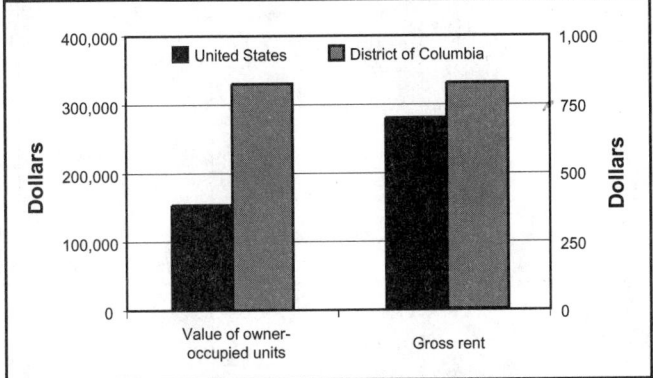

Median Household Income, 1984–2004 (2004 Dollars)

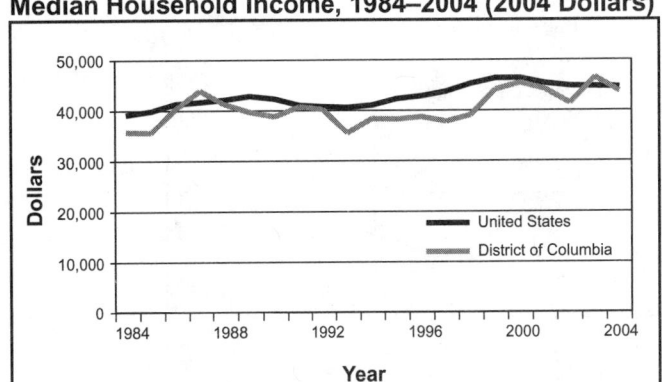

Table DC-6. Household Income and Poverty Status, 1980–2004

(2004 CPI-U-RS adjusted dollars, rate.)

Year	City Median household income (2004 dollars)	City Poverty rate	U.S. Median household income (2004 dollars)	U.S. Poverty rate
2004	43 426	16.7	44 389	12.7
2003	46 255	16.8	44 482	12.5
2002	41 039	17.0	44 546	12.1
2001	43 932	18.2	45 062	11.7
2000	45 216	15.2	46 058	11.3
1999	43 832	14.7	46 129	11.9
1998	38 693	22.3	45 003	12.7
1997	37 392	21.8	43 430	13.3
1996	38 317	24.1	42 544	13.7
1995	37 847	22.2	41 943	13.8
1994	37 969	21.2	40 677	14.5
1993	35 149	26.4	40 217	15.1
1992	39 909	20.3	40 422	14.8
1991	40 420	18.6	40 746	14.2
1990	38 388	21.1	41 963	13.5
1989	39 355	18.0	42 524	12.8
1988	41 029	15.2	41 771	13.0
1987	43 658	14.9	41 322	13.4
1986	39 994	12.8	40 939	13.6
1985	35 289	20.4	39 545	14.0
1984	35 310	21.1	38 782	14.4
1983	. . .	21.5	. . .	15.2
1982	. . .	19.3	. . .	15.0
1981	. . .	18.1	. . .	14.0
1980	. . .	20.9	. . .	13.0

. . . = Not available.

Table DC-7. Employment Status by Demographic Group, 2004

(Numbers in thousands, rate.)

Characteristic	Civilian noninstitutional population	Civilian labor force		Employed	Unemployment rate
		Number	Participation rate		
SEX AND AGE					
Total	443	299	67.6	275	8.2
16 to 19 years	24	7	28.6	5	30.4
20 to 24 years	42	30	71.5	25	18.3
25 to 34 years	100	85	85.1	79	7.5
35 to 44 years	88	74	84.0	69	6.8
45 to 54 years	67	54	80.1	50	7.2
55 to 64 years	58	40	68.0	39	2.9
65 years and over	63	9	14.9	9	6.4
Men	203	150	73.9	136	9.0
16 to 19 years	11	3	30.5	2	31.8
20 to 24 years	20	15	76.0	12	23.5
25 to 34 years	46	41	89.6	38	8.0
35 to 44 years	43	38	88.5	35	6.3
45 to 54 years	33	27	83.3	25	7.4
55 to 64 years	26	19	73.3	19	3.6
65 years and over	24	6	23.3	5	9.1
Women	240	149	62.3	138	7.4
16 to 19 years	12	3	26.9	2	28.9
20 to 24 years	22	15	67.5	13	13.0
25 to 34 years	54	44	81.3	41	7.0
35 to 44 years	46	36	79.7	34	7.4
45 to 54 years	34	26	76.9	24	6.9
55 to 64 years	32	20	63.7	20	2.3
65 years and over	39	4	9.8	4	2.5
MARITAL STATUS					
Married men, spouse present	63	48	76.4	46	4.2
Married women, spouse present	64	42	66.0	40	4.9
Women who maintain families	42	25	58.5	22	10.1
RACE, HISPANIC ORIGIN, AND SEX					
White	177	140	79.1	135	3.5
Men	88	74	84.6	72	3.2
Women	89	65	73.8	63	3.8
Black	247	147	59.5	128	13.0
Men	107	70	65.3	59	15.6
Women	139	77	55.1	69	10.5
Hispanic or Latino[1]	36	28	76.4	26	7.4
Men	18	15	82.7	13	9.7
Women	18	13	70.2	12	4.9
RACE, HISPANIC ORIGIN, AND AGE					
White					
25 to 34 years	55	49	90.3	48	2.7
35 to 44 years	34	31	91.6	30	2.4
45 to 54 years	22	20	91.2	19	4.3
55 to 64 years	23	19	79.0	18	1.3
Black					
25 to 34 years	40	31	79.0	27	15.5
35 to 44 years	51	41	79.9	37	10.3
45 to 54 years	43	32	74.1	29	9.4
65 years and over	42	5	11.4	5	3.2

Note: Data in Table 7 are from the Current Population Survey (CPS) and do not match Bureau of Labor Statistics estimates in Table 8. See notes and definitions for more details.

[1]May be of any race.

Table DC-8. Employment Status, 1990–2004

(Numbers in thousands, rate.)

Year	Civilian labor force	Employed	Unemployed	Unemployment rate
2004	298 958	274 465	24 493	8.2
2003	297 906	276 595	21 311	7.2
2002	300 605	280 302	20 303	6.8
2001	306 561	287 552	19 009	6.2
2000	309 496	291 833	17 663	5.7
1999	308 085	288 016	20 069	6.5
1998	293 820	270 242	23 578	8.0
1997	286 548	262 789	23 759	8.3
1996	290 498	265 734	24 764	8.5
1995	299 491	273 764	25 727	8.6
1994	310 099	285 207	24 892	8.0
1993	314 299	287 731	26 568	8.5
1992	317 326	290 103	27 223	8.6
1991	322 584	297 828	24 756	7.7
1990	331 700	311 838	19 862	6.0

Note: Population age 16 years and over.

Unemployment Rate, 1980–2004

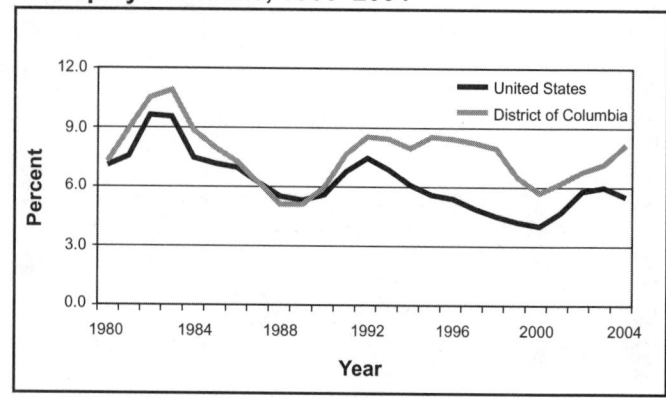

Table DC-9. Employment and Average Wages by Industry, 2001–2004

(Estimates are based on the 2002 North American Industry Classification System [NAICS].)

Industry	2001	2002	2003	2004	Annual average percent change, 2001–2004
			Number of jobs		
TOTAL EMPLOYMENT BY PLACE OF WORK	759 933	773 834	777 086	782 509	1.0
Farm Employment	0	0	0	0	X
Nonfarm Employment	759 933	773 834	777 086	782 509	1.0
Private employment	514 524	522 883	525 137	531 467	1.1
Forestry, fishing, hunting, and other[1]	D	D	9 853	9 853	. . .
Mining	D	D	568	578	. . .
Utilities	D	D	2 624	2 555	. . .
Construction	13 680	14 493	15 322	14 602	2.2
Manufacturing	3 874	D	2 943	2 803	-10.2
Durable goods manufacturing	1 526	D	1 087	1 002	-13.1
Nondurable goods manufacturing	2 348	D	1 856	1 801	-8.5
Wholesale trade	4 787	4 677	4 961	5 041	1.7
Retail trade	20 261	20 291	20 387	20 701	0.7
Transportation and warehousing	D	D	7 823	7 614	. . .
Information	D	27 884	27 161	26 364	. . .
Finance and insurance	21 668	21 516	21 124	20 650	-1.6
Real estate and rental and leasing	17 138	17 171	17 790	18 344	2.3
Professional and technical services	114 029	116 867	117 962	120 466	1.8
Management of companies and enterprises	2 559	2 494	1 738	1 574	-15.0
Administrative and waste services	45 721	45 699	46 885	46 716	0.7
Educational services	42 720	43 775	44 679	46 633	3.0
Health care and social assistance	56 885	60 724	59 061	58 999	1.2
Arts, entertainment, and recreation	10 290	10 760	11 069	11 027	2.3
Accommodation and food services	D	44 649	46 269	47 850	. . .
Other services, except public administration	64 956	67 963	66 918	69 097	2.1
Government and government enterprises	245 409	250 951	251 949	251 042	0.8
			Dollars		
AVERAGE WAGES AND SALARIES BY PLACE OF WORK	55 379	57 394	59 858	63 685	4.8
Farm Earnings	0	0	0	0	X
Nonfarm Earnings	55 379	57 394	59 858	63 685	4.8
Private earnings	53 257	54 338	56 349	59 831	4.0
Forestry, fishing, hunting, and other[1]	D	D	106 203	107 452	. . .
Mining	D	D	159 022	142 233	. . .
Utilities	D	D	68 114	72 318	. . .
Construction	43 417	45 886	46 471	48 780	4.0
Manufacturing	63 161	D	64 952	73 701	5.3
Durable goods manufacturing	73 697	D	83 689	103 187	11.9
Nondurable goods manufacturing	56 450	D	54 129	57 657	0.7
Wholesale trade	63 317	64 661	72 021	75 820	6.2
Retail trade	25 659	26 257	26 699	27 918	2.9
Transportation and warehousing	D	D	46 570	47 992	. . .
Information	D	75 754	78 905	84 534	. . .
Finance and insurance	97 394	94 982	99 043	111 492	4.6
Real estate and rental and leasing	46 074	47 565	51 264	57 105	7.4
Professional and technical services	82 229	84 246	86 935	93 024	4.2
Management of companies and enterprises	131 568	129 441	130 058	144 548	3.2
Administrative and waste services	28 218	29 161	30 470	32 988	5.3
Educational services	33 034	35 444	37 382	37 750	4.5
Health care and social assistance	40 272	40 515	44 048	47 145	5.4
Arts, entertainment, and recreation	49 575	45 779	42 965	41 284	-5.9
Accommodation and food services	D	24 421	25 235	26 536	. . .
Other services, except public administration	47 662	49 644	52 431	55 057	4.9
Government and government enterprises	59 357	63 062	66 334	70 888	6.1

Note: Average wages and salaries are a calculation by the editors of wage and salary disbursements divided by full- and part-time wage and salary employment. Data may not add to total or may appear as zero due to rounding.

[1] "Other" consists of the number of jobs held by U.S. residents employed by international organizations and foreign embassies and consulates in the United States.
D = Suppressed to avoid disclosure of data of individual companies.
X = Not applicable.
. . . = Not available.

LABOR MARKET

The District of Columbia had the highest unemployment rate in 2004, but experienced a sizable increase in jobs from 2000 to 2004. Both the labor force participation rate and the employment/population ratio were relatively low, suggesting an under performing labor market. Government was by far the largest employment sector in 2004, accounting for 33 percent of total employment. Professional and technical services was the second largest employment sector, and educational services had the highest growth rate from 2001 to 2004. The District of Columbia's average wages and salaries were the highest in the nation and experienced the highest rate of growth from 2001 to 2004.

Employment by Industry, 2004

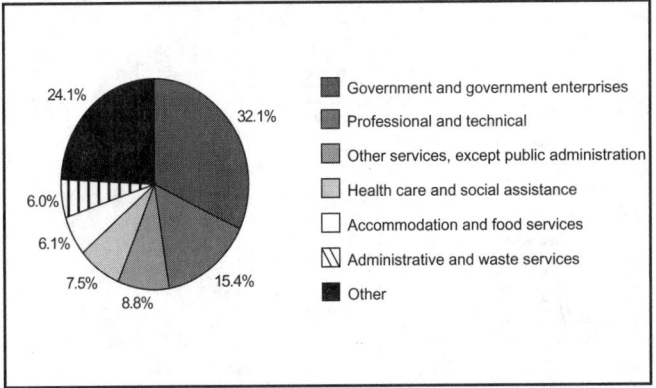

Table DC-10. Personal Income by Major Source, Selected Years 1980–2004

(Millions of dollars, except where noted.)

Item	1980	1990	2000	2001	2002	2003	2004	Average annual percent change, 2000–2004
Earnings by Place of Work	16 125	32 860	48 999	52 256	55 075	57 333	61 908	6.0
Wage and salary disbursements	12 471	24 905	37 046	39 052	41 116	42 921	45 863	5.5
Supplements to wages and salaries	2 910	6 391	9 228	10 160	10 933	11 280	12 612	8.1
Proprietors' income[1]	744	1 564	2 725	3 044	3 026	3 132	3 433	5.9
Farm proprietors' income	0	0	0	0	0	0	0	X
Nonfarm proprietors' income	744	1 564	2 725	3 044	3 026	3 132	3 433	5.9
(-) Contributions for government social insurance[2]	859	2 813	4 493	4 921	5 260	5 481	5 776	6.5
(+) Adjustment for residence[3]	-9 728	-19 150	-28 346	-28 871	-31 030	-32 226	-34 782	5.2
(=) Net Earnings by Place of Residence	5 538	10 897	16 160	18 465	18 786	19 626	21 350	7.2
(+) Dividends, interest, and rent[4]	1 283	3 393	4 124	4 094	3 859	3 936	4 041	-0.5
(+) Personal current transfer receipts	1 025	1 734	2 818	2 966	3 292	3 360	3 448	5.2
Personal income	7 845	16 025	23 102	25 525	25 937	26 922	28 839	5.7
Farm income	7 845	16 025	23 102	25 525	25 937	26 922	28 839	5.7
Nonfarm income	0	0	0	0	0	0	0	X
Per Capita Personal Income (Dollars)[5]	12 291	26 473	40 456	44 827	45 935	48 280	52 101	6.5

Note: Data may not add to total or may appear as zero due to rounding.

[1]Proprietors' income includes the inventory valuation adjustment and the capital consumption adjustment.
[2]Contributions for government social insurance are included in earnings by type and industry, but they are excluded from personal income.
[3]The adjustment for residence is the net inflow of the earnings of interarea commuters.
[4]Rental income of persons includes the capital consumption adjustment.
[5]Per capita personal income is total personal income divided by total midyear population.
X = Not applicable.

Per Capita Personal Income, 1980–2004 (Current Dollars)

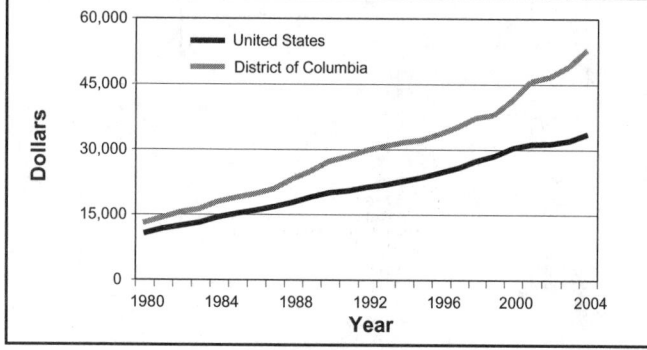

ECONOMIC ACTIVITY

Despite the 2001 recession, the city's gross state product (GSP) had an above average rate of growth during the 2001–2004 period, partly due to increased in federal spending. Over the 2003–2004 period, the GSP grew by 6.2 percent, increasing more quickly than the national average rate of 4.3 percent. The government sector was the leading contributor to the GSP, followed by professional and technical services. The median value of the city's owner-occupied housing totaled $334,702, the third highest amount in the nation in 2004. This represented an increase of over 112 percent from its 2000 level. This may have been one factor behind the city's population loss, as people sought more affordable housing in the areas outside the District of Columbia.

Table DC-11. Real Gross State Product, 1997–2004

(Millions of chained 2000 dollars, percent.)

Industry	1997	1998	1999	2000	2001	2002	2003	2004	Average annual percent change, 2001–2004
GROSS STATE PRODUCT	54 686	55 204	58 012	58 425	61 087	62 582	64 137	68 129	3.7
As a percent of U.S. gross product	0.6	0.6	0.6	0.6	0.6	0.6	0.6	0.6	X
Private Industries	33 277	34 531	37 023	38 167	39 603	40 468	42 035	44 680	4.1
Agriculture, forestry, fishing, and hunting	0	0	0	0	0	0	0	2	X
Mining	30	35	27	17	18	20	11	8	-23.7
Utilities	394	391	410	540	505	521	592	618	7.0
Construction	570	573	537	574	589	639	655	616	1.5
Manufacturing	206	297	233	215	219	199	201	221	0.3
As a percent of gross state product	0.4	0.5	0.4	0.4	0.4	0.3	0.3	0.3	X
Wholesale trade	530	578	630	614	628	634	686	712	4.3
Retail trade	846	867	899	904	923	953	998	1 072	5.1
Transportation and warehousing	420	384	460	522	484	453	463	448	-2.5
Information	3 367	3 025	3 946	3 544	3 999	4 325	4 675	5 175	9.0
Finance and insurance	2 395	2 631	2 947	2 968	3 331	3 313	3 614	4 016	6.4
Real estate and rental and leasing	4 321	4 491	4 697	4 727	4 812	4 874	5 126	5 386	3.8
Services	20 227	21 312	22 230	23 534	24 105	24 562	25 077	26 525	3.2
As a percent of gross state product	37.0	38.6	38.3	40.3	39.5	39.2	39.1	38.9	X
Professional and technical services	9 279	10 037	10 798	11 552	12 008	12 375	12 733	13 542	4.1
Management of companies and enterprises	333	386	361	447	508	505	430	411	-6.8
Administrative and waste services	1 418	1 517	1 424	1 442	1 541	1 607	1 735	1 809	5.5
Educational services	1 554	1 704	1 708	1 610	1 494	1 477	1 475	1 453	-0.9
Health care and social assistance	2 428	2 404	2 440	2 546	2 730	2 821	2 867	2 949	2.6
Arts, entertainment, and recreation	211	251	308	373	401	392	375	350	-4.4
Accommodation and food services	1 647	1 543	1 629	1 926	1 789	1 779	1 861	2 009	3.9
Other services, except public administration	3 357	3 470	3 562	3 638	3 634	3 606	3 601	4 002	3.3
Government	21 456	20 698	20 997	20 258	21 486	22 115	22 118	23 451	3.0
As a percent of gross state product	39.2	37.5	36.2	34.7	35.2	35.3	34.5	34.4	X

X = Not applicable.

Table DC-12. Government Transfer Payments, Selected Years 1980–2004

(Millions of dollars, percent.)

Item	1980	1990	2000	2001	2002	2003	2004	Average annual percent change, 2000–2004
CURRENT TRANSFER PAYMENTS TO INDIVIDUALS	985	1 665	2 709	2 845	3 190	3 271	3 362	5.5
Retirement and Disability Insurance Benefits	292	466	609	634	657	663	683	2.9
Old-age, survivors, and disability insurance (OASDI) benefits	269	430	579	603	624	633	651	3.0
Railroad retirement and disability benefits	14	15	12	12	12	11	12	-0.8
Workers' compensation	9	20	17	17	19	18	18	1.5
Other government retirement and disability insurance benefits	1	1	1	1	1	1	1	7.6
Medical Benefits	322	777	1 502	1 581	1 743	1 837	1 893	5.9
Medicare benefits	152	339	578	633	669	697	752	6.8
Public assistance medical care benefits	164	430	913	931	1 050	1 120	1 118	5.2
Military medical insurance benefits	7	8	11	17	24	20	22	18.3
Income Maintenance Benefits	208	244	426	426	469	477	500	4.1
Supplemental Security Income (SSI) benefits	31	55	93	98	102	105	110	4.2
Family assistance	93	87	110	119	129	119	120	2.2
Food stamps	41	45	75	71	77	95	97	6.8
Other income maintenance benefits	43	58	148	138	161	157	173	4.0
Unemployment Insurance Compensation	80	89	63	74	160	117	73	3.7
Veterans' Benefits	56	58	60	71	102	115	130	21.0
Federal Education and Training Assistance	26	29	42	51	53	49	52	5.2
Other Payments to Individuals	-	1	5	9	7	13	32	55.6

Note: See notes and definitions for more details. Data may not add to total or may appear as zero due to rounding.

* = Less than $500,000.

EXPORTS

In 2004, the District of Columbia's exports were valued at more than $1.1 billion, ranking 46th in the nation. Exports increased by 12.6 percent between 2001 and 2004, which was a rate of growth slightly above the national average. As a city, the District of Columbia is not directly comparable to the states, because data reflect origin of movement rather than product origin (see notes and definitions for more information). Transportation equipment accounted for over half of the city's exports. Most of the export data reported for the District of Columbia reflected the city as a site where export contracts were finalized

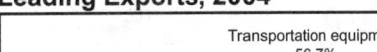

Leading Exports, 2004

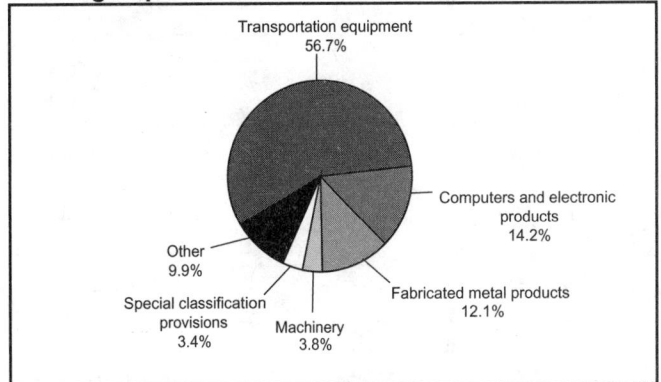

Table DC-13. Exports of Goods by Leading Products and Destinations, 2001–2004

(Millions of dollars, percent, rank based on 2004 dollar values.)

Product and market	2001	2002	2003	2004	Percent share of total, 2004	Average annual percent change, 2001–2004
Total Goods						
Total	1 034	1 066	809	1 164	100.0	4.0
Manufactures	959	997	737	1 111	95.4	5.0
Agriculture and livestock	2	8	2	1	0.1	-18.5
Other commodities	73	61	70	52	4.5	-10.7
Five Leading Exports (NAICS Code)						
Transportation equipment (336)	576	546	341	660	56.7	4.6
Computers and electronic products (334)	90	85	109	165	14.2	22.3
Fabricated metal products (332)	147	251	127	141	12.1	-1.4
Machinery manufactures (333)	20	12	27	44	3.8	30.0
Special classification provisions (990)	29	29	50	39	3.4	11.2
Five Leading Markets	562	438	418	1 043	89.6	22.9
Greece	1	6	2	393	33.7	632.4
United Kingdom	300	180	123	282	24.3	-2.0
Taiwan	56	41	41	64	5.5	4.6
United Arab Emirates	1	2	8	55	4.7	328.8
New Zealand	2	3	11	24	2.0	120.2

AGRICULTURE

Note: The Department of Agriculture does not collect separate data for the District of Columbia. In the 2002 Census of Agriculture, the city was included with Maryland.

ENERGY

In 2001, energy prices in the District of Columbia were the highest in the country. The city ranked 19th in the nation for expenditures per person. The District of Columbia's per capita consumption was well below the national average, largely because of its small population base and small industrial sector. More than 60 percent of energy was consumed by the city's commercial sector. The city's largest source of energy was electricity from other states, followed by petroleum and natural gas.

Energy Consumption by Source, 2001

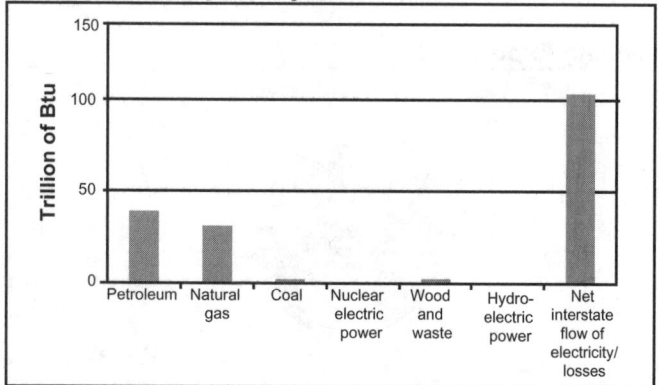

Energy Consumption by Sector, 2001

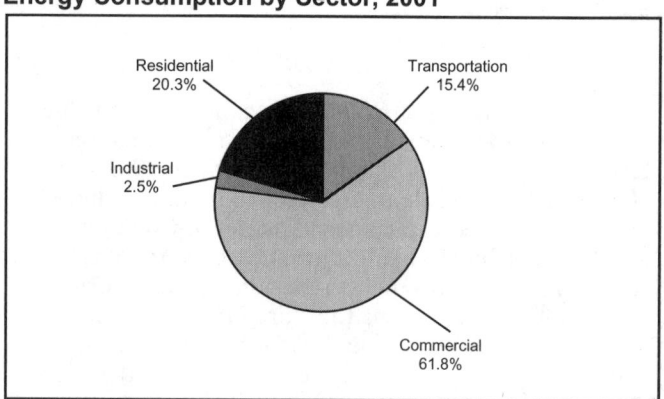

Table DC-15. Energy Consumption, Expenditures, and Prices, Selected Years 1960–2001
(Dollars, Btu [British Thermal Unit], percent distribution.)

Item	1960	1965	1970	1975	1980	1985	1990	1995	2000	2001
Total Consumption (Billion Btu)	119 873	159 179	205 914	163 282	152 627	165 939	176 173	184 444	186 534	168 231
Consumption per capita (million Btu)	156.9	199.7	272.1	231.0	239.1	261.5	290.3	334.6	326.1	293.7
Consumption by Sector (Percent Distribution)										
Residential	20.2	16.8	16.5	19.0	21.8	22.7	19.8	20.2	19.6	20.3
Commercial	27.0	34.3	36.3	32.2	32.0	42.6	45.2	63.2	63.6	61.8
Industrial	28.8	27.6	31.2	26.2	28.3	17.7	19.5	1.9	1.9	2.5
Transportation	24.0	21.2	16.0	22.7	18.0	17.0	15.5	14.7	14.8	15.4
Consumption by Source (Billion Btu)										
Coal	27 792	13 804	28 427	10 142	3 284	3 489	1 733	143	177	748
Natural gas	12 951	17 315	26 402	26 210	27 952	29 336	29 094	33 201	34 377	30 578
Petroleum	59 885	92 330	129 410	75 960	47 702	39 526	37 962	37 005	34 492	33 464
Nuclear electric power	0	0	0	0	0	0	0	0	0	0
Hydroelectric power[1]	32	32	8	8	0	0	0	0	0	0
Wood and waste	123	88	105	123	2 000	2 959	1 623	2 006	1 338	1 130
Other	0	0	0	0	0	0	0	0	1	1
Net interstate flow of electricity/losses[2]	19 091	35 611	21 562	50 839	71 689	90 629	105 760	112 090	116 148	102 311
Total Expenditures (Thousands of Dollars)	. . .	. . .	277 400	500 500	815 200	1 143 900	1 079 100	1 274 800	1 533 900	1 479 300
Expenditures per capita (dollars)	. . .	. . .	367	708	1 277	1 803	1 778	2 312	2 681	2 583
Prices by Sector (Dollars Per Million Btu)										
Total	. . .	. . .	1.72	4.33	8.71	11.57	11.09	12.36	14.86	15.57
Residential	. . .	. . .	2.00	3.79	7.10	9.69	9.46	11.12	13.50	15.00
Commercial	. . .	. . .	1.41	4.63	8.51	12.67	11.59	13.86	16.27	17.17
Industrial	. . .	. . .	1.19	4.29	10.20	17.08	14.68	11.01	11.95	12.39
Transportation	. . .	. . .	2.74	4.43	9.44	9.92	10.24	10.52	13.40	13.14

[1]A negative number in this row results from pumped storage for which, overall, more electricity is expended than created to provide electricity during peak demand periods.
[2]Net interstate flow of electricity is the difference between the amount of energy in the electricity sold within a state (including associated losses) and the energy input at the electric utilities within the state. A positive number indicates that more electricity (including associated losses) came into the state than went out of the state during the year; conversely, a negative number indicates that more electricity (including associated losses) went out of the state than came into the state.
. . . = Not available.

Table DC-16. Taxes, Fiscal 2004

(Dollars, percent distribution.)

Item	Thousands of dollars	Percent distribution	Dollars per capita	
			City	U.S.
TOTAL TAXES	3 933 860	100.0	7 097.8	2 024.8
Property Taxes	1 023 246	26.0	1 846.2	38.9
Sales and Gross Receipts	1 121 558	28.5	2 023.6	1 003.4
General sales and gross receipts	754 544	19.2	1 361.4	677.0
Selective sales taxes	367 014	9.3	662.2	326.4
Alcoholic beverages	4 955	0.1	8.9	15.7
Insurance premiums	47 373	1.2	85.5	47.0
Motor fuels	27 318	0.7	49.3	114.6
Public utilities	170 851	4.3	308.3	39.2
Tobacco products	21 258	0.5	38.4	42.0
Other selective sales	95 259	2.4	171.9	49.8
Licenses	145 886	3.7	263.2	134.9
Corporation	65 864	1.7	118.8	21.6
Motor vehicle	24 442	0.6	44.1	59.4
Motor vehicle operators	4 907	0.1	8.8	6.4
Occupation and business, not elsewhere classified	18 992	0.5	34.3	37.1
Other licenses	31 681	0.8	57.2	2.6
Other Taxes	1 643 170	41.8	2 964.7	847.6
Individual income	1 080 365	27.5	1 949.3	673.6
Corporation net income	169 842	4.3	306.4	105.1
Death and gift	21 284	0.5	38.4	19.6
Documentary and stock transfer	336 506	8.6	607.2	27.1
Other	35 173	0.9	63.5	0.8

GOVERNMENT FINANCE

The District's revenues outpaced spending and it registered a budget surplus, an encouraging trend in most recent years. Dependent in large part on revenues from the federal government, revenues totaled over $6.9 billion in 2001–2002, the latest year for which data are available. Spending per capita was substaintially above national averages for most major expediture categories, especially education, public welfare, health, and hospitals. Taxes were also substaintially above the national average, particularly property taxes, sales taxes, and individual income taxes

Per Capita State Taxes, Fiscal 2004

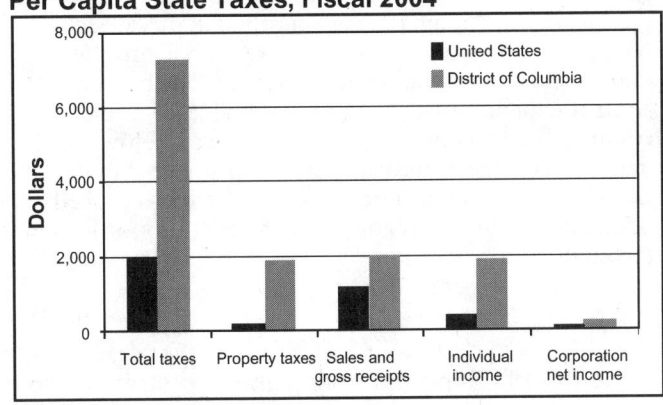

Table DC-17. Government Finances, 2001–2002

(Dollars, percent distribution.)

Item	Millions of dollars	Percent distribution	Dollars per capita	
			City	U.S.
GENERAL REVENUE	6 922 336	100.0	12 102.0	5 987.0
Intergovernmental revenue	2 840 094	41.0	4 965.2	1 281.2
Taxes	3 227 909	46.6	5 643.2	3 216.2
General sales	558 480	8.1	976.4	792.4
Selective sales	377 359	5.5	659.7	359.4
License taxes	50 189	0.7	87.7	130.5
Individual income tax	949 175	13.7	1 659.4	720.7
Corporate income tax	211 249	3.1	369.3	100.0
Other taxes	278 068	4.0	486.1	121.1
Current charges	301 694	4.4	527.4	899.7
Miscellaneous general revenue	552 639	8.0	966.2	590.0
GENERAL EXPENDITURE	7 832 123	100.0	13 692.5	7 289.9
Intergovernmental expenditure	0	0.0	0.0	15.6
Direct expenditure	7 832 123	100.0	13 692.5	7 274.3
Expenditure by Function				
Education	1 174 741	15.0	2 053.7	2 113.2
Public welfare	1 462 362	18.7	2 556.6	999.1
Hospitals	176 920	2.3	309.3	311.3
Health	377 946	4.8	660.7	211.3
Highways	69 235	0.9	121.0	409.7
Police protection	384 690	4.9	672.5	229.0
Correction	173 818	2.2	303.9	194.1
Natural resources	0	0.0	0.0	78.2
Parks and recreation	303 049	3.9	529.8	107.0
Government administration	382 844	4.9	669.3	329.7
Interest on general debt	235 875	3.0	412.4	267.5
Other and unallocable	854 664	10.9	1 494.2	354.6
DEBT AT END OF FISCAL YEAR	5 436 087	X	9 503.6	5 974.6
CASH AND SECURITY HOLDINGS	5 693 635	X	9 953.9	12 972.5

X = Not applicable.

Table DC-18. Education Indicators, 2000–2004

(Percent, number.)

Item	City	U.S.
Total Population 25 Years and Over (Thousands), 2004	397	186 877
Educational Attainment, 2004		
Percent high school graduate or more	86.4	85.2
Percent college graduate or more	45.7	27.7
Elementary and Secondary Schools, 2002–2003		
Total students	76 166	48 202 324
Percent of students eligible for free or reduced-price lunch ..	61.7	40.6
Percent of students who were English language learners	7.3	7.8
Total schools	203	92 330
Student/teacher ratio	13.8	15.9
Per student expenditures	11 847	8 041
Higher Education, 2002–2003		
Total enrollment	92 620	17 035 027
Bachelor's degrees awarded	8 900	1 348 503
Percent women	59.5	57.5

Educational Attainment, 2004

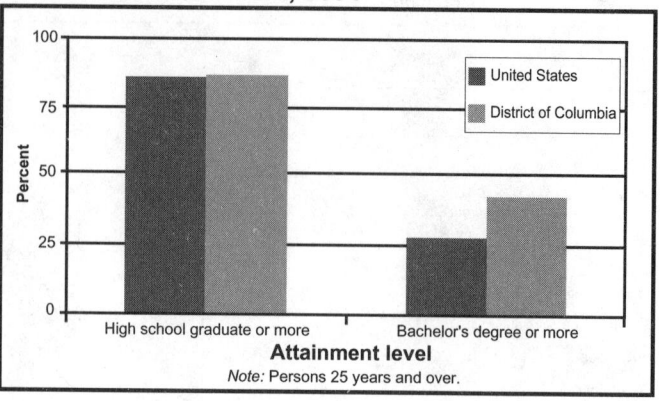

Attainment level

Note: Persons 25 years and over.

EDUCATION

Although educational attainment rates were above the national average, particularly at the college level, the performance of the city's public schools has been relatively poor, especially at the high school level. Many children in the District of Columbia were enrolled in private schools, giving the city a level of private school enrollment that was far above the national average. The city's per student expenditures of $11,847 ranked third in the country. The student/teacher ratio was well below the national average. Nearly 62 percent of students in the District of Columbia were eligible for free or reduced-price lunch, which was among the highest proportions in the country.

VOTER PARTICIPATION

Despite the fact that participation in national elections was limited to voting for the president and a delegate to the U.S. House of Representatives, the District of Columbia's voter turnout was well above the national average. In 2000, 65.6 percent of eligible voters cast ballots; this proportion fell to 62 percent in 2004. The male participation rate stayed about the same, but the participation rate for women fell by more than 6 percentage points. However, the female participation rate remained above that of men. The city voted overwhelmingly Democrat, with nearly 90 percent of voters casting ballots for the Democratic presidential candidate in 2004, according to the official tally by the Clerk of the U.S. House of Representatives.

Table DC-19. Reported Voting and Registration, November 2000 and November 2004

(Numbers in thousands, percent.)

Characteristic	Total population 18 years and over	Total citizen		Total registered		Total voted	
		Number	Percent	Number	Percent	Number	Percent
NOVEMBER 2000							
Total	407	373	91.5	295	72.4	267	65.6
Male	191	173	90.6	130	67.8	114	59.8
Female	216	200	92.4	165	76.6	153	70.8
NOVEMBER 2004							
Total	435	390	89.6	293	67.4	270	62.0
Male	199	176	88.1	130	65.0	118	59.3
Female	236	214	90.8	164	69.4	152	64.3
Race and Hispanic Origin							
White alone	179	149	83.3	122	68.1	116	64.8
Non-Hispanic White alone	150	140	93.5	115	77.1	110	73.4
Black alone	240	229	95.6	163	68.2	146	61.0
Asian alone	9	5	B	4	B	3	B
Hispanic or Latino[1]	38	15	B	10	B	9	B
White alone or in combination	184	153	83.4	124	67.7	118	64.6
Non-Hispanic White alone or in combination	151	141	93.4	116	77.1	111	73.4
Black alone or in combination	242	231	95.6	165	68.4	148	61.2
Asian alone or in combination	10	6	B	5	B	4	B
Age							
18 to 24 years	51	48	B	29	B	26	B
25 to 44 years	192	161	83.6	125	65.0	118	61.5
45 to 64 years	131	123	93.3	97	73.8	91	69.1
65 to 74 years	29	28	B	21	B	18	B
75 years and over	32	31	B	22	B	17	B

[1]May be of any race.
B = Base is too small to show derived measure.

At a Glance:

- Florida's population in 2004 was 17.4 million, making it the fourth most populous state in the country.

- From 2000 to 2004, the state's population grew by 8.8 percent, which was the third highest growth rate in the nation.

- In 2004, non-Hispanic Whites accounted for 62.8 percent of the population, and Blacks made up 15.4 percent. Hispanics (of any race) were a significant proportion of the population at 19.0 percent. Florida ranked seventh in the nation in terms of its proportion of this ethnic group.

- Florida's median household income was below the national average, reflecting the number of retirees on reduced income. With a large proportion of the state's population receiving retirement benefits, Florida's poverty rate was below the U.S. average.

- The unemployment rate in 2004 was 4.8 percent, well below the national average of 5.5 percent.

- In 2004, the proportion of the population without health insurance was quite high at nearly 20 percent, which is notable for a state with such a high population of elderly residents.

- Florida had one of the ten lowest voter participation rates in 2004.

Table FL-1. Population by Sex and Age, 1990, 2000, and 2004

(Number, percent.)

Sex and age	1990	2000	2004	Percent distribution, 2004	Average annual percent change, 2000–2004
Total Population	12 937 926	15 982 378	17 397 161	X	2.1
Percent of total U.S. population	5.2	5.7	5.9	X	X
Sex					
Male	6 261 719	7 797 715	8 524 398	49.0	2.3
Female	6 676 207	8 184 663	8 872 763	51.0	2.0
Age					
Under 5 years	849 596	945 823	1 091 292	6.3	1.6
5 to 17 years	2 016 641	2 700 517	2 911 998	16.7	2.7
18 years and over	2 559 201	12 336 038	13 393 871	77.0	2.1
18 to 24 years	10 071 689	1 330 602	1 549 324	8.9	1.7
25 to 44 years	1 215 657	4 569 347	4 671 734	26.9	1.3
45 to 64 years	3 927 400	3 628 492	4 245 230	24.4	3.7
65 years and over	2 369 431	2 807 597	2 927 583	16.8	1.6
85 years and over	210 110	331 287	379 572	2.2	4.5
Median age (years)	36.2	38.7	39.3	X	X

X = Not applicable.

Average Annual Rate of Population Growth, 1980–2004

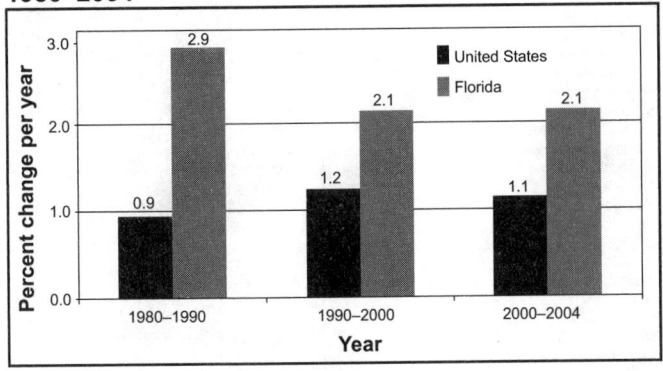

POPULATION

Florida was a retirement haven for many Americans, and its net immigration from other states totaled 791,900 during the 2000–2004 period, the highest number in the country. It also attracted immigrants from other countries. Total net international immigration was 445,000 over the period, ranking fourth in the country. The mix of immigration resulted in a population that is generally older than the national average—it had the highest proportion of population age 65 years and over (16.8 percent), as well as a substantial number of younger persons. More than 90 percent of the population lived in Florida's large metropolitan areas: Miami and Tampa were the state's largest cities.

Table FL-2. Population by Race and Hispanic Origin, 1990, 2000, and 2004

(Number, percent.)

Race and Hispanic origin	1990	2000	2004
Total Population	12 937 926	15 982 378	17 397 161
Non-Hispanic (Percent)			
One race[1]			
White	73.2	65.8	62.8
Black	13.1	14.5	14.9
American Indian, Alaska Native[2]	0.3	0.3	0.3
Asian and Pacific Islander[2]	1.2	1.7	2.0
Other race[2]	1.8	. . .	. . .
Two or more races	. . .	0.9	1.0
Hispanic or Latino[3] (Percent)	12.2	16.8	19.0

[1]Individuals could report only one race in the 1990 census and could report one or more races on the 2000 census. Data on race in 2000 and 2004 are not comparable to 1990.
[2]Data for 1990 include people of Hispanic or Latino origin.
[3]May be of any race.
. . . = Not available.

Minority Population as a Percent of Total Population, 2004

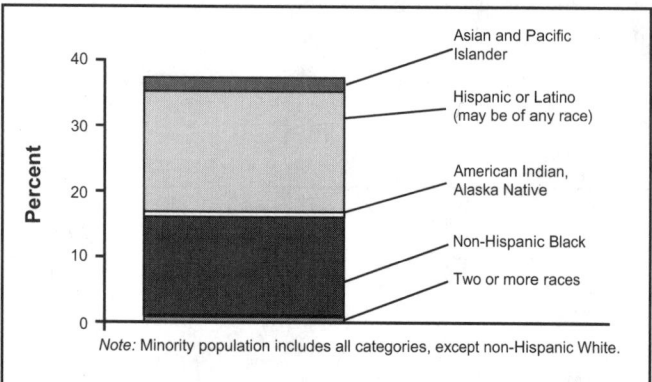

Note: Minority population includes all categories, except non-Hispanic White.

Age-Adjusted Death Rates, Average 2000–2002

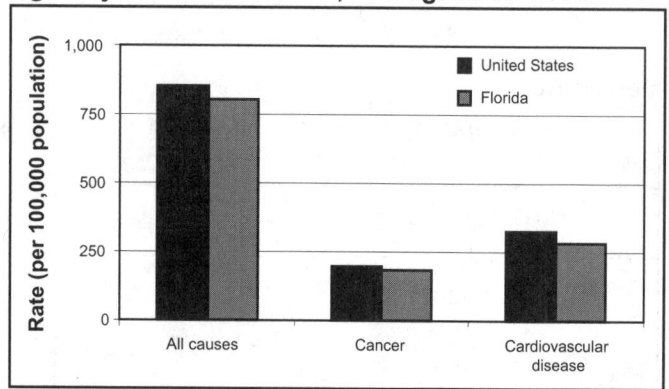

HEALTH

Florida's health insurance coverage was the third lowest in the nation. Considering the extensive health insurance coverage of the elderly population by Medicare, this suggests a lack of adequate coverage for Florida's younger age groups. More than 15 percent of children lacked health insurance, the sixth highest proportion in the country. The state's age-adjusted death rates were lower than the national averages.

Table FL-3. Health Characteristics, 2000–2004

(Number, rate, percent.)

Item	State	U.S.
Births, 2003–2004		
Number of births	212 250	4 089 950
Birth rate (per 1,000 population)	12.5	14.1
Teenage birth rate (per 1,000 women age 15–19 years)	42.5	41.6
Mortality Rates, Average 2000–2002		
Infant mortality rate (per 1,000 live births)	7.2	6.9
Age-adjusted mortality rate (per 100,000 population)		
All races	796.4	853.3
Non-Hispanic White	796.1	843.1
Black	1 046.1	1 097.7
American Indian, Alaska Native	. . .	687.0
Asian and Pacific Islander	323.5	486.0
Hispanic or Latino[1]	623.6	642.7
Health Insurance, 2004		
Percent of all persons without health insurance	19.9	15.7
Percent of children without health insurance	15.1	11.2
Percent of low-income children without health insurance	9.1	7.1

[1]May be of any race.
. . . = Not available.

Table FL-4. Leading Causes of Death, Average 2000–2002

(Number, rate per 100,000 population.)

Cause	Number of deaths	Age-adjusted death rates	
		State	U.S.
ALL CAUSES	166 493	796.4	853.3
Leading Causes			
Major cardiovascular diseases	64 641	297.3	326.5
Cancer	39 138	187.3	196.0
Chronic lower respiratory diseases	8 887	40.5	43.7
Unintentional injuries	6 877	39.9	35.7
Diabetes (underlying cause)	4 554	21.6	25.2
Influenza and pneumonia	3 324	15.3	22.7
Alzheimer's disease	3 653	16.1	19.0
Motor vehicle accidents	3 065	18.5	15.0
Nephritis, nephrotic syndrome, and nephrosis ..	2 087	9.6	13.8
Septicemia	1 656	7.8	11.4
Suicides	2 246	13.1	10.7
Firearm-related	1 798	10.7	10.3
Cirrhosis	2 079	11.1	9.5
Drug-induced	1 703	10.7	7.9
Alcohol-induced	1 370	7.8	6.9
Homicides	970	6.1	6.0
Falls	1 058	5.0	5.2
HIV	1 728	10.8	5.0
Viral hepatitis	447	2.5	2.0
Anemias	278	1.4	1.6
Drownings	373	2.3	1.3
Fire deaths	136	0.8	1.2

Note: The rates are age-adjusted to the U.S. 2000 standard population.

Table FL-5. Households and Housing Characteristics, 1990, 2000, and 2004

(Number, percent, and dollars.)

Characteristic	1990	2000	2004	Average annual percent change, 2000–2004
Total Households	5 134 869	6 337 929	6 819 280	1.8
Family households	3 511 825	4 210 760	4 475 033	1.5
Married-couple family	2 791 734	3 192 266	3 294 267	0.8
Other family	720 091	1 018 494	1 180 766	3.8
Male householder, no wife present	171 535	259 494	319 011	5.3
Female householder, no husband present	548 556	759 000	861 755	3.2
Nonfamily households	1 623 044	2 127 169	2 344 247	2.5
Householder living alone	1 309 954	1 687 303	1 890 864	2.9
Householder not living alone	313 090	439 866	453 383	0.8
Housing Characteristics				
Average size	2.46	2.46	2.49	X
Housing units	6 100 262	7 302 947	8 009 427	2.3
Occupied housing units	5 134 869	6 337 929	6 819 280	1.8
Owner-occupied	3 452 160	4 441 799	4 808 029	2.0
Renter-occupied	1 682 709	1 896 130	2 011 251	1.5
Median gross rent of renter-occupied housing units (dollars)	481	641	766	4.6
Median value of owner-occupied housing units (dollars)	76 500	105 500	149 291	9.1

X = Not applicable.

Median Housing Value and Median Rent, 2004

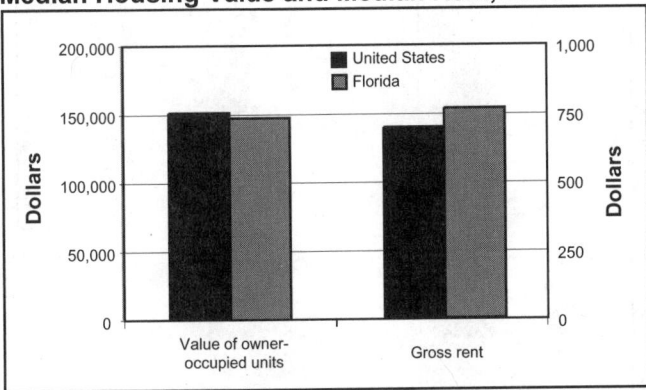

Median Household Income, 1984–2004 (2004 Dollars)

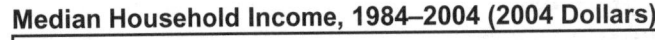
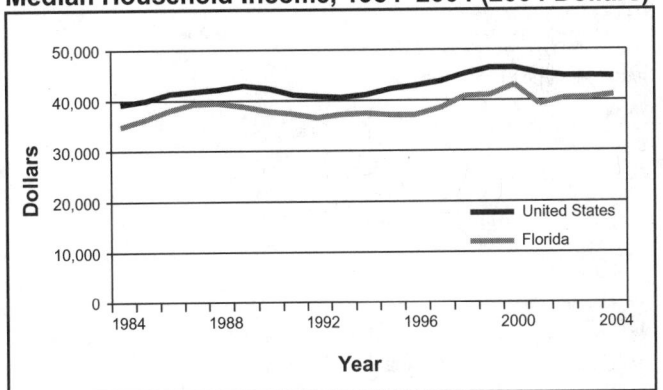

Table FL-6. Household Income and Poverty Status, 1980–2004

(2004 CPI-U-RS adjusted dollars, rate.)

Year	State		U.S.	
	Median household income (2004 dollars)	Poverty rate	Median household income (2004 dollars)	Poverty rate
2004	40 554	11.6	44 389	12.7
2003	40 019	12.7	44 482	12.5
2002	39 940	12.6	44 546	12.1
2001	38 865	12.7	45 062	11.7
2000	42 621	11.0	46 058	11.3
1999	40 614	12.4	46 129	11.9
1998	40 402	13.1	45 003	12.7
1997	38 090	14.3	43 430	13.3
1996	36 729	14.2	42 544	13.7
1995	36 612	16.2	41 943	13.8
1994	36 933	14.9	40 677	14.5
1993	36 753	17.8	40 217	15.1
1992	36 085	15.6	40 422	14.8
1991	36 859	15.4	40 746	14.2
1990	37 397	14.4	41 963	13.5
1989	38 374	12.5	42 524	12.8
1988	38 980	13.6	41 771	13.0
1987	38 942	12.4	41 322	13.4
1986	37 572	11.4	40 939	13.6
1985	35 736	13.4	39 545	14.0
1984	34 232	15.1	38 782	14.4
1983	. . .	14.7	. . .	15.2
1982	. . .	15.2	. . .	15.0
1981	. . .	16.6	. . .	14.0
1980	. . .	16.7	. . .	13.0

. . . = Not available.

Table FL-7. Employment Status by Demographic Group, 2004

(Numbers in thousands, rate.)

Characteristic	Civilian noninstitutional population	Civilian labor force		Employed	Unemployment rate
		Number	Participation rate		
SEX AND AGE					
Total	13 521	8 411	62.2	8 021	4.6
16 to 19 years	889	353	39.8	299	15.4
20 to 24 years	1 054	785	74.5	723	7.9
25 to 34 years	1 997	1 674	83.8	1 600	4.4
35 to 44 years	2 524	2 104	83.3	2 027	3.7
45 to 54 years	2 460	2 017	82.0	1 951	3.3
55 to 64 years	1 863	1 130	60.6	1 089	3.6
65 years and over	2 734	347	12.7	332	4.3
Men	6 480	4 507	69.6	4 302	4.5
16 to 19 years	450	174	38.6	144	17.2
20 to 24 years	518	413	79.7	386	6.5
25 to 34 years	986	910	92.3	871	4.2
35 to 44 years	1 256	1 157	92.1	1 112	3.9
45 to 54 years	1 189	1 055	88.7	1 019	3.4
55 to 64 years	891	600	67.3	577	3.9
65 years and over	1 190	199	16.7	193	2.9
Women	7 041	3 904	55.4	3 719	4.7
16 to 19 years	439	180	41.0	155	13.7
20 to 24 years	536	372	69.5	337	9.4
25 to 34 years	1 011	764	75.6	728	4.7
35 to 44 years	1 268	946	74.6	915	3.4
45 to 54 years	1 270	962	75.8	932	3.1
55 to 64 years	972	530	54.6	512	3.4
65 years and over	1 544	148	9.6	139	6.3
MARITAL STATUS					
Married men, spouse present	3 633	2 584	71.1	2 507	3.0
Married women, spouse present	3 563	1 963	55.1	1 902	3.1
Women who maintain families	785	547	69.6	518	5.2
RACE, HISPANIC ORIGIN, AND SEX					
White	11 164	6 860	61.5	6 591	3.9
Men	5 399	3 741	69.3	3 590	4.0
Women	5 764	3 119	54.1	3 000	3.8
Black	1 908	1 245	65.3	1 137	8.6
Men	869	602	69.3	553	8.2
Women	1 039	643	61.9	584	9.1
Asian	275	184	67.0	177	3.8
Men	129	100	77.7	97	3.1
Women	146	84	57.6	80	4.7
Hispanic or Latino[1]	2 533	1 654	65.3	1 572	5.0
Men	1 287	980	76.1	928	5.3
Women	1 247	674	54.1	643	4.6
RACE, HISPANIC ORIGIN, AND AGE					
White					
25 to 34 years	1 533	1 290	84.2	1 242	3.7
35 to 44 years	2 051	1 711	83.4	1 658	3.1
45 to 54 years	2 043	1 690	82.7	1 638	3.1
55 to 64 years	1 625	989	60.9	953	3.6

Note: Data in Table 7 are from the Current Population Survey (CPS) and do not match Bureau of Labor Statistics estimates in Table 8. See notes and definitions for more details.

[1]May be of any race.

Table FL-8. Employment Status, 1990–2004

(Numbers in thousands, rate.)

Year	Civilian labor force	Employed	Unemployed	Unemployment rate
2004	8 396 433	7 997 077	399 356	4.8
2003	8 194 768	7 763 860	430 908	5.3
2002	8 072 864	7 615 730	457 134	5.7
2001	8 005 054	7 633 728	371 326	4.6
2000	7 858 656	7 558 636	300 020	3.8
1999	7 710 988	7 401 659	309 329	4.0
1998	7 572 631	7 232 345	340 286	4.5
1997	7 408 862	7 040 660	368 202	5.0
1996	7 207 707	6 826 997	380 710	5.3
1995	7 045 431	6 655 500	389 931	5.5
1994	6 970 074	6 502 124	467 950	6.7
1993	6 786 938	6 297 070	489 868	7.2
1992	6 692 592	6 133 417	559 175	8.4
1991	6 551 675	6 055 255	496 420	7.6
1990	6 465 579	6 060 994	404 585	6.3

Note: Population age 16 years and over.

Unemployment Rate, 1980–2004

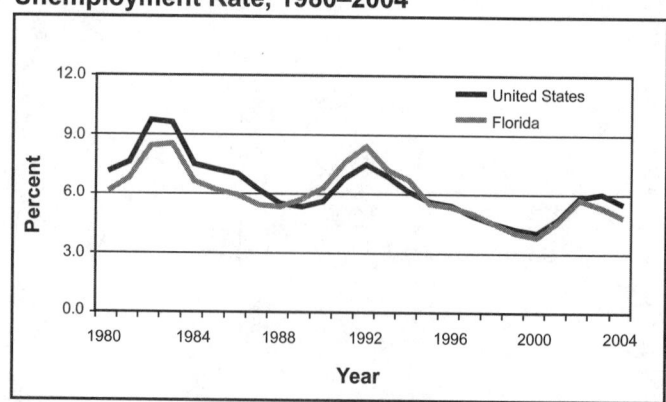

Table FL-9. Employment and Average Wages by Industry, 2001–2004

(Estimates are based on the 2002 North American Industry Classification System [NAICS].)

Industry	2001	2002	2003	2004	Annual average percent change, 2001–2004
	Number of jobs				
TOTAL EMPLOYMENT BY PLACE OF WORK	9 112 069	9 204 887	9 395 491	9 695 687	2.1
Farm Employment	94 516	93 743	97 589	92 134	-0.8
Nonfarm Employment	9 017 553	9 111 144	9 297 902	9 603 553	2.1
Private employment	7 903 700	7 988 050	8 154 634	8 452 914	2.3
Forestry, fishing, hunting, and other[1]	92 234	93 099	90 263	89 249	-1.1
Mining	13 219	11 746	13 209	13 644	1.1
Utilities	29 159	26 161	25 383	25 013	-5.0
Construction	583 527	585 036	618 625	672 783	4.9
Manufacturing	454 256	429 972	409 634	411 641	-3.2
Durable goods manufacturing	301 807	282 943	267 398	271 692	-3.4
Nondurable goods manufacturing	152 449	147 029	142 236	139 949	-2.8
Wholesale trade	344 832	341 856	342 923	353 990	0.9
Retail trade	1 095 740	1 091 807	1 093 339	1 123 205	0.8
Transportation and warehousing	286 730	284 369	277 313	281 201	-0.6
Information	212 528	199 093	195 808	191 180	-3.5
Finance and insurance	441 613	451 762	462 693	474 949	2.5
Real estate and rental and leasing	397 190	418 070	450 320	477 530	6.3
Professional and technical services	553 987	559 276	577 039	603 158	2.9
Management of companies and enterprises	63 451	72 809	71 403	73 029	4.8
Administrative and waste services	906 992	914 918	965 442	1 005 962	3.5
Educational services	119 632	128 412	134 332	141 410	5.7
Health care and social assistance	856 918	879 750	906 619	930 964	2.8
Arts, entertainment, and recreation	243 688	245 485	243 127	252 688	1.2
Accommodation and food services	662 193	673 602	688 900	729 218	3.3
Other services, except public administration	545 811	580 827	588 262	602 100	3.3
Government and government enterprises	1 113 853	1 123 094	1 143 268	1 150 639	1.1
	Dollars				
AVERAGE WAGES AND SALARIES BY PLACE OF WORK	31 297	32 259	33 331	34 940	3.7
Farm Earnings	18 113	19 747	15 421	21 947	6.6
Nonfarm Earnings	31 391	32 346	33 465	35 026	3.7
Private earnings	30 929	31 718	32 781	34 260	3.5
Forestry, fishing, hunting, and other[1]	14 954	15 618	15 997	16 681	3.7
Mining	44 615	45 812	45 853	46 799	1.6
Utilities	59 401	54 247	56 698	65 693	3.4
Construction	33 487	34 035	35 220	36 637	3.0
Manufacturing	37 877	39 258	40 826	42 403	3.8
Durable goods manufacturing	39 128	40 939	42 452	44 049	4.0
Nondurable goods manufacturing	35 366	35 971	37 721	39 152	3.4
Wholesale trade	45 368	45 969	47 858	50 339	3.5
Retail trade	22 662	23 255	23 951	24 841	3.1
Transportation and warehousing	34 671	35 491	36 719	38 137	3.2
Information	46 427	46 035	47 392	50 984	3.2
Finance and insurance	48 862	50 640	53 585	56 206	4.8
Real estate and rental and leasing	30 323	31 397	33 575	35 787	5.7
Professional and technical services	49 635	50 107	50 758	53 059	2.2
Management of companies and enterprises	60 907	63 931	68 374	71 435	5.5
Administrative and waste services	22 916	24 731	24 702	25 758	4.0
Educational services	25 769	26 405	27 584	28 828	3.8
Health care and social assistance	33 100	34 349	35 705	37 448	4.2
Arts, entertainment, and recreation	27 606	27 943	29 566	30 889	3.8
Accommodation and food services	15 546	15 736	16 309	17 048	3.1
Other services, except public administration	21 333	21 591	22 624	23 481	3.2
Government and government enterprises	34 074	35 972	37 389	39 545	5.1

Note: Average wages and salaries are a calculation by the editors of wage and salary disbursements divided by full- and part-time wage and salary employment. Data may not add to total or may appear as zero due to rounding.

[1] "Other" consists of the number of jobs held by U.S. residents employed by international organizations and foreign embassies and consulates in the United States.

LABOR MARKET

Florida's unemployment rate declined as economic activity in the state increased, following a period of slower growth in 2001. Wage and salary employment increased 6.4 percent from 2001 to 2004, the fourth slowest growth rate in the nation. The industries with the highest rates of growth were real estate, educational services, and construction. Florida's largest industry employers were retail trade, government and government enterprises, administrative and waste services, and health care. It should be noted, however, that the employment mix in 2004 may have been affected by the recent hurricanes. Average wages and salaries were below the national averages across most industries.

Employment by Industry, 2004

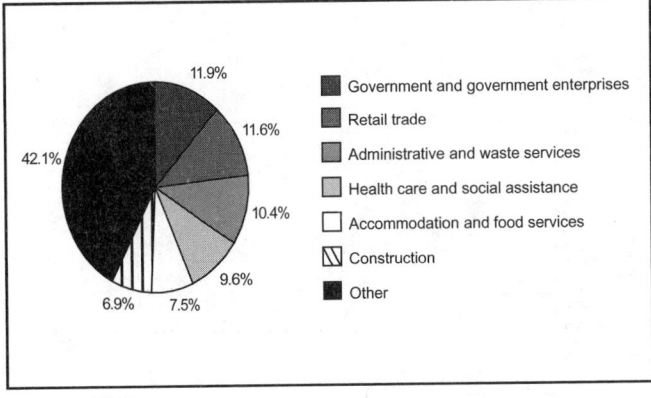

Table FL-10. Personal Income by Major Source, Selected Years 1980–2004

(Millions of dollars, except where noted.)

Item	1980	1990	2000	2001	2002	2003	2004	Average annual percent change, 2000–2004
Earnings by Place of Work	66 169	162 431	303 505	315 310	328 637	346 347	375 381	5.5
Wage and salary disbursements	49 560	123 231	228 447	239 228	247 077	258 555	278 996	5.1
Supplements to wages and salaries	9 071	25 927	45 107	47 556	51 829	56 386	62 798	8.6
Proprietors' income[1]	7 538	13 273	29 951	28 526	29 731	31 405	33 587	2.9
Farm proprietors' income	1 151	1 231	772	891	685	697	759	-0.4
Nonfarm proprietors' income	6 387	12 042	29 180	27 635	29 045	30 708	32 828	3.0
(-) Contributions for government social insurance[2]	5 915	17 966	33 266	35 508	37 117	39 030	42 165	6.1
(+) Adjustment for residence[3]	16	637	1 514	1 572	1 549	1 543	1 610	1.5
(=) Net Earnings by Place of Residence	60 270	145 102	271 753	281 373	293 070	308 860	334 825	5.4
(+) Dividends, interest, and rent[4]	24 129	75 602	117 914	122 897	121 968	118 176	118 400	0.1
(+) Personal current transfer receipts	13 341	34 280	67 872	74 367	80 391	84 915	94 086	8.5
Personal income	97 741	254 984	457 539	478 637	495 429	511 951	547 312	4.6
Farm income	96 106	252 953	455 840	476 653	493 600	510 268	545 292	4.6
Nonfarm income	1 635	2 030	1 700	1 984	1 829	1 683	2 019	4.4
Per Capita Personal Income (Dollars)[5]	9 933	19 564	28 509	29 268	29 700	30 116	31 460	2.5

Note: Data may not add to total or may appear as zero due to rounding.

[1]Proprietors' income includes the inventory valuation adjustment and the capital consumption adjustment.
[2]Contributions for government social insurance are included in earnings by type and industry, but they are excluded from personal income.
[3]The adjustment for residence is the net inflow of the earnings of interarea commuters.
[4]Rental income of persons includes the capital consumption adjustment.
[5]Per capita personal income is total personal income divided by total midyear population.

Per Capita Personal Income, 1980–2004 (Current Dollars)

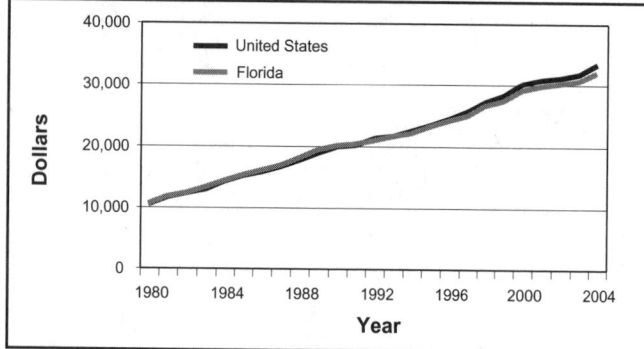

ECONOMIC ACTIVITY

Florida's economy proved to be immune from the 2001 recession: in each year over the 2001–2004 period, its growth rate was well above the national average. From 2003 to 2004, the state's economy grew by 5.9 percent, one of the highest rates of increase in the country. The chief contributing sectors were real estate, government, retail trade, and finance and insurance. Housing price appreciation was among the highest in the nation during the 2000–2004 period, but the median value of owner-occupied housing ranked 22nd in the nation in 2004, reflecting the disparity between the sharp appreciation in coastal areas and the slower growth in inland parts of the state.

Table FL-11. Real Gross State Product, 1997–2004

(Millions of chained 2000 dollars, percent.)

Industry	1997	1998	1999	2000	2001	2002	2003	2004	Average annual percent change, 2001–2004
GROSS STATE PRODUCT	414 710	434 523	453 108	470 120	484 433	497 740	517 855	548 299	4.2
As a percent of U.S. gross product	4.8	4.8	4.8	4.8	4.9	5.0	5.0	5.1	X
Private Industries	360 459	379 604	397 582	412 849	427 515	440 015	458 914	486 624	4.4
Agriculture, forestry, fishing, and hunting	4 511	5 027	5 336	5 815	5 120	5 597	4 999	4 596	-3.5
Mining	550	609	697	652	601	618	597	568	-1.9
Utilities	8 951	8 845	8 815	9 415	8 468	8 445	9 199	10 430	7.2
Construction	22 976	23 879	24 141	24 886	25 777	25 693	26 748	29 081	4.1
Manufacturing	26 277	27 837	28 140	29 896	28 717	29 492	30 976	32 843	4.6
As a percent of gross state product	6.3	6.4	6.2	6.4	5.9	5.9	6.0	6.0	X
Wholesale trade	26 495	29 531	31 423	32 237	34 741	35 545	35 292	37 199	2.3
Retail trade	33 206	35 826	37 581	39 424	42 960	44 458	47 401	51 037	5.9
Transportation and warehousing	13 121	13 821	14 296	15 042	14 722	14 748	15 891	16 463	3.8
Information	15 762	17 132	19 434	20 687	22 293	22 965	24 598	27 304	7.0
Finance and insurance	25 779	26 599	28 726	29 386	32 032	34 458	37 311	40 447	8.1
Real estate and rental and leasing	64 323	66 690	70 335	71 537	76 168	77 558	80 302	82 981	2.9
Services	119 047	123 974	128 757	133 871	136 094	140 736	146 051	154 333	4.3
As a percent of gross state product	28.7	28.5	28.4	28.5	28.1	28.3	28.2	28.1	X
Professional and technical services	21 642	24 097	25 630	28 683	29 622	30 522	31 443	33 529	4.2
Management of companies and enterprises	5 812	5 539	5 469	5 389	5 768	6 323	6 834	6 893	6.1
Administrative and waste services	19 565	21 608	24 133	24 638	24 250	26 268	27 871	29 300	6.5
Educational services	2 622	2 733	2 824	2 944	2 976	2 991	2 958	3 017	0.5
Health care and social assistance	32 044	31 963	32 031	32 890	34 379	35 615	36 972	38 435	3.8
Arts, entertainment, and recreation	8 147	7 989	8 292	8 454	8 569	8 499	8 528	8 963	1.5
Accommodation and food services	16 218	16 778	17 285	17 804	17 647	17 746	18 460	20 159	4.5
Other services, except public administration	12 997	13 267	13 093	13 069	12 883	12 772	12 985	14 037	2.9
Government	54 351	54 958	55 529	57 271	56 930	57 755	59 023	61 774	2.8
As a percent of gross state product	13.1	12.6	12.3	12.2	11.8	11.6	11.4	11.3	X

X = Not applicable.

Table FL-12. Government Transfer Payments, Selected Years 1980–2004

(Millions of dollars, percent.)

Item	1980	1990	2000	2001	2002	2003	2004	Average annual percent change, 2000–2004
CURRENT TRANSFER PAYMENTS TO INDIVIDUALS	12 685	32 590	64 208	70 160	76 553	81 297	87 150	7.9
Retirement and Disability Insurance Benefits	7 475	17 280	29 551	31 319	32 950	34 283	36 080	5.1
Old-age, survivors, and disability insurance (OASDI) benefits	7 155	16 656	28 712	30 468	32 043	33 332	35 094	5.1
Railroad retirement and disability benefits	221	367	434	442	456	470	478	2.4
Workers' compensation	66	143	263	255	278	279	289	2.3
Other government retirement and disability insurance benefits	34	113	142	153	173	203	219	11.4
Medical Benefits	2 824	11 011	26 285	29 547	32 740	35 434	38 886	10.3
Medicare benefits	2 332	7 971	18 049	20 045	21 507	22 773	25 075	8.6
Public assistance medical care benefits	417	2 729	7 917	9 022	10 562	12 101	13 147	13.5
Military medical insurance benefits	75	312	318	479	671	560	664	20.2
Income Maintenance Benefits	1 054	2 147	5 144	5 394	6 075	6 748	7 626	10.3
Supplemental Security Income (SSI) benefits	294	666	1 649	1 753	1 824	1 928	2 016	5.1
Family assistance	203	448	511	638	675	638	650	6.2
Food stamps	445	660	771	787	891	1 036	1 504	18.2
Other income maintenance benefits	111	372	2 213	2 216	2 685	3 147	3 457	11.8
Unemployment Insurance Compensation	223	518	698	1 035	1 692	1 622	1 175	13.9
Veterans' Benefits	960	1 316	1 919	2 046	2 258	2 419	2 548	7.3
Federal Education and Training Assistance	146	304	559	719	795	752	799	9.3
Other Payments to Individuals	3	13	51	100	43	39	38	-7.4

Note: See notes and definitions for more details. Data may not add to total or may appear as zero due to rounding.

EXPORTS

As one of the nation's top exporters, Florida exported goods worth just under $29 billion in 2004, which reflected a strong recovery after a fall-off in sales in 2002. The chief exports were computers and electronic products and transportation equipment, which increased by over 31 percent from 2001 and 2004. Chemicals and machinery manufactures are also among the state's leading exports. Agricultural and livestock exports increased by 15 percent from 2001 to 2004; however, they made up just 3 percent of the state's total exports. Ten percent of Florida's exports went to Brazil, one-third of which were computers and electronic products.

Leading Exports, 2004

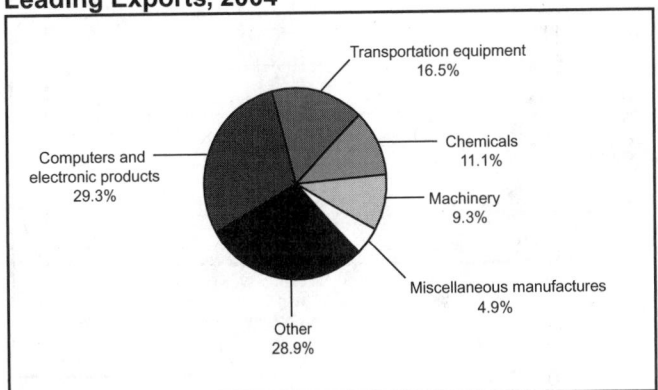

Table FL-13. Exports of Goods by Leading Products and Destinations, 2001–2004

(Millions of dollars, percent, rank based on 2004 dollar values.)

Product and market	2001	2002	2003	2004	Percent share of total, 2004	Average annual percent change, 2001–2004
Total Goods						
Total	27 185	24 544	24 953	28 982	100.0	2.2
Manufactures	25 513	23 022	23 305	27 069	93.4	2.0
Agriculture and livestock	777	769	783	897	3.1	4.9
Other commodities	895	754	865	1 016	3.5	4.3
Five Leading Exports (NAICS Code)						
Computers and electronic products (334)	8 383	7 226	7 287	8 479	29.3	0.4
Transportation equipment (336)	3 650	3 638	3 728	4 794	16.5	9.5
Chemical manufactures (325)	2 570	2 673	2 921	3 224	11.1	7.9
Machinery manufactures (333)	3 129	2 354	2 249	2 709	9.3	-4.7
Miscellaneous manufactures (339)	1 210	1 272	1 314	1 407	4.9	5.2
Five Leading Markets	21 144	18 936	19 006	21 598	74.5	0.7
Brazil	3 625	2 782	2 537	2 905	10.0	-7.1
Canada	2 588	2 294	2 369	2 500	8.6	-1.1
Mexico	1 695	1 477	1 815	1 795	6.2	1.9
Venezuela	1 641	1 233	776	1 500	5.2	-2.9
Colombia	1 010	961	1 018	1 104	3.8	3.0

Table FL-14. Agriculture, 1997 and 2002

(Number, acres, and dollars.)

Item	1997	2002
Number of farms	45 808	44 081
Land in farms (acres)	10 659 777	10 414 877
Farm Size		
Average size of farm (acres)	233	236
Farms by size (percent distribution)		
Fewer than 50 acres	64.0	64.9
50 to 499 acres	29.7	28.3
500 acres or more	6.4	6.8
Market Value of Land and Equipment (Dollars)		
Land and buildings average value per farm	540 572	665 376
Average value per acre	2 344	2 836
Machinery and equipment average value per farm	35 239	39 884
Value of Sales (Thousands of Dollars)		
Agricultural products sold	6 137 802	6 242 272
Crops	4 853 417	5 041 433
Livestock, poultry, and their products	1 284 385	1 200 839
Average per farm (dollars)	133 990	141 609
Value of sales (percent distribution)		
Less than $10,000	64.9	63.4
$10,000 to $99,999	23.3	25.0
$100,000 or more	11.7	11.6
Government Payments		
Payments (thousands of dollars)	11 759	21 818
Percent of farms receiving government payments	9.6	5.8
Farm operators whose principal occupation is farming (percent)	41.9	52.2

AGRICULTURE

Cash receipts from farming totaled over $6.2 billion in 2002. Oranges and greenhouse and nursery items were Florida's major crops. Farming was relatively small-scale, as 63.4 percent of farms had values of cash receipts less than $10,000. Nearly 65 percent of farms spanned fewer than 50 acres. Only New Jersey and Hawaii had higher proportions of small farms. Just over 52 percent of Florida's farm operators considered farming as their chief occupation.

ENERGY

Energy prices in Florida were the 12th highest in the nation. Due to the state's favorable climate, expenditures per person ranked last, at about $500 below the U.S. average. The chief consuming sector was transportation, followed by the residential sector. Florida's leading source of energy was petroleum, which accounted for about half of total energy consumption. The state's consumption per capita of 253 Btu was low, ranking which ranked 45th in the nation.

Energy Consumption by Source, 2001

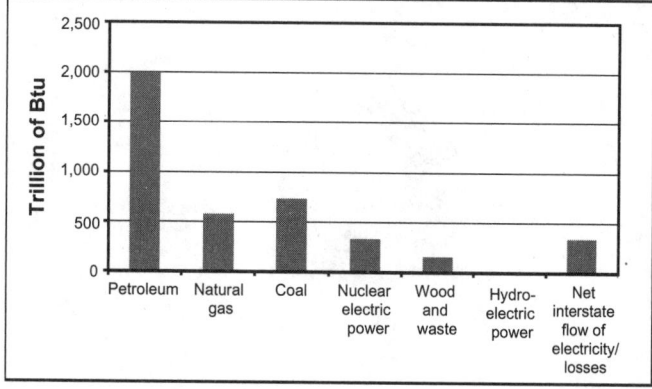

Energy Consumption by Sector, 2001

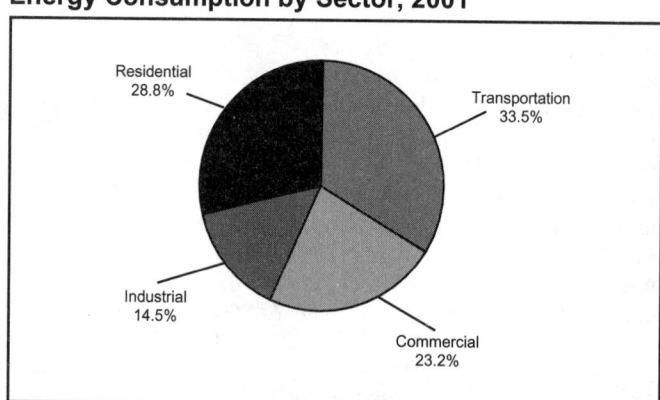

Table FL-15. Energy Consumption, Expenditures, and Prices, Selected Years 1960–2001

(Dollars, Btu [British Thermal Unit], percent distribution.)

Item	1960	1965	1970	1975	1980	1985	1990	1995	2000	2001
Total Consumption (Billion Btu)	810 454	1 115 514	1 581 422	1 945 116	2 511 814	2 703 299	3 276 908	3 653 423	4 137 819	4 134 776
Consumption per capita (million Btu)	163.7	187.4	232.9	228.3	257.7	238.2	253.3	257.5	258.9	252.8
Consumption by Sector (Percent Distribution)										
Residential	16.8	17.5	22.2	23.6	23.8	26.2	26.7	28.3	28.4	28.8
Commercial	12.4	13.5	15.8	17.1	15.2	20.6	21.9	21.7	22.8	23.2
Industrial	27.9	28.0	23.5	20.9	23.1	17.9	16.7	16.8	14.8	14.5
Transportation	42.9	40.9	38.5	38.4	37.8	35.3	34.7	33.2	34.0	33.5
Consumption by Source (Billion Btu)										
Coal	27 176	55 189	116 720	133 463	225 457	472 352	633 393	686 921	760 448	726 066
Natural gas	142 900	191 669	350 626	292 139	329 568	305 060	341 994	574 460	569 758	569 758
Petroleum	612 793	826 642	1 069 395	1 381 996	1 661 856	1 334 125	1 582 135	1 611 790	1 960 475	1 989 711
Nuclear electric power	0	0	0	92 177	182 563	249 204	230 471	301 978	336 766	329 983
Hydroelectric power[1]	2 990	3 118	3 061	2 438	2 229	2 549	1 816	2 380	885	1 503
Wood and waste	32 690	36 798	47 974	47 568	73 843	101 492	151 310	187 338	162 238	149 979
Other	0	0	0	0	0	0	0	27 480	32 634	31 693
Net interstate flow of electricity/losses[2]	-8 096	2 098	-6 354	-4 665	36 297	238 518	308 309	251 072	310 512	336 083
Total Expenditures (Thousands of Dollars)	...	...	2 633 200	6 042 800	14 856 600	18 554 000	20 975 400	22 961 300	30 660 500	31 605 300
Expenditures per capita (dollars)	...	...	388	709	1 524	1 635	1 621	1 619	1 918	1 932
Prices by Sector (Dollars Per Million Btu)										
Total	...	...	2.34	4.59	8.78	10.73	10.18	10.04	12.04	12.48
Residential	...	...	4.54	8.91	14.16	20.44	21.02	21.57	21.97	24.41
Commercial	...	...	3.53	7.13	12.25	15.66	15.02	15.67	16.06	18.28
Industrial	...	...	0.97	2.70	5.42	7.03	5.14	4.57	6.40	6.76
Transportation	...	...	2.19	3.79	8.39	8.19	7.94	7.66	10.16	9.52

[1]A negative number in this row results from pumped storage for which, overall, more electricity is expended than created to provide electricity during peak demand periods.
[2]Net interstate flow of electricity is the difference between the amount of energy in the electricity sold within a state (including associated losses) and the energy input at the electric utilities within the state. A positive number indicates that more electricity (including associated losses) came into the state than went out of the state during the year; conversely, a negative number indicates that more electricity (including associated losses) went out of the state than came into the state.
... = Not available.

Table FL-16. State Taxes, Fiscal 2004

(Dollars, percent distribution.)

Item	Thousands of dollars	Percent distribution	Dollars per capita	
			State	U.S.
TOTAL TAXES	30 767 561	100.0	1 768.6	2 024.8
Property Taxes	261 690	0.9	15.0	38.9
Sales and Gross Receipts	23 707 430	77.1	1 362.7	1 003.4
General sales and gross receipts	17 355 404	56.4	997.6	677.0
Selective sales taxes	6 352 026	20.6	365.1	326.4
Alcoholic beverages	591 551	1.9	34.0	15.7
Insurance premiums	573 100	1.9	32.9	47.0
Motor fuels	1 823 349	5.9	104.8	114.6
Public utilities	2 504 220	8.1	144.0	39.2
Tobacco products	446 406	1.5	25.7	42.0
Other selective sales	386 651	1.3	22.2	49.8
Licenses	1 774 881	5.8	102.0	134.9
Corporation	161 423	0.5	9.3	21.6
Motor vehicle	1 124 851	3.7	64.7	59.4
Occupation and business, not elsewhere classified	255 501	0.8	14.7	37.1
Other Taxes	5 023 560	16.3	288.8	847.6
Corporation net income	1 345 780	4.4	77.4	105.1
Death and gift	383 030	1.2	22.0	19.6
Documentary and stock transfer	3 250 670	10.6	186.8	27.1

GOVERNMENT FINANCE

Florida's revenues fell slightly short of expenditures during 2003, partly due to the need for increased spending on hurricane-related costs. However, expenditures per capita were the lowest in the nation in 2003. The per capita revenue also ranked last among the 50 states. Florida's total taxes per person were well below average, ranking 35th in the nation. Although Florida had a relatively high sales tax rate—which affected tourists as well as residents—the state did not have individual state income taxes. Florida's property taxes were relatively low when compared to the U.S. average. The state's debt per capita of less than $1,300 was also relatively low.

Per Capita State Taxes, Fiscal 2004

Table FL-17. State Government Finances, 2003

(Dollars, percent distribution.)

Item	Millions of dollars	Percent distribution	Dollars per capita	
			State	U.S.
GENERAL REVENUE	49 584 279	100.0	2 916.9	3 832.6
Intergovernmental revenue	12 850 982	25.9	756.0	1 246.0
Taxes	26 993 487	54.4	1 588.0	1 891.6
General sales	14 963 444	30.2	880.2	636.0
Selective sales	5 611 868	11.3	330.1	307.4
License taxes	1 756 585	3.5	103.3	123.6
Individual income tax	0	0.0	0.0	626.8
Corporate income tax	1 226 980	2.5	72.2	97.8
Other taxes	3 434 610	6.9	202.0	99.9
Current charges	3 364 671	6.8	197.9	366.5
Miscellaneous general revenue	6 375 139	12.9	375.0	328.6
GENERAL EXPENDITURE	50 217 755	100.0	2 954.2	4 010.5
Intergovernmental expenditure	14 460 722	28.8	850.7	1 316.9
Direct expenditure	35 757 033	71.2	2 103.5	2 693.6
Expenditure by Function				
Education	16 326 315	32.5	960.4	1 416.4
Public welfare	13 399 713	26.7	788.3	1 083.3
Hospitals	224 631	0.4	13.2	132.3
Health	2 902 463	5.8	170.7	173.0
Highways	4 943 244	9.8	290.8	295.4
Police protection	415 772	0.8	24.5	38.4
Correction	2 141 271	4.3	126.0	135.0
Natural resources	1 697 840	3.4	99.9	64.0
Parks and recreation	197 185	0.4	11.6	20.1
Government administration	1 864 022	3.7	109.6	151.3
Interest on general debt	1 016 285	2.0	59.8	107.8
Other and unallocable	5 089 014	10.1	299.4	393.4
DEBT AT END OF FISCAL YEAR	21 993 221	X	1 293.8	2 404.7
CASH AND SECURITY HOLDINGS	138 711 144	X	8 160.0	8 938.4

X = Not applicable.

Table FL-18. Education Indicators, 2000–2004

(Percent, number.)

Item	State	U.S.
Total Population 25 Years and Over (Thousands), 2004	11 489	186 877
Educational Attainment, 2004		
Percent high school graduate or more	85.9	85.2
Percent college graduate or more	26.0	27.7
Elementary and Secondary Schools, 2002–2003		
Total students	2 539 929	48 202 324
Percent of students eligible for free or reduced-price lunch ..	45.8	40.6
Percent of students who were English language learners	7.6	7.8
Total schools	3 382	92 330
Student/teacher ratio	17.9	15.9
Per student expenditures	6 439	8 041
Dropouts, Grades 9–12, 2000–2001 (Percent)	3.7	. . .
Higher Education, 2002–2003		
Total enrollment	850 711	17 035 027
Bachelor's degrees awarded	58 933	1 348 503
Percent women	57.6	57.5

. . . = Not available.

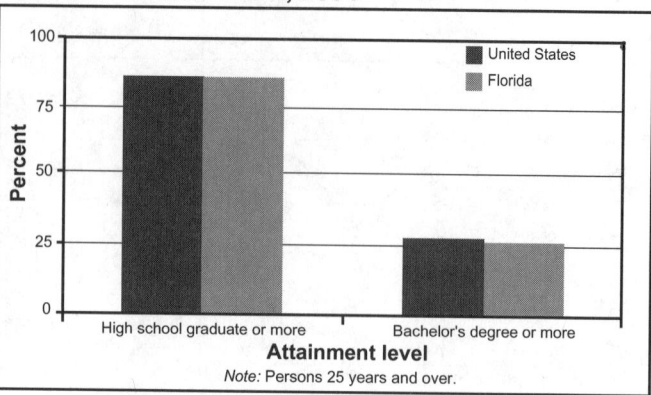

Educational Attainment, 2004

Note: Persons 25 years and over.

EDUCATION

The educational attainment of the population largely reflected its age composition. The proportion of the population holding high school diplomas was above average in 2004; however, the state's college attainment level was below average, reflecting the fact that fewer older persons were college graduates. Florida had the ninth highest student/teacher ratio in the nation, with 17.9 students per teacher. The state's per student expenditures, at $6,439, ranked among the 10 lowest in the nation. The state's dropout rate was 3.6 percent, which was below average among the 46 states reporting dropout data.

VOTER PARTICIPATION

Turnout among eligible voters for the most recent presidential elections was 51.6 percent in 2000 and 56.1 percent in 2004. Florida ranked 43rd in the nation for voter turnout in the 2004 election. Close to 66 percent of eligible women voted in 2004. Non-Hispanic Whites also had relatively high voter turnout. Of the popular vote cast for president in 2000, 48.8 percent went to each of the two major candidates. In 2004, 52.1 percent voted for the Republican candidate and 47.1 voted for the Democratic candidate, according to the official tally by the Clerk of the U.S. House of Representatives.

Table FL-19. Reported Voting and Registration, November 2000 and November 2004

(Numbers in thousands, percent.)

Characteristic	Total population 18 years and over	Total citizen		Total registered		Total voted	
		Number	Percent	Number	Percent	Number	Percent
NOVEMBER 2000							
Total	11 633	10 081	86.7	7 043	60.5	6 006	51.6
Male	5 533	4 749	85.8	3 228	58.3	2 740	49.5
Female	6 100	5 332	87.4	3 816	62.6	3 266	53.5
NOVEMBER 2004							
Total	13 133	11 469	87.3	8 219	62.6	7 372	56.1
Male	6 266	5 393	86.1	3 784	60.4	3 375	53.9
Female	6 867	6 075	88.5	4 434	64.6	3 997	58.2
Race and Hispanic Origin							
White alone	10 871	9 635	88.6	7 030	64.7	6 349	58.4
Non-Hispanic White alone	8 594	8 279	96.3	6 169	71.8	5 577	64.9
Black alone	1 832	1 490	81.3	965	52.6	815	44.5
Asian alone[1]	260	185	71.4	97	37.2	86	33.1
Hispanic or Latino[1]	2 422	1 444	59.6	924	38.2	824	34.0
White alone or in combination	11 011	9 770	88.7	7 135	64.8	6 450	58.6
Non-Hispanic White alone or in combination	8 701	8 384	96.4	6 251	71.8	5 656	65.0
Black alone or in combination	1 873	1 528	81.6	994	53.1	841	44.9
Asian alone or in combination	277	203	73.2	112	40.2	99	35.7
Age							
18 to 24 years	1 503	1 257	83.7	712	47.4	581	38.7
25 to 44 years	4 522	3 658	80.9	2 488	55.0	2 173	48.1
45 to 64 years	4 374	3 970	90.8	2 916	66.7	2 693	61.6
65 to 74 years	1 345	1 258	93.5	988	73.5	922	68.6
75 years and over	1 390	1 326	95.4	1 115	80.2	1 003	72.2

[1]May be of any race.

At a Glance:

- Georgia's population was just over 8.8 million in 2004, ranking it as the ninth most populous state in the nation.

- Non-Hispanic Whites totaled 60.2 percent of the population, and Blacks made up 29.7 percent of residents, which was the fourth largest proportion of this racial group in the United States.

- Georgia had the fifth highest birth rate in the nation. In 2004, 9.6 percent of the state's population was age 65 years and over, which was the third lowest proportion of this age group in the country.

- Median household income ranked 37th in the nation. The poverty rate was 13.1 percent, which was only slightly above the national average and ranked as the 19th highest in the country.

- Georgia's unemployment rate was 4.6 percent in 2004, ranking as the 13th lowest in the nation.

- The gross state product, which has grown steadily in recent years, ranked 10th in the country.

- In 2004, 17.4 percent of the state's population lacked health insurance, giving Georgia one of the highest proportions of uninsured residents in the nation.

Table GA-1. Population by Sex and Age, 1990, 2000, and 2004

(Number, percent.)

Sex and age	1990	2000	2004	Percent distribution, 2004	Average annual percent change, 2000–2004
Total Population	6 478 216	8 186 453	8 829 383	X	1.9
Percent of total U.S. population	2.6	2.9	3.0	X	X
Sex					
Male	3 144 503	4 027 113	4 365 423	49.4	2.0
Female	3 333 713	4 159 340	4 463 960	50.6	1.8
Age					
Under 5 years	495 535	595 150	679 064	7.7	2.1
5 to 17 years	1 231 768	1 574 084	1 653 503	18.7	2.1
18 years and over	1 167 465	6 017 219	6 496 816	73.6	2.3
18 to 24 years	4 750 913	837 732	901 607	10.2	1.4
25 to 44 years	738 584	2 652 764	2 755 988	31.2	1.7
45 to 64 years	2 190 594	1 741 448	1 992 139	22.6	3.9
65 years and over	654 270	785 275	847 082	9.6	1.9
85 years and over	57 244	87 857	95 273	1.1	3.9
Median age (years)	31.4	33.4	33.8	X	X

X = Not applicable.

Average Annual Rate of Population Growth, 1980–2004

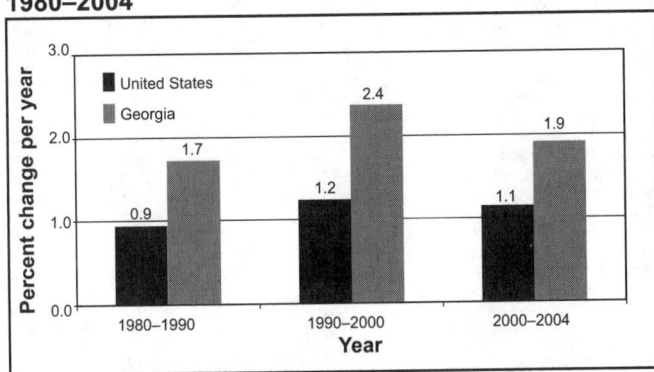

POPULATION

Georgia's population has grown steadily in recent years. Between 2000 and 2004, its rate of increase was the fifth fastest in the country. During this time, the state experienced high rates of immigration. Georgia was the fourth leading destination for people moving from other states; more than 181,000 people moved to the state from 2000 to 2004. Another 161,000 moved to Georgia from other countries. An above average birth rate also contributed to the high population growth. The population growth has largely been centered around Atlanta, which has drawn large numbers of working-age people.

Table GA-2. Population by Race and Hispanic Origin, 1990, 2000, and 2004

(Number, percent.)

Race and Hispanic origin	1990	2000	2004
Total Population	6 478 216	8 186 453	8 829 383
Non-Hispanic (Percent)			
One race[1]			
White	70.1	62.8	60.2
Black	26.8	28.6	29.2
American Indian, Alaska Native[2]	0.2	0.2	0.2
Asian and Pacific Islander[2]	1.2	2.2	2.6
Other race[2]	0.7	. . .	. . .
Two or more races	. . .	0.8	0.9
Hispanic or Latino[3] (Percent)	1.7	5.3	6.8

[1]Individuals could report only one race in the 1990 census and could report one or more races on the 2000 census. Data on race in 2000 and 2004 are not comparable to 1990.
[2]Data for 1990 include people of Hispanic or Latino origin.
[3]May be of any race.
. . . = Not available.

Minority Population as a Percent of Total Population, 2004

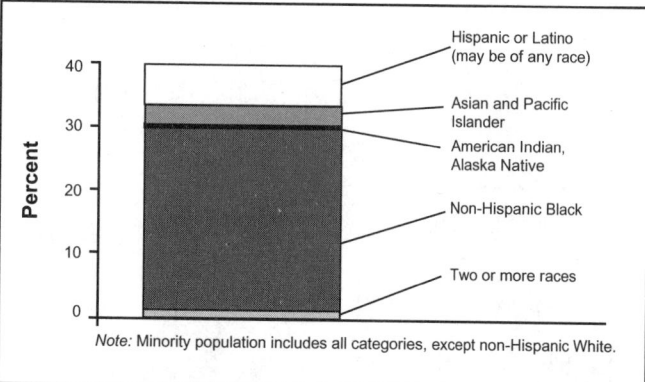

Note: Minority population includes all categories, except non-Hispanic White.

Age-Adjusted Death Rates, Average 2000–2002

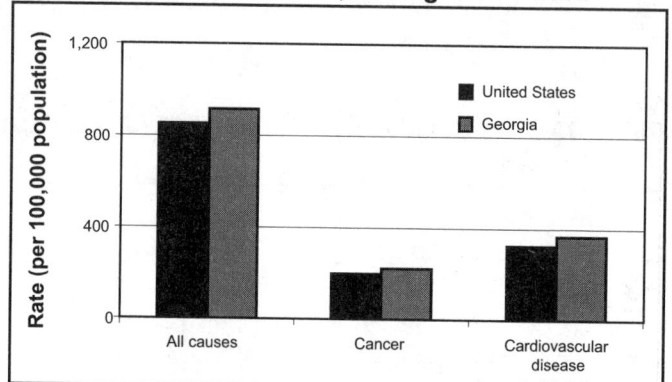

HEALTH

Georgia's infant mortality rate of 8.7 deaths per 1,000 live births was the eighth highest rate in the nation. The state's birth rate for teenage mothers was the ninth highest in the United States. The age-adjusted death rates in Georgia were above average for most of the leading causes of death.

Table GA-3. Health Characteristics, 2000–2004

(Number, rate, percent.)

Item	State	U.S.
Births, 2003–2004		
Number of births	135 979	4 089 950
Birth rate (per 1,000 population)	15.7	14.1
Teenage birth rate (per 1,000 women age 15–19 years)	53.5	41.6
Mortality Rates, Average 2000–2002		
Infant mortality rate (per 1,000 live births)	8.7	6.9
Age-adjusted mortality rate (per 100,000 population)		
All races	958.9	853.3
Non-Hispanic White	919.9	843.1
Black	1 136.7	1 097.7
American Indian, Alaska Native	. . .	687.0
Asian and Pacific Islander	410.2	486.0
Hispanic or Latino[1]	366.5	642.7
Health Insurance, 2004		
Percent of all persons without health insurance	17.4	15.7
Percent of children without health insurance	11.7	11.2
Percent of low-income children without health insurance	8.3	7.1

[1]May be of any race.
. . . = Not available.

Table GA-4. Leading Causes of Death, Average 2000–2002

(Number, rate per 100,000 population.)

Cause	Number of deaths	Age-adjusted death rates	
		State	U.S.
ALL CAUSES	64 601	958.9	853.3
Leading Causes			
Major cardiovascular diseases	23 621	363.7	326.5
Cancer	13 828	202.3	196.0
Chronic lower respiratory diseases	3 109	48.1	43.7
Unintentional injuries	3 277	42.0	35.7
Diabetes (underlying cause)	1 504	22.3	25.2
Influenza and pneumonia	1 699	27.0	22.7
Alzheimer's disease	1 393	23.1	19.0
Motor vehicle accidents	1 526	18.5	15.0
Nephritis, nephrotic syndrome, and nephrosis ..	1 320	20.3	13.8
Septicemia	1 259	19.1	11.4
Suicides	897	11.0	10.7
Firearm-related	1 118	13.4	10.3
Cirrhosis	660	8.8	9.5
Drug-induced	550	6.5	7.9
Alcohol-induced	490	6.1	6.9
Homicides	669	7.7	6.0
Falls	400	6.1	5.2
HIV	725	8.5	5.0
Viral Hepatitis	124	1.6	2.0
Anemias	132	1.9	1.6
Drownings	124	1.4	1.3
Fire deaths	128	1.7	1.2

Note: The rates are age-adjusted to the U.S. 2000 standard population.

Table GA-5. Households and Housing Characteristics, 1990, 2000, and 2004

(Number, percent, and dollars.)

Characteristic	1990	2000	2004	Average annual percent change, 2000–2004
Total Households	2 366 615	3 006 369	3 210 006	1.7
Family households	1 713 072	2 111 647	2 217 238	1.2
Married-couple family	1 306 756	1 548 800	1 583 309	0.6
Other family	406 316	562 847	633 929	3.0
Male householder, no wife present	76 675	127 437	149 025	4.0
Female householder, no husband present	329 641	435 410	484 904	2.7
Nonfamily households	653 543	894 722	992 768	2.6
Householder living alone	537 702	710 523	826 300	3.8
Householder not living alone	115 841	184 199	166 468	-2.5
Housing Characteristics				
Average size	2.66	2.65	2.67	X
Housing units	2 638 418	3 281 737	3 672 677	2.9
Occupied housing units	2 366 615	3 006 369	3 210 006	1.7
Owner-occupied	1 536 759	2 029 154	2 172 266	1.7
Renter-occupied	829 856	977 215	1 037 740	1.5
Median gross rent of renter-occupied housing units (dollars) ...	433	613	677	2.5
Median value of owner-occupied housing units (dollars)	70 700	111 200	136 912	5.3

X = Not applicable.

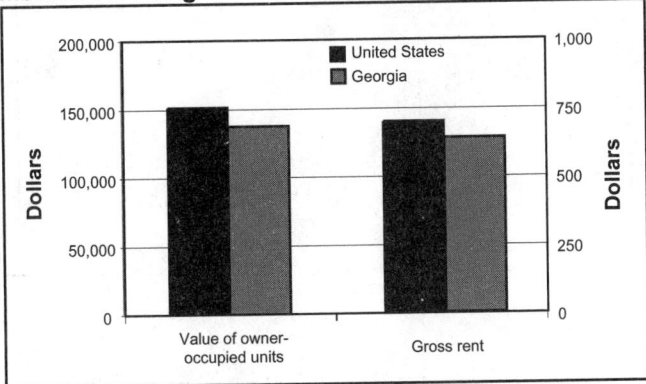

Median Housing Value and Median Rent, 2004

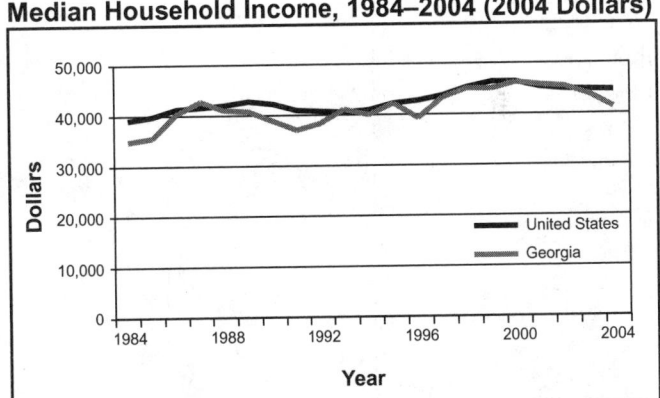

Median Household Income, 1984–2004 (2004 Dollars)

Table GA-6. Household Income and Poverty Status, 1980–2004

(2004 CPI-U-RS adjusted dollars, rate.)

Year	State		U.S.	
	Median household income (2004 dollars)	Poverty rate	Median household income (2004 dollars)	Poverty rate
2004	40 970	13.1	44 389	12.7
2003	43 579	11.9	44 482	12.5
2002	45 103	11.2	44 546	12.1
2001	45 433	12.9	45 062	11.7
2000	45 961	12.1	46 058	11.3
1999	44 688	12.8	46 129	11.9
1998	44 749	13.5	45 003	12.7
1997	43 029	14.5	43 430	13.3
1996	38 953	14.8	42 544	13.7
1995	41 972	12.1	41 943	13.8
1994	39 673	14.0	40 677	14.5
1993	40 760	13.5	40 217	15.1
1992	37 995	17.7	40 422	14.8
1991	36 804	17.2	40 746	14.2
1990	38 625	15.8	41 963	13.5
1989	40 518	15.0	42 524	12.8
1988	40 760	14.0	41 771	13.0
1987	42 480	14.6	41 322	13.4
1986	40 073	14.6	40 939	13.6
1985	35 244	17.7	39 545	14.0
1984	34 576	16.9	38 782	14.4
1983	. . .	18.8	. . .	15.2
1982	. . .	19.6	. . .	15.0
1981	. . .	16.3	. . .	14.0
1980	. . .	13.9	. . .	13.0

. . . = Not available.

Table GA-7. Employment Status by Demographic Group, 2004

(Numbers in thousands, rate.)

Characteristic	Civilian noninstitutional population	Civilian labor force		Employed	Unemployment rate
		Number	Participation rate		
SEX AND AGE					
Total	6 534	4 399	67.3	4 194	4.7
16 to 19 years	436	160	36.7	134	16.3
20 to 24 years	637	461	72.4	427	7.3
25 to 34 years	1 323	1 088	82.2	1 037	4.7
35 to 44 years	1 364	1 154	84.6	1 115	3.4
45 to 54 years	1 187	947	79.7	907	4.2
55 to 64 years	813	486	59.7	473	2.5
65 years and over	773	103	13.3	99	3.3
Men	3 142	2 389	76.0	2 280	4.6
16 to 19 years	211	88	41.7	74	15.5
20 to 24 years	314	253	80.6	234	7.6
25 to 34 years	659	606	91.9	582	4.0
35 to 44 years	678	618	91.2	597	3.4
45 to 54 years	555	475	85.6	452	4.7
55 to 64 years	406	283	69.7	277	2.0
Women	3 392	2 010	59.2	1 914	4.8
16 to 19 years	225	72	32.0	60	17.2
20 to 24 years	324	208	64.3	194	7.0
25 to 34 years	664	483	72.7	456	5.6
35 to 44 years	687	536	78.1	518	3.4
45 to 54 years	633	472	74.6	454	3.7
55 to 64 years	407	203	49.8	196	3.3
MARITAL STATUS					
Married men, spouse present	1 778	1 424	80.1	1 394	2.1
Married women, spouse present	1 740	1 054	60.6	1 020	3.3
Women who maintain families	497	354	71.3	328	7.6
RACE, HISPANIC ORIGIN, AND SEX					
White	4 558	3 052	67.0	2 946	3.5
Men	2 244	1 732	77.2	1 677	3.2
Women	2 314	1 320	57.1	1 270	3.8
Black	1 738	1 178	67.8	1 087	7.7
Men	773	560	72.5	512	8.6
Women	965	618	64.1	575	7.0
Asian	164	118	71.5	113	3.8
Hispanic or Latino[1]	383	299	78.1	285	4.6
Men	228	208	91.5	202	2.9
Women	155	91	58.4	83	8.5
RACE, HISPANIC ORIGIN, AND AGE					
White					
20 to 24 years	421	297	70.7	280	5.8
25 to 34 years	881	718	81.5	695	3.2
35 to 44 years	929	789	84.9	768	2.7
45 to 54 years	839	681	81.1	658	3.3
55 to 64 years	611	385	62.9	376	2.2
65 years and over	615	80	13.0	78	2.6
Black					
25 to 34 years	378	314	83.0	288	8.1
35 to 44 years	390	328	84.0	310	5.2
45 to 54 years	309	233	75.4	218	6.4

Note: Data in Table 7 are from the Current Population Survey (CPS) and do not match Bureau of Labor Statistics estimates in Table 8. See notes and definitions for more details.

[1]May be of any race.

Table GA-8. Employment Status, 1990–2004

(Numbers in thousands, rate.)

Year	Civilian labor force	Employed	Unemployed	Unemployment rate
2004	4 390 395	4 188 271	202 124	4.6
2003	4 340 666	4 134 525	206 141	4.7
2002	4 308 229	4 100 119	208 110	4.8
2001	4 277 967	4 107 109	170 858	4.0
2000	4 233 388	4 084 062	149 326	3.5
1999	4 106 678	3 951 684	154 994	3.8
1998	4 029 245	3 861 646	167 599	4.2
1997	3 926 801	3 751 699	175 102	4.5
1996	3 812 908	3 638 219	174 689	4.6
1995	3 699 727	3 522 905	176 822	4.8
1994	3 594 682	3 412 606	182 076	5.1
1993	3 485 592	3 278 794	206 798	5.9
1992	3 410 412	3 182 777	227 635	6.7
1991	3 298 665	3 132 596	166 069	5.0
1990	3 300 136	3 129 389	170 747	5.2

Unemployment Rate, 1980–2004

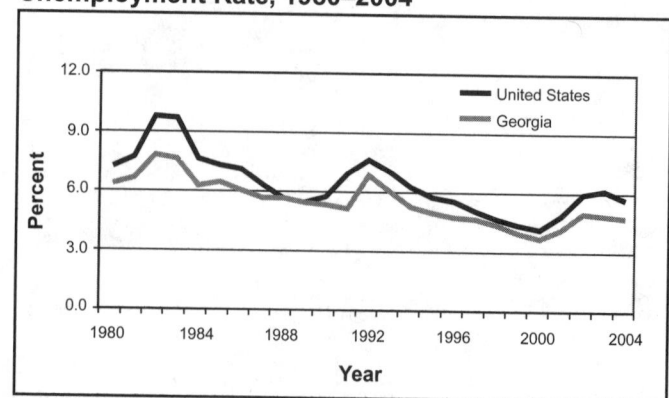

Note: Population age 16 years and over.

Table GA-9. Employment and Average Wages by Industry, 2001–2004

(Estimates are based on the 2002 North American Industry Classification System [NAICS].)

Industry	2001	2002	2003	2004	Annual average percent change, 2001–2004
	Number of jobs				
TOTAL EMPLOYMENT BY PLACE OF WORK	4 907 675	4 893 437	4 921 409	5 016 893	0.7
Farm Employment	65 561	67 281	66 664	66 868	0.7
Nonfarm Employment	4 842 114	4 826 156	4 854 745	4 950 025	0.7
Private employment	4 133 251	4 102 109	4 120 414	4 208 712	0.6
Forestry, fishing, hunting, and other¹	28 210	27 760	26 317	26 126	-2.5
Mining	9 784	8 940	9 168	9 160	-2.2
Utilities	21 270	21 141	21 001	20 806	-0.7
Construction	313 109	302 188	309 926	316 573	0.4
Manufacturing	520 835	488 989	464 210	464 534	-3.7
Durable goods manufacturing	236 716	219 824	207 381	210 751	-3.8
Nondurable goods manufacturing	284 119	269 165	256 829	253 783	-3.7
Wholesale trade	229 213	222 484	219 647	222 069	-1.0
Retail trade	549 060	543 125	539 380	544 756	-0.3
Transportation and warehousing	194 108	188 829	187 008	190 539	-0.6
Information	154 864	142 527	134 328	131 307	-5.4
Finance and insurance	203 359	205 441	207 635	210 611	1.2
Real estate and rental and leasing	156 853	162 974	175 923	184 537	5.6
Professional and technical services	293 582	290 802	295 784	298 668	0.6
Management of companies and enterprises	66 917	61 516	53 699	55 377	-6.1
Administrative and waste services	315 065	321 483	325 819	352 174	3.8
Educational services	76 906	81 934	84 524	86 445	4.0
Health care and social assistance	360 418	374 107	389 800	401 782	3.7
Arts, entertainment, and recreation	71 067	71 453	72 826	73 743	1.2
Accommodation and food services	316 370	320 923	333 297	345 994	3.0
Other services, except public administration	252 261	265 493	270 122	273 511	2.7
Government and government enterprises	708 863	724 047	734 331	741 313	1.5
	Dollars				
AVERAGE WAGES AND SALARIES BY PLACE OF WORK	34 559	35 178	36 112	37 353	2.6
Farm Earnings	18 190	17 737	14 890	17 224	-1.8
Nonfarm Earnings	34 623	35 249	36 202	37 440	2.6
Private earnings	35 201	35 598	36 444	37 806	2.4
Forestry, fishing, hunting, and other¹	22 184	21 825	22 339	23 758	2.3
Mining	45 474	47 437	49 315	51 606	4.3
Utilities	64 169	67 151	68 230	68 384	2.1
Construction	35 749	36 058	36 893	38 424	2.4
Manufacturing	37 394	38 287	39 507	41 420	3.5
Durable goods manufacturing	39 792	40 346	41 580	43 481	3.0
Nondurable goods manufacturing	35 415	36 623	37 852	39 726	3.9
Wholesale trade	52 838	52 659	53 609	56 319	2.1
Retail trade	22 518	22 907	23 609	24 148	2.4
Transportation and warehousing	42 938	43 747	44 577	46 167	2.4
Information	57 265	56 979	59 675	61 395	2.3
Finance and insurance	54 820	56 296	58 297	61 277	3.8
Real estate and rental and leasing	35 008	36 413	37 293	40 117	4.6
Professional and technical services	55 967	56 315	56 886	58 771	1.6
Management of companies and enterprises	58 141	60 179	65 052	72 482	7.6
Administrative and waste services	24 553	25 228	26 754	27 499	3.8
Educational services	26 829	27 425	28 364	29 566	3.3
Health care and social assistance	33 588	34 789	35 580	37 066	3.3
Arts, entertainment, and recreation	27 602	30 417	29 296	28 150	0.7
Accommodation and food services	14 262	14 319	14 465	14 937	1.6
Other services, except public administration	22 255	22 682	23 519	24 262	2.9
Government and government enterprises	31 819	33 629	35 102	35 766	4.0

Note: Average wages and salaries are a calculation by the editors of wage and salary disbursements divided by full- and part-time wage and salary employment. Data may not add to total or may appear as zero due to rounding.

¹ "Other" consists of the number of jobs held by U.S. residents employed by international organizations and foreign embassies and consulates in the United States.

LABOR MARKET

Georgia's unemployment rate has been below average in recent years. The state also had a relatively high labor force participation rate, indicating a reasonably active labor market. The government sector was the largest employer in 2004, followed by retail trade, manufacturing, and health care services. As in many other states, manufacturing employment declined between 2001 and 2003. It appeared to have stabilized in 2004, as factory jobs edged up, although it remained well below its employment level from 2001. Georgia's average wages and salaries were below the national average across most industries, and the earnings growth rate was also slower than average.

Employment by Industry, 2004

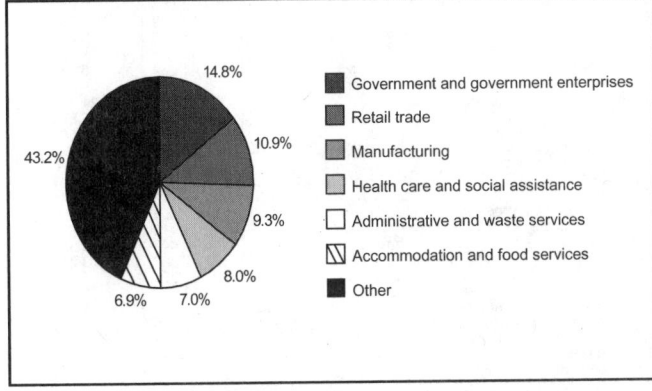

- 14.8% Government and government enterprises
- 10.9% Retail trade
- 9.3% Manufacturing
- 8.0% Health care and social assistance
- 7.0% Administrative and waste services
- 6.9% Accommodation and food services
- 43.2% Other

Table GA-10. Personal Income by Major Source, Selected Years 1980–2004

(Millions of dollars, except where noted.)

Item	1980	1990	2000	2001	2002	2003	2004	Average annual percent change, 2000–2004
Earnings by Place of Work	38 260	91 991	187 035	194 091	197 039	203 388	216 335	3.7
Wage and salary disbursements	29 805	69 654	140 529	143 845	144 592	147 807	155 166	2.5
Supplements to wages and salaries	5 567	14 407	27 348	28 842	31 727	33 825	37 477	8.2
Proprietors' income[1]	2 889	7 931	19 158	21 404	20 719	21 757	23 692	5.5
Farm proprietors' income	-135	1 018	1 361	1 656	1 126	1 591	1 730	6.2
Nonfarm proprietors' income	3 024	6 912	17 797	19 748	19 593	20 166	21 961	5.4
(-) Contributions for government social insurance[2]	3 309	9 719	19 367	20 178	20 579	21 073	22 782	4.1
(+) Adjustment for residence[3]	-114	-113	-728	-766	-811	-812	-840	X
(=) Net Earnings by Place of Residence	34 837	82 159	166 940	173 148	175 649	181 504	192 713	3.7
(+) Dividends, interest, and rent[4]	5 901	19 906	37 570	38 767	36 731	36 235	37 362	-0.1
(+) Personal current transfer receipts	5 454	12 577	25 845	28 702	32 568	32 924	35 462	8.2
Personal income	46 192	114 643	230 356	240 616	244 948	250 662	265 538	3.6
Farm income	46 167	113 400	228 722	238 650	243 503	248 792	263 476	3.6
Nonfarm income	25	1 243	1 634	1 967	1 445	1 870	2 062	6.0
Per Capita Personal Income (Dollars)[5]	8 420	17 603	27 989	28 675	28 683	28 890	30 074	1.8

Note: Data may not add to total or may appear as zero due to rounding.

[1]Proprietors' income includes the inventory valuation adjustment and the capital consumption adjustment.
[2]Contributions for government social insurance are included in earnings by type and industry, but they are excluded from personal income.
[3]The adjustment for residence is the net inflow of the earnings of interarea commuters.
[4]Rental income of persons includes the capital consumption adjustment.
[5]Per capita personal income is total personal income divided by total midyear population.
X = Not applicable.

Per Capita Personal Income, 1980–2004 (Current Dollars)

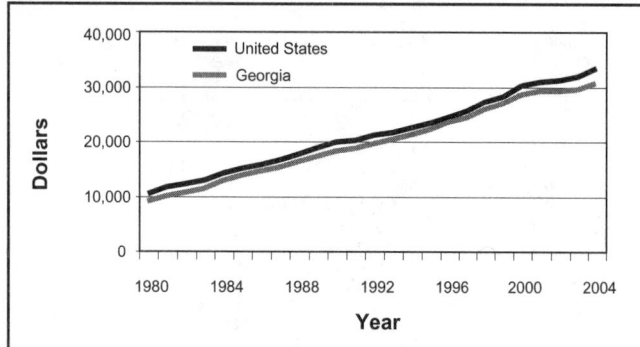

ECONOMIC ACTIVITY

Georgia had the 10th largest gross state product in 2004. However, its growth rate over the 2001–2004 period ranked 37th in the nation. From 2003 to 2004, the state's economic activity began to see some improvement with an above average rate of growth. Manufacturing, information, real estate and related activities, and finance and insurance were the strongest contributors to this growth. Housing prices rose substantially in the urban areas of Georgia, particularly in the Atlanta metropolitan area, but statewide housing price appreciation was relatively low. In 2004, the median value of owner-occupied housing in Georgia ranked 27th in the country and was well below the national average.

Table GA-11. Real Gross State Product, 1997–2004

(Millions of chained 2000 dollars, percent.)

Industry	1997	1998	1999	2000	2001	2002	2003	2004	Average annual percent change, 2001–2004
GROSS STATE PRODUCT	250 758	265 886	283 096	291 014	292 880	294 780	302 966	316 652	2.6
As a percent of U.S. gross product	2.9	3.0	3.0	3.0	3.0	2.9	2.9	2.9	X
Private Industries	218 721	232 971	249 530	256 521	257 693	258 854	265 704	278 496	2.6
Agriculture, forestry, fishing, and hunting	2 558	2 650	2 871	3 036	2 979	2 548	3 299	2 714	-3.1
Mining	809	932	1 010	1 028	946	917	946	866	-2.9
Utilities	5 289	5 277	5 408	5 871	5 457	5 517	5 906	6 020	3.3
Construction	12 923	13 723	14 553	14 385	14 048	13 327	13 379	13 738	-0.7
Manufacturing	41 062	43 135	46 830	46 223	42 251	42 204	42 996	45 707	2.7
As a percent of gross state product	16.4	16.2	16.5	15.9	14.4	14.3	14.2	14.4	X
Wholesale trade	19 008	21 775	23 181	23 275	24 957	24 624	23 689	24 475	-0.6
Retail trade	16 838	17 874	19 274	19 864	21 085	21 789	22 810	23 921	4.3
Transportation and warehousing	9 864	10 566	11 501	12 287	11 646	12 109	12 547	13 293	4.5
Information	13 141	14 990	17 441	18 766	20 169	20 304	21 311	23 047	4.5
Finance and insurance	13 151	13 776	14 990	16 174	16 812	17 216	18 795	20 170	6.3
Real estate and rental and leasing	27 320	28 637	29 919	31 254	32 428	32 413	32 616	34 211	1.8
Services	57 197	59 841	62 599	64 358	65 019	66 027	67 603	70 784	2.9
As a percent of gross state product	22.8	22.5	22.1	22.1	22.2	22.4	22.3	22.4	X
Professional and technical services	14 013	15 770	16 638	17 876	18 257	18 366	18 786	19 227	1.7
Management of companies and enterprises	6 442	6 356	6 380	6 128	5 898	5 691	5 705	6 218	1.8
Administrative and waste services	7 828	8 274	9 061	8 866	8 700	9 088	9 618	10 453	6.3
Educational services	1 372	1 437	1 571	1 611	2 137	2 093	1 987	1 958	-2.9
Health care and social assistance	13 315	13 346	13 902	14 411	14 950	15 686	16 238	16 896	4.2
Arts, entertainment, and recreation	1 757	1 686	1 915	1 920	1 991	2 094	2 004	1 919	-1.2
Accommodation and food services	6 425	6 790	7 171	7 474	7 284	7 185	7 384	7 872	2.6
Other services, except public administration	6 045	6 182	5 961	6 072	5 802	5 824	5 881	6 241	2.5
Government	32 110	32 952	33 567	34 493	35 183	35 907	37 223	38 154	2.7
As a percent of gross state product	12.8	12.4	11.9	11.9	12.0	12.2	12.3	12.0	X

X = Not applicable.

Table GA-12. Government Transfer Payments, Selected Years 1980–2004

(Millions of dollars, percent.)

Item	1980	1990	2000	2001	2002	2003	2004	Average annual percent change, 2000–2004
CURRENT TRANSFER PAYMENTS TO INDIVIDUALS	5 083	11 769	23 696	26 218	30 392	30 899	33 272	8.9
Retirement and Disability Insurance Benefits	2 442	5 303	9 822	10 506	11 172	11 706	12 352	5.9
Old-age, survivors, and disability insurance (OASDI) benefits	2 322	5 068	9 506	10 177	10 807	11 324	11 959	5.9
Railroad retirement and disability benefits	101	162	207	214	225	233	238	3.5
Workers' compensation	14	48	71	74	89	89	91	6.6
Other government retirement and disability insurance benefits	4	25	37	41	52	60	65	14.9
Medical Benefits	1 127	4 032	9 623	10 863	13 497	12 845	14 450	10.7
Medicare benefits	614	2 233	4 982	5 559	5 993	6 385	7 083	9.2
Public assistance medical care benefits	479	1 668	4 490	5 071	7 173	6 177	7 023	11.8
Military medical insurance benefits	35	131	150	234	330	283	344	23.0
Income Maintenance Benefits	737	1 415	2 806	2 954	3 283	3 827	4 202	10.6
Supplemental Security Income (SSI) benefits	234	415	785	826	854	887	928	4.3
Family assistance	138	335	266	275	193	292	298	2.9
Food stamps	274	407	489	534	648	820	960	18.4
Other income maintenance benefits	92	257	1 265	1 319	1 588	1 828	2 016	12.4
Unemployment Insurance Compensation	264	324	332	630	1 040	1 038	674	19.4
Veterans' Benefits	433	551	823	891	999	1 080	1 157	8.9
Federal Education and Training Assistance	78	140	271	336	385	379	401	10.3
Other Payments to Individuals	1	3	20	38	17	23	35	14.4

Note: See notes and definitions for more details. Data may not add to total or may appear as zero due to rounding.

EXPORTS

In 2004, Georgia ranked 11th in the nation for the value of its exports, which totaled $19.6 billion. Exports grew by 34 percent over the 2001–2004 period. Transportation equipment, computers and electronic products, machinery, and chemical manufactures were the leading exports. The value of Georgia's transportation exports more than doubled from 2001 to 2004. Computers and electronic product exports increased 43 percent during the same period. Canada, Japan, and Mexico were the largest of Georgia's export markets. Exports to China have doubled since 2001, and the country became Georgia's sixth leading export market.

Leading Exports, 2004

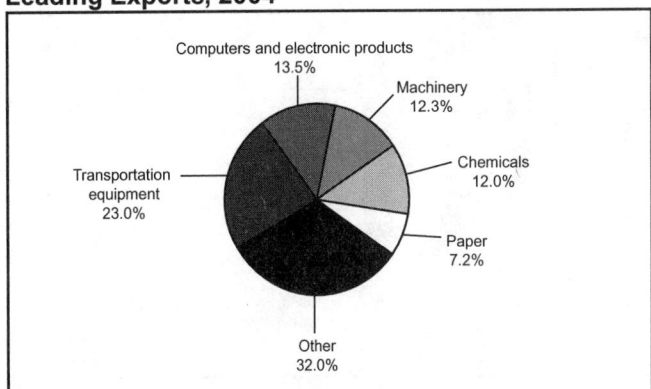

Table GA-13. Exports of Goods by Leading Products and Destinations, 2001–2004

(Millions of dollars, percent, rank based on 2004 dollar values.)

Product and market	2001	2002	2003	2004	Percent share of total, 2004	Average annual percent change, 2001–2004
Total Goods						
Total	14 644	14 413	16 286	19 633	100.0	10.3
Manufactures	13 498	13 193	14 964	18 124	92.3	10.3
Agriculture and livestock	838	903	979	1 092	5.6	9.3
Other commodities	308	317	343	416	2.1	10.6
Five Leading Exports (NAICS Code)						
Transportation equipment (336)	2 174	2 542	3 132	4 517	23.0	27.6
Computers and electronic products (334)	1 860	1 869	2 469	2 658	13.5	12.6
Machinery manufactures (333)	1 755	1 362	1 556	2 414	12.3	11.2
Chemical manufactures (325)	1 740	1 873	2 096	2 347	12.0	10.5
Paper products (322)	1 401	1 341	1 362	1 405	7.2	0.1
Five Leading Markets	11 937	11 989	13 672	16 383	83.4	11.1
Canada	3 751	3 638	3 962	4 265	21.7	4.4
Japan	1 367	1 249	1 517	1 546	7.9	4.2
Mexico	948	1 091	1 163	1 495	7.6	16.4
United Kingdom	783	954	1 036	1 111	5.7	12.4
Netherlands	425	626	893	833	4.2	25.1

Table GA-14. Agriculture, 1997 and 2002

(Number, acres, and dollars.)

Item	1997	2002
Number of farms	49 343	49 311
Land in farms (acres)	11 262 838	10 744 239
Farm Size		
Average size of farm (acres)	228	218
Farms by size (percent distribution)		
Fewer than 50 acres	35.7	39.2
50 to 499 acres	54.0	50.9
500 acres or more	10.3	9.9
Market Value of Land and Equipment (Dollars)		
Land and buildings average value per farm	362 690	457 427
Average value per acre	1 550	2 112
Machinery and equipment average value per farm	42 061	51 847
Value of Sales (Thousands of Dollars)		
Agricultural products sold	5 182 676	4 911 752
Crops	1 995 404	1 579 596
Livestock, poultry, and their products	3 187 272	3 332 156
Average per farm (dollars)	105 034	99 608
Value of sales (percent distribution)		
Less than $10,000	65.6	69.3
$10,000 to $99,999	19.3	18.0
$100,000 or more	15.1	12.7
Government Payments		
Payments (thousands of dollars)	68 579	118 535
Percent of farms receiving government payments	34.5	31.5
Farm operators whose principal occupation is farming (percent)	40.2	50.9

AGRICULTURE

Cash receipts from the sale of farm products totaled $4.9 billion in 2002, a decrease from the last farm census in 1997. Georgia's major products were poultry, cotton, and peanuts. Crops made up about 32 percent of the total value of agricultural products sold. More than 69 percent of farms had sales of less than $10,000. About half of farm operators considered farming to be their primary occupation. Just over 39 percent of farms spanned fewer than 50 acres.

ENERGY

Energy prices were below average in Georgia. The state ranked 37th in the nation by expenditures per person in 2001, the latest year for which data are available from the Department of Energy. Georgia's per capita consumption dropped to 343 Btu, which ranked 26th in the country. The highest consumption was in the industrial sector, followed by the transportation sector. In 2001, petroleum accounted for about 35 percent of energy consumption, followed by coal at 26.8 percent.

Energy Consumption by Source, 2001

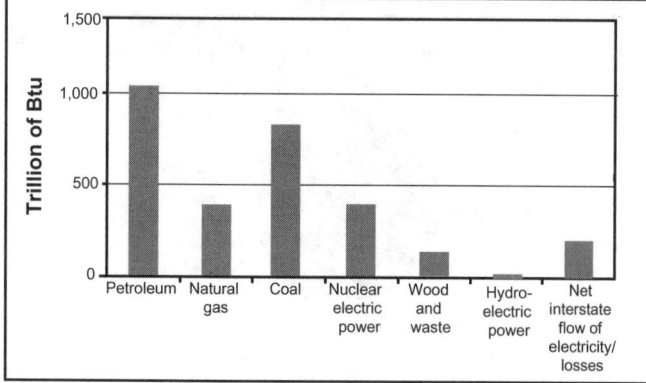

Energy Consumption by Sector, 2001

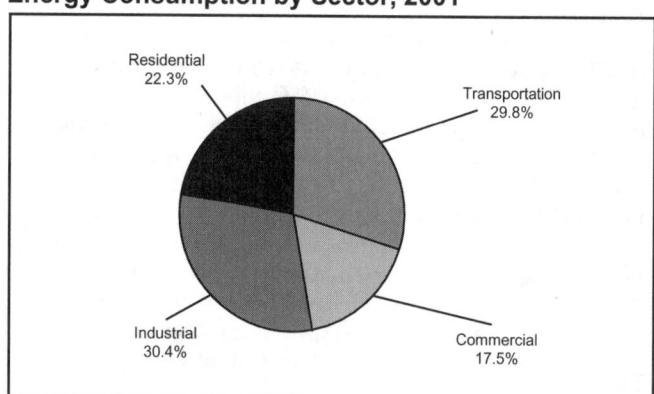

Table GA-15. Energy Consumption, Expenditures, and Prices, Selected Years 1960–2001

(Dollars, Btu [British Thermal Unit], percent distribution.)

Item	1960	1965	1970	1975	1980	1985	1990	1995	2000	2001
Total Consumption (Billion Btu)	701 822	918 235	1 280 960	1 493 402	1 727 617	1 941 712	2 305 073	2 658 073	2 983 994	2 880 617
Consumption per capita (million Btu)	178.0	212.0	279.2	294.9	316.2	325.6	355.8	369.8	364.5	343.1
Consumption by Sector (Percent Distribution)										
Residential	23.4	21.0	21.1	20.9	20.7	20.2	20.0	20.8	22.6	22.3
Commercial	9.4	9.9	11.4	12.9	12.0	13.6	14.5	14.8	16.8	17.5
Industrial	37.4	41.1	36.2	33.6	35.5	35.8	36.0	34.6	31.8	30.4
Transportation	29.7	28.0	31.3	32.6	31.8	30.4	29.6	29.8	28.8	29.8
Consumption by Source (Billion Btu)										
Coal	88 950	152 600	193 155	311 988	521 518	725 678	714 130	723 828	819 542	772 042
Natural gas	188 460	219 774	342 834	335 376	325 288	289 696	319 413	383 519	421 336	362 696
Petroleum	302 233	391 416	553 595	658 275	707 328	782 317	833 290	960 154	1 041 135	1 034 027
Nuclear electric power	0	0	0	34 063	92 015	107 602	262 401	322 151	338 660	351 907
Hydroelectric power[1]	24 810	33 808	26 430	45 103	45 942	29 522	51 295	48 819	23 727	20 620
Wood and waste	71 206	74 215	71 792	78 324	91 793	113 751	190 845	204 892	192 167	164 511
Other	0	0	0	0	0	0	0	147	331	348
Net interstate flow of electricity/losses[2]	26 163	46 422	93 155	30 272	-56 267	-106 855	-66 446	14 497	147 096	174 466
Total Expenditures (Thousands of Dollars)	...	...	1 769 100	3 954 700	8 862 000	11 094 600	13 011 900	14 694 600	19 764 100	19 361 300
Expenditures per capita (dollars)	...	...	386	781	1 622	1 861	2 009	2 044	2 414	2 306
Prices by Sector (Dollars Per Million Btu)										
Total	...	...	1.85	3.64	7.26	8.35	8.26	7.97	9.87	10.08
Residential	...	...	2.28	4.27	7.78	11.79	13.99	14.11	15.27	16.82
Commercial	...	...	2.62	4.97	7.68	12.14	14.49	14.64	14.99	16.01
Industrial	...	...	0.88	2.26	4.83	6.26	5.01	4.67	5.55	5.97
Transportation	...	...	2.33	4.11	8.73	7.90	7.67	7.09	9.79	9.15

[1]A negative number in this row results from pumped storage for which, overall, more electricity is expended than created to provide electricity during peak demand periods.
[2]Net interstate flow of electricity is the difference between the amount of energy in the electricity sold within a state (including associated losses) and the energy input at the electric utilities within the state. A positive number indicates that more electricity (including associated losses) came into the state than went out of the state during the year; conversely, a negative number indicates that more electricity (including associated losses) went out of the state than came into the state.
... = Not available.

Table GA-16. State Taxes, Fiscal 2004

(Dollars, percent distribution.)

Item	Thousands of dollars	Percent distribution	Dollars per capita	
			State	U.S.
TOTAL TAXES	14 570 573	100.0	1 650.3	2 024.8
Property Taxes	65 118	0.4	7.4	38.9
Sales and Gross Receipts	6 468 785	44.4	732.7	1 003.4
General sales and gross receipts	4 921 337	33.8	557.4	677.0
Selective sales taxes	1 547 448	10.6	175.3	326.4
Alcoholic beverages	149 801	1.0	17.0	15.7
Insurance premiums	317 463	2.2	36.0	47.0
Motor fuels	755 994	5.2	85.6	114.6
Tobacco products	227 348	1.6	25.8	42.0
Other selective sales	96 842	0.7	11.0	49.8
Licenses	617 663	4.2	70.0	134.9
Motor vehicle	279 991	1.9	31.7	59.4
Occupation and business, not elsewhere classified	117 376	0.8	13.3	37.1
Other licenses	103 811	0.7	11.8	2.6
Other Taxes	7 419 007	50.9	840.3	847.6
Individual income	6 830 486	46.9	773.6	673.6
Corporation net income	494 701	3.4	56.0	105.1

GOVERNMENT FINANCE

State revenues amounted to over $26.3 billion in 2003. Revenues per person, at $3,033, were well below the U.S. average and ranked 46th in the nation. The state's expenditures per capita were slightly higher at $3,376, but ranked among the 10 lowest in the country. Georgia's per capita taxes of $1,650 ranked 42nd in the country. Individual income taxes accounted for $774 of this total, and ranked 16th in the nation among the 43 states with such taxes. The other major component of state revenues was sales taxes; property taxes were very low. Georgia's debt per capita was among the lowest in the nation.

Per Capita State Taxes, Fiscal 2004

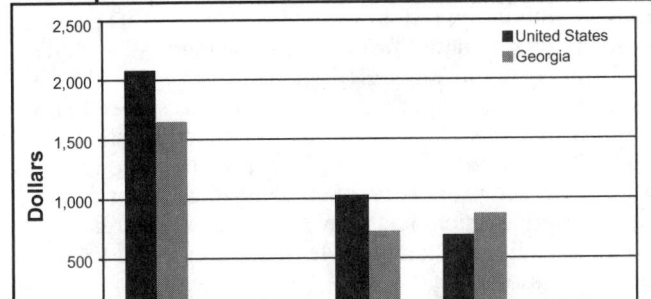

Table GA-17. State Government Finances, 2003

(Dollars, percent distribution.)

Item	Millions of dollars	Percent distribution	Dollars per capita	
			State	U.S.
GENERAL REVENUE	26 320 141	100.0	3 033.7	3 832.6
Intergovernmental revenue	9 028 114	34.3	1 040.6	1 246.0
Taxes	13 411 632	51.0	1 545.8	1 891.6
General sales	4 770 869	18.1	549.9	636.0
Selective sales	1 256 542	4.8	144.8	307.4
License taxes	452 513	1.7	52.2	123.6
Individual income tax	6 271 374	23.8	722.8	626.8
Corporate income tax	484 139	1.8	55.8	97.8
Other taxes	176 195	0.7	20.3	99.9
Current charges	1 970 480	7.5	227.1	366.5
Miscellaneous general revenue	1 909 915	7.3	220.1	328.6
GENERAL EXPENDITURE	29 291 099	100.0	3 376.1	4 010.5
Intergovernmental expenditure	9 016 458	30.8	1 039.2	1 316.9
Direct expenditure	20 274 641	69.2	2 336.9	2 693.6
Expenditure by Function				
Education	12 748 724	43.5	1 469.4	1 416.4
Public welfare	8 059 442	27.5	928.9	1 083.3
Hospitals	686 804	2.3	79.2	132.3
Health	884 198	3.0	101.9	173.0
Highways	1 842 562	6.3	212.4	295.4
Police protection	263 366	0.9	30.4	38.4
Correction	1 271 565	4.3	146.6	135.0
Natural resources	498 380	1.7	57.4	64.0
Parks and recreation	152 957	0.5	17.6	20.1
Government administration	687 028	2.3	79.2	151.3
Interest on general debt	429 906	1.5	49.6	107.8
Other and unallocable	1 766 167	6.0	203.6	393.4
DEBT AT END OF FISCAL YEAR	8 890 184	X	1 024.7	2 404.7
CASH AND SECURITY HOLDINGS	61 859 351	X	7 129.9	8 938.4

X = Not applicable.

Table GA-18. Education Indicators, 2000–2004

(Percent, number.)

Item	State	U.S.
Total Population 25 Years and Over (Thousands), 2004	5 525	186 877
Educational Attainment, 2004		
Percent high school graduate or more	85.2	85.2
Percent college graduate or more	27.6	27.7
Elementary and Secondary Schools, 2002–2003		
Total students	1 496 012	48 202 324
Percent of students eligible for free or reduced-price lunch ..	46.4	40.6
Percent of students who were English language learners	4.3	7.8
Total schools	2 003	92 330
Student/teacher ratio	15.7	15.9
Per student expenditures	7 774	8 041
Dropouts, Grades 9–12, 2000–2001 (Percent)	6.5	. . .
Higher Education, 2002–2003		
Total enrollment	406 171	17 035 027
Bachelor's degrees awarded	31 974	1 348 503
Percent women	58.7	57.5

. . . = Not available.

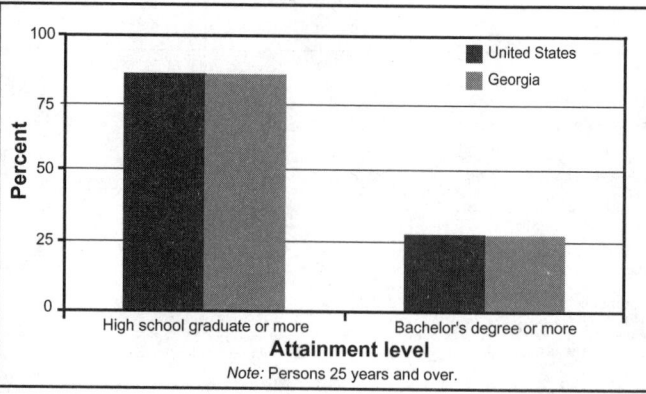

Educational Attainment, 2004

Note: Persons 25 years and over.

EDUCATION

Georgia matched the national average with 85.2 percent of its population holding high school diplomas. The state ranked 18th in the nation with 27.6 percent of its population having graduated from college. Among the 46 states reporting dropout rates, Georgia had one of the 10 highest rates. Georgia's per student expenditures were below the U.S. average. The student/teacher ratio was slightly below the national average of 15.9. The state had an above average proportion of students eligible for free or reduced-price lunch. Just over 4 percent of Georgia's students were English language learners, compared to 7.8 percent nationally.

VOTER PARTICIPATION

Georgia's voter participation rates tended to be well below the national average. In 2000, it was among 5 states with voter turnouts of less than 50 percent. In 2004, 52.6 of eligible Georgia residents voted. Asians and Hispanics had the lowest voter turnout, with less than 20 percent of eligible voters in each group turning out. According to the official tally by the Clerk of the U.S. House of Representatives, 55 percent of the state's residents voted for the Republican presidential candidate in 2000 and 58 percent voted similarly in 2004. The only group with an over 60 percent turnout rate was persons age 65 to 74 years, who had a turnout rate of over 69 percent.

Table GA-19. Reported Voting and Registration, November 2000 and November 2004

(Numbers in thousands, percent.)

Characteristic	Total population 18 years and over	Total citizen		Total registered		Total voted	
		Number	Percent	Number	Percent	Number	Percent
NOVEMBER 2000							
Total	5 775	5 553	96.1	3 528	61.1	2 827	49.0
Male	2 697	2 584	95.8	1 609	59.7	1 270	47.1
Female	3 078	2 969	96.5	1 919	62.3	1 557	50.6
NOVEMBER 2004							
Total	6 338	5 866	92.6	3 948	62.3	3 332	52.6
Male	3 070	2 793	91.0	1 791	58.4	1 503	49.0
Female	3 268	3 074	94.1	2 157	66.0	1 829	56.0
Race and Hispanic Origin							
White alone	4 390	4 068	92.7	2 788	63.5	2 351	53.6
Non-Hispanic White alone	4 051	3 993	98.6	2 753	68.0	2 327	57.4
Black alone	1 688	1 598	94.7	1 083	64.2	919	54.4
Asian alone	194	133	68.5	43	22.1	31	16.1
Hispanic or Latino[1]	376	86	22.8	36	9.6	26	7.0
White alone or in combination	4 431	4 110	92.8	2 808	63.4	2 368	53.4
Non-Hispanic White alone or in combination	4 093	4 035	98.6	2 773	67.8	2 343	57.3
Black alone or in combination	1 703	1 614	94.8	1 089	64.0	925	54.3
Asian alone or in combination	194	133	68.5	43	22.1	31	16.1
Age							
18 to 24 years	856	777	90.7	457	53.4	361	42.2
25 to 44 years	2 668	2 344	87.9	1 550	58.1	1 316	49.3
45 to 64 years	2 004	1 948	97.2	1 338	66.7	1 136	56.7
65 to 74 years	520	508	97.7	393	75.5	361	69.4
75 years and over	289	289	100.0	211	73.0	157	54.3

[1]May be of any race.

At a Glance:

- Hawaii's population was close to 1.3 million in 2004, ranking it as the 42nd most populous state in the country.

- Hawaii was one of a few states with a minority group as the largest racial group in the state. In 2004, Asian and Pacific Islanders of one race represented 49.4 percent of the population—the highest proportion of this racial group in the nation. Among persons reporting two or more races, the majority included Asian and Pacific Islander.

- Median household income in Hawaii was the third highest in the nation. However, this figure is overstated, as income figures are not adjusted for cost of living. (Hawaii's cost of living was among the highest in the United States, due to its reliance on imports of most goods.)

- In 2004, Hawaii's unemployment rate was 3.3 percent, the lowest in the country.

- The proportion of people lacking health insurance was very low—only 9.6 percent, compared with 15.7 percent for the nation as a whole.

Table HI-1. Population by Sex and Age, 1990, 2000, and 2004

(Number, percent.)

Sex and age	1990	2000	2004	Percent distribution, 2004	Average annual percent change, 2000–2004
Total Population	1 108 229	1 211 537	1 262 840	X	1.0
Percent of total U.S. population	0.4	0.4	0.4	X	X
Sex					
Male	563 891	608 671	630 025	49.9	0.9
Female	544 338	602 866	632 815	50.1	1.2
Age					
Under 5 years	83 223	78 163	88 759	7.0	0.3
5 to 17 years	196 903	217 604	209 934	16.6	0.5
18 years and over	202 878	915 770	964 147	76.3	1.1
18 to 24 years	828 103	114 893	126 248	10.0	0.2
25 to 44 years	121 185	362 336	341 359	27.0	-0.7
45 to 64 years	379 035	277 940	324 532	25.7	3.5
65 years and over	125 005	160 601	172 008	13.6	2.4
85 years and over	10 397	17 564	25 344	2.0	6.8
Median age (years)	32.5	36.2	37.7	X	X

X = Not applicable.

Average Annual Rate of Population Growth, 1980–2004

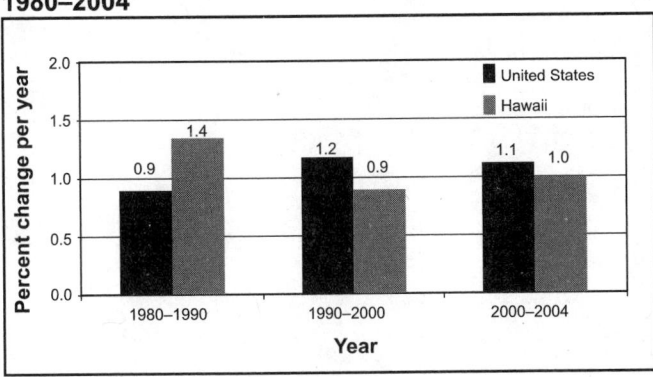

POPULATION

Hawaii's population's growth rate of 4.2 percent from 2000 to 2004 was slightly below the national average. Although net international immigration, largely from the Far East, drew in over 24,000 new residents, Hawaii's out-migration to other states was also strong—nearly 12,000 residents left the state during the 2000–2004 period. The median age of the population, at 37.7 years, was the 14th highest in the nation. Over 70 percent of the state's population was based in Honolulu. Non-Hispanic Whites comprised 23.3 percent of Hawaii's population, the lowest proportion of this racial group in the nation.

Table HI-2. Population by Race and Hispanic Origin, 1990, 2000, and 2004

(Number, percent.)

Race and Hispanic origin	1990	2000	2004
Total Population	1 108 229	1 211 537	1 262 840
Non-Hispanic (Percent)			
One race[1]			
White	31.4	23.3	23.3
Black	2.3	1.7	2.0
American Indian, Alaska Native[2]	0.5	0.2	0.2
Asian and Pacific Islander[2]	61.8	50.2	49.4
Other race[2]	1.9	. . .	. . .
Two or more races	. . .	17.3	17.1
Hispanic or Latino[3] (Percent)	7.3	7.2	7.9

[1]Individuals could report only one race in the 1990 census and could report one or more races on the 2000 census. Data on race in 2000 and 2004 are not comparable to 1990.
[2]Data for 1990 include people of Hispanic or Latino origin.
[3]May be of any race.
. . . = Not available.

Minority Population as a Percent of Total Population, 2004

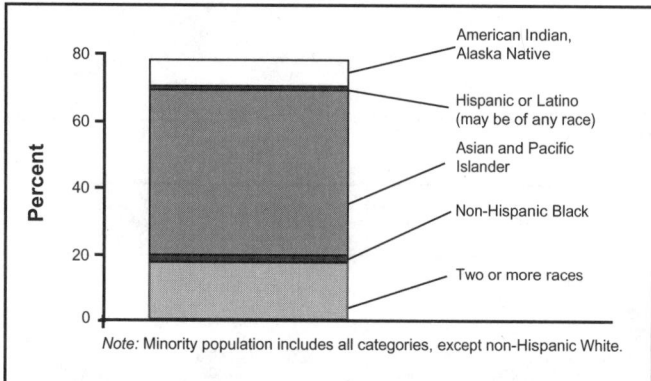

Note: Minority population includes all categories, except non-Hispanic White.

Age-Adjusted Death Rates, Average 2000–2002

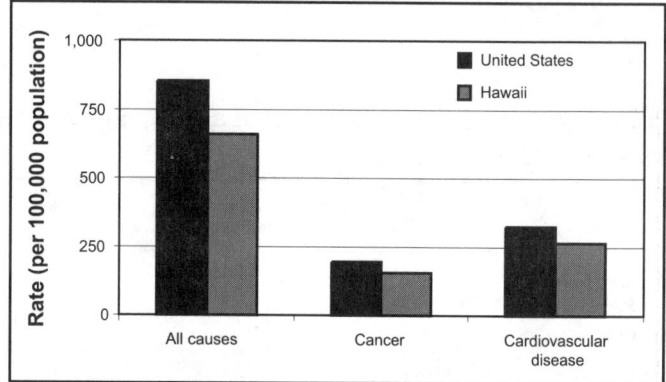

HEALTH

Hawaii's infant mortality rate was above the U.S. average. However, the state's age-adjusted death rate for all causes was the lowest in the nation. Hawaii's birth rate was slightly above average, but its birth rate for teenage mothers was below average.

Table HI-3. Health Characteristics, 2000–2004

(Number, rate, percent.)

Item	State	U.S.
Births, 2003–2004		
Number of births	18 100	4 089 950
Birth rate (per 1,000 population)	14.4	14.1
Teenage birth rate (per 1,000 women age 15–19 years)	37.3	41.6
Mortality Rates, Average 2000–2002		
Infant mortality rate (per 1,000 live births)	7.2	6.9
Age-adjusted mortality rate (per 100,000 population)		
All races	660.1	853.3
Non-Hispanic White	674.0	843.1
Black	427.7	1 097.7
American Indian, Alaska Native	. . .	687.0
Asian and Pacific Islander	652.4	486.0
Hispanic or Latino[1]	1 107.2	642.7
Health Insurance, 2004		
Percent of all persons without health insurance	9.6	15.7
Percent of children without health insurance	5.4	11.2
Percent of low-income children without health insurance	2.4	7.1

[1]May be of any race.
. . . = Not available.

Table HI-4. Leading Causes of Death, Average 2000–2002

(Number, rate per 100,000 population.)

Cause	Number of deaths	Age-adjusted death rates	
		State	U.S.
ALL CAUSES	8 495	660.1	853.3
Leading Causes			
Major cardiovascular diseases	3 380	262.7	326.5
Cancer	1 971	151.9	196.0
Chronic lower respiratory diseases	274	21.1	43.7
Unintentional injuries	369	29.4	35.7
Diabetes (underlying cause)	193	14.9	25.2
Influenza and pneumonia	225	17.5	22.7
Alzheimer's disease	127	10.0	19.0
Motor vehicle accidents	121	9.7	15.0
Nephritis, nephrotic syndrome, and nephrosis ..	124	9.6	13.8
Septicemia	148	11.5	11.4
Suicides	131	10.5	10.7
Firearm-related	45	3.6	10.3
Cirrhosis	83	6.4	9.5
Drug-induced	77	6.2	7.9
Alcohol-induced	38	3.0	6.9
Homicides	35	2.9	6.0
Falls	74	5.8	5.2
HIV	26	2.1	5.0
Viral hepatitis	19	1.5	2.0
Anemias	19	1.5	1.6
Drownings	32	2.6	1.3
Fire deaths	*	*	1.2

Note: The rates are age-adjusted to the U.S. 2000 standard population.

Table HI-5. Households and Housing Characteristics, 1990, 2000, and 2004

(Number, percent, and dollars.)

Characteristic	1990	2000	2004	Average annual percent change, 2000–2004
Total Households	356 267	403 240	427 673	1.5
Family households	263 456	287 068	295 350	0.7
Married-couple family	210 468	216 077	223 999	0.9
Other family	52 988	70 991	71 351	0.1
Male householder, no wife present	15 579	21 068	21 238	0.2
Female householder, no husband present	37 409	49 923	50 113	0.1
Nonfamily households	92 811	116 172	132 323	3.3
Householder living alone	68 985	88 153	104 002	4.2
Householder not living alone	23 826	28 019	28 321	0.3
Housing Characteristics				
Average size	3.01	2.92	2.87	X
Housing units	389 810	460 542	482 873	1.2
Occupied housing units	356 267	403 240	427 673	1.5
Owner-occupied	191 911	227 888	251 808	2.5
Renter-occupied	164 356	175 352	175 865	0.1
Median gross rent of renter-occupied housing units (dollars) ...	650	779	871	2.8
Median value of owner-occupied housing units (dollars)	242 600	272 700	364 840	7.5

X = Not applicable.

Median Housing Value and Median Rent, 2004

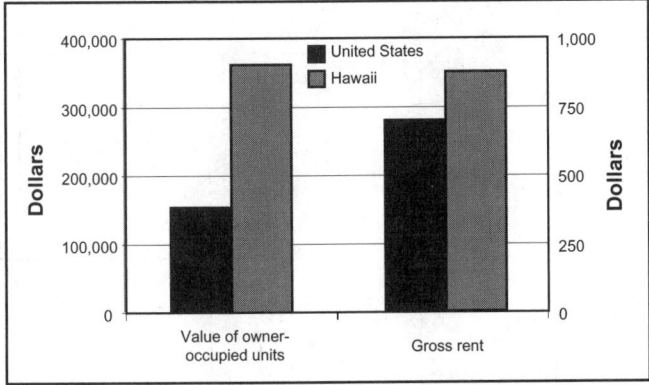

Median Household Income, 1984–2004 (2004 Dollars)

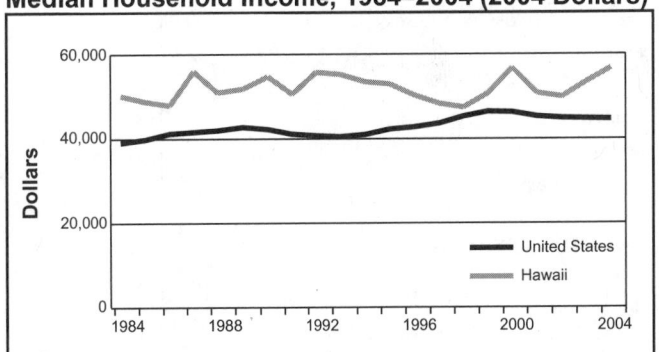

Table HI-6. Household Income and Poverty Status, 1980–2004

(2004 CPI-U-RS adjusted dollars, rate.)

Year	State Median household income (2004 dollars)	State Poverty rate	U.S. Median household income (2004 dollars)	U.S. Poverty rate
2004	56 454	8.4	44 389	12.7
2003	53 227	9.3	44 482	12.5
2002	49 687	11.3	44 546	12.1
2001	50 622	11.4	45 062	11.7
2000	56 540	8.9	46 058	11.3
1999	50 445	10.8	46 129	11.9
1998	47 251	10.9	45 003	12.7
1997	48 042	13.9	43 430	13.3
1996	50 072	12.1	42 544	13.7
1995	52 744	10.3	41 943	13.8
1994	53 274	8.7	40 677	14.5
1993	54 920	8.0	40 217	15.1
1992	55 565	11.2	40 422	14.8
1991	50 375	7.7	40 746	14.2
1990	54 545	11.0	41 963	13.5
1989	51 541	11.3	42 524	12.8
1988	50 669	11.1	41 771	13.0
1987	55 691	8.8	41 322	13.4
1986	47 691	10.7	40 939	13.6
1985	48 492	10.7	39 545	14.0
1984	49 963	9.3	38 782	14.4
1983	. . .	12.9	. . .	15.2
1982	. . .	13.2	. . .	15.0
1981	. . .	11.3	. . .	14.0
1980	. . .	8.5	. . .	13.0

. . . = Not available.

Table HI-7. Employment Status by Demographic Group, 2004

(Numbers in thousands, rate.)

Characteristic	Civilian noninstitutional population	Civilian labor force		Employed	Unemployment rate
		Number	Participation rate		
SEX AND AGE					
Total	946	612	64.7	591	3.4
16 to 19 years	59	21	36.5	18	15.0
20 to 24 years	80	61	76.4	56	8.6
25 to 34 years	152	129	84.4	125	3.1
35 to 44 years	167	141	84.3	138	2.3
45 to 54 years	173	147	85.3	144	2.0
55 to 64 years	131	85	64.9	84	1.8
65 years and over	184	27	14.8	26	2.7
Men	455	317	69.7	304	4.1
20 to 24 years	39	31	80.3	28	9.6
25 to 34 years	76	69	90.5	66	4.2
35 to 44 years	80	72	90.6	71	2.3
45 to 54 years	87	77	87.6	75	2.6
55 to 64 years	63	43	68.7	42	1.9
Women	491	295	60.1	287	2.7
20 to 24 years	41	30	72.7	28	7.6
25 to 34 years	76	60	78.4	59	1.8
35 to 44 years	88	69	78.6	67	2.2
45 to 54 years	85	71	82.8	70	1.3
55 to 64 years	68	42	61.4	41	1.8
MARITAL STATUS					
Married men, spouse present	248	175	70.7	171	2.2
Married women, spouse present	253	161	63.6	158	1.9
Women who maintain families	49	29	59.1	28	3.9
RACE, HISPANIC ORIGIN, AND SEX					
White	205	138	67.1	134	2.7
Men	104	74	71.6	72	2.7
Women	101	63	62.6	62	2.7
Asian	482	297	61.7	290	2.3
Men	218	147	67.3	142	2.9
Women	264	151	57.1	148	1.8
Hispanic or Latino[1]	54	38	69.7	35	6.7
Men	27	20	75.9	19	6.6
Women	27	17	63.7	16	6.8
RACE, HISPANIC ORIGIN, AND AGE					
White					
25 to 34 years	31	25	80.3	24	3.8
35 to 44 years	40	33	81.8	33	1.3
45 to 54 years	44	37	85.6	37	2.3
55 to 64 years	35	23	64.4	22	2.0
Asian					
20 to 24 years	34	27	79.0	25	6.1
25 to 34 years	66	57	86.5	56	2.2
35 to 44 years	78	67	85.3	66	1.6
45 to 54 years	87	77	88.8	76	1.9
55 to 64 years	69	46	66.1	45	1.5
65 years and over	125	16	12.9	16	1.7

Note: Data in Table 7 are from the Current Population Survey (CPS) and do not match Bureau of Labor Statistics estimates in Table 8. See notes and definitions for more details.

[1]May be of any race.

Table HI-8. Employment Status, 1990–2004

(Numbers in thousands, rate.)

Year	Civilian labor force	Employed	Unemployed	Unemployment rate
2004	615 811	595 772	20 039	3.3
2003	612 498	588 637	23 861	3.9
2002	608 779	584 054	24 725	4.1
2001	613 012	586 754	26 258	4.3
2000	607 764	583 197	24 567	4.0
1999	606 660	576 314	30 346	5.0
1998	604 302	570 152	34 150	5.7
1997	601 664	566 766	34 898	5.8
1996	596 753	561 683	35 070	5.9
1995	589 479	557 042	32 437	5.5
1994	585 818	555 749	30 069	5.1
1993	581 745	556 331	25 414	4.4
1992	576 009	551 563	24 446	4.2
1991	563 044	547 351	15 693	2.8
1990	551 028	537 620	13 408	2.4

Note: Population age 16 years and over.

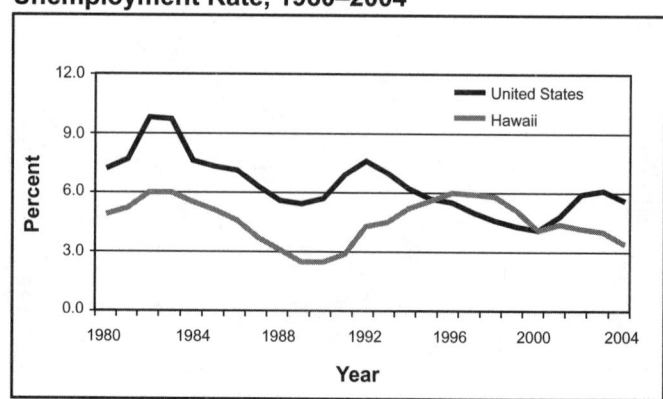

Unemployment Rate, 1980–2004

Table HI-9. Employment and Average Wages by Industry, 2001–2004

(Estimates are based on the 2002 North American Industry Classification System [NAICS].)

Industry	2001	2002	2003	2004	Annual average percent change, 2001–2004
	Number of jobs				
TOTAL EMPLOYMENT BY PLACE OF WORK	767 161	770 187	786 058	808 434	1.8
Farm Employment	12 137	12 259	12 178	12 051	-0.2
Nonfarm Employment	755 024	757 928	773 880	796 383	1.8
Private employment	586 471	588 079	602 990	623 494	2.1
Forestry, fishing, hunting, and other1	4 630	4 942	4 296	3 987	-4.9
Mining	532	469	552	580	2.9
Utilities	2 720	2 745	2 753	2 791	0.9
Construction	33 051	33 919	36 614	38 353	5.1
Manufacturing	19 604	18 545	18 087	18 733	-1.5
Durable goods manufacturing	D	D	D	6 150	. . .
Nondurable goods manufacturing	D	D	D	12 583	. . .
Wholesale trade	20 341	20 145	20 556	21 040	1.1
Retail trade	85 020	82 668	83 487	86 827	0.7
Transportation and warehousing	28 945	26 941	27 486	28 932	0.0
Information	13 496	13 049	12 146	12 458	-2.6
Finance and insurance	23 793	23 847	23 853	24 352	0.8
Real estate and rental and leasing	33 427	33 542	35 779	37 324	3.7
Professional and technical services	38 267	39 129	40 243	41 166	2.5
Management of companies and enterprises	6 175	6 802	6 905	7 020	4.4
Administrative and waste services	46 085	48 597	51 134	52 630	4.5
Educational services	14 905	15 444	16 205	16 633	3.7
Health care and social assistance	61 625	62 962	64 991	67 180	2.9
Arts, entertainment, and recreation	19 970	20 299	20 417	21 045	1.8
Accommodation and food services	91 618	90 258	92 612	96 631	1.8
Other services, except public administration	42 267	43 776	44 874	45 812	2.7
Government and government enterprises	168 553	169 849	170 890	172 889	0.9
	Dollars				
AVERAGE WAGES AND SALARIES BY PLACE OF WORK	31 304	32 897	34 138	35 750	4.5
Farm Earnings	24 330	24 480	23 406	26 549	3.0
Nonfarm Earnings	31 382	32 991	34 257	35 847	4.5
Private earnings	30 072	31 181	32 244	33 885	4.1
Forestry, fishing, hunting, and other1	23 785	25 189	24 076	22 988	-1.1
Mining	57 968	63 751	67 191	79 461	11.1
Utilities	65 795	66 355	70 691	73 448	3.7
Construction	47 082	49 093	49 526	50 901	2.6
Manufacturing	29 974	30 612	31 353	32 467	2.7
Durable goods manufacturing	D	D	D	38 756	. . .
Nondurable goods manufacturing	D	D	D	30 010	. . .
Wholesale trade	37 997	38 892	40 427	42 343	3.7
Retail trade	21 981	22 766	24 005	24 587	3.8
Transportation and warehousing	36 286	36 850	36 492	36 545	0.2
Information	43 225	43 091	45 358	48 417	3.9
Finance and insurance	46 723	50 758	51 087	54 351	5.2
Real estate and rental and leasing	30 650	32 359	34 569	37 172	6.6
Professional and technical services	45 512	47 424	49 496	51 138	4.0
Management of companies and enterprises	55 320	60 243	60 713	84 119	15.0
Administrative and waste services	21 945	22 995	24 094	25 567	5.2
Educational services	25 229	25 294	26 309	27 557	3.0
Health care and social assistance	34 346	34 830	35 924	37 319	2.8
Arts, entertainment, and recreation	20 626	21 232	22 188	23 047	3.8
Accommodation and food services	21 534	22 267	23 197	24 595	4.5
Other services, except public administration	23 394	23 901	24 667	25 646	3.1
Government and government enterprises	34 953	37 885	39 783	41 335	5.7

Note: Average wages and salaries are a calculation by the editors of wage and salary disbursements divided by full- and part-time wage and salary employment. Data may not add to total or may appear as zero due to rounding.

1 "Other" consists of the number of jobs held by U.S. residents employed by international organizations and foreign embassies and consulates in the United States.
D = Suppressed to avoid disclosure of data of individual companies.
. . . = Not available.

LABOR MARKET

After a period of high unemployment during the late 1990s, Hawaii's unemployment rate fell dramatically to become the lowest in the nation in 2004. This appears to have been partly due to the number of people who dropped out of the labor force (that is, who were not employed or seeking a job). This was indicated by relatively low labor force participation rates. Another reason for this precipitous decline was the relatively strong growth in employment over the 2001–2004 period. Wage and salary employment was concentrated in retail trade, health care, tourism (accommodation and food services industries), and government. Average wages and salaries in most industries were below the national averages.

Employment by Industry, 2004

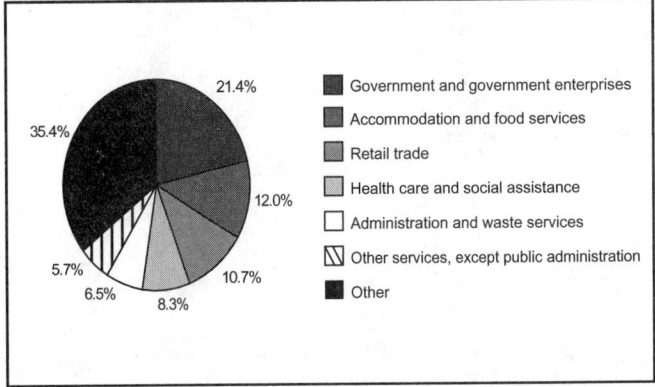

Table HI-10. Personal Income by Major Source, Selected Years 1980–2004

(Millions of dollars, except where noted.)

Item	1980	1990	2000	2001	2002	2003	2004	Average annual percent change, 2000–2004
Earnings by Place of Work	9 158	20 225	26 478	26 960	28 602	30 508	33 012	5.7
Wage and salary disbursements	6 692	14 492	19 267	19 889	20 922	22 092	23 715	5.3
Supplements to wages and salaries	1 550	3 487	4 325	4 664	5 322	5 882	6 516	10.8
Proprietors' income[1]	916	2 247	2 887	2 407	2 358	2 534	2 781	-0.9
Farm proprietors' income	228	65	11	15	18	26	6	-13.0
Nonfarm proprietors' income	688	2 182	2 876	2 391	2 340	2 508	2 774	-0.9
(-) Contributions for government social insurance[2]	781	2 113	2 668	2 786	2 987	3 220	3 388	6.2
(+) Adjustment for residence[3]	0	0	0	0	0	0	0	X
(=) Net Earnings by Place of Residence	8 377	18 112	23 810	24 174	25 615	27 288	29 624	5.6
(+) Dividends, interest, and rent[4]	1 733	4 505	6 567	6 596	6 045	5 946	6 279	-1.1
(+) Personal current transfer receipts	962	2 087	4 074	4 357	4 712	4 892	5 272	6.7
Personal income	11 073	24 704	34 451	35 126	36 371	38 125	41 176	4.6
Farm income	10 699	24 455	34 252	34 925	36 164	37 918	40 970	4.6
Nonfarm income	374	249	199	202	207	208	205	0.8
Per Capita Personal Income (Dollars)[5]	11 443	22 186	28 422	28 745	29 462	30 531	32 606	3.5

Note: Data may not add to total or may appear as zero due to rounding.

[1]Proprietors' income includes the inventory valuation adjustment and the capital consumption adjustment.
[2]Contributions for government social insurance are included in earnings by type and industry, but they are excluded from personal income.
[3]The adjustment for residence is the net inflow of the earnings of interarea commuters.
[4]Rental income of persons includes the capital consumption adjustment.
[5]Per capita personal income is total personal income divided by total midyear population.
X = Not applicable.

Per Capita Personal Income, 1980–2004 (Current Dollars)

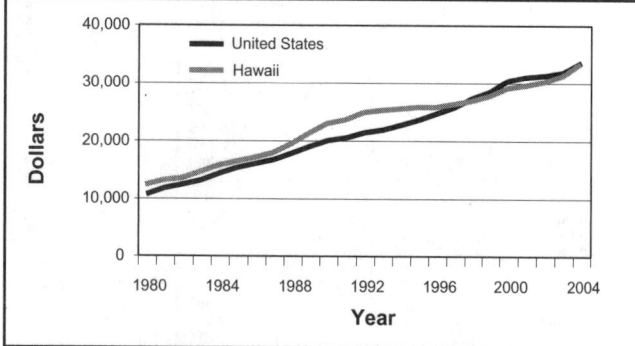

ECONOMIC ACTIVITY

Hawaii's economy recovered at an above average rate from the 2001 recession, as the service industries' growth rates picked up considerably. Particular growth was seen in tourism, a cyclically sensitive industry, and health care. Jobs in construction also grew substantially. The state's gross state product (GSP) ranked 41st in the nation. From 2003 to 2004, the GSP grew 6 percent, which was the 5th highest rate of growth in the country. Housing prices appreciated considerably in Honolulu and surrounding areas, placing these homes among the most expensive properties in the United States. In 2004, the median value of owner-occupied housing in Hawaii was the second highest in the nation.

Table HI-11. Real Gross State Product, 1997–2004

(Millions of chained 2000 dollars, percent.)

Industry	1997	1998	1999	2000	2001	2002	2003	2004	Average annual percent change, 2001–2004
GROSS STATE PRODUCT	40 412	39 629	39 821	40 176	40 532	41 398	42 964	45 556	4.0
As a percent of U.S. gross product	0.5	0.4	0.4	0.4	0.4	0.4	0.4	0.4	X
Private Industries	31 335	30 662	30 917	31 480	31 765	32 327	33 782	35 707	4.0
Agriculture, forestry, fishing, and hunting	283	295	348	365	323	376	345	255	-7.6
Mining	14	15	16	18	16	14	16	17	2.0
Utilities	834	813	831	829	780	741	798	848	2.8
Construction	2 032	1 879	1 734	1 817	1 777	1 863	1 970	2 022	4.4
Manufacturing	901	857	874	838	761	779	776	815	2.3
As a percent of gross state product	2.2	2.2	2.2	2.1	1.9	1.9	1.8	1.8	X
Wholesale trade	1 294	1 373	1 399	1 372	1 506	1 574	1 604	1 658	3.3
Retail trade	2 933	2 850	2 895	3 018	3 221	3 311	3 626	3 891	6.5
Transportation and warehousing	1 662	1 611	1 731	1 847	1 986	1 765	1 770	1 880	-1.8
Information	1 116	1 165	1 255	1 328	1 343	1 305	1 336	1 519	4.2
Finance and insurance	1 896	1 744	1 715	1 863	1 893	1 943	2 022	2 196	5.1
Real estate and rental and leasing	6 701	6 607	6 778	6 674	6 747	6 825	7 093	7 421	3.2
Services	11 741	11 494	11 348	11 510	11 431	11 835	12 430	13 231	5.0
As a percent of gross state product	29.1	29.0	28.5	28.6	28.2	28.6	28.9	29.0	X
Professional and technical services	1 732	1 739	1 701	1 710	1 794	1 879	2 012	2 069	4.9
Management of companies and enterprises	601	547	497	431	412	488	495	654	16.7
Administrative and waste services	1 108	1 074	1 135	1 166	1 196	1 347	1 492	1 559	9.2
Educational services	417	409	395	403	388	384	384	380	-0.7
Health care and social assistance	2 637	2 645	2 609	2 666	2 702	2 749	2 871	2 966	3.2
Arts, entertainment, and recreation	549	541	511	492	487	510	517	532	3.0
Accommodation and food services	3 526	3 357	3 366	3 560	3 400	3 453	3 613	3 946	5.1
Other services, except public administration	1 171	1 182	1 134	1 082	1 052	1 025	1 046	1 125	2.3
Government	9 080	8 972	8 906	8 696	8 767	9 069	9 192	9 849	4.0
As a percent of gross state product	22.5	22.6	22.4	21.6	21.6	21.9	21.4	21.6	X

X = Not applicable.

Table HI-12. Government Transfer Payments, Selected Years 1980–2004

(Millions of dollars, percent.)

Item	1980	1990	2000	2001	2002	2003	2004	Average annual percent change, 2000–2004
CURRENT TRANSFER PAYMENTS TO INDIVIDUALS	902	1 960	3 844	4 100	4 485	4 689	5 072	7.2
Retirement and Disability Insurance Benefits	378	918	1 654	1 779	1 890	1 973	2 086	6.0
Old-age, survivors, and disability insurance (OASDI) benefits	366	894	1 629	1 752	1 856	1 940	2 051	5.9
Railroad retirement and disability benefits	2	3	2	2	2	2	2	2.5
Workers' compensation	9	18	19	20	25	25	26	8.0
Other government retirement and disability insurance benefits	*	2	5	5	7	6	7	9.6
Medical Benefits	210	617	1 340	1 442	1 614	1 723	1 992	10.4
Medicare benefits	98	346	682	760	819	870	962	9.0
Public assistance medical care benefits	107	240	640	655	760	829	1 000	11.8
Military medical insurance benefits	5	31	18	27	36	25	30	13.2
Income Maintenance Benefits	200	279	572	544	573	612	640	2.8
Supplemental Security Income (SSI) benefits	20	52	104	107	111	113	118	3.2
Family assistance	91	100	141	126	114	106	102	-7.7
Food stamps	62	85	162	149	152	156	154	-1.2
Other income maintenance benefits	27	42	166	162	196	237	266	12.5
Unemployment Insurance Compensation	51	46	106	147	202	168	121	3.3
Veterans' Benefits	52	68	129	139	155	168	182	9.0
Federal Education and Training Assistance	11	19	38	43	46	42	44	3.7
Other Payments to Individuals	1	13	4	6	3	3	6	9.7

Note: See notes and definitions for more details. Data may not add to total or may appear as zero due to rounding.

EXPORTS

Hawaii ranked the lowest in the country in terms of the value of its exports ($405 million) in 2004. Petroleum and coal products were the leading export, followed by transportation equipment. Waste and scrap exports, which ranked third, grew 149 percent from 2001 to 2004. Beverage and tobacco exports grew from less than $1 million in 2001 to over $25 million in 2004, and were Hawaii's sixth leading export. Due to Hawaii's location, Japan, Singapore, and South Korea were the state's largest export markets. Exports to Singapore and China have experienced the highest rates of growth in recent years.

Leading Exports, 2004

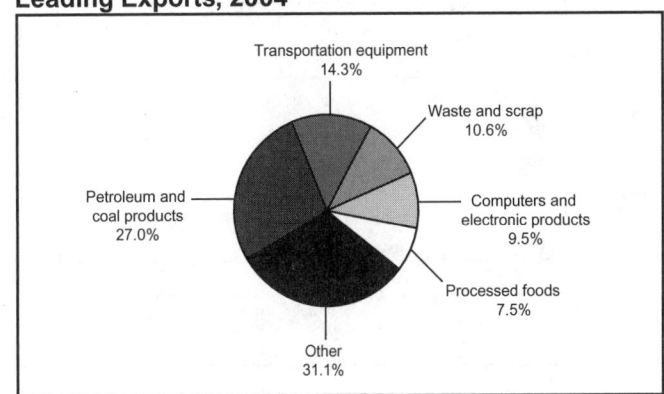

Table HI-13. Exports of Goods by Leading Products and Destinations, 2001–2004

(Millions of dollars, percent, rank based on 2004 dollar values.)

Product and market	2001	2002	2003	2004	Percent share of total, 2004	Average annual percent change, 2001–2004
Total Goods						
Total	370	514	368	405	100.0	3.1
Manufactures	302	420	290	310	76.6	0.9
Agriculture and livestock	30	26	26	29	7.2	-1.0
Other commodities	38	68	52	66	16.2	20.3
Five Leading Exports (NAICS Code)						
Petroleum and coal products (324)	92	77	75	109	27.0	5.8
Transportation equipment (336)	80	244	93	58	14.3	-10.0
Waste and scrap (910)	17	23	31	43	10.6	35.6
Computers and electronic products (334)	59	29	29	39	9.5	-13.4
Processed foods (311)	26	24	24	30	7.5	5.0
Five Leading Markets	359	501	299	399	98.6	3.6
Japan	140	164	148	117	28.9	-5.8
Singapore	7	77	6	48	11.9	93.7
South Korea	56	23	34	44	10.9	-7.4
China	13	8	13	34	8.4	36.3
Canada	24	19	20	24	5.9	-0.7

Table HI-14. Agriculture, 1997 and 2002
(Number, acres, and dollars.)

Item	1997	2002
Number of farms	5 473	5 398
Land in farms (acres)	1 439 071	1 300 499
Farm Size		
Average size of farm (acres)	263	241
Farms by size (percent distribution)		
Fewer than 50 acres	89.0	88.0
50 to 499 acres	8.4	8.9
500 acres or more	2.6	3.1
Market Value of Land and Equipment (Dollars)		
Land and buildings average value per farm	632 281	842 875
Average value per acre	2 405	3 507
Machinery and equipment average value per farm	38 709	35 568
Value of Sales (Thousands of Dollars)		
Agricultural products sold	496 935	533 423
Crops	401 411	445 356
Livestock, poultry, and their products	95 524	88 067
Average per farm (dollars)	90 798	98 819
Value of sales (percent distribution)		
Less than $10,000	58.1	56.3
$10,000 to $99,999	33.7	34.8
$100,000 or more	8.2	9.0
Government Payments		
Payments (thousands of dollars)	625	886
Percent of farms receiving government payments	2.1	2.1
Farm operators whose principal occupation is farming (percent)	55.8	57.9

AGRICULTURE

Despite its pineapple, sugar cane, and macadamia nut crop production, Hawaii was not a major farming state. In 2002, cash receipts from farming totaled only $553 million, which ranked 41st in the nation. Only 9 percent of farms had sales of $100,000 or more. In 2002, 88 percent of farms spanned fewer than 50 acres, which was the highest proportion of farms of this size in the nation. However, this proportion reflected the high market value of land and buildings, which ranked seventh with an average of nearly $843,000 per farm.

ENERGY

Energy prices per Btu in Hawaii were the second highest in the nation, due to its need to import products from the mainland and from abroad. However, expenditures per person were relatively low, ranking only 39th in the nation. Hawaii's per capita consumption was also well below the national average, ranking 48th in the country.

Energy Consumption by Source, 2001

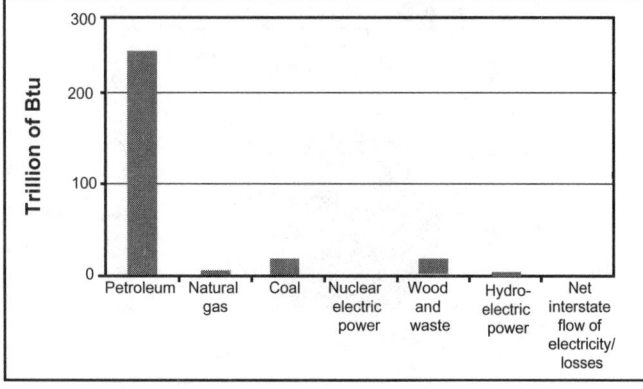

Energy Consumption by Sector, 2001

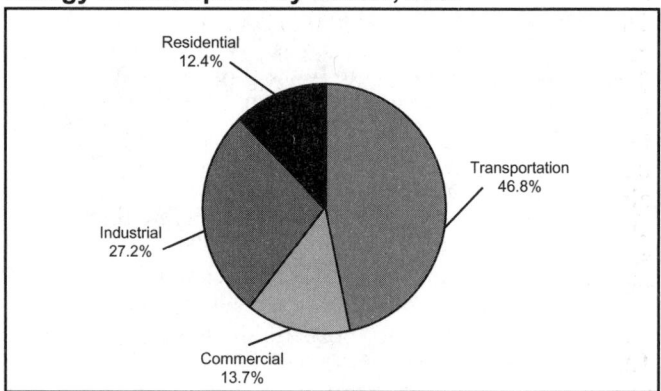

Table HI-15. Energy Consumption, Expenditures, and Prices, Selected Years 1960–2001
(Dollars, Btu [British Thermal Unit], percent distribution.)

Item	1960	1965	1970	1975	1980	1985	1990	1995	2000	2001
Total Consumption (Billion Btu)	94 861	130 602	196 964	214 414	265 428	251 417	324 389	302 508	280 034	282 163
Consumption per capita (million Btu)	149.9	185.5	255.8	242.0	275.1	241.8	292.7	256.3	231.1	230.3
Consumption by Sector (Percent Distribution)										
Residential	7.7	7.8	8.3	9.1	8.8	8.3	9.7	10.8	12.6	12.4
Commercial	5.5	5.2	5.9	6.5	7.8	8.0	12.1	12.4	13.9	13.7
Industrial	21.7	26.6	22.2	23.5	28.1	26.8	30.5	31.1	28.8	27.2
Transportation	65.1	60.5	63.6	60.9	55.3	56.8	47.6	45.7	44.7	46.8
Consumption by Source (Billion Btu)										
Coal	0	0	0	0	0	1 124	721	19 914	17 654	17 551
Natural gas	0	0	0	0	3 015	2 687	2 983	2 906	2 976	2 919
Petroleum	94 569	129 337	195 404	212 916	249 605	232 095	292 730	252 556	235 194	239 834
Nuclear electric power	0	0	0	0	0	0	0	0	0	0
Hydroelectric power[1]	292	1 093	1 131	929	898	893	827	1 009	1 055	1 025
Wood and waste	0	172	429	569	11 910	14 217	25 924	19 803	16 101	15 121
Other	0	0	0	0	0	401	1 204	6 320	7 054	5 713
Net interstate flow of electricity/losses[2]	0	0	0	0	0	0	0	0	0	0
Total Expenditures (Thousands of Dollars)	...	...	276 900	654 200	1 727 300	1 907 400	2 116 400	2 203 700	2 592 100	2 811 500
Expenditures per capita (dollars)	...	...	360	738	1 790	1 835	1 910	1 867	2 140	2 295
Prices by Sector (Dollars Per Million Btu)										
Total	...	...	1.74	3.97	8.70	10.22	9.91	11.14	14.55	15.41
Residential	...	...	7.07	13.13	20.08	30.90	28.45	37.17	44.26	44.26
Commercial	...	...	5.65	12.66	17.85	25.74	16.14	26.52	35.78	37.18
Industrial	...	...	1.60	4.94	8.58	12.24	10.81	12.12	18.26	19.05
Transportation	...	...	1.34	2.96	7.40	7.81	7.91	7.44	8.61	9.88

[1]A negative number in this row results from pumped storage for which, overall, more electricity is expended than created to provide electricity during peak demand periods.
[2]Net interstate flow of electricity is the difference between the amount of energy in the electricity sold within a state (including associated losses) and the energy input at the electric utilities within the state. A positive number indicates that more electricity (including associated losses) came into the state than went out of the state during the year; conversely, a negative number indicates that more electricity (including associated losses) went out of the state than came into the state.
. . . = Not available.

Table HI-16. State Taxes, Fiscal 2004

(Dollars, percent distribution.)

Item	Thousands of dollars	Percent distribution	Dollars per capita	
			State	U.S.
TOTAL TAXES	3 849 135	100.0	3 047.6	2 024.8
Property Taxes	X	X	X	38.9
Sales and Gross Receipts	2 470 299	64.2	1 955.9	1 003.4
General sales and gross receipts	1 900 377	49.4	1 504.6	677.0
Selective sales taxes	569 922	14.8	451.2	326.4
Alcoholic beverages	41 250	1.1	32.7	15.7
Insurance premiums	81 916	2.1	64.9	47.0
Motor fuels	84 378	2.2	66.8	114.6
Public utilities	99 504	2.6	78.8	39.2
Tobacco products	79 387	2.1	62.9	42.0
Other selective sales	183 487	4.8	145.3	49.8
Licenses	123 257	3.2	97.6	134.9
Motor vehicle	89 268	2.3	70.7	59.4
Occupation and business, not elsewhere classified	19 484	0.5	15.4	37.1
Other Taxes	1 255 579	32.6	994.1	847.6
Individual income	1 169 205	30.4	925.7	673.6
Corporation net income	58 119	1.5	46.0	105.1

X = Not applicable.

GOVERNMENT FINANCE

Due to its small population base, Hawaii's revenues per person were high in comparison to the national average. They amounted to over $5,100 in 2003, ranking 6th in the country. Hawaii also had high per capita expenditures of $5,486. In fiscal year 2004, per capita taxes amounted to nearly $3,048. The largest revenue source by far was sales taxes, which raised revenue from tourists as well as residents. The state's individual income taxes amounted to almost $926 per person, which was the 10th highest amount in the nation. Hawaii had no property taxes. The state's per capita debt was among the highest in the nation.

Per Capita State Taxes, Fiscal 2004

Table HI-17. State Government Finances, 2003

(Dollars, percent distribution.)

Item	Millions of dollars	Percent distribution	Dollars per capita	
			State	U.S.
GENERAL REVENUE	6 377 451	100.0	5 106.0	3 832.6
Intergovernmental revenue	1 537 997	24.1	1 231.4	1 246.0
Taxes	3 569 824	56.0	2 858.2	1 891.6
General sales	1 792 698	28.1	1 435.3	636.0
Selective sales	556 897	8.7	445.9	307.4
License taxes	124 430	2.0	99.6	123.6
Individual income tax	1 037 854	16.3	831.0	626.8
Corporate income tax	30 603	0.5	24.5	97.8
Other taxes	27 342	0.4	21.9	99.9
Current charges	865 199	13.6	692.7	366.5
Miscellaneous general revenue	404 431	6.3	323.8	328.6
GENERAL EXPENDITURE	6 851 905	100.0	5 485.9	4 010.5
Intergovernmental expenditure	125 434	1.8	100.4	1 316.9
Direct expenditure	6 726 471	98.2	5 385.5	2 693.6
Expenditure by Function				
Education	2 331 771	34.0	1 866.9	1 416.4
Public welfare	1 216 609	17.8	974.1	1 083.3
Hospitals	214 517	3.1	171.8	132.3
Health	448 818	6.6	359.3	173.0
Highways	259 303	3.8	207.6	295.4
Police protection	10 349	0.2	8.3	38.4
Correction	135 034	2.0	108.1	135.0
Natural resources	109 274	1.6	87.5	64.0
Parks and recreation	54 643	0.8	43.8	20.1
Government administration	471 175	6.9	377.2	151.3
Interest on general debt	353 448	5.2	283.0	107.8
Other and unallocable	1 246 964	18.2	998.4	393.4
DEBT AT END OF FISCAL YEAR	5 652 531	X	4 525.6	2 404.7
CASH AND SECURITY HOLDINGS	13 311 649	X	10 657.8	8 938.4

X = Not applicable.

Table HI-18. Education Indicators, 2000–2004

(Percent, number.)

Item	State	U.S.
Total Population 25 Years and Over (Thousands), 2004	823	186 877
Educational Attainment, 2004		
Percent high school graduate or more	88.0	85.2
Percent college graduate or more	26.6	27.7
Elementary and Secondary Schools, 2002–2003		
Total students	183 829	48 202 324
Percent of students eligible for free or reduced-price lunch ..	42.5	40.6
Percent of students who were English language learners	7.0	7.8
Total schools	283	92 330
Student/teacher ratio	16.5	15.9
Per student expenditures	8 100	8 041
Dropouts, Grades 9–12, 2000–2001 (Percent)	5.1	. . .
Higher Education, 2002–2003		
Total enrollment	66 071	17 035 027
Bachelor's degrees awarded	5 047	1 348 503
Percent women	60.8	57.5

. . . = Not available.

Educational Attainment, 2004

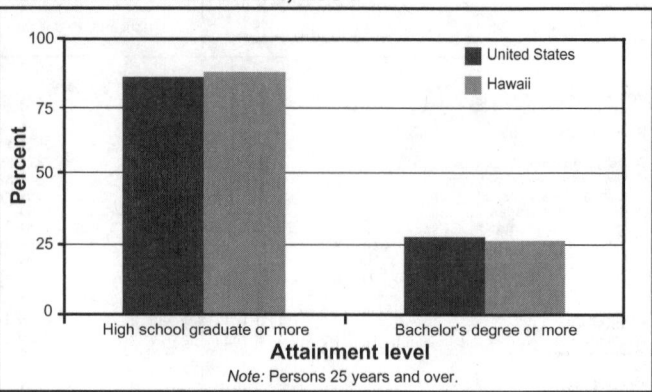

Note: Persons 25 years and over.

EDUCATION

Hawaii had an above average proportion of high school graduates in 2004, ranking 18th in the nation. The state's college attainment level was slightly below the U.S. average. The student/teacher ratio was higher than average, with 16.5 students per teacher. The state's per student expenditures of $8,100 were above the U.S. average. The dropout rate was 5.1 percent, which was the 14th highest among the 46 states reporting data. Hawaii had a slightly above average proportion of students eligible for free or reduced-price lunches. More than 60 percent of bachelor's degrees were awarded to women in Hawaii, which was well above the U.S. average.

VOTER PARTICIPATION

Hawaii ranked last for voter registration and voter turnout in both the 2000 and 2004 elections. This may be partly due to the time zone difference, which could have caused vote outcomes to be projected before Hawaiians went the polls. Non-Hispanic Whites reported voting at a rate of over 62 percent, while Asians, who were the state's majority population, had a rate of about 42 percent. According to the official tally by the Clerk of the U.S. House of Representatives, 55.8 percent of Hawaiians voted for the Democratic candidate for president in 2000, and 54 percent voted Democrat in 2004.

Table HI-19. Reported Voting and Registration, November 2000 and November 2004

(Numbers in thousands, percent.)

Characteristic	Total population 18 years and over	Total citizen		Total registered		Total voted	
		Number	Percent	Number	Percent	Number	Percent
NOVEMBER 2000							
Total	855	771	90.1	402	47.0	340	39.7
Male	413	372	90.0	183	44.3	154	37.3
Female	442	399	90.2	219	49.5	186	42.0
NOVEMBER 2004							
Total	938	852	90.8	497	53.0	433	46.2
Male	448	414	92.3	228	50.9	196	43.7
Female	490	438	89.4	269	54.9	237	48.4
Race and Hispanic Origin							
White alone	208	196	94.0	148	71.2	130	62.5
Non-Hispanic White alone	186	178	95.9	139	74.7	121	65.2
Black alone	17	17	B	7	B	6	B
Asian alone	475	411	86.4	228	48.0	200	42.0
Hispanic or Latino[1]	55	48	B	23	B	19	B
White alone or in combination	321	309	96.1	207	64.3	181	56.4
Non-Hispanic White alone or in combination	284	276	97.3	190	66.8	166	58.4
Black alone or in combination	21	21	B	9	B	8	B
Asian alone or in combination	602	536	89.1	294	48.8	257	42.7
Age							
18 to 24 years	98	91	B	37	B	27	B
25 to 44 years	338	293	86.7	150	44.4	128	37.9
45 to 64 years	302	279	92.4	187	61.9	169	56.0
65 to 74 years	79	74	B	55	B	51	B
75 years and over	121	115	94.8	68	56.4	58	47.9

[1]May be of any race.
B = Base is too small to show derived measure.

At a Glance:

- Idaho was a relatively sparsely populated state. Its population of fewer than 1.4 million people ranked 39th in the nation in 2004.

- More than 87 percent of the state's population was non-Hispanic White, which was the 10th highest proportion of this racial group in the nation. Hispanics (of any race) made up nearly 9 percent of the population.

- Median household income was just above the U.S. average and ranked 22nd in the nation. Idaho's poverty rate, at 9.9 percent in 2004, was relatively low compared to the rest of the country.

- In 2004, the state's unemployment rate was 4.7 percent, which was well below the U.S. average.

- Idaho's gross state product was the ninth smallest in the country, but experienced above average growth in recent years.

- Idaho had the ninth highest proportion of high school graduates age 25 years and over; however, the percentage of people holding bachelor's degrees or more was well below the U.S. average, ranking only 38th in 2004.

Table ID-1. Population by Sex and Age, 1990, 2000, and 2004

(Number, percent.)

Sex and age	1990	2000	2004	Percent distribution, 2004	Average annual percent change, 2000–2004
Total Population	1 006 749	1 293 953	1 393 262	X	1.9
Percent of total U.S. population	0.4	0.5	0.5	X	X
Sex					
Male	500 956	648 660	698 624	50.1	1.9
Female	505 793	645 293	694 638	49.9	1.9
Age					
Under 5 years	80 193	97 643	103 482	7.4	1.7
5 to 17 years	228 212	271 387	268 929	19.3	1.2
18 years and over	176 864	924 923	1 020 851	73.3	2.8
18 to 24 years	698 344	138 829	156 734	11.2	3.4
25 to 44 years	98 247	362 401	376 582	27.0	1.6
45 to 64 years	301 968	277 777	328 840	23.6	4.6
65 years and over	121 265	145 916	158 695	11.4	2.0
85 years and over	11 398	18 057	22 478	1.6	5.1
Median age (years)	31.5	33.2	34.1	X	X

X = Not applicable.

Average Annual Rate of Population Growth, 1980–2004

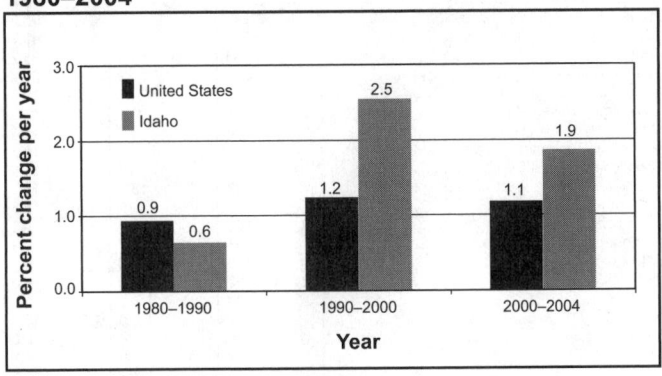

POPULATION

Like the other Rocky Mountain states, Idaho has benefited in recent years from an influx of new residents, due in part to its summer and winter recreational opportunities. The state's population growth rate of 7.7 percent from 2000 to 2004 was the 6th highest in the nation. Idaho's high birth rate contributed to this growth, along with an influx of over 40,000 people from other states. Another 12,000 people moved to Idaho from outside the United States. The state's median age of 34.1 years was among the lowest in the country, and it had among the highest proportion of population under 18 years of age in the nation.

Table ID-2. Population by Race and Hispanic Origin, 1990, 2000, and 2004

(Number, percent.)

Race and Hispanic origin	1990	2000	2004
Total Population	1 006 749	1 293 953	1 393 262
Non-Hispanic (Percent)			
One race[1]			
White	92.2	88.4	87.2
Black	0.3	0.4	0.4
American Indian, Alaska Native[2]	1.4	1.2	1.2
Asian and Pacific Islander[2]	0.9	1.0	1.1
Other race[2]	3.0	. . .	. . .
Two or more races	. . .	1.1	1.2
Hispanic or Latino[3] (Percent)	5.3	7.9	8.9

[1]Individuals could report only one race in the 1990 census and could report one or more races on the 2000 census. Data on race in 2000 and 2004 are not comparable to 1990.
[2]Data for 1990 include people of Hispanic or Latino origin.
[3]May be of any race.
. . . = Not available.

Minority Population as a Percent of Total Population, 2004

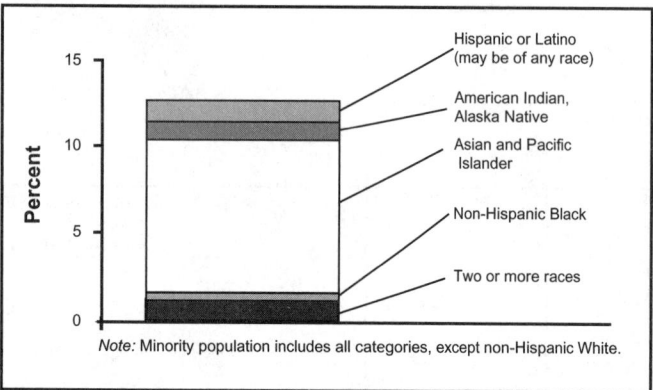

Note: Minority population includes all categories, except non-Hispanic White.

Age-Adjusted Death Rates, Average 2000–2002

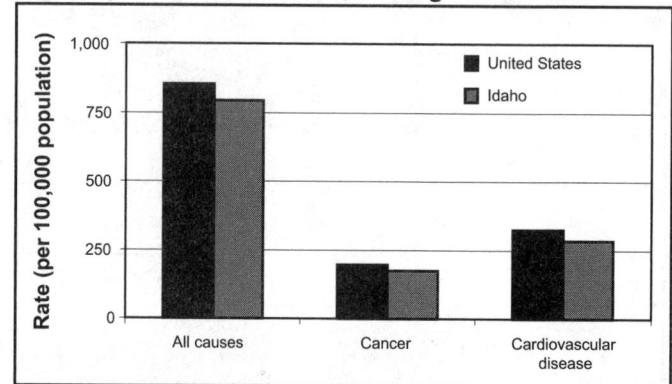

HEALTH

Despite a high overall birth rate, Idaho's birth rate for teenage mothers was below the national average. The state's infant mortality rate and age-adjusted death rate for all causes were also below the U.S. averages. Idaho ranked 34th in the nation for its proportion of residents lacking health insurance.

Table ID-3. Health Characteristics, 2000–2004

(Number, rate, percent.)

Item	State	U.S.
Births, 2003–2004		
Number of births	21 800	4 089 950
Birth rate (per 1,000 population)	16.0	14.1
Teenage birth rate (per 1,000 women age 15–19 years)	39.3	41.6
Mortality Rates, Average 2000–2002		
Infant mortality rate (per 1,000 live births)	6.6	6.9
Age-adjusted mortality rate (per 100,000 population)		
All races	797.8	853.3
Non-Hispanic White	797.8	843.1
Black	1 163.2	1 097.7
American Indian, Alaska Native	960.8	687.0
Asian and Pacific Islander	579.1	486.0
Hispanic or Latino[1]	607.6	642.7
Health Insurance, 2004		
Percent of all persons without health insurance	15.4	15.7
Percent of children without health insurance	8.6	11.2
Percent of low-income children without health insurance	5.3	7.1

[1]May be of any race.

Table ID-4. Leading Causes of Death, Average 2000–2002

(Number, rate per 100,000 population.)

Cause	Number of deaths	Age-adjusted death rates	
		State	U.S.
ALL CAUSES	9 746	797.8	853.3
Leading Causes			
Major cardiovascular diseases	3 471	286.4	326.5
Cancer	2 120	174.5	196.0
Chronic lower respiratory diseases	582	48.5	43.7
Unintentional injuries	566	44.0	35.7
Diabetes (underlying cause)	315	25.9	25.2
Influenza and pneumonia	264	21.7	22.7
Alzheimer's disease	291	24.1	19.0
Motor vehicle accidents	264	20.0	15.0
Nephritis, nephrotic syndrome, and nephrosis ..	92	7.6	13.8
Septicemia	58	4.7	11.4
Suicides	193	15.0	10.7
Firearm-related	155	12.0	10.3
Cirrhosis	106	8.6	9.5
Drug-induced	97	7.7	7.9
Alcohol-induced	115	9.2	6.9
Homicides	32	2.5	6.0
Falls	100	8.2	5.2
HIV	11	0.9	5.0
Viral hepatitis	18	1.4	2.0
Anemias	12	1.0	1.6
Drownings	21	1.6	1.3
Fire deaths	10	0.8	1.2

Note: The rates are age-adjusted to the U.S. 2000 standard population.

Table ID-5. Households and Housing Characteristics, 1990, 2000, and 2004

(Number, percent, and dollars.)

Characteristic	1990	2000	2004	Average annual percent change, 2000–2004
Total Households	360 723	469 645	515 252	2.3
Family households	263 194	335 588	366 550	2.2
Married-couple family	224 198	276 511	298 544	1.9
Other family	38 996	59 077	68 006	3.6
Male householder, no wife present	10 113	18 228	19 410	1.6
Female householder, no husband present	28 883	40 849	48 596	4.4
Nonfamily households	97 529	134 057	148 702	2.6
Householder living alone	80 800	105 175	117 662	2.8
Householder not living alone	16 729	28 882	31 040	1.8
Housing Characteristics				
Average size	2.73	2.69	2.64	X
Housing units	413 327	527 824	578 774	2.3
Occupied housing units	360 723	469 645	515 252	2.3
Owner-occupied	252 734	339 960	373 005	2.3
Renter-occupied	107 989	129 685	142 247	2.3
Median gross rent of renter-occupied housing units (dollars) ...	330	515	566	2.4
Median value of owner-occupied housing units (dollars)	58 000	106 300	120 825	3.3

X = Not applicable.

Median Housing Value and Median Rent, 2004

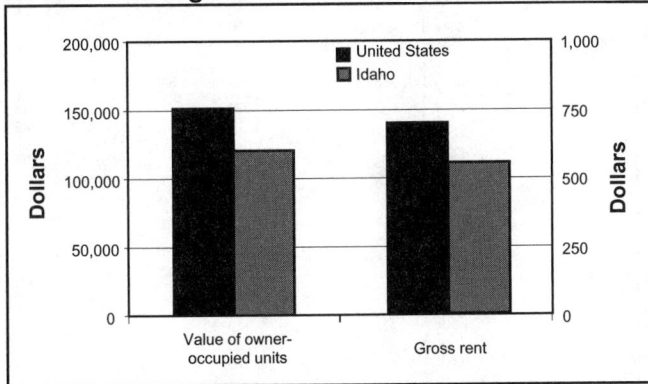

Median Household Income, 1984–2004 (2004 Dollars)

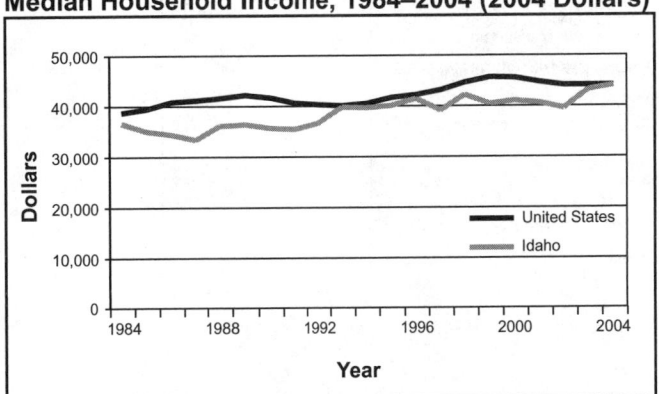

Table ID-6. Household Income and Poverty Status, 1980–2004

(2004 CPI-U-RS adjusted dollars, rate.)

Year	State		U.S.	
	Median household income (2004 dollars)	Poverty rate	Median household income (2004 dollars)	Poverty rate
2004	44 430	9.9	44 389	12.7
2003	43 511	10.2	44 482	12.5
2002	39 616	11.3	44 546	12.1
2001	40 807	11.5	45 062	11.7
2000	41 255	12.5	46 058	11.3
1999	40 579	14.1	46 129	11.9
1998	42 451	13.0	45 003	12.7
1997	39 204	14.7	43 430	13.3
1996	41 605	11.9	42 544	13.7
1995	40 220	14.5	41 943	13.8
1994	39 760	12.0	40 677	14.5
1993	39 920	13.1	40 217	15.1
1992	36 553	15.2	40 422	14.8
1991	35 322	13.9	40 746	14.2
1990	35 463	14.9	41 963	13.5
1989	36 269	12.4	42 524	12.8
1988	35 979	12.5	41 771	13.0
1987	33 004	15.1	41 322	13.4
1986	34 119	18.5	40 939	13.6
1985	34 762	16.0	39 545	14.0
1984	36 493	17.3	38 782	14.4
1983	. . .	17.7	. . .	15.2
1982	. . .	15.6	. . .	15.0
1981	. . .	17.7	. . .	14.0
1980	. . .	14.7	. . .	13.0

. . . = Not available.

Table ID-7. Employment Status by Demographic Group, 2004

(Numbers in thousands, rate.)

Characteristic	Civilian noninstitutional population	Civilian labor force		Employed	Unemployment rate
		Number	Participation rate		
SEX AND AGE					
Total	1 039	706	68.0	669	5.3
16 to 19 years	83	45	55.0	38	16.9
20 to 24 years	107	82	77.2	76	7.3
25 to 34 years	189	154	81.4	146	5.0
35 to 44 years	181	152	84.0	146	3.6
45 to 54 years	182	159	87.0	153	3.6
55 to 64 years	136	88	65.0	85	4.2
65 years and over	162	26	15.8	24	4.8
Men	512	383	74.8	361	5.8
16 to 19 years	43	24	55.1	20	16.3
20 to 24 years	50	41	82.6	38	8.6
25 to 34 years	96	89	92.6	84	5.4
35 to 44 years	91	84	91.5	80	3.9
45 to 54 years	88	80	90.5	76	4.3
55 to 64 years	66	49	73.6	47	4.5
65 years and over	77	17	22.2	16	6.4
Women	527	323	61.3	307	4.7
16 to 19 years	40	22	54.8	18	17.5
20 to 24 years	57	41	72.5	39	6.0
25 to 34 years	93	65	69.8	62	4.3
35 to 44 years	89	68	76.4	66	3.3
45 to 54 years	94	79	83.6	77	2.8
55 to 64 years	70	39	56.8	38	3.8
MARITAL STATUS					
Married men, spouse present	314	244	77.6	235	3.5
Married women, spouse present	310	192	61.9	187	2.8
Women who maintain families	49	35	71.1	33	6.4
RACE, HISPANIC ORIGIN, AND SEX					
White	981	674	68.7	640	5.0
Men	485	366	75.4	346	5.5
Women	497	308	62.0	294	4.4
Hispanic or Latino[1]	79	56	70.1	51	8.0
Men	41	34	83.5	32	6.4
Women	38	21	55.8	19	10.5
RACE, HISPANIC ORIGIN, AND AGE					
White					
16 to 19 years	75	43	57.1	36	16.1
20 to 24 years	101	80	79.1	74	7.0
25 to 34 years	177	145	82.2	139	4.3
35 to 44 years	169	142	84.3	137	3.5
45 to 54 years	175	153	87.5	148	3.5
55 to 64 years	129	86	66.6	83	4.1
65 years and over	156	24	15.7	23	5.0
Hispanic or Latino[1]					
25 to 34 years	27	20	75.3	19	7.3

Note: Data in Table 7 are from the Current Population Survey (CPS) and do not match Bureau of Labor Statistics estimates in Table 8. See notes and definitions for more details.

[1]May be of any race.

Table ID-8. Employment Status, 1990–2004

(Numbers in thousands, rate.)

Year	Civilian labor force	Employed	Unemployed	Unemployment rate
2004	703 067	669 728	33 339	4.7
2003	690 800	654 222	36 578	5.3
2002	682 861	645 958	36 903	5.4
2001	675 828	642 908	32 920	4.9
2000	661 599	630 934	30 665	4.6
1999	652 884	620 962	31 922	4.9
1998	647 873	614 748	33 125	5.1
1997	629 839	598 004	31 835	5.1
1996	613 888	581 191	32 697	5.3
1995	598 984	567 558	31 426	5.2
1994	584 129	552 354	31 775	5.4
1993	549 763	516 307	33 456	6.1
1992	527 566	493 767	33 799	6.4
1991	506 654	476 531	30 123	5.9
1990	494 121	467 102	27 019	5.5

Note: Population age 16 years and over.

Unemployment Rate, 1980–2004

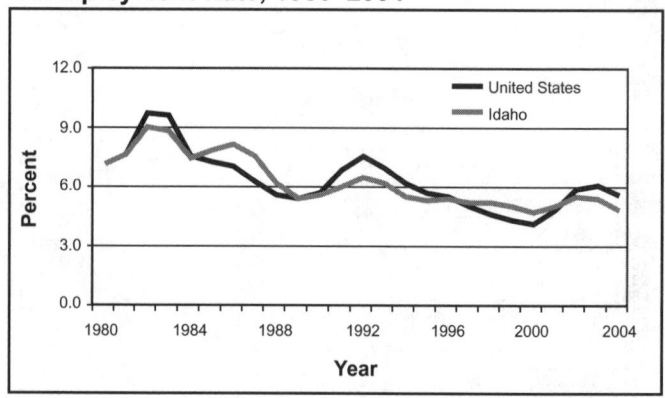

Table ID-9. Employment and Average Wages by Industry, 2001–2004

(Estimates are based on the 2002 North American Industry Classification System [NAICS].)

Industry	2001	2002	2003	2004	Annual average percent change, 2001–2004
	Number of jobs				
TOTAL EMPLOYMENT BY PLACE OF WORK	795 644	802 022	811 772	834 456	1.6
Farm Employment	40 207	41 404	39 880	40 150	0.0
Nonfarm Employment	755 437	760 618	771 892	794 306	1.7
Private employment	636 182	639 489	648 836	669 653	1.7
Forestry, fishing, hunting, and other[1]	16 309	16 802	16 157	15 878	-0.9
Mining	3 047	2 592	2 803	3 041	-0.1
Utilities	1 916	2 020	1 999	1 999	1.4
Construction	58 954	57 061	58 704	62 391	1.9
Manufacturing	72 880	69 256	66 463	66 157	-3.2
Durable goods manufacturing	46 008	43 284	41 142	41 590	-3.3
Nondurable goods manufacturing	26 872	25 972	25 321	24 567	-2.9
Wholesale trade	28 144	27 602	27 143	28 162	0.0
Retail trade	95 130	95 613	96 595	98 699	1.2
Transportation and warehousing	22 728	22 393	22 460	22 865	0.2
Information	11 605	10 899	11 136	11 900	0.8
Finance and insurance	26 746	27 823	28 492	29 146	2.9
Real estate and rental and leasing	26 184	26 681	28 581	30 438	5.1
Professional and technical services	45 698	45 623	46 504	47 523	1.3
Management of companies and enterprises	8 046	7 974	7 604	7 645	-1.7
Administrative and waste services	40 381	42 967	44 625	48 110	6.0
Educational services	9 250	10 014	10 432	10 920	5.7
Health care and social assistance	65 950	68 815	71 567	74 417	4.1
Arts, entertainment, and recreation	13 703	14 488	14 933	15 275	3.7
Accommodation and food services	50 506	50 444	51 682	53 065	1.7
Other services, except public administration	39 005	40 422	40 956	42 022	2.5
Government and government enterprises	119 255	121 129	123 056	124 653	1.5
	Dollars				
AVERAGE WAGES AND SALARIES BY PLACE OF WORK	27 188	27 725	28 201	29 328	2.6
Farm Earnings	21 553	24 881	23 098	21 996	0.7
Nonfarm Earnings	27 336	27 801	28 328	29 510	2.6
Private earnings	27 281	27 583	28 086	29 229	2.3
Forestry, fishing, hunting, and other[1]	19 106	20 191	20 832	22 341	5.4
Mining	38 731	40 126	43 361	44 127	4.4
Utilities	47 910	68 328	53 569	53 412	3.7
Construction	31 055	31 060	30 671	31 037	0.0
Manufacturing	37 580	38 176	39 464	41 479	3.3
Durable goods manufacturing	41 684	42 663	44 412	46 666	3.8
Nondurable goods manufacturing	30 670	30 804	31 586	32 861	2.3
Wholesale trade	34 408	34 510	35 458	36 916	2.4
Retail trade	20 224	20 576	21 378	22 284	3.3
Transportation and warehousing	29 778	30 321	30 605	31 890	2.3
Information	33 098	33 416	34 449	36 233	3.1
Finance and insurance	37 056	37 554	39 417	40 404	2.9
Real estate and rental and leasing	20 787	21 364	21 882	23 678	4.4
Professional and technical services	41 956	42 174	43 256	45 300	2.6
Management of companies and enterprises	63 690	60 777	61 074	68 320	2.4
Administrative and waste services	17 933	18 489	19 873	20 968	5.3
Educational services	19 699	20 930	21 776	22 745	4.9
Health care and social assistance	27 077	27 791	28 332	29 267	2.6
Arts, entertainment, and recreation	18 485	19 524	15 829	15 553	-5.6
Accommodation and food services	10 697	10 981	11 244	11 682	3.0
Other services, except public administration	17 621	17 809	18 261	18 843	2.3
Government and government enterprises	27 561	28 677	29 288	30 642	3.6

Note: Average wages and salaries are a calculation by the editors of wage and salary disbursements divided by full- and part-time wage and salary employment. Data may not add to total or may appear as zero due to rounding.

1 "Other" consists of the number of jobs held by U.S. residents employed by international organizations and foreign embassies and consulates in the United States.

LABOR MARKET

Idaho's unemployment rate has been below the national average since 2000, but its pattern of change has reflected national trends. Wage and salary employment was concentrated in a variety of private nonfarm industries, including retail trade, health care, manufacturing, and construction. The state's largest overall employer was the government sector. Employment grew steadily over the 2001–2004 period. Idaho had the ninth highest rate of growth from 2001 to 2004. A loss of manufacturing jobs was more than offset by the strong employment growth in construction and in several service-providing sectors. Average wages and salaries in Idaho were below the national average across most industries, and their growth rates were also lower than average.

Employment by Industry, 2004

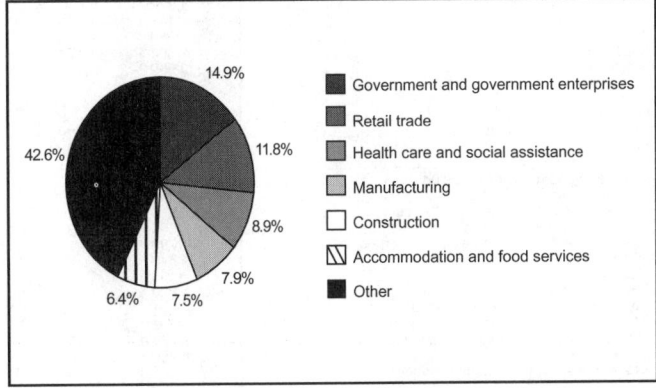

14.9% 11.8% 8.9% 7.9% 7.5% 6.4% 42.6%

- Government and government enterprises
- Retail trade
- Health care and social assistance
- Manufacturing
- Construction
- Accommodation and food services
- Other

Table ID-10. Personal Income by Major Source, Selected Years 1980–2004

(Millions of dollars, except where noted.)

Item	1980	1990	2000	2001	2002	2003	2004	Average annual percent change, 2000–2004
Earnings by Place of Work	6 442	12 089	23 453	24 484	25 072	25 806	28 154	4.7
Wage and salary disbursements	4 488	7 964	16 551	16 880	17 254	17 669	18 848	3.3
Supplements to wages and salaries	898	1 828	3 549	3 647	4 041	4 310	4 747	7.5
Proprietors' income[1]	1 057	2 296	3 353	3 957	3 777	3 827	4 559	8.0
Farm proprietors' income	246	772	471	646	487	368	742	12.1
Nonfarm proprietors' income	810	1 525	2 883	3 311	3 290	3 460	3 817	7.3
(-) Contributions for government social insurance[2]	605	1 358	2 676	2 723	2 812	2 914	3 094	3.7
(+) Adjustment for residence[3]	61	152	524	530	542	559	589	2.9
(=) Net Earnings by Place of Residence	5 899	10 884	21 302	22 291	22 801	23 451	25 649	4.8
(+) Dividends, interest, and rent[4]	1 365	3 067	5 909	6 195	6 051	5 951	6 101	0.8
(+) Personal current transfer receipts	934	1 968	4 079	4 568	4 971	5 257	5 644	8.5
Personal income	8 198	15 918	31 290	33 054	33 823	34 660	37 394	4.6
Farm income	7 804	14 942	30 448	32 039	32 905	33 915	36 285	4.5
Nonfarm income	394	977	842	1 015	918	745	1 108	7.1
Per Capita Personal Income (Dollars)[5]	8 648	15 724	24 075	25 018	25 181	25 354	26 839	2.8

Note: Data may not add to total or may appear as zero due to rounding.

[1]Proprietors' income includes the inventory valuation adjustment and the capital consumption adjustment.
[2]Contributions for government social insurance are included in earnings by type and industry, but they are excluded from personal income.
[3]The adjustment for residence is the net inflow of the earnings of interarea commuters.
[4]Rental income of persons includes the capital consumption adjustment.
[5]Per capita personal income is total personal income divided by total midyear population.

Per Capita Personal Income, 1980–2004 (Current Dollars)

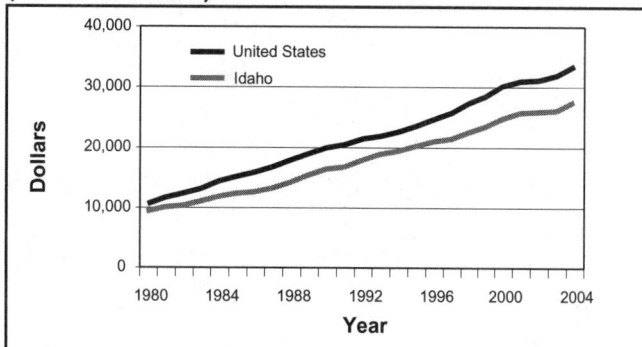

ECONOMIC ACTIVITY

Idaho's economy was not significantly affected by the 2001 recession: it grew at a rate well above the national average in each of the years from 2001 to 2004. Over this period, Idaho's real gross state product grew by 13.6 percent. This was the sixth highest rate of growth in the nation. The largest contributors to growth from 2003 to 2004 were manufacturing, real estate activities, retail trade, information services, and government. Housing prices appreciated substantially in areas of the state associated with recreational activities, but the median value of owner-occupied housing in the state ranked only 30th in the nation in 2004.

Table ID-11. Real Gross State Product, 1997–2004

(Millions of chained 2000 dollars, percent.)

Industry	1997	1998	1999	2000	2001	2002	2003	2004	Average annual percent change, 2001–2004
GROSS STATE PRODUCT	28 781	30 080	32 955	35 206	36 182	37 413	38 849	41 107	4.3
As a percent of U.S. gross product	0.3	0.3	0.4	0.4	0.4	0.4	0.4	0.4	X
Private Industries	24 322	25 507	28 234	30 379	31 259	32 415	33 839	35 874	4.7
Agriculture, forestry, fishing, and hunting	1 370	1 511	1 712	1 854	1 841	2 082	1 919	1 707	-2.5
Mining	143	147	152	140	111	101	110	109	-0.6
Utilities	560	562	576	646	691	796	792	816	5.7
Construction	2 302	2 243	2 289	2 273	2 355	2 217	2 205	2 323	-0.5
Manufacturing	2 959	3 217	4 593	5 807	5 926	6 187	7 090	7 839	9.8
As a percent of gross state product	10.3	10.7	13.9	16.5	16.4	16.5	18.3	19.1	X
Wholesale trade	1 647	1 829	1 956	1 936	2 113	2 131	2 098	2 203	1.4
Retail trade	2 419	2 535	2 706	2 836	3 000	3 212	3 507	3 762	7.8
Transportation and warehousing	999	997	1 015	1 033	995	1 027	1 059	1 096	3.3
Information	507	588	663	725	768	772	849	1 024	10.1
Finance and insurance	1 156	1 314	1 310	1 369	1 409	1 502	1 610	1 689	6.2
Real estate and rental and leasing	3 409	3 536	3 783	3 901	4 059	4 137	4 232	4 631	4.5
Services	7 191	7 282	7 551	7 859	7 986	8 260	8 531	8 979	4.0
As a percent of gross state product	25.0	24.2	22.9	22.3	22.1	22.1	22.0	21.8	X
Professional and technical services	1 865	1 937	2 037	2 232	2 281	2 342	2 456	2 550	3.8
Management of companies and enterprises	790	757	744	733	639	607	576	610	-1.5
Administrative and waste services	648	670	766	775	821	910	1 014	1 116	10.8
Educational services	146	146	154	161	166	168	164	165	-0.2
Health care and social assistance	1 888	1 921	1 978	2 082	2 197	2 318	2 407	2 519	4.7
Arts, entertainment, and recreation	291	222	259	267	315	356	320	322	0.7
Accommodation and food services	802	843	855	879	855	868	901	950	3.6
Other services, except public administration	761	786	758	730	712	691	693	747	1.6
Government	4 486	4 593	4 726	4 827	4 923	5 002	5 028	5 255	2.2
As a percent of gross state product	15.6	15.3	14.3	13.7	13.6	13.4	12.9	12.8	X

X = Not applicable.

Table ID-12. Government Transfer Payments, Selected Years 1980–2004

(Millions of dollars, percent.)

Item	1980	1990	2000	2001	2002	2003	2004	Average annual percent change, 2000–2004
CURRENT TRANSFER PAYMENTS TO INDIVIDUALS	870	1 842	3 804	4 258	4 690	4 997	5 381	9.1
Retirement and Disability Insurance Benefits	482	1 056	1 854	1 996	2 128	2 252	2 384	6.5
Old-age, survivors, and disability insurance (OASDI) benefits	440	954	1 698	1 829	1 953	2 062	2 186	6.5
Railroad retirement and disability benefits	32	54	67	68	71	72	74	2.5
Workers' compensation	10	47	88	97	102	115	120	8.1
Other government retirement and disability insurance benefits	*	1	2	3	3	4	4	16.1
Medical Benefits	153	477	1 360	1 570	1 714	1 818	2 082	11.2
Medicare benefits	99	283	696	779	843	902	1 003	9.5
Public assistance medical care benefits	50	181	644	762	834	885	1 041	12.8
Military medical insurance benefits	3	13	20	29	37	31	38	17.7
Income Maintenance Benefits	87	128	286	299	343	401	443	11.5
Supplemental Security Income (SSI) benefits	14	33	85	90	94	98	103	5.0
Family assistance	24	20	22	22	20	22	25	3.6
Food stamps	30	41	47	50	64	80	95	19.6
Other income maintenance benefits	19	34	133	137	165	201	219	13.4
Unemployment Insurance Compensation	76	72	111	165	249	252	177	12.4
Veterans' Benefits	57	69	129	142	162	176	191	10.4
Federal Education and Training Assistance	15	35	58	76	86	90	95	13.2
Other Payments to Individuals	1	5	6	10	7	8	9	11.6

Note: See notes and definitions for more details. Data may not add to total or may appear as zero due to rounding.

EXPORTS

Exports of goods increased substantially over the 2001–2004 period, although Idaho remained among the 15 states with the smallest values of exports. In 2004, the state's exports totaled $2.9 billion. Computers and electronic products were the leading export. These exports increased by 45 percent from 2001 to 2004 and made up more than 65 percent of total exports in 2004. Processed food exports ranked second, accounting for 8.4 percent of the total. The United Kingdom was Idaho's leading export market, followed closely by Canada. Exports to Taiwan, which consisted primarily of computers and electronic products, grew 160 percent from 2001 to 2004.

Leading Exports, 2004

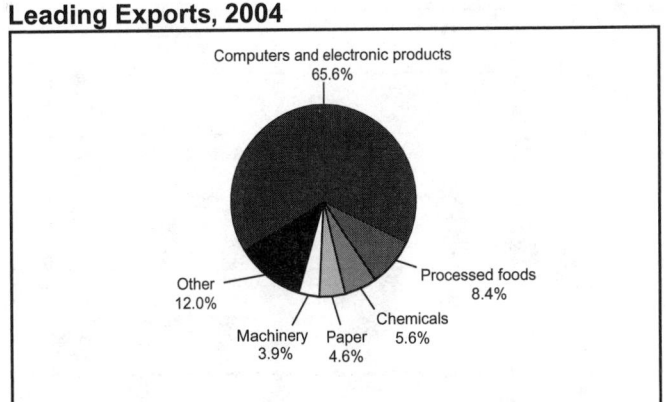

Table ID-13. Exports of Goods by Leading Products and Destinations, 2001–2004

(Millions of dollars, percent, rank based on 2004 dollar values.)

Product and market	2001	2002	2003	2004	Percent share of total, 2004	Average annual percent change, 2001–2004
Total Goods						
Total	2 122	1 967	2 096	2 915	100.0	11.2
Manufactures	1 961	1 818	1 941	2 728	93.6	11.6
Agriculture and livestock	143	132	138	163	5.6	4.5
Other commodities	18	17	17	24	0.8	9.1
Five Leading Exports (NAICS Code)						
Computers and electronic products (334)	1 311	1 170	1 206	1 911	65.6	13.4
Processed foods (311)	267	258	269	244	8.4	-3.0
Chemical manufactures (325)	113	96	153	162	5.6	12.8
Paper products (322)	98	106	113	136	4.6	11.3
Machinery manufactures (333)	59	80	76	113	3.9	24.1
Five Leading Markets	2 011	1 874	2 006	2 822	96.8	12.0
United Kingdom	288	322	350	459	15.8	16.8
Canada	354	295	362	436	14.9	7.2
Singapore	373	173	204	393	13.5	1.8
Taiwan	123	100	131	320	11.0	37.5
Japan	235	260	269	268	9.2	4.4

Table ID-14. Agriculture, 1997 and 2002

(Number, acres, and dollars.)

Item	1997	2002
Number of farms	25 590	25 017
Land in farms (acres)	12 057 001	11 767 294
Farm Size		
Average size of farm (acres)	471	470
Farms by size (percent distribution)		
Fewer than 50 acres	43.7	49.2
50 to 499 acres	36.4	32.8
500 acres or more	19.9	18.0
Market Value of Land and Equipment (Dollars)		
Land and buildings average value per farm	487 885	613 303
Average value per acre	1 035	1 270
Machinery and equipment average value per farm	72 191	91 746
Value of Sales (Thousands of Dollars)		
Agricultural products sold	3 388 296	3 908 262
Crops	1 816 769	1 787 172
Livestock, poultry, and their products	1 571 526	2 121 090
Average per farm (dollars)	132 407	156 224
Value of sales (percent distribution)		
Less than $10,000	52.5	62.8
$10,000 to $99,999	28.6	21.6
$100,000 or more	18.9	15.6
Government Payments		
Payments (thousands of dollars)	76 428	93 934
Percent of farms receiving government payments	37.3	28.4
Farm operators whose principal occupation is farming (percent)	50.0	55.4

AGRICULTURE

Cash receipts from farming totaled $3.9 million in 2002, a 16.8 percent increase over the previous farm census in 1997. Idaho's chief products were dairy, cattle, and potatoes. Most of the state's farming was small-scale: nearly 85 percent of farms had sales of under $100,000. However, more than 50 percent of farms spanned 50 acres or more. Just over 55 percent of farm operators reported farming as their principal occupation.

ENERGY

Energy prices per Btu in Idaho were among the 10 lowest in the nation. Total expenditures reached $3.1 billion, or $2,378 per capita, in 2001. The state's per capita consumption was 379.2 million Btu in 2001, ranking Idaho 19th in the nation. However, this was down considerably from the previous year, when the per capita consumption reached 414.7 Btu. Major sources of energy in the state were petroleum, natural gas, and imports of electricity.

Energy Consumption by Source, 2001

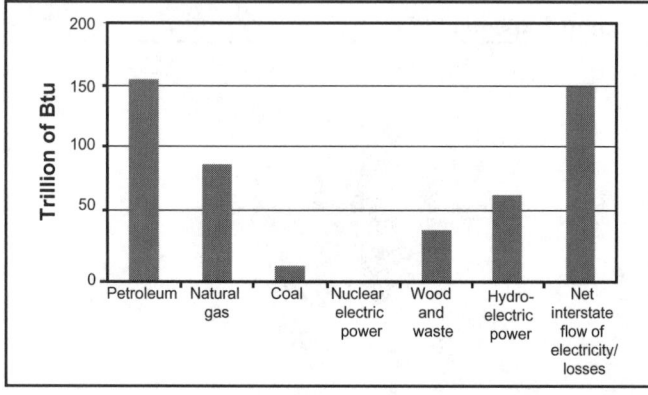

Energy Consumption by Sector, 2001

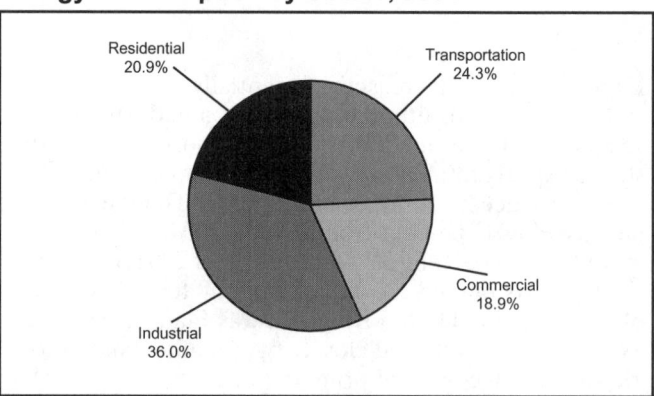

Table ID-15. Energy Consumption, Expenditures, and Prices, Selected Years 1960–2001

(Dollars, Btu [British Thermal Unit], percent distribution.)

Item	1960	1965	1970	1975	1980	1985	1990	1995	2000	2001
Total Consumption (Billion Btu)	190 746	234 862	296 418	359 071	348 094	354 560	402 923	458 992	536 642	501 019
Consumption per capita (million Btu)	286.0	342.4	415.7	431.6	368.8	356.7	400.2	394.0	414.7	379.2
Consumption by Sector (Percent Distribution)										
Residential	19.5	17.1	16.4	20.2	20.9	23.1	19.6	19.4	20.1	20.9
Commercial	13.2	12.3	12.0	16.8	17.1	18.4	17.9	16.7	18.9	18.9
Industrial	45.1	49.5	49.4	41.0	38.1	36.0	40.1	39.8	37.8	36.0
Transportation	22.2	21.1	22.2	22.0	23.9	22.5	22.4	24.1	23.2	24.3
Consumption by Source (Billion Btu)										
Coal	16 845	15 863	7 935	13 416	9 610	8 870	10 086	8 946	13 732	11 223
Natural gas	22 776	36 092	49 411	63 776	51 646	41 115	46 786	65 686	74 519	81 782
Petroleum	73 725	86 910	105 134	125 462	112 703	101 933	120 059	140 907	167 182	155 253
Nuclear electric power	0	0	0	0	0	0	0	0	0	0
Hydroelectric power[1]	66 333	69 417	74 260	106 908	98 760	113 491	94 814	113 322	111 871	73 488
Wood and waste	11 354	10 361	11 476	11 103	14 650	17 792	23 376	25 433	27 616	28 728
Other	0	-2	-2	0	0	190	900	532	1 738	1 522
Net interstate flow of electricity/losses[2]	-287	16 221	48 206	38 406	60 724	71 171	106 902	104 165	139 983	149 022
Total Expenditures (Thousands of Dollars)	...	...	348 800	735 100	1 465 800	1 686 500	1 837 100	2 219 900	3 108 300	3 142 100
Expenditures per capita (dollars)	...	...	489	884	1 553	1 697	1 825	1 906	2 402	2 378
Prices by Sector (Dollars Per Million Btu)										
Total	...	...	1.76	3.00	6.64	8.03	7.43	7.51	8.94	9.63
Residential	...	...	2.50	3.42	7.16	10.28	10.72	11.02	11.38	13.09
Commercial	...	...	2.19	2.89	6.43	9.10	9.12	9.61	9.78	11.81
Industrial	...	...	0.98	1.95	4.38	5.45	4.40	4.50	4.96	5.92
Transportation	...	...	2.47	4.25	8.98	9.06	9.01	8.93	12.06	11.20

[1]A negative number in this row results from pumped storage for which, overall, more electricity is expended than created to provide electricity during peak demand periods.
[2]Net interstate flow of electricity is the difference between the amount of energy in the electricity sold within a state (including associated losses) and the energy input at the electric utilities within the state. A positive number indicates that more electricity (including associated losses) came into the state than went out of the state during the year; conversely, a negative number indicates that more electricity (including associated losses) went out of the state than came into the state.
. . . = Not available.

Table ID-16. State Taxes, Fiscal 2004

(Dollars, percent distribution.)

Item	Thousands of dollars	Percent distribution	Dollars per capita	
			State	U.S.
TOTAL TAXES	2 647 790	100.0	1 900.8	2 024.8
Property Taxes	X	X	X	38.9
Sales and Gross Receipts	1 403 155	53.0	1 007.3	1 003.4
General sales and gross receipts	1 036 924	39.2	744.4	677.0
Selective sales taxes	366 231	13.8	262.9	326.4
Insurance premiums	82 283	3.1	59.1	47.0
Motor fuels	218 019	8.2	156.5	114.6
Tobacco products	52 271	2.0	37.5	42.0
Licenses	220 800	8.3	158.5	134.9
Hunting and fishing	29 455	1.1	21.2	4.2
Motor vehicle	107 269	4.1	77.0	59.4
Public utility	28 350	1.1	20.4	1.5
Occupation and business, not elsewhere classified	42 094	1.6	30.2	37.1
Other Taxes	1 023 835	38.7	735.0	847.6
Individual income	907 795	34.3	651.7	673.6
Corporation net income	103 784	3.9	74.5	105.1

X = Not applicable.

GOVERNMENT FINANCE

State revenues per person in 2003 were low compared to the rest of the country. Idaho's per capita expenditures were also low, ranking 41st in the nation. Expenditures on highways and natural resources, on a per capita basis, were significantly higher than the U.S. average. In fiscal year 2004, per capita taxes were $1,900, which were below the national average and ranked 32nd in the nation. More than $651 of per capita taxes were derived from individual income taxes. General sales taxes averaged out to $744 per person. Idaho had no property taxes. The state's debt per person of $1,904 was well below the U.S. average of $2,405.

Per Capita State Taxes, Fiscal, 2004

Table ID-17. State Government Finances, 2003

(Dollars, percent distribution.)

Item	Millions of dollars	Percent distribution	Dollars per capita	
			State	U.S.
GENERAL REVENUE	4 616 599	100.0	3 377.2	3 832.6
Intergovernmental revenue	1 455 705	31.5	1 064.9	1 246.0
Taxes	2 344 344	50.8	1 715.0	1 891.6
General sales	842 006	18.2	616.0	636.0
Selective sales	325 471	7.1	238.1	307.4
License taxes	221 200	4.8	161.8	123.6
Individual income tax	843 780	18.3	617.2	626.8
Corporate income tax	93 490	2.0	68.4	97.8
Other taxes	18 397	0.4	13.5	99.9
Current charges	411 858	8.9	301.3	366.5
Miscellaneous general revenue	404 692	8.8	296.0	328.6
GENERAL EXPENDITURE	4 759 455	100.0	3 481.7	4 010.5
Intergovernmental expenditure	1 449 076	30.4	1 060.0	1 316.9
Direct expenditure	3 310 379	69.6	2 421.6	2 693.6
Expenditure by Function				
Education	1 886 421	39.6	1 380.0	1 416.4
Public welfare	1 092 616	23.0	799.3	1 083.3
Hospitals	45 747	1.0	33.5	132.3
Health	116 088	2.4	84.9	173.0
Highways	521 746	11.0	381.7	295.4
Police protection	40 953	0.9	30.0	38.4
Correction	164 813	3.5	120.6	135.0
Natural resources	162 831	3.4	119.1	64.0
Parks and recreation	29 487	0.6	21.6	20.1
Government administration	199 568	4.2	146.0	151.3
Interest on general debt	141 690	3.0	103.6	107.8
Other and unallocable	357 495	7.5	261.5	393.4
DEBT AT END OF FISCAL YEAR	2 602 620	X	1 903.9	2 404.7
CASH AND SECURITY HOLDINGS	10 508 819	X	7 687.5	8 938.4

X = Not applicable.

Table ID-18. Education Indicators, 2000–2004

(Percent, number.)

Item	State	U.S.
Total Population 25 Years and Over (Thousands), 2004	852	186 877
Educational Attainment, 2004		
Percent high school graduate or more	87.9	85.2
Percent college graduate or more	23.8	27.7
Elementary and Secondary Schools, 2002–2003		
Total students	248 515	48 202 324
Percent of students eligible for free or reduced-price lunch ..	37.0	40.6
Percent of students who were English language learners	7.8	7.8
Total schools	660	92 330
Student/teacher ratio	17.9	15.9
Per student expenditures	6 081	8 041
Dropouts, Grades 9–12, 2000–2001 (Percent)	3.9	. . .
Higher Education, 2002–2003		
Total enrollment	73 167	17 035 027
Bachelor's degrees awarded	5 975	1 348 503
Percent women	54.3	57.5

. . . = Not available.

Educational Attainment, 2004

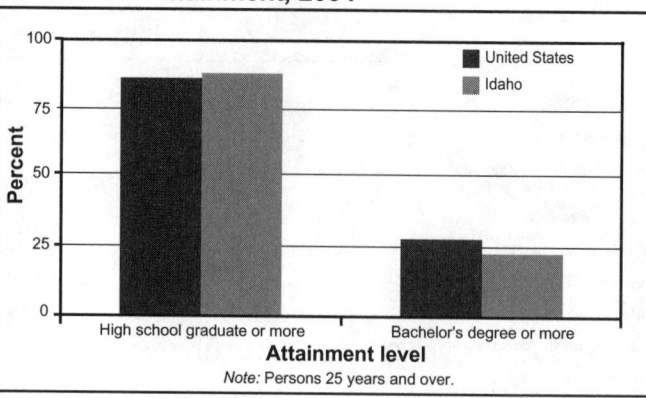

Note: Persons 25 years and over.

EDUCATION

Idaho's high school attainment level reached 87.9 percent in 2004, which was higher than the U.S. average of 85.2 percent. However, the state's proportion of college graduates was among the 10 lowest in the nation. This may be a reflection of the occupational mix of the state's economy, in which many jobs did not require a higher level of education. Idaho had the eighth highest student/teacher ratio, reflecting the high population growth and a high proportion of student-age population. Not surprisingly, per student expenditures were low, ranking 49th in the country. Idaho's dropout rate of 3.9 percent was slightly lower than the average of the 46 reporting states.

VOTER PARTICIPATION

Voter participation levels were close to the national average: 53.9 percent of eligible Idaho residents voted in 2000 and 58.7 percent voted in 2004. The state ranked 34th for proportion of voters in 2004. About 65 percent of eligible non-Hispanic Whites voted in the 2004 elections. Close to 46 percent of eligible voters age 18 to 24 years reported voting. This was a higher proportion for that age group than the national average. The state voted overwhelmingly Republican. According to the official tally by the Clerk of the U.S. House of Representatives, 67.2 percent of voters in Idaho voted Republican in 2000, and 68.4 percent voted similarly in 2004.

Table ID-19. Reported Voting and Registration, November 2000 and November 2004

(Numbers in thousands, percent.)

Characteristic	Total population 18 years and over	Total citizen		Total registered		Total voted	
		Number	Percent	Number	Percent	Number	Percent
NOVEMBER 2000							
Total	927	892	96.1	569	61.4	500	53.9
Male	447	426	95.3	265	59.3	232	51.9
Female	480	465	96.9	304	63.3	268	55.8
NOVEMBER 2004							
Total	996	948	95.3	663	66.5	585	58.7
Male	487	462	94.9	317	65.2	273	56.1
Female	509	487	95.6	345	67.9	311	61.2
Race and Hispanic Origin							
White alone	942	897	95.3	644	68.4	571	60.7
Non-Hispanic White alone	857	848	99.0	626	73.1	558	65.2
Black alone	5	5	B	-	B	-	B
Asian alone	15	12	B	4	B	2	B
Hispanic or Latino[1]	89	53	B	19	B	14	B
White alone or in combination	960	916	95.4	654	68.1	580	60.4
Non-Hispanic White alone or in combination	872	864	99.0	636	72.9	567	65.0
Black alone or in combination	7	7	B	1	B	-	B
Asian alone or in combination	17	14	B	5	B	4	B
Age							
18 to 24 years	151	143	94.7	82	54.7	69	45.8
25 to 44 years	359	338	94.1	218	60.7	190	53.0
45 to 64 years	334	320	95.7	242	72.5	219	65.6
65 to 74 years	74	72	B	58	B	53	B
75 years and over	78	76	B	62	B	53	B

[1]May be of any race.
- = Represents zero or rounds to zero.
B = Base is too small to show derived measure.

At a Glance:

- Illinois's population was over 12.7 million in 2004, ranking the state as the fifth most populous in the nation.

- Non-Hispanic Whites made up 66.2 percent of the state's population. Illinois ranked among the top 15 states for its proportions of Blacks, Asian and Pacific Islanders, and Hispanics.

- Illinois was the fifth leading destination among the states for immigrants from other countries.

- Median household income was above the national average, ranking 18th in the country. Illinois's poverty rate was slightly below the U.S. average.

- In 2004, Illinois's unemployment rate reached 6.2 percent, which was higher than the rates of all but five states.

- Illinois was among four states with lower employment in 2004 than in 2001. This was primarily caused by the loss of over 118,000 manufacturing jobs.

- The state's economy was the nation's fifth largest, as measured by real gross state product (GSP); however, GSP growth from 2001 to 2004 was the second lowest in the nation.

Table IL-1. Population by Sex and Age, 1990, 2000, and 2004

(Number, percent.)

Sex and age	1990	2000	2004	Percent distribution, 2004	Average annual percent change, 2000–2004
Total Population	11 430 602	12 419 293	12 713 634	X	0.6
Percent of total U.S. population	4.6	4.4	4.3	X	X
Sex					
Male	5 552 233	6 080 336	6 243 216	49.1	0.7
Female	5 878 369	6 338 957	6 470 418	50.9	0.5
Age					
Under 5 years	848 141	876 549	890 545	7.0	0.2
5 to 17 years	2 098 225	2 368 902	2 347 605	18.5	0.8
18 years and over	2 141 412	9 173 842	9 475 484	74.5	0.8
18 to 24 years	8 484 236	1 210 898	1 260 365	9.9	0.2
25 to 44 years	1 212 950	3 795 544	3 703 357	29.1	0.0
45 to 64 years	3 693 329	2 667 375	2 991 133	23.5	2.4
65 years and over	1 436 545	1 500 025	1 520 629	12.0	0.4
85 years and over	147 549	192 031	219 387	1.7	3.0
Median age (years)	32.7	34.7	35.3	X	X

X = Not applicable.

Average Annual Rate of Population Growth, 1980–2004

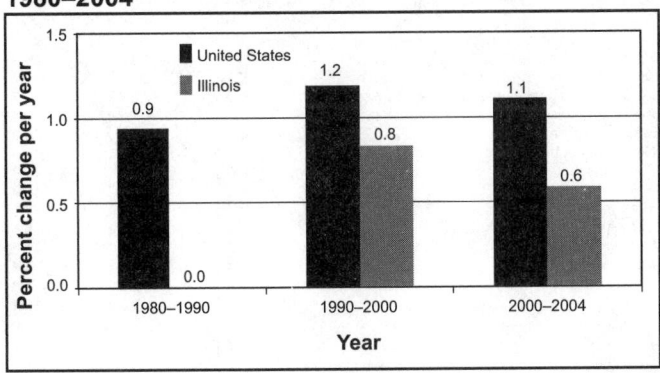

POPULATION

Illinois's population grew by 2.4 percent between 2000 and 2004, a rate equal to just half of the national rate but only slightly lower than the rates of neighboring states (with the exception of Iowa, which had a much slower rate of growth). Illinois had a net loss of over 300,000 residents to other states. This was offset by the addition of nearly 277,000 new residents from other countries. The remaining population growth was due to natural increase (the number of births minus the number of deaths). Illinois's population was concentrated around the Chicago area, which ranks among the most highly populated areas of the United States.

Table IL-2. Population by Race and Hispanic Origin, 1990, 2000, and 2004

(Number, percent.)

Race and Hispanic origin	1990	2000	2004
Total Population	11 430 602	12 419 293	12 713 634
Non-Hispanic (Percent)			
One race[1]			
White	74.8	68.2	66.2
Black	14.6	15.0	14.8
American Indian, Alaska Native[2]	0.2	0.2	0.2
Asian and Pacific Islander[2]	2.5	3.5	3.9
Other race[2]	4.2	. . .	. . .
Two or more races	. . .	0.8	0.9
Hispanic or Latino[3] (Percent)	7.9	12.3	14.0

[1]Individuals could report only one race in the 1990 census and could report one or more races on the 2000 census. Data on race in 2000 and 2004 are not comparable to 1990.
[2]Data for 1990 include people of Hispanic or Latino origin.
[3]May be of any race.
. . . = Not available.

Minority Population as a Percent of Total Population, 2004

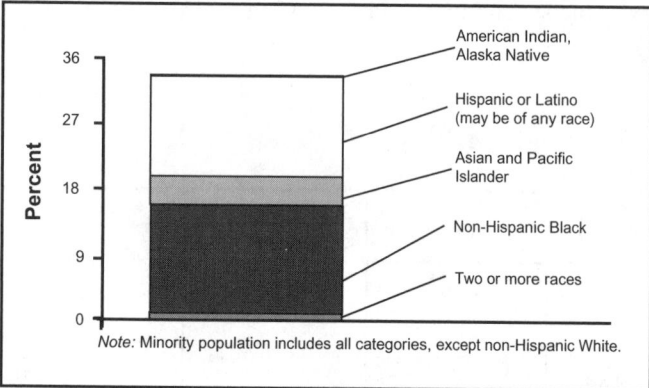

Note: Minority population includes all categories, except non-Hispanic White.

Age-Adjusted Death Rates, Average 2000–2002

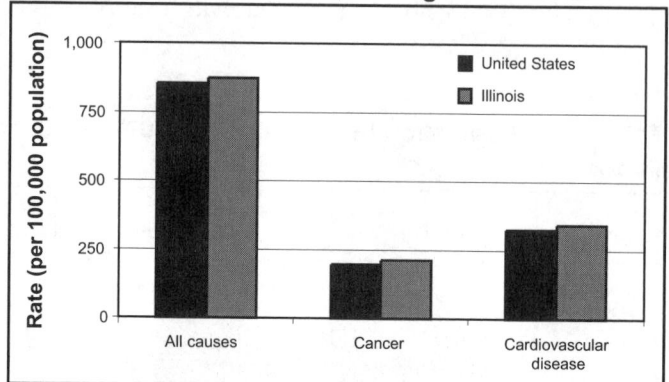

HEALTH

Illinois's rate of health insurance coverage was better than the national average. In 2004, 14 percent of the state's population lacked health insurance. Illinois's birth rate and infant mortality rate were above the U.S. averages. However, the state's teenage birth rate was slightly below average.

Table IL-3. Health Characteristics, 2000–2004

(Number, rate, percent.)

Item	State	U.S.
Births, 2003–2004		
Number of births	182 495	4 089 950
Birth rate (per 1,000 population)	14.4	14.1
Teenage birth rate (per 1,000 women age 15–19 years)	40.4	41.6
Mortality Rates, Average 2000–2002		
Infant mortality rate (per 1,000 live births)	7.8	6.9
Age-adjusted mortality rate (per 100,000 population)		
All races	863.9	853.3
Non-Hispanic White	835.7	843.1
Black	1 163.1	1 097.7
American Indian, Alaska Native	. . .	687.0
Asian and Pacific Islander	413.1	486.0
Hispanic or Latino[1]	535.2	642.7
Health Insurance, 2004		
Percent of all persons without health insurance	14.0	15.7
Percent of children without health insurance	11.4	11.2
Percent of low-income children without health insurance	7.4	7.1

[1]May be of any race.
. . . = Not available.

Table IL-4. Leading Causes of Death, Average 2000–2002

(Number, rate per 100,000 population.)

Cause	Number of deaths	Age-adjusted death rates	
		State	U.S.
ALL CAUSES	106 244	863.9	853.3
Leading Causes			
Major cardiovascular diseases	40 980	332.3	326.5
Cancer	24 960	206.0	196.0
Chronic lower respiratory diseases	4 790	39.4	43.7
Unintentional injuries	4 113	33.0	35.7
Diabetes (underlying cause)	3 033	24.9	25.2
Influenza and pneumonia	2 839	22.8	22.7
Alzheimer's disease	2 238	17.9	19.0
Motor vehicle accidents	1 539	12.3	15.0
Nephritis, nephrotic syndrome, and nephrosis ..	2 211	18.0	13.8
Septicemia	1 966	16.0	11.4
Suicides	1 096	8.8	10.7
Firearm-related	1 217	9.6	10.3
Cirrhosis	1 079	8.9	9.5
Drug-induced	956	7.6	7.9
Alcohol-induced	584	4.8	6.9
Homicides	1 028	8.1	6.0
Falls	526	4.3	5.2
HIV	496	4.0	5.0
Viral hepatitis	144	1.2	2.0
Anemias	241	1.9	1.6
Drownings	117	0.9	1.3
Fire deaths	155	1.2	1.2

Note: The rates are age-adjusted to the U.S. 2000 standard population.

Table IL-5. Households and Housing Characteristics, 1990, 2000, and 2004

(Number, percent, and dollars.)

Characteristic	1990	2000	2004	Average annual percent change, 2000–2004
Total Households	4 202 240	4 591 779	4 659 791	0.4
Family households	2 924 880	3 105 513	3 096 322	-0.1
Married-couple family	2 271 962	2 353 892	2 338 931	-0.2
Other family	652 918	751 621	757 391	0.2
Male householder, no wife present	147 173	187 903	186 071	-0.2
Female householder, no husband present	505 745	563 718	571 320	0.3
Nonfamily households	1 277 360	1 486 266	1 563 469	1.3
Householder living alone	1 081 113	1 229 807	1 309 497	1.6
Householder not living alone	196 247	256 459	253 972	-0.2
Housing Characteristics				
Average size	2.65	2.63	2.66	X
Housing units	4 506 275	4 885 615	5 094 186	1.1
Occupied housing units	4 202 240	4 591 779	4 659 791	0.4
Owner-occupied	2 699 182	3 088 884	3 226 646	1.1
Renter-occupied	1 503 058	1 502 895	1 433 145	-1.2
Median gross rent of renter-occupied housing units (dollars)	445	605	698	3.6
Median value of owner-occupied housing units (dollars)	80 100	130 800	167 711	6.4

X = Not applicable.

Median Housing Value and Median Rent, 2004

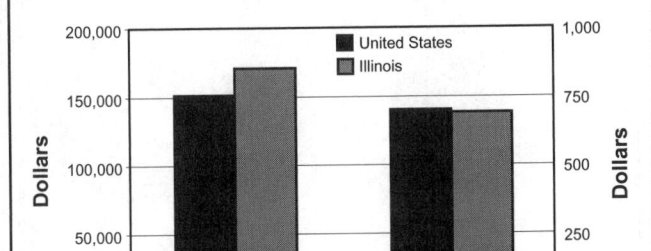

Median Household Income, 1984–2004 (2004 Dollars)

Table IL-6. Household Income and Poverty Status, 1980–2004

(2004 CPI-U-RS adjusted dollars, rate.)

Year	State Median household income (2004 dollars)	State Poverty rate	U.S. Median household income (2004 dollars)	U.S. Poverty rate
2004	46 132	12.2	44 389	12.7
2003	46 367	12.6	44 482	12.5
2002	44 863	12.8	44 546	12.1
2001	49 269	10.1	45 062	11.7
2000	50 527	10.7	46 058	11.3
1999	52 515	9.9	46 129	11.9
1998	49 972	10.1	45 003	12.7
1997	48 451	11.2	43 430	13.3
1996	47 413	12.1	42 544	13.7
1995	46 861	12.4	41 943	13.8
1994	44 229	12.4	40 677	14.5
1993	42 297	13.6	40 217	15.1
1992	41 629	15.6	40 422	14.8
1991	43 123	13.5	40 746	14.2
1990	45 605	13.7	41 963	13.5
1989	46 046	12.7	42 524	12.8
1988	45 299	12.7	41 771	13.0
1987	43 068	14.4	41 322	13.4
1986	43 593	13.3	40 939	13.6
1985	41 642	15.6	39 545	14.0
1984	41 095	15.0	38 782	14.4
1983	. . .	14.3	. . .	15.2
1982	. . .	13.4	. . .	15.0
1981	. . .	12.1	. . .	14.0
1980	. . .	12.3	. . .	13.0

. . . = Not available.

Table IL-7. Employment Status by Demographic Group, 2004

(Numbers in thousands, rate.)

Characteristic	Civilian noninstitutional population	Civilian labor force		Employed	Unemployment rate
		Number	Participation rate		
SEX AND AGE					
Total	9 641	6 386	66.2	5 997	6.1
16 to 19 years	706	316	44.8	259	18.0
20 to 24 years	902	657	72.9	593	9.7
25 to 34 years	1 737	1 442	83.0	1 357	5.8
35 to 44 years	1 882	1 592	84.6	1 508	5.2
45 to 54 years	1 715	1 433	83.5	1 377	3.9
55 to 64 years	1 179	723	61.3	684	5.4
65 years and over	1 520	224	14.7	217	3.0
Men	4 650	3 408	73.3	3 203	6.0
16 to 19 years	367	167	45.4	140	16.0
20 to 24 years	457	350	76.5	317	9.4
25 to 34 years	843	778	92.3	731	6.0
35 to 44 years	945	876	92.7	827	5.6
45 to 54 years	844	745	88.2	718	3.6
55 to 64 years	556	372	67.0	354	4.9
65 years and over	638	120	18.8	116	2.8
Women	4 991	2 979	59.7	2 794	6.2
16 to 19 years	339	149	44.1	119	20.3
20 to 24 years	445	308	69.1	277	10.2
25 to 34 years	893	664	74.3	626	5.6
35 to 44 years	937	715	76.4	681	4.7
45 to 54 years	871	688	79.0	660	4.1
55 to 64 years	623	350	56.2	330	5.8
65 years and over	882	104	11.8	101	3.3
MARITAL STATUS					
Married men, spouse present	2 556	1 998	78.2	1 933	3.3
Married women, spouse present	2 541	1 561	61.4	1 504	3.6
Women who maintain families	569	412	72.4	374	9.0
RACE, HISPANIC ORIGIN, AND SEX					
White	7 893	5 282	66.9	5 011	5.1
Men	3 865	2 891	74.8	2 743	5.1
Women	4 028	2 391	59.4	2 268	5.2
Black	1 330	825	62.0	718	12.9
Men	582	360	61.9	308	14.4
Women	747	464	62.1	410	11.8
Asian	333	223	67.1	214	3.9
Men	163	125	76.3	121	3.2
Women	169	99	58.2	94	4.8
Hispanic or Latino[1]	1 085	752	69.3	704	6.4
Men	588	485	82.4	461	4.9
Women	496	268	53.9	243	9.1
RACE, HISPANIC ORIGIN, AND AGE					
White					
25 to 34 years	1 369	1 154	84.3	1 103	4.4
35 to 44 years	1 522	1 300	85.4	1 241	4.6
45 to 54 years	1 402	1 193	85.1	1 155	3.2
55 to 64 years	994	622	62.6	589	5.3

Note: Data in Table 7 are from the Current Population Survey (CPS) and do not match Bureau of Labor Statistics estimates in Table 8. See notes and definitions for more details.

[1]May be of any race.

Table IL-8. Employment Status, 1990–2004

(Numbers in thousands, rate.)

Year	Civilian labor force	Employed	Unemployed	Unemployment rate
2004	6 395 785	6 000 140	395 645	6.2
2003	6 361 478	5 934 131	427 347	6.7
2002	6 378 608	5 961 248	417 360	6.5
2001	6 473 035	6 121 940	351 095	5.4
2000	6 471 796	6 181 302	290 494	4.5
1999	6 429 466	6 143 130	286 336	4.5
1998	6 330 665	6 047 050	283 615	4.5
1997	6 290 774	5 988 296	302 478	4.8
1996	6 239 028	5 907 278	331 750	5.3
1995	6 178 774	5 857 677	321 097	5.2
1994	6 121 285	5 766 671	354 614	5.8
1993	6 073 634	5 625 103	448 531	7.4
1992	6 018 149	5 546 722	471 427	7.8
1991	5 923 409	5 493 554	429 855	7.3
1990	5 931 619	5 560 548	371 071	6.3

Note: Population age 16 years and over.

Unemployment Rate, 1980–2004

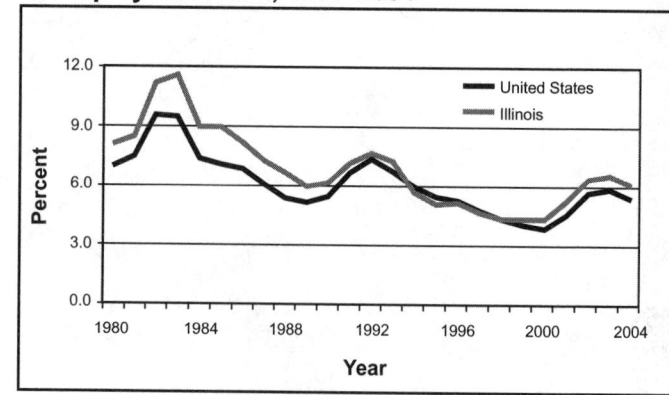

Table IL-9. Employment and Average Wages by Industry, 2001–2004

(Estimates are based on the 2002 North American Industry Classification System [NAICS].)

Industry	2001	2002	2003	2004	Annual average percent change, 2001–2004
	Number of jobs				
TOTAL EMPLOYMENT BY PLACE OF WORK	7 371 122	7 284 020	7 257 217	7 300 134	-0.3
Farm Employment	97 702	92 690	92 524	90 181	-2.6
Nonfarm Employment	7 273 420	7 191 330	7 164 693	7 209 953	-0.3
Private employment	6 372 163	6 282 117	6 264 066	6 317 089	-0.3
Forestry, fishing, hunting, and other[1]	14 375	15 245	13 860	13 491	-2.1
Mining	18 423	17 049	18 339	18 672	0.4
Utilities	30 156	28 717	25 226	24 600	-6.6
Construction	386 449	382 617	388 447	385 193	-0.1
Manufacturing	834 764	774 620	735 176	716 746	-5.0
Durable goods manufacturing	516 995	468 453	440 781	432 273	-5.8
Nondurable goods manufacturing	317 769	306 167	294 395	284 473	-3.6
Wholesale trade	333 748	321 985	319 923	320 148	-1.4
Retail trade	766 596	758 115	757 486	760 901	-0.2
Transportation and warehousing	291 744	282 328	278 713	281 835	-1.1
Information	171 025	152 809	144 165	138 068	-6.9
Finance and insurance	444 589	442 120	441 362	440 445	-0.3
Real estate and rental and leasing	225 656	228 791	239 077	247 880	3.2
Professional and technical services	515 743	499 723	490 606	494 432	-1.4
Management of companies and enterprises	77 234	87 993	86 160	88 301	4.6
Administrative and waste services	450 674	444 420	450 855	482 054	2.3
Educational services	141 420	145 456	150 991	156 353	3.4
Health care and social assistance	708 129	720 382	731 431	741 719	1.6
Arts, entertainment, and recreation	133 889	138 687	139 956	141 177	1.8
Accommodation and food services	434 290	434 393	441 922	451 957	1.3
Other services, except public administration	393 259	406 667	410 371	413 117	1.7
Government and government enterprises	901 257	909 213	900 627	892 864	-0.3
	Dollars				
AVERAGE WAGES AND SALARIES BY PLACE OF WORK	38 475	39 140	40 002	41 742	2.8
Farm Earnings	18 102	20 935	23 283	29 914	18.2
Nonfarm Earnings	38 541	39 187	40 051	41 772	2.7
Private earnings	38 951	39 438	40 282	41 996	2.5
Forestry, fishing, hunting, and other[1]	24 058	24 219	24 323	25 433	1.9
Mining	50 122	51 346	51 161	53 285	2.1
Utilities	78 025	79 086	78 888	82 501	1.9
Construction	47 573	48 520	49 135	50 239	1.8
Manufacturing	43 715	44 819	46 212	48 587	3.6
Durable goods manufacturing	44 173	45 027	46 376	49 116	3.6
Nondurable goods manufacturing	42 969	44 500	45 966	47 783	3.6
Wholesale trade	52 960	53 499	54 728	57 645	2.9
Retail trade	22 844	23 465	23 782	24 397	2.2
Transportation and warehousing	40 017	40 746	40 843	42 296	1.9
Information	52 958	52 322	54 063	56 781	2.4
Finance and insurance	65 802	66 319	69 334	74 326	4.1
Real estate and rental and leasing	39 681	41 699	41 372	44 168	3.6
Professional and technical services	63 895	64 266	65 722	68 809	2.5
Management of companies and enterprises	87 690	82 191	86 013	95 158	2.8
Administrative and waste services	25 229	25 456	26 063	26 789	2.0
Educational services	29 194	30 159	31 939	33 005	4.2
Health care and social assistance	32 974	34 093	35 213	36 525	3.5
Arts, entertainment, and recreation	25 641	27 047	26 991	27 569	2.4
Accommodation and food services	14 473	14 477	14 749	15 310	1.9
Other services, except public administration	24 608	25 761	26 517	27 544	3.8
Government and government enterprises	36 115	37 753	38 731	40 476	3.9

Note: Average wages and salaries are a calculation by the editors of wage and salary disbursements divided by full- and part-time wage and salary employment. Data may not add to total or may appear as zero due to rounding.

[1] "Other" consists of the number of jobs held by U.S. residents employed by international organizations and foreign embassies and consulates in the United States.

LABOR MARKET

The unemployment rate in Illinois has been higher than the national average since 2000, and it rose substantially as a result of the 2001 recession. Employment was spread across many sectors. Government was the largest employer, accounting for 12.2 percent of total jobs in the state, followed by retail trade, health care services, and manufacturing (largely durable goods manufacturing). Over the 2001–2004 period, manufacturing employment declined at a rate of about 5 percent per year. Job growth during this time period was mostly limited to the service sector, although many of these industries experienced slow employment growth, with the notable exceptions of management and health care.

Employment by Industry, 2004

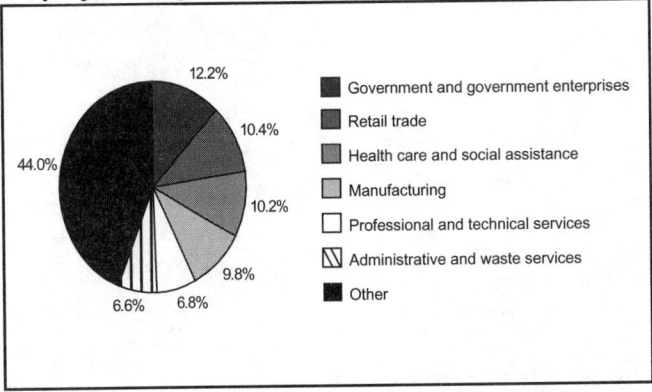

- Government and government enterprises
- Retail trade
- Health care and social assistance
- Manufacturing
- Professional and technical services
- Administrative and waste services
- Other

44.0%   12.2%   10.4%   10.2%   9.8%   6.8%   6.6%

Table IL-10. Personal Income by Major Source, Selected Years 1980–2004

(Millions of dollars, except where noted.)

Item	1980	1990	2000	2001	2002	2003	2004	Average annual percent change, 2000–2004
Earnings by Place of Work	99 797	184 815	313 024	318 172	324 661	339 273	350 954	2.9
Wage and salary disbursements	76 481	138 488	236 026	240 335	240 088	242 647	253 110	1.8
Supplements to wages and salaries	14 534	27 778	45 399	47 402	52 112	62 552	59 597	7.0
Proprietors' income[1]	8 782	18 550	31 599	30 435	32 461	34 074	38 248	4.9
Farm proprietors' income	88	1 393	963	709	255	925	2 404	25.7
Nonfarm proprietors' income	8 694	17 157	30 636	29 725	32 206	33 149	35 843	4.0
(-) Contributions for government social insurance[2]	8 955	19 637	33 038	33 984	34 477	35 214	37 243	3.0
(+) Adjustment for residence[3]	262	-281	-1 343	-1 505	-1 443	-1 418	-1 355	X
(=) Net Earnings by Place of Residence	91 104	164 897	278 642	282 683	288 741	302 641	312 356	2.9
(+) Dividends, interest, and rent[4]	20 148	47 026	76 913	76 281	73 143	70 261	72 690	-1.4
(+) Personal current transfer receipts	14 585	26 576	44 818	48 290	52 107	54 310	56 439	5.9
Personal income	125 838	238 499	400 373	407 254	413 991	427 212	441 485	2.5
Farm income	125 503	236 795	399 055	406 144	413 372	425 843	438 595	2.4
Nonfarm income	335	1 704	1 319	1 109	619	1 369	2 891	21.7
Per Capita Personal Income (Dollars)[5]	11 005	20 824	32 185	32 532	32 895	33 774	34 725	1.9

Note: Data may not add to total or may appear as zero due to rounding.

[1]Proprietors' income includes the inventory valuation adjustment and the capital consumption adjustment.
[2]Contributions for government social insurance are included in earnings by type and industry, but they are excluded from personal income.
[3]The adjustment for residence is the net inflow of the earnings of interarea commuters.
[4]Rental income of persons includes the capital consumption adjustment.
[5]Per capita personal income is total personal income divided by total midyear population.
X = Not applicable.

Per Capita Personal Income, 1980–2004 (Current Dollars)

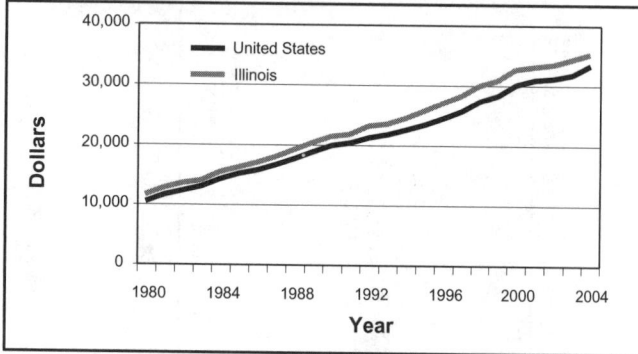

ECONOMIC ACTIVITY

Illinois's economy grew very slowly between 2001 and 2004, and only began to show signs of more robust growth in 2004. Gross state product grew just 2.9 percent from 2001 to 2004, as compared to the U.S. growth rate of 9.1 percent. The sectors with the highest rates of growth between 2003 and 2004 were information, administrative and waste services, and management. Housing price appreciation was below the national average over the 2000–2004 period, despite some significant price increases in the suburban areas of Chicago. Illinois ranked 19th in the nation for median value of owner-occupied housing in 2004.

Table IL-11. Real Gross State Product, 1997–2004

(Millions of chained 2000 dollars, percent.)

Industry	1997	1998	1999	2000	2001	2002	2003	2004	Average annual percent change, 2001–2004
GROSS STATE PRODUCT	425 023	439 794	452 784	464 257	465 299	465 826	470 101	478 966	1.0
As a percent of U.S. gross product	4.9	4.9	4.8	4.8	4.7	4.7	4.6	4.5	X
Private Industries	383 409	397 519	409 735	420 225	420 880	421 246	426 283	440 605	1.5
Agriculture, forestry, fishing, and hunting	2 887	2 343	1 545	2 090	2 038	2 592	2 810	3 001	13.8
Mining	931	1 047	1 171	1 052	1 048	1 009	982	903	-4.8
Utilities	9 428	9 389	9 809	10 430	9 675	10 162	10 377	10 715	3.5
Construction	19 805	20 076	20 643	20 952	20 976	20 598	20 298	19 680	-2.1
Manufacturing	64 992	66 250	66 383	68 984	64 978	65 322	66 223	68 093	1.6
As a percent of gross state product	15.3	15.1	14.7	14.9	14.0	14.0	14.1	14.2	X
Wholesale trade	28 716	31 462	33 073	33 252	35 030	35 135	33 980	34 840	-0.2
Retail trade	23 659	24 392	25 643	27 356	29 239	30 296	31 442	32 783	3.9
Transportation and warehousing	15 245	15 755	16 486	17 172	17 041	17 177	17 671	18 301	2.4
Information	15 737	16 784	18 719	17 822	18 792	19 609	20 498	22 176	5.7
Finance and insurance	39 613	41 481	42 836	45 243	45 145	43 708	46 760	49 393	3.0
Real estate and rental and leasing	52 004	53 242	55 767	57 579	59 363	57 991	55 934	57 591	-1.0
Services	110 442	115 346	117 806	118 291	117 693	117 870	119 762	123 960	1.7
As a percent of gross state product	26.0	26.2	26.0	25.5	25.3	25.3	25.5	25.9	X
Professional and technical services	32 061	35 305	36 808	38 550	38 493	37 971	38 107	39 039	0.5
Management of companies and enterprises	10 605	10 435	10 751	9 571	9 645	9 748	10 237	10 929	4.3
Administrative and waste services	13 902	14 754	14 967	13 951	13 182	13 257	13 813	14 786	3.9
Educational services	3 826	3 908	3 977	4 020	3 994	3 962	4 012	3 981	-0.1
Health care and social assistance	25 116	25 315	25 998	26 810	27 484	28 070	28 596	29 058	1.9
Arts, entertainment, and recreation	3 927	3 733	3 862	3 859	4 019	4 232	4 189	4 149	1.1
Accommodation and food services	9 850	10 351	10 194	10 423	10 133	9 950	10 140	10 685	1.8
Other services, except public administration	11 155	11 545	11 249	11 107	10 743	10 680	10 668	11 333	1.8
Government	41 659	42 288	43 051	44 032	44 417	44 575	43 868	38 770	-4.4
As a percent of gross state product	9.8	9.6	9.5	9.5	9.5	9.6	9.3	8.1	X

X = Not applicable.

Table IL-12. Government Transfer Payments, Selected Years 1980–2004

(Millions of dollars, percent.)

Item	1980	1990	2000	2001	2002	2003	2004	Average annual percent change, 2000–2004
CURRENT TRANSFER PAYMENTS TO INDIVIDUALS	13 711	24 898	41 726	44 905	49 041	51 500	53 598	6.5
Retirement and Disability Insurance Benefits	6 422	12 364	18 188	19 089	19 994	20 585	21 500	4.3
Old-age, survivors, and disability insurance (OASDI) benefits	5 956	11 766	17 538	18 406	19 202	19 759	20 648	4.2
Railroad retirement and disability benefits	332	473	527	535	553	561	571	2.0
Workers' compensation	29	36	56	61	74	74	76	7.8
Other government retirement and disability insurance benefits	105	90	66	87	166	192	205	32.8
Medical Benefits	3 504	7 741	16 887	18 234	19 931	21 339	22 842	7.8
Medicare benefits	2 078	5 032	9 206	10 154	10 813	11 397	12 481	7.9
Public assistance medical care benefits	1 413	2 647	7 624	7 998	9 008	9 850	10 250	7.7
Military medical insurance benefits	13	62	57	83	110	93	111	18.3
Income Maintenance Benefits	1 699	2 974	4 363	4 463	4 786	5 197	5 621	6.5
Supplemental Security Income (SSI) benefits	233	652	1 204	1 238	1 276	1 297	1 356	3.0
Family assistance	722	866	656	626	630	650	648	-0.3
Food stamps	414	865	783	832	941	1 088	1 265	12.7
Other income maintenance benefits	330	592	1 720	1 768	1 939	2 163	2 352	8.1
Unemployment Insurance Compensation	1 441	957	1 212	1 915	3 038	3 023	2 165	15.6
Veterans' Benefits	450	506	599	625	685	738	791	7.2
Federal Education and Training Assistance	193	330	428	506	567	583	623	9.9
Other Payments to Individuals	3	26	51	73	39	34	55	2.1

Note: See notes and definitions for more details. Data may not add to total or may appear as zero due to rounding.

EXPORTS

Although Illinois was one of the country's leading exporters (ranking seventh in 2004), the value of its exports declined significantly between 2001 and 2003. Despite a large increase in 2004, they remained below the 2001 value. Transportation equipment suffered the largest loss from 2001 to 2004, with a decline of nearly 48 percent, or $2.9 billion. Among the leading exports, chemicals and machinery manufactures had the highest rates of growth during the 2001–2004 period. Canada was the chief foreign market for the state's exports; however, exports to this country were down nearly 19 percent between 2001 and 2004. Among the top markets, exports to the Netherlands increased the most significantly (48.7 percent).

Leading Exports, 2004

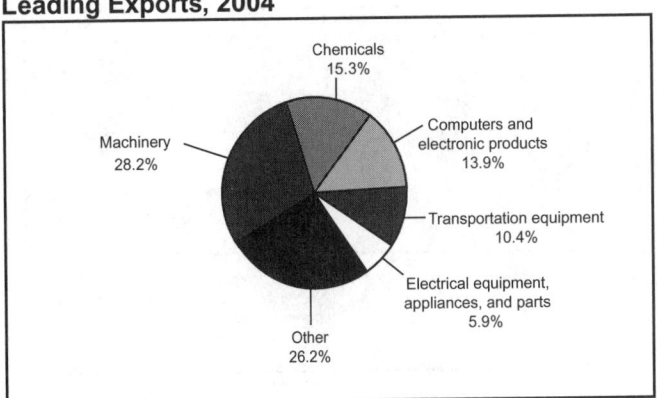

Table IL-13. Exports of Goods by Leading Products and Destinations, 2001–2004

(Millions of dollars, percent, rank based on 2004 dollar values.)

Product and market	2001	2002	2003	2004	Percent share of total, 2004	Average annual percent change, 2001–2004
Total Goods	30 434	25 686	26 473	30 214	100.0	-0.2
Total	29 434	24 696	25 336	28 943	95.8	-0.6
Manufactures	340	435	507	662	2.2	24.9
Agriculture and livestock	660	555	629	609	2.0	-2.7
Other commodities						
Five Leading Exports (NAICS Code)						
Machinery manufactures (333)	7 109	6 528	6 893	8 528	28.2	6.3
Chemical manufactures (325)	3 763	3 518	3 891	4 617	15.3	7.1
Computers and electronic products (334)	4 367	3 940	3 664	4 210	13.9	-1.2
Transportation equipment (336)	6 037	3 254	2 950	3 146	10.4	-19.5
Electrical equipment, appliances, and parts (335)	1 885	1 625	1 711	1 792	5.9	-1.7
Five Leading Markets	27 582	23 365	23 806	27 105	89.7	-0.6
Canada	11 436	8 175	8 559	9 282	30.7	-6.7
Mexico	2 260	2 103	2 153	2 417	8.0	2.3
United Kingdom	1 674	1 605	1 544	1 859	6.2	3.5
Japan	2 089	2 090	1 964	1 856	6.1	-3.9
Germany	1 368	1 176	1 210	1 420	4.7	1.2

Table IL-14. Agriculture, 1997 and 2002
(Number, acres, and dollars.)

Item	1997	2002
Number of farms	79 112	73 027
Land in farms (acres)	27 673 285	27 310 833
Farm Size		
Average size of farm (acres)	350	374
Farms by size (percent distribution)		
Fewer than 50 acres	25.7	26.9
50 to 499 acres	51.0	49.1
500 acres or more	23.3	24.0
Market Value of Land and Equipment (Dollars)		
Land and buildings average value per farm	736 255	913 251
Average value per acre	2 136	2 425
Machinery and equipment average value per farm	86 662	102 242
Value of Sales (Thousands of Dollars)		
Agricultural products sold	8 634 730	7 676 239
Crops	6 602 817	5 871 542
Livestock, poultry, and their products	2 031 913	1 804 697
Average per farm (dollars)	109 146	105 115
Value of sales (percent distribution)		
Less than $10,000	36.1	41.4
$10,000 to $99,999	34.5	31.9
$100,000 or more	29.4	26.7
Government Payments		
Payments (thousands of dollars)	372 268	412 636
Percent of farms receiving government payments	69.0	65.5
Farm operators whose principal occupation is farming (percent)	54.4	64.1

AGRICULTURE

With cash receipts of close to $7.7 billion in 2002, Illinois ranked among the top 10 states for farming, although there was a decline in value in this sector from the previous farm census in 1997. The state's chief crops were corn and soybeans. More than three-quarters of the state's agricultural sales were crops. Large scale farming was evident: over 30 percent of farms had sales of $100,000 or more, and 64 percent of all farm operators classified farming as their principal occupation. In 2002, 24 percent of farms had 500 acres or more, which was among the highest proportions in the nation.

ENERGY

Energy expenditures per person were relatively low, ranking only 36th in the country. Per capita consumption ranked 35th. The state's price per million Btu was $11.01, which was among the 20 highest prices in the nation. The chief source of energy was petroleum. The largest energy consumer was the industry sector.

Energy Consumption by Source, 2001

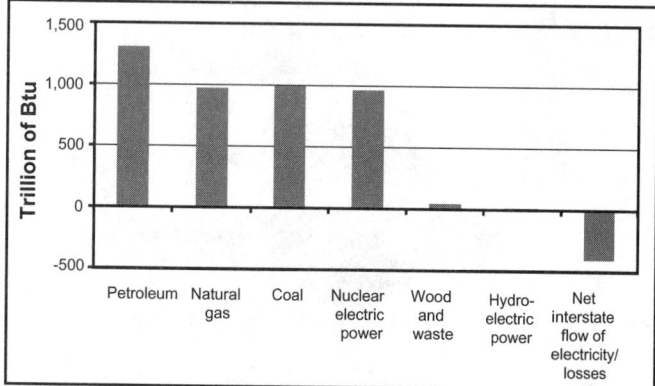

Energy Consumption by Sector, 2001

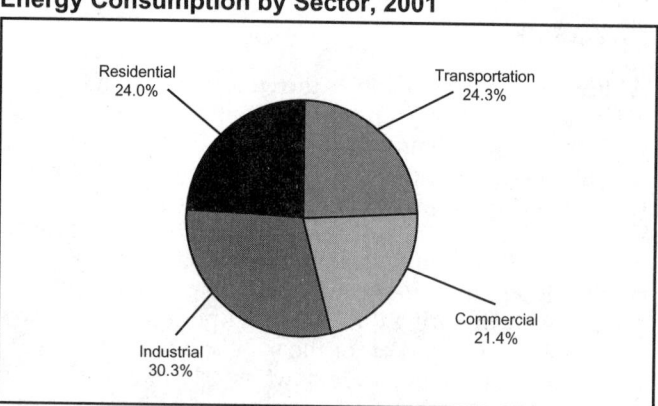

Table IL-15. Energy Consumption, Expenditures, and Prices, Selected Years 1960–2001
(Dollars, Btu [British Thermal Unit], percent distribution.)

Item	1960	1965	1970	1975	1980	1985	1990	1995	2000	2001
Total Consumption (Billion Btu)	2 527 029	3 035 628	3 708 788	3 877 709	3 834 667	3 450 688	3 574 916	3 872 501	4 006 102	3 870 148
Consumption per capita (million Btu)	250.7	283.9	333.8	343.4	335.6	302.7	312.7	325.8	322.6	309.2
Consumption by Sector (Percent Distribution)										
Residential	23.2	22.9	23.3	24.0	24.0	25.5	24.5	25.3	24.0	24.0
Commercial	12.6	14.0	15.1	16.1	16.7	18.2	18.7	18.9	20.5	21.4
Industrial	44.3	43.4	40.2	37.2	37.8	35.3	35.0	35.1	31.4	30.3
Transportation	20.0	19.7	21.3	22.8	21.4	21.0	21.7	20.7	24.2	24.3
Consumption by Source (Billion Btu)										
Coal	914 648	1 014 492	920 303	845 574	844 481	811 110	748 167	826 687	1 016 571	993 588
Natural gas	536 127	778 662	1 203 225	1 123 588	1 113 694	1 000 521	960 187	1 099 670	1 053 319	970 672
Petroleum	1 105 006	1 225 970	1 498 912	1 636 987	1 478 060	1 115 762	1 154 464	1 217 034	1 332 800	1 304 066
Nuclear electric power	2 958	11 393	27 600	245 760	302 604	415 387	760 711	824 598	932 749	964 961
Hydroelectric power[1]	1 986	1 827	1 747	1 274	1 438	1 422	1 497	1 278	1 467	1 465
Wood and waste	31 033	33 209	39 317	41 624	87 370	93 451	68 164	53 775	41 123	38 700
Other	0	0	0	0	0	0	323	437	655	736
Net interstate flow of electricity/losses[2]	-64 729	-29 925	17 684	-17 097	7 018	13 035	-118 597	-150 977	-372 582	-404 041
Total Expenditures (Thousands of Dollars)	...	...	4 939 900	9 300 400	18 614 900	21 009 300	21 561 600	23 200 200	29 189 500	29 386 500
Expenditures per capita (dollars)	...	...	445	824	1 629	1 843	1 886	1 952	2 350	2 348
Prices by Sector (Dollars Per Million Btu)										
Total	...	...	1.70	3.16	6.71	8.45	8.62	8.59	10.43	11.01
Residential	...	...	1.89	3.06	6.01	8.97	9.56	9.71	11.30	12.91
Commercial	...	...	1.94	3.61	7.35	10.20	11.10	11.69	12.92	13.87
Industrial	...	...	0.97	2.26	4.99	6.75	6.23	6.02	7.28	7.65
Transportation	...	...	2.47	4.07	9.00	9.01	9.19	8.96	11.42	11.23

[1]A negative number in this row results from pumped storage for which, overall, more electricity is expended than created to provide electricity during peak demand periods.
[2]Net interstate flow of electricity is the difference between the amount of energy in the electricity sold within a state (including associated losses) and the energy input at the electric utilities within the state. A positive number indicates that more electricity (including associated losses) came into the state than went out of the state during the year; conversely, a negative number indicates that more electricity (including associated losses) went out of the state than came into the state.
. . . = Not available.

Table IL-16. State Taxes, Fiscal 2004

(Dollars, percent distribution.)

Item	Thousands of dollars	Percent distribution	Dollars per capita	
			State	U.S.
TOTAL TAXES	25 490 593	100.0	2 004.9	2 024.8
Property Taxes	57 084	0.2	4.5	38.9
Sales and Gross Receipts	12 526 542	49.1	985.3	1 003.4
General sales and gross receipts	6 922 587	27.2	544.5	677.0
Selective sales taxes	5 603 955	22.0	440.8	326.4
Alcoholic beverages	147 883	0.6	11.6	15.7
Amusements	785 922	3.1	61.8	17.0
Insurance premiums	378 517	1.5	29.8	47.0
Motor fuels	1 421 927	5.6	111.8	114.6
Public utilities	1 704 655	6.7	134.1	39.2
Tobacco products	760 226	3.0	59.8	42.0
Other selective sales	392 783	1.5	30.9	49.8
Licenses	2 385 596	9.4	187.6	134.9
Corporation	169 449	0.7	13.3	21.6
Motor vehicle	1 370 405	5.4	107.8	59.4
Occupation and business, not elsewhere classified	718 979	2.8	56.6	37.1
Other Taxes	10 521 371	41.3	827.5	847.6
Individual income	8 139 558	31.9	640.2	673.6
Corporation net income	2 068 574	8.1	162.7	105.1
Death and gift	221 733	0.9	17.4	19.6

GOVERNMENT FINANCE

In 2003, state revenues per person were well below the national average, as were expenditures per person. By both measures, Illinois ranked among the lowest 10 states in the country. The state's debt per capita was $3,691, which was well above the U.S. average and ranked 11th in the nation. Illinois's per capita taxes collected in fiscal year 2004 amounted to $2,005, which was the 24th highest in nation. The largest share was derived from individual income taxes, which were $640 per person. The state's per capita general sales and gross receipts and selective sales taxes amounted to $545 and $441, respectively.

Per Capita State Taxes, Fiscal 2004

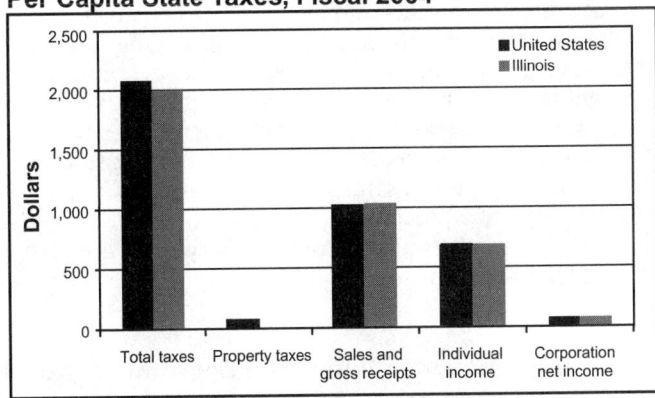

Table IL-17. State Government Finances, 2003

(Dollars, percent distribution.)

Item	Millions of dollars	Percent distribution	Dollars per capita	
			State	U.S.
GENERAL REVENUE	40 815 713	100.0	3 226.8	3 832.6
Intergovernmental revenue	12 027 338	29.5	950.8	1 246.0
Taxes	22 211 693	54.4	1 756.0	1 891.6
General sales	6 558 746	16.1	518.5	636.0
Selective sales	4 826 429	11.8	381.6	307.4
License taxes	1 845 165	4.5	145.9	123.6
Individual income tax	7 340 982	18.0	580.4	626.8
Corporate income tax	1 293 188	3.2	102.2	97.8
Other taxes	347 183	0.9	27.4	99.9
Current charges	2 884 353	7.1	228.0	366.5
Miscellaneous general revenue	3 692 329	9.0	291.9	328.6
GENERAL EXPENDITURE	43 954 103	100.0	3 474.9	4 010.5
Intergovernmental expenditure	13 369 662	30.4	1 057.0	1 316.9
Direct expenditure	30 584 441	69.6	2 417.9	2 693.6
Expenditure by Function				
Education	14 118 807	32.1	1 116.2	1 416.4
Public welfare	11 478 589	26.1	907.5	1 083.3
Hospitals	958 446	2.2	75.8	132.3
Health	2 569 793	5.8	203.2	173.0
Highways	3 834 256	8.7	303.1	295.4
Police protection	407 932	0.9	32.2	38.4
Correction	1 369 510	3.1	108.3	135.0
Natural resources	422 712	1.0	33.4	64.0
Parks and recreation	554 371	1.3	43.8	20.1
Government administration	1 387 596	3.2	109.7	151.3
Interest on general debt	2 071 586	4.7	163.8	107.8
Other and unallocable	4 780 505	10.9	377.9	393.4
DEBT AT END OF FISCAL YEAR	46 688 761	X	3 691.1	2 404.7
CASH AND SECURITY HOLDINGS	87 544 459	X	6 921.1	8 938.4

X = Not applicable.

Table IL-18. Education Indicators, 2000–2004

(Percent, number.)

Item	State	U.S.
Total Population 25 Years and Over (Thousands), 2004	8 090	186 877
Educational Attainment, 2004		
Percent high school graduate or more	86.8	85.2
Percent college graduate or more	27.4	27.7
Elementary and Secondary Schools, 2002–2003		
Total students	2 084 187	48 202 324
Percent of students eligible for free or reduced-price lunch ..	38.8	40.6
Percent of students who were English language learners	. . .	7.8
Total schools	4 271	92 330
Student/teacher ratio	16.5	15.9
Per student expenditures	8 287	8 041
Dropouts, Grades 9–12, 2000–2001 (Percent)	6.4	. . .
Higher Education, 2002–2003		
Total enrollment	788 613	17 035 027
Bachelor's degrees awarded	59 569	1 348 503
Percent women	57.1	57.5

. . . = Not available.

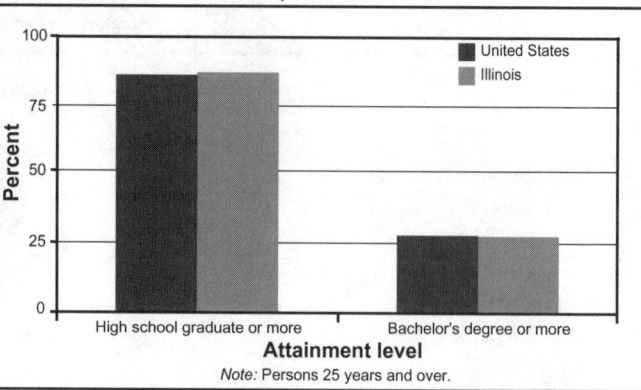

Educational Attainment, 2004

Note: Persons 25 years and over.

EDUCATION

Illinois ranked 29th in the country for its proportion of population age 25 years and over that had completed high school. The proportion with college degrees was 27.4 percent, just below the national average. Illinois's student/teacher ratio was slightly above the U.S. average ratio of 15.9. The state's per student expenditures of $8,287 surpassed the national average. Of the 46 states reporting dropout rates, Illinois is 1 of 9 states with a dropout rate of 6 percent or more. The state had a slightly below average proportion of students eligible for free or reduced-price lunch.

VOTER PARTICIPATION

Illinois turned out 56.8 percent of eligible voters in 2000 and 61 percent in 2004, rates only slightly higher than the national averages for those years. Illinois ranked 28th in the nation for voter turnout in the 2004 election. Asians and Hispanics had the lowest voter participation rates in Illinois. For persons age 45 to 74 years, the voter turnout exceeded 70 percent. Less than 37 percent of persons age 18 to 24 years in Illinois reported voting in the 2004 election. According to the official tally by the Clerk of the U.S. House of Representatives, 54.6 percent voted for the Democratic presidential candidate in 2000 and 54.8 percent voted Democrat in 2004.

Table IL-19. Reported Voting and Registration, November 2000 and November 2004

(Numbers in thousands, percent.)

Characteristic	Total population 18 years and over	Total citizen		Total registered		Total voted	
		Number	Percent	Number	Percent	Number	Percent
NOVEMBER 2000							
Total	8 859	8 118	91.6	5 911	66.7	5 030	56.8
Male	4 207	3 812	90.6	2 726	64.8	2 310	54.9
Female	4 652	4 306	92.6	3 185	68.5	2 720	58.5
NOVEMBER 2004							
Total	9 303	8 640	92.9	6 437	69.2	5 672	61.0
Male	4 469	4 143	92.7	3 049	68.2	2 640	59.1
Female	4 835	4 497	93.0	3 388	70.1	3 032	62.7
Race and Hispanic Origin							
White alone	7 648	7 112	93.0	5 376	70.3	4 708	61.6
Non-Hispanic White alone	6 676	6 524	97.7	5 037	75.4	4 418	66.2
Black alone	1 277	1 268	99.3	919	72.0	855	66.9
Asian alone	277	201	72.5	99	35.6	75	27.1
Hispanic or Latino[1]	1 031	608	59.0	343	33.2	294	28.5
White alone or in combination	7 685	7 147	93.0	5 404	70.3	4 733	61.6
Non-Hispanic White alone or in combination	6 714	6 558	97.7	5 064	75.4	4 443	66.2
Black alone or in combination	1 289	1 280	99.3	926	71.8	860	66.7
Asian alone or in combination	283	204	72.1	102	36.0	78	27.6
Age							
18 to 24 years	1 140	1 024	89.9	565	49.6	421	36.9
25 to 44 years	3 723	3 352	90.0	2 490	66.9	2 194	58.9
45 to 64 years	2 934	2 793	95.2	2 219	75.6	2 056	70.1
65 to 74 years	718	699	97.3	571	79.5	510	71.0
75 years and over	788	772	98.0	592	75.2	491	62.3

[1]May be of any race.

At a Glance:

- Indiana's population was just over 6.2 million in 2004, ranking the state as the 14th most populous in the nation.

- Non-Hispanic Whites made up nearly 85 percent of the population, which was the 15th highest proportion of this racial group in the country. Blacks made up over 9 percent of the population and Hispanics (of any race) represented just over 4 percent of residents, both well below U.S. averages.

- Median household income was below the national average—Indiana was 30th in the state rankings. The state's poverty rate of 11.6 percent was below the national average.

- The unemployment rate in 2004 was 5.2 percent of residents, ranking 25th in the country.

- Real gross state product was the 15th largest in the country and had an above average rate of growth from 2001 to 2004.

- Indiana had among the 5 lowest proportions of residents age 25 years and over with college degrees.

- Indiana had above average per capita energy consumption and expenditures.

Table IN-1. Population by Sex and Age, 1990, 2000, and 2004

(Number, percent.)

Sex and age	1990	2000	2004	Percent distribution, 2004	Average annual percent change, 2000–2004
Total Population	5 544 159	6 080 485	6 237 569	X	0.6
Percent of total U.S. population	2.2	2.2	2.1	X	X
Sex					
Male	2 688 281	2 982 474	3 068 975	49.2	0.7
Female	2 855 878	3 098 011	3 168 594	50.8	0.6
Age					
Under 5 years	398 656	423 215	430 557	6.9	0.4
5 to 17 years	1 057 308	1 151 181	1 169 738	18.8	0.7
18 years and over	1 052 847	4 506 089	4 637 274	74.3	0.9
18 to 24 years	4 088 195	614 721	632 427	10.1	0.3
25 to 44 years	604 882	1 791 828	1 733 724	27.8	0.0
45 to 64 years	1 734 270	1 346 709	1 499 113	24.0	2.6
65 years and over	696 196	752 831	772 010	12.4	0.8
85 years and over	71 751	91 558	104 873	1.7	2.8
Median age (years)	32.7	35.2	35.7	X	X

X = Not applicable.

Average Annual Rate of Population Growth, 1980–2004

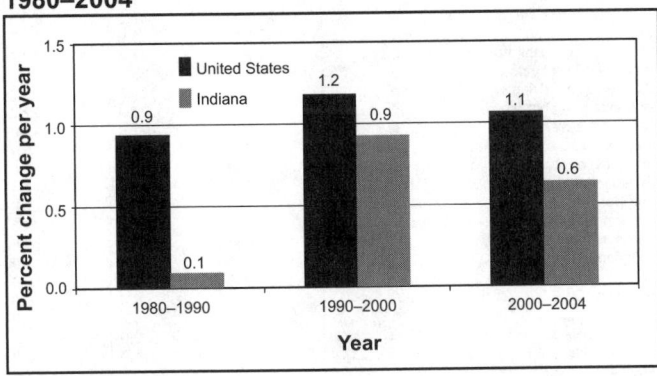

POPULATION

From 2000 to 2004, Indiana's population grew by 2.6 percent, which was well below the U.S. rate of 4.3 percent. Most of its neighboring states also had below average rates of population change. Indiana lost over 18,000 residents to other states during the 2000–2004 period. However, this was more than offset by the migration of over 47,000 people from other countries into the state. In 2004, 25.7 percent of the state's population was under 18 years old. This was the 12th highest proportion in the nation. Indiana's largest population center was Indianapolis, which has experienced steady growth since 2000.

Table IN-2. Population by Race and Hispanic Origin, 1990, 2000, and 2004

(Number, percent.)

Race and Hispanic origin	1990	2000	2004
Total Population	5 544 159	6 080 485	6 237 569
Non-Hispanic (Percent)			
One race[1]			
White	89.6	86.0	84.6
Black	7.7	8.4	8.6
American Indian, Alaska Native[2]	0.2	0.2	0.2
Asian and Pacific Islander[2]	0.7	1.0	1.2
Other race[2]	0.7	. . .	. . .
Two or more races	. . .	0.9	1.0
Hispanic or Latino[3] (Percent)	1.8	3.5	4.3

[1]Individuals could report only one race in the 1990 census and could report one or more races on the 2000 census. Data on race in 2000 and 2004 are not comparable to 1990.
[2]Data for 1990 include people of Hispanic or Latino origin.
[3]May be of any race.
. . . = Not available.

Minority Population as a Percent of Total Population, 2004

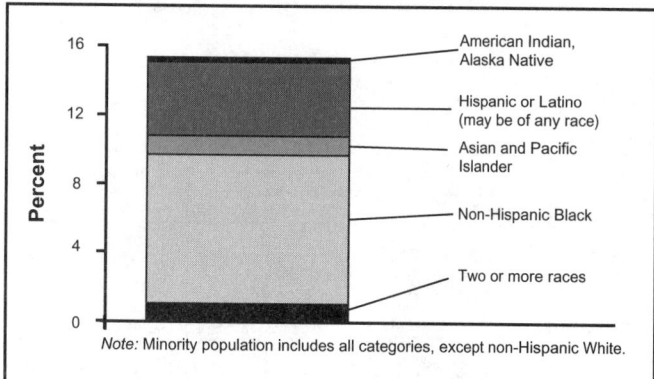

Note: Minority population includes all categories, except non-Hispanic White.

Age-Adjusted Death Rates, Average 2000–2002

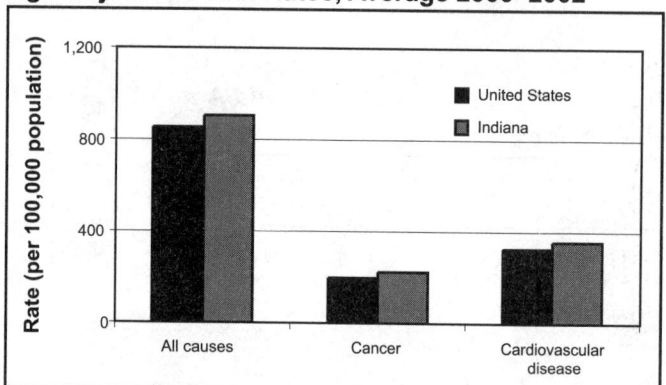

HEALTH

In 2004, 14.3 percent of Indiana's population lacked health insurance, compared with 15 percent nationally. The state's infant mortality rate was relatively high, as was the age-adjusted death rate (both rates ranked 16th highest in the country). Indiana's birth rate almost exactly matched the U.S. average rate.

Table IN-3. Health Characteristics, 2000–2004

(Number, rate, percent.)

Item	State	U.S.
Births, 2003–2004		
Number of births	86 434	4 089 950
Birth rate (per 1,000 population)	14.0	14.1
Teenage birth rate (per 1,000 women age 15–19 years)	43.5	41.6
Mortality Rates, Average 2000–2002		
Infant mortality rate (per 1,000 live births)	7.7	6.9
Age-adjusted mortality rate (per 100,000 population)		
All races	910.8	853.3
Non-Hispanic White	899.9	843.1
Black	1 152.1	1 097.7
American Indian, Alaska Native	. . .	687.0
Asian and Pacific Islander	305.7	486.0
Hispanic or Latino[1]	591.7	642.7
Health Insurance, 2004		
Percent of all persons without health insurance	14.2	15.7
Percent of children without health insurance	8.9	11.2
Percent of low-income children without health insurance	5.9	7.1

[1]May be of any race.
. . . = Not available.

Table IN-4. Leading Causes of Death, Average 2000–2002

(Number, rate per 100,000 population.)

Cause	Number of deaths	Age-adjusted death rates	
		State	U.S.
ALL CAUSES	55 354	910.8	853.3
Leading Causes			
Major cardiovascular diseases	21 096	347.0	326.5
Cancer	12 846	211.9	196.0
Chronic lower respiratory diseases	3 109	51.4	43.7
Unintentional injuries	2 157	35.2	35.7
Diabetes (underlying cause)	1 679	27.7	25.2
Influenza and pneumonia	1 271	20.9	22.7
Alzheimer's disease	1 305	21.4	19.0
Motor vehicle accidents	917	14.9	15.0
Nephritis, nephrotic syndrome, and nephrosis ..	1 152	19.0	13.8
Septicemia	810	13.4	11.4
Suicides	714	11.7	10.7
Firearm-related	706	11.5	10.3
Cirrhosis	488	8.0	9.5
Drug-induced	327	5.4	7.9
Alcohol-induced	323	5.3	6.9
Homicides	396	6.4	6.0
Falls	261	4.3	5.2
HIV	118	2.0	5.0
Viral hepatitis	82	1.3	2.0
Anemias	94	1.6	1.6
Drownings	73	1.2	1.3
Fire deaths	89	1.5	1.2

Note: The rates are age-adjusted to the U.S. 2000 standard population.

Table IN-5. Households and Housing Characteristics, 1990, 2000, and 2004

(Number, percent, and dollars.)

Characteristic	1990	2000	2004	Average annual percent change, 2000–2004
Total Households	2 065 355	2 336 306	2 412 885	0.8
Family households	1 480 351	1 602 501	1 621 912	0.3
Married-couple family	1 202 020	1 251 458	1 259 245	0.2
Other family	278 331	351 043	362 667	0.8
Male householder, no wife present	60 703	91 671	91 242	-0.1
Female householder, no husband present	217 628	259 372	271 425	1.1
Nonfamily households	585 004	733 805	790 973	1.9
Householder living alone	496 841	605 428	666 240	2.4
Householder not living alone	88 163	128 377	124 733	-0.7
Housing Characteristics				
Average size	2.61	2.53	2.51	X
Housing units	2 246 046	2 532 319	2 690 619	1.5
Occupied housing units	2 065 355	2 336 306	2 412 885	0.8
Owner-occupied	1 450 898	1 669 162	1 733 447	0.9
Renter-occupied	614 457	667 144	679 438	0.5
Median gross rent of renter-occupied housing units (dollars)	374	521	589	3.1
Median value of owner-occupied housing units (dollars)	53 500	94 300	110 020	3.9

X = Not applicable.

Median Housing Value and Median Rent, 2004

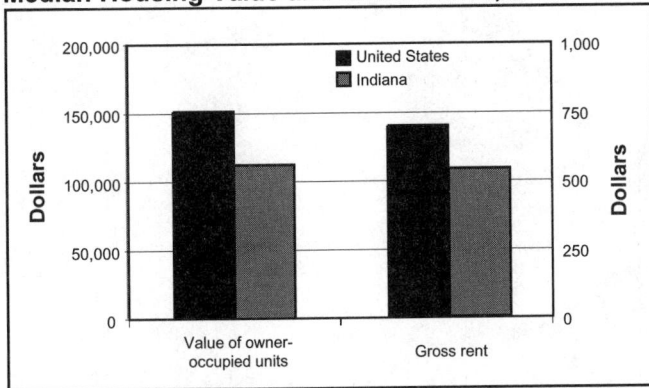

Median Household Income, 1984–2004 (2004 Dollars)

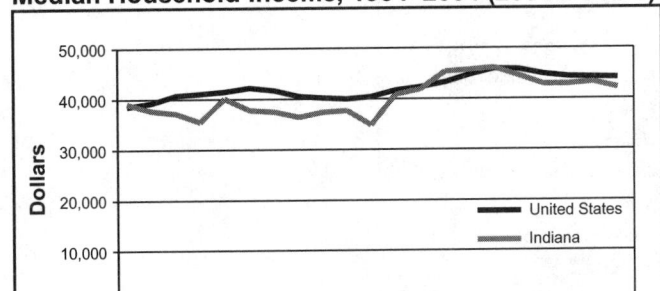

Table IN-6. Household Income and Poverty Status, 1980–2004

(2004 CPI-U-RS adjusted dollars, rate.)

Year	State Median household income (2004 dollars)	State Poverty rate	U.S. Median household income (2004 dollars)	U.S. Poverty rate
2004	42 327	11.6	44 389	12.7
2003	43 565	9.9	44 482	12.5
2002	43 116	9.1	44 546	12.1
2001	43 089	8.5	45 062	11.7
2000	44 824	8.5	46 058	11.3
1999	46 290	6.7	46 129	11.9
1998	45 982	9.4	45 003	12.7
1997	45 641	8.8	43 430	13.3
1996	42 130	7.5	42 544	13.7
1995	41 093	9.6	41 943	13.8
1994	35 123	13.7	40 677	14.5
1993	37 944	12.2	40 217	15.1
1992	37 643	11.8	40 422	14.8
1991	36 638	15.7	40 746	14.2
1990	37 738	13.0	41 963	13.5
1989	38 099	13.7	42 524	12.8
1988	40 341	10.1	41 771	13.0
1987	35 809	11.1	41 322	13.4
1986	37 373	12.7	40 939	13.6
1985	37 966	12.0	39 545	14.0
1984	39 396	12.9	38 782	14.4
1983	. . .	16.1	. . .	15.2
1982	. . .	12.6	. . .	15.0
1981	. . .	12.6	. . .	14.0
1980	. . .	11.8	. . .	13.0

. . . = Not available.

Table IN-7. Employment Status by Demographic Group, 2004
(Numbers in thousands, rate.)

Characteristic	Civilian noninstitutional population	Civilian labor force		Employed	Unemployment rate
		Number	Participation rate		
SEX AND AGE					
Total	4 725	3 160	66.9	2 993	5.3
16 to 19 years	345	162	46.8	138	14.4
20 to 24 years	385	296	76.7	267	9.8
25 to 34 years	807	665	82.4	630	5.2
35 to 44 years	970	830	85.6	796	4.1
45 to 54 years	878	725	82.6	698	3.7
55 to 64 years	604	369	61.1	353	4.4
65 years and over	736	113	15.4	111	1.9
Men	2 290	1 674	73.1	1 588	5.2
16 to 19 years	181	85	46.8	74	13.2
20 to 24 years	184	145	78.5	130	9.9
25 to 34 years	409	378	92.4	358	5.3
35 to 44 years	481	446	92.7	428	4.0
45 to 54 years	432	368	85.2	355	3.5
55 to 64 years	280	187	66.8	178	5.0
65 years and over	323	66	20.5	65	1.6
Women	2 435	1 486	61.0	1 406	5.4
16 to 19 years	164	77	46.8	65	15.7
20 to 24 years	201	151	75.1	136	9.8
25 to 34 years	398	287	72.1	272	5.1
35 to 44 years	489	385	78.6	368	4.2
45 to 54 years	446	357	80.2	343	4.0
55 to 64 years	323	182	56.3	175	3.7
65 years and over	413	47	11.4	46	2.4
MARITAL STATUS					
Married men, spouse present	1 339	1 041	77.7	1 014	2.6
Married women, spouse present	1 319	831	63.0	802	3.5
Women who maintain families	268	186	69.4	171	7.7
RACE, HISPANIC ORIGIN, AND SEX					
White	4 250	2 855	67.2	2 717	4.8
Men	2 066	1 526	73.9	1 453	4.8
Women	2 184	1 328	60.8	1 263	4.9
Black	361	233	64.4	209	10.0
Men	163	105	64.4	95	10.0
Women	198	128	64.4	115	10.1
Hispanic or Latino[1]	167	126	75.6	114	9.2
Men	87	76	87.7	71	7.2
Women	80	50	62.4	44	12.3
RACE, HISPANIC ORIGIN, AND AGE					
White					
16 to 19 years	309	150	48.5	131	12.7
20 to 24 years	335	260	77.6	238	8.4
25 to 34 years	706	591	83.7	563	4.6
35 to 44 years	868	746	85.9	717	3.8
45 to 54 years	786	657	83.6	633	3.6
55 to 64 years	555	346	62.3	330	4.5
65 years and over	691	105	15.3	104	1.6

Note: Data in Table 7 are from the Current Population Survey (CPS) and do not match Bureau of Labor Statistics estimates in Table 8. See notes and definitions for more details.

[1]May be of any race.

Table IN-8. Employment Status, 1990–2004
(Numbers in thousands, rate.)

Year	Civilian labor force	Employed	Unemployed	Unemployment rate
2004	3 170 404	3 005 247	165 157	5.2
2003	3 169 207	3 000 784	168 423	5.3
2002	3 152 158	2 989 544	162 614	5.2
2001	3 151 395	3 020 287	131 108	4.2
2000	3 142 881	3 051 413	91 468	2.9
1999	3 136 581	3 046 922	89 659	2.9
1998	3 124 509	3 033 444	91 065	2.9
1997	3 117 935	3 014 499	103 436	3.3
1996	3 102 990	2 982 750	120 240	3.9
1995	3 112 286	2 977 440	134 846	4.3
1994	3 049 880	2 911 781	138 099	4.5
1993	2 948 331	2 800 739	147 592	5.0
1992	2 877 772	2 703 403	174 369	6.1
1991	2 816 248	2 657 957	158 291	5.6
1990	2 830 551	2 688 858	141 693	5.0

Note: Population age 16 years and over.

Unemployment Rate, 1980–2004

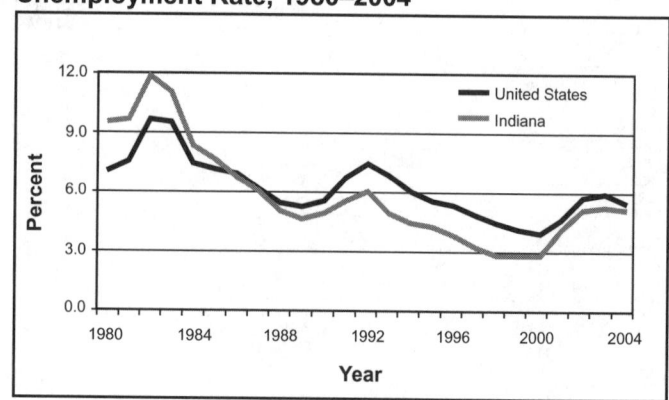

Table IN-9. Employment and Average Wages by Industry, 2001–2004

(Estimates are based on the 2002 North American Industry Classification System [NAICS].)

Industry	2001	2002	2003	2004	Annual average percent change, 2001–2004
	Number of jobs				
TOTAL EMPLOYMENT BY PLACE OF WORK	3 611 302	3 584 868	3 594 283	3 641 313	0.3
Farm Employment	77 322	73 466	71 684	70 454	-3.1
Nonfarm Employment	3 533 980	3 511 402	3 522 599	3 570 859	0.3
Private employment	3 103 167	3 077 354	3 081 971	3 128 640	0.3
Forestry, fishing, hunting, and other[1]	8 373	8 368	7 821	7 866	-2.1
Mining	9 518	9 172	9 563	9 779	0.9
Utilities	15 373	15 069	14 756	14 856	-1.1
Construction	213 719	209 395	212 487	216 944	0.5
Manufacturing	627 897	600 983	585 038	584 342	-2.4
Durable goods manufacturing	465 038	441 950	428 011	427 472	-2.8
Nondurable goods manufacturing	162 859	159 033	157 027	156 870	-1.2
Wholesale trade	132 877	129 583	127 153	128 795	-1.0
Retail trade	429 915	423 353	419 599	420 256	-0.8
Transportation and warehousing	138 859	133 028	131 369	133 975	-1.2
Information	51 676	48 127	47 059	47 127	-3.0
Finance and insurance	138 268	137 265	138 542	137 227	-0.3
Real estate and rental and leasing	98 379	98 944	103 584	108 575	3.3
Professional and technical services	142 377	142 545	144 336	148 293	1.4
Management of companies and enterprises	27 527	27 922	27 633	27 780	0.3
Administrative and waste services	168 862	177 957	181 738	195 510	5.0
Educational services	58 615	61 710	64 138	66 305	4.2
Health care and social assistance	338 122	343 088	350 765	356 420	1.8
Arts, entertainment, and recreation	67 327	68 372	69 366	69 958	1.3
Accommodation and food services	235 016	235 777	238 260	242 605	1.1
Other services, except public administration	200 467	206 696	208 764	212 027	1.9
Government and government enterprises	430 813	434 048	440 628	442 219	0.9
	Dollars				
AVERAGE WAGES AND SALARIES BY PLACE OF WORK	31 129	31 960	32 770	34 098	3.1
Farm Earnings	18 106	20 943	22 489	30 418	18.9
Nonfarm Earnings	31 191	32 002	32 811	34 111	3.0
Private earnings	31 481	32 277	33 099	34 415	3.0
Forestry, fishing, hunting, and other[1]	15 927	18 031	18 462	19 980	7.9
Mining	45 874	46 664	47 977	49 739	2.7
Utilities	58 328	59 043	60 496	62 834	2.5
Construction	36 701	37 563	38 486	39 331	2.3
Manufacturing	42 033	43 894	45 403	47 588	4.2
Durable goods manufacturing	42 086	44 240	46 082	48 190	4.6
Nondurable goods manufacturing	41 881	42 927	43 546	45 941	3.1
Wholesale trade	41 447	42 530	44 078	46 079	3.6
Retail trade	19 705	20 394	20 931	21 451	2.9
Transportation and warehousing	33 134	34 818	35 472	36 508	3.3
Information	38 043	38 922	40 462	43 220	4.3
Finance and insurance	44 386	44 252	45 614	48 479	3.0
Real estate and rental and leasing	25 418	26 672	27 765	28 873	4.3
Professional and technical services	42 066	42 756	43 661	45 028	2.3
Management of companies and enterprises	65 325	61 706	61 541	66 792	0.7
Administrative and waste services	21 142	21 373	21 907	22 729	2.4
Educational services	21 493	22 126	22 670	23 506	3.0
Health care and social assistance	31 195	32 271	33 055	34 455	3.4
Arts, entertainment, and recreation	25 091	26 008	26 571	27 508	3.1
Accommodation and food services	11 634	11 864	11 967	12 306	1.9
Other services, except public administration	20 941	21 811	22 526	23 321	3.7
Government and government enterprises	29 434	30 372	31 136	32 331	3.2

Note: Average wages and salaries are a calculation by the editors of wage and salary disbursements divided by full- and part-time wage and salary employment. Data may not add to total or may appear as zero due to rounding.

[1] "Other" consists of the number of jobs held by U.S. residents employed by international organizations and foreign embassies and consulates in the United States.

LABOR MARKET

The unemployment rate, which dropped to a low of 2.9 percent in the late 1990s, rose to 5.2 percent in 2004 but remained somewhat below the national average. From 2001 to 2004, total wage and salary employment growth was sluggish. In 2004, employment was concentrated in the manufacturing industries (particularly durable goods manufacturing), followed by government, retail trade, and health care services. Between 2001 and 2004, manufacturing employment declined significantly, with a loss of over 43,000 jobs. Administrative and waste services, educational services, and professional and technical services had the highest rates of growth, helping to give Indiana an overall increase in jobs from 2001 to 2004.

Employment by Industry, 2004

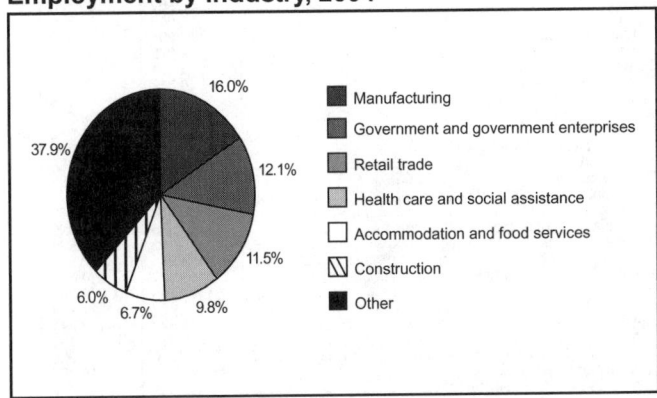

Table IN-10. Personal Income by Major Source, Selected Years 1980–2004

(Millions of dollars, except where noted.)

Item	1980	1990	2000	2001	2002	2003	2004	Average annual percent change, 2000–2004
Earnings by Place of Work	40 505	73 278	125 272	126 310	130 639	137 419	144 238	3.6
Wage and salary disbursements	31 256	55 721	94 821	95 058	96 457	98 679	103 540	2.2
Supplements to wages and salaries	5 906	11 314	19 629	20 232	23 199	26 575	26 906	8.2
Proprietors' income[1]	3 343	6 243	10 822	11 020	10 983	12 165	13 792	6.3
Farm proprietors' income	187	611	292	179	-139	334	944	34.1
Nonfarm proprietors' income	3 157	5 632	10 530	10 842	11 121	11 831	12 848	5.1
(-) Contributions for government social insurance[2]	3 725	8 221	13 888	14 113	14 519	15 024	15 815	3.3
(+) Adjustment for residence[3]	667	1 513	3 374	3 472	3 385	3 415	3 514	1.0
(=) Net Earnings by Place of Residence	37 447	66 570	114 757	115 669	119 505	125 810	131 936	3.5
(+) Dividends, interest, and rent[4]	7 937	18 516	28 997	28 530	27 685	26 892	27 864	-1.0
(+) Personal current transfer receipts	6 085	12 127	21 531	23 682	25 202	26 113	27 765	6.6
Personal income	51 469	97 213	165 285	167 881	172 392	178 815	187 565	3.2
Farm income	51 116	96 387	164 745	167 425	172 278	178 198	186 275	3.1
Nonfarm income	353	826	540	457	114	617	1 290	24.3
Per Capita Personal Income (Dollars)[5]	9 374	17 491	27 132	27 397	27 993	28 843	30 070	2.6

Note: Data may not add to total or may appear as zero due to rounding.

[1]Proprietors' income includes the inventory valuation adjustment and the capital consumption adjustment.
[2]Contributions for government social insurance are included in earnings by type and industry, but they are excluded from personal income.
[3]The adjustment for residence is the net inflow of the earnings of interarea commuters.
[4]Rental income of persons includes the capital consumption adjustment.
[5]Per capita personal income is total personal income divided by total midyear population.

Per Capita Personal Income, 1980–2004 (Current Dollars)

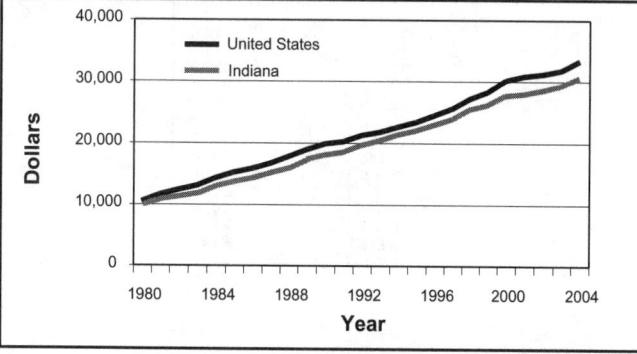

ECONOMIC ACTIVITY

Real gross state product (GSP) declined significantly as a result of the 2001 recession, but growth subsequently recovered at rates slightly above the national average. Manufacturing growth—both durable and nondurable—was particularly strong during recovery. Real estate services, government, and retail trade were also major contributors to Indiana's GSP. Agriculture had the highest rate of growth, but still represented only a small proportion of the state's economy. Housing price appreciation was well below the national average. In 2004, the median value of owner-occupied housing ranked 38th in the country. The real estate industry did not contribute significantly to the state's economic activity.

Table IN-11. Real Gross State Product, 1997–2004

(Millions of chained 2000 dollars, percent.)

Industry	1997	1998	1999	2000	2001	2002	2003	2004	Average annual percent change, 2001–2004
GROSS STATE PRODUCT	176 853	184 979	189 519	194 683	190 876	194 993	201 263	208 834	3.0
As a percent of U.S. gross product	2.1	2.1	2.0	2.0	1.9	1.9	2.0	1.9	X
Private Industries	158 952	166 685	171 013	175 724	172 137	176 583	182 703	189 865	3.3
Agriculture, forestry, fishing, and hunting	1 688	1 336	884	1 216	1 283	1 323	1 791	1 728	10.4
Mining	554	639	702	630	627	704	720	679	2.7
Utilities	4 072	3 888	4 079	4 406	4 181	4 150	4 466	4 733	4.2
Construction	9 491	9 741	9 417	8 986	8 698	8 499	8 478	8 499	-0.8
Manufacturing	48 812	52 714	54 353	57 875	52 462	56 018	58 358	61 182	5.3
As a percent of gross state product	27.6	28.5	28.7	29.7	27.5	28.7	29.0	29.3	X
Wholesale trade	9 045	9 918	10 372	10 335	10 915	11 205	10 978	11 304	1.2
Retail trade	11 422	11 842	12 371	12 561	13 372	13 985	14 969	15 485	5.0
Transportation and warehousing	6 139	6 343	6 536	6 679	6 461	6 559	6 762	6 944	2.4
Information	3 839	4 038	4 243	4 244	4 434	4 557	4 938	5 629	8.3
Finance and insurance	10 270	10 755	10 765	11 149	11 275	10 811	12 026	12 432	3.3
Real estate and rental and leasing	17 350	17 675	18 703	19 146	19 818	19 557	19 132	19 834	0.0
Services	36 314	37 858	38 666	38 495	38 628	39 367	40 344	41 834	2.7
As a percent of gross state product	20.5	20.5	20.4	19.8	20.2	20.2	20.0	20.0	X
Professional and technical services	5 962	6 534	6 903	6 798	6 981	7 107	7 391	7 629	3.0
Management of companies and enterprises	2 978	2 911	2 704	2 475	2 350	2 269	2 273	2 341	-0.1
Administrative and waste services	4 208	4 485	4 743	4 498	4 345	4 721	4 957	5 365	7.3
Educational services	1 169	1 201	1 218	1 190	1 238	1 242	1 211	1 201	-1.0
Health care and social assistance	11 673	11 774	11 842	12 299	12 679	13 056	13 395	13 732	2.7
Arts, entertainment, and recreation	1 823	2 211	2 406	2 447	2 543	2 559	2 608	2 612	0.9
Accommodation and food services	3 931	4 103	4 245	4 245	4 170	4 144	4 218	4 376	1.6
Other services, except public administration	4 570	4 639	4 605	4 543	4 322	4 269	4 291	4 578	1.9
Government	17 925	18 302	18 506	18 958	18 739	18 428	18 599	19 019	0.5
As a percent of gross state product	10.1	9.9	9.8	9.7	9.8	9.5	9.2	9.1	X

X = Not applicable.

Table IN-12. Government Transfer Payments, Selected Years 1980–2004

(Millions of dollars, percent.)

Item	1980	1990	2000	2001	2002	2003	2004	Average annual percent change, 2000–2004
CURRENT TRANSFER PAYMENTS TO INDIVIDUALS	5 681	11 338	20 081	22 082	23 722	24 684	26 316	7.0
Retirement and Disability Insurance Benefits	3 140	6 206	9 703	10 233	10 740	11 199	11 723	4.8
Old-age, survivors, and disability insurance (OASDI) benefits	2 950	5 931	9 384	9 905	10 389	10 778	11 287	4.7
Railroad retirement and disability benefits	130	197	236	242	254	258	263	2.7
Workers' compensation	14	20	26	28	29	28	29	2.6
Other government retirement and disability insurance benefits	46	58	56	58	68	135	145	26.7
Medical Benefits	1 121	3 747	7 789	8 805	9 416	9 555	10 637	8.1
Medicare benefits	730	2 120	4 101	4 536	4 849	5 131	5 636	8.3
Public assistance medical care benefits	380	1 596	3 658	4 226	4 503	4 369	4 936	7.8
Military medical insurance benefits	11	31	30	43	64	56	66	21.5
Income Maintenance Benefits	465	779	1 658	1 738	1 942	2 148	2 337	9.0
Supplemental Security Income (SSI) benefits	60	177	386	403	427	444	465	4.7
Family assistance	139	173	298	275	251	225	243	-5.0
Food stamps	169	240	276	336	419	500	572	20.0
Other income maintenance benefits	98	189	698	724	845	978	1 058	10.9
Unemployment Insurance Compensation	602	145	300	596	874	961	746	25.6
Veterans' Benefits	266	300	382	404	443	476	505	7.3
Federal Education and Training Assistance	87	156	236	279	296	334	355	10.7
Other Payments to Individuals	1	5	13	27	12	12	13	0.2

Note: See notes and definitions for more details. Data may not add to total or may appear as zero due to rounding.

EXPORTS

Exports of goods rose substantially between 2001 and 2004. Indiana was the 13th largest exporter among the states in 2004. Transportation equipment was the state's largest export, followed by chemicals and machinery manufactures. Indiana exported over $8.5 billion of goods to Canada, about half of which were transportation equipment. Canada was the destination for over 44 percent of Indiana's exports. Exports from Indiana to all the top markets have shown significant growth since 2001, except for Japan, where exports remained flat. Among the state's leading exports, chemical manufactures have shown the most growth, increasing nearly 61 percent from 2001 to 2004.

Leading Exports, 2004

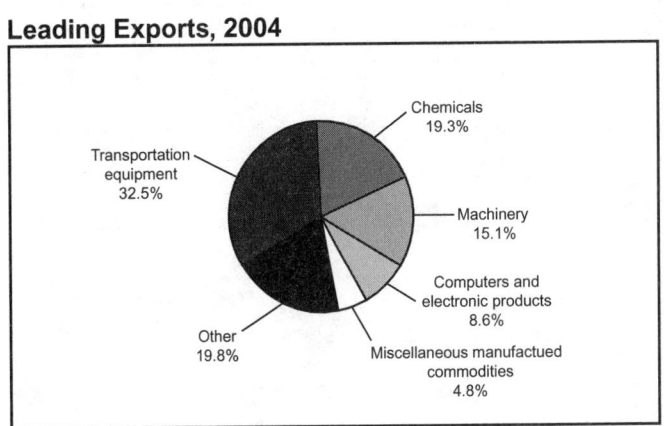

Table IN-13. Exports of Goods by Leading Products and Destinations, 2001–2004

(Millions of dollars, percent, rank based on 2004 dollar values.)

Product and market	2001	2002	2003	2004	Percent share of total, 2004	Average annual percent change, 2001–2004
Total Goods						
Total	14 365	14 923	16 402	19 109	100.0	10.0
Manufactures	14 051	14 603	16 120	18 783	98.3	10.2
Agriculture and livestock	94	72	75	91	0.5	-1.0
Other commodities	220	248	207	235	1.2	2.3
Five Leading Exports (NAICS Code)						
Transportation equipment (336)	4 511	4 786	5 273	6 207	32.5	11.2
Chemical manufactures (325)	2 287	2 441	3 005	3 679	19.3	17.2
Machinery manufactures (333)	2 223	2 351	2 441	2 884	15.1	9.1
Computers and electronic products (334)	1 449	1 530	1 589	1 641	8.6	4.2
Miscellaneous manufactures (339)	586	594	679	908	4.8	15.7
Five Leading Markets	13 473	14 209	15 613	18 100	94.7	10.3
Canada	6 201	6 819	7 459	8 535	44.7	11.2
Mexico	1 770	1 943	2 105	2 543	13.3	12.8
United Kingdom	941	1 007	1 209	1 282	6.7	10.9
France	669	638	922	1 178	6.2	20.8
Japan	701	714	630	720	3.8	0.9

Table IN-14. Agriculture, 1997 and 2002

(Number, acres, and dollars.)

Item	1997	2002
Number of farms	66 707	60 296
Land in farms (acres)	15 525 154	15 058 670
Farm Size		
Average size of farm (acres)	233	250
Farms by size (percent distribution)		
Fewer than 50 acres	35.5	39.9
50 to 499 acres	51.5	46.4
500 acres or more	13.0	13.8
Market Value of Land and Equipment (Dollars)		
Land and buildings average value per farm	486 171	637 645
Average value per acre	2 097	2 567
Machinery and equipment average value per farm	58 614	80 240
Value of Sales (Thousands of Dollars)		
Agricultural products sold	5 323 116	4 783 158
Crops	3 297 312	2 992 747
Livestock, poultry, and their products	2 025 804	1 790 411
Average per farm (dollars)	79 798	79 328
Value of sales (percent distribution)		
Less than $10,000	48.8	54.0
$10,000 to $99,999	32.7	28.8
$100,000 or more	18.4	17.2
Government Payments		
Payments (thousands of dollars)	194 246	224 701
Percent of farms receiving government payments	56.9	44.5
Farm operators whose principal occupation is farming (percent)	43.1	55.7

AGRICULTURE

Cash receipts from farming totaled close to $4.8 billion in 2004, a decline of 10 percent from the 1997 farm census. Indiana's leading products were corn and soybeans. In 2002, 54 percent of farms had sales of less than $10,000, and 55.7 percent of farm operators considered farming to be their principal occupation. Nearly 40 percent of farms spanned fewer than 50 acres. The average value of land and buildings per farm was over $637,000, which was about $100,000 more than the U.S. average.

ENERGY

Energy prices in Indiana were among the lowest in the nation. However, the state's energy expenditures per person of $2,786 were the eighth highest in the nation. Per capita consumption ranked seventh. Both of these measures reflected Indiana's industrial sector, which accounted for over 46 percent of the state's energy use. The largest source of energy was coal.

Energy Consumption by Source, 2001

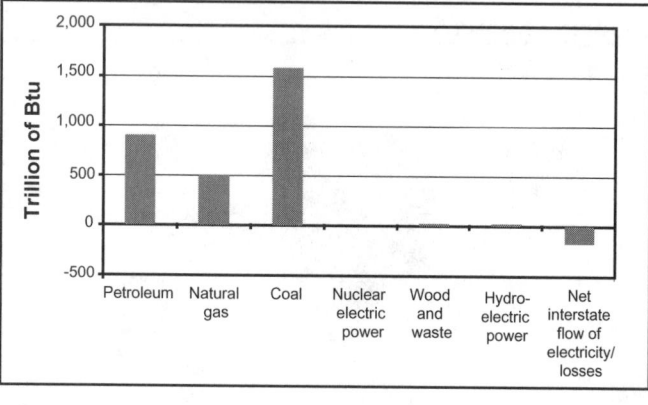

Energy Consumption by Sector, 2001

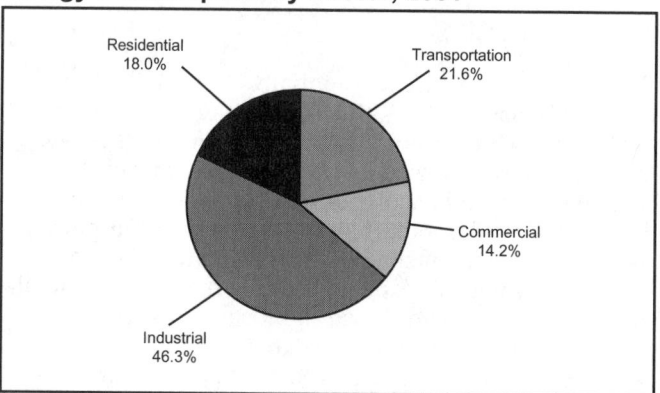

Table IN-15. Energy Consumption, Expenditures, and Prices, Selected Years 1960–2001

(Dollars, Btu [British Thermal Unit], percent distribution.)

Item	1960	1965	1970	1975	1980	1985	1990	1995	2000	2001
Total Consumption (Billion Btu)	1 531 524	1 804 319	2 226 578	2 387 166	2 410 390	2 312 101	2 512 931	2 645 462	2 914 190	2 801 669
Consumption per capita (million Btu)	328.5	366.6	428.6	444.9	439.0	423.5	453.3	456.8	479.3	457.3
Consumption by Sector (Percent Distribution)										
Residential	18.4	17.6	18.8	18.8	18.9	18.3	17.4	18.7	17.8	18.0
Commercial	7.0	7.4	8.5	9.3	9.3	10.4	11.2	11.9	12.1	14.2
Industrial	57.2	58.3	55.7	53.9	53.4	49.0	48.4	45.8	47.5	46.3
Transportation	17.3	16.6	17.0	18.0	18.3	22.3	22.9	23.5	22.6	21.6
Consumption by Source (Billion Btu)										
Coal	794 942	900 562	1 006 824	1 061 168	1 156 965	1 193 273	1 361 823	1 344 404	1 595 052	1 567 104
Natural gas	219 758	357 502	548 640	472 567	483 872	436 421	459 073	541 632	584 850	513 745
Petroleum	601 732	653 293	737 744	822 995	751 293	728 988	831 576	841 372	895 969	837 314
Nuclear electric power	0	0	0	0	0	0	0	0	0	0
Hydroelectric power[1]	1 079	979	5 199	4 623	4 928	4 451	4 588	4 818	6 001	5 806
Wood and waste	23 477	22 081	23 295	26 719	49 485	53 822	46 156	37 983	31 487	31 175
Other	0	0	0	0	0	0	0	515	752	1 158
Net interstate flow of electricity/losses[2]	-109 465	-130 098	-95 125	-906	-36 153	-104 854	-190 799	-125 500	-200 233	-154 633
Total Expenditures (Thousands of Dollars)	...	...	2 564 300	5 201 000	10 075 100	11 796 300	12 144 500	12 766 700	16 858 100	17 066 200
Expenditures per capita (dollars)	...	...	494	969	1 835	2 161	2 190	2 204	2 772	2 786
Prices by Sector (Dollars Per Million Btu)										
Total	...	...	1.44	2.83	5.65	6.91	6.69	6.85	8.20	8.78
Residential	...	...	2.00	3.19	6.38	9.76	10.03	10.20	11.42	13.57
Commercial	...	...	1.81	3.02	6.15	8.65	9.46	9.35	10.27	11.48
Industrial	...	...	0.76	2.03	3.69	4.86	4.31	4.56	5.10	5.80
Transportation	...	...	2.66	4.35	9.25	8.27	8.04	7.63	10.58	10.10

[1]A negative number in this row results from pumped storage for which, overall, more electricity is expended than created to provide electricity during peak demand periods.
[2]Net interstate flow of electricity is the difference between the amount of energy in the electricity sold within a state (including associated losses) and the energy input at the electric utilities within the state. A positive number indicates that more electricity (including associated losses) came into the state than went out of the state during the year; conversely, a negative number indicates that more electricity (including associated losses) went out of the state than came into the state.
... = Not available.

Table IN-16. State Taxes, Fiscal 2004

(Dollars, percent distribution.)

Item	Thousands of dollars	Percent distribution	Dollars per capita	
			State	U.S.
TOTAL TAXES	11 957 470	100.0	1 916.9	2 024.8
Property Taxes	8 923	0.1	1.4	38.9
Sales and Gross Receipts	6 906 954	57.8	1 107.2	1 003.4
General sales and gross receipts	4 759 445	39.8	763.0	677.0
Selective sales taxes	2 147 509	18.0	344.3	326.4
Amusements	765 707	6.4	122.8	17.0
Insurance premiums	178 303	1.5	28.6	47.0
Motor fuels	802 168	6.7	128.6	114.6
Tobacco products	338 716	2.8	54.3	42.0
Licenses	448 387	3.7	71.9	134.9
Motor vehicle	158 542	1.3	25.4	59.4
Motor vehicle operators	211 999	1.8	34.0	6.4
Other Taxes	4 593 206	38.4	736.3	847.6
Individual income	3 807 861	31.8	610.4	673.6
Corporation net income	644 787	5.4	103.4	105.1
Death and gift	139 995	1.2	22.4	19.6

GOVERNMENT FINANCE

State revenues per capita were below the national average in 2003, as were expenditures per person. Indiana ranked among the bottom 10 states for both measures. In fiscal year 2004, per capita taxes amounted to $1,917. General sales receipts were the largest source of revenues, followed by individual income taxes. The state's per capita income tax of $610 ranked 32nd out of the 43 states with such a tax. Indiana's debt per capita was relatively low and ranked 32nd in the country. The state's property taxes were among the lowest in the nation.

Per Capita State Taxes, Fiscal 2004

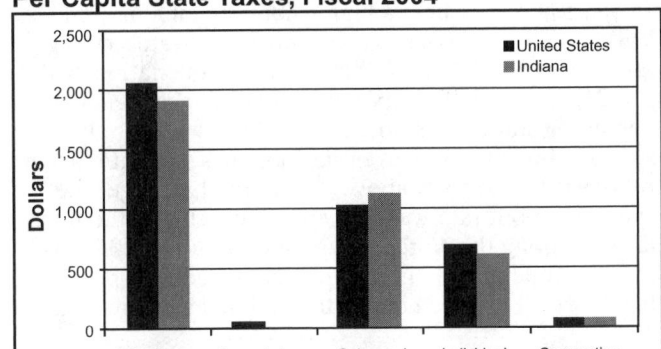

Table IN-17. State Government Finances, 2003

(Dollars, percent distribution.)

Item	Millions of dollars	Percent distribution	Dollars per capita	
			State	U.S.
GENERAL REVENUE	21 674 754	100.0	3 495.9	3 832.6
Intergovernmental revenue	6 346 679	29.3	1 023.7	1 246.0
Taxes	11 216 456	51.7	1 809.1	1 891.6
General sales	4 210 262	19.4	679.1	636.0
Selective sales	2 014 361	9.3	324.9	307.4
License taxes	415 373	1.9	67.0	123.6
Individual income tax	3 644 159	16.8	587.8	626.8
Corporate income tax	729 164	3.4	117.6	97.8
Other taxes	203 137	0.9	32.8	99.9
Current charges	2 512 554	11.6	405.2	366.5
Miscellaneous general revenue	1 599 065	7.4	257.9	328.6
GENERAL EXPENDITURE	21 295 408	100.0	3 434.7	4 010.5
Intergovernmental expenditure	6 760 945	31.7	1 090.5	1 316.9
Direct expenditure	14 534 463	68.3	2 344.3	2 693.6
Expenditure by Function				
Education	8 639 690	40.6	1 393.5	1 416.4
Public welfare	5 377 805	25.3	867.4	1 083.3
Hospitals	282 438	1.3	45.6	132.3
Health	545 088	2.6	87.9	173.0
Highways	1 712 840	8.0	276.3	295.4
Police protection	196 066	0.9	31.6	38.4
Correction	654 475	3.1	105.6	135.0
Natural resources	277 385	1.3	44.7	64.0
Parks and recreation	50 581	0.2	8.2	20.1
Government administration	521 250	2.4	84.1	151.3
Interest on general debt	447 431	2.1	72.2	107.8
Other and unallocable	2 590 359	12.2	417.8	393.4
DEBT AT END OF FISCAL YEAR	11 853 847	X	1 911.9	2 404.7
CASH AND SECURITY HOLDINGS	33 490 856	X	5 401.8	8 938.4

X = Not applicable.

Table IN-18. Education Indicators, 2000–2004

(Percent, number.)

Item	State	U.S.
Total Population 25 Years and Over (Thousands), 2004	4 010	186 877
Educational Attainment, 2004		
Percent high school graduate or more	87.2	85.2
Percent college graduate or more	21.1	27.7
Elementary and Secondary Schools, 2002–2003		
Total students	1 003 875	48 202 324
Percent of students eligible for free or reduced-price lunch ..	34.9	40.6
Percent of students who were English language learners	4.2	7.8
Total schools	1 909	92 330
Student/teacher ratio	16.9	15.9
Per student expenditures	8 057	8 041
Dropouts, Grades 9–12, 2000–2001 (Percent)	2.3	. . .
Higher Education, 2002–2003		
Total enrollment	344 438	17 035 027
Bachelor's degrees awarded	35 284	1 348 503
Percent women	54.4	57.5

. . . = Not available.

Educational Attainment, 2004

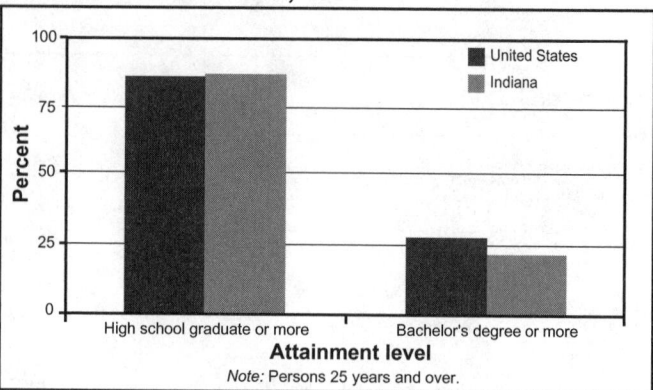

Note: Persons 25 years and over.

EDUCATION

In Indiana, more than 87 percent of the population age 25 years and over held a high school diploma in 2004. This was above the national average. The state's college attainment level was the third lowest in the nation, with just 21.1 percent of the population holding a bachelor's degree or more. Per student expenditures were only slightly above the U.S. average. Indiana's student/teacher ratio was also slightly above the national average. The state's dropout rate was 2.3 percent, which was the third lowest among the 46 reporting states. Less than 35 percent of students are eligible for free or reduced-price lunch, which was well below the national average.

VOTER PARTICIPATION

Voter turnout was higher than the national average in the 2000 election, but was much lower in 2004. Hispanics had the lowest voter turnout, with less than 23 percent of eligible voters casting ballots in 2004. Persons 75 years old and over had the highest voter participation, with 76.1 percent of those eligible voting. The proportion of women casting votes fell from 60.6 percent in 2000 to 57.4 percent in 2004. The official tally by the Clerk of the U.S. House of Representatives showed that the majority of voters in Indiana voted for the Republican presidential candidate, with proportions of 56.6 percent in 2000 and 59.9 percent in 2004.

Table IN-19. Reported Voting and Registration, November 2000 and November 2004

(Numbers in thousands, percent.)

Characteristic	Total population 18 years and over	Total citizen		Total registered		Total voted	
		Number	Percent	Number	Percent	Number	Percent
NOVEMBER 2000							
Total	4 380	4 303	98.3	3 000	68.5	2 564	58.5
Male	2 157	2 121	98.3	1 424	66.0	1 217	56.4
Female	2 223	2 183	98.2	1 576	70.9	1 347	60.6
NOVEMBER 2004							
Total	4 536	4 435	97.8	3 031	66.8	2 598	57.3
Male	2 182	2 132	97.7	1 473	67.5	1 247	57.1
Female	2 354	2 303	97.8	1 558	66.2	1 351	57.4
Race and Hispanic Origin							
White alone	4 088	3 999	97.8	2 755	67.4	2 364	57.8
Non-Hispanic White alone	3 905	3 881	99.4	2 698	69.1	2 323	59.5
Black alone	368	368	100.0	229	62.3	198	53.8
Asian alone	22	10	B	5	B	5	B
Hispanic or Latino[1]	182	118	64.8	57	31.5	41	22.6
White alone or in combination	4 133	4 044	97.8	2 784	67.4	2 386	57.7
Non-Hispanic White alone or in combination	3 950	3 926	99.4	2 726	69.0	2 344	59.3
Black alone or in combination	376	376	100.0	233	62.0	202	53.7
Asian alone or in combination	22	10	B	5	B	5	B
Age							
18 to 24 years	571	564	98.8	296	51.8	232	40.7
25 to 44 years	1 740	1 659	95.3	1 041	59.8	868	49.9
45 to 64 years	1 523	1 512	99.3	1 119	73.5	975	64.1
65 to 74 years	370	368	99.7	295	79.8	269	72.7
75 years and over	333	331	99.6	280	84.2	253	76.1

[1]May be of any race.
B = Base is too small to show derived measure.

IOWA

At a Glance:

- Iowa's population was just under 3 million in 2004, ranking the state 30th in the nation.
- Nearly 92 percent of the state's residents were non-Hispanic White, which was the fifth highest proportion of this racial group in the nation.
- Iowa's median household income of $43,015 was just below the national average and ranked 26th in the nation. The state's poverty rate was also below the U.S. average.
- The unemployment rate was 4.4 percent, well below the national average of 5.5 percent.
- The state's economy, as measured by real gross state product (GSP), was the 29th largest in the country. The GSP grew 5.5 percent from 2003 to 2004, which was the 5th highest rate of growth in the nation.
- Nearly 90 percent of Iowa's population age 25 years and over held a high school diploma; this was the among the top 10 proportions in the country.
- Only 9.5 percent of the state's residents lacked health insurance. This was the second lowest proportion in the country.

Table IA-1. Population by Sex and Age, 1990, 2000, and 2004

(Number, percent.)

Sex and age	1990	2000	2004	Percent distribution, 2004	Average annual percent change, 2000–2004
Total Population	2 776 755	2 926 324	2 954 451	X	0.2
Percent of total U.S. population	1.1	1.0	1.0	X	X
Sex					
Male	1 344 802	1 435 515	1 454 107	49.2	0.3
Female	1 431 953	1 490 809	1 500 344	50.8	0.2
Age					
Under 5 years	193 203	188 413	180 839	6.1	-0.6
5 to 17 years	525 677	545 225	499 598	16.9	-0.4
18 years and over	524 116	2 192 686	2 274 014	77.0	0.7
18 to 24 years	2 057 875	298 008	316 404	10.7	0.8
25 to 44 years	283 713	808 259	787 033	26.6	-0.3
45 to 64 years	823 940	650 206	737 438	25.0	2.5
65 years and over	426 106	436 213	433 139	14.7	0.1
85 years and over	55 255	65 118	72 373	2.4	2.0
Median age (years)	34.0	36.6	38.0	X	X

X = Not applicable.

Average Annual Rate of Population Growth, 1980–2004

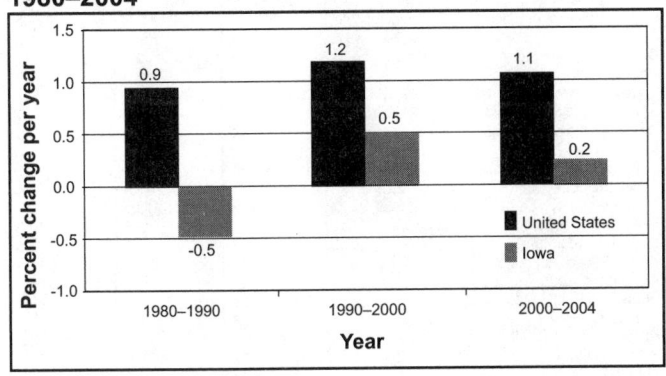

POPULATION

From 2000 to 2004, Iowa's population grew by 1 percent, which was among the 5 lowest growth rates in the nation. During this period, the state lost over 37,000 residents to other states. Immigration from other countries added nearly 25,000 new residents. Iowa's below average birth rate also contributed to the slow rate of population growth. The composition of the population was somewhat older than that of the country as a whole. Iowa's median age in 2004 was 38 years, which was among the 10 highest in the nation. Close to 15 percent of the state's population was 65 years old and over, which was the 5th highest proportion of this age group in the country.

Table IA-2. Population by Race and Hispanic Origin, 1990, 2000, and 2004

(Number, percent.)

Race and Hispanic origin	1990	2000	2004
Total Population	2 776 755	2 926 324	2 954 451
Non-Hispanic (Percent)			
One race[1]			
White	95.9	92.8	91.7
Black	1.7	2.1	2.2
American Indian, Alaska Native[2]	0.3	0.3	0.3
Asian and Pacific Islander[2]	0.9	1.3	1.4
Other race[2]	0.5	. . .	. . .
Two or more races	. . .	0.7	0.8
Hispanic or Latino[3] (Percent)	1.2	2.8	3.5

[1]Individuals could report only one race in the 1990 census and could report one or more races on the 2000 census. Data on race in 2000 and 2004 are not comparable to 1990.
[2]Data for 1990 include people of Hispanic or Latino origin.
[3]May be of any race.
. . . = Not available.

Minority Population as a Percent of Total Population, 2004

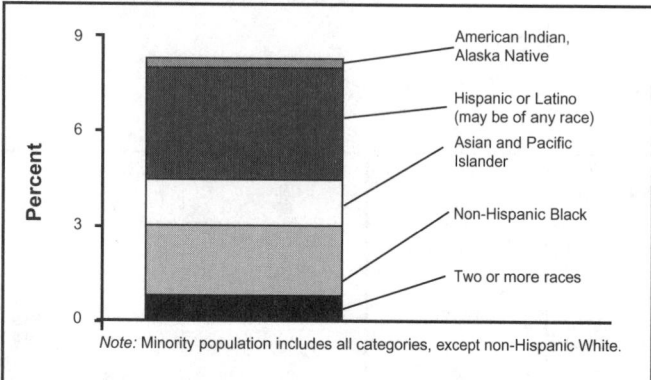

Note: Minority population includes all categories, except non-Hispanic White.

Age-Adjusted Death Rates, Average 2000–2002

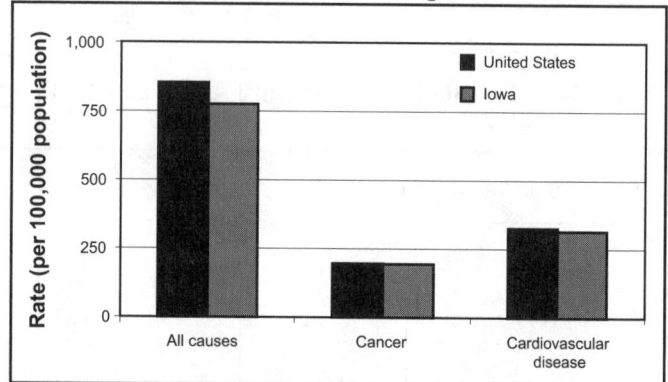

HEALTH

The state's birth rate and its birth rate for teenage mothers were both well below the U.S. averages. Iowa had a low infant mortality rate, and its age-adjusted death rate for all causes was among the 10 lowest in the nation.

Table IA-3. Health Characteristics, 2000–2004

(Number, rate, percent.)

Item	State	U.S.
Births, 2003–2004		
Number of births	38 174	4 089 950
Birth rate (per 1,000 population)	13.0	14.1
Teenage birth rate (per 1,000 women age 15–19 years)	31.9	41.6
Mortality Rates, Average 2000–2002		
Infant mortality rate (per 1,000 live births)	5.8	6.9
Age-adjusted mortality rate (per 100,000 population)		
All races	781.4	853.3
Non-Hispanic White	779.2	843.1
Black	1 085.6	1 097.7
American Indian, Alaska Native	. . .	687.0
Asian and Pacific Islander	477.1	486.0
Hispanic or Latino[1]	631.2	642.7
Health Insurance, 2004		
Percent of all persons without health insurance	9.5	15.7
Percent of children without health insurance	6.0	11.2
Percent of low-income children without health insurance	4.9	7.1

[1]May be of any race.
. . . = Not available.

Table IA-4. Leading Causes of Death, Average 2000–2002

(Number, rate per 100,000 population.)

Cause	Number of deaths	Age-adjusted death rates	
		State	U.S.
ALL CAUSES	27 943	781.4	853.3
Leading Causes			
Major cardiovascular diseases	11 334	305.3	326.5
Cancer	6 442	189.7	196.0
Chronic lower respiratory diseases	1 548	43.5	43.7
Unintentional injuries	1 071	33.0	35.7
Diabetes (underlying cause)	691	19.6	25.2
Influenza and pneumonia	919	23.8	22.7
Alzheimer's disease	844	21.2	19.0
Motor vehicle accidents	432	14.2	15.0
Nephritis, nephrotic syndrome, and nephrosis ..	265	7.2	13.8
Septicemia	245	7.0	11.4
Suicides	302	10.2	10.7
Firearm-related	194	6.5	10.3
Cirrhosis	208	6.5	9.5
Drug-induced	90	3.1	7.9
Alcohol-induced	151	4.9	6.9
Homicides	58	2.0	6.0
Falls	226	6.1	5.2
HIV	23	0.8	5.0
Viral hepatitis	27	0.9	2.0
Anemias	44	1.2	1.6
Drownings	35	1.2	1.3
Fire deaths	31	1.0	1.2

Note: The rates are age-adjusted to the U.S. 2000 standard population.

Table IA-5. Households and Housing Characteristics, 1990, 2000, and 2004

(Number, percent, and dollars.)

Characteristic	1990	2000	2004	Average annual percent change, 2000–2004
Total Households	1 064 325	1 149 276	1 175 771	0.6
Family households	740 819	769 684	773 898	0.1
Married-couple family	629 893	633 254	630 131	-0.1
Other family	110 926	136 430	143 767	1.3
Male householder, no wife present	25 785	38 160	41 103	1.9
Female householder, no husband present	85 141	98 270	102 664	1.1
Nonfamily households	323 506	379 592	401 873	1.4
Householder living alone	275 466	313 083	337 368	1.9
Householder not living alone	48 040	66 509	64 505	-0.8
Housing Characteristics				
Average size	2.52	2.46	2.42	X
Housing units	1 143 669	1 232 511	1 292 976	1.2
Occupied housing units	1 064 325	1 149 276	1 175 771	0.6
Owner-occupied	745 377	831 419	867 585	1.1
Renter-occupied	318 948	317 857	308 186	-0.8
Median gross rent of renter-occupied housing units (dollars)	336	470	533	3.2
Median value of owner-occupied housing units (dollars)	45 500	82 500	95 901	3.8

X = Not applicable.

Median Housing Value and Median Rent, 2004

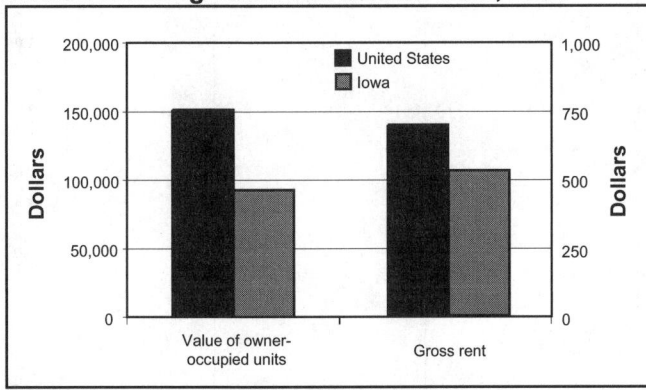

Median Household Income, 1984–2004 (2004 Dollars)

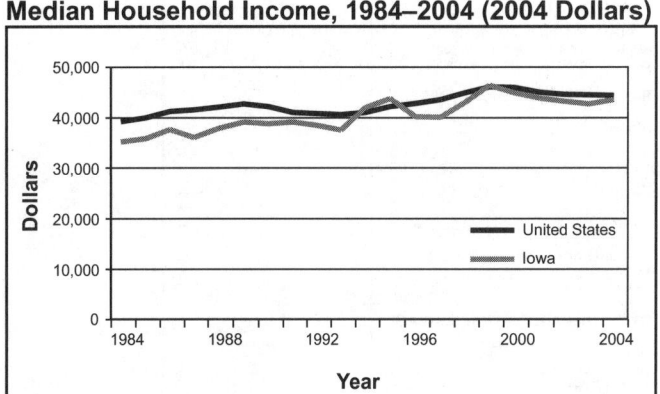

Table IA-6. Household Income and Poverty Status, 1980–2004

(2004 CPI-U-RS adjusted dollars, rate.)

Year	State Median household income (2004 dollars)	State Poverty rate	U.S. Median household income (2004 dollars)	U.S. Poverty rate
2004	43 512	10.8	44 389	12.7
2003	42 496	8.9	44 482	12.5
2002	43 118	9.2	44 546	12.1
2001	43 726	7.4	45 062	11.7
2000	44 963	8.3	46 058	11.3
1999	46 585	7.4	46 129	11.9
1998	42 844	9.1	45 003	12.7
1997	39 649	9.6	43 430	13.3
1996	39 807	9.6	42 544	13.7
1995	43 719	12.2	41 943	13.8
1994	41 705	10.7	40 677	14.5
1993	36 898	10.3	40 217	15.1
1992	37 924	11.5	40 422	14.8
1991	38 618	9.6	40 746	14.2
1990	38 242	10.4	41 963	13.5
1989	38 639	10.3	42 524	12.8
1988	37 291	9.4	41 771	13.0
1987	35 286	14.5	41 322	13.4
1986	36 930	12.9	40 939	13.6
1985	35 040	17.9	39 545	14.0
1984	34 367	14.6	38 782	14.4
1983	. . .	16.7	. . .	15.2
1982	. . .	13.4	. . .	15.0
1981	. . .	13.1	. . .	14.0
1980	. . .	10.8	. . .	13.0

. . . = Not available.

Table IA-7. Employment Status by Demographic Group, 2004

(Numbers in thousands, rate.)

Characteristic	Civilian noninstitutional population	Civilian labor force		Employed	Unemployment rate
		Number	Participation rate		
SEX AND AGE					
Total	2 307	1 620	70.2	1 545	4.6
16 to 19 years	170	104	61.1	91	12.2
20 to 24 years	233	192	82.4	175	8.7
25 to 34 years	370	321	86.7	307	4.3
35 to 44 years	397	353	88.9	341	3.5
45 to 54 years	450	397	88.2	385	3.1
55 to 64 years	267	186	69.8	181	2.7
65 years and over	420	68	16.1	65	3.4
Men	1 124	846	75.3	809	4.4
16 to 19 years	87	52	60.1	45	13.6
20 to 24 years	119	102	85.9	95	7.5
25 to 34 years	189	175	92.3	166	4.6
35 to 44 years	195	185	95.2	180	3.0
45 to 54 years	225	203	90.0	198	2.3
55 to 64 years	130	94	72.1	91	3.3
65 years and over	179	36	19.9	34	3.4
Women	1 183	774	65.4	736	4.9
16 to 19 years	83	51	62.2	46	10.7
20 to 24 years	114	89	78.7	80	10.1
25 to 34 years	181	146	80.8	141	3.8
35 to 44 years	203	168	82.8	161	4.1
45 to 54 years	225	194	86.5	187	3.9
55 to 64 years	137	92	67.6	90	2.1
65 years and over	241	32	13.3	31	3.4
MARITAL STATUS					
Married men, spouse present	660	506	76.7	495	2.2
Married women, spouse present	670	461	68.8	447	3.0
Women who maintain families	105	80	76.5	72	9.9
RACE, HISPANIC ORIGIN, AND SEX					
White	2 193	1 542	70.3	1 474	4.4
Men	1 065	801	75.2	768	4.1
Women	1 129	741	65.6	706	4.7
Black	44	28	63.5	22	19.6
Asian	40	30	75.9	30	1.4
Hispanic or Latino[1]	80	64	79.0	59	7.4
Men	43	39	89.8	36	6.0
Women	37	25	66.5	22	9.7
RACE, HISPANIC ORIGIN, AND AGE					
White					
16 to 19 years	159	98	61.8	86	12.2
20 to 24 years	215	179	83.5	165	8.2
25 to 34 years	340	297	87.2	285	4.0
35 to 44 years	376	337	89.5	325	3.4
45 to 54 years	435	385	88.3	374	2.8
55 to 64 years	258	180	69.8	175	2.7
65 years and over	410	66	16.1	64	3.2

Note: Data in Table 7 are from the Current Population Survey (CPS) and do not match Bureau of Labor Statistics estimates in Table 8. See notes and definitions for more details.

[1]May be of any race.

Table IA-8. Employment Status, 1990–2004

(Numbers in thousands, rate.)

Year	Civilian labor force	Employed	Unemployed	Unemployment rate
2004	1 623 844	1 545 412	78 432	4.8
2003	1 620 030	1 548 215	71 815	4.4
2002	1 638 042	1 573 701	64 341	3.9
2001	1 622 634	1 569 541	53 093	3.3
2000	1 605 212	1 561 129	44 083	2.7
1999	1 602 634	1 560 848	41 786	2.6
1998	1 602 865	1 556 479	46 386	2.9
1997	1 606 503	1 555 837	50 666	3.2
1996	1 609 270	1 551 200	58 070	3.6
1995	1 585 287	1 527 972	57 315	3.6
1994	1 569 124	1 510 253	58 871	3.8
1993	1 545 272	1 480 417	64 855	4.2
1992	1 509 146	1 441 414	67 732	4.5
1991	1 476 380	1 408 730	67 650	4.6
1990	1 458 858	1 393 302	65 556	4.5

Note: Population age 16 years and over.

Unemployment Rate, 1980–2004

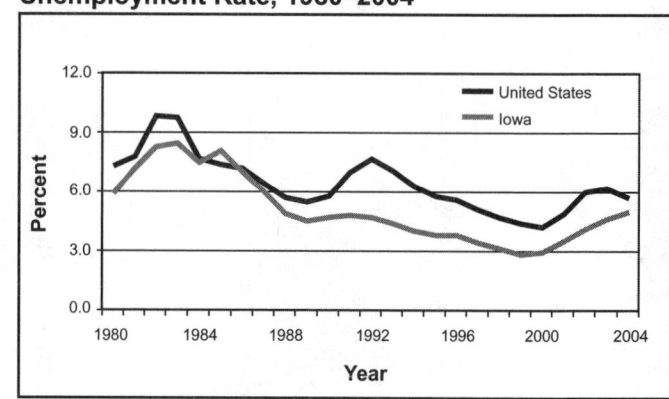

Table IA-9. Employment and Average Wages by Industry, 2001–2004

(Estimates are based on the 2002 North American Industry Classification System [NAICS].)

Industry	2001	2002	2003	2004	Annual average percent change, 2001–2004
			Number of jobs		
TOTAL EMPLOYMENT BY PLACE OF WORK	1 916 252	1 905 591	1 904 045	1 934 816	0.3
Farm Employment	106 615	106 741	103 611	103 492	-1.0
Nonfarm Employment	1 809 637	1 798 850	1 800 434	1 831 324	0.4
Private employment	1 552 778	1 541 887	1 542 476	1 572 818	0.4
Forestry, fishing, hunting, and other[1]	11 415	12 045	10 986	11 785	1.1
Mining	2 801	2 612	2 742	2 959	1.8
Utilities	8 545	8 918	8 986	8 940	1.5
Construction	102 367	101 362	104 377	108 924	2.1
Manufacturing	246 817	234 078	226 598	229 743	-2.4
Durable goods manufacturing	150 646	140 423	135 131	140 178	-2.4
Nondurable goods manufacturing	96 171	93 655	91 467	89 565	-2.3
Wholesale trade	73 468	72 035	70 657	71 711	-0.8
Retail trade	234 507	232 351	232 404	234 278	0.0
Transportation and warehousing	63 637	64 111	63 914	65 678	1.1
Information	41 291	38 173	37 012	37 087	-3.5
Finance and insurance	100 313	102 845	103 718	105 710	1.8
Real estate and rental and leasing	42 572	42 508	43 077	44 759	1.7
Professional and technical services	64 303	64 390	65 525	66 990	1.4
Management of companies and enterprises	7 779	8 154	8 917	9 306	6.2
Administrative and waste services	80 743	80 688	81 343	84 565	1.6
Educational services	37 374	37 535	38 367	39 729	2.1
Health care and social assistance	191 174	191 165	192 977	195 236	0.7
Arts, entertainment, and recreation	32 939	33 804	33 974	34 366	1.4
Accommodation and food services	112 334	112 794	113 914	116 299	1.2
Other services, except public administration	98 399	102 319	102 988	104 753	2.1
Government and government enterprises	256 859	256 963	257 958	258 506	0.2
			Dollars		
AVERAGE WAGES AND SALARIES BY PLACE OF WORK	28 159	28 953	30 046	31 418	3.7
Farm Earnings	22 944	21 088	27 694	31 106	10.7
Nonfarm Earnings	28 210	29 030	30 069	31 421	3.7
Private earnings	28 070	28 866	29 907	31 328	3.7
Forestry, fishing, hunting, and other[1]	14 156	16 015	16 672	20 859	13.8
Mining	36 711	39 090	39 213	40 481	3.3
Utilities	55 712	57 667	59 525	64 867	5.2
Construction	34 073	34 778	35 514	36 294	2.1
Manufacturing	37 114	38 181	39 830	42 124	4.3
Durable goods manufacturing	38 829	39 896	41 847	44 224	4.4
Nondurable goods manufacturing	34 439	35 620	36 867	38 855	4.1
Wholesale trade	36 845	38 262	39 320	41 495	4.0
Retail trade	18 871	19 539	19 947	20 382	2.6
Transportation and warehousing	33 067	33 516	34 551	36 177	3.0
Information	34 890	34 830	36 676	38 576	3.4
Finance and insurance	41 556	42 823	45 675	48 304	5.1
Real estate and rental and leasing	25 390	26 744	27 738	28 577	4.0
Professional and technical services	37 908	38 885	40 076	41 172	2.8
Management of companies and enterprises	46 935	50 060	53 664	56 784	6.6
Administrative and waste services	19 406	19 835	20 824	21 724	3.8
Educational services	18 471	19 517	20 402	21 162	4.6
Health care and social assistance	27 380	28 592	29 526	30 982	4.2
Arts, entertainment, and recreation	16 616	17 007	17 571	18 038	2.8
Accommodation and food services	10 426	10 644	10 738	11 058	2.0
Other services, except public administration	18 953	19 498	20 022	20 829	3.2
Government and government enterprises	28 895	29 829	30 846	31 878	3.3

Note: Average wages and salaries are a calculation by the editors of wage and salary disbursements divided by full- and part-time wage and salary employment. Data may not add to total or may appear as zero due to rounding.

[1] "Other" consists of the number of jobs held by U.S. residents employed by international organizations and foreign embassies and consulates in the United States.

LABOR MARKET

Iowa's unemployment rate has been well below the national average in recent years, despite rising noticeably following the 2001 recession. Total wage and salary employment declined sharply in 2002 and recovered only moderately in the subsequent two years. The government sector was the state's largest employer, accounting for over 13 percent of employment. Retail trade, manufacturing, and health care services also employed large numbers of people. The farming sector, long associated with Iowa, has lost employment steadily over the years. In 2004, it represented just over 5 percent of total jobs. Average wages and salaries were well below the national averages across most industries, but their growth rates exceeded U.S. averages.

Employment by Industry, 2004

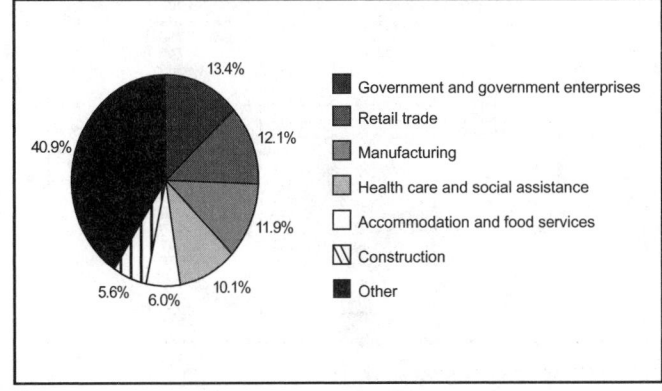

- Government and government enterprises
- Retail trade
- Manufacturing
- Health care and social assistance
- Accommodation and food services
- Construction
- Other

13.4% · 12.1% · 11.9% · 40.9% · 10.1% · 6.0% · 5.6%

Table IA-10. Personal Income by Major Source, Selected Years 1980–2004

(Millions of dollars, except where noted.)

Item	1980	1990	2000	2001	2002	2003	2004	Average annual percent change, 2000–2004
Earnings by Place of Work	20 838	34 963	57 336	58 302	60 293	62 522	69 373	4.9
Wage and salary disbursements	15 198	24 541	42 216	43 233	43 986	45 456	48 134	3.3
Supplements to wages and salaries	2 868	5 063	8 556	8 960	9 988	10 910	11 810	8.4
Proprietors' income[1]	2 772	5 360	6 564	6 109	6 319	6 157	9 430	9.5
Farm proprietors' income	383	1 945	1 316	907	1 167	771	3 524	27.9
Nonfarm proprietors' income	2 389	3 415	5 248	5 203	5 151	5 386	5 906	3.0
(-) Contributions for government social insurance[2]	2 067	4 010	6 609	6 820	7 009	7 307	7 692	3.9
(+) Adjustment for residence[3]	92	323	832	783	836	867	869	1.1
(=) **Net Earnings by Place of Residence**	18 863	31 276	51 560	52 265	54 121	56 082	62 550	4.9
(+) Dividends, interest, and rent[4]	5 661	10 473	15 416	15 556	15 478	15 096	15 533	0.2
(+) Personal current transfer receipts	3 405	6 609	10 787	11 635	12 888	12 851	13 416	5.6
Personal income	27 930	48 358	77 763	79 456	82 487	84 029	91 500	4.2
Farm income	27 259	46 124	76 124	78 182	80 980	82 827	87 492	3.5
Nonfarm income	671	2 234	1 638	1 274	1 507	1 202	4 008	25.1
Per Capita Personal Income (Dollars)[5]	9 585	17 389	26 554	27 103	28 107	28 562	30 970	3.9

Note: Data may not add to total or may appear as zero due to rounding.

[1]Proprietors' income includes the inventory valuation adjustment and the capital consumption adjustment.
[2]Contributions for government social insurance are included in earnings by type and industry, but they are excluded from personal income.
[3]The adjustment for residence is the net inflow of the earnings of interarea commuters.
[4]Rental income of persons includes the capital consumption adjustment.
[5]Per capita personal income is total personal income divided by total midyear population.

Per Capita Personal Income, 1980–2004 (Current Dollars)

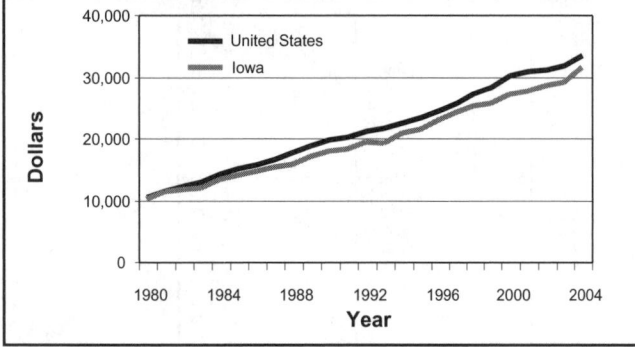

ECONOMIC ACTIVITY

Iowa's economy recovered quite well from the fall-off in activity during the 2001 recession. Between 2003 and 2004, it had one of the highest growth rates in the nation at 5.5 percent. Manufacturing—for both durable and nondurable goods—was the largest source of economic growth during this period. Management, finance and insurance, and utilities were the sectors with the highest rates of growth from 2001 to 2004. Government transfer payments grew at a below average rate from 2000 to 2004. Iowa was one of 10 states with a median value of owner-occupied housing of less than $100,000. Housing did not play a significant role in the state's economic activity.

Table IA-11. Real Gross State Product, 1997–2004

(Millions of chained 2000 dollars, percent.)

Industry	1997	1998	1999	2000	2001	2002	2003	2004	Average annual percent change, 2001–2004
GROSS STATE PRODUCT	85 692	86 525	88 009	90 815	90 306	93 227	95 569	100 853	3.8
As a percent of U.S. gross product	1.0	1.0	0.9	0.9	0.9	0.9	0.9	0.9	X
Private Industries	75 516	76 097	77 433	80 129	79 503	82 502	84 873	90 019	4.2
Agriculture, forestry, fishing, and hunting	3 982	3 004	1 947	2 449	2 554	3 626	3 067	3 992	16.1
Mining	139	167	173	184	166	165	164	164	-0.4
Utilities	1 760	1 814	2 056	2 030	1 972	2 053	2 244	2 515	8.4
Construction	3 745	3 911	3 859	3 543	3 515	3 468	3 523	3 646	1.2
Manufacturing	18 989	18 789	18 955	19 918	19 453	19 622	20 510	21 873	4.0
As a percent of gross state product	22.2	21.7	21.5	21.9	21.5	21.0	21.5	21.7	X
Wholesale trade	5 244	5 649	6 054	5 608	5 898	6 074	5 830	6 073	1.0
Retail trade	5 456	5 778	6 081	6 222	6 638	6 980	7 293	7 567	4.5
Transportation and warehousing	2 649	2 792	2 962	3 116	3 056	3 111	3 215	3 368	3.3
Information	2 369	2 665	2 938	3 076	3 069	3 084	3 323	3 737	6.8
Finance and insurance	6 996	7 191	7 348	8 884	7 887	8 857	9 932	10 572	10.3
Real estate and rental and leasing	7 570	7 691	8 245	8 536	8 855	8 708	8 645	8 787	-0.3
Services	16 111	16 488	16 859	16 562	16 457	16 774	17 172	17 721	2.5
As a percent of gross state product	18.8	19.1	19.2	18.2	18.2	18.0	18.0	17.6	X
Professional and technical services	2 740	2 764	2 868	2 769	2 794	2 850	2 965	3 039	2.8
Management of companies and enterprises	547	558	574	521	464	517	605	630	10.7
Administrative and waste services	1 976	1 998	2 118	1 745	1 752	1 808	1 906	1 987	4.3
Educational services	732	725	728	727	704	699	684	682	-1.1
Health care and social assistance	5 395	5 481	5 637	5 830	5 976	6 125	6 230	6 393	2.3
Arts, entertainment, and recreation	1 009	1 063	1 035	926	921	949	967	962	1.5
Accommodation and food services	1 637	1 727	1 754	1 897	1 851	1 860	1 859	1 931	1.4
Other services, except public administration	2 075	2 172	2 145	2 147	1 995	1 966	1 956	2 097	1.7
Government	10 172	10 432	10 579	10 686	10 802	10 734	10 716	10 874	0.2
As a percent of gross state product	11.9	12.1	12.0	11.8	12.0	11.5	11.2	10.8	X

X = Not applicable.

Table IA-12. Government Transfer Payments, Selected Years 1980–2004

(Millions of dollars, percent.)

Item	1980	1990	2000	2001	2002	2003	2004	Average annual percent change, 2000–2004
CURRENT TRANSFER PAYMENTS TO INDIVIDUALS	3 186	6 196	10 046	10 822	12 157	12 173	12 730	6.1
Retirement and Disability Insurance Benefits	1 793	3 450	5 059	5 319	5 527	5 673	5 901	3.9
Old-age, survivors, and disability insurance (OASDI) benefits	1 697	3 294	4 892	5 152	5 352	5 495	5 718	4.0
Railroad retirement and disability benefits	79	116	131	133	138	141	143	2.3
Workers' compensation	4	8	11	10	12	12	12	3.2
Other government retirement and disability insurance benefits	12	33	25	24	25	26	28	2.3
Medical Benefits	704	1 869	3 746	4 077	5 004	4 736	5 088	8.0
Medicare benefits	460	1 178	2 034	2 243	2 388	2 510	2 736	7.7
Public assistance medical care benefits	240	680	1 701	1 817	2 593	2 206	2 330	8.2
Military medical insurance benefits	4	11	11	17	22	19	23	20.8
Income Maintenance Benefits	286	446	684	721	767	857	938	8.2
Supplemental Security Income (SSI) benefits	38	101	175	184	191	193	202	3.6
Family assistance	144	153	108	107	109	116	116	1.9
Food stamps	58	112	101	111	132	153	188	16.9
Other income maintenance benefits	46	81	301	318	335	395	431	9.5
Unemployment Insurance Compensation	200	151	211	314	441	468	334	12.2
Veterans' Benefits	150	172	213	221	239	255	270	6.1
Federal Education and Training Assistance	53	105	124	156	173	176	187	10.9
Other Payments to Individuals	*	3	10	15	7	8	12	3.8

Note: See notes and definitions for more details. Data may not add to total or may appear as zero due to rounding.

EXPORTS

Iowa ranked 28th in the country in terms of the value of goods exported. Of the $6.4 billion of exported goods in 2004, the leading export was machinery manufactures, followed by processed food and chemicals. The value of machinery manufactures exports increased by 63 percent from 2001 to 2004. Agricultural exports made up just 6.1 percent of total exports. In 2004, the state's main export markets were Canada and Mexico, both of which have grown substantially since 2001. Australia became one of the state's top five markets in 2004, as exports to this country more than doubled since 2001. The leading export to Australia was machinery manufactures.

Leading Exports, 2004

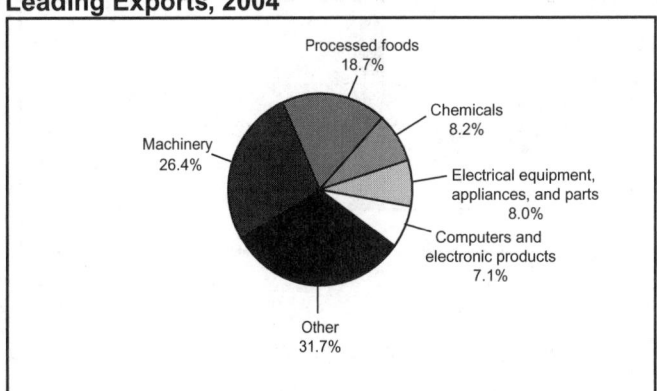

Table IA-13. Exports of Goods by Leading Products and Destinations, 2001–2004

(Millions of dollars, percent, rank based on 2004 dollar values.)

Product and market	2001	2002	2003	2004	Percent share of total, 2004	Average annual percent change, 2001–2004
Total Goods						
Total	4 660	4 755	5 236	6 394	100.0	11.1
Manufactures	4 378	4 493	4 888	5 967	93.3	10.9
Agriculture and livestock	232	221	314	389	6.1	18.8
Other commodities	50	40	33	38	0.6	-8.5
Five Leading Exports (NAICS Code)						
Machinery manufactures (333)	1 034	1 216	1 298	1 687	26.4	17.7
Processed foods (311)	951	939	1 061	1 195	18.7	7.9
Chemical manufactures (325)	427	448	444	523	8.2	7.1
Electrical equipment, appliances, and parts (335)	390	394	447	511	8.0	9.4
Computers and electronic products (334)	409	435	432	452	7.1	3.4
Five Leading Markets	4 259	4 358	4 805	5 899	92.3	11.5
Canada	1 582	1 676	1 871	2 293	35.9	13.2
Mexico	372	396	670	820	12.8	30.1
Japan	647	605	576	632	9.9	-0.8
United Kingdom	207	192	211	254	4.0	7.0
Australia	115	115	144	251	3.9	29.7

Table IA-14. Agriculture, 1997 and 2002

(Number, acres, and dollars.)

Item	1997	2002
Number of farms	96 705	90 655
Land in farms (acres)	32 313 119	31 729 490
Farm Size		
Average size of farm (acres)	334	350
Farms by size (percent distribution)		
Fewer than 50 acres	19.8	23.3
50 to 499 acres	58.2	54.0
500 acres or more	22.0	22.7
Market Value of Land and Equipment (Dollars)		
Land and buildings average value per farm	559 678	707 730
Average value per acre	1 698	2 005
Machinery and equipment average value per farm	79 607	100 422
Value of Sales (Thousands of Dollars)		
Agricultural products sold	12 162 165	12 273 634
Crops	6 381 676	6 071 272
Livestock, poultry, and their products	5 780 489	6 202 362
Average per farm (dollars)	125 766	135 388
Value of sales (percent distribution)		
Less than $10,000	29.0	35.4
$10,000 to $99,999	38.1	34.4
$100,000 or more	32.9	30.2
Government Payments		
Payments (thousands of dollars)	562 555	538 896
Percent of farms receiving government payments	78.7	69.6
Farm operators whose principal occupation is farming (percent)	60.1	68.3

AGRICULTURE

With 90,655 farms in 2002, Iowa had the third largest number of farms in the country, behind only Texas and Missouri. Sales were valued at close to $12.3 billion, which was the third highest value in the nation. Iowa was not a state with large-scale farming: about 70 percent of farms had sales of less than $100,000. However, less than 24 percent of farms spanned fewer than 50 acres, which was among the smallest proportions of farms of this size in the nation. The state received significant support from the federal government, with nearly 70 percent of farms collecting government payments. The state's chief products were corn, hogs, and soybeans. Over 68 percent of farm operators in Iowa considered farming to be their principal occupation.

ENERGY

In 2001, Iowa ranked ninth in terms of expenditures per person, although its energy prices were below average. The state's per capita consumption was among the 15 highest in the nation.

Energy Consumption by Source, 2001

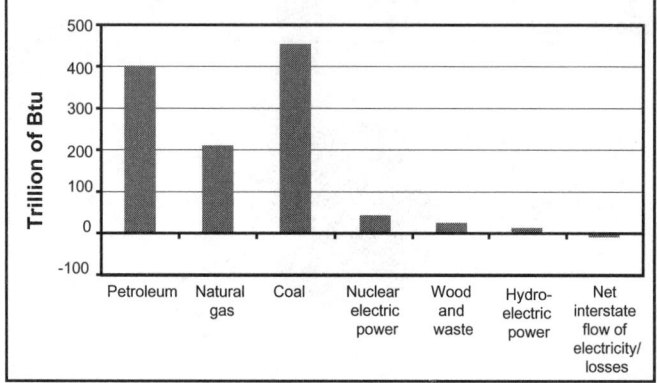

Energy Consumption by Sector, 2001

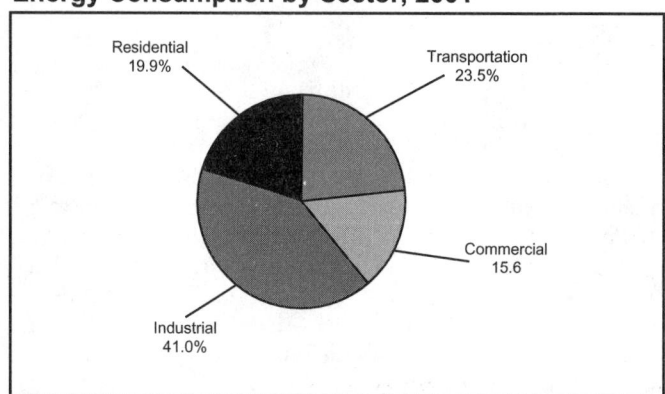

Table IA-15. Energy Consumption, Expenditures, and Prices, Selected Years 1960–2001

(Dollars, Btu [British Thermal Unit], percent distribution.)

Item	1960	1965	1970	1975	1980	1985	1990	1995	2000	2001
Total Consumption (Billion Btu)	602 917	698 124	850 559	944 534	1 009 295	933 569	962 153	1 110 786	1 175 967	1 150 675
Consumption per capita (million Btu)	218.6	254.6	301.0	327.9	346.4	329.9	346.5	391.0	401.9	392.4
Consumption by Sector (Percent Distribution)										
Residential	26.7	26.4	25.6	24.5	24.1	24.0	22.3	21.5	20.1	19.9
Commercial	11.6	12.4	13.4	14.8	12.5	14.4	14.6	14.2	14.7	15.6
Industrial	36.7	37.9	36.4	34.4	39.8	38.2	38.9	41.1	42.1	41.0
Transportation	25.0	23.2	24.7	26.3	23.6	23.5	24.2	23.2	23.1	23.5
Consumption by Source (Billion Btu)										
Coal	115 945	126 638	130 867	131 562	234 425	268 806	335 002	372 313	445 896	444 883
Natural gas	193 688	249 988	351 800	348 564	270 390	228 388	220 396	262 505	233 736	225 240
Petroleum	285 885	295 267	346 448	375 799	373 111	320 833	307 871	370 324	414 835	400 885
Nuclear electric power	0	0	0	25 235	27 955	20 467	31 868	39 191	46 439	40 253
Hydroelectric power[1]	9 481	9 698	9 816	9 142	9 828	10 334	9 103	10 343	9 222	8 599
Wood and waste	6 404	5 462	6 264	7 887	50 828	56 771	47 500	41 359	30 141	30 673
Other	0	0	0	0	0	3 614	72	198	5 361	5 327
Net interstate flow of electricity/losses[2]	-8 485	11 071	5 365	46 345	42 758	24 356	10 340	14 554	-9 663	-5 184
Total Expenditures (Thousands of Dollars)	...	...	1 259 600	2 364 300	5 002 500	5 410 600	5 195 900	6 052 100	8 289 000	8 160 500
Expenditures per capita (dollars)	...	...	446	821	1 717	1 912	1 871	2 130	2 833	2 783
Prices by Sector (Dollars Per Million Btu)										
Total	...	...	1.80	3.12	6.68	8.02	7.60	7.56	9.88	10.02
Residential	...	...	2.06	3.44	6.82	9.59	10.20	10.47	12.94	14.11
Commercial	...	...	1.81	2.94	6.31	9.24	8.52	9.21	11.05	11.38
Industrial	...	...	1.05	2.02	4.67	5.93	4.57	5.06	7.16	7.34
Transportation	...	...	2.60	4.24	9.34	8.95	9.22	8.53	11.36	10.80

[1]A negative number in this row results from pumped storage for which, overall, more electricity is expended than created to provide electricity during peak demand periods.
[2]Net interstate flow of electricity is the difference between the amount of energy in the electricity sold within a state (including associated losses) and the energy input at the electric utilities within the state. A positive number indicates that more electricity (including associated losses) came into the state than went out of the state during the year; conversely, a negative number indicates that more electricity (including associated losses) went out of the state than came into the state.
. . . = Not available.

Table IA-16. State Taxes, Fiscal 2004

(Dollars, percent distribution.)

Item	Thousands of dollars	Percent distribution	Dollars per capita	
			State	U.S.
TOTAL TAXES	5 133 126	100.0	1 737.7	2 024.8
Property Taxes	X	X	X	38.9
Sales and Gross Receipts	2 437 323	47.5	825.1	1 003.4
General sales and gross receipts	1 617 505	31.5	547.6	677.0
Selective sales taxes	819 818	16.0	277.5	326.4
Amusements	213 522	4.2	72.3	17.0
Insurance premiums	138 229	2.7	46.8	47.0
Motor fuels	357 835	7.0	121.1	114.6
Tobacco products	94 282	1.8	31.9	42.0
Licenses	565 515	11.0	191.4	134.9
Corporation	38 999	0.8	13.2	21.6
Motor vehicle	377 672	7.4	127.8	59.4
Occupation and business, not elsewhere classified	75 977	1.5	25.7	37.1
Other Taxes	2 130 288	41.5	721.2	847.6
Individual income	1 958 697	38.2	663.1	673.6
Corporation net income	89 826	1.7	30.4	105.1
Death and gift	67 896	1.3	23.0	19.6

X = Not applicable.

GOVERNMENT FINANCE

In 2003, Iowa was not far off the national averages, with state revenues per capita amounting to $3,772. The state's expenditures per person exceeded revenue, but were below the national average. Per capita expenditures were higher than average for education, hospitals, and highways. The state's debt per capita amounted to about $1,455, which was among the 15 lowest amounts in the nation. In fiscal year 2004, Iowa had below average per capita taxes of $1,738. Of this amount, the largest share of revenue was from individual income taxes, which totaled $663 per person. General sales taxes had the second largest intake with $548. Iowa had no property taxes.

Per Capita State Taxes, Fiscal, 2004

Table IA-17. State Government Finances, 2003

(Dollars, percent distribution.)

Item	Millions of dollars	Percent distribution	Dollars per capita	
			State	U.S.
GENERAL REVENUE	11 096 904	100.0	3 771.9	3 832.6
Intergovernmental revenue	3 534 400	31.9	1 201.4	1 246.0
Taxes	4 922 455	44.4	1 673.2	1 891.6
General sales	1 589 917	14.3	540.4	636.0
Selective sales	779 069	7.0	264.8	307.4
License taxes	537 574	4.8	182.7	123.6
Individual income tax	1 791 129	16.1	608.8	626.8
Corporate income tax	140 031	1.3	47.6	97.8
Other taxes	84 735	0.8	28.8	99.9
Current charges	1 530 512	13.8	520.2	366.5
Miscellaneous general revenue	1 109 537	10.0	377.1	328.6
GENERAL EXPENDITURE	11 714 669	100.0	3 981.9	4 010.5
Intergovernmental expenditure	3 442 552	29.4	1 170.1	1 316.9
Direct expenditure	8 272 117	70.6	2 811.7	2 693.6
Expenditure by Function				
Education	4 589 923	39.2	1 560.1	1 416.4
Public welfare	2 795 400	23.9	950.2	1 083.3
Hospitals	759 789	6.5	258.3	132.3
Health	241 311	2.1	82.0	173.0
Highways	1 356 482	11.6	461.1	295.4
Police protection	86 332	0.7	29.3	38.4
Correction	294 911	2.5	100.2	135.0
Natural resources	243 227	2.1	82.7	64.0
Parks and recreation	23 027	0.2	7.8	20.1
Government administration	503 328	4.3	171.1	151.3
Interest on general debt	122 471	1.0	41.6	107.8
Other and unallocable	698 468	6.0	237.4	393.4
DEBT AT END OF FISCAL YEAR	4 279 448	X	1 454.6	2 404.7
CASH AND SECURITY HOLDINGS	25 147 636	X	8 547.8	8 938.4

X = Not applicable.

Table IA-18. Education Indicators, 2000–2004

(Percent, number.)

Item	State	U.S.
Total Population 25 Years and Over (Thousands), 2004	1 923	186 877
Educational Attainment, 2004		
Percent high school graduate or more	89.8	85.2
Percent college graduate or more	24.3	27.7
Elementary and Secondary Schools, 2002–2003		
Total students	482 210	48 202 324
Percent of students eligible for free or reduced-price lunch ..	30.0	40.6
Percent of students who were English language learners	3.2	7.8
Total schools	1 500	92 330
Student/teacher ratio	13.8	15.9
Per student expenditures	7 574	8 041
Dropouts, Grades 9–12, 2000–2001 (Percent)	2.4	. . .
Higher Education, 2002–2003		
Total enrollment	203 923	17 035 027
Bachelor's degrees awarded	20 034	1 348 503
Percent women	57.0	57.5

. . . = Not available.

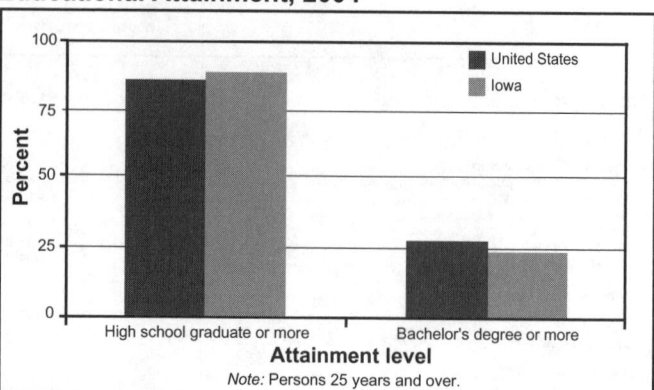

Educational Attainment, 2004

Note: Persons 25 years and over.

EDUCATION

Iowa ranked 9th in the nation for high school attainment, with 89.8 percent of its residents age 25 years and over holding high school diplomas. Nationally, 85.2 percent of the population in this age group had graduated from high school. However, Iowa had a below average proportion (24.3 percent) of college graduates. The state's educational expenditures per student were below the national average, ranking 26th in the nation. Of the 46 states with dropout data, Iowa was among 4 states with rates under 2.5 percent. Iowa's student/teacher ratio of 13.8 was well below the U.S. average of 15.9. This may reflect the state's low proportion of school-age population.

VOTER PARTICIPATION

Perhaps because of the state's central role in the election primary process, Iowa's voter turnout was much higher than the national average in both 2000 and 2004. The state's voter turnout ranked 9th in 2000 and 8th in 2004. More than 75 percent of the eligible population age 65 years and over voted in the 2004 election. Among residents age 18 to 24 years, this proportion was 58 percent, which was among the highest in the nation for this age group. In 2000, 47.2 percent of voters in Iowa cast their ballots for the Democratic presidential candidate; in 2004, 49.9 percent of votes were for the Republican candidate.

Table IA-19. Reported Voting and Registration, November 2000 and November 2004

(Numbers in thousands, percent.)

Characteristic	Total population 18 years and over	Total citizen		Total registered		Total voted	
		Number	Percent	Number	Percent	Number	Percent
NOVEMBER 2000							
Total	2 110	2 008	95.2	1 524	72.2	1 353	64.1
Male	1 049	992	94.5	733	69.9	650	62.0
Female	1 061	1 017	95.8	790	74.5	703	66.3
NOVEMBER 2004							
Total	2 212	2 136	96.6	1 674	75.7	1 522	68.8
Male	1 073	1 034	96.4	788	73.5	708	66.0
Female	1 139	1 102	96.8	886	77.8	814	71.5
Race and Hispanic Origin							
White alone	2 120	2 061	97.2	1 620	76.4	1 473	69.5
Non-Hispanic White alone	2 052	2 038	99.3	1 608	78.4	1 463	71.3
Black alone	37	36	B	24	B	23	B
Asian alone	27	15	B	11	B	11	B
Hispanic or Latino[1]	69	24	B	13	B	12	B
White alone or in combination	2 136	2 077	97.3	1 634	76.5	1 484	69.5
Non-Hispanic White alone or in combination	2 068	2 055	99.3	1 622	78.5	1 474	71.3
Black alone or in combination	41	40	B	28	B	26	B
Asian alone or in combination	30	18	B	12	B	11	B
Age							
18 to 24 years	315	294	93.4	209	66.3	183	58.0
25 to 44 years	756	713	94.4	538	71.2	474	62.7
45 to 64 years	715	705	98.5	574	80.2	541	75.7
65 to 74 years	191	188	98.7	152	79.8	144	75.3
75 years and over	235	235	100.0	201	85.5	181	76.8

[1]May be of any race.
B = Base is too small to show derived measure.

At a Glance:

- With 2.7 million residents, Kansas's population ranked 33rd in the nation in 2004.

- Nearly 82 percent of the population was non-Hispanic White and just over 8 percent was Hispanic (of any race).

- Kansas ranked low for median household income, but its poverty rate was well below the national average.

- The state's real gross state product ranked 32nd in the country. Kansas had the third lowest state debt per capita in 2003.

- Kansas had an unemployment rate that was close to the U.S. average, but its total employment grew just 0.5 percent from 2001 to 2004, among the smallest rates in the nation.

- Among the population age 25 years and over, Kansas ranked 6th for proportion of high school graduates and 16th for proportion with a bachelor's degree or more.

- Just 11.1 percent of the state's population lacked health insurance, which was among the smallest proportions in the nation.

Table KS-1. Population by Sex and Age, 1990, 2000, and 2004

(Number, percent.)

Sex and age	1990	2000	2004	Percent distribution, 2004	Average annual percent change, 2000–2004
Total Population	2 477 574	2 688 418	2 735 502	X	0.4
Percent of total U.S. population	1.0	1.0	0.9	X	X
Sex					
Male	1 214 645	1 328 474	1 358 381	49.7	0.6
Female	1 262 929	1 359 944	1 377 121	50.3	0.3
Age					
Under 5 years	188 390	188 708	188 782	6.9	-0.1
5 to 17 years	473 224	524 285	494 709	18.1	0.3
18 years and over	444 397	1 975 425	2 052 011	75.0	0.9
18 to 24 years	1 815 960	275 592	299 476	10.9	1.1
25 to 44 years	254 493	769 204	746 056	27.3	-0.3
45 to 64 years	774 499	574 400	651 900	23.8	2.8
65 years and over	342 571	356 229	354 579	13.0	0.3
85 years and over	42 241	51 770	55 055	2.0	2.0
Median age (years)	32.8	35.2	35.8	X	X

X = Not applicable.

Average Annual Rate of Population Growth, 1980–2004

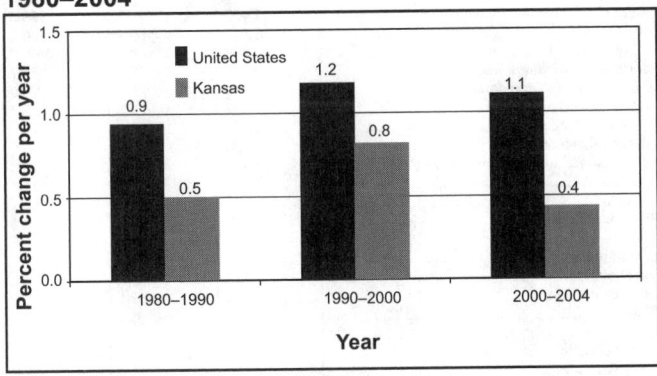

POPULATION

From 2000 to 2004, Kansas's population grew 1.7 percent, which was well below the national average growth rate of 4.3 percent. Kansas's growth rate was also lower than those of all of its neighboring states. The state lost over 48,000 residents to other states during the 2000–2004 period. Kansas's above average birth rate and immigration from other countries gave the state a net increase of population during this period. In 2004, 13 percent of the state's population was age 65 years and over, which was above average; however, Kansas's median age of 35.8 years was slightly below the U.S. average.

Table KS-2. Population by Race and Hispanic Origin, 1990, 2000, and 2004

(Number, percent.)

Race and Hispanic origin	1990	2000	2004
Total Population	2 477 574	2 688 418	2 735 502
Non-Hispanic (Percent)			
One race[1]			
White	88.4	83.3	81.9
Black	5.7	5.7	5.7
American Indian, Alaska Native[2]	0.9	0.8	0.8
Asian and Pacific Islander[2]	1.3	1.8	2.1
Other race[2]	2.0	. . .	. . .
Two or more races	. . .	1.4	1.5
Hispanic or Latino[3] (Percent)	3.8	7.0	8.1

[1]Individuals could report only one race in the 1990 census and could report one or more races on the 2000 census. Data on race in 2000 and 2004 are not comparable to 1990.
[2]Data for 1990 include people of Hispanic or Latino origin.
[3]May be of any race.
. . . = Not available.

Minority Population as a Percent of Total Population, 2004

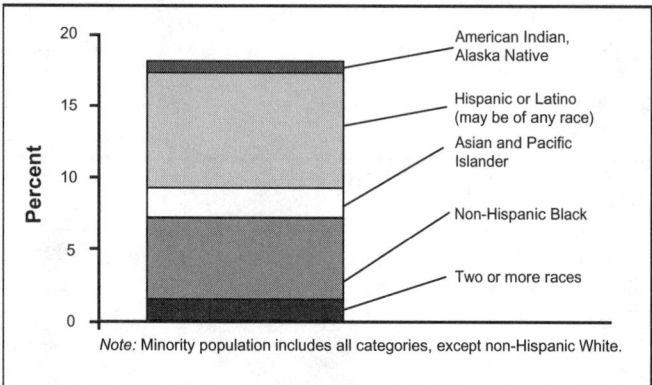

Note: Minority population includes all categories, except non-Hispanic White.

Age-Adjusted Death Rates, Average 2000–2002

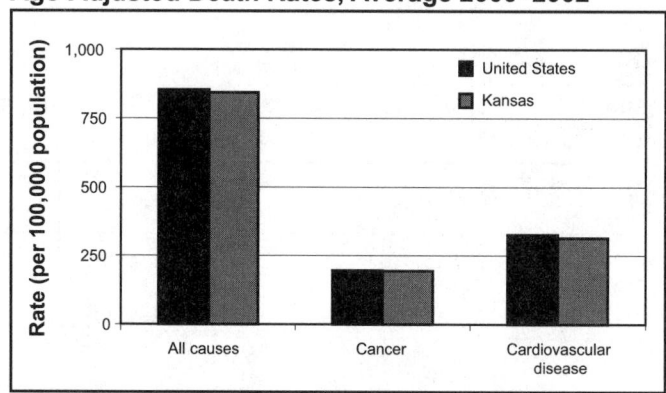

HEALTH

Kansas's infant mortality and age-adjusted death rates were close to the U.S. averages. Despite having the 13th highest birth rate in the nation, Kansas's birth rate for teenage mothers was below the U.S. average. The state ranked sixth highest in the country for the percentage of the population with health insurance coverage.

Table KS-3. Health Characteristics, 2000–2004

(Number, rate, percent.)

Item	State	U.S.
Births, 2003–2004		
Number of births	39 476	4 089 950
Birth rate (per 1,000 population)	14.5	14.1
Teenage birth rate (per 1,000 women age 15–19 years)	41.2	41.6
Mortality Rates, Average 2000–2002		
Infant mortality rate (per 1,000 live births)	7.0	6.9
Age-adjusted mortality rate (per 100,000 population)		
All races	843.6	853.3
Non-Hispanic White	825.6	843.1
Black	1 178.3	1 097.7
American Indian, Alaska Native	. . .	687.0
Asian and Pacific Islander	307.5	486.0
Hispanic or Latino[1]	595.8	642.7
Health Insurance, 2004		
Percent of all persons without health insurance	11.1	15.7
Percent of children without health insurance	6.5	11.2
Percent of low-income children without health insurance	5.0	7.1

[1]May be of any race.
. . . = Not available.

Table KS-4. Leading Causes of Death, Average 2000–2002

(Number, rate per 100,000 population.)

Cause	Number of deaths	Age-adjusted death rates State	Age-adjusted death rates U.S.
ALL CAUSES	24 795	843.6	853.3
Leading Causes			
Major cardiovascular diseases	9 400	311.5	326.5
Cancer	5 344	189.4	196.0
Chronic lower respiratory diseases	1 407	48.6	43.7
Unintentional injuries	1 116	39.9	35.7
Diabetes (underlying cause)	718	24.9	25.2
Influenza and pneumonia	667	21.5	22.7
Alzheimer's disease	676	21.3	19.0
Motor vehicle accidents	520	18.9	15.0
Nephritis, nephrotic syndrome, and nephrosis ..	498	16.6	13.8
Septicemia	280	9.5	11.4
Suicides	321	11.9	10.7
Firearm-related	278	10.2	10.3
Cirrhosis	190	7.0	9.5
Drug-induced	149	5.7	7.9
Alcohol-induced	152	5.7	6.9
Homicides	138	5.1	6.0
Falls	180	6.0	5.2
HIV	34	1.3	5.0
Viral hepatitis	38	1.4	2.0
Anemias	59	1.9	1.6
Drownings	29	1.1	1.3
Fire deaths	39	1.4	1.2

Note: The rates are age-adjusted to the U.S. 2000 standard population.

Table KS-5. Households and Housing Characteristics, 1990, 2000, and 2004

(Number, percent, and dollars.)

Characteristic	1990	2000	2004	Average annual percent change, 2000–2004
Total Households	944 726	1 037 891	1 076 366	0.9
Family households	658 600	701 547	707 663	0.2
Married-couple family	552 495	567 924	570 071	0.1
Other family	106 105	133 623	137 592	0.7
Male householder, no wife present	24 672	36 962	37 754	0.5
Female householder, no husband present	81 433	96 661	99 838	0.8
Nonfamily households	286 126	336 344	368 703	2.3
Householder living alone	245 156	280 387	308 574	2.4
Householder not living alone	40 970	55 957	60 129	1.8
Housing Characteristics				
Average size	2.53	2.51	2.47	X
Housing units	1 044 112	1 131 200	1 185 114	1.2
Occupied housing units	944 726	1 037 891	1 076 366	0.9
Owner-occupied	641 762	718 703	748 354	1.0
Renter-occupied	302 964	319 188	328 012	0.7
Median gross rent of renter-occupied housing units (dollars) ...	372	498	567	3.3
Median value of owner-occupied housing units (dollars)	51 800	83 500	102 458	5.2

X = Not applicable.

Median Housing Value and Median Rent, 2004

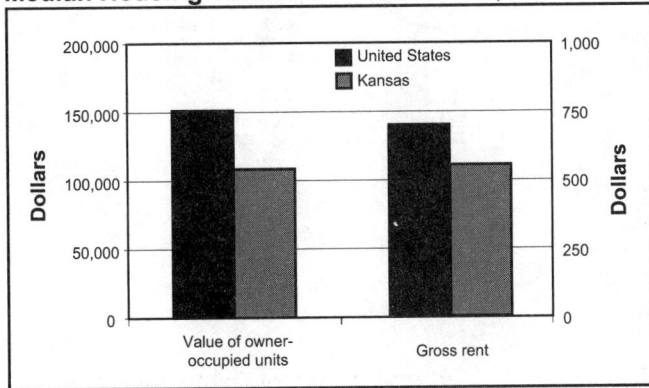

Median Household Income, 1984–2004 (2004 Dollars)

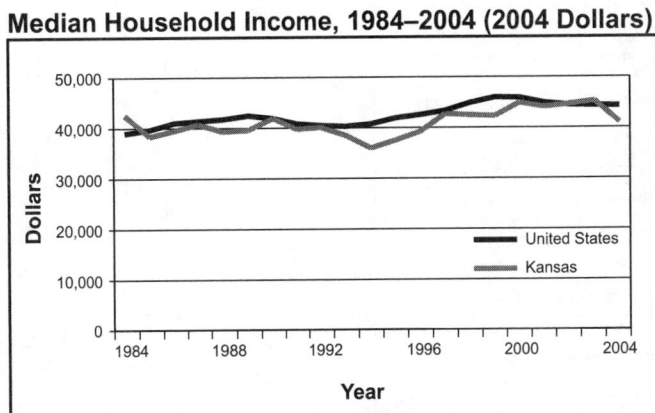

Table KS-6. Household Income and Poverty Status, 1980–2004

(2004 CPI-U-RS adjusted dollars, rate.)

Year	State		U.S.	
	Median household income (2004 dollars)	Poverty rate	Median household income (2004 dollars)	Poverty rate
2004	40 987	11.4	44 389	12.7
2003	45 421	10.8	44 482	12.5
2002	44 767	10.1	44 546	12.1
2001	44 194	10.1	45 062	11.7
2000	45 037	8.0	46 058	11.3
1999	42 334	12.3	46 129	11.9
1998	42 487	9.6	45 003	12.7
1997	42 804	9.7	43 430	13.3
1996	39 059	11.2	42 544	13.7
1995	37 346	10.8	41 943	13.8
1994	35 708	14.9	40 677	14.5
1993	38 323	13.1	40 217	15.1
1992	40 039	11.1	40 422	14.8
1991	39 622	12.3	40 746	14.2
1990	41 926	10.3	41 963	13.5
1989	39 517	10.8	42 524	12.8
1988	39 226	8.1	41 771	13.0
1987	40 681	9.2	41 322	13.4
1986	39 343	11.1	40 939	13.6
1985	38 156	13.8	39 545	14.0
1984	42 613	10.7	38 782	14.4
1983	. . .	13.6	. . .	15.2
1982	. . .	10.4	. . .	15.0
1981	. . .	11.7	. . .	14.0
1980	. . .	9.4	. . .	13.0

. . . = Not available.

Table KS-7. Employment Status by Demographic Group, 2004

(Numbers in thousands, rate.)

Characteristic	Civilian noninstitutional population	Civilian labor force		Employed	Unemployment rate
		Number	Participation rate		
SEX AND AGE					
Total	2 069	1 480	71.5	1 398	5.5
16 to 19 years	161	91	56.3	77	15.2
20 to 24 years	193	156	80.9	142	8.8
25 to 34 years	359	310	86.4	292	5.8
35 to 44 years	381	334	87.6	318	4.8
45 to 54 years	403	350	86.8	337	3.5
55 to 64 years	249	174	70.0	169	3.1
65 years and over	323	65	20.2	63	3.4
Men	1 008	795	78.9	754	5.2
16 to 19 years	83	47	55.9	39	15.4
20 to 24 years	101	86	85.7	79	8.3
25 to 34 years	180	168	93.3	160	4.7
35 to 44 years	184	172	93.4	164	4.5
45 to 54 years	203	186	91.6	178	4.3
55 to 64 years	122	96	78.8	94	2.5
65 years and over	135	40	29.6	39	3.0
Women	1 061	685	64.5	644	5.9
16 to 19 years	78	44	56.8	38	15.0
20 to 24 years	92	70	75.8	63	9.4
25 to 34 years	179	142	79.4	132	7.2
35 to 44 years	197	162	82.1	153	5.2
45 to 54 years	200	164	82.0	159	2.7
55 to 64 years	127	78	61.4	75	3.9
65 years and over	189	25	13.5	24	4.0
MARITAL STATUS					
Married men, spouse present	590	490	83.1	474	3.3
Married women, spouse present	579	395	68.2	382	3.3
Women who maintain families	109	82	75.5	72	12.1
RACE, HISPANIC ORIGIN, AND SEX					
White	1 834	1 321	72.0	1 259	4.7
Men	892	710	79.7	676	4.8
Women	942	610	64.8	583	4.5
Black	107	71	66.3	59	17.4
Men	51	35	67.4	30	12.1
Women	56	36	65.2	28	22.5
Asian	57	40	70.1	38	5.8
Hispanic or Latino[1]	109	86	78.6	80	7.0
Men	63	54	86.6	50	7.2
Women	47	32	67.9	30	6.5
RACE, HISPANIC ORIGIN, AND AGE					
White					
16 to 19 years	139	81	57.9	70	13.1
20 to 24 years	168	137	81.9	126	8.0
25 to 34 years	305	267	87.7	254	4.9
35 to 44 years	331	294	88.9	283	3.6
45 to 54 years	361	319	88.3	309	3.2
55 to 64 years	227	161	71.0	157	2.7
65 years and over	304	62	20.3	60	2.8

Note: Data in Table 7 are from the Current Population Survey (CPS) and do not match Bureau of Labor Statistics estimates in Table 8. See notes and definitions for more details.

[1]May be of any race.

Table KS-8. Employment Status, 1990–2004

(Numbers in thousands, rate.)

Year	Civilian labor force	Employed	Unemployed	Unemployment rate
2004	1 463 943	1 383 654	80 289	5.5
2003	1 447 478	1 366 061	81 417	5.6
2002	1 425 342	1 351 738	73 604	5.2
2001	1 408 800	1 348 506	60 294	4.3
2000	1 408 587	1 356 326	52 261	3.7
1999	1 409 556	1 359 908	49 648	3.5
1998	1 401 588	1 348 793	52 795	3.8
1997	1 383 486	1 329 797	53 689	3.9
1996	1 371 948	1 311 843	60 105	4.4
1995	1 355 850	1 296 202	59 648	4.4
1994	1 344 443	1 279 098	65 345	4.9
1993	1 325 075	1 257 847	67 228	5.1
1992	1 304 907	1 244 438	60 469	4.6
1991	1 283 125	1 225 007	58 118	4.5
1990	1 270 352	1 215 102	55 250	4.3

Note: Population age 16 years and over.

Unemployment Rate, 1980–2004

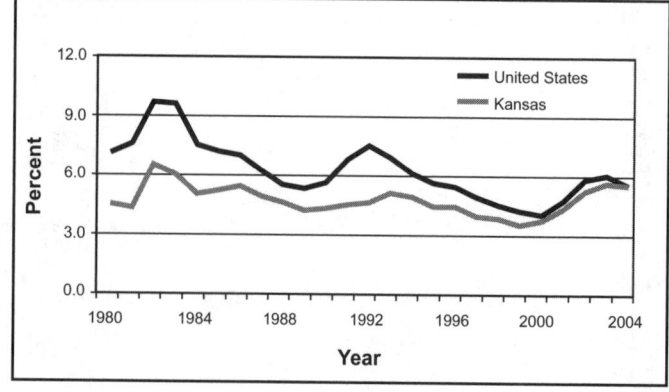

Table KS-9. Employment and Average Wages by Industry, 2001–2004

(Estimates are based on the 2002 North American Industry Classification System [NAICS].)

Industry	2001	2002	2003	2004	Annual average percent change, 2001–2004
	Number of jobs				
TOTAL EMPLOYMENT BY PLACE OF WORK	1 782 308	1 772 881	1 765 678	1 791 396	0.2
Farm Employment	78 519	78 346	77 312	78 615	0.0
Nonfarm Employment	1 703 789	1 694 535	1 688 366	1 712 781	0.2
Private employment	1 420 488	1 408 064	1 401 272	1 424 278	0.1
Forestry, fishing, hunting, and other[1]	8 594	9 606	8 931	8 916	1.2
Mining	19 678	17 635	20 229	21 610	3.2
Utilities	7 641	7 130	7 271	7 361	-1.2
Construction	93 353	90 807	92 513	93 441	0.0
Manufacturing	200 628	189 662	179 661	182 288	-3.1
Durable goods manufacturing	127 971	116 478	108 586	110 848	-4.7
Nondurable goods manufacturing	72 657	73 184	71 075	71 440	-0.6
Wholesale trade	66 127	66 090	64 505	65 151	-0.5
Retail trade	200 983	199 540	198 178	199 651	-0.2
Transportation and warehousing	56 611	55 774	55 655	55 740	-0.5
Information	54 564	50 342	48 086	45 135	-6.1
Finance and insurance	77 725	79 595	79 723	80 157	1.0
Real estate and rental and leasing	45 743	46 120	48 400	50 695	3.5
Professional and technical services	83 682	82 848	83 411	86 771	1.2
Management of companies and enterprises	13 228	11 948	10 504	9 970	-9.0
Administrative and waste services	81 224	82 537	82 067	86 455	2.1
Educational services	21 469	22 301	22 955	24 184	4.0
Health care and social assistance	167 656	169 874	171 527	175 534	1.5
Arts, entertainment, and recreation	25 578	26 174	25 845	26 553	1.3
Accommodation and food services	103 325	103 642	103 990	105 965	0.8
Other services, except public administration	92 679	96 439	97 821	98 701	2.1
Government and government enterprises	283 301	286 471	287 094	288 503	0.6
	Dollars				
AVERAGE WAGES AND SALARIES BY PLACE OF WORK	29 540	30 216	30 942	32 216	2.9
Farm Earnings	27 648	27 118	26 817	32 361	5.4
Nonfarm Earnings	29 558	30 242	30 979	32 215	2.9
Private earnings	30 174	30 737	31 450	32 646	2.7
Forestry, fishing, hunting, and other[1]	17 557	17 951	18 277	18 689	2.1
Mining	38 347	36 514	39 510	41 997	3.1
Utilities	60 553	65 523	58 595	62 092	0.8
Construction	33 658	34 125	34 210	34 751	1.1
Manufacturing	39 232	40 530	41 223	42 978	3.1
Durable goods manufacturing	41 697	43 405	44 106	45 982	3.3
Nondurable goods manufacturing	34 885	35 955	36 829	38 330	3.2
Wholesale trade	41 443	42 602	43 642	45 810	3.4
Retail trade	19 598	19 965	20 401	20 852	2.1
Transportation and warehousing	35 014	35 407	36 435	37 477	2.3
Information	45 525	47 695	51 086	55 959	7.1
Finance and insurance	41 858	43 011	45 662	47 014	3.9
Real estate and rental and leasing	24 871	26 209	26 827	27 772	3.7
Professional and technical services	41 912	42 291	42 292	44 156	1.8
Management of companies and enterprises	50 430	50 149	53 111	58 178	4.9
Administrative and waste services	22 639	23 202	24 140	24 738	3.0
Educational services	20 225	20 421	21 000	21 711	2.4
Health care and social assistance	28 103	28 829	29 807	30 932	3.2
Arts, entertainment, and recreation	14 057	14 525	15 235	15 697	3.7
Accommodation and food services	11 442	11 497	11 754	12 267	2.3
Other services, except public administration	19 553	20 232	20 926	21 403	3.1
Government and government enterprises	27 067	28 295	29 157	30 539	4.1

Note: Average wages and salaries are a calculation by the editors of wage and salary disbursements divided by full- and part-time wage and salary employment. Data may not add to total or may appear as zero due to rounding.

[1] "Other" consists of the number of jobs held by U.S. residents employed by international organizations and foreign embassies and consulates in the United States.

LABOR MARKET

Kansas's unemployment rate was below the national average until 2004, when its rate of 5.5 percent matched the U.S. average. Employment grew very slowly, increasing by just 0.5 percent over the 2001–2004 period. Jobs in manufacturing, particularly in durable goods, fell by over 54,000 during this period. Management and information also had high rates of job losses. The largest employer in Kansas was the government sector, which accounted for 16 percent of total employment. This was followed by retail trade, manufacturing, and health care. Educational services, real estate, and mining had the highest rates of job growth from 2001 to 2004. Kansas's average wages and salaries were below the U.S. averages in most categories.

Employment by Industry, 2004

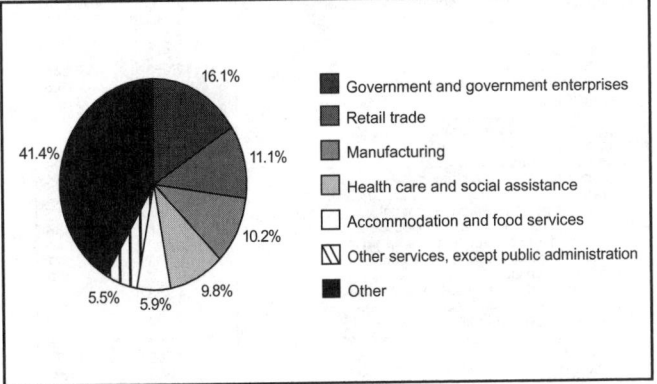

Table KS-10. Personal Income by Major Source, Selected Years 1980–2004

(Millions of dollars, except where noted.)

Item	1980	1990	2000	2001	2002	2003	2004	Average annual percent change, 2000–2004
Earnings by Place of Work	17 755	32 867	55 796	58 258	59 207	61 762	65 154	4.0
Wage and salary disbursements	13 317	23 447	41 289	42 571	43 092	43 612	45 847	2.7
Supplements to wages and salaries	2 634	5 014	8 470	8 923	10 061	10 803	11 766	8.6
Proprietors' income[1]	1 804	4 406	6 036	6 764	6 054	7 347	7 541	5.7
Farm proprietors' income	-82	1 145	344	376	-112	818	435	6.0
Nonfarm proprietors' income	1 886	3 261	5 692	6 388	6 166	6 529	7 106	5.7
(-) Contributions for government social insurance[2]	1 760	3 708	6 259	6 496	6 659	6 809	7 185	3.5
(+) Adjustment for residence[3]	729	975	1 103	993	975	855	842	-6.5
(=) Net Earnings by Place of Residence	16 724	30 134	50 640	52 755	53 524	55 808	58 811	3.8
(+) Dividends, interest, and rent[4]	4 098	9 174	14 437	14 350	13 818	13 556	14 087	-0.6
(+) Personal current transfer receipts	2 756	5 568	9 492	10 459	11 214	11 428	11 912	5.8
Personal income	23 578	44 876	74 570	77 564	78 556	80 792	84 810	3.3
Farm income	23 491	43 516	73 885	76 807	78 328	79 622	83 909	3.2
Nonfarm income	87	1 360	684	757	228	1 170	901	7.1
Per Capita Personal Income (Dollars)[5]	9 953	18 085	27 694	28 714	28 956	29 651	31 003	2.9

Note: Data may not add to total or may appear as zero due to rounding.

[1]Proprietors' income includes the inventory valuation adjustment and the capital consumption adjustment.
[2]Contributions for government social insurance are included in earnings by type and industry, but they are excluded from personal income.
[3]The adjustment for residence is the net inflow of the earnings of interarea commuters.
[4]Rental income of persons includes the capital consumption adjustment.
[5]Per capita personal income is total personal income divided by total midyear population.

Per Capita Personal Income, 1980–2004
(Current Dollars)

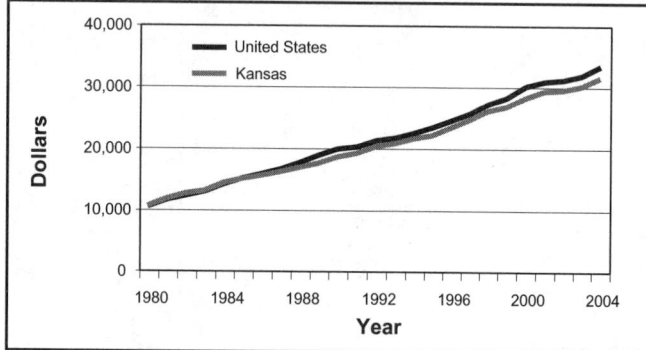

ECONOMIC ACTIVITY

Real gross state product increased 6.2 percent over the 2001–2004 period, ranking among the lowest growth rates in the nation. From 2001 to 2004, information, finance and insurance, administrative and waste services, and utilities had the highest rates of growth. Educational services and agriculture had the biggest declines. Manufacturing and government remained the leading sectors of Kansas's economy. From 2003 to 2004, growth was boosted by improved activity in manufacturing, wholesale and retail trade, and information services. The median value of owner-occupied housing in Kansas was well below the national average and not a significant factor in the state's economic activity.

Table KS-11. Real Gross State Product, 1997–2004

(Millions of chained 2000 dollars, percent.)

Industry	1997	1998	1999	2000	2001	2002	2003	2004	Average annual percent change, 2001–2004
GROSS STATE PRODUCT	76 095	79 620	81 263	83 427	84 696	85 765	86 814	89 941	2.0
As a percent of U.S. gross product	0.9	0.9	0.9	0.9	0.9	0.9	0.8	0.8	X
Private Industries	65 346	68 589	70 149	72 176	73 375	74 480	75 291	77 946	2.0
Agriculture, forestry, fishing, and hunting	2 100	1 846	1 687	1 652	1 742	1 613	1 929	1 617	-2.5
Mining	1 264	1 065	1 000	939	856	917	834	870	0.5
Utilities	1 695	1 664	1 776	1 726	1 830	1 864	1 937	2 089	4.5
Construction	3 612	3 667	3 765	3 721	3 570	3 433	3 381	3 333	-2.3
Manufacturing	12 253	13 224	12 916	13 932	13 545	13 425	12 943	13 699	0.4
As a percent of gross state product	16.1	16.6	15.9	16.7	16.0	15.7	14.9	15.2	X
Wholesale trade	4 885	5 372	5 510	5 436	5 791	5 949	5 708	5 879	0.5
Retail trade	5 552	5 917	6 159	6 218	6 657	6 939	7 251	7 532	4.2
Transportation and warehousing	2 836	2 877	2 938	3 142	3 161	3 227	3 380	3 418	2.6
Information	3 346	3 745	5 224	6 246	6 317	6 839	7 445	8 002	8.2
Finance and insurance	4 457	4 586	4 684	4 790	4 828	5 161	5 496	5 672	5.5
Real estate and rental and leasing	7 192	7 645	7 406	7 637	8 050	7 892	7 612	7 865	-0.8
Services	16 315	17 117	17 124	16 737	17 049	17 300	17 511	18 209	2.2
As a percent of gross state product	21.4	21.5	21.1	20.1	20.1	20.2	20.2	20.2	X
Professional and technical services	3 088	3 486	3 527	3 552	3 778	3 814	3 862	4 094	2.7
Management of companies and enterprises	1 092	1 040	995	927	905	866	851	838	-2.5
Administrative and waste services	2 240	2 277	2 293	2 019	2 046	2 172	2 233	2 335	4.5
Educational services	402	433	436	436	417	403	382	385	-2.6
Health care and social assistance	4 983	5 117	5 209	5 339	5 509	5 667	5 773	5 947	2.6
Arts, entertainment, and recreation	408	381	401	402	414	428	423	431	1.4
Accommodation and food services	1 945	2 115	2 040	2 013	1 989	1 970	1 989	2 088	1.6
Other services, except public administration	2 157	2 268	2 223	2 049	1 991	1 980	1 998	2 091	1.6
Government	10 760	11 035	11 114	11 252	11 322	11 290	11 523	11 987	1.9
As a percent of gross state product	14.1	13.9	13.7	13.5	13.4	13.2	13.3	13.3	X

X = Not applicable.

Table KS-12. Government Transfer Payments, Selected Years 1980–2004

(Millions of dollars, percent.)

Item	1980	1990	2000	2001	2002	2003	2004	Average annual percent change, 2000–2004
CURRENT TRANSFER PAYMENTS TO INDIVIDUALS	2 591	5 255	8 908	9 693	10 526	10 790	11 264	6.0
Retirement and Disability Insurance Benefits	1 417	2 829	4 286	4 508	4 690	4 818	5 008	4.0
Old-age, survivors, and disability insurance (OASDI) benefits	1 294	2 625	4 060	4 276	4 444	4 565	4 750	4.0
Railroad retirement and disability benefits	111	169	203	208	217	223	227	2.8
Workers' compensation	7	29	17	16	16	17	17	0.0
Other government retirement and disability insurance benefits	6	5	5	8	13	13	14	30.3
Medical Benefits	648	1 656	3 470	3 905	4 294	4 188	4 566	7.1
Medicare benefits	420	1 072	1 903	2 096	2 229	2 344	2 555	7.6
Public assistance medical care benefits	216	537	1 519	1 740	1 974	1 768	1 924	6.1
Military medical insurance benefits	12	47	48	69	90	75	87	15.7
Income Maintenance Benefits	198	349	623	638	703	822	887	9.3
Supplemental Security Income (SSI) benefits	28	66	151	158	164	170	178	4.1
Family assistance	88	103	122	123	118	128	140	3.6
Food stamps	41	100	85	95	118	145	164	18.0
Other income maintenance benefits	41	80	265	261	302	379	405	11.2
Unemployment Insurance Compensation	139	151	175	247	415	522	333	17.4
Veterans' Benefits	141	168	233	244	268	289	308	7.2
Federal Education and Training Assistance	46	95	112	135	148	142	152	7.9
Other Payments to Individuals	2	5	10	16	8	9	11	2.1

Note: See notes and definitions for more details. Data may not add to total or may appear as zero due to rounding.

EXPORTS

In 2004, Kansas ranked 30th in the nation for value of its exports. Exports from the state declined sharply between 2001 and 2003, but recovered somewhat in 2004. This was primarily due to a large drop in processed food exports. Kansas's leading exports were transportation equipment (airplanes), processed foods, and computers and electronic products. Canada was the largest of Kansas's export markets, followed by Mexico and the United Kingdom. Exports to Japan, the state's fifth leading market, fell by 72 percent from 2001 to 2004. This was also due to the drastic decline in processed food exports.

Leading Exports, 2004

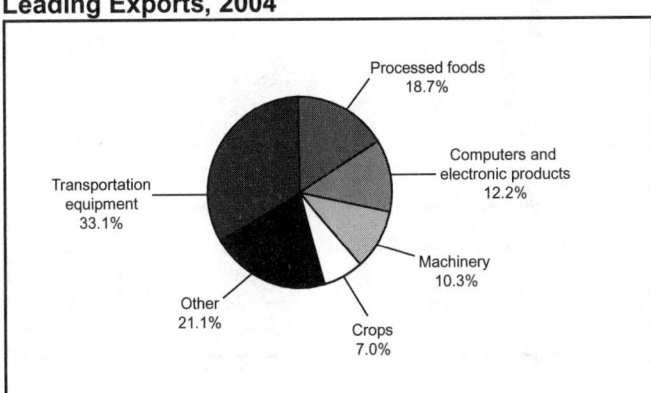

Table KS-13. Exports of Goods by Leading Products and Destinations, 2001–2004

(Millions of dollars, percent, rank based on 2004 dollar values.)

Product and market	2001	2002	2003	2004	Percent share of total, 2004	Average annual percent change, 2001–2004
Total Goods						
Total	5 005	4 988	4 553	4 931	100.0	-0.5
Manufactures	4 530	4 484	4 149	4 453	90.3	-0.6
Agriculture and livestock	300	366	282	390	7.9	9.2
Other commodities	175	139	123	88	1.8	-20.3
Five Leading Exports (NAICS Code)						
Transportation equipment (336)	1 657	1 678	1 271	1 632	33.1	-0.5
Processed foods (311)	1 298	1 316	1 304	804	16.3	-14.7
Computers and electronic products (334)	341	277	339	600	12.2	20.8
Machinery manufactures (333)	437	415	415	507	10.3	5.1
Crop production (111)	285	350	259	345	7.0	6.7
Five Leading Markets	4 440	4 337	4 117	4 354	88.3	-0.6
Canada	1 217	1 271	1 021	1 310	26.6	2.5
Mexico	547	664	602	645	13.1	5.6
United Kingdom	304	233	249	287	5.8	-1.9
China	259	200	176	211	4.3	-6.7
Japan	709	528	543	199	4.0	-34.6

Table KS-14. Agriculture, 1997 and 2002

(Number, acres, and dollars.)

Item	1997	2002
Number of farms	65 476	64 414
Land in farms (acres)	46 650 618	47 227 944
Farm Size		
Average size of farm (acres)	712	733
Farms by size (percent distribution)		
Fewer than 50 acres	16.9	17.4
50 to 499 acres	47.7	48.0
500 acres or more	35.4	34.6
Market Value of Land and Equipment (Dollars)		
Land and buildings average value per farm	417 704	505 999
Average value per acre	586	687
Machinery and equipment average value per farm	72 488	95 124
Value of Sales (Thousands of Dollars)		
Agricultural products sold	9 312 865	8 746 244
Crops	3 352 243	2 418 447
Livestock, poultry, and their products	5 960 622	6 327 797
Average per farm (dollars)	142 233	135 782
Value of sales (percent distribution)		
Less than $10,000	39.7	48.3
$10,000 to $99,999	39.8	34.5
$100,000 or more	20.5	17.1
Government Payments		
Payments (thousands of dollars)	355 024	328 244
Percent of farms receiving government payments	67.9	60.8
Farm operators whose principal occupation is farming (percent)	54.7	63.1

AGRICULTURE

Cash receipts from farming totaled $8.7 billion in 2002, the fifth highest amount in the nation, but less than the total reported in the previous farm census in 1997. Crop sales amounted to less than 28 percent of total sales. Kansas's leading products were cattle, wheat, and corn. Just 17.4 percent of farms spanned fewer than 50 acres, which was among the lowest proportions of farms of this size in the country. Nonetheless, more than 48 percent of farms had sales of less than $10,000, compared with 59.3 percent nationally. Just over 63 percent of farm operators reported farming as their principal occupation.

ENERGY

Energy expenditures per person in Kansas were higher than the average, ranking 14th in the country. The state's energy prices were slightly less than the U.S. average. Kansas ranked 15th in the nation for per capita consumption. Its main energy sources were petroleum and coal.

Energy Consumption by Source, 2001

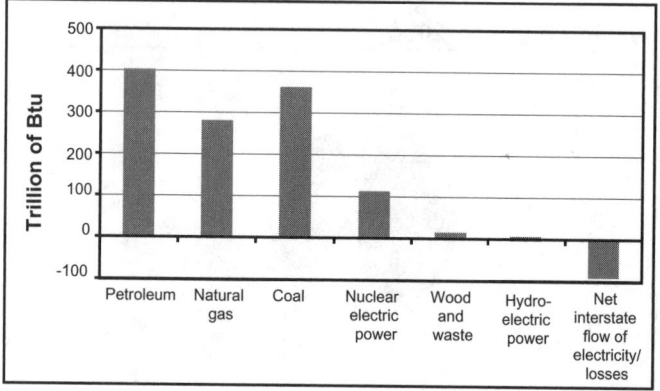

Energy Consumption by Sector, 2001

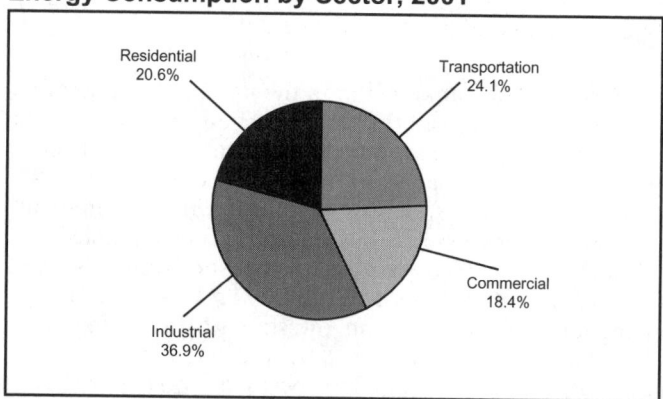

Table KS-15. Energy Consumption, Expenditures, and Prices, Selected Years 1960–2001

(Dollars, Btu [British Thermal Unit], percent distribution.)

Item	1960	1965	1970	1975	1980	1985	1990	1995	2000	2001
Total Consumption (Billion Btu)	632 347	724 845	874 212	926 780	1 027 609	1 017 083	1 051 607	1 052 013	1 094 654	1 043 701
Consumption per capita (million Btu)	290.2	328.6	388.7	406.4	434.7	419.0	424.5	406.7	407.2	386.5
Consumption by Sector (Percent Distribution)										
Residential	19.6	20.7	20.6	19.7	18.2	18.3	18.0	19.4	20.6	20.6
Commercial	10.8	10.4	11.9	13.2	13.9	15.2	16.0	16.9	17.7	18.4
Industrial	42.2	41.8	38.7	38.1	40.7	40.2	39.4	37.6	37.0	36.9
Transportation	27.3	27.2	28.7	29.0	27.2	26.2	26.6	26.1	24.7	24.1
Consumption by Source (Billion Btu)										
Coal	15 724	15 282	10 701	62 280	191 574	259 501	271 739	289 714	362 806	354 632
Natural gas	373 664	440 802	574 542	490 748	481 990	354 756	352 645	367 750	314 869	273 849
Petroleum	253 444	278 035	302 798	385 589	375 698	400 672	405 104	358 909	405 547	390 967
Nuclear electric power	0	0	0	0	0	40 960	83 328	105 723	94 495	108 102
Hydroelectric power[1]	211	140	71	48	86	93	138	116	156	260
Wood and waste	3 912	3 358	3 659	5 763	10 787	10 283	11 461	10 873	8 428	7 767
Other	0	0	0	0	0	0	80	179	284	710
Net interstate flow of electricity/losses[2]	-14 607	-12 773	-17 560	-17 648	-32 526	-49 181	-72 887	-81 250	-91 931	-92 587
Total Expenditures (Thousands of Dollars)	...	...	918 300	1 730 100	4 093 500	5 148 700	5 285 200	5 286 000	7 374 400	7 082 000
Expenditures per capita (dollars)	...	...	408	759	1 732	2 121	2 133	2 043	2 743	2 622
Prices by Sector (Dollars Per Million Btu)										
Total	...	...	1.56	2.89	5.99	7.26	7.56	7.70	10.38	10.58
Residential	...	...	1.68	2.53	5.45	8.62	10.04	10.40	12.86	13.89
Commercial	...	...	1.56	2.75	5.62	8.51	9.20	10.04	12.61	13.43
Industrial	...	...	0.81	1.87	4.02	5.35	5.02	4.90	7.81	7.67
Transportation	...	...	2.34	4.13	8.58	8.40	8.52	8.15	10.94	10.70

[1]A negative number in this row results from pumped storage for which, overall, more electricity is expended than created to provide electricity during peak demand periods.
[2]Net interstate flow of electricity is the difference between the amount of energy in the electricity sold within a state (including associated losses) and the energy input at the electric utilities within the state. A positive number indicates that more electricity (including associated losses) came into the state than went out of the state during the year; conversely, a negative number indicates that more electricity (including associated losses) went out of the state than came into the state.
... = Not available.

Table KS-16. State Taxes, Fiscal 2004

(Dollars, percent distribution.)

Item	Thousands of dollars	Percent distribution	Dollars per capita	
			State	U.S.
TOTAL TAXES	5 283 676	100.0	1 931.2	2 024.8
Property Taxes	57 554	1.1	21.0	38.9
Sales and Gross Receipts	2 723 152	51.5	995.3	1 003.4
General sales and gross receipts	1 932 927	36.6	706.5	677.0
Selective sales taxes	790 225	15.0	288.8	326.4
Alcoholic beverages	87 637	1.7	32.0	15.7
Insurance premiums	121 827	2.3	44.5	47.0
Motor fuels	428 985	8.1	156.8	114.6
Tobacco products	124 586	2.4	45.5	42.0
Licenses	274 619	5.2	100.4	134.9
Corporation	47 170	0.9	17.2	21.6
Motor vehicle	161 497	3.1	59.0	59.4
Other Taxes	2 228 351	42.2	814.5	847.6
Individual income	1 915 530	36.3	700.1	673.6
Corporation net income	166 609	3.2	60.9	105.1
Death and gift	48 064	0.9	17.6	19.6
Severance	98 148	1.9	35.9	21.5

GOVERNMENT FINANCE

Kansas ranked 36th in the nation for both per capita state revenues and per capita expenditures in 2003. Spending was above average on highways and education and below average on public welfare. The state's debt per person was $907, which was the third lowest in the nation. The U.S. average debt per person in 2003 was $2,405. In fiscal year 2004, tax collections per person amounted to $1,931, which was slightly below average. The largest tax source, general sales taxes, was followed closely by individual income taxes. Kansas's individual income taxes ranked 22nd among the 43 states with such taxes. The state's property taxes were below average.

Per Capita State Taxes, Fiscal 2004

Table KS-17. State Government Finances, 2003

(Dollars, percent distribution.)

Item	Millions of dollars	Percent distribution	Dollars per capita	
			State	U.S.
GENERAL REVENUE	9 752 078	100.0	3 578.7	3 832.6
Intergovernmental revenue	3 266 719	33.5	1 198.8	1 246.0
Taxes	5 008 411	51.4	1 838.0	1 891.6
General sales	1 888 543	19.4	693.0	636.0
Selective sales	775 840	8.0	284.7	307.4
License taxes	256 372	2.6	94.1	123.6
Individual income tax	1 776 884	18.2	652.1	626.8
Corporate income tax	124 519	1.3	45.7	97.8
Other taxes	186 253	1.9	68.4	99.9
Current charges	808 541	8.3	296.7	366.5
Miscellaneous general revenue	668 407	6.9	245.3	328.6
GENERAL EXPENDITURE	9 843 383	100.0	3 612.2	4 010.5
Intergovernmental expenditure	2 925 220	29.7	1 073.5	1 316.9
Direct expenditure	6 918 163	70.3	2 538.8	2 693.6
Expenditure by Function				
Education	4 210 861	42.8	1 545.3	1 416.4
Public welfare	1 905 638	19.4	699.3	1 083.3
Hospitals	102 323	1.0	37.6	132.3
Health	524 233	5.3	192.4	173.0
Highways	1 094 228	11.1	401.6	295.4
Police protection	72 321	0.7	26.5	38.4
Correction	336 268	3.4	123.4	135.0
Natural resources	184 607	1.9	67.8	64.0
Parks and recreation	6 072	0.1	2.2	20.1
Government administration	533 689	5.4	195.8	151.3
Interest on general debt	128 976	1.3	47.3	107.8
Other and unallocable	744 167	7.6	273.1	393.4
DEBT AT END OF FISCAL YEAR	2 471 939	X	907.1	2 404.7
CASH AND SECURITY HOLDINGS	12 194 362	X	4 475.0	8 938.4

X = Not applicable.

Table KS-18. Education Indicators, 2000–2004
(Percent, number.)

Item	State	U.S.
Total Population 25 Years and Over (Thousands), 2004	1 717	186 877
Educational Attainment, 2004		
Percent high school graduate or more	89.6	85.2
Percent college graduate or more	30.0	27.7
Elementary and Secondary Schools, 2002–2003		
Total students	470 957	48 202 324
Percent of students eligible for free or reduced-price lunch ..	37.4	40.6
Percent of students who were English language learners	4.8	7.8
Total schools	1 431	92 330
Student/teacher ratio	14.4	15.9
Per student expenditures	7 454	8 041
Dropouts, Grades 9–12, 2000–2001 (Percent)	3.1	. . .
Higher Education, 2002–2003		
Total enrollment	193 841	17 035 027
Bachelor's degrees awarded	15 744	1 348 503
Percent women	56.2	57.5

. . . = Not available.

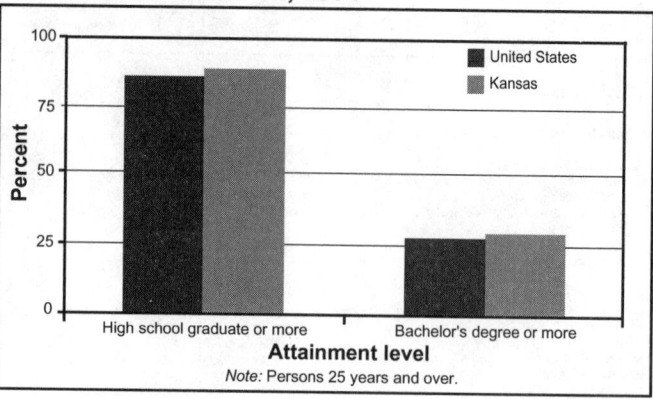

Educational Attainment, 2004

Note: Persons 25 years and over.

EDUCATION

Kansas has above average educational attainment levels. In 2004, 89.6 percent of the state's population age 25 years and over had graduated from high school. Kansas was among 13 states and the District of Columbia with 30 percent or more of residents holding bachelor's degrees or more. The state's expenditures per student for K–12 public schools were below the U.S. average. Kansas's student/teacher ratio of 14.4 was well below the national average of 15.9. The dropout rate of 3.1 percent ranked among the 10 lowest of the 46 states reporting data.

VOTER PARTICIPATION

Voter turnout was well above the national average in 2000, but only slightly above the national average in 2004. The state voted overwhelmingly for the Republican presidential candidate in both elections. According to the official tally by the Clerk of the U.S. House of Representatives, 58 percent of eligible voters in Kansas in 2000 and 62 percent in 2004 voted for the Republican presidential candidate. More than 78 percent of eligible residents age 65 to 74 years reported voting in the 2004 election, while about 35 percent of persons age 18 to 24 years voted. Less than 22 percent of eligible Hispanics voted.

Table KS-19. Reported Voting and Registration, November 2000 and November 2004
(Numbers in thousands, percent.)

Characteristic	Total population 18 years and over	Total citizen		Total registered		Total voted	
		Number	Percent	Number	Percent	Number	Percent
NOVEMBER 2000							
Total	1 908	1 861	97.5	1 293	67.7	1 148	60.2
Male	927	904	97.5	600	64.7	528	57.0
Female	981	958	97.6	693	70.6	620	63.2
NOVEMBER 2004							
Total	1 990	1 851	93.1	1 338	67.2	1 188	59.7
Male	970	896	92.4	633	65.3	554	57.1
Female	1 019	955	93.7	704	69.1	633	62.1
Race and Hispanic Origin							
White alone	1 768	1 671	94.5	1 224	69.2	1 101	62.2
Non-Hispanic White alone	1 649	1 624	98.5	1 198	72.7	1 076	65.3
Black alone	99	97	B	64	B	53	B
Asian alone	73	34	B	14	B	11	B
Hispanic or Latino[1]	132	55	41.6	30	22.7	28	21.5
White alone or in combination	1 803	1 706	94.6	1 250	69.3	1 117	62.0
Non-Hispanic White alone or in combination	1 682	1 657	98.5	1 223	72.7	1 091	64.9
Black alone or in combination	102	100	98.3	66	64.3	54	52.6
Asian alone or in combination	73	34	B	14	B	11	B
Age							
18 to 24 years	286	248	86.6	139	48.4	101	35.1
25 to 44 years	723	643	89.1	421	58.2	371	51.3
45 to 64 years	668	655	98.0	525	78.6	488	73.0
65 to 74 years	133	129	97.4	112	84.2	105	78.7
75 years and over	179	175	97.8	141	78.8	124	69.0

[1]May be of any race.
B = Base is too small to show derived measure.

At a Glance:

- Kentucky's population of over 4.2 million people ranked 26th in the nation in 2004.

- Non-Hispanic Whites made up 88.7 percent of the population. Hispanics (of any race) accounted for 1.9 percent of Kentucky's residents, which was among the smallest proportions of this ethnic group in the nation.

- Kentucky's median household income was among the five lowest in the nation, and the state's poverty rate of 17.7 percent was the second highest in the country.

- The state's unemployment rate was 5.3 percent in 2004, just below the national average, and real gross state product ranked 26th in the country.

- Among the population age 25 years and over, Kentucky ranked 44th for high school attainment and 48th for college attainment.

- Kentucky's age-adjusted death rate for all causes was the sixth highest in the country.

- The state's property taxes were among the 10 highest in the nation.

Table KY-1. Population by Sex and Age, 1990, 2000, and 2004

(Number, percent.)

Sex and age	1990	2000	2004	Percent distribution, 2004	Average annual percent change, 2000–2004
Total Population	3 685 296	4 041 769	4 145 922	X	0.6
Percent of total U.S. population	1.5	1.4	1.4	X	X
Sex					
Male	1 785 235	1 975 368	2 033 894	49.1	0.7
Female	1 900 061	2 066 401	2 112 028	50.9	0.5
Age					
Under 5 years	250 871	265 901	266 614	6.4	0.3
5 to 17 years	703 223	728 917	713 573	17.2	0.1
18 years and over	705 186	3 046 951	3 165 735	76.4	1.1
18 to 24 years	2 731 202	401 858	412 635	10.0	0.2
25 to 44 years	399 989	1 210 773	1 189 512	28.7	0.2
45 to 64 years	1 159 182	929 527	1 044 261	25.2	2.9
65 years and over	466 845	504 793	519 327	12.5	0.8
85 years and over	46 367	58 261	59 024	1.4	1.8
Median age (years)	32.9	35.9	37.0	X	X

X = Not applicable.

Average Annual Rate of Population Growth, 1980–2004

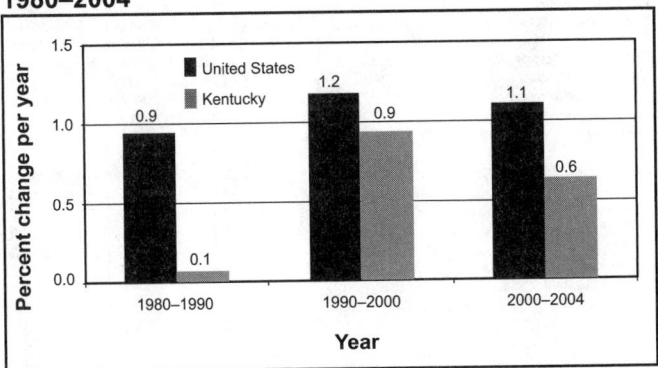

POPULATION

Kentucky's population increased by 2.6 percent over the 2000–2004 period, which was below the national average. In 2002, South Carolina overtook Kentucky to become the 25th most populous state in the nation, and that state's population growth continues to outpace Kentucky's. From 2000 to 2004, over 22,000 new residents moved to Kentucky from other states, and an additional 22,700 people moved in from other countries. While Kentucky had a below average proportion of its population under 18 years old, the state's age distribution was fairly close to that of the nation as a whole. Kentucky had among the smallest proportions of Asian and Pacific Islander and American Indian populations.

Table KY-2. Population by Race and Hispanic Origin, 1990, 2000, and 2004

(Number, percent.)

Race and Hispanic origin	1990	2000	2004
Total Population	3 685 296	4 041 769	4 145 922
Non-Hispanic (Percent)			
One race[1]			
White	91.7	89.4	88.7
Black	7.1	7.3	7.4
American Indian, Alaska Native[2]	0.2	0.2	0.2
Asian and Pacific Islander[2]	0.5	0.8	0.2
Other race[2]	0.2	. . .	0.9
Two or more races	. . .	0.8	. . .
			0.9
Hispanic or Latino[3] (Percent)	0.6	1.5	1.9

[1]Individuals could report only one race in the 1990 census and could report one or more races on the 2000 census. Data on race in 2000 and 2004 are not comparable to 1990.
[2]Data for 1990 include people of Hispanic or Latino origin.
[3]May be of any race.
. . . = Not available.

Minority Population as a Percent of Total Population, 2004

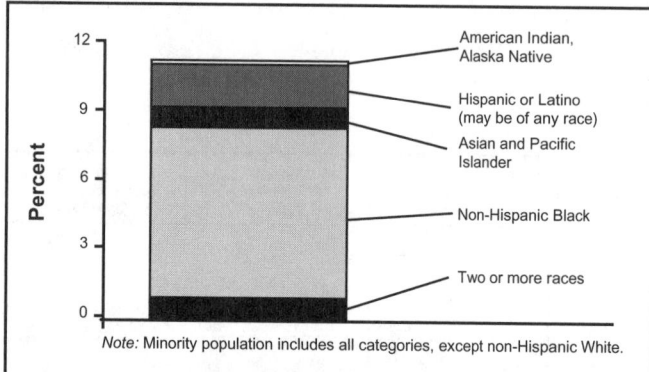

Note: Minority population includes all categories, except non-Hispanic White.

Age-Adjusted Death Rates, Average 2000–2002

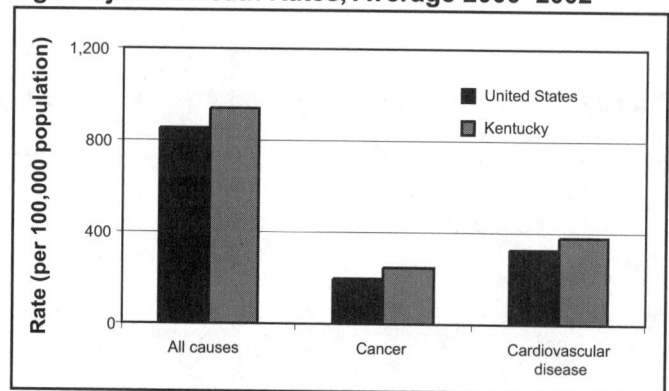

HEALTH

In 2004, Kentucky's health insurance coverage rate was well above the national average for all persons and for children. The state's birth rate was below the U.S. average; however, its birth rate for teenage mothers was the 14th highest in the country.

Table KY-3. Health Characteristics, 2000–2004

(Number, rate, percent.)

Item	State	U.S.
Births, 2003–2004		
Number of births	55 236	4 089 950
Birth rate (per 1,000 population)	13.4	14.1
Teenage birth rate (per 1,000 women age 15–19 years)	49.6	41.6
Mortality Rates, Average 2000–2002		
Infant mortality rate (per 1,000 live births)	6.7	6.9
Age-adjusted mortality rate (per 100,000 population)		
All races	991.7	853.3
Non-Hispanic White	984.1	843.1
Black	1 176.0	1 097.7
American Indian, Alaska Native	. . .	687.0
Asian and Pacific Islander	427.8	486.0
Hispanic or Latino[1]	843.7	642.7
Health Insurance, 2004		
Percent of all persons without health insurance	14.3	15.7
Percent of children without health insurance	8.4	11.2
Percent of low-income children without health insurance	6.3	7.1

[1]May be of any race.
. . . = Not available.

Table KY-4. Leading Causes of Death, Average 2000–2002

(Number, rate per 100,000 population.)

Cause	Number of deaths	Age-adjusted death rates State	Age-adjusted death rates U.S.
ALL CAUSES	40 021	991.7	853.3
Leading Causes			
Major cardiovascular diseases	15 157	378.3	326.5
Cancer	9 334	227.3	196.0
Chronic lower respiratory diseases	2 279	56.5	43.7
Unintentional injuries	1 973	48.2	35.7
Diabetes (underlying cause)	1 157	28.5	25.2
Influenza and pneumonia	1 169	29.6	22.7
Alzheimer's disease	941	24.1	19.0
Motor vehicle accidents	833	20.2	15.0
Nephritis, nephrotic syndrome, and nephrosis ..	792	19.8	13.8
Septicemia	607	15.1	11.4
Suicides	519	12.5	10.7
Firearm-related	537	12.9	10.3
Cirrhosis	378	9.0	9.5
Drug-induced	359	8.7	7.9
Alcohol-induced	248	5.9	6.9
Homicides	206	5.0	6.0
Falls	177	4.4	5.2
HIV	84	2.0	5.0
Viral hepatitis	62	1.5	2.0
Anemias	77	1.9	1.6
Drownings	63	1.6	1.3
Fire deaths	78	1.9	1.2

Note: The rates are age-adjusted to the U.S. 2000 standard population.

Table KY-5. Households and Housing Characteristics, 1990, 2000, and 2004

(Number, percent, and dollars.)

Characteristic	1990	2000	2004	Average annual percent change, 2000–2004
Total Households	1 379 782	1 590 647	1 647 464	0.9
Family households	1 015 998	1 104 398	1 142 281	0.8
Married-couple family	816 732	857 944	872 550	0.4
Other family	199 266	246 454	269 731	2.3
Male householder, no wife present	39 606	58 497	74 318	6.2
Female householder, no husband present	159 660	187 957	195 413	1.0
Nonfamily households	363 784	486 249	505 183	1.0
Householder living alone	321 247	414 095	431 710	1.0
Householder not living alone	42 537	72 154	73 473	0.5
Housing Characteristics				
Average size	2.60	2.47	2.45	X
Housing units	1 506 845	1 750 927	1 842 971	1.3
Occupied housing units	1 379 782	1 590 647	1 647 464	0.9
Owner-occupied	960 469	1 125 397	1 155 568	0.7
Renter-occupied	419 313	465 250	491 896	1.4
Median gross rent of renter-occupied housing units (dollars)	319	445	503	3.1
Median value of owner-occupied housing units (dollars)	50 100	86 700	98 438	3.2

X = Not applicable.

Median Housing Value and Median Rent, 2004

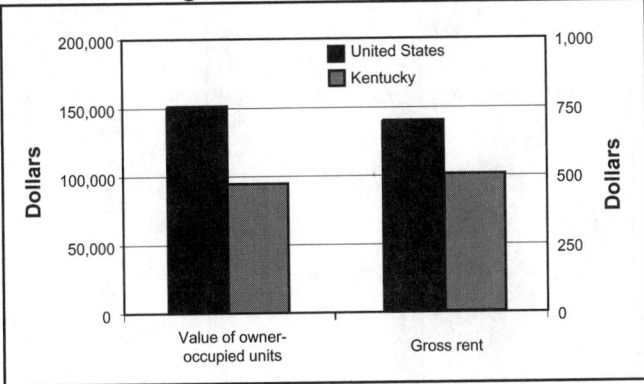

Median Household Income, 1984–2004 (2004 Dollars)

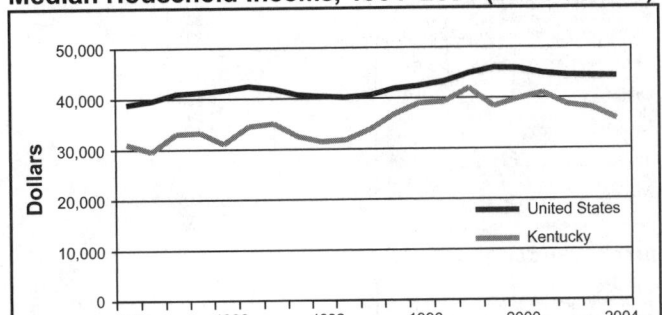

Table KY-6. Household Income and Poverty Status, 1980–2004

(2004 CPI-U-RS adjusted dollars, rate.)

Year	State		U.S.	
	Median household income (2004 dollars)	Poverty rate	Median household income (2004 dollars)	Poverty rate
2004	35 643	17.7	44 389	12.7
2003	37 929	14.4	44 482	12.5
2002	38 615	14.2	44 546	12.1
2001	41 016	12.6	45 062	11.7
2000	39 779	12.6	46 058	11.3
1999	38 242	12.1	46 129	11.9
1998	41 956	13.5	45 003	12.7
1997	39 260	15.9	43 430	13.3
1996	38 853	17.0	42 544	13.7
1995	36 692	14.7	41 943	13.8
1994	33 530	18.5	40 677	14.5
1993	31 380	20.4	40 217	15.1
1992	30 987	19.7	40 422	14.8
1991	32 141	18.8	40 746	14.2
1990	34 727	17.3	41 963	13.5
1989	34 252	16.1	42 524	12.8
1988	30 543	17.6	41 771	13.0
1987	32 874	17.3	41 322	13.4
1986	32 680	17.7	40 939	13.6
1985	29 069	19.4	39 545	14.0
1984	30 590	19.1	38 782	14.4
1983	. . .	17.9	. . .	15.2
1982	. . .	16.2	. . .	15.0
1981	. . .	19.3	. . .	14.0
1980	. . .	19.3	. . .	13.0

. . . = Not available.

Table KY-7. Employment Status by Demographic Group, 2004

(Numbers in thousands, rate.)

Characteristic	Civilian noninstitutional population	Civilian labor force		Employed	Unemployment rate
		Number	Participation rate		
SEX AND AGE					
Total	3 194	1 977	61.9	1 874	5.2
16 to 19 years	237	113	47.6	88	21.7
20 to 24 years	256	197	76.7	178	9.3
25 to 34 years	539	427	79.1	404	5.3
35 to 44 years	636	517	81.3	499	3.5
45 to 54 years	566	426	75.2	411	3.4
55 to 64 years	432	225	51.9	220	2.0
65 years and over	526	73	13.9	73	0.6
Men	1 534	1 057	68.9	998	5.6
16 to 19 years	130	66	50.8	52	21.5
20 to 24 years	117	95	81.4	84	11.6
25 to 34 years	274	244	89.2	232	5.1
35 to 44 years	306	263	86.2	252	4.2
45 to 54 years	286	230	80.3	221	3.6
55 to 64 years	200	116	58.0	115	1.3
65 years and over	223	43	19.4	43	0.7
Women	1 660	920	55.4	876	4.8
16 to 19 years	107	47	43.9	37	21.9
20 to 24 years	140	102	72.9	95	7.1
25 to 34 years	266	183	68.8	172	5.6
35 to 44 years	331	254	76.8	247	2.8
45 to 54 years	281	196	70.0	190	3.1
55 to 64 years	232	109	46.7	106	2.7
MARITAL STATUS					
Married men, spouse present	893	644	72.1	626	2.8
Married women, spouse present	899	522	58.0	508	2.5
Women who maintain families	207	121	58.7	108	10.7
RACE, HISPANIC ORIGIN, AND SEX					
White	2 893	1 781	61.6	1 698	4.7
Men	1 393	957	68.7	910	5.0
Women	1 499	824	54.9	788	4.3
Black	228	147	64.6	131	11.2
Men	105	70	67.3	61	13.7
Women	124	77	62.3	70	9.0
Hispanic or Latino[1]	48	33	68.7	30	7.2
RACE, HISPANIC ORIGIN, AND AGE					
White					
16 to 19 years	209	102	48.8	81	20.1
20 to 24 years	230	181	78.5	167	7.8
25 to 34 years	475	379	79.7	362	4.4
35 to 44 years	564	458	81.1	442	3.4
45 to 54 years	507	379	74.9	368	3.1
55 to 64 years	411	212	51.5	207	2.0
65 years and over	497	71	14.3	71	0.6
Black					
25 to 34 years	42	33	78.8	29	13.6
35 to 44 years	53	44	83.9	42	6.0
45 to 54 years	48	37	77.8	35	6.6

Note: Data in Table 7 are from the Current Population Survey (CPS) and do not match Bureau of Labor Statistics estimates in Table 8. See notes and definitions for more details.

[1] May be of any race.

Table KY-8. Employment Status, 1990–2004

(Numbers in thousands, rate.)

Year	Civilian labor force	Employed	Unemployed	Unemployment rate
2004	1 973 944	1 870 249	103 695	5.3
2003	1 979 004	1 856 204	122 800	6.2
2002	1 949 646	1 838 151	111 495	5.7
2001	1 957 166	1 854 296	102 870	5.3
2000	1 953 154	1 870 819	82 335	4.2
1999	1 944 384	1 854 270	90 114	4.6
1998	1 920 292	1 832 775	87 517	4.6
1997	1 912 591	1 809 785	102 806	5.4
1996	1 880 267	1 777 259	103 008	5.5
1995	1 860 896	1 757 111	103 785	5.6
1994	1 829 325	1 729 483	99 842	5.5
1993	1 804 000	1 689 100	114 900	6.4
1992	1 782 402	1 658 511	123 891	7.0
1991	1 770 336	1 639 343	130 993	7.4
1990	1 747 605	1 640 875	106 730	6.1

Note: Population age 16 years and over.

Unemployment Rate, 1980–2004

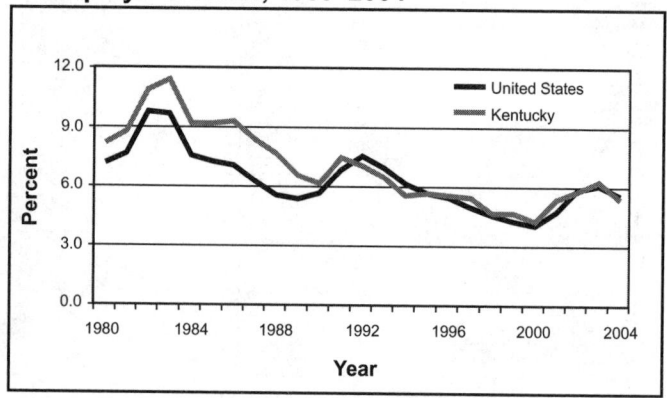

Table KY-9. Employment and Average Wages by Industry, 2001–2004

(Estimates are based on the 2002 North American Industry Classification System [NAICS].)

Industry	2001	2002	2003	2004	Annual average percent change, 2001–2004
	Number of jobs				
TOTAL EMPLOYMENT BY PLACE OF WORK	2 305 386	2 292 088	2 306 485	2 332 983	0.4
Farm Employment	111 347	111 224	113 070	110 577	-0.2
Nonfarm Employment	2 194 039	2 180 864	2 193 415	2 222 406	0.4
Private employment	1 845 278	1 834 001	1 845 373	1 875 791	0.5
Forestry, fishing, hunting, and other[1]	17 529	17 320	15 966	15 867	-3.3
Mining	23 283	22 855	22 696	23 623	0.5
Utilities	7 333	6 881	6 654	6 586	-3.5
Construction	137 491	131 159	134 508	135 605	-0.5
Manufacturing	299 516	282 327	273 103	271 133	-3.3
Durable goods manufacturing	190 636	177 634	169 831	169 373	-3.9
Nondurable goods manufacturing	108 880	104 693	103 272	101 760	-2.2
Wholesale trade	78 547	77 352	78 467	80 221	0.7
Retail trade	265 399	263 425	263 385	265 818	0.1
Transportation and warehousing	99 143	96 864	95 585	96 516	-0.9
Information	37 305	35 173	34 268	32 971	-4.0
Finance and insurance	79 808	82 655	83 950	86 022	2.5
Real estate and rental and leasing	56 171	56 518	59 206	61 516	3.1
Professional and technical services	91 311	91 384	91 959	93 105	0.7
Management of companies and enterprises	14 440	14 350	14 215	15 856	3.2
Administrative and waste services	106 053	108 637	110 955	118 548	3.8
Educational services	30 756	31 601	33 019	34 272	3.7
Health care and social assistance	210 763	218 196	224 361	227 380	2.6
Arts, entertainment, and recreation	30 031	31 125	31 340	32 283	2.4
Accommodation and food services	142 582	143 172	146 837	152 233	2.2
Other services, except public administration	117 817	123 007	124 899	126 236	2.3
Government and government enterprises	348 761	346 863	348 042	346 615	-0.2
	Dollars				
AVERAGE WAGES AND SALARIES BY PLACE OF WORK	29 334	30 303	31 229	32 517	3.5
Farm Earnings	13 308	16 898	14 168	15 801	5.9
Nonfarm Earnings	29 476	30 419	31 415	32 694	3.5
Private earnings	29 526	30 279	31 197	32 430	3.2
Forestry, fishing, hunting, and other[1]	20 201	20 182	20 284	22 274	3.3
Mining	45 204	45 770	46 259	48 507	2.4
Utilities	61 052	56 777	56 745	58 288	-1.5
Construction	32 785	33 281	34 129	34 456	1.7
Manufacturing	38 009	39 597	41 316	43 152	4.3
Durable goods manufacturing	39 413	41 056	42 877	44 832	4.4
Nondurable goods manufacturing	35 555	37 123	38 755	40 361	4.3
Wholesale trade	40 192	41 302	42 419	44 953	3.8
Retail trade	19 030	19 726	20 344	20 897	3.2
Transportation and warehousing	39 212	39 677	41 679	43 805	3.8
Information	35 098	35 275	35 725	37 946	2.6
Finance and insurance	40 224	41 733	44 061	46 212	4.7
Real estate and rental and leasing	23 806	25 034	25 784	26 838	4.1
Professional and technical services	41 998	42 082	43 147	45 121	2.4
Management of companies and enterprises	64 192	68 690	70 841	73 876	4.8
Administrative and waste services	18 407	19 546	19 946	20 472	3.6
Educational services	17 816	18 293	18 942	19 812	3.6
Health care and social assistance	30 454	31 348	32 228	33 728	3.5
Arts, entertainment, and recreation	17 166	18 047	19 171	19 514	4.4
Accommodation and food services	12 200	12 695	12 708	12 912	1.9
Other services, except public administration	19 764	20 403	21 323	22 086	3.8
Government and government enterprises	29 260	31 032	32 365	33 864	5.0

Note: Average wages and salaries are a calculation by the editors of wage and salary disbursements divided by full- and part-time wage and salary employment. Data may not add to total or may appear as zero due to rounding.

[1] "Other" consists of the number of jobs held by U.S. residents employed by international organizations and foreign embassies and consulates in the United States.

LABOR MARKET

The unemployment rate increased significantly as a result of the 2001 recession. However, by 2004, it was below the national average and about in line with those of its neighboring states. (Ohio and Illinois, which had higher rates, were exceptions.) The government sector was Kentucky's largest employer, followed by manufacturing, retail trade, and health care services. Total wage and salary employment recovered slowly from the 2001 recession. Government employment declined between 2001 and 2004. Information and manufacturing (particularly durable goods) were hardest hit, as 2004 employment levels in these sectors remained below those of 2001. Average wages and salaries in Kentucky were markedly lower than the national average across most industries.

Employment by Industry, 2004

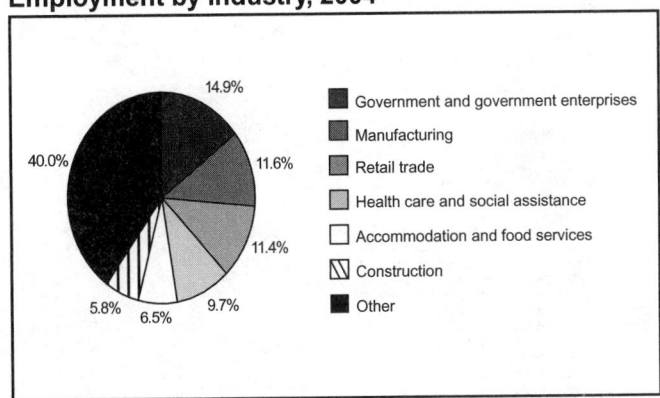

- Government and government enterprises
- Manufacturing
- Retail trade
- Health care and social assistance
- Accommodation and food services
- Construction
- Other

Table KY-10. Personal Income by Major Source, Selected Years 1980–2004

(Millions of dollars, except where noted.)

Item	1980	1990	2000	2001	2002	2003	2004	Average annual percent change, 2000–2004
Earnings by Place of Work	23 488	42 475	73 872	75 456	77 534	81 228	85 485	3.7
Wage and salary disbursements	17 000	30 977	54 278	55 816	57 006	58 872	61 792	3.3
Supplements to wages and salaries	3 638	6 944	11 865	12 327	14 001	15 745	16 315	8.3
Proprietors' income[1]	2 851	4 555	7 730	7 314	6 527	6 612	7 378	-1.2
Farm proprietors' income	396	845	1 240	700	-151	19	225	-34.7
Nonfarm proprietors' income	2 455	3 710	6 490	6 614	6 678	6 592	7 152	2.5
(-) Contributions for government social insurance[2]	2 064	4 677	8 182	8 478	8 808	9 124	9 590	4.1
(+) Adjustment for residence[3]	28	-101	-719	-976	-1 054	-1 323	-1 436	X
(=) Net Earnings by Place of Residence	21 453	37 697	64 972	66 002	67 672	70 782	74 458	3.5
(+) Dividends, interest, and rent[4]	4 059	10 361	17 137	17 191	16 449	15 810	16 502	-0.9
(+) Personal current transfer receipts	4 453	8 968	16 736	18 153	19 498	20 097	21 606	6.6
Personal income	29 965	57 026	98 845	101 346	103 619	106 688	112 566	3.3
Farm income	29 422	55 992	97 416	100 405	103 477	106 358	112 001	3.5
Nonfarm income	543	1 034	1 430	942	142	330	564	-20.7
Per Capita Personal Income (Dollars)[5]	8 178	15 437	24 412	24 914	25 335	25 907	27 151	2.7

Note: Data may not add to total or may appear as zero due to rounding.

[1]Proprietors' income includes the inventory valuation adjustment and the capital consumption adjustment.
[2]Contributions for government social insurance are included in earnings by type and industry, but they are excluded from personal income.
[3]The adjustment for residence is the net inflow of the earnings of interarea commuters.
[4]Rental income of persons includes the capital consumption adjustment.
[5]Per capita personal income is total personal income divided by total midyear population.
X = Not applicable.

Per Capita Personal Income, 1980–2004 (Current Dollars)

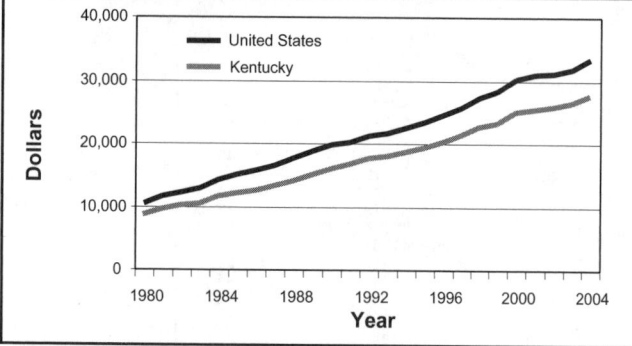

ECONOMIC ACTIVITY

Real gross state product (GSP) grew at a rate slightly above the national average during its recovery from the 2001 recession. However, GSP grew at a below average rate from 2003 to 2004. The sectors with the highest rates of growth from 2001 to 2004 were information, administrative and waste services, and retail trade. Kentucky's largest sector in 2004 was manufacturing, which accounted for 22.3 percent of the GSP. Agriculture, mining, and construction have fared poorly since 2000. There was appreciation in housing prices in some areas of the state, primarily in areas associated with horse farm estates; however, the median value of owner-occupied housing in Kentucky remained well below the national average.

Table KY-11. Real Gross State Product, 1997–2004

(Millions of chained 2000 dollars, percent.)

Industry	1997	1998	1999	2000	2001	2002	2003	2004	Average annual percent change, 2001–2004
GROSS STATE PRODUCT	111 576	114 350	116 689	112 737	113 530	116 269	120 508	125 021	3.3
As a percent of U.S. gross product	1.3	1.3	1.2	1.2	1.2	1.2	1.2	1.2	X
Private Industries	95 725	98 570	100 810	97 146	97 983	100 469	103 728	107 601	3.2
Agriculture, forestry, fishing, and hunting	1 603	1 599	1 600	2 274	1 798	1 597	1 725	1 505	-5.8
Mining	2 078	2 257	2 352	2 232	2 300	2 303	2 181	2 091	-3.1
Utilities	1 784	1 767	1 793	1 795	1 715	1 730	1 814	1 856	2.7
Construction	5 168	5 216	5 241	5 120	4 987	4 724	4 777	4 681	-2.1
Manufacturing	30 733	30 930	30 550	25 046	24 245	25 244	26 519	27 867	4.8
As a percent of gross state product	27.5	27.0	26.2	22.2	21.4	21.7	22.0	22.3	X
Wholesale trade	5 557	6 322	6 644	6 668	7 170	7 392	7 236	7 616	2.0
Retail trade	7 251	7 578	7 857	8 081	8 430	9 005	9 483	9 912	5.5
Transportation and warehousing	4 476	4 870	5 217	5 386	5 318	5 415	5 803	6 052	4.4
Information	2 221	2 361	2 477	2 659	2 974	3 157	3 293	3 591	6.5
Finance and insurance	4 195	4 227	4 386	4 753	5 502	5 637	5 871	6 312	4.7
Real estate and rental and leasing	9 146	9 322	9 907	10 097	10 626	10 686	10 713	10 988	1.1
Services	21 568	22 111	22 786	23 037	22 959	23 686	24 484	25 441	3.5
As a percent of gross state product	19.3	19.3	19.5	20.4	20.2	20.4	20.3	20.3	X
Professional and technical services	3 923	4 148	4 415	4 762	4 843	4 920	5 274	5 450	4.0
Management of companies and enterprises	1 571	1 493	1 469	1 449	1 200	1 248	1 264	1 391	5.0
Administrative and waste services	2 146	2 217	2 337	2 348	2 236	2 444	2 546	2 703	6.5
Educational services	488	502	522	549	554	551	538	542	-0.7
Health care and social assistance	7 595	7 622	7 927	7 843	8 199	8 514	8 771	8 987	3.1
Arts, entertainment, and recreation	586	598	623	634	631	670	679	691	3.1
Accommodation and food services	2 764	2 947	2 920	2 917	2 883	2 949	2 975	3 097	2.4
Other services, except public administration	2 495	2 584	2 573	2 535	2 413	2 390	2 437	2 580	2.3
Government	15 873	15 784	15 876	15 591	15 547	15 804	16 762	17 396	3.8
As a percent of gross state product	14.2	13.8	13.6	13.8	13.7	13.6	13.9	13.9	X

X = Not applicable.

Table KY-12. Government Transfer Payments, Selected Years 1980–2004

(Millions of dollars, percent.)

Item	1980	1990	2000	2001	2002	2003	2004	Average annual percent change, 2000–2004
CURRENT TRANSFER PAYMENTS TO INDIVIDUALS	4 200	8 475	15 778	17 069	18 460	19 060	20 546	6.8
Retirement and Disability Insurance Benefits	2 165	4 123	6 686	7 054	7 411	7 724	8 045	4.7
Old-age, survivors, and disability insurance (OASDI) benefits	1 805	3 658	6 205	6 581	6 936	7 249	7 568	5.1
Railroad retirement and disability benefits	110	170	211	218	228	234	238	3.0
Workers' compensation	50	128	146	138	130	127	132	-2.5
Other government retirement and disability insurance benefits	200	168	123	118	116	114	107	-3.4
Medical Benefits	767	2 675	6 439	7 007	7 631	7 677	8 764	8.0
Medicare benefits	443	1 543	3 065	3 401	3 645	3 865	4 252	8.5
Public assistance medical care benefits	314	1 076	3 309	3 514	3 860	3 699	4 381	7.3
Military medical insurance benefits	10	56	65	92	126	112	131	19.1
Income Maintenance Benefits	594	1 022	1 764	1 861	2 032	2 228	2 399	8.0
Supplemental Security Income (SSI) benefits	163	350	758	797	822	838	876	3.7
Family assistance	139	184	137	148	142	141	149	2.1
Food stamps	222	345	337	360	421	501	563	13.7
Other income maintenance benefits	69	143	532	556	647	748	812	11.2
Unemployment Insurance Compensation	341	213	290	453	643	646	499	14.6
Veterans' Benefits	268	319	424	447	493	532	571	7.7
Federal Education and Training Assistance	64	121	168	230	243	246	258	11.4
Other Payments to Individuals	1	2	8	16	7	8	11	6.2

Note: See notes and definitions for more details. Data may not add to total or may appear as zero due to rounding.

EXPORTS

Kentucky's exports ranked 19th in the nation, with a total value of nearly $13 billion. Total exports increased nearly 43 percent from 2001 to 2004. The state's chief export product was transportation equipment, followed by chemical and machinery manufactures. Exports of computers and electronic products recovered somewhat in 2004; however, they remained well below their 2001 value. Canada was the top market for Kentucky's exports, receiving over 35 percent of the state's exported goods. In 2004, France became the second leading market for Kentucky's exports. Transportation equipment made up more than 88 percent of exports to France.

Leading Exports, 2004

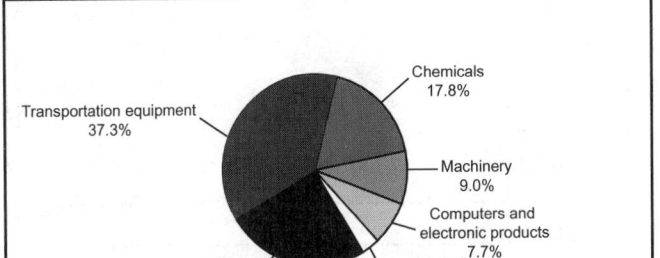

Table KY-13. Exports of Goods by Leading Products and Destinations, 2001–2004

(Millions of dollars, percent, rank based on 2004 dollar values.)

Product and market	2001	2002	2003	2004	Percent share of total, 2004	Average annual percent change, 2001–2004
Total Goods						
Total	9 048	10 607	10 734	12 992	100.0	12.8
Manufactures	8 433	10 146	10 039	12 489	96.1	14.0
Agriculture and livestock	449	307	527	305	2.4	-12.0
Other commodities	167	153	167	197	1.5	5.8
Five Leading Exports (NAICS Code)						
Transportation equipment (336)	3 036	4 466	3 707	4 852	37.3	16.9
Chemical manufactures (325)	1 341	1 766	2 017	2 314	17.8	19.9
Machinery manufactures (333)	747	824	917	1 163	9.0	15.9
Computers and electronic products (334)	1 132	827	740	999	7.7	-4.1
Fabricated metal products (332)	302	330	341	394	3.0	9.2
Five Leading Markets	8 201	9 871	10 054	12 308	94.7	14.5
Canada	2 954	3 652	3 424	4 633	35.7	16.2
France	432	795	741	1 084	8.3	35.9
United Kingdom	802	824	850	959	7.4	6.1
Japan	838	1 003	983	865	6.7	1.0
Mexico	434	469	518	786	6.1	21.9

Table KY-14. Agriculture, 1997 and 2002

(Number, acres, and dollars.)

Item	1997	2002
Number of farms	91 198	86 541
Land in farms (acres)	13 940 180	13 843 706
Farm Size		
Average size of farm (acres)	153	160
Farms by size (percent distribution)		
Fewer than 50 acres	35.7	34.8
50 to 499 acres	58.9	59.6
500 acres or more	5.4	5.6
Market Value of Land and Equipment (Dollars)		
Land and buildings average value per farm	222 914	294 056
Average value per acre	1 470	1 824
Machinery and equipment average value per farm	32 604	41 458
Value of Sales (Thousands of Dollars)		
Agricultural products sold	3 158 783	3 080 080
Crops	1 610 935	1 110 209
Livestock, poultry, and their products	1 547 847	1 969 871
Average per farm (dollars)	34 637	35 591
Value of sales (percent distribution)		
Less than $10,000	58.9	67.3
$10,000 to $99,999	34.8	26.8
$100,000 or more	6.3	5.9
Government Payments		
Payments (thousands of dollars)	58 730	94 053
Percent of farms receiving government payments	27.6	26.4
Farm operators whose principal occupation is farming (percent)	39.5	54.2

AGRICULTURE

Although Kentucky had a large number of horse farms with sizable acreage, cash receipts from farming totaled only about $3 billion, the 28th highest in the nation. Crops made up about 36 percent of total sales. In 2002, over two-thirds of the farms had receipts of less than $10,000. Horses, tobacco, and cattle were Kentucky's chief products. Only 5.6 percent of farms spanned 500 acres or more, which was among the smallest proportions of large farms in the nation. The average farm in Kentucky was 160 acres, compared with the national average of 441 acres.

ENERGY

Kentucky's energy prices per million Btu were among the lowest in the nation. However, the state's energy expenditures per person of $2,709 ranked 12th in the nation. The state's per capita consumption ranked sixth in the country in 2001. Coal was the leading energy source, followed by petroleum.

Energy Consumption by Source, 2001

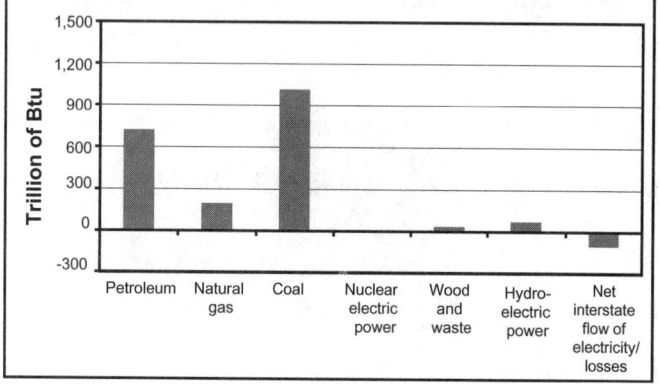

Energy Consumption by Sector, 2001

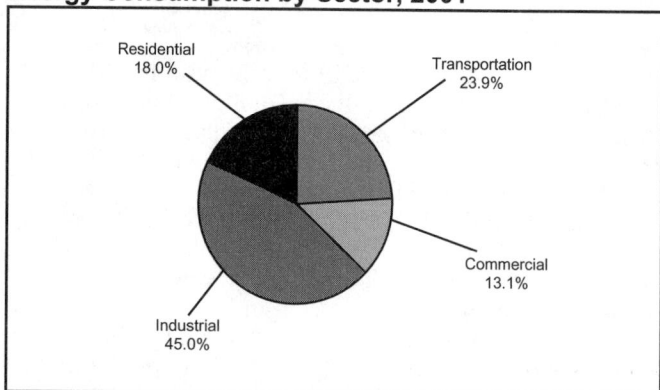

Table KY-15. Energy Consumption, Expenditures, and Prices, Selected Years 1960–2001

(Dollars, Btu [British Thermal Unit], percent distribution.)

Item	1960	1965	1970	1975	1980	1985	1990	1995	2000	2001
Total Consumption (Billion Btu)	824 101	905 928	1 116 534	1 293 836	1 399 146	1 332 836	1 494 862	1 786 151	1 877 796	1 879 463
Consumption per capita (million Btu)	271.3	288.5	346.7	373.1	382.2	360.7	405.6	463.3	464.6	462.1
Consumption by Sector (Percent Distribution)										
Residential	16.4	16.0	19.1	17.5	18.6	20.0	18.4	18.4	18.6	18.0
Commercial	6.3	6.6	9.0	10.0	11.8	12.0	11.9	11.5	13.2	13.1
Industrial	58.6	56.2	48.5	50.2	46.4	44.0	44.5	46.4	44.7	45.0
Transportation	18.6	21.2	23.4	22.3	23.2	24.0	25.2	23.6	23.5	23.9
Consumption by Source (Billion Btu)										
Coal	286 738	415 492	527 054	558 334	641 685	716 929	803 502	929 390	997 627	1 010 706
Natural gas	153 807	176 734	252 265	209 199	204 104	177 685	191 707	245 578	234 180	216 707
Petroleum	201 268	262 060	369 314	429 923	516 302	451 652	507 091	597 287	699 774	704 310
Nuclear electric power	0	0	0	0	0	0	0	0	0	0
Hydroelectric power[1]	28 333	25 760	33 303	36 035	30 538	30 727	32 874	35 303	23 713	39 226
Wood and waste	22 418	21 678	23 719	30 821	19 649	35 991	16 738	16 499	10 815	9 685
Other	0	0	0	0	0	0	0	240	601	676
Net interstate flow of electricity/losses[2]	131 538	4 205	-89 122	29 523	-13 131	-80 149	-57 290	-38 310	-88 914	-101 846
Total Expenditures (Thousands of Dollars)	...	...	1 305 300	2 706 700	6 217 500	6 789 100	7 342 400	8 171 200	10 995 100	11 017 800
Expenditures per capita (dollars)	...	...	405	780	1 698	1 838	1 992	2 120	2 720	2 709
Prices by Sector (Dollars Per Million Btu)										
Total	...	...	1.66	3.26	6.74	7.92	7.81	7.28	9.22	9.29
Residential	...	...	1.84	3.19	6.84	9.94	10.23	10.06	11.90	13.07
Commercial	...	...	1.54	2.54	5.92	7.83	9.67	9.18	10.67	11.72
Industrial	...	...	1.01	2.64	5.24	6.90	5.65	4.97	6.46	6.61
Transportation	...	...	2.58	4.34	8.82	8.19	8.70	8.37	10.96	10.36

[1]A negative number in this row results from pumped storage for which, overall, more electricity is expended than created to provide electricity during peak demand periods.
[2]Net interstate flow of electricity is the difference between the amount of energy in the electricity sold within a state (including associated losses) and the energy input at the electric utilities within the state. A positive number indicates that more electricity (including associated losses) came into the state than went out of the state during the year; conversely, a negative number indicates that more electricity (including associated losses) went out of the state than came into the state.
... = Not available.

Table KY-16. State Taxes, Fiscal 2004

(Dollars, percent distribution.)

Item	Thousands of dollars	Percent distribution	Dollars per capita	
			State	U.S.
TOTAL TAXES	8 463 400	100.0	2 041.3	2 024.8
Property Taxes	455 460	5.4	109.9	38.9
Sales and Gross Receipts	4 006 307	47.3	966.3	1 003.4
General sales and gross receipts	2 466 033	29.1	594.8	677.0
Selective sales taxes	1 540 274	18.2	371.5	326.4
Alcoholic beverages	79 104	0.9	19.1	15.7
Insurance premiums	331 903	3.9	80.0	47.0
Motor fuels	476 605	5.6	115.0	114.6
Other selective sales	616 337	7.3	148.7	49.8
Licenses	542 480	6.4	130.8	134.9
Corporation	198 245	2.3	47.8	21.6
Motor vehicle	205 314	2.4	49.5	59.4
Occupation and business, not elsewhere classified	85 419	1.0	20.6	37.1
Other Taxes	3 459 153	40.9	834.3	847.6
Individual income	2 819 393	33.3	680.0	673.6
Corporation net income	381 538	4.5	92.0	105.1
Death and gift	67 679	0.8	16.3	19.6
Severance	187 109	2.2	45.1	21.5

GOVERNMENT FINANCE

Kentucky ranked 22nd in the nation for both per capita expenditures and per capita revenue. Both of these dollar figures were above the U.S. averages. Expenditures on highway and public spending were above average on a per capita basis. The state's taxes per person in fiscal year 2004 amounted to $2,041, just above the U.S. average. The largest share of revenue was derived from individual income taxes, followed by general sales taxes. Kentucky's property taxes ranked 9th in the nation among the 37 states with such taxes. The state's debt per capita was $1,726, which ranked 36th in the country.

Per Capita State Taxes, Fiscal 2004

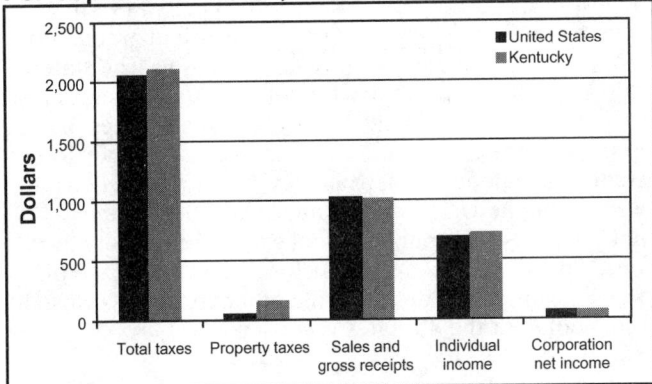

Table KY-17. State Government Finances, 2003

(Dollars, percent distribution.)

Item	Millions of dollars	Percent distribution	Dollars per capita	
			State	U.S.
GENERAL REVENUE	16 525 770	100.0	4 013.1	3 832.6
Intergovernmental revenue	5 330 212	32.3	1 294.4	1 246.0
Taxes	8 318 707	50.3	2 020.1	1 891.6
General sales	2 387 206	14.4	579.7	636.0
Selective sales	1 496 639	9.1	363.4	307.4
License taxes	536 797	3.2	130.4	123.6
Individual income tax	2 813 947	17.0	683.3	626.8
Corporate income tax	369 572	2.2	89.8	97.8
Other taxes	714 546	4.3	173.5	99.9
Current charges	1 645 971	10.0	399.7	366.5
Miscellaneous general revenue	1 230 880	7.4	298.9	328.6
GENERAL EXPENDITURE	16 857 615	100.0	4 093.6	4 010.5
Intergovernmental expenditure	3 693 634	21.9	897.0	1 316.9
Direct expenditure	13 163 981	78.1	3 196.7	2 693.6
Expenditure by Function				
Education	6 096 709	36.2	1 480.5	1 416.4
Public welfare	4 964 095	29.4	1 205.5	1 083.3
Hospitals	523 447	3.1	127.1	132.3
Health	519 701	3.1	126.2	173.0
Highways	1 816 167	10.8	441.0	295.4
Police protection	188 584	1.1	45.8	38.4
Correction	474 334	2.8	115.2	135.0
Natural resources	316 167	1.9	76.8	64.0
Parks and recreation	130 579	0.8	31.7	20.1
Government administration	678 823	4.0	164.8	151.3
Interest on general debt	436 241	2.6	105.9	107.8
Other and unallocable	712 768	4.2	173.1	393.4
DEBT AT END OF FISCAL YEAR	7 108 634	X	1 726.2	2 404.7
CASH AND SECURITY HOLDINGS	32 921 671	X	7 994.6	8 938.4

X = Not applicable.

Table KY-18. Education Indicators, 2000–2004

(Percent, number.)

Item	State	U.S.
Total Population 25 Years and Over (Thousands), 2004	2 754	186 877
Educational Attainment, 2004		
Percent high school graduate or more	81.8	85.2
Percent college graduate or more	21.0	27.7
Elementary and Secondary Schools, 2002–2003		
Total students	660 782	48 202 324
Percent of students eligible for free or reduced-price lunch ..	. . .	40.6
Percent of students who were English language learners	1.3	7.8
Total schools	1 381	92 330
Student/teacher ratio	16.1	15.9
Per student expenditures	6 661	8 041
Dropouts, Grades 9–12, 2000–2001 (Percent)	4.0	. . .
Higher Education, 2002–2003		
Total enrollment	227 268	17 035 027
Bachelor's degrees awarded	16 254	1 348 503
Percent women	59.4	57.5

. . . = Not available.

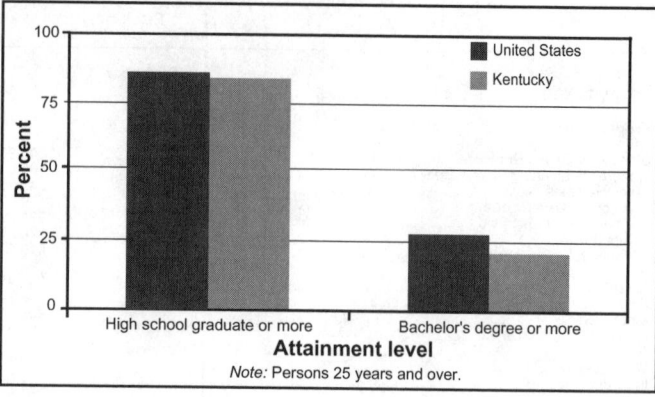

Educational Attainment, 2004

Note: Persons 25 years and over.

EDUCATION

Kentucky's educational attainment rates were among the lowest in the nation. In 2004, only 81.8 percent of the state's population age 25 years and over had graduated from high school, ranking 44th in the nation. The state ranked 48th in the country for college attainment, as just 21 percent of its residents held bachelor's degrees or more. Despite having a lower than average proportion of student-age population, Kentucky's student/teacher ratio was above the U.S. average and ranked 16th in the nation. The state's public school expenditures per student were $6,661, which was well below the U.S. average of $8,041. Kentucky's dropout rate of 4 percent was close to the median of the 46 states reporting data.

VOTER PARTICIPATION

Voter turnout was below the national average in 2000, but significantly above the national average in 2004. The proportion of women voting increased 10 percentage points from 2000 to 2004. Persons age 45 to 74 years had the highest voter participation rates, with a turnout of over 70 percent. More than 53 percent of eligible voters age 18 to 24 years reported voting in the 2004 election. Nationally, just 41.9 percent of this age group voted in 2004. Blacks had a voter turnout of about 68 percent, which was above the non-Hispanic White participation rate of less than 64 percent. The Republican presidential ticket took 56.5 percent of the vote in 2000, and 59.5 percent of the vote in 2004.

Table KY-19. Reported Voting and Registration, November 2000 and November 2004

(Numbers in thousands, percent.)

Characteristic	Total population 18 years and over	Total citizen		Total registered		Total voted	
		Number	Percent	Number	Percent	Number	Percent
NOVEMBER 2000							
Total	2 996	2 918	97.4	2 087	69.7	1 645	54.9
Male	1 398	1 356	97.0	963	68.8	760	54.3
Female	1 597	1 562	97.8	1 125	70.4	886	55.5
NOVEMBER 2004							
Total	3 042	2 969	97.6	2 231	73.3	1 930	63.4
Male	1 454	1 407	96.8	1 039	71.5	884	60.8
Female	1 588	1 562	98.4	1 192	75.1	1 046	65.9
Race and Hispanic Origin							
White alone	2 775	2 729	98.4	2 041	73.6	1 765	63.6
Non-Hispanic White alone	2 736	2 709	99.0	2 024	74.0	1 749	63.9
Black alone	204	198	97.2	158	77.3	140	68.5
Asian alone	27	6	B	6	B	6	B
Hispanic or Latino[1]	44	20	B	18	B	16	B
White alone or in combination	2 799	2 754	98.4	2 061	73.6	1 778	63.5
Non-Hispanic White alone or in combination	2 760	2 733	99.0	2 044	74.0	1 763	63.9
Black alone or in combination	205	200	97.2	158	76.8	140	68.0
Asian alone or in combination	27	6	B	6	B	6	B
Age							
18 to 24 years	362	346	95.5	229	63.1	198	53.1
25 to 44 years	1 147	1 098	95.8	778	67.8	686	59.8
45 to 64 years	1 012	1 006	99.4	811	80.1	710	70.1
65 to 74 years	296	296	100.0	243	82.0	216	72.8
75 years and over	224	222	99.3	171	76.2	126	56.2

[1]May be of any race.
B = Base is too small to show derived measure.

At a Glance:

- The population of Louisiana was just over 4.5 million in 2004, ranking it as the 24th most populous state in the nation. However, since Hurricane Katrina struck in August 2005, the demographic and economic profile of the state has been dramatically impacted. Therefore, the data in *State Profiles* provide a portrait of Louisiana prior to the hurricane. Data from 2005 and beyond may show an entirely different picture of the state.

- In 2004, the population of Louisiana was 61.8 percent non-Hispanic White and nearly 33 percent Black, giving the state the third highest proportion of this racial group in the country.

- The median household income in Louisiana was well below the national average in 2004, reflecting earnings trends throughout the Gulf region. Louisiana's poverty rate was the fourth highest in the nation.

- Among persons age 25 years and over, Louisiana ranked 50th for the proportion of its population with a high school diploma and 45th for the proportion with a bachelor's degree or more.

- Louisiana's age-adjusted mortality rate for all causes of death was the third highest in the nation.

Table LA-1. Population by Sex and Age, 1990, 2000, and 2004

(Number, percent.)

Sex and age	1990	2000	2004	Percent distribution, 2004	Average annual percent change, 2000–2004
Total Population	4 219 973	4 468 976	4 515 770	X	0.3
Percent of total U.S. population	1.7	1.6	1.5	X	X
Sex					
Male	2 031 386	2 162 903	2 193 983	48.6	0.4
Female	2 188 587	2 306 073	2 321 787	51.4	0.2
Age					
Under 5 years	334 650	317 392	323 991	7.2	-0.4
5 to 17 years	892 619	902 407	840 970	18.6	-0.4
18 years and over	749 344	3 249 177	3 350 809	74.2	0.8
18 to 24 years	2 992 704	473 801	503 192	11.1	0.5
25 to 44 years	464 511	1 293 128	1 239 938	27.5	-0.4
45 to 64 years	1 309 858	965 319	1 080 035	23.9	2.7
65 years and over	468 991	516 929	527 644	11.7	0.9
85 years and over	43 633	58 676	60 321	1.3	2.5
Median age (years)	30.9	34.0	34.9	X	X

X = Not applicable.

Average Annual Rate of Population Growth, 1980–2004

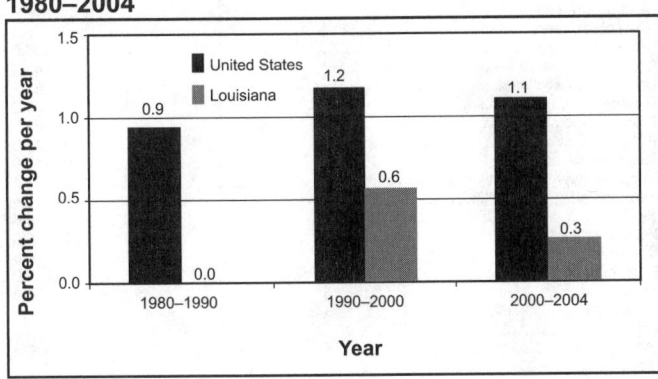

POPULATION

A sizable proportion of the resident population evacuated in the aftermath of Hurricanes Katrina and Rita; consequently, accurate estimates for Louisiana and the other Gulf States will remain difficult to ascertain for some time. Although some signs favor the return of many of its residents, this is by no means certain. The widespread devastation, uncertainties of future protection from strong hurricane forces, and difficulties in streamlining insurance reimbursements and obtaining financing for rebuilding destroyed properties will all influence future population movements. Before the storms, Louisiana's population had been growing quite slowly, increasing just 1.0 percent from 2000 to 2004.

Table LA-2. Population by Race and Hispanic Origin, 1990, 2000, and 2004

(Number, percent.)

Race and Hispanic origin	1990	2000	2004
Total Population	4 219 973	4 468 976	4 515 770
Non-Hispanic (Percent)			
One race[1]			
White	65.8	62.7	61.8
Black	30.6	32.4	32.8
American Indian, Alaska Native[2]	0.4	0.5	0.6
Asian and Pacific Islander[2]	1.0	1.3	1.4
Other race[2]	0.5	. . .	. . .
Two or more races	. . .	0.7	0.8
Hispanic or Latino[3] (Percent)	2.2	2.4	2.8

[1]Individuals could report only one race in the 1990 census and could report one or more races on the 2000 census. Data on race in 2000 and 2004 are not comparable to 1990.
[2]Data for 1990 include people of Hispanic or Latino origin.
[3]May be of any race.
. . . = Not available.

Minority Population as a Percent of Total Population, 2004

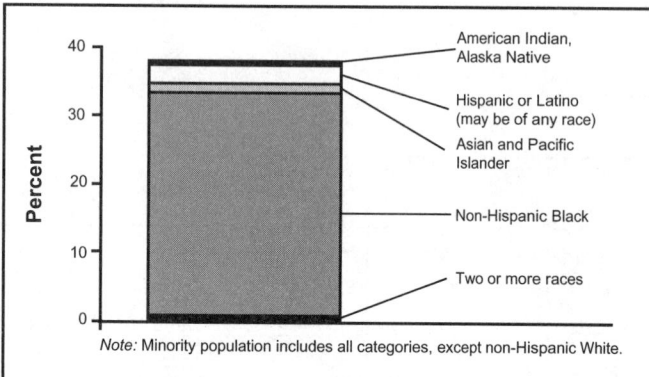

Note: Minority population includes all categories, except non-Hispanic White.

Age-Adjusted Death Rates, Average 2000–2002

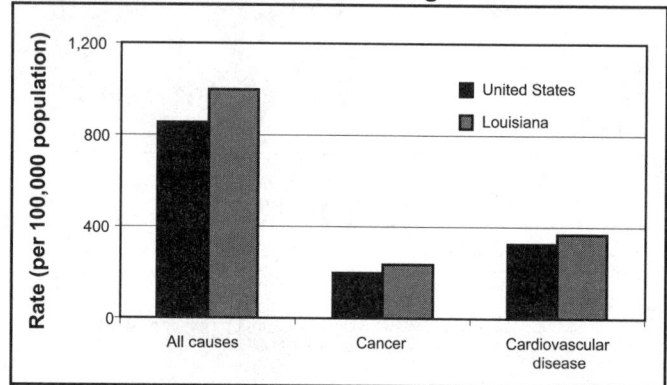

HEALTH

Although health insurance coverage in Louisiana expanded to more residents in recent years, it remained low in comparison to most other states. Louisiana's infant mortality rate was the third highest in the nation. The teenage birth rate was among the 10 highest in the nation.

Table LA-3. Health Characteristics, 2000–2004

(Number, rate, percent.)

Item	State	U.S.
Births, 2003–2004		
Number of births	65 040	4 089 950
Birth rate (per 1,000 population)	14.5	14.1
Teenage birth rate (per 1,000 women age 15–19 years)	56.0	41.6
Mortality Rates, Average 2000–2002		
Infant mortality rate (per 1,000 live births)	9.8	6.9
Age-adjusted mortality rate (per 100,000 population)		
All races	1 002.7	853.3
Non-Hispanic White	940.0	843.1
Black	1 205.9	1 097.7
American Indian, Alaska Native	. . .	687.0
Asian and Pacific Islander	492.2	486.0
Hispanic or Latino[1]	539.0	642.7
Health Insurance, 2004		
Percent of all persons without health insurance	17.2	15.7
Percent of children without health insurance	8.0	11.2
Percent of low-income children without health insurance	6.8	7.1

[1]May be of any race.
. . . = Not available.

Table LA-4. Leading Causes of Death, Average 2000–2002

(Number, rate per 100,000 population.)

Cause	Number of deaths	Age-adjusted death rates	
		State	U.S.
ALL CAUSES	41 626	1 002.7	853.3
Leading Causes			
Major cardiovascular diseases	14 919	364.8	326.5
Cancer	9 453	225.9	196.0
Chronic lower respiratory diseases	1 714	41.8	43.7
Unintentional injuries	2 050	46.8	35.7
Diabetes (underlying cause)	1 734	41.7	25.2
Influenza and pneumonia	956	23.8	22.7
Alzheimer's disease	960	24.3	19.0
Motor vehicle accidents	957	21.4	15.0
Nephritis, nephrotic syndrome, and nephrosis ..	965	23.5	13.8
Septicemia	785	19.2	11.4
Suicides	487	11.1	10.7
Firearm-related	816	18.2	10.3
Cirrhosis	353	8.2	9.5
Drug-induced	385	8.8	7.9
Alcohol-induced	221	5.1	6.9
Homicides	582	12.8	6.0
Falls	140	3.4	5.2
HIV	385	8.9	5.0
Viral hepatitis	144	3.3	2.0
Anemias	111	2.7	1.6
Drownings	119	2.7	1.3
Fire deaths	103	2.4	1.2

Note: The rates are age-adjusted to the U.S. 2000 standard population.

Table LA-5. Households and Housing Characteristics, 1990, 2000, and 2004

(Number, percent, and dollars.)

Characteristic	1990	2000	2004	Average annual percent change, 2000–2004
Total Households	1 499 269	1 656 053	1 713 680	0.9
Family households	1 089 882	1 156 438	1 170 815	0.3
Married-couple family	803 282	809 498	803 838	-0.2
Other family	286 600	346 940	366 977	1.4
Male householder, no wife present	52 471	71 865	76 662	1.6
Female householder, no husband present	234 129	275 075	290 315	1.4
Nonfamily households	409 387	499 615	542 865	2.1
Householder living alone	356 060	419 200	457 447	2.2
Householder not living alone	53 327	80 415	85 418	1.5
Housing Characteristics				
Average size	2.74	2.62	2.56	X
Housing units	1 716 241	1 847 181	1 919 859	1.0
Occupied housing units	1 499 269	1 656 053	1 713 680	0.9
Owner-occupied	987 919	1 125 135	1 134 672	0.2
Renter-occupied	511 350	530 918	579 008	2.2
Median gross rent of renter-occupied housing units (dollars)	352	466	540	3.8
Median value of owner-occupied housing units (dollars)	58 000	85 000	95 910	3.1

X = Not applicable.

Median Housing Value and Median Rent, 2004

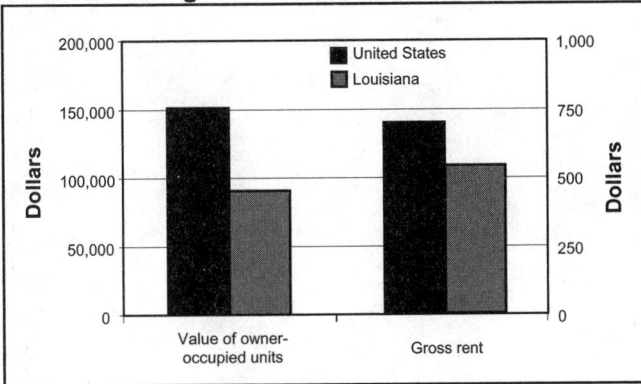

Median Household Income, 1984–2004 (2004 Dollars)

Table LA-6. Household Income and Poverty Status, 1980–2004

(2004 CPI-U-RS adjusted dollars, rate.)

Year	State		U.S.	
	Median household income (2004 dollars)	Poverty rate	Median household income (2004 dollars)	Poverty rate
2004	36 440	16.7	44 389	12.7
2003	34 408	17.0	44 482	12.5
2002	35 722	17.5	44 546	12.1
2001	35 558	16.2	45 062	11.7
2000	33 694	17.2	46 058	11.3
1999	37 013	19.2	46 129	11.9
1998	36 728	19.1	45 003	12.7
1997	39 035	16.3	43 430	13.3
1996	36 275	20.5	42 544	13.7
1995	34 402	19.7	41 943	13.8
1994	32 372	25.7	40 677	14.5
1993	33 872	26.4	40 217	15.1
1992	33 565	24.5	40 422	14.8
1991	34 217	19.0	40 746	14.2
1990	31 399	23.6	41 963	13.5
1989	33 631	23.3	42 524	12.8
1988	31 449	22.8	41 771	13.0
1987	33 949	25.1	41 322	13.4
1986	34 351	22.0	40 939	13.6
1985	35 462	18.1	39 545	14.0
1984	32 785	20.6	38 782	14.4
1983	. . .	21.5	. . .	15.2
1982	. . .	22.7	. . .	15.0
1981	. . .	22.0	. . .	14.0
1980	. . .	20.3	. . .	13.0

. . . = Not available.

Table LA-7. Employment Status by Demographic Group, 2004
(Numbers in thousands, rate.)

Characteristic	Civilian noninstitutional population	Civilian labor force		Employed	Unemployment rate
		Number	Participation rate		
SEX AND AGE					
Total	3 377	2 058	60.9	1 934	6.0
16 to 19 years	262	90	34.2	71	21.2
20 to 24 years	372	257	68.9	229	10.6
25 to 34 years	570	444	78.0	415	6.6
35 to 44 years	607	475	78.3	458	3.5
45 to 54 years	619	481	77.8	461	4.3
55 to 64 years	432	251	58.1	241	4.0
65 years and over	516	60	11.7	59	1.7
Men	1 589	1 075	67.7	1 008	6.3
20 to 24 years	184	138	74.9	122	12.0
25 to 34 years	274	243	88.6	226	6.8
35 to 44 years	275	235	85.5	228	3.1
45 to 54 years	293	251	85.8	242	3.6
55 to 64 years	216	137	63.2	130	4.9
Women	1 788	982	54.9	926	5.7
16 to 19 years	124	50	40.6	42	17.1
20 to 24 years	188	118	63.0	108	9.0
25 to 34 years	296	202	68.1	189	6.4
35 to 44 years	332	240	72.2	230	3.9
45 to 54 years	326	230	70.6	219	5.0
55 to 64 years	215	114	53.0	111	2.9
MARITAL STATUS					
Married men, spouse present	862	640	74.3	623	2.6
Married women, spouse present	846	466	55.1	451	3.2
Women who maintain families	290	197	68.2	183	7.3
RACE, HISPANIC ORIGIN, AND SEX					
White	2 305	1 434	62.2	1 372	4.4
Men	1 119	796	71.1	760	4.5
Women	1 186	639	53.8	612	4.2
Black	1 015	594	58.5	533	10.3
Men	448	268	60.0	237	11.7
Women	568	325	57.3	296	9.1
Hispanic or Latino[1]	69	48	69.7	46	5.6
RACE, HISPANIC ORIGIN, AND AGE					
White					
16 to 19 years	158	60	38.0	52	14.0
20 to 24 years	229	168	73.4	156	7.4
25 to 34 years	384	306	79.8	293	4.2
35 to 44 years	403	328	81.5	319	2.8
45 to 54 years	427	334	78.3	321	3.9
55 to 64 years	306	190	62.1	185	3.0
65 years and over	398	47	11.8	46	2.1
Black					
20 to 24 years	136	86	63.6	71	17.1
25 to 34 years	177	133	75.3	117	12.5
35 to 44 years	198	144	72.5	137	5.1
45 to 54 years	181	138	76.7	131	5.4
55 to 64 years	112	52	46.0	47	8.5

Note: Data in Table 7 are from the Current Population Survey (CPS) and do not match Bureau of Labor Statistics estimates in Table 8. See notes and definitions for more details.

[1]May be of any race.

Table LA-8. Employment Status, 1990–2004
(Numbers in thousands, rate.)

Year	Civilian labor force	Employed	Unemployed	Unemployment rate
2004	2 057 526	1 940 315	117 211	5.7
2003	2 042 390	1 914 550	127 840	6.3
2002	2 022 326	1 902 957	119 369	5.9
2001	2 029 738	1 921 056	108 682	5.4
2000	2 028 123	1 927 360	100 763	5.0
1999	2 022 162	1 926 732	95 430	4.7
1998	2 027 265	1 918 907	108 358	5.3
1997	2 004 792	1 890 102	114 690	5.7
1996	1 980 714	1 855 474	125 240	6.3
1995	1 950 958	1 820 359	130 599	6.7
1994	1 931 434	1 785 654	145 780	7.5
1993	1 878 274	1 738 570	139 704	7.4
1992	1 940 080	1 787 541	152 539	7.9
1991	1 922 022	1 789 796	132 226	6.9
1990	1 877 388	1 767 306	110 082	5.9

Note: Population age 16 years and over.

Unemployment Rate, 1980–2004

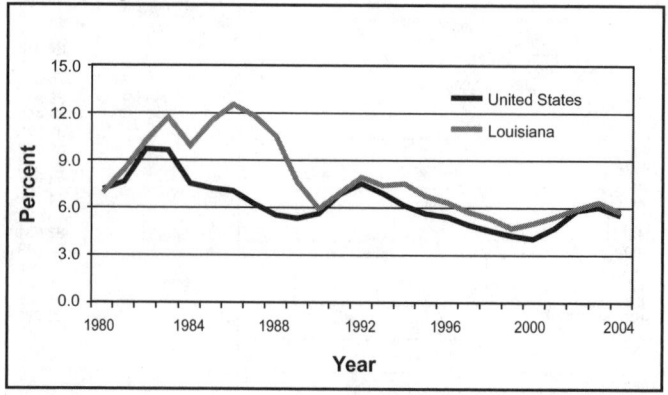

Table LA-9. Employment and Average Wages by Industry, 2001–2004

(Estimates are based on the 2002 North American Industry Classification System [NAICS].)

Industry	2001	2002	2003	2004	Annual average percent change, 2001–2004
	Number of jobs				
TOTAL EMPLOYMENT BY PLACE OF WORK	2 409 298	2 411 642	2 435 031	2 462 290	0.7
Farm Employment	37 436	37 132	34 006	34 498	-2.7
Nonfarm Employment	2 371 862	2 374 510	2 401 025	2 427 792	0.8
Private employment	1 963 544	1 961 047	1 985 181	2 010 348	0.8
Forestry, fishing, hunting, and other[1]	22 574	24 656	22 002	21 292	-1.9
Mining	58 655	54 350	55 363	54 013	-2.7
Utilities	10 211	10 275	10 129	9 967	-0.8
Construction	170 565	164 013	168 452	167 064	-0.7
Manufacturing	178 444	167 313	161 644	158 261	-3.9
Durable goods manufacturing	91 138	84 704	81 700	80 924	-3.9
Nondurable goods manufacturing	87 306	82 609	79 944	77 337	-4.0
Wholesale trade	83 188	83 219	81 957	82 184	-0.4
Retail trade	272 071	271 062	270 774	272 732	0.1
Transportation and warehousing	91 750	90 488	90 313	89 238	-0.9
Information	34 619	32 874	33 588	34 180	-0.4
Finance and insurance	86 297	88 642	90 097	91 338	1.9
Real estate and rental and leasing	73 859	74 295	77 576	80 760	3.0
Professional and technical services	114 990	116 562	119 061	123 209	2.3
Management of companies and enterprises	23 325	23 627	22 722	22 998	-0.5
Administrative and waste services	118 110	119 734	122 386	126 842	2.4
Educational services	39 689	41 659	43 735	45 786	4.9
Health care and social assistance	225 106	232 176	241 972	247 672	3.2
Arts, entertainment, and recreation	55 347	55 113	53 867	55 125	-0.1
Accommodation and food services	167 281	167 714	174 111	179 820	2.4
Other services, except public administration	137 463	143 275	145 432	147 867	2.5
Government and government enterprises	408 318	413 463	415 844	417 444	0.7
	Dollars				
AVERAGE WAGES AND SALARIES BY PLACE OF WORK ...	28 548	29 491	30 271	31 334	3.2
Farm Earnings	19 438	19 633	17 667	22 259	4.6
Nonfarm Earnings	28 590	29 536	30 315	31 367	3.1
Private earnings	28 879	29 618	30 233	31 267	2.7
Forestry, fishing, hunting, and other[1]	25 013	25 309	26 272	26 337	1.7
Mining	55 071	55 342	57 676	59 993	2.9
Utilities	53 419	55 108	56 955	61 947	5.1
Construction	32 207	33 032	33 077	34 200	2.0
Manufacturing	41 718	43 942	45 397	47 739	4.6
Durable goods manufacturing	36 379	38 377	39 892	41 988	4.9
Nondurable goods manufacturing	47 226	49 586	51 020	53 694	4.4
Wholesale trade	37 780	38 543	39 849	41 757	3.4
Retail trade	18 772	19 491	20 146	20 524	3.0
Transportation and warehousing	37 218	38 001	38 673	40 455	2.8
Information	36 866	37 836	36 595	37 811	0.8
Finance and insurance	36 857	37 430	38 287	39 895	2.7
Real estate and rental and leasing	29 497	29 555	30 273	31 345	2.0
Professional and technical services	42 384	42 523	43 171	44 341	1.5
Management of companies and enterprises	46 180	47 405	47 731	50 324	2.9
Administrative and waste services	19 159	20 561	21 821	23 065	6.4
Educational services	22 820	23 822	23 550	24 133	1.9
Health care and social assistance	27 322	28 355	28 854	29 974	3.1
Arts, entertainment, and recreation	22 938	24 383	26 304	26 844	5.4
Accommodation and food services	12 534	12 935	13 112	13 418	2.3
Other services, except public administration	19 243	19 816	20 615	21 445	3.7
Government and government enterprises	27 447	29 220	30 630	31 751	5.0

Note: Average wages and salaries are a calculation by the editors of wage and salary disbursements divided by full- and part-time wage and salary employment. Data may not add to total or may appear as zero due to rounding.

[1] "Other" consists of the number of jobs held by U.S. residents employed by international organizations and foreign embassies and consulates in the United States.

LABOR MARKET

Louisiana's unemployment rate was above the national average in recent years, despite being lower than the rates of its neighbors, Mississippi and Texas, in 2004. Employment was concentrated in the government sector, followed by retail trade, health care, tourism-related sectors (accommodation and food services), and construction. Over the 2001–2004 period, wage and salary employment grew slowly. The manufacturing sector lost jobs during this time, but health care, real estate, and other service sectors helped offset this decline. Average wages and salaries were below the national averages for most industries, but the rate of growth of earnings somewhat outpaced the national averages in many industries.

Employment by Industry, 2004

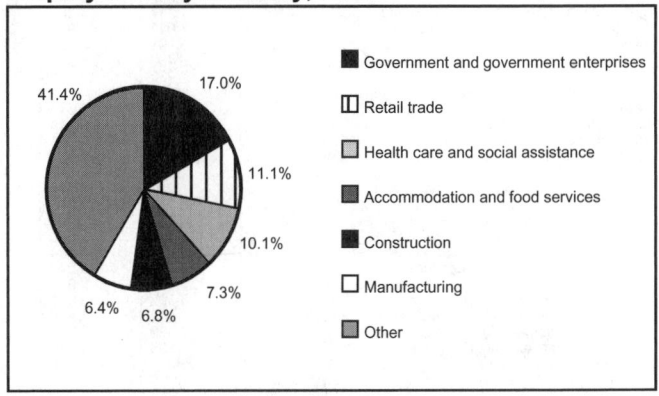

41.4%   17.0%   11.1%   10.1%   7.3%   6.8%   6.4%

- ■ Government and government enterprises
- ▯ Retail trade
- ▨ Health care and social assistance
- ▦ Accommodation and food services
- ■ Construction
- ▢ Manufacturing
- ■ Other

Table LA-10. Personal Income by Major Source, Selected Years 1980–2004

(Millions of dollars, except where noted.)

Item	1980	1990	2000	2001	2002	2003	2004	Average annual percent change, 2000–2004
Earnings by Place of Work	30 869	47 414	75 415	80 392	82 707	86 874	91 176	4.9
Wage and salary disbursements	23 669	34 491	55 572	58 061	59 571	61 344	63 861	3.5
Supplements to wages and salaries	4 441	7 423	11 521	12 187	13 747	15 121	16 104	8.7
Proprietors' income[1]	2 759	5 501	8 322	10 143	9 389	10 409	11 211	7.7
Farm proprietors' income	43	209	306	255	23	507	429	8.8
Nonfarm proprietors' income	2 716	5 292	8 015	9 888	9 366	9 902	10 782	7.7
(-) Contributions for government social insurance[2]	2 595	4 569	7 380	7 845	8 138	8 400	8 746	4.3
(+) Adjustment for residence[3]	-339	-119	-260	-139	-130	-164	-140	X
(=) **Net Earnings by Place of Residence**	27 934	42 726	67 775	72 408	74 439	78 310	82 290	5.0
(+) Dividends, interest, and rent[4]	4 857	11 456	17 700	17 429	16 539	15 999	16 597	-1.6
(+) Personal current transfer receipts	4 276	9 870	17 676	20 420	21 732	21 867	24 026	8.0
Personal income	37 067	64 052	103 151	110 256	112 709	116 176	122 913	4.5
Farm income	36 905	63 681	102 660	109 800	112 489	115 533	122 304	4.5
Nonfarm income	162	371	490	456	220	643	609	5.6
Per Capita Personal Income (Dollars)[5]	8 777	15 173	23 078	24 685	25 175	25 853	27 219	4.2

Note: Data may not add to total or may appear as zero due to rounding.

[1]Proprietors' income includes the inventory valuation adjustment and the capital consumption adjustment.
[2]Contributions for government social insurance are included in earnings by type and industry, but they are excluded from personal income.
[3]The adjustment for residence is the net inflow of the earnings of interarea commuters.
[4]Rental income of persons includes the capital consumption adjustment.
[5]Per capita personal income is total personal income divided by total midyear population.
X = Not applicable.

Per Capita Personal Income, 1980–2004 (Current Dollars)

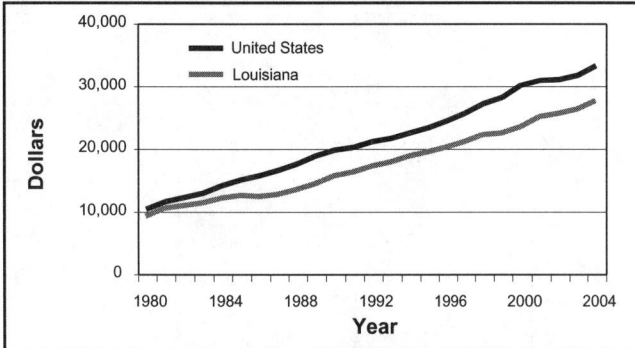

ECONOMIC ACTIVITY

Real gross state product (GSP) experienced declines following the 2001 recession and did not recover until 2004. The GSP growth rate of 2.2 percent was well below the national average. The state's share of the U.S. gross product fell from 1.5 percent in 1999 to 1.2 percent in 2004. Information, administrative and waste services, finance and insurance, and real estate had the highest rates of growth over the 2001–2004 period. While housing prices rose substantially in some pockets of the state, overall appreciation was below the national average from 2000 to 2004. The median value of owner-occupied housing was among the lowest 10 in 2004.

Table LA-11. Real Gross State Product, 1997–2004

(Millions of chained 2000 dollars, percent.)

Industry	1997	1998	1999	2000	2001	2002	2003	2004	Average annual percent change, 2001–2004
GROSS STATE PRODUCT	128 936	136 213	139 382	134 755	132 355	130 596	130 733	133 607	0.3
As a percent of U.S. gross product	1.5	1.5	1.5	1.4	1.3	1.3	1.3	1.2	X
Private Industries	113 597	120 433	123 557	118 914	116 487	114 326	114 065	116 402	0.0
Agriculture, forestry, fishing, and hunting	1 217	982	1 131	1 122	1 098	1 079	1 320	1 219	3.5
Mining	17 048	23 950	25 137	23 010	21 943	15 712	14 007	13 676	-14.6
Utilities	3 197	3 184	3 214	3 537	3 584	3 841	3 712	3 965	3.4
Construction	6 430	6 979	6 468	6 089	5 756	5 465	5 378	5 246	-3.0
Manufacturing	17 932	17 985	19 357	16 671	13 208	14 264	14 082	13 962	1.9
As a percent of gross state product	13.9	13.2	13.9	12.4	10.0	10.9	10.8	10.5	X
Wholesale trade	6 380	7 014	6 848	6 646	7 254	7 536	7 300	7 437	0.8
Retail trade	8 229	8 614	8 820	8 893	9 640	10 259	10 803	11 201	5.1
Transportation and warehousing	4 626	4 781	4 738	4 847	4 900	4 956	5 099	5 143	1.6
Information	2 407	2 604	2 711	2 911	3 367	3 591	3 763	4 161	7.3
Finance and insurance	4 568	4 679	4 807	4 810	4 823	5 041	5 242	5 518	4.6
Real estate and rental and leasing	11 340	11 706	11 983	12 407	12 513	13 169	13 223	13 894	3.6
Services	28 021	27 996	28 587	27 968	28 539	29 254	30 136	31 214	3.0
As a percent of gross state product	21.7	20.6	20.5	20.8	21.6	22.4	23.1	23.4	X
Professional and technical services	5 529	5 570	5 700	5 565	5 844	5 849	6 060	6 272	2.4
Management of companies and enterprises	1 884	1 784	1 725	1 555	1 900	1 921	1 982	2 007	1.8
Administrative and waste services	3 026	3 040	3 071	2 796	2 780	2 981	3 175	3 330	6.2
Educational services	843	911	931	915	914	933	889	886	-1.0
Health care and social assistance	8 502	8 211	8 185	8 160	8 218	8 536	8 823	9 091	3.4
Arts, entertainment, and recreation	1 562	1 436	2 041	1 986	2 091	2 160	2 184	2 193	1.6
Accommodation and food services	3 569	3 735	3 823	3 894	3 820	3 902	4 015	4 202	3.2
Other services, except public administration	3 106	3 309	3 111	3 097	2 972	2 972	3 008	3 233	2.8
Government	15 311	15 771	15 840	15 840	15 869	16 253	16 639	17 164	2.6
As a percent of gross state product	11.9	11.6	11.4	11.8	12.0	12.4	12.7	12.8	X

X = Not applicable.

Table LA-12. Government Transfer Payments, Selected Years 1980–2004

(Millions of dollars, percent.)

Item	1980	1990	2000	2001	2002	2003	2004	Average annual percent change, 2000–2004
CURRENT TRANSFER PAYMENTS TO INDIVIDUALS	3 985	9 333	16 582	19 174	20 515	20 796	22 933	8.4
Retirement and Disability Insurance Benefits	1 812	3 830	6 064	6 407	6 757	6 983	7 275	4.7
Old-age, survivors, and disability insurance (OASDI) benefits	1 737	3 690	5 911	6 251	6 588	6 809	7 097	4.7
Railroad retirement and disability benefits	64	102	117	119	123	126	128	2.4
Workers' compensation	9	34	30	32	39	38	39	6.5
Other government retirement and disability insurance benefits	1	4	6	6	7	10	11	13.9
Medical Benefits	918	3 503	7 456	9 471	9 884	9 700	11 312	11.0
Medicare benefits	475	1 929	4 140	4 578	4 901	5 182	5 681	8.2
Public assistance medical care benefits	427	1 503	3 242	4 785	4 841	4 404	5 500	14.1
Military medical insurance benefits	16	71	74	108	141	114	131	15.5
Income Maintenance Benefits	672	1 353	2 204	2 295	2 636	2 848	3 101	8.9
Supplemental Security Income (SSI) benefits	222	377	716	742	761	769	804	3.0
Family assistance	124	187	88	100	119	106	106	4.9
Food stamps	250	562	448	506	615	689	783	15.0
Other income maintenance benefits	77	227	952	947	1 141	1 284	1 408	10.3
Unemployment Insurance Compensation	236	134	177	236	397	400	321	16.1
Veterans' Benefits	276	340	455	479	530	571	608	7.5
Federal Education and Training Assistance	71	170	217	265	303	285	302	8.6
Other Payments to Individuals	1	3	11	21	8	9	14	7.0

Note: See notes and definitions for more details. Data may not add to total or may appear as zero due to rounding.

EXPORTS

In 2004, Louisiana was the 10th largest exporter in the country; however, this ranking may be overstated. As explained in the notes and definitions section of this book, data denote the transportation origin and not necessarily the state where the exported goods were actually grown or manufactured. Therefore, many products exported from the port of New Orleans were attributed to Louisiana, when they were actually produced by inland states along the Mississippi River. The leading export products reported were crops, chemical manufactures, and petroleum. Exports of petroleum and transportation equipment grew considerably from 2001 to 2004. Exports to China have tripled during this period. Louisiana's other leading export markets were Japan, Mexico, and Canada.

Leading Exports, 2004

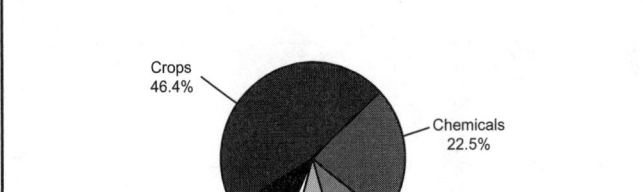

Table LA-13. Exports of Goods by Leading Products and Destinations, 2001–2004

(Millions of dollars, percent, rank based on 2004 dollar values.)

Product and market	2001	2002	2003	2004	Percent share of total, 2004	Average annual percent change, 2001–2004
Total Goods						
Total	16 589	17 567	18 390	19 922	100.0	6.3
Manufactures	8 809	8 748	8 819	10 318	51.8	5.4
Agriculture and livestock	7 661	8 701	9 481	9 438	47.4	7.2
Other commodities	120	118	90	166	0.8	11.5
Five Leading Exports (NAICS Code)						
Crop production (111)	7 559	8 603	9 379	9 248	46.4	7.0
Chemical manufactures (325)	3 442	3 038	3 708	4 478	22.5	9.2
Petroleum and coal products (324)	1 188	1 091	1 206	1 922	9.6	17.4
Processed foods (311)	2 347	2 348	2 112	1 861	9.3	-7.4
Transportation equipment (336)	282	729	305	497	2.5	20.9
Five Leading Markets	12 700	13 464	14 652	15 616	78.4	7.1
Japan	2 137	2 521	2 482	2 361	11.8	3.4
China	683	768	2 117	2 194	11.0	47.6
Mexico	1 524	1 632	1 776	1 949	9.8	8.5
Canada	1 028	1 037	1 247	1 434	7.2	11.7
South Korea	550	548	626	729	3.7	9.9

Table LA-14. Agriculture, 1997 and 2002

(Number, acres, and dollars.)

Item	1997	2002
Number of farms	30 425	27 413
Land in farms (acres)	8 367 843	7 830 664
Farm Size		
Average size of farm (acres)	275	286
Farms by size (percent distribution)		
Fewer than 50 acres	39.5	41.2
50 to 499 acres	46.6	44.9
500 acres or more	13.9	13.9
Market Value of Land and Equipment (Dollars)		
Land and buildings average value per farm	338 828	444 007
Average value per acre	1 236	1 534
Machinery and equipment average value per farm	54 406	64 379
Value of Sales (Thousands of Dollars)		
Agricultural products sold	2 142 630	1 815 803
Crops	1 457 793	1 065 611
Livestock, poultry, and their products	684 837	750 192
Average per farm (dollars)	70 423	66 239
Value of sales (percent distribution)		
Less than $10,000	65.2	66.5
$10,000 to $99,999	20.3	21.0
$100,000 or more	14.5	12.5
Government Payments		
Payments (thousands of dollars)	72 271	123 599
Percent of farms receiving government payments	30.0	27.6
Farm operators whose principal occupation is farming (percent) ...	43.8	54.0

AGRICULTURE

Cash receipts from farm products totaled $1.8 billion in 2002, somewhat less than those reported on the 1997 farm census. Sales of livestock, poultry, and their products increased 17 percent, while crop sales fell about 27 percent. Total sales ranked 33rd in the nation. Cane sugar, poultry, cotton, and rice were Louisiana's main products. Nearly two-thirds of farms had sales of less than $10,000. More than 41 percent of farms spanned fewer than 50 acres, a proportion that has increased since the 1997 census.

ENERGY

Energy expenditures per person were the third highest in the nation, most likely due to the intensive use of petroleum and natural gas in the state's manufacturing sector. However, Louisiana's energy prices were the third lowest in the nation, behind only Alaska and North Dakota. The state's per capita consumption level also ranked third in the nation. Louisiana's industrial sector accounted for 61 percent of total consumption.

Energy Consumption by Source, 2001

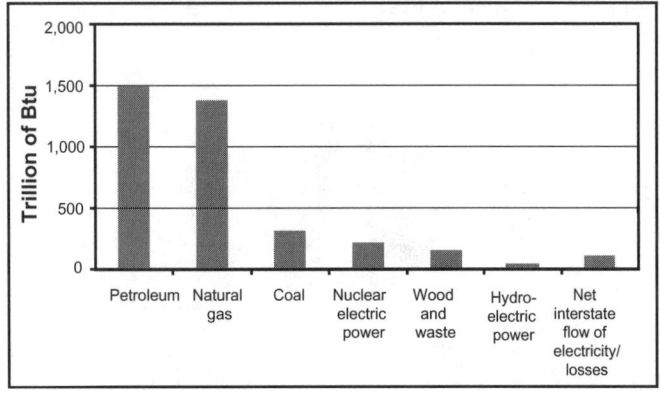

Energy Consumption by Sector, 2001

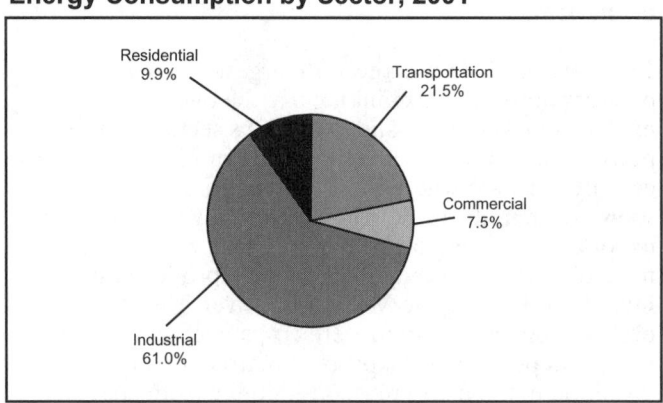

Table LA-15. Energy Consumption, Expenditures, and Prices, Selected Years 1960–2001

(Dollars, Btu [British Thermal Unit], percent distribution.)

Item	1960	1965	1970	1975	1980	1985	1990	1995	2000	2001
Total Consumption (Billion Btu)	1 506 983	1 765 768	2 703 130	3 004 415	3 647 551	3 144 749	3 591 473	3 850 312	3 971 383	3 499 524
Consumption per capita (million Btu)	462.7	505.1	741.7	773.1	867.2	713.4	851.1	889.6	888.7	783.6
Consumption by Sector (Percent Distribution)										
Residential	7.2	7.8	7.9	8.4	7.9	9.6	8.6	8.7	9.4	9.9
Commercial	4.6	5.2	6.8	6.2	7.8	7.6	6.1	5.9	7.0	7.5
Industrial	71.2	69.4	70.8	68.4	66.6	64.2	66.0	65.5	62.1	61.0
Transportation	17.0	17.6	14.5	17.0	17.7	18.6	19.2	19.9	21.5	21.5
Consumption by Source (Billion Btu)										
Coal	0	0	0	0	2 456	159 097	208 868	216 823	253 270	240 000
Natural gas	1 003 771	1 156 449	1 894 224	1 854 766	1 862 179	1 441 820	1 654 692	1 737 257	1 625 863	1 339 493
Petroleum	471 751	569 766	766 484	1 101 146	1 588 977	1 229 769	1 380 984	1 507 998	1 645 034	1 491 376
Nuclear electric power	0	0	0	0	0	26 102	150 230	164 812	164 734	181 128
Hydroelectric power[1]	0	0	0	0	0	0	6 829	9 819	5 430	7 450
Wood and waste	38 992	38 299	41 620	42 358	72 378	77 861	121 134	143 024	137 550	129 999
Other	0	0	0	0	0	0	186	336	515	563
Net interstate flow of electricity/losses[2]	-7 531	1 253	801	6 145	121 560	210 101	68 549	70 242	138 988	109 515
Total Expenditures (Thousands of Dollars)	. . .	. . .	1 702 600	4 098 700	11 333 400	12 837 800	13 307 500	13 055 100	20 178 500	18 026 000
Expenditures per capita (dollars)	. . .	. . .	467	1 055	2 695	2 912	3 154	3 016	4 515	4 036
Prices by Sector (Dollars Per Million Btu)										
Total	. . .	. . .	0.95	2.04	4.54	6.47	5.86	5.20	7.68	8.19
Residential	. . .	. . .	2.27	3.29	7.71	12.89	14.50	14.72	17.04	18.31
Commercial	. . .	. . .	1.62	2.89	5.54	13.09	14.95	15.35	16.28	17.67
Industrial	. . .	. . .	0.48	1.40	3.32	4.80	4.00	3.30	5.75	6.02
Transportation	. . .	. . .	1.97	3.28	6.87	7.19	6.87	6.27	8.37	8.45

[1]A negative number in this row results from pumped storage for which, overall, more electricity is expended than created to provide electricity during peak demand periods.
[2]Net interstate flow of electricity is the difference between the amount of energy in the electricity sold within a state (including associated losses) and the energy input at the electric utilities within the state. A positive number indicates that more electricity (including associated losses) came into the state than went out of the state during the year; conversely, a negative number indicates that more electricity (including associated losses) went out of the state than came into the state.
. . . = Not available.

Table LA-16. State Taxes, Fiscal 2004

(Dollars, percent distribution.)

Item	Thousands of dollars	Percent distribution	Dollars per capita	
			State	U.S.
TOTAL TAXES	8 025 507	100.0	1 777.1	2 024.8
Property Taxes	39 739	0.5	8.8	38.9
Sales and Gross Receipts	4 610 512	57.4	1 020.9	1 003.4
General sales and gross receipts	2 680 716	33.4	593.6	677.0
Selective sales taxes	1 929 796	24.0	427.3	326.4
Alcoholic beverages	53 422	0.7	11.8	15.7
Amusements	524 119	6.5	116.1	17.0
Insurance premiums	342 353	4.3	75.8	47.0
Motor fuels	560 769	7.0	124.2	114.6
Tobacco products	101 040	1.3	22.4	42.0
Other selective sales	320 206	4.0	70.9	49.8
Licenses	429 068	5.3	95.0	134.9
Corporation	186 912	2.3	41.4	21.6
Motor vehicle	114 090	1.4	25.3	59.4
Occupation and business, not elsewhere classified	76 956	1.0	17.0	37.1
Other Taxes	2 946 188	36.7	652.0	847.6
Individual income	2 187 050	27.3	484.3	673.6
Corporation net income	236 745	2.9	52.4	105.1
Death and gift	45 784	0.6	10.1	19.6
Severance	476 609	5.9	105.5	21.5

GOVERNMENT FINANCE

Louisiana's revenues of $4,067 per person were above the national average in 2003. However, the state's per capita expenditures of $3,632 were below the U.S. average. Particularly low were expenditures per capita for public welfare. The state's hospital expenditures were more than twice the national average. Louisiana's taxes per person were lower than average. In fiscal year 2004, general sales receipts were the largest tax revenue source, followed by individual income taxes. Louisiana's individual income tax per person ranked 38th in the nation. The state's property taxes were well below the U.S. average. Debt per capita amounted to $2,175, which ranked 26th in the country.

Per Capita State Taxes, Fiscal 2004

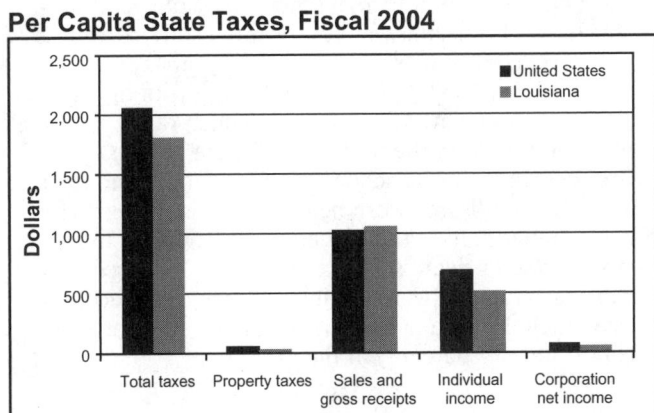

Table LA-17. State Government Finances, 2003

(Dollars, percent distribution.)

Item	Millions of dollars	Percent distribution	Dollars per capita	
			State	U.S.
GENERAL REVENUE	18 276 111	100.0	4 066.8	3 832.6
Intergovernmental revenue	6 501 978	35.6	1 446.8	1 246.0
Taxes	7 449 507	40.8	1 657.7	1 891.6
General sales	2 488 627	13.6	553.8	636.0
Selective sales	1 886 110	10.3	419.7	307.4
License taxes	426 741	2.3	95.0	123.6
Individual income tax	1 867 150	10.2	415.5	626.8
Corporate income tax	198 716	1.1	44.2	97.8
Other taxes	582 163	3.2	129.5	99.9
Current charges	2 362 867	12.9	525.8	366.5
Miscellaneous general revenue	1 961 759	10.7	436.5	328.6
GENERAL EXPENDITURE	16 323 015	100.0	3 632.2	4 010.5
Intergovernmental expenditure	4 329 053	26.5	963.3	1 316.9
Direct expenditure	11 993 962	73.5	2 668.9	2 693.6
Expenditure by Function				
Education	6 235 015	38.2	1 387.4	1 416.4
Public welfare	2 800 278	17.2	623.1	1 083.3
Hospitals	1 507 432	9.2	335.4	132.3
Health	418 057	2.6	93.0	173.0
Highways	1 142 621	7.0	254.2	295.4
Police protection	262 317	1.6	58.4	38.4
Correction	619 414	3.8	137.8	135.0
Natural resources	393 305	2.4	87.5	64.0
Parks and recreation	240 501	1.5	53.5	20.1
Government administration	614 142	3.8	136.7	151.3
Interest on general debt	570 949	3.5	127.0	107.8
Other and unallocable	1 518 984	9.3	338.0	393.4
DEBT AT END OF FISCAL YEAR	9 773 279	X	2 174.7	2 404.7
CASH AND SECURITY HOLDINGS	36 968 929	X	8 226.3	8 938.4

X = Not applicable.

Table LA-18. Education Indicators, 2000–2004

(Percent, number.)

Item	State	U.S.
Total Population 25 Years and Over (Thousands), 2004	2 758	186 877
Educational Attainment, 2004		
Percent high school graduate or more	78.7	85.2
Percent college graduate or more	22.4	27.7
Elementary and Secondary Schools, 2002–2003		
Total students	730 464	48 202 324
Percent of students eligible for free or reduced-price lunch ..	61.4	40.6
Percent of students who were English language learners	1.7	7.8
Total schools	1 522	92 330
Student/teacher ratio	14.4	15.9
Per student expenditures	6 922	8 041
Dropouts, Grades 9–12, 2000–2001 (Percent)	7.0	. . .
Higher Education, 2002–2003		
Total enrollment	238 102	17 035 027
Bachelor's degrees awarded	21 182	1 348 503
Percent women	60.7	57.5

. . . = Not available.

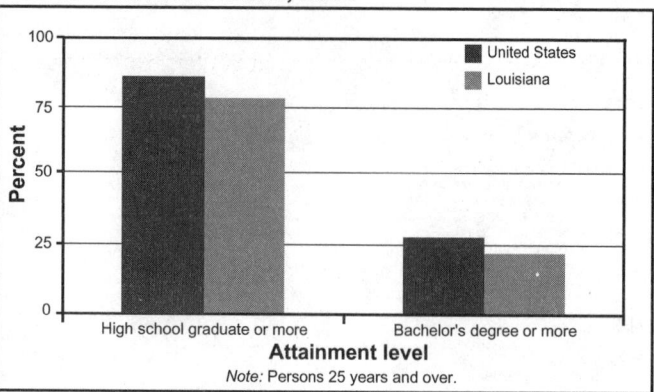

Educational Attainment, 2004

Note: Persons 25 years and over.

EDUCATION

Louisiana had very low high school and college attainment levels. Louisiana was one of three states with less than 80 percent of its residents age 25 years and over holding high school diplomas. The state's proportion of college graduates was 22.4 percent, which ranked among the seven lowest in the nation. Louisiana had an above average proportion of school-age population, and its per student expenditures were below the U.S. average. The state also had one of the highest proportion of students who attended private schools. More than 61 percent of Louisiana students were eligible for free or reduced-price lunch. Louisiana had the fifth highest reported dropout rate (7 percent) in the nation.

VOTER PARTICIPATION

Louisiana had above average voter turnout in both the 2000 and 2004 elections. In 2004, the participation rates of men and women were nearly identical, with about 63 percent of each group turning out to vote. In the 2000 election, 66 percent of eligible women and 63 percent of eligible men voted. Nationally, women had a higher turnout rate than men. Nearly 78 percent of eligible persons age 65 to 74 years voted, while just 46 percent of the population age 18 to 24 years voted. In 2000, 52.6 percent of eligible voters cast their ballots for the Republican presidential ticket; this proportion increased to 57.6 percent in 2004.

Table LA-19. Reported Voting and Registration, November 2000 and November 2004

(Numbers in thousands, percent.)

Characteristic	Total population 18 years and over	Total citizen		Total registered		Total voted	
		Number	Percent	Number	Percent	Number	Percent
NOVEMBER 2000							
Total	3 143	3 091	98.4	2 369	75.4	2 030	64.6
Male	1 434	1 401	97.7	1 049	73.2	903	63.0
Female	1 709	1 690	98.9	1 320	77.2	1 127	66.0
NOVEMBER 2004							
Total	3 277	3 218	98.2	2 413	73.6	2 067	63.1
Male	1 528	1 502	98.3	1 132	74.1	963	63.0
Female	1 749	1 716	98.1	1 281	73.2	1 104	63.1
Race and Hispanic Origin							
White alone	2 260	2 210	97.8	1 697	75.1	1 446	64.0
Non-Hispanic White alone	2 191	2 180	99.5	1 678	76.6	1 430	65.2
Black alone	976	966	99.0	693	71.1	606	62.1
Asian alone	8	8	B	2	B	2	B
Hispanic or Latino[1]	68	30	B	19	B	16	B
White alone or in combination	2 272	2 223	97.8	1 709	75.2	1 453	64.0
Non-Hispanic White alone or in combination	2 204	2 193	99.5	1 690	76.7	1 437	65.2
Black alone or in combination	985	976	99.0	703	71.3	613	62.2
Asian alone or in combination	8	8	B	2	B	2	B
Age							
18 to 24 years	495	481	97.2	288	58.1	227	46.0
25 to 44 years	1 206	1 160	96.2	898	74.5	779	64.6
45 to 64 years	1 105	1 105	100.0	848	76.7	741	67.0
65 to 74 years	229	229	100.0	187	81.6	178	77.9
75 years and over	242	242	100.0	192	79.4	142	58.6

[1]May be of any race.
B = Base is too small to show derived measure.

At a Glance:

- Maine's population in 2004 was just over 1.3 million, ranking it as the 40th most populous state in the nation.

- As with most of its New England neighbors, Maine's population was predominately non-Hispanic White—96.1 percent. This was the highest proportion of this racial group in the country.

- Median household income was below the national average, ranking 32nd in the country. Maine's poverty rate of 11.6 percent was also below the national average.

- Maine's unemployment rate was 4.6 percent, the 14th lowest in the country.

- Real gross state product was among the nation's smallest, ranking 44th, but its economic growth from 2001 to 2004 was slightly above average.

- Maine had an above average proportion of its population age 25 years and over holding high school diplomas, but a below average proportion with bachelor's degrees or more. The state ranked 40th in the nation for proportion of college graduates.

- In 2004, only 10 percent of the population lacked health insurance—the fourth lowest proportion in the nation.

Table ME-1. Population by Sex and Age, 1990, 2000, and 2004

(Number, percent.)

Sex and age	1990	2000	2004	Percent distribution, 2004	Average annual percent change, 2000–2004
Total Population	1 227 928	1 274 923	1 317 253	X	0.8
Percent of total U.S. population	0.5	0.5	0.4	X	X
Sex					
Male	597 850	620 309	643 143	48.8	0.9
Female	630 078	654 614	674 110	51.2	0.7
Age					
Under 5 years	85 722	70 726	67 628	5.1	-1.8
5 to 17 years	223 280	230 512	214 501	16.3	-0.3
18 years and over	233 201	973 685	1 035 124	78.6	0.9
18 to 24 years	918 926	103 903	124 451	9.4	0.0
25 to 44 years	123 772	370 597	350 442	26.6	-0.9
45 to 64 years	398 580	315 783	370 480	28.1	3.4
65 years and over	163 373	183 402	189 751	14.4	1.1
85 years and over	18 226	23 316	25 091	1.9	2.4
Median age (years)	33.8	38.6	40.6	X	X

X = Not applicable.

Average Annual Rate of Population Growth, 1980–2004

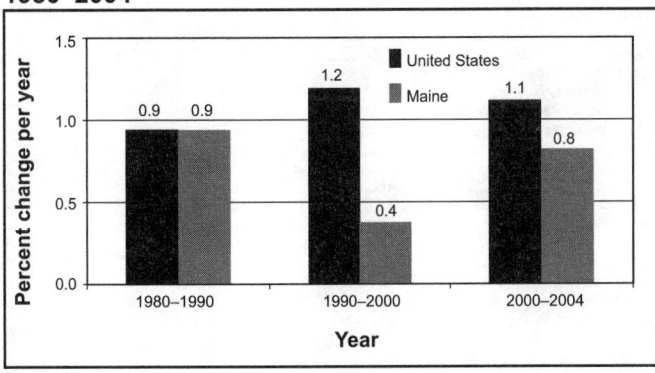

POPULATION

Maine's population increase of 3.3 percent from 2000 to 2004 was slower than the national average. Its population growth was faster than Vermont's, but considerably slower than New Hampshire's. The proportion of the population under 18 years old was the third lowest in the nation, behind only the District of Columbia and West Virginia. In 2004, residents age 65 years and over represented 14.4 percent of the population, compared with 12.4 percent nationally. More than 80 percent of the state's population growth during the 2000–2004 period was through in-migration from other states. Natural increase (births minus deaths) and international immigration only added small numbers to the state's population.

Table ME-2. Population by Race and Hispanic Origin, 1990, 2000, and 2004

(Number, percent.)

Race and Hispanic origin	1990	2000	2004
Total Population	1 227 928	1 274 923	1 317 253
Non-Hispanic (Percent)			
One race[1]			
White	98.0	96.6	96.1
Black	0.4	0.5	0.7
American Indian, Alaska Native[2]	0.5	0.5	0.6
Asian and Pacific Islander[2]	0.5	0.7	0.8
Other race[2]	0.1	. . .	. . .
Two or more races	. . .	0.8	0.9
Hispanic or Latino[3] (Percent)	0.6	0.7	0.9

[1]Individuals could report only one race in the 1990 census and could report one or more races on the 2000 census. Data on race in 2000 and 2004 are not comparable to 1990.
[2]Data for 1990 include people of Hispanic or Latino origin.
[3]May be of any race.
. . . = Not available.

Minority Population as a Percent of Total Population, 2004

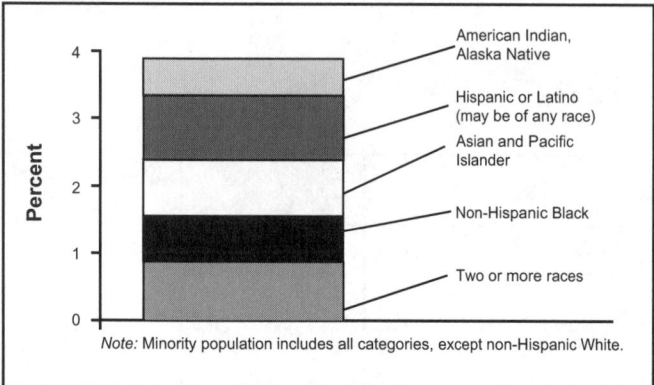

Note: Minority population includes all categories, except non-Hispanic White.

Age-Adjusted Death Rates, Average 2000–2002

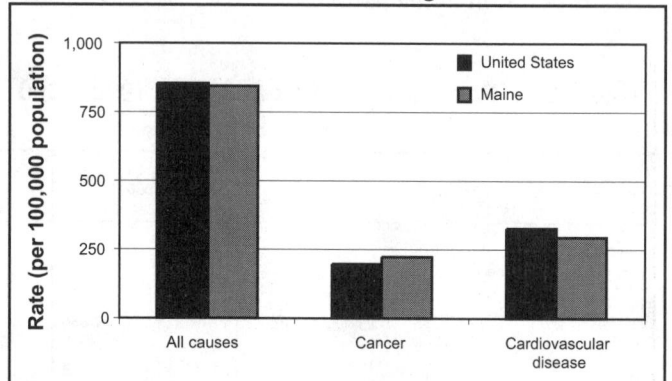

HEALTH

Maine's rate of health insurance coverage was well above the national average in 2004. The infant mortality rate was the third lowest in the nation. Maine's birth rate matched Vermont's as the lowest in the nation. The state's age-adjusted death rates were close to the national averages.

Table ME-3. Health Characteristics, 2000–2004

(Number, rate, percent.)

Item	State	U.S.
Births, 2003–2004		
Number of births	13 855	4 089 950
Birth rate (per 1,000 population)	10.6	14.1
Teenage birth rate (per 1,000 women age 15–19 years)	24.9	41.6
Mortality Rates, Average 2000–2002		
Infant mortality rate (per 1,000 live births)	5.1	6.9
Age-adjusted mortality rate (per 100,000 population)		
All races	847.9	853.3
Non-Hispanic White	845.3	843.1
Black	773.1	1 097.1
American Indian, Alaska Native	. . .	687.0
Asian and Pacific Islander	494.8	486.0
Hispanic or Latino[1]	. . .	642.7
Health Insurance, 2004		
Percent of all persons without health insurance	10.0	15.7
Percent of children without health insurance	5.8	11.2
Percent of low-income children without health insurance	3.2	7.1

[1]May be of any race.
. . . = Not available.

Table ME-4. Leading Causes of Death, Average 2000–2002

(Number, rate per 100,000 population.)

Cause	Number of deaths	Age-adjusted death rates	
		State	U.S.
ALL CAUSES	12 490	847.9	853.3
Leading Causes			
Major cardiovascular diseases	4 409	294.9	326.5
Cancer	3 107	211.4	196.0
Chronic lower respiratory diseases	786	53.1	43.7
Unintentional injuries	469	34.8	35.7
Diabetes (underlying cause)	386	26.2	25.2
Influenza and pneumonia	307	20.3	22.7
Alzheimer's disease	483	31.8	19.0
Motor vehicle accidents	186	14.2	15.0
Nephritis, nephrotic syndrome, and nephrosis ..	205	13.7	13.8
Septicemia	126	8.5	11.4
Suicides	160	12.0	10.7
Firearm-related	99	7.3	10.3
Cirrhosis	117	8.1	9.5
Drug-induced	100	7.7	7.9
Alcohol-induced	97	6.8	6.9
Homicides	16	1.2	6.0
Falls	80	5.4	5.2
HIV	14	1.0	5.0
Viral hepatitis	16	1.1	2.0
Anemias	24	1.6	1.6
Drownings	21	1.6	1.3
Fire deaths	13	1.0	1.2

Note: The rates are age-adjusted to the U.S. 2000 standard population.

Table ME-5. Households and Housing Characteristics, 1990, 2000, and 2004

(Number, percent, and dollars.)

Characteristic	1990	2000	2004	Average annual percent change, 2000–2004
Total Households	465 312	518 200	534 412	0.8
Family households	328 685	340 685	349 902	0.7
Married-couple family	270 565	272 152	274 552	0.2
Other family	58 120	68 533	75 350	2.4
Male householder, no wife present	13 760	19 511	23 986	5.3
Female householder, no husband present	44 360	49 022	51 364	1.2
Nonfamily households	136 627	177 515	184 510	1.0
Householder living alone	108 474	139 969	144 777	0.8
Householder not living alone	28 153	37 546	39 733	1.4
Housing Characteristics				
Average size	2.56	2.39	2.39	X
Housing units	587 045	651 901	676 667	0.9
Occupied housing units	465 312	518 200	534 412	0.8
Owner-occupied	327 888	370 905	389 781	1.2
Renter-occupied	137 424	147 295	144 631	-0.5
Median gross rent of renter-occupied housing units (dollars)	419	497	582	4.0
Median value of owner-occupied housing units (dollars)	87 300	98 700	143 182	9.7

X = Not applicable.

Median Housing Value and Median Rent, 2004

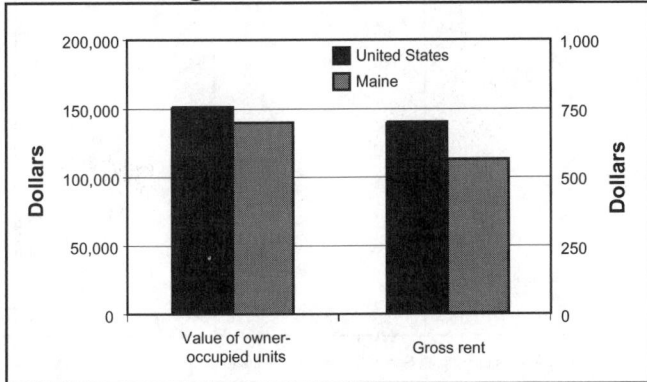

Median Household Income, 1984–2004 (2004 Dollars)

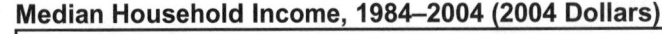
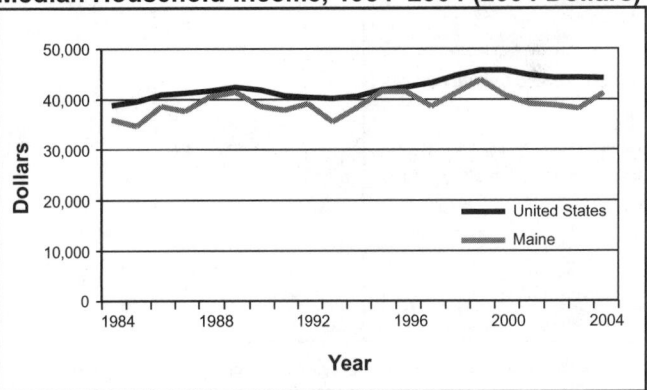

Table ME-6. Household Income and Poverty Status, 1980–2004

(2004 CPI-U-RS adjusted dollars, rate.)

Year	State Median household income (2004 dollars)	State Poverty rate	U.S. Median household income (2004 dollars)	U.S. Poverty rate
2004	41 363	11.6	44 389	12.7
2003	38 110	11.6	44 482	12.5
2002	38 710	13.4	44 546	12.1
2001	39 069	10.3	45 062	11.7
2000	40 877	10.1	46 058	11.3
1999	44 050	10.6	46 129	11.9
1998	41 248	10.4	45 003	12.7
1997	38 462	10.1	43 430	13.3
1996	41 590	11.2	42 544	13.7
1995	41 675	11.2	41 943	13.8
1994	38 222	9.4	40 677	14.5
1993	35 321	15.4	40 217	15.1
1992	39 077	13.5	40 422	14.8
1991	37 692	14.1	40 746	14.2
1990	38 489	13.1	41 963	13.5
1989	41 517	10.4	42 524	12.8
1988	40 509	13.2	41 771	13.0
1987	37 528	11.7	41 322	13.4
1986	38 517	10.2	40 939	13.6
1985	34 357	11.9	39 545	14.0
1984	35 725	13.0	38 782	14.4
1983	. . .	12.4	. . .	15.2
1982	. . .	13.7	. . .	15.0
1981	. . .	16.0	. . .	14.0
1980	. . .	14.6	. . .	13.0

. . . = Not available.

Table ME-7. Employment Status by Demographic Group, 2004

(Numbers in thousands, rate.)

Characteristic	Civilian noninstitutional population	Civilian labor force		Employed	Unemployment rate
		Number	Participation rate		
SEX AND AGE					
Total	1 055	696	66.0	664	4.7
16 to 19 years	70	36	51.3	31	13.9
20 to 24 years	85	67	79.1	63	6.3
25 to 34 years	154	129	83.9	122	5.1
35 to 44 years	196	166	84.8	160	3.7
45 to 54 years	204	170	83.2	164	3.7
55 to 64 years	155	102	65.6	99	3.0
65 years and over	191	27	14.1	26	4.1
Men	507	362	71.4	344	5.1
16 to 19 years	35	18	51.4	16	13.0
20 to 24 years	43	36	84.2	33	7.3
25 to 34 years	75	68	90.4	64	5.9
35 to 44 years	95	86	90.3	83	3.9
45 to 54 years	106	91	86.1	87	4.4
55 to 64 years	71	47	67.0	46	2.6
65 years and over	82	15	18.7	15	5.2
Women	547	334	61.0	320	4.2
16 to 19 years	35	18	51.1	15	14.8
20 to 24 years	42	31	73.8	29	5.1
25 to 34 years	78	61	77.5	58	4.2
35 to 44 years	101	80	79.6	78	3.5
45 to 54 years	98	79	80.1	76	2.9
55 to 64 years	84	54	64.4	52	3.3
65 years and over	109	12	10.7	11	2.7
MARITAL STATUS					
Married men, spouse present	284	208	73.1	201	3.4
Married women, spouse present	281	181	64.5	177	2.5
Women who maintain families	51	34	65.9	32	4.3
RACE, HISPANIC ORIGIN, AND SEX					
White	1 018	674	66.3	644	4.6
Men	489	350	71.7	333	5.0
Women	529	324	61.3	311	4.1
RACE, HISPANIC ORIGIN, AND AGE					
White					
16 to 19 years	67	35	52.5	30	13.6
20 to 24 years	82	65	79.1	61	6.1
25 to 34 years	147	124	84.2	118	4.9
35 to 44 years	188	160	85.4	154	3.7
45 to 54 years	197	165	83.9	159	3.8
55 to 64 years	150	99	66.0	96	2.8
65 years and over	188	27	14.3	26	4.2

Note: Data in Table 7 are from the Current Population Survey (CPS) and do not match Bureau of Labor Statistics estimates in Table 8. See notes and definitions for more details.

Table ME-8. Employment Status, 1990–2004

(Numbers in thousands, rate.)

Year	Civilian labor force	Employed	Unemployed	Unemployment rate
2004	699 342	667 223	32 119	4.6
2003	694 313	659 579	34 734	5.0
2002	684 691	654 522	30 169	4.4
2001	676 291	649 955	26 336	3.9
2000	674 395	651 183	23 212	3.4
1999	667 673	641 351	26 322	3.9
1998	657 415	627 920	29 495	4.5
1997	658 153	624 410	33 743	5.1
1996	651 669	617 479	34 190	5.2
1995	638 695	601 565	37 130	5.8
1994	629 671	589 073	40 598	6.4
1993	631 404	589 800	41 604	6.6
1992	639 622	594 082	45 540	7.1
1991	638 870	590 604	48 266	7.6
1990	631 147	597 902	33 245	5.3

Note: Population age 16 years and over.

Unemployment Rate, 1980–2004

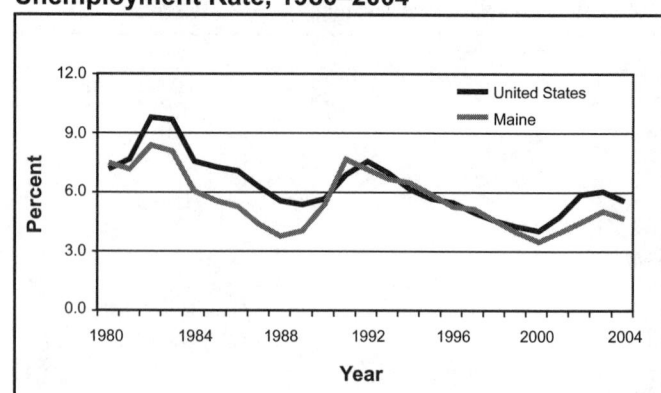

Table ME-9. Employment and Average Wages by Industry, 2001–2004

(Estimates are based on the 2002 North American Industry Classification System [NAICS].)

Industry	2001	2002	2003	2004	Annual average percent change, 2001–2004
	Number of jobs				
TOTAL EMPLOYMENT BY PLACE OF WORK	796 702	799 455	803 584	814 376	0.7
Farm Employment	10 908	10 980	10 975	10 320	-1.8
Nonfarm Employment	785 794	788 475	792 609	804 056	0.8
Private employment	676 297	677 818	680 928	692 485	0.8
Forestry, fishing, hunting, and other[1]	16 816	17 994	15 243	14 769	-4.2
Mining	494	423	499	513	1.3
Utilities	2 360	2 308	2 083	1 991	-5.5
Construction	54 758	54 130	57 336	58 367	2.2
Manufacturing	79 315	72 789	68 589	67 790	-5.1
Durable goods manufacturing	42 070	38 645	36 748	36 690	-4.5
Nondurable goods manufacturing	37 245	34 144	31 841	31 100	-5.8
Wholesale trade	22 859	22 638	23 378	24 118	1.8
Retail trade	106 703	107 191	107 447	110 055	1.0
Transportation and warehousing	20 026	19 821	19 330	19 606	-0.7
Information	13 938	13 100	13 111	12 951	-2.4
Finance and insurance	33 434	33 471	33 164	32 848	-0.6
Real estate and rental and leasing	21 077	21 730	23 130	24 423	5.0
Professional and technical services	40 152	39 791	39 687	40 673	0.4
Management of companies and enterprises	6 222	6 565	6 081	5 922	-1.6
Administrative and waste services	32 169	32 997	33 970	33 914	1.8
Educational services	14 414	14 803	15 269	15 699	2.9
Health care and social assistance	101 687	104 693	107 048	111 325	3.1
Arts, entertainment, and recreation	17 015	17 928	18 343	18 491	2.8
Accommodation and food services	53 768	54 591	55 717	56 918	1.9
Other services, except public administration	39 090	40 855	41 503	42 112	2.5
Government and government enterprises	109 497	110 657	111 681	111 571	0.6
	Dollars				
AVERAGE WAGES AND SALARIES BY PLACE OF WORK ...	28 306	29 276	30 333	31 565	3.7
Farm Earnings	18 557	24 387	20 179	26 136	12.1
Nonfarm Earnings	28 369	29 307	30 400	31 595	3.7
Private earnings	28 136	28 946	29 943	31 109	3.4
Forestry, fishing, hunting, and other[1]	27 304	27 812	28 658	31 254	4.6
Mining	27 114	29 696	29 308	29 505	2.9
Utilities	49 851	51 797	53 969	56 457	4.2
Construction	32 488	32 644	33 591	34 496	2.0
Manufacturing	36 322	38 029	40 121	40 956	4.1
Durable goods manufacturing	35 821	37 474	39 172	40 847	4.5
Nondurable goods manufacturing	36 871	38 639	41 178	41 081	3.7
Wholesale trade	39 929	41 118	42 572	43 946	3.2
Retail trade	19 841	20 549	21 358	21 928	3.4
Transportation and warehousing	29 769	30 115	31 295	32 650	3.1
Information	36 038	37 182	38 457	40 162	3.7
Finance and insurance	41 196	42 796	45 546	47 711	5.0
Real estate and rental and leasing	24 424	25 932	27 052	27 813	4.4
Professional and technical services	39 920	42 037	43 001	44 818	3.9
Management of companies and enterprises	51 210	52 073	52 422	66 388	9.0
Administrative and waste services	22 976	23 369	23 633	25 101	3.0
Educational services	23 666	25 271	26 147	27 179	4.7
Health care and social assistance	28 712	29 704	30 813	32 126	3.8
Arts, entertainment, and recreation	17 773	17 740	18 480	18 982	2.2
Accommodation and food services	13 165	13 696	14 007	14 568	3.4
Other services, except public administration	18 302	18 748	19 539	20 398	3.7
Government and government enterprises	29 479	31 002	32 523	33 881	4.7

Note: Average wages and salaries are a calculation by the editors of wage and salary disbursements divided by full- and part-time wage and salary employment. Data may not add to total or may appear as zero due to rounding.

[1] "Other" consists of the number of jobs held by U.S. residents employed by international organizations and foreign embassies and consulates in the United States.

LABOR MARKET

Maine's unemployment rate has been below the national average since the mid–1990s; however, it was higher than the rates in neighboring Vermont and New Hampshire. The largest employment sectors in 2004 were government, health care services, and retail trade. Wage and salary employment rose throughout the 2001–2004 period, with particularly strong gains between 2003 and 2004. The employment losses that occurred in manufacturing were offset by large increases in construction, retail trade, health care, tourism, real estate and related activities, and government. Average wages and salaries were significantly below the national average in all major industry groupings.

Employment by Industry, 2004

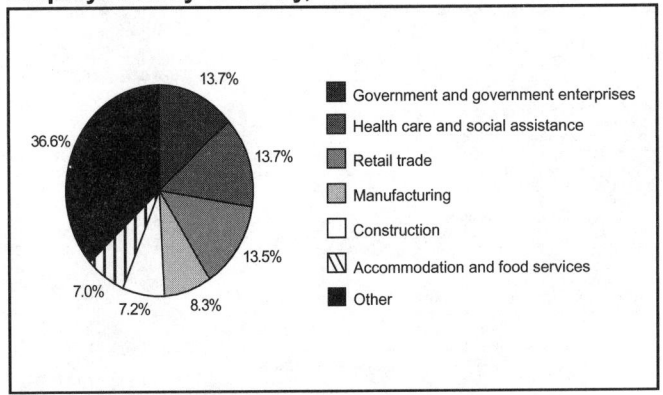

- 13.7% Government and government enterprises
- 13.7% Health care and social assistance
- 13.5% Retail trade
- 8.3% Manufacturing
- 7.2% Construction
- 7.0% Accommodation and food services
- 36.6% Other

Table ME-10. Personal Income by Major Source, Selected Years 1980–2004

(Millions of dollars, except where noted.)

Item	1980	1990	2000	2001	2002	2003	2004	Average annual percent change, 2000–2004
Earnings by Place of Work	7 189	15 907	23 371	24 837	25 545	26 631	28 228	4.8
Wage and salary disbursements	5 272	11 392	17 195	17 983	18 552	19 250	20 191	4.1
Supplements to wages and salaries	1 141	2 699	3 773	4 058	4 422	4 631	5 036	7.5
Proprietors' income[1]	776	1 816	2 404	2 795	2 571	2 750	3 001	5.7
Farm proprietors' income	-1	99	57	27	-60	-23	-26	X
Nonfarm proprietors' income	776	1 717	2 347	2 768	2 631	2 773	3 028	6.6
(-) Contributions for government social insurance[2]	670	1 704	2 666	2 812	2 857	2 941	3 079	3.7
(+) Adjustment for residence[3]	-14	58	701	726	710	706	756	1.9
(=) Net Earnings by Place of Residence	6 504	14 261	21 406	22 751	23 398	24 396	25 905	4.9
(+) Dividends, interest, and rent[4]	1 431	4 135	6 179	6 338	6 089	5 834	6 078	-0.4
(+) Personal current transfer receipts	1 471	3 006	5 588	6 018	6 477	7 021	7 499	7.6
Personal income	9 406	21 402	33 173	35 107	35 965	37 251	39 482	4.4
Farm income	9 362	21 240	33 032	34 996	35 918	37 182	39 410	4.5
Nonfarm income	44	162	141	111	47	69	72	-15.4
Per Capita Personal Income (Dollars)[5]	8 347	17 376	25 969	27 286	27 713	28 453	29 973	3.6

Note: Data may not add to total or may appear as zero due to rounding.

[1]Proprietors' income includes the inventory valuation adjustment and the capital consumption adjustment.
[2]Contributions for government social insurance are included in earnings by type and industry, but they are excluded from personal income.
[3]The adjustment for residence is the net inflow of the earnings of interarea commuters.
[4]Rental income of persons includes the capital consumption adjustment.
[5]Per capita personal income is total personal income divided by total midyear population.
X = Not applicable.

Per Capita Personal Income, 1980–2004 (Current Dollars)

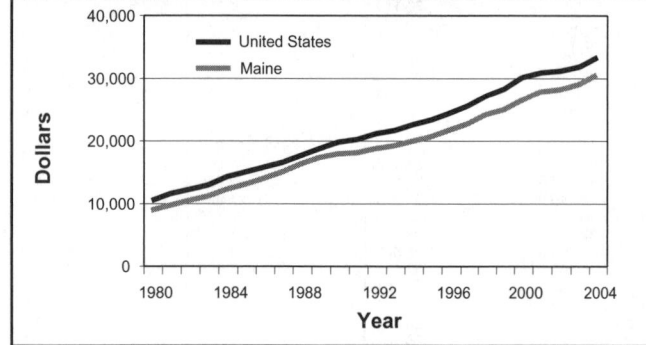

ECONOMIC ACTIVITY

The growth in gross state product withstood the 2001 recession, but in the most recent period of 2003–2004, the state's increase of 3.9 percent was below the national average and the growth rates of both Vermont and New Hampshire. Retail sales, real estate activity, health care, and government were the largest contributors to growth during this most recent period. Retail trade, management, and utilities had the highest rates of growth; however, the latter two sectors represented small portions of Maine's economy. Housing price appreciation has been at the national average rate of increase since 2000, and the median value of owner-occupied housing remained below average, ranking 25th in the nation.

Table ME-11. Real Gross State Product, 1997–2004

(Millions of chained 2000 dollars, percent.)

Industry	1997	1998	1999	2000	2001	2002	2003	2004	Average annual percent change, 2001–2004
GROSS STATE PRODUCT	33 355	33 566	34 435	35 662	36 138	37 110	38 097	39 564	3.1
As a percent of U.S. gross product	0.4	0.4	0.4	0.4	0.4	0.4	0.4	0.4	X
Private Industries	28 713	28 886	29 681	30 757	31 109	31 997	32 926	34 239	3.2
Agriculture, forestry, fishing, and hunting	416	455	543	644	540	545	585	554	0.9
Mining	3	4	4	4	4	4	4	4	0.0
Utilities	707	685	663	747	736	820	816	831	4.1
Construction	1 409	1 495	1 639	1 637	1 613	1 529	1 600	1 617	0.1
Manufacturing	4 824	4 821	4 974	5 402	4 730	4 771	4 918	5 104	2.6
As a percent of gross state product	14.5	14.4	14.4	15.1	13.1	12.9	12.9	12.9	X
Wholesale trade	1 556	1 731	1 808	1 776	1 977	2 046	2 113	2 181	3.3
Retail trade	2 761	2 950	3 066	3 177	3 483	3 730	3 987	4 237	6.8
Transportation and warehousing	768	792	802	862	842	849	906	932	3.4
Information	819	881	999	973	1 045	1 108	1 189	1 299	7.5
Finance and insurance	3 417	2 608	2 407	2 475	2 545	2 579	2 618	2 694	1.9
Real estate and rental and leasing	4 171	4 275	4 366	4 425	4 820	4 967	4 971	5 187	2.5
Services	7 936	8 211	8 419	8 636	8 779	9 065	9 255	9 654	3.2
As a percent of gross state product	23.8	24.5	24.4	24.2	24.3	24.4	24.3	24.4	X
Professional and technical services	1 336	1 430	1 481	1 578	1 626	1 679	1 713	1 773	2.9
Management of companies and enterprises	516	493	464	460	412	436	409	474	4.8
Administrative and waste services	775	821	811	801	799	837	865	864	2.6
Educational services	318	323	330	319	317	323	313	308	-1.0
Health care and social assistance	2 908	3 006	3 198	3 328	3 467	3 593	3 704	3 876	3.8
Arts, entertainment, and recreation	239	245	266	265	289	304	313	307	2.0
Accommodation and food services	977	1 010	1 053	1 094	1 087	1 123	1 148	1 206	3.5
Other services, except public administration	867	883	816	791	782	770	790	846	2.7
Government	4 643	4 681	4 754	4 904	5 028	5 113	5 175	5 329	2.0
As a percent of gross state product	13.9	13.9	13.8	13.8	13.9	13.8	13.6	13.5	X

X = Not applicable.

Table ME-12. Government Transfer Payments, Selected Years 1980–2004

(Millions of dollars, percent.)

Item	1980	1990	2000	2001	2002	2003	2004	Average annual percent change, 2000–2004
CURRENT TRANSFER PAYMENTS TO INDIVIDUALS	1 387	2 836	5 307	5 707	6 190	6 757	7 234	8.1
Retirement and Disability Insurance Benefits	666	1 296	2 137	2 262	2 388	2 498	2 610	5.1
Old-age, survivors, and disability insurance (OASDI) benefits	640	1 246	2 076	2 200	2 322	2 429	2 539	5.2
Railroad retirement and disability benefits	25	42	46	47	49	49	50	1.7
Workers' compensation	1	7	12	12	15	15	15	6.7
Other government retirement and disability insurance benefits	*	1	3	3	3	5	5	20.1
Medical Benefits	331	943	2 250	2 497	2 774	3 146	3 487	11.6
Medicare benefits	180	456	1 002	1 113	1 197	1 269	1 394	8.6
Public assistance medical care benefits	145	472	1 234	1 364	1 550	1 855	2 068	13.8
Military medical insurance benefits	6	16	14	20	27	21	25	15.4
Income Maintenance Benefits	191	317	565	536	538	594	614	2.1
Supplemental Security Income (SSI) benefits	29	57	125	132	138	155	162	6.7
Family assistance	60	104	99	93	94	93	100	0.3
Food stamps	61	67	81	89	101	128	146	15.8
Other income maintenance benefits	41	88	259	222	204	217	206	-5.5
Unemployment Insurance Compensation	76	123	85	112	156	166	139	13.1
Veterans' Benefits	100	126	222	241	271	293	314	9.0
Federal Education and Training Assistance	22	27	45	53	59	56	59	7.2
Other Payments to Individuals	*	3	4	6	3	5	11	28.8

Note: See notes and definitions for more details. Data may not add to total or may appear as zero due to rounding.

* = Less than $500,000.

EXPORTS

The value of Maine's exports ranked 40th in the nation in 2004. Computers and electronic products were the state's leading exports, followed by paper products. Lobsters were among the state's top five commodity exports. Canada was the largest export market, and imported a large share of Maine's fishing, hunting, and trapping goods, as well as forestry and logging products. Exports to Brazil, primarily consisting of transportation equipment, grew from $16 million in 2003 to $263 million in 2004. As a result, Brazil became the state's third largest market. Exports to Malaysia, Singapore, and China have all grown considerably in recent years. However, Canada remained the destination for 34 percent of the Maine's total exports.

Leading Exports, 2004

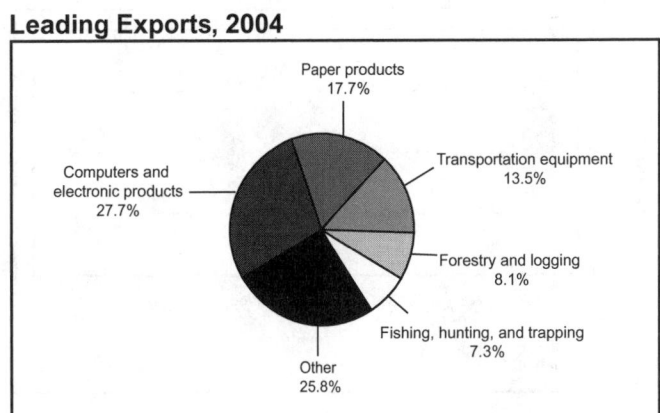

Table ME-13. Exports of Goods by Leading Products and Destinations, 2001–2004

(Millions of dollars, percent, rank based on 2004 dollar values.)

Product and market	2001	2002	2003	2004	Percent share of total, 2004	Average annual percent change, 2001–2004
Total Goods						
Total	1 812	1 973	2 188	2 432	100.0	10.3
Manufactures	1 294	1 539	1 722	1 954	80.4	14.7
Agriculture and livestock	466	393	415	421	17.3	-3.3
Other commodities	52	42	52	56	2.3	2.5
Five Leading Exports (NAICS Code)						
Computers and electronic products (334)	347	535	605	675	27.7	24.8
Paper products (322)	354	385	415	429	17.7	6.6
Transportation equipment (336)	80	101	164	327	13.5	60.2
Forestry and logging (113)	187	185	185	197	8.1	1.8
Fishing, hunting, and trapping (114)	149	166	181	177	7.3	5.9
Five Leading Markets	1 683	1 857	2 049	2 326	95.6	11.4
Canada	846	791	821	827	34.0	-0.8
Malaysia	133	168	237	339	13.9	36.6
Brazil	23	15	16	263	10.8	126.8
Singapore	105	248	224	234	9.6	30.6
China	34	48	78	113	4.6	48.8

Table ME-14. Agriculture, 1997 and 2002

(Number, acres, and dollars.)

Item	1997	2002
Number of farms	7 404	7 196
Land in farms (acres)	1 313 066	1 369 768
Farm Size		
Average size of farm (acres)	177	190
Farms by size (percent distribution)		
Fewer than 50 acres	34.0	38.6
50 to 499 acres	58.7	53.4
500 acres or more	7.3	8.0
Market Value of Land and Equipment (Dollars)		
Land and buildings average value per farm	230 120	322 690
Average value per acre	1 267	1 637
Machinery and equipment average value per farm	44 285	54 316
Value of Sales (Thousands of Dollars)		
Agricultural products sold	450 278	463 603
Crops	219 600	222 356
Livestock, poultry, and their products	230 678	241 247
Average per farm (dollars)	60 815	64 425
Value of sales (percent distribution)		
Less than $10,000	65.1	70.8
$10,000 to $99,999	24.3	19.8
$100,000 or more	10.6	9.4
Government Payments		
Payments (thousands of dollars)	3 383	8 664
Percent of farms receiving government payments	18.5	17.3
Farm operators whose principal occupation is farming (percent)	44.9	47.4

AGRICULTURE

Total cash receipts from farming amounted to $463.6 million in 2002, an increase of about 5.8 percent from the 1997 farm census. The chief products were potatoes and dairy products. More than 70 percent of farms in Maine had sales of less than $10,000. Just 9.4 percent had sales of $100,000 or more. The state's farms tended to be smaller, averaging 190 acres, compared with 441 acres nationally. Just over 47 percent of farm operators considered farming to be their principal occupation.

ENERGY

Maine's energy expenditures per capita were the seventh highest in the nation in 2001, according to the latest available data from the Department of Energy. However, the state's energy prices were slightly below the national average. In terms of consumption, the state ranked 17th on a per capita basis. Usage of petroleum was particularly high, because (like many states in New England) home heating in Maine was supplied by oil. Wood and waste was the second leading source of fuel in Maine.

Energy Consumption by Source, 2001

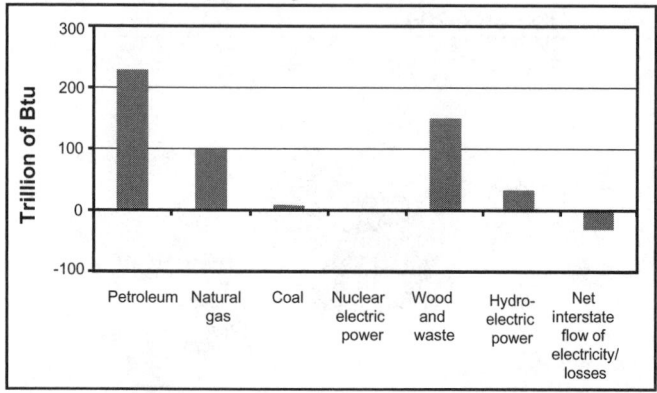

Energy Consumption by Sector, 2001

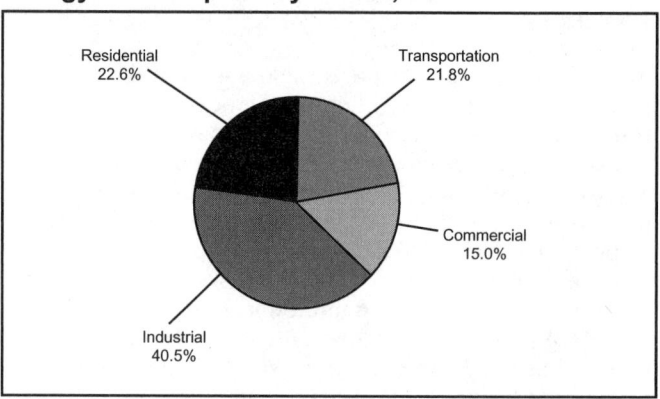

Table ME-15. Energy Consumption, Expenditures, and Prices, Selected Years 1960–2001

(Dollars, Btu [British Thermal Unit], percent distribution.)

Item	1960	1965	1970	1975	1980	1985	1990	1995	2000	2001
Total Consumption (Billion Btu)	232 411	232 387	302 735	324 743	379 416	423 171	467 312	495 877	532 368	490 686
Consumption per capita (million Btu)	239.8	233.1	304.6	302.9	337.4	363.9	380.6	400.7	417.6	381.9
Consumption by Sector (Percent Distribution)										
Residential	27.6	29.8	27.2	27.0	22.0	19.8	19.4	20.5	18.9	22.6
Commercial	7.0	8.5	8.2	9.7	9.9	10.1	13.7	11.4	13.5	15.0
Industrial	36.7	32.1	35.7	34.8	46.2	47.9	42.1	47.5	45.1	40.5
Transportation	28.7	29.6	29.0	28.4	22.0	22.2	24.7	20.6	22.5	21.8
Consumption by Source (Billion Btu)										
Coal	20 408	7 992	2 166	1 311	3 008	5 093	10 413	10 995	9 980	7 882
Natural gas	0	0	1 315	1 976	2 322	2 620	4 572	5 634	48 048	101 190
Petroleum	152 420	171 630	231 305	222 133	198 320	209 045	247 287	244 482	265 386	233 407
Nuclear electric power	0	0	0	49 586	48 040	56 875	51 436	2 076	0	0
Hydroelectric power[1]	30 607	21 625	29 942	27 719	25 106	28 118	42 550	34 586	36 630	26 911
Wood and waste	29 178	30 050	29 478	32 705	93 497	107 245	108 799	127 823	139 729	140 359
Other	508	755	1 760	4 900	12 827	2 345	7 674	15 800	17 313	15 817
Net interstate flow of electricity/losses[2]	-709	335	6 769	-15 587	-3 706	11 831	-5 419	54 481	15 280	-34 880
Total Expenditures (Thousands of Dollars)	...	...	439 400	875 100	1 785 700	2 189 900	2 645 300	2 855 700	3 809 200	3 625 000
Expenditures per capita (dollars)	...	...	442	816	1 588	1 883	2 154	2 308	2 988	2 822
Prices by Sector (Dollars Per Million Btu)										
Total	...	...	1.93	3.70	7.93	8.86	8.08	7.66	9.65	10.05
Residential	...	...	2.12	4.06	8.98	11.13	12.15	11.55	14.94	15.20
Commercial	...	...	2.40	5.06	9.09	11.73	9.46	13.16	14.68	17.12
Industrial	...	...	1.06	2.55	5.26	6.10	4.49	3.91	4.57	4.60
Transportation	...	...	2.28	3.95	8.99	9.06	9.11	9.40	11.93	11.35

[1]A negative number in this row results from pumped storage for which, overall, more electricity is expended than created to provide electricity during peak demand periods.
[2]Net interstate flow of electricity is the difference between the amount of energy in the electricity sold within a state (including associated losses) and the energy input at the electric utilities within the state. A positive number indicates that more electricity (including associated losses) came into the state than went out of the state during the year; conversely, a negative number indicates that more electricity (including associated losses) went out of the state than came into the state.
... = Not available.

Table ME-16. State Taxes, Fiscal 2004

(Dollars, percent distribution.)

Item	Thousands of dollars	Percent distribution	Dollars per capita	
			State	U.S.
TOTAL TAXES	2 896 759	100.0	2 199.5	2 024.8
Property Taxes	45 308	1.6	34.4	38.9
Sales and Gross Receipts	1 360 152	47.0	1 032.8	1 003.4
General sales and gross receipts	917 248	31.7	696.5	677.0
Selective sales taxes	442 904	15.3	336.3	326.4
Alcoholic beverages	39 279	1.4	29.8	15.7
Insurance premiums	77 770	2.7	59.0	47.0
Motor fuels	220 410	7.6	167.4	114.6
Tobacco products	92 626	3.2	70.3	42.0
Licenses	158 199	5.5	120.1	134.9
Motor vehicle	81 740	2.8	62.1	59.4
Occupation and business, not elsewhere classified	49 464	1.7	37.6	37.1
Other Taxes	1 333 100	46.0	1 012.2	847.6
Individual income	1 160 028	40.0	880.8	673.6
Corporation net income	111 616	3.9	84.8	105.1
Death and gift	32 076	1.1	24.4	19.6
Documentary and stock transfer	29 380	1.0	22.3	27.1

GOVERNMENT FINANCE

Maine's state revenues per person were the 10th highest in the nation. Expenditures per person, of $4,639, ranked 12th. Spending on public welfare, health care, and natural resources was well above the national average. Maine's debt per person was $3,375, which ranked 12th in the nation. As a result, the state spent more per person on interest on general debt than most states. Taxes per person amounted to $2,199 in fiscal year 2004. Individual income taxes were the largest source of revenue, followed by general sales taxes. The state's property taxes were slightly below the average of the 37 states with such taxes.

Per Capita State Taxes, Fiscal 2004

Table ME-17. State Government Finances, 2003

(Dollars, percent distribution.)

Item	Millions of dollars	Percent distribution	Dollars per capita	
			State	U.S.
GENERAL REVENUE	6 093 384	100.0	4 655.0	3 832.6
Intergovernmental revenue	2 062 560	33.8	1 575.7	1 246.0
Taxes	2 697 275	44.3	2 060.6	1 891.6
General sales	857 495	14.1	655.1	636.0
Selective sales	423 947	7.0	323.9	307.4
License taxes	150 171	2.5	114.7	123.6
Individual income tax	1 074 826	17.6	821.1	626.8
Corporate income tax	91 188	1.5	69.7	97.8
Other taxes	99 648	1.6	76.1	99.9
Current charges	490 682	8.1	374.8	366.5
Miscellaneous general revenue	842 867	13.8	643.9	328.6
GENERAL EXPENDITURE	6 072 093	100.0	4 638.7	4 010.5
Intergovernmental expenditure	1 051 164	17.3	803.0	1 316.9
Direct expenditure	5 020 929	82.7	3 835.7	2 693.6
Expenditure by Function				
Education	1 574 270	25.9	1 202.6	1 416.4
Public welfare	1 990 470	32.8	1 520.6	1 083.3
Hospitals	50 970	0.8	38.9	132.3
Health	400 804	6.6	306.2	173.0
Highways	492 304	8.1	376.1	295.4
Police protection	68 212	1.1	52.1	38.4
Correction	107 345	1.8	82.0	135.0
Natural resources	156 234	2.6	119.4	64.0
Parks and recreation	10 566	0.2	8.1	20.1
Government administration	243 158	4.0	185.8	151.3
Interest on general debt	233 917	3.9	178.7	107.8
Other and unallocable	743 843	12.3	568.2	393.4
DEBT AT END OF FISCAL YEAR	4 417 481	X	3 374.7	2 404.7
CASH AND SECURITY HOLDINGS	11 979 579	X	9 151.7	8 938.4

X = Not applicable.

Table ME-18. Education Indicators, 2000–2004

(Percent, number.)

Item	State	U.S.
Total Population 25 Years and Over (Thousands), 2004	881	186 877
Educational Attainment, 2004		
Percent high school graduate or more	87.1	85.2
Percent college graduate or more	24.2	27.7
Elementary and Secondary Schools, 2002–2003		
Total students	204 337	48 202 324
Percent of students eligible for free or reduced-price lunch ..	32.8	40.6
Percent of students who were English language learners	1.4	7.8
Total schools	672	92 330
Student/teacher ratio	11.5	15.9
Per student expenditures	9 344	8 041
Dropouts, Grades 9–12, 2000–2001 (Percent)	2.8	. . .
Higher Education, 2002–2003		
Total enrollment	64 086	17 035 027
Bachelor's degrees awarded	6 158	1 348 503
Percent women	59.6	57.5

. . . = Not available.

Educational Attainment, 2004

Note: Persons 25 years and over.

EDUCATION

In 2004, more than 87 percent of the state's population age 25 years and over had graduated from high school. However, this contrasted with a below average college completion rate. Just 24.2 percent of Maine's residents held bachelor's degrees or more. This may have reflected the relatively large concentration of older residents in Maine, for whom college attendance was not as prevalent. Expenditures per student in grades K–12 were the 10th highest in the nation at $9,344. The state's student/teacher ratio of 11.5 was second lowest in the country behind only Vermont. Both of these measures reflected the state's relatively low proportion of student-age population.

VOTER PARTICIPATION

Voter turnout in both the 2000 and 2004 elections was among the highest in the country. More than 70 percent of those eligible to vote in Maine went to the polls in 2004. In 2000, 49.1 percent of votes were for the Democratic presidential candidate, and in 2004, that proportion increased to 53.6 percent. Among persons age 18 to 24 years, 58.6 percent of the eligible population voted. This was among the highest proportions for that age group in the nation. More than 77 percent of eligible persons age 45 to 64 years turned out to vote in the 2004 election.

Table ME-19. Reported Voting and Registration, November 2000 and November 2004

(Numbers in thousands, percent.)

Characteristic	Total population 18 years and over	Total citizen		Total registered		Total voted	
		Number	Percent	Number	Percent	Number	Percent
NOVEMBER 2000							
Total	979	966	98.7	786	80.3	677	69.2
Male	465	461	99.1	374	80.4	315	67.7
Female	514	505	98.3	412	80.3	362	70.5
NOVEMBER 2004							
Total	1 022	1 007	98.5	824	80.6	736	72.0
Male	493	484	98.2	390	79.0	346	70.2
Female	529	523	98.9	434	82.1	390	73.7
Race and Hispanic Origin							
White alone	990	977	98.7	799	80.7	714	72.1
Non-Hispanic White alone	984	970	98.7	793	80.6	708	72.0
Black alone	8	8	B	6	B	5	B
Asian alone	9	7	B	6	B	5	B
Hispanic or Latino[1]	9	9	B	7	B	7	B
White alone or in combination	1 002	989	98.7	809	80.8	723	72.2
Non-Hispanic White alone or in combination	995	982	98.7	803	80.7	717	72.0
Black alone or in combination	8	8	B	6	B	5	B
Asian alone or in combination	9	8	B	6	B	5	B
Age							
18 to 24 years	127	125	98.6	88	69.4	74	58.6
25 to 44 years	340	334	98.1	267	78.3	238	69.8
45 to 64 years	368	362	98.6	312	84.9	285	77.4
65 to 74 years	88	87	B	75	B	68	B
75 years and over	99	98	B	82	B	71	B

[1]May be of any race.
B = Base is too small to show derived measure.

At a Glance:

- Maryland's population totaled just under 5.6 million in 2004, ranking it as the 19th most populous state in the nation, despite its relatively small land size.

- About 60 percent of the population was non-Hispanic White. Blacks accounted for over 28 percent of residents, which was the sixth highest proportion of this racial group in the nation. Just over 5 percent of Maryland's population was Asian and Pacific Islander, ranking the state eighth in the country for its proportion of this racial group.

- In 2004, median household income was the highest in the nation. Correspondingly, the state's poverty rate of 9.8 percent was relatively low.

- Maryland is unemployment rate was 4.2 percent, which ranked among the 10 lowest in the nation.

- The state had the fifth highest proportion of population age 25 years and over holding a bachelor's degree or more.

- In Maryland, 14.6 percent of residents lacked health insurance, ranking 21st in the nation but still below the national average.

Table MD-1. Population by Sex and Age, 1990, 2000, and 2004

(Number, percent.)

Sex and age	1990	2000	2004	Percent distribution, 2004	Average annual percent change, 2000–2004
Total Population	4 781 468	5 296 486	5 558 058	X	1.2
Percent of total U.S. population	1.9	1.9	1.9	X	X
Sex					
Male	2 318 671	2 557 794	2 690 901	48.4	1.3
Female	2 462 797	2 738 692	2 867 157	51.6	1.2
Age					
Under 5 years	357 818	353 393	374 578	6.7	0.2
5 to 17 years	804 423	1 002 779	1 020 230	18.4	1.7
18 years and over	919 268	3 940 314	4 163 250	74.9	1.0
18 to 24 years	3 619 227	450 922	521 202	9.4	0.1
25 to 44 years	505 373	1 664 677	1 605 417	28.9	-0.3
45 to 64 years	1 677 104	1 225 408	1 401 888	25.2	3.1
65 years and over	517 482	599 307	634 743	11.4	1.5
85 years and over	46 496	66 902	82 752	1.5	4.3
Median age (years)	32.9	36.0	36.9	X	X

X = Not applicable.

Average Annual Rate of Population Growth, 1980–2004

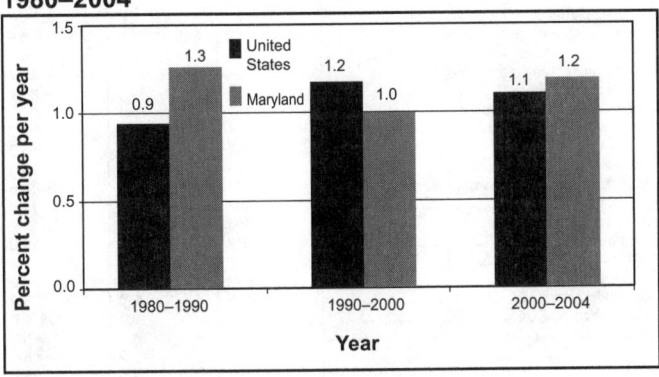

POPULATION

From 2000 to 2004, Maryland's population increased by 4.9 percent, which was above the national average but below the rate of neighboring Virginia. More than one-third of this growth was the result of international immigration, which far surpassed the number of new residents from other states. The metropolitan counties close to the District of Columbia and Baltimore were home to the largest proportion of the state's population, although counties further from these urban centers experienced rapid growth. Maryland had a below average proportion of population age 65 years and over. However, the state's median age of 36.9 years was above the national median age.

Table MD-2. Population by Race and Hispanic Origin, 1990, 2000, and 2004

(Number, percent.)

Race and Hispanic origin	1990	2000	2004
Total Population	4 781 468	5 296 486	5 558 058
Non-Hispanic (Percent)			
One race[1]			
White	69.6	62.3	59.8
Black	24.6	27.9	28.6
American Indian, Alaska Native[2]	0.3	0.3	0.3
Asian and Pacific Islander[2]	2.9	4.1	4.6
Other race[2]	0.9	. . .	. . .
Two or more races	. . .	1.2	1.3
Hispanic or Latino[3] (Percent)	2.6	4.3	5.4

[1]Individuals could report only one race in the 1990 census and could report one or more races on the 2000 census. Data on race in 2000 and 2004 are not comparable to 1990.
[2]Data for 1990 include people of Hispanic or Latino origin.
[3]May be of any race.
. . . = Not available.

Minority Population as a Percent of Total Population, 2004

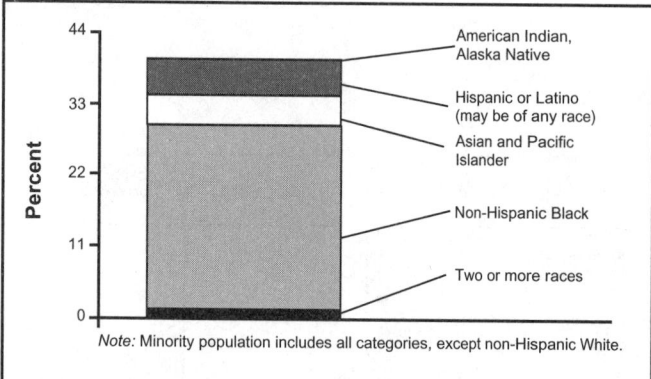

Note: Minority population includes all categories, except non-Hispanic White.

Age-Adjusted Death Rates, Average 2000–2002

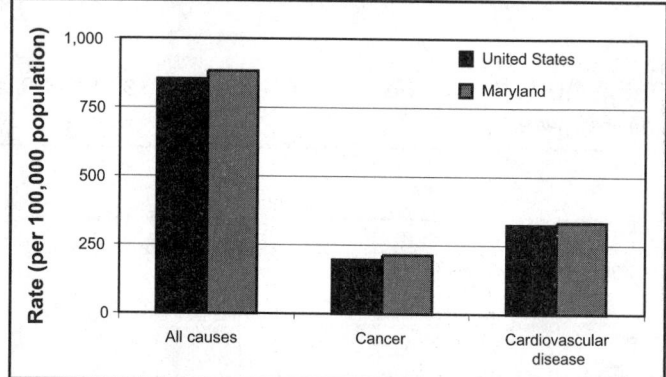

HEALTH

Maryland ranked 21st in the nation for its proportion of residents who lacked health insurance. The infant mortality rate and age-adjusted death rates were above the national average, ranking 16th and 18th, respectively. Maryland's birth rate and teenage birth rate were slightly below average.

Table MD-3. Health Characteristics, 2000–2004

(Number, rate, percent.)

Item	State	U.S.
Births, 2003–2004		
Number of births	74 930	4 089 950
Birth rate (per 1,000 population)	13.6	14.1
Teenage birth rate (per 1,000 women age 15–19 years)	33.3	41.6
Mortality Rates, Average 2000–2002		
Infant mortality rate (per 1,000 live births)	7.7	6.9
Age-adjusted mortality rate (per 100,000 population)		
All races	881.8	853.3
Non-Hispanic White	838.6	843.1
Black	1 094.5	1 097.7
American Indian, Alaska Native	. . .	687.0
Asian and Pacific Islander	402.4	486.0
Hispanic or Latino[1]	280.2	642.7
Health Insurance, 2004		
Percent of all persons without health insurance	14.6	15.7
Percent of children without health insurance	9.6	11.2
Percent of low-income children without health insurance	5.9	7.1

[1]May be of any race.
. . . = Not available.

Table MD-4. Leading Causes of Death, Average 2000–2002

(Number, rate per 100,000 population.)

Cause	Number of deaths	Age-adjusted death rates State	Age-adjusted death rates U.S.
ALL CAUSES	43 854	881.8	853.3
Leading Causes			
Major cardiovascular diseases	16 049	329.0	326.5
Cancer	10 336	204.8	196.0
Chronic lower respiratory diseases	1 926	39.6	43.7
Unintentional injuries	1 284	24.6	35.7
Diabetes (underlying cause)	1 497	30.1	25.2
Influenza and pneumonia	1 055	21.9	22.7
Alzheimer's disease	875	18.7	19.0
Motor vehicle accidents	664	12.5	15.0
Nephritis, nephrotic syndrome, and nephrosis ..	606	12.3	13.8
Septicemia	994	20.1	11.4
Suicides	468	8.7	10.7
Firearm-related	613	11.6	10.3
Cirrhosis	456	8.5	9.5
Drug-induced	697	12.5	7.9
Alcohol-induced	285	5.2	6.9
Homicides	516	9.7	6.0
Falls	215	4.4	5.2
HIV	578	10.2	5.0
Viral hepatitis	105	1.9	2.0
Anemias	102	2.1	1.6
Drownings	48	0.9	1.3
Fire deaths	49	0.9	1.2

Note: The rates are age-adjusted to the U.S. 2000 standard population.

Table MD-5. Households and Housing Characteristics, 1990, 2000, and 2004

(Number, percent, and dollars.)

Characteristic	1990	2000	2004	Average annual percent change, 2000–2004
Total Households	1 748 991	1 980 859	2 077 900	1.2
Family households	1 245 814	1 359 318	1 383 478	0.4
Married-couple family	948 563	994 549	994 244	0.0
Other family	297 251	364 769	389 234	1.6
Male householder, no wife present	65 362	84 893	80 735	-1.2
Female householder, no husband present	231 889	279 876	308 499	2.5
Nonfamily households	503 177	621 541	694 422	2.8
Householder living alone	394 572	495 459	566 334	3.4
Householder not living alone	108 605	126 082	128 088	0.4
Housing Characteristics				
Average size	2.67	2.61	2.61	X
Housing units	1 891 917	2 145 283	2 250 339	1.2
Occupied housing units	1 748 991	1 980 859	2 077 900	1.2
Owner-occupied	1 137 296	1 341 751	1 443 955	1.9
Renter-occupied	611 695	639 108	633 945	-0.2
Median gross rent of renter-occupied housing units (dollars) ...	548	689	837	5.0
Median value of owner-occupied housing units (dollars)	115 500	146 000	216 529	10.4

X = Not applicable.

Median Housing Value and Median Rent, 2004

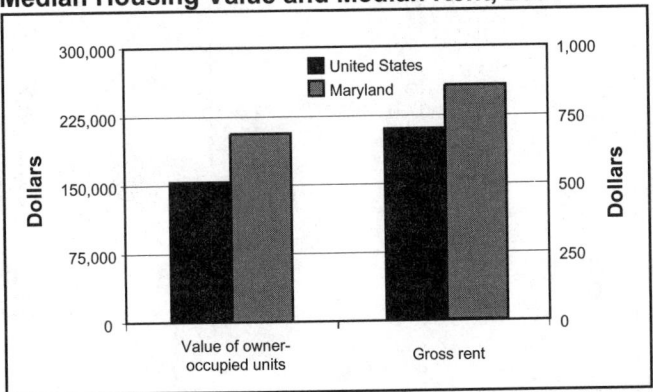

Median Household Income, 1984–2004 (2004 Dollars)

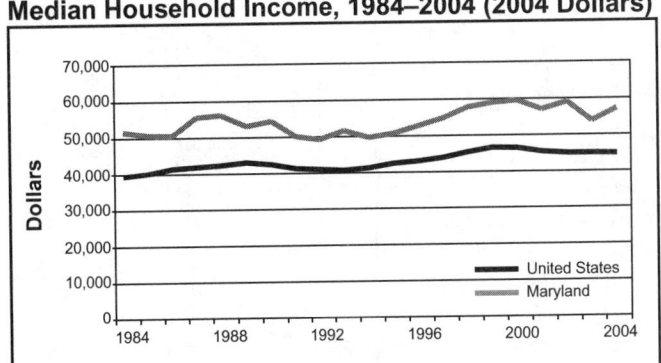

Table MD-6. Household Income and Poverty Status, 1980–2004

(2004 CPI-U-RS adjusted dollars, rate.)

Year	State		U.S.	
	Median household income (2004 dollars)	Poverty rate	Median household income (2004 dollars)	Poverty rate
2004	57 319	9.8	44 389	12.7
2003	53 720	8.6	44 482	12.5
2002	59 250	7.4	44 546	12.1
2001	57 122	7.2	45 062	11.7
2000	59 819	7.4	46 058	11.3
1999	59 174	7.3	46 129	11.9
1998	57 886	7.2	45 003	12.7
1997	54 791	8.4	43 430	13.3
1996	52 734	10.3	42 544	13.7
1995	50 516	10.1	41 943	13.8
1994	49 420	10.7	40 677	14.5
1993	51 414	9.7	40 217	15.1
1992	49 087	11.8	40 422	14.8
1991	49 978	9.1	40 746	14.2
1990	54 455	9.9	41 963	13.5
1989	52 984	9.0	42 524	12.8
1988	56 082	9.8	41 771	13.0
1987	55 608	9.2	41 322	13.4
1986	50 324	9.2	40 939	13.6
1985	50 459	8.7	39 545	14.0
1984	51 400	8.7	38 782	14.4
1983	. . .	8.7	. . .	15.2
1982	. . .	12.3	. . .	15.0
1981	. . .	10.7	. . .	14.0
1980	. . .	9.5	. . .	13.0

. . . = Not available.

Table MD-7. Employment Status by Demographic Group, 2004

(Numbers in thousands, rate.)

Characteristic	Civilian noninstitutional population	Civilian labor force		Employed	Unemployment rate
		Number	Participation rate		
SEX AND AGE					
Total	4 223	2 883	68.3	2 762	4.2
16 to 19 years	306	137	44.7	117	14.6
20 to 24 years	325	244	75.1	224	8.0
25 to 34 years	661	565	85.5	546	3.4
35 to 44 years	928	787	84.8	765	2.9
45 to 54 years	788	668	84.8	645	3.4
55 to 64 years	572	380	66.4	365	3.8
65 years and over	643	102	15.9	99	2.8
Men	1 986	1 489	75.0	1 431	3.9
16 to 19 years	145	61	42.4	51	16.4
20 to 24 years	173	135	78.1	124	8.4
25 to 34 years	322	300	93.0	292	2.7
35 to 44 years	428	402	93.9	393	2.3
45 to 54 years	377	336	89.3	326	3.1
55 to 64 years	276	200	72.7	193	3.7
65 years and over	265	54	20.2	52	2.1
Women	2 237	1 394	62.3	1 331	4.6
16 to 19 years	161	76	46.8	66	13.2
20 to 24 years	151	108	71.6	100	7.5
25 to 34 years	339	265	78.3	254	4.2
35 to 44 years	500	385	77.1	372	3.4
45 to 54 years	411	331	80.6	319	3.7
55 to 64 years	296	180	60.6	172	4.0
65 years and over	378	49	12.9	47	3.6
MARITAL STATUS					
Married men, spouse present	1 060	840	79.3	825	1.8
Married women, spouse present	1 074	687	64.0	665	3.2
Women who maintain families	276	214	77.5	202	5.6
RACE, HISPANIC ORIGIN, AND SEX					
White	2 862	1 939	67.7	1 871	3.5
Men	1 387	1 052	75.9	1 018	3.2
Women	1 475	886	60.1	853	3.8
Black	1 119	773	69.1	725	6.2
Men	493	355	72.0	335	5.8
Women	625	418	66.9	391	6.5
Asian	178	123	69.4	120	2.5
Hispanic or Latino[1]	289	232	80.3	222	4.4
Men	168	154	91.2	148	3.9
Women	121	79	65.0	74	5.2
RACE, HISPANIC ORIGIN, AND AGE					
White					
16 to 19 years	190	100	52.3	87	12.8
20 to 24 years	202	158	78.3	149	5.5
25 to 34 years	427	368	86.3	358	2.6
35 to 44 years	593	501	84.5	489	2.3
45 to 54 years	541	466	86.1	453	2.8
55 to 64 years	397	267	67.2	258	3.4
65 years and over	513	80	15.5	77	3.4

Note: Data in Table 7 are from the Current Population Survey (CPS) and do not match Bureau of Labor Statistics estimates in Table 8. See notes and definitions for more details.

[1]May be of any race.

Table MD-8. Employment Status, 1990–2004

(Numbers in thousands, rate.)

Year	Civilian labor force	Employed	Unemployed	Unemployment rate
2004	2 882 638	2 761 015	121 623	4.2
2003	2 879 654	2 751 455	128 199	4.5
2002	2 862 890	2 735 130	127 760	4.5
2001	2 833 516	2 719 498	114 018	4.0
2000	2 802 403	2 702 823	99 580	3.6
1999	2 787 870	2 687 843	100 027	3.6
1998	2 780 009	2 661 192	118 817	4.3
1997	2 778 202	2 646 200	132 002	4.8
1996	2 751 738	2 615 584	136 154	4.9
1995	2 709 899	2 572 708	137 191	5.1
1994	2 684 166	2 545 413	138 753	5.2
1993	2 660 795	2 501 515	159 280	6.0
1992	2 659 659	2 484 910	174 749	6.6
1991	2 629 882	2 466 378	163 504	6.2
1990	2 582 827	2 465 249	117 578	4.6

Note: Population age 16 years and over.

Unemployment Rate, 1980–2004

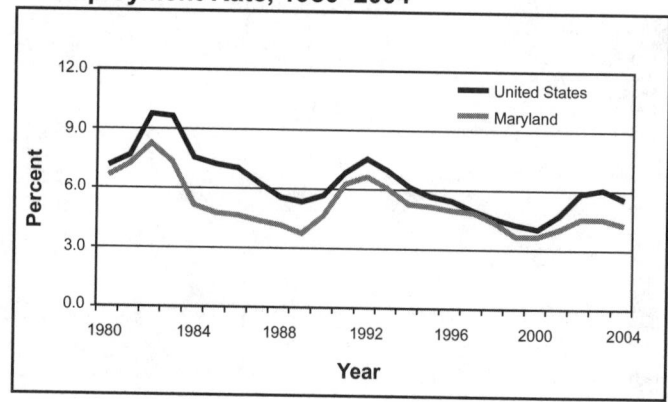

Table MD-9. Employment and Average Wages by Industry, 2001–2004

(Estimates are based on the 2002 North American Industry Classification System [NAICS].)

Industry	2001	2002	2003	2004	Annual average percent change, 2001–2004
	Number of jobs				
TOTAL EMPLOYMENT BY PLACE OF WORK	3 128 757	3 162 131	3 198 086	3 245 769	1.2
Farm Employment	18 727	18 942	17 651	17 597	-2.1
Nonfarm Employment	3 110 030	3 143 189	3 180 435	3 228 172	1.3
Private employment	2 590 126	2 613 359	2 648 601	2 703 236	1.4
Forestry, fishing, hunting, and other[1]	6 858	7 746	7 107	7 106	1.2
Mining	2 991	2 623	2 881	3 064	0.8
Utilities	11 203	10 293	9 943	9 748	-4.5
Construction	214 170	213 894	219 863	229 732	2.4
Manufacturing	175 143	163 075	153 593	149 755	-5.1
Durable goods manufacturing	94 903	87 199	81 294	79 715	-5.6
Nondurable goods manufacturing	80 240	75 876	72 299	70 040	-4.4
Wholesale trade	101 829	100 848	98 907	100 240	-0.5
Retail trade	353 357	352 699	355 822	361 158	0.7
Transportation and warehousing	91 500	90 477	89 030	90 510	-0.4
Information	69 644	63 735	61 655	60 333	-4.7
Finance and insurance	140 828	143 724	147 196	147 467	1.5
Real estate and rental and leasing	115 749	118 490	125 690	130 848	4.2
Professional and technical services	286 305	288 995	295 716	303 178	1.9
Management of companies and enterprises	11 237	11 408	10 249	12 318	3.1
Administrative and waste services	187 740	190 528	194 872	202 241	2.5
Educational services	69 507	75 652	78 209	81 736	5.6
Health care and social assistance	324 676	335 629	346 441	352 821	2.8
Arts, entertainment, and recreation	62 439	65 583	66 473	69 424	3.6
Accommodation and food services	187 733	193 520	197 935	202 257	2.5
Other services, except public administration	177 217	184 440	187 019	189 300	2.2
Government and government enterprises	519 904	529 830	531 834	524 936	0.3
	Dollars				
AVERAGE WAGES AND SALARIES BY PLACE OF WORK	37 640	38 841	40 202	42 117	3.8
Farm Earnings	18 601	23 732	23 623	26 015	11.8
Nonfarm Earnings	37 687	38 879	40 238	42 151	3.8
Private earnings	36 675	37 466	38 774	40 607	3.5
Forestry, fishing, hunting, and other[1]	21 651	21 963	22 982	24 276	3.9
Mining	50 836	47 871	47 999	48 546	-1.5
Utilities	66 757	68 629	72 890	76 437	4.6
Construction	40 376	41 220	42 285	44 058	3.0
Manufacturing	47 099	48 388	50 135	53 289	4.2
Durable goods manufacturing	52 083	54 357	56 581	60 607	5.2
Nondurable goods manufacturing	41 235	41 566	42 943	45 026	3.0
Wholesale trade	51 987	52 679	54 834	57 571	3.5
Retail trade	24 021	24 665	25 421	26 242	3.0
Transportation and warehousing	35 837	36 571	37 563	39 120	3.0
Information	55 830	56 233	57 814	60 987	3.0
Finance and insurance	57 959	60 067	64 071	66 818	4.9
Real estate and rental and leasing	35 769	37 785	39 764	44 268	7.4
Professional and technical services	58 653	60 473	61 789	65 377	3.7
Management of companies and enterprises	52 829	54 356	65 178	67 086	8.3
Administrative and waste services	25 639	26 851	27 753	28 991	4.2
Educational services	30 354	31 157	32 817	34 186	4.0
Health care and social assistance	34 486	35 582	36 851	38 592	3.8
Arts, entertainment, and recreation	23 432	23 333	23 599	24 303	1.2
Accommodation and food services	16 598	16 479	17 131	17 610	2.0
Other services, except public administration	24 653	25 406	26 612	27 768	4.0
Government and government enterprises	41 764	44 475	46 040	48 440	5.1

Note: Average wages and salaries are a calculation by the editors of wage and salary disbursements divided by full- and part-time wage and salary employment. Data may not add to total or may appear as zero due to rounding.

[1] "Other" consists of the number of jobs held by U.S. residents employed by international organizations and foreign embassies and consulates in the United States.

LABOR MARKET

In recent years, Maryland's unemployment rate has been below the national average. Employment grew steadily over the 2001–2004 period at an annual rate of 1.2 percent, which was double the national average rate. The service industries, particularly education, health care, and real estate and related activities, had strong growth. Utilities, manufacturing, and information had significant declines in employment from 2001 to 2004. In 2004, government, retail trade, health care, and professional and technical services were the largest employers. Average wages and salaries in Maryland were higher than the national average.

Employment by Industry, 2004

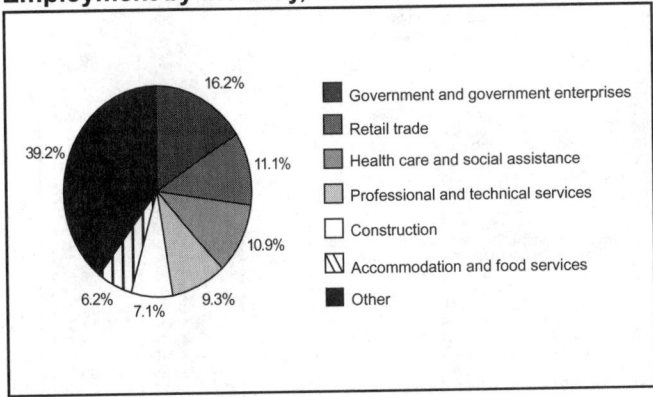

Table MD-10. Personal Income by Major Source, Selected Years 1980–2004

(Millions of dollars, except where noted.)

Item	1980	1990	2000	2001	2002	2003	2004	Average annual percent change, 2000–2004
Earnings by Place of Work	32 902	75 579	124 435	132 158	138 693	145 105	155 168	5.7
Wage and salary disbursements	25 469	57 367	93 833	98 643	102 369	106 327	112 383	4.6
Supplements to wages and salaries	5 116	12 362	19 668	21 104	23 451	24 912	27 570	8.8
Proprietors' income[1]	2 318	5 850	10 934	12 411	12 874	13 866	15 215	8.6
Farm proprietors' income	-23	249	214	151	-48	122	199	-1.8
Nonfarm proprietors' income	2 341	5 601	10 720	12 260	12 922	13 744	15 017	8.8
(-) Contributions for government social insurance[2]	2 861	8 417	13 613	14 628	15 350	15 976	17 122	5.9
(+) Adjustment for residence[3]	5 961	12 546	19 892	20 321	21 042	21 978	23 895	4.7
(=) Net Earnings by Place of Residence	36 002	79 708	130 715	137 851	144 386	151 107	161 941	5.5
(+) Dividends, interest, and rent[4]	6 767	20 088	32 998	33 910	32 939	32 512	34 292	1.0
(+) Personal current transfer receipts	4 526	9 890	18 245	19 896	21 460	22 896	24 028	7.1
Personal income	47 296	109 686	181 957	191 657	198 785	206 515	220 261	4.9
Farm income	47 243	109 342	181 612	191 373	198 663	206 247	219 904	4.9
Nonfarm income	53	344	345	284	122	268	357	0.8
Per Capita Personal Income (Dollars)[5]	11 187	22 852	34 257	35 628	36 531	37 464	39 629	3.7

Note: Data may not add to total or may appear as zero due to rounding.

[1]Proprietors' income includes the inventory valuation adjustment and the capital consumption adjustment.
[2]Contributions for government social insurance are included in earnings by type and industry, but they are excluded from personal income.
[3]The adjustment for residence is the net inflow of the earnings of interarea commuters.
[4]Rental income of persons includes the capital consumption adjustment.
[5]Per capita personal income is total personal income divided by total midyear population.

Per Capita Personal Income, 1980–2004 (Current Dollars)

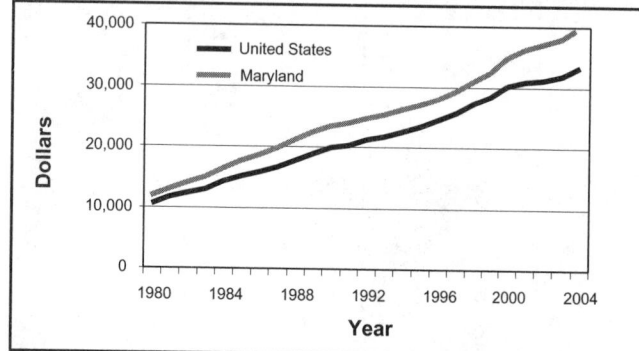

ECONOMIC ACTIVITY

Maryland did not suffer any fall-off in economic activity during the 2001–2004 period, as the national recession did not dampen the gross state product (GSP) growth. From 2003 to 2004, the GSP grew by 4.8 percent, which was higher than the national average rate of growth. Government, real estate, professional and technical services, and retail trade were the largest contributors to the GSP. Management services had the highest rate of growth from 2001 to 2004. Housing prices in many parts of Maryland were among the highest in the nation over the 2000–2004 period. The median value of owner-occupied housing was the 10th highest in the nation in 2004.

Table MD-11. Real Gross State Product, 1997–2004

(Millions of chained 2000 dollars, percent.)

Industry	1997	1998	1999	2000	2001	2002	2003	2004	Average annual percent change, 2001–2004
GROSS STATE PRODUCT	162 706	168 683	175 064	179 978	187 245	192 482	198 334	207 797	3.5
As a percent of U.S. gross product	1.9	1.9	1.9	1.8	1.9	1.9	1.9	1.9	X
Private Industries	133 113	138 056	144 315	148 859	155 494	160 136	166 128	174 698	4.0
Agriculture, forestry, fishing, and hunting	466	514	560	670	572	526	615	608	2.1
Mining	102	111	111	126	126	134	133	134	2.1
Utilities	4 773	4 588	4 672	4 943	4 947	4 903	5 205	5 469	3.4
Construction	9 364	9 458	9 770	9 866	10 176	10 138	10 256	10 723	1.8
Manufacturing	11 895	12 366	12 683	12 751	12 908	13 065	13 528	14 099	3.0
As a percent of gross state product	7.3	7.3	7.2	7.1	6.9	6.8	6.8	6.8	X
Wholesale trade	8 551	9 440	10 008	10 069	10 994	11 213	11 007	11 387	1.2
Retail trade	11 205	11 618	12 013	12 448	13 460	14 234	15 044	15 976	5.9
Transportation and warehousing	3 691	3 766	4 003	4 222	4 017	4 191	4 350	4 520	4.0
Information	5 623	6 041	6 536	7 219	7 681	7 519	7 887	8 663	4.1
Finance and insurance	9 474	10 242	11 012	11 276	12 015	12 968	14 053	14 610	6.7
Real estate and rental and leasing	23 830	24 308	25 676	26 649	28 230	28 724	29 389	30 980	3.1
Services	44 296	45 649	47 295	48 621	50 425	52 623	54 828	57 782	4.6
As a percent of gross state product	27.2	27.1	27.0	27.0	26.9	27.3	27.6	27.8	X
Professional and technical services	13 989	14 915	15 805	16 739	17 928	19 107	20 096	21 458	6.2
Management of companies and enterprises	719	693	678	726	900	961	1 100	1 325	13.8
Administrative and waste services	5 288	5 579	5 830	5 417	5 383	5 731	6 035	6 311	5.4
Educational services	1 662	1 753	1 844	1 979	1 978	2 003	1 983	2 001	0.4
Health care and social assistance	11 799	11 771	12 010	12 424	12 947	13 469	13 972	14 386	3.6
Arts, entertainment, and recreation	1 504	1 378	1 408	1 437	1 397	1 432	1 427	1 501	2.4
Accommodation and food services	4 616	4 759	4 947	5 008	5 096	5 140	5 345	5 559	2.9
Other services, except public administration	4 719	4 801	4 773	4 891	4 796	4 780	4 870	5 241	3.0
Government	29 629	30 661	30 754	31 120	31 753	32 354	32 263	33 178	1.5
As a percent of gross state product	18.2	18.2	17.6	17.3	17.0	16.8	16.3	16.0	X

X = Not applicable.

Table MD-12. Government Transfer Payments, Selected Years 1980–2004

(Millions of dollars, percent.)

Item	1980	1990	2000	2001	2002	2003	2004	Average annual percent change, 2000–2004
CURRENT TRANSFER PAYMENTS TO INDIVIDUALS	4 217	9 223	16 981	18 474	20 146	21 663	22 778	7.6
Retirement and Disability Insurance Benefits	1 985	4 295	7 045	7 479	7 864	8 175	8 592	5.1
Old-age, survivors, and disability insurance (OASDI) benefits	1 851	3 877	6 625	7 061	7 432	7 720	8 122	5.2
Railroad retirement and disability benefits	87	144	152	153	156	156	159	1.0
Workers' compensation	29	249	250	246	255	263	273	2.3
Other government retirement and disability insurance benefits	18	25	18	18	19	20	36	19.6
Medical Benefits	1 149	3 397	7 499	8 331	9 157	10 182	10 862	9.7
Medicare benefits	633	1 965	4 259	4 737	5 084	5 386	5 942	8.7
Public assistance medical care benefits	503	1 371	3 198	3 531	3 981	4 713	4 820	10.8
Military medical insurance benefits	13	61	43	62	91	83	101	23.9
Income Maintenance Benefits	540	857	1 548	1 541	1 669	1 780	1 901	5.3
Supplemental Security Income (SSI) benefits	83	191	407	428	442	450	471	3.7
Family assistance	217	307	248	232	219	190	236	-1.2
Food stamps	145	214	196	194	220	266	296	10.9
Other income maintenance benefits	95	145	697	686	788	874	898	6.5
Unemployment Insurance Compensation	240	277	275	441	721	754	529	17.8
Veterans' Benefits	234	292	429	457	508	544	573	7.5
Federal Education and Training Assistance	69	101	168	200	212	197	210	5.7
Other Payments to Individuals	2	4	16	26	15	31	111	61.3

Note: See notes and definitions for more details. Data may not add to total or may appear as zero due to rounding.

EXPORTS

The value of Maryland's exports ranked 29th in the nation in 2004. The state's chief export products were chemicals, computers and electronic products, and transportation equipment (airplanes and helicopter parts). Canada was Maryland's leading export market, as the destination for 19 percent of the state's goods. Exports to Egypt have increased from $66 million in 2001 to $383 million in 2004. Transportation equipment accounted for more than 60 percent of total exports to Egypt. Japan also became a leading destination for Maryland's exports. In 2004, leather and related products made up about 60 percent of the state's exports to Japan.

Leading Exports, 2004

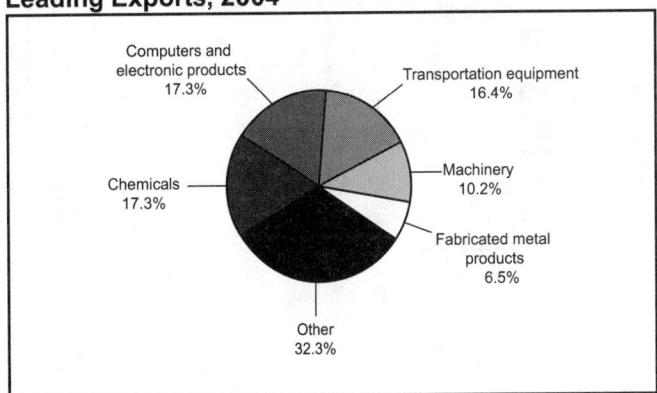

Table MD-13. Exports of Goods by Leading Products and Destinations, 2001–2004

(Millions of dollars, percent, rank based on 2004 dollar values.)

Product and market	2001	2002	2003	2004	Percent share of total, 2004	Average annual percent change, 2001–2004
Total Goods						
Total	4 975	4 474	4 941	5 746	100.0	4.9
Manufactures	4 620	4 173	4 585	5 367	93.4	5.1
Agriculture and livestock	146	67	81	143	2.5	-0.6
Other commodities	208	234	274	236	4.1	4.2
Five Leading Exports (NAICS Code)						
Chemical manufactures (325)	628	707	838	996	17.3	16.6
Computers and electronic products (334)	1 242	808	744	991	17.3	-7.2
Transportation equipment (336)	803	914	1 019	942	16.4	5.5
Machinery manufactures (333)	611	424	488	588	10.2	-1.3
Fabricated metal products (332)	241	279	246	371	6.5	15.4
Five Leading Markets	4 249	3 794	4 240	4 962	86.4	5.3
Canada	869	824	943	1 092	19.0	7.9
Egypt	66	38	328	383	6.7	79.4
Japan	213	262	311	360	6.3	19.1
Mexico	131	242	301	341	5.9	37.7
United Kingdom	313	331	325	323	5.6	1.0

Table MD-14. Agriculture, 1997 and 2002

(Number, acres, and dollars.)

Item	1997	2002
Number of farms	13 254	12 198
Land in farms (acres)	2 193 063	2 077 630
Farm Size		
Average size of farm (acres)	165	170
Farms by size (percent distribution)		
Fewer than 50 acres	46.3	47.8
50 to 499 acres	46.3	44.4
500 acres or more	7.4	7.8
Market Value of Land and Equipment (Dollars)		
Land and buildings average value per farm	537 600	694 061
Average value per acre	3 247	4 084
Machinery and equipment average value per farm	57 316	74 528
Value of Sales (Thousands of Dollars)		
Agricultural products sold	1 371 374	1 293 303
Crops	456 523	450 202
Livestock, poultry, and their products	914 851	843 101
Average per farm (dollars)	103 469	106 026
Value of sales (percent distribution)		
Less than $10,000	53.5	60.5
$10,000 to $99,999	26.5	22.3
$100,000 or more	20.0	17.2
Government Payments		
Payments (thousands of dollars)	14 470	33 131
Percent of farms receiving government payments	22.7	27.6
Farm operators whose principal occupation is farming (percent) ...	49.2	57.2

AGRICULTURE

Cash receipts from farming in Maryland were $1.3 billion in 2002, a slight decline from the previous farm census in 1997. The state's chief products were poultry, greenhouse/nursery products, and dairy products. About 60 percent of Maryland's farms had sales of less than $100,000. Nearly 48 percent of the state's farms spanned fewer than 50 acres. The proportion of farm operators reporting farming as their principal occupation was 57.2 percent in 2002.

ENERGY

Energy prices per Btu in Maryland ranked 13th in the nation. However, the state's energy expenditures per person were among the lowest in the country in 2001, the latest year for which data are available from the Department of Energy. This may reflect a less than average industrial sector, and, consequently, less consumption of energy. Maryland's energy consumption per capita was also low, ranking 42nd in the nation. Petroleum and coal were the state's leading energy sources.

Energy Consumption by Source, 2001

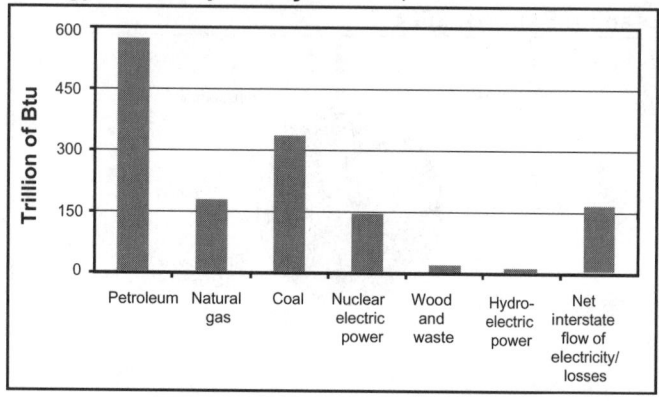

Energy Consumption by Sector, 2001

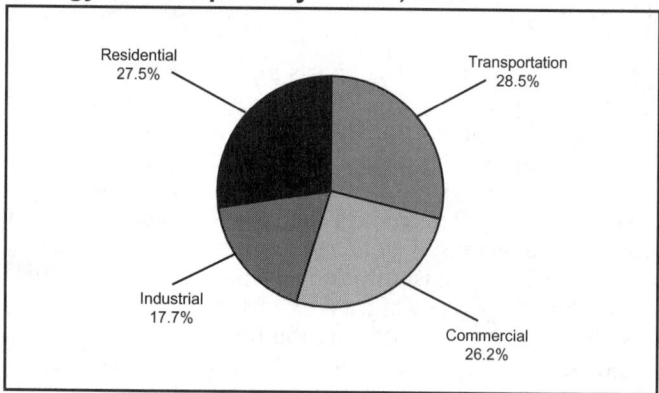

Table MD-15. Energy Consumption, Expenditures, and Prices, Selected Years 1960–2001

(Dollars, Btu [British Thermal Unit], percent distribution.)

Item	1960	1965	1970	1975	1980	1985	1990	1995	2000	2001
Total Consumption (Billion Btu)	697 463	863 099	1 073 600	1 069 928	1 153 202	1 159 826	1 261 768	1 333 014	1 443 606	1 420 356
Consumption per capita (million Btu)	224.9	239.7	273.6	258.5	273.5	262.8	263.9	265.3	272.6	263.8
Consumption by Sector (Percent Distribution)										
Residential	20.5	20.4	22.1	23.5	24.3	25.2	26.2	28.4	27.7	27.5
Commercial	10.6	10.6	12.2	14.4	14.3	13.1	13.6	25.8	26.1	26.2
Industrial	44.1	43.8	40.3	34.3	33.8	34.2	34.0	19.6	18.2	17.7
Transportation	24.8	25.2	25.4	27.8	27.6	27.4	26.3	26.2	27.9	28.5
Consumption by Source (Billion Btu)										
Coal	226 566	327 393	311 292	197 160	235 710	256 210	286 482	289 558	312 162	317 322
Natural gas	73 315	100 979	159 584	141 854	163 449	155 966	180 591	199 201	219 360	191 405
Petroleum	353 374	413 403	534 447	593 623	532 968	484 432	510 496	490 550	557 303	568 131
Nuclear electric power	0	0	0	48 307	119 409	105 434	13 242	135 939	144 204	142 681
Hydroelectric power[1]	14 609	11 925	20 009	24 049	13 189	15 919	23 913	14 870	17 674	12 041
Wood and waste	23 838	27 094	31 772	31 785	27 785	37 028	28 833	38 114	36 617	28 008
Other	0	0	0	0	0	0	114	141	164	303
Net interstate flow of electricity/losses[2]	5 761	-17 695	16 495	33 150	60 692	104 837	218 096	164 640	156 122	160 464
Total Expenditures (Thousands of Dollars)	. . .	. . .	1 527 300	3 256 100	6 432 700	7 393 800	8 047 100	8 986 600	11 581 700	11 445 500
Expenditures per capita (dollars)	. . .	. . .	389	787	1 525	1 675	1 683	1 789	2 187	2 126
Prices by Sector (Dollars Per Million Btu)										
Total	. . .	. . .	1.78	4.00	7.66	9.02	9.40	10.21	12.11	12.09
Residential	. . .	. . .	2.31	4.57	8.45	11.46	12.31	13.64	15.09	15.78
Commercial	. . .	. . .	2.60	5.76	9.75	12.91	11.87	12.65	13.86	14.15
Industrial	. . .	. . .	0.91	2.78	4.96	6.31	6.50	5.25	6.93	6.80
Transportation	. . .	. . .	2.30	4.30	8.92	9.02	9.61	9.69	12.12	11.63

[1]A negative number in this row results from pumped storage for which, overall, more electricity is expended than created to provide electricity during peak demand periods.
[2]Net interstate flow of electricity is the difference between the amount of energy in the electricity sold within a state (including associated losses) and the energy input at the electric utilities within the state. A positive number indicates that more electricity (including associated losses) came into the state than went out of the state during the year; conversely, a negative number indicates that more electricity (including associated losses) went out of the state than came into the state.
. . . = Not available.

Table MD-16. State Taxes, Fiscal 2004

(Dollars, percent distribution.)

Item	Thousands of dollars	Percent distribution	Dollars per capita	
			State	U.S.
TOTAL TAXES	12 314 799	100.0	2 215.7	2 024.8
Property Taxes	478 796	3.9	86.2	38.9
Sales and Gross Receipts	5 212 424	42.3	937.8	1 003.4
General sales and gross receipts	2 945 060	23.9	529.9	677.0
Selective sales taxes	2 267 364	18.4	408.0	326.4
Insurance premiums	279 089	2.3	50.2	47.0
Motor fuels	746 044	6.1	134.2	114.6
Public utilities	137 373	1.1	24.7	39.2
Tobacco products	272 066	2.2	49.0	42.0
Other selective sales	792 469	6.4	142.6	49.8
Licenses	511 559	4.2	92.0	134.9
Motor vehicle	282 167	2.3	50.8	59.4
Occupation and business, not elsewhere classified	131 948	1.1	23.7	37.1
Other Taxes	6 112 020	49.6	1 099.7	847.6
Individual income	5 277 844	42.9	949.6	673.6
Corporation net income	447 487	3.6	80.5	105.1
Death and gift	152 251	1.2	27.4	19.6
Documentary and stock transfer	183 189	1.5	33.0	27.1

GOVERNMENT FINANCE

Despite being a high-income state, Maryland's revenues per person were low relative to the national average. The state's per capita expenditures in 2003 also ranked below average. On a per capita basis, Maryland spent more on health, corrections, and law enforcement, and less on education and public welfare. The state's debt per person was above the national average. The state's taxes per person were above average, ranking 15th in the country. Among the 37 states with property taxes, Maryland ranked 10th. The state's individual income taxes were the largest tax source and were the eighth highest in the nation.

Per Capita State Taxes, Fiscal 2004

Table MD-17. State Government Finances, 2003

(Dollars, percent distribution.)

Item	Millions of dollars	Percent distribution	Dollars per capita	
			State	U.S.
GENERAL REVENUE	20 538 540	100.0	3 726.2	3 832.6
Intergovernmental revenue	5 829 817	28.4	1 057.7	1 246.0
Taxes	10 980 324	53.5	1 992.1	1 891.6
General sales	2 720 162	13.2	493.5	636.0
Selective sales	2 144 312	10.4	389.0	307.4
License taxes	440 705	2.1	80.0	123.6
Individual income tax	4 681 860	22.8	849.4	626.8
Corporate income tax	379 020	1.8	68.8	97.8
Other taxes	614 265	3.0	111.4	99.9
Current charges	2 102 109	10.2	381.4	366.5
Miscellaneous general revenue	1 626 290	7.9	295.0	328.6
GENERAL EXPENDITURE	21 789 034	100.0	3 953.0	4 010.5
Intergovernmental expenditure	5 358 342	24.6	972.1	1 316.9
Direct expenditure	16 430 692	75.4	2 980.9	2 693.6
Expenditure by Function				
Education	7 271 618	33.4	1 319.2	1 416.4
Public welfare	5 051 914	23.2	916.5	1 083.3
Hospitals	411 021	1.9	74.6	132.3
Health	1 507 476	6.9	273.5	173.0
Highways	1 715 935	7.9	311.3	295.4
Police protection	397 090	1.8	72.0	38.4
Correction	1 050 389	4.8	190.6	135.0
Natural resources	429 907	2.0	78.0	64.0
Parks and recreation	271 547	1.2	49.3	20.1
Government administration	819 463	3.8	148.7	151.3
Interest on general debt	860 049	3.9	156.0	107.8
Other and unallocable	2 002 625	9.2	363.3	393.4
DEBT AT END OF FISCAL YEAR	12 950 949	X	2 349.6	2 404.7
CASH AND SECURITY HOLDINGS	40 693 869	X	7 382.8	8 938.4

X = Not applicable.

Table MD-18. Education Indicators, 2000–2004

(Percent, number.)

Item	State	U.S.
Total Population 25 Years and Over (Thousands), 2004	3 609	186 877
Educational Attainment, 2004		
Percent high school graduate or more	87.4	85.2
Percent college graduate or more	35.2	27.7
Elementary and Secondary Schools, 2002–2003		
Total students	866 743	48 202 324
Percent of students eligible for free or reduced-price lunch ..	31.4	40.6
Percent of students who were English language learners	3.2	7.8
Total schools	1 359	92 330
Student/teacher ratio	15.8	15.9
Per student expenditures	9 153	8 041
Dropouts, Grades 9–12, 2000–2001 (Percent)	3.9	. . .
Higher Education, 2002–2003		
Total enrollment	309 052	17 035 027
Bachelor's degrees awarded	24 537	1 348 503
Percent women	57.2	57.5

. . . = Not available.

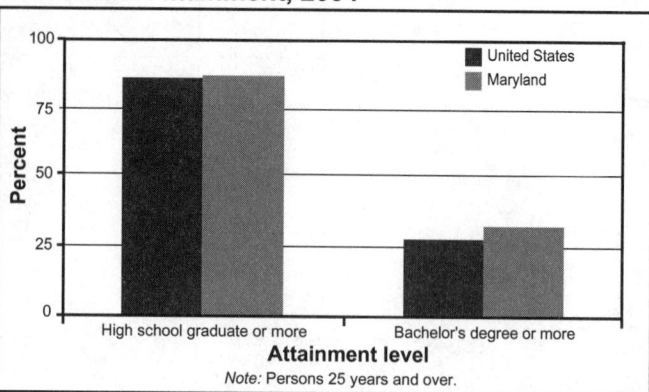

Educational Attainment, 2004

Note: Persons 25 years and over.

EDUCATION

In 2004, more than 35 percent of Maryland residents held a bachelor's degree or more, ranking the state fifth in the nation. The state's high school attainment level was also above the U.S. average and ranked 24th. Among the 46 states with dropout data, Maryland ranked 22nd with 3.9 percent. The state's per student expenditures of $9,153 were the 11th highest in the nation. Just over 31 percent of elementary and secondary students were eligible for free or reduced-price lunch, compared with over 40 percent nationally. The state's student/teacher ratio nearly equaled the U.S. average.

VOTER PARTICIPATION

Voter turnout was about average for both the 2000 and 2004 elections. In 2004, residents age 45 to 64 years had the highest voter turnout, with 70.9 percent casting ballots. Less than 43 percent of eligible residents age 18 to 24 years voted in the 2004 election. Among the different race and ethnic groups, non-Hispanic Whites had the highest rates of voter participation and Hispanics had the lowest. In the 2000 election, 56.5 percent of the eligible population voted for the Democratic presidential ticket, according to the official tally by the Clerk of the U.S. House of Representatives. In 2004, this proportion increased to 56 percent.

Table MD-19. Reported Voting and Registration, November 2000 and November 2004

(Numbers in thousands, percent.)

Characteristic	Total population 18 years and over	Total citizen		Total registered		Total voted	
		Number	Percent	Number	Percent	Number	Percent
NOVEMBER 2000							
Total	3 812	3 565	93.5	2 499	65.6	2 178	57.1
Male	1 838	1 681	91.5	1 129	61.4	970	52.8
Female	1 974	1 883	95.4	1 371	69.5	1 208	61.2
NOVEMBER 2004							
Total	4 043	3 678	91.0	2 676	66.2	2 413	59.7
Male	1 906	1 699	89.2	1 221	64.1	1 112	58.3
Female	2 137	1 978	92.6	1 454	68.1	1 301	60.9
Race and Hispanic Origin							
White alone	2 737	2 529	92.4	1 913	69.9	1 733	63.3
Non-Hispanic White alone	2 504	2 449	97.8	1 868	74.6	1 689	67.5
Black alone	1 070	990	92.6	668	62.4	598	55.9
Asian alone	168	104	61.6	52	30.7	50	29.8
Hispanic or Latino¹	282	100	35.4	58	20.6	53	19.0
White alone or in combination	2 777	2 557	92.1	1 934	69.7	1 750	63.0
Non-Hispanic White alone or in combination	2 531	2 476	97.8	1 889	74.6	1 706	67.4
Black alone or in combination	1 094	1 002	91.6	676	61.8	604	55.2
Asian alone or in combination	172	107	62.4	55	32.1	53	30.6
Age							
18 to 24 years	433	371	85.7	207	47.8	186	42.9
25 to 44 years	1 581	1 362	86.1	952	60.2	830	52.5
45 to 64 years	1 425	1 348	94.6	1 072	75.2	1 011	70.9
65 to 74 years	312	310	99.3	241	77.2	212	67.9
75 years and over	290	287	98.9	204	70.3	174	60.1

¹May be of any race.

At a Glance:

- In 2004, Massachusetts's population was over 6.4 million, making it the 13th most populous state in the country.

- Similiar to the trends of its New England neighbors, non-Hispanic Whites represented the majority of Massachusetts's population (80.8 percent) in 2004. Asian and Pacific Islanders made up 4.6 percent of the state's population, which was the ninth highest proportion of this racial group in the nation.

- Massachusetts's median household income of $52,830 was the eighth highest in the nation. The state's poverty rate of 9.2 percent was well below the national average.

- The unemployment rate was 5.1 percent, which was below the national average. The real gross state product ranked as the 13th largest in the nation.

- The state's infant mortality rate was the lowest in the country.

- Massachusetts ranked 28th in the country for the proportion of its population age 25 years and over who had completed high school. More than 36 percent of the state's population held bachelor's degrees or more, which was the second highest proportion in the nation.

Table MA-1. Population by Sex and Age, 1990, 2000, and 2004

(Number, percent.)

Sex and age	1990	2000	2004	Percent distribution, 2004	Average annual percent change, 2000–2004
Total Population	6 016 425	6 349 097	6 416 505	X	0.3
Percent of total U.S. population	2.4	2.3	2.2	X	X
Sex					
Male	2 888 745	3 058 816	3 106 345	48.4	0.4
Female	3 127 680	3 290 281	3 310 160	51.6	0.2
Age					
Under 5 years	412 473	397 268	395 662	6.2	-0.4
5 to 17 years	940 602	1 102 796	1 068 527	16.7	0.9
18 years and over	1 115 150	4 849 033	4 952 316	77.2	0.4
18 to 24 years	4 663 350	579 328	598 047	9.3	-1.3
25 to 44 years	709 099	1 989 783	1 910 811	29.8	-0.4
45 to 64 years	2 019 817	1 419 760	1 589 115	24.8	2.6
65 years and over	819 284	860 162	854 343	13.3	0.3
85 years and over	92 209	116 692	136 125	2.1	3.0
Median age (years)	33.4	36.5	37.8	X	X

X = Not applicable.

Average Annual Rate of Population Growth, 1980–2004

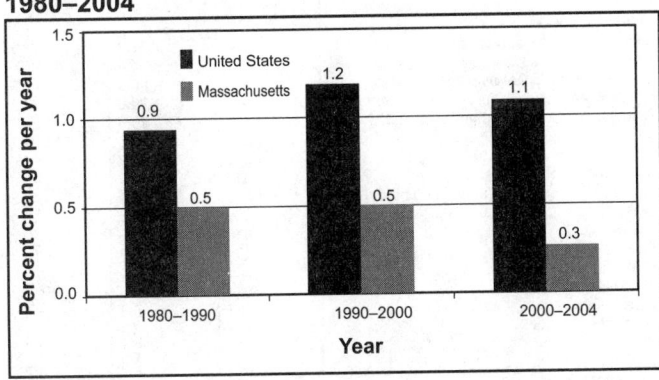

POPULATION

From 2000 to 2004, Massachusetts's population grew by 1.1 percent, among the lowest rates of population growth in the nation. This increase was considerably below those of Vermont, New Hampshire, and Connecticut; however, it was similar to that of New York. During this period, more than 173,000 residents of Massachusetts moved to other states. An influx of 137,000 people from abroad, combined with the state's natural increase (births minus deaths), prevented the state from experiencing a population loss. Massachusetts had a below average proportion of its population under 18 years old, but its proportion of population over 65 years of age was the 13th highest in the nation.

Table MA-2. Population by Race and Hispanic Origin, 1990, 2000, and 2004

(Number, percent.)

Race and Hispanic origin	1990	2000	2004
Total Population	6 016 425	6 349 097	6 416 505
Non-Hispanic (Percent)			
One race[1]			
White	87.8	82.8	80.8
Black	4.6	5.5	5.7
American Indian, Alaska Native[2]	0.2	0.2	0.2
Asian and Pacific Islander[2]	2.4	3.9	4.6
Other race[2]	2.6	. . .	. . .
Two or more races	. . .	0.9	1.1
Hispanic or Latino[3] (Percent)	4.8	6.8	7.7

[1]Individuals could report only one race in the 1990 census and could report one or more races on the 2000 census. Data on race in 2000 and 2004 are not comparable to 1990.
[2]Data for 1990 include people of Hispanic or Latino origin.
[3]May be of any race.
. . . = Not available.

Minority Population as a Percent of Total Population, 2004

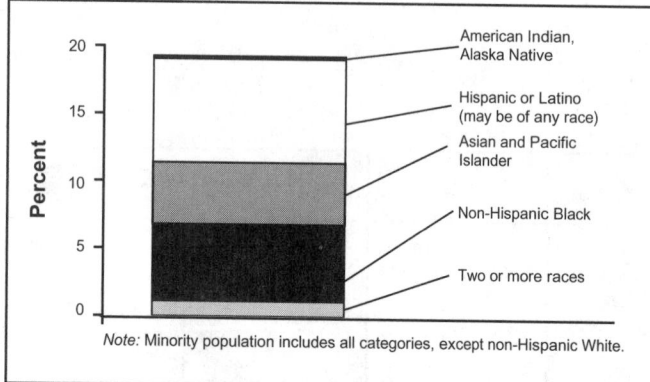

Note: Minority population includes all categories, except non-Hispanic White.

Age-Adjusted Death Rates, Average 2000–2002

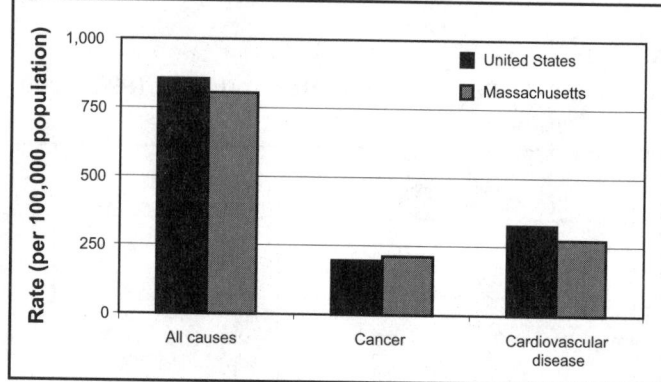

HEALTH

In 2004, 11.7 percent of Massachusetts's population lacked health insurance. This was among the 15 lowest proportions in the nation. The state's birth rate was well below the U.S. average, and its birth rate for teenage mothers was the third lowest in the nation.

Table MA-3. Health Characteristics, 2000–2004

(Number, rate, percent.)

Item	State	U.S.
Births, 2003–2004		
Number of births	80 184	4 089 950
Birth rate (per 1,000 population)	12.5	14.1
Teenage birth rate (per 1,000 women age 15–19 years)	23.0	41.6
Mortality Rates, Average 2000–2002		
Infant mortality rate (per 1,000 live births)	4.8	6.9
Age-adjusted mortality rate (per 100,000 population)		
All races	801.8	853.3
Non-Hispanic White	804.0	843.1
Black	878.1	1 097.7
American Indian, Alaska Native	. . .	687.0
Asian and Pacific Islander	379.6	486.0
Hispanic or Latino[1]	582.0	642.7
Health Insurance, 2004		
Percent of all persons without health insurance	11.7	15.7
Percent of children without health insurance	6.5	11.2
Percent of low-income children without health insurance	2.7	7.1

[1]May be of any race.
. . . = Not available.

Table MA-4. Leading Causes of Death, Average 2000–2002

(Number, rate per 100,000 population.)

Cause	Number of deaths	Age-adjusted death rates	
		State	U.S.
ALL CAUSES	56 788	801.8	853.3
Leading Causes			
Major cardiovascular diseases	20 042	277.7	326.5
Cancer	13 897	201.5	196.0
Chronic lower respiratory diseases	2 827	40.0	43.7
Unintentional injuries	1 425	20.8	35.7
Diabetes (underlying cause)	1 402	20.0	25.2
Influenza and pneumonia	1 978	26.8	22.7
Alzheimer's disease	1 512	20.2	19.0
Motor vehicle accidents	517	7.9	15.0
Nephritis, nephrotic syndrome, and nephrosis ..	1 245	17.4	13.8
Septicemia	956	13.5	11.4
Suicides	416	6.3	10.7
Firearm-related	191	2.9	10.3
Cirrhosis	566	8.4	9.5
Drug-induced	644	9.7	7.9
Alcohol-induced	352	5.3	6.9
Homicides	154	2.4	6.0
Falls	220	3.1	5.2
HIV	235	3.5	5.0
Viral hepatitis	98	1.5	2.0
Anemias	111	1.5	1.6
Drownings	49	0.8	1.3
Fire deaths	54	0.8	1.2

Note: The rates are age-adjusted to the U.S. 2000 standard population.

Table MA-5. Households and Housing Characteristics, 1990, 2000, and 2004

(Number, percent, and dollars.)

Characteristic	1990	2000	2004	Average annual percent change, 2000–2004
Total Households	2 247 110	2 443 580	2 435 421	-0.1
Family households	1 514 746	1 576 696	1 565 568	-0.2
Married-couple family	1 170 275	1 197 917	1 176 009	-0.5
Other family	344 471	378 779	389 559	0.7
Male householder, no wife present	73 548	88 835	94 089	1.4
Female householder, no husband present	270 923	289 944	295 470	0.5
Nonfamily households	732 364	866 884	869 853	0.1
Householder living alone	580 774	684 345	691 173	0.2
Householder not living alone	151 590	182 539	178 680	-0.5
Housing Characteristics				
Average size	2.58	2.51	2.55	X
Housing units	2 472 711	2 621 989	2 672 061	0.5
Occupied housing units	2 247 110	2 443 580	2 435 421	-0.1
Owner-occupied	1 331 493	1 508 052	1 572 183	1.0
Renter-occupied	915 617	935 528	863 238	-2.0
Median gross rent of renter-occupied housing units (dollars) ...	580	684	852	5.6
Median value of owner-occupied housing units (dollars)	162 200	185 700	331 200	15.6

X = Not applicable.

Median Housing Value and Median Rent, 2004

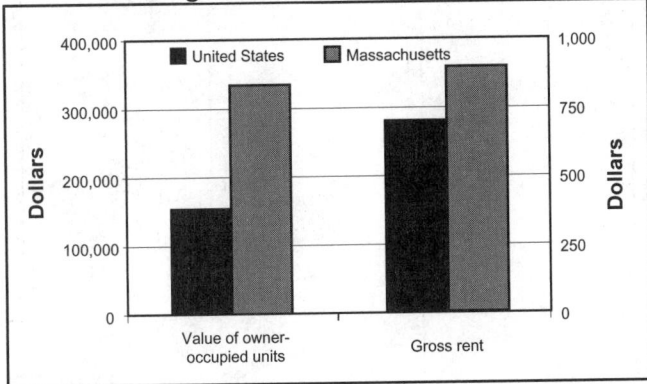

Median Household Income, 1984–2004 (2004 Dollars)

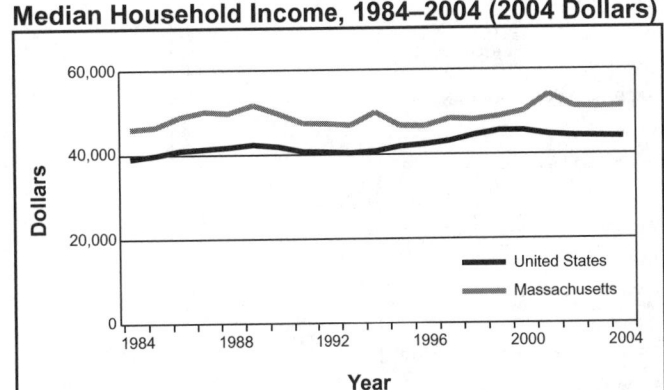

Table MA-6. Household Income and Poverty Status, 1980–2004

(2004 CPI-U-RS adjusted dollars, rate.)

Year	State		U.S.	
	Median household income (2004 dollars)	Poverty rate	Median household income (2004 dollars)	Poverty rate
2004	52 370	9.2	44 389	12.7
2003	52 324	10.3	44 482	12.5
2002	52 368	10.0	44 546	12.1
2001	55 760	8.9	45 062	11.7
2000	51 283	9.8	46 058	11.3
1999	49 880	11.8	46 129	11.9
1998	49 008	8.7	45 003	12.7
1997	49 320	12.2	43 430	13.3
1996	47 341	10.1	42 544	13.7
1995	47 480	11.0	41 943	13.8
1994	51 061	9.7	40 677	14.5
1993	47 713	10.7	40 217	15.1
1992	47 973	10.3	40 422	14.8
1991	48 303	11.0	40 746	14.2
1990	50 798	10.7	41 963	13.5
1989	53 087	8.8	42 524	12.8
1988	50 959	8.5	41 771	13.0
1987	51 269	8.2	41 322	13.4
1986	49 888	9.2	40 939	13.6
1985	47 229	9.2	39 545	14.0
1984	46 644	8.9	38 782	14.4
1983	. . .	7.7	. . .	15.2
1982	. . .	10.3	. . .	15.0
1981	. . .	8.9	. . .	14.0
1980	. . .	9.5	. . .	13.0

. . . = Not available.

Table MA-7. Employment Status by Demographic Group, 2004

(Numbers in thousands, rate.)

Characteristic	Civilian noninstitutional population	Civilian labor force		Employed	Unemployment rate
		Number	Participation rate		
SEX AND AGE					
Total	5 036	3 399	67.5	3 226	5.1
16 to 19 years	362	171	47.2	148	13.4
20 to 24 years	420	318	75.7	289	9.0
25 to 34 years	867	733	84.5	702	4.2
35 to 44 years	1 004	855	85.2	820	4.2
45 to 54 years	925	773	83.5	743	3.9
55 to 64 years	609	426	69.9	406	4.7
65 years and over	848	123	14.5	119	3.4
Men	2 402	1 769	73.7	1 665	5.9
16 to 19 years	184	78	42.2	65	16.1
20 to 24 years	217	172	79.4	154	10.4
25 to 34 years	425	383	90.1	362	5.4
35 to 44 years	483	443	91.8	422	4.8
45 to 54 years	453	402	88.6	382	5.0
55 to 64 years	301	226	75.1	215	4.6
65 years and over	339	66	19.4	64	2.9
Women	2 634	1 629	61.9	1 562	4.2
16 to 19 years	178	93	52.3	83	11.1
20 to 24 years	203	145	71.8	135	7.3
25 to 34 years	442	350	79.2	340	2.9
35 to 44 years	522	412	79.1	398	3.5
45 to 54 years	472	371	78.6	361	2.8
55 to 64 years	308	200	64.8	190	4.9
65 years and over	509	57	11.2	55	4.0
MARITAL STATUS					
Married men, spouse present	1 252	975	77.8	937	3.9
Married women, spouse present	1 211	774	64.0	751	3.1
Women who maintain families	329	232	70.4	217	6.5
RACE, HISPANIC ORIGIN, AND SEX					
White	4 478	3 041	67.9	2 900	4.6
Men	2 143	1 585	74.0	1 497	5.5
Women	2 335	1 456	62.4	1 402	3.7
Black	308	201	65.2	181	9.7
Men	142	103	72.4	94	8.3
Women	166	98	59.0	87	11.2
Asian	204	127	62.3	119	6.7
Hispanic or Latino[1]	321	235	73.1	214	8.7
Men	147	116	78.7	106	9.1
Women	173	119	68.4	109	8.3
RACE, HISPANIC ORIGIN, AND AGE					
White					
16 to 19 years	300	142	47.4	126	11.2
20 to 24 years	356	274	76.9	254	7.3
25 to 34 years	740	634	85.6	610	3.7
35 to 44 years	898	773	86.1	742	4.0
45 to 54 years	841	710	84.4	683	3.8
55 to 64 years	552	393	71.1	373	5.0
65 years and over	790	116	14.6	111	3.7

Note: Data in Table 7 are from the Current Population Survey (CPS) and do not match Bureau of Labor Statistics estimates in Table 8. See notes and definitions for more details.

[1]May be of any race.

Table MA-8. Employment Status, 1990–2004

(Numbers in thousands, rate.)

Year	Civilian labor force	Employed	Unemployed	Unemployment rate
2004	3 393 122	3 219 487	173 635	5.1
2003	3 413 782	3 215 624	198 158	5.8
2002	3 427 900	3 247 094	180 806	5.3
2001	3 400 624	3 274 561	126 063	3.7
2000	3 366 582	3 276 737	89 845	2.7
1999	3 355 324	3 245 761	109 563	3.3
1998	3 321 662	3 208 988	112 674	3.4
1997	3 293 415	3 158 851	134 564	4.1
1996	3 231 053	3 083 332	147 721	4.6
1995	3 204 888	3 029 360	175 528	5.5
1994	3 187 813	2 989 123	198 690	6.2
1993	3 172 904	2 940 565	232 339	7.3
1992	3 180 740	2 899 718	281 022	8.8
1991	3 198 883	2 916 293	282 590	8.8
1990	3 226 368	3 022 393	203 975	6.3

Note: Population age 16 years and over.

Unemployment Rate, 1980–2004

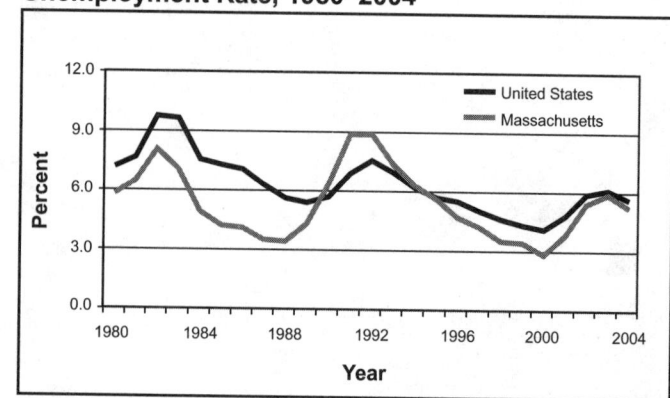

Table MA-9. Employment and Average Wages by Industry, 2001–2004

(Estimates are based on the 2002 North American Industry Classification System [NAICS].)

Industry	2001	2002	2003	2004	Annual average percent change, 2001–2004
			Number of jobs		
TOTAL EMPLOYMENT BY PLACE OF WORK	4 125 438	4 064 960	4 029 906	4 044 476	-0.7
Farm Employment	10 916	10 882	10 940	10 117	-2.5
Nonfarm Employment	4 114 522	4 054 078	4 018 966	4 034 359	-0.7
Private employment	3 656 412	3 598 389	3 573 794	3 599 771	-0.5
Forestry, fishing, hunting, and other[1]	13 450	14 993	13 785	13 372	-0.2
Mining	2 554	2 452	2 864	3 036	5.9
Utilities	12 388	11 380	10 952	10 422	-5.6
Construction	218 776	217 361	219 566	222 851	0.6
Manufacturing	401 126	361 759	337 581	325 241	-6.8
Durable goods manufacturing	269 925	238 952	219 805	212 725	-7.6
Nondurable goods manufacturing	131 201	122 807	117 776	112 516	-5.0
Wholesale trade	151 796	145 960	145 414	145 762	-1.3
Retail trade	416 841	416 947	415 769	418 569	0.1
Transportation and warehousing	101 171	96 017	94 351	93 250	-2.7
Information	123 109	110 019	102 785	98 632	-7.1
Finance and insurance	234 116	233 036	227 864	223 369	-1.6
Real estate and rental and leasing	119 848	122 358	129 757	135 516	4.2
Professional and technical services	372 367	357 445	352 473	361 229	-1.0
Management of companies and enterprises	70 397	68 677	65 555	65 438	-2.4
Administrative and waste services	211 313	202 982	205 879	215 362	0.6
Educational services	188 017	190 832	193 130	197 276	1.6
Health care and social assistance	485 521	495 673	500 928	508 797	1.6
Arts, entertainment, and recreation	85 429	90 168	91 893	94 033	3.3
Accommodation and food services	251 812	255 968	257 909	260 935	1.2
Other services, except public administration	196 381	204 362	205 339	206 681	1.7
Government and government enterprises	458 110	455 689	445 172	434 588	-1.7
			Dollars		
AVERAGE WAGES AND SALARIES BY PLACE OF WORK	43 842	43 888	45 257	47 873	3.0
Farm Earnings	18 565	24 385	20 182	26 139	12.1
Nonfarm Earnings	43 879	43 917	45 296	47 901	3.0
Private earnings	44 730	44 534	45 795	48 389	2.7
Forestry, fishing, hunting, and other[1]	37 462	38 926	40 596	47 013	7.9
Mining	46 902	47 822	48 731	49 615	1.9
Utilities	76 740	77 636	81 537	83 896	3.0
Construction	50 803	52 168	51 501	52 178	0.9
Manufacturing	54 363	55 356	58 270	60 791	3.8
Durable goods manufacturing	59 757	60 835	64 022	67 329	4.1
Nondurable goods manufacturing	43 222	44 647	47 506	48 395	3.8
Wholesale trade	61 789	60 996	64 292	66 949	2.7
Retail trade	24 801	25 202	26 102	27 053	2.9
Transportation and warehousing	35 932	36 898	37 498	38 825	2.6
Information	66 892	66 437	68 251	72 694	2.8
Finance and insurance	87 349	85 355	87 941	102 806	5.6
Real estate and rental and leasing	43 446	44 624	44 984	48 196	3.5
Professional and technical services	74 201	72 765	74 532	79 673	2.4
Management of companies and enterprises	67 494	64 103	67 844	74 972	3.6
Administrative and waste services	30 350	30 822	31 698	32 734	2.6
Educational services	31 329	33 342	34 701	36 115	4.9
Health care and social assistance	35 607	37 012	39 223	40 717	4.6
Arts, entertainment, and recreation	28 736	29 074	29 954	30 820	2.4
Accommodation and food services	17 244	17 360	17 778	18 473	2.3
Other services, except public administration	24 531	25 487	26 306	27 153	3.4
Government and government enterprises	38 251	39 909	42 034	44 641	5.3

Note: Average wages and salaries are a calculation by the editors of wage and salary disbursements divided by full- and part-time wage and salary employment. Data may not add to total or may appear as zero due to rounding.

[1] "Other" consists of the number of jobs held by U.S. residents employed by international organizations and foreign embassies and consulates in the United States.

LABOR MARKET

Massachusetts's unemployment rate was below the national average in 2004 (ranking 24th), and has been below the U.S. average since the mid-1990s. Employment declined during the 2001–2003 period, as the state lost about 95,600 jobs. Massachusetts experienced only a slight increase in jobs in 2004. From 2001 to 2004, employment in manufacturing and finance and insurance declined significantly, which was partially offset by increases in service sector jobs. Wage and salary jobs in the state were concentrated in health care, government, retail trade, professional and technical services, and manufacturing. Average wages and salaries in most industries were generally well above the national averages.

Employment by Industry, 2004

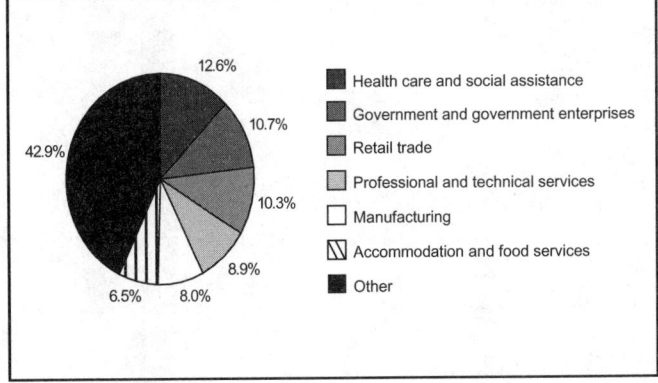

Table MA-10. Personal Income by Major Source, Selected Years 1980–2004

(Millions of dollars, except where noted.)

Item	1980	1990	2000	2001	2002	2003	2004	Average annual percent change, 2000–2004
Earnings by Place of Work	48 283	108 748	195 839	200 721	200 829	204 741	218 375	2.8
Wage and salary disbursements	37 582	83 129	150 842	153 131	150 108	151 998	160 157	1.5
Supplements to wages and salaries	6 869	16 326	27 664	28 432	30 813	32 345	35 916	6.7
Proprietors' income[1]	3 833	9 292	17 333	19 158	19 908	20 398	22 302	6.5
Farm proprietors' income	47	66	6	-15	-34	-13	-16	X
Nonfarm proprietors' income	3 786	9 226	17 327	19 172	19 942	20 412	22 318	6.5
(-) Contributions for government social insurance[2]	4 217	11 227	20 551	21 152	21 023	21 316	22 977	2.8
(+) Adjustment for residence[3]	-483	-2 089	-5 116	-5 074	-4 911	-4 877	-5 104	X
(=) **Net Earnings by Place of Residence**	43 583	95 432	170 173	174 495	174 895	178 548	190 295	2.8
(+) Dividends, interest, and rent[4]	9 165	26 109	42 108	43 988	41 670	42 764	44 381	1.3
(+) Personal current transfer receipts	8 172	17 241	27 928	30 613	33 363	34 064	35 469	6.2
Personal income	60 920	138 782	240 209	249 095	249 928	255 375	270 145	3.0
Farm income	60 818	138 636	240 099	249 006	249 831	255 275	270 038	3.0
Nonfarm income	102	146	110	89	98	101	106	-0.9
Per Capita Personal Income (Dollars)[5]	10 602	23 043	37 756	38 949	38 975	39 776	42 102	2.8

Note: Data may not add to total or may appear as zero due to rounding.

[1]Proprietors' income includes the inventory valuation adjustment and the capital consumption adjustment.
[2]Contributions for government social insurance are included in earnings by type and industry, but they are excluded from personal income.
[3]The adjustment for residence is the net inflow of the earnings of interarea commuters.
[4]Rental income of persons includes the capital consumption adjustment.
[5]Per capita personal income is total personal income divided by total midyear population.
X = Not applicable.

Per Capita Personal Income, 1980–2004 (Current Dollars)

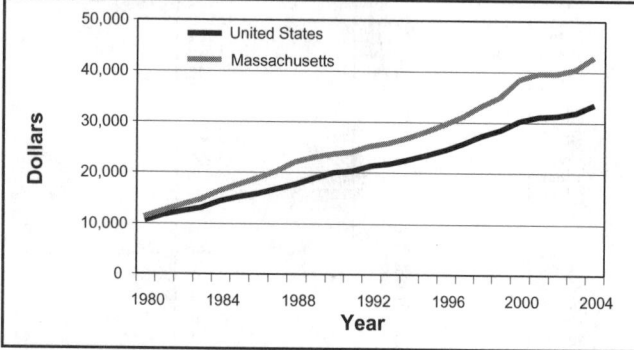

ECONOMIC ACTIVITY

The growth rate of Massachusetts's real gross state product (GSP) was adversely affected by the 2001 recession, and the state's economic activity did not show any strength until 2004. The GSP's growth rate was the 14th highest in the nation from 2003 to 2004. Professional and technical services, real estate and related activities, and retail trade contributed to the renewal of growth from 2003 to 2004. Housing price appreciation has been significant in the eastern areas of the state, particularly in the areas surrounding Boston. Overall, Massachusetts ranked fourth in the nation in 2004 for median value of owner-occupied housing.

Table MA-11. Real Gross State Product, 1997–2004

(Millions of chained 2000 dollars, percent.)

Industry	1997	1998	1999	2000	2001	2002	2003	2004	Average annual percent change, 2001–2004
GROSS STATE PRODUCT	227 074	241 535	256 659	276 786	279 434	278 213	284 286	298 066	2.2
As a percent of U.S. gross product	2.6	2.7	2.7	2.8	2.8	2.8	2.8	2.8	X
Private Industries	204 714	218 929	233 424	253 492	255 947	254 795	261 066	274 528	2.4
Agriculture, forestry, fishing, and hunting	442	385	469	540	587	679	713	734	7.7
Mining	67	81	93	97	103	94	105	102	-0.3
Utilities	3 319	3 348	3 223	3 455	3 161	3 104	3 371	3 384	2.3
Construction	10 193	10 954	11 645	12 168	13 299	13 217	12 704	12 703	-1.5
Manufacturing	24 737	27 888	30 063	37 132	34 972	35 255	37 957	39 611	4.2
As a percent of gross state product	10.9	11.5	11.7	13.4	12.5	12.7	13.4	13.3	X
Wholesale trade	14 359	16 243	17 878	16 335	18 065	17 593	17 492	17 777	-0.5
Retail trade	12 130	12 791	13 677	14 557	15 768	16 550	17 493	18 511	5.5
Transportation and warehousing	4 352	4 559	4 769	5 180	5 071	4 941	5 012	5 009	-0.4
Information	9 764	10 360	12 049	12 986	13 629	13 422	13 630	14 951	3.1
Finance and insurance	21 589	24 339	26 971	30 333	30 227	30 546	33 237	37 584	7.5
Real estate and rental and leasing	32 268	32 966	34 607	35 978	38 599	37 830	36 949	38 612	0.0
Services	72 767	75 609	78 339	84 728	82 408	81 549	82 915	86 476	1.6
As a percent of gross state product	32.0	31.3	30.5	30.6	29.5	29.3	29.2	29.0	X
Professional and technical services	20 551	22 525	24 640	28 469	28 505	27 408	27 652	29 523	1.2
Management of companies and enterprises	6 985	6 786	6 870	7 506	6 151	5 767	5 767	6 006	-0.8
Administrative and waste services	7 646	8 066	8 252	8 382	7 392	7 305	7 631	8 025	2.8
Educational services	5 575	5 594	5 602	5 934	5 866	5 913	5 740	5 665	-1.2
Health care and social assistance	19 716	19 588	19 505	20 374	20 480	21 075	21 918	22 360	3.0
Arts, entertainment, and recreation	1 796	1 841	1 908	1 913	2 026	2 139	2 187	2 239	3.4
Accommodation and food services	5 555	6 026	6 258	6 605	6 522	6 552	6 634	6 953	2.2
Other services, except public administration	4 943	5 183	5 304	5 545	5 466	5 390	5 386	5 705	1.4
Government	22 491	22 664	23 264	23 293	23 487	23 417	23 261	23 631	0.2
As a percent of gross state product	9.9	9.4	9.1	8.4	8.4	8.4	8.2	7.9	X

X = Not applicable.

Table MA-12. Government Transfer Payments, Selected Years 1980–2004

(Millions of dollars, percent.)

Item	1980	1990	2000	2001	2002	2003	2004	Average annual percent change, 2000–2004
CURRENT TRANSFER PAYMENTS TO INDIVIDUALS	7 769	16 385	26 471	29 013	31 974	32 815	34 226	6.6
Retirement and Disability Insurance Benefits	3 396	6 367	9 875	10 349	10 752	11 096	11 515	3.9
Old-age, survivors, and disability insurance (OASDI) benefits	3 301	6 228	9 701	10 166	10 545	10 816	11 219	3.7
Railroad retirement and disability benefits	61	76	70	70	70	70	71	0.4
Workers' compensation	33	52	87	91	100	99	103	4.2
Other government retirement and disability insurance benefits	1	11	17	22	37	111	121	64.4
Medical Benefits	2 279	6 653	12 813	14 196	15 423	15 873	17 395	7.9
Medicare benefits	1 200	3 190	6 188	6 814	7 248	7 602	8 267	7.5
Public assistance medical care benefits	1 061	3 431	6 602	7 351	8 136	8 239	9 090	8.3
Military medical insurance benefits	17	32	23	30	39	32	38	13.6
Income Maintenance Benefits	1 097	1 616	2 170	2 232	2 334	2 504	2 643	5.1
Supplemental Security Income (SSI) benefits	242	400	812	837	853	857	895	2.5
Family assistance	516	696	599	587	598	634	635	1.5
Food stamps	172	222	176	180	213	267	319	16.0
Other income maintenance benefits	168	299	583	628	670	746	794	8.0
Unemployment Insurance Compensation	394	1 067	785	1 356	2 526	2 366	1 517	17.9
Veterans' Benefits	460	525	579	600	651	690	704	5.0
Federal Education and Training Assistance	142	151	236	254	273	242	260	2.5
Other Payments to Individuals	1	6	14	26	15	44	194	92.8

Note: See notes and definitions for more details. Data may not add to total or may appear as zero due to rounding.

EXPORTS

Massachusetts's exported goods were worth $21.8 billion in 2004, ranking ninth in the country. By far, the largest export was computers and electronic products, which accounted for over 34 percent of total exports. Chemical manufactures and machinery manufactures together made up over 33 percent of exports. Canada, Germany, and the Netherlands were the state's chief export markets. Exports to the Netherlands tripled from 2001 to 2004, primarily as a result of increased chemical manufactures exports. Exports to China doubled during this period, and the country became the seventh largest market for Massachusetts's exports. Computers and electronic products and machinery manufactures were the major types of exports to China.

Leading Exports, 2004

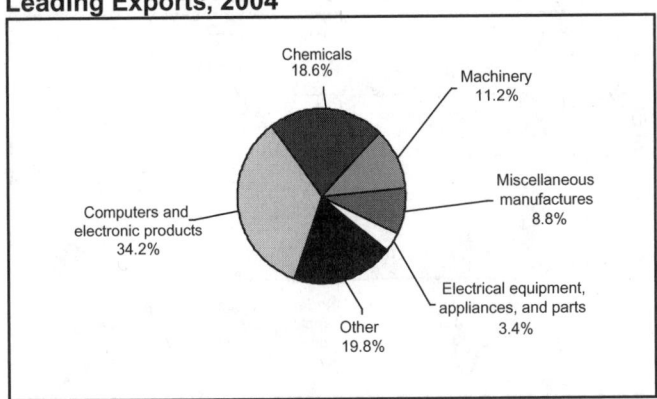

Table MA-13. Exports of Goods by Leading Products and Destinations, 2001–2004

(Millions of dollars, percent, rank based on 2004 dollar values.)

Product and market	2001	2002	2003	2004	Percent share of total, 2004	Average annual percent change, 2001–2004
Total Goods						
Total	17 490	16 708	18 663	21 837	100.0	7.7
Manufactures	16 612	15 874	17 736	20 737	95.0	7.7
Agriculture and livestock	254	282	301	363	1.7	12.6
Other commodities	624	552	626	737	3.4	5.7
Five Leading Exports (NAICS Code)						
Computers and electronic products (334)	8 122	7 024	7 688	7 475	34.2	-2.7
Chemical manufactures (325)	1 534	2 267	3 216	4 907	22.5	47.4
Machinery manufactures (333)	2 044	1 786	1 668	2 456	11.2	6.3
Miscellaneous manufactures (339)	1 213	1 210	1 571	1 927	8.8	16.7
Electrical equipment, appliances, and parts (335)	691	649	592	752	3.4	2.8
Five Leading Markets	16 222	15 229	17 261	20 494	93.8	8.1
Canada	2 845	2 710	2 642	2 899	13.3	0.6
Germany	1 401	1 199	1 599	2 516	11.5	21.6
Netherlands	820	1 054	1 759	2 515	11.5	45.3
Japan	1 964	1 599	1 636	1 815	8.3	-2.6
United Kingdom	1 851	1 579	1 430	1 503	6.9	-6.7

Table MA-14. Agriculture, 1997 and 2002

(Number, acres, and dollars.)

Item	1997	2002
Number of farms	7 307	6 075
Land in farms (acres)	577 637	518 570
Farm Size		
Average size of farm (acres)	79	85
Farms by size (percent distribution)		
Fewer than 50 acres	60.2	60.0
50 to 499 acres	37.8	37.3
500 acres or more	2.0	2.7
Market Value of Land and Equipment (Dollars)		
Land and buildings average value per farm	418 750	755 254
Average value per acre	5 543	9 234
Machinery and equipment average value per farm	36 684	50 243
Value of Sales (Thousands of Dollars)		
Agricultural products sold	483 529	384 314
Crops	384 933	277 069
Livestock, poultry, and their products	98 596	107 244
Average per farm (dollars)	66 173	63 262
Value of sales (percent distribution)		
Less than $10,000	59.4	63.6
$10,000 to $99,999	27.9	25.1
$100,000 or more	12.7	11.4
Government Payments		
Payments (thousands of dollars)	1 330	4 268
Percent of farms receiving government payments	8.0	6.8
Farm operators whose principal occupation is farming (percent)	49.3	54.0

AGRICULTURE

Cash receipts from farming in 2002 showed a decline from the previous farm census in 1997, with sales dropping from $484 million to $384 million. Massachusetts ranked 47th for overall value of agricultural sales in 2002. Greenhouse/nursery products were the state's leading farm crops. More than 63 percent of farms in Massachusetts had sales of less than $10,000, and just over half of all farm operators considered farming to be their principal occupation. The majority of farms spanned fewer than 50 acres. Just 2.7 percent of Massachusetts's farms were 500 acres or more.

ENERGY

As a cold-climate state, Massachusetts had above average energy expenditures per person. Energy prices in the state were the third highest in the nation in 2001. However, its per capita energy consumption of 242 million Btu ranked 47th in the country. The industrial sector used just 16.9 percent of total energy, which was among the smallest proportions of consumption by this sector in the nation.

Energy Consumption by Source, 2001

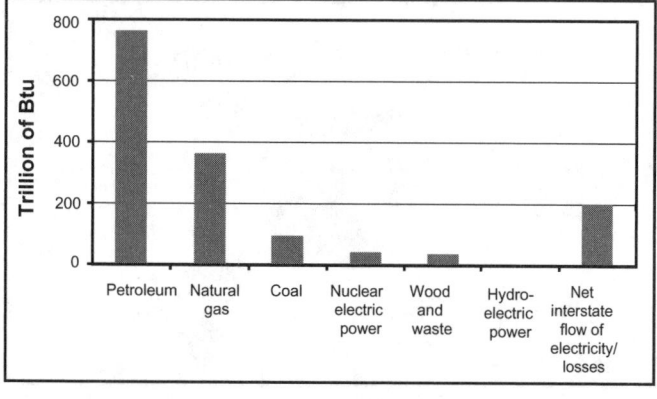

Energy Consumption by Sector, 2001

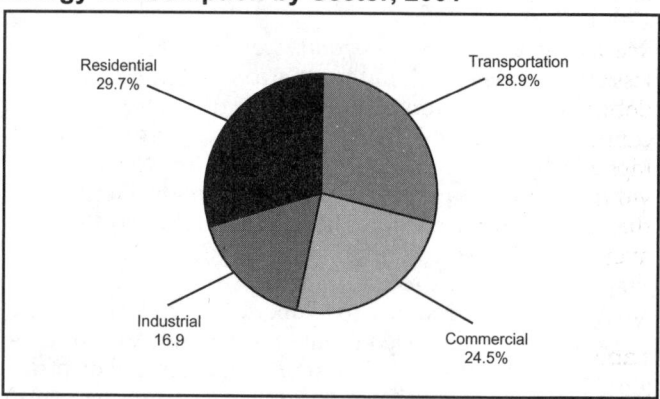

Table MA-15. Energy Consumption, Expenditures, and Prices, Selected Years 1960–2001

(Dollars, Btu [British Thermal Unit], percent distribution.)

Item	1960	1965	1970	1975	1980	1985	1990	1995	2000	2001
Total Consumption (Billion Btu)	1 054 345	1 246 656	1 466 008	1 422 825	1 258 975	1 321 208	1 417 001	1 436 942	1 547 266	1 548 818
Consumption per capita (million Btu)	204.8	226.6	257.7	247.1	219.4	224.7	235.5	237.0	243.7	242.0
Consumption by Sector (Percent Distribution)										
Residential	32.9	30.5	30.0	31.8	31.7	30.0	30.4	30.1	29.5	29.7
Commercial	18.1	19.2	20.6	21.6	22.6	21.2	24.6	25.9	24.1	24.5
Industrial	28.0	28.8	25.5	20.6	17.2	19.9	16.3	16.1	17.0	16.9
Transportation	20.9	21.5	23.8	26.0	28.5	28.9	28.7	28.0	29.3	28.9
Consumption by Source (Billion Btu)										
Coal	118 745	127 922	21 393	24 484	22 845	110 246	114 005	105 362	114 656	109 032
Natural gas	80 612	115 712	149 074	154 583	185 508	224 794	273 910	391 647	357 744	364 114
Petroleum	804 268	957 676	1 242 008	1 126 475	917 188	799 060	814 542	683 705	764 187	762 404
Nuclear electric power	394	11 407	13 272	41 636	35 255	65 141	53 647	47 133	57 487	53 745
Hydroelectric power[1]	10 570	6 938	7 904	4 342	1 642	2 740	6 030	644	3 721	-90
Wood and waste	42 784	48 698	57 139	48 983	59 790	59 754	51 229	65 058	58 328	56 074
Other	0	0	0	0	0	14 710	6 769	6 444	6 417	3 072
Net interstate flow of electricity/losses[2]	-3 029	-21 696	-24 782	22 322	36 746	44 762	96 870	136 949	184 727	200 468
Total Expenditures (Thousands of Dollars)	. . .	. . .	2 298 500	4 701 900	8 253 100	9 661 900	10 783 100	11 642 700	14 648 800	15 956 700
Expenditures per capita (dollars)	. . .	. . .	404	817	1 439	1 643	1 792	1 920	2 307	2 493
Prices by Sector (Dollars Per Million Btu)										
Total	. . .	. . .	1.89	4.12	8.78	9.92	10.35	11.03	13.01	14.18
Residential	. . .	. . .	2.22	4.19	8.40	10.63	11.40	12.06	13.64	15.64
Commercial	. . .	. . .	1.64	4.51	9.31	12.66	12.36	13.23	15.92	20.70
Industrial	. . .	. . .	1.06	3.36	8.15	8.44	9.43	9.58	10.75	11.66
Transportation	. . .	. . .	2.38	4.25	9.03	8.87	8.93	9.58	12.20	11.47

[1]A negative number in this row results from pumped storage for which, overall, more electricity is expended than created to provide electricity during peak demand periods.
[2]Net interstate flow of electricity is the difference between the amount of energy in the electricity sold within a state (including associated losses) and the energy input at the electric utilities within the state. A positive number indicates that more electricity (including associated losses) came into the state than went out of the state during the year; conversely, a negative number indicates that more electricity (including associated losses) went out of the state than came into the state.
. . . = Not available.

Table MA-16. State Taxes, Fiscal 2004

(Dollars, percent distribution.)

Item	Thousands of dollars	Percent distribution	Dollars per capita	
			State	U.S.
TOTAL TAXES	16 698 723	100.0	2 602.3	2 024.8
Property Taxes	51	0.0	0.0	38.9
Sales and Gross Receipts	5 462 094	32.7	851.2	1 003.4
General sales and gross receipts	3 743 204	22.4	583.3	677.0
Selective sales taxes	1 718 890	10.3	267.9	326.4
Insurance premiums	399 764	2.4	62.3	47.0
Motor fuels	684 242	4.1	106.6	114.6
Tobacco products	425 421	2.5	66.3	42.0
Other selective sales	129 989	0.8	20.3	49.8
Licenses	664 556	4.0	103.6	134.9
Motor vehicle	292 688	1.8	45.6	59.4
Motor vehicle operators	90 605	0.5	14.1	6.4
Occupation and business, not elsewhere classified	140 493	0.8	21.9	37.1
Other licenses	105 127	0.6	16.4	2.6
Other Taxes	10 572 022	63.3	1 647.5	847.6
Individual income	8 830 334	52.9	1 376.1	673.6
Corporation net income	1 301 076	7.8	202.8	105.1
Death and gift	194 706	1.2	30.3	19.6
Documentary and stock transfer	245 906	1.5	38.3	27.1

GOVERNMENT FINANCE

The state's per capita revenues of $4,208 were above the national average in 2003. Expenditures per person were 17th highest in the nation. The state spent higher than average amounts on health and highways, and relatively less on education and public welfare. Massachusetts's debt per person of $7,551 was second only to Alaska. Per capita taxes amounted to $2,602 in fiscal year 2004. A high proportion of revenue was collected through individual income taxes, which were the highest per capita in the nation. Sales taxes per person were below the U.S. average.

Per Capita State Taxes, Fiscal 2004

Table MA-17. State Government Finances, 2003

(Dollars, percent distribution.)

Item	Millions of dollars	Percent distribution	Dollars per capita	
			State	U.S.
GENERAL REVENUE	27 012 438	100.0	4 207.5	3 832.6
Intergovernmental revenue	5 130 127	19.0	799.1	1 246.0
Taxes	15 608 027	57.8	2 431.2	1 891.6
General sales	3 708 069	13.7	577.6	636.0
Selective sales	1 702 851	6.3	265.2	307.4
License taxes	597 079	2.2	93.0	123.6
Individual income tax	8 026 149	29.7	1 250.2	626.8
Corporate income tax	1 184 610	4.4	184.5	97.8
Other taxes	389 269	1.4	60.6	99.9
Current charges	2 191 938	8.1	341.4	366.5
Miscellaneous general revenue	4 082 346	15.1	635.9	328.6
GENERAL EXPENDITURE	27 870 663	100.0	4 341.2	4 010.5
Intergovernmental expenditure	6 435 841	23.1	1 002.5	1 316.9
Direct expenditure	21 434 822	76.9	3 338.8	2 693.6
Expenditure by Function				
Education	6 774 160	24.3	1 055.2	1 416.4
Public welfare	5 292 878	19.0	824.4	1 083.3
Hospitals	507 129	1.8	79.0	132.3
Health	1 878 337	6.7	292.6	173.0
Highways	2 429 436	8.7	378.4	295.4
Police protection	424 923	1.5	66.2	38.4
Correction	1 049 512	3.8	163.5	135.0
Natural resources	266 116	1.0	41.4	64.0
Parks and recreation	342 004	1.2	53.3	20.1
Government administration	1 290 558	4.6	201.0	151.3
Interest on general debt	2 476 785	8.9	385.8	107.8
Other and unallocable	5 138 825	18.4	800.4	393.4
DEBT AT END OF FISCAL YEAR	48 478 722	X	7 551.2	2 404.7
CASH AND SECURITY HOLDINGS	59 207 225	X	9 222.3	8 938.4

X = Not applicable.

Table MA-18. Education Indicators, 2000–2004

(Percent, number.)

Item	State	U.S.
Total Population 25 Years and Over (Thousands), 2004	4 344	186 877
Educational Attainment, 2004		
Percent high school graduate or more	86.9	85.2
Percent college graduate or more	36.7	27.7
Elementary and Secondary Schools, 2002–2003		
Total students	982 989	48 202 324
Percent of students eligible for free or reduced-price lunch ..	27.2	40.6
Percent of students who were English language learners	5.0	7.8
Total schools	1 894	92 330
Student/teacher ratio	13.6	15.9
Per student expenditures	10 460	8 041
Higher Education, 2002–2003		
Total enrollment	440 448	17 035 027
Bachelor's degrees awarded	44 726	1 348 503
Percent women	57.6	57.5

Educational Attainment, 2004

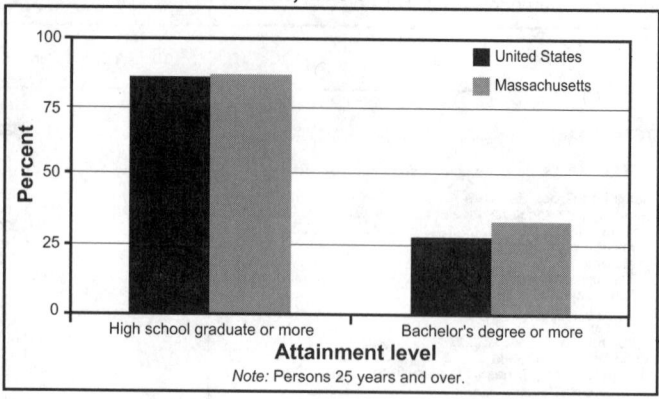

Note: Persons 25 years and over.

EDUCATION

Nearly 87 percent of the state's population age 25 years and over had graduated from high school. This was the 28th highest proportion in the nation. Over 36 percent of residents were college graduates, second only to the proportion in the District of Columbia. Massachusetts's student/teacher ratio was below average. Expenditures per student reached $10,640, which was the fifth highest rate of spending in the nation. Both of these measures reflected a below average proportion of student-age population. Just 27.2 percent of the state's students were eligible for free or reduced-price lunch; about 40 percent of students were eligible nationally.

VOTER PARTICIPATION

Voter turnout was well above the national average in both the 2000 and 2004 elections. In 2004, 63.7 percent of eligible voters turned out, which was up from 60.1 percent in 2000. The state ranked among the top 16 for voter participation rates in each election. More than 70 percent of eligible voters age 45 years and over turned out in 2004. About 42 percent of residents age 18 to 24 years voted, a rate similar to the national average for this age group. Massachusetts voted overwhelmingly Democrat; in 2000, 59.1 percent of voters cast ballots for the Democratic presidential ticket, and in 2004, this proportion increased to 61.6 percent.

Table MA-19. Reported Voting and Registration, November 2000 and November 2004

(Numbers in thousands, percent.)

Characteristic	Total population 18 years and over	Total citizen		Total registered		Total voted	
		Number	Percent	Number	Percent	Number	Percent
NOVEMBER 2000							
Total	4 614	4 246	92.0	3 244	70.3	2 772	60.1
Male	2 212	2 009	90.8	1 519	68.7	1 296	58.6
Female	2 403	2 237	93.1	1 725	71.8	1 476	61.4
NOVEMBER 2004							
Total	4 840	4 497	92.9	3 483	72.0	3 085	63.7
Male	2 299	2 115	92.0	1 641	71.4	1 429	62.2
Female	2 541	2 382	93.7	1 842	72.5	1 656	65.2
Race and Hispanic Origin							
White alone	4 297	4 049	94.2	3 234	75.3	2 880	67.0
Non-Hispanic White alone	4 046	3 896	96.3	3 131	77.4	2 807	69.4
Black alone	292	273	93.5	148	50.7	127	43.5
Asian alone	199	128	64.1	76	38.2	59	29.4
Hispanic or Latino[1]	323	212	65.7	140	43.5	106	32.9
White alone or in combination	4 318	4 065	94.2	3 249	75.2	2 894	67.0
Non-Hispanic White alone or in combination	4 066	3 913	96.2	3 145	77.4	2 822	69.4
Black alone or in combination	292	273	93.5	148	50.7	127	43.5
Asian alone or in combination	210	138	65.9	85	40.3	67	32.0
Age							
18 to 24 years	662	606	91.5	348	52.6	277	41.8
25 to 44 years	1 781	1 601	89.9	1 196	67.1	1 044	58.6
45 to 64 years	1 552	1 476	95.1	1 248	80.4	1 140	73.4
65 to 74 years	428	415	97.0	360	84.2	330	77.2
75 years and over	417	399	95.8	331	79.4	294	70.6

[1]May be of any race.

At a Glance:

- Michigan's population was about 10.1 million in 2004, the eighth highest in the country.

- Non-Hispanic Whites made up over 78 percent of the population. Blacks accounted for 14.2 percent of residents, which was the 16th highest proportion of this racial group in the nation.

- The state's median household income of $42,328 was below the U.S. average and ranked 29th in the nation. Michigan's poverty rate of 13.3 percent was the 17th highest in the country.

- In 2004, Michigan's unemployment rate was 7.1 percent, the fourth highest in the country. The state's real gross state product was the ninth largest of the states, but its growth rate in recent years was among the lowest in the nation.

- Michigan ranked 19th for proportion of residents age 25 years and over with a high school diploma and 37th for those with a bachelor's degree or more.

- The state's infant mortality rate of 8.1 deaths per 1,000 live births was the 11th highest in the nation.

Table MI-1. Population by Sex and Age, 1990, 2000, and 2004

(Number, percent.)

Sex and age	1990	2000	2004	Percent distribution, 2004	Average annual percent change, 2000–2004
Total Population	9 295 297	9 938 444	10 112 620	X	0.4
Percent of total U.S. population	3.7	3.5	3.4	X	X
Sex					
Male	4 512 781	4 873 095	4 968 663	49.1	0.5
Female	4 782 516	5 065 349	5 143 957	50.9	0.4
Age					
Under 5 years	702 554	672 005	649 842	6.4	-0.7
5 to 17 years	1 756 211	1 923 762	1 883 597	18.6	0.5
18 years and over	1 742 842	7 342 677	7 579 181	74.9	0.7
18 to 24 years	6 836 532	932 137	996 571	9.9	-0.1
25 to 44 years	1 004 527	2 960 544	2 819 898	27.9	-0.4
45 to 64 years	2 980 702	2 230 978	2 516 117	24.9	2.7
65 years and over	1 108 461	1 219 018	1 246 595	12.3	0.9
85 years and over	106 907	142 460	175 067	1.7	3.7
Median age (years)	32.5	35.5	36.6	X	X

X = Not applicable.

Average Annual Rate of Population Growth, 1980–2004

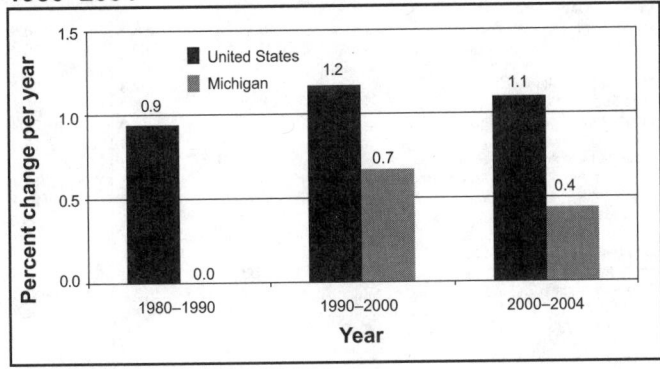

POPULATION

Michigan is a state whose fortunes have long been tied to the auto industry. This affects the state's economic activity and labor market, as well as influencing changes in the population, which fluctuates according to perceptions of economic opportunities. Michigan's population grew by only 1.8 percent between 2000 and 2004, an increase equal to about half of the national growth rate. This increase was higher than that in Ohio, but far less than those in Indiana and Illinois. Over the period, the state experienced an out-migration of over 116,000 residents, which contributed to its slow growth rate. An influx of nearly 104,000 new residents from abroad prevented the state from experiencing a population loss.

Table MI-2. Population by Race and Hispanic Origin, 1990, 2000, and 2004

(Number, percent.)

Race and Hispanic origin	1990	2000	2004
Total Population	9 295 297	9 938 444	10 112 620
Non-Hispanic (Percent)			
One race[1]			
White	82.3	79.0	78.1
Black	13.8	14.2	14.2
American Indian, Alaska Native[2]	0.6	0.5	0.5
Asian and Pacific Islander[2]	1.1	1.8	2.2
Other race[2]	0.9	. . .	. . .
Two or more races	. . .	1.2	1.3
Hispanic or Latino[3] (Percent)	2.2	3.3	3.7

[1]Individuals could report only one race in the 1990 census and could report one or more races on the 2000 census. Data on race in 2000 and 2004 are not comparable to 1990.
[2]Data for 1990 include people of Hispanic or Latino origin.
[3]May be of any race.
. . . = Not available.

Minority Population as a Percent of Total Population, 2004

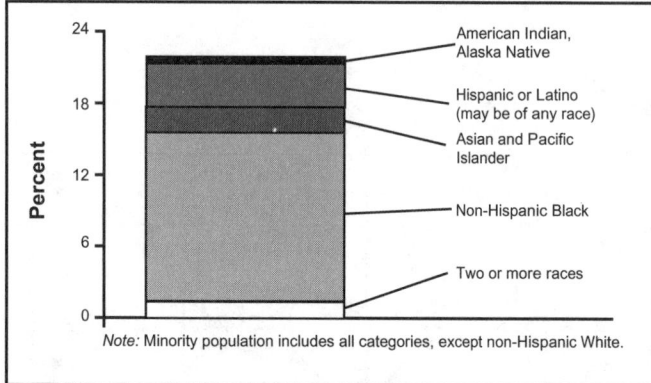

Note: Minority population includes all categories, except non-Hispanic White.

Age-Adjusted Death Rates, Average 2000–2002

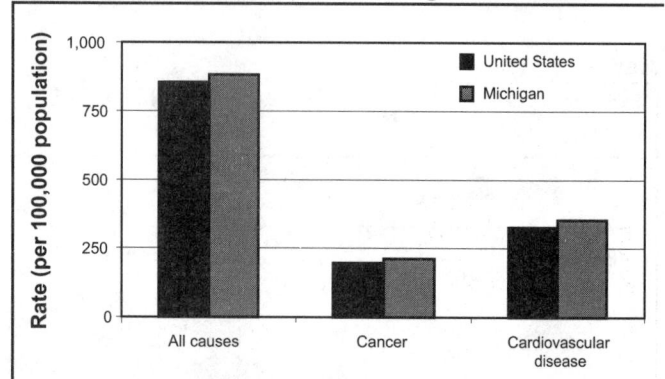

HEALTH

Michigan's health insurance coverage rate was above average, with just 11.6 percent of residents lacking coverage. The state's birth rate was below the national average, and its birth rate for teenage mothers was also below average. The infant mortality rate and age-adjusted death rates were well above the U.S. averages.

Table MI-3. Health Characteristics, 2000–2004

(Number, rate, percent.)

Item	State	U.S.
Births, 2003–2004		
Number of births	131 094	4 089 950
Birth rate (per 1,000 population)	13.0	14.1
Teenage birth rate (per 1,000 women age 15–19 years)	34.4	41.6
Mortality Rates, Average 2000–2002		
Infant mortality rate (per 1,000 live births)	8.1	6.9
Age-adjusted mortality rate (per 100,000 population)		
All races	884.0	853.3
Non-Hispanic White	841.5	843.1
Black	1 161.8	1 097.7
American Indian, Alaska Native	. . .	687.0
Asian and Pacific Islander	397.5	486.0
Hispanic or Latino[1]	658.5	642.7
Health Insurance, 2004		
Percent of all persons without health insurance	11.6	15.7
Percent of children without health insurance	6.8	11.2
Percent of low-income children without health insurance	4.5	7.1

[1]May be of any race.
. . . = Not available.

Table MI-4. Leading Causes of Death, Average 2000–2002

(Number, rate per 100,000 population.)

Cause	Number of deaths	Age-adjusted death rates	
		State	U.S.
ALL CAUSES	87 057	884.0	853.3
Leading Causes			
Major cardiovascular diseases	35 008	356.6	326.5
Cancer	19 824	200.5	196.0
Chronic lower respiratory diseases	4 310	44.0	43.7
Unintentional injuries	3 265	32.8	35.7
Diabetes (underlying cause)	2 681	27.2	25.2
Influenza and pneumonia	2 052	21.0	22.7
Alzheimer's disease	1 802	18.5	19.0
Motor vehicle accidents	1 379	13.8	15.0
Nephritis, nephrotic syndrome, and nephrosis ..	1 528	15.6	13.8
Septicemia	953	9.7	11.4
Suicides	1 044	10.4	10.7
Firearm-related	1 080	10.8	10.3
Cirrhosis	1 029	10.2	9.5
Drug-induced	968	9.6	7.9
Alcohol-induced	680	6.7	6.9
Homicides	701	7.0	6.0
Falls	480	4.9	5.2
HIV	247	2.5	5.0
Viral hepatitis	155	1.5	2.0
Anemias	198	2.0	1.6
Drownings	127	1.3	1.3
Fire deaths	134	1.3	1.2

Note: The rates are age-adjusted to the U.S. 2000 standard population.

Table MI-5. Households and Housing Characteristics, 1990, 2000, and 2004

(Number, percent, and dollars.)

Characteristic	1990	2000	2004	Average annual percent change, 2000–2004
Total Households	3 419 331	3 785 661	3 923 135	0.9
Family households	2 439 171	2 575 699	2 629 211	0.5
Married-couple family	1 883 143	1 947 710	1 978 547	0.4
Other family	556 028	627 989	650 664	0.9
Male householder, no wife present	113 789	154 187	151 026	-0.5
Female householder, no husband present	442 239	473 802	499 638	1.3
Nonfamily households	980 160	1 209 962	1 293 924	1.7
Householder living alone	809 449	993 607	1 097 613	2.5
Householder not living alone	170 711	216 355	196 311	-2.4
Housing Characteristics				
Average size	2.66	2.56	2.51	X
Housing units	3 847 926	4 234 279	4 433 482	1.2
Occupied housing units	3 419 331	3 785 661	3 923 135	0.9
Owner-occupied	2 427 643	2 793 124	2 928 862	1.2
Renter-occupied	991 688	992 537	994 273	0.0
Median gross rent of renter-occupied housing units (dollars) ...	423	546	628	3.6
Median value of owner-occupied housing units (dollars)	60 100	115 600	145 177	5.9

X = Not applicable.

Median Housing Value and Median Rent, 2004

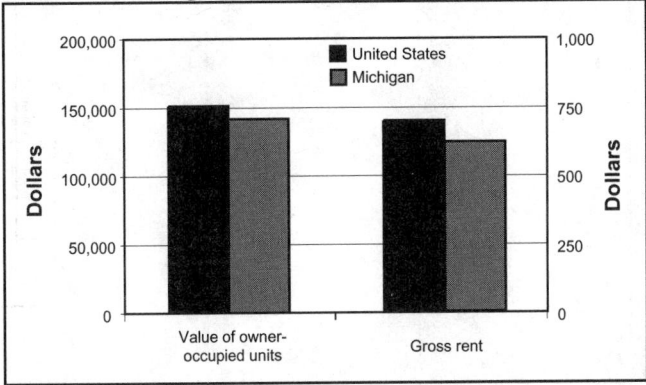

Median Household Income, 1984–2004 (2004 Dollars)

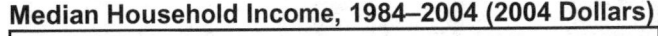
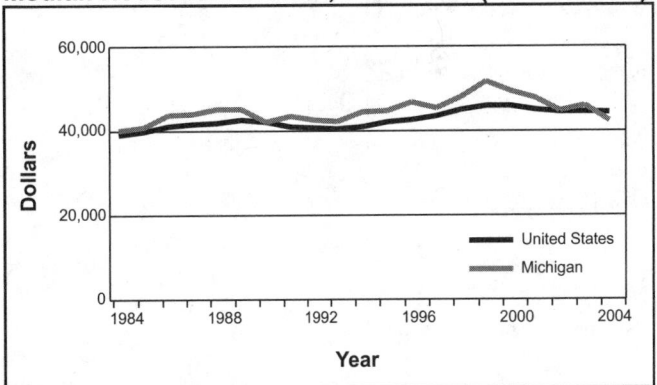

Table MI-6. Household Income and Poverty Status, 1980–2004

(2004 CPI-U-RS adjusted dollars, rate.)

Year	State Median household income (2004 dollars)	State Poverty rate	U.S. Median household income (2004 dollars)	U.S. Poverty rate
2004	42 328	13.3	44 389	12.7
2003	46 232	11.4	44 482	12.5
2002	44 868	11.6	44 546	12.1
2001	48 070	9.4	45 062	11.7
2000	49 922	9.9	46 058	11.3
1999	52 242	9.7	46 129	11.9
1998	48 401	11.0	45 003	12.7
1997	45 469	10.3	43 430	13.3
1996	47 019	11.2	42 544	13.7
1995	44 836	12.2	41 943	13.8
1994	44 485	14.1	40 677	14.5
1993	42 046	15.4	40 217	15.1
1992	42 574	13.6	40 422	14.8
1991	43 438	14.1	40 746	14.2
1990	41 955	14.3	41 963	13.5
1989	45 274	13.2	42 524	12.8
1988	45 219	12.1	41 771	13.0
1987	44 051	12.2	41 322	13.4
1986	43 748	13.9	40 939	13.6
1985	40 590	14.5	39 545	14.0
1984	39 734	16.7	38 782	14.4
1983	. . .	16.8	. . .	15.2
1982	. . .	16.2	. . .	15.0
1981	. . .	13.0	. . .	14.0
1980	. . .	12.9	. . .	13.0

. . . = Not available.

Table MI-7. Employment Status by Demographic Group, 2004

(Numbers in thousands, rate.)

Characteristic	Civilian noninstitutional population	Civilian labor force		Employed	Unemployment rate
		Number	Participation rate		
SEX AND AGE					
Total	7 748	5 114	66.0	4 758	7.0
16 to 19 years	568	283	49.9	230	18.9
20 to 24 years	683	531	77.8	475	10.6
25 to 34 years	1 295	1 060	81.9	991	6.5
35 to 44 years	1 499	1 242	82.8	1 167	6.0
45 to 54 years	1 515	1 239	81.8	1 175	5.2
55 to 64 years	1 018	601	59.0	570	5.1
65 years and over	1 170	157	13.5	150	5.0
Men	3 738	2 720	72.8	2 516	7.5
16 to 19 years	292	145	49.7	114	21.1
20 to 24 years	345	282	81.8	250	11.4
25 to 34 years	625	568	90.9	525	7.6
35 to 44 years	750	682	90.9	639	6.2
45 to 54 years	746	643	86.3	610	5.2
55 to 64 years	480	309	64.4	292	5.7
65 years and over	500	90	17.9	85	4.8
Women	4 010	2 394	59.7	2 241	6.4
16 to 19 years	276	138	50.1	115	16.5
20 to 24 years	338	249	73.7	225	9.7
25 to 34 years	671	492	73.4	466	5.3
35 to 44 years	749	560	74.7	528	5.7
45 to 54 years	769	596	77.5	565	5.2
55 to 64 years	538	291	54.2	279	4.4
65 years and over	670	68	10.1	64	5.2
MARITAL STATUS					
Married men, spouse present	2 148	1 631	75.9	1 562	4.3
Married women, spouse present	2 061	1 248	60.6	1 195	4.3
Women who maintain families	518	355	68.5	323	9.0
RACE, HISPANIC ORIGIN, AND SEX					
White	6 434	4 291	66.7	4 041	5.8
Men	3 138	2 327	74.2	2 178	6.4
Women	3 296	1 964	59.6	1 863	5.2
Black	1 005	610	60.7	523	14.4
Men	446	273	61.2	228	16.4
Women	559	337	60.3	294	12.7
Asian	169	121	71.7	114	6.1
Hispanic or Latino[1]	230	159	69.4	140	12.3
Men	118	96	80.7	82	14.4
Women	111	64	57.4	58	9.3
RACE, HISPANIC ORIGIN, AND AGE					
White					
16 to 19 years	460	244	52.9	204	16.2
20 to 24 years	541	435	80.5	400	8.1
25 to 34 years	1 018	843	82.8	798	5.3
35 to 44 years	1 229	1 030	83.8	980	4.8
45 to 54 years	1 280	1 074	83.9	1 024	4.6
55 to 64 years	875	530	60.6	504	4.9
65 years and over	1 032	136	13.2	131	3.9

Note: Data in Table 7 are from the Current Population Survey (CPS) and do not match Bureau of Labor Statistics estimates in Table 8. See notes and definitions for more details.

[1]May be of any race.

Table MI-8. Employment Status, 1990–2004

(Numbers in thousands, rate.)

Year	Civilian labor force	Employed	Unemployed	Unemployment rate
2004	5 078 979	4 719 343	359 636	7.1
2003	5 053 506	4 695 148	358 358	7.1
2002	5 038 821	4 724 036	314 785	6.2
2001	5 131 908	4 864 600	267 308	5.2
2000	5 157 374	4 967 218	190 156	3.7
1999	5 089 421	4 897 144	192 277	3.8
1998	5 007 953	4 809 503	198 450	4.0
1997	4 963 077	4 748 691	214 386	4.3
1996	4 888 192	4 647 116	241 076	4.9
1995	4 834 939	4 576 521	258 418	5.3
1994	4 804 463	4 508 900	295 563	6.2
1993	4 711 598	4 364 545	347 053	7.4
1992	4 661 696	4 234 783	426 913	9.2
1991	4 588 881	4 162 074	426 807	9.3
1990	4 619 988	4 262 409	357 579	7.7

Note: Population age 16 years and over.

Unemployment Rate, 1980–2004

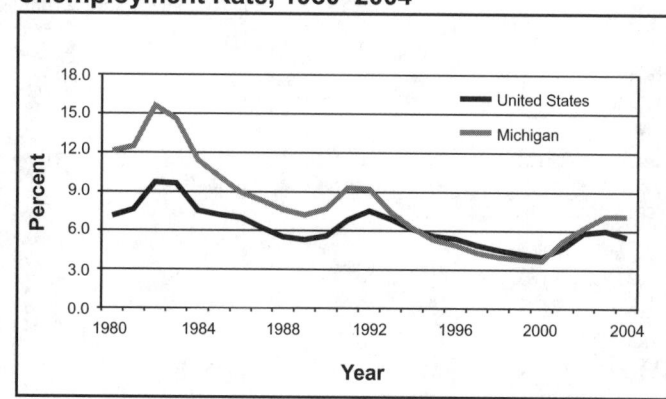

Table MI-9. Employment and Average Wages by Industry, 2001–2004

(Estimates are based on the 2002 North American Industry Classification System [NAICS].)

Industry	2001	2002	2003	2004	Annual average percent change, 2001–2004
	Number of jobs				
TOTAL EMPLOYMENT BY PLACE OF WORK	5 539 887	5 482 838	5 450 988	5 466 794	-0.4
Farm Employment	72 906	72 733	72 601	74 259	0.6
Nonfarm Employment	5 466 981	5 410 105	5 378 387	5 392 535	-0.5
Private employment	4 767 485	4 709 470	4 681 618	4 700 629	-0.5
Forestry, fishing, hunting, and other[1]	16 835	16 462	15 318	15 609	-2.5
Mining	14 278	12 691	13 682	14 049	-0.5
Utilities	21 698	20 965	21 108	21 019	-1.1
Construction	304 276	295 876	291 737	294 286	-1.1
Manufacturing	843 743	779 467	737 845	717 055	-5.3
Durable goods manufacturing	670 371	615 829	579 117	562 364	-5.7
Nondurable goods manufacturing	173 372	163 638	158 728	154 691	-3.7
Wholesale trade	196 162	189 835	187 291	185 213	-1.9
Retail trade	654 619	640 847	632 131	631 789	-1.2
Transportation and warehousing	134 666	132 822	129 645	130 209	-1.1
Information	87 123	83 468	81 382	79 392	-3.0
Finance and insurance	207 866	212 416	216 461	216 004	1.3
Real estate and rental and leasing	167 758	172 048	181 608	189 866	4.2
Professional and technical services	366 306	360 440	354 617	352 592	-1.3
Management of companies and enterprises	68 848	70 687	69 615	69 775	0.4
Administrative and waste services	322 152	325 326	333 519	344 597	2.3
Educational services	73 183	77 763	81 854	86 531	5.7
Health care and social assistance	551 775	567 008	580 209	589 115	2.2
Arts, entertainment, and recreation	100 369	102 854	103 706	104 547	1.4
Accommodation and food services	350 383	354 602	356 380	361 552	1.1
Other services, except public administration	285 445	293 893	293 510	297 429	1.4
Government and government enterprises	699 496	700 635	696 769	691 906	-0.4
	Dollars				
AVERAGE WAGES AND SALARIES BY PLACE OF WORK	36 756	37 520	38 784	39 745	2.6
Farm Earnings	29 132	31 696	22 650	25 457	-4.4
Nonfarm Earnings	36 786	37 542	38 851	39 810	2.7
Private earnings	37 244	37 859	39 174	40 119	2.5
Forestry, fishing, hunting, and other[1]	18 452	19 063	19 837	20 854	4.2
Mining	44 359	44 174	47 339	50 493	4.4
Utilities	67 292	69 505	74 000	73 139	2.8
Construction	42 726	42 968	43 118	43 762	0.8
Manufacturing	49 656	51 950	55 391	55 998	4.1
Durable goods manufacturing	51 663	54 131	57 784	58 366	4.2
Nondurable goods manufacturing	41 788	43 619	46 545	47 279	4.2
Wholesale trade	50 950	51 506	53 455	55 719	3.0
Retail trade	21 669	22 477	22 981	23 569	2.8
Transportation and warehousing	40 866	42 021	43 817	45 482	3.6
Information	47 228	47 155	49 127	51 385	2.9
Finance and insurance	48 867	49 654	51 540	52 871	2.7
Real estate and rental and leasing	28 728	29 505	29 364	29 964	1.4
Professional and technical services	60 358	60 343	62 727	64 653	2.3
Management of companies and enterprises	84 414	77 616	82 550	91 821	2.8
Administrative and waste services	26 551	27 838	28 488	29 646	3.7
Educational services	22 646	23 044	23 851	24 469	2.6
Health care and social assistance	33 398	34 556	35 532	36 826	3.3
Arts, entertainment, and recreation	23 299	24 814	25 135	25 927	3.6
Accommodation and food services	12 237	12 497	12 691	13 018	2.1
Other services, except public administration	23 159	23 385	24 106	24 828	2.3
Government and government enterprises	34 177	35 781	37 072	38 106	3.7

Note: Average wages and salaries are a calculation by the editors of wage and salary disbursements divided by full- and part-time wage and salary employment. Data may not add to total or may appear as zero due to rounding.

[1] "Other" consists of the number of jobs held by U.S. residents employed by international organizations and foreign embassies and consulates in the United States.

LABOR MARKET

Michigan's unemployment rate has been above the national average since 2001; in 2004, it was the seventh highest in the nation. This was partly due to the state's economic reliance on the auto industry, which has recently experienced hard times. Manufacturing was the largest employer of wage and salary workers in Michigan, accounting for 13 percent of total jobs in 2004. However, manufacturing employment was down 15 percent from 2001. Job losses also occurred in information services, professional and technical services, retail trade, and construction. Average wages and salaries were above the national average, particularly in manufacturing, construction, and management, but their rate of growth was somewhat below average.

Employment by Industry, 2004

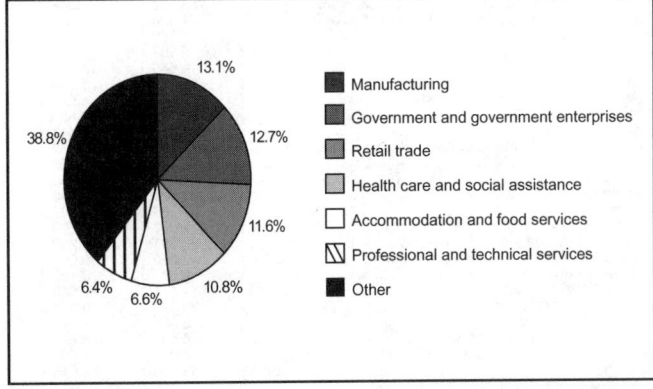

- Manufacturing
- Government and government enterprises
- Retail trade
- Health care and social assistance
- Accommodation and food services
- Professional and technical services
- Other

13.1%
38.8%
12.7%
11.6%
10.8%
6.6%
6.4%

Table MI-10. Personal Income by Major Source, Selected Years 1980–2004

(Millions of dollars, except where noted.)

Item	1980	1990	2000	2001	2002	2003	2004	Average annual percent change, 2000–2004
Earnings by Place of Work	75 853	135 305	231 181	233 875	238 530	251 867	253 959	2.4
Wage and salary disbursements	57 828	102 779	175 327	173 102	173 457	176 653	180 245	0.7
Supplements to wages and salaries	13 177	22 152	37 854	37 180	42 252	49 606	46 394	5.2
Proprietors' income[1]	4 848	10 375	18 000	23 593	22 820	25 608	27 319	11.0
Farm proprietors' income	330	371	-60	-278	-208	118	194	X
Nonfarm proprietors' income	4 519	10 003	18 060	23 871	23 029	25 490	27 126	10.7
(-) Contributions for government social insurance[2]	7 181	15 869	26 411	26 358	26 746	27 496	28 217	1.7
(+) Adjustment for residence[3]	355	457	1 005	1 063	1 131	1 202	1 282	6.3
(=) Net Earnings by Place of Residence	69 026	119 893	205 775	208 580	212 914	225 573	227 024	2.5
(+) Dividends, interest, and rent[4]	12 625	32 537	49 515	47 635	45 766	45 883	48 154	-0.7
(+) Personal current transfer receipts	13 809	23 758	38 938	43 327	44 855	47 035	48 956	5.9
Personal income	95 460	176 189	294 227	299 542	303 535	318 491	324 134	2.4
Farm income	94 945	175 455	293 710	299 226	303 145	317 913	323 380	2.4
Nonfarm income	514	734	517	316	390	578	754	9.9
Per Capita Personal Income (Dollars)[5]	10 314	18 922	29 552	29 940	30 225	31 589	32 052	2.1

Note: Data may not add to total or may appear as zero due to rounding.

[1]Proprietors' income includes the inventory valuation adjustment and the capital consumption adjustment.
[2]Contributions for government social insurance are included in earnings by type and industry, but they are excluded from personal income.
[3]The adjustment for residence is the net inflow of the earnings of interarea commuters.
[4]Rental income of persons includes the capital consumption adjustment.
[5]Per capita personal income is total personal income divided by total midyear population.
X = Not applicable.

Per Capita Personal Income, 1980–2004 (Current Dollars)

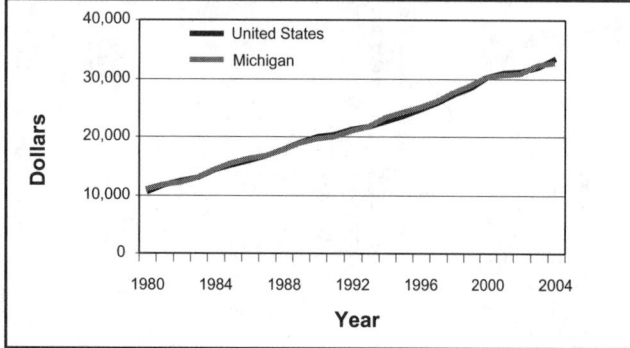

ECONOMIC ACTIVITY

Real gross state product (GSP) declined sharply during the 2001 recession and recovered slowly in subsequent years. From 2003 to 2004, Michigan's GSP grew just 1.2 percent, which was the lowest rate of growth in the nation. The construction and mining sectors declined considerably from 2001 to 2004. Retail trade and the service industries of information, real estate, and "other" services (a sector that supplies temporary workers to other industries) were the chief contributors to growth during the 2003–2004 period. The rate of housing price appreciation was less than half the national average rate. In 2004, the median value of owner-occupied housing in Michigan ranked 24th in the nation, totaling $145,177.

Table MI-11. Real Gross State Product, 1997–2004

(Millions of chained 2000 dollars, percent.)

Industry	1997	1998	1999	2000	2001	2002	2003	2004	Average annual percent change, 2001–2004
GROSS STATE PRODUCT	317 263	322 475	333 567	337 185	328 228	333 714	340 972	344 954	1.7
As a percent of U.S. gross product	3.7	3.6	3.5	3.5	3.3	3.3	3.3	3.2	X
Private Industries	283 962	289 842	300 384	303 519	294 722	300 245	307 525	311 493	1.9
Agriculture, forestry, fishing, and hunting	1 396	1 397	1 631	1 587	1 455	1 700	1 632	1 558	2.3
Mining	682	695	662	649	594	586	551	537	-3.3
Utilities	5 907	5 931	6 411	6 438	6 619	6 501	7 193	7 202	2.9
Construction	14 640	15 269	15 778	15 888	14 857	14 206	13 544	13 281	-3.7
Manufacturing	69 880	71 109	75 290	76 326	68 573	72 065	76 418	76 646	3.8
As a percent of gross state product	22.0	22.1	22.6	22.6	20.9	21.6	22.4	22.2	X
Wholesale trade	17 702	19 654	20 402	19 833	20 392	20 713	20 308	20 285	-0.2
Retail trade	20 518	21 447	21 983	22 841	24 414	25 063	25 985	26 828	3.2
Transportation and warehousing	7 652	7 532	8 139	8 367	7 776	8 293	8 778	9 016	5.1
Information	7 430	7 955	8 725	8 769	9 325	9 377	10 005	10 810	5.0
Finance and insurance	15 424	16 180	16 860	17 290	17 461	18 899	19 761	20 009	4.6
Real estate and rental and leasing	41 580	39 546	39 191	38 200	39 709	38 747	37 597	38 225	-1.3
Services	81 688	83 399	85 369	87 332	83 549	84 281	86 320	87 765	1.7
As a percent of gross state product	25.7	25.9	25.6	25.9	25.5	25.3	25.3	25.4	X
Professional and technical services	23 481	25 297	26 392	28 273	26 430	26 385	27 130	26 945	0.6
Management of companies and enterprises	10 356	10 002	9 787	9 033	7 831	7 425	7 753	8 122	1.2
Administrative and waste services	9 580	10 136	10 799	10 578	9 898	10 541	11 089	11 473	5.0
Educational services	1 479	1 528	1 532	1 557	1 521	1 534	1 515	1 518	-0.1
Health care and social assistance	20 420	19 968	20 302	20 828	21 015	21 653	22 159	22 460	2.2
Arts, entertainment, and recreation	2 014	2 043	2 251	2 585	2 683	2 836	2 815	2 786	1.3
Accommodation and food services	6 422	6 724	6 792	7 121	6 885	6 859	6 903	7 125	1.1
Other services, except public administration	7 936	7 701	7 514	7 357	7 286	7 048	6 956	7 336	0.2
Government	33 350	32 645	33 182	33 665	33 500	33 480	33 496	33 519	0.0
As a percent of gross state product	10.5	10.1	9.9	10.0	10.2	10.0	9.8	9.7	X

X = Not applicable.

Table MI-12. Government Transfer Payments, Selected Years 1980–2004

(Millions of dollars, percent.)

Item	1980	1990	2000	2001	2002	2003	2004	Average annual percent change, 2000–2004
CURRENT TRANSFER PAYMENTS TO INDIVIDUALS	13 112	22 414	36 675	40 833	42 807	45 147	47 080	6.4
Retirement and Disability Insurance Benefits	5 234	10 366	16 231	17 176	18 004	18 659	19 490	4.7
Old-age, survivors, and disability insurance (OASDI) benefits	5 001	10 014	15 900	16 835	17 650	18 252	19 069	4.6
Railroad retirement and disability benefits	108	171	218	223	231	236	240	2.5
Workers' compensation	103	139	60	64	63	65	67	2.7
Other government retirement and disability insurance benefits	23	42	53	54	59	107	115	21.4
Medical Benefits	2 866	7 049	14 891	17 165	17 185	18 305	19 614	7.1
Medicare benefits	1 653	4 337	8 178	9 051	9 676	10 227	11 213	8.2
Public assistance medical care benefits	1 200	2 678	6 679	8 063	7 436	8 017	8 328	5.7
Military medical insurance benefits	14	35	35	51	73	62	73	20.8
Income Maintenance Benefits	1 973	3 035	3 729	3 850	4 163	4 487	4 781	6.4
Supplemental Security Income (SSI) benefits	236	486	1 086	1 102	1 098	1 166	1 219	2.9
Family assistance	1 079	1 244	915	855	884	824	807	-3.1
Food stamps	287	696	456	536	658	813	950	20.2
Other income maintenance benefits	371	610	1 272	1 357	1 522	1 684	1 806	9.2
Unemployment Insurance Compensation	2 421	1 181	905	1 613	2 355	2 563	1 992	21.8
Veterans' Benefits	448	476	566	591	644	690	726	6.4
Federal Education and Training Assistance	166	297	332	395	437	425	455	8.2
Other Payments to Individuals	3	9	21	43	19	18	22	0.9

Note: See notes and definitions for more details. Data may not add to total or may appear as zero due to rounding.

EXPORTS

One bright spot in the state's economy was the export sector, in which the value of goods increased at a 3.2 percent annual rate between 2001 and 2004. Michigan ranked fourth in the country for exports in 2004, with total exports valued at over $35.6 billion. Transportation equipment accounted for nearly 52 percent of total exports. The value of these exports improved from a slump in 2003, but remained slightly below their 2001 level. Other chief exports in 2004 were machinery manufactures and chemical manufactures. Canada was by far the state's largest export market, followed distantly by Mexico. Exports to China have more than doubled since 2001, with the country becoming Michigan's seventh largest market in 2004.

Leading Exports, 2004

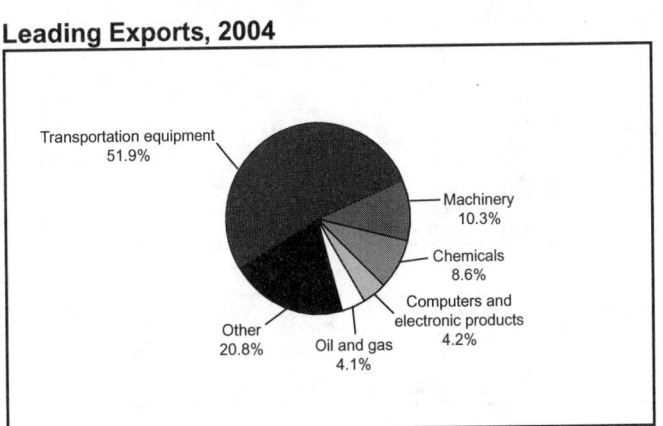

Table MI-13. Exports of Goods by Leading Products and Destinations, 2001–2004

(Millions of dollars, percent, rank based on 2004 dollar values.)

Product and market	2001	2002	2003	2004	Percent share of total, 2004	Average annual percent change, 2001–2004
Total Goods						
Total	32 366	33 775	32 941	35 625	100.0	3.2
Manufactures	31 401	32 685	31 535	33 286	93.4	2.0
Agriculture and livestock	607	721	991	1 910	5.4	46.5
Other commodities	358	369	415	429	1.2	6.2
Five Leading Exports (NAICS Code)						
Transportation equipment (336)	18 559	19 583	18 086	18 499	51.9	-0.1
Machinery manufactures (333)	3 489	3 584	3 372	3 680	10.3	1.8
Chemical manufactures (325)	2 524	2 823	2 785	3 059	8.6	6.6
Computers and electronic products (334)	1 464	1 404	1 444	1 503	4.2	0.9
Oil and gas extraction (211)	191	319	526	1 470	4.1	97.3
Five Leading Markets	30 921	32 338	31 503	34 059	95.6	3.3
Canada	17 562	19 801	19 799	21 486	60.3	7.0
Mexico	4 791	4 239	4 006	4 173	11.7	-4.5
Japan	1 204	1 116	1 100	1 069	3.0	-3.9
Germany	928	989	973	1 010	2.8	2.8
United Kingdom	946	779	706	660	1.9	-11.3

Table MI-14. Agriculture, 1997 and 2002

(Number, acres, and dollars.)

Item	1997	2002
Number of farms	53 519	53 315
Land in farms (acres)	10 443 935	10 142 958
Farm Size		
Average size of farm (acres)	195	190
Farms by size (percent distribution)		
Fewer than 50 acres	34.8	41.1
50 to 499 acres	55.9	49.9
500 acres or more	9.3	9.0
Market Value of Land and Equipment (Dollars)		
Land and buildings average value per farm	335 580	509 299
Average value per acre	1 704	2 667
Machinery and equipment average value per farm	62 011	73 910
Value of Sales (Thousands of Dollars)		
Agricultural products sold	3 694 670	3 772 435
Crops	2 314 487	2 362 628
Livestock, poultry, and their products	1 380 183	1 409 807
Average per farm (dollars)	69 035	70 757
Value of sales (percent distribution)		
Less than $10,000	54.7	62.2
$10,000 to $99,999	31.3	25.7
$100,000 or more	14.0	12.2
Government Payments		
Payments (thousands of dollars)	97 638	144 771
Percent of farms receiving government payments	45.2	34.0
Farm operators whose principal occupation is farming (percent)	45.1	54.5

AGRICULTURE

Cash receipts from farming totaled $3.8 billion in 2002, an increase of 5.6 percent from the 1997 farm census. The state ranked 22nd in the nation for value of agricultural sales. Michigan's chief products were dairy, greenhouse/nursery products, and soybeans. In 2002, 62.2 percent of farms had sales of less than $10,000, up from 54.7 percent in 1997. The proportion of farms spanning fewer than 50 acres increased from 34.8 percent to 41.1 percent during this period. The proportion of farm operators reporting farming as their principal occupation rose to 54.5 percent in 2002.

ENERGY

Energy expenditures per person were relatively low, ranking 40th in the country in 2001. Michigan's energy prices were also among the lowest in the nation. The state's per capita energy consumption of 312 Btu was the 34th highest in the nation. The industrial sector was the largest consumer of energy.

Energy Consumption by Source, 2001

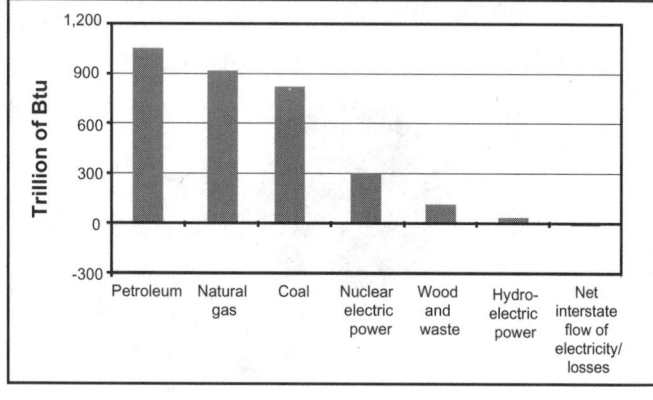

Energy Consumption by Sector, 2001

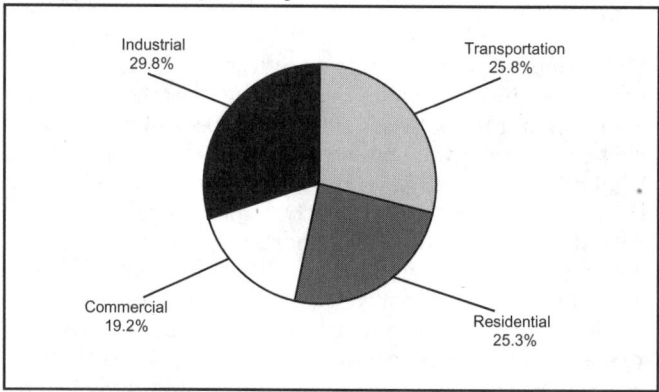

Table MI-15. Energy Consumption, Expenditures, and Prices, Selected Years 1960–2001

(Dollars, Btu [British Thermal Unit], percent distribution.)

Item	1960	1965	1970	1975	1980	1985	1990	1995	2000	2001
Total Consumption (Billion Btu)	1 852 172	2 291 403	2 725 983	2 889 369	2 882 254	2 655 806	2 850 637	3 104 634	3 252 097	3 119 999
Consumption per capita (million Btu)	236.8	274.2	306.9	316.9	311.2	292.6	306.7	321.4	327.2	311.8
Consumption by Sector (Percent Distribution)										
Residential	26.1	24.4	25.8	25.6	26.4	26.2	24.9	25.3	24.4	25.3
Commercial	9.6	10.6	12.1	13.7	14.6	15.0	15.7	19.0	19.4	19.2
Industrial	43.4	44.6	40.4	37.9	37.4	35.8	35.6	31.1	31.1	29.8
Transportation	20.9	20.4	21.8	22.9	21.5	23.0	23.8	24.6	25.1	25.8
Consumption by Source (Billion Btu)										
Coal	653 141	830 191	828 881	750 983	759 026	781 884	788 030	786 695	799 792	796 467
Natural gas	382 980	563 563	821 261	894 795	874 654	719 871	898 849	992 718	984 345	928 650
Petroleum	713 863	804 654	979 111	1 098 861	965 363	836 004	904 545	982 585	1 064 028	1 041 719
Nuclear electric power	0	2 132	4 113	79 031	173 339	142 886	228 682	256 879	196 925	279 074
Hydroelectric power[1]	21 839	18 954	17 878	11 553	12 464	10 416	9 704	8 924	3 815	4 427
Wood and waste	37 260	36 904	36 432	35 906	87 606	95 367	78 992	90 377	92 269	79 452
Other	4 264	-1 410	-1 365	1 091	19 396	1 334	-36 443	20 748	282	-5 688
Net interstate flow of electricity/losses[2]	38 824	36 415	39 673	17 150	-9 593	68 043	-21 722	-34 292	110 641	-4 103
Total Expenditures (Thousands of Dollars)	...	...	3 737 300	7 611 200	14 414 500	16 365 400	16 709 900	17 815 200	22 483 100	21 912 700
Expenditures per capita (dollars)	...	...	421	835	1 556	1 803	1 798	1 844	2 262	2 190
Prices by Sector (Dollars Per Million Btu)										
Total	...	...	1.70	3.33	6.59	8.43	7.99	7.88	9.63	9.77
Residential	...	...	1.73	3.13	5.53	8.75	8.46	8.43	9.50	10.39
Commercial	...	...	2.14	3.40	6.37	10.08	10.09	10.50	11.76	12.04
Industrial	...	...	1.02	2.54	4.97	6.96	6.27	5.69	6.51	6.60
Transportation	...	...	2.50	4.46	9.63	8.96	8.53	8.16	11.41	10.86

[1]A negative number in this row results from pumped storage for which, overall, more electricity is expended than created to provide electricity during peak demand periods.
[2]Net interstate flow of electricity is the difference between the amount of energy in the electricity sold within a state (including associated losses) and the energy input at the electric utilities within the state. A positive number indicates that more electricity (including associated losses) came into the state than went out of the state during the year; conversely, a negative number indicates that more electricity (including associated losses) went out of the state than came into the state.
. . . = Not available.

Table MI-16. State Taxes, Fiscal 2004

(Dollars, percent distribution.)

Item	Thousands of dollars	Percent distribution	Dollars per capita	
			State	U.S.
TOTAL TAXES	24 061 065	100.0	2 379.2	2 024.8
Property Taxes	2 803 017	11.6	277.2	38.9
Sales and Gross Receipts	10 844 250	45.1	1 072.3	1 003.4
General sales and gross receipts	7 894 458	32.8	780.6	677.0
Selective sales taxes	2 949 792	12.3	291.7	326.4
Alcoholic beverages	149 424	0.6	14.8	15.7
Insurance premiums	230 272	1.0	22.8	47.0
Motor fuels	1 081 259	4.5	106.9	114.6
Tobacco products	992 793	4.1	98.2	42.0
Other selective sales	356 203	1.5	35.2	49.8
Licenses	1 545 457	6.4	152.8	134.9
Motor vehicle	1 064 774	4.4	105.3	59.4
Occupation and business, not elsewhere classified	171 844	0.7	17.0	37.1
Other licenses	146 089	0.6	14.4	2.6
Other Taxes	8 868 341	36.9	876.9	847.6
Individual income	6 576 065	27.3	650.3	673.6
Corporation net income	1 841 010	7.7	182.0	105.1
Documentary and stock transfer	317 480	1.3	31.4	27.1

GOVERNMENT FINANCE

In 2003, Michigan was above the national averages for state revenues and expenditures per person, ranking 15th and 17th in the nation, respectively. Per capita spending on education and health was also above the national average, while public welfare expenditures were below average. In fiscal year 2004, Michigan's per capita taxes amounted to $2,379, making them the 11th highest in the country. The largest component of these taxes was sales receipts. Individual taxes per person amounted to $650, which ranked 28th in the nation and below the U.S. average. The state's property taxes were the third highest among the 37 states with property taxes.

Per Capita State Taxes, Fiscal 2004

Table MI-17. State Government Finances, 2003

(Dollars, percent distribution.)

Item	Millions of dollars	Percent distribution	Dollars per capita	
			State	U.S.
GENERAL REVENUE	43 010 240	100.0	4 266.0	3 832.6
Intergovernmental revenue	12 221 555	28.4	1 212.2	1 246.0
Taxes	22 748 159	52.9	2 256.3	1 891.6
General sales	7 685 308	17.9	762.3	636.0
Selective sales	2 508 924	5.8	248.8	307.4
License taxes	1 339 579	3.1	132.9	123.6
Individual income tax	6 519 643	15.2	646.7	626.8
Corporate income tax	1 843 072	4.3	182.8	97.8
Other taxes	2 851 633	6.6	282.8	99.9
Current charges	5 218 416	12.1	517.6	366.5
Miscellaneous general revenue	2 822 110	6.6	279.9	328.6
GENERAL EXPENDITURE	44 522 173	100.0	4 416.0	4 010.5
Intergovernmental expenditure	19 851 778	44.6	1 969.0	1 316.9
Direct expenditure	24 670 395	55.4	2 447.0	2 693.6
Expenditure by Function				
Education	19 262 143	43.3	1 910.6	1 416.4
Public welfare	9 138 181	20.5	906.4	1 083.3
Hospitals	1 672 783	3.8	165.9	132.3
Health	3 748 496	8.4	371.8	173.0
Highways	2 786 999	6.3	276.4	295.4
Police protection	320 612	0.7	31.8	38.4
Correction	1 678 957	3.8	166.5	135.0
Natural resources	489 925	1.1	48.6	64.0
Parks and recreation	137 989	0.3	13.7	20.1
Government administration	910 980	2.0	90.4	151.3
Interest on general debt	1 044 621	2.3	103.6	107.8
Other and unallocable	3 330 487	7.5	330.3	393.4
DEBT AT END OF FISCAL YEAR	22 478 857	X	2 229.6	2 404.7
CASH AND SECURITY HOLDINGS	65 431 886	X	6 490.0	8 938.4

X = Not applicable.

Table MI-18. Education Indicators, 2000–2004

(Percent, number.)

Item	State	U.S.
Total Population 25 Years and Over (Thousands), 2004	6 444	186 877
Educational Attainment, 2004		
Percent high school graduate or more	87.9	85.2
Percent college graduate or more	24.4	27.7
Elementary and Secondary Schools, 2002–2003		
Total students	1 785 160	48 202 324
Percent of students eligible for free or reduced-price lunch ..	34.4	40.6
Percent of students who were English language learners	3.5	7.8
Total schools	3 871	92 330
Student/teacher ratio	18.1	15.9
Per student expenditures	8 781	8 041
Higher Education, 2002–2003		
Total enrollment	615 527	17 035 027
Bachelor's degrees awarded	50 178	1 348 503
Percent women	57.5	57.5

Educational Attainment, 2004

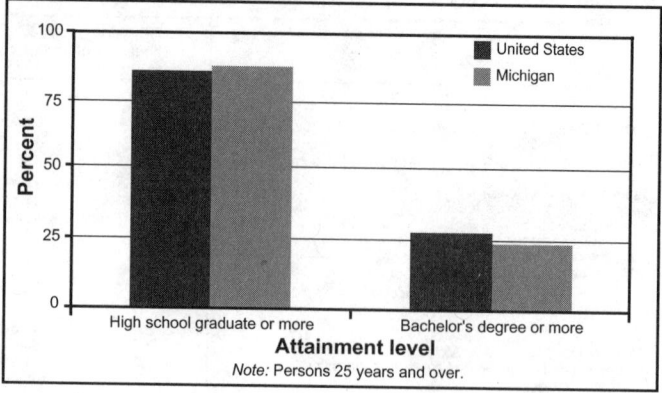

Note: Persons 25 years and over.

EDUCATION

Michigan had an above average proportion of high school graduates age 25 years and over in 2004. The state's proportion of college graduates in that age group ranked 37th in the nation, with 24.4 percent of residents holding a bachelor's degree or more. The state's per student expenditures of $8,781 were the 15th highest in the nation. The student/teacher ratio of 18.1 was the 7th highest in the country, well above the national average of 15.9. Over 34 percent of the state's students were eligible for free or reduced-price lunch, which was below the U.S. proportion of 40.6 percent.

VOTER PARTICIPATION

Voter turnout was much higher than the national average for both the 2000 and 2004 elections. Nearly two-thirds of eligible women in Michigan voted in the 2004 election. The participation rates for non-Hispanic Whites and for Blacks were both over 62 percent. Voter turnout among Asians and Hispanics was low, at 21.2 percent and 35.5 percent, respectively. In 2004, more than 50 percent of eligible voters age 18 to 24 years cast ballots, which was much higher than the national proportion of 41.9 percent for this age group. In 2000, 51.3 percent of eligible residents voted for the Democratic presidential ticket. In 2004, that proportion declined slightly to 51.2 percent.

Table MI-19. Reported Voting and Registration, November 2000 and November 2004

(Numbers in thousands, percent.)

Characteristic	Total population 18 years and over	Total citizen		Total registered		Total voted	
		Number	Percent	Number	Percent	Number	Percent
NOVEMBER 2000							
Total	7 231	6 963	96.3	4 996	69.1	4 343	60.1
Male	3 517	3 387	96.3	2 387	67.9	2 057	58.5
Female	3 713	3 576	96.3	2 609	70.3	2 287	61.6
NOVEMBER 2004							
Total	7 452	7 177	96.3	5 364	72.0	4 818	64.7
Male	3 604	3 451	95.7	2 519	69.9	2 261	62.7
Female	3 848	3 726	96.8	2 845	73.9	2 558	66.5
Race and Hispanic Origin							
White alone	6 163	6 023	97.7	4 526	73.4	4 083	66.3
Non-Hispanic White alone	5 984	5 895	98.5	4 462	74.6	4 021	67.2
Black alone	957	928	97.0	676	70.7	599	62.6
Asian alone	173	73	42.3	41	23.7	37	21.2
Hispanic or Latino[1]	201	144	71.3	73	36.5	71	35.5
White alone or in combination	6 230	6 090	97.8	4 582	73.5	4 128	66.3
Non-Hispanic White alone or in combination	6 051	5 962	98.5	4 517	74.7	4 066	67.2
Black alone or in combination	968	940	97.1	686	70.9	609	62.9
Asian alone or in combination	180	80	44.6	48	26.7	44	24.2
Age							
18 to 24 years	1 046	986	94.2	644	61.6	539	51.5
25 to 44 years	2 671	2 530	94.7	1 865	69.8	1 631	61.1
45 to 64 years	2 543	2 486	97.8	1 928	75.8	1 788	70.3
65 to 74 years	638	626	98.1	488	76.5	462	72.5
75 years and over	554	549	99.1	438	79.2	398	71.8

[1]May be of any race.

At a Glance:

- In 2004, Minnesota's population was just over 5.1 million, making it the 21st most populous state in the nation.

- Non-Hispanic Whites were the overwhelming majority in the state, accounting for about 87 per cent of the population (the 12th highest proportion of this racial group in the nation). American Indians made up 1.1 percent of the state's population, which was among the 15 highest proportions of this racial group in the country.

- Minnesota's median household income of $56,125 was the fourth highest in the country. The state's poverty rate of 7.0 percent was the second lowest in the nation, behind only New Hampshire.

- The unemployment rate was 4.7 percent, which was below the national average. Real gross state product was the 17th largest in the country.

- In 2004, over 92 percent of Minnesota's residents age 25 years and over held a high school diploma. This was the highest proportion in the country. The state ranked 10th for proportion of college graduates in that same age group

- Less than 9 percent of Minnesota's residents lacked health insurance, which was the lowest proportion in the country.

Table MN-1. Population by Sex and Age, 1990, 2000, and 2004

(Number, percent.)

Sex and age	1990	2000	2004	Percent distribution, 2004	Average annual percent change, 2000–2004
Total Population	4 375 099	4 919 479	5 100 958	X	0.9
Percent of total U.S. population	1.8	1.7	1.7	X	X
Sex					
Male	2 145 183	2 435 631	2 531 918	49.6	1.0
Female	2 229 916	2 483 848	2 569 040	50.4	0.8
Age					
Under 5 years	336 800	329 594	332 024	6.5	-0.2
5 to 17 years	829 983	957 300	908 256	17.8	0.7
18 years and over	772 746	3 632 585	3 860 678	75.7	1.3
18 to 24 years	3 208 316	470 434	530 997	10.4	1.3
25 to 44 years	442 809	1 497 320	1 471 584	28.8	0.1
45 to 64 years	1 445 827	1 070 565	1 242 918	24.4	3.5
65 years and over	546 934	594 266	615 179	12.1	0.9
85 years and over	68 835	85 601	98 215	1.9	2.7
Median age (years)	32.4	35.4	36.4	X	X

X = Not applicable.

Average Annual Rate of Population Growth, 1980–2004

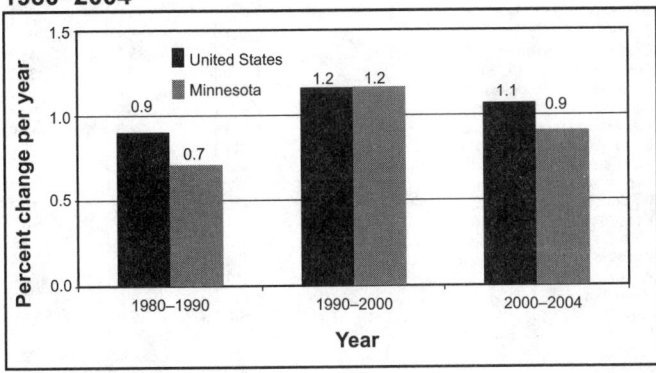

POPULATION

Minnesota's population increased 3.7 percent between 2000 and 2004, a rate of growth that ranked below the national average. However, this increase was greater than those of its neighbors, Wisconsin, South Dakota, North Dakota, and Iowa. Minnesota gained more than 60,000 new residents from abroad, while losing just 7,700 to other states. With just 4 percent of the state's population made up of Blacks, Minnesota ranked 33rd in the nation for proportion of this racial group. The state had a below average proportions of population under 18 years old and over 65 years old, giving it an above average proportion of working-age population.

Table MN-2. Population by Race and Hispanic Origin, 1990, 2000, and 2004

(Number, percent.)

Race and Hispanic origin	1990	2000	2004
Total Population	4 375 099	4 919 479	5 100 958
Non-Hispanic (Percent)			
One race[1]			
White	93.7	88.3	86.7
Black	2.1	3.6	4.0
American Indian, Alaska Native[2]	1.1	1.1	1.1
Asian and Pacific Islander[2]	1.8	1.1	1.1
Other race[2]	0.5	3.0	3.4
Two or more races	. . .	. . .	. . .
		1.2	1.3
Hispanic or Latino[3] (Percent)	1.2	2.9	3.5

[1]Individuals could report only one race in the 1990 census and could report one or more races on the 2000 census. Data on race in 2000 and 2004 are not comparable to 1990.
[2]Data for 1990 include people of Hispanic or Latino origin.
[3]May be of any race.
. . . = Not available.

Minority Population as a Percent of Total Population, 2004

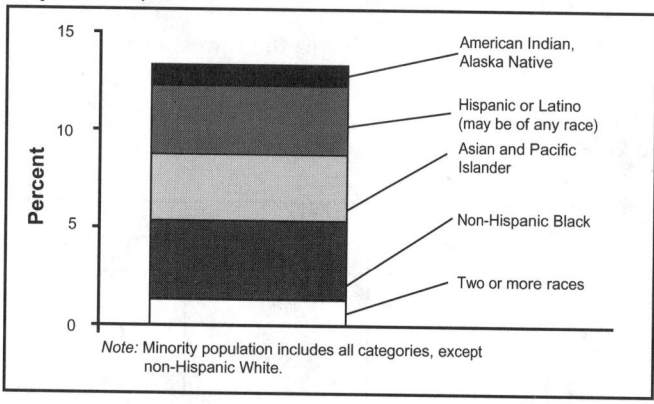

Note: Minority population includes all categories, except non-Hispanic White.

Age-Adjusted Death Rates, Average 2000–2002

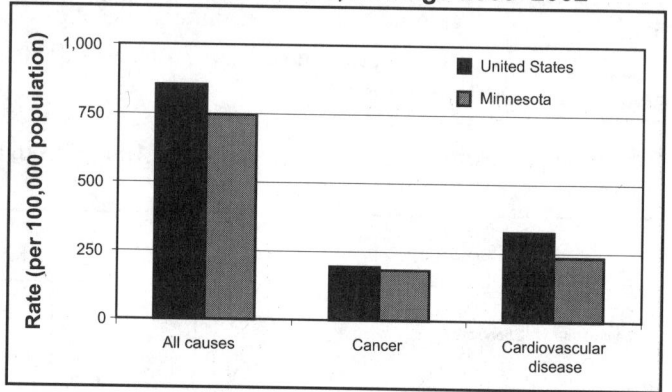

HEALTH

Minnesota's infant mortality rate was well below the U.S. average. The state's age-adjusted death rate was the second lowest in the nation. It's birth rate was slightly below average, and its birth rate for teenage mothers was the seventh lowest in the country.

Table MN-3. Health Characteristics, 2000–2004

(Number, rate, percent.)

Item	State	U.S.
Births, 2003–2004		
Number of births	70 050	4 089 950
Birth rate (per 1,000 population)	13.8	14.1
Teenage birth rate (per 1,000 women age 15–19 years)	26.6	41.6
Mortality Rates, Average 2000–2002		
Infant mortality rate (per 1,000 live births)	5.5	6.9
Age-adjusted mortality rate (per 100,000 population)		
All races	749.2	853.3
Non-Hispanic White	734.5	843.1
Black	969.0	1 097.7
American Indian, Alaska Native	1 205.4	687.0
Asian and Pacific Islander	532.4	486.0
Hispanic or Latino[1]	579.0	642.7
Health Insurance, 2004		
Percent of all persons without health insurance	8.9	15.7
Percent of children without health insurance	6.8	11.2
Percent of low-income children without health insurance	4.1	7.1

[1]May be of any race.

Table MN-4. Leading Causes of Death, Average 2000–2002

(Number, rate per 100,000 population.)

Cause	Number of deaths	Age-adjusted death rates	
		State	U.S.
ALL CAUSES	37 978	749.2	853.3
Leading Causes			
Major cardiovascular diseases	12 637	245.9	326.5
Cancer	9 131	186.2	196.0
Chronic lower respiratory diseases	1 927	38.8	43.7
Unintentional injuries	1 812	35.5	35.7
Diabetes (underlying cause)	1 246	24.9	25.2
Influenza and pneumonia	858	16.2	22.7
Alzheimer's disease	1 173	22.0	19.0
Motor vehicle accidents	644	12.8	15.0
Nephritis, nephrotic syndrome, and nephrosis ..	680	13.3	13.8
Septicemia	247	4.9	11.4
Suicides	472	9.4	10.7
Firearm-related	314	6.2	10.3
Cirrhosis	343	7.0	9.5
Drug-induced	208	4.1	7.9
Alcohol-induced	319	6.4	6.9
Homicides	131	2.6	6.0
Falls	467	9.0	5.2
HIV	59	1.2	5.0
Viral hepatitis	61	1.2	2.0
Anemias	98	1.8	1.6
Drownings	62	1.2	1.3
Fire deaths	39	0.8	1.2

Note: The rates are age-adjusted to the U.S. 2000 standard population.

Table MN-5. Households and Housing Characteristics, 1990, 2000, and 2004

(Number, percent, and dollars.)

Characteristic	1990	2000	2004	Average annual percent change, 2000–2004
Total Households	1 647 853	1 895 127	2 054 900	2.0
Family households	1 130 683	1 255 141	1 363 340	2.1
Married-couple family	942 524	1 018 245	1 105 557	2.1
Other family	188 159	236 896	257 783	2.1
Male householder, no wife present	46 605	68 114	77 669	3.3
Female householder, no husband present	141 554	168 782	180 114	1.6
Nonfamily households	517 170	639 986	691 560	2.0
Householder living alone	413 531	509 468	561 313	2.5
Householder not living alone	103 639	130 518	130 247	-0.1
Housing Characteristics				
Average size	2.58	2.52	2.41	X
Housing units	1 848 445	2 065 946	2 212 701	1.7
Occupied housing units	1 647 853	1 895 127	2 054 900	2.0
Owner-occupied	1 183 673	1 412 865	1 547 452	2.3
Renter-occupied	464 180	482 262	507 448	1.3
Median gross rent of renter-occupied housing units (dollars)	422	566	673	4.4
Median value of owner-occupied housing units (dollars)	73 700	122 400	181 135	10.3

X = Not applicable.

Median Housing Value and Median Rent, 2004

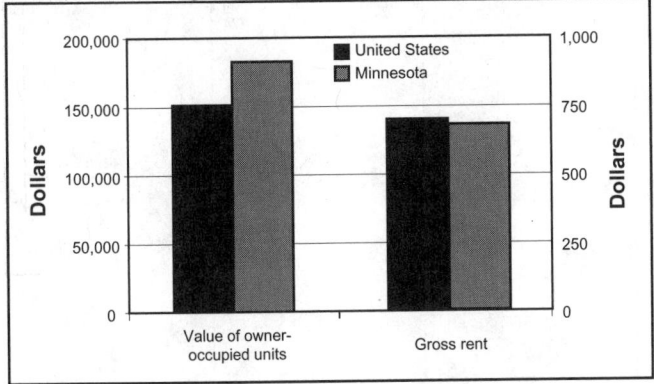

Median Household Income, 1984–2004 (2004 Dollars)

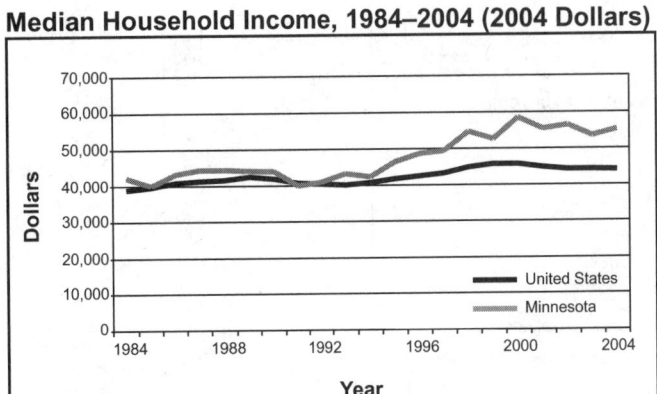

Table MN-6. Household Income and Poverty Status, 1980–2004

(2004 CPI-U-RS adjusted dollars, rate.)

Year	State		U.S.	
	Median household income (2004 dollars)	Poverty rate	Median household income (2004 dollars)	Poverty rate
2004	56 125	7.0	44 389	12.7
2003	54 243	7.4	44 482	12.5
2002	57 375	6.5	44 546	12.1
2001	56 216	7.4	45 062	11.7
2000	59 507	5.7	46 058	11.3
1999	53 317	7.3	46 129	11.9
1998	55 467	10.3	45 003	12.7
1997	49 955	9.6	43 430	13.3
1996	49 136	9.8	42 544	13.7
1995	46 691	9.2	41 943	13.8
1994	42 417	11.7	40 677	14.5
1993	43 359	11.6	40 217	15.1
1992	40 877	13.0	40 422	14.8
1991	39 871	12.9	40 746	14.2
1990	44 096	12.0	41 963	13.5
1989	44 406	11.2	42 524	12.8
1988	44 628	11.6	41 771	13.0
1987	44 655	11.3	41 322	13.4
1986	43 482	12.5	40 939	13.6
1985	39 944	12.6	39 545	14.0
1984	42 279	9.1	38 782	14.4
1983	. . .	12.1	. . .	15.2
1982	. . .	13.3	. . .	15.0
1981	. . .	10.9	. . .	14.0
1980	. . .	8.7	. . .	13.0

. . . = Not available.

Table MN-7. Employment Status by Demographic Group, 2004

(Numbers in thousands, rate.)

Characteristic	Civilian noninstitutional population	Civilian labor force		Employed	Unemployment rate
		Number	Participation rate		
SEX AND AGE					
Total	3 943	2 941	74.6	2 800	4.8
16 to 19 years	290	173	59.7	152	12.4
20 to 24 years	373	321	86.0	297	7.4
25 to 34 years	645	563	87.3	532	5.5
35 to 44 years	822	728	88.6	707	3.0
45 to 54 years	810	713	88.0	686	3.8
55 to 64 years	481	345	71.7	333	3.5
65 years and over	523	98	18.8	95	3.1
Men	1 937	1 556	80.3	1 470	5.5
16 to 19 years	144	86	59.4	73	14.6
20 to 24 years	193	176	91.0	160	8.9
25 to 34 years	325	301	92.6	281	6.7
35 to 44 years	412	389	94.5	376	3.3
45 to 54 years	406	377	92.8	362	4.1
55 to 64 years	230	175	76.1	167	4.6
65 years and over	227	53	23.4	51	3.3
Women	2 006	1 384	69.0	1 330	3.9
16 to 19 years	146	88	60.1	79	10.3
20 to 24 years	180	145	80.7	137	5.6
25 to 34 years	320	262	81.9	251	4.1
35 to 44 years	410	339	82.7	330	2.6
45 to 54 years	404	336	83.2	324	3.5
55 to 64 years	251	170	67.7	166	2.4
65 years and over	296	45	15.2	44	2.9
MARITAL STATUS					
Married men, spouse present	1 125	931	82.8	898	3.5
Married women, spouse present	1 115	795	71.3	774	2.6
Women who maintain families	169	127	75.5	119	6.3
RACE, HISPANIC ORIGIN, AND SEX					
White	3 589	2 681	74.7	2 566	4.3
Men	1 769	1 419	80.2	1 347	5.0
Women	1 820	1 263	69.4	1 219	3.4
Black	124	94	75.7	82	12.9
Men	63	54	85.9	47	14.0
Women	61	39	65.2	35	11.5
Asian	166	123	74.4	117	5.0
Men	79	65	82.6	62	4.7
Women	87	58	66.9	55	5.4
Hispanic or Latino[1]	102	81	78.9	76	6.4
RACE, HISPANIC ORIGIN, AND AGE					
White					
16 to 19 years	253	153	60.4	136	10.9
20 to 24 years	323	281	86.9	261	7.0
25 to 34 years	545	482	88.5	457	5.3
35 to 44 years	742	661	89.1	645	2.5
45 to 54 years	764	678	88.7	655	3.4
55 to 64 years	459	333	72.4	321	3.4
65 years and over	503	93	18.6	91	2.4

Note: Data in Table 7 are from the Current Population Survey (CPS) and do not match Bureau of Labor Statistics estimates in Table 8. See notes and definitions for more details.

[1]May be of any race.

Table MN-8. Employment Status, 1990–2004

(Numbers in thousands, rate.)

Year	Civilian labor force	Employed	Unemployed	Unemployment rate
2004	2 951 682	2 813 831	137 851	4.7
2003	2 929 371	2 786 091	143 280	4.9
2002	2 899 623	2 767 058	132 565	4.6
2001	2 875 568	2 764 353	111 215	3.9
2000	2 823 168	2 733 110	90 058	3.2
1999	2 763 825	2 686 942	76 883	2.8
1998	2 731 716	2 656 674	75 042	2.7
1997	2 694 348	2 605 673	88 675	3.3
1996	2 670 174	2 565 808	104 366	3.9
1995	2 626 995	2 529 464	97 531	3.7
1994	2 576 491	2 471 516	104 975	4.1
1993	2 515 074	2 391 055	124 019	4.9
1992	2 467 219	2 341 011	126 208	5.1
1991	2 427 046	2 300 781	126 265	5.2
1990	2 390 010	2 275 853	114 157	4.8

Note: Population age 16 years and over.

Unemployment Rate, 1980–2004

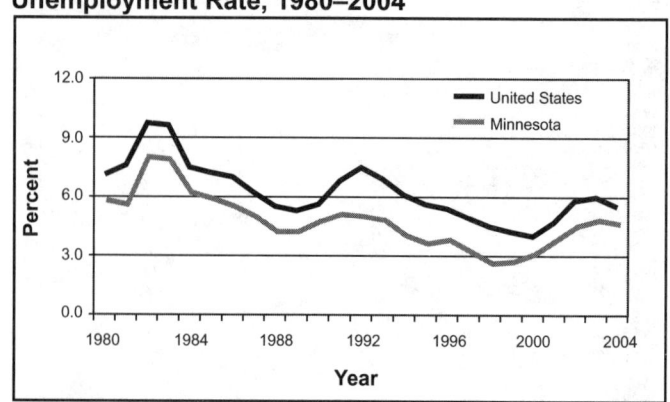

Table MN-9. Employment and Average Wages by Industry, 2001–2004

(Estimates are based on the 2002 North American Industry Classification System [NAICS].)

Industry	2001	2002	2003	2004	Annual average percent change, 2001–2004
	Number of jobs				
TOTAL EMPLOYMENT BY PLACE OF WORK	3 363 442	3 362 183	3 378 332	3 423 684	0.6
Farm Employment	100 729	101 094	99 960	99 189	-0.5
Nonfarm Employment	3 262 713	3 261 089	3 278 372	3 324 495	0.6
Private employment	2 854 359	2 851 720	2 870 979	2 916 519	0.7
Forestry, fishing, hunting, and other[1]	13 290	14 503	13 440	13 488	0.5
Mining	7 726	7 129	7 061	7 128	-2.6
Utilities	12 922	12 490	12 259	12 211	-1.9
Construction	181 710	182 596	188 365	193 061	2.0
Manufacturing	392 053	370 852	358 747	357 013	-3.1
Durable goods manufacturing	251 081	234 917	226 219	228 926	-3.0
Nondurable goods manufacturing	140 972	135 935	132 528	128 087	-3.1
Wholesale trade	141 171	138 156	137 671	139 264	-0.5
Retail trade	376 856	375 739	377 318	380 402	0.3
Transportation and warehousing	112 014	105 374	104 030	105 918	-1.8
Information	77 164	73 523	69 404	67 894	-4.2
Finance and insurance	174 765	177 945	181 242	181 744	1.3
Real estate and rental and leasing	90 350	92 899	99 118	103 960	4.8
Professional and technical services	190 046	187 145	186 893	189 493	-0.1
Management of companies and enterprises	65 333	62 122	60 725	64 490	-0.4
Administrative and waste services	152 275	150 964	154 256	160 964	1.9
Educational services	61 852	65 957	67 973	70 109	4.3
Health care and social assistance	351 553	366 718	380 728	390 438	3.6
Arts, entertainment, and recreation	65 561	69 183	70 101	70 499	2.5
Accommodation and food services	203 449	205 877	207 871	212 914	1.5
Other services, except public administration	184 269	192 548	193 777	195 529	2.0
Government and government enterprises	408 354	409 369	407 393	407 976	0.0
	Dollars				
AVERAGE WAGES AND SALARIES BY PLACE OF WORK	35 801	36 670	37 789	39 551	3.4
Farm Earnings	29 130	31 689	24 309	27 981	-1.3
Nonfarm Earnings	35 843	36 700	37 880	39 626	3.4
Private earnings	36 351	37 046	38 212	40 060	3.3
Forestry, fishing, hunting, and other[1]	17 929	19 248	19 538	20 605	4.7
Mining	49 222	49 361	54 336	56 567	4.7
Utilities	67 141	69 623	67 949	75 382	3.9
Construction	44 084	44 738	45 334	46 464	1.8
Manufacturing	42 437	44 332	46 550	49 074	5.0
Durable goods manufacturing	44 505	46 508	49 305	52 235	5.5
Nondurable goods manufacturing	38 762	40 582	41 871	43 451	3.9
Wholesale trade	51 390	52 661	54 500	57 277	3.7
Retail trade	21 084	21 737	22 148	23 063	3.0
Transportation and warehousing	41 619	42 175	43 081	44 055	1.9
Information	47 344	47 605	49 590	53 310	4.0
Finance and insurance	60 430	60 163	64 252	67 948	4.0
Real estate and rental and leasing	32 021	33 587	34 834	35 015	3.0
Professional and technical services	56 083	56 628	58 398	60 696	2.7
Management of companies and enterprises	77 691	79 571	79 149	88 483	4.4
Administrative and waste services	24 662	25 493	26 250	27 064	3.1
Educational services	22 233	22 541	23 392	24 372	3.1
Health care and social assistance	32 742	34 020	35 053	36 471	3.7
Arts, entertainment, and recreation	22 478	23 306	24 225	24 695	3.2
Accommodation and food services	12 530	12 749	13 075	13 394	2.2
Other services, except public administration	21 724	22 769	23 572	24 606	4.2
Government and government enterprises	32 914	34 728	35 976	37 119	4.1

Note: Average wages and salaries are a calculation by the editors of wage and salary disbursements divided by full- and part-time wage and salary employment. Data may not add to total or may appear as zero due to rounding.

[1] "Other" consists of the number of jobs held by U.S. residents employed by international organizations and foreign embassies and consulates in the United States.

LABOR MARKET

The state's unemployment rate has been low relative to the national average since the mid-1990s. Wage and salary employment was concentrated in government, health care, retail trade, and manufacturing. Employment growth stagnated in 2002, following the previous year's recession, but grew steadily in both 2003 and 2004. Manufacturing employment declined throughout the 2001–2004 period, but this was offset by job growth in the services sector, particularly in health care, real estate, administrative services, educational services, and tourist-related activities. Average wages and salaries were generally higher than the national average in goods-producing industries, but lower than average in many service-providing industries.

Employment by Industry, 2004

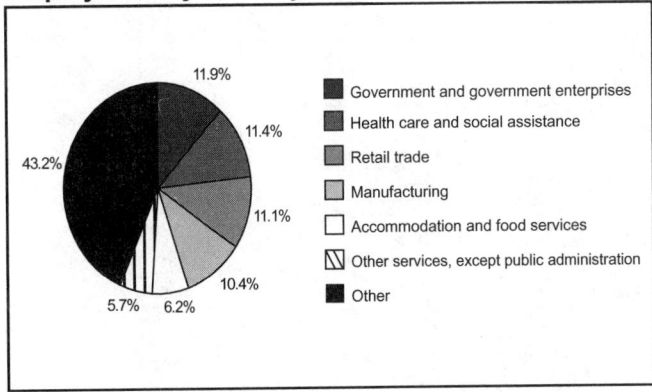

- Government and government enterprises
- Health care and social assistance
- Retail trade
- Manufacturing
- Accommodation and food services
- Other services, except public administration
- Other

Table MN-10. Personal Income by Major Source, Selected Years 1980–2004

(Millions of dollars, except where noted.)

Item	1980	1990	2000	2001	2002	2003	2004	Average annual percent change, 2000–2004
Earnings by Place of Work	33 418	68 073	125 416	129 156	133 352	138 386	148 042	4.2
Wage and salary disbursements	25 327	50 978	96 448	99 663	101 354	104 250	110 065	3.4
Supplements to wages and salaries	4 702	10 201	18 346	19 508	21 613	23 268	25 398	8.5
Proprietors' income[1]	3 389	6 894	10 623	9 984	10 385	10 868	12 579	4.3
Farm proprietors' income	702	1 572	455	-137	-1	417	1 117	25.2
Nonfarm proprietors' income	2 688	5 322	10 168	10 121	10 386	10 452	11 461	3.0
(-) Contributions for government social insurance[2]	3 111	7 823	14 734	15 342	15 760	16 412	17 357	4.2
(+) Adjustment for residence[3]	-92	-469	-1 040	-1 136	-1 131	-1 168	-1 231	X
(=) Net Earnings by Place of Residence	30 215	59 781	109 642	112 677	116 461	120 806	129 454	4.2
(+) Dividends, interest, and rent[4]	6 826	17 517	31 339	30 918	29 926	30 876	32 232	0.7
(+) Personal current transfer receipts	4 857	10 020	16 983	18 982	20 594	21 619	22 829	7.7
Personal income	41 898	87 318	157 964	162 578	166 980	173 300	184 515	4.0
Farm income	40 973	85 422	156 988	162 166	166 415	172 400	182 864	3.9
Nonfarm income	924	1 896	976	412	565	900	1 651	14.1
Per Capita Personal Income (Dollars)[5]	10 256	19 891	32 017	32 609	33 229	34 221	36 173	3.1

Note: Data may not add to total or may appear as zero due to rounding.

[1]Proprietors' income includes the inventory valuation adjustment and the capital consumption adjustment.
[2]Contributions for government social insurance are included in earnings by type and industry, but they are excluded from personal income.
[3]The adjustment for residence is the net inflow of the earnings of interarea commuters.
[4]Rental income of persons includes the capital consumption adjustment.
[5]Per capita personal income is total personal income divided by total midyear population.
X = Not applicable.

Per Capita Personal Income, 1980–2004 (Current Dollars)

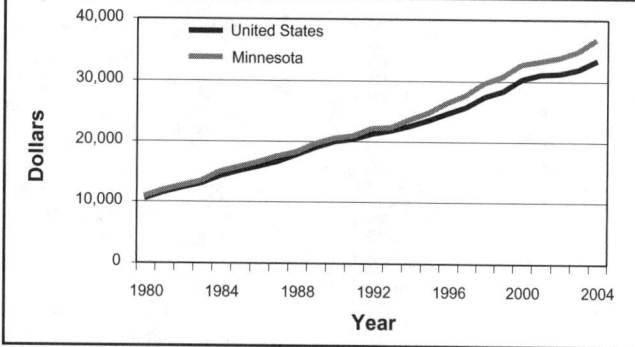

ECONOMIC ACTIVITY

Minnesota's real gross state product was the 17th largest in the nation in 2004. From 2001 to 2004, it grew by 10.5 percent, a rate above the national average. The main sectors contributing to this increase were durable goods manufacturing, real estate and related activities, and transportation and warehousing. Agriculture also showed a high rate of growth during this period. Housing price appreciation was close to the national average. The median value of owner-occupied housing in Minnesota was $181,135, the 15th highest in the nation and nearly $30,000 above the U.S. average.

Table MN-11. Real Gross State Product, 1997–2004

(Millions of chained 2000 dollars, percent.)

Industry	1997	1998	1999	2000	2001	2002	2003	2004	Average annual percent change, 2001–2004
GROSS STATE PRODUCT	163 072	172 257	176 736	185 431	186 611	191 718	198 526	206 216	3.4
As a percent of U.S. gross product	1.9	1.9	1.9	1.9	1.9	1.9	1.9	1.9	X
Private Industries	144 969	154 248	158 287	166 186	167 414	172 303	179 234	186 711	3.7
Agriculture, forestry, fishing, and hunting	2 328	2 491	1 933	2 120	2 061	2 600	2 623	2 506	6.7
Mining	525	595	576	614	448	459	475	438	-0.7
Utilities	2 538	2 565	2 682	2 664	2 561	2 743	2 837	3 155	7.2
Construction	7 835	8 401	8 947	9 135	9 218	9 098	9 109	9 179	-0.1
Manufacturing	24 045	25 853	25 493	28 013	25 943	27 001	28 807	30 503	5.5
As a percent of gross state product	14.7	15.0	14.4	15.1	13.9	14.1	14.5	14.8	X
Wholesale trade	11 137	12 234	12 673	12 606	13 772	14 302	14 331	14 836	2.5
Retail trade	9 991	10 882	11 516	12 370	12 901	13 853	14 675	15 510	6.3
Transportation and warehousing	5 809	5 711	6 179	6 764	6 516	6 495	7 025	7 315	3.9
Information	5 307	5 709	6 400	6 595	6 767	7 249	7 436	8 346	7.2
Finance and insurance	13 625	15 342	15 462	17 071	18 063	18 511	20 863	21 802	6.5
Real estate and rental and leasing	18 801	19 662	20 196	20 857	22 282	22 105	22 134	22 204	-0.1
Services	43 172	44 735	46 305	47 380	46 902	47 962	49 128	51 354	3.1
As a percent of gross state product	26.5	26.0	26.2	25.6	25.1	25.0	24.7	24.9	X
Professional and technical services	9 447	10 234	10 909	11 387	11 335	11 422	11 740	12 087	2.2
Management of companies and enterprises	7 544	7 243	7 212	7 274	6 778	6 628	6 536	7 316	2.6
Administrative and waste services	4 374	4 678	4 870	4 420	4 209	4 344	4 569	4 746	4.1
Educational services	1 265	1 315	1 366	1 378	1 317	1 312	1 275	1 266	-1.3
Health care and social assistance	11 209	11 519	12 113	12 733	13 249	14 062	14 666	15 150	4.6
Arts, entertainment, and recreation	1 427	1 485	1 446	1 513	1 502	1 614	1 657	1 631	2.8
Accommodation and food services	3 380	3 577	3 872	4 214	4 075	4 147	4 255	4 426	2.8
Other services, except public administration	4 526	4 684	4 517	4 461	4 437	4 433	4 430	4 732	2.2
Government	18 155	18 011	18 450	19 245	19 198	19 425	19 342	19 583	0.7
As a percent of gross state product	11.1	10.5	10.4	10.4	10.3	10.1	9.7	9.5	X

X = Not applicable.

Table MN-12. Government Transfer Payments, Selected Years 1980–2004

(Millions of dollars, percent.)

Item	1980	1990	2000	2001	2002	2003	2004	Average annual percent change, 2000–2004
CURRENT TRANSFER PAYMENTS TO INDIVIDUALS	4 552	9 376	15 748	17 618	19 342	20 441	21 633	8.3
Retirement and Disability Insurance Benefits	2 234	4 447	7 001	7 427	7 807	8 131	8 523	5.0
Old-age, survivors, and disability insurance (OASDI) benefits	2 068	4 103	6 636	7 051	7 419	7 715	8 093	5.1
Railroad retirement and disability benefits	136	208	239	241	246	250	254	1.6
Workers' compensation	29	131	111	118	122	121	126	3.3
Other government retirement and disability insurance benefits	1	5	16	17	20	46	50	33.6
Medical Benefits	1 240	3 268	6 539	7 541	8 370	8 992	10 008	11.2
Medicare benefits	605	1 576	2 921	3 236	3 464	3 662	4 025	8.3
Public assistance medical care benefits	628	1 679	3 604	4 281	4 873	5 305	5 954	13.4
Military medical insurance benefits	7	13	15	23	33	25	30	19.7
Income Maintenance Benefits	444	863	1 254	1 346	1 435	1 568	1 601	6.3
Supplemental Security Income (SSI) benefits	52	156	350	371	391	409	427	5.0
Family assistance	211	363	305	329	330	339	298	-0.6
Food stamps	67	174	165	177	204	232	258	11.8
Other income maintenance benefits	114	171	434	468	510	588	619	9.3
Unemployment Insurance Compensation	314	342	393	663	1 039	1 032	730	16.8
Veterans' Benefits	236	282	379	405	449	484	523	8.4
Federal Education and Training Assistance	81	163	164	209	226	218	233	9.3
Other Payments to Individuals	4	12	19	27	16	17	14	-7.1

Note: See notes and definitions for more details. Data may not add to total or may appear as zero due to rounding.

EXPORTS

Minnesota ranked as the 21st largest exporter of goods in 2004. Since 2001, the value of the state's exports has grown by over 20 percent. The chief exports were computers and electronic products and machinery manufactures. About one-fourth of the state's exports went to Canada, followed by Ireland and Japan. Exports to Ireland doubled from 2001 to 2004, primarily as a result of the increase in miscellaneous manufactures exports, which were the state's third largest export. The value of exports to Japan fell from 2001 to 2003, as the country dropped to become Minnesota's third largest market. Exports to the Netherlands and China have increased significantly since 2001.

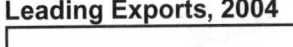

Leading Exports, 2004

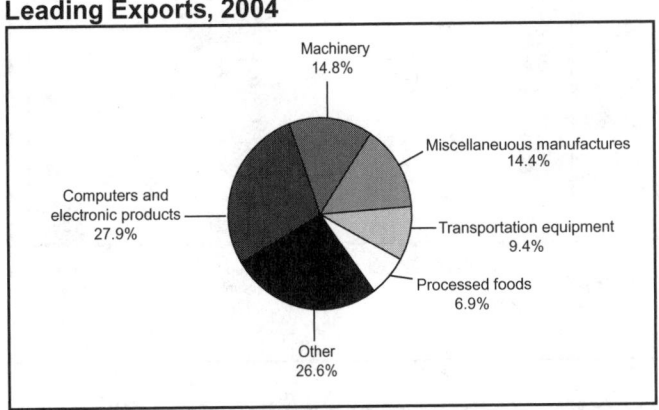

Table MN-13. Exports of Goods by Leading Products and Destinations, 2001–2004

(Millions of dollars, percent, rank based on 2004 dollar values.)

Product and market	2001	2002	2003	2004	Percent share of total, 2004	Average annual percent change, 2001–2004
Total Goods						
Total	10 524	10 402	11 266	12 678	100.0	6.4
Manufactures	9 730	9 518	10 455	11 764	92.8	6.5
Agriculture and livestock	621	731	648	675	5.3	2.8
Other commodities	174	153	162	239	1.9	11.2
Five Leading Exports (NAICS Code)						
Computers and electronic products (334)	3 875	3 279	3 355	3 533	27.9	-3.0
Machinery manufactures (333)	1 420	1 374	1 491	1 882	14.8	9.8
Miscellaneous manufactures (339)	769	1 112	1 694	1 828	14.4	33.5
Transportation equipment (336)	844	1 061	1 141	1 189	9.4	12.1
Processed foods (311)	666	700	731	871	6.9	9.3
Five Leading Markets	9 757	9 708	10 498	11 711	92.4	6.3
Canada	2 635	2 819	2 902	3 213	25.3	6.8
Ireland	649	767	1 204	1 312	10.3	26.4
Japan	1 053	840	846	880	6.9	-5.8
Netherlands	389	407	575	670	5.3	19.9
United Kingdom	519	587	579	598	4.7	4.8

Table MN-14. Agriculture, 1997 and 2002

(Number, acres, and dollars.)

Item	1997	2002
Number of farms	78 755	80 839
Land in farms (acres)	27 560 621	27 512 270
Farm Size		
Average size of farm (acres)	350	340
Farms by size (percent distribution)		
Fewer than 50 acres	20.0	24.9
50 to 499 acres	59.8	56.1
500 acres or more	20.2	19.0
Market Value of Land and Equipment (Dollars)		
Land and buildings average value per farm	398 576	517 132
Average value per acre	1 148	1 513
Machinery and equipment average value per farm ...	81 809	86 369
Value of Sales (Thousands of Dollars)		
Agricultural products sold	8 404 722	8 575 627
Crops	4 312 433	4 562 882
Livestock, poultry, and their products	4 092 288	4 012 745
Average per farm (dollars)	106 720	106 083
Value of sales (percent distribution)		
Less than $10,000	39.8	48.2
$10,000 to $99,999	34.2	28.9
$100,000 or more	26.0	22.9
Government Payments		
Payments (thousands of dollars)	336 311	350 709
Percent of farms receiving government payments ...	66.6	54.3
Farm operators whose principal occupation is farming (percent) ...	57.3	62.9

AGRICULTURE

Minnesota was a major farming state. In 2002, cash receipts from farming totaled nearly $8.6 billion, a 3.4 percent increase from the previous farm census in 1997. The state ranked sixth in the nation for the value of total sales. Dairy, soybeans, and corn were the state's leading products. Over half of Minnesota's farms had sales of $10,000 or more. More than 75 percent of the state's farms spanned 50 acres or more, which was among the highest proportions of farms of this size in the nation. Nearly 63 percent of farm operators reported farming as their principal occupation.

ENERGY

Energy expenditures per person reached nearly $2,500, ranking 20th in the nation in 2001. Minnesota's per capita energy consumption was above average, but down from the previous year. Energy prices in the state were slightly below average. Petroleum, coal, and natural gas were Minnesota's chief sources of energy.

Energy Consumption by Source, 2001

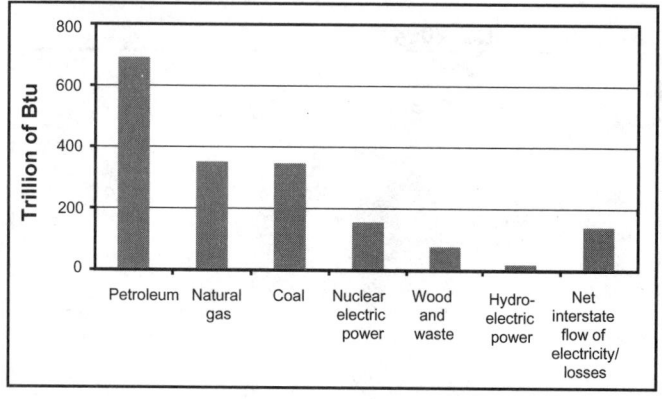

Energy Consumption by Sector, 2001

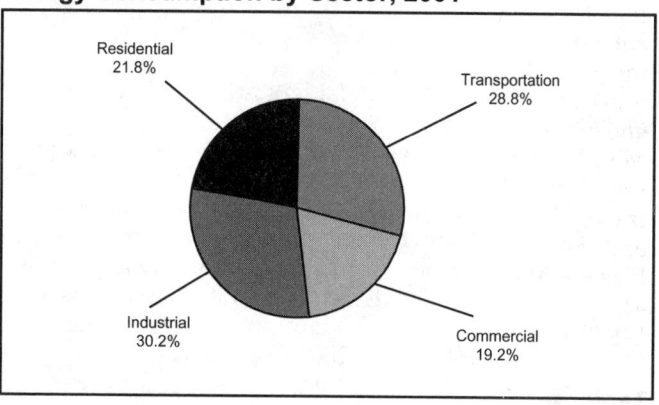

Table MN-15. Energy Consumption, Expenditures, and Prices, Selected Years 1960–2001

(Dollars, Btu [British Thermal Unit], percent distribution.)

Item	1960	1965	1970	1975	1980	1985	1990	1995	2000	2001
Total Consumption (Billion Btu)	723 854	866 352	1 107 673	1 246 044	1 228 328	1 255 450	1 386 575	1 633 922	1 787 959	1 744 512
Consumption per capita (million Btu) ...	212.0	241.2	291.0	316.9	301.4	300.0	316.9	354.8	363.4	349.9
Consumption by Sector (Percent Distribution)										
Residential	27.2	27.6	26.9	25.2	24.8	24.5	23.1	22.4	21.3	21.8
Commercial	9.0	8.5	12.6	13.5	11.8	14.9	14.4	13.6	13.8	19.2
Industrial	38.8	40.0	35.8	35.7	36.4	34.3	38.2	37.4	36.2	30.2
Transportation	25.1	23.9	24.7	25.6	27.0	26.4	24.3	26.6	28.7	28.8
Consumption by Source (Billion Btu)										
Coal	131 265	159 987	179 727	191 490	242 420	226 094	325 471	337 973	373 768	353 127
Natural gas	186 121	248 244	343 007	331 518	284 988	258 510	291 828	357 690	367 462	345 002
Petroleum	382 101	425 139	512 161	556 237	498 382	481 441	502 581	604 136	677 965	673 540
Nuclear electric power	0	1 693	0	107 372	109 374	122 923	128 458	139 149	135 160	123 172
Hydroelectric power[1]	9 542	11 420	9 379	9 539	8 169	10 169	8 915	11 324	9 501	8 461
Wood and waste	25 415	23 366	23 443	27 410	49 653	54 279	48 334	57 776	58 749	57 155
Other	308	380	432	630	3 250	9 104	2 976	29 953	34 850	37 862
Net interstate flow of electricity/losses[2] ...	-10 898	-3 877	39 525	21 848	32 091	92 930	78 012	95 920	130 504	146 194
Total Expenditures (Thousands of Dollars)	...	...	1 649 700	3 093 200	6 063 100	7 345 400	7 558 300	8 758 500	12 224 200	12 446 700
Expenditures per capita (dollars)	...	...	433	787	1 488	1 756	1 728	1 902	2 485	2 497
Prices by Sector (Dollars Per Million Btu)										
Total	...	...	1.87	3.18	6.89	8.38	8.01	7.72	9.86	10.43
Residential	...	...	2.15	3.36	6.86	9.26	9.13	9.24	11.63	12.95
Commercial	...	...	1.44	2.55	5.35	7.80	7.62	7.58	9.78	11.57
Industrial	...	...	1.12	2.34	5.07	6.92	6.09	5.75	6.98	6.96
Transportation	...	...	2.64	4.13	8.88	9.15	9.23	8.60	11.19	11.04

[1]A negative number in this row results from pumped storage for which, overall, more electricity is expended than created to provide electricity during peak demand periods.
[2]Net interstate flow of electricity is the difference between the amount of energy in the electricity sold within a state (including associated losses) and the energy input at the electric utilities within the state. A positive number indicates that more electricity (including associated losses) came into the state than went out of the state during the year; conversely, a negative number indicates that more electricity (including associated losses) went out of the state than came into the state.
... = Not available.

Table MN-16. State Taxes, Fiscal 2004

(Dollars, percent distribution.)

Item	Thousands of dollars	Percent distribution	Dollars per capita	
			State	U.S.
TOTAL TAXES	14 734 921	100.0	2 888.6	2 024.8
Property Taxes	607 863	4.1	119.2	38.9
Sales and Gross Receipts	6 384 318	43.3	1 251.6	1 003.4
General sales and gross receipts	4 066 790	27.6	797.2	677.0
Selective sales taxes	2 317 528	15.7	454.3	326.4
Insurance premiums	265 970	1.8	52.1	47.0
Motor fuels	648 428	4.4	127.1	114.6
Tobacco products	190 116	1.3	37.3	42.0
Other selective sales	1 086 194	7.4	212.9	49.8
Licenses	941 783	6.4	184.6	134.9
Motor vehicle	517 447	3.5	101.4	59.4
Occupation and business, not elsewhere classified	283 517	1.9	55.6	37.1
Other Taxes	6 800 957	46.2	1 333.3	847.6
Individual income	5 709 584	38.7	1 119.3	673.6
Corporation net income	637 183	4.3	124.9	105.1
Death and gift	87 022	0.6	17.1	19.6
Documentary and stock transfer	352 354	2.4	69.1	27.1

GOVERNMENT FINANCE

Per capita state expenditures exceeded $5,000 in 2003, ranking ninth in the nation. The state's per capita revenue was slightly lower, at $4,556, but ranked among the top 15 in the country. Spending per capita was significantly higher than average for education, public welfare, and highways, but was lower for health and hospitals. Minnesota's taxes per person amounted to $2,889, which was the fourth highest amount in the nation. The largest tax source was individual income taxes, followed by general sales receipts. Individual income taxes were the fifth highest in the nation. Minnesota's per capita debt ranked 41st in the nation, totaling nearly $1,000 less than the U.S. average.

Per Capita State Taxes, Fiscal, 2004

Table MN-17. State Government Finances, 2003

(Dollars, percent distribution.)

Item	Millions of dollars	Percent distribution	Dollars per capita	
			State	U.S.
GENERAL REVENUE	23 072 489	100.0	4 556.2	3 832.6
Intergovernmental revenue	5 982 225	25.9	1 181.3	1 246.0
Taxes	13 981 287	60.6	2 760.9	1 891.6
General sales	3 903 717	16.9	770.9	636.0
Selective sales	2 162 044	9.4	426.9	307.4
License taxes	909 927	3.9	179.7	123.6
Individual income tax	5 374 550	23.3	1 061.3	626.8
Corporate income tax	596 584	2.6	117.8	97.8
Other taxes	1 034 465	4.5	204.3	99.9
Current charges	1 736 359	7.5	342.9	366.5
Miscellaneous general revenue	1 372 618	5.9	271.0	328.6
GENERAL EXPENDITURE	25 383 926	100.0	5 012.6	4 010.5
Intergovernmental expenditure	9 618 471	37.9	1 899.4	1 316.9
Direct expenditure	15 765 455	62.1	3 113.2	2 693.6
Expenditure by Function				
Education	9 727 645	38.3	1 920.9	1 416.4
Public welfare	7 890 539	31.1	1 558.2	1 083.3
Hospitals	204 374	0.8	40.4	132.3
Health	560 327	2.2	110.6	173.0
Highways	1 839 550	7.2	363.3	295.4
Police protection	225 726	0.9	44.6	38.4
Correction	403 527	1.6	79.7	135.0
Natural resources	531 913	2.1	105.0	64.0
Parks and recreation	130 431	0.5	25.8	20.1
Government administration	664 777	2.6	131.3	151.3
Interest on general debt	385 954	1.5	76.2	107.8
Other and unallocable	2 819 163	11.1	556.7	393.4
DEBT AT END OF FISCAL YEAR	7 150 401	X	1 412.0	2 404.7
CASH AND SECURITY HOLDINGS	50 295 826	X	9 932.0	8 938.4

X = Not applicable.

Table MN-18. Education Indicators, 2000–2004

(Percent, number.)

Item	State	U.S.
Total Population 25 Years and Over (Thousands), 2004	3 337	186 877
Educational Attainment, 2004		
Percent high school graduate or more	92.3	85.2
Percent college graduate or more	32.5	27.7
Elementary and Secondary Schools, 2002–2003		
Total students	846 891	48 202 324
Percent of students eligible for free or reduced-price lunch ..	28.2	40.6
Percent of students who were English language learners	6.3	7.8
Total schools	2 182	92 330
Student/teacher ratio	16.3	15.9
Per student expenditures	8 109	8 041
Dropouts, Grades 9–12, 2000–2001 (Percent)	3.8	. . .
Higher Education, 2002–2003		
Total enrollment	325 370	17 035 027
Bachelor's degrees awarded	25 783	1 348 503
Percent women	58.4	57.5

. . . = Not available.

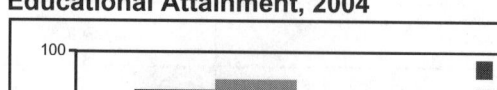

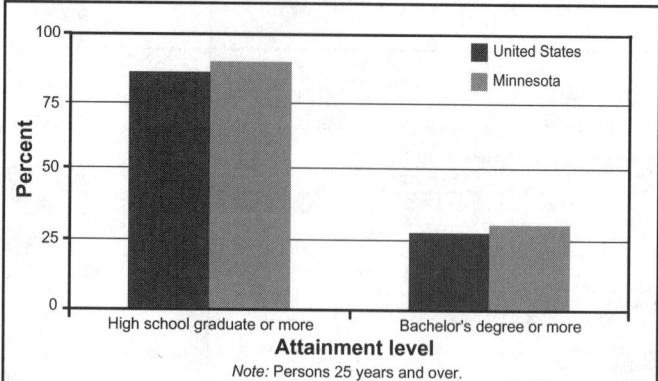

Educational Attainment, 2004

Note: Persons 25 years and over.

EDUCATION

Minnesota had some of the highest educational attainment levels in the nation. The state ranked 1st in the nation for proportion of high school graduates age 25 years and over and 10th for proportion of college graduates age 25 years and over. Despite having a below average proportion of student-age population, Minnesota's student/teacher ratio exceeded the national average and was the 15th highest in the nation. The state's expenditures per student were $8,109, which ranked 20th in the nation. The dropout rate was 3.8 percent, which was slightly below the average of the 46 states that reported such data. Just over 28 percent of Minnesota's students were eligible for free or reduced-price lunch. This was well below the U.S. proportion of 40.6 percent.

VOTER PARTICIPATION

Minnesota had high voter turnout rates for both the 2000 and 2004 elections. In 2004, nearly 78 percent of eligible voters cast ballots, the highest proportion in the nation. Nearly 4 in 5 eligible women voted in the 2004 election. Among persons age 45 to 74 years, more than 81 percent voted. Nearly 66 percent of eligible voters age 18 to 24 years cast ballots. This was the highest proportion of voters among this age group in the nation. Asian and Hispanics had turnout rates close to 45 percent. Democrats garnered 47.9 percent of the vote in 2000 and 51.1 percent of the vote in 2004.

Table MN-19. Reported Voting and Registration, November 2000 and November 2004

(Numbers in thousands, percent.)

Characteristic	Total population 18 years and over	Total citizen		Total registered		Total voted	
		Number	Percent	Number	Percent	Number	Percent
NOVEMBER 2000							
Total	3 506	3 407	97.2	2 688	76.7	2 376	67.8
Male	1 721	1 661	96.5	1 257	73.0	1 119	65.0
Female	1 785	1 746	97.8	1 431	80.2	1 257	70.4
NOVEMBER 2004							
Total	3 766	3 645	96.8	3 080	81.8	2 887	76.7
Male	1 858	1 792	96.5	1 471	79.2	1 374	74.0
Female	1 908	1 853	97.1	1 608	84.3	1 513	79.3
Race and Hispanic Origin							
White alone	3 435	3 377	98.3	2 884	83.9	2 703	78.7
Non-Hispanic White alone	3 333	3 307	99.2	2 835	85.0	2 658	79.7
Black alone	128	107	83.3	83	64.7	83	64.7
Asian alone	137	96	70.0	69	50.4	56	41.1
Hispanic or Latino[1]	108	73	68.0	53	48.9	49	45.6
White alone or in combination	3 469	3 410	98.3	2 908	83.8	2 728	78.6
Non-Hispanic White alone or in combination	3 367	3 341	99.2	2 860	84.9	2 683	79.7
Black alone or in combination	136	115	84.3	91	66.8	91	66.8
Asian alone or in combination	142	101	71.1	72	50.5	59	41.6
Age							
18 to 24 years	572	547	95.7	407	71.1	376	65.8
25 to 44 years	1 364	1 302	95.4	1 090	79.9	1 031	75.5
45 to 64 years	1 305	1 274	97.7	1 128	86.5	1 059	81.2
65 to 74 years	250	249	99.5	222	88.8	206	82.5
75 years and over	275	273	99.3	233	84.8	214	78.0

[1]May be of any race.

At a Glance:

- The Gulf Coast region of Mississippi was severely damaged by Hurricanes Katrina and Rita. As of autumn 2005, a considerable number of residents have been unable to return to their homes and jobs and economic activity countinues to be adversely affected. Therefore, what follows is a profile of the state pre-hurricanes.

- In 2004, Mississippi's population was 2.9 million, ranking it as the 31st most populous in the nation. Blacks accounted for nearly 37 percent of the population, which was the second highest proportion of this racial group in the country (behind only the District of Columbia).

- Mississippi's median household income of $34,930 was the third lowest in the country. The state's poverty rate of 18.6 percent was the highest in the nation and nearly 6 percentage points higher than the U.S. poverty rate.

- The unemployment rate was 6.2 percent, the sixth highest in the nation. Real gross state product was 35th, below those of neighboring Louisiana and Alabama.

- In 2004, 20.1 percent of state residents age 25 years and over were college graduates. This was the third lowest proportion in the nation.

Table MS-1. Population by Sex and Age, 1990, 2000, and 2004

(Number, percent.)

Sex and age	1990	2000	2004	Percent distribution, 2004	Average annual percent change, 2000–2004
Total Population	2 573 216	2 844 658	2 902 966	X	0.5
Percent of total U.S. population	1.0	1.0	1.0	X	X
Sex					
Male	1 230 617	1 373 554	1 408 733	48.5	0.6
Female	1 342 599	1 471 104	1 494 233	51.5	0.4
Age					
Under 5 years	195 365	204 364	208 354	7.2	0.3
5 to 17 years	551 396	570 823	541 215	18.6	-0.1
18 years and over	462 241	2 069 471	2 153 397	74.2	1.2
18 to 24 years	1 826 455	310 974	323 150	11.1	0.7
25 to 44 years	293 346	807 170	796 095	27.4	0.4
45 to 64 years	749 584	607 804	681 285	23.5	2.8
65 years and over	321 284	343 523	352 867	12.2	0.7
85 years and over	32 335	42 891	39 632	1.4	1.7
Median age (years)	31.1	33.8	34.7	X	X

X = Not applicable.

Average Annual Rate of Population Growth, 1980–2004

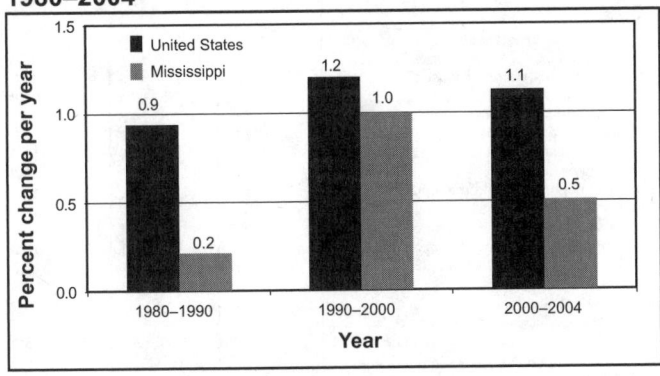

POPULATION

Mississippi's population increased 2.0 percent between 2000 and 2004. This rate of growth was faster than those in neighboring Alabama and Louisiana, but only about half of the national growth rate. Over that period, Mississippi lost over 10,000 residents to other states, while over 8,700 people moved into the state from other countries. The state's above average birth rate offset what would have otherwise been a net population loss. Mississippi had the 10th highest proportion of residents under 18 years old. The state's median age was among the 10 lowest in the nation.

Table MS-2. Population by Race and Hispanic Origin, 1990, 2000, and 2004

(Number, percent.)

Race and Hispanic origin	1990	2000	2004
Total Population	2 573 216	2 844 658	2 902 966
Non-Hispanic (Percent)			
One race[1]			
White	63.1	60.8	59.9
Black	35.4	36.2	36.6
American Indian, Alaska Native[2]	0.3	0.4	0.4
Asian and Pacific Islander[2]	0.5	0.7	0.7
Other race[2]	0.1	. . .	. . .
Two or more races	. . .	0.5	0.6
Hispanic or Latino[3] (Percent)	0.6	1.4	1.7

[1]Individuals could report only one race in the 1990 census and could report one or more races on the 2000 census. Data on race in 2000 and 2004 are not comparable to 1990.
[2]Data for 1990 include people of Hispanic or Latino origin.
[3]May be of any race.
. . . = Not available.

Minority Population as a Percent of Total Population, 2004

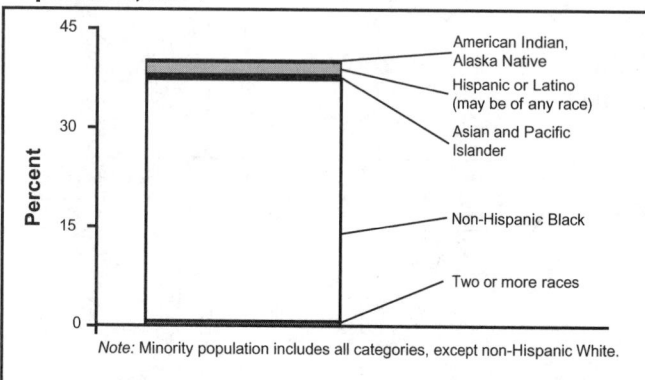

Note: Minority population includes all categories, except non-Hispanic White.

Age-Adjusted Death Rates, Average 2000–2002

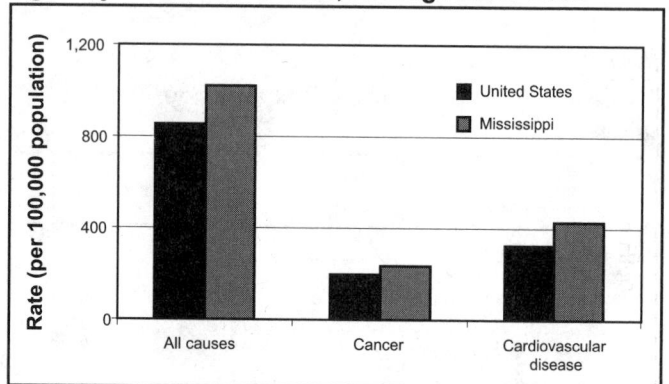

HEALTH

More than 17 percent of Mississippi's population lacked health insurance in 2004. The state's infant mortality rate was the second highest in the nation. Mississippi's age-adjusted death rate also ranked second. The state's birth rate was above average, and its birth rate for teenage mothers was the third highest in the nation.

Table MS-3. Health Characteristics, 2000–2004

(Number, rate, percent.)

Item	State	U.S.
Births, 2003–2004		
Number of births	42 380	4 089 950
Birth rate (per 1,000 population)	14.7	14.1
Teenage birth rate (per 1,000 women age 15–19 years)	62.5	41.6
Mortality Rates, Average 2000–2002		
Infant mortality rate (per 1,000 live births)	10.5	6.9
Age-adjusted mortality rate (per 100,000 population)		
All races	1 035.2	853.3
Non-Hispanic White	975.3	843.1
Black	1 194.8	1 097.7
American Indian, Alaska Native	. . .	687.0
Asian and Pacific Islander	499.1	486.0
Hispanic or Latino[1]	221.9	642.7
Health Insurance, 2004		
Percent of all persons without health insurance	17.1	15.7
Percent of children without health insurance	14.2	11.2
Percent of low-income children without health insurance	9.0	7.1

[1]May be of any race.
. . . = Not available.

Table MS-4. Leading Causes of Death, Average 2000–2002

(Number, rate per 100,000 population.)

Cause	Number of deaths	Age-adjusted death rates	
		State	U.S.
ALL CAUSES	28 589	1 035.2	853.3
Leading Causes			
Major cardiovascular diseases	11 686	425.1	326.5
Cancer	6 034	219.2	196.0
Chronic lower respiratory diseases	1 323	48.3	43.7
Unintentional injuries	1 622	57.4	35.7
Diabetes (underlying cause)	669	24.3	25.2
Influenza and pneumonia	788	28.6	22.7
Alzheimer's disease	489	17.9	19.0
Motor vehicle accidents	853	29.8	15.0
Nephritis, nephrotic syndrome, and nephrosis ..	598	21.8	13.8
Septicemia	514	18.7	11.4
Suicides	322	11.4	10.7
Firearm-related	488	17.1	10.3
Cirrhosis	247	8.9	9.5
Drug-induced	169	6.1	7.9
Alcohol-induced	158	5.7	6.9
Homicides	314	11.0	6.0
Falls	172	6.3	5.2
HIV	182	6.7	5.0
Viral hepatitis	44	1.6	2.0
Anemias	58	2.1	1.6
Drownings	78	2.7	1.3
Fire deaths	97	3.5	1.2

Note: The rates are age-adjusted to the U.S. 2000 standard population.

Table MS-5. Households and Housing Characteristics, 1990, 2000, and 2004

(Number, percent, and dollars.)

Characteristic	1990	2000	2004	Average annual percent change, 2000–2004
Total Households	911 374	1 046 434	1 074 503	0.7
Family households	674 378	747 159	756 074	0.3
Married-couple family	498 240	520 844	508 581	-0.6
Other family	176 138	226 315	247 493	2.3
Male householder, no wife present	30 917	45 610	57 610	6.0
Female householder, no husband present	145 221	180 705	189 883	1.2
Nonfamily households	236 996	299 275	318 429	1.6
Householder living alone	212 949	257 708	273 878	1.5
Householder not living alone	24 047	41 567	44 551	1.7
Housing Characteristics				
Average size	2.75	2.63	2.61	X
Housing units	1 010 423	1 161 953	1 221 240	1.3
Occupied housing units	911 374	1 046 434	1 074 503	0.7
Owner-occupied	651 587	756 967	748 043	-0.3
Renter-occupied	259 787	289 467	326 460	3.1
Median gross rent of renter-occupied housing units (dollars) ...	309	439	529	4.8
Median value of owner-occupied housing units (dollars)	45 100	71 400	79 023	2.6

X = Not applicable.

Median Housing Value and Median Rent, 2004

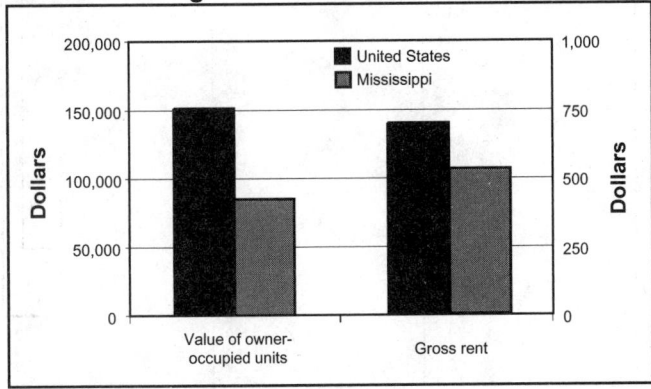

Median Household Income, 1984–2004 (2004 Dollars)

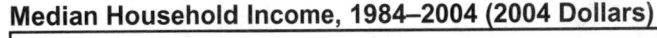
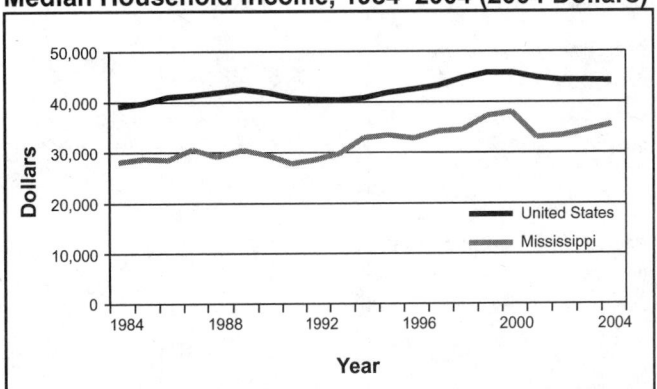

Table MS-6. Household Income and Poverty Status, 1980–2004

(2004 CPI-U-RS adjusted dollars, rate.)

Year	State Median household income (2004 dollars)	State Poverty rate	U.S. Median household income (2004 dollars)	U.S. Poverty rate
2004	34 930	18.6	44 389	12.7
2003	33 608	16.0	44 482	12.5
2002	32 438	18.4	44 546	12.1
2001	32 185	19.3	45 062	11.7
2000	37 622	14.9	46 058	11.3
1999	36 814	16.2	46 129	11.9
1998	33 702	17.6	45 003	12.7
1997	33 447	16.7	43 430	13.3
1996	31 978	20.6	42 544	13.7
1995	32 665	23.5	41 943	13.8
1994	32 024	19.9	40 677	14.5
1993	28 567	24.7	40 217	15.1
1992	27 141	24.6	40 422	14.8
1991	26 340	23.7	40 746	14.2
1990	28 278	25.7	41 963	13.5
1989	29 300	22.0	42 524	12.8
1988	27 872	27.2	41 771	13.0
1987	29 439	25.0	41 322	13.4
1986	27 153	26.6	40 939	13.6
1985	27 482	25.1	39 545	14.0
1984	26 697	25.1	38 782	14.4
1983	. . .	27.0	. . .	15.2
1982	. . .	22.9	. . .	15.0
1981	. . .	25.7	. . .	14.0
1980	. . .	24.3	. . .	13.0

. . . = Not available.

Table MS-7. Employment Status by Demographic Group, 2004

(Numbers in thousands, rate.)

Characteristic	Civilian noninstitutional population	Civilian labor force		Employed	Unemployment rate
		Number	Participation rate		
SEX AND AGE					
Total	2 169	1 335	61.6	1 252	6.2
16 to 19 years	166	57	34.5	45	20.7
20 to 24 years	186	124	66.8	105	15.2
25 to 34 years	400	326	81.6	308	5.7
35 to 44 years	409	330	80.6	315	4.4
45 to 54 years	383	294	76.7	282	3.9
55 to 64 years	283	157	55.5	152	3.0
65 years and over	342	47	13.7	44	6.0
Men	1 021	698	68.4	659	5.6
16 to 19 years	83	28	34.0	22	21.9
20 to 24 years	96	72	75.0	61	15.1
25 to 34 years	179	162	90.3	155	4.3
35 to 44 years	202	174	86.5	168	3.7
45 to 54 years	186	151	81.2	145	3.5
55 to 64 years	144	87	60.6	85	2.9
Women	1 147	637	55.5	593	6.8
16 to 19 years	82	29	34.9	23	19.5
20 to 24 years	90	52	58.0	44	15.3
25 to 34 years	221	165	74.5	153	7.0
35 to 44 years	207	155	74.8	147	5.2
45 to 54 years	197	143	72.6	137	4.4
55 to 64 years	139	70	50.3	68	3.1
MARITAL STATUS					
Married men, spouse present	558	411	73.6	401	2.5
Married women, spouse present	559	336	60.1	323	3.7
Women who maintain families	181	117	64.5	107	8.9
RACE, HISPANIC ORIGIN, AND SEX					
White	1 377	862	62.6	827	4.1
Men	668	482	72.2	463	4.0
Women	709	380	53.6	364	4.3
Black	743	441	59.4	396	10.3
Men	330	201	60.8	181	9.9
Women	412	241	58.3	215	10.7
Hispanic or Latino[1]	35	26	76.2	25	6.2
RACE, HISPANIC ORIGIN, AND AGE					
White					
16 to 19 years	83	37	44.1	32	12.3
20 to 24 years	108	78	71.7	70	10.3
25 to 34 years	236	191	81.0	185	3.2
35 to 44 years	246	195	79.3	190	2.7
45 to 54 years	246	197	80.1	192	2.9
55 to 64 years	198	124	62.8	121	2.9
65 years and over	259	40	15.4	38	5.8
Black					
20 to 24 years	74	43	58.1	32	24.9
25 to 34 years	151	125	82.9	113	9.7
35 to 44 years	153	128	83.6	119	6.7
45 to 54 years	127	89	70.2	83	6.4
55 to 64 years	81	31	38.5	30	3.0

Note: Data in Table 7 are from the Current Population Survey (CPS) and do not match Bureau of Labor Statistics estimates in Table 8. See notes and definitions for more details.

[1]May be of any race.

Table MS-8. Employment Status, 1990–2004

(Numbers in thousands, rate.)

Year	Civilian labor force	Employed	Unemployed	Unemployment rate
2004	1 330 184	1 248 056	82 128	6.2
2003	1 321 809	1 237 198	84 611	6.4
2002	1 306 820	1 219 060	87 760	6.7
2001	1 303 306	1 229 964	73 342	5.6
2000	1 318 082	1 243 959	74 123	5.6
1999	1 291 684	1 223 725	67 959	5.3
1998	1 281 362	1 211 535	69 827	5.4
1997	1 278 015	1 200 845	77 170	6.0
1996	1 266 609	1 187 018	79 591	6.3
1995	1 257 567	1 175 278	82 289	6.5
1994	1 242 550	1 159 959	82 591	6.6
1993	1 211 182	1 126 904	84 278	7.0
1992	1 197 633	1 097 672	99 961	8.3
1991	1 190 725	1 084 695	106 030	8.9
1990	1 175 744	1 085 419	90 325	7.7

Note: Population age 16 years and over.

Unemployment Rate, 1980–2004

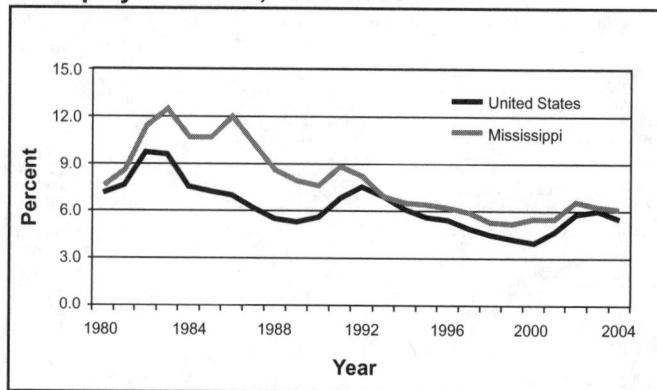

Table MS-9. Employment and Average Wages by Industry, 2001–2004

(Estimates are based on the 2002 North American Industry Classification System [NAICS].)

Industry	2001	2002	2003	2004	Annual average percent change, 2001–2004
	Number of jobs				
TOTAL EMPLOYMENT BY PLACE OF WORK	1 469 614	1 472 950	1 472 814	1 489 777	0.5
Farm Employment	53 062	53 668	51 039	50 907	-1.4
Nonfarm Employment	1 416 552	1 419 282	1 421 775	1 438 870	0.5
Private employment	1 141 298	1 141 491	1 140 974	1 157 429	0.5
Forestry, fishing, hunting, and other[1]	20 056	19 785	18 040	17 738	-4.0
Mining	8 904	7 929	8 699	8 993	0.3
Utilities	8 156	8 231	8 127	8 139	-0.1
Construction	86 020	86 907	85 527	84 957	-0.4
Manufacturing	205 517	192 684	183 578	184 245	-3.6
Durable goods manufacturing	128 009	121 073	116 088	119 473	-2.3
Nondurable goods manufacturing	77 508	71 611	67 490	64 772	-5.8
Wholesale trade	39 102	38 809	38 753	38 906	-0.2
Retail trade	172 384	172 266	171 230	172 478	0.0
Transportation and warehousing	48 992	49 480	49 461	50 249	0.8
Information	19 226	17 885	17 151	16 652	-4.7
Finance and insurance	47 128	47 570	47 585	47 803	0.5
Real estate and rental and leasing	32 070	32 830	34 494	36 009	3.9
Professional and technical services	48 081	48 680	50 059	51 836	2.5
Management of companies and enterprises	10 898	11 022	10 801	10 237	-2.1
Administrative and waste services	54 206	57 282	59 538	64 451	5.9
Educational services	17 685	18 346	19 059	19 929	4.1
Health care and social assistance	111 908	116 158	120 127	122 968	3.2
Arts, entertainment, and recreation	27 404	21 148	20 250	20 356	-9.4
Accommodation and food services	106 631	114 468	117 361	119 525	3.9
Other services, except public administration	76 930	80 011	81 134	81 958	2.1
Government and government enterprises	275 254	277 791	280 801	281 441	0.7
	Dollars				
AVERAGE WAGES AND SALARIES BY PLACE OF WORK ...	25 414	26 203	27 192	28 167	3.5
Farm Earnings	19 437	19 626	17 684	22 269	4.6
Nonfarm Earnings	25 462	26 255	27 249	28 205	3.5
Private earnings	25 414	26 099	26 916	27 803	3.0
Forestry, fishing, hunting, and other[1]	21 642	22 126	23 264	23 934	3.4
Mining	41 597	43 398	44 544	45 980	3.4
Utilities	46 740	49 170	51 575	56 010	6.2
Construction	28 388	29 762	29 523	29 409	1.2
Manufacturing	29 353	30 348	31 933	33 198	4.2
Durable goods manufacturing	29 815	30 747	32 546	33 879	4.4
Nondurable goods manufacturing	28 591	29 674	30 879	31 942	3.8
Wholesale trade	35 517	36 566	37 834	40 098	4.1
Retail trade	18 008	18 462	19 163	19 645	2.9
Transportation and warehousing	31 627	32 141	33 239	34 493	2.9
Information	36 434	35 371	35 009	35 667	-0.7
Finance and insurance	35 146	36 365	37 973	39 348	3.8
Real estate and rental and leasing	20 783	22 440	21 502	22 710	3.0
Professional and technical services	38 491	39 485	40 023	40 968	2.1
Management of companies and enterprises	46 523	49 286	51 722	54 790	5.6
Administrative and waste services	16 740	17 564	18 592	19 316	4.9
Educational services	17 383	17 936	19 000	19 876	4.6
Health care and social assistance	28 702	29 737	30 712	31 960	3.6
Arts, entertainment, and recreation	21 117	20 611	21 011	21 889	1.2
Accommodation and food services	14 165	14 784	14 957	15 249	2.5
Other services, except public administration	18 016	18 478	19 191	19 780	3.2
Government and government enterprises	25 626	26 774	28 341	29 528	4.8

Note: Average wages and salaries are a calculation by the editors of wage and salary disbursements divided by full- and part-time wage and salary employment. Data may not add to total or may appear as zero due to rounding.

[1] "Other" consists of the number of jobs held by U.S. residents employed by international organizations and foreign embassies and consulates in the United States.

LABOR MARKET

Mississippi's unemployment rate has been above average in recent years; in 2004, it ranked sixth in the nation. Government was the state's largest employer, followed by manufacturing, retail trade, health care, and accommodation and food services. From 2001 to 2004, wage and salary employment rose just 1.4 percent. The service-providing sector had the largest employment growth, with particular gains in health care, administrative and waste services, accommodation and food services, and real estate and related activities. Manufacturing and retail trade employment declined between 2001 and 2003, but rose slightly in 2004. Average wages and salaries were well below national averages, particularly in goods-producing industries.

Employment by Industry, 2004

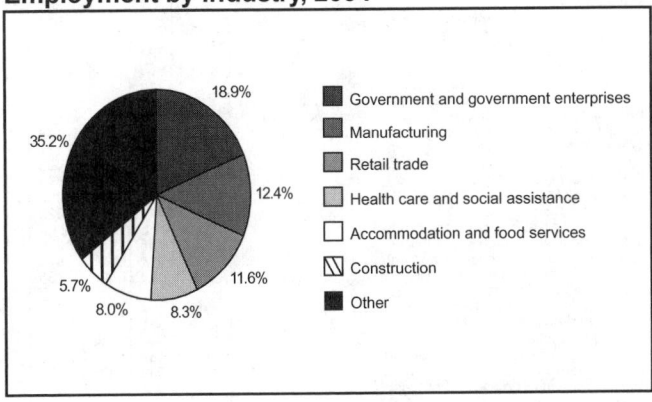

- 18.9% Government and government enterprises
- Manufacturing
- 12.4% Retail trade
- Health care and social assistance
- Accommodation and food services
- Construction
- Other

35.2% 5.7% 8.0% 8.3% 11.6%

Table MS-10. Personal Income by Major Source, Selected Years 1980–2004

(Millions of dollars, except where noted.)

Item	1980	1990	2000	2001	2002	2003	2004	Average annual percent change, 2000–2004
Earnings by Place of Work	13 346	24 001	41 991	43 237	44 153	46 726	49 622	4.3
Wage and salary disbursements	10 019	17 555	30 748	31 081	31 900	32 859	34 276	2.8
Supplements to wages and salaries	1 943	3 954	6 740	7 012	7 844	8 605	9 285	8.3
Proprietors' income[1]	1 384	2 491	4 503	5 145	4 409	5 262	6 060	7.7
Farm proprietors' income	28	238	529	693	108	747	1 147	21.4
Nonfarm proprietors' income	1 356	2 253	3 974	4 452	4 300	4 515	4 913	5.4
(-) Contributions for government social insurance[2]	1 216	2 712	4 707	4 819	5 019	5 202	5 457	3.8
(+) Adjustment for residence[3]	425	754	1 506	1 658	1 693	1 738	1 853	5.3
(=) Net Earnings by Place of Residence	12 555	22 042	38 790	40 077	40 827	43 262	46 018	4.4
(+) Dividends, interest, and rent[4]	2 275	5 754	9 547	9 782	9 207	8 967	9 239	-0.8
(+) Personal current transfer receipts	2 865	5 958	11 500	12 880	13 889	14 435	15 512	7.8
Personal income	17 695	33 754	59 837	62 739	63 923	66 664	70 770	4.3
Farm income	17 527	33 332	59 124	61 846	63 619	65 781	69 442	4.1
Nonfarm income	168	422	713	893	304	883	1 328	16.8
Per Capita Personal Income (Dollars)[5]	7 007	13 089	21 005	21 950	22 291	23 126	24 379	3.8

Note: Data may not add to total or may appear as zero due to rounding.

[1]Proprietors' income includes the inventory valuation adjustment and the capital consumption adjustment.
[2]Contributions for government social insurance are included in earnings by type and industry, but they are excluded from personal income.
[3]The adjustment for residence is the net inflow of the earnings of interarea commuters.
[4]Rental income of persons includes the capital consumption adjustment.
[5]Per capita personal income is total personal income divided by total midyear population.

Per Capita Personal Income, 1980–2004 (Current Dollars)

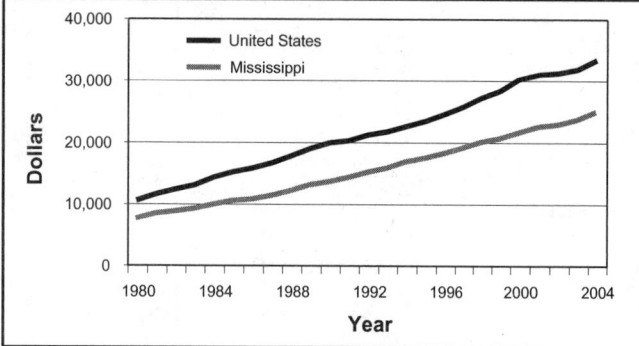

ECONOMIC ACTIVITY

Real gross state product declined in the 2001 recession, and its subsequent recovery has been gradual. The largest contributions to recovery came from the government sector, durable goods manufacturing, real estate and related activities, utilities, and heath care. The arts, entertainment, and recreation sector experienced significant declines. Construction has also dropped in recent years. The median value of owner-occupied housing in Mississippi was the second lowest in the country. Housing price appreciation has been about half the national average and has not been a significant factor in the state's overall economic activity.

Table MS-11. Real Gross State Product, 1997–2004

(Millions of chained 2000 dollars, percent.)

Industry	1997	1998	1999	2000	2001	2002	2003	2004	Average annual percent change, 2001–2004
GROSS STATE PRODUCT	61 648	63 149	64 593	64 133	63 736	65 222	66 646	68 816	2.6
As a percent of U.S. gross product	0.7	0.7	0.7	0.7	0.6	0.7	0.6	0.6	X
Private Industries	51 652	52 845	53 982	53 308	52 927	54 365	55 586	57 341	2.7
Agriculture, forestry, fishing, and hunting	1 641	1 511	1 605	1 583	1 682	1 442	1 823	1 818	2.6
Mining	749	621	652	636	610	732	744	748	7.0
Utilities	1 627	1 645	1 699	1 782	1 657	1 691	1 792	1 958	5.7
Construction	2 969	3 245	3 091	2 865	2 661	2 743	2 574	2 467	-2.5
Manufacturing	12 115	11 891	12 177	11 445	10 736	10 806	10 947	11 294	1.7
As a percent of gross state product	19.7	18.8	18.9	17.8	16.8	16.6	16.4	16.4	X
Wholesale trade	2 971	3 450	3 517	3 439	3 554	3 653	3 613	3 746	1.8
Retail trade	4 974	5 478	5 733	5 674	5 962	6 269	6 576	6 869	4.8
Transportation and warehousing	2 081	2 137	2 191	2 230	2 154	2 211	2 332	2 400	3.7
Information	1 459	1 495	1 517	1 811	1 899	1 887	1 902	1 978	1.4
Finance and insurance	2 591	2 598	2 616	2 707	2 749	2 866	2 945	3 044	3.5
Real estate and rental and leasing	5 216	5 302	5 592	5 767	5 917	6 292	6 207	6 446	2.9
Services	13 341	13 520	13 604	13 368	13 369	13 789	14 183	14 665	3.1
As a percent of gross state product	21.6	21.4	21.1	20.8	21.0	21.1	21.3	21.3	X
Professional and technical services	1 783	1 955	1 972	2 042	2 147	2 175	2 277	2 365	3.3
Management of companies and enterprises	911	844	777	752	698	719	738	700	0.1
Administrative and waste services	1 193	1 188	1 180	1 054	992	1 091	1 176	1 280	8.9
Educational services	310	317	323	327	320	321	318	323	0.3
Health care and social assistance	4 177	4 069	4 023	4 111	4 224	4 432	4 602	4 753	4.0
Arts, entertainment, and recreation	1 331	1 241	1 249	1 000	967	722	717	715	-9.6
Accommodation and food services	1 949	2 166	2 408	2 593	2 504	2 813	2 822	2 910	5.1
Other services, except public administration	1 687	1 740	1 672	1 489	1 517	1 516	1 533	1 619	2.2
Government	9 992	10 301	10 609	10 824	10 810	10 861	11 066	11 473	2.0
As a percent of gross state product	16.2	16.3	16.4	16.9	17.0	16.7	16.6	16.7	X

X = Not applicable.

Table MS-12. Government Transfer Payments, Selected Years 1980–2004

(Millions of dollars, percent.)

Item	1980	1990	2000	2001	2002	2003	2004	Average annual percent change, 2000–2004
CURRENT TRANSFER PAYMENTS TO INDIVIDUALS	2 662	5 596	10 803	12 095	13 216	13 836	14 902	8.4
Retirement and Disability Insurance Benefits	1 211	2 463	4 213	4 490	4 768	4 959	5 170	5.3
Old-age, survivors, and disability insurance (OASDI) benefits	1 160	2 375	4 104	4 376	4 645	4 829	5 038	5.3
Railroad retirement and disability benefits	44	67	82	86	91	95	96	4.0
Workers' compensation	7	19	24	25	29	28	29	4.6
Other government retirement and disability insurance benefits	1	2	3	3	4	6	7	24.9
Medical Benefits	559	1 703	4 485	5 297	5 838	6 100	6 869	11.2
Medicare benefits	330	1 003	2 350	2 609	2 798	2 968	3 259	8.5
Public assistance medical care benefits	221	665	2 099	2 631	2 959	3 065	3 529	13.9
Military medical insurance benefits	8	35	37	57	81	67	81	21.5
Income Maintenance Benefits	500	927	1 453	1 535	1 708	1 847	1 982	8.1
Supplemental Security Income (SSI) benefits	171	298	512	530	543	550	575	2.9
Family assistance	61	86	59	89	86	74	80	7.9
Food stamps	208	360	231	264	302	342	373	12.7
Other income maintenance benefits	60	182	651	652	777	881	955	10.0
Unemployment Insurance Compensation	115	116	126	192	271	269	191	11.1
Veterans' Benefits	217	275	340	354	387	413	428	5.9
Federal Education and Training Assistance	57	106	170	207	232	235	247	9.7
Other Payments to Individuals	2	6	15	20	12	14	14	-1.0

Note: See notes and definitions for more details. Data may not add to total or may appear as zero due to rounding.

EXPORTS

The value of Mississippi's exports ranked 36th in the nation in 2004, after rebounding from a slump in 2003. Chemical manufactures, machinery manufactures, and paper products were the state's leading exports in 2004. Transportation equipment exports fell by about 75 percent from 2001 to 2004; however, the value of these exports increased from 2003 to 2004. Canada was the state's leading market, although exports to this country declined 19 percent from 2001 to 2004. Nigeria became the fourth leading market in 2004, due to a sudden significant increase in demand for machinery manufactures exports. Other major markets were Canada and Mexico.

Leading Exports, 2004

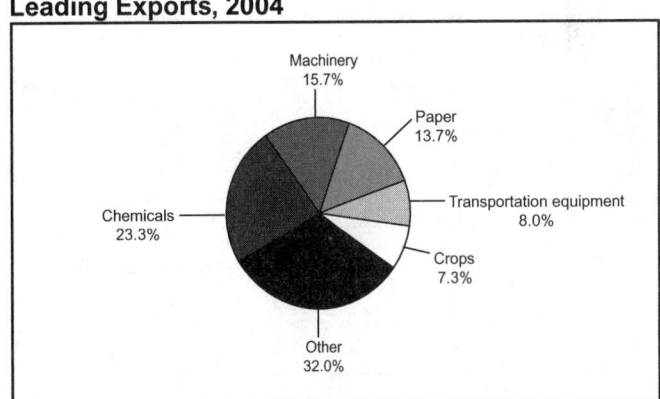

Machinery 15.7%
Paper 13.7%
Transportation equipment 8.0%
Crops 7.3%
Other 32.0%
Chemicals 23.3%

Table MS-13. Exports of Goods by Leading Products and Destinations, 2001–2004

(Millions of dollars, percent, rank based on 2004 dollar values.)

Product and market	2001	2002	2003	2004	Percent share of total, 2004	Average annual percent change, 2001–2004
Total Goods						
Total	3 557	3 058	2 558	3 179	100.0	-3.7
Manufactures	3 420	2 513	2 354	2 916	91.7	-5.2
Agriculture and livestock	122	128	191	247	7.8	26.4
Other commodities	15	418	14	16	0.5	3.0
Five Leading Exports (NAICS Code)						
Chemical manufactures (325)	576	618	614	741	23.3	8.7
Machinery manufactures (333)	314	305	301	499	15.7	16.7
Paper products (322)	391	354	308	435	13.7	3.6
Transportation equipment (336)	1 019	123	151	255	8.0	-37.0
Crop production (111)	108	113	180	232	7.3	29.0
Five Leading Markets	2 666	2 291	2 101	2 759	86.8	1.2
Canada	887	492	584	719	22.6	-6.8
Mexico	453	462	256	466	14.7	1.0
Belgium	179	194	208	242	7.6	10.5
Nigeria	12	3	4	203	6.4	159.7
China	90	138	109	116	3.6	8.9

Table MS-14. Agriculture, 1997 and 2002

(Number, acres, and dollars.)

Item	1997	2002
Number of farms	42 150	42 186
Land in farms (acres)	11 436 287	11 097 543
Farm Size		
Average size of farm (acres)	271	263
Farms by size (percent distribution)		
Fewer than 50 acres	27.6	30.0
50 to 499 acres	60.8	60.1
500 acres or more	11.6	9.9
Market Value of Land and Equipment (Dollars)		
Land and buildings average value per farm	299 460	370 689
Average value per acre	1 075	1 381
Machinery and equipment average value per farm	46 228	51 839
Value of Sales (Thousands of Dollars)		
Agricultural products sold	3 485 867	3 116 295
Crops	1 345 448	1 025 385
Livestock, poultry, and their products	2 140 420	2 090 909
Average per farm (dollars)	82 701	73 870
Value of sales (percent distribution)		
Less than $10,000	72.6	74.1
$10,000 to $99,999	15.7	15.5
$100,000 or more	11.7	10.3
Government Payments		
Payments (thousands of dollars)	103 371	145 508
Percent of farms receiving government payments	37.0	29.4
Farm operators whose principal occupation is farming (percent)	36.8	48.8

AGRICULTURE

The value of farm sales totaled over $3.1 billion in 2002, a slight decline from the previous farm census in 1997. The state ranked 27th in the nation for agricultural receipts in 2002. Poultry and cotton were the chief products. About 90 percent of Mississippi's farms spanned fewer than 500 acres. Over 74 percent of farms had sales of less than $10,000. In 2002, nearly 49 percent of farm operators reporting farming as their principal occupation, which was an increase from 1997.

ENERGY

Energy prices were slightly lower than the U.S. average in 2001, the latest year for which state-level data are available from the Department of Energy. Per capita consumption reached 410 Btu, which ranked 12th in the nation. Mississippi ranked 15th in the country in terms of energy expenditures per person. Petroleum and natural gas were the chief sources of energy. The industrial sector accounted for over 36 percent of energy used in the state.

Energy Consumption by Source, 2001

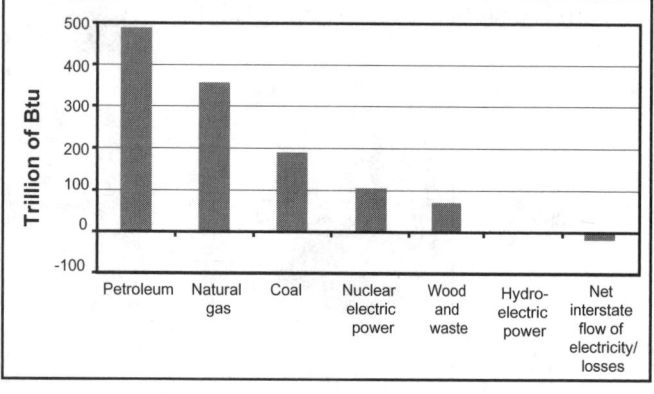

Energy Consumption by Sector, 2001

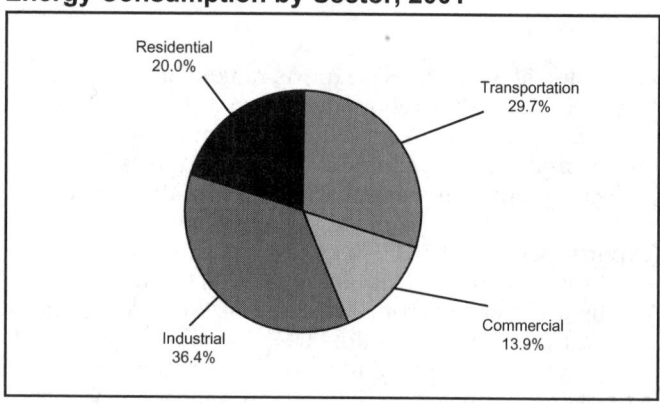

Table MS-15. Energy Consumption, Expenditures, and Prices, Selected Years 1960–2001

(Dollars, Btu [British Thermal Unit], percent distribution.)

Item	1960	1965	1970	1975	1980	1985	1990	1995	2000	2001
Total Consumption (Billion Btu)	405 725	512 530	746 852	772 195	830 793	836 245	1 016 783	1 105 092	1 227 143	1 172 648
Consumption per capita (million Btu)	186.3	228.2	336.9	321.8	329.6	323.1	395.1	410.7	431.4	410.3
Consumption by Sector (Percent Distribution)										
Residential	21.5	19.1	19.9	19.7	19.4	20.0	17.8	18.2	19.4	20.0
Commercial	8.3	7.6	8.7	10.5	12.6	11.1	10.5	10.5	13.4	13.9
Industrial	38.3	41.8	42.5	39.9	36.6	38.9	43.0	40.9	37.8	36.4
Transportation	31.9	31.6	28.9	29.9	31.4	30.0	28.7	30.4	29.3	29.7
Consumption by Source (Billion Btu)										
Coal	753	1 020	13 225	33 355	74 997	109 381	103 943	103 785	147 479	198 273
Natural gas	187 874	250 626	369 391	235 345	270 909	233 010	261 921	295 377	312 077	340 787
Petroleum	143 048	175 139	272 551	377 587	382 592	315 063	376 436	400 803	461 820	485 528
Nuclear electric power	0	0	0	0	0	46 014	78 541	84 196	111 534	103 685
Hydroelectric power[1]	0	0	0	0	0	0	0	0	0	0
Wood and waste	46 565	37 759	33 527	31 152	34 334	48 996	84 421	94 905	75 664	57 480
Other	0	0	0	0	0	0	0	29	274	309
Net interstate flow of electricity/losses[2]	27 484	47 986	58 158	94 756	67 962	83 782	111 492	125 899	118 296	-13 413
Total Expenditures (Thousands of Dollars)	...	...	838 700	1 618 000	3 810 700	4 293 500	4 938 500	5 372 500	7 465 200	7 458 700
Expenditures per capita (dollars)	...	...	378	674	1 512	1 659	1 919	1 997	2 624	2 610
Prices by Sector (Dollars Per Million Btu)										
Total	...	...	1.71	3.19	7.27	8.13	7.80	7.63	9.53	10.13
Residential	...	...	2.36	4.37	9.01	11.88	13.46	14.14	15.83	17.44
Commercial	...	...	1.96	3.34	6.70	12.04	13.42	13.35	14.36	15.81
Industrial	...	...	0.73	1.93	4.81	5.93	4.61	4.55	5.62	6.52
Transportation	...	...	2.64	3.91	8.71	7.98	8.15	7.56	9.92	9.36

[1]A negative number in this row results from pumped storage for which, overall, more electricity is expended than created to provide electricity during peak demand periods.
[2]Net interstate flow of electricity is the difference between the amount of energy in the electricity sold within a state (including associated losses) and the energy input at the electric utilities within the state. A positive number indicates that more electricity (including associated losses) came into the state than went out of the state during the year; conversely, a negative number indicates that more electricity (including associated losses) went out of the state than came into the state.
... = Not available.

Table MS-16. State Taxes, Fiscal 2004

(Dollars, percent distribution.)

Item	Thousands of dollars	Percent distribution	Dollars per capita	
			State	U.S.
TOTAL TAXES	5 124 730	100.0	1 765.3	2 024.8
Property Taxes	40 241	0.8	13.9	38.9
Sales and Gross Receipts	3 391 202	66.2	1 168.2	1 003.4
General sales and gross receipts	2 482 908	48.4	855.3	677.0
Selective sales taxes	908 294	17.7	312.9	326.4
Alcoholic beverages	39 793	0.8	13.7	15.7
Amusements	167 327	3.3	57.6	17.0
Insurance premiums	161 201	3.1	55.5	47.0
Motor fuels	464 748	9.1	160.1	114.6
Tobacco products	55 587	1.1	19.2	42.0
Licenses	318 488	6.2	109.7	134.9
Corporation	89 763	1.8	30.9	21.6
Motor vehicle	117 892	2.3	40.6	59.4
Occupation and business, not elsewhere classified	59 525	1.2	20.5	37.1
Other Taxes	1 374 799	26.8	473.6	847.6
Individual income	1 061 704	20.7	365.7	673.6
Corporation net income	243 846	4.8	84.0	105.1
Severance	53 809	1.0	18.5	21.5

GOVERNMENT FINANCE

In 2003, Mississippi's expenditures per person of $4,118 were above the U.S. average. The state's revenues per person of $4,195 were also above the national average, ranking 20th in the nation. Spending was above average for public welfare, hospitals, and highways, and below average for education and health. Mississippi's per capita taxes of $1,765 in fiscal year 2004 were below the U.S. average, ranking 35th in the nation. Individual income taxes amounted to nearly $366 per person, which ranked 40th among the 43 states with such taxes. The largest tax source was sales taxes, which exceeded the national per capita average.

Per Capita State Taxes, Fiscal 2004

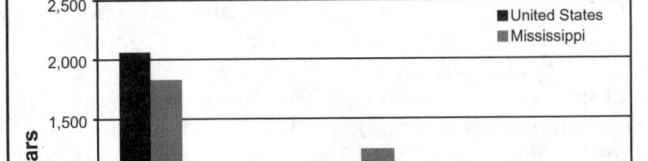

Table MS-17. State Government Finances, 2003

(Dollars, percent distribution.)

Item	Millions of dollars	Percent distribution	Dollars per capita	
			State	U.S.
GENERAL REVENUE	11 873 033	100.0	4 118.3	3 832.6
Intergovernmental revenue	5 086 417	42.8	1 764.3	1 246.0
Taxes	4 999 144	42.1	1 734.0	1 891.6
General sales	2 459 984	20.7	853.3	636.0
Selective sales	844 894	7.1	293.1	307.4
License taxes	314 482	2.6	109.1	123.6
Individual income tax	1 020 028	8.6	353.8	626.8
Corporate income tax	288 778	2.4	100.2	97.8
Other taxes	70 978	0.6	24.6	99.9
Current charges	1 245 075	10.5	431.9	366.5
Miscellaneous general revenue	542 397	4.6	188.1	328.6
GENERAL EXPENDITURE	12 094 517	100.0	4 195.1	4 010.5
Intergovernmental expenditure	3 665 580	30.3	1 271.4	1 316.9
Direct expenditure	8 428 937	69.7	2 923.7	2 693.6
Expenditure by Function				
Education	4 028 841	33.3	1 397.4	1 416.4
Public welfare	3 712 507	30.7	1 287.7	1 083.3
Hospitals	667 307	5.5	231.5	132.3
Health	285 729	2.4	99.1	173.0
Highways	974 381	8.1	338.0	295.4
Police protection	68 338	0.6	23.7	38.4
Correction	295 629	2.4	102.5	135.0
Natural resources	214 849	1.8	74.5	64.0
Parks and recreation	43 360	0.4	15.0	20.1
Government administration	259 811	2.1	90.1	151.3
Interest on general debt	199 916	1.7	69.3	107.8
Other and unallocable	1 343 849	11.1	466.1	393.4
DEBT AT END OF FISCAL YEAR	4 166 614	X	1 445.2	2 404.7
CASH AND SECURITY HOLDINGS	22 100 380	X	7 665.8	8 938.4

X = Not applicable.

Table MS-18. Education Indicators, 2000–2004

(Percent, number.)

Item	State	U.S.
Total Population 25 Years and Over (Thousands), 2004	1 786	186 877
Educational Attainment, 2004		
Percent high school graduate or more	83.0	85.2
Percent college graduate or more	20.1	27.7
Elementary and Secondary Schools, 2002–2003		
Total students	492 645	48 202 324
Percent of students eligible for free or reduced-price lunch ..	64.3	40.6
Percent of students who were English language learners	0.6	7.8
Total schools	887	92 330
Student/teacher ratio	15.1	15.9
Per student expenditures	5 792	8 041
Dropouts, Grades 9–12, 2000–2001 (Percent)	3.9	...
Higher Education, 2002–2003		
Total enrollment	148 211	17 035 027
Bachelor's degrees awarded	11 797	1 348 503
Percent women	60.6	57.5

. . . = Not available.

Educational Attainment, 2004

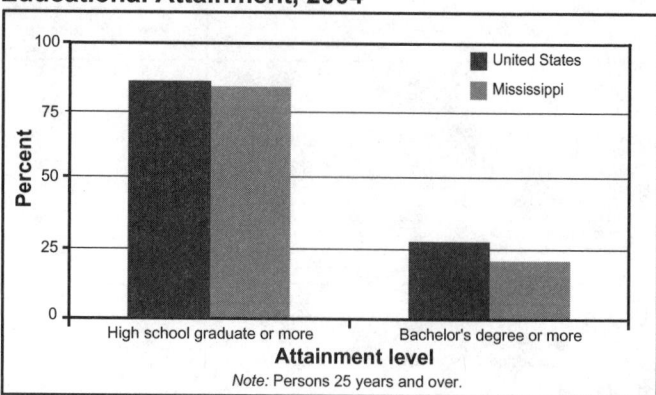

Note: Persons 25 years and over.

EDUCATION

In 2004, just 83 percent of Mississippi's residents age 25 years and over held high school diplomas, which ranked 40th in the nation. The proportion of the state's population age 25 years and over with bachelor's degrees or more was 20.1 percent. Only Arkansas and West Virginia had smaller proportions of college graduates. Along with Mississippi's low educational attainment rates, per student expenditures of $5,792 were the second lowest in the nation. Despite the state's above average proportion of student-age population, the student/teacher ratio was smaller than the national average. Among the 46 states reporting dropout rates, Mississippi's rate of 3.6 percent was about average.

VOTER PARTICIPATION

Voter turnout was higher than the national average for both the 2000 and 2004 elections. In 2004, more than 60 percent of eligible voters cast ballots. The participation rate for women was 65.4 percent, while 55.4 percent of men voted. Among the different age groups, persons 65 years old and over had a participation rate exceeding 70 percent, while just 50 percent of eligible voters between the ages of 18 and 24 years voted. Blacks had a higher turnout rate than non-Hispanic Whites. In 2000, 57.6 percent of Mississippi's voters cast ballots for the Republican presidential ticket; 59 percent voted Republican in 2004.

Table MS-19. Reported Voting and Registration, November 2000 and November 2004

(Numbers in thousands, percent.)

Characteristic	Total population 18 years and over	Total citizen		Total registered		Total voted	
		Number	Percent	Number	Percent	Number	Percent
NOVEMBER 2000							
Total	2 029	2 001	98.6	1 465	72.2	1 213	59.8
Male	943	929	98.6	655	69.5	535	56.8
Female	1 086	1 072	98.7	809	74.5	678	62.4
NOVEMBER 2004							
Total	2 081	2 049	98.4	1 510	72.5	1 263	60.7
Male	972	954	98.2	677	69.6	538	55.4
Female	1 109	1 094	98.7	833	75.1	725	65.4
Race and Hispanic Origin							
White alone	1 335	1 310	98.1	965	72.3	786	58.9
Non-Hispanic White alone	1 288	1 285	99.7	949	73.6	773	60.0
Black alone	698	698	100.0	531	76.1	466	66.8
Asian alone	8	-	B	-	B	-	B
Hispanic or Latino[1]	46	25	B	16	B	12	B
White alone or in combination	1 353	1 328	98.2	974	72.0	795	58.7
Non-Hispanic White alone or in combination	1 306	1 302	99.7	958	73.3	782	59.9
Black alone or in combination	700	700	100.0	533	76.2	466	66.6
Asian alone or in combination	8	-	B	-	B	-	B
Age							
18 to 24 years	280	270	96.3	178	63.5	140	50.0
25 to 44 years	794	771	97.2	554	69.8	456	57.4
45 to 64 years	673	673	100.0	500	74.2	430	63.8
65 to 74 years	171	171	100.0	145	84.7	120	70.2
75 years and over	163	163	100.0	133	81.8	117	71.9

[1]May be of any race.
- = Represents zero or rounds to zero.
B = Base is too small to show derived measure.

At a Glance:

- The population of Missouri was over 5.7 million, ranking it as the 17th most populous state in the nation.

- Just over 83 percent of the population was non-Hispanic White, and 11.4 percent was Black.

- Median household income was below the national average, ranking 31st in the nation. The state's poverty rate of 12.6 percent was also below the U.S. average.

- Missouri's unemployment rate in 2004 was 5.7 percent, which was above the national average and ranked 13th in the nation.

- The state's real gross state product was the 21st largest in the nation in 2004, but has experienced one of the lowest growth rates in recent years.

- Missouri had above average high school and college attainment levels in 2004.

- In 2004, 12.6 percent of Missouri residents lacked health insurance, compared with 15.7 percent nationally.

Table MO-1. Population by Sex and Age, 1990, 2000, and 2004

(Number, percent.)

Sex and age	1990	2000	2004	Percent distribution, 2004	Average annual percent change, 2000–2004
Total Population	5 117 073	5 595 211	5 754 618	X	0.7
Percent of total U.S. population	2.1	2.0	2.0	X	X
Sex					
Male	2 464 315	2 720 177	2 810 852	48.8	0.8
Female	2 652 758	2 875 034	2 943 766	51.2	0.6
Age					
Under 5 years	369 244	369 898	371 469	6.5	-0.1
5 to 17 years	945 582	1 057 794	1 013 073	17.6	0.5
18 years and over	980 562	4 167 519	4 370 076	75.9	1.0
18 to 24 years	3 802 247	535 978	589 309	10.2	0.9
25 to 44 years	517 191	1 626 302	1 596 315	27.7	0.1
45 to 64 years	1 586 813	1 249 860	1 418 760	24.7	2.7
65 years and over	717 681	755 379	765 692	13.3	0.5
85 years and over	81 217	98 571	100 379	1.7	1.6
Median age (years)	33.4	36.1	37.0	X	X

X = Not applicable.

Average Annual Rate of Population Growth, 1980–2004

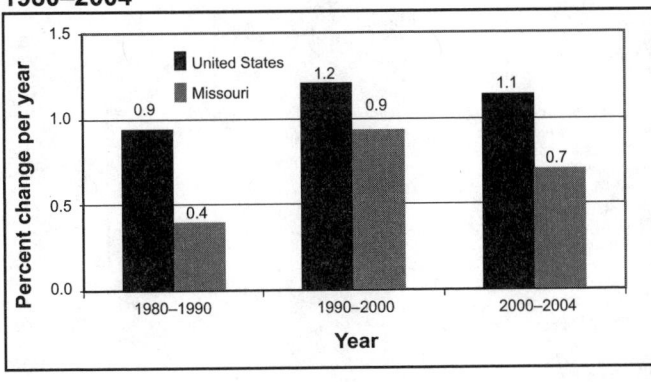

POPULATION

Missouri's population increased 2.8 percent between 2000 and 2004, a rate that lagged far behind the national growth rate of 4.3 percent. However, the state's growth rate was above those of Illinois, Iowa, and Kansas, but below that of Arkansas. Missouri gained nearly 36,000 residents from other countries and more than 20,000 new residents from other states. The age distribution of the population was slightly higher than the nation as a whole, with a lower proportion of population under 18 years old and a higher proportion age 65 years and over. St. Louis and Kansas City were the state's largest metropolitan areas.

Table MO-2. Population by Race and Hispanic Origin, 1990, 2000, and 2004

(Number, percent.)

Race and Hispanic origin	1990	2000	2004
Total Population	5 117 073	5 595 211	5 754 618
Non-Hispanic (Percent)			
One race[1]			
White	86.9	83.9	83.1
Black	10.7	11.2	11.4
American Indian, Alaska Native[2]	0.4	0.4	0.4
Asian and Pacific Islander[2]	0.8	1.2	1.3
Other race[2]	0.4	. . .	. . .
Two or more races	. . .	1.1	1.2
Hispanic or Latino[3] (Percent)	1.2	2.1	2.6

[1]Individuals could report only one race in the 1990 census and could report one or more races on the 2000 census. Data on race in 2000 and 2004 are not comparable to 1990.
[2]Data for 1990 include people of Hispanic or Latino origin.
[3]May be of any race.
. . . = Not available.

Minority Population as a Percent of Total Population, 2004

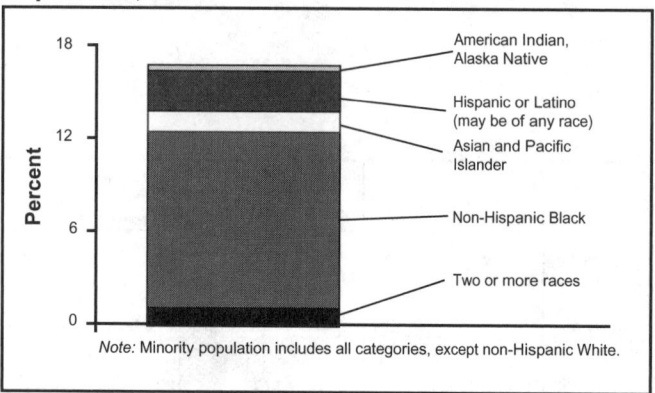

Note: Minority population includes all categories, except non-Hispanic White.

Age-Adjusted Death Rates, Average 2000–2002

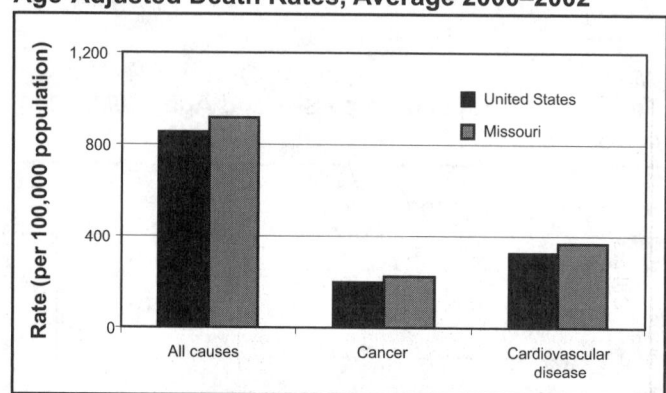

HEALTH

Missouri's health insurance coverage rate was better than the national rate. The state's infant mortality rate and age-adjusted death rates were above average, ranking 16th and 14th in the country, respectively. Missouri's birth rate for teenage mothers was also slightly above the national average.

Table MO-3. Health Characteristics, 2000–2004

(Number, rate, percent.)

Item	State	U.S.
Births, 2003–2004		
Number of births	77 045	4 089 950
Birth rate (per 1,000 population)	13.5	14.1
Teenage birth rate (per 1,000 women age 15–19 years)	43.2	41.6
Mortality Rates, Average 2000–2002		
Infant mortality rate (per 1,000 live births)	7.7	6.9
Age-adjusted mortality rate (per 100,000 population)		
All races	914.2	853.3
Non-Hispanic White	892.7	843.1
Black	1 167.9	1 097.7
American Indian, Alaska Native	. . .	687.0
Asian and Pacific Islander	421.3	486.0
Hispanic or Latino[1]	735.4	642.7
Health Insurance, 2004		
Percent of all persons without health insurance	12.6	15.7
Percent of children without health insurance	8.5	11.2
Percent of low-income children without health insurance	5.1	7.1

[1]May be of any race.
. . . = Not available.

Table MO-4. Leading Causes of Death, Average 2000–2002

(Number, rate per 100,000 population.)

Cause	Number of deaths	Age-adjusted death rates	
		State	U.S.
ALL CAUSES	55 262	914.2	853.3
Leading Causes			
Major cardiovascular diseases	22 021	359.4	326.5
Cancer	12 277	205.5	196.0
Chronic lower respiratory diseases	2 850	47.2	43.7
Unintentional injuries	2 498	43.1	35.7
Diabetes (underlying cause)	1 539	25.6	25.2
Influenza and pneumonia	1 617	26.1	22.7
Alzheimer's disease	1 130	18.0	19.0
Motor vehicle accidents	1 116	19.6	15.0
Nephritis, nephrotic syndrome, and nephrosis ..	991	16.2	13.8
Septicemia	671	11.1	11.4
Suicides	706	12.4	10.7
Firearm-related	727	12.8	10.3
Cirrhosis	426	7.3	9.5
Drug-induced	382	6.8	7.9
Alcohol-induced	338	5.9	6.9
Homicides	400	7.1	6.0
Falls	399	6.5	5.2
HIV	144	2.6	5.0
Viral hepatitis	96	1.7	2.0
Anemias	99	1.6	1.6
Drownings	68	1.2	1.3
Fire deaths	96	1.7	1.2

Note: The rates are age-adjusted to the U.S. 2000 standard population.

Table MO-5. Households and Housing Characteristics, 1990, 2000, and 2004

(Number, percent, and dollars.)

Characteristic	1990	2000	2004	Average annual percent change, 2000–2004
Total Households	1 961 206	2 194 594	2 309 205	1.3
Family households	1 368 334	1 476 516	1 537 309	1.0
Married-couple family	1 104 723	1 140 866	1 186 645	1.0
Other family	263 611	335 650	350 664	1.1
Male householder, no wife present	55 436	81 890	84 867	0.9
Female householder, no husband present	208 175	253 760	265 797	1.2
Nonfamily households	592 872	718 078	771 896	1.8
Householder living alone	510 684	599 808	652 778	2.1
Householder not living alone	82 188	118 270	119 118	0.2
Housing Characteristics				
Average size	2.54	2.48	2.42	X
Housing units	2 199 129	2 442 017	2 564 340	1.2
Occupied housing units	1 961 206	2 194 594	2 309 205	1.3
Owner-occupied	1 348 746	1 542 149	1 635 404	1.5
Renter-occupied	612 460	652 445	673 801	0.8
Median gross rent of renter-occupied housing units (dollars)	368	484	567	4.0
Median value of owner-occupied housing units (dollars)	59 300	89 900	117 033	6.8

X = Not applicable.

Median Housing Value and Median Rent, 2004

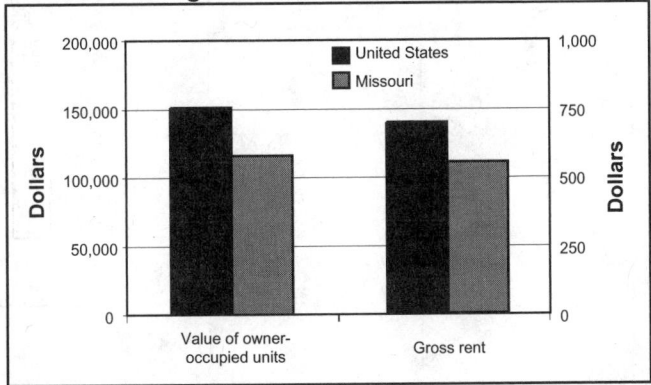

Median Household Income, 1984–2004 (2004 Dollars)

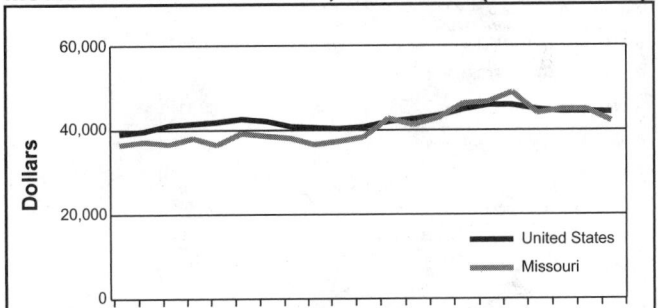

Table MO-6. Household Income and Poverty Status, 1980–2004

(2004 CPI-U-RS adjusted dollars, rate.)

Year	State		U.S.	
	Median household income (2004 dollars)	Poverty rate	Median household income (2004 dollars)	Poverty rate
2004	42 094	12.2	44 389	12.7
2003	44 938	10.7	44 482	12.5
2002	44 932	9.9	44 546	12.1
2001	44 113	9.7	45 062	11.7
2000	49 466	9.2	46 058	11.3
1999	46 908	11.7	46 129	11.9
1998	46 526	9.8	45 003	12.7
1997	42 900	11.8	43 430	13.3
1996	41 073	9.5	42 544	13.7
1995	42 865	9.4	41 943	13.8
1994	38 063	15.6	40 677	14.5
1993	36 923	16.1	40 217	15.1
1992	36 101	15.7	40 422	14.8
1991	37 770	14.8	40 746	14.2
1990	38 304	13.4	41 963	13.5
1989	38 980	12.6	42 524	12.8
1988	35 969	12.7	41 771	13.0
1987	37 719	14.0	41 322	13.4
1986	36 052	14.4	40 939	13.6
1985	36 734	13.7	39 545	14.0
1984	35 945	14.5	38 782	14.4
1983	. . .	16.7	. . .	15.2
1982	. . .	14.6	. . .	15.0
1981	. . .	13.2	. . .	14.0
1980	. . .	13.0	. . .	13.0

. . . = Not available.

Table MO-7. Employment Status by Demographic Group, 2004

(Numbers in thousands, rate.)

Characteristic	Civilian noninstitutional population	Civilian labor force		Employed	Unemployment rate
		Number	Participation rate		
SEX AND AGE					
Total	4 424	3 017	68.2	2 844	5.7
16 to 19 years	313	175	55.9	145	17.4
20 to 24 years	401	328	81.8	295	9.9
25 to 34 years	764	661	86.5	620	6.2
35 to 44 years	822	706	85.9	678	3.9
45 to 54 years	798	669	83.8	644	3.8
55 to 64 years	574	366	63.7	353	3.4
65 years and over	751	113	15.0	109	3.0
Men	2 120	1 572	74.1	1 479	5.9
16 to 19 years	139	76	54.8	61	20.1
20 to 24 years	213	183	86.0	165	9.9
25 to 34 years	381	354	93.0	329	7.1
35 to 44 years	403	371	91.9	359	3.3
45 to 54 years	395	343	86.9	329	4.0
55 to 64 years	267	182	68.0	176	3.0
65 years and over	322	63	19.4	60	3.9
Women	2 303	1 445	62.7	1 365	5.6
16 to 19 years	175	99	56.8	84	15.4
20 to 24 years	188	145	76.9	130	9.9
25 to 34 years	383	307	80.0	291	5.2
35 to 44 years	419	335	80.1	320	4.6
45 to 54 years	403	326	80.8	314	3.5
55 to 64 years	307	184	59.9	177	3.9
65 years and over	429	50	11.6	49	1.9
MARITAL STATUS					
Married men, spouse present	1 224	930	76.0	904	2.8
Married women, spouse present	1 190	752	63.2	731	2.8
Women who maintain families	258	197	76.4	176	10.8
RACE, HISPANIC ORIGIN, AND SEX					
White	3 834	2 606	68.0	2 479	4.9
Men	1 850	1 374	74.2	1 300	5.4
Women	1 984	1 232	62.1	1 179	4.3
Black	458	325	70.9	282	13.1
Men	200	146	72.6	128	12.4
Women	257	179	69.6	155	13.8
Asian	59	36	61.1	36	1.7
Hispanic or Latino[1]	124	97	77.9	90	7.1
Men	72	65	90.6	61	6.1
RACE, HISPANIC ORIGIN, AND AGE					
White					
16 to 19 years	263	152	57.7	131	13.9
20 to 24 years	331	275	83.0	251	8.6
25 to 34 years	653	565	86.5	535	5.2
35 to 44 years	703	607	86.3	587	3.4
45 to 54 years	688	578	84.0	560	3.2
55 to 64 years	514	328	64.0	318	3.3
65 years and over	682	101	14.7	97	3.4

Note: Data in Table 7 are from the Current Population Survey (CPS) and do not match Bureau of Labor Statistics estimates in Table 8. See notes and definitions for more details.

[1]May be of any race.

Table MO-8. Employment Status, 1990–2004

(Numbers in thousands, rate.)

Year	Civilian labor force	Employed	Unemployed	Unemployment rate
2004	3 031 105	2 858 897	172 208	5.7
2003	3 013 856	2 845 802	168 054	5.6
2002	2 994 522	2 837 544	156 978	5.2
2001	2 990 992	2 856 402	134 590	4.5
2000	2 950 404	2 854 164	96 240	3.3
1999	2 911 190	2 819 853	91 337	3.1
1998	2 910 871	2 794 869	116 002	4.0
1997	2 904 214	2 780 185	124 029	4.3
1996	2 869 406	2 734 860	134 546	4.7
1995	2 822 199	2 690 210	131 989	4.7
1994	2 758 661	2 622 286	136 375	4.9
1993	2 705 747	2 539 792	165 955	6.1
1992	2 662 447	2 502 779	159 668	6.0
1991	2 647 068	2 474 167	172 901	6.5
1990	2 607 584	2 456 998	150 586	5.8

Note: Population age 16 years and over.

Unemployment Rate, 1980–2004

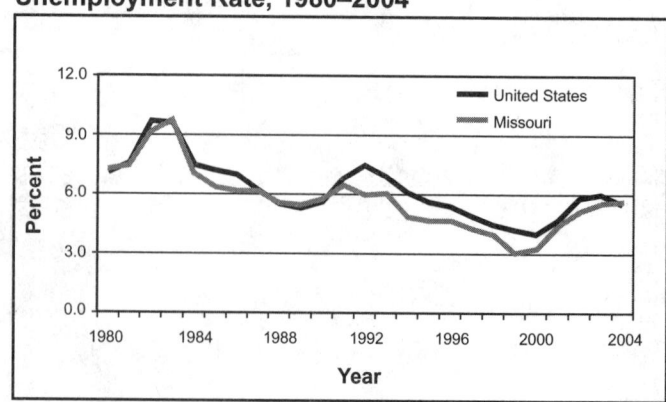

Table MO-9. Employment and Average Wages by Industry, 2001–2004

(Estimates are based on the 2002 North American Industry Classification System [NAICS].)

Industry	2001	2002	2003	2004	Annual average percent change, 2001–2004
	Number of jobs				
TOTAL EMPLOYMENT BY PLACE OF WORK	3 481 232	3 470 932	3 477 470	3 513 088	0.3
Farm Employment	122 119	122 649	117 859	116 655	-1.5
Nonfarm Employment	3 359 113	3 348 283	3 359 611	3 396 433	0.4
Private employment	2 888 336	2 877 222	2 885 492	2 922 662	0.4
Forestry, fishing, hunting, and other[1]	12 385	13 416	12 735	12 767	1.0
Mining	7 070	6 363	6 845	7 325	1.2
Utilities	13 025	12 971	12 310	12 171	-2.2
Construction	208 448	204 629	209 244	213 186	0.8
Manufacturing	352 593	334 566	322 388	324 046	-2.8
Durable goods manufacturing	217 572	205 105	198 493	201 895	-2.5
Nondurable goods manufacturing	135 021	129 461	123 895	122 151	-3.3
Wholesale trade	130 128	128 014	127 041	128 538	-0.4
Retail trade	387 987	391 847	394 063	397 205	0.8
Transportation and warehousing	129 133	126 797	122 398	121 447	-2.0
Information	81 522	76 568	74 373	72 054	-4.0
Finance and insurance	155 565	157 780	159 640	159 555	0.8
Real estate and rental and leasing	108 881	110 668	116 559	120 884	3.5
Professional and technical services	172 952	171 536	173 220	176 375	0.7
Management of companies and enterprises	73 267	70 073	67 521	65 159	-3.8
Administrative and waste services	164 880	163 558	166 941	174 039	1.8
Educational services	67 904	71 119	71 621	74 425	3.1
Health care and social assistance	335 565	340 606	345 995	350 434	1.5
Arts, entertainment, and recreation	66 635	68 514	68 226	70 239	1.8
Accommodation and food services	227 007	230 359	234 185	239 934	1.9
Other services, except public administration	193 389	197 838	200 187	202 879	1.6
Government and government enterprises	470 777	471 061	474 119	473 771	0.2
	Dollars				
AVERAGE WAGES AND SALARIES BY PLACE OF WORK	31 740	32 527	33 297	34 365	2.7
Farm Earnings	23 012	21 199	24 671	26 891	5.3
Nonfarm Earnings	31 775	32 572	33 328	34 388	2.7
Private earnings	32 255	32 956	33 676	34 760	2.5
Forestry, fishing, hunting, and other[1]	19 781	21 372	28 369	25 256	8.5
Mining	46 001	47 911	52 895	57 606	7.8
Utilities	63 974	70 520	59 424	63 275	-0.4
Construction	39 046	39 472	39 378	40 020	0.8
Manufacturing	38 521	39 966	41 320	42 604	3.4
Durable goods manufacturing	39 061	40 695	42 468	43 707	3.8
Nondurable goods manufacturing	37 655	38 813	39 487	40 786	2.7
Wholesale trade	44 096	44 595	45 902	48 132	3.0
Retail trade	20 369	20 884	21 418	21 781	2.3
Transportation and warehousing	35 627	37 736	38 036	38 053	2.2
Information	45 126	44 790	46 659	49 534	3.2
Finance and insurance	44 878	45 669	47 747	49 027	3.0
Real estate and rental and leasing	27 735	27 831	28 482	29 630	2.2
Professional and technical services	50 327	51 260	53 099	54 719	2.8
Management of companies and enterprises	62 346	64 057	64 443	70 540	4.2
Administrative and waste services	21 760	22 912	23 421	25 066	4.8
Educational services	27 060	27 628	28 772	29 804	3.3
Health care and social assistance	30 434	31 417	32 399	33 682	3.4
Arts, entertainment, and recreation	26 254	28 416	29 239	29 195	3.6
Accommodation and food services	12 547	12 823	12 979	13 248	1.8
Other services, except public administration	21 764	22 244	22 948	23 724	2.9
Government and government enterprises	29 353	30 652	31 611	32 545	3.5

Note: Average wages and salaries are a calculation by the editors of wage and salary disbursements divided by full- and part-time wage and salary employment. Data may not add to total or may appear as zero due to rounding.

[1] "Other" consists of the number of jobs held by U.S. residents employed by international organizations and foreign embassies and consulates in the United States.

LABOR MARKET

The state's unemployment rate was just above the national average in 2004. Wage and salary employment declined in 2001, and its recovery was slow. From 2001 to 2003, employment grew by just 0.9 percent. Missouri's largest employers were government, retail trade, health care, manufacturing, and the tourism-related sector of accommodation and food services. From 2001 to 2003, manufacturing employment declined sharply; despite recovering somewhat in 2004, it remained well below its 2001 level. This weakness was offset by job gains in retail trade and several service-providing sectors. Average wages and salaries in Missouri were well below the national averages in most industries. The earnings growth rate was also below the national average.

Employment by Industry, 2004

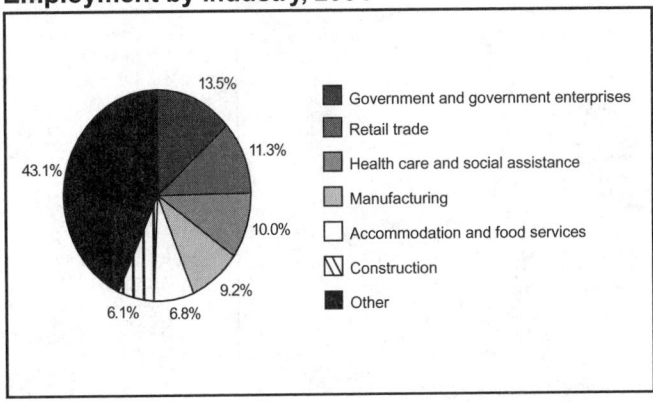

Table MO-10. Personal Income by Major Source, Selected Years 1980–2004

(Millions of dollars, except where noted.)

Item	1980	1990	2000	2001	2002	2003	2004	Average annual percent change, 2000–2004
Earnings by Place of Work	36 843	69 849	118 429	120 956	124 622	128 855	135 473	3.4
Wage and salary disbursements	28 140	52 616	88 781	90 686	92 126	93 927	97 382	2.3
Supplements to wages and salaries	5 140	10 640	17 894	18 677	21 166	23 027	24 271	7.9
Proprietors' income[1]	3 564	6 592	11 753	11 593	11 330	11 901	13 819	4.1
Farm proprietors' income	49	481	391	264	-51	256	1 251	33.7
Nonfarm proprietors' income[2]	3 515	6 111	11 362	11 329	11 381	11 645	12 569	2.6
(-) Contributions for government social insurance[2]	3 284	7 670	12 842	13 288	13 672	14 047	14 593	3.2
(+) Adjustment for residence[3]	-1 524	-2 626	-4 056	-3 938	-3 993	-3 895	-3 995	X
(=) **Net Earnings by Place of Residence**	32 034	59 553	101 530	103 729	106 957	110 913	116 884	3.6
(+) Dividends, interest, and rent[4]	7 778	19 014	29 030	28 768	27 904	28 726	29 770	0.6
(+) Personal current transfer receipts	6 082	11 839	22 162	24 439	26 231	27 359	28 957	6.9
Personal income	45 893	90 407	152 722	156 937	161 093	166 998	175 611	3.6
Farm income	45 676	89 735	152 080	156 396	160 892	166 479	174 110	3.4
Nonfarm income	218	671	642	542	201	519	1 501	23.7
Per Capita Personal Income (Dollars)[5]	9 324	17 627	27 241	27 813	28 363	29 199	30 516	2.9

Note: Data may not add to total or may appear as zero due to rounding.

[1]Proprietors' income includes the inventory valuation adjustment and the capital consumption adjustment.
[2]Contributions for government social insurance are included in earnings by type and industry, but they are excluded from personal income.
[3]The adjustment for residence is the net inflow of the earnings of interarea commuters.
[4]Rental income of persons includes the capital consumption adjustment.
[5]Per capita personal income is total personal income divided by total midyear population.
X = Not applicable.

Per Capita Personal Income, 1980–2004 (Current Dollars)

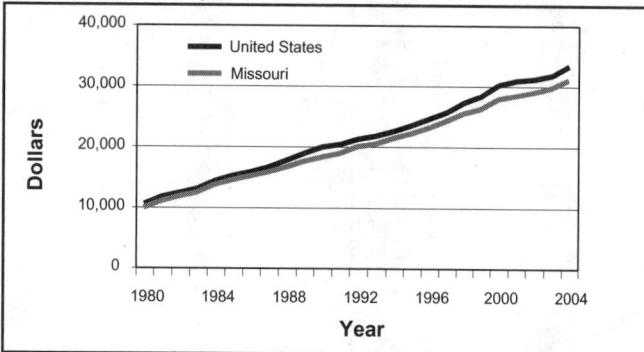

ECONOMIC ACTIVITY

Missouri's real gross state product (GSP) was the 21st largest in the nation in 2004. Its growth slowed considerably during the recession in 2001, and its subsequent recovery has been slower than the national average. From 2001 to 2004, Missouri's GSP grew 4.8 percent (compared with the national growth rate of 9.1 percent). The chief contributors to recent performance were durable goods manufacturing, retail trade, and information services. Real estate and construction had the largest declines from 2001 to 2004. Housing price appreciation was about 40 percent below the U.S. average. The median value of owner-occupied housing in Missouri ranked 33rd in the country.

Table MO-11. Real Gross State Product, 1997–2004

(Millions of chained 2000 dollars, percent.)

Industry	1997	1998	1999	2000	2001	2002	2003	2004	Average annual percent change, 2001–2004
GROSS STATE PRODUCT	168 205	170 468	172 973	176 443	177 460	178 589	181 638	186 018	1.6
As a percent of U.S. gross product	2.0	1.9	1.8	1.8	1.8	1.8	1.8	1.7	X
Private Industries	149 293	151 381	153 513	156 173	157 311	158 700	161 562	165 538	1.7
Agriculture, forestry, fishing, and hunting	1 715	1 396	1 104	1 567	1 541	1 601	2 059	2 148	11.7
Mining	321	362	400	387	360	335	355	369	0.8
Utilities	2 954	2 944	3 115	3 017	3 316	3 368	3 266	3 429	1.1
Construction	7 880	7 923	8 353	8 380	8 395	8 061	7 933	7 898	-2.0
Manufacturing	32 045	30 670	29 312	29 337	27 659	28 451	28 844	30 039	2.8
As a percent of gross state product	19.1	18.0	16.9	16.6	15.6	15.9	15.9	16.1	X
Wholesale trade	10 074	11 035	11 347	11 216	11 941	12 116	11 754	12 082	0.4
Retail trade	11 266	11 647	12 124	12 209	13 180	13 951	14 697	15 199	4.9
Transportation and warehousing	6 464	6 742	6 759	6 961	7 100	7 247	7 401	7 142	0.2
Information	7 300	7 676	8 037	9 288	9 211	8 799	9 236	10 159	3.3
Finance and insurance	9 869	10 302	10 501	10 251	10 455	10 645	11 617	11 902	4.4
Real estate and rental and leasing	15 352	15 861	17 063	17 568	18 615	18 053	17 700	17 453	-2.1
Services	43 974	44 764	45 442	45 993	45 564	46 142	46 856	48 007	1.8
As a percent of gross state product	26.1	26.3	26.3	26.1	25.7	25.8	25.8	25.8	X
Professional and technical services	8 596	9 132	9 280	10 017	9 852	10 021	10 405	10 638	2.6
Management of companies and enterprises	6 703	6 492	6 685	6 675	6 536	6 323	6 255	6 229	-1.6
Administrative and waste services	4 122	4 238	4 477	4 167	4 089	4 268	4 441	4 744	5.1
Educational services	1 780	1 844	1 814	1 882	1 841	1 829	1 764	1 764	-1.4
Health care and social assistance	11 611	11 747	11 817	11 999	12 171	12 462	12 714	12 928	2.0
Arts, entertainment, and recreation	2 388	2 259	2 250	2 168	2 199	2 359	2 329	2 337	2.0
Accommodation and food services	4 150	4 363	4 495	4 548	4 462	4 513	4 562	4 712	1.8
Other services, except public administration	4 624	4 689	4 624	4 537	4 414	4 367	4 386	4 655	1.8
Government	18 910	19 082	19 457	20 270	20 151	19 900	20 094	20 492	0.6
As a percent of gross state product	11.2	11.2	11.2	11.5	11.4	11.1	11.1	11.0	X

X = Not applicable.

Table MO-12. Government Transfer Payments, Selected Years 1980–2004

(Millions of dollars, percent.)

Item	1980	1990	2000	2001	2002	2003	2004	Average annual percent change, 2000–2004
CURRENT TRANSFER PAYMENTS TO INDIVIDUALS	5 746	11 182	20 904	23 039	24 964	26 186	27 778	7.4
Retirement and Disability Insurance Benefits	3 057	5 877	9 226	9 790	10 298	10 665	11 113	4.8
Old-age, survivors, and disability insurance (OASDI) benefits	2 870	5 585	8 885	9 418	9 874	10 218	10 652	4.6
Railroad retirement and disability benefits	167	242	274	280	290	296	301	2.4
Workers' compensation	12	39	55	62	76	82	85	11.7
Other government retirement and disability insurance benefits	8	11	12	30	58	68	74	58.3
Medical Benefits	1 261	3 484	8 798	10 030	10 937	11 538	12 602	9.4
Medicare benefits	901	2 429	4 495	4 973	5 315	5 613	6 139	8.1
Public assistance medical care benefits	345	1 022	4 247	4 976	5 513	5 828	6 347	10.6
Military medical insurance benefits	14	33	56	82	110	96	116	19.8
Income Maintenance Benefits	558	971	1 820	1 928	2 121	2 302	2 512	8.4
Supplemental Security Income (SSI) benefits	140	239	497	522	542	555	580	3.9
Family assistance	182	235	253	271	248	182	192	-6.6
Food stamps	151	327	364	413	484	595	687	17.2
Other income maintenance benefits	85	169	706	722	846	970	1 053	10.5
Unemployment Insurance Compensation	477	306	326	475	730	777	579	15.5
Veterans' Benefits	311	372	500	526	579	625	674	7.7
Federal Education and Training Assistance	82	168	217	259	283	262	278	6.4
Other Payments to Individuals	1	5	17	30	16	19	20	5.1

Note: See notes and definitions for more details. Data may not add to total or may appear as zero due to rounding.

EXPORTS

In 2004, the value of Missouri's exports totaled nearly $9 billion, ranking 25th in the nation. The state's leading exports were transportation equipment and chemical manufactures, both of which grew rapidly over the 2001–2004 period. Canada was the largest market for the state's exports, accounting for 44 percent of the total. Mexico was also a significant market for Missouri's goods. China became the fourth largest market in 2004, with exports to this country more than tripling from 2001 to 2004. China was the state's fastest-growing export market. Exports to Belgium and Italy also grew considerably.

Leading Exports, 2004

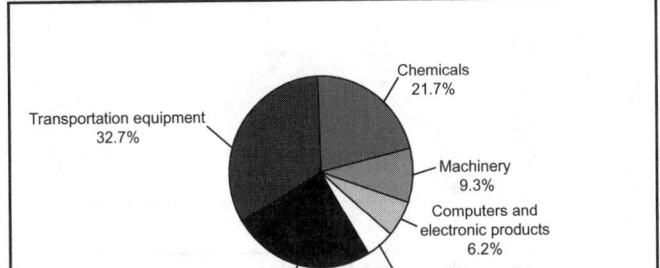

Table MO-13. Exports of Goods by Leading Products and Destinations, 2001–2004

(Millions of dollars, percent, rank based on 2004 dollar values.)

Product and market	2001	2002	2003	2004	Percent share of total, 2004	Average annual percent change, 2001–2004
Total Goods						
Total	6 173	6 791	7 234	8 997	100.0	13.4
Manufactures	5 963	6 584	6 981	8 565	95.2	12.8
Agriculture and livestock	115	109	154	293	3.3	36.5
Other commodities	95	98	100	140	1.6	13.6
Five Leading Exports (NAICS Code)						
Transportation equipment (336)	1 802	2 290	2 187	2 942	32.7	17.8
Chemical manufactures (325)	1 010	1 207	1 499	1 953	21.7	24.6
Machinery manufactures (333)	740	676	741	833	9.3	4.0
Computers and electronic products (334)	444	444	484	554	6.2	7.7
Electrical equipment, appliances, and parts (335)	307	338	372	433	4.8	12.1
Five Leading Markets	5 555	6 302	6 729	8 391	93.3	14.7
Canada	2 518	3 117	3 081	3 962	44.0	16.3
Mexico	673	693	748	946	10.5	12.0
Japan	311	311	420	434	4.8	11.8
China	108	130	260	366	4.1	50.1
United Kingdom	284	336	295	344	3.8	6.6

Table MO-14. Agriculture, 1997 and 2002

(Number, acres, and dollars.)

Item	1997	2002
Number of farms	110 986	106 797
Land in farms (acres)	30 202 772	29 946 035
Farm Size		
Average size of farm (acres)	272	280
Farms by size (percent distribution)		
Fewer than 50 acres	22.2	23.1
50 to 499 acres	63.7	62.9
500 acres or more	14.1	14.0
Market Value of Land and Equipment (Dollars)		
Land and buildings average value per farm	294 636	424 347
Average value per acre	1 084	1 508
Machinery and equipment average value per farm ...	39 084	49 940
Value of Sales (Thousands of Dollars)		
Agricultural products sold	5 466 009	4 983 255
Crops	2 389 939	1 992 446
Livestock, poultry, and their products	3 076 070	2 990 809
Average per farm (dollars)	49 250	46 661
Value of sales (percent distribution)		
Less than $10,000	59.0	59.0
$10,000 to $99,999	31.2	32.2
$100,000 or more	9.7	8.8
Government Payments		
Payments (thousands of dollars)	211 414	264 475
Percent of farms receiving government payments	37.5	40.6
Farm operators whose principal occupation is farming (percent) ...	42.8	57.2

AGRICULTURE

Missouri ranked 12th in the nation for value of agricultural sales. In 2003, cash receipts from farming totaled $4.9 billion, which was significantly less than the sales reported on the 1997 farm census. Most of the decline was due to a drop in crop sales. In 2002, 59 percent of farms in the state had sales of less than $10,000. About 23 percent of farms spanned fewer than 50 acres, which was among the lowest proportions of farms this size in the nation. About 57 percent of farm operators reported farming as their principal occupation, which was a significant increase from 1997. The state's chief products were cattle, soybeans, and hogs.

ENERGY

Missouri's energy expenditures per person were slightly above the national average in 2001. Energy prices in the state were also above average, ranking 17th in the country. The transportation sector was the leading consumer of energy.

Energy Consumption by Source, 2001

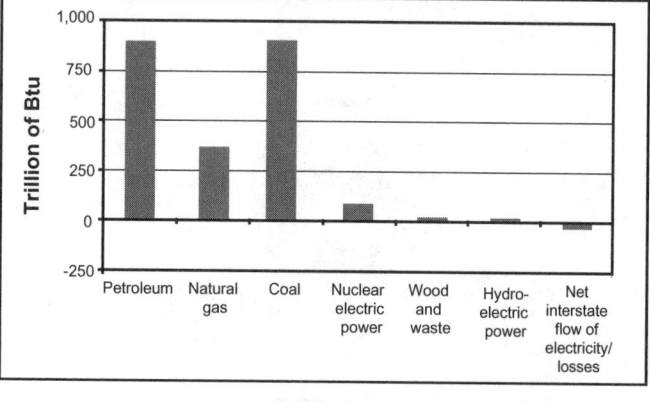

Energy Consumption by Sector, 2001

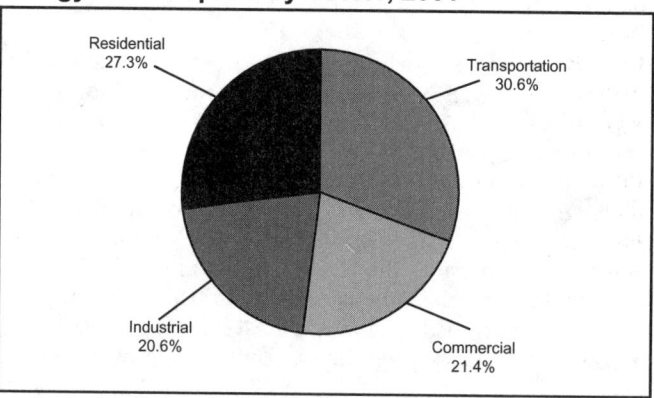

Table MO-15. Energy Consumption, Expenditures, and Prices, Selected Years 1960–2001

(Dollars, Btu [British Thermal Unit], percent distribution.)

Item	1960	1965	1970	1975	1980	1985	1990	1995	2000	2001
Total Consumption (Billion Btu)	900 908	1 049 540	1 319 009	1 415 952	1 464 019	1 427 638	1 517 714	1 684 789	1 785 092	1 815 043
Consumption per capita (million Btu)	208.5	235.0	282.0	294.5	297.8	285.5	296.6	316.4	319.0	322.0
Consumption by Sector (Percent Distribution)										
Residential	26.1	24.3	24.8	26.4	28.1	26.5	26.0	26.6	27.0	27.3
Commercial	12.4	11.6	14.2	14.3	16.7	17.5	19.4	19.8	21.4	21.4
Industrial	33.3	35.2	31.4	29.3	27.2	25.9	23.3	21.6	20.5	20.6
Transportation	28.2	29.0	29.6	30.0	28.0	30.1	31.3	32.1	31.2	30.6
Consumption by Source (Billion Btu)										
Coal	170 906	189 620	279 245	430 226	531 438	529 684	539 583	593 732	688 904	716 108
Natural gas	270 074	347 967	432 532	371 837	322 908	264 318	241 335	281 059	289 045	288 618
Petroleum	404 618	468 405	581 320	616 009	597 007	570 555	618 196	683 088	681 728	718 851
Nuclear electric power	0	0	0	0	0	85 290	84 635	86 597	104 205	87 599
Hydroelectric power[1]	7 807	8 387	9 733	13 315	5 797	31 272	22 425	19 114	4 160	8 529
Wood and waste	33 634	27 017	23 611	27 099	28 789	28 704	17 338	17 352	13 026	11 106
Other	0	0	0	0	0	0	0	211	193	184
Net interstate flow of electricity/losses[2]	13 868	8 144	-7 432	-42 534	-21 920	-82 186	-6 010	3 626	3 831	-15 951
Total Expenditures (Thousands of Dollars)	...	...	1 947 400	3 648 300	7 666 700	8 543 100	9 427 800	10 047 500	13 219 800	13 821 700
Expenditures per capita (dollars)	...	...	416	759	1 559	1 708	1 842	1 887	2 363	2 452
Prices by Sector (Dollars Per Million Btu)										
Total	...	...	1.84	3.32	7.19	8.28	8.82	8.51	10.97	11.12
Residential	...	...	2.07	3.37	6.82	9.58	11.10	11.12	13.33	14.66
Commercial	...	...	1.67	2.87	6.86	10.24	11.27	11.10	12.37	13.40
Industrial	...	...	1.14	2.41	5.42	6.40	6.37	6.00	7.69	7.63
Transportation	...	...	2.32	4.07	8.76	8.19	8.30	7.72	10.91	10.33

[1]A negative number in this row results from pumped storage for which, overall, more electricity is expended than created to provide electricity during peak demand periods.
[2]Net interstate flow of electricity is the difference between the amount of energy in the electricity sold within a state (including associated losses) and the energy input at the electric utilities within the state. A positive number indicates that more electricity (including associated losses) came into the state than went out of the state during the year; conversely, a negative number indicates that more electricity (including associated losses) went out of the state than came into the state.
. . . = Not available.

Table MO-16. State Taxes, Fiscal 2004

(Dollars, percent distribution.)

Item	Thousands of dollars	Percent distribution	Dollars per capita	
			State	U.S.
TOTAL TAXES	9 119 664	100.0	1 584.6	2 024.8
Property Taxes	22 763	0.2	4.0	38.9
Sales and Gross Receipts	4 468 508	49.0	776.5	1 003.4
General sales and gross receipts	2 950 055	32.3	512.6	677.0
Selective sales taxes	1 518 453	16.7	263.8	326.4
Amusements	307 062	3.4	53.4	17.0
Insurance premiums	304 848	3.3	53.0	47.0
Motor fuels	726 705	8.0	126.3	114.6
Tobacco products	109 653	1.2	19.0	42.0
Licenses	605 590	6.6	105.2	134.9
Corporation	90 862	1.0	15.8	21.6
Motor vehicle	254 740	2.8	44.3	59.4
Occupation and business, not elsewhere classified	135 328	1.5	23.5	37.1
Other licenses	53 814	0.6	9.4	2.6
Other Taxes	4 022 803	44.1	699.0	847.6
Individual income	3 720 749	40.8	646.5	673.6
Corporation net income	224 366	2.5	39.0	105.1
Death and gift	69 657	0.8	12.1	19.6

GOVERNMENT FINANCE

Per capita revenues were well below the U.S. average in 2003. Missouri's per capita expenditures of $3,346 ranked as the 42nd lowest in the nation. With the exceptions of hospitals and highways, Missouri's per capita expenditures for major categories were lower than the national averages. In 2004, per capita taxes amounted to $1,585, which was the 6th lowest amount in the country. The largest share of these taxes came from individual income taxes, which amounted to $647 per person in fiscal year 2004. Missouri's debt per person was $2,422, which was above the national average and ranked 20th in the country.

Per Capita State Taxes, Fiscal 2004

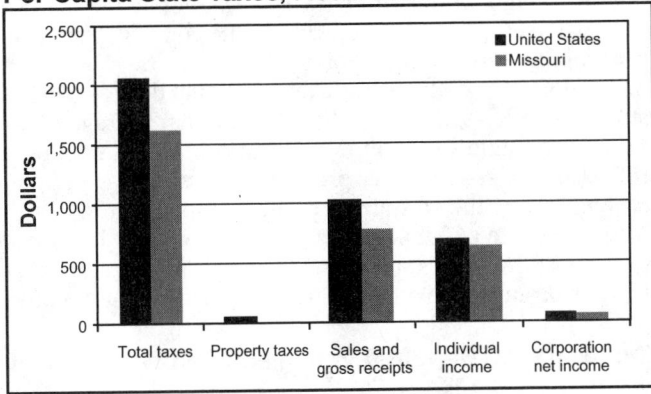

Table MO-17. State Government Finances, 2003

(Dollars, percent distribution.)

Item	Millions of dollars	Percent distribution	Dollars per capita	
			State	U.S.
GENERAL REVENUE	19 135 079	100.0	3 345.9	3 832.6
Intergovernmental revenue	7 172 806	37.5	1 254.2	1 246.0
Taxes	8 627 396	45.1	1 508.6	1 891.6
General sales	2 819 814	14.7	493.1	636.0
Selective sales	1 406 582	7.4	246.0	307.4
License taxes	562 934	2.9	98.4	123.6
Individual income tax	3 519 844	18.4	615.5	626.8
Corporate income tax	205 729	1.1	36.0	97.8
Other taxes	112 493	0.6	19.7	99.9
Current charges	1 705 748	8.9	298.3	366.5
Miscellaneous general revenue	1 629 129	8.5	284.9	328.6
GENERAL EXPENDITURE	19 137 212	100.0	3 346.2	4 010.5
Intergovernmental expenditure	5 159 094	27.0	902.1	1 316.9
Direct expenditure	13 978 118	73.0	2 444.2	2 693.6
Expenditure by Function				
Education	6 732 710	35.2	1 177.2	1 416.4
Public welfare	5 591 971	29.2	977.8	1 083.3
Hospitals	893 540	4.7	156.2	132.3
Health	585 878	3.1	102.4	173.0
Highways	1 854 329	9.7	324.2	295.4
Police protection	162 920	0.9	28.5	38.4
Correction	656 273	3.4	114.8	135.0
Natural resources	290 176	1.5	50.7	64.0
Parks and recreation	56 018	0.3	9.8	20.1
Government administration	774 406	4.0	135.4	151.3
Interest on general debt	604 950	3.2	105.8	107.8
Other and unallocable	934 041	4.9	163.3	393.4
DEBT AT END OF FISCAL YEAR	13 855 016	X	2 422.6	2 404.7
CASH AND SECURITY HOLDINGS	49 558 702	X	8 665.6	8 938.4

X = Not applicable.

Table MO-18. Education Indicators, 2000–2004

(Percent, number.)

Item	State	U.S.
Total Population 25 Years and Over (Thousands), 2004	3 698	186 877
Educational Attainment, 2004		
Percent high school graduate or more	87.9	85.2
Percent college graduate or more	28.1	27.7
Elementary and Secondary Schools, 2002–2003		
Total students	924 445	48 202 324
Percent of students eligible for free or reduced-price lunch ..	37.5	40.6
Percent of students who were English language learners	1.6	7.8
Total schools	2 286	92 330
Student/teacher ratio	13.9	15.9
Per student expenditures	7 349	8 041
Dropouts, Grades 9–12, 2000–2001 (Percent)	3.6	. . .
Higher Education, 2002–2003		
Total enrollment	352 337	17 035 027
Bachelor's degrees awarded	33 291	1 348 503
Percent women	57.1	57.5

. . . = Not available.

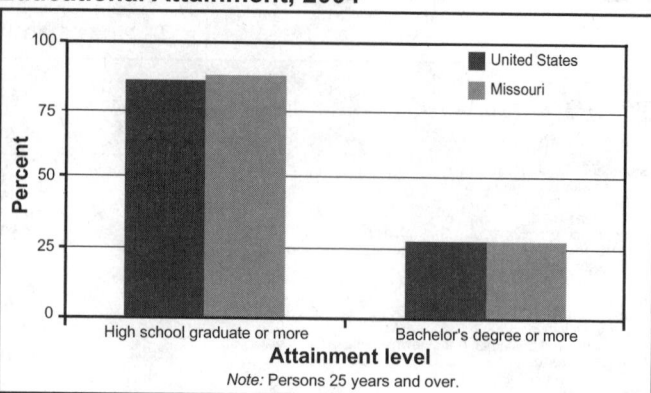

Educational Attainment, 2004

Legend: United States, Missouri

Note: Persons 25 years and over.

EDUCATION

Nearly 88 percent of the state's residents age 25 years and over held high school diplomas. This was above the national average and ranked 19th in the country. The proportion of the population holding bachelor's degrees or more also exceeded the U.S. average. Expenditures per student of $7,349 were less than the national average of $8,041. The state's student/teacher ratio was 13.9, in part reflecting the state's lower proportion of school-age population. Among the 46 states reporting dropout rates, Missouri's rate of 3.6 percent was about average. Just 1.6 percent of the state's students were English language learners, compared with 7.8 percent of students nationally.

VOTER PARTICIPATION

Voter turnout was higher than average for both the 2000 and 2004 elections. In 2004, the voter turnout rate was 66.3 percent, which was the 10th highest proportion in the nation. Blacks had a voter participation rate close to 74 percent in 2004, while about 67 percent of eligible Whites voted. Just 30 percent of eligible Hispanic voters participated in the 2004 election. Among the different age groups, persons age 65 years and over had the highest voter participation rate. In 2000, 50.4 percent of eligible voters in Missouri cast ballots for the Republican presidential candidate, and 53.3 percent voted similarly in 2004.

Table MO-19. Reported Voting and Registration, November 2000 and November 2004

(Numbers in thousands, percent.)

Characteristic	Total population 18 years and over	Total citizen		Total registered		Total voted	
		Number	Percent	Number	Percent	Number	Percent
NOVEMBER 2000							
Total	4 066	3 987	98.1	3 023	74.3	2 659	65.4
Male	1 902	1 872	98.4	1 386	72.9	1 217	64.0
Female	2 165	2 115	97.7	1 637	75.6	1 442	66.6
NOVEMBER 2004							
Total	4 243	4 106	96.8	3 336	78.6	2 815	66.3
Male	2 023	1 933	95.6	1 540	76.1	1 299	64.2
Female	2 219	2 173	97.9	1 796	80.9	1 516	68.3
Race and Hispanic Origin							
White alone	3 636	3 538	97.3	2 865	78.8	2 424	66.7
Non-Hispanic White alone	3 544	3 483	98.3	2 822	79.6	2 393	67.5
Black alone	433	433	100.0	382	88.2	324	74.7
Asian alone	55	27	B	13	B	13	B
Hispanic or Latino[1]	115	68	58.8	50	43.3	35	30.1
White alone or in combination	3 702	3 604	97.4	2 917	78.8	2 468	66.7
Non-Hispanic White alone or in combination	3 610	3 549	98.3	2 874	79.6	2 437	67.5
Black alone or in combination	455	455	100.0	399	87.6	335	73.6
Asian alone or in combination	57	29	B	15	B	15	B
Age							
18 to 24 years	540	519	96.2	343	63.6	269	49.9
25 to 44 years	1 576	1 483	94.1	1 193	75.7	965	61.2
45 to 64 years	1 317	1 305	99.1	1 110	84.3	966	73.3
65 to 74 years	452	441	97.6	373	82.4	342	75.7
75 years and over	357	357	100.0	316	88.6	273	76.3

[1]May be of any race.
B = Base is too small to show derived measure.

At a Glance:

- In 2004, Montana had an estimated population of nearly 927,000, ranking it 44th in the country.

- Over 89 percent of the population was non-Hispanic White. Over 6 percent of the state's residents were American Indian, which was the fifth largest proportion of this racial group in the nation.

- Montana's median household income of less than $34,000 was the second lowest in the country. The state's poverty rate of 14.1 percent was above the national average.

- The unemployment rate was among the lowest in the country, at 4.4 percent in 2004. Real gross state product was among the nation's smallest, but it had an above average rate of growth from 2001 to 2004.

- In 2004, nearly 92 percent of the state's residents age 25 years and over held high school diplomas, ranking second in the nation.

- Over 19 percent of Montana's population lacked health insurance in 2004. This was the fifth highest proportion in the nation.

Table MT-1. Population by Sex and Age, 1990, 2000, and 2004

(Number, percent.)

Sex and age	1990	2000	2004	Percent distribution, 2004	Average annual percent change, 2000–2004
Total Population	799 065	902 195	926 865	X	0.7
Percent of total U.S. population	0.3	0.3	0.3	X	X
Sex					
Male	395 769	449 480	462 265	49.9	0.7
Female	403 296	452 715	464 600	50.1	0.6
Age					
Under 5 years	59 257	54 869	52 510	5.7	-1.0
5 to 17 years	162 847	175 193	155 583	16.8	-0.3
18 years and over	150 627	672 133	718 772	77.5	1.6
18 to 24 years	576 961	85 757	99 049	10.7	2.5
25 to 44 years	70 011	245 220	234 483	25.3	-0.5
45 to 64 years	249 826	220 207	258 691	27.9	4.0
65 years and over	106 497	120 949	126 549	13.7	1.3
85 years and over	10 676	15 337	18 233	2.0	4.0
Median age (years)	33.8	37.5	39.5	X	X

X = Not applicable.

Average Annual Rate of Population Growth, 1980–2004

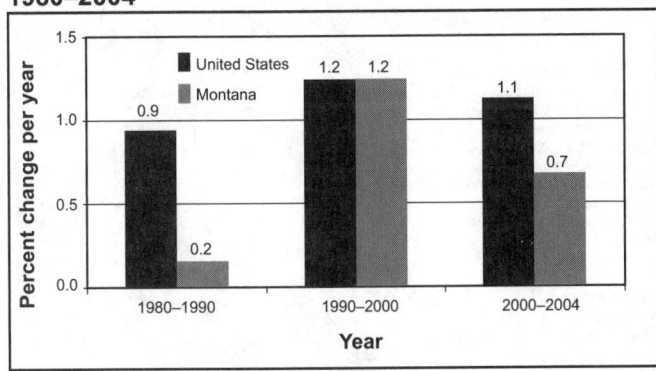

POPULATION

Montana is a large, sparsely populated state, with one of the lowest population density rates in the nation. From 2000 to 2004, the state's population increased 2.7 percent, which was well below the national population growth rate. The state benefited from the in-migration of over 13,000 new residents from other states. However, Montana ranked last for the number of new residents from other countries. The state had one of the smallest proportions of population age 18 years and under. Montana also had the fourth highest median age in the nation. Blacks made up just 0.3 percent of the state's population, the lowest proportion of this racial group in the country.

Table MT-2. Population by Race and Hispanic Origin, 1990, 2000, and 2004

(Number, percent.)

Race and Hispanic origin	1990	2000	2004
Total Population	799 065	902 195	926 865
Non-Hispanic (Percent)			
One race[1]			
White	91.8	89.7	89.1
Black	0.3	0.3	0.3
American Indian, Alaska Native[2]	6.0	6.0	6.2
Asian and Pacific Islander[2]	0.5	0.6	0.6
Other race[2]	0.5	. . .	. . .
Two or more races	. . .	1.4	1.4
Hispanic or Latino[3] (Percent)	1.5	2.0	2.4

[1]Individuals could report only one race in the 1990 census and could report one or more races on the 2000 census. Data on race in 2000 and 2004 are not comparable to 1990.
[2]Data for 1990 include people of Hispanic or Latino origin.
[3]May be of any race.
. . . = Not available.

Minority Population as a Percent of Total Population, 2004

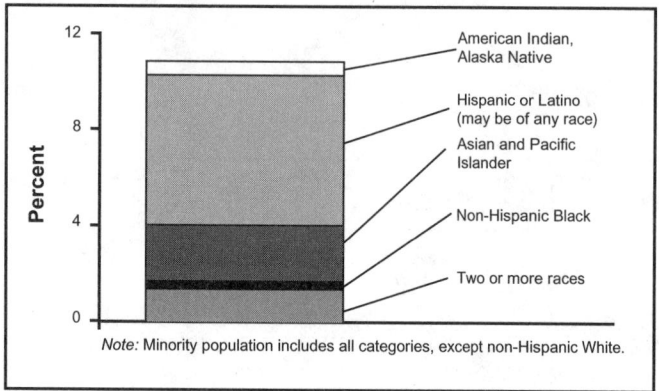

Note: Minority population includes all categories, except non-Hispanic White.

Age-Adjusted Death Rates, Average 2000–2002

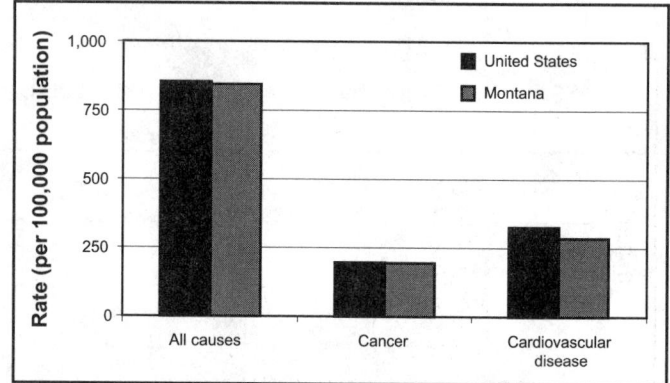

HEALTH

Montana's infant mortality rate was the same as the national average. Its age-adjusted death rate for all causes was slightly below average, and its death rate for cardiovascular diseases was well below the U.S. average. Montana's birth rate was among the lowest in the nation, contributing to the state's slower population growth.

Table MT-3. Health Characteristics, 2000–2004

(Number, rate, percent.)

Item	State	U.S.
Births, 2003–2004		
Number of births	11 422	4 089 950
Birth rate (per 1,000 population)	12.4	14.1
Teenage birth rate (per 1,000 women age 15–19 years)	35.0	41.6
Mortality Rates, Average 2000–2002		
Infant mortality rate (per 1,000 live births)	6.9	6.9
Age-adjusted mortality rate (per 100,000 population)		
All races	842.8	853.3
Non-Hispanic White	821.9	843.1
Black	1 091.9	1 097.7
American Indian, Alaska Native	1 271.6	687.0
Asian and Pacific Islander	. . .	486.0
Hispanic or Latino[1]	725.7	642.7
Health Insurance, 2004		
Percent of all persons without health insurance	19.1	15.7
Percent of children without health insurance	15.4	11.2
Percent of low-income children without health insurance	10.6	7.1

[1]May be of any race.
. . . = Not available.

Table MT-4. Leading Causes of Death, Average 2000–2002

(Number, rate per 100,000 population.)

Cause	Number of deaths	Age-adjusted death rates	
		State	U.S.
ALL CAUSES	8 289	842.8	853.3
Leading Causes			
Major cardiovascular diseases	2 762	277.0	326.5
Cancer	1 911	194.2	196.0
Chronic lower respiratory diseases	559	56.7	43.7
Unintentional injuries	496	53.0	35.7
Diabetes (underlying cause)	222	22.5	25.2
Influenza and pneumonia	217	21.7	22.7
Alzheimer's disease	251	24.8	19.0
Motor vehicle accidents	225	24.7	15.0
Nephritis, nephrotic syndrome, and nephrosis ..	116	11.7	13.8
Septicemia	69	7.0	11.4
Suicides	172	18.8	10.7
Firearm-related	143	15.6	10.3
Cirrhosis	105	10.8	9.5
Drug-induced	64	7.0	7.9
Alcohol-induced	98	10.1	6.9
Homicides	30	3.3	6.0
Falls	110	11.1	5.2
HIV	7	0.8	5.0
Viral hepatitis	13	1.3	2.0
Anemias	17	1.7	1.6
Drownings	20	2.2	1.3
Fire deaths	7	0.8	1.2

Note: The rates are age-adjusted to the U.S. 2000 standard population.

Table MT-5. Households and Housing Characteristics, 1990, 2000, and 2004

(Number, percent, and dollars.)

Characteristic	1990	2000	2004	Average annual percent change, 2000–2004
Total Households	306 163	358 667	368 530	0.7
Family households	211 666	237 407	238 947	0.2
Married-couple family	176 526	192 067	193 352	0.2
Other family	35 140	45 340	45 595	0.1
Male householder, no wife present	8 743	13 324	14 486	2.1
Female householder, no husband present	26 397	32 016	31 109	-0.7
Nonfamily households	94 497	121 260	129 583	1.7
Householder living alone	80 491	98 422	106 502	2.0
Householder not living alone	14 006	22 838	23 081	0.3
Housing Characteristics				
Average size	2.53	2.45	2.45	X
Housing units	361 155	412 633	423 262	0.6
Occupied housing units	306 163	358 667	368 530	0.7
Owner-occupied	205 899	247 723	252 597	0.5
Renter-occupied	100 264	110 944	115 933	1.1
Median gross rent of renter-occupied housing units (dollars) ...	311	447	520	3.9
Median value of owner-occupied housing units (dollars)	56 500	99 500	119 319	4.6

X = Not applicable.

Median Housing Value and Median Rent, 2004

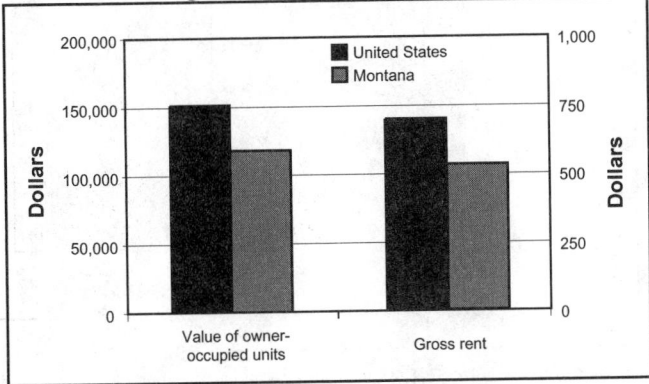

Median Household Income, 1984–2004 (2004 Dollars)

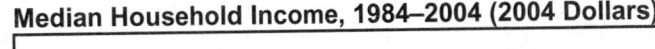
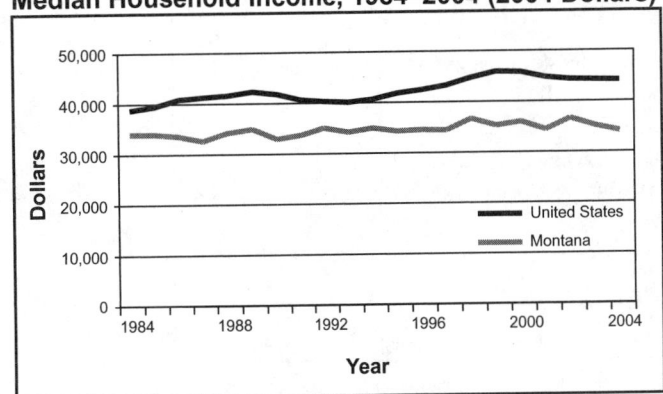

Table MT-6. Household Income and Poverty Status, 1980–2004

(2004 CPI-U-RS adjusted dollars, rate.)

Year	State		U.S.	
	Median household income (2004 dollars)	Poverty rate	Median household income (2004 dollars)	Poverty rate
2004	33 987	14.1	44 389	12.7
2003	35 025	15.1	44 482	12.5
2002	36 591	13.5	44 546	12.1
2001	34 282	13.3	45 062	11.7
2000	35 953	14.1	46 058	11.3
1999	35 182	15.8	46 129	11.9
1998	36 545	16.6	45 003	12.7
1997	34 284	15.6	43 430	13.3
1996	34 383	17.0	42 544	13.7
1995	34 165	15.3	41 943	13.8
1994	34 836	11.5	40 677	14.5
1993	34 075	14.9	40 217	15.1
1992	34 998	13.8	40 422	14.8
1991	33 579	15.4	40 746	14.2
1990	32 758	16.3	41 963	13.5
1989	34 854	15.6	42 524	12.8
1988	34 109	14.6	41 771	13.0
1987	32 557	18.0	41 322	13.4
1986	33 426	16.5	40 939	13.6
1985	33 883	16.0	39 545	14.0
1984	33 801	13.8	38 782	14.4
1983	. . .	15.4	. . .	15.2
1982	. . .	17.0	. . .	15.0
1981	. . .	13.1	. . .	14.0
1980	. . .	13.2	. . .	13.0

. . . = Not available.

Table MT-7. Employment Status by Demographic Group, 2004
(Numbers in thousands, rate.)

Characteristic	Civilian noninstitutional population	Civilian labor force		Employed	Unemployment rate
		Number	Participation rate		
SEX AND AGE					
Total	730	486	66.5	462	4.9
16 to 19 years	60	30	49.6	26	11.0
20 to 24 years	57	47	83.3	43	9.8
25 to 34 years	105	89	84.3	84	5.2
35 to 44 years	131	114	87.0	110	3.6
45 to 54 years	143	120	83.7	116	3.5
55 to 64 years	107	68	62.9	65	3.4
65 years and over	127	19	14.8	18	4.5
Men	359	256	71.2	242	5.6
16 to 19 years	33	16	49.4	14	12.6
20 to 24 years	29	25	87.6	23	9.8
25 to 34 years	53	48	90.5	45	6.0
35 to 44 years	61	56	91.5	54	3.6
45 to 54 years	71	62	86.7	59	3.7
55 to 64 years	56	38	67.4	36	4.7
65 years and over	55	10	18.6	10	6.6
Women	370	230	62.0	220	4.3
16 to 19 years	27	13	50.0	12	9.0
20 to 24 years	28	22	78.7	20	9.9
25 to 34 years	52	40	77.9	39	4.3
35 to 44 years	69	58	83.0	56	3.6
45 to 54 years	72	58	80.8	57	3.4
55 to 64 years	51	30	57.9	29	1.7
MARITAL STATUS					
Married men, spouse present	199	146	73.6	142	2.9
Married women, spouse present	203	131	64.7	128	2.6
Women who maintain families	33	25	74.7	23	6.2
RACE, HISPANIC ORIGIN, AND SEX					
White	673	449	66.8	430	4.3
Men	332	239	72.0	227	4.9
Women	341	210	61.7	203	3.7
Hispanic or Latino[1]	16	11	66.5	10	6.4
RACE, HISPANIC ORIGIN, AND AGE					
White					
16 to 19 years	50	27	53.5	24	10.5
20 to 24 years	48	41	84.3	37	8.2
25 to 34 years	95	82	86.1	78	4.6
35 to 44 years	119	103	87.0	100	2.7
45 to 54 years	135	114	84.3	110	3.4
55 to 64 years	102	65	63.9	63	3.3
65 years and over	124	18	14.6	17	4.5

Note: Data in Table 7 are from the Current Population Survey (CPS) and do not match Bureau of Labor Statistics estimates in Table 8. See notes and definitions for more details.

[1]May be of any race.

Table MT-8. Employment Status, 1990–2004
(Numbers in thousands, rate.)

Year	Civilian labor force	Employed	Unemployed	Unemployment rate
2004	483 043	461 746	21 297	4.4
2003	473 473	452 493	20 980	4.4
2002	469 254	448 459	20 795	4.4
2001	468 097	447 213	20 884	4.5
2000	468 277	445 881	22 396	4.8
1999	465 256	440 646	24 610	5.3
1998	460 837	435 156	25 681	5.6
1997	451 617	427 504	24 113	5.3
1996	447 141	422 458	24 683	5.5
1995	441 705	417 770	23 935	5.4
1994	434 774	410 957	23 817	5.5
1993	422 579	397 257	25 322	6.0
1992	417 262	390 362	26 900	6.4
1991	409 649	383 776	25 873	6.3
1990	408 301	383 706	24 595	6.0

Note: Population age 16 years and over.

Unemployment Rate, 1980–2004

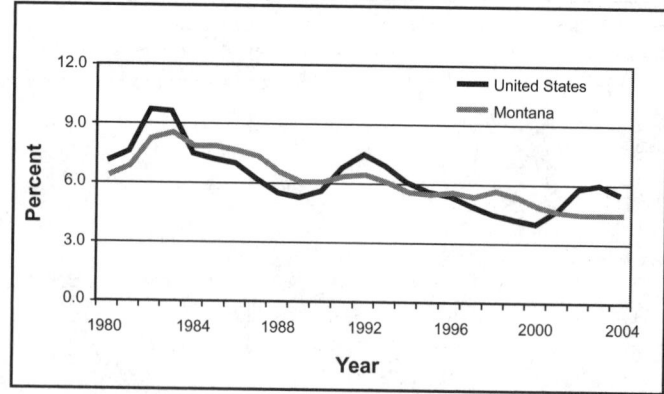

Table MT-9. Employment and Average Wages by Industry, 2001–2004

(Estimates are based on the 2002 North American Industry Classification System [NAICS].)

Industry	2001	2002	2003	2004	Annual average percent change, 2001–2004
	Number of jobs				
TOTAL EMPLOYMENT BY PLACE OF WORK	565 989	572 341	581 668	596 758	1.8
Farm Employment	32 047	32 535	31 655	31 785	-0.3
Nonfarm Employment	533 942	539 806	550 013	564 973	1.9
Private employment	443 701	450 300	457 843	472 667	2.1
Forestry, fishing, hunting, and other¹	7 617	8 424	7 660	7 482	-0.6
Mining	7 060	6 722	6 956	8 272	5.4
Utilities	3 259	2 990	2 909	2 992	-2.8
Construction	38 351	38 550	41 308	43 354	4.2
Manufacturing	24 601	23 380	22 349	22 609	-2.8
Durable goods manufacturing	16 553	15 346	14 366	14 325	-4.7
Nondurable goods manufacturing	8 048	8 034	7 983	8 284	1.0
Wholesale trade	17 301	17 224	17 290	17 897	1.1
Retail trade	70 766	71 207	71 262	73 191	1.1
Transportation and warehousing	17 493	17 366	17 006	17 076	-0.8
Information	9 412	9 085	9 163	9 276	-0.5
Finance and insurance	20 602	21 293	21 779	22 352	2.8
Real estate and rental and leasing	18 958	19 202	20 469	21 736	4.7
Professional and technical services	29 092	29 769	30 329	31 046	2.2
Management of companies and enterprises	1 364	1 480	1 429	1 177	-4.8
Administrative and waste services	21 296	21 576	22 816	24 008	4.1
Educational services	5 785	6 180	6 384	6 709	5.1
Health care and social assistance	57 654	59 746	60 340	62 119	2.5
Arts, entertainment, and recreation	14 583	15 499	16 518	17 094	5.4
Accommodation and food services	46 393	47 293	48 168	49 708	2.3
Other services, except public administration	32 114	33 314	33 708	34 569	2.5
Government and government enterprises	90 241	89 506	92 170	92 306	0.8
	Dollars				
AVERAGE WAGES AND SALARIES BY PLACE OF WORK ...	24 959	25 923	26 815	27 720	3.6
Farm Earnings	21 575	24 902	23 149	22 030	0.7
Nonfarm Earnings	25 010	25 939	26 866	27 801	3.6
Private earnings	24 317	24 992	25 851	26 804	3.3
Forestry, fishing, hunting, and other¹	19 370	21 434	21 418	22 256	4.7
Mining	52 592	52 619	53 134	53 910	0.8
Utilities	53 033	56 240	59 201	58 462	3.3
Construction	30 529	30 635	31 716	32 282	1.9
Manufacturing	32 433	33 374	34 534	35 263	2.8
Durable goods manufacturing	31 420	32 266	33 207	33 994	2.7
Nondurable goods manufacturing	34 530	35 516	36 896	37 419	2.7
Wholesale trade	32 262	33 539	34 194	36 039	3.8
Retail trade	18 480	19 319	20 075	20 698	3.8
Transportation and warehousing	33 592	33 919	34 670	36 106	2.4
Information	31 113	32 761	33 331	34 993	4.0
Finance and insurance	35 262	36 086	38 020	39 243	3.6
Real estate and rental and leasing	18 186	18 694	20 066	21 528	5.8
Professional and technical services	34 118	35 000	36 779	38 119	3.8
Management of companies and enterprises	35 575	36 316	37 182	41 046	4.9
Administrative and waste services	17 197	18 221	18 923	20 117	5.4
Educational services	16 312	16 533	17 387	18 134	3.6
Health care and social assistance	26 451	27 523	28 747	29 927	4.2
Arts, entertainment, and recreation	14 569	14 796	15 337	15 335	1.7
Accommodation and food services	10 878	11 157	11 394	11 683	2.4
Other services, except public administration	17 694	18 134	18 998	19 789	3.8
Government and government enterprises	27 489	29 394	30 506	31 473	4.6

Note: Average wages and salaries are a calculation by the editors of wage and salary disbursements divided by full- and part-time wage and salary employment. Data may not add to total or may appear as zero due to rounding.

¹ "Other" consists of the number of jobs held by U.S. residents employed by international organizations and foreign embassies and consulates in the United States.

LABOR MARKET

Montana's unemployment rate has been below the national average since 2000. Wage and salary employment was concentrated in government, retail trade, health care, tourism-related sectors, and construction. Employment grew steadily during the 2001–2004 period, at the sixth highest rate in the nation. Declines in manufacturing and utilities were offset by increases in construction, wholesale and retail trade, and most service sector industries. Average wages and salaries were the lowest in the country and below average across all major industry groupings. However, the state's average wages and salaries grew by 11.1 percent over the 2001–2004 period, which was among the 15 highest rates of growth in the nation.

Employment by Industry, 2004

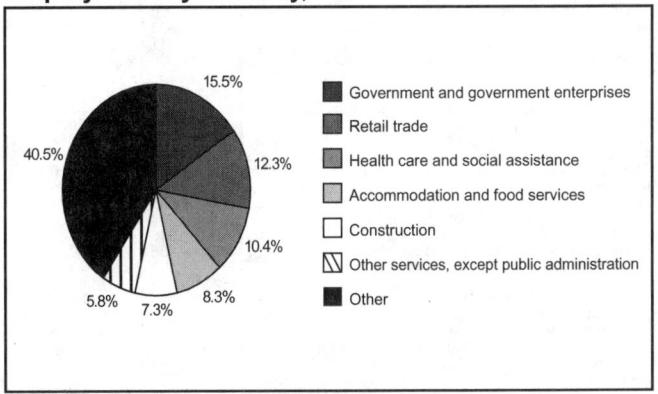

- Government and government enterprises
- Retail trade
- Health care and social assistance
- Accommodation and food services
- Construction
- Other services, except public administration
- Other

40.5% 15.5% 12.3% 10.4% 8.3% 7.3% 5.8%

Table MT-10. Personal Income by Major Source, Selected Years 1980–2004

(Millions of dollars, except where noted.)

Item	1980	1990	2000	2001	2002	2003	2004	Average annual percent change, 2000–2004
Earnings by Place of Work	5 322	8 483	14 321	15 581	16 019	17 247	18 445	6.5
Wage and salary disbursements	3 870	5 701	9 963	10 458	10 948	11 489	12 156	5.1
Supplements to wages and salaries	783	1 411	2 306	2 451	2 749	3 004	3 283	9.2
Proprietors' income[1]	668	1 371	2 052	2 672	2 322	2 754	3 007	10.0
Farm proprietors' income	-14	279	82	128	46	275	287	36.9
Nonfarm proprietors' income	682	1 092	1 970	2 544	2 276	2 479	2 720	8.4
(-) Contributions for government social insurance[2] ...	537	1 077	1 733	1 853	1 970	2 077	2 201	6.2
(+) Adjustment for residence[3]	14	-4	26	32	31	29	30	3.3
(=) Net Earnings by Place of Residence	4 799	7 402	12 614	13 760	14 080	15 199	16 274	6.6
(+) Dividends, interest, and rent[4]	1 453	2 935	4 763	4 995	4 974	4 979	5 157	2.0
(+) Personal current transfer receipts	892	2 024	3 339	3 605	3 789	3 919	4 212	6.0
Personal income	7 144	12 361	20 716	22 359	22 843	24 096	25 643	5.5
Farm income	7 032	11 982	20 483	22 083	22 627	23 672	25 212	5.3
Nonfarm income	112	379	233	276	216	424	431	16.6
Per Capita Personal Income (Dollars)[5]	9 058	15 448	22 929	24 672	25 083	26 244	27 666	4.8

Note: Data may not add to total or may appear as zero due to rounding.

[1]Proprietors' income includes the inventory valuation adjustment and the capital consumption adjustment.
[2]Contributions for government social insurance are included in earnings by type and industry, but they are excluded from personal income.
[3]The adjustment for residence is the net inflow of the earnings of interarea commuters.
[4]Rental income of persons includes the capital consumption adjustment.
[5]Per capita personal income is total personal income divided by total midyear population.

Per Capita Personal Income, 1980–2004 (Current Dollars)

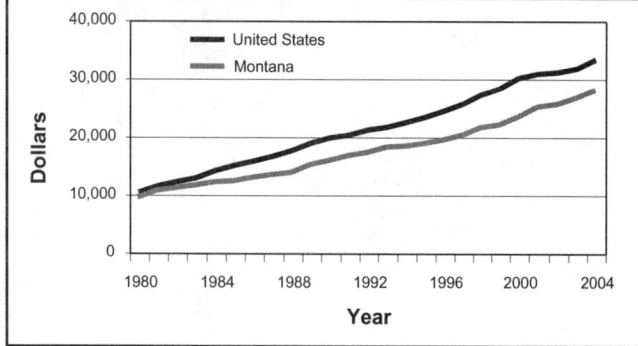

ECONOMIC ACTIVITY

Montana's economy was dominated by the service sector, and the state's economic growth was faster than the national average throughout the 2001–2004 period. Real gross state product ranked 48th in the nation in 2004, but grew by 12.2 percent from 2001 to 2004. The main sectors contributing to growth were real estate and related activities, health care, information services, construction, and wholesale and retail trade. Housing price appreciation has been strong in recent years—at about the national average growth rate—and even higher in the recreational areas of the state. Still, the median value of owner-occupied housing in Montana ranked 31st in the nation.

Table MT-11. Real Gross State Product, 1997–2004

(Millions of chained 2000 dollars, percent.)

Industry	1997	1998	1999	2000	2001	2002	2003	2004	Average annual percent change, 2001–2004
GROSS STATE PRODUCT	20 098	20 587	20 916	21 367	21 838	22 621	23 493	24 506	3.9
As a percent of U.S. gross product	0.2	0.2	0.2	0.2	0.2	0.2	0.2	0.2	X
Private Industries	16 608	17 074	17 393	17 732	18 213	18 968	19 704	20 625	4.2
Agriculture, forestry, fishing, and hunting	756	722	736	753	757	917	900	900	5.9
Mining	636	648	717	728	694	650	660	713	0.9
Utilities	811	788	859	871	801	812	867	888	3.5
Construction	1 208	1 239	1 215	1 155	1 179	1 163	1 252	1 302	3.4
Manufacturing	1 232	1 393	1 204	1 260	1 225	1 236	1 228	1 231	0.2
As a percent of gross state product	6.1	6.8	5.8	5.9	5.6	5.5	5.2	5.0	X
Wholesale trade	1 135	1 226	1 227	1 246	1 317	1 389	1 370	1 442	3.1
Retail trade	1 553	1 589	1 649	1 667	1 805	1 992	2 131	2 275	8.0
Transportation and warehousing	980	984	1 005	1 017	964	984	1 026	1 062	3.3
Information	484	534	578	605	687	741	796	878	8.5
Finance and insurance	903	910	964	1 005	1 077	1 139	1 220	1 298	6.4
Real estate and rental and leasing	2 211	2 278	2 378	2 430	2 566	2 586	2 672	2 880	3.9
Services	4 695	4 777	4 864	4 994	5 156	5 397	5 620	5 809	4.1
As a percent of gross state product	23.4	23.2	23.3	23.4	23.6	23.9	23.9	23.7	X
Professional and technical services	846	860	884	942	1 029	1 082	1 150	1 185	4.8
Management of companies and enterprises	65	60	74	65	129	154	169	142	3.3
Administrative and waste services	393	411	429	411	410	439	483	515	7.9
Educational services	75	80	83	83	81	81	77	77	-1.7
Health care and social assistance	1 725	1 750	1 796	1 863	1 895	1 996	2 048	2 117	3.8
Arts, entertainment, and recreation	285	271	270	280	284	300	324	323	4.4
Accommodation and food services	720	735	754	777	752	776	791	826	3.2
Other services, except public administration ...	586	610	574	573	576	569	578	624	2.7
Government	3 494	3 513	3 523	3 635	3 625	3 654	3 790	3 883	2.3
As a percent of gross state product	17.4	17.1	16.8	17.0	16.6	16.2	16.1	15.8	X

X = Not applicable.

Table MT-12. Government Transfer Payments, Selected Years 1980–2004

(Millions of dollars, percent.)

Item	1980	1990	2000	2001	2002	2003	2004	Average annual percent change, 2000–2004
CURRENT TRANSFER PAYMENTS TO INDIVIDUALS	836	1 916	3 127	3 366	3 573	3 717	4 008	6.4
Retirement and Disability Insurance Benefits	469	1 098	1 540	1 625	1 715	1 785	1 872	5.0
Old-age, survivors, and disability insurance (OASDI) benefits	400	845	1 376	1 452	1 527	1 584	1 665	4.9
Railroad retirement and disability benefits	43	73	92	94	97	98	100	2.1
Workers' compensation	23	177	71	78	89	100	104	10.1
Other government retirement and disability insurance benefits	3	2	2	2	2	2	2	9.9
Medical Benefits	169	521	1 095	1 198	1 254	1 277	1 476	7.8
Medicare benefits	101	296	551	611	656	695	765	8.5
Public assistance medical care benefits	66	212	526	561	562	554	681	6.6
Military medical insurance benefits	2	13	17	25	35	28	30	15.0
Income Maintenance Benefits	68	142	251	267	295	328	343	8.1
Supplemental Security Income (SSI) benefits	11	29	57	61	63	64	67	3.8
Family assistance	19	40	28	32	36	34	26	-1.9
Food stamps	20	42	52	54	59	72	82	12.3
Other income maintenance benefits	19	31	114	120	137	159	168	10.2
Unemployment Insurance Compensation	56	48	70	82	96	104	82	4.1
Veterans' Benefits	53	66	119	127	142	153	166	8.6
Federal Education and Training Assistance	14	33	41	54	61	57	60	10.1
Other Payments to Individuals	6	9	11	13	10	12	9	-3.2

Note: See notes and definitions for more details. Data may not add to total or may appear as zero due to rounding.

EXPORTS

The value of Montana's exports was the second lowest in the country in 2004. However, exports increased nearly 15.6 percent from 2001 to 2004. Exports of chemical manufactures increased significantly and became the state's leading export in 2003. In 2004, chemical manufactures accounted for more than 20 percent of total exports. Mining and paper product exports more than doubled from 2001 to 2004. Over half of the state's exports went to Canada. Exports of animal products to Canada fell from nearly $92 million in 2001 to less than $2 million in 2004. Exports to Japan, South Korea, and China more than doubled between 2001 and 2004.

Leading Exports, 2004

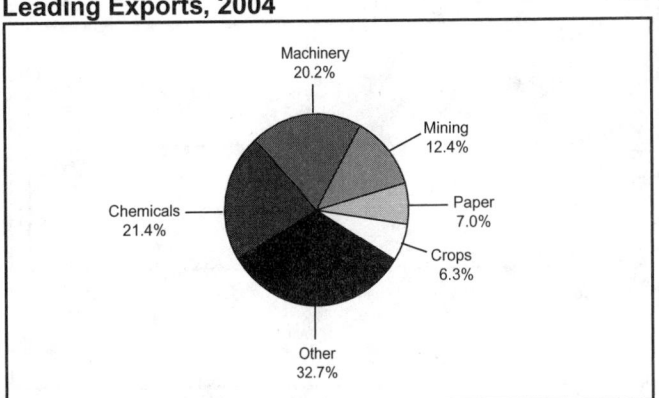

Table MT-13. Exports of Goods by Leading Products and Destinations, 2001–2004

(Millions of dollars, percent, rank based on 2004 dollar values.)

Product and market	2001	2002	2003	2004	Percent share of total, 2004	Average annual percent change, 2001–2004
Total Goods						
Total	489	386	361	565	100.0	4.9
Manufactures	295	290	273	432	76.5	13.6
Agriculture and livestock	171	79	66	116	20.6	-12.1
Other commodities	23	17	23	17	3.0	-9.7
Five Leading Exports (NAICS Code)						
Chemical manufactures (325)	51	60	65	121	21.4	33.5
Machinery manufactures (333)	101	72	59	114	20.2	4.0
Mining (212)	35	25	31	70	12.4	25.9
Paper products (322)	19	30	28	40	7.0	27.9
Crop production (111)	36	27	23	36	6.3	-0.1
Five Leading Markets	476	374	352	553	97.8	5.1
Canada	303	235	222	297	52.6	-0.6
Japan	22	27	27	54	9.6	34.2
Mexico	34	15	11	34	6.1	0.4
South Korea	8	7	8	27	4.9	53.3
Taiwan	23	14	9	27	4.8	5.3

Table MT-14. Agriculture, 1997 and 2002

(Number, acres, and dollars.)

Item	1997	2002
Number of farms	27 632	27 870
Land in farms (acres)	58 445 339	59 612 403
Farm Size		
Average size of farm (acres)	2 115	2 139
Farms by size (percent distribution)		
Fewer than 50 acres	21.2	23.3
50 to 499 acres	30.6	30.4
500 acres or more	48.2	46.4
Market Value of Land and Equipment (Dollars)		
Land and buildings average value per farm	650 281	835 250
Average value per acre	309	386
Machinery and equipment average value per farm	73 526	83 976
Value of Sales (Thousands of Dollars)		
Agricultural products sold	1 921 771	1 882 114
Crops	952 468	733 324
Livestock, poultry, and their products	969 303	1 148 791
Average per farm (dollars)	69 549	67 532
Value of sales (percent distribution)		
Less than $10,000	43.4	50.4
$10,000 to $99,999	36.8	31.5
$100,000 or more	19.8	18.0
Government Payments		
Payments (thousands of dollars)	185 547	210 749
Percent of farms receiving government payments	53.3	44.5
Farm operators whose principal occupation is farming (percent) ...	61.0	63.5

AGRICULTURE

The value of Montana's farm products totaled $1.9 billion in 2002, somewhat higher than the total value reported on the previous farm census in 1997. The state ranked 32nd in the nation for these cash receipts in 2002. The value of crop sales declined from 1997 to 2002, but sales of livestock, poultry, and their products increased. The state's leading products were cattle and wheat. Over 63 percent of farm operators considered farming to be their principal occupation—a significantly higher proportion than in many other farming states.

ENERGY

Energy expenditures per person were high in Montana, ranking 10th in the nation. However, energy prices were close to the national average. The state's per capita consumption of 403.5 Btu ranked 13th in the nation, but was down significantly from earlier years. Coal and petroleum were the chief energy sources. Hydroelectric power was also a significant contributor to Montana's energy sources.

Energy Consumption by Source, 2001

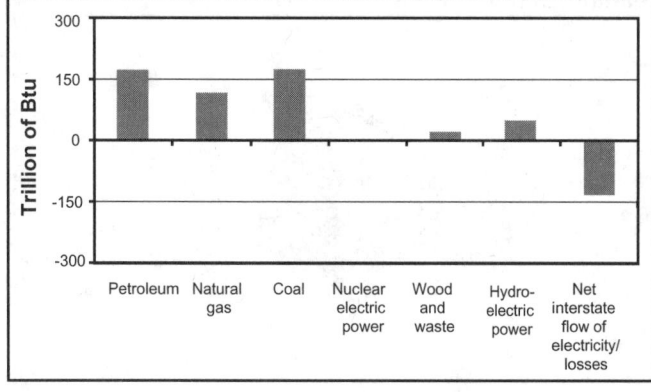

Energy Consumption by Sector, 2001

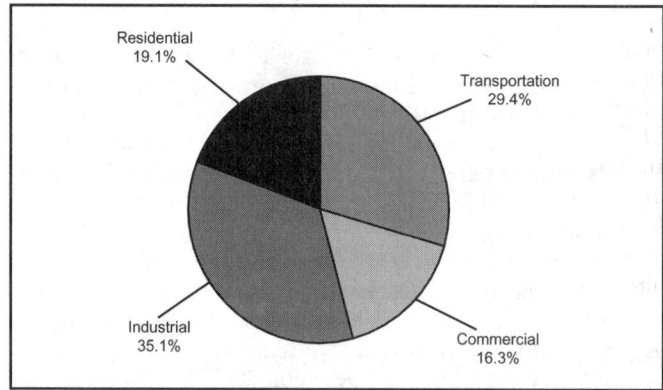

Table MT-15. Energy Consumption, Expenditures, and Prices, Selected Years 1960–2001

(Dollars, Btu [British Thermal Unit], percent distribution.)

Item	1960	1965	1970	1975	1980	1985	1990	1995	2000	2001
Total Consumption (Billion Btu)	227 594	259 004	322 786	345 477	360 491	370 206	350 089	384 822	407 621	365 571
Consumption per capita (million Btu)	337.2	366.9	464.8	461.7	458.2	450.2	438.1	443.1	451.8	403.5
Consumption by Sector (Percent Distribution)										
Residential	16.4	16.2	15.9	17.3	17.1	18.3	17.7	17.1	17.3	19.1
Commercial	11.5	11.4	11.5	12.8	11.7	18.6	14.9	13.9	15.1	16.3
Industrial	46.5	50.1	51.5	46.2	46.6	41.1	44.1	43.4	41.6	35.1
Transportation	25.6	22.3	21.1	23.8	24.7	22.0	23.4	25.6	26.0	29.4
Consumption by Source (Billion Btu)										
Coal	3 999	5 537	12 023	18 630	60 228	99 055	168 852	175 306	176 783	184 287
Natural gas	57 638	70 795	90 601	81 190	61 453	47 312	44 377	59 571	69 589	66 482
Petroleum	107 103	110 841	126 134	154 554	163 629	151 704	142 344	155 528	165 204	167 984
Nuclear electric power	0	0	0	0	0	0	0	0	0	0
Hydroelectric power[1]	62 415	87 692	91 769	105 784	103 522	106 294	111 476	110 811	98 167	67 285
Wood and waste	7 520	7 813	6 627	6 223	11 089	13 970	11 572	16 565	15 756	13 173
Other	-2	-3	-4	-6	-7	238	287	126	274	284
Net interstate flow of electricity/losses[2]	-11 079	-23 672	-4 365	-20 898	-39 422	-48 366	-128 819	-133 086	-118 152	-133 926
Total Expenditures (Thousands of Dollars)	. . .	. . .	334 400	658 300	1 409 400	1 741 100	1 684 500	1 983 700	2 544 000	2 483 500
Expenditures per capita (dollars)	. . .	. . .	482	880	1 792	2 117	2 108	2 284	2 820	2 741
Prices by Sector (Dollars Per Million Btu)										
Total	. . .	. . .	1.56	2.78	6.03	7.39	7.67	7.84	9.71	10.23
Residential	. . .	. . .	1.86	2.72	5.35	8.22	8.86	9.52	10.93	12.06
Commercial	. . .	. . .	1.51	2.39	5.12	8.21	8.38	9.58	10.47	12.43
Industrial	. . .	. . .	0.82	1.80	3.72	5.70	5.21	4.99	6.40	6.54
Transportation	. . .	. . .	2.34	4.02	8.92	8.44	9.36	9.56	12.21	11.65

[1]A negative number in this row results from pumped storage for which, overall, more electricity is expended than created to provide electricity during peak demand periods.
[2]Net interstate flow of electricity is the difference between the amount of energy in the electricity sold within a state (including associated losses) and the energy input at the electric utilities within the state. A positive number indicates that more electricity (including associated losses) came into the state than went out of the state during the year; conversely, a negative number indicates that more electricity (including associated losses) went out of the state than came into the state.
. . . = Not available.

Table MT-16. State Taxes, Fiscal 2004

(Dollars, percent distribution.)

Item	Thousands of dollars	Percent distribution	Dollars per capita	
			State	U.S.
TOTAL TAXES	1 625 692	100.0	1 753.7	2 024.8
Property Taxes	183 937	11.3	198.4	38.9
Sales and Gross Receipts	437 051	26.9	471.5	1 003.4
Selective sales taxes	437 051	26.9	471.5	326.4
Alcoholic beverages	20 570	1.3	22.2	15.7
Amusements	50 496	3.1	54.5	17.0
Insurance premiums	61 063	3.8	65.9	47.0
Motor fuels	197 605	12.2	213.2	114.6
Public utilities	28 169	1.7	30.4	39.2
Tobacco products	45 209	2.8	48.8	42.0
Other selective sales	33 842	2.1	36.5	49.8
Licenses	233 372	14.4	251.8	134.9
Hunting and fishing	37 208	2.3	40.1	4.2
Motor vehicle	144 651	8.9	156.0	59.4
Occupation and business, not elsewhere classified	37 855	2.3	40.8	37.1
Other Taxes	771 332	47.4	832.1	847.6
Individual income	605 582	37.3	653.3	673.6
Corporation net income	67 723	4.2	73.1	105.1
Death and gift	11 431	0.7	12.3	19.6
Severance	83 503	5.1	90.1	21.5

GOVERNMENT FINANCE

State revenues and expenditures per person were above the national average in 2003. Montana's expenditures per person were the 15th highest in the nation. Spending on health, highways, and natural resources was much higher than average, while spending on public welfare and hospitals was below average. Taxes per person amounted to $1,754 in fiscal year 2004, ranking 37th in the nation. Individual income taxes were the largest source of revenue, but remained lower than the national average. Montana's property taxes were the 6th highest of the 37 states with such taxes. The state's per capita debt was also above the national average.

Per Capita State Taxes, Fiscal 2004

Table MT-17. State Government Finances, 2003

(Dollars, percent distribution.)

Item	Millions of dollars	Percent distribution	Dollars per capita	
			State	U.S.
GENERAL REVENUE	3 967 788	100.0	4 322.2	3 832.6
Intergovernmental revenue	1 582 665	39.9	1 724.0	1 246.0
Taxes	1 487 019	37.5	1 619.8	1 891.6
General sales	0	0.0	0.0	636.0
Selective sales	385 840	9.7	420.3	307.4
License taxes	207 449	5.2	226.0	123.6
Individual income tax	535 830	13.5	583.7	626.8
Corporate income tax	44 137	1.1	48.1	97.8
Other taxes	313 763	7.9	341.8	99.9
Current charges	428 806	10.8	467.1	366.5
Miscellaneous general revenue	469 298	11.8	511.2	328.6
GENERAL EXPENDITURE	3 917 125	100.0	4 267.0	4 010.5
Intergovernmental expenditure	938 000	23.9	1 021.8	1 316.9
Direct expenditure	2 979 125	76.1	3 245.2	2 693.6
Expenditure by Function				
Education	1 372 442	35.0	1 495.0	1 416.4
Public welfare	663 613	16.9	722.9	1 083.3
Hospitals	42 815	1.1	46.6	132.3
Health	262 645	6.7	286.1	173.0
Highways	495 515	12.6	539.8	295.4
Police protection	45 678	1.2	49.8	38.4
Correction	103 384	2.6	112.6	135.0
Natural resources	187 761	4.8	204.5	64.0
Parks and recreation	6 319	0.2	6.9	20.1
Government administration	240 176	6.1	261.6	151.3
Interest on general debt	125 218	3.2	136.4	107.8
Other and unallocable	371 559	9.5	404.8	393.4
DEBT AT END OF FISCAL YEAR	2 879 317	X	3 136.5	2 404.7
CASH AND SECURITY HOLDINGS	9 802 395	X	10 678.0	8 938.4

X = Not applicable.

Table MT-18. Education Indicators, 2000–2004

(Percent, number.)

Item	State	U.S.
Total Population 25 Years and Over (Thousands), 2004	623	186 877
Educational Attainment, 2004		
Percent high school graduate or more	91.9	85.2
Percent college graduate or more	25.5	27.7
Elementary and Secondary Schools, 2002–2003		
Total students	149 995	48 202 324
Percent of students eligible for free or reduced-price lunch ..	33.7	40.6
Percent of students who were English language learners	4.5	7.8
Total schools	865	92 330
Student/teacher ratio	14.4	15.9
Per student expenditures	7 496	8 041
Dropouts, Grades 9–12, 2000–2001 (Percent)	3.9	. . .
Higher Education, 2002–2003		
Total enrollment	45 286	17 035 027
Bachelor's degrees awarded	5 238	1 348 503
Percent women	53.8	57.5

. . . = Not available.

Educational Attainment, 2004

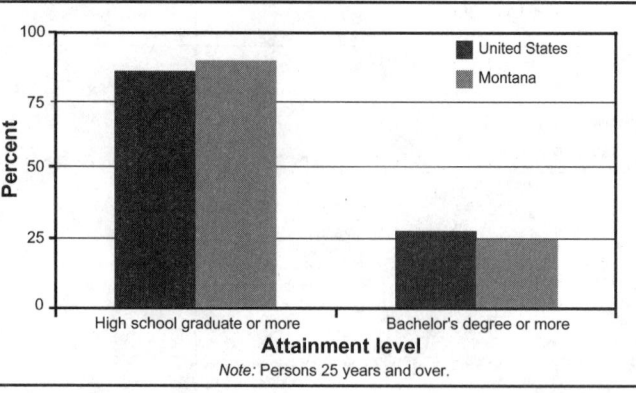

Attainment level

Note: Persons 25 years and over.

EDUCATION

In 2004, 91.9 percent of Montana's residents age 25 years and over held high school diplomas. Only Minnesota had a higher proportion of high school graduates. Montana ranked 26th in the nation for college attainment, with 25.5 percent of its population age 25 years and over holding bachelor's degrees or more. The state's per student expenditures of $7,496 were below the U.S. average of $8,041. The student/teacher ratio was also lower than the national average, partly due to the state's smaller proportion of school-age population. Montana's dropout rate of 3.9 percent was about average among the 46 states reporting such data.

VOTER PARTICIPATION

Montana ranked much higher than the national average for voter turnout for both the 2000 and 2004 elections. In 2004, the state had the sixth highest voter participation rate in the nation. More than 71 percent of eligible female voters in Montana turned out for the 2004 election. This was an increase of more than 7 percentage points from this group's turnout rate in 2000. The male turnout rate increased 8 percentage points from the 2000 to the 2004 election. Montana voted overwhelmingly Republican. In 2000, 58.4 percent cast their ballots for the Republican presidential candidate; in 2004, 59.1 percent voted similarly.

Table MT-19. Reported Voting and Registration, November 2000 and November 2004

(Numbers in thousands, percent.)

Characteristic	Total population 18 years and over	Total citizen		Total registered		Total voted	
		Number	Percent	Number	Percent	Number	Percent
NOVEMBER 2000							
Total	658	650	98.9	461	70.0	409	62.2
Male	329	327	99.4	224	68.0	198	60.1
Female	329	323	98.3	237	72.1	212	64.3
NOVEMBER 2004							
Total	690	687	99.6	519	75.1	482	69.9
Male	339	338	99.8	252	74.5	231	68.1
Female	352	350	99.4	266	75.7	252	71.6
Race and Hispanic Origin							
White alone	647	646	99.8	493	76.1	461	71.1
Non-Hispanic White alone	637	636	99.8	486	76.3	456	71.5
Asian alone	3	1	B	-	B	-	B
Hispanic or Latino[1]	12	12	B	6	B	5	B
White alone or in combination	657	655	99.8	498	75.9	465	70.8
Non-Hispanic White alone or in combination	646	645	99.8	492	76.1	460	71.2
Asian alone or in combination	4	2	B	-	B	-	B
Age							
18 to 24 years	90	90	B	52	B	41	B
25 to 44 years	222	220	99.3	152	68.6	139	62.8
45 to 64 years	254	254	100.0	207	81.6	198	77.8
65 to 74 years	61	61	B	53	B	53	B
75 years and over	63	62	B	54	B	52	B

[1]May be of any race.
- = Represents zero or rounds to zero.
B = Base is too small to show derived measure.

At a Glance:

- In 2004, Nebraska's population was over 1.7 million. Like many of its neighbors, the state had below average population growth from 2001 to 2004.

- The state lost nearly 24,000 residents to other states from 2001 to 2004, but an above average birth rate helped prevent a net population loss.

- Nearly 86 percent of Nebraska's population was non-Hispanic White. This was the 14th highest proportion of this racial group in the nation. More than 4 percent of the population was Black and 7 percent was Hispanic (of any race).

- Median household income was just below the national average, ranking 24th in the country. Nebraska's poverty rate of 9.4 percent was well below the U.S. average.

- In 2004, the state's unemployment rate was 3.8 percent, the sixth lowest in the nation.

- More than 91 percent of the state's residents age 25 years and over held high school diplomas, the fourth highest proportion in the nation.

- Nebraska ranked fourth in the nation for the value of its agricultural sales.

Table NE-1. Population by Sex and Age, 1990, 2000, and 2004

(Number, percent.)

Sex and age	1990	2000	2004	Percent distribution, 2004	Average annual percent change, 2000–2004
Total Population	1 578 385	1 711 263	1 747 214	X	0.5
Percent of total U.S. population	0.6	0.6	0.6	X	X
Sex					
Male	769 439	843 351	863 628	49.4	0.6
Female	808 946	867 912	883 586	50.6	0.4
Age					
Under 5 years	119 606	117 048	122 049	7.0	0.1
5 to 17 years	309 406	333 194	312 517	17.9	0.1
18 years and over	284 398	1 261 021	1 312 648	75.1	1.0
18 to 24 years	1 149 373	174 425	190 767	10.9	1.4
25 to 44 years	155 887	487 107	473 637	27.1	-0.2
45 to 64 years	486 020	367 294	416 441	23.8	2.8
65 years and over	223 068	232 195	231 803	13.3	0.3
85 years and over	29 202	33 953	35 910	2.1	1.6
Median age (years)	32.9	35.3	35.9	X	X

X = Not applicable.

Average Annual Rate of Population Growth, 1980–2004

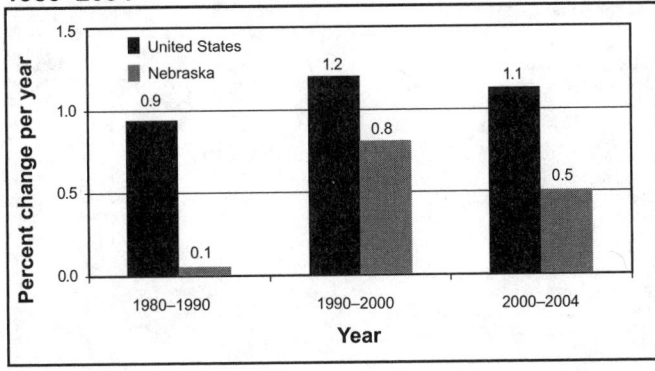

POPULATION

Nebraska's population increased 2.1 percent from 2000 to 2004, which was well below the national growth rate of 4.3 percent. Despite a net loss of population to other states, Nebraska gained nearly 19,000 new residents from other countries. The largest concentration of population was in the city of Omaha. The state's proportion of school-age residents was close to the U.S. average. However, Nebraska had the 16th highest proportion of population age 65 years and over. Having fewer working-age residents contributed to the state's low unemployment rate. Nebraska had the 17th highest proportion of American Indian residents in the nation.

Table NE-2. Population by Race and Hispanic Origin, 1990, 2000, and 2004

(Number, percent.)

Race and Hispanic origin	1990	2000	2004
Total Population	1 578 385	1 711 263	1 747 214
Non-Hispanic (Percent)			
One race[1]			
White	92.5	87.5	85.7
Black	3.6	4.0	4.1
American Indian, Alaska Native[2]	0.8	0.8	0.8
Asian and Pacific Islander[2]	0.8	1.3	1.5
Other race[2]	1.0	. . .	. . .
Two or more races	. . .	0.9	1.0
Hispanic or Latino[3] (Percent)	2.3	5.5	6.9

[1]Individuals could report only one race in the 1990 census and could report one or more races on the 2000 census. Data on race in 2000 and 2004 are not comparable to 1990.
[2]Data for 1990 include people of Hispanic or Latino origin.
[3]May be of any race.
. . . = Not available.

Minority Population as a Percent of Total Population, 2004

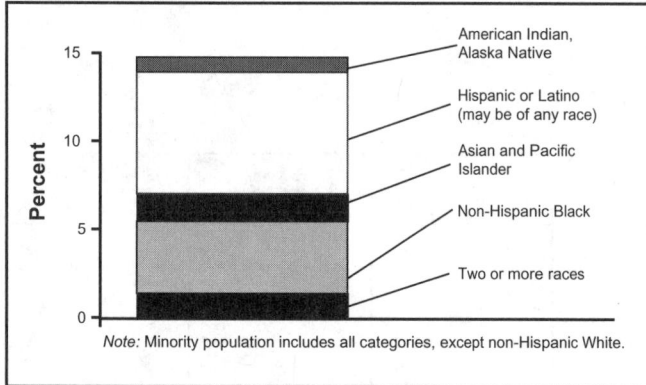

Note: Minority population includes all categories, except non-Hispanic White.

Age-Adjusted Death Rates, Average 2000–2002

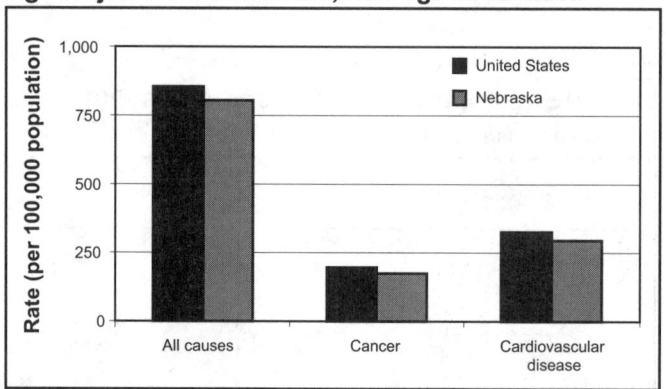

HEALTH

Just 11.4 percent of Nebraska's residents lacked health insurance, well below the U.S. proportion of 15.7 percent. The state's infant mortality rate was close to the national average, and its age-adjusted death rate was slightly below average.

Table NE-3. Health Characteristics, 2000–2004

(Number, rate, percent.)

Item	State	U.S.
Births, 2003–2004		
Number of births	25 917	4 089 950
Birth rate (per 1,000 population)	14.9	14.1
Teenage birth rate (per 1,000 women age 15–19 years)	36.0	41.6
Mortality Rates, Average 2000–2002		
Infant mortality rate (per 1,000 live births)	7.0	6.9
Age-adjusted mortality rate (per 100,000 population)		
All races	799.9	853.3
Non-Hispanic White	787.3	843.1
Black	1 112.3	1 097.7
American Indian, Alaska Native	1 199.8	687.0
Asian and Pacific Islander	439.7	486.0
Hispanic or Latino[1]	554.0	642.7
Health Insurance, 2004		
Percent of all persons without health insurance	11.4	15.7
Percent of children without health insurance	6.0	11.2
Percent of low-income children without health insurance	4.6	7.1

[1]May be of any race.

Table NE-4. Leading Causes of Death, Average 2000–2002

(Number, rate per 100,000 population.)

Cause	Number of deaths	Age-adjusted death rates	
		State	U.S.
ALL CAUSES	15 301	799.9	853.3
Leading Causes			
Major cardiovascular diseases	5 738	291.1	326.5
Cancer	3 401	185.5	196.0
Chronic lower respiratory diseases	885	46.8	43.7
Unintentional injuries	678	37.1	35.7
Diabetes (underlying cause)	401	21.3	25.2
Influenza and pneumonia	382	18.8	22.7
Alzheimer's disease	414	20.0	19.0
Motor vehicle accidents	283	16.1	15.0
Nephritis, nephrotic syndrome, and nephrosis ..	273	14.0	13.8
Septicemia	132	7.1	11.4
Suicides	194	11.3	10.7
Firearm-related	149	8.6	10.3
Cirrhosis	108	6.2	9.5
Drug-induced	63	3.7	7.9
Alcohol-induced	87	5.1	6.9
Homicides	53	3.1	6.0
Falls	149	7.5	5.2
HIV	26	1.6	5.0
Viral hepatitis	19	1.1	2.0
Anemias	26	1.3	1.6
Drownings	18	1.0	1.3
Fire deaths	17	0.9	1.2

Note: The rates are age-adjusted to the U.S. 2000 standard population.

Table NE-5. Households and Housing Characteristics, 1990, 2000, and 2004

(Number, percent, and dollars.)

Characteristic	1990	2000	2004	Average annual percent change, 2000–2004
Total Households	602 363	666 184	687 456	0.8
Family households	415 427	443 411	449 933	0.4
Married-couple family	350 514	360 996	366 636	0.4
Other family	64 913	82 415	83 297	0.3
Male householder, no wife present	14 738	22 072	24 694	2.8
Female householder, no husband present	50 175	60 343	58 603	-0.7
Nonfamily households	186 936	222 773	237 523	1.6
Householder living alone	159 671	183 550	194 328	1.4
Householder not living alone	27 265	39 223	43 195	2.4
Housing Characteristics				
Average size	2.54	2.49	2.47	X
Housing units	660 621	722 668	757 743	1.2
Occupied housing units	602 363	666 184	687 456	0.8
Owner-occupied	400 394	449 317	470 233	1.1
Renter-occupied	201 969	216 867	217 223	0.0
Median gross rent of renter-occupied housing units (dollars)	348	491	547	2.7
Median value of owner-occupied housing units (dollars)	50 000	88 000	106 656	4.9

X = Not applicable.

Median Housing Value and Median Rent, 2004

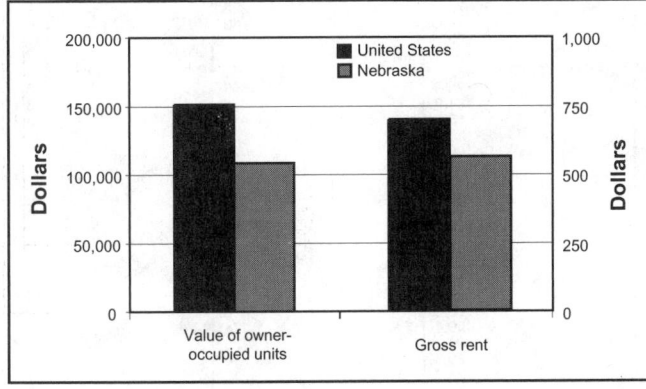

Median Household Income, 1984–2004 (2004 Dollars)

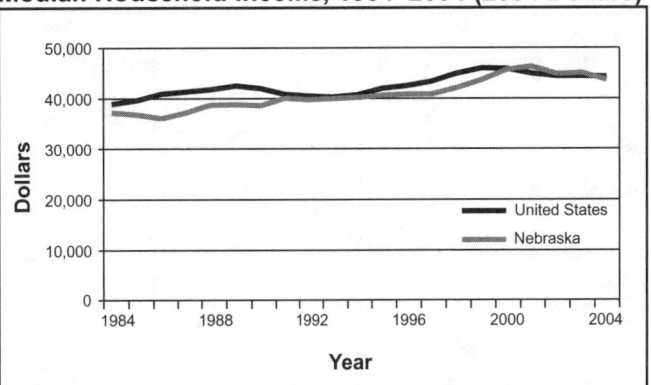

Table NE-6. Household Income and Poverty Status, 1980–2004

(2004 CPI-U-RS adjusted dollars, rate.)

Year	State		U.S.	
	Median household income (2004 dollars)	Poverty rate	Median household income (2004 dollars)	Poverty rate
2004	43 761	9.4	44 389	12.7
2003	45 156	9.8	44 482	12.5
2002	44 953	10.6	44 546	12.1
2001	46 538	9.4	45 062	11.7
2000	45 795	8.6	46 058	11.3
1999	43 782	11.0	46 129	11.9
1998	42 142	12.3	45 003	12.7
1997	40 716	9.8	43 430	13.3
1996	40 772	10.2	42 544	13.7
1995	40 531	9.6	41 943	13.8
1994	40 085	8.8	40 677	14.5
1993	39 917	10.3	40 217	15.1
1992	39 646	10.6	40 422	14.8
1991	39 965	9.5	40 746	14.2
1990	38 514	10.3	41 963	13.5
1989	38 718	12.8	42 524	12.8
1988	38 601	10.3	41 771	13.0
1987	37 000	11.9	41 322	13.4
1986	35 801	13.6	40 939	13.6
1985	36 500	14.8	39 545	14.0
1984	37 021	13.3	38 782	14.4
1983	. . .	15.2	. . .	15.2
1982	. . .	13.6	. . .	15.0
1981	. . .	14.0	. . .	14.0
1980	. . .	13.0	. . .	13.0

. . . = Not available.

Table NE-7. Employment Status by Demographic Group, 2004

(Numbers in thousands, rate.)

Characteristic	Civilian noninstitutional population	Civilian labor force		Employed	Unemployment rate
		Number	Participation rate		
SEX AND AGE					
Total	1 331	990	74.4	953	3.8
16 to 19 years	100	64	63.9	56	12.6
20 to 24 years	133	110	82.3	102	6.7
25 to 34 years	218	196	89.5	189	3.4
35 to 44 years	249	226	90.6	218	3.3
45 to 54 years	264	235	88.8	231	1.7
55 to 64 years	159	120	76.0	117	2.5
65 years and over	207	40	19.5	39	2.2
Men	649	524	80.7	504	3.7
16 to 19 years	51	32	63.6	28	13.1
20 to 24 years	68	58	86.4	55	6.3
25 to 34 years	110	105	94.9	101	3.8
35 to 44 years	123	118	95.4	114	3.1
45 to 54 years	134	124	92.6	122	1.3
55 to 64 years	77	63	80.9	61	2.5
65 years and over	86	24	27.9	23	2.9
Women	682	467	68.5	449	3.8
16 to 19 years	49	32	64.3	28	12.0
20 to 24 years	65	51	78.1	47	7.2
25 to 34 years	108	91	84.1	88	3.1
35 to 44 years	126	108	85.8	104	3.5
45 to 54 years	131	111	84.9	108	2.1
55 to 64 years	81	58	71.2	57	2.4
MARITAL STATUS					
Married men, spouse present	387	319	82.5	313	2.1
Married women, spouse present	399	287	72.0	282	1.7
Women who maintain families	57	43	75.0	40	6.4
RACE, HISPANIC ORIGIN, AND SEX					
White	1 222	914	74.8	885	3.2
Men	597	485	81.3	470	3.1
Women	625	428	68.6	414	3.3
Black	48	32	66.9	29	11.5
Hispanic or Latino[1]	79	62	78.5	58	7.3
Men	43	36	84.5	34	5.9
Women	36	26	71.4	24	9.3
RACE, HISPANIC ORIGIN, AND AGE					
White					
16 to 19 years	85	56	66.3	51	10.2
20 to 24 years	120	100	83.6	95	5.3
25 to 34 years	198	179	90.4	174	2.8
35 to 44 years	226	205	90.7	199	2.8
45 to 54 years	245	220	89.8	216	1.7
55 to 64 years	148	113	76.7	110	2.4
65 years and over	200	40	19.9	39	2.2

Note: Data in Table 7 are from the Current Population Survey (CPS) and do not match Bureau of Labor Statistics estimates in Table 8. See notes and definitions for more details.

[1]May be of any race.

Table NE-8. Employment Status, 1990–2004

(Numbers in thousands, rate.)

Year	Civilian labor force	Employed	Unemployed	Unemployment rate
2004	985 340	947 882	37 458	3.8
2003	975 639	936 736	38 903	4.0
2002	959 363	923 620	35 743	3.7
2001	956 879	926 926	29 953	3.1
2000	952 057	925 898	26 159	2.7
1999	942 189	916 270	25 919	2.8
1998	938 106	914 644	23 462	2.5
1997	926 814	904 492	22 322	2.4
1996	921 521	896 132	25 389	2.8
1995	906 351	882 603	23 748	2.6
1994	885 932	862 659	23 273	2.6
1993	861 406	837 361	24 045	2.8
1992	841 928	817 915	24 013	2.9
1991	832 215	810 181	22 034	2.6
1990	816 703	797 799	18 904	2.3

Note: Population age 16 years and over.

Unemployment Rate, 1980–2004

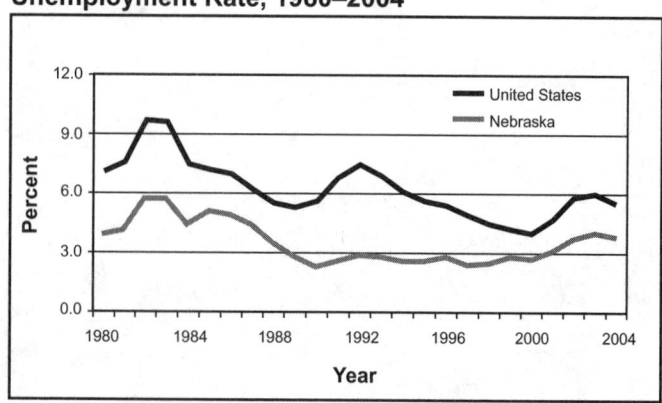

Table NE-9. Employment and Average Wages by Industry, 2001–2004

(Estimates are based on the 2002 North American Industry Classification System [NAICS].)

Industry	2001	2002	2003	2004	Annual average percent change, 2001–2004
	Number of jobs				
TOTAL EMPLOYMENT BY PLACE OF WORK	1 182 375	1 179 899	1 187 214	1 201 762	0.5
Farm Employment	62 362	61 639	60 192	59 882	-1.3
Nonfarm Employment	1 120 013	1 118 260	1 127 022	1 141 880	0.6
Private employment	955 853	950 474	957 757	971 512	0.5
Forestry, fishing, hunting, and other[1]	8 609	8 520	7 762	8 079	-2.1
Mining	2 346	2 172	2 484	2 520	2.4
Utilities	1 599	1 800	2 035	2 008	7.9
Construction	65 442	65 067	67 971	69 549	2.0
Manufacturing	113 892	109 291	105 378	103 810	-3.0
Durable goods manufacturing	55 363	51 732	48 871	48 545	-4.3
Nondurable goods manufacturing	58 529	57 559	56 507	55 265	-1.9
Wholesale trade	45 625	44 740	44 051	43 998	-1.2
Retail trade	139 535	136 241	136 830	138 048	-0.4
Transportation and warehousing	52 085	53 840	54 717	55 803	2.3
Information	25 384	24 198	23 609	23 373	-2.7
Finance and insurance	65 427	65 198	66 039	66 658	0.6
Real estate and rental and leasing	26 038	26 418	27 566	28 989	3.6
Professional and technical services	51 565	51 264	51 740	53 748	1.4
Management of companies and enterprises	13 350	14 484	14 026	14 837	3.6
Administrative and waste services	62 465	59 565	58 483	59 093	-1.8
Educational services	19 242	20 059	20 719	21 429	3.7
Health care and social assistance	112 387	114 838	118 824	121 142	2.5
Arts, entertainment, and recreation	18 084	18 569	18 757	19 016	1.7
Accommodation and food services	70 928	70 134	71 166	72 570	0.8
Other services, except public administration	61 850	64 076	65 600	66 842	2.6
Government and government enterprises	164 160	167 786	169 265	170 368	1.2
	Dollars				
AVERAGE WAGES AND SALARIES BY PLACE OF WORK	28 456	29 466	30 436	31 570	3.5
Farm Earnings	27 631	26 939	29 237	32 039	5.1
Nonfarm Earnings	28 468	29 500	30 452	31 564	3.5
Private earnings	28 212	29 172	30 051	31 171	3.4
Forestry, fishing, hunting, and other[1]	12 796	14 308	15 254	13 891	2.8
Mining	34 749	35 542	37 943	40 616	5.3
Utilities	59 275	63 799	69 761	77 992	9.6
Construction	32 186	33 160	33 524	34 149	2.0
Manufacturing	32 464	33 407	34 641	35 764	3.3
Durable goods manufacturing	33 756	34 796	36 320	38 145	4.2
Nondurable goods manufacturing	31 252	32 170	33 205	33 698	2.5
Wholesale trade	36 502	37 680	38 676	41 149	4.1
Retail trade	18 293	19 081	19 545	20 269	3.5
Transportation and warehousing	41 933	41 271	41 027	41 778	-0.1
Information	40 561	41 490	43 485	44 581	3.2
Finance and insurance	39 660	41 292	42 976	44 828	4.2
Real estate and rental and leasing	23 762	24 596	25 196	26 337	3.5
Professional and technical services	42 224	42 771	44 645	45 745	2.7
Management of companies and enterprises	51 928	53 935	56 217	58 132	3.8
Administrative and waste services	20 749	22 698	22 558	23 777	4.6
Educational services	22 304	22 486	23 626	24 747	3.5
Health care and social assistance	29 462	30 405	31 609	32 943	3.8
Arts, entertainment, and recreation	13 723	13 691	14 042	14 415	1.7
Accommodation and food services	10 614	10 765	10 932	11 284	2.1
Other services, except public administration	18 795	19 358	20 480	21 301	4.3
Government and government enterprises	29 684	31 007	32 289	33 364	4.0

Note: Average wages and salaries are a calculation by the editors of wage and salary disbursements divided by full- and part-time wage and salary employment. Data may not add to total or may appear as zero due to rounding.

1 "Other" consists of the number of jobs held by U.S. residents employed by international organizations and foreign embassies and consulates in the United States.

LABOR MARKET

Along with a low unemployment rate, Nebraska had an above average labor force participation rate, suggesting a relatively robust labor market. Total wage and salary employment growth was low over the 2001–2004 period. Manufacturing employment declined from 2001 to 2004. Jobs in nondurable goods industries, which tend to be less cyclically sensitive, experienced less of a drop than jobs in durable goods production. Average wages and salaries were well below the national averages across all major industry groupings, despite having an above average overall rate of growth.

Employment by Industry, 2004

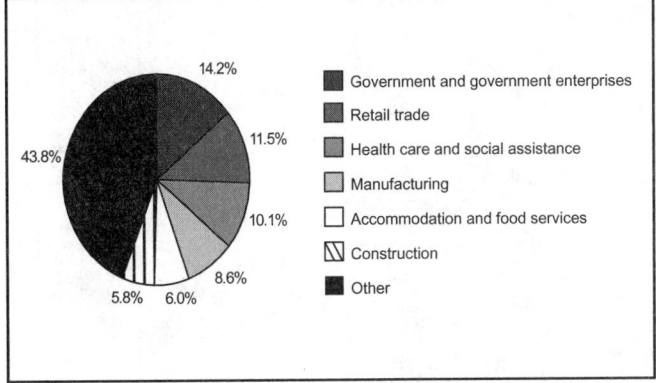

- Government and government enterprises — 14.2%
- Retail trade — 11.5%
- Health care and social assistance — 10.1%
- Manufacturing — 8.6%
- Accommodation and food services — 6.0%
- Construction — 5.8%
- Other — 43.8%

Table NE-10. Personal Income by Major Source, Selected Years 1980–2004

(Millions of dollars, except where noted.)

Item	1980	1990	2000	2001	2002	2003	2004	Average annual percent change, 2000–2004
Earnings by Place of Work	11 151	21 918	36 120	37 672	38 522	41 489	43 878	5.0
Wage and salary disbursements	8 483	14 979	26 540	27 316	28 087	29 112	30 431	3.5
Supplements to wages and salaries	1 496	3 125	5 317	5 612	6 361	6 832	7 344	8.4
Proprietors' income[1]	1 172	3 814	4 264	4 744	4 073	5 545	6 103	9.4
Farm proprietors' income	-105	1 933	609	792	291	1 563	1 741	30.0
Nonfarm proprietors' income	1 277	1 881	3 654	3 951	3 782	3 981	4 362	4.5
(-) Contributions for government social insurance[2]	1 051	2 372	4 031	4 200	4 379	4 549	4 738	4.1
(+) Adjustment for residence[3]	-215	-382	-825	-833	-887	-927	-963	X
(=) Net Earnings by Place of Residence	9 885	19 164	31 263	32 639	33 255	36 013	38 176	5.1
(+) Dividends, interest, and rent[4]	2 824	5 915	9 991	9 998	10 023	10 036	10 474	1.2
(+) Personal current transfer receipts	1 693	3 365	6 075	6 666	7 069	7 378	7 743	6.3
Personal income	14 403	28 444	47 329	49 303	50 347	53 427	56 393	4.5
Farm income	14 313	26 275	46 386	48 124	49 702	51 463	54 219	4.0
Nonfarm income	90	2 169	943	1 180	644	1 964	2 175	23.2
Per Capita Personal Income (Dollars)[5]	9 160	17 983	27 625	28 684	29 162	30 750	32 276	4.0

Note: Data may not add to total or may appear as zero due to rounding.

[1]Proprietors' income includes the inventory valuation adjustment and the capital consumption adjustment.
[2]Contributions for government social insurance are included in earnings by type and industry, but they are excluded from personal income.
[3]The adjustment for residence is the net inflow of the earnings of interarea commuters.
[4]Rental income of persons includes the capital consumption adjustment.
[5]Per capita personal income is total personal income divided by total midyear population.
 X = Not applicable.

Per Capita Personal Income, 1980–2004 (Current Dollars)

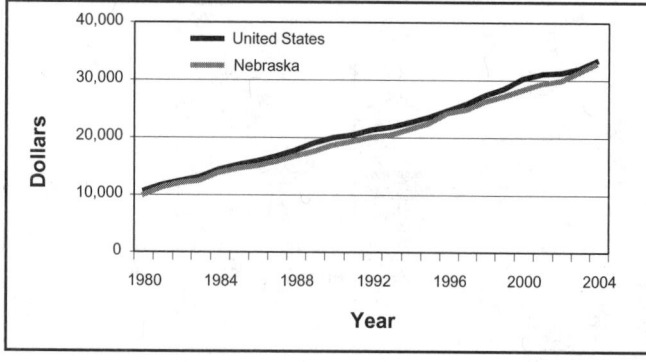

ECONOMIC ACTIVITY

Nebraska's gross state product (GSP) ranked 37th in the nation, but its growth rate from 2003 to 2004 was just 1.5 percent, which was the second lowest growth rate in the country. This was partly due to declines in agricultural-related industries and construction, as well as to the only moderate recoveries in manufacturing and many service-providing industries. Housing price appreciation was well below the national average, and the median value of owner-occupied housing ranked 39th in the country at $106,696. Housing activity played an insignificant role in the state's economic activity during this period.

Table NE-11. Real Gross State Product, 1997–2004

(Millions of chained 2000 dollars, percent.)

Industry	1997	1998	1999	2000	2001	2002	2003	2004	Average annual percent change, 2001–2004
GROSS STATE PRODUCT	52 781	53 814	54 594	55 727	56 158	57 599	60 672	61 596	3.1
As a percent of U.S. gross product	0.6	0.6	0.6	0.6	0.6	0.6	0.6	0.6	X
Private Industries	44 755	45 696	46 631	47 831	48 000	49 280	52 195	52 882	3.3
Agriculture, forestry, fishing, and hunting	2 515	2 296	1 887	1 962	2 182	2 232	3 614	2 625	6.4
Mining	40	41	55	44	41	43	45	44	2.4
Utilities	646	654	604	619	687	672	756	805	5.4
Construction	2 373	2 521	2 614	2 532	2 394	2 348	2 407	2 424	0.4
Manufacturing	6 514	6 654	6 976	7 550	7 345	7 522	7 843	8 047	3.1
As a percent of gross state product	12.3	12.4	12.8	13.5	13.1	13.1	12.9	13.1	X
Wholesale trade	3 411	3 691	3 823	3 831	4 054	4 235	4 118	4 306	2.0
Retail trade	3 463	3 506	3 673	3 673	3 990	4 229	4 530	4 772	6.1
Transportation and warehousing	3 497	3 740	3 904	3 914	4 048	4 211	4 251	4 349	2.4
Information	1 984	1 741	1 947	1 839	1 896	2 063	2 282	2 511	9.8
Finance and insurance	4 329	4 644	4 715	5 184	4 519	4 624	4 984	5 193	4.7
Real estate and rental and leasing	4 653	4 760	4 970	5 024	5 246	5 196	5 067	5 234	-0.1
Services	11 170	11 389	11 477	11 660	11 597	11 937	12 317	12 762	3.2
As a percent of gross state product	21.2	21.2	21.0	20.9	20.7	20.7	20.3	20.7	X
Professional and technical services	2 132	2 215	2 242	2 352	2 339	2 430	2 563	2 692	4.8
Management of companies and enterprises	1 020	967	928	1 028	850	943	926	953	3.9
Administrative and waste services	1 790	1 770	1 661	1 454	1 469	1 501	1 488	1 515	1.0
Educational services	395	385	390	408	423	401	400	401	-1.8
Health care and social assistance	3 159	3 328	3 523	3 671	3 752	3 884	4 067	4 183	3.7
Arts, entertainment, and recreation	323	320	317	310	336	347	358	357	2.0
Accommodation and food services	1 042	1 084	1 140	1 188	1 173	1 180	1 210	1 258	2.4
Other services, except public administration	1 309	1 320	1 276	1 249	1 255	1 251	1 305	1 403	3.8
Government	8 041	8 130	7 965	7 896	8 158	8 319	8 489	8 717	2.2
As a percent of gross state product	15.2	15.1	14.6	14.2	14.5	14.4	14.0	14.2	X

X = Not applicable.

Table NE-12. Government Transfer Payments, Selected Years 1980–2004

(Millions of dollars, percent.)

Item	1980	1990	2000	2001	2002	2003	2004	Average annual percent change, 2000–2004
CURRENT TRANSFER PAYMENTS TO INDIVIDUALS	1 582	3 159	5 694	6 245	6 693	7 033	7 397	6.8
Retirement and Disability Insurance Benefits	930	1 787	2 696	2 833	2 953	3 033	3 150	4.0
Old-age, survivors, and disability insurance (OASDI) benefits	856	1 666	2 534	2 665	2 775	2 850	2 963	4.0
Railroad retirement and disability benefits	72	116	153	159	167	172	175	3.3
Workers' compensation	2	5	7	8	8	8	8	3.6
Other government retirement and disability insurance benefits	*	1	1	1	2	4	4	34.6
Medical Benefits	351	924	2 259	2 582	2 740	2 885	3 071	8.0
Medicare benefits	238	555	1 162	1 282	1 367	1 435	1 562	7.7
Public assistance medical care benefits	107	346	1 074	1 268	1 329	1 411	1 463	8.0
Military medical insurance benefits	6	23	23	32	45	39	46	18.9
Income Maintenance Benefits	117	230	427	449	527	602	665	11.7
Supplemental Security Income (SSI) benefits	24	48	92	96	99	102	106	3.8
Family assistance	43	61	49	49	61	67	72	10.2
Food stamps	27	61	60	65	76	94	112	16.8
Other income maintenance benefits	24	61	227	239	291	339	374	13.3
Unemployment Insurance Compensation	54	34	54	88	148	170	133	25.2
Veterans' Benefits	97	120	189	204	231	252	280	10.4
Federal Education and Training Assistance	31	62	65	82	90	87	93	9.4
Other Payments to Individuals	1	2	4	7	3	3	5	4.2

Note: See notes and definitions for more details. Data may not add to total or may appear as zero due to rounding.

* = Less than $500,000.

EXPORTS

Nebraska was not a major force in the goods export market. The value of its exports was $2.3 billion in 2004, ranking 42nd in the nation. From 2001 to 2004, exports dropped by 14.3 percent. This was primarily due to a decline in processed food exports, which fell from over $1 billion in 2001 to $563 million in 2004. Growth in machinery manufactures and chemical manufactures exports could not offset this loss. Crop production and transportation exports, which were the state's fourth and fifth leading exports, respectively, also declined during this period. Exports to Japan fell considerably from 2001 to 2004, mostly due to the drop in processed food exports.

Leading Exports, 2004

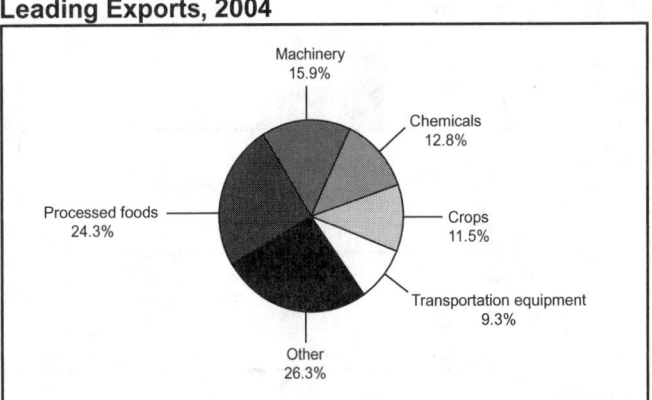

Table NE-13. Exports of Goods by Leading Products and Destinations, 2001–2004

(Millions of dollars, percent, rank based on 2004 dollar values.)

Product and market	2001	2002	2003	2004	Percent share of total, 2004	Average annual percent change, 2001–2004
Total Goods						
Total	2 702	2 528	2 724	2 316	100.0	-5.0
Manufactures	2 266	2 226	2 249	1 934	83.5	-5.1
Agriculture and livestock	406	271	429	345	14.9	-5.3
Other commodities	29	31	46	37	1.6	8.0
Five Leading Exports (NAICS Code)						
Processed foods (311)	1 070	1 053	955	563	24.3	-19.3
Machinery manufactures (333)	269	284	294	368	15.9	11.0
Chemical manufactures (325)	166	217	249	295	12.8	21.3
Crop production (111)	334	257	294	266	11.5	-7.3
Transportation equipment (336)	259	211	235	215	9.3	-5.9
Five Leading Markets	2 493	2 338	2 514	2 119	91.5	-5.3
Canada	572	561	701	690	29.8	6.4
Mexico	449	465	472	418	18.1	-2.3
Japan	621	429	358	193	8.4	-32.2
China	69	76	84	88	3.8	8.5
Netherlands	101	74	99	86	3.7	-5.1

Table NE-14. Agriculture, 1997 and 2002

(Number, acres, and dollars.)

Item	1997	2002
Number of farms	54 539	49 355
Land in farms (acres)	45 853 656	45 903 116
Farm Size		
Average size of farm (acres)	841	930
Farms by size (percent distribution)		
Fewer than 50 acres	15.5	14.8
50 to 499 acres	44.2	43.5
500 acres or more	40.3	41.6
Market Value of Land and Equipment (Dollars)		
Land and buildings average value per farm	550 705	723 863
Average value per acre	658	776
Machinery and equipment average value per farm	83 079	111 776
Value of Sales (Thousands of Dollars)		
Agricultural products sold	9 937 248	9 703 657
Crops	3 881 119	3 388 265
Livestock, poultry, and their products	6 056 130	6 315 392
Average per farm (dollars)	182 204	196 609
Value of sales (percent distribution)		
Less than $10,000	25.1	30.5
$10,000 to $99,999	40.9	37.5
$100,000 or more	34.0	32.0
Government Payments		
Payments (thousands of dollars)	326 937	347 517
Percent of farms receiving government payments	72.0	64.9
Farm operators whose principal occupation is farming (percent) ...	67.8	73.0

AGRICULTURE

Nebraska was a large farming state. In 2002, the value of its agricultural sales ranked fourth in the nation. About 35 percent of these sales came from crops, while the remaining proportion was from livestock, poultry, and their products. The state's chief products were cattle, hogs, and wheat. Nearly one-third of farms in Nebraska had sales of $100,000 or more, and 73 percent of all farm operators regarded farming as their principal occupation. Less than 15 percent of farms in the state spanned fewer than 50 acres, which was among the smallest proportions of farms of this size in the nation.

ENERGY

In 2001, energy expenditures per person in Nebraska were relatively high, ranking 18th in the nation. Per capita consumption was also above average, though down slightly from 2000. Energy prices were below the U.S. average. In 2001, coal overtook petroleum to become the state's leading source of energy.

Energy Consumption by Source, 2001

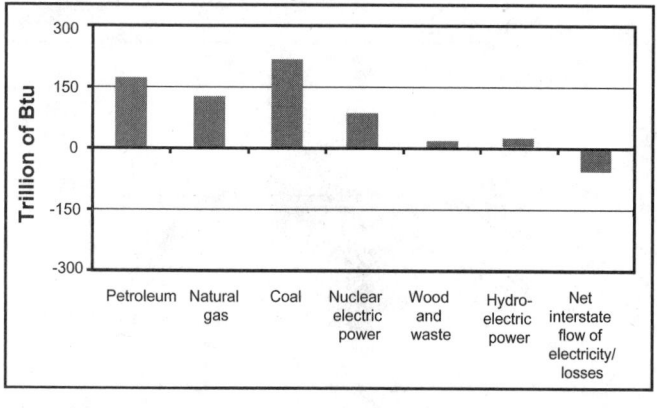

Energy Consumption by Sector, 2001

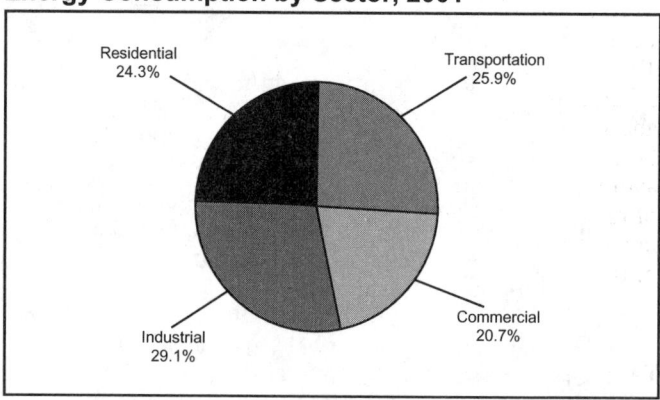

Table NE-15. Energy Consumption, Expenditures, and Prices, Selected Years 1960–2001

(Dollars, Btu [British Thermal Unit], percent distribution.)

Item	1960	1965	1970	1975	1980	1985	1990	1995	2000	2001
Total Consumption (Billion Btu)	308 314	349 227	487 332	525 733	508 749	500 267	522 291	586 745	630 929	627 081
Consumption per capita (million Btu)	218.5	237.4	328.1	340.7	324.1	315.7	330.9	358.8	368.7	364.8
Consumption by Sector (Percent Distribution)										
Residential	25.4	27.3	25.9	23.6	24.9	25.6	24.2	23.5	23.1	24.3
Commercial	13.9	15.2	19.4	17.3	18.3	22.0	21.5	21.3	20.8	20.7
Industrial	30.2	28.2	26.1	30.6	29.1	24.5	25.6	27.3	28.8	29.1
Transportation	30.6	29.2	28.6	28.5	27.7	27.9	28.6	27.9	27.4	25.9
Consumption by Source (Billion Btu)										
Coal	20 010	20 815	29 716	32 886	93 942	115 478	142 024	179 482	206 940	227 495
Natural gas	140 430	164 719	224 114	217 521	159 491	123 864	109 174	133 690	127 599	124 057
Petroleum	136 476	141 138	192 052	208 101	189 582	189 218	206 232	212 188	224 468	217 783
Nuclear electric power	0	-64	0	65 153	63 082	43 911	79 485	78 650	89 988	91 170
Hydroelectric power[1]	10 317	11 663	14 383	12 624	13 875	15 051	11 859	14 706	15 309	11 437
Wood and waste	3 108	1 901	1 567	2 775	7 069	6 656	4 273	4 508	4 896	4 376
Other	0	0	0	0	0	0	89	199	335	394
Net interstate flow of electricity/losses[2]	-2 026	9 055	25 500	-13 327	-18 292	6 088	-30 844	-36 677	-38 606	-49 631
Total Expenditures (Thousands of Dollars)	...	...	666 900	1 202 200	2 454 300	2 929 000	3 130 100	3 333 500	4 310 700	4 412 300
Expenditures per capita (dollars)	...	...	449	779	1 563	1 848	1 983	2 039	2 519	2 567
Prices by Sector (Dollars Per Million Btu)										
Total	...	...	1.72	2.89	6.51	8.01	8.35	7.97	9.90	10.25
Residential	...	...	1.84	2.95	5.79	8.74	9.34	9.69	11.26	12.36
Commercial	...	...	1.37	2.36	5.00	8.27	8.86	8.84	10.85	11.91
Industrial	...	...	0.88	1.77	4.50	6.21	6.15	5.24	6.95	7.24
Transportation	...	...	2.51	4.15	9.20	8.72	9.13	8.74	11.07	10.84

[1]A negative number in this row results from pumped storage for which, overall, more electricity is expended than created to provide electricity during peak demand periods.
[2]Net interstate flow of electricity is the difference between the amount of energy in the electricity sold within a state (including associated losses) and the energy input at the electric utilities within the state. A positive number indicates that more electricity (including associated losses) came into the state than went out of the state during the year; conversely, a negative number indicates that more electricity (including associated losses) went out of the state than came into the state.
... = Not available.

Table NE-16. State Taxes, Fiscal 2004

(Dollars, percent distribution.)

Item	Thousands of dollars	Percent distribution	Dollars per capita	
			State	U.S.
TOTAL TAXES	3 639 811	100.0	2 083.5	2 024.8
Property Taxes	2 336	0.1	1.3	38.9
Sales and Gross Receipts	1 988 078	54.6	1 138.0	1 003.4
General sales and gross receipts	1 524 591	41.9	872.7	677.0
Selective sales taxes	463 487	12.7	265.3	326.4
Alcoholic beverages	23 159	0.6	13.3	15.7
Insurance premiums	38 460	1.1	22.0	47.0
Motor fuels	302 899	8.3	173.4	114.6
Tobacco products	71 220	2.0	40.8	42.0
Other selective sales	18 210	0.5	10.4	49.8
Licenses	201 921	5.5	115.6	134.9
Motor vehicle	88 780	2.4	50.8	59.4
Occupation and business, not elsewhere classified	63 980	1.8	36.6	37.1
Other licenses	20 165	0.6	11.5	2.6
Other Taxes	1 447 476	39.8	828.6	847.6
Individual income	1 242 603	34.1	711.3	673.6
Corporation net income	167 429	4.6	95.8	105.1
Death and gift	26 423	0.7	15.1	19.6

GOVERNMENT FINANCE

State revenues per person were slightly above the national average in 2003, while expenditures per person were below average. However, Nebraska was among just 12 states where expenditures did not exceed revenue. The state's debt per person of $1,229 was among the seven lowest in the nation. Expenditures on hospitals and health were above average. In fiscal year 2004, total taxes per person amounted to $2,083, which was above average and ranked 18th in the nation. The chief sources of revenue were sales receipts and individual income taxes. The state's property taxes were among the lowest of the 37 states with such taxes.

Per Capita State Taxes, Fiscal 2004

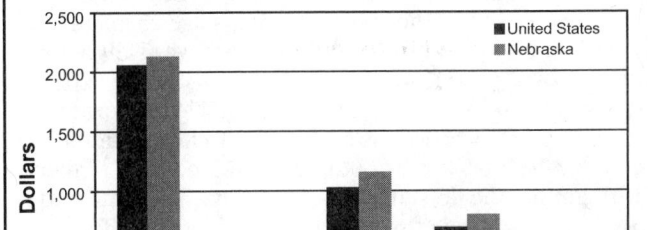

Table NE-17. State Government Finances, 2003

(Dollars, percent distribution.)

Item	Millions of dollars	Percent distribution	Dollars per capita	
			State	U.S.
GENERAL REVENUE	6 749 800	100.0	3 885.9	3 832.6
Intergovernmental revenue	2 139 810	31.7	1 231.9	1 246.0
Taxes	3 347 700	49.6	1 927.3	1 891.6
General sales	1 426 914	21.1	821.5	636.0
Selective sales	459 812	6.8	264.7	307.4
License taxes	199 584	3.0	114.9	123.6
Individual income tax	1 122 893	16.6	646.5	626.8
Corporate income tax	111 597	1.7	64.2	97.8
Other taxes	26 900	0.4	15.5	99.9
Current charges	623 152	9.2	358.8	366.5
Miscellaneous general revenue	639 138	9.5	368.0	328.6
GENERAL EXPENDITURE	6 493 783	100.0	3 738.5	4 010.5
Intergovernmental expenditure	1 784 749	27.5	1 027.5	1 316.9
Direct expenditure	4 709 034	72.5	2 711.0	2 693.6
Expenditure by Function				
Education	2 233 120	34.4	1 285.6	1 416.4
Public welfare	1 809 391	27.9	1 041.7	1 083.3
Hospitals	191 539	2.9	110.3	132.3
Health	391 150	6.0	225.2	173.0
Highways	557 869	8.6	321.2	295.4
Police protection	69 707	1.1	40.1	38.4
Correction	182 378	2.8	105.0	135.0
Natural resources	164 263	2.5	94.6	64.0
Parks and recreation	32 494	0.5	18.7	20.1
Government administration	184 353	2.8	106.1	151.3
Interest on general debt	107 132	1.6	61.7	107.8
Other and unallocable	570 387	8.8	328.4	393.4
DEBT AT END OF FISCAL YEAR	2 135 502	X	1 229.4	2 404.7
CASH AND SECURITY HOLDINGS	8 609 609	X	4 956.6	8 938.4

X = Not applicable.

Table NE-18. Education Indicators, 2000–2004

(Percent, number.)

Item	State	U.S.
Total Population 25 Years and Over (Thousands), 2004	1 103	186 877
Educational Attainment, 2004		
Percent high school graduate or more	91.3	85.2
Percent college graduate or more	24.8	27.7
Elementary and Secondary Schools, 2002–2003		
Total students	285 402	48 202 324
Percent of students eligible for free or reduced-price lunch ..	33.9	40.6
Percent of students who were English language learners	5.5	7.8
Total schools	1 250	92 330
Student/teacher ratio	13.6	15.9
Per student expenditures	8 074	8 041
Dropouts, Grades 9–12, 2000–2001 (Percent)	4.2	...
Higher Education, 2002–2003		
Total enrollment	117 621	17 035 027
Bachelor's degrees awarded	11 025	1 348 503
Percent women	55.3	57.5

. . . = Not available.

Educational Attainment, 2004

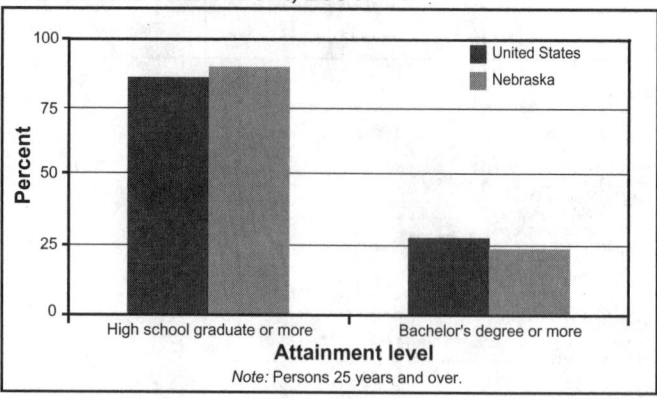

Note: Persons 25 years and over.

EDUCATION

Nebraska was one of eight states that had a high school attainment rate of more than 90 percent in 2004. Less than 25 percent of the state's residents age 25 years and over had graduated from college, which was well below the national proportion. Nebraska's per student expenditures of $8,074 were slightly above the U.S. average. The student/teacher ratio was among the 15 lowest in the country. Nebraska's dropout rate of 4.2 percent ranked 18th among the 46 states reporting data. The state had a lower than average proportion of students qualifying for free or reduced-price lunch.

VOTER PARTICIPATION

Voter turnout in Nebraska for both the 2000 and 2004 elections was just above the national average. More than 61 percent of eligible voters participated in the 2004 election. Among eligible voters age 45 years and over, the participation rate exceeded 70 percent. Hispanics had the lowest voter turnout in the state, with just over 16 percent of eligible voters casting ballots in 2004. The majority of the state's voters cast ballots for the Republican presidential candidate in both elections. In 2000, 62.2 percent of residents voted for the Republican presidential ticket; in 2004, this proportion increased to 65.9 percent.

Table NE-19. Reported Voting and Registration, November 2000 and November 2004

(Numbers in thousands, percent.)

Characteristic	Total population 18 years and over	Total citizen		Total registered		Total voted	
		Number	Percent	Number	Percent	Number	Percent
NOVEMBER 2000							
Total	1 205	1 176	97.6	865	71.8	710	58.9
Male	579	567	97.9	394	68.1	331	57.2
Female	626	609	97.3	471	75.2	379	60.5
NOVEMBER 2004							
Total	1 294	1 215	93.9	918	70.9	793	61.3
Male	628	585	93.2	431	68.7	367	58.4
Female	667	630	94.5	487	73.0	426	64.0
Race and Hispanic Origin							
White alone	1 181	1 127	95.4	865	73.3	755	63.9
Non-Hispanic White alone	1 089	1 084	99.6	845	77.6	741	68.1
Black alone	51	47	B	31	B	21	B
Asian alone	16	7	B	2	B	2	B
Hispanic or Latino[1]	119	56	47.2	27	23.0	19	16.2
White alone or in combination	1 198	1 143	95.4	877	73.2	762	63.6
Non-Hispanic White alone or in combination	1 103	1 099	99.6	854	77.4	748	67.8
Black alone or in combination	53	49	B	31	B	21	B
Asian alone or in combination	16	7	B	2	B	2	B
Age							
18 to 24 years	203	186	91.8	102	50.3	78	38.6
25 to 44 years	457	412	90.2	300	65.6	252	55.1
45 to 64 years	420	405	96.5	336	79.9	301	71.8
65 to 74 years	107	106	98.4	87	80.7	79	73.9
75 years and over	107	106	99.1	94	87.4	82	76.6

[1]May be of any race.
B = Base is too small to show derived measure.

At a Glance:

- Nevada's population grew nearly 17 percent from 2000 to 2004, making it the fastest-growing state in the nation. In 2004, its population was over 2.3 million, ranking 35th in the country.

- In 2004, 61.2 percent of the state's population was non-Hispanic White. Nearly 23 percent of residents were Hispanic (of any race), which was the fifth highest proportion of this ethnic group in the nation.

- Median household income was well above the national average, ranking 17th in the country. Nevada's poverty rate of 10.9 percent was below average.

- The state's unemployment rate was 4.3 percent in 2004 (the 11th lowest in the nation). Real gross state product ranked 31st in the country, but had the highest rate of growth in the nation from 2000 to 2004.

- For persons age 25 years and over, Nevada ranked 33rd for proportion of high school graduates and 35th for proportion of college graduates.

- More than 18 percent of the state's residents lacked health insurance in 2004.

Table NV-1. Population by Sex and Age, 1990, 2000, and 2004

(Number, percent.)

Sex and age	1990	2000	2004	Percent distribution, 2004	Average annual percent change, 2000–2004
Total Population	1 201 833	1 998 257	2 334 771	X	4.0
Percent of total U.S. population	0.5	0.7	0.8	X	X
Sex					
Male	611 880	1 018 051	1 188 803	50.9	4.0
Female	589 953	980 206	1 145 968	49.1	4.0
Age					
Under 5 years	92 217	145 817	169 018	7.2	4.2
5 to 17 years	204 731	365 982	434 578	18.6	5.5
18 years and over	244 017	1 486 458	1 731 175	74.1	4.8
18 to 24 years	904 885	179 708	209 851	9.0	4.0
25 to 44 years	118 945	628 572	710 299	30.4	3.9
45 to 64 years	414 292	459 249	548 946	23.5	6.0
65 years and over	127 631	218 929	262 079	11.2	5.3
85 years and over	7 463	16 989	24 000	1.0	8.8
Median age (years)	33.2	35.0	35.0	X	X

X = Not applicable.

Average Annual Rate of Population Growth, 1980–2004

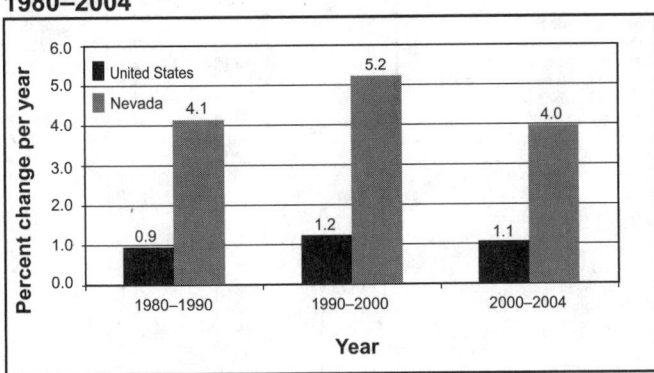

POPULATION

Nevada has seen an enormous increase in its population in recent years. The population increased by 16.9 percent between 2000 and 2004, and has been among the fastest growing in the nation for many years. A substantial share of this increase has been caused by immigration from other states and from foreign countries. During the 2000–2004 period, over 216,000 people moved into Nevada from other states, along with nearly 56,000 new residents from other countries. The state had the ninth highest proportion of population under 18 years old, and the sixth lowest proportion of population 65 years old and over. Las Vegas was the largest metropolitan area.

Table NV-2. Population by Race and Hispanic Origin, 1990, 2000, and 2004

(Number, percent.)

Race and Hispanic origin	1990	2000	2004
Total Population	1 201 833	1 998 257	2 334 771
Non-Hispanic (Percent)			
One race[1]			
White	78.7	65.7	61.2
Black	6.4	6.7	7.0
American Indian, Alaska Native[2]	1.6	1.1	1.0
Asian and Pacific Islander[2]	3.2	4.9	5.8
Other race[2]	4.4	. . .	. . .
Two or more races	. . .	1.9	2.1
Hispanic or Latino[3] (Percent)	10.4	19.7	22.8

[1]Individuals could report only one race in the 1990 census and could report one or more races on the 2000 census. Data on race in 2000 and 2004 are not comparable to 1990.
[2]Data for 1990 include people of Hispanic or Latino origin.
[3]May be of any race.
. . . = Not available.

Minority Population as a Percent of Total Population, 2004

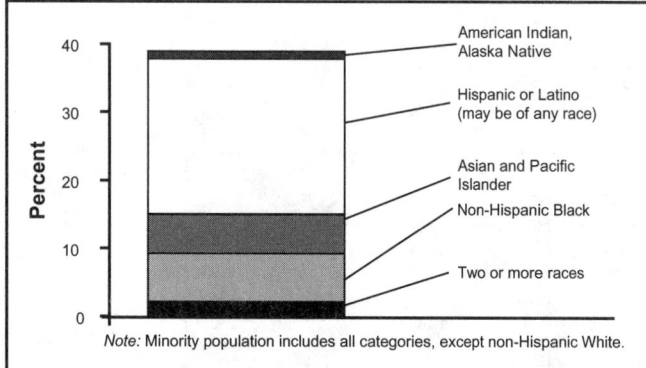

Note: Minority population includes all categories, except non-Hispanic White.

Age-Adjusted Death Rates, Average 2000–2002

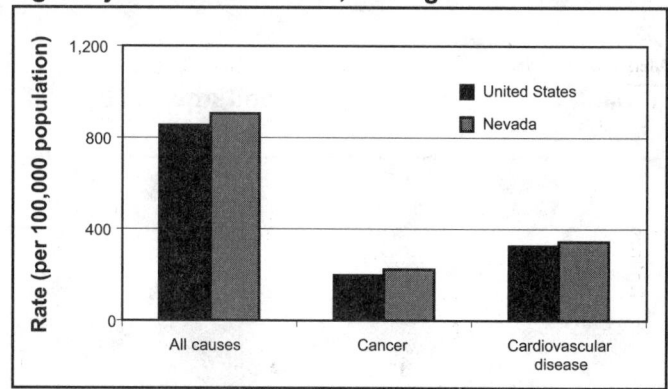

HEALTH

The relatively low rate of health insurance coverage partly reflected the state's large service-providing economy and a high number of jobs that were less likely to provide workers with health insurance. Nevada's birth rate was the ninth highest in the nation.

Table NV-3. Health Characteristics, 2000–2004

(Number, rate, percent.)

Item	State	U.S.
Births, 2003–2004		
Number of births	33 647	4 089 950
Birth rate (per 1,000 population)	15.0	14.1
Teenage birth rate (per 1,000 women age 15–19 years)	53.0	41.6
Mortality Rates, Average 2000–2002		
Infant mortality rate (per 1,000 live births)	6.0	6.9
Age-adjusted mortality rate (per 100,000 population)		
All races	915.9	853.1
Non-Hispanic White	952.3	843.1
Black	1 082.4	1 097.7
American Indian, Alaska Native	706.0	687.0
Asian and Pacific Islander	560.8	486.0
Hispanic or Latino[1]	532.5	642.7
Health Insurance, 2004		
Percent of all persons without health insurance	18.5	15.7
Percent of children without health insurance	16.1	11.2
Percent of low-income children without health insurance	10.1	7.1

[1]May be of any race.

Table NV-4. Leading Causes of Death, Average 2000–2002

(Number, rate per 100,000 population.)

Cause	Number of deaths	Age-adjusted death rates	
		State	U.S.
ALL CAUSES	16 158	915.9	853.3
Leading Causes			
Major cardiovascular diseases	5 595	330.2	326.5
Cancer	3 838	206.4	196.0
Chronic lower respiratory diseases	1 100	64.0	43.7
Unintentional injuries	776	39.2	35.7
Diabetes (underlying cause)	314	16.8	25.2
Influenza and pneumonia	347	21.7	22.7
Alzheimer's disease	220	15.3	19.0
Motor vehicle accidents	331	16.2	15.0
Nephritis, nephrotic syndrome, and nephrosis ..	359	20.9	13.8
Septicemia	351	20.3	11.4
Suicides	403	19.6	10.7
Firearm-related	352	17.1	10.3
Cirrhosis	285	13.8	9.5
Drug-induced	294	14.0	7.9
Alcohol-induced	224	10.6	6.9
Homicides	161	7.7	6.0
Falls	79	4.7	5.2
HIV	80	3.8	5.0
Viral hepatitis	45	2.2	2.0
Anemias	30	1.8	1.6
Drownings	26	1.3	1.3
Fire deaths	16	0.8	1.2

Note: The rates are age-adjusted to the U.S. 2000 standard population.

Table NV-5. Households and Housing Characteristics, 1990, 2000, and 2004

(Number, percent, and dollars.)

Characteristic	1990	2000	2004	Average annual percent change, 2000–2004
Total Households	466 297	751 165	871 915	3.8
Family households	307 400	498 333	560 310	3.0
Married-couple family	239 573	373 201	415 049	2.7
Other family	67 827	125 132	145 261	3.8
Male householder, no wife present	20 318	41 650	35 899	-3.6
Female householder, no husband present	47 509	83 482	109 362	7.0
Nonfamily households	158 897	252 832	311 605	5.4
Householder living alone	119 627	186 745	244 846	7.0
Householder not living alone	39 270	66 087	66 759	0.3
Housing Characteristics				
Average size	2.53	2.62	2.64	X
Housing units	518 858	827 457	976 446	4.2
Occupied housing units	466 297	751 165	871 915	3.8
Owner-occupied	255 388	457 247	533 755	3.9
Renter-occupied	210 909	293 918	338 160	3.6
Median gross rent of renter-occupied housing units (dollars) ...	509	699	787	3.0
Median value of owner-occupied housing units (dollars)	95 300	142 000	202 937	9.3

X = Not applicable.

Median Housing Value and Median Rent, 2004

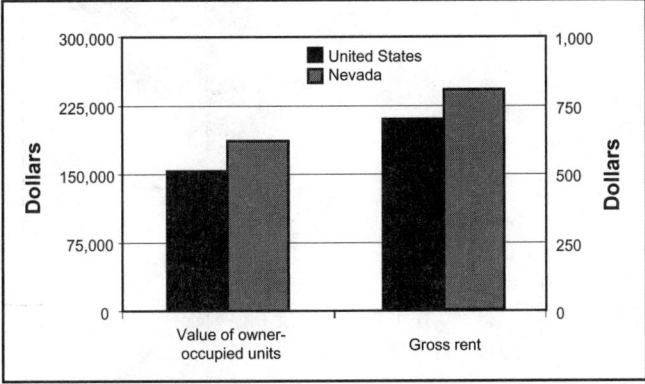

Median Household Income, 1984–2004 (2004 Dollars)

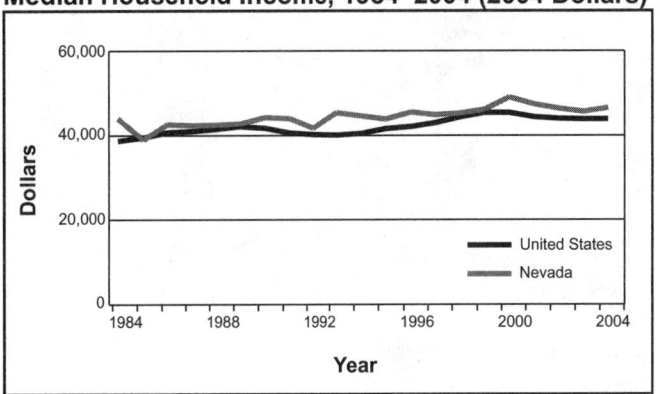

Table NV-6. Household Income and Poverty Status, 1980–2004

(2004 CPI-U-RS adjusted dollars, rate.)

	State		U.S.	
Year	Median household income (2004 dollars)	Poverty rate	Median household income (2004 dollars)	Poverty rate
2004	47 330	10.9	44 389	12.7
2003	46 398	10.9	44 482	12.5
2002	47 224	8.9	44 546	12.1
2001	48 450	7.1	45 062	11.7
2000	50 191	8.8	46 058	11.3
1999	46 996	11.3	46 129	11.9
1998	46 011	10.6	45 003	12.7
1997	45 600	11.0	43 430	13.3
1996	46 198	8.1	42 544	13.7
1995	44 415	11.1	41 943	13.8
1994	45 225	11.1	40 677	14.5
1993	46 104	9.8	40 217	15.1
1992	42 100	14.7	40 422	14.8
1991	44 548	11.4	40 746	14.2
1990	44 878	9.8	41 963	13.5
1989	43 163	10.8	42 524	12.8
1988	42 934	8.6	41 771	13.0
1987	42 741	10.4	41 322	13.4
1986	43 110	8.1	40 939	13.6
1985	38 969	14.4	39 545	14.0
1984	44 597	10.5	38 782	14.4
1983	. . .	9.7	. . .	15.2
1982	. . .	7.8	. . .	15.0
1981	. . .	10.5	. . .	14.0
1980	. . .	8.3	. . .	13.0

. . . = Not available.

Table NV-7. Employment Status by Demographic Group, 2004

(Numbers in thousands, rate.)

Characteristic	Civilian noninstitutional population	Civilian labor force		Employed	Unemployment rate
		Number	Participation rate		
SEX AND AGE					
Total	1 759	1 175	66.8	1 125	4.2
16 to 19 years	120	55	45.8	48	13.0
20 to 24 years	151	116	77.0	108	7.2
25 to 34 years	336	284	84.5	273	3.7
35 to 44 years	351	294	83.8	285	2.8
45 to 54 years	310	253	81.6	246	2.8
55 to 64 years	226	135	59.8	129	4.8
65 years and over	266	38	14.3	37	3.9
Men	886	657	74.2	629	4.2
16 to 19 years	63	29	45.5	24	16.0
20 to 24 years	73	62	84.1	58	6.4
25 to 34 years	175	167	95.5	160	4.1
35 to 44 years	180	169	93.4	165	2.2
45 to 54 years	157	137	87.3	133	2.9
55 to 64 years	108	70	65.5	67	4.9
65 years and over	129	23	17.9	22	5.8
Women	874	518	59.3	496	4.2
16 to 19 years	58	27	46.1	24	9.8
20 to 24 years	77	54	70.2	50	8.2
25 to 34 years	160	116	72.6	113	3.2
35 to 44 years	170	125	73.6	121	3.7
45 to 54 years	153	116	75.7	112	2.7
55 to 64 years	119	65	54.6	62	4.8
MARITAL STATUS					
Married men, spouse present	482	363	75.4	355	2.4
Married women, spouse present	451	263	58.3	255	2.9
Women who maintain families	102	73	71.4	68	6.5
RACE, HISPANIC ORIGIN, AND SEX					
White	1 483	986	66.5	948	3.9
Men	755	562	74.3	540	3.9
Women	728	425	58.4	408	3.8
Black	112	73	64.9	68	6.2
Men	54	38	70.4	36	6.3
Women	58	35	59.8	33	6.1
Asian	99	70	70.8	67	4.7
Men	46	34	75.3	32	7.1
Women	53	36	66.9	35	2.3
Hispanic or Latino[1]	301	220	73.1	211	3.8
Men	162	143	88.2	138	3.6
Women	138	77	55.5	74	4.1
RACE, HISPANIC ORIGIN, AND AGE					
White					
20 to 24 years	125	97	77.4	90	7.4
25 to 34 years	274	231	84.4	223	3.3
35 to 44 years	292	242	82.8	236	2.4
45 to 54 years	266	216	81.4	211	2.6
55 to 64 years	197	119	60.5	114	4.5
65 years and over	229	33	14.6	32	3.6

Note: Data in Table 7 are from the Current Population Survey (CPS) and do not match Bureau of Labor Statistics estimates in Table 8. See notes and definitions for more details.

[1]May be of any race.

Table NV-8. Employment Status, 1990–2004

(Numbers in thousands, rate.)

Year	Civilian labor force	Employed	Unemployed	Unemployment rate
2004	1 177 558	1 126 346	51 212	4.3
2003	1 148 519	1 089 709	58 810	5.1
2002	1 124 629	1 061 900	62 729	5.6
2001	1 102 370	1 043 911	58 459	5.3
2000	1 064 015	1 016 072	47 943	4.5
1999	1 022 584	978 969	43 615	4.3
1998	982 065	938 662	43 403	4.4
1997	937 803	895 258	42 545	4.5
1996	893 556	847 274	46 282	5.2
1995	852 622	805 286	47 336	5.6
1994	814 221	764 451	49 770	6.1
1993	765 898	714 032	51 866	6.8
1992	727 558	677 076	50 482	6.9
1991	693 695	650 324	43 371	6.3
1990	655 896	622 516	33 380	5.1

Unemployment Rate, 1980–2004

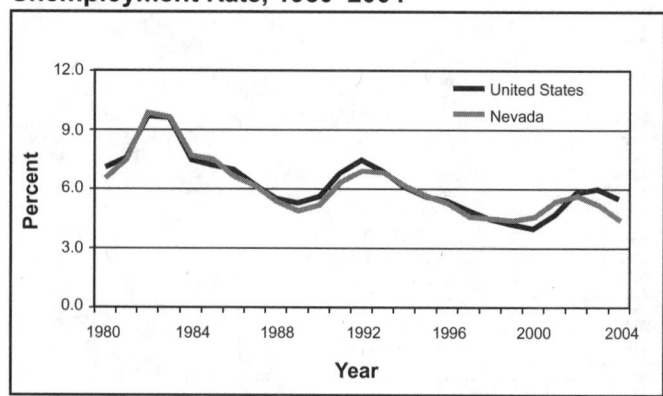

Note: Population age 16 years and over.

Table NV-9. Employment and Average Wages by Industry, 2001–2004

(Estimates are based on the 2002 North American Industry Classification System [NAICS].)

Industry	2001	2002	2003	2004	Annual average percent change, 2001–2004
	Number of jobs				
TOTAL EMPLOYMENT BY PLACE OF WORK	1 288 792	1 303 692	1 353 836	1 430 271	3.5
Farm Employment	5 512	4 986	5 349	5 225	-1.8
Nonfarm Employment	1 283 280	1 298 706	1 348 487	1 425 046	3.6
Private employment	1 147 539	1 157 533	1 202 651	1 274 664	3.6
Forestry, fishing, hunting, and other[1]	1 650	1 839	1 729	1 743	1.8
Mining	11 858	10 825	11 299	12 381	1.4
Utilities	4 621	5 163	5 179	5 243	4.3
Construction	107 640	108 285	117 368	136 527	8.2
Manufacturing	46 643	46 065	47 018	49 435	2.0
Durable goods manufacturing	31 237	31 137	32 109	34 172	3.0
Nondurable goods manufacturing	15 406	14 928	14 909	15 263	-0.3
Wholesale trade	38 269	38 469	37 799	39 026	0.7
Retail trade	137 236	140 058	145 761	153 322	3.8
Transportation and warehousing	42 490	42 191	42 518	44 706	1.7
Information	21 990	19 706	19 023	18 108	-6.3
Finance and insurance	62 252	63 871	66 104	68 483	3.2
Real estate and rental and leasing	59 131	62 993	68 338	72 758	7.2
Professional and technical services	63 994	66 476	70 456	74 089	5.0
Management of companies and enterprises	9 129	9 167	9 384	11 326	7.5
Administrative and waste services	80 825	80 733	86 127	94 712	5.4
Educational services	6 035	6 828	7 479	8 287	11.1
Health care and social assistance	77 185	81 030	84 886	89 587	5.1
Arts, entertainment, and recreation	42 457	43 791	45 215	46 138	2.8
Accommodation and food services	284 409	277 958	283 870	293 234	1.0
Other services, except public administration	49 725	52 085	53 098	55 559	3.8
Government and government enterprises	135 741	141 173	145 836	150 382	3.5
	Dollars				
AVERAGE WAGES AND SALARIES BY PLACE OF WORK ...	33 572	34 514	35 840	37 616	3.9
Farm Earnings	21 564	30 906	22 468	23 046	2.2
Nonfarm Earnings	33 600	34 521	35 869	37 644	3.9
Private earnings	32 869	33 705	34 990	36 778	3.8
Forestry, fishing, hunting, and other[1]	18 366	22 335	22 036	21 984	6.2
Mining	58 696	62 210	62 864	63 308	2.6
Utilities	68 537	70 375	73 808	80 130	5.3
Construction	39 775	40 812	41 745	42 622	2.3
Manufacturing	39 522	39 185	41 522	42 550	2.5
Durable goods manufacturing	42 114	41 279	44 237	45 026	2.3
Nondurable goods manufacturing	34 200	34 742	35 567	36 892	2.6
Wholesale trade	45 927	46 295	47 783	50 761	3.4
Retail trade	25 211	25 649	26 062	27 202	2.6
Transportation and warehousing	31 370	32 510	33 681	35 110	3.8
Information	45 059	45 138	45 995	47 645	1.9
Finance and insurance	46 007	47 130	50 737	53 691	5.3
Real estate and rental and leasing	29 629	30 772	31 721	34 359	5.1
Professional and technical services	52 651	54 173	56 665	57 862	3.2
Management of companies and enterprises	98 753	105 825	123 507	147 783	14.4
Administrative and waste services	23 450	23 959	24 486	25 069	2.3
Educational services	26 610	28 026	28 037	29 519	3.5
Health care and social assistance	37 539	38 709	39 992	41 640	3.5
Arts, entertainment, and recreation	24 483	24 796	26 008	27 457	3.9
Accommodation and food services	26 151	26 945	27 648	28 863	3.3
Other services, except public administration	23 343	23 745	24 371	25 742	3.3
Government and government enterprises	38 734	40 026	41 810	43 684	4.1

Note: Average wages and salaries are a calculation by the editors of wage and salary disbursements divided by full- and part-time wage and salary employment. Data may not add to total or may appear as zero due to rounding.

[1] "Other" consists of the number of jobs held by U.S. residents employed by international organizations and foreign embassies and consulates in the United States.

LABOR MARKET

Nevada's unemployment rate has been slightly below the national average since 2000. This was accompanied by a relatively high labor force participation rate, suggesting that Nevada's labor market has been successful in providing jobs for those seeking work. Wage and salary employment was concentrated in tourism-related sectors (accommodation and food services), retail trade, government, and construction. Unlike most other states, a relatively small proportion of jobs were in manufacturing industries. Employment increased each year between 2001 and 2004, with Nevada's labor market appearing to be largely immune to the 2001 recession. Average wages and salaries for most industries were slightly below the national averages.

Employment by Industry, 2004

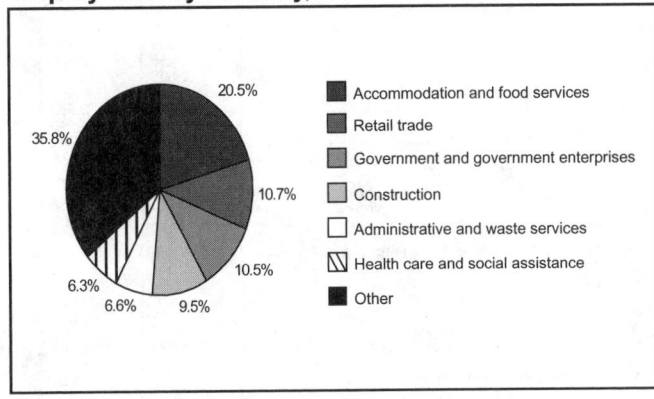

- 20.5% Accommodation and food services
- 35.8%
- 10.7% Retail trade
- 10.5% Government and government enterprises
- 9.5% Construction
- 6.6% Administrative and waste services
- 6.3% Health care and social assistance
- Other

Table NV-10. Personal Income by Major Source, Selected Years 1980–2004

(Millions of dollars, except where noted.)

Item	1980	1990	2000	2001	2002	2003	2004	Average annual percent change, 2000–2004
Earnings by Place of Work	8 022	19 912	47 401	49 487	50 995	55 068	61 538	6.7
Wage and salary disbursements	6 302	15 082	35 138	36 670	37 800	40 631	45 171	6.5
Supplements to wages and salaries	1 112	3 149	6 844	7 331	7 991	8 794	9 992	9.9
Proprietors' income[1]	607	1 680	5 419	5 487	5 205	5 643	6 376	4.1
Farm proprietors' income	31	45	34	39	14	28	39	3.0
Nonfarm proprietors' income	576	1 635	5 384	5 447	5 191	5 615	6 337	4.2
(-) Contributions for government social insurance[2]	775	2 387	4 701	4 988	5 245	5 627	6 180	7.1
(+) Adjustment for residence[3]	-160	-381	-339	-302	-305	-361	-449	X
(=) Net Earnings by Place of Residence	7 087	17 144	42 361	44 198	45 445	49 079	54 909	6.7
(+) Dividends, interest, and rent[4]	1 529	5 085	13 067	13 351	13 545	14 392	15 108	3.7
(+) Personal current transfer receipts	863	2 607	5 999	6 819	7 658	8 160	8 859	10.2
Personal income	9 480	24 837	61 428	64 367	66 649	71 632	78 876	6.4
Farm income	9 424	24 760	61 334	64 270	66 569	71 545	78 780	6.5
Nonfarm income	56	76	94	98	80	87	96	0.5
Per Capita Personal Income (Dollars)[5]	11 700	20 346	30 437	30 721	30 738	31 947	33 783	2.6

Note: Data may not add to total or may appear as zero due to rounding.

[1]Proprietors' income includes the inventory valuation adjustment and the capital consumption adjustment.
[2]Contributions for government social insurance are included in earnings by type and industry, but they are excluded from personal income.
[3]The adjustment for residence is the net inflow of the earnings of interarea commuters.
[4]Rental income of persons includes the capital consumption adjustment.
[5]Per capita personal income is total personal income divided by total midyear population.
X = Not applicable.

Per Capita Personal Income, 1980–2004 (Current Dollars)

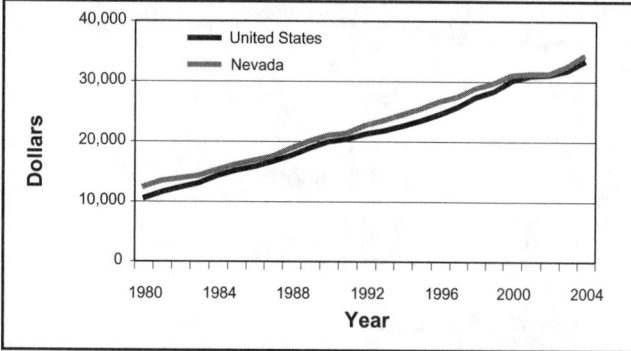

ECONOMIC ACTIVITY

From 2001 to 2004, Nevada's real gross state product (GSP) grew by over 20 percent, more than double the national rate growth of 9.1 percent. The largest contributors to this increase were real estate and related activities, tourism, retail trade, transportation and warehousing, management services, and government. Mining was the only industry that experienced declines from 2001 to 2004. Housing price appreciation over recent years has been among the fastest in the country. In 2004, the median value of owner-occupied housing in the state, totaling nearly $203,000, was the 13th highest in the nation. Housing contributed to the state's employment and economic growth during the period.

Table NV-11. Real Gross State Product, 1997–2004

(Millions of chained 2000 dollars, percent.)

Industry	1997	1998	1999	2000	2001	2002	2003	2004	Average annual percent change, 2001–2004
GROSS STATE PRODUCT	64 480	67 242	71 311	74 797	75 892	78 167	83 603	91 418	6.4
As a percent of U.S. gross product	0.7	0.7	0.8	0.8	0.8	0.8	0.8	0.9	X
Private Industries	57 816	60 140	63 999	67 247	68 207	70 411	75 565	82 915	6.7
Agriculture, forestry, fishing, and hunting	134	167	171	204	188	189	194	163	-4.6
Mining	1 196	1 258	1 308	1 348	1 158	1 127	1 197	1 157	0.0
Utilities	1 308	1 305	1 371	1 385	1 372	1 478	1 614	1 793	9.3
Construction	7 456	7 686	7 488	6 940	6 785	6 796	7 283	8 254	6.8
Manufacturing	2 305	2 531	2 404	2 787	2 756	2 780	3 069	3 323	6.4
As a percent of gross state product	3.6	3.8	3.4	3.7	3.6	3.6	3.7	3.6	X
Wholesale trade	2 617	2 993	3 138	3 194	3 530	3 616	3 547	3 770	2.2
Retail trade	4 641	4 949	5 406	5 783	6 386	6 781	7 479	8 303	9.1
Transportation and warehousing	2 051	2 124	2 296	2 572	2 174	2 434	2 987	3 241	14.2
Information	1 318	1 486	1 862	2 107	2 211	2 165	2 255	2 326	1.7
Finance and insurance	3 397	3 458	4 186	5 459	5 597	5 913	6 855	7 816	11.8
Real estate and rental and leasing	8 456	8 819	9 131	9 254	9 695	10 039	10 329	11 409	5.6
Services	23 110	23 468	25 289	26 214	26 389	27 147	28 849	31 443	6.0
As a percent of gross state product	35.8	34.9	35.5	35.0	34.8	34.7	34.5	34.4	X
Professional and technical services	2 933	3 135	3 260	3 340	3 562	3 806	4 259	4 518	8.2
Management of companies and enterprises	1 085	1 073	1 127	908	1 314	1 313	1 633	2 285	20.3
Administrative and waste services	1 977	2 115	2 338	2 325	2 338	2 391	2 632	2 887	7.3
Educational services	102	114	124	130	138	144	143	156	4.2
Health care and social assistance	2 874	2 927	3 107	3 336	3 584	3 809	4 035	4 305	6.3
Arts, entertainment, and recreation	2 174	2 242	2 177	2 245	2 232	2 167	2 281	2 361	1.9
Accommodation and food services	10 613	10 467	11 751	12 585	11 883	12 210	12 523	13 411	4.1
Other services, except public administration	1 352	1 395	1 405	1 345	1 338	1 307	1 343	1 520	4.3
Government	6 664	7 106	7 312	7 550	7 685	7 759	8 051	8 528	3.5
As a percent of gross state product	10.3	10.6	10.3	10.1	10.1	9.9	9.6	9.3	X

X = Not applicable.

Table NV-12. Government Transfer Payments, Selected Years 1980–2004

(Millions of dollars, percent.)

Item	1980	1990	2000	2001	2002	2003	2004	Average annual percent change, 2000–2004
CURRENT TRANSFER PAYMENTS TO INDIVIDUALS	809	2 460	5 588	6 343	7 223	7 751	8 440	10.9
Retirement and Disability Insurance Benefits	456	1 428	2 684	2 949	3 211	3 443	3 723	8.5
Old-age, survivors, and disability insurance (OASDI) benefits	327	1 051	2 610	2 869	3 123	3 351	3 628	8.6
Railroad retirement and disability benefits	17	34	49	50	52	53	54	2.7
Workers' compensation	111	341	21	23	28	29	29	8.2
Other government retirement and disability insurance benefits	1	3	5	6	8	11	12	26.2
Medical Benefits	187	675	2 044	2 363	2 706	2 941	3 390	13.5
Medicare benefits	121	447	1 327	1 509	1 657	1 797	2 039	11.3
Public assistance medical care benefits	54	193	678	795	967	1 075	1 268	16.9
Military medical insurance benefits	12	35	39	58	82	69	84	21.2
Income Maintenance Benefits	51	145	407	441	548	629	654	12.6
Supplemental Security Income (SSI) benefits	11	33	109	121	133	144	151	8.6
Family assistance	11	28	41	42	59	57	45	2.8
Food stamps	17	44	58	71	100	114	123	20.6
Other income maintenance benefits	12	40	200	207	257	313	335	13.8
Unemployment Insurance Compensation	52	87	197	296	434	390	285	9.6
Veterans' Benefits	52	93	199	221	249	272	307	11.4
Federal Education and Training Assistance	9	28	47	50	56	59	63	8.0
Other Payments to Individuals	2	4	10	22	19	16	18	15.7

Note: See notes and definitions for more details. Data may not add to total or may appear as zero due to rounding.

EXPORTS

As Nevada's economy was largely based around service-providing industries, exports did not play a very significant role in the overall economy. In 2004, the state ranked 40th in the nation for value of exports, which amounted to $2.9 billion. The leading export was primary metal manufactures, which increased from $32 million in 2001 to nearly $1.3 billion in 2004. Transportation equipment exports fell from being the second leading export in 2001 to the sixth in 2004. All of Nevada's other leading exports have had sizable gains in recent years. Switzerland became the state's leading export market in 2003, as a result of its demand for Nevada's primary metal manufactures exports (mainly gold).

Leading Exports, 2004

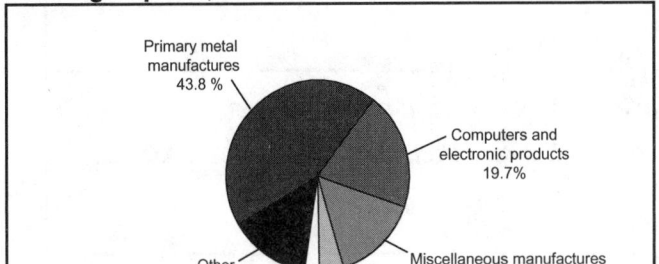

Table NV-13. Exports of Goods by Leading Products and Destinations, 2001–2004

(Millions of dollars, percent, rank based on 2004 dollar values.)

Product and market	2001	2002	2003	2004	Percent share of total, 2004	Average annual percent change, 2001–2004
Total Goods						
Total	1 423	1 177	2 033	2 907	100.0	26.9
Manufactures	1 324	1 098	1 937	2 795	96.2	28.3
Agriculture and livestock	44	41	46	54	1.9	7.0
Other commodities	55	37	49	57	2.0	1.2
Five Leading Exports (NAICS Code)						
Primary metal manufactures (331)	32	27	672	1 275	43.8	242.2
Computers and electronic products (334)	457	413	491	571	19.7	7.7
Miscellaneous manufactures (339)	240	301	366	436	15.0	22.1
Machinery manufactures (333)	82	74	107	129	4.5	16.3
Fabricated metal products (332)	59	51	77	85	2.9	12.9
Five Leading Markets	1 324	1 079	1 889	2 768	95.2	27.9
Switzerland	9	9	658	1 260	43.4	429.3
Canada	581	380	468	583	20.1	0.2
Mexico	125	71	105	118	4.0	-2.0
Japan	85	76	79	101	3.5	5.8
Israel	26	36	50	71	2.5	39.5

Table NV-14. Agriculture, 1997 and 2002

(Number, acres, and dollars.)

Item	1997	2002
Number of farms	3 198	2 989
Land in farms (acres)	6 397 569	6 330 622
Farm Size		
Average size of farm (acres)	2 000	2 118
Farms by size (percent distribution)		
Fewer than 50 acres	43.7	46.7
50 to 499 acres	33.3	29.1
500 acres or more	23.0	24.2
Market Value of Land and Equipment (Dollars)		
Land and buildings average value per farm	794 743	953 619
Average value per acre	398	446
Machinery and equipment average value per farm	65 749	110 619
Value of Sales (Thousands of Dollars)		
Agricultural products sold	358 869	446 989
Crops	153 225	157 730
Livestock, poultry, and their products	205 643	289 259
Average per farm (dollars)	112 217	149 545
Value of sales (percent distribution)		
Less than $10,000	52.4	55.4
$10,000 to $99,999	31.5	25.2
$100,000 or more	16.1	19.4
Government Payments		
Payments (thousands of dollars)	1 343	4 322
Percent of farms receiving government payments	9.6	14.7
Farm operators whose principal occupation is farming (percent)	52.4	58.7

AGRICULTURE

In 2002, Nevada's cash receipts from farming totaled $447 million, which ranked among the five lowest amounts in the nation. Cattle was the chief product, as very little in the way of crops was grown in this largely desert state. More than 55 percent of farms had less than $10,000 in sales. Nearly 47 percent of farms spanned fewer than 50 acres, which was the 15th highest proportion of farms of this size in the country.

ENERGY

Energy expenditures per person were slightly above the national average in 2001. Energy prices in Nevada were the 10th highest in the nation. The state's per capita consumption was well below average, ranking 37th in the nation. Petroleum, coal, and natural gas were the state's main energy sources. The transportation sector was the largest consumer of energy, accounting for almost to 33 percent of total energy used. Nevada was a large exporter of electricity.

Energy Consumption by Source, 2001

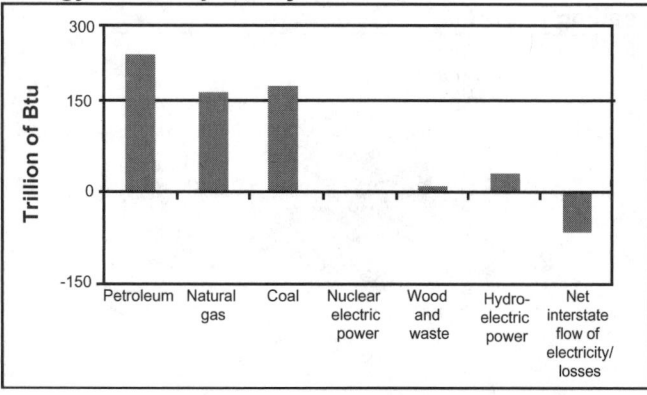

Energy Consumption by Sector, 2001

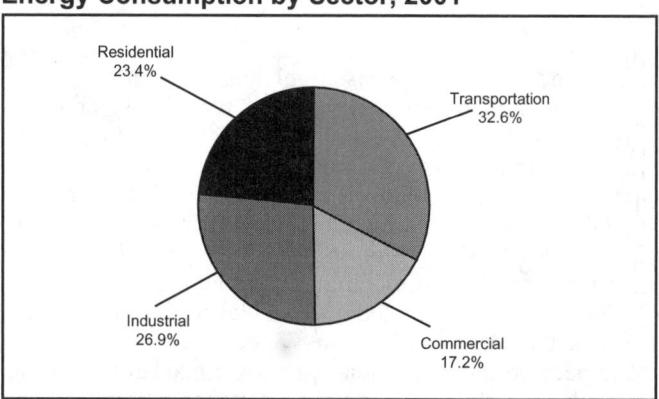

Table NV-15. Energy Consumption, Expenditures, and Prices, Selected Years 1960–2001

(Dollars, Btu [British Thermal Unit], percent distribution.)

Item	1960	1965	1970	1975	1980	1985	1990	1995	2000	2001
Total Consumption (Billion Btu)	91 152	130 310	190 113	238 223	291 603	302 576	399 442	497 439	626 495	629 370
Consumption per capita (million Btu)	319.8	293.5	389.0	384.2	364.3	318.2	332.4	326.0	313.5	300.5
Consumption by Sector (Percent Distribution)										
Residential	15.7	18.9	19.6	20.3	21.4	22.5	21.8	20.5	22.9	23.4
Commercial	11.5	14.8	19.5	21.5	11.7	18.0	17.6	17.4	17.5	17.2
Industrial	26.6	23.4	22.4	19.5	27.1	22.8	27.4	29.6	26.8	26.9
Transportation	46.2	42.9	38.4	38.7	39.8	36.7	33.1	32.4	32.7	32.6
Consumption by Source (Billion Btu)										
Coal	3 962	7 892	17 290	101 298	93 216	126 210	165 309	162 496	199 344	188 568
Natural gas	12 883	29 395	56 868	65 355	62 020	41 630	66 887	112 502	194 127	181 258
Petroleum	54 537	70 005	90 407	115 885	147 098	135 587	168 773	208 168	235 826	250 166
Nuclear electric power	0	0	0	0	0	0	0	0	0	0
Hydroelectric power[1]	21 164	16 668	17 271	17 583	24 643	45 386	18 048	20 021	24 783	25 575
Wood and waste	946	876	1 051	1 244	2 764	4 118	2 733	3 474	4 124	3 480
Other	0	0	0	0	0	99	16 914	33 572	30 431	26 959
Net interstate flow of electricity/losses[2]	-2 340	5 474	7 226	-63 142	-38 138	-50 454	-39 224	-42 794	-62 140	-46 635
Total Expenditures (Thousands of Dollars)	. . .	. . .	278 500	614 100	1 659 700	1 856 600	2 395 400	3 030 400	4 708 700	5 126 900
Expenditures per capita (dollars)	. . .	. . .	570	990	2 073	1 952	1 993	1 986	2 356	2 448
Prices by Sector (Dollars Per Million Btu)										
Total	. . .	. . .	1.96	3.52	8.17	8.94	8.96	9.21	11.70	12.70
Residential	. . .	. . .	2.67	4.28	8.69	12.44	11.11	13.39	13.83	17.23
Commercial	. . .	. . .	2.17	3.87	7.73	11.16	10.46	11.24	11.86	15.85
Industrial	. . .	. . .	1.02	2.18	7.20	7.67	7.90	8.10	10.15	12.40
Transportation	. . .	. . .	2.08	3.66	8.44	7.79	8.37	7.94	11.53	10.47

[1]A negative number in this row results from pumped storage for which, overall, more electricity is expended than created to provide electricity during peak demand periods.
[2]Net interstate flow of electricity is the difference between the amount of energy in the electricity sold within a state (including associated losses) and the energy input at the electric utilities within the state. A positive number indicates that more electricity (including associated losses) came into the state than went out of the state during the year; conversely, a negative number indicates that more electricity (including associated losses) went out of the state than came into the state.
. . . = Not available.

Table NV-16. State Taxes, Fiscal 2004

(Dollars, percent distribution.)

Item	Thousands of dollars	Percent distribution	Dollars per capita	
			State	U.S.
TOTAL TAXES	4 738 877	100.0	2 029.5	2 024.8
Property Taxes	132 468	2.8	56.7	38.9
Sales and Gross Receipts	3 824 602	80.7	1 638.0	1 003.4
General sales and gross receipts	2 264 749	47.8	969.9	677.0
Selective sales taxes	1 559 853	32.9	668.0	326.4
Alcoholic beverages	33 867	0.7	14.5	15.7
Amusements	861 511	18.2	369.0	17.0
Insurance premiums	194 228	4.1	83.2	47.0
Motor fuels	293 595	6.2	125.7	114.6
Tobacco products	129 055	2.7	55.3	42.0
Other selective sales	37 946	0.8	16.2	49.8
Licenses	623 400	13.2	267.0	134.9
Amusements	95 668	2.0	41.0	0.8
Corporation	52 760	1.1	22.6	21.6
Motor vehicle	139 467	2.9	59.7	59.4
Occupation and business, not elsewhere classified	308 850	6.5	132.3	37.1
Other Taxes	158 407	3.3	67.8	847.6
Death and gift	24 548	0.5	10.5	19.6
Documentary and stock transfer	96 704	2.0	41.4	27.1
Severance	37 155	0.8	15.9	21.5

GOVERNMENT FINANCE

In 2003, Nevada's revenues and expenditures per person were lower than the national averages, ranking 49th in the country for both amounts. Spending on health was the only category in which the state ranked higher than the national average. In fiscal year 2004, per capita taxes amounted to $2,029, an amount that ranked 22nd in the country and was close to the national average. The state had no individual income or corporate income taxes. Thus, the largest sources of revenue were sales receipts and licenses, which brought in a high amount of income due to the large number of casinos in the state. Nevada's property taxes ranked 14th among the 37 states with such taxes.

Per Capita State Taxes, Fiscal 2004

Table NV-17. State Government Finances, 2003

(Dollars, percent distribution.)

Item	Millions of dollars	Percent distribution	Dollars per capita	
			State	U.S.
GENERAL REVENUE	6 548 496	100.0	2 920.8	3 832.6
Intergovernmental revenue	1 498 008	22.9	668.2	1 246.0
Taxes	4 129 137	63.1	1 841.7	1 891.6
General sales	2 192 321	33.5	977.8	636.0
Selective sales	1 309 644	20.0	584.1	307.4
License taxes	449 224	6.9	200.4	123.6
Individual income tax	0	0.0	0.0	626.8
Corporate income tax	0	0.0	0.0	97.8
Other taxes	177 948	2.7	79.4	99.9
Current charges	587 136	9.0	261.9	366.5
Miscellaneous general revenue	334 215	5.1	149.1	328.6
GENERAL EXPENDITURE	6 705 536	100.0	2 990.9	4 010.5
Intergovernmental expenditure	2 648 660	39.5	1 181.4	1 316.9
Direct expenditure	4 056 876	60.5	1 809.5	2 693.6
Expenditure by Function				
Education	2 666 071	39.8	1 189.2	1 416.4
Public welfare	1 190 018	17.7	530.8	1 083.3
Hospitals	128 511	1.9	57.3	132.3
Health	198 602	3.0	88.6	173.0
Highways	705 996	10.5	314.9	295.4
Police protection	58 925	0.9	26.3	38.4
Correction	216 356	3.2	96.5	135.0
Natural resources	109 909	1.6	49.0	64.0
Parks and recreation	17 379	0.3	7.8	20.1
Government administration	201 305	3.0	89.8	151.3
Interest on general debt	132 342	2.0	59.0	107.8
Other and unallocable	1 080 122	16.1	481.8	393.4
DEBT AT END OF FISCAL YEAR	3 604 272	X	1 607.6	2 404.7
CASH AND SECURITY HOLDINGS	19 162 163	X	8 546.9	8 938.4

X = Not applicable.

Table NV-18. Education Indicators, 2000–2004

(Percent, number.)

Item	State	U.S.
Total Population 25 Years and Over (Thousands), 2004	1 464	186 877
Educational Attainment, 2004		
Percent high school graduate or more	86.3	85.2
Percent college graduate or more	24.5	27.7
Elementary and Secondary Schools, 2002–2003		
Total students	369 498	48 202 324
Percent of students eligible for free or reduced-price lunch ..	41.6	40.6
Percent of students who were English language learners	18.1	7.8
Total schools	527	92 330
Student/teacher ratio	19.0	15.9
Per student expenditures	6 092	8 041
Dropouts, Grades 9–12, 2000–2001 (Percent)	6.4	. . .
Higher Education, 2002–2003		
Total enrollment	96 883	17 035 027
Bachelor's degrees awarded	4 877	1 348 503
Percent women	59.5	57.5

. . . = Not available.

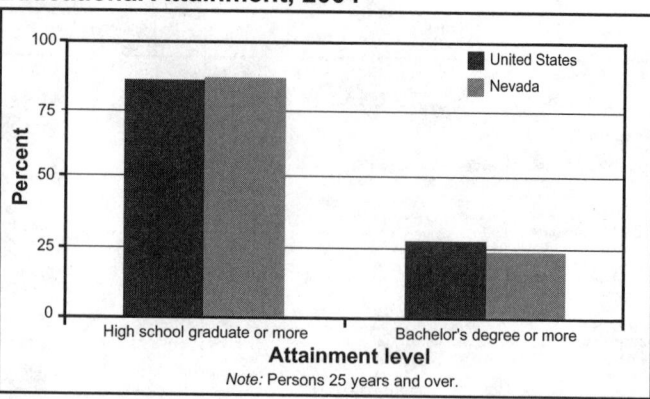

Educational Attainment, 2004

Note: Persons 25 years and over.

EDUCATION

The proportion of Nevada's residents age 25 years and over with a high school diploma increased to 86.3 percent in 2004, which exceeded the national average. The proportion of college graduates among the same age group remained lower than the U.S. average. The rapid influx of new residents also impacted other education measures. The state's student/teacher ratio was the sixth highest in the nation. Nevada's per student expenditures amounted to $6,092, nearly $2,000 less than the national average. Nevada ranked seventh out of the 46 states with dropout data, with a rate of 6.4 percent.

VOTER PARTICIPATION

Nevada had one of the lowest voter turnout rates in the country for both the 2000 and 2004 elections. In 2004, 51.3 percent of eligible voters turned out, ranking 48th in the nation. This participation rate was a slight improvement over the 46.5 percent that voted in 2000. Less than 24 percent of eligible Hispanic voters cast ballots in 2004. Persons age 45 to 75 years had the highest participation rate, exceeding 60 percent. Less than 39 percent of eligible voters age 18 to 24 years cast ballots in 2004. The Republican presidential candidate won 49.5 percent of the vote in 2000 and 50.8 percent of the vote in 2004.

Table NV-19. Reported Voting and Registration, November 2000 and November 2004

(Numbers in thousands, percent.)

Characteristic	Total population 18 years and over	Total citizen		Total registered		Total voted	
		Number	Percent	Number	Percent	Number	Percent
NOVEMBER 2000							
Total	1 377	1 229	89.3	720	52.3	641	46.5
Male	693	623	89.9	349	50.3	310	44.7
Female	683	606	88.7	371	54.2	331	48.4
NOVEMBER 2004							
Total	1 699	1 477	87.0	965	56.8	871	51.3
Male	856	743	86.8	471	55.0	421	49.2
Female	842	734	87.1	494	58.7	450	53.4
Race and Hispanic Origin							
White alone	1 445	1 260	87.2	844	58.4	763	52.8
Non-Hispanic White alone	1 168	1 123	96.1	770	65.9	696	59.6
Black alone	113	108	95.7	61	54.1	56	49.6
Asian alone	84	64	B	31	B	29	B
Hispanic or Latino[1]	301	151	50.2	83	27.6	72	23.8
White alone or in combination	1 465	1 280	87.4	859	58.7	775	52.9
Non-Hispanic White alone or in combination	1 182	1 137	96.2	780	66.0	705	59.7
Black alone or in combination	122	117	96.0	69	56.8	63	52.0
Asian alone or in combination	88	68	B	35	B	32	B
Age							
18 to 24 years	215	187	87.0	103	47.8	83	38.4
25 to 44 years	673	535	79.4	329	48.9	291	43.3
45 to 64 years	544	501	92.0	359	65.9	335	61.5
65 to 74 years	153	144	94.3	106	69.4	99	64.6
75 years and over	113	110	97.6	68	60.2	63	55.9

[1]May be of any race.
B = Base is too small to show derived measure.

At a Glance:

- In 2004, New Hampshire's population reached nearly 1.4 million, ranking it as the 41st most populous state in the country.

- Non-Hispanic Whites made up over 94 percent of the population, the fifth highest proportion of this racial group in the nation.

- New Hampshire's median household income of $56,886 was the second highest in the country; the state's poverty rate was the lowest of all the states.

- The unemployment rate was 3.8 percent in 2004 (the 7th lowest in the nation) and real gross state product ranked 40th.

- The educational attainment of New Hampshire residents was high: the state ranked sixth for the proportion of population age 25 years and over with a high school diploma and fourth for the population with a bachelor's degree or more.

- Like its New England neighbors, New Hampshire had a below average proportion of residents without health insurance.

Table NH-1. Population by Sex and Age, 1990, 2000, and 2004

(Number, percent.)

Sex and age	1990	2000	2004	Percent distribution, 2004	Average annual percent change, 2000–2004
Total Population	1 109 252	1 235 786	1 299 500	X	1.3
Percent of total U.S. population	0.4	0.4	0.4	X	X
Sex					
Male	543 544	607 687	640 940	49.3	1.3
Female	565 708	628 099	658 560	50.7	1.2
Age					
Under 5 years	84 565	75 685	72 678	5.6	-1.2
5 to 17 years	194 190	233 877	232 316	17.9	1.3
18 years and over	200 411	926 224	994 506	76.5	1.3
18 to 24 years	830 497	103 369	122 278	9.4	0.2
25 to 44 years	117 602	381 240	364 920	28.1	-0.4
45 to 64 years	387 455	293 645	350 636	27.0	4.1
65 years and over	125 029	147 970	156 672	12.1	1.7
85 years and over	13 286	18 231	21 723	1.7	3.7
Median age (years)	32.7	37.1	38.8	X	X

X = Not applicable.

Average Annual Rate of Population Growth, 1980–2004

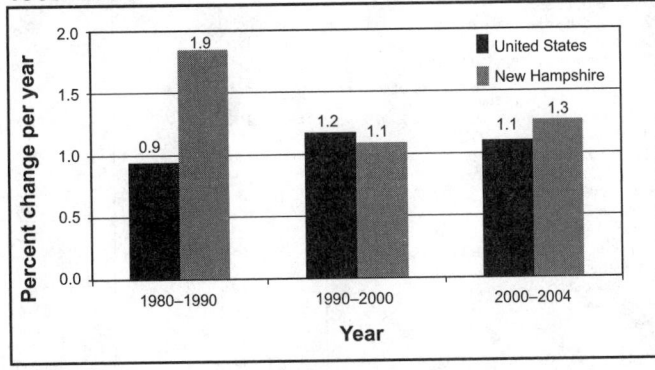

POPULATION

New Hampshire's population increased by 5.2 percent between 2000 and 2004. This was the 14th highest growth rate in the nation and above the growth rates of the other New England states. Over half of its growth was due to an influx of new residents from other states. Another 9,600 people moved to New Hampshire from other countries. The state's birth rate was the third lowest in the nation and did not contribute greatly to the state's population growth. New Hampshire had a below average proportion of its population under 18 years old.

Table NH-2. Population by Race and Hispanic Origin, 1990, 2000, and 2004

(Number, percent.)

Race and Hispanic origin	1990	2000	2004
Total Population	1 109 252	1 235 786	1 299 500
Non-Hispanic (Percent)			
One race[1]			
White	97.3	95.3	94.3
Black	0.6	0.7	0.8
American Indian, Alaska Native[2]	0.2	0.2	0.2
Asian and Pacific Islander[2]	0.8	1.3	1.7
Other race[2]	0.3	. . .	. . .
Two or more races	. . .	0.8	0.9
Hispanic or Latino[3] (Percent)	1.0	1.7	2.1

[1]Individuals could report only one race in the 1990 census and could report one or more races on the 2000 census. Data on race in 2000 and 2004 are not comparable to 1990.
[2]Data for 1990 include people of Hispanic or Latino origin.
[3]May be of any race.
. . . = Not available.

Minority Population as a Percent of Total Population, 2004

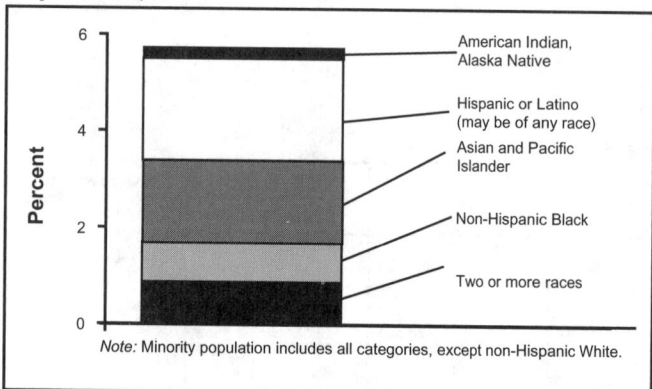

Note: Minority population includes all categories, except non-Hispanic White.

Age-Adjusted Death Rates, Average 2000–2002

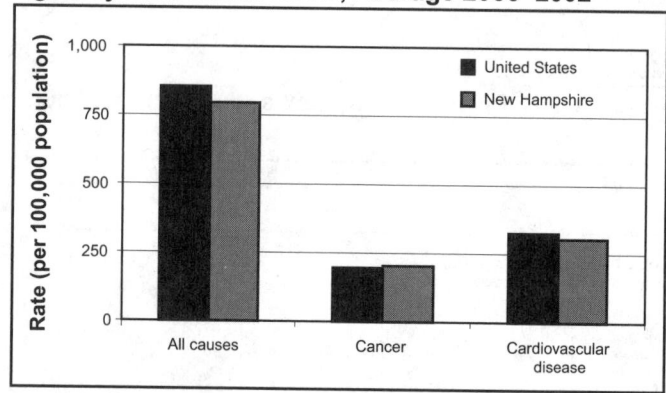

HEALTH

New Hampshire's infant mortality rate was the second lowest in the nation, and its birth rate for teenage mother was the lowest in the country. The state's age-adjusted death rates were below the national averages for most of the leading causes of death.

Table NH-3. Health Characteristics, 2000–2004

(Number, rate, percent.)

Item	State	U.S.
Births, 2003–2004		
Number of births	14 393	4 089 950
Birth rate (per 1,000 population)	11.2	14.1
Teenage birth rate (per 1,000 women age 15–19 years)	18.2	41.6
Mortality Rates, Average 2000–2002		
Infant mortality rate (per 1,000 live births)	4.9	6.9
Age-adjusted mortality rate (per 100,000 population)		
All races	796.2	853.3
Non-Hispanic White	785.8	843.1
Black	796.2	1 097.7
American Indian, Alaska Native	. . .	687.0
Asian and Pacific Islander	373.3	486.0
Hispanic or Latino[1]	392.7	642.7
Health Insurance, 2004		
Percent of all persons without health insurance	11.7	15.7
Percent of children without health insurance	7.8	11.2
Percent of low-income children without health insurance	4.1	7.1

[1]May be of any race.
. . . = Not available.

Table NH-4. Leading Causes of Death, Average 2000–2002

(Number, rate per 100,000 population.)

Cause	Number of deaths	Age-adjusted death rates	
		State	U.S.
ALL CAUSES	9 788	796.2	853.3
Leading Causes			
Major cardiovascular diseases	3 696	301.6	326.5
Cancer	2 470	199.8	196.0
Chronic lower respiratory diseases	591	48.8	43.7
Unintentional injuries	351	28.0	35.7
Diabetes (underlying cause)	300	24.4	25.2
Influenza and pneumonia	216	17.7	22.7
Alzheimer's disease	296	24.3	19.0
Motor vehicle accidents	126	10.0	15.0
Nephritis, nephrotic syndrome, and nephrosis ..	128	10.5	13.8
Septicemia	68	5.6	11.4
Suicides	143	11.2	10.7
Firearm-related	82	6.4	10.3
Cirrhosis	105	8.3	9.5
Drug-induced	82	6.3	7.9
Alcohol-induced	96	7.3	6.9
Homicides	14	1.1	6.0
Falls	61	5.0	5.2
HIV	13	1.0	5.0
Viral hepatitis	16	1.2	2.0
Anemias	16	1.2	1.6
Drownings	12	1.0	1.3
Fire deaths	14	1.1	1.2

Note: The rates are age-adjusted to the U.S. 2000 standard population.

Table NH-5. Households and Housing Characteristics, 1990, 2000, and 2004

(Number, percent, and dollars.)

Characteristic	1990	2000	2004	Average annual percent change, 2000–2004
Total Households	411 186	474 606	491 589	0.9
Family households	292 601	323 651	332 472	0.7
Married-couple family	245 307	262 438	267 910	0.5
Other family	47 294	61 213	64 562	1.3
Male householder, no wife present	12 517	18 261	17 866	-0.5
Female householder, no husband present	34 777	42 952	46 696	2.1
Nonfamily households	118 585	150 955	159 117	1.3
Householder living alone	90 364	116 014	123 869	1.7
Householder not living alone	28 221	34 941	35 248	0.2
Housing Characteristics				
Average size	2.62	2.53	2.57	X
Housing units	503 904	547 024	575 671	1.3
Occupied housing units	411 186	474 606	491 589	0.9
Owner-occupied	280 372	330 700	356 649	1.9
Renter-occupied	130 814	143 906	134 940	-1.6
Median gross rent of renter-occupied housing units (dollars) ...	549	646	810	5.8
Median value of owner-occupied housing units (dollars)	129 300	133 300	216 639	12.9

X = Not applicable.

Median Housing Value and Median Rent, 2004

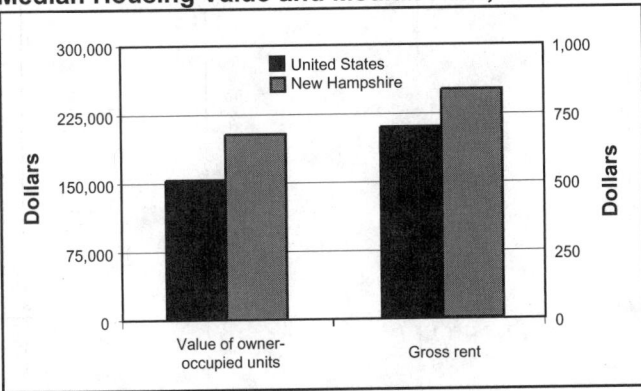

Median Household Income, 1984–2004 (2004 Dollars)

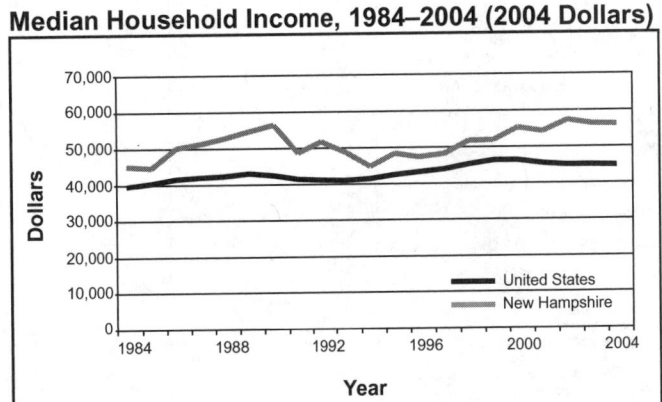

Table NH-6. Household Income and Poverty Status, 1980–2004

(2004 CPI-U-RS adjusted dollars, rate.)

Year	State		U.S.	
	Median household income (2004 dollars)	Poverty rate	Median household income (2004 dollars)	Poverty rate
2004	56 886	5.4	44 389	12.7
2003	57 060	5.8	44 482	12.5
2002	58 109	5.8	44 546	12.1
2001	54 776	6.5	45 062	11.7
2000	55 860	4.5	46 058	11.3
1999	52 203	7.6	46 129	11.9
1998	52 032	9.8	45 003	12.7
1997	48 117	9.1	43 430	13.3
1996	47 237	6.4	42 544	13.7
1995	48 215	5.3	41 943	13.8
1994	44 436	7.7	40 677	14.5
1993	48 872	9.9	40 217	15.1
1992	52 033	8.7	40 422	14.8
1991	48 734	7.3	40 746	14.2
1990	57 185	6.3	41 963	13.5
1989	55 214	7.7	42 524	12.8
1988	53 125	6.7	41 771	13.0
1987	51 423	4.8	41 322	13.4
1986	50 232	3.7	40 939	13.6
1985	44 209	6.0	39 545	14.0
1984	44 836	7.1	38 782	14.4
1983	. . .	8.1	. . .	15.2
1982	. . .	10.3	. . .	15.0
1981	. . .	7.6	. . .	14.0
1980	. . .	7.0	. . .	13.0

. . . = Not available.

Table NH-7. Employment Status by Demographic Group, 2004

(Numbers in thousands, rate.)

Characteristic	Civilian noninstitutional population	Civilian labor force		Employed	Unemployment rate
		Number	Participation rate		
SEX AND AGE					
Total	1 018	724	71.1	698	3.7
16 to 19 years	76	40	52.9	35	12.3
20 to 24 years	80	64	79.8	60	5.7
25 to 34 years	159	134	84.7	130	3.5
35 to 44 years	208	181	87.0	177	2.4
45 to 54 years	207	182	88.0	178	2.7
55 to 64 years	139	100	72.2	97	3.5
65 years and over	149	22	15.0	22	3.2
Men	497	387	77.9	372	4.0
16 to 19 years	41	20	48.9	17	14.6
20 to 24 years	41	33	80.4	31	6.8
25 to 34 years	76	71	93.6	69	3.2
35 to 44 years	101	96	94.8	94	2.4
45 to 54 years	107	101	94.3	98	3.1
55 to 64 years	69	54	79.2	52	4.5
65 years and over	62	12	19.0	12	2.4
Women	521	337	64.7	326	3.3
16 to 19 years	34	20	57.7	18	10.0
20 to 24 years	39	31	79.2	29	4.5
25 to 34 years	83	63	76.5	61	3.8
35 to 44 years	107	85	79.6	83	2.4
45 to 54 years	100	82	81.2	80	2.2
55 to 64 years	70	46	65.3	45	2.4
MARITAL STATUS					
Married men, spouse present	298	244	81.9	239	2.3
Married women, spouse present	288	192	66.7	189	1.7
Women who maintain families	45	32	70.5	30	5.6
RACE, HISPANIC ORIGIN, AND SEX					
White	979	695	71.0	670	3.6
Men	477	370	77.6	355	4.0
Women	502	325	64.8	315	3.3
Asian	17	12	67.6	11	3.0
Hispanic or Latino[1]	16	13	81.8	13	5.3
RACE, HISPANIC ORIGIN, AND AGE					
White					
16 to 19 years	73	39	53.1	34	12.4
20 to 24 years	76	61	80.6	58	5.3
25 to 34 years	147	125	85.2	121	3.5
35 to 44 years	198	172	87.0	168	2.3
45 to 54 years	202	178	88.1	173	2.7
55 to 64 years	136	98	72.1	94	3.6
65 years and over	147	22	14.9	21	3.3

Note: Data in Table 7 are from the Current Population Survey (CPS) and do not match Bureau of Labor Statistics estimates in Table 8. See notes and definitions for more details.

[1]May be of any race.

Table NH-8. Employment Status, 1990–2004

(Numbers in thousands, rate.)

Year	Civilian labor force	Employed	Unemployed	Unemployment rate
2004	723 028	695 739	27 289	3.8
2003	717 297	685 366	31 931	4.5
2002	713 903	681 509	32 394	4.5
2001	704 821	680 587	24 234	3.4
2000	695 300	677 071	18 229	2.6
1999	684 904	666 066	18 838	2.8
1998	670 560	651 292	19 268	2.9
1997	656 094	635 469	20 625	3.1
1996	641 246	617 629	23 617	3.7
1995	631 050	605 929	25 121	4.0
1994	624 566	594 935	29 631	4.7
1993	619 307	580 137	39 170	6.3
1992	615 648	568 909	46 739	7.6
1991	614 452	569 621	44 831	7.3
1990	620 037	585 032	35 005	5.6

Note: Population age 16 years and over.

Unemployment Rate, 1980–2004

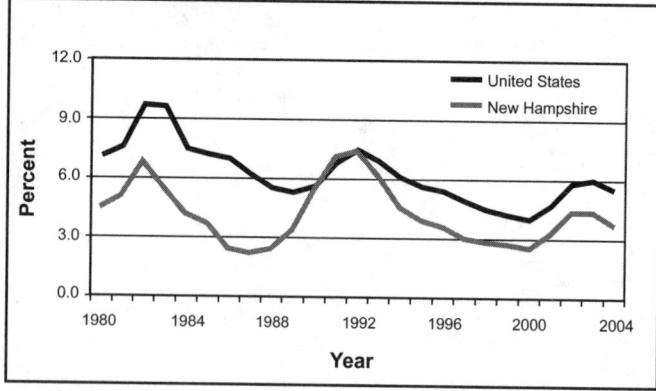

Table NH-9. Employment and Average Wages by Industry, 2001–2004

(Estimates are based on the 2002 North American Industry Classification System [NAICS].)

Industry	2001	2002	2003	2004	Annual average percent change, 2001–2004
	Number of jobs				
TOTAL EMPLOYMENT BY PLACE OF WORK	795 229	794 563	804 072	819 201	1.0
Farm Employment	5 092	5 114	5 126	4 823	-1.8
Nonfarm Employment	790 137	789 449	798 946	814 378	1.0
Private employment	702 058	698 447	705 577	721 094	0.9
Forestry, fishing, hunting, and other[1]	3 665	3 738	3 265	3 202	-4.4
Mining	885	798	877	935	1.8
Utilities	2 897	3 005	2 944	2 886	-0.1
Construction	52 143	52 732	55 920	57 117	3.1
Manufacturing	101 748	89 212	84 430	84 251	-6.1
Durable goods manufacturing	76 720	66 067	62 366	63 246	-6.2
Nondurable goods manufacturing	25 028	23 145	22 064	21 005	-5.7
Wholesale trade	29 355	29 380	29 354	30 117	0.9
Retail trade	112 822	114 704	115 507	117 120	1.3
Transportation and warehousing	16 992	16 820	16 945	16 725	-0.5
Information	15 642	14 634	14 300	14 617	-2.2
Finance and insurance	35 046	35 988	36 224	36 513	1.4
Real estate and rental and leasing	26 491	27 008	28 707	30 252	4.5
Professional and technical services	47 977	47 162	47 461	49 214	0.9
Management of companies and enterprises	7 369	6 673	6 502	7 215	-0.7
Administrative and waste services	33 430	33 489	35 138	37 178	3.6
Educational services	23 938	25 331	26 276	27 225	4.4
Health care and social assistance	80 845	83 064	85 238	86 715	2.4
Arts, entertainment, and recreation	18 406	19 189	19 552	20 314	3.3
Accommodation and food services	52 925	54 128	54 702	56 660	2.3
Other services, except public administration	39 482	41 392	42 235	42 838	2.8
Government and government enterprises	88 079	91 002	93 369	93 284	1.9
	Dollars				
AVERAGE WAGES AND SALARIES BY PLACE OF WORK	34 689	35 373	36 533	38 354	3.4
Farm Earnings	18 503	24 382	20 164	26 155	12.2
Nonfarm Earnings	34 736	35 404	36 580	38 383	3.4
Private earnings	35 485	36 096	37 199	39 003	3.2
Forestry, fishing, hunting, and other[1]	27 513	27 925	30 243	31 981	5.1
Mining	43 916	46 929	43 470	47 328	2.5
Utilities	64 404	66 469	69 012	79 212	7.1
Construction	42 169	43 797	42 080	43 410	1.0
Manufacturing	44 670	46 061	48 184	50 648	4.3
Durable goods manufacturing	46 509	48 212	50 637	53 171	4.6
Nondurable goods manufacturing	38 954	39 836	41 165	42 933	3.3
Wholesale trade	59 829	59 285	60 375	62 891	1.7
Retail trade	23 163	23 907	25 081	25 590	3.4
Transportation and warehousing	30 561	31 045	31 526	33 564	3.2
Information	55 892	54 697	56 208	59 149	1.9
Finance and insurance	53 788	56 624	61 054	64 027	6.0
Real estate and rental and leasing	30 276	34 585	36 673	38 433	8.3
Professional and technical services	56 708	56 715	57 376	59 605	1.7
Management of companies and enterprises	69 027	67 336	71 872	91 382	9.8
Administrative and waste services	28 190	29 093	29 565	31 454	3.7
Educational services	26 328	28 139	30 052	31 222	5.8
Health care and social assistance	32 800	34 436	35 743	37 365	4.4
Arts, entertainment, and recreation	17 601	17 435	18 485	19 387	3.3
Accommodation and food services	14 994	15 324	15 738	16 186	2.6
Other services, except public administration	22 830	23 928	24 598	25 482	3.7
Government and government enterprises	29 990	31 220	32 941	34 669	5.0

Note: Average wages and salaries are a calculation by the editors of wage and salary disbursements divided by full- and part-time wage and salary employment. Data may not add to total or may appear as zero due to rounding.

[1] "Other" consists of the number of jobs held by U.S. residents employed by international organizations and foreign embassies and consulates in the United States.

LABOR MARKET

New Hampshire's unemployment rate has been below the national average since the mid-1990s. In 2004, it was roughly equal to that of Vermont, but was lower than those of the other New England states (Connecticut, Maine, Massachusetts, and Rhode Island). Employment was concentrated in retail trade, government, health care, manufacturing, construction, and tourism-related industries (accommodation and food services). Manufacturing employment decreased quite dramatically during the 2001–2003 period, but the rate of decline slowed in 2004. These losses were offset by employment gains in health care, tourism, and government. Overall, average wages and salaries were only slightly below the national average.

Employment by Industry, 2004

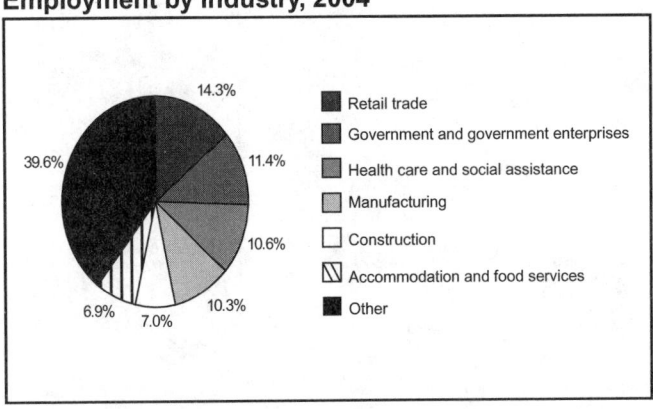

- 14.3% Retail trade
- 11.4% Government and government enterprises
- 10.6% Health care and social assistance
- 10.3% Manufacturing
- 7.0% Construction
- 6.9% Accommodation and food services
- 39.6% Other

Table NH-10. Personal Income by Major Source, Selected Years 1980–2004

(Millions of dollars, except where noted.)

Item	1980	1990	2000	2001	2002	2003	2004	Average annual percent change, 2000–2004
Earnings by Place of Work	6 410	15 817	29 405	30 353	31 173	32 479	34 913	4.4
Wage and salary disbursements	4 891	11 781	21 875	22 469	22 733	23 557	25 064	3.5
Supplements to wages and salaries	876	2 275	4 039	4 291	4 700	5 053	5 593	8.5
Proprietors' income[1]	644	1 761	3 491	3 593	3 739	3 869	4 257	5.1
Farm proprietors' income	-2	20	0	-3	-15	-3	-2	X
Nonfarm proprietors' income	646	1 741	3 491	3 596	3 754	3 871	4 259	5.1
(-) Contributions for government social insurance[2]	560	1 720	3 210	3 354	3 423	3 558	3 815	4.4
(+) Adjustment for residence[3]	849	2 004	4 043	4 015	3 903	3 890	4 059	0.1
(=) **Net Earnings by Place of Residence**	6 699	16 101	30 239	31 014	31 652	32 812	35 157	3.8
(+) Dividends, interest, and rent[4]	1 435	4 568	6 986	7 044	6 794	6 629	6 938	-0.2
(+) Personal current transfer receipts	969	2 149	4 204	4 566	4 994	5 080	5 566	7.3
Personal income	9 104	22 817	41 429	42 624	43 441	44 521	47 661	3.6
Farm income	9 091	22 775	41 389	42 588	43 409	44 483	47 620	3.6
Nonfarm income	13	42	40	36	32	38	41	1.0
Per Capita Personal Income (Dollars)[5]	9 850	20 512	33 396	33 850	34 055	34 547	36 676	2.4

Note: Data may not add to total or may appear as zero due to rounding.

[1]Proprietors' income includes the inventory valuation adjustment and the capital consumption adjustment.
[2]Contributions for government social insurance are included in earnings by type and industry, but they are excluded from personal income.
[3]The adjustment for residence is the net inflow of the earnings of interarea commuters.
[4]Rental income of persons includes the capital consumption adjustment.
[5]Per capita personal income is total personal income divided by total midyear population.
X = Not applicable.

Per Capita Personal Income, 1980–2004 (Current Dollars)

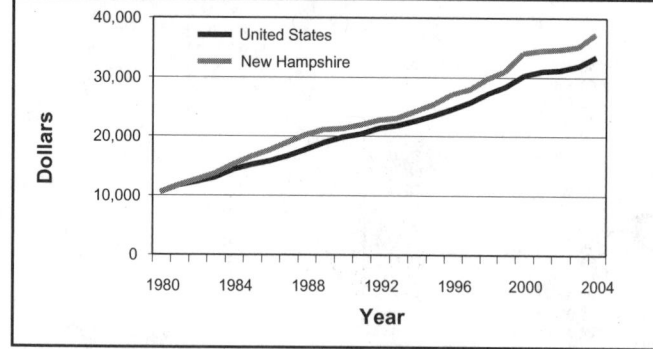

ECONOMIC ACTIVITY

Real gross state product (GSP) slowed during the 2001 recession, but recovered in subsequent years. Between 2003 and 2004, New Hampshire's GSP growth rate of 5.4 percent was the 10th fastest in the country. The chief contributors to this increase were durable goods manufacturing, real estate and related activities, information services, retail trade, and utilities. Housing prices have appreciated slightly faster than average over recent years. In 2004, the median value of owner-occupied housing in the state was the 9th highest in the country, having increased by over 60 percent from 2000 to 2004.

Table NH-11. Real Gross State Product, 1997–2004

(Millions of chained 2000 dollars, percent.)

Industry	1997	1998	1999	2000	2001	2002	2003	2004	Average annual percent change, 2001–2004
GROSS STATE PRODUCT	36 607	39 493	40 636	43 584	43 691	44 475	45 874	48 353	3.4
As a percent of U.S. gross product	0.4	0.4	0.4	0.4	0.4	0.4	0.4	0.5	X
Private Industries	33 173	35 976	37 052	39 815	39 882	40 610	41 903	44 277	3.5
Agriculture, forestry, fishing, and hunting	147	171	201	221	188	189	206	206	3.1
Mining	21	29	29	30	33	33	32	33	0.0
Utilities	1 135	1 115	1 097	1 234	1 153	1 350	1 429	1 603	11.6
Construction	1 757	1 957	1 973	1 921	2 174	2 231	2 218	2 281	1.6
Manufacturing	6 220	7 038	6 452	7 200	6 295	6 143	6 609	7 049	3.8
As a percent of gross state product	17.0	17.8	15.9	16.5	14.4	13.8	14.4	14.6	X
Wholesale trade	2 060	2 412	2 580	2 770	3 076	3 115	3 032	3 140	0.7
Retail trade	2 922	3 093	3 321	3 465	3 837	4 209	4 566	4 790	7.7
Transportation and warehousing	572	641	699	757	718	743	815	833	5.1
Information	811	944	1 193	1 308	1 368	1 391	1 460	1 695	7.4
Finance and insurance	2 627	3 089	3 499	4 077	4 062	3 958	3 942	4 050	-0.1
Real estate and rental and leasing	5 253	5 247	5 575	5 703	6 013	6 080	6 131	6 443	2.3
Services	9 701	10 170	10 456	11 128	10 940	11 109	11 456	12 184	3.7
As a percent of gross state product	26.5	25.8	25.7	25.5	25.0	25.0	25.0	25.2	X
Professional and technical services	2 118	2 340	2 527	2 893	2 788	2 734	2 820	2 992	2.4
Management of companies and enterprises	737	784	720	850	612	541	553	735	6.3
Administrative and waste services	1 053	1 085	1 088	1 051	1 039	1 083	1 149	1 244	6.2
Educational services	585	584	607	626	624	652	661	660	1.9
Health care and social assistance	2 741	2 794	2 927	3 050	3 199	3 366	3 494	3 598	4.0
Arts, entertainment, and recreation	338	337	355	357	380	402	417	442	5.2
Accommodation and food services	1 098	1 173	1 189	1 244	1 272	1 314	1 341	1 422	3.8
Other services, except public administration	1 031	1 073	1 043	1 057	1 026	1 017	1 021	1 091	2.1
Government	3 451	3 519	3 585	3 769	3 809	3 865	3 972	4 082	2.3
As a percent of gross state product	9.4	8.9	8.8	8.6	8.7	8.7	8.7	8.4	X

X = Not applicable.

Table NH-12. Government Transfer Payments, Selected Years 1980–2004

(Millions of dollars, percent.)

Item	1980	1990	2000	2001	2002	2003	2004	Average annual percent change, 2000–2004
CURRENT TRANSFER PAYMENTS TO INDIVIDUALS	906	1 999	3 918	4 249	4 708	4 816	5 301	7.8
Retirement and Disability Insurance Benefits	507	1 105	1 877	2 000	2 117	2 223	2 340	5.7
Old-age, survivors, and disability insurance (OASDI) benefits	494	1 032	1 850	1 971	2 085	2 187	2 302	5.6
Railroad retirement and disability benefits	10	13	13	13	13	13	13	1.4
Workers' compensation	3	58	11	11	13	13	13	5.1
Other government retirement and disability insurance benefits	*	3	4	6	6	11	12	27.6
Medical Benefits	194	596	1 602	1 760	1 972	1 934	2 316	9.7
Medicare benefits	122	344	754	839	903	960	1 061	8.9
Public assistance medical care benefits	71	242	841	911	1 055	962	1 240	10.2
Military medical insurance benefits	1	10	8	11	14	12	14	17.5
Income Maintenance Benefits	84	121	239	232	260	288	303	6.1
Supplemental Security Income (SSI) benefits	13	26	61	64	68	70	73	4.5
Family assistance	27	35	49	41	47	46	43	-3.1
Food stamps	23	23	28	29	36	41	45	13.1
Other income maintenance benefits	22	37	101	99	109	131	142	8.8
Unemployment Insurance Compensation	32	64	27	65	153	154	97	37.6
Veterans' Benefits	72	94	139	147	161	172	179	6.5
Federal Education and Training Assistance	17	18	31	39	44	40	43	8.5
Other Payments to Individuals	*	1	2	5	3	5	22	75.2

Note: See notes and definitions for more details. Data may not add to total or may appear as zero due to rounding.

* = Less than $500,000.

EXPORTS

The value of New Hampshire's exports totaled close to $2.3 billion in 2004, ranking 42nd in the country. The state's leading exports were computers and electronic products and machinery manufactures, which combined to equal more than half of New Hampshire's exports. The value of the state's three leading exports fell from 2001 to 2004, resulting in a decline of total exports. New Hampshire's chief export market was Canada, followed distantly by Japan and the United Kingdom. Exports to the United Kingdom fell significantly from 2001 to 2004, due to a drop in demand for computers and electronic products and machinery manufactures. Exports to China doubled from 2001 to 2004, ranking the country as New Hampshire's sixth leading export market.

Leading Exports, 2004

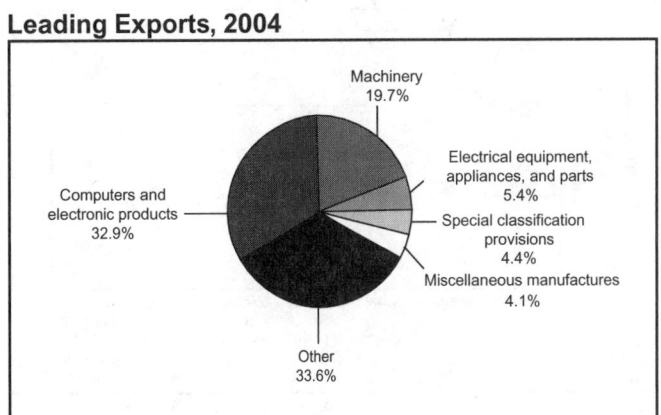

Table NH-13. Exports of Goods by Leading Products and Destinations, 2001–2004

(Millions of dollars, percent, rank based on 2004 dollar values.)

Product and market	2001	2002	2003	2004	Percent share of total, 2004	Average annual percent change, 2001–2004
Total Goods						
Total	2 401	1 863	1 931	2 286	100.0	-1.6
Manufactures	2 269	1 700	1 762	2 065	90.4	-3.1
Agriculture and livestock	45	43	38	42	1.8	-2.4
Other commodities	87	120	131	179	7.8	27.2
Five Leading Exports (NAICS Code)						
Computers and electronic products (334)	885	570	614	751	32.9	-5.3
Machinery manufactures (333)	466	385	389	449	19.7	-1.3
Electrical equipment, appliances, and parts (335)	205	100	95	124	5.4	-15.5
Special classification provisions (990)	69	97	91	100	4.4	13.2
Miscellaneous manufactures (339)	67	75	81	93	4.1	11.5
Five Leading Markets	2 169	1 706	1 758	2 073	90.7	-1.5
Canada	594	514	506	541	23.7	-3.1
Japan	198	127	139	201	8.8	0.4
United Kingdom	366	164	160	167	7.3	-22.9
Germany	143	128	109	144	6.3	0.0
Netherlands	82	90	128	138	6.0	18.9

Table NH-14. Agriculture, 1997 and 2002

(Number, acres, and dollars.)

Item	1997	2002
Number of farms	3 928	3 363
Land in farms (acres)	463 383	444 879
Farm Size		
Average size of farm (acres)	118	132
Farms by size (percent distribution)		
Fewer than 50 acres	46.2	45.9
50 to 499 acres	50.0	49.0
500 acres or more	3.8	5.2
Market Value of Land and Equipment (Dollars)		
Land and buildings average value per farm	295 677	400 943
Average value per acre	2 448	3 131
Machinery and equipment average value per farm	34 541	40 868
Value of Sales (Thousands of Dollars)		
Agricultural products sold	155 698	144 835
Crops	78 033	83 149
Livestock, poultry, and their products	77 665	61 686
Average per farm (dollars)	39 638	43 067
Value of sales (percent distribution)		
Less than $10,000	72.5	73.8
$10,000 to $99,999	20.2	18.6
$100,000 or more	7.3	7.5
Government Payments		
Payments (thousands of dollars)	897	3 823
Percent of farms receiving government payments	11.5	10.7
Farm operators whose principal occupation is farming (percent)	40.2	48.6

AGRICULTURE

In 2002, cash receipts from farming totaled only $145 million, ranking 48th in the nation. This also represented a decline in sales from the 1997 agricultural census. The number of farms fell by 14 percent from 1997 to 2002. Farm production was concentrated in dairy and greenhouse/nursery products. In 2002, nearly 74 percent of farms in the state had sales of less than $10,000, and just 5 percent of farms spanned 500 acres or more. Less than half of New Hampshire's farm operators reported farming as their primary occupation.

ENERGY

Energy expenditures per person were slightly above the national average. New Hampshire's energy prices were the eighth highest in the country. The state's per capita consumption fell from 2001 to 2002; it ranked as the ninth lowest in the nation in 2002. The transportation sector was New Hampshire's largest consumer of energy.

Energy Consumption by Source, 2001

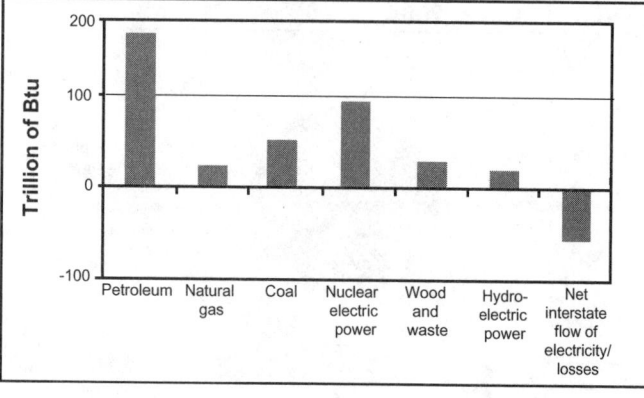

Energy Consumption by Sector, 2001

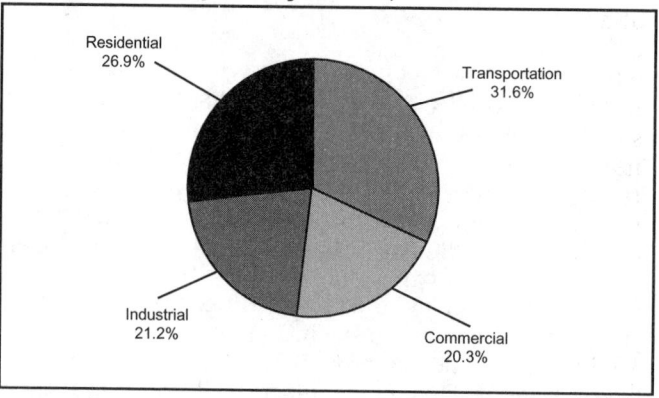

Table NH-15. Energy Consumption, Expenditures, and Prices, Selected Years 1960–2001

(Dollars, Btu [British Thermal Unit], percent distribution.)

Item	1960	1965	1970	1975	1980	1985	1990	1995	2000	2001
Total Consumption (Billion Btu)	112 252	131 436	187 197	202 064	208 304	234 017	264 241	272 074	328 091	322 163
Consumption per capita (million Btu)	184.9	194.4	253.8	243.9	226.3	234.8	238.2	237.5	265.5	255.9
Consumption by Sector (Percent Distribution)										
Residential	36.0	37.6	34.6	34.7	30.4	30.3	29.8	30.4	26.5	26.9
Commercial	7.3	7.7	8.2	8.7	12.8	12.3	16.4	20.3	20.2	20.3
Industrial	26.7	26.3	30.1	28.6	29.0	30.6	26.2	19.6	22.3	21.2
Transportation	30.0	28.4	27.1	28.0	27.8	26.9	27.6	29.7	31.0	31.6
Consumption by Source (Billion Btu)										
Coal	5 390	11 171	27 149	26 187	29 275	39 719	31 545	35 577	44 033	40 132
Natural gas	2 952	4 133	6 796	7 707	9 663	10 916	14 474	20 136	26 397	24 849
Petroleum	83 475	96 472	140 451	137 518	134 644	130 203	159 054	151 091	181 791	178 318
Nuclear electric power	0	0	0	0	0	0	43 182	88 042	82 617	90 822
Hydroelectric power[1]	14 775	11 003	13 006	13 013	10 666	11 811	19 567	14 126	14 559	10 078
Wood and waste	10 855	11 015	12 315	12 840	19 755	21 456	27 061	25 788	24 983	23 921
Other	0	0	0	0	0	3 046	153	4 396	5 383	1 437
Net interstate flow of electricity/losses[2]	-5 194	-2 359	-12 521	4 799	4 301	16 865	-30 795	-67 082	-51 673	-47 394
Total Expenditures (Thousands of Dollars)	...	...	317 600	644 600	1 313 200	1 627 800	2 014 100	2 299 400	3 248 600	3 127 900
Expenditures per capita (dollars)	...	...	430	778	1 426	1 633	1 816	2 007	2 629	2 484
Prices by Sector (Dollars Per Million Btu)										
Total	...	...	2.18	4.32	9.32	10.31	10.81	11.75	13.53	13.29
Residential	...	...	2.23	4.57	9.77	11.54	13.00	13.48	16.20	16.41
Commercial	...	...	3.11	6.16	9.43	12.91	11.88	16.36	16.66	17.59
Industrial	...	...	1.21	3.43	7.88	9.53	9.79	9.68	10.46	10.37
Transportation	...	...	2.60	4.27	9.62	9.16	9.43	9.73	12.28	11.34

[1]A negative number in this row results from pumped storage for which, overall, more electricity is expended than created to provide electricity during peak demand periods.
[2]Net interstate flow of electricity is the difference between the amount of energy in the electricity sold within a state (including associated losses) and the energy input at the electric utilities within the state. A positive number indicates that more electricity (including associated losses) came into the state than went out of the state during the year; conversely, a negative number indicates that more electricity (including associated losses) went out of the state than came into the state.
... = Not available.

Table NH-16. State Taxes, Fiscal 2004

(Dollars, percent distribution.)

Item	Thousands of dollars	Percent distribution	Dollars per capita State	Dollars per capita U.S.
TOTAL TAXES	2 005 389	100.0	1 542.6	2 024.8
Property Taxes	493 589	24.6	379.7	38.9
Sales and Gross Receipts	674 354	33.6	518.7	1 003.4
Selective sales taxes	674 354	33.6	518.7	326.4
Alcoholic beverages	12 239	0.6	9.4	15.7
Insurance premiums	79 450	4.0	61.1	47.0
Motor fuels	129 913	6.5	99.9	114.6
Public utilities	65 581	3.3	50.4	39.2
Tobacco products	100 014	5.0	76.9	42.0
Other selective sales	281 265	14.0	216.4	49.8
Licenses	199 170	9.9	153.2	134.9
Alcoholic beverages	17 514	0.9	13.5	1.3
Motor vehicle	84 431	4.2	65.0	59.4
Motor vehicle operators	13 051	0.7	10.0	6.4
Occupation and business, not elsewhere classified	61 597	3.1	47.4	37.1
Other Taxes	638 276	31.8	491.0	847.6
Individual income	54 769	2.7	42.1	673.6
Corporation net income	407 603	20.3	313.5	105.1
Death and gift	30 536	1.5	23.5	19.6
Documentary and stock transfer	145 368	7.2	111.8	27.1

GOVERNMENT FINANCE

New Hampshire's revenues and expenditures per person were below the national averages in 2003. Spending was also below average for most categories of outlays. In fiscal year 2004, New Hampshire's per capita taxes amounted to $1,543. This was among the five lowest amounts in the nation. Individual income taxes of only $42 per person were among the lowest of the 43 states with such taxes. New Hampshire had no general sales tax. As a result, the state relied more heavily on corporate income taxes and property taxes. New Hampshire had the second highest per capita property taxes in the nation.

Per Capita State Taxes, Fiscal 2004

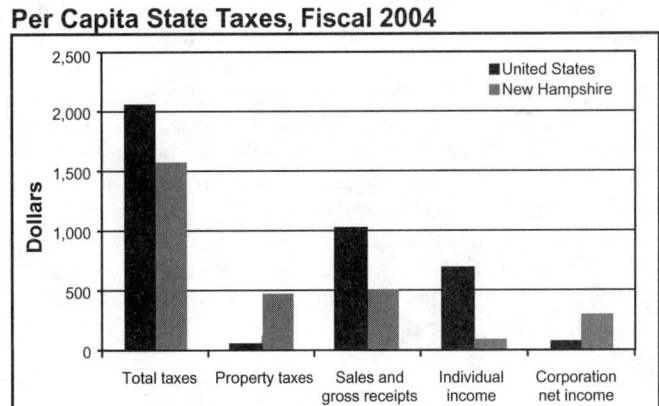

Table NH-17. State Government Finances, 2003

(Dollars, percent distribution.)

Item	Millions of dollars	Percent distribution	Dollars per capita State	Dollars per capita U.S.
GENERAL REVENUE	4 566 307	100.0	3 542.5	3 832.6
Intergovernmental revenue	1 464 454	32.1	1 136.1	1 246.0
Taxes	1 959 211	42.9	1 520.0	1 891.6
General sales	0	0.0	0.0	636.0
Selective sales	632 757	13.9	490.9	307.4
License taxes	192 420	4.2	149.3	123.6
Individual income tax	55 118	1.2	42.8	626.8
Corporate income tax	396 162	8.7	307.3	97.8
Other taxes	682 754	15.0	529.7	99.9
Current charges	544 869	11.9	422.7	366.5
Miscellaneous general revenue	597 773	13.1	463.8	328.6
GENERAL EXPENDITURE	4 591 789	100.0	3 562.3	4 010.5
Intergovernmental expenditure	1 283 091	27.9	995.4	1 316.9
Direct expenditure	3 308 698	72.1	2 566.9	2 693.6
Expenditure by Function				
Education	1 635 389	35.6	1 268.7	1 416.4
Public welfare	1 185 850	25.8	920.0	1 083.3
Hospitals	48 940	1.1	38.0	132.3
Health	175 661	3.8	136.3	173.0
Highways	374 780	8.2	290.8	295.4
Police protection	41 749	0.9	32.4	38.4
Correction	95 637	2.1	74.2	135.0
Natural resources	70 642	1.5	54.8	64.0
Parks and recreation	11 249	0.2	8.7	20.1
Government administration	202 094	4.4	156.8	151.3
Interest on general debt	310 212	6.8	240.7	107.8
Other and unallocable	439 586	9.6	341.0	393.4
DEBT AT END OF FISCAL YEAR	5 594 078	X	4 339.9	2 404.7
CASH AND SECURITY HOLDINGS	8 837 120	X	6 855.8	8 938.4

X = Not applicable.

Table NH-18. Education Indicators, 2000–2004

(Percent, number.)

Item	State	U.S.
Total Population 25 Years and Over (Thousands), 2004	828	186 877
Educational Attainment, 2004		
Percent high school graduate or more	90.8	85.2
Percent college graduate or more	35.4	27.7
Elementary and Secondary Schools, 2002–2003		
Total students	207 671	48 202 324
Percent of students eligible for free or reduced-price lunch ..	16.3	40.6
Percent of students who were English language learners	1.3	7.8
Total schools	473	92 330
Student/teacher ratio	13.7	15.9
Per student expenditures	8 579	8 041
Dropouts, Grades 9–12, 2000–2001 (Percent)	4.0	. . .
Higher Education, 2002–2003		
Total enrollment	69 147	17 035 027
Bachelor's degrees awarded	7 563	1 348 503
Percent women	58.3	57.5

. . . = Not available.

Educational Attainment, 2004

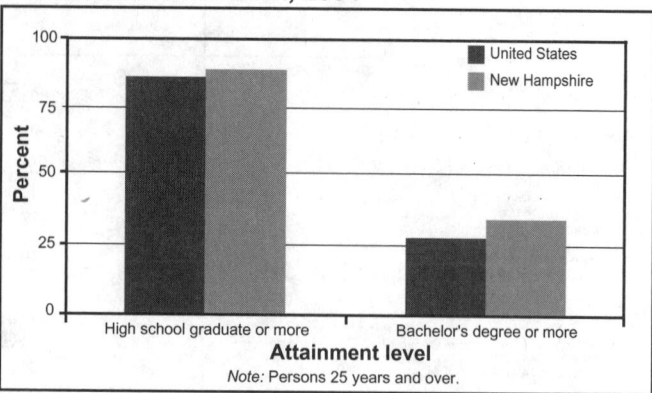

Note: Persons 25 years and over.

EDUCATION

New Hampshire had one the highest educational attainment levels in the nation. In 2004, more than 90 percent of its population age 25 years and over held high school diplomas. More than 35 percent of this age group held bachelor's degrees or more, giving the state the fourth largest proportion of college graduates in the nation. New Hampshire's per student expenditures of $8,579 ranked 17th in the country. The state's student/teacher ratio was well below average, partly reflecting the below average proportion of student-age population. Among the 46 states reporting dropout data, New Hampshire ranked 17th with a rate of 4.0 percent.

VOTER PARTICIPATION

Voter turnout was very high in New Hampshire, particularly for the 2004 election, when its turnout rate of 68.9 percent ranked seventh in the nation. This may have been influenced by the state's position of holding the first presidential primary in the country. Nearly 75 percent of eligible voters between the ages of 45 and 64 years cast ballots in the 2004 election. Nearly 53 percent of those age 18 to 24 years voted. As with most states, the proportion of women voters exceeded that of men. In 2000, 48.1 percent of eligible voters cast ballots for the Republican presidential ticket. In 2004, the Democratic presidential ticket received 50.2 percent of the state's votes.

Table NH-19. Reported Voting and Registration, November 2000 and November 2004

(Numbers in thousands, percent.)

Characteristic	Total population 18 years and over	Total citizen		Total registered		Total voted	
		Number	Percent	Number	Percent	Number	Percent
NOVEMBER 2000							
Total	902	857	95.0	628	69.6	571	63.3
Male	442	421	95.3	301	68.1	271	61.3
Female	461	437	94.8	327	70.9	300	65.2
NOVEMBER 2004							
Total	982	948	96.5	716	72.9	677	68.9
Male	479	461	96.1	341	71.2	320	66.7
Female	503	487	96.8	375	74.6	358	71.1
Race and Hispanic Origin							
White alone	943	922	97.7	699	74.1	663	70.3
Non-Hispanic White alone	932	914	98.0	695	74.5	659	70.6
Black alone	6	3	B	2	B	1	B
Asian alone	17	8	B	5	B	5	B
Hispanic or Latino[1]	11	9	B	5	B	5	B
White alone or in combination	956	935	97.8	708	74.0	670	70.1
Non-Hispanic White alone or in combination	945	926	98.0	703	74.4	665	70.4
Black alone or in combination	7	4	B	3	B	2	B
Asian alone or in combination	18	9	B	6	B	6	B
Age							
18 to 24 years	103	97	94.3	58	56.2	54	52.8
25 to 44 years	377	361	95.7	259	68.7	241	64.1
45 to 64 years	334	325	97.5	260	77.9	249	74.7
65 to 74 years	87	83	B	74	B	70	B
75 years and over	82	81	B	66	B	62	B

[1]May be of any race.
B = Base is too small to show derived measure.

At a Glance:

- New Jersey's population was nearly 8.7 million in 2004, making it the 10th most populous state in the nation. It was also the most densely populated state (though the District of Columbia had a higher population density).

- Non-Hispanic Whites made up nearly 64 percent of the state's population. Hispanics (of any race) accounted for nearly 15 percent of residents.

- The state's median household income was quite high, ranking fifth in the country. New Jersey's poverty rate was correspondingly low at 8 percent, giving the state one of the five lowest rates in the nation.

- New Jersey's unemployment rate was 4.8 percent in 2004 and was well below the national average.

- Real gross state product was the eighth largest in the country in 2004, but grew at a slower than average rate during the 2001–2004 period.

- In 2004, 34.6 percent of New Jersey's population age 25 years and over held bachelor's degrees or more, the sixth highest proportion in the nation.

Table NJ-1. Population by Sex and Age, 1990, 2000, and 2004

(Number, percent.)

Sex and age	1990	2000	2004	Percent distribution, 2004	Average annual percent change, 2000–2004
Total Population	7 730 188	8 414 350	8 698 879	X	0.8
Percent of total U.S. population	3.1	3.0	3.0	X	X
Sex					
Male	3 735 685	4 082 813	4 235 853	48.7	0.9
Female	3 994 503	4 331 537	4 463 026	51.3	0.8
Age					
Under 5 years	532 637	563 785	581 467	6.7	0.4
5 to 17 years	1 266 825	1 523 773	1 574 592	18.1	1.6
18 years and over	1 562 207	6 326 792	6 542 820	75.2	0.7
18 to 24 years	5 930 726	676 628	743 937	8.6	-0.4
25 to 44 years	779 184	2 624 146	2 511 298	28.9	-0.1
45 to 64 years	2 557 310	1 912 882	2 161 444	24.8	2.4
65 years and over	1 032 025	1 113 136	1 126 141	12.9	0.7
85 years and over	95 547	135 999	162 808	1.9	4.1
Median age (years)	34.3	36.7	37.7	X	X

X = Not applicable.

Average Annual Rate of Population Growth, 1980–2004

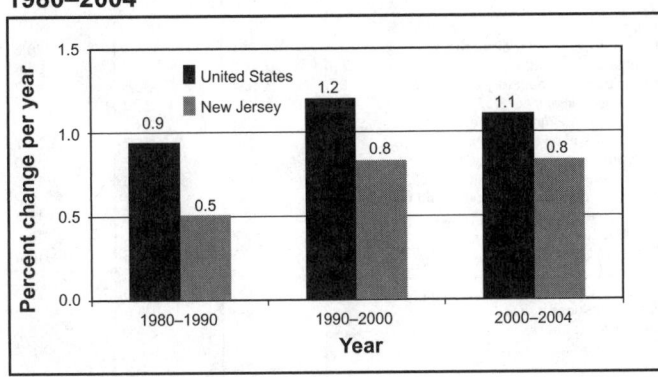

POPULATION

New Jersey's population increased 3.4 percent between 2000 and 2004, which was below the national average rate, but higher than those of neighboring New York and Pennsylvania. Between 2000 and 2004, international immigration to the state totaled 245,000, the sixth highest influx of international immigrants in the country. This more than offset the loss of 135,000 residents to other states. New Jersey's population was slightly older than the nation as a whole, with a median age of 37.7 years. New Jersey had the third largest proportion of Asian and Pacific Islander residents and the ninth largest proportion of Hispanic residents (of any race) in the nation.

Table NJ-2. Population by Race and Hispanic Origin, 1990, 2000, and 2004

(Number, percent.)

Race and Hispanic origin	1990	2000	2004
Total Population	7 730 188	8 414 350	8 698 879
Non-Hispanic (Percent)			
One race[1]			
White	74.0	66.6	63.8
Black	12.7	13.3	13.3
American Indian, Alaska Native[2]	0.2	0.1	0.1
Asian and Pacific Islander[2]	3.5	5.8	6.9
Other race[2]	3.6	. . .	. . .
Two or more races	. . .	0.9	1.0
Hispanic or Latino[3] (Percent)	9.6	13.3	14.9

[1]Individuals could report only one race in the 1990 census and could report one or more races on the 2000 census. Data on race in 2000 and 2004 are not comparable to 1990.
[2]Data for 1990 include people of Hispanic or Latino origin.
[3]May be of any race.
. . . = Not available.

Minority Population as a Percent of Total Population, 2004

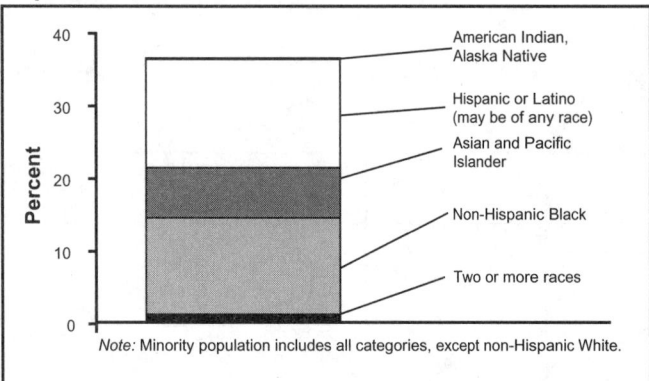

Note: Minority population includes all categories, except non-Hispanic White.

Age-Adjusted Death Rates, Average 2000–2002

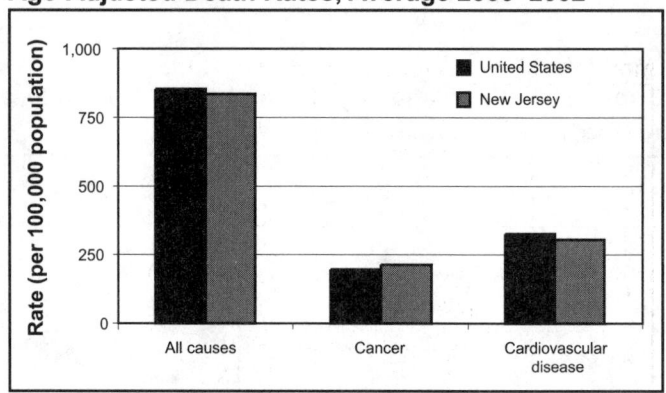

HEALTH

In 2004, 15.3 percent of New Jersey's population lacked health insurance coverage, a rate that was just below the national average. The state's infant mortality rate and age-adjusted death rates were also below the national averages. The state's birth rate for teenage mothers was the sixth lowest in the nation.

Table NJ-3. Health Characteristics, 2000–2004

(Number, rate, percent.)

Item	State	U.S.
Births, 2003–2004		
Number of births	116 983	4 089 950
Birth rate (per 1,000 population)	13.5	14.1
Teenage birth rate (per 1,000 women age 15–19 years)	25.5	41.6
Mortality Rates, Average 2000–2002		
Infant mortality rate (per 1,000 live births)	6.1	6.9
Age-adjusted mortality rate (per 100,000 population)		
All races	829.4	853.3
Non-Hispanic White	819.8	843.1
Black	1 077.0	1 097.7
American Indian, Alaska Native	. . .	687.0
Asian and Pacific Islander	372.5	486.0
Hispanic or Latino[1]	567.6	642.7
Health Insurance, 2004		
Percent of all persons without health insurance	15.3	15.7
Percent of children without health insurance	11.7	11.2
Percent of low-income children without health insurance	5.1	7.1

[1]May be of any race.
. . . = Not available.

Table NJ-4. Leading Causes of Death, Average 2000–2002

(Number, rate per 100,000 population.)

Cause	Number of deaths	Age-adjusted death rates	
		State	U.S.
ALL CAUSES	74 506	829.4	853.3
Leading Causes			
Major cardiovascular diseases	28 801	318.1	326.5
Cancer	18 022	201.7	196.0
Chronic lower respiratory diseases	2 934	32.6	43.7
Unintentional injuries	2 429	27.9	35.7
Diabetes (underlying cause)	2 524	28.2	25.2
Influenza and pneumonia	1 970	21.7	22.7
Alzheimer's disease	1 388	15.2	19.0
Motor vehicle accidents	750	8.8	15.0
Nephritis, nephrotic syndrome, and nephrosis ..	1 551	17.2	13.8
Septicemia	1 853	20.5	11.4
Suicides	567	6.5	10.7
Firearm-related	375	4.5	10.3
Cirrhosis	758	8.5	9.5
Drug-induced	825	9.5	7.9
Alcohol-induced	492	5.5	6.9
Homicides	337	4.0	6.0
Falls	267	3.0	5.2
HIV	792	9.0	5.0
Viral hepatitis	171	1.9	2.0
Anemias	200	2.2	1.6
Drownings	74	0.9	1.3
Fire deaths	76	0.9	1.2

Note: The rates are age-adjusted to the U.S. 2000 standard population.

Table NJ-5. Households and Housing Characteristics, 1990, 2000, and 2004

(Number, percent, and dollars.)

Characteristic	1990	2000	2004	Average annual percent change, 2000–2004
Total Households	2 794 711	3 064 645	3 134 481	0.6
Family households	2 021 346	2 154 539	2 200 082	0.5
Married-couple family	1 578 702	1 638 322	1 655 479	0.3
Other family	442 644	516 217	544 603	1.3
Male householder, no wife present	104 189	129 205	134 496	1.0
Female householder, no husband present	338 455	387 012	410 107	1.5
Nonfamily households	773 365	910 106	934 399	0.7
Householder living alone	646 171	751 287	769 393	0.6
Householder not living alone	127 194	158 819	165 006	1.0
Housing Characteristics				
Average size	2.70	2.68	2.71	X
Housing units	3 075 310	3 310 275	3 414 739	0.8
Occupied housing units	2 794 711	3 064 645	3 134 481	0.6
Owner-occupied	1 813 381	2 011 473	2 134 253	1.5
Renter-occupied	981 330	1 053 172	1 000 228	-1.3
Median gross rent of renter-occupied housing units (dollars) ...	592	751	877	4.0
Median value of owner-occupied housing units (dollars)	161 200	170 800	291 294	14.3

X = Not applicable.

Median Housing Value and Median Rent, 2004

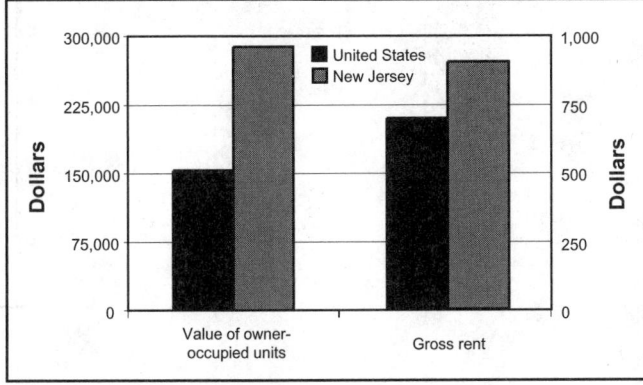

Median Household Income, 1984–2004 (2004 Dollars)

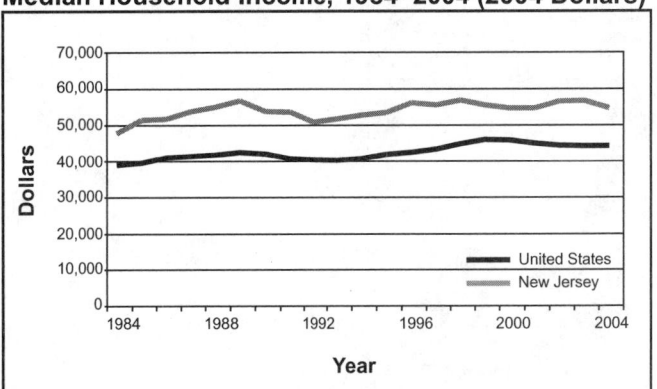

Table NJ-6. Household Income and Poverty Status, 1980–2004

(2004 CPI-U-RS adjusted dollars, rate.)

Year	State		U.S.	
	Median household income (2004 dollars)	Poverty rate	Median household income (2004 dollars)	Poverty rate
2004	55 446	8.0	44 389	12.7
2003	57 551	8.6	44 482	12.5
2002	57 318	7.9	44 546	12.1
2001	55 245	8.1	45 062	11.7
2000	55 289	7.3	46 058	11.3
1999	56 373	7.8	46 129	11.9
1998	57 666	8.6	45 003	12.7
1997	56 359	9.3	43 430	13.3
1996	56 900	9.2	42 544	13.7
1995	54 065	7.8	41 943	13.8
1994	53 305	9.2	40 677	14.5
1993	52 136	10.9	40 217	15.1
1992	51 458	10.3	40 422	14.8
1991	54 167	9.7	40 746	14.2
1990	54 283	9.2	41 963	13.5
1989	57 550	8.2	42 524	12.8
1988	55 675	6.2	41 771	13.0
1987	54 449	8.3	41 322	13.4
1986	52 151	8.9	40 939	13.6
1985	51 872	8.3	39 545	14.0
1984	48 058	10.1	38 782	14.4
1983	. . .	11.1	. . .	15.2
1982	. . .	12.2	. . .	15.0
1981	. . .	10.0	. . .	14.0
1980	. . .	9.0	. . .	13.0

. . . = Not available.

Table NJ-7. Employment Status by Demographic Group, 2004

(Numbers in thousands, rate.)

Characteristic	Civilian noninstitutional population	Civilian labor force		Employed	Unemployment rate
		Number	Participation rate		
SEX AND AGE					
Total	6 666	4 388	65.8	4 178	4.8
16 to 19 years	489	178	36.3	153	13.8
20 to 24 years	569	416	73.0	384	7.6
25 to 34 years	1 011	847	83.8	809	4.5
35 to 44 years	1 370	1 135	82.9	1 093	3.7
45 to 54 years	1 273	1 064	83.5	1 018	4.3
55 to 64 years	875	603	68.9	579	4.0
65 years and over	1 078	146	13.5	141	3.5
Men	3 183	2 356	74.0	2 245	4.7
16 to 19 years	258	95	36.8	82	13.2
20 to 24 years	269	203	75.5	186	8.7
25 to 34 years	505	475	94.1	457	3.8
35 to 44 years	674	631	93.6	608	3.6
45 to 54 years	627	569	90.7	547	3.9
55 to 64 years	407	305	74.9	290	4.9
65 years and over	442	77	17.5	75	3.7
Women	3 483	2 032	58.4	1 933	4.9
16 to 19 years	231	83	35.7	71	14.4
20 to 24 years	300	212	70.8	198	6.6
25 to 34 years	506	372	73.5	352	5.3
35 to 44 years	696	504	72.5	485	3.8
45 to 54 years	646	494	76.5	471	4.7
55 to 64 years	469	298	63.7	289	3.0
65 years and over	636	68	10.8	66	3.3
MARITAL STATUS					
Married men, spouse present	1 802	1 432	79.4	1 386	3.2
Married women, spouse present	1 758	1 072	61.0	1 034	3.5
Women who maintain families	369	254	68.9	235	7.5
RACE, HISPANIC ORIGIN, AND SEX					
White	5 303	3 489	65.8	3 343	4.2
Men	2 558	1 895	74.1	1 815	4.2
Women	2 745	1 594	58.1	1 528	4.1
Black	894	583	65.2	530	9.1
Men	398	274	69.0	249	9.2
Women	496	308	62.2	281	9.0
Asian	400	266	66.5	257	3.3
Men	194	162	83.6	158	2.6
Women	205	103	50.3	99	4.5
Hispanic or Latino[1]	860	621	72.2	592	4.6
Men	426	347	81.6	334	3.7
Women	434	273	62.9	258	5.7
RACE, HISPANIC ORIGIN, AND AGE					
White					
25 to 34 years	757	642	84.8	619	3.6
35 to 44 years	1 071	889	83.0	859	3.4
45 to 54 years	1 031	871	84.5	839	3.7
55 to 64 years	712	491	69.0	473	3.7

Note: Data in Table 7 are from the Current Population Survey (CPS) and do not match Bureau of Labor Statistics estimates in Table 8. See notes and definitions for more details.

[1]May be of any race.

Table NJ-8. Employment Status, 1990–2004

(Numbers in thousands, rate.)

Year	Civilian labor force	Employed	Unemployed	Unemployment rate
2004	4 388 042	4 176 230	211 812	4.8
2003	4 370 977	4 115 123	255 854	5.9
2002	4 371 573	4 117 644	253 929	5.8
2001	4 295 771	4 111 546	184 225	4.3
2000	4 286 660	4 129 103	157 557	3.7
1999	4 284 555	4 092 714	191 841	4.5
1998	4 242 366	4 047 062	195 304	4.6
1997	4 257 440	4 031 022	226 418	5.3
1996	4 184 052	3 925 794	258 258	6.2
1995	4 111 828	3 846 322	265 506	6.5
1994	4 067 486	3 789 960	277 526	6.8
1993	4 034 585	3 727 262	307 323	7.6
1992	4 051 920	3 709 471	342 449	8.5
1991	4 050 380	3 776 632	273 748	6.8
1990	4 072 494	3 864 958	207 536	5.1

Note: Population age 16 years and over.

Unemployment Rate, 1980–2004

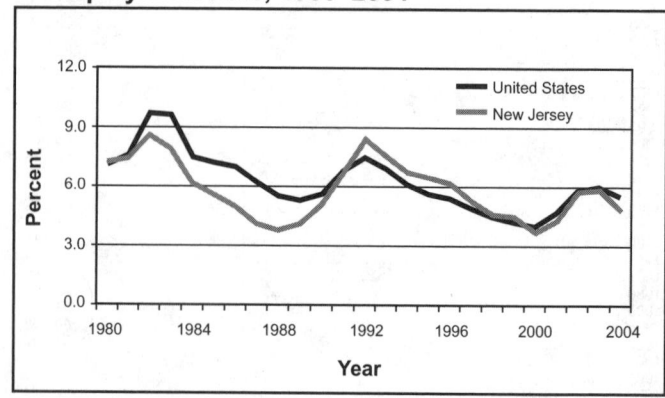

Table NJ-9. Employment and Average Wages by Industry, 2001–2004

(Estimates are based on the 2002 North American Industry Classification System [NAICS].)

Industry	2001	2002	2003	2004	Annual average percent change, 2001–2004
	Number of jobs				
TOTAL EMPLOYMENT BY PLACE OF WORK	4 789 296	4 805 562	4 837 532	4 894 023	0.7
Farm Employment	18 529	19 100	17 560	17 496	-1.9
Nonfarm Employment	4 770 767	4 786 462	4 819 972	4 876 527	0.7
Private employment	4 158 047	4 162 677	4 185 402	4 230 876	0.6
Forestry, fishing, hunting, and other[1]	6 607	6 943	6 309	6 264	-1.8
Mining	3 090	2 515	2 872	2 977	-1.2
Utilities	16 461	16 035	15 494	15 234	-2.5
Construction	226 454	228 275	231 253	239 080	1.8
Manufacturing	410 358	378 665	360 982	350 385	-5.1
Durable goods manufacturing	187 252	168 324	160 508	156 735	-5.8
Nondurable goods manufacturing	223 106	210 341	200 474	193 650	-4.6
Wholesale trade	259 217	249 684	248 129	249 039	-1.3
Retail trade	535 187	538 549	545 282	548 746	0.8
Transportation and warehousing	200 132	193 392	191 664	191 826	-1.4
Information	136 055	122 162	114 341	110 076	-6.8
Finance and insurance	275 661	279 552	280 415	280 709	0.6
Real estate and rental and leasing	165 991	173 486	187 515	197 295	5.9
Professional and technical services	402 822	392 657	389 741	394 545	-0.7
Management of companies and enterprises	66 335	69 283	67 941	67 046	0.4
Administrative and waste services	296 558	306 899	303 726	314 906	2.0
Educational services	95 084	102 322	105 649	107 206	4.1
Health care and social assistance	478 685	496 581	509 814	519 159	2.7
Arts, entertainment, and recreation	82 276	87 373	89 542	92 643	4.0
Accommodation and food services	275 416	281 074	291 539	296 483	2.5
Other services, except public administration	225 658	237 230	243 194	247 257	3.1
Government and government enterprises	612 720	623 785	634 570	645 651	1.8
	Dollars				
AVERAGE WAGES AND SALARIES BY PLACE OF WORK	43 497	44 315	45 583	47 217	2.8
Farm Earnings	18 617	23 738	23 630	26 005	11.8
Nonfarm Earnings	43 552	44 363	45 627	47 259	2.8
Private earnings	43 549	44 208	45 420	46 982	2.6
Forestry, fishing, hunting, and other[1]	19 994	21 177	20 937	21 763	2.9
Mining	52 606	53 292	52 058	56 308	2.3
Utilities	72 183	74 051	77 136	79 866	3.4
Construction	49 739	50 358	50 335	51 215	1.0
Manufacturing	51 075	52 990	56 040	58 945	4.9
Durable goods manufacturing	48 013	49 626	51 815	53 862	3.9
Nondurable goods manufacturing	53 631	55 665	59 401	63 030	5.5
Wholesale trade	60 196	60 600	64 248	64 717	2.4
Retail trade	26 784	27 614	28 143	28 365	1.9
Transportation and warehousing	37 995	39 016	40 090	42 098	3.5
Information	64 826	66 988	68 840	72 263	3.7
Finance and insurance	75 091	77 033	78 398	82 656	3.3
Real estate and rental and leasing	39 851	41 681	43 096	47 543	6.1
Professional and technical services	67 160	67 812	69 116	72 182	2.4
Management of companies and enterprises	85 642	88 690	94 349	101 887	6.0
Administrative and waste services	28 538	29 222	30 876	32 189	4.1
Educational services	30 712	30 973	32 885	31 182	0.5
Health care and social assistance	36 642	37 912	39 125	40 944	3.8
Arts, entertainment, and recreation	26 989	27 666	28 612	27 799	1.0
Accommodation and food services	19 124	19 578	19 698	20 242	1.9
Other services, except public administration	25 296	25 849	26 763	27 889	3.3
Government and government enterprises	43 574	45 218	46 746	48 742	3.8

Note: Average wages and salaries are a calculation by the editors of wage and salary disbursements divided by full- and part-time wage and salary employment. Data may not add to total or may appear as zero due to rounding.

[1] "Other" consists of the number of jobs held by U.S. residents employed by international organizations and foreign embassies and consulates in the United States.

LABOR MARKET

New Jersey's unemployment rate rose sharply after the 2001 recession, reflecting the national pattern. However, in 2004, the unemployment rate was below the national average. Employment growth was relatively slow over the 2001–2004 period, as manufacturing employment declined and several service industries also experienced losses in jobs. Retail trade was one of the state's largest employers, and its job growth was sluggish during the early 2000s. Employment was stronger in health care and educational services. Average wages and salaries were above the national average across all major industries, although their rate of growth between 2001 and 2004 was only average.

Employment by Industry, 2004

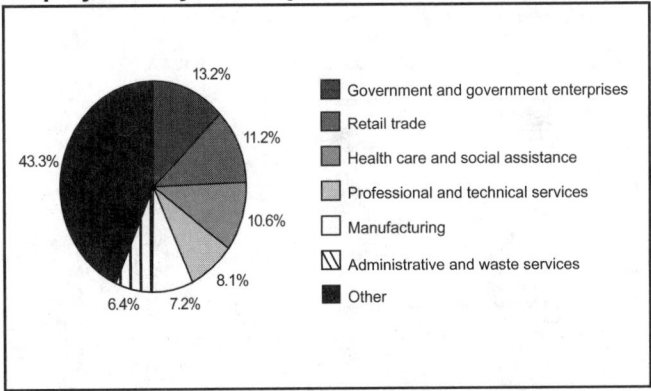

- Government and government enterprises
- Retail trade
- Health care and social assistance
- Professional and technical services
- Manufacturing
- Administrative and waste services
- Other

43.3% — 13.2% — 11.2% — 10.6% — 8.1% — 7.2% — 6.4%

Table NJ-10. Personal Income by Major Source, Selected Years 1980–2004

(Millions of dollars, except where noted.)

Item	1980	1990	2000	2001	2002	2003	2004	Average annual percent change, 2000–2004
Earnings by Place of Work	62 549	139 821	233 441	238 440	245 449	252 476	265 521	3.3
Wage and salary disbursements	47 913	105 863	175 899	178 335	181 215	186 204	194 057	2.5
Supplements to wages and salaries	9 543	21 398	32 316	33 542	37 226	38 965	41 773	6.6
Proprietors' income[1]	5 093	12 560	25 226	26 562	27 009	27 306	29 690	4.2
Farm proprietors' income	37	115	108	65	-15	13	6	-50.7
Nonfarm proprietors' income	5 056	12 446	25 118	26 497	27 023	27 293	29 684	4.3
(-) Contributions for government social insurance[2]	6 325	16 641	26 854	27 970	28 635	29 198	30 241	3.0
(+) Adjustment for residence[3]	7 159	10 556	25 657	27 219	24 819	24 734	27 371	1.6
(=) **Net Earnings by Place of Residence**	63 384	133 736	232 244	237 689	241 633	248 011	262 650	3.1
(+) Dividends, interest, and rent[4]	13 209	37 702	56 234	56 587	54 151	52 305	54 806	-0.6
(+) Personal current transfer receipts	9 763	19 315	35 076	38 676	42 089	43 105	44 734	6.3
Personal income	86 355	190 753	323 554	332 951	337 873	343 421	362 190	2.9
Farm income	86 246	190 527	323 262	332 700	337 645	343 200	361 958	2.9
Nonfarm income	109	226	292	252	228	221	232	-5.6
Per Capita Personal Income (Dollars)[5]	11 707	24 572	38 365	39 142	39 392	39 737	41 636	2.1

Note: Data may not add to total or may appear as zero due to rounding.

[1]Proprietors' income includes the inventory valuation adjustment and the capital consumption adjustment.
[2]Contributions for government social insurance are included in earnings by type and industry, but they are excluded from personal income.
[3]The adjustment for residence is the net inflow of the earnings of interarea commuters.
[4]Rental income of persons includes the capital consumption adjustment.
[5]Per capita personal income is total personal income divided by total midyear population.

Per Capita Personal Income, 1980–2004 (Current Dollars)

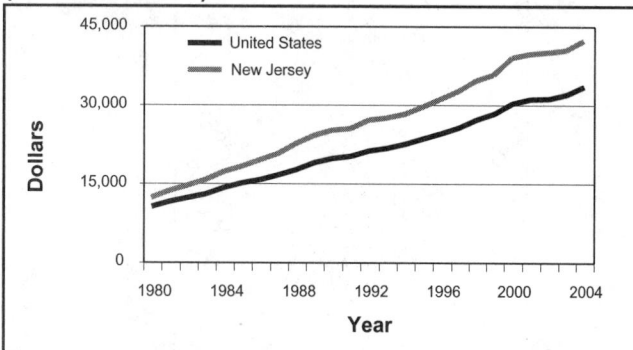

ECONOMIC ACTIVITY

Real gross state product (GSP) did not decline during the 2001 recession, but growth since then has been slower than the growth in most other states. Over the 2003–2004 period, New Jersey's GSP grew 3.4 percent, ranking 38th in the country. Contributing to this slow growth were the modest gains in manufacturing, construction, and retail trade. Real estate, finance and insurance, and government were the strongest sectors. Housing prices have appreciated substantially over recent years, particularly 1-1 in areas around New York City. In 2004, the median value of owner-occupied housing in New Jersey was the fifth highest in the nation.

Table NJ-11. Real Gross State Product, 1997–2004

(Millions of chained 2000 dollars, percent.)

Industry	1997	1998	1999	2000	2001	2002	2003	2004	Average annual percent change, 2001–2004
GROSS STATE PRODUCT	316 128	325 271	332 926	343 959	354 390	363 045	371 806	384 466	2.8
As a percent of U.S. gross product	3.7	3.6	3.5	3.5	3.6	3.6	3.6	3.6	X
Private Industries	281 981	291 959	299 648	310 296	320 207	328 450	336 435	347 931	2.8
Agriculture, forestry, fishing, and hunting	449	480	515	639	545	611	547	456	-5.8
Mining	163	197	212	204	204	157	168	164	-7.0
Utilities	6 290	6 178	6 328	6 726	6 488	6 592	7 070	7 309	4.1
Construction	12 891	13 000	12 936	13 265	14 269	14 314	13 976	14 222	-0.1
Manufacturing	37 105	36 362	38 639	40 614	39 878	41 028	43 274	44 220	3.5
As a percent of gross state product	11.7	11.2	11.6	11.8	11.3	11.3	11.6	11.5	X
Wholesale trade	25 719	28 674	29 177	29 873	32 265	32 153	32 041	31 506	-0.8
Retail trade	19 286	20 182	21 065	22 368	24 277	26 065	27 472	28 248	5.2
Transportation and warehousing	10 227	10 523	11 009	11 242	10 545	10 664	11 486	11 766	3.7
Information	15 320	15 610	16 121	16 646	17 741	17 646	18 003	19 389	3.0
Finance and insurance	21 009	22 810	24 392	26 949	29 038	30 837	32 519	34 447	5.9
Real estate and rental and leasing	48 233	49 414	49 365	51 004	54 084	54 828	54 945	58 641	2.7
Services	85 892	88 922	90 012	90 767	90 956	93 701	95 268	97 963	2.5
As a percent of gross state product	27.2	27.3	27.0	26.4	25.7	25.8	25.6	25.5	X
Professional and technical services	25 405	27 693	29 296	29 918	30 118	30 145	30 273	31 206	1.2
Management of companies and enterprises	9 177	8 878	8 627	8 616	7 544	8 268	8 202	8 204	2.8
Administrative and waste services	10 661	10 871	11 094	10 265	10 294	11 071	11 512	12 040	5.4
Educational services	2 532	2 639	2 756	2 868	2 861	2 836	2 812	2 501	-4.4
Health care and social assistance	20 570	20 845	20 590	21 102	22 043	23 013	23 658	24 380	3.4
Arts, entertainment, and recreation	2 546	2 643	2 527	2 545	2 890	2 988	3 094	3 070	2.0
Accommodation and food services	8 348	8 498	8 475	8 699	8 475	8 667	8 875	9 186	2.7
Other services, except public administration	6 653	6 855	6 647	6 754	6 731	6 713	6 842	7 376	3.1
Government	34 249	33 341	33 285	33 662	34 187	34 610	35 389	36 535	2.2
As a percent of gross state product	10.8	10.3	10.0	9.8	9.6	9.5	9.5	9.5	X

X = Not applicable.

Table NJ-12. Government Transfer Payments, Selected Years 1980–2004

(Millions of dollars, percent.)

Item	1980	1990	2000	2001	2002	2003	2004	Average annual percent change, 2000–2004
CURRENT TRANSFER PAYMENTS TO INDIVIDUALS	9 180	18 215	33 092	36 484	40 129	41 282	42 896	6.7
Retirement and Disability Insurance Benefits	4 686	9 068	14 328	15 142	15 850	16 301	17 103	4.5
Old-age, survivors, and disability insurance (OASDI) benefits	4 372	8 465	13 525	14 227	14 840	15 236	15 904	4.1
Railroad retirement and disability benefits	116	149	151	151	154	154	157	1.1
Workers' compensation	52	137	231	252	224	235	244	1.4
Other government retirement and disability insurance benefits	147	317	421	511	631	676	798	17.3
Medical Benefits	2 001	6 148	14 805	16 742	18 112	18 575	18 736	6.1
Medicare benefits	1 224	3 497	7 991	8 818	9 397	9 876	10 791	7.8
Public assistance medical care benefits	770	2 623	6 787	7 888	8 668	8 655	7 891	3.8
Military medical insurance benefits	7	28	27	36	47	44	54	18.5
Income Maintenance Benefits	1 131	1 405	2 063	2 194	2 380	2 549	2 725	7.2
Supplemental Security Income (SSI) benefits	156	347	674	702	723	733	766	3.2
Family assistance	562	504	250	333	370	386	406	12.9
Food stamps	235	308	299	295	314	348	395	7.2
Other income maintenance benefits	177	247	840	864	973	1 083	1 159	8.4
Unemployment Insurance Compensation	880	1 028	1 127	1 577	2 867	2 681	1 978	15.1
Veterans' Benefits	365	415	487	506	553	588	613	5.9
Federal Education and Training Assistance	114	138	262	284	318	302	322	5.3
Other Payments to Individuals	3	13	20	38	50	286	1 418	189.6

Note: See notes and definitions for more details. Data may not add to total or may appear as zero due to rounding.

EXPORTS

The value of New Jersey's exports was $19.2 billion in 2004, the 12th highest in the nation. Chemical manufactures were the state's leading export, accounting for 27.2 percent of total exports, followed by computers and electronic products. With the exception of chemical manufactures, the state's other leading exports all declined from 2001 to 2004. Canada was the largest export market for New Jersey's goods. Exports to Japan fell by over 34 percent from 2001 to 2002, primarily as a result of a drop in computers and electronic products and machinery manufactures exports. However, by 2004, exports to Japan had risen to over $1.1 billion, which was still below the 2001 value of exports to that country.

Leading Exports, 2004

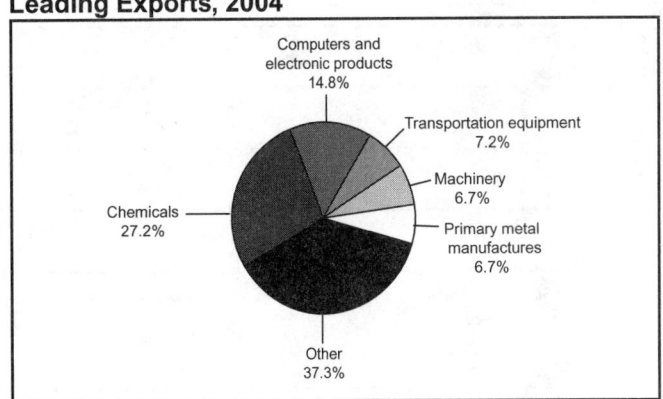

Table NJ-13. Exports of Goods by Leading Products and Destinations, 2001–2004

(Millions of dollars, percent, rank based on 2004 dollar values.)

Product and market	2001	2002	2003	2004	Percent share of total, 2004	Average annual percent change, 2001–2004
Total Goods						
Total	18 946	17 002	16 818	19 192	100.0	0.4
Manufactures	17 562	15 610	15 312	17 292	90.1	-0.5
Agriculture and livestock	312	268	307	346	1.8	3.5
Other commodities	1 072	1 124	1 199	1 554	8.1	13.2
Five Leading Exports (NAICS Code)						
Chemical manufactures (325)	4 924	4 508	4 591	5 229	27.2	2.0
Computers and electronic products (334)	3 586	2 589	2 555	2 843	14.8	-7.5
Transportation equipment (336)	1 564	1 557	1 397	1 388	7.2	-3.9
Machinery manufactures (333)	1 317	1 033	1 123	1 290	6.7	-0.7
Primary metal manufactures (331)	1 491	1 113	1 009	1 287	6.7	-4.8
Five Leading Markets	16 885	15 168	14 998	17 044	88.8	0.3
Canada	3 914	3 705	3 757	4 164	21.7	2.1
United Kingdom	1 639	1 336	1 407	1 772	9.2	2.6
Japan	1 470	930	936	1 149	6.0	-7.9
Mexico	1 107	862	831	1 140	5.9	1.0
Germany	1 037	911	1 022	1 058	5.5	0.7

Table NJ-14. Agriculture, 1997 and 2002
(Number, acres, and dollars.)

Item	1997	2002
Number of farms	10 045	9 924
Land in farms (acres)	856 909	805 682
Farm Size		
Average size of farm (acres)	85	81
Farms by size (percent distribution)		
Fewer than 50 acres	68.5	70.5
50 to 499 acres	28.0	26.1
500 acres or more	3.5	3.5
Market Value of Land and Equipment (Dollars)		
Land and buildings average value per farm	572 273	741 808
Average value per acre	6 710	9 245
Machinery and equipment average value per farm	46 233	53 954
Value of Sales (Thousands of Dollars)		
Agricultural products sold	707 161	749 872
Crops	600 547	657 494
Livestock, poultry, and their products	106 613	92 378
Average per farm (dollars)	70 399	75 561
Value of sales (percent distribution)		
Less than $10,000	63.3	71.0
$10,000 to $99,999	24.9	18.3
$100,000 or more	11.7	10.7
Government Payments		
Payments (thousands of dollars)	3 001	4 441
Percent of farms receiving government payments	7.1	5.9
Farm operators whose principal occupation is farming (percent)	41.9	52.3

AGRICULTURE

Cash receipts from farming amounted to $750 million in 2002, according to the Department of Agriculture's Census of Agriculture. This was an increase of 7.6 percent from the previous farm census in 1997. The leading agricultural products were greenhouse/nursery goods and horses. More than 70 percent of New Jersey's farms had less than $10,000 in sales. About 70 percent of farms spanned fewer than 50 acres, which was the second highest proportion of farms this size in the nation. Over 52 percent of farm operators reported farming as their primary occupation.

ENERGY

In 2001, energy expenditures per person were $2,373, an amount lower than the national average. The state's energy prices were above average. New Jersey's per capita consumption was below the national average. The chief sources of energy were petroleum, natural gas, and nuclear power. The transportation sector was the state's largest consumer of energy.

Energy Consumption by Source, 2001

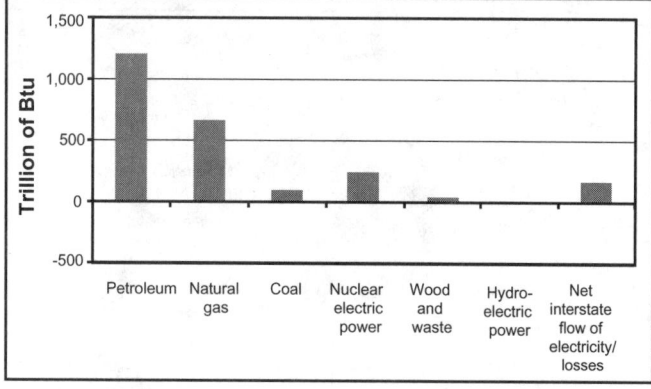

Energy Consumption by Sector, 2001

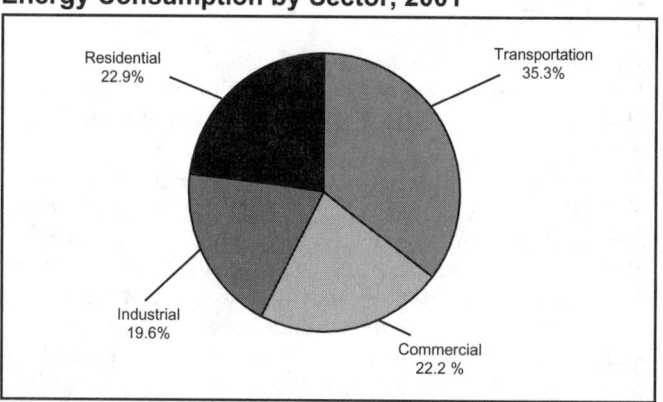

Table NJ-15. Energy Consumption, Expenditures, and Prices, Selected Years 1960–2001
(Dollars, Btu [British Thermal Unit], percent distribution.)

Item	1960	1965	1970	1975	1980	1985	1990	1995	2000	2001
Total Consumption (Billion Btu)	1 302 630	1 597 260	2 028 018	1 939 119	2 134 403	2 214 577	2 336 426	2 563 653	2 523 014	2 500 366
Consumption per capita (million Btu)	214.7	236.0	282.8	264.3	289.8	292.7	302.2	321.8	299.8	294.0
Consumption by Sector (Percent Distribution)										
Residential	23.8	24.6	24.5	25.7	24.1	22.6	21.6	21.3	23.0	22.9
Commercial	12.8	13.4	16.1	16.7	18.1	17.4	20.9	20.1	22.6	22.2
Industrial	37.4	37.0	35.0	30.9	31.3	24.0	23.3	25.2	18.5	19.6
Transportation	25.9	25.0	24.3	26.8	26.5	36.0	34.2	33.5	35.9	35.3
Consumption by Source (Billion Btu)										
Coal	168 775	236 647	123 291	60 498	68 692	103 310	80 800	79 902	114 733	112 217
Natural gas	144 132	219 196	331 247	251 669	351 039	389 090	458 050	720 661	626 483	585 825
Petroleum	956 293	1 099 673	1 489 793	1 323 581	1 325 505	1 258 062	1 234 459	1 247 885	1 251 133	1 246 307
Nuclear electric power	0	0	37 917	34 645	83 192	188 752	251 538	176 576	298 041	318 913
Hydroelectric power[1]	480	-326	-4 228	-2 834	-2 934	-2 550	-1 229	-862	-1 291	-1 259
Wood and waste	20 034	24 019	30 134	33 783	58 433	48 820	21 157	43 764	38 554	36 777
Other	0	0	0	0	0	0	435	575	665	683
Net interstate flow of electricity/losses[2]	12 916	18 051	19 864	237 776	250 477	229 092	291 216	295 151	194 697	201 474
Total Expenditures (Thousands of Dollars)	...	...	3 094 000	6 243 700	13 177 900	16 118 500	16 088 000	17 436 800	20 758 000	20 178 400
Expenditures per capita (dollars)	...	...	432	851	1 789	2 130	2 081	2 189	2 467	2 373
Prices by Sector (Dollars Per Million Btu)										
Total	...	...	1.95	4.28	8.35	9.53	9.21	9.04	11.03	11.00
Residential	...	...	2.27	4.47	8.75	11.71	11.83	12.86	12.80	13.24
Commercial	...	...	2.01	5.18	9.20	13.65	12.50	14.50	13.71	15.26
Industrial	...	...	1.20	3.51	7.15	9.31	7.80	6.36	9.26	9.29
Transportation	...	...	2.39	4.32	8.60	7.54	7.56	6.97	9.91	9.20

[1]A negative number in this row results from pumped storage for which, overall, more electricity is expended than created to provide electricity during peak demand periods.
[2]Net interstate flow of electricity is the difference between the amount of energy in the electricity sold within a state (including associated losses) and the energy input at the electric utilities within the state. A positive number indicates that more electricity (including associated losses) came into the state than went out of the state during the year; conversely, a negative number indicates that more electricity (including associated losses) went out of the state than came into the state.
... = Not available.

Table NJ-16. State Taxes, Fiscal 2004

(Dollars, percent distribution.)

Item	Thousands of dollars	Percent distribution	Dollars per capita	
			State	U.S.
TOTAL TAXES	20 981 428	100.0	2 411.9	2 024.8
Property Taxes	3 660	0.0	0.4	38.9
Sales and Gross Receipts	9 740 284	46.4	1 119.7	1 003.4
General sales and gross receipts	6 261 700	29.8	719.8	677.0
Selective sales taxes	3 478 584	16.6	399.9	326.4
Amusements	468 072	2.2	53.8	17.0
Insurance premiums	417 873	2.0	48.0	47.0
Motor fuels	546 952	2.6	62.9	114.6
Public utilities	942 744	4.5	108.4	39.2
Tobacco products	777 512	3.7	89.4	42.0
Other selective sales	238 074	1.1	27.4	49.8
Licenses	1 177 242	5.6	135.3	134.9
Corporation	249 969	1.2	28.7	21.6
Motor vehicle	398 691	1.9	45.8	59.4
Occupation and business, not elsewhere classified	407 712	1.9	46.9	37.1
Other Taxes	10 060 242	47.9	1 156.5	847.6
Individual income	7 400 733	35.3	850.8	673.6
Corporation net income	1 896 998	9.0	218.1	105.1
Death and gift	516 008	2.5	59.3	19.6
Documentary and stock transfer	246 503	1.2	28.3	27.1

GOVERNMENT FINANCE

In 2003, state revenues per person were much higher than the national average, ranking 12th in the country. Expenditures per capita were only slightly above the national average. The state had one of the largest differences between per capita expenditures and per capita revenues. New Jersey's per capita debt amounted to $3,889, which was among the 10 highest amounts in the country. Spending per resident on hospitals and correctional facilities was above average, while outlays on education, public welfare, and health were below average. In fiscal year 2004, taxes per person were well above average, ranking eighth in the nation.

Per Capita State Taxes, Fiscal 2004

Table NJ-17. State Government Finances, 2003

(Dollars, percent distribution.)

Item	Millions of dollars	Percent distribution	Dollars per capita	
			State	U.S.
GENERAL REVENUE	38 819 455	100.0	4 492.0	3 832.6
Intergovernmental revenue	9 064 614	23.4	1 048.9	1 246.0
Taxes	19 936 266	51.4	2 306.9	1 891.6
General sales	5 936 057	15.3	686.9	636.0
Selective sales	3 085 383	7.9	357.0	307.4
License taxes	1 169 923	3.0	135.4	123.6
Individual income tax	6 735 282	17.4	779.4	626.8
Corporate income tax	2 397 043	6.2	277.4	97.8
Other taxes	612 578	1.6	70.9	99.9
Current charges	3 940 368	10.2	456.0	366.5
Miscellaneous general revenue	5 878 207	15.1	680.2	328.6
GENERAL EXPENDITURE	34 859 788	100.0	4 033.8	4 010.5
Intergovernmental expenditure	8 997 417	25.8	1 041.1	1 316.9
Direct expenditure	25 862 371	74.2	2 992.6	2 693.6
Expenditure by Function				
Education	11 215 395	32.2	1 297.8	1 416.4
Public welfare	7 005 033	20.1	810.6	1 083.3
Hospitals	1 402 133	4.0	162.2	132.3
Health	882 500	2.5	102.1	173.0
Highways	2 559 450	7.3	296.2	295.4
Police protection	390 817	1.1	45.2	38.4
Correction	1 294 773	3.7	149.8	135.0
Natural resources	371 247	1.1	43.0	64.0
Parks and recreation	362 743	1.0	42.0	20.1
Government administration	1 317 210	3.8	152.4	151.3
Interest on general debt	1 151 253	3.3	133.2	107.8
Other and unallocable	6 907 234	19.8	799.3	393.4
DEBT AT END OF FISCAL YEAR	33 608 678	X	3 889.0	2 404.7
CASH AND SECURITY HOLDINGS	84 400 619	X	9 766.3	8 938.4

X = Not applicable.

Table NJ-18. Education Indicators, 2000–2004

(Percent, number.)

Item	State	U.S.
Total Population 25 Years and Over (Thousands), 2004	5 655	186 877
Educational Attainment, 2004		
Percent high school graduate or more	87.6	85.2
Percent college graduate or more	34.6	27.7
Elementary and Secondary Schools, 2002–2003		
Total students	1 367 438	48 202 324
Percent of students eligible for free or reduced-price lunch ..	25.6	40.6
Percent of students who were English language learners	4.2	7.8
Total schools	2 414	92 330
Student/teacher ratio	12.7	15.9
Per student expenditures	12 568	8 041
Dropouts, Grades 9–12, 2000–2001 (Percent)	2.5	...
Higher Education, 2002–2003		
Total enrollment	380 051	17 035 027
Bachelor's degrees awarded	29 604	1 348 503
Percent women	57.9	57.5

. . . = Not available.

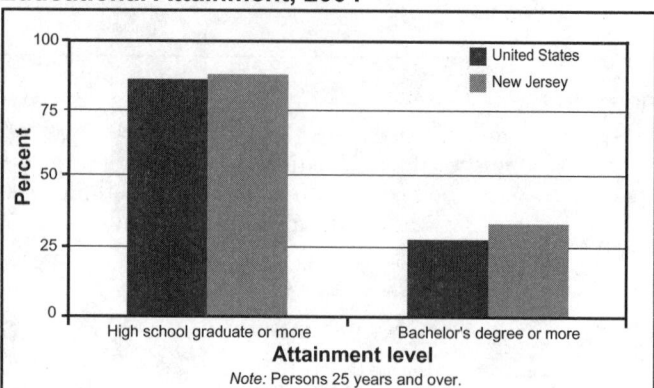

Educational Attainment, 2004

Note: Persons 25 years and over.

EDUCATION

Over 87 percent of New Jersey residents age 25 years and over held high school diplomas. Close to 35 percent of the population in this age group held bachelor's degrees or more, which was the sixth highest proportion in the nation. The state's per student expenditures of $12,568 were the highest in the nation, and more than $4,500 above the national average. New Jersey's student/teacher ratio was the third lowest in the country. Among the 46 states reporting dropout data, New Jersey had the fifth lowest rate at 2.5 percent. Less than 26 percent of students were eligible for free or reduced-price lunch, which was well below the national average.

VOTER PARTICIPATION

Voter turnout was slightly below average for both the 2000 and 2004 elections. In 2000, 55.2 percent of eligible residents voted; this proportion increased to 57.6 percent in 2004. Asians and Hispanics had the lowest voter participation rates in 2004. Nearly 70 percent of eligible residents age 65 to 74 years old voted. This proportion fell to 43.1 percent for persons age 18 to 24 years old. In 2000, 56.1 percent of voters voted for the Democratic presidential candidate, a proportion that fell to 52.9 percent in 2004, according to the official tally by the Clerk of the U.S. House of Representatives.

Table NJ-19. Reported Voting and Registration, November 2000 and November 2004

(Numbers in thousands, percent.)

Characteristic	Total population 18 years and over	Total citizen		Total registered		Total voted	
		Number	Percent	Number	Percent	Number	Percent
NOVEMBER 2000							
Total	6 109	5 458	89.3	3 859	63.2	3 374	55.2
Male	2 919	2 598	89.0	1 820	62.4	1 602	54.9
Female	3 190	2 860	89.7	2 039	63.9	1 772	55.5
NOVEMBER 2004							
Total	6 413	5 591	87.2	4 085	63.7	3 693	57.6
Male	3 052	2 621	85.9	1 852	60.7	1 676	54.9
Female	3 361	2 971	88.4	2 233	66.4	2 017	60.0
Race and Hispanic Origin							
White alone	5 174	4 621	89.3	3 410	65.9	3 086	59.7
Non-Hispanic White alone	4 354	4 189	96.2	3 108	71.4	2 839	65.2
Black alone	845	732	86.7	523	61.9	462	54.7
Asian alone	335	194	58.1	115	34.3	107	32.1
Hispanic or Latino[1]	906	475	52.4	331	36.6	277	30.6
White alone or in combination	5 227	4 658	89.1	3 443	65.9	3 120	59.7
Non-Hispanic White alone or in combination	4 374	4 210	96.2	3 125	71.4	2 856	65.3
Black alone or in combination	858	745	86.9	535	62.3	473	55.2
Asian alone or in combination	337	197	58.3	115	34.1	107	31.8
Age							
18 to 24 years	753	643	85.4	388	51.6	324	43.1
25 to 44 years	2 405	1 939	80.6	1 374	57.1	1 239	51.5
45 to 64 years	2 228	2 023	90.8	1 546	69.4	1 440	64.6
65 to 74 years	569	547	96.0	439	77.1	398	69.8
75 years and over	458	439	96.0	338	73.9	293	63.9

[1]May be of any race.

At a Glance:

- In 2004, New Mexico's population was 1.9 million, ranking it as the 36th most populous state in the nation.

- New Mexico is one of just a few states in which non-Hispanic Whites made up less than 50 percent of the population. Hispanics (of any race) made up 43.3 percent of the population, which was the highest proportion of this ethnic group in the country. The state also had the second highest proportion of American Indians (9.2 percent) in the nation.

- New Mexico was among 11 states with median household incomes of less than $40,000. The state's poverty rate of 16.5 percent was the sixth highest in the nation.

- While New Mexico's real gross state product ranked 38th in the nation in 2004, its growth rate from 2001 to 2004 was among the highest in the country.

- The state ranked 41st in the nation for its proportion of high school graduates and 31st for college graduates.

- The state had a very high proportion of population lacking health insurance. In 2004, it ranked 50th in the nation for rate of health insurance coverage, with only Texas having a lower proportion of insured population.

Table NM-1. Population by Sex and Age, 1990, 2000, and 2004

(Number, percent.)

Sex and age	1990	2000	2004	Percent distribution, 2004	Average annual percent change, 2000–2004
Total Population	1 515 069	1 819 046	1 903 289	X	1.1
Percent of total U.S. population	0.6	0.6	0.6	X	X
Sex					
Male	745 253	894 317	936 067	49.2	1.1
Female	769 816	924 729	967 222	50.8	1.1
Age					
Under 5 years	125 878	130 628	133 366	7.0	0.2
5 to 17 years	320 863	377 946	358 921	18.9	0.8
18 years and over	268 976	1 310 472	1 411 002	74.1	2.0
18 to 24 years	1 068 328	177 576	206 085	10.8	2.2
25 to 44 years	151 824	516 100	501 746	26.4	0.3
45 to 64 years	484 466	404 571	473 697	24.9	4.2
65 years and over	163 062	212 225	229 474	12.1	2.5
85 years and over	14 232	23 306	26 817	1.4	4.8
Median age (years)	31.1	34.6	35.7	X	X

X = Not applicable.

Average Annual Rate of Population Growth, 1980–2004

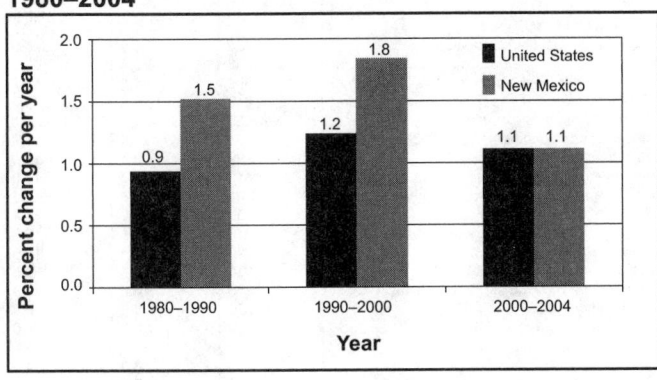

POPULATION

New Mexico's population increased 4.6 percent between 2000 and 2004. This rate was above the national average, but below those of neighboring states—particularly Arizona, whose rate of growth was nearly twice that of New Mexico. The state attracted cross-border immigrants as well as residents from other states. New Mexico received about 23,000 immigrants from outside the United States; this accounted for more than one-fourth of the state's total population growth. New Mexico also had an above average birth rate, which further supported its population growth. The state had the eighth highest proportion of population under 18 years old in the country. Its largest metropolitan area was Albuquerque.

Table NM-2. Population by Race and Hispanic Origin, 1990, 2000, and 2004

(Number, percent.)

Race and Hispanic origin	1990	2000	2004
Total Population	1 515 069	1 819 046	1 903 289
Non-Hispanic (Percent)			
One race[1]			
White	50.4	45.2	43.5
Black	1.8	1.7	1.8
American Indian, Alaska Native[2]	8.9	8.9	9.2
Asian and Pacific Islander[2]	0.9	1.1	1.2
Other race[2]	12.6	. . .	. . .
Two or more races	. . .	1.0	1.1
Hispanic or Latino[3] (Percent)	38.2	42.1	43.3

[1]Individuals could report only one race in the 1990 census and could report one or more races on the 2000 census. Data on race in 2000 and 2004 are not comparable to 1990.
[2]Data for 1990 include people of Hispanic or Latino origin.
[3]May be of any race.
. . . = Not available.

Minority Population as a Percent of Total Population, 2004

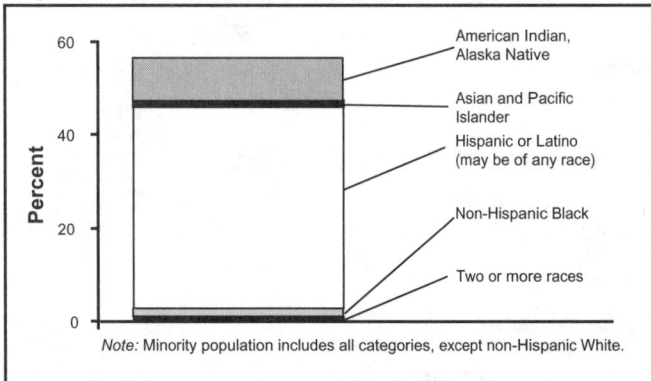

Note: Minority population includes all categories, except non-Hispanic White.

Age-Adjusted Death Rates, Average 2000–2002

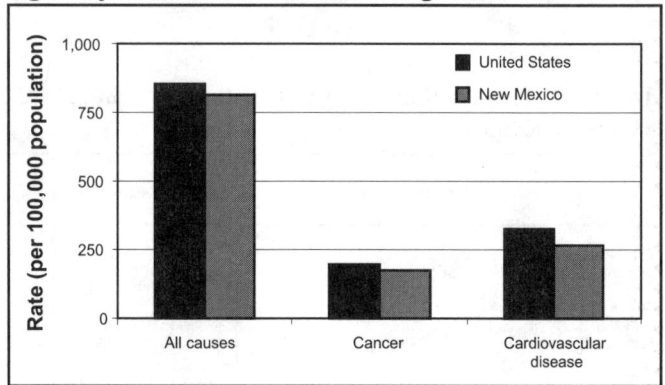

HEALTH

New Mexico had the second highest birth rate for teenage mothers in the country. The state's overall birth rate was also above average. A high proportion of the state's residents lacked health insurance, which partly reflected high immigration rates and high rates of employment in industries that did not provide health insurance.

Table NM-3. Health Characteristics, 2000–2004

(Number, rate, percent.)

Item	State	U.S.
Births, 2003–2004		
Number of births	27 821	4 089 950
Birth rate (per 1,000 population)	14.8	14.1
Teenage birth rate (per 1,000 women age 15–19 years)	62.7	41.6
Mortality Rates, Average 2000–2002		
Infant mortality rate (per 1,000 live births)	6.4	6.9
Age-adjusted mortality rate (per 100,000 population)		
All races	815.0	853.3
Non-Hispanic White	799.8	843.1
Black	881.7	1 097.7
American Indian, Alaska Native	894.7	687.0
Asian and Pacific Islander	537.3	486.0
Hispanic or Latino[1]	795.7	642.7
Health Insurance, 2004		
Percent of all persons without health insurance	21.0	15.7
Percent of children without health insurance	15.3	11.2
Percent of low-income children without health insurance	8.4	7.1

[1]May be of any race.

Table NM-4. Leading Causes of Death, Average 2000–2002

(Number, rate per 100,000 population.)

Cause	Number of deaths	Age-adjusted death rates	
		State	U.S.
ALL CAUSES	13 966	815.0	853.3
Leading Causes			
Major cardiovascular diseases	4 423	263.0	326.5
Cancer	2 958	170.4	196.0
Chronic lower respiratory diseases	800	47.2	43.7
Unintentional injuries	1 040	58.5	35.7
Diabetes (underlying cause)	535	31.1	25.2
Influenza and pneumonia	353	21.3	22.7
Alzheimer's disease	299	18.4	19.0
Motor vehicle accidents	413	22.7	15.0
Nephritis, nephrotic syndrome, and nephrosis ..	181	10.8	13.8
Septicemia	120	7.0	11.4
Suicides	346	19.2	10.7
Firearm-related	290	16.0	10.3
Cirrhosis	320	17.7	9.5
Drug-induced	286	16.0	7.9
Alcohol-induced	326	18.0	6.9
Homicides	150	8.2	6.0
Falls	181	10.8	5.2
HIV	35	2.0	5.0
Viral hepatitis	53	2.9	2.0
Anemias	22	1.3	1.6
Drownings	21	1.2	1.3
Fire deaths	18	1.0	1.2

Note: The rates are age-adjusted to the U.S. 2000 standard population.

Table NM-5. Households and Housing Characteristics, 1990, 2000, and 2004

(Number, percent, and dollars.)

Characteristic	1990	2000	2004	Average annual percent change, 2000–2004
Total Households	542 709	677 971	711 827	1.2
Family households	391 487	466 515	459 803	-0.4
Married-couple family	303 789	341 818	327 601	-1.1
Other family	87 698	124 697	132 202	1.5
Male householder, no wife present	23 143	35 075	38 254	2.2
Female householder, no husband present	64 555	89 622	93 948	1.2
Nonfamily households	151 222	211 456	252 024	4.5
Householder living alone	124 883	172 181	204 638	4.4
Householder not living alone	26 339	39 275	47 386	4.8
Housing Characteristics				
Average size	2.74	2.63	2.62	X
Housing units	632 058	780 579	825 540	1.4
Occupied housing units	542 709	677 971	711 827	1.2
Owner-occupied	365 965	474 445	493 009	1.0
Renter-occupied	176 744	203 526	218 818	1.8
Median gross rent of renter-occupied housing units (dollars) ...	372	503	546	2.1
Median value of owner-occupied housing units (dollars)	69 800	108 100	110 788	0.6

X = Not applicable.

Median Housing Value and Median Rent, 2004

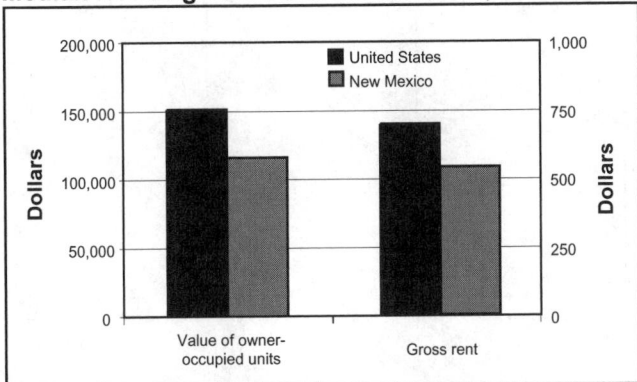

Median Household Income, 1984–2004 (2004 Dollars)

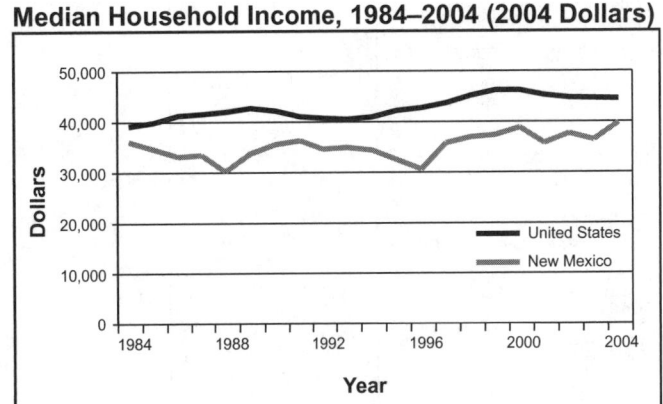

Table NM-6. Household Income and Poverty Status, 1980–2004

(2004 CPI-U-RS adjusted dollars, rate.)

Year	State		U.S.	
	Median household income (2004 dollars)	Poverty rate	Median household income (2004 dollars)	Poverty rate
2004	39 467	16.5	44 389	12.7
2003	36 048	18.1	44 482	12.5
2002	37 244	17.9	44 546	12.1
2001	35 347	18.0	45 062	11.7
2000	38 493	17.5	46 058	11.3
1999	36 923	20.9	46 129	11.9
1998	36 506	20.4	45 003	12.7
1997	35 310	21.2	43 430	13.3
1996	30 070	25.5	42 544	13.7
1995	31 992	25.3	41 943	13.8
1994	33 921	21.1	40 677	14.5
1993	34 446	17.4	40 217	15.1
1992	34 120	21.6	40 422	14.8
1991	35 896	22.4	40 746	14.2
1990	35 090	20.9	41 963	13.5
1989	33 250	19.5	42 524	12.8
1988	29 606	23.0	41 771	13.0
1987	33 009	19.4	41 322	13.4
1986	32 632	21.3	40 939	13.6
1985	34 196	18.5	39 545	14.0
1984	35 694	19.5	38 782	14.4
1983	. . .	24.5	. . .	15.2
1982	. . .	22.4	. . .	15.0
1981	. . .	18.6	. . .	14.0
1980	. . .	20.6	. . .	13.0

. . . = Not available.

Table NM-7. Employment Status by Demographic Group, 2004

(Numbers in thousands, rate.)

Characteristic	Civilian noninstitutional population	Civilian labor force		Employed	Unemployment rate
		Number	Participation rate		
SEX AND AGE					
Total	1 436	911	63.5	860	5.6
16 to 19 years	110	44	40.0	36	18.9
20 to 24 years	139	93	66.9	85	8.8
25 to 34 years	254	200	78.7	187	6.4
35 to 44 years	238	193	81.4	184	4.8
45 to 54 years	268	211	78.8	202	4.4
55 to 64 years	201	130	64.9	127	2.2
65 years and over	226	39	17.3	39	0.5
Men	692	484	69.9	457	5.4
20 to 24 years	66	47	72.1	45	5.2
25 to 34 years	128	114	89.3	107	6.5
35 to 44 years	115	102	89.0	98	4.5
45 to 54 years	132	109	82.5	103	5.7
55 to 64 years	93	66	71.5	65	2.2
Women	744	427	57.5	403	5.8
20 to 24 years	74	46	62.2	40	12.6
25 to 34 years	126	86	68.0	81	6.3
35 to 44 years	123	91	74.3	86	5.2
45 to 54 years	136	102	75.2	99	3.0
55 to 64 years	108	64	59.1	62	2.2
65 years and over	124	18	14.8	18	1.0
MARITAL STATUS					
Married men, spouse present	365	267	73.2	261	2.6
Married women, spouse present	362	210	57.8	202	3.6
Women who maintain families	102	65	63.9	61	6.7
RACE, HISPANIC ORIGIN, AND SEX					
White	1 226	783	63.9	744	5.0
Men	594	420	70.6	400	4.7
Women	631	363	57.6	344	5.2
Black	31	19	62.6	17	13.7
Hispanic or Latino[1]	577	369	63.9	341	7.5
Men	283	201	70.8	185	7.6
Women	294	168	57.3	156	7.5
RACE, HISPANIC ORIGIN, AND AGE					
White					
16 to 19 years	91	40	43.6	33	17.6
20 to 24 years	114	77	67.3	71	7.8
25 to 34 years	206	164	79.6	154	5.8
35 to 44 years	199	163	81.8	155	4.7
45 to 54 years	235	187	79.5	181	3.2
55 to 64 years	179	118	65.7	115	2.4
65 years and over	202	36	17.6	35	0.5
Black					
20 to 24 years	69	47	67.2	42	10.6
25 to 34 years	122	97	79.4	89	7.7
35 to 44 years	102	79	77.7	74	6.0
45 to 54 years	92	72	77.5	67	6.2
55 to 64 years	72	44	61.5	43	4.0

Note: Data in Table 7 are from the Current Population Survey (CPS) and do not match Bureau of Labor Statistics estimates in Table 8. See notes and definitions for more details.

[1]May be of any race.

Table NM-8. Employment Status, 1990–2004

(Numbers in thousands, rate.)

Year	Civilian labor force	Employed	Unemployed	Unemployment rate
2004	911 940	859 962	51 978	5.7
2003	893 396	840 858	52 538	5.9
2002	875 389	827 533	47 856	5.5
2001	861 626	819 413	42 213	4.9
2000	850 846	808 544	42 302	5.0
1999	839 988	793 052	46 936	5.6
1998	835 879	783 661	52 218	6.2
1997	822 627	768 596	54 031	6.6
1996	812 862	751 826	61 036	7.5
1995	798 621	744 557	54 064	6.8
1994	776 827	725 387	51 440	6.6
1993	755 053	700 258	54 795	7.3
1992	735 447	680 463	54 984	7.5
1991	719 243	667 698	51 545	7.2
1990	711 891	663 698	48 193	6.8

Note: Population age 16 years and over.

Unemployment Rate, 1980–2004

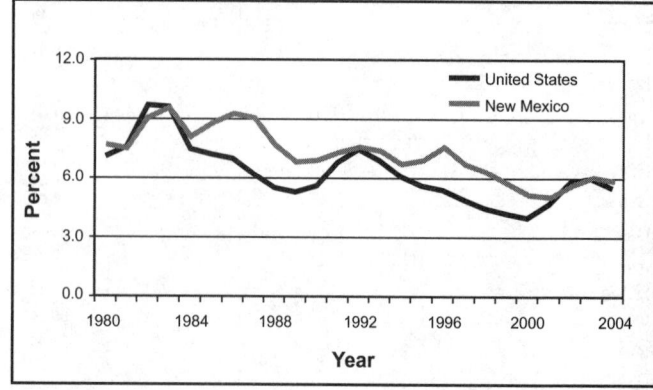

Table NM-9. Employment and Average Wages by Industry, 2001–2004

(Estimates are based on the 2002 North American Industry Classification System [NAICS].)

Industry	2001	2002	2003	2004	Annual average percent change, 2001–2004
	Number of jobs				
TOTAL EMPLOYMENT BY PLACE OF WORK	977 815	987 924	1 015 263	1 038 426	2.0
Farm Employment	24 091	24 038	23 925	24 169	0.1
Nonfarm Employment	953 724	963 886	991 338	1 014 257	2.1
Private employment	748 250	755 004	778 412	797 876	2.2
Forestry, fishing, hunting, and other[1]	7 019	7 282	7 013	6 954	-0.3
Mining	19 469	17 549	19 065	20 231	1.3
Utilities	4 272	4 097	4 107	4 039	-1.9
Construction	63 144	61 091	64 383	67 879	2.4
Manufacturing	46 001	43 550	41 626	41 248	-3.6
Durable goods manufacturing	32 671	30 495	28 693	28 418	-4.5
Nondurable goods manufacturing	13 330	13 055	12 933	12 830	-1.3
Wholesale trade	27 970	27 179	26 721	26 742	-1.5
Retail trade	111 250	111 915	114 122	116 508	1.6
Transportation and warehousing	23 854	23 927	24 138	24 780	1.3
Information	19 331	18 590	18 068	17 128	-4.0
Finance and insurance	30 996	31 083	31 767	32 091	1.2
Real estate and rental and leasing	29 117	29 486	33 171	35 029	6.4
Professional and technical services	60 386	61 028	64 674	66 124	3.1
Management of companies and enterprises	6 083	5 923	5 401	5 268	-4.7
Administrative and waste services	52 659	53 800	53 484	55 280	1.6
Educational services	11 826	12 539	13 470	14 118	6.1
Health care and social assistance	89 614	96 306	103 175	107 519	6.3
Arts, entertainment, and recreation	18 570	19 498	20 619	21 301	4.7
Accommodation and food services	76 403	77 912	79 611	80 702	1.8
Other services, except public administration	50 286	52 249	53 797	54 935	3.0
Government and government enterprises	205 474	208 882	212 926	216 381	1.7
	Dollars				
AVERAGE WAGES AND SALARIES BY PLACE OF WORK	28 718	29 676	30 471	31 638	3.3
Farm Earnings	26 593	31 862	25 927	24 312	-2.9
Nonfarm Earnings	28 736	29 659	30 509	31 701	3.3
Private earnings	27 621	28 109	28 864	29 988	2.8
Forestry, fishing, hunting, and other[1]	13 584	14 543	15 015	15 883	5.3
Mining	46 615	47 456	48 614	51 284	3.2
Utilities	54 346	53 518	54 130	57 000	1.6
Construction	30 138	30 019	30 528	31 326	1.3
Manufacturing	38 079	37 680	39 409	40 503	2.1
Durable goods manufacturing	42 513	41 939	44 349	45 180	2.0
Nondurable goods manufacturing	27 123	27 624	28 466	30 132	3.6
Wholesale trade	36 316	37 467	38 223	39 913	3.2
Retail trade	20 744	21 166	21 689	22 599	2.9
Transportation and warehousing	33 577	34 217	34 795	36 972	3.3
Information	32 828	31 782	33 155	34 872	2.0
Finance and insurance	35 701	37 537	39 250	40 193	4.0
Real estate and rental and leasing	24 300	29 987	25 872	27 264	3.9
Professional and technical services	48 977	50 737	52 804	54 605	3.7
Management of companies and enterprises	41 264	43 093	42 073	46 929	4.4
Administrative and waste services	22 485	23 111	24 737	26 042	5.0
Educational services	21 725	21 752	22 432	23 325	2.4
Health care and social assistance	28 010	28 968	29 531	30 492	2.9
Arts, entertainment, and recreation	16 934	17 123	17 723	17 858	1.8
Accommodation and food services	11 888	12 279	12 517	13 019	3.1
Other services, except public administration	18 424	18 992	19 630	20 380	3.4
Government and government enterprises	31 935	34 071	35 162	36 562	4.6

Note: Average wages and salaries are a calculation by the editors of wage and salary disbursements divided by full- and part-time wage and salary employment. Data may not add to total or may appear as zero due to rounding.

[1] "Other" consists of the number of jobs held by U.S. residents employed by international organizations and foreign embassies and consulates in the United States.

LABOR MARKET

From 2001 to 2004, New Mexico's employment grew by 6.2 percent, which was the fifth highest rate of increase in the nation. Declines in manufacturing jobs were more than offset by employment increases in the state's largest industries—government and government enterprises, retail trade, health services, and tourist-related industries. The unemployment rate rose following the 2001 recession; in 2004, it was 5.7 percent, just above the national average and above the rate of neighboring Arizona, but below the rate of Texas. Average wages and salaries grew by over 10 percent during the 2001–2004 period, but remained below the U.S. average, ranking 37th in the nation.

Employment by Industry, 2004

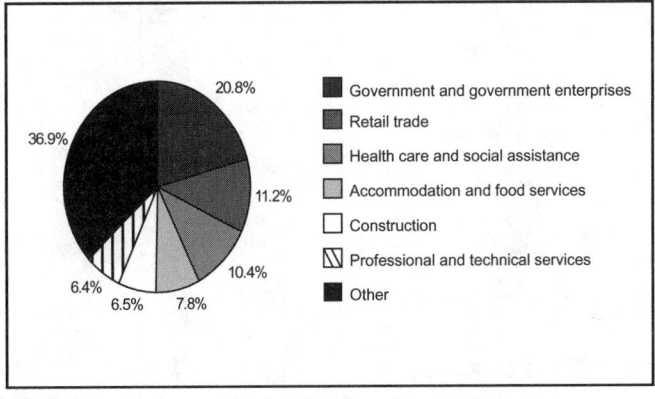

Table NM-10. Personal Income by Major Source, Selected Years 1980–2004

(Millions of dollars, except where noted.)

Item	1980	1990	2000	2001	2002	2003	2004	Average annual percent change, 2000–2004
Earnings by Place of Work	8 740	16 822	29 196	31 946	33 147	34 669	37 190	6.2
Wage and salary disbursements	6 602	12 297	21 769	23 021	24 041	25 038	26 497	5.0
Supplements to wages and salaries	1 302	2 831	4 668	4 997	5 567	6 026	6 612	9.1
Proprietors' income[1]	836	1 694	2 759	3 928	3 540	3 604	4 080	10.3
Farm proprietors' income	107	308	305	515	292	368	522	14.4
Nonfarm proprietors' income	729	1 386	2 454	3 413	3 248	3 236	3 558	9.7
(-) Contributions for government social insurance[2]	740	1 737	3 115	3 337	3 520	3 693	3 874	5.6
(+) Adjustment for residence[3]	-3	51	250	251	259	265	281	2.9
(=) Net Earnings by Place of Residence	7 996	15 136	26 332	28 860	29 885	31 241	33 597	6.3
(+) Dividends, interest, and rent[4]	1 623	4 525	7 545	8 080	7 190	7 123	7 128	-1.4
(+) Personal current transfer receipts	1 310	3 046	6 441	7 198	7 906	8 418	9 053	8.9
Personal income	10 929	22 708	40 318	44 138	44 982	46 782	49 778	5.4
Farm income	10 752	22 298	39 826	43 439	44 478	46 227	49 073	5.4
Nonfarm income	176	409	492	699	504	555	704	9.4
Per Capita Personal Income (Dollars)[5]	8 346	14 924	22 135	24 088	24 247	24 903	26 154	4.3

Note: Data may not add to total or may appear as zero due to rounding.

[1]Proprietors' income includes the inventory valuation adjustment and the capital consumption adjustment.
[2]Contributions for government social insurance are included in earnings by type and industry, but they are excluded from personal income.
[3]The adjustment for residence is the net inflow of the earnings of interarea commuters.
[4]Rental income of persons includes the capital consumption adjustment.
[5]Per capita personal income is total personal income divided by total midyear population.

Per Capita Personal Income, 1980–2004 (Current Dollars)

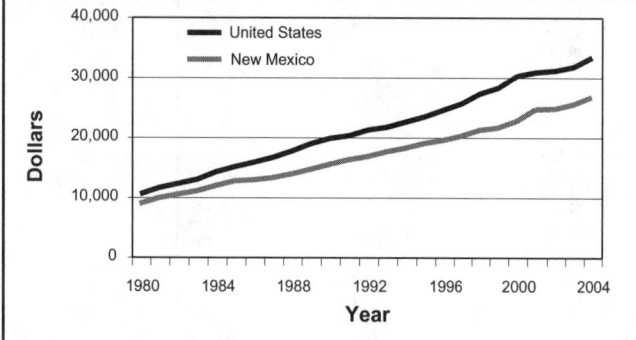

ECONOMIC ACTIVITY

New Mexico's real gross state product (GSP) recovered steadily after the 2001 recession. Over the 2001–2004 period, the GSP rose by 12 percent, the 11th fastest rate of growth in the country. The principal contributors to this growth were government, retail trade, real estate and related activities, and health care services. Manufacturing has also rebounded in recent years, contributing to the rise in the GSP. The median value of owner-occupied housing in New Mexico in 2004 ranked 36th in the nation. From 2000 to 2004, this amount increased by just 2.5 percent, which was the lowest rate of growth in the nation.

Table NM-11. Real Gross State Product, 1997–2004

(Millions of chained 2000 dollars, percent.)

Industry	1997	1998	1999	2000	2001	2002	2003	2004	Average annual percent change, 2001–2004
GROSS STATE PRODUCT	45 762	45 987	50 006	50 419	50 465	52 506	54 183	56 512	3.8
As a percent of U.S. gross product	0.5	0.5	0.5	0.5	0.5	0.5	0.5	0.5	X
Private Industries	36 886	36 958	40 941	41 188	40 861	42 582	44 101	45 982	4.0
Agriculture, forestry, fishing, and hunting	689	743	874	887	944	913	935	799	-5.4
Mining	3 503	3 485	3 575	3 482	3 454	3 437	3 305	3 398	-0.5
Utilities	1 161	1 066	1 095	1 184	1 050	1 076	1 163	1 235	5.6
Construction	2 204	2 182	2 073	2 116	2 198	2 070	2 125	2 211	0.2
Manufacturing	5 447	4 987	7 233	7 108	5 646	5 980	7 090	7 606	10.4
As a percent of gross state product	11.9	10.8	14.5	14.1	11.2	11.4	13.1	13.5	X
Wholesale trade	1 821	1 974	2 022	1 952	2 090	2 132	2 041	2 085	-0.1
Retail trade	3 412	3 496	3 630	3 649	3 860	4 150	4 302	4 609	6.1
Transportation and warehousing	1 198	1 281	1 314	1 369	1 310	1 353	1 456	1 554	5.9
Information	1 107	1 209	1 416	1 549	1 627	1 614	1 691	1 757	2.6
Finance and insurance	1 466	1 632	1 789	1 694	1 807	1 897	2 041	2 110	5.3
Real estate and rental and leasing	4 982	5 065	5 277	5 362	5 725	6 214	6 029	6 330	3.4
Services	10 317	10 546	10 644	10 836	11 039	11 646	12 087	12 563	4.4
As a percent of gross state product	22.5	22.9	21.3	21.5	21.9	22.2	22.3	22.2	X
Professional and technical services	2 925	3 012	3 067	3 181	3 228	3 370	3 585	3 666	4.3
Management of companies and enterprises	404	385	346	338	322	324	291	298	-2.5
Administrative and waste services	1 179	1 177	1 344	1 325	1 397	1 483	1 550	1 622	5.1
Educational services	220	229	228	221	226	228	218	218	-1.2
Health care and social assistance	2 594	2 707	2 702	2 806	2 943	3 197	3 373	3 537	6.3
Arts, entertainment, and recreation	378	413	372	361	340	390	391	396	5.2
Accommodation and food services	1 472	1 487	1 512	1 536	1 513	1 586	1 599	1 662	3.2
Other services, except public administration	1 145	1 136	1 073	1 068	1 070	1 068	1 080	1 164	2.8
Government	8 904	9 073	9 064	9 231	9 598	9 921	10 091	10 532	3.1
As a percent of gross state product	19.5	19.7	18.1	18.3	19.0	18.9	18.6	18.6	X

X = Not applicable.

Table NM-12. Government Transfer Payments, Selected Years 1980–2004

(Millions of dollars, percent.)

Item	1980	1990	2000	2001	2002	2003	2004	Average annual percent change, 2000–2004
CURRENT TRANSFER PAYMENTS TO INDIVIDUALS	1 218	2 840	6 014	6 697	7 448	7 974	8 601	9.4
Retirement and Disability Insurance Benefits	579	1 333	2 402	2 553	2 697	2 816	2 973	5.5
Old-age, survivors, and disability insurance (OASDI) benefits	529	1 244	2 303	2 452	2 590	2 709	2 864	5.6
Railroad retirement and disability benefits	35	55	68	69	71	72	73	2.0
Workers' compensation	11	28	26	26	29	28	29	2.7
Other government retirement and disability insurance benefits	4	6	5	6	6	6	6	6.2
Medical Benefits	218	798	2 345	2 778	3 193	3 468	3 839	13.1
Medicare benefits	140	459	1 043	1 163	1 257	1 340	1 487	9.3
Public assistance medical care benefits	74	311	1 268	1 562	1 863	2 069	2 284	15.9
Military medical insurance benefits	4	28	34	54	73	60	68	18.7
Income Maintenance Benefits	193	393	758	769	841	930	1 023	7.8
Supplemental Security Income (SSI) benefits	42	90	193	205	217	223	233	4.8
Family assistance	42	65	122	117	101	98	103	-4.1
Food stamps	84	123	139	138	159	190	229	13.4
Other income maintenance benefits	26	115	304	308	365	419	458	10.8
Unemployment Insurance Compensation	48	60	84	106	175	180	146	14.9
Veterans' Benefits	122	155	268	294	332	364	409	11.2
Federal Education and Training Assistance	26	59	93	114	128	120	127	8.0
Other Payments to Individuals	31	43	64	83	82	97	83	7.0

Note: See notes and definitions for more details. Data may not add to total or may appear as zero due to rounding.

EXPORTS

New Mexico's exports totaled over $2 billion in 2004. This was down from the 2003 value of exports, but up considerably from 2001 and 2002 levels. These changes were the result of a fluctuating market for computers and electronic products exports. Products in this category were the state's leading export in 2004, accounting for nearly 64 percent of total exports. From 2003 to 2004, exports of machinery manufactures doubled, making them the state's second leading export. The state's chief export market was Mexico, with fabricated metal products and machinery manufactures as the leading exports to this country. Exports to China increased rapidly from 2001 to 2004.

Leading Exports, 2004

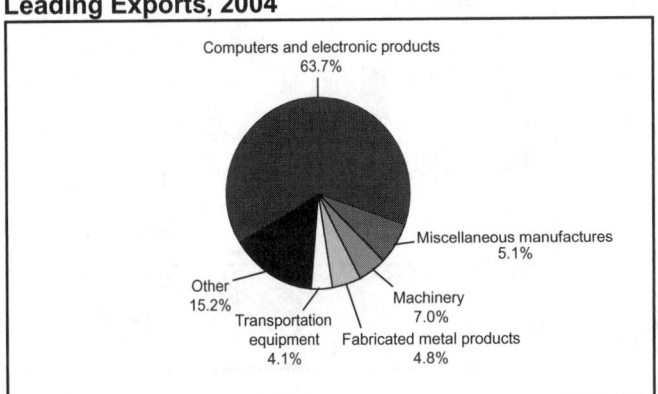

Table NM-13. Exports of Goods by Leading Products and Destinations, 2001–2004

(Millions of dollars, percent, rank based on 2004 dollar values.)

Product and market	2001	2002	2003	2004	Percent share of total, 2004	Average annual percent change, 2001–2004
Total Goods						
Total	1 405	1 196	2 326	2 046	100.0	13.4
Manufactures	1 353	1 077	2 241	1 945	95.1	12.9
Agriculture and livestock	27	38	45	49	2.4	22.1
Other commodities	25	82	45	53	2.6	28.2
Five Leading Exports (NAICS Code)						
Computers and electronic products (334)	1 107	788	1 813	1 304	63.7	5.6
Machinery manufactures (333)	53	79	73	143	7.0	39.2
Miscellaneous manufactures (339)	21	17	15	105	5.1	71.3
Fabricated metal products (332)	18	13	65	99	4.8	75.8
Transportation equipment (336)	31	58	87	84	4.1	39.4
Five Leading Markets	1 281	1 092	2 245	1 996	97.6	15.9
Mexico	112	117	242	358	17.5	47.4
Costa Rica	87	123	104	232	11.3	38.7
Malaysia	168	92	225	225	11.0	10.2
China	35	48	207	221	10.8	85.4
Philippines	259	180	441	203	9.9	-7.7

Table NM-14. Agriculture, 1997 and 2002

(Number, acres, and dollars.)

Item	1997	2002
Number of farms	17 876	15 170
Land in farms (acres)	46 177 267	44 810 083
Farm Size		
Average size of farm (acres)	2 583	2 954
Farms by size (percent distribution)		
Fewer than 50 acres	41.2	44.7
50 to 499 acres	28.5	26.5
500 acres or more	30.3	28.8
Market Value of Land and Equipment (Dollars)		
Land and buildings average value per farm	542 530	698 908
Average value per acre	208	234
Machinery and equipment average value per farm	40 733	58 262
Value of Sales (Thousands of Dollars)		
Agricultural products sold	1 664 133	1 700 030
Crops	496 240	397 257
Livestock, poultry, and their products	1 167 893	1 302 773
Average per farm (dollars)	93 093	112 065
Value of sales (percent distribution)		
Less than $10,000	67.2	68.3
$10,000 to $99,999	22.6	21.2
$100,000 or more	10.2	10.5
Government Payments		
Payments (thousands of dollars)	32 341	50 201
Percent of farms receiving government payments	21.1	21.4
Farm operators whose principal occupation is farming (percent)	46.8	55.9

AGRICULTURE

Cash receipts from farming totaled $1.7 billion in 2002, according to the Department of Agriculture's Census of Agriculture. Crop sales declined from 1997 to 2002, but sales of livestock, poultry, and their products increased by about $135 million. New Mexico's chief products were dairy items and cattle. More than half of all farms spanned 50 acres or more, although about 68 percent of farms had sales of less than $10,000.

ENERGY

The price of energy was relatively high in New Mexico, ranking 15th in the country. Total expenditures per person amounted to $2,358 in 2001, an amount well below the national average due to an absence of heavy industrial consumers. However, the industrial sector and transportation sector each consumed about one-third of the state's energy. Per capita consumption ranked 20th in the nation. The chief sources of energy were coal, natural gas, and petroleum.

Energy Consumption by Source, 2001

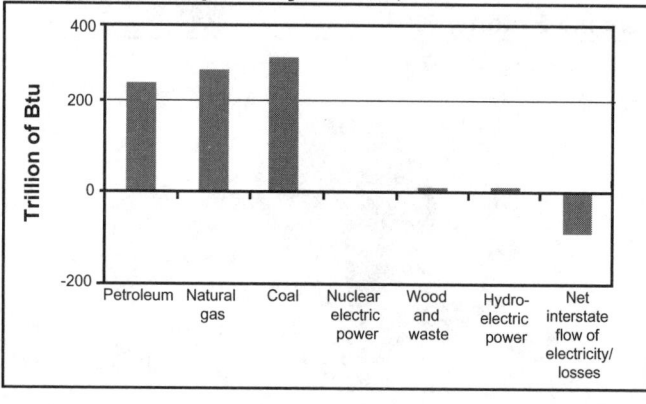

Energy Consumption by Sector, 2001

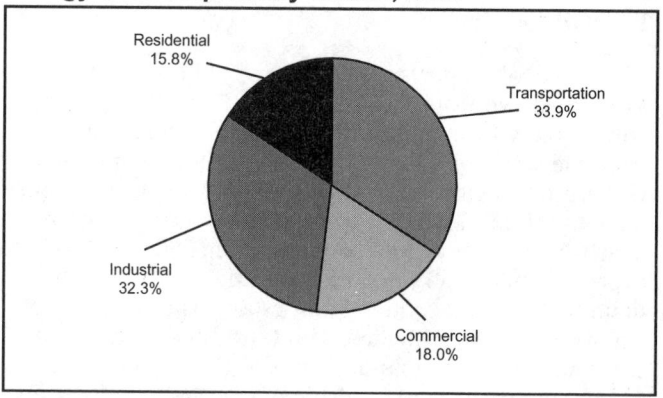

Table NM-15. Energy Consumption, Expenditures, and Prices, Selected Years 1960–2001

(Dollars, Btu [British Thermal Unit], percent distribution.)

Item	1960	1965	1970	1975	1980	1985	1990	1995	2000	2001
Total Consumption (Billion Btu)	329 022	353 847	458 794	459 712	481 125	464 491	597 982	585 437	676 785	679 202
Consumption per capita (million Btu)	346.0	349.7	451.1	396.3	369.3	322.9	394.7	348.0	372.1	371.3
Consumption by Sector (Percent Distribution)										
Residential	13.2	13.9	13.6	13.4	14.1	15.6	13.4	14.1	15.0	15.8
Commercial	7.0	9.3	14.0	12.8	14.9	16.2	16.0	17.2	18.2	18.0
Industrial	51.9	44.2	42.2	39.4	34.4	33.1	32.3	35.3	33.3	32.3
Transportation	27.8	32.5	30.2	34.4	36.6	35.1	38.3	33.4	33.5	33.9
Consumption by Source (Billion Btu)										
Coal	4 064	44 277	99 380	132 535	202 870	268 374	275 665	275 216	305 515	297 121
Natural gas	207 301	224 253	292 522	255 637	231 330	162 312	251 470	219 476	259 018	262 105
Petroleum	107 205	128 635	155 819	199 652	201 607	188 189	211 954	209 033	247 231	250 988
Nuclear electric power	0	0	0	0	0	0	0	0	0	0
Hydroelectric power[1]	745	448	690	660	977	1 336	2 137	2 722	2 256	2 414
Wood and waste	6 628	5 627	4 858	5 343	5 250	7 220	3 745	4 257	4 539	4 017
Other	0	0	0	0	0	0	703	764	1 148	1 143
Net interstate flow of electricity/losses[2]	3 079	-49 392	-94 475	-134 115	-160 910	-162 940	-147 693	-126 030	-142 921	-138 587
Total Expenditures (Thousands of Dollars)	. . .	. . .	462 400	902 600	2 206 500	2 535 700	2 930 600	2 901 100	4 075 700	4 312 600
Expenditures per capita (dollars)	. . .	. . .	455	778	1 694	1 763	1 934	1 724	2 241	2 358
Prices by Sector (Dollars Per Million Btu)										
Total	. . .	. . .	1.46	2.88	7.10	9.32	9.29	9.03	10.80	11.24
Residential	. . .	. . .	1.77	3.04	6.64	10.99	10.96	11.43	12.22	13.85
Commercial	. . .	. . .	1.37	2.74	6.77	12.65	11.68	12.08	12.56	14.43
Industrial	. . .	. . .	0.65	1.52	4.99	7.80	7.63	6.12	7.59	8.45
Transportation	. . .	. . .	2.28	4.03	8.69	8.47	8.70	8.92	11.11	10.43

[1]A negative number in this row results from pumped storage for which, overall, more electricity is expended than created to provide electricity during peak demand periods.
[2]Net interstate flow of electricity is the difference between the amount of energy in the electricity sold within a state (including associated losses) and the energy input at the electric utilities within the state. A positive number indicates that more electricity (including associated losses) came into the state than went out of the state during the year; conversely, a negative number indicates that more electricity (including associated losses) went out of the state than came into the state.
. . . = Not available.

Table NM-16. State Taxes, Fiscal 2004

(Dollars, percent distribution.)

Item	Thousands of dollars	Percent distribution	Dollars per capita	
			State	U.S.
TOTAL TAXES	4 001 780	100.0	2 102.9	2 024.8
Property Taxes	53 074	1.3	27.9	38.9
Sales and Gross Receipts	2 038 440	50.9	1 071.2	1 003.4
General sales and gross receipts	1 443 300	36.1	758.4	677.0
Selective sales taxes	595 140	14.9	312.7	326.4
Alcoholic beverages	37 503	0.9	19.7	15.7
Amusements	38 543	1.0	20.2	17.0
Insurance premiums	87 448	2.2	46.0	47.0
Motor fuels	210 863	5.3	110.8	114.6
Tobacco products	52 718	1.3	27.7	42.0
Other selective sales	148 736	3.7	78.2	49.8
Licenses	169 805	4.2	89.2	134.9
Motor vehicle	121 246	3.0	63.7	59.4
Occupation and business, not elsewhere classified	21 575	0.5	11.3	37.1
Other Taxes	1 740 461	43.5	914.6	847.6
Individual income	1 007 248	25.2	529.3	673.6
Corporation net income	138 196	3.5	72.6	105.1
Severance	587 625	14.7	308.8	21.5

GOVERNMENT FINANCE

In 2003, state revenues per person were well above the national average, ranking ninth in the nation. New Mexico's expenditures per resident were the seventh highest in the country. Expenditures per capita on education, public welfare, hospitals, and highways were significantly above the national averages, while health spending was below average. The largest share of taxes came from general sales taxes, followed by individual income taxes and severance, which are taxes imposed on the removal of natural resources such as coal, natural gas, minerals, and timber. Notable shares of taxes derived from severance can also be found in other western states.

Per Capita State Taxes, Fiscal 2004

Table NM-17. State Government Finances, 2003

(Dollars, percent distribution.)

Item	Millions of dollars	Percent distribution	Dollars per capita	
			State	U.S.
GENERAL REVENUE	9 007 272	100.0	4 793.6	3 832.6
Intergovernmental revenue	3 220 765	35.8	1 714.1	1 246.0
Taxes	3 607 156	40.0	1 919.7	1 891.6
General sales	1 368 200	15.2	728.2	636.0
Selective sales	505 220	5.6	268.9	307.4
License taxes	152 092	1.7	80.9	123.6
Individual income tax	923 113	10.2	491.3	626.8
Corporate income tax	101 546	1.1	54.0	97.8
Other taxes	556 985	6.2	296.4	99.9
Current charges	693 076	7.7	368.8	366.5
Miscellaneous general revenue	1 486 275	16.5	791.0	328.6
GENERAL EXPENDITURE	9 713 782	100.0	5 169.7	4 010.5
Intergovernmental expenditure	2 951 328	30.4	1 570.7	1 316.9
Direct expenditure	6 762 454	69.6	3 599.0	2 693.6
Expenditure by Function				
Education	3 677 414	37.9	1 957.1	1 416.4
Public welfare	2 410 880	24.8	1 283.1	1 083.3
Hospitals	446 538	4.6	237.6	132.3
Health	290 949	3.0	154.8	173.0
Highways	818 750	8.4	435.7	295.4
Police protection	109 352	1.1	58.2	38.4
Correction	264 845	2.7	141.0	135.0
Natural resources	179 821	1.9	95.7	64.0
Parks and recreation	55 581	0.6	29.6	20.1
Government administration	363 784	3.7	193.6	151.3
Interest on general debt	175 261	1.8	93.3	107.8
Other and unallocable	920 607	9.5	490.0	393.4
DEBT AT END OF FISCAL YEAR	4 601 117	X	2 448.7	2 404.7
CASH AND SECURITY HOLDINGS	29 826 816	X	15 873.8	8 938.4

X = Not applicable.

Table NM-18. Education Indicators, 2000–2004

(Percent, number.)

Item	State	U.S.
Total Population 25 Years and Over (Thousands), 2004	1 181	186 877
Educational Attainment, 2004		
Percent high school graduate or more	82.9	85.2
Percent college graduate or more	25.1	27.7
Elementary and Secondary Schools, 2002–2003		
Total students	320 234	48 202 324
Percent of students eligible for free or reduced-price lunch ..	58.2	40.6
Percent of students who were English language learners	16.9	7.8
Total schools	801	92 330
Student/teacher ratio	15.0	15.9
Per student expenditures	7 125	8 041
Dropouts, Grades 9–12, 2000–2001 (Percent)	5.2	. . .
Higher Education, 2002–2003		
Total enrollment	121 606	17 035 027
Bachelor's degrees awarded	7 027	1 348 503
Percent women	58.9	57.5

. . . = Not available.

Educational Attainment, 2004

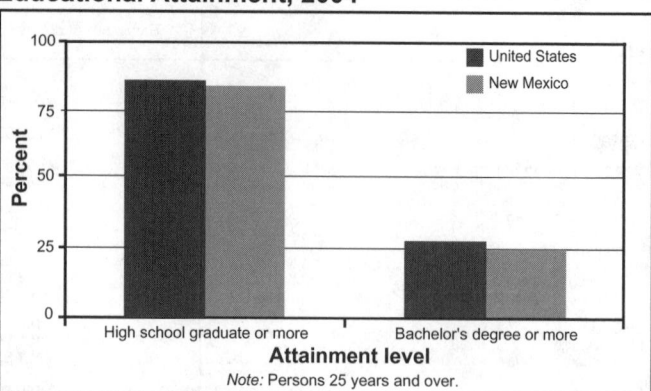

Note: Persons 25 years and over.

EDUCATION

New Mexico's school-age population has grown rapidly in recent years, and its proportion of population under 18 years old was the ninth highest in the nation. Despite above average per capita spending on education, expenditures per student in New Mexico were well below the national average. However, the student/teacher ratio was also below average. New Mexico had below average educational attainment levels. More than 58 percent of the state's students were eligible for free or reduced-price lunch, which was among the five highest proportions in the nation. Nearly 17 percent of students were English language learners, which was also well above the national average rate.

VOTER PARTICIPATION

New Mexico's voter turnout was below the national average for both the 2000 and 2004 elections. However, the proportion of the population that voted increased from 51.3 percent in 2000 to 60.9 percent in 2004. Non-Hispanic Whites had the highest voter participation rates, while just over 50 percent of eligible Hispanics cast ballots in the 2004 election. Less than 40 percent of eligible voters age 18 to 24 years turned out to vote. In 2000, 56.1 percent of eligible residents voted for the Democratic presidential candidate; this proportion fell to 52.9 percent in 2004, according to the official tally by the Clerk of the U.S. House of Representatives.

Table NM-19. Reported Voting and Registration, November 2000 and November 2004

(Numbers in thousands, percent.)

Characteristic	Total population 18 years and over	Total citizen		Total registered		Total voted	
		Number	Percent	Number	Percent	Number	Percent
NOVEMBER 2000							
Total	1 261	1 188	94.3	750	59.5	647	51.3
Male	591	559	94.7	332	56.1	286	48.3
Female	670	629	93.9	419	62.5	361	53.9
NOVEMBER 2004							
Total	1 375	1 301	94.6	936	68.1	837	60.9
Male	658	621	94.4	436	66.2	392	59.6
Female	717	680	94.7	501	69.8	445	62.0
Race and Hispanic Origin							
White alone	1 151	1 087	94.4	792	68.8	715	62.1
Non-Hispanic White alone	660	653	98.9	509	77.1	471	71.4
Black alone	34	34	B	23	B	23	B
Asian alone	11	3	B	3	B	3	B
Hispanic or Latino[1]	544	486	89.2	316	58.0	276	50.6
White alone or in combination	1 181	1 115	94.4	807	68.3	728	61.7
Non-Hispanic White alone or in combination	677	669	98.9	519	76.7	480	70.9
Black alone or in combination	39	39	B	26	B	26	B
Asian alone or in combination	11	3	B	3	B	3	B
Age							
18 to 24 years	187	177	94.2	93	49.5	74	39.7
25 to 44 years	491	442	90.0	319	64.9	284	57.8
45 to 64 years	483	471	97.4	352	72.9	323	66.8
65 to 74 years	109	108	99.0	92	84.7	83	76.4
75 years and over	105	103	99.0	80	76.6	73	69.7

[1]May be of any race.
B = Base is too small to show derived measure.

At a Glance:

- New York's population exceeded 19.2 million in 2004, giving it the third largest population in the country.
- Non-Hispanic Whites represented 61.1 percent of the population. The state had the fifth highest proportion of Asians and Pacific Islanders in the nation and the eighth highest proportion of Hispanics (of any race).
- Median household income was slightly above the national average, ranking 21st in the country. New York's poverty rate of 15 percent was among the 10 highest in the nation.
- Average wages and salaries increased by 6.9 percent from 2001 to 2004, which was the second lowest growth rate in the nation.
- In 2004, real gross state product (GSP) was the second largest in the country, behind only California. Its rate of growth from 2001 to 2004 was very slow.
- New York had the second highest per student expenditures and the third highest dropout rate (among the 46 states reporting such data) in the country.

Table NY-1. Population by Sex and Age, 1990, 2000, and 2004

(Number, percent.)

Sex and age	1990	2000	2004	Percent distribution, 2004	Average annual percent change, 2000–2004
Total Population	17 990 455	18 976 457	19 227 088	X	0.3
Percent of total U.S. population	7.2	6.7	6.5	X	X
Sex					
Male	8 625 673	9 146 748	9 304 581	48.4	0.4
Female	9 364 782	9 829 709	9 922 507	51.6	0.2
Age					
Under 5 years	1 255 764	1 239 417	1 246 045	6.5	-0.3
5 to 17 years	3 003 785	3 450 690	3 326 318	17.3	0.7
18 years and over	3 550 887	14 286 350	14 654 725	76.2	0.5
18 to 24 years	13 730 906	1 765 453	1 825 192	9.5	-0.6
25 to 44 years	1 953 424	5 831 622	5 626 026	29.3	-0.3
45 to 64 years	5 862 873	4 240 923	4 710 691	24.5	2.1
65 years and over	2 363 722	2 448 352	2 492 816	13.0	0.5
85 years and over	248 173	311 488	353 883	1.8	2.8
Median age (years)	33.7	35.9	37.1	X	X

X = Not applicable.

Average Annual Rate of Population Growth, 1980–2004

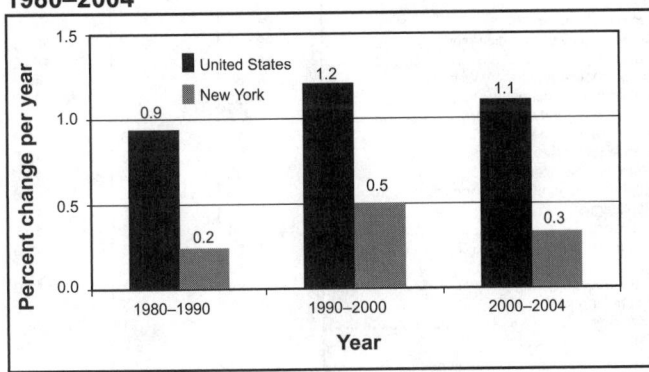

POPULATION

New York's population increased by only 1.3 percent between 2000 and 2004, which was among the 11 lowest rates of growth in the nation. Florida is projected to overtake New York by 2015 to become the nation's third most populous state. From 2000 to 2004, New York had the second highest influx of immigrants from abroad, with over 562,000 new residents arriving from other countries. However, this was offset by a loss of nearly 772,000 residents to other states. A below average birth rate also contributed to slow population growth. The state had an above average proportion of elderly residents and a below average proportion of school-age population.

Table NY-2. Population by Race and Hispanic Origin, 1990, 2000, and 2004

(Number, percent.)

Race and Hispanic origin	1990	2000	2004
Total Population	17 990 455	18 976 457	19 227 088
Non-Hispanic (Percent)			
One race[1]			
White	69.3	62.6	61.1
Black	14.3	15.2	15.1
American Indian, Alaska Native[2]	0.3	0.3	0.3
Asian and Pacific Islander[2]	3.9	5.8	6.4
Other race[2]	5.5	. . .	. . .
Two or more races	. . .	1.0	1.1
Hispanic or Latino[3] (Percent)	12.3	15.1	16.0

[1]Individuals could report only one race in the 1990 census and could report one or more races on the 2000 census. Data on race in 2000 and 2004 are not comparable to 1990.
[2]Data for 1990 include people of Hispanic or Latino origin.
[3]May be of any race.
. . . = Not available.

Minority Population as a Percent of Total Population, 2004

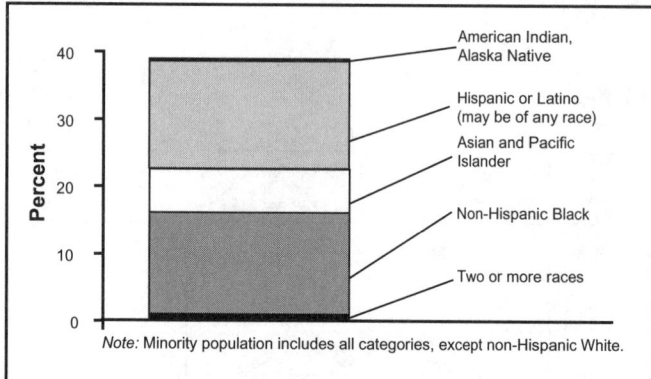

Note: Minority population includes all categories, except non-Hispanic White.

Age-Adjusted Death Rates, Average 2000–2002

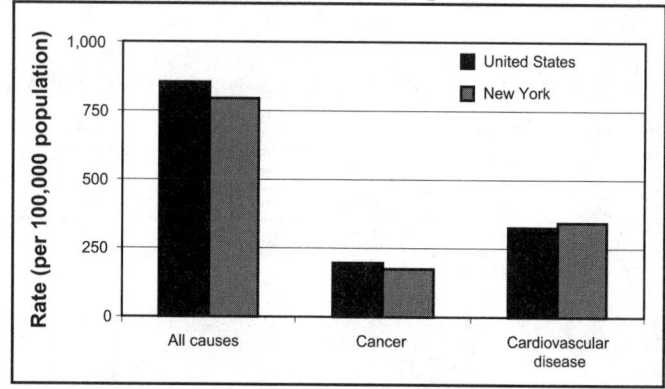

HEALTH

In 2004, 14.2 percent of New Yorkers lacked health insurance, which was below the national average. However, neighboring Pennsylvania and Connecticut had higher rates of coverage. New York's infant mortality and age-adjusted death rates were below the national averages.

Table NY-3. Health Characteristics, 2000–2004

(Number, rate, percent.)

Item	State	U.S.
Births, 2003–2004		
Number of births	253 714	4 089 950
Birth rate (per 1,000 population)	13.2	14.1
Teenage birth rate (per 1,000 women age 15–19 years)	28.2	41.6
Mortality Rates, Average 2000–2002		
Infant mortality rate (per 1,000 live births)	6.1	6.9
Age-adjusted mortality rate (per 100,000 population)		
All races	797.2	853.3
Non-Hispanic White	791.0	843.1
Black	870.5	1 097.7
American Indian, Alaska Native	. . .	687.0
Asian and Pacific Islander	401.7	486.0
Hispanic or Latino[1]	608.0	642.7
Health Insurance, 2004		
Percent of all persons without health insurance	14.2	15.7
Percent of children without health insurance	8.6	11.2
Percent of low-income children without health insurance	5.5	7.1

[1]May be of any race.
. . . = Not available.

Table NY-4. Leading Causes of Death, Average 2000–2002

(Number, rate per 100,000 population.)

Cause	Number of deaths	Age-adjusted death rates	
		State	U.S.
ALL CAUSES	158 520	797.2	853.3
Leading Causes			
Major cardiovascular diseases	68 207	339.9	326.5
Cancer	36 945	187.6	196.0
Chronic lower respiratory diseases	6 885	34.7	43.7
Unintentional injuries	4 630	23.7	35.7
Diabetes (underlying cause)	3 885	19.6	25.2
Influenza and pneumonia	5 218	25.8	22.7
Alzheimer's disease	1 682	8.2	19.0
Motor vehicle accidents	1 585	8.2	15.0
Nephritis, nephrotic syndrome, and nephrosis ..	2 442	12.2	13.8
Septicemia	2 311	11.6	11.4
Suicides	1 204	6.2	10.7
Firearm-related	1 052	5.5	10.3
Cirrhosis	1 412	7.2	9.5
Drug-induced	1 099	5.7	7.9
Alcohol-induced	1 122	5.7	6.9
Homicides	988	5.1	6.0
Falls	910	4.6	5.2
HIV	2 099	10.8	5.0
Viral hepatitis	439	2.2	2.0
Anemias	270	1.4	1.6
Drownings	134	0.7	1.3
Fire deaths	189	1.0	1.2

Note: The rates are age-adjusted to the U.S. 2000 standard population.

Table NY-5. Households and Housing Characteristics, 1990, 2000, and 2004

(Number, percent, and dollars.)

Characteristic	1990	2000	2004	Average annual percent change, 2000–2004
Total Households	6 639 322	7 056 860	7 087 566	0.1
Family households	4 489 312	4 639 387	4 614 684	-0.1
Married-couple family	3 315 845	3 289 514	3 250 893	-0.3
Other family	1 173 467	1 349 873	1 363 791	0.3
Male householder, no wife present	254 201	311 697	343 190	2.4
Female householder, no husband present	919 266	1 038 176	1 020 601	-0.4
Nonfamily households	2 150 010	2 417 473	2 472 882	0.6
Householder living alone	1 806 263	1 982 742	2 039 618	0.7
Householder not living alone	343 747	434 731	433 264	-0.1
Housing Characteristics				
Average size	2.63	2.61	2.63	X
Housing units	7 226 891	7 679 307	7 819 359	0.5
Occupied housing units	6 639 322	7 056 860	7 087 566	0.1
Owner-occupied	3 464 436	3 739 166	3 941 494	1.3
Renter-occupied	3 174 886	3 317 694	3 146 072	-1.3
Median gross rent of renter-occupied housing units (dollars) ...	486	672	796	4.3
Median value of owner-occupied housing units (dollars)	130 400	148 700	220 981	10.4

X = Not applicable.

Median Housing Value and Median Rent, 2004

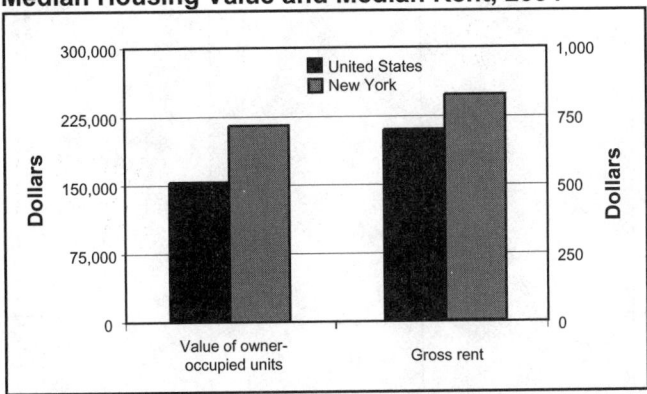

Median Household Income, 1984–2004 (2004 Dollars)

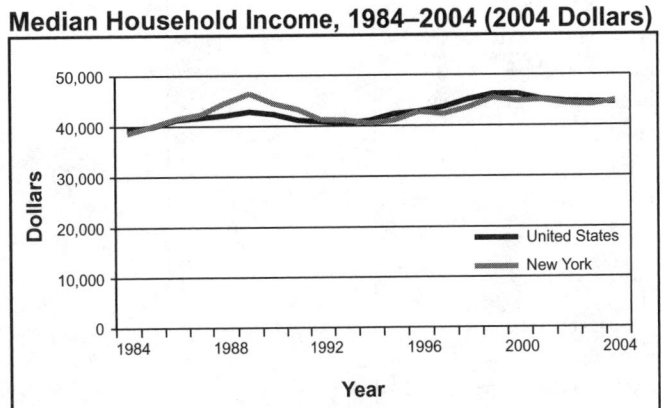

Table NY-6. Household Income and Poverty Status, 1980–2004

(2004 CPI-U-RS adjusted dollars, rate.)

Year	State Median household income (2004 dollars)	State Poverty rate	U.S. Median household income (2004 dollars)	U.S. Poverty rate
2004	44 664	15.0	44 389	12.7
2003	43 938	14.3	44 482	12.5
2002	44 081	14.0	44 546	12.1
2001	44 940	14.2	45 062	11.7
2000	44 692	13.9	46 058	11.3
1999	45 327	14.2	46 129	11.9
1998	43 278	16.7	45 003	12.7
1997	42 014	16.5	43 430	13.3
1996	42 446	16.7	42 544	13.7
1995	40 653	16.5	41 943	13.8
1994	40 217	17.0	40 677	14.5
1993	40 804	16.4	40 217	15.1
1992	40 969	15.7	40 422	14.8
1991	43 002	15.3	40 746	14.2
1990	44 272	14.3	41 963	13.5
1989	46 334	12.6	42 524	12.8
1988	44 364	13.4	41 771	13.0
1987	41 955	14.3	41 322	13.4
1986	41 150	13.2	40 939	13.6
1985	39 581	15.8	39 545	14.0
1984	38 111	16.0	38 782	14.4
1983	. . .	16.0	. . .	15.2
1982	. . .	14.8	. . .	15.0
1981	. . .	14.4	. . .	14.0
1980	. . .	13.8	. . .	13.0

. . . = Not available.

Table NY-7. Employment Status by Demographic Group, 2004

(Numbers in thousands, rate.)

Characteristic	Civilian noninstitutional population	Civilian labor force		Employed	Unemployment rate
		Number	Participation rate		
SEX AND AGE					
Total	14 906	9 370	62.9	8 823	5.8
16 to 19 years	1 061	387	36.5	324	16.3
20 to 24 years	1 321	895	67.8	802	10.4
25 to 34 years	2 610	2 108	80.8	1 980	6.0
35 to 44 years	2 857	2 339	81.9	2 216	5.3
45 to 54 years	2 684	2 155	80.3	2 074	3.7
55 to 64 years	1 924	1 173	61.0	1 125	4.1
65 years and over	2 449	314	12.8	301	4.2
Men	7 065	4 965	70.3	4 671	5.9
16 to 19 years	535	189	35.4	151	20.0
20 to 24 years	656	474	72.2	416	12.2
25 to 34 years	1 290	1 159	89.8	1 095	5.5
35 to 44 years	1 384	1 252	90.5	1 196	4.5
45 to 54 years	1 287	1 100	85.4	1 058	3.8
55 to 64 years	909	621	68.4	594	4.5
65 years and over	1 003	169	16.9	161	4.5
Women	7 841	4 406	56.2	4 151	5.8
16 to 19 years	526	198	37.5	172	12.8
20 to 24 years	664	421	63.4	386	8.4
25 to 34 years	1 320	949	71.9	885	6.7
35 to 44 years	1 473	1 087	73.8	1 020	6.1
45 to 54 years	1 397	1 055	75.5	1 016	3.6
55 to 64 years	1 015	551	54.3	532	3.6
65 years and over	1 446	145	10.0	140	3.8
MARITAL STATUS					
Married men, spouse present	3 670	2 757	75.1	2 664	3.4
Married women, spouse present	3 487	2 035	58.4	1 956	3.9
Women who maintain families	1 082	738	68.2	674	8.7
RACE, HISPANIC ORIGIN, AND SEX					
White	11 230	7 136	63.5	6 774	5.1
Men	5 393	3 835	71.1	3 633	5.3
Women	5 837	3 301	56.5	3 141	4.8
Black	2 491	1 481	59.4	1 330	10.1
Men	1 084	693	64.0	623	10.2
Women	1 407	787	55.9	708	10.1
Asian	979	621	63.5	597	4.0
Men	487	367	75.5	352	4.0
Women	492	254	51.6	244	3.8
Hispanic or Latino[1]	2 138	1 354	63.3	1 249	7.7
Men	1 012	729	72.0	673	7.7
Women	1 126	625	55.5	576	7.8
RACE, HISPANIC ORIGIN, AND AGE					
White					
25 to 34 years	1 833	1 527	83.3	1 453	4.9
35 to 44 years	2 090	1 730	82.8	1 651	4.6
45 to 54 years	2 029	1 662	81.9	1 606	3.4
55 to 64 years	1 534	939	61.2	906	3.4

Note: Data in Table 7 are from the Current Population Survey (CPS) and do not match Bureau of Labor Statistics estimates in Table 8. See notes and definitions for more details.

[1]May be of any race.

Table NY-8. Employment Status, 1990–2004

(Numbers in thousands, rate.)

Year	Civilian labor force	Employed	Unemployed	Unemployment rate
2004	9 355 135	8 811 784	543 351	5.8
2003	9 300 309	8 705 319	594 990	6.4
2002	9 311 417	8 732 103	579 314	6.2
2001	9 177 563	8 729 849	447 714	4.9
2000	9 180 368	8 763 571	416 797	4.5
1999	9 134 079	8 657 431	476 648	5.2
1998	9 058 800	8 546 550	512 250	5.7
1997	8 997 511	8 416 544	580 967	6.5
1996	8 780 545	8 228 913	551 632	6.3
1995	8 676 837	8 125 798	551 039	6.4
1994	8 681 987	8 080 243	601 744	6.9
1993	8 698 934	8 013 498	685 436	7.9
1992	8 734 942	7 979 726	755 216	8.6
1991	8 754 679	8 112 503	642 176	7.3
1990	8 808 856	8 339 800	469 056	5.3

Note: Population age 16 years and over.

Unemployment Rate, 1980–2004

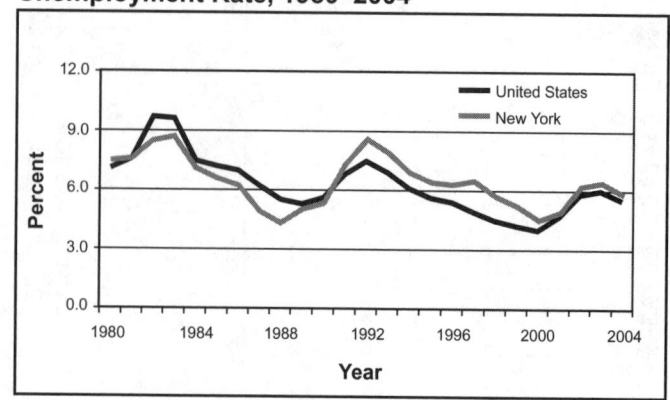

Table NY-9. Employment and Average Wages by Industry, 2001–2004

(Estimates are based on the 2002 North American Industry Classification System [NAICS].)

Industry	2001	2002	2003	2004	Annual average percent change, 2001–2004
	Number of jobs				
TOTAL EMPLOYMENT BY PLACE OF WORK	10 491 096	10 414 954	10 451 749	10 562 849	0.2
Farm Employment	59 730	59 916	59 666	55 260	-2.6
Nonfarm Employment	10 431 366	10 355 038	10 392 083	10 507 589	0.2
Private employment	8 946 637	8 849 617	8 892 973	9 010 297	0.2
Forestry, fishing, hunting, and other[1]	23 689	24 448	22 598	22 371	-1.9
Mining	9 876	8 731	10 077	10 704	2.7
Utilities	43 796	43 279	42 158	40 427	-2.6
Construction	462 822	449 274	456 622	461 326	-0.1
Manufacturing	734 909	680 327	641 302	624 664	-5.3
Durable goods manufacturing	422 884	388 120	362 696	355 527	-5.6
Nondurable goods manufacturing	312 025	292 207	278 606	269 137	-4.8
Wholesale trade	399 253	387 065	384 737	387 223	-1.0
Retail trade	1 026 415	1 021 831	1 025 444	1 041 922	0.5
Transportation and warehousing	324 632	310 972	312 059	317 732	-0.7
Information	358 650	325 907	309 761	304 514	-5.3
Finance and insurance	726 286	698 078	687 712	690 084	-1.7
Real estate and rental and leasing	358 530	361 036	379 557	394 084	3.2
Professional and technical services	798 205	782 921	793 362	807 450	0.4
Management of companies and enterprises	122 454	127 627	126 362	124 811	0.6
Administrative and waste services	523 064	512 034	513 483	530 077	0.4
Educational services	339 070	350 808	364 154	376 506	3.6
Health care and social assistance	1 322 903	1 358 553	1 395 025	1 416 239	2.3
Arts, entertainment, and recreation	258 204	269 074	271 150	281 622	2.9
Accommodation and food services	554 968	558 746	572 367	586 550	1.9
Other services, except public administration	558 911	578 906	585 043	591 991	1.9
Government and government enterprises	1 484 729	1 505 421	1 499 110	1 497 292	0.3
	Dollars				
AVERAGE WAGES AND SALARIES BY PLACE OF WORK	46 024	45 629	46 585	49 198	2.2
Farm Earnings	18 619	24 397	20 195	26 117	11.9
Nonfarm Earnings	46 090	45 681	46 652	49 247	2.2
Private earnings	47 104	46 446	47 334	50 121	2.1
Forestry, fishing, hunting, and other[1]	69 260	70 052	70 676	72 087	1.3
Mining	43 674	44 432	47 084	47 219	2.6
Utilities	70 196	77 658	78 982	82 533	5.5
Construction	46 559	47 676	48 618	49 179	1.8
Manufacturing	44 856	46 155	48 166	50 072	3.7
Durable goods manufacturing	47 731	48 777	50 790	52 583	3.3
Nondurable goods manufacturing	40 940	42 644	44 731	46 734	4.5
Wholesale trade	54 672	55 787	57 636	60 219	3.3
Retail trade	24 228	24 968	25 654	26 473	3.0
Transportation and warehousing	36 719	37 336	38 032	39 042	2.1
Information	67 381	66 503	70 261	73 507	2.9
Finance and insurance	136 371	124 296	124 378	142 979	1.6
Real estate and rental and leasing	41 453	42 035	42 854	45 709	3.3
Professional and technical services	68 487	68 512	69 935	73 301	2.3
Management of companies and enterprises	106 178	112 637	107 423	115 199	2.8
Administrative and waste services	30 288	30 900	32 389	33 822	3.7
Educational services	29 963	31 139	32 234	33 372	3.7
Health care and social assistance	32 812	33 683	35 250	36 620	3.7
Arts, entertainment, and recreation	36 615	36 889	38 239	39 326	2.4
Accommodation and food services	18 276	18 542	18 936	19 727	2.6
Other services, except public administration	24 059	25 040	26 034	26 954	3.9
Government and government enterprises	41 032	42 002	43 371	45 013	3.1

Note: Average wages and salaries are a calculation by the editors of wage and salary disbursements divided by full- and part-time wage and salary employment. Data may not add to total or may appear as zero due to rounding.

[1] "Other" consists of the number of jobs held by U.S. residents employed by international organizations and foreign embassies and consulates in the United States.

LABOR MARKET

New York's unemployment rate has been higher than the national average for a number of years. In 2004, its joblessness rate of 5.8 percent ranked 12th in the nation. Employment growth over the 2001–2004 period was slow, as job losses occurred in many key industries, including information, finance and insurance, construction, and manufacturing. Jobs in educational services; arts, entertainment, and recreation; and health care increased during this period. Average wages and salaries were substantially above the national average, particularly in finance and insurance, management, and several other service industries. However, average wages and salaries grew very slowly between 2001 and 2004.

Employment by Industry, 2004

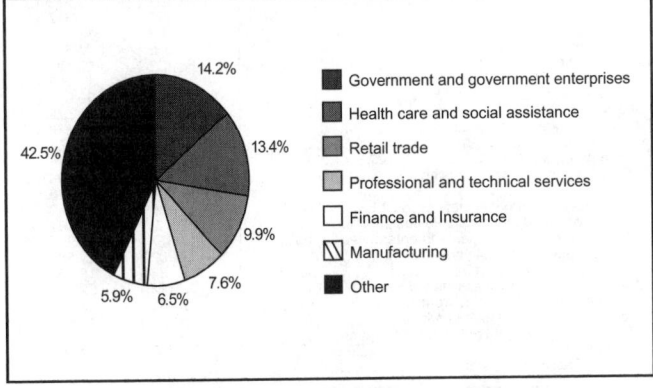

- 14.2% Government and government enterprises
- 13.4% Health care and social assistance
- 9.9% Retail trade
- 7.6% Professional and technical services
- 6.5% Finance and Insurance
- 5.9% Manufacturing
- 42.5% Other

Table NY-10. Personal Income by Major Source, Selected Years 1980–2004

(Millions of dollars, except where noted.)

Item	1980	1990	2000	2001	2002	2003	2004	Average annual percent change, 2000–2004
Earnings by Place of Work	156 988	333 212	538 623	551 151	549 391	558 590	596 293	2.6
Wage and salary disbursements	117 240	248 311	400 389	409 929	400 141	406 464	431 455	1.9
Supplements to wages and salaries	24 287	47 641	70 860	74 190	81 052	85 779	92 298	6.8
Proprietors' income[1]	15 461	37 261	67 373	67 031	68 199	66 347	72 539	1.9
Farm proprietors' income	260	376	294	365	-108	166	135	-17.6
Nonfarm proprietors' income	15 201	36 885	67 078	66 666	68 307	66 181	72 404	1.9
(-) Contributions for government social insurance[2]	15 326	37 849	57 239	59 470	60 133	61 993	64 650	3.1
(+) Adjustment for residence[3]	-8 203	-14 083	-34 495	-35 416	-32 385	-32 131	-35 360	X
(=) **Net Earnings by Place of Residence**	133 459	281 280	446 888	456 264	456 873	464 465	496 282	2.7
(+) Dividends, interest, and rent[4]	32 079	84 547	115 784	113 585	103 078	103 127	107 765	-1.8
(+) Personal current transfer receipts	27 955	58 069	100 334	110 036	116 904	122 772	132 991	7.3
Personal income	193 492	423 897	663 005	679 886	676 856	690 365	737 039	2.7
Farm income	192 985	423 184	662 280	679 088	676 403	689 718	736 384	2.7
Nonfarm income	507	713	726	797	453	647	655	-2.5
Per Capita Personal Income (Dollars)[5]	11 015	23 523	34 897	35 622	35 343	35 933	38 333	2.4

Note: Data may not add to total or may appear as zero due to rounding.

[1]Proprietors' income includes the inventory valuation adjustment and the capital consumption adjustment.
[2]Contributions for government social insurance are included in earnings by type and industry, but they are excluded from personal income.
[3]The adjustment for residence is the net inflow of the earnings of interarea commuters.
[4]Rental income of persons includes the capital consumption adjustment.
[5]Per capita personal income is total personal income divided by total midyear population.
X = Not applicable.

Per Capita Personal Income, 1980–2004 (Current Dollars)

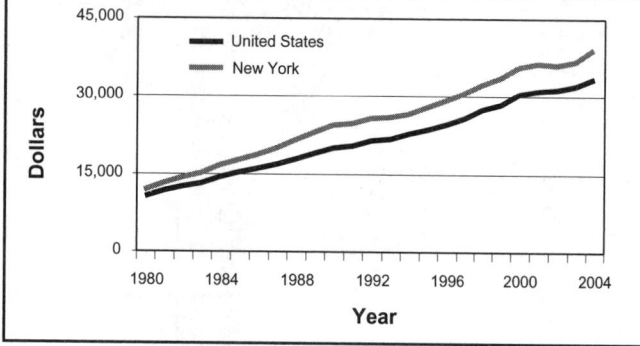

ECONOMIC ACTIVITY

After the 2001 recession, New York's real gross state product (GSP) experienced a period of slow growth; however, over the 2003–2004 period, the GSP increased 4.7 percent, a rate well above the national average. This rate was the 15th fastest in the country. The strongest contributions to the GSP were from finance and insurance, real estate and related activities, retail trade, and professional and technical services. Housing prices have appreciated at a rate above the national average in recent years, particularly in areas surrounding New York City. In 2004, the median value of owner-occupied housing in New York was the eighth highest in the country.

Table NY-11. Real Gross State Product, 1997–2004

(Millions of chained 2000 dollars, percent.)

Industry	1997	1998	1999	2000	2001	2002	2003	2004	Average annual percent change, 2001–2004
GROSS STATE PRODUCT	670 980	698 377	732 371	769 403	783 183	777 099	801 038	838 912	2.3
As a percent of U.S. gross product	7.8	7.8	7.8	7.9	8.0	7.8	7.8	7.8	X
Private Industries	595 730	621 035	653 465	690 213	704 090	698 676	722 736	759 851	2.6
Agriculture, forestry, fishing, and hunting	1 063	1 313	1 532	1 695	1 711	1 640	1 626	1 366	-7.2
Mining	291	337	368	378	372	359	369	366	-0.5
Utilities	13 259	13 173	13 846	13 907	14 291	15 022	15 899	16 293	4.5
Construction	21 308	22 539	23 351	24 025	24 621	23 678	23 494	23 031	-2.2
Manufacturing	53 133	57 124	56 973	60 252	57 252	58 216	60 626	62 780	3.1
As a percent of gross state product	7.9	8.2	7.8	7.8	7.3	7.5	7.6	7.5	X
Wholesale trade	36 394	39 982	41 588	40 768	43 732	44 492	43 792	44 734	0.8
Retail trade	34 935	36 522	38 787	40 505	43 270	45 426	48 633	51 534	6.0
Transportation and warehousing	13 809	14 376	14 437	14 972	15 036	14 745	15 569	15 878	1.8
Information	41 024	44 455	47 575	49 893	54 439	53 314	56 960	62 371	4.6
Finance and insurance	91 628	98 006	108 965	130 921	137 518	130 193	138 273	157 594	4.6
Real estate and rental and leasing	100 800	97 508	101 498	101 658	100 804	99 091	99 894	101 625	0.3
Services	191 064	197 428	205 504	211 238	211 335	212 544	218 379	225 217	2.1
As a percent of gross state product	28.5	28.3	28.1	27.5	27.0	27.4	27.3	26.8	X
Professional and technical services	53 793	58 351	62 777	67 016	65 756	64 473	65 983	68 364	1.3
Management of companies and enterprises	17 677	17 227	17 091	18 267	21 078	21 563	22 069	22 060	1.5
Administrative and waste services	18 902	19 586	21 498	19 937	19 137	19 334	20 344	21 172	3.4
Educational services	9 532	10 265	10 010	10 349	10 217	10 208	10 090	10 025	-0.6
Health care and social assistance	52 412	52 241	52 979	53 840	54 508	56 238	58 539	59 825	3.2
Arts, entertainment, and recreation	7 991	8 150	8 363	8 104	8 181	8 380	8 448	8 895	2.8
Accommodation and food services	15 025	15 592	16 830	17 812	16 934	17 017	17 396	18 344	2.7
Other services, except public administration	15 732	16 016	15 956	15 913	15 524	15 331	15 510	16 532	2.1
Government	75 463	77 494	78 969	79 190	79 107	78 439	78 467	79 425	0.1
As a percent of gross state product	11.2	11.1	10.8	10.3	10.1	10.1	9.8	9.5	X

X = Not applicable.

Table NY-12. Government Transfer Payments, Selected Years 1980–2004

(Millions of dollars, percent.)

Item	1980	1990	2000	2001	2002	2003	2004	Average annual percent change, 2000–2004
CURRENT TRANSFER PAYMENTS TO INDIVIDUALS	26 283	55 232	95 735	102 344	112 332	118 430	128 601	7.7
Retirement and Disability Insurance Benefits	11 280	20 218	30 862	32 366	33 644	34 991	36 495	4.3
Old-age, survivors, and disability insurance (OASDI) benefits	10 689	19 044	28 701	30 155	31 382	32 214	33 574	4.0
Railroad retirement and disability benefits	278	340	344	350	361	365	372	1.9
Workers' compensation	281	787	1 755	1 782	1 800	1 846	1 930	2.4
Other government retirement and disability insurance benefits	32	47	62	79	101	566	620	77.8
Medical Benefits	8 109	24 134	49 723	53 143	59 300	63 191	69 215	8.6
Medicare benefits	3 478	9 789	17 805	19 671	20 997	22 073	24 124	7.9
Public assistance medical care benefits	4 618	14 285	31 873	33 409	38 218	41 043	45 004	9.0
Military medical insurance benefits	13	60	45	63	86	74	87	17.6
Income Maintenance Benefits	4 130	7 375	11 277	11 758	12 381	13 067	14 020	5.6
Supplemental Security Income (SSI) benefits	789	1 580	3 212	3 333	3 420	3 408	3 560	2.6
Family assistance	1 656	2 428	2 700	2 825	2 842	3 085	3 126	3.7
Food stamps	751	1 123	1 346	1 387	1 496	1 725	1 951	9.7
Other income maintenance benefits	934	2 244	4 020	4 212	4 623	4 849	5 383	7.6
Unemployment Insurance Compensation	1 310	1 791	1 651	2 659	4 272	3 949	2 641	12.5
Veterans' Benefits	963	1 068	1 134	1 179	1 290	1 371	1 408	5.6
Federal Education and Training Assistance	483	625	1 028	1 137	1 272	1 153	1 222	4.4
Other Payments to Individuals	8	21	59	102	174	710	3 600	179.3

Note: See notes and definitions for more details. Data may not add to total or may appear as zero due to rounding.

EXPORTS

In 2004, the value of New York's exports was $44.4 billion, ranking third in the nation behind Texas and California. Miscellaneous manufactures became the state's leading export in 2003, as their value increased by nearly 52 percent from 2001 to 2004. Computers and electronic products and machinery manufactures were New York's other leading export products. Canada was New York's largest export market, followed distantly by Israel and the United Kingdom. China has been the state's most rapidly growing export market in recent years, as exports to this country increased by more than 80 percent from 2001 to 2004.

Leading Exports, 2004

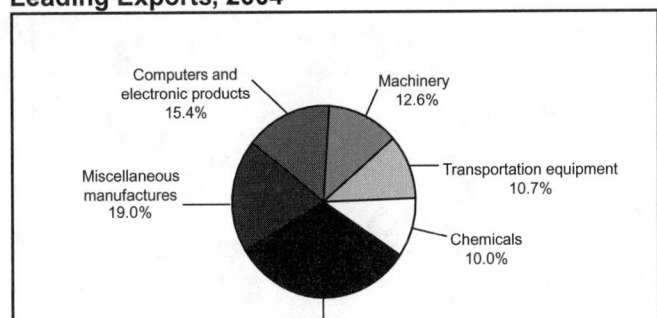

Table NY-13. Exports of Goods by Leading Products and Destinations, 2001–2004

(Millions of dollars, percent, rank based on 2004 dollar values.)

Product and market	2001	2002	2003	2004	Percent share of total, 2004	Average annual percent change, 2001–2004
Total Goods						
Total	42 172	36 977	39 181	44 401	100.0	1.7
Manufactures	36 399	32 275	34 481	38 603	86.9	2.0
Agriculture and livestock	425	479	420	470	1.1	3.4
Other commodities	5 348	4 222	4 280	5 329	12.0	-0.1
Five Leading Exports (NAICS Code)						
Miscellaneous manufactures (339)	5 551	5 611	6 399	8 426	19.0	14.9
Computers and electronic products (334)	6 538	6 297	6 306	6 857	15.4	1.6
Machinery manufactures (333)	4 824	4 181	4 138	5 590	12.6	5.0
Transportation equipment (336)	4 467	4 509	4 533	4 754	10.7	2.1
Chemical manufactures (325)	4 407	3 940	4 315	4 450	10.0	0.3
Five Leading Markets	38 550	33 342	35 435	39 626	89.2	0.9
Canada	9 760	9 221	9 041	10 081	22.7	1.1
Israel	2 021	2 140	2 372	3 734	8.4	22.7
United Kingdom	3 131	2 369	3 283	2 845	6.4	-3.1
Japan	3 613	2 823	2 625	2 425	5.5	-12.5
Mexico	1 852	1 898	1 705	2 168	4.9	5.4

Table NY-14. Agriculture, 1997 and 2002

(Number, acres, and dollars.)

Item	1997	2002
Number of farms	38 264	37 255
Land in farms (acres)	7 788 241	7 660 969
Farm Size		
Average size of farm (acres)	204	206
Farms by size (percent distribution)		
Fewer than 50 acres	28.3	30.4
50 to 499 acres	62.7	60.3
500 acres or more	9.0	9.4
Market Value of Land and Equipment (Dollars)		
Land and buildings average value per farm	272 670	345 504
Average value per acre	1 327	1 708
Machinery and equipment average value per farm	56 522	96 252
Value of Sales (Thousands of Dollars)		
Agricultural products sold	2 930 569	3 117 834
Crops	1 066 347	1 135 129
Livestock, poultry, and their products	1 864 222	1 982 706
Average per farm (dollars)	76 588	83 689
Value of sales (percent distribution)		
Less than $10,000	51.6	55.9
$10,000 to $99,999	29.9	26.8
$100,000 or more	18.5	17.3
Government Payments		
Payments (thousands of dollars)	32 789	110 234
Percent of farms receiving government payments	27.2	26.6
Farm operators whose principal occupation is farming (percent) ...	53.9	60.8

AGRICULTURE

Cash receipts from farming totaled $3.1 billion in 2002, according to the Department of Agriculture's Census of Agriculture. Dairy products were New York's leading agricultural product. Nearly 56 percent of farms had sales of less than $10,000, indicating that farming was relatively small-scale. About 30 percent of farms spanned fewer than 50 acres. Nearly 60 percent of farm operators in New York indicated that farming was their principal occupation, an increase of nearly 7 percentage points from 1997.

ENERGY

New York had the sixth highest energy prices in the nation. However, energy expenditures per person amounted to $2,092 in 2001, the fourth lowest amount in the country. The state's per capita consumption was the second lowest in the nation, behind only Rhode Island. The state's primary energy sources were petroleum and natural gas, followed distantly by nuclear power. The commercial sector was the largest consumer of energy.

Energy Consumption by Source, 2001

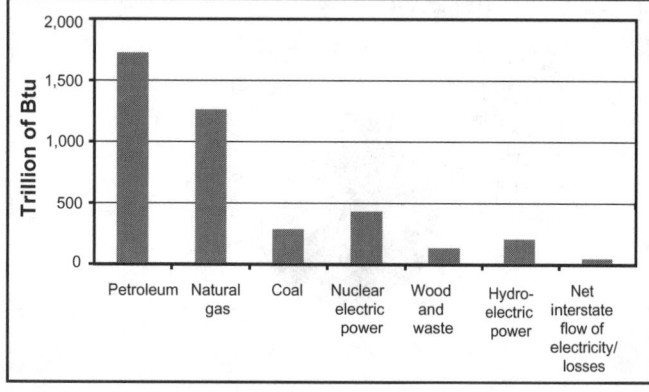

Energy Consumption by Sector, 2001

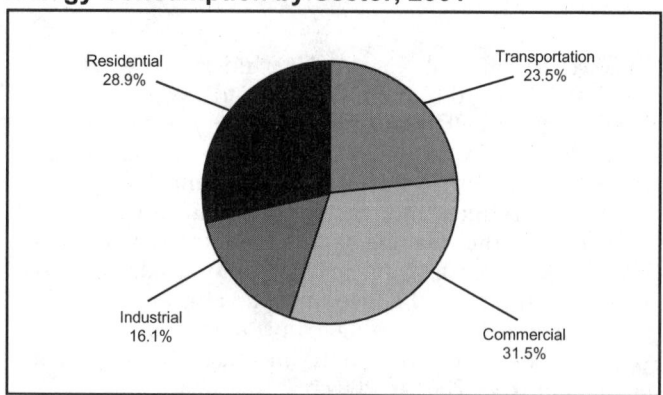

Table NY-15. Energy Consumption, Expenditures, and Prices, Selected Years 1960–2001

(Dollars, Btu [British Thermal Unit], percent distribution.)

Item	1960	1965	1970	1975	1980	1985	1990	1995	2000	2001
Total Consumption (Billion Btu)	2 989 563	3 672 883	4 320 205	3 945 970	3 919 617	3 526 039	3 757 078	3 873 176	4 245 982	4 134 644
Consumption per capita (million Btu)	178.1	207.1	236.8	219.2	223.2	198.2	208.8	213.4	223.7	216.8
Consumption by Sector (Percent Distribution)										
Residential	24.4	24.5	24.9	26.6	26.4	28.3	27.7	28.0	28.7	28.9
Commercial	19.0	20.0	21.6	22.2	22.9	26.3	28.0	29.3	31.5	31.5
Industrial	29.8	31.5	28.1	24.6	24.5	21.4	19.6	19.2	16.8	16.1
Transportation	26.8	24.1	25.4	26.6	26.2	24.0	24.7	23.6	22.9	23.5
Consumption by Source (Billion Btu)										
Coal	691 728	755 238	598 940	312 508	313 708	301 368	349 774	305 275	330 843	314 998
Natural gas	434 127	558 658	725 813	585 536	755 879	784 737	895 362	1 295 399	1 279 694	1 205 905
Petroleum	1 700 551	2 117 508	2 663 414	2 594 616	2 168 653	1 695 644	1 815 463	1 480 821	1 710 532	1 712 489
Nuclear electric power	0	8 585	46 908	144 387	210 259	255 910	249 982	276 714	328 597	422 047
Hydroelectric power[1]	130 051	204 632	262 884	294 729	275 016	284 044	282 249	256 059	243 999	225 389
Wood and waste	59 263	58 111	62 607	60 171	147 164	123 192	104 651	127 881	173 225	152 059
Other	12 361	1 690	3 222	5 567	24 454	58 985	2 775	30 985	30 529	27 581
Net interstate flow of electricity/losses[2]	-38 518	-31 539	-43 583	-51 544	24 485	22 160	56 822	100 042	148 564	74 176
Total Expenditures (Thousands of Dollars)	. . .	. . .	6 378 200	12 656 900	23 340 600	25 951 100	27 897 900	31 214 900	40 262 800	39 903 200
Expenditures per capita (dollars)	. . .	. . .	350	703	1 329	1 459	1 551	1 720	2 122	2 092
Prices by Sector (Dollars Per Million Btu)										
Total	. . .	. . .	1.81	4.10	8.01	10.24	10.42	11.12	13.16	13.41
Residential	. . .	. . .	2.18	4.37	8.19	11.63	12.29	13.67	15.10	16.18
Commercial	. . .	. . .	1.98	5.41	9.22	13.48	12.85	14.56	15.89	17.05
Industrial	. . .	. . .	0.97	2.84	5.36	6.89	7.16	6.24	7.35	7.41
Transportation	. . .	. . .	2.14	4.02	8.87	8.85	8.90	9.36	12.07	10.88

[1]A negative number in this row results from pumped storage for which, overall, more electricity is expended than created to provide electricity during peak demand periods.
[2]Net interstate flow of electricity is the difference between the amount of energy in the electricity sold within a state (including associated losses) and the energy input at the electric utilities within the state. A positive number indicates that more electricity (including associated losses) came into the state than went out of the state during the year; conversely, a negative number indicates that more electricity (including associated losses) went out of the state than came into the state.
. . . = Not available.

Table NY-16. State Taxes, Fiscal 2004

(Dollars, percent distribution.)

Item	Thousands of dollars	Percent distribution	Dollars per capita	
			State	U.S.
TOTAL TAXES	45 833 652	100.0	2 383.8	2 024.8
Property Taxes	X	X	X	38.9
Sales and Gross Receipts	16 478 965	36.0	857.1	1 003.4
General sales and gross receipts	10 050 291	21.9	522.7	677.0
Selective sales taxes	6 428 674	14.0	334.4	326.4
Insurance premiums	833 073	1.8	43.3	47.0
Motor fuels	518 557	1.1	27.0	114.6
Public utilities	821 911	1.8	42.8	39.2
Tobacco products	1 009 595	2.2	52.5	42.0
Other selective sales	3 017 773	6.6	157.0	49.8
Licenses	1 200 242	2.6	62.4	134.9
Motor vehicle	793 597	1.7	41.3	59.4
Other Taxes	28 154 445	61.4	1 464.3	847.6
Individual income	24 647 225	53.8	1 281.9	673.6
Corporation net income	2 044 504	4.5	106.3	105.1
Death and gift	736 004	1.6	38.3	19.6
Documentary and stock transfer	726 712	1.6	37.8	27.1

X = Not applicable.

GOVERNMENT FINANCE

State revenues and expenditures per person were among the highest in the country in 2003. Per capita revenues amounted to $5,145, ranking fifth in the nation, and per capita expenditures of $5,300 were sixth highest in the country. Spending per capita on education was nearly twice the national average, and expenditures on health and hospitals were also above average. Taxes per person were above average in fiscal year 2004 and ranked 10th in the country. Individual income taxes, the second highest in the nation, were the largest source of tax revenue.

Per Capita State Taxes, Fiscal 2004

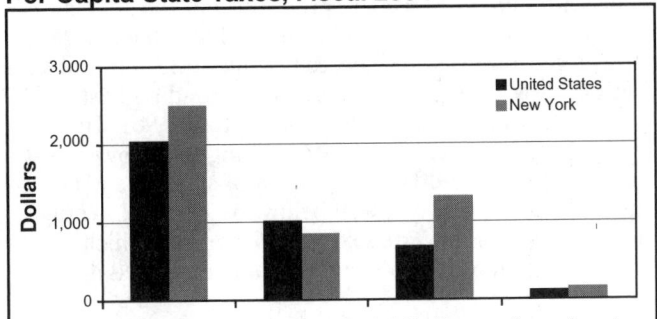

Table NY-17. State Government Finances, 2003

(Dollars, percent distribution.)

Item	Millions of dollars	Percent distribution	Dollars per capita	
			State	U.S.
GENERAL REVENUE	98 842 100	100.0	5 144.8	3 832.6
Intergovernmental revenue	43 442 351	44.0	2 261.2	1 246.0
Taxes	42 253 291	42.7	2 199.3	1 891.6
General sales	8 841 872	8.9	460.2	636.0
Selective sales	6 303 581	6.4	328.1	307.4
License taxes	1 043 227	1.1	54.3	123.6
Individual income tax	22 648 364	22.9	1 178.9	626.8
Corporate income tax	2 089 104	2.1	108.7	97.8
Other taxes	1 327 143	1.3	69.1	99.9
Current charges	5 692 910	5.8	296.3	366.5
Miscellaneous general revenue	7 453 548	7.5	388.0	328.6
GENERAL EXPENDITURE	101 825 036	100.0	5 300.1	4 010.5
Intergovernmental expenditure	40 874 514	40.1	2 127.6	1 316.9
Direct expenditure	60 950 522	59.9	3 172.5	2 693.6
Expenditure by Function				
Education	27 209 154	26.7	1 416.3	1 416.4
Public welfare	38 893 504	38.2	2 024.4	1 083.3
Hospitals	3 646 135	3.6	189.8	132.3
Health	5 027 482	4.9	261.7	173.0
Highways	3 881 359	3.8	202.0	295.4
Police protection	587 382	0.6	30.6	38.4
Correction	2 535 996	2.5	132.0	135.0
Natural resources	390 580	0.4	20.3	64.0
Parks and recreation	466 127	0.5	24.3	20.1
Government administration	4 269 212	4.2	222.2	151.3
Interest on general debt	3 522 330	3.5	183.3	107.8
Other and unallocable	11 395 775	11.2	593.2	393.4
DEBT AT END OF FISCAL YEAR	91 634 857	X	4 769.7	2 404.7
CASH AND SECURITY HOLDINGS	229 310 901	X	11 935.8	8 938.4

X = Not applicable.

Table NY-18. Education Indicators, 2000–2004

(Percent, number.)

Item	State	U.S.
Total Population 25 Years and Over (Thousands), 2004	12 508	186 877
Educational Attainment, 2004		
Percent high school graduate or more	85.4	85.2
Percent college graduate or more	30.6	27.7
Elementary and Secondary Schools, 2002–2003		
Total students	2 888 233	48 202 324
Percent of students eligible for free or reduced-price lunch ..	...	40.6
Percent of students who were English language learners	...	7.8
Total schools	4 470	92 330
Student/teacher ratio	13.3	15.9
Per student expenditures	11 961	8 041
Dropouts, Grades 9–12, 2000–2001 (Percent)	7.1	...
Higher Education, 2002–2003		
Total enrollment	1 136 922	17 035 027
Bachelor's degrees awarded	106 188	1 348 503
Percent women	58.7	57.5

. . . = Not available.

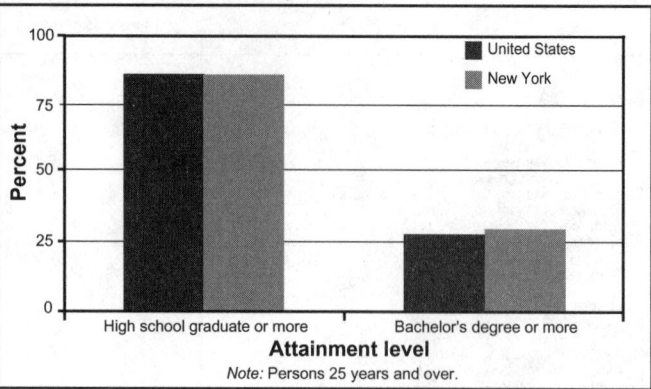

Educational Attainment, 2004

Note: Persons 25 years and over.

EDUCATION

In 2004, New York exceeded the national average educational attainment rates. The proportion of the state's population age 25 years and over holding a bachelor's degree or more was 30.6 percent, ranking 13th in the nation. New York had the country's second highest expenditures per student, amounting to $11,961. The state's student/teacher ratio was among the 6 lowest ratios in the nation. The proportion of student-age population in New York was well below the national average. The state's dropout rate exceeded 7 percent, which ranked 3rd among the 46 states reporting such data.

VOTER PARTICIPATION

The voter turnout for eligible New Yorkers was below the national average for both the 2000 and 2004 elections. In 2004, the state ranked 45th in the nation for voter participation. Non-Hispanic Whites had the highest rates of voter turnout, while less than 26 percent of eligible Asians and just 31 percent of eligible Hispanics voted. According to the official tally by the Clerk of the U.S. House of Representatives, 59 percent of New Yorkers cast their ballots for the Democratic presidential candidate in 2000, and 56.1 percent voted similarly in 2004.

Table NY-19. Reported Voting and Registration, November 2000 and November 2004

(Numbers in thousands, percent.)

Characteristic	Total population 18 years and over	Total citizen		Total registered		Total voted	
		Number	Percent	Number	Percent	Number	Percent
NOVEMBER 2000							
Total	13 725	11 877	86.5	8 047	58.6	7 004	51.0
Male	6 613	5 689	86.0	3 710	56.1	3 251	49.2
Female	7 112	6 189	87.0	4 337	61.0	3 753	52.8
NOVEMBER 2004							
Total	14 492	12 779	88.2	8 624	59.5	7 698	53.1
Male	6 865	6 043	88.0	3 965	57.8	3 561	51.9
Female	7 627	6 736	88.3	4 659	61.1	4 137	54.2
Race and Hispanic Origin							
White alone	11 055	10 122	91.6	7 090	64.1	6 366	57.6
Non-Hispanic White alone	9 389	9 005	95.9	6 457	68.8	5 846	62.3
Black alone	2 354	1 924	81.7	1 188	50.5	1 042	44.3
Asian alone	939	614	65.3	287	30.5	241	25.7
Hispanic or Latino[1]	1 976	1 346	68.1	754	38.2	613	31.0
White alone or in combination	11 130	10 190	91.6	7 118	64.0	6 389	57.4
Non-Hispanic White alone or in combination	9 444	9 059	95.9	6 485	68.7	5 870	62.2
Black alone or in combination	2 421	1 981	81.8	1 203	49.7	1 055	43.6
Asian alone or in combination	953	627	65.8	297	31.2	246	25.8
Age							
18 to 24 years	1 979	1 682	85.0	909	45.9	771	39.0
25 to 44 years	5 366	4 469	83.3	2 919	54.4	2 569	47.9
45 to 64 years	4 710	4 317	91.7	3 077	65.3	2 855	60.6
65 to 74 years	1 280	1 220	95.3	891	69.6	806	62.9
75 years and over	1 156	1 091	94.4	828	71.6	697	60.4

[1]May be of any race.

At a Glance:

- North Carolina's population was over 8.5 million in 2004. Its growth rate in recent years was above average, and the state is projected to replace New Jersey as the 10th most populous state by 2010.

- Non-Hispanic Whites made up more than 68 percent of the population, followed by Blacks at nearly 22 percent, which was the sixth highest proportion of this racial group in the nation.

- Despite concentrations of high income earners in some parts of the state, the overall median household income was low, ranking 39th in the nation.

- The state's poverty rate of 14.6 percent was the 12th highest in the country. North Carolina's unemployment rate of 5.5 percent was identical to the national average rate.

- In 2004, North Carolina had the 11th largest real gross state product, which grew at an above average rate from 2001 to 2004.

- North Carolina ranked among the lowest 10 for both the high school and college attainment levels of its population age 25 years and over.

Table NC-1. Population by Sex and Age, 1990, 2000, and 2004

(Number, percent.)

Sex and age	1990	2000	2004	Percent distribution, 2004	Average annual percent change, 2000–2004
Total Population	6 628 637	8 049 313	8 541 221	X	1.5
Percent of total U.S. population	2.7	2.9	2.9	X	X
Sex					
Male	3 214 290	3 942 695	4 198 851	49.2	1.6
Female	3 414 347	4 106 618	4 342 370	50.8	1.4
Age					
Under 5 years	458 955	539 509	600 113	7.0	1.8
5 to 17 years	1 147 194	1 424 538	1 518 379	17.8	2.0
18 years and over	1 285 608	6 085 266	6 422 729	75.2	1.8
18 to 24 years	5 022 488	806 821	828 100	9.7	0.4
25 to 44 years	781 053	2 500 535	2 531 063	29.6	1.2
45 to 64 years	2 151 486	1 808 862	2 031 317	23.8	3.4
65 years and over	804 341	969 048	1 032 249	12.1	1.8
85 years and over	69 969	105 461	120 640	1.4	4.1
Median age (years)	33.0	35.3	35.7	X	X

X = Not applicable.

Average Annual Rate of Population Growth, 1980–2004

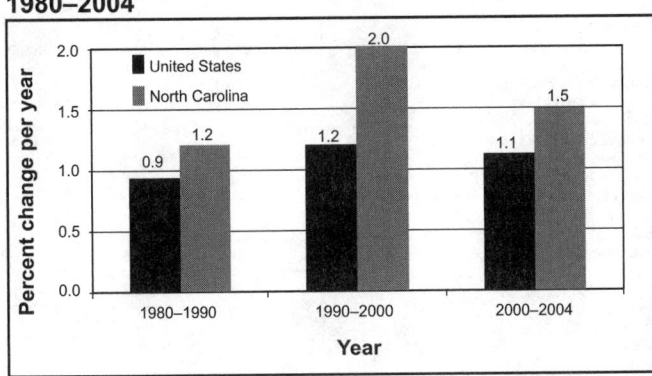

POPULATION

North Carolina's population increased by 6.1 percent between 2000 and 2004, which was the ninth fastest growth rate in the country. Both domestic and international immigration added significantly to the state's population base. During the 2000–2004 period, immigration from other states added nearly 167,000 new residents, and another 132,000 new residents arrived from abroad. The state had a slightly younger population than the nation as a whole, with a smaller proportion of residents age 65 years and over. American Indians made up 1.2 percent of North Carolina's population, which was the 11th highest proportion of this racial group in the nation.

Table NC-2. Population by Race and Hispanic Origin, 1990, 2000, and 2004

(Number, percent.)

Race and Hispanic origin	1990	2000	2004
Total Population	6 628 637	8 049 313	8 541 221
Non-Hispanic (Percent)			
One race[1]			
White	75.0	70.3	68.6
Black	21.9	21.5	21.5
American Indian, Alaska Native[2]	1.2	1.2	1.2
Asian and Pacific Islander[2]	0.8	1.5	1.7
Other race[2]	0.5	. . .	. . .
Two or more races	. . .	0.8	0.9
Hispanic or Latino[3] (Percent)	1.2	4.7	6.1

[1]Individuals could report only one race in the 1990 census and could report one or more races on the 2000 census. Data on race in 2000 and 2004 are not comparable to 1990.
[2]Data for 1990 include people of Hispanic or Latino origin.
[3]May be of any race.
. . . = Not available.

Minority Population as a Percent of Total Population, 2004

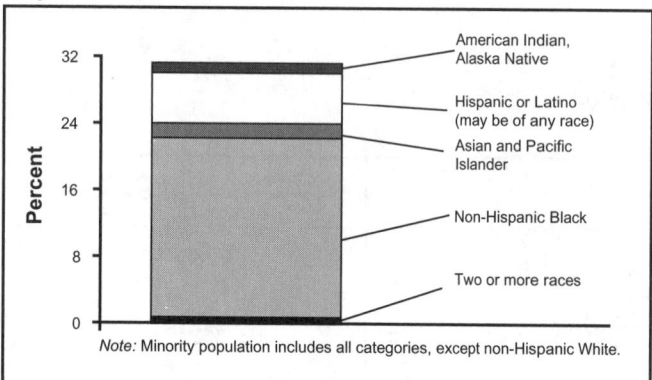

Note: Minority population includes all categories, except non-Hispanic White.

Age-Adjusted Death Rates, Average 2000–2002

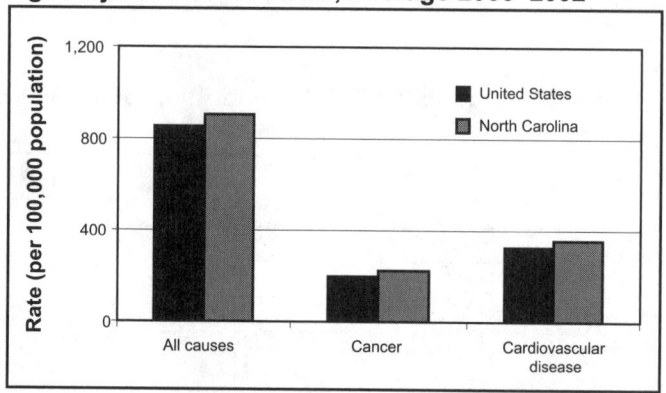

HEALTH

In 2004, 15.7 percent of North Carolina's residents lacked health insurance, matching the national rate. The state's infant mortality rate was the ninth highest in the country, and the age-adjusted death rate was also above average. The birth rate for teenage mothers was the 15th highest in the nation.

Table NC-3. Health Characteristics, 2000–2004

(Number, rate, percent.)

Item	State	U.S.
Births, 2003–2004		
Number of births	118 323	4 089 950
Birth rate (per 1,000 population)	14.1	14.1
Teenage birth rate (per 1,000 women age 15–19 years)	49.0	41.6
Mortality Rates, Average 2000–2002		
Infant mortality rate (per 1,000 live births)	8.4	6.9
Age-adjusted mortality rate (per 100,000 population)		
All races	920.2	853.3
Non-Hispanic White	879.4	843.1
Black	1 133.5	1 097.7
American Indian, Alaska Native	946.5	687.0
Asian and Pacific Islander	367.5	486.0
Hispanic or Latino[1]	295.7	642.7
Health Insurance, 2004		
Percent of all persons without health insurance	15.7	15.7
Percent of children without health insurance	11.2	11.2
Percent of low-income children without health insurance	7.6	7.1

[1]May be of any race.

Table NC-4. Leading Causes of Death, Average 2000–2002

(Number, rate per 100,000 population.)

Cause	Number of deaths	Age-adjusted death rates	
		State	U.S.
ALL CAUSES	71 632	920.2	853.3
Leading Causes			
Major cardiovascular diseases	26 225	341.9	326.5
Cancer	16 020	202.0	196.0
Chronic lower respiratory diseases	3 629	46.8	43.7
Unintentional injuries	3 554	44.1	35.7
Diabetes (underlying cause)	2 157	27.5	25.2
Influenza and pneumonia	1 874	24.9	22.7
Alzheimer's disease	1 824	24.7	19.0
Motor vehicle accidents	1 638	19.9	15.0
Nephritis, nephrotic syndrome, and nephrosis ..	1 361	17.7	13.8
Septicemia	1 094	14.1	11.4
Suicides	985	11.9	10.7
Firearm-related	1 114	13.5	10.3
Cirrhosis	749	9.2	9.5
Drug-induced	600	7.3	7.9
Alcohol-induced	650	7.9	6.9
Homicides	633	7.6	6.0
Falls	443	5.8	5.2
HIV	472	5.7	5.0
Viral hepatitis	134	1.6	2.0
Anemias	164	2.1	1.6
Drownings	115	1.4	1.3
Fire deaths	127	1.6	1.2

Note: The rates are age-adjusted to the U.S. 2000 standard population.

Table NC-5. Households and Housing Characteristics, 1990, 2000, and 2004

(Number, percent, and dollars.)

Characteristic	1990	2000	2004	Average annual percent change, 2000–2004
Total Households	2 517 026	3 132 013	3 340 330	1.6
Family households	1 812 053	2 158 869	2 280 086	1.4
Married-couple family	1 424 206	1 645 346	1 680 713	0.5
Other family	387 847	513 523	599 373	3.9
Male householder, no wife present	77 971	123 526	150 483	5.1
Female householder, no husband present	309 876	389 997	448 890	3.6
Nonfamily households	704 973	973 144	1 060 244	2.2
Householder living alone	596 959	795 271	892 329	2.9
Householder not living alone	108 014	177 873	167 915	-1.4
Housing Characteristics				
Average size	2.54	2.49	2.48	X
Housing units	2 818 193	3 523 944	3 860 078	2.3
Occupied housing units	2 517 026	3 132 013	3 340 330	1.6
Owner-occupied	1 711 817	2 172 355	2 305 212	1.5
Renter-occupied	805 209	959 658	1 035 118	1.9
Median gross rent of renter-occupied housing units (dollars) ...	382	548	610	2.7
Median value of owner-occupied housing units (dollars)	65 300	108 300	117 771	2.1

X = Not applicable.

Median Housing Value and Median Rent, 2004

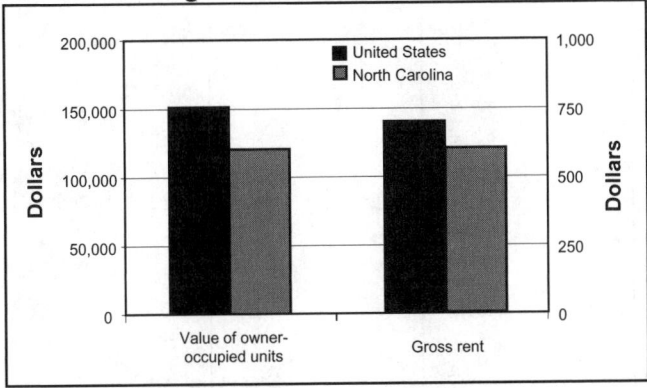

Median Household Income, 1984–2004 (2004 Dollars)

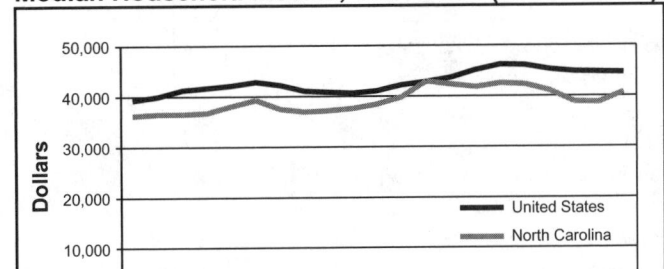

Table NC-6. Household Income and Poverty Status, 1980–2004

(2004 CPI-U-RS adjusted dollars, rate.)

Year	State		U.S.	
	Median household income (2004 dollars)	Poverty rate	Median household income (2004 dollars)	Poverty rate
2004	40 365	14.6	44 389	12.7
2003	38 281	15.7	44 482	12.5
2002	38 355	14.3	44 546	12.1
2001	40 723	12.5	45 062	11.7
2000	42 030	12.5	46 058	11.3
1999	42 227	13.8	46 129	11.9
1998	41 477	14.0	45 003	12.7
1997	42 063	11.4	43 430	13.3
1996	42 675	12.2	42 544	13.7
1995	39 362	12.6	41 943	13.8
1994	37 967	14.2	40 677	14.5
1993	37 101	14.4	40 217	15.1
1992	36 642	15.8	40 422	14.8
1991	36 319	14.5	40 746	14.2
1990	36 898	13.0	41 963	13.5
1989	38 846	12.2	42 524	12.8
1988	37 460	12.6	41 771	13.0
1987	36 192	13.8	41 322	13.4
1986	35 947	14.3	40 939	13.6
1985	35 917	14.2	39 545	14.0
1984	35 588	14.6	38 782	14.4
1983	. . .	15.8	. . .	15.2
1982	. . .	20.3	. . .	15.0
1981	. . .	17.5	. . .	14.0
1980	. . .	15.0	. . .	13.0

. . . = Not available.

Table NC-7. Employment Status by Demographic Group, 2004

(Numbers in thousands, rate.)

Characteristic	Civilian noninstitutional population	Civilian labor force		Employed	Unemployment rate
		Number	Participation rate		
SEX AND AGE					
Total	6 439	4 243	65.9	4 016	5.4
16 to 19 years	433	185	42.8	150	19.2
20 to 24 years	600	454	75.7	412	9.3
25 to 34 years	1 183	991	83.7	943	4.8
35 to 44 years	1 222	1 035	84.7	997	3.7
45 to 54 years	1 157	919	79.4	882	4.1
55 to 64 years	861	510	59.2	489	4.1
65 years and over	983	148	15.1	142	4.1
Men	3 082	2 270	73.6	2 154	5.1
16 to 19 years	215	93	43.5	77	17.9
20 to 24 years	292	241	82.5	216	10.6
25 to 34 years	587	553	94.1	532	3.8
35 to 44 years	611	569	93.1	548	3.7
45 to 54 years	565	479	84.8	459	4.2
55 to 64 years	395	257	65.0	249	3.3
65 years and over	417	78	18.6	74	4.1
Women	3 357	1 973	58.8	1 862	5.6
16 to 19 years	218	92	42.2	73	20.5
20 to 24 years	308	213	69.2	197	7.8
25 to 34 years	596	438	73.5	412	5.9
35 to 44 years	612	467	76.3	449	3.7
45 to 54 years	592	440	74.3	423	4.0
55 to 64 years	465	252	54.2	240	4.9
65 years and over	566	71	12.5	68	4.1
MARITAL STATUS					
Married men, spouse present	1 780	1 361	76.5	1 321	2.9
Married women, spouse present	1 763	1 064	60.4	1 030	3.2
Women who maintain families	405	273	67.3	248	9.0
RACE, HISPANIC ORIGIN, AND SEX					
White	4 836	3 216	66.5	3 089	3.9
Men	2 360	1 787	75.7	1 720	3.8
Women	2 477	1 429	57.7	1 370	4.2
Black	1 308	837	64.0	749	10.5
Men	583	386	66.2	344	10.8
Women	725	451	62.2	405	10.3
Asian	128	84	65.4	82	2.0
Hispanic or Latino[1]	429	319	74.5	303	5.1
Men	260	233	89.5	220	5.2
Women	169	87	51.4	83	4.9
RACE, HISPANIC ORIGIN, AND AGE					
White					
16 to 19 years	288	138	47.9	118	14.3
20 to 24 years	413	330	79.9	310	6.1
25 to 34 years	887	745	84.0	720	3.4
35 to 44 years	899	769	85.5	749	2.6
45 to 54 years	861	688	79.9	668	3.0
55 to 64 years	686	421	61.3	403	4.1
65 years and over	802	126	15.7	122	3.6

Note: Data in Table 7 are from the Current Population Survey (CPS) and do not match Bureau of Labor Statistics estimates in Table 8. See notes and definitions for more details.

[1]May be of any race.

Table NC-8. Employment Status, 1990–2004

(Numbers in thousands, rate.)

Year	Civilian labor force	Employed	Unemployed	Unemployment rate
2004	4 256 340	4 020 788	235 552	5.5
2003	4 230 241	3 957 077	273 164	6.5
2002	4 201 385	3 921 819	279 566	6.7
2001	4 182 974	3 948 692	234 282	5.6
2000	4 113 790	3 959 389	154 401	3.8
1999	4 053 949	3 921 244	132 705	3.3
1998	3 985 573	3 844 792	140 781	3.5
1997	3 962 777	3 809 601	153 176	3.9
1996	3 875 125	3 704 108	171 017	4.4
1995	3 748 853	3 582 647	166 206	4.4
1994	3 672 907	3 511 339	161 568	4.4
1993	3 621 196	3 434 311	186 885	5.2
1992	3 595 919	3 372 068	223 851	6.2
1991	3 539 623	3 330 035	209 588	5.9
1990	3 497 568	3 352 165	145 403	4.2

Note: Population age 16 years and over.

Unemployment Rate, 1980–2004

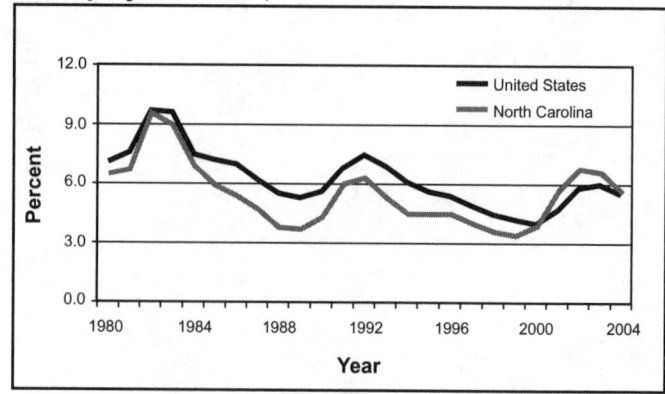

Table NC-9. Employment and Average Wages by Industry, 2001–2004

(Estimates are based on the 2002 North American Industry Classification System [NAICS].)

Industry	2001	2002	2003	2004	Annual average percent change, 2001–2004
	Number of jobs				
TOTAL EMPLOYMENT BY PLACE OF WORK	4 885 069	4 878 093	4 887 821	4 974 274	0.6
Farm Employment	82 772	84 803	81 140	76 533	-2.6
Nonfarm Employment	4 802 297	4 793 290	4 806 681	4 897 741	0.7
Private employment	4 053 784	4 031 867	4 032 526	4 111 753	0.5
Forestry, fishing, hunting, and other[1]	27 709	29 538	26 954	26 121	-1.9
Mining	6 381	5 572	5 887	6 018	-1.9
Utilities	D	14 836	14 772	14 204	...
Construction	344 336	330 634	329 917	341 021	-0.3
Manufacturing	720 461	662 403	621 455	599 904	-5.9
Durable goods manufacturing	367 284	329 493	309 061	307 514	-5.7
Nondurable goods manufacturing	353 177	332 910	312 394	292 390	-6.1
Wholesale trade	175 366	176 793	178 452	184 535	1.7
Retail trade	544 721	539 599	536 973	545 518	0.0
Transportation and warehousing	148 922	139 648	138 072	142 014	-1.6
Information	D	87 532	85 244	82 361	...
Finance and insurance	178 903	183 071	183 828	187 918	1.7
Real estate and rental and leasing	143 514	148 220	156 119	163 992	4.5
Professional and technical services	234 853	234 345	237 053	244 901	1.4
Management of companies and enterprises	62 936	65 363	63 168	65 077	1.1
Administrative and waste services	269 396	276 704	288 205	300 713	3.7
Educational services	65 491	71 918	75 161	78 789	6.4
Health care and social assistance	394 025	411 352	426 691	442 417	3.9
Arts, entertainment, and recreation	77 962	80 649	81 199	82 832	2.0
Accommodation and food services	296 520	304 827	311 332	325 738	3.2
Other services, except public administration	255 593	268 863	272 044	277 680	2.8
Government and government enterprises	748 513	761 423	774 155	785 988	1.6
	Dollars				
AVERAGE WAGES AND SALARIES BY PLACE OF WORK	31 505	32 141	33 031	34 363	2.9
Farm Earnings	17 950	19 252	17 649	22 185	7.3
Nonfarm Earnings	31 594	32 232	33 134	34 435	2.9
Private earnings	31 628	32 175	32 986	34 311	2.8
Forestry, fishing, hunting, and other[1]	18 864	20 579	21 153	22 399	5.9
Mining	45 282	43 039	45 373	49 805	3.2
Utilities	D	59 712	60 859	65 691	...
Construction	31 977	31 979	32 639	33 764	1.8
Manufacturing	37 056	38 280	39 517	41 617	3.9
Durable goods manufacturing	39 548	40 016	41 221	43 538	3.3
Nondurable goods manufacturing	34 486	36 576	37 848	39 611	4.7
Wholesale trade	43 350	44 578	46 522	48 885	4.1
Retail trade	21 171	21 561	21 952	22 521	2.1
Transportation and warehousing	35 241	35 826	36 142	36 888	1.5
Information	D	46 609	48 524	51 468	...
Finance and insurance	52 596	54 185	57 926	60 056	4.5
Real estate and rental and leasing	28 173	28 724	29 686	31 688	4.0
Professional and technical services	48 204	48 328	49 550	51 314	2.1
Management of companies and enterprises	61 564	65 373	67 992	73 912	6.3
Administrative and waste services	20 990	21 994	22 320	23 580	4.0
Educational services	28 225	28 199	28 752	29 779	1.8
Health care and social assistance	31 276	31 792	32 410	33 544	2.4
Arts, entertainment, and recreation	23 689	23 737	24 784	25 801	2.9
Accommodation and food services	12 717	12 811	12 972	13 255	1.4
Other services, except public administration	21 185	21 359	21 850	22 566	2.1
Government and government enterprises	31 438	32 480	33 757	34 956	3.6

Note: Average wages and salaries are a calculation by the editors of wage and salary disbursements divided by full- and part-time wage and salary employment. Data may not add to total or may appear as zero due to rounding.

[1] "Other" consists of the number of jobs held by U.S. residents employed by international organizations and foreign embassies and consulates in the United States.
D = Suppressed to avoid disclosure of data of individual companies.
... = Not available.

LABOR MARKET

North Carolina's labor market was adversely affected by the 2001 recession, causing sharp increases in the state's unemployment rate. This rate only began to show improvement in 2004. Employment growth was subdued over the 2001–2004 period, as a sharp drop in jobs in manufacturing and sluggish employment growth in retail trade largely negated the job gains in educational services, real estate and related activities, health care, accommodation and food services, and government. North Carolina's average wages and salaries were about 11 percent lower than national average in 2004, but grew at a rate close to the U.S. average.

Employment by Industry, 2004

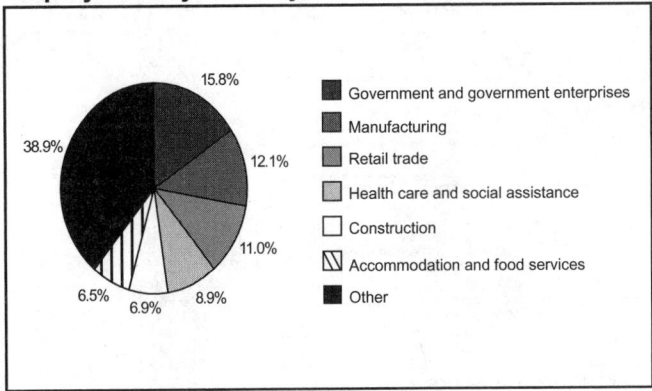

Table NC-10. Personal Income by Major Source, Selected Years 1980–2004

(Millions of dollars, except where noted.)

Item	1980	1990	2000	2001	2002	2003	2004	Average annual percent change, 2000–2004
Earnings by Place of Work	39 580	90 212	168 771	173 298	176 122	181 782	193 782	3.5
Wage and salary disbursements	30 571	67 674	127 449	129 705	131 196	134 042	141 282	2.6
Supplements to wages and salaries	5 669	13 910	25 491	26 406	29 185	31 848	34 492	7.9
Proprietors' income[1]	3 340	8 628	15 831	17 187	15 741	15 892	18 008	3.3
Farm proprietors' income	369	1 758	2 121	2 231	672	990	1 748	-4.7
Nonfarm proprietors' income	2 971	6 869	13 710	14 956	15 069	14 902	16 260	4.4
(-) Contributions for government social insurance[2]	3 727	10 017	18 748	19 564	19 908	20 912	21 929	4.0
(+) Adjustment for residence[3]	23	-447	-885	-781	-769	-733	-776	X
(=) Net Earnings by Place of Residence	35 875	79 748	149 137	152 953	155 445	160 137	171 077	3.5
(+) Dividends, interest, and rent[4]	6 599	21 605	39 633	39 156	37 195	36 822	38 664	-0.6
(+) Personal current transfer receipts	5 870	13 573	29 898	33 286	35 980	37 585	40 544	7.9
Personal income	48 344	114 926	218 668	225 395	228 621	234 544	250 286	3.4
Farm income	47 720	112 822	216 113	222 651	227 359	233 042	247 972	3.5
Nonfarm income	624	2 104	2 555	2 744	1 262	1 502	2 314	-2.4
Per Capita Personal Income (Dollars)[5]	8 195	17 246	27 068	27 493	27 505	27 852	29 303	2.0

Note: Data may not add to total or may appear as zero due to rounding.

[1]Proprietors' income includes the inventory valuation adjustment and the capital consumption adjustment.
[2]Contributions for government social insurance are included in earnings by type and industry, but they are excluded from personal income.
[3]The adjustment for residence is the net inflow of the earnings of interarea commuters.
[4]Rental income of persons includes the capital consumption adjustment.
[5]Per capita personal income is total personal income divided by total midyear population.
X = Not applicable.

Per Capita Personal Income, 1980–2004 (Current Dollars)

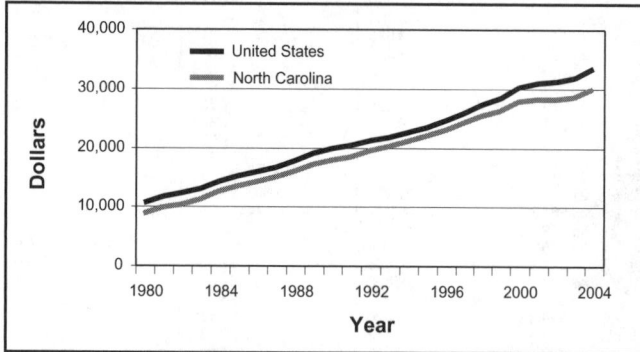

ECONOMIC ACTIVITY

Real gross state product grew at an above average rate throughout the 2001–2004 period. Its growth of 10.4 percent during this period ranked 22nd in the country. Contributors to this increase were manufacturing, retail trade, finance and insurance, information, and real estate and related activities. Agriculture, mining, construction, and educational services experienced declines from 2001 to 2004. Housing values rose at a below average rate, increasing just 8.7 percent from 2000 to 2004, compared with 26.6 percent nationally. In 2004, the median value of owner-occupied housing in North Carolina totaled $117,771, ranking 32nd in the country.

Table NC-11. Real Gross State Product, 1997–2004

(Millions of chained 2000 dollars, percent.)

Industry	1997	1998	1999	2000	2001	2002	2003	2004	Average annual percent change, 2001–2004
GROSS STATE PRODUCT	239 698	250 885	261 778	274 306	279 893	286 943	295 897	308 970	3.3
As a percent of U.S. gross product	2.8	2.8	2.8	2.8	2.8	2.9	2.9	2.9	X
Private Industries	208 324	218 690	228 837	240 723	246 304	252 934	260 466	271 810	3.3
Agriculture, forestry, fishing, and hunting	3 279	2 831	2 812	3 852	3 628	2 517	2 645	2 906	-7.1
Mining	415	482	521	512	488	470	446	439	-3.5
Utilities	4 321	4 252	4 483	4 784	4 640	4 861	5 378	5 609	6.5
Construction	12 504	13 024	13 213	12 784	12 434	11 637	11 396	11 710	-2.0
Manufacturing	58 922	59 825	64 466	67 325	66 102	67 367	68 740	69 869	1.9
As a percent of gross state product	24.6	23.8	24.6	24.5	23.6	23.5	23.2	22.6	X
Wholesale trade	12 707	14 030	14 851	14 742	15 726	16 656	16 834	17 724	4.1
Retail trade	15 568	16 310	17 307	17 978	19 150	20 280	21 793	22 903	6.1
Transportation and warehousing	7 007	7 196	7 288	7 398	7 401	7 149	7 538	7 749	1.5
Information	6 747	7 490	8 083	8 553	9 154	9 248	9 927	10 879	5.9
Finance and insurance	15 491	19 212	22 660	22 271	24 555	27 978	29 123	31 075	8.2
Real estate and rental and leasing	23 218	23 874	20 063	26 645	27 817	27 714	27 789	29 271	1.7
Services	48 122	50 428	53 177	53 876	55 278	57 240	59 182	61 991	3.9
As a percent of gross state product	20.1	20.1	20.3	19.6	19.7	19.9	20.0	20.1	X
Professional and technical services	9 189	10 290	11 526	12 662	12 991	13 093	13 931	14 577	3.9
Management of companies and enterprises	5 741	5 649	5 634	5 025	5 395	5 959	5 965	6 295	5.3
Administrative and waste services	6 043	6 501	7 113	6 466	6 227	6 766	7 102	7 508	6.4
Educational services	1 546	1 621	1 678	1 725	1 756	1 737	1 678	1 685	-1.4
Health care and social assistance	12 961	13 141	13 660	14 256	15 335	15 910	16 476	17 103	3.7
Arts, entertainment, and recreation	1 448	1 562	1 673	1 725	1 858	1 891	1 908	1 946	1.6
Accommodation and food services	5 494	5 766	5 987	6 206	6 044	6 209	6 444	6 804	4.0
Other services, except public administration	5 700	5 898	5 906	5 811	5 672	5 675	5 678	6 073	2.3
Government	31 433	32 225	32 952	33 583	33 593	34 025	35 427	37 137	3.4
As a percent of gross state product	13.1	12.8	12.6	12.2	12.0	11.9	12.0	12.0	X

X = Not applicable.

Table NC-12. Government Transfer Payments, Selected Years 1980–2004

(Millions of dollars, percent.)

Item	1980	1990	2000	2001	2002	2003	2004	Average annual percent change, 2000–2004
CURRENT TRANSFER PAYMENTS TO INDIVIDUALS	5 469	12 732	28 108	31 277	34 199	36 004	38 907	8.5
Retirement and Disability Insurance Benefits	2 823	6 413	11 871	12 692	13 552	14 226	14 980	6.0
Old-age, survivors, and disability insurance (OASDI) benefits	2 739	6 253	11 654	12 463	13 294	13 963	14 710	6.0
Railroad retirement and disability benefits	68	112	141	145	152	157	159	3.1
Workers' compensation	8	32	52	56	69	68	70	7.5
Other government retirement and disability insurance benefits	8	16	24	27	38	38	40	14.1
Medical Benefits	1 093	3 879	11 413	13 078	13 976	14 648	16 634	9.9
Medicare benefits	654	2 194	5 588	6 236	6 726	7 162	7 923	9.1
Public assistance medical care benefits	417	1 569	5 674	6 635	6 964	7 241	8 413	10.3
Military medical insurance benefits	22	117	150	207	286	245	297	18.6
Income Maintenance Benefits	744	1 395	3 137	3 195	3 674	4 095	4 497	9.4
Supplemental Security Income (SSI) benefits	233	467	859	908	941	967	1 010	4.1
Family assistance	154	260	263	285	273	266	256	-0.7
Food stamps	242	301	390	449	555	677	782	19.0
Other income maintenance benefits	114	367	1 626	1 553	1 904	2 186	2 448	10.8
Unemployment Insurance Compensation	254	323	511	972	1 508	1 420	1 020	18.9
Veterans' Benefits	446	547	884	954	1 078	1 177	1 302	10.2
Federal Education and Training Assistance	108	150	268	344	387	417	443	13.4
Other Payments to Individuals	2	26	23	42	23	20	31	7.5

Note: See notes and definitions for more details. Data may not add to total or may appear as zero due to rounding.

EXPORTS

North Carolina's exports totaled $18.1 billion in 2004, making it the 15th largest exporter in the country. After a decline following the 2001 recession, total goods exports rebounded, growing 23 percent from 2002 to 2004. Chemical manufactures were the state's chief export, followed by computers and electronic products, which together accounted for over one-third of exports. Canada, as the destination for about 25 percent of North Carolina's goods, was by far the state's largest export market. Mexico and Japan were the other leading markets, while Italy, China, France, and Honduras were all rapidly growing markets.

Leading Exports, 2004

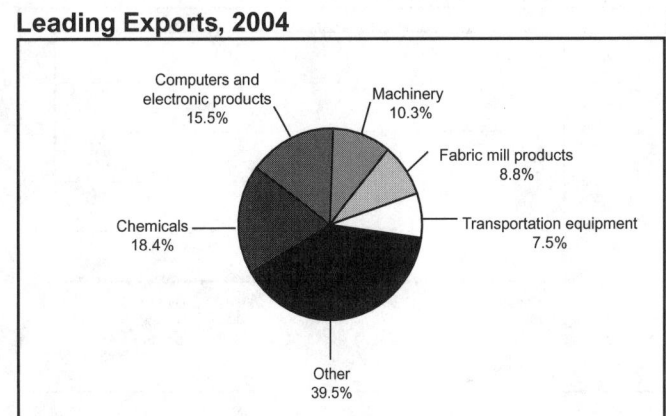

Computers and electronic products 15.5%

Machinery 10.3%

Fabric mill products 8.8%

Transportation equipment 7.5%

Chemicals 18.4%

Other 39.5%

Table NC-13. Exports of Goods by Leading Products and Destinations, 2001–2004

(Millions of dollars, percent, rank based on 2004 dollar values.)

Product and market	2001	2002	2003	2004	Percent share of total, 2004	Average annual percent change, 2001–2004
Total Goods						
Total	16 799	14 719	16 199	18 115	100.0	2.5
Manufactures	15 726	13 817	15 319	17 136	94.6	2.9
Agriculture and livestock	842	697	654	708	3.9	-5.6
Other commodities	231	204	225	271	1.5	5.5
Five Leading Exports (NAICS Code)						
Chemical manufactures (325)	2 314	2 356	3 025	3 337	18.4	13.0
Computers and electronic products (334)	2 813	2 400	2 706	2 816	15.5	0.0
Machinery manufactures (333)	1 658	1 450	1 557	1 858	10.3	3.9
Fabric mill products (313)	1 205	1 297	1 376	1 591	8.8	9.7
Transportation equipment (336)	906	856	1 164	1 359	7.5	14.5
Five Leading Markets	14 682	12 876	14 328	15 901	87.8	2.7
Canada	4 086	3 739	3 896	4 486	24.8	3.2
Mexico	1 626	1 330	1 464	1 582	8.7	-0.9
Japan	1 372	1 417	1 591	1 462	8.1	2.1
United Kingdom	970	735	687	812	4.5	-5.7
Honduras	428	575	696	671	3.7	16.2

Table NC-14. Agriculture, 1997 and 2002

(Number, acres, and dollars.)

Item	1997	2002
Number of farms	59 120	53 930
Land in farms (acres)	9 444 867	9 079 001
Farm Size		
Average size of farm (acres)	160	168
Farms by size (percent distribution)		
Fewer than 50 acres	45.0	45.6
50 to 499 acres	48.2	47.1
500 acres or more	6.8	7.2
Market Value of Land and Equipment (Dollars)		
Land and buildings average value per farm	349 841	518 719
Average value per acre	2 127	3 088
Machinery and equipment average value per farm	47 411	63 902
Value of Sales (Thousands of Dollars)		
Agricultural products sold	7 832 362	6 961 686
Crops	2 600 655	2 008 634
Livestock, poultry, and their products	5 231 707	4 953 052
Average per farm (dollars)	132 482	129 087
Value of sales (percent distribution)		
Less than $10,000	59.7	63.7
$10,000 to $99,999	22.9	20.0
$100,000 or more	17.4	16.3
Government Payments		
Payments (thousands of dollars)	52 546	97 696
Percent of farms receiving government payments	27.2	22.8
Farm operators whose principal occupation is farming (percent) ...	45.6	58.7

AGRICULTURE

Cash receipts from farming totaled about $7 billion in 2002, according to the Department of Agriculture's Census of Agriculture. This was a significant decline from the previous farm census in 1997, mostly reflecting a drop in crop sales (including tobacco). The state's leading farm products were hogs and chickens. Nearly 64 percent of farms had sales of less than $10,000. More than 45 percent of North Carolina's farms spanned fewer than 50 acres. Nearly 59 percent of farm operators reported farming as their principal occupation—an increase from 1997, when this proportion was 45.6 percent.

ENERGY

North Carolina's energy prices were the 12th highest in the country. However, per capita consumption was below the national average. Total energy expenditures per person of $2,302 in 2001 were also below average. Petroleum, coal, and nuclear power were the state's chief energy sources.

Energy Consumption by Source, 2001

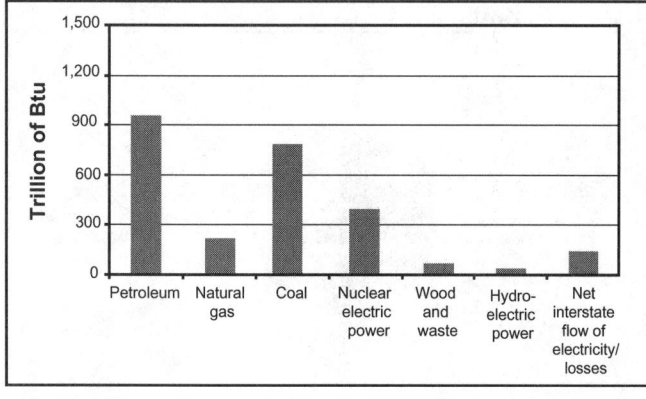

Energy Consumption by Sector, 2001

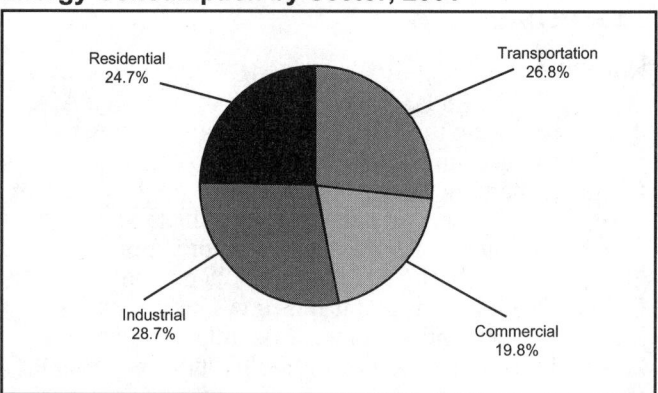

Table NC-15. Energy Consumption, Expenditures, and Prices, Selected Years 1960–2001

(Dollars, Btu [British Thermal Unit], percent distribution.)

Item	1960	1965	1970	1975	1980	1985	1990	1995	2000	2001
Total Consumption (Billion Btu)	826 970	1 002 219	1 345 155	1 463 000	1 671 264	1 801 546	2 087 652	2 393 769	2 668 806	2 590 457
Consumption per capita (million Btu)	181.5	206.1	264.6	263.7	284.1	288.1	314.9	333.1	331.6	316.1
Consumption by Sector (Percent Distribution)										
Residential	28.5	26.1	25.6	24.0	24.1	23.6	22.8	23.8	24.6	24.7
Commercial	7.0	8.9	11.6	12.2	12.9	15.1	16.6	17.2	19.1	19.8
Industrial	36.5	37.2	35.7	34.9	36.5	34.0	34.9	33.8	30.0	28.7
Transportation	28.0	27.9	27.1	29.0	26.6	27.3	25.7	25.2	26.4	26.8
Consumption by Source (Billion Btu)										
Coal	231 342	325 866	491 383	476 522	624 696	550 505	568 300	662 876	786 127	756 545
Natural gas	47 032	78 245	154 856	116 889	155 156	138 375	166 745	212 010	240 730	215 600
Petroleum	419 419	496 338	620 585	639 452	667 880	699 989	732 487	836 201	963 838	949 615
Nuclear electric power	0	0	0	15 477	62 997	205 037	274 130	377 308	408 054	394 673
Hydroelectric power[1]	53 782	56 294	45 896	73 417	56 992	42 766	72 809	58 656	33 112	26 409
Wood and waste	73 725	67 314	65 900	66 411	71 876	90 772	100 948	108 963	93 783	92 063
Other	0	0	0	0	0	0	288	318	335	345
Net interstate flow of electricity/losses[2]	1 670	-21 837	-33 466	74 832	31 667	74 103	171 946	137 437	142 826	155 207
Total Expenditures (Thousands of Dollars)	. . .	. . .	1 906 300	3 998 300	8 585 800	10 828 900	12 630 100	14 401 100	19 254 000	18 865 000
Expenditures per capita (dollars)	. . .	. . .	375	721	1 460	1 732	1 905	2 004	2 392	2 302
Prices by Sector (Dollars Per Million Btu)										
Total	. . .	. . .	2.00	4.06	7.93	9.34	9.58	9.40	11.34	11.43
Residential	. . .	. . .	2.35	5.03	9.49	13.44	16.03	16.06	17.54	18.62
Commercial	. . .	. . .	2.57	5.13	8.46	12.51	13.42	13.75	14.77	15.41
Industrial	. . .	. . .	1.03	2.90	5.21	6.99	5.89	5.77	6.95	7.10
Transportation	. . .	. . .	2.52	4.27	9.35	8.62	9.10	8.49	11.00	10.35

[1]A negative number in this row results from pumped storage for which, overall, more electricity is expended than created to provide electricity during peak demand periods.
[2]Net interstate flow of electricity is the difference between the amount of energy in the electricity sold within a state (including associated losses) and the energy input at the electric utilities within the state. A positive number indicates that more electricity (including associated losses) came into the state than went out of the state during the year; conversely, a negative number indicates that more electricity (including associated losses) went out of the state than came into the state.
. . . = Not available.

Table NC-16. State Taxes, Fiscal 2004
(Dollars, percent distribution.)

Item	Thousands of dollars	Percent distribution	Dollars per capita	
			State	U.S.
TOTAL TAXES	16 576 316	100.0	1 940.8	2 024.8
Property Taxes	X	X	X	38.9
Sales and Gross Receipts	7 269 203	43.9	851.1	1 003.4
General sales and gross receipts	4 351 823	26.3	509.5	677.0
Selective sales taxes	2 917 380	17.6	341.6	326.4
Alcoholic beverages	212 224	1.3	24.8	15.7
Insurance premiums	432 975	2.6	50.7	47.0
Motor fuels	1 272 611	7.7	149.0	114.6
Public utilities	319 731	1.9	37.4	39.2
Other selective sales	624 602	3.8	73.1	49.8
Licenses	1 017 247	6.1	119.1	134.9
Corporation	337 740	2.0	39.5	21.6
Motor vehicle	440 180	2.7	51.5	59.4
Occupation and business, not elsewhere classified	131 728	0.8	15.4	37.1
Other Taxes	8 289 866	50.0	970.6	847.6
Individual income	7 250 837	43.7	848.9	673.6
Corporation net income	837 085	5.0	98.0	105.1
Death and gift	145 109	0.9	17.0	19.6

X = Not applicable.

GOVERNMENT FINANCE

State revenues and expenditures per person were both below the national average in 2003; North Carolina ranked 35th in the nation for both measures. Spending per capita on education and health fell significantly below average, while outlays on highways and police protection were above the national averages. Taxation relied primarily on individual income tax collections, general sales, and motor fuel taxes. While total per capita taxes were below average, per capita individual income taxes amounted to $849, which was the 14th highest amount in the nation. North Carolina's debt per person was $1,442, which was among the lowest in the country.

Per Capita State Taxes, Fiscal 2004

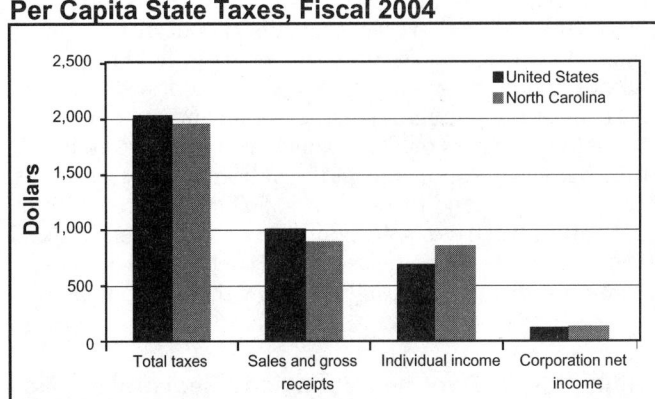

Table NC-17. State Government Finances, 2003
(Dollars, percent distribution.)

Item	Millions of dollars	Percent distribution	Dollars per capita	
			State	U.S.
GENERAL REVENUE	30 171 034	100.0	3 582.8	3 832.6
Intergovernmental revenue	10 278 725	34.1	1 220.6	1 246.0
Taxes	15 848 650	52.5	1 882.0	1 891.6
General sales	4 005 124	13.3	475.6	636.0
Selective sales	2 746 998	9.1	326.2	307.4
License taxes	937 372	3.1	111.3	123.6
Individual income tax	7 089 142	23.5	841.8	626.8
Corporate income tax	898 369	3.0	106.7	97.8
Other taxes	171 645	0.6	20.4	99.9
Current charges	2 560 135	8.5	304.0	366.5
Miscellaneous general revenue	1 483 524	4.9	176.2	328.6
GENERAL EXPENDITURE	30 428 323	100.0	3 613.4	4 010.5
Intergovernmental expenditure	10 356 152	34.0	1 229.8	1 316.9
Direct expenditure	20 072 171	66.0	2 383.6	2 693.6
Expenditure by Function				
Education	12 376 047	40.7	1 469.7	1 416.4
Public welfare	7 813 094	25.7	927.8	1 083.3
Hospitals	1 052 927	3.5	125.0	132.3
Health	1 026 171	3.4	121.9	173.0
Highways	2 722 986	8.9	323.4	295.4
Police protection	359 016	1.2	42.6	38.4
Correction	942 711	3.1	112.0	135.0
Natural resources	563 816	1.9	67.0	64.0
Parks and recreation	130 528	0.4	15.5	20.1
Government administration	766 185	2.5	91.0	151.3
Interest on general debt	446 717	1.5	53.0	107.8
Other and unallocable	2 228 125	7.3	264.6	393.4
DEBT AT END OF FISCAL YEAR	12 141 890	X	1 441.9	2 404.7
CASH AND SECURITY HOLDINGS	65 591 853	X	7 789.1	8 938.4

X = Not applicable.

Table NC-18. Education Indicators, 2000–2004

(Percent, number.)

Item	State	U.S.
Total Population 25 Years and Over (Thousands), 2004	5 313	186 877
Educational Attainment, 2004		
Percent high school graduate or more	80.9	85.2
Percent college graduate or more	23.4	27.7
Elementary and Secondary Schools, 2002–2003		
Total students	1 335 954	48 202 324
Percent of students eligible for free or reduced-price lunch ..	44.5	40.6
Percent of students who were English language learners	4.5	7.8
Total schools	2 245	92 330
Student/teacher ratio	15.1	15.9
Per student expenditures	6 562	8 041
Dropouts, Grades 9–12, 2000–2001 (Percent)	5.7	. . .
Higher Education, 2002–2003		
Total enrollment	449 841	17 035 027
Bachelor's degrees awarded	37 272	1 348 503
Percent women	59.1	57.5

. . . = Not available.

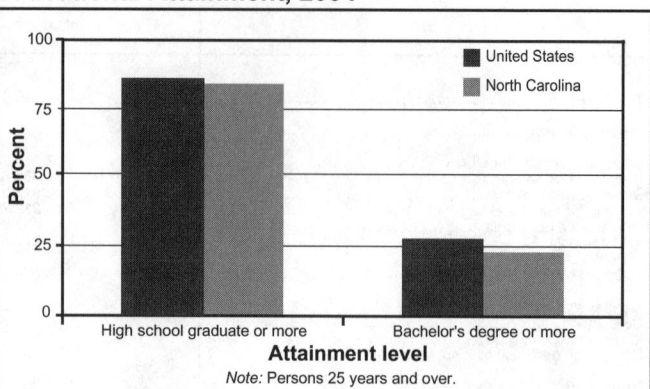

Educational Attainment, 2004

Note: Persons 25 years and over.

EDUCATION

North Carolina's educational attainment levels were well below the national averages. In 2004, about 81 percent of the state's residents age 25 years and over held high school diplomas, ranking 47th in the nation. Just over 23 percent of the population age 25 years and over held bachelor's degrees or more, which also ranked among the 10 lowest proportions in the nation. North Carolina's per student expenditures were $6,562 and ranked 40th in the nation. The state's dropout rate of 5.7 percent ranked 11th among the 46 states reporting such data. The student/teacher ratio was slightly below the national average.

VOTER PARTICIPATION

Voter turnout was below average for the 2000 election, but nearly identical to the national average for the 2004 election. Just 8.2 percent of eligible Hispanics voted in 2004. For non-Hispanic Whites and Blacks, participation rates were close to 62 percent. Persons age 65 to 74 years had the highest voter turnout, while less than 39 percent of voters age 18 to 24 years cast ballots in 2004. According to the official tally by the Clerk of the U.S. House of Representatives, 56 percent of North Carolina's voters cast ballots for the Republican presidential candidate in both the 2000 and 2004 elections.

Table NC-19. Reported Voting and Registration, November 2000 and November 2004

(Numbers in thousands, percent.)

Characteristic	Total population 18 years and over	Total citizen		Total registered		Total voted	
		Number	Percent	Number	Percent	Number	Percent
NOVEMBER 2000							
Total	5 629	5 335	94.8	3 720	66.1	2 995	53.2
Male	2 626	2 442	93.0	1 693	64.5	1 361	51.8
Female	3 003	2 893	96.3	2 026	67.5	1 633	54.4
NOVEMBER 2004							
Total	6 250	5 923	94.8	4 292	68.7	3 639	58.2
Male	2 979	2 806	94.2	1 958	65.7	1 626	54.6
Female	3 271	3 117	95.3	2 334	71.3	2 013	61.5
Race and Hispanic Origin							
White alone	4 709	4 461	94.7	3 268	69.4	2 736	58.1
Non-Hispanic White alone	4 408	4 355	98.8	3 227	73.2	2 713	61.5
Black alone	1 241	1 213	97.7	874	70.4	784	63.1
Asian alone	125	85	67.6	43	34.4	43	34.4
Hispanic or Latino[1]	327	109	33.4	44	13.4	27	8.2
White alone or in combination	4 750	4 502	94.8	3 296	69.4	2 758	58.1
Non-Hispanic White alone or in combination	4 449	4 396	98.8	3 255	73.2	2 735	61.5
Black alone or in combination	1 259	1 230	97.7	887	70.4	792	62.9
Asian alone or in combination	130	89	68.7	47	36.5	47	36.5
Age							
18 to 24 years	808	729	90.2	419	51.9	310	38.4
25 to 44 years	2 430	2 233	91.9	1 589	65.4	1 327	54.6
45 to 64 years	1 938	1 901	98.1	1 439	74.3	1 261	65.1
65 to 74 years	610	606	99.3	491	80.5	446	73.1
75 years and over	463	454	98.1	353	76.3	295	63.6

[1]May be of any race.

At a Glance:

- North Dakota's population was estimated to be 634,366 in 2004. Only the District of Columbia, Vermont, and Wyoming had fewer residents.

- Over 91 percent of the population was non-Hispanic White. About 5 percent of North Dakota's residents were American Indian, which was the sixth highest proportion of this racial group in the nation.

- Less than 22 percent of North Dakota's population was under 18 years old, and the state had the fourth highest proportion of population over 65 years old.

- The state's median household income ranked 42nd in the nation, but its poverty rate was well below the national average.

- The unemployment rate in 2004 was 3.3 percent, the second lowest in the country.

- Real gross state product was the nation's smallest, but its growth rate from 2001 to 2004 was the 13th highest in the nation.

- North Dakota had the second lowest dropout rate of the 46 states reporting such data.

Table ND-1. Population by Sex and Age, 1990, 2000, and 2004

(Number, percent.)

Sex and age	1990	2000	2004	Percent distribution, 2004	Average annual percent change, 2000–2004
Total Population	638 800	642 200	634 366	X	-0.3
Percent of total U.S. population	0.3	0.2	0.2	X	X
Sex					
Male	318 201	320 524	316 631	49.9	-0.3
Female	320 599	321 676	317 735	50.1	-0.3
Age					
Under 5 years	47 845	39 400	35 754	5.6	-2.2
5 to 17 years	127 540	121 449	103 201	16.3	-1.5
18 years and over	110 472	481 351	495 411	78.1	0.5
18 to 24 years	463 415	73 118	76 665	12.1	0.8
25 to 44 years	67 853	174 891	165 758	26.1	-1.1
45 to 64 years	194 035	138 864	159 817	25.2	2.7
65 years and over	91 055	94 478	93 171	14.7	0.2
85 years and over	11 240	14 726	16 413	2.6	2.8
Median age (years)	32.3	36.2	37.9	X	X

X = Not applicable.

Average Annual Rate of Population Growth, 1980–2004

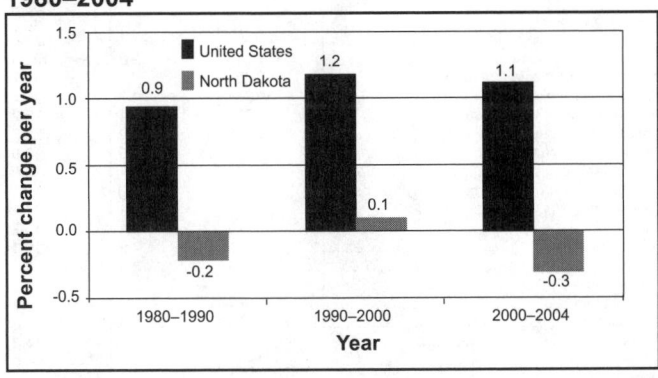

POPULATION

North Dakota's population declined by 1.2 percent between 2000 and 2004. It was the only state to lose residents. (The District of Columbia also experienced a population loss during this period.) Vermont, which currently has fewer residents, is projected to surpass North Dakota in population by 2010. The major reason for North Dakota's population loss was the migration of nearly 18,000 residents to other locations. Many of these migrants were younger, resulting in the state having an above average proportion of older residents. North Dakota added about 3,000 people from other countries, which was the third smallest influx of foreign immigrants in the nation.

Table ND-2. Population by Race and Hispanic Origin, 1990, 2000, and 2004

(Number, percent.)

Race and Hispanic origin	1990	2000	2004
Total Population	638 800	642 200	634 366
Non-Hispanic (Percent)			
One race[1]			
White	94.2	91.9	91.1
Black	0.5	0.6	0.7
American Indian, Alaska Native[2]	4.1	4.8	5.1
Asian and Pacific Islander[2]	0.5	0.6	0.7
Other race[2]	0.3	. . .	. . .
Two or more races	. . .	0.9	0.9
Hispanic or Latino[3] (Percent)	0.7	1.2	1.5

[1]Individuals could report only one race in the 1990 census and could report one or more races on the 2000 census. Data on race in 2000 and 2004 are not comparable to 1990.
[2]Data for 1990 include people of Hispanic or Latino origin.
[3]May be of any race.
. . . = Not available.

Minority Population as a Percent of Total Population, 2004

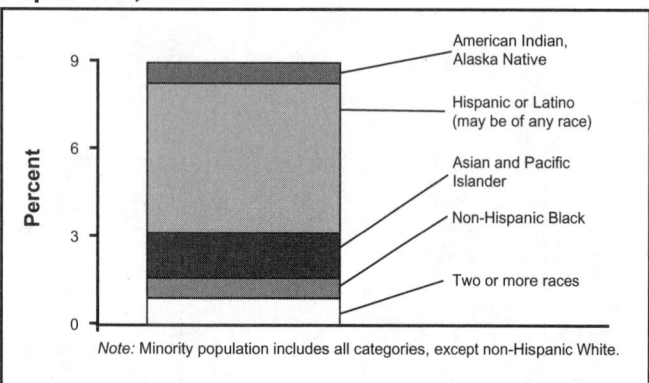

Note: Minority population includes all categories, except non-Hispanic White.

Age-Adjusted Death Rates, Average 2000–2002

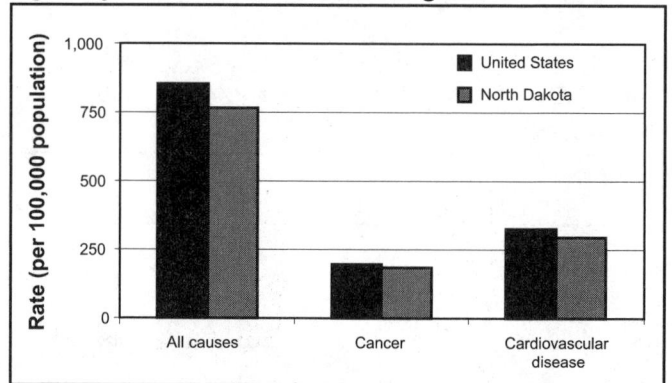

HEALTH

Just 11.2 percent of North Dakota's population lacked health insurance, which partly reflected the state's low unemployment rate and the relatively large proportion of population over 65 years old (which was covered by Medicare). The state's age-adjusted death rate was the third lowest in the nation.

Table ND-3. Health Characteristics, 2000–2004

(Number, rate, percent.)

Item	State	U.S.
Births, 2003–2004		
Number of births	7 972	4 089 950
Birth rate (per 1,000 population)	12.6	14.1
Teenage birth rate (per 1,000 women age 15–19 years)	26.8	41.6
Mortality Rates, Average 2000–2002		
Infant mortality rate (per 1,000 live births)	7.8	6.9
Age-adjusted mortality rate (per 100,000 population)		
All races	761.8	853.3
Non-Hispanic White	724.4	843.1
Black	. . .	1 097.7
American Indian, Alaska Native	1 438.4	687.0
Asian and Pacific Islander	. . .	486.0
Hispanic or Latino[1]	. . .	642.7
Health Insurance, 2004		
Percent of all persons without health insurance	11.2	15.7
Percent of children without health insurance	9.6	11.2
Percent of low-income children without health insurance	7.3	7.1

[1]May be of any race.
. . . = Not available.

Table ND-4. Leading Causes of Death, Average 2000–2002

(Number, rate per 100,000 population.)

Cause	Number of deaths	Age-adjusted death rates	
		State	U.S.
ALL CAUSES	5 932	761.8	853.3
Leading Causes			
Major cardiovascular diseases	2 331	287.1	326.5
Cancer	1 343	182.2	196.0
Chronic lower respiratory diseases	308	39.9	43.7
Unintentional injuries	244	34.7	35.7
Diabetes (underlying cause)	204	26.4	25.2
Influenza and pneumonia	163	18.9	22.7
Alzheimer's disease	242	27.5	19.0
Motor vehicle accidents	104	15.7	15.0
Nephritis, nephrotic syndrome, and nephrosis ..	58	7.0	13.8
Septicemia	41	5.4	11.4
Suicides	79	12.4	10.7
Firearm-related	49	7.8	10.3
Cirrhosis	58	8.6	9.5
Drug-induced	19	2.9	7.9
Alcohol-induced	62	9.4	6.9
Homicides	9	1.6	6.0
Falls	57	6.9	5.2
HIV	*	*	5.0
Viral hepatitis	*	*	2.0
Anemias	11	1.3	1.6
Drownings	*	*	1.3
Fire deaths	8	1.3	1.2

Note: The rates are age-adjusted to the U.S. 2000 standard population.

* = Unreliable data.

Table ND-5. Households and Housing Characteristics, 1990, 2000, and 2004

(Number, percent, and dollars.)

Characteristic	1990	2000	2004	Average annual percent change, 2000–2004
Total Households	240 878	257 152	262 585	0.5
Family households	166 270	166 150	166 312	0.0
Married-couple family	142 374	137 433	136 049	-0.3
Other family	23 896	28 717	30 263	1.3
Male householder, no wife present	6 373	8 569	10 553	5.3
Female householder, no husband present	17 523	20 148	19 710	-0.5
Nonfamily households	74 608	91 002	96 273	1.4
Householder living alone	63 953	75 420	79 849	1.4
Householder not living alone	10 655	15 582	16 424	1.3
Housing Characteristics				
Average size	2.55	2.41	2.32	X
Housing units	276 340	289 677	300 815	0.9
Occupied housing units	240 878	257 152	262 585	0.5
Owner-occupied	157 950	171 299	178 727	1.1
Renter-occupied	82 928	85 853	83 858	-0.6
Median gross rent of renter-occupied housing units (dollars) ...	313	412	466	3.1
Median value of owner-occupied housing units (dollars)	50 500	74 400	84 354	3.2

X = Not applicable.

Median Housing Value and Median Rent, 2004

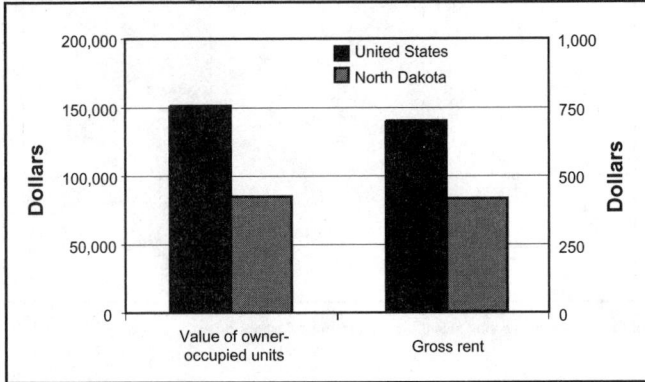

Median Household Income, 1984–2004 (2004 Dollars)

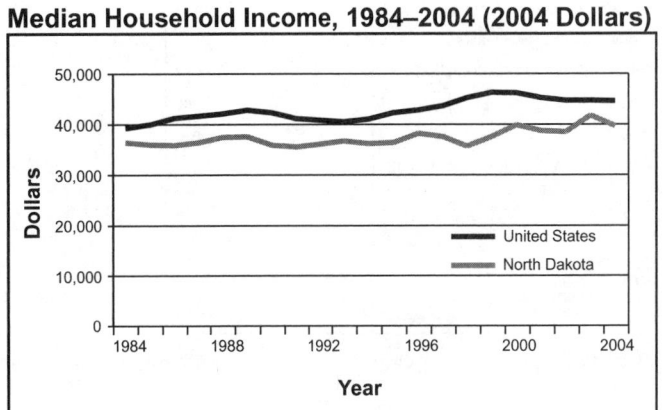

Table ND-6. Household Income and Poverty Status, 1980–2004

(2004 CPI-U-RS adjusted dollars, rate.)

Year	State		U.S.	
	Median household income (2004 dollars)	Poverty rate	Median household income (2004 dollars)	Poverty rate
2004	39 261	9.7	44 389	12.7
2003	41 496	9.7	44 482	12.5
2002	38 025	11.6	44 546	12.1
2001	38 195	13.8	45 062	11.7
2000	39 484	10.4	46 058	11.3
1999	37 023	13.1	46 129	11.9
1998	35 072	15.1	45 003	12.7
1997	37 158	13.6	43 430	13.3
1996	37 723	11.0	42 544	13.7
1995	35 805	12.0	41 943	13.8
1994	35 652	10.4	40 677	14.5
1993	36 197	11.2	40 217	15.1
1992	35 570	12.1	40 422	14.8
1991	35 019	14.5	40 746	14.2
1990	35 406	13.7	41 963	13.5
1989	37 115	12.2	42 524	12.8
1988	36 964	11.6	41 771	13.0
1987	35 900	11.4	41 322	13.4
1986	35 367	13.5	40 939	13.6
1985	35 505	15.9	39 545	14.0
1984	35 938	15.4	38 782	14.4
1983	. . .	15.0	. . .	15.2
1982	. . .	12.9	. . .	15.0
1981	. . .	14.2	. . .	14.0
1980	. . .	15.5	. . .	13.0

. . . = Not available.

Table ND-7. Employment Status by Demographic Group, 2004

(Numbers in thousands, rate.)

Characteristic	Civilian noninstitutional population	Civilian labor force		Employed	Unemployment rate
		Number	Participation rate		
SEX AND AGE					
Total	497	359	72.3	347	3.4
16 to 19 years	40	22	56.0	20	10.9
20 to 24 years	51	43	83.9	40	7.6
25 to 34 years	77	68	88.5	66	3.6
35 to 44 years	83	75	90.6	74	2.0
45 to 54 years	98	87	89.3	86	2.1
55 to 64 years	64	47	73.9	47	1.5
65 years and over	83	15	18.3	15	1.3
Men	245	189	77.1	181	4.2
16 to 19 years	21	12	56.2	10	13.2
20 to 24 years	27	23	84.9	20	10.1
25 to 34 years	39	37	94.7	35	4.2
35 to 44 years	41	39	94.3	38	1.9
45 to 54 years	50	46	91.6	44	3.0
55 to 64 years	31	25	79.5	25	1.5
Women	252	170	67.6	166	2.5
16 to 19 years	19	11	55.7	10	8.3
20 to 24 years	25	20	82.8	19	4.8
25 to 34 years	38	31	82.1	30	2.9
35 to 44 years	42	37	87.0	36	2.0
45 to 54 years	48	42	86.9	41	1.0
55 to 64 years	33	23	68.7	22	1.5
MARITAL STATUS					
Married men, spouse present	143	113	79.0	111	1.7
Married women, spouse present	144	105	72.6	103	1.6
Women who maintain families	19	15	75.7	14	4.4
RACE, HISPANIC ORIGIN, AND SEX					
White	465	339	73.0	330	2.9
Men	229	178	77.8	172	3.4
Women	236	161	68.3	157	2.3
RACE, HISPANIC ORIGIN, AND AGE					
White					
16 to 19 years	36	21	58.3	19	9.4
20 to 24 years	47	40	86.0	38	6.6
25 to 34 years	69	63	90.9	61	3.1
35 to 44 years	77	71	91.6	70	1.6
45 to 54 years	92	83	90.5	82	1.5
55 to 64 years	62	46	74.6	46	1.5
65 years and over	82	15	18.5	15	1.3

Note: Data in Table 7 are from the Current Population Survey (CPS) and do not match Bureau of Labor Statistics estimates in Table 8. See notes and definitions for more details.

Table ND-8. Employment Status, 1990–2004

(Numbers in thousands, rate.)

Year	Civilian labor force	Employed	Unemployed	Unemployment rate
2004	354 325	342 221	12 104	3.4
2003	351 467	338 809	12 658	3.6
2002	348 758	336 430	12 328	3.5
2001	346 497	336 939	9 558	2.8
2000	346 855	336 925	9 930	2.9
1999	347 634	336 481	11 153	3.2
1998	347 020	336 642	10 378	3.0
1997	345 855	335 854	10 001	2.9
1996	345 068	334 086	10 982	3.2
1995	342 559	331 252	11 307	3.3
1994	340 030	327 377	12 653	3.7
1993	323 208	308 915	14 293	4.4
1992	320 263	305 056	15 207	4.7
1991	318 866	305 007	13 859	4.3
1990	318 795	305 935	12 860	4.0

Note: Population age 16 years and over.

Unemployment Rate, 1980–2004

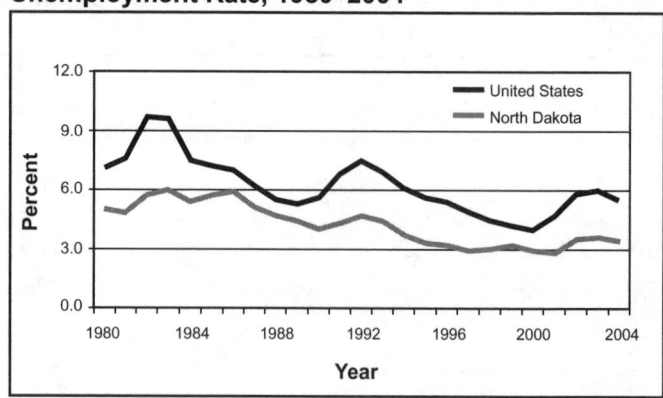

Table ND-9. Employment and Average Wages by Industry, 2001–2004

(Estimates are based on the 2002 North American Industry Classification System [NAICS].)

Industry	2001	2002	2003	2004	Annual average percent change, 2001–2004
			Number of jobs		
TOTAL EMPLOYMENT BY PLACE OF WORK	448 897	451 242	453 699	463 652	1.1
Farm Employment	37 682	37 667	35 385	35 876	-1.6
Nonfarm Employment	411 215	413 575	418 314	427 776	1.3
Private employment	333 807	334 582	338 156	347 258	1.3
Forestry, fishing, hunting, and other[1]	4 186	4 643	4 371	4 426	1.9
Mining	4 282	3 895	4 150	4 457	1.3
Utilities	3 437	3 419	3 395	3 393	-0.4
Construction	23 285	22 479	23 770	25 231	2.7
Manufacturing	25 253	25 032	24 733	25 920	0.9
Durable goods manufacturing	16 618	16 384	16 072	17 072	0.9
Nondurable goods manufacturing	8 635	8 648	8 661	8 848	0.8
Wholesale trade	19 606	19 153	19 127	19 602	0.0
Retail trade	51 888	52 177	52 799	53 626	1.1
Transportation and warehousing	13 458	13 567	13 489	13 733	0.7
Information	9 302	8 594	8 424	8 444	-3.2
Finance and insurance	19 775	20 237	20 498	20 792	1.7
Real estate and rental and leasing	9 437	9 338	9 443	9 817	1.3
Professional and technical services	14 762	14 788	15 444	16 104	2.9
Management of companies and enterprises	3 016	3 116	3 057	3 113	1.1
Administrative and waste services	16 311	16 204	15 487	16 179	-0.3
Educational services	4 325	4 732	4 964	5 207	6.4
Health care and social assistance	52 472	52 715	53 927	54 643	1.4
Arts, entertainment, and recreation	5 871	6 248	6 336	6 565	3.8
Accommodation and food services	28 753	29 015	29 196	29 987	1.4
Other services, except public administration	24 388	25 230	25 546	26 019	2.2
Government and government enterprises	77 408	78 993	80 158	80 518	1.3
			Dollars		
AVERAGE WAGES AND SALARIES BY PLACE OF WORK	25 365	26 269	27 401	28 731	4.2
Farm Earnings	27 634	27 048	27 355	30 440	3.3
Nonfarm Earnings	25 329	26 258	27 402	28 712	4.3
Private earnings	25 237	25 968	27 050	28 416	4.0
Forestry, fishing, hunting, and other[1]	16 227	16 827	17 029	18 127	3.8
Mining	48 304	48 970	50 724	52 673	2.9
Utilities	56 585	57 913	62 057	66 640	5.6
Construction	31 879	31 845	32 523	34 250	2.4
Manufacturing	31 561	32 446	34 041	35 849	4.3
Durable goods manufacturing	32 689	33 762	35 652	37 436	4.6
Nondurable goods manufacturing	29 365	29 910	31 008	32 741	3.7
Wholesale trade	33 204	34 455	36 100	38 330	4.9
Retail trade	18 202	18 781	19 278	19 807	2.9
Transportation and warehousing	33 957	33 962	35 037	36 722	2.6
Information	32 182	34 190	37 202	40 262	7.8
Finance and insurance	34 055	34 853	36 657	38 629	4.3
Real estate and rental and leasing	17 869	18 873	19 896	21 066	5.6
Professional and technical services	33 189	35 647	35 988	36 695	3.4
Management of companies and enterprises	44 834	44 813	46 914	51 790	4.9
Administrative and waste services	16 388	17 300	17 924	18 878	4.8
Educational services	18 837	18 779	19 559	20 447	2.8
Health care and social assistance	26 928	28 167	29 121	30 707	4.5
Arts, entertainment, and recreation	11 605	12 304	12 568	12 467	2.4
Accommodation and food services	9 624	9 957	10 259	10 449	2.8
Other services, except public administration	16 718	17 233	18 152	18 450	3.3
Government and government enterprises	25 646	27 233	28 574	29 715	5.0

Note: Average wages and salaries are a calculation by the editors of wage and salary disbursements divided by full- and part-time wage and salary employment. Data may not add to total or may appear as zero due to rounding.

[1] "Other" consists of the number of jobs held by U.S. residents employed by international organizations and foreign embassies and consulates in the United States.

LABOR MARKET

North Dakota's unemployment rate has been below the national average for many years. Combined with the state's high labor force participation rate, this suggested that residents who sought jobs were successful. Employment grew by 3.3 percent during the 2001–2004 period, which was among the top 15 rates in the nation. The state's largest employers were government, health care, and tourism-related industries (accommodation and food services). North Dakota was one of two states that experienced gains in manufacturing employment after the 2001 recession. Average wages and salaries were substantially below the national average, although their growth rate of 13.3 percent from 2001 to 2004 was the fourth highest in the nation.

Employment by Industry, 2004

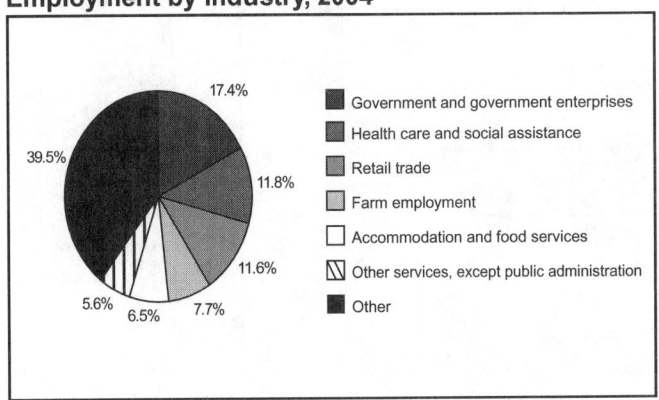

- Government and government enterprises — 39.5%
- Health care and social assistance — 17.4%
- Retail trade — 11.8%
- Farm employment — 11.6%
- Accommodation and food services — 7.7%
- Other services, except public administration — 6.5%
- Other — 5.6%

Table ND-10. Personal Income by Major Source, Selected Years 1980–2004

(Millions of dollars, except where noted.)

Item	1980	1990	2000	2001	2002	2003	2004	Average annual percent change, 2000–2004
Earnings by Place of Work	3 837	7 465	12 322	12 601	12 953	14 493	14 808	4.7
Wage and salary disbursements	3 194	4 957	8 425	8 833	9 169	9 621	10 294	5.1
Supplements to wages and salaries	611	1 162	1 929	2 008	2 244	2 475	2 727	9.0
Proprietors' income[1]	32	1 347	1 967	1 760	1 540	2 397	1 787	-2.4
Farm proprietors' income	-478	656	817	377	220	1 045	306	-21.8
Nonfarm proprietors' income	510	690	1 151	1 383	1 320	1 352	1 481	6.5
(-) Contributions for government social insurance[2]	448	908	1 503	1 559	1 632	1 732	1 841	5.2
(+) Adjustment for residence[3]	-153	-194	-428	-461	-488	-515	-562	X
(=) Net Earnings by Place of Residence	3 235	6 363	10 391	10 581	10 833	12 246	12 405	4.5
(+) Dividends, interest, and rent[4]	1 216	2 231	3 244	3 352	3 256	3 204	3 289	0.3
(+) Personal current transfer receipts	723	1 573	2 462	2 531	2 675	2 744	2 860	3.8
Personal income	5 174	10 166	16 097	16 465	16 764	18 194	18 553	3.6
Farm income	5 574	9 421	15 144	15 933	16 405	17 044	18 116	4.6
Nonfarm income	-400	745	953	532	359	1 150	437	-17.7
Per Capita Personal Income (Dollars)[5]	7 907	15 943	25 106	25 876	26 450	28 725	29 247	3.9

Note: Data may not add to total or may appear as zero due to rounding.

[1]Proprietors' income includes the inventory valuation adjustment and the capital consumption adjustment.
[2]Contributions for government social insurance are included in earnings by type and industry, but they are excluded from personal income.
[3]The adjustment for residence is the net inflow of the earnings of interarea commuters.
[4]Rental income of persons includes the capital consumption adjustment.
[5]Per capita personal income is total personal income divided by total midyear population.
X = Not applicable.

Per Capita Personal Income, 1980–2004 (Current Dollars)

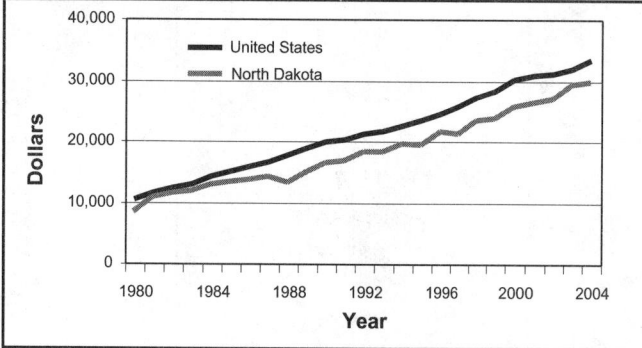

ECONOMIC ACTIVITY

Real gross state product (GSP) increased by 11.7 percent over the 2001–2004 period. However, from 2003 to 2004, the GSP growth rate slowed to 2.1 percent, which was well below the national growth rate of 4.3 percent. Gains in many industries, such as wholesale and retail trade, durable goods manufacturing, and information services, were largely offset by a significant decrease in the agriculture, forestry, fishing, and hunting sector from 2003 to 2004. Housing values have increased moderately in recent years, but at a rate below the national average. In 2004, the value of owner-occupied housing in North Dakota was $84,354, among the lowest in the country.

Table ND-11. Real Gross State Product, 1997–2004

(Millions of chained 2000 dollars, percent.)

Industry	1997	1998	1999	2000	2001	2002	2003	2004	Average annual percent change, 2001–2004
GROSS STATE PRODUCT	17 032	18 066	17 578	18 076	18 198	19 037	19 909	20 335	3.8
As a percent of U.S. gross product	0.2	0.2	0.2	0.2	0.2	0.2	0.2	0.2	X
Private Industries	14 162	15 224	14 985	15 263	15 348	16 119	16 898	17 197	3.9
Agriculture, forestry, fishing, and hunting	808	1 105	779	979	847	1 170	1 409	866	0.7
Mining	416	430	450	426	382	433	375	378	-0.4
Utilities	480	512	523	479	473	516	535	568	6.3
Construction	873	899	967	844	783	740	779	839	2.3
Manufacturing	1 695	2 001	1 819	1 828	1 902	2 009	2 121	2 309	6.7
As a percent of gross state product	10.0	11.1	10.3	10.1	10.5	10.6	10.7	11.4	X
Wholesale trade	1 255	1 351	1 383	1 389	1 503	1 571	1 630	1 716	4.5
Retail trade	1 343	1 372	1 399	1 433	1 515	1 597	1 708	1 798	5.9
Transportation and warehousing	769	751	757	853	779	736	780	811	1.4
Information	458	495	542	556	599	639	717	827	11.4
Finance and insurance	834	953	1 028	1 155	1 151	1 232	1 253	1 343	5.3
Real estate and rental and leasing	1 445	1 468	1 507	1 522	1 617	1 584	1 570	1 644	0.6
Services	3 831	3 823	3 846	3 801	3 812	3 913	4 061	4 228	3.5
As a percent of gross state product	22.5	21.2	21.9	21.0	20.9	20.6	20.4	20.8	X
Professional and technical services	634	658	667	598	642	679	757	802	7.7
Management of companies and enterprises	182	177	169	185	158	162	166	176	3.7
Administrative and waste services	291	295	308	298	308	324	321	340	3.3
Educational services	75	71	76	77	73	73	72	72	-0.5
Health care and social assistance	1 549	1 539	1 558	1 592	1 611	1 648	1 697	1 748	2.8
Arts, entertainment, and recreation	106	96	97	92	96	110	110	110	4.6
Accommodation and food services	500	511	506	506	482	485	496	513	2.1
Other services, except public administration	494	476	465	453	442	432	442	467	1.9
Government	2 882	2 846	2 591	2 814	2 850	2 920	3 014	3 137	3.2
As a percent of gross state product	16.9	15.8	14.7	15.6	15.7	15.3	15.1	15.4	X

X = Not applicable.

Table ND-12. Government Transfer Payments, Selected Years 1980–2004

(Millions of dollars, percent.)

Item	1980	1990	2000	2001	2002	2003	2004	Average annual percent change, 2000–2004
CURRENT TRANSFER PAYMENTS TO INDIVIDUALS	676	1 487	2 322	2 378	2 540	2 616	2 732	4.1
Retirement and Disability Insurance Benefits	372	809	1 142	1 142	1 165	1 196	1 239	2.1
Old-age, survivors, and disability insurance (OASDI) benefits	332	653	973	1 022	1 056	1 082	1 121	3.6
Railroad retirement and disability benefits	23	39	50	51	52	53	54	1.6
Workers' compensation	17	116	119	69	56	61	64	-14.3
Other government retirement and disability insurance benefits	*	*	*	*	*	*	*	X
Medical Benefits	161	467	880	913	1 005	1 017	1 094	5.6
Medicare benefits	111	254	429	472	501	525	569	7.3
Public assistance medical care benefits	48	206	437	422	478	471	500	3.4
Military medical insurance benefits	2	6	14	19	25	21	26	17.3
Income Maintenance Benefits	51	95	153	156	172	199	206	7.7
Supplemental Security Income (SSI) benefits	10	18	32	33	34	34	35	2.5
Family assistance	16	24	24	20	23	30	24	0.3
Food stamps	10	26	26	28	32	38	41	12.7
Other income maintenance benefits	16	27	71	75	83	97	105	10.2
Unemployment Insurance Compensation	38	25	33	36	60	59	45	8.0
Veterans' Benefits	34	42	61	65	72	78	85	8.7
Federal Education and Training Assistance	15	34	32	44	49	42	45	8.9
Other Payments to Individuals	5	15	21	22	18	23	17	-5.2

Note: See notes and definitions for more details. Data may not add to total or may appear as zero due to rounding.

* = Less than $500,000.
X = Not applicable.

EXPORTS

The value of North Dakota's exports totaled $1 billion in 2004, ranking the state as one of the nation's smallest exporters. The state's exports increased by 25 percent from 2001 to 2004, as oil and gas extraction and processed food exports rose significantly. In 2004, the state's largest exports were machinery manufactures, crops, and processed foods, which together totaled three-lst quarters of the state's exports. Canada accounted for 47.6 percent of North Dakota's exports; Belgium and Australia had lesser shares. Exports to Australia have tripled since 2001, with machinery manufactures making up nearly all of exports to this country.

Leading Exports, 2004

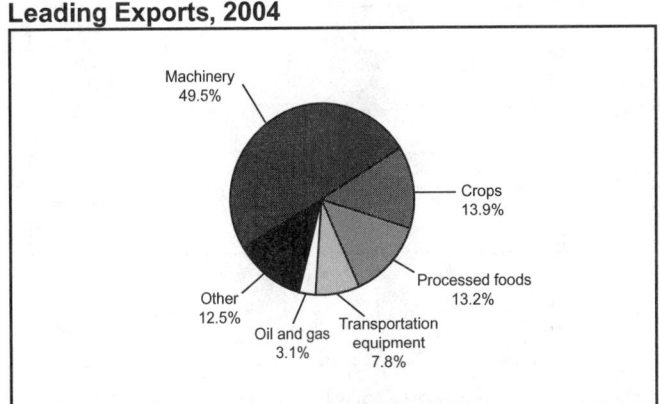

Table ND-13. Exports of Goods by Leading Products and Destinations, 2001–2004

(Millions of dollars, percent, rank based on 2004 dollar values.)

Product and market	2001	2002	2003	2004	Percent share of total, 2004	Average annual percent change, 2001–2004
Total Goods						
Total	806	859	854	1 008	100.0	7.7
Manufactures	632	645	626	804	79.8	8.3
Agriculture and livestock	150	193	202	179	17.8	6.1
Other commodities	24	22		26	25	2.5	1.6
Five Leading Exports (NAICS Code)						
Machinery manufactures (333)	401	425	405	499	49.5	7.5
Crop production (111)	129	175	172	140	13.9	2.8
Processed foods (311)	87	106	106	133	13.2	15.4
Transportation equipment (336)	75	57	53	79	7.8	1.5
Oil and gas extraction (211)	10	10	20	32	3.1	45.1
Five Leading Markets	766	827	802	954	94.6	7.6
Canada	394	440	476	480	47.6	6.8
Belgium	156	158	101	101	10.0	-13.5
Australia	25	47	47	77	7.6	45.0
Mexico	38	39	32	47	4.7	7.3
Italy	30	27	22	41	4.1	11.3

Table ND-14. Agriculture, 1997 and 2002

(Number, acres, and dollars.)

Item	1997	2002
Number of farms	32 348	30 619
Land in farms (acres)	39 678 169	39 294 879
Farm Size		
Average size of farm (acres)	1 227	1 283
Farms by size (percent distribution)		
Fewer than 50 acres	7.1	6.7
50 to 499 acres	31.7	36.5
500 acres or more	61.2	56.8
Market Value of Land and Equipment (Dollars)		
Land and buildings average value per farm	495 730	517 448
Average value per acre	406	404
Machinery and equipment average value per farm	108 745	124 298
Value of Sales (Thousands of Dollars)		
Agricultural products sold	2 908 049	3 233 366
Crops	2 229 835	2 460 372
Livestock, poultry, and their products	678 214	772 994
Average per farm (dollars)	89 899	105 600
Value of sales (percent distribution)		
Less than $10,000	27.8	38.5
$10,000 to $99,999	45.1	32.7
$100,000 or more	27.0	28.8
Government Payments		
Payments (thousands of dollars)	274 621	293 067
Percent of farms receiving government payments	83.5	78.0
Farm operators whose principal occupation is farming (percent)	72.3	70.7

AGRICULTURE

Cash receipts from farming totaled $3.2 billion in 2002, according to the Department of Agriculture's Census of Agriculture. This represented only a small increase from the previous farm census in 1997. The state's chief agricultural product was wheat. Unlike many other states, farming tended to be large-scale: more than 60 percent of farms had sales of $10,000 or more, and over 70 percent of farm operators reported farming as their principal occupation. Just 6.7 percent of farms spanned fewer than 50 acres, which was the smallest proportion of farms this size in the nation.

ENERGY

North Dakota had the lowest energy prices in the country. However, the state's cold climate helped to increase per capita energy consumption, which ranked fourth in the nation in 2001. Expenditures per person were also the fourth highest in the country. The chief energy sources were coal and petroleum. The industrial sector accounted for almost half of the state's energy consumption.

Energy Consumption by Source, 2001

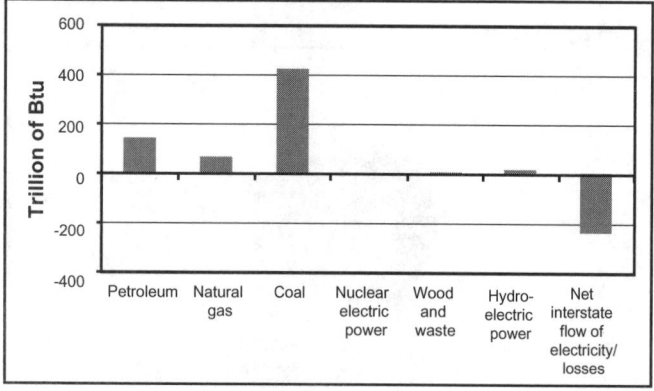

Energy Consumption by Sector, 2001

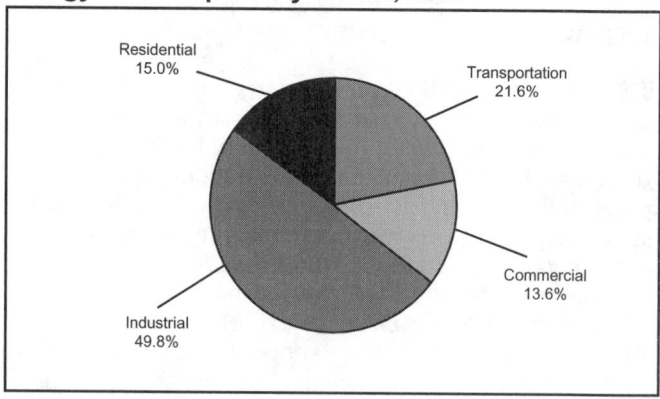

Table ND-15. Energy Consumption, Expenditures, and Prices, Selected Years 1960–2001

(Dollars, Btu [British Thermal Unit], percent distribution.)

Item	1960	1965	1970	1975	1980	1985	1990	1995	2000	2001
Total Consumption (Billion Btu)	159 636	169 618	191 062	206 451	223 221	303 330	314 540	353 387	382 835	406 879
Consumption per capita (million Btu)	252.6	261.4	309.3	323.1	342.0	448.1	492.4	550.8	596.1	639.5
Consumption by Sector (Percent Distribution)										
Residential	19.6	18.2	20.2	20.5	22.7	18.4	16.9	16.6	15.8	15.0
Commercial	7.8	9.8	11.2	13.9	15.0	13.0	12.8	13.0	12.9	13.6
Industrial	46.5	44.1	40.2	35.0	29.8	46.0	49.7	49.8	50.3	49.8
Transportation	26.1	27.9	28.4	30.5	32.5	22.6	20.7	20.6	21.1	21.6
Consumption by Source (Billion Btu)										
Coal	30 531	24 746	57 471	67 943	163 322	301 957	374 518	399 755	424 568	419 791
Natural gas	27 356	32 437	33 731	36 862	24 037	29 838	33 529	47 689	58 513	62 583
Petroleum	101 870	107 106	115 285	116 763	126 840	118 180	111 999	114 329	119 727	138 033
Nuclear electric power	0	0	0	0	0	0	0	0	0	0
Hydroelectric power[1]	11 407	26 105	29 536	34 806	26 107	22 699	17 799	25 341	21 652	13 553
Wood and waste	473	333	386	456	2 933	2 803	1 862	2 739	2 377	2 124
Other	0	-2	1 000	3 979	9 726	9 025	151	2 638	2 442	2 206
Net interstate flow of electricity/losses[2]	-12 000	-21 107	-46 347	-54 358	-129 744	-181 172	-225 319	-239 104	-246 445	-231 411
Total Expenditures (Thousands of Dollars)	...	...	290 400	543 500	1 246 300	1 647 500	1 582 400	1 588 000	2 076 600	2 243 200
Expenditures per capita (dollars)	...	...	470	851	1 909	2 434	2 477	2 475	3 234	3 526
Prices by Sector (Dollars Per Million Btu)										
Total	...	...	1.99	3.49	7.33	7.07	6.57	5.99	7.43	7.53
Residential	...	...	2.52	3.94	7.50	10.15	10.10	9.97	11.72	12.47
Commercial	...	...	1.77	2.23	5.36	8.64	8.84	8.81	10.19	11.06
Industrial	...	...	1.55	3.18	6.02	4.95	4.03	3.30	4.09	4.34
Transportation	...	...	2.19	3.95	8.74	8.66	9.31	8.74	11.59	10.98

[1]A negative number in this row results from pumped storage for which, overall, more electricity is expended than created to provide electricity during peak demand periods.
[2]Net interstate flow of electricity is the difference between the amount of energy in the electricity sold within a state (including associated losses) and the energy input at the electric utilities within the state. A positive number indicates that more electricity (including associated losses) came into the state than went out of the state during the year; conversely, a negative number indicates that more electricity (including associated losses) went out of the state than came into the state.
... = Not available.

Table ND-16. State Taxes, Fiscal 2004

(Dollars, percent distribution.)

Item	Thousands of dollars	Percent distribution	Dollars per capita	
			State	U.S.
TOTAL TAXES	1 228 890	100.0	1 938.3	2 024.8
Property Taxes	1 478	0.1	2.3	38.9
Sales and Gross Receipts	666 738	54.3	1 051.6	1 003.4
General sales and gross receipts	367 304	29.9	579.3	677.0
Selective sales taxes	299 434	24.4	472.3	326.4
Amusements	10 079	0.8	15.9	17.0
Insurance premiums	30 928	2.5	48.8	47.0
Motor fuels	118 744	9.7	187.3	114.6
Public utilities	34 098	2.8	53.8	39.2
Tobacco products	21 167	1.7	33.4	42.0
Other selective sales	75 923	6.2	119.8	49.8
Licenses	118 377	9.6	186.7	134.9
Hunting and fishing	12 838	1.0	20.2	4.2
Motor vehicle	54 707	4.5	86.3	59.4
Occupation and business, not elsewhere classified	46 226	3.8	72.9	37.1
Other Taxes	442 297	36.0	697.6	847.6
Individual income	213 982	17.4	337.5	673.6
Corporation net income	49 807	4.1	78.6	105.1
Severance	175 625	14.3	277.0	21.5

GOVERNMENT FINANCE

Per capita state revenues and expenditures were well above the U.S. average in 2003. North Dakota had the eighth highest revenues per person. Per capita spending was below average on public welfare, hospitals, and education, but nearly twice the national average on highways. In fiscal year 2004, taxes per person were slightly below average, ranking 28th in the country. The state's per capita individual income taxes were the second lowest of the 43 states with such taxes. The state derived a significant amount of revenue from severance (taxes paid on the removal of natural resources). These taxes were prevalent among many western states.

Per Capita State Taxes, Fiscal 2004

Table ND-17. State Government Finances, 2003

(Dollars, percent distribution.)

Item	Millions of dollars	Percent distribution	Dollars per capita	
			State	U.S.
GENERAL REVENUE	3 035 526	100.0	4 795.5	3 832.6
Intergovernmental revenue	1 128 029	37.2	1 782.0	1 246.0
Taxes	1 177 727	38.8	1 860.6	1 891.6
General sales	360 831	11.9	570.0	636.0
Selective sales	288 775	9.5	456.2	307.4
License taxes	102 750	3.4	162.3	123.6
Individual income tax	199 390	6.6	315.0	626.8
Corporate income tax	55 989	1.8	88.4	97.8
Other taxes	169 992	5.6	268.6	99.9
Current charges	509 411	16.8	804.8	366.5
Miscellaneous general revenue	220 359	7.3	348.1	328.6
GENERAL EXPENDITURE	2 897 516	100.0	4 577.4	4 010.5
Intergovernmental expenditure	606 096	20.9	957.5	1 316.9
Direct expenditure	2 291 420	79.1	3 619.9	2 693.6
Expenditure by Function				
Education	1 021 351	35.2	1 613.5	1 416.4
Public welfare	651 385	22.5	1 029.0	1 083.3
Hospitals	43 184	1.5	68.2	132.3
Health	49 426	1.7	78.1	173.0
Highways	365 282	12.6	577.1	295.4
Police protection	12 645	0.4	20.0	38.4
Correction	44 526	1.5	70.3	135.0
Natural resources	129 769	4.5	205.0	64.0
Parks and recreation	17 302	0.6	27.3	20.1
Government administration	108 038	3.7	170.7	151.3
Interest on general debt	85 195	2.9	134.6	107.8
Other and unallocable	369 413	12.7	583.6	393.4
DEBT AT END OF FISCAL YEAR	1 599 233	X	2 526.4	2 404.7
CASH AND SECURITY HOLDINGS	6 904 921	X	10 908.2	8 938.4

X = Not applicable.

Table ND-18. Education Indicators, 2000–2004

(Percent, number.)

Item	State	U.S.
Total Population 25 Years and Over (Thousands), 2004	414	186 877
Educational Attainment, 2004		
Percent high school graduate or more	89.5	85.2
Percent college graduate or more	25.2	27.7
Elementary and Secondary Schools, 2002–2003		
Total students	104 225	48 202 324
Percent of students eligible for free or reduced-price lunch ..	28.3	40.6
Percent of students who were English language learners	1.6	7.8
Total schools	528	92 330
Student/teacher ratio	12.7	15.9
Per student expenditures	6 870	8 041
Dropouts, Grades 9–12, 2000–2001 (Percent)	2.0	. . .
Higher Education, 2002–2003		
Total enrollment	46 068	17 035 027
Bachelor's degrees awarded	4 882	1 348 503
Percent women	52.7	57.5

. . . = Not available.

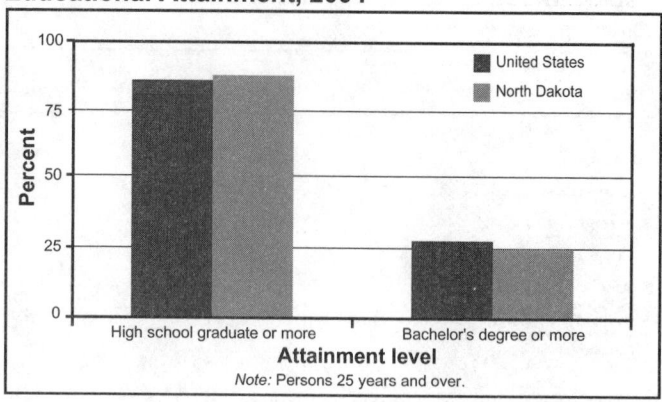

Educational Attainment, 2004

Note: Persons 25 years and over.

EDUCATION

North Dakota's proportion of high school graduates among its population age 25 years and over was the 12th highest in the nation in 2004. The proportion of college graduates within the same age group fell short of the national average, ranking 30th in the nation. North Dakota's student/teacher ratio was among the five lowest in the nation, which was partly due to the state's low proportion of student-age population. Per student expenditures of $6,820 were well below the national average, ranking 38th in the nation. The state's dropout rate of just 2.0 percent was the second lowest of the 46 states reporting such data.

VOTER PARTICIPATION

Voter turnout was the highest in the country for the 2000 election and the fourth highest for the 2004 election. More than 88.5 percent of North Dakota's eligible population was registered to vote, which was the highest proportion in the nation. In 2004, 70.8 percent of eligible residents turned out to vote. The proportion of male voters dropped slightly from 2000 to 2004, but the proportion of female voters increased nearly 3 percentage points. According to the official tally by the Clerk of the U.S. House of Representatives, 60.7 percent of the state's voters cast ballots for the Republican presidential candidate in 2000; this proportion increased to 62.9 percent in 2004.

Table ND-19. Reported Voting and Registration, November 2000 and November 2004

(Numbers in thousands, percent.)

Characteristic	Total population 18 years and over	Total citizen		Total registered		Total voted	
		Number	Percent	Number	Percent	Number	Percent
NOVEMBER 2000							
Total	449	445	99.0	409	91.1	313	69.8
Male	222	219	98.9	202	91.0	155	69.7
Female	228	226	99.2	208	91.2	159	69.8
NOVEMBER 2004							
Total	466	462	99.1	412	88.5	330	70.8
Male	228	226	99.3	199	87.6	158	69.2
Female	238	235	98.8	213	89.3	172	72.4
Race and Hispanic Origin							
White alone	443	440	99.4	393	88.8	318	71.9
Non-Hispanic White alone	439	436	99.4	390	89.0	317	72.3
Black alone	3	3	B	2	B	1	B
Hispanic or Latino[1]	6	6	B	4	B	2	B
White alone or in combination	447	444	99.3	397	88.7	321	71.8
Non-Hispanic White alone or in combination	442	439	99.3	393	89.0	319	72.2
Black alone or in combination	4	4	B	3	B	2	B
Age							
18 to 24 years	77	75	B	62	B	39	B
25 to 44 years	144	143	99.2	129	89.6	100	69.3
45 to 64 years	164	163	99.4	147	89.7	126	77.0
65 to 74 years	33	33	B	30	B	27	B
75 years and over	47	47	B	44	B	38	B

[1]May be of any race.
B = Base is too small to show derived measure.

At a Glance:

- Ohio's population was close to 11.5 million in 2004, making it the seventh most populous state in the nation; however, the state's rate of population growth from 2000 to 2004 ranked among the five lowest in the country.

- Non-Hispanic Whites made up 83.3 percent of the population; the next largest racial group was Blacks, who represented 11.7 percent of the state's residents.

- Ohio's median household income of less than $43,000 was below the national average. The state's poverty rate of 11.4 percent was also below the national average.

- The state's unemployment rate was 6.1 percent in 2004, which was the 10th highest in the country.

- Economic activity was severely impacted by the 2001 recession, and it recovered very slowly. However, in 2004, Ohio's gross state product was the seventh largest in the nation.

- Just 11.4 percent of Ohio's population lacked health insurance, which was among the lowest proportions in the nation.

- The state had an above average proportion of residents age 25 years and over that had graduated from high school, but a below average proportion that had graduated from college.

Table OH-1. Population by Sex and Age, 1990, 2000, and 2004

(Number, percent.)

Sex and age	1990	2000	2004	Percent distribution, 2004	Average annual percent change, 2000–2004
Total Population	10 847 115	11 353 140	11 459 011	X	0.2
Percent of total U.S. population	4.4	4.0	3.9	X	X
Sex					
Male	5 226 340	5 512 262	5 580 635	48.7	0.3
Female	5 620 775	5 840 878	5 878 376	51.3	0.2
Age					
Under 5 years	785 149	754 930	730 035	6.4	-0.6
5 to 17 years	2 014 595	2 133 409	2 049 177	17.9	0.1
18 years and over	2 092 949	8 464 801	8 679 799	75.7	0.5
18 to 24 years	8 047 371	1 056 544	1 127 662	9.8	-0.1
25 to 44 years	1 136 418	3 325 210	3 147 813	27.5	-0.6
45 to 64 years	3 411 043	2 575 290	2 879 408	25.1	2.3
65 years and over	1 406 961	1 507 757	1 524 916	13.3	0.6
85 years and over	138 030	176 796	208 433	1.8	3.1
Median age (years)	33.3	36.2	37.3	X	X

X = Not applicable.

Average Annual Rate of Population Growth, 1980–2004

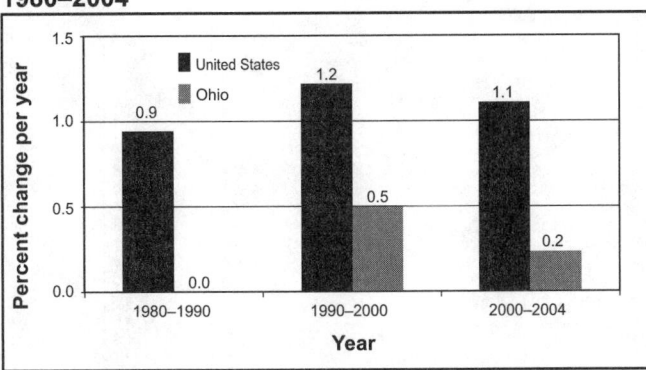

POPULATION

Ohio's population increased by only 0.9 percent between 2000 and 2004, which was the fourth lowest growth rate in the nation; however, it was similar to those of its neighbors, Pennsylvania and West Virginia. From 2000 to 2004, the state lost over 133,000 residents to other locations. During this period, 64,000 people moved into Ohio from other countries. As out-migration tended to occur more frequently among younger people, the proportion of older residents in Ohio was higher than the national average. In 2004, 13.3 percent of the state's population was age 65 years and over, compared with 12.4 percent nationally.

Table OH-2. Population by Race and Hispanic Origin, 1990, 2000, and 2004

(Number, percent.)

Race and Hispanic origin	1990	2000	2004
Total Population	10 847 115	11 353 140	11 459 011
Non-Hispanic (Percent)			
One race[1]			
White	87.1	84.2	83.3
Black	10.6	11.5	11.7
American Indian, Alaska Native[2]	0.2	0.2	0.2
Asian and Pacific Islander[2]	0.8	1.2	1.4
Other race[2]	0.5	. . .	. . .
Two or more races	. . .	1.0	1.2
Hispanic or Latino[3] (Percent)	1.3	1.9	2.2

[1]Individuals could report only one race in the 1990 census and could report one or more races on the 2000 census. Data on race in 2000 and 2004 are not comparable to 1990.
[2]Data for 1990 include people of Hispanic or Latino origin.
[3]May be of any race.
. . . = Not available.

Minority Population as a Percent of Total Population, 2004

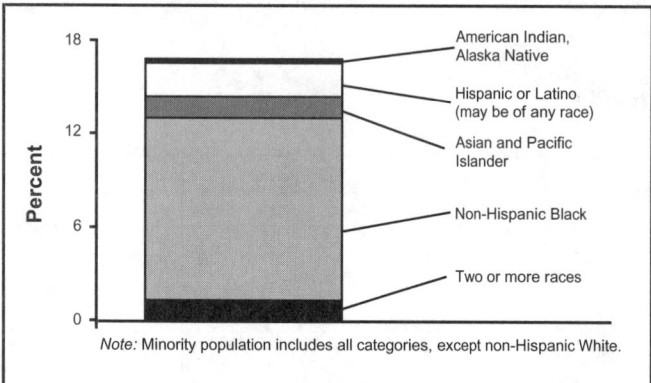

Note: Minority population includes all categories, except non-Hispanic White.

Age-Adjusted Death Rates, Average 2000–2002

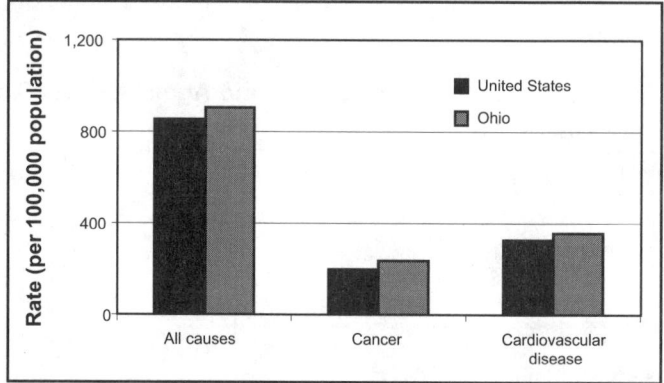

HEALTH

Ohio's birth rate was below the national average. The state's infant mortality rate was well above average, and its age-adjusted death rate for all causes was the 15th highest in the country. The state's health insurance coverage rate was better than those of most other states.

Table OH-3. Health Characteristics, 2000–2004

(Number, rate, percent.)

Item	State	U.S.
Births, 2003–2004		
Number of births	149 679	4 089 950
Birth rate (per 1,000 population)	13.1	14.1
Teenage birth rate (per 1,000 women age 15–19 years)	39.4	41.6
Mortality Rates, Average 2000–2002		
Infant mortality rate (per 1,000 live births)	7.7	6.9
Age-adjusted mortality rate (per 100,000 population)		
All races	910.9	853.3
Non-Hispanic White	888.9	843.1
Black	1 143.2	1 097.7
American Indian, Alaska Native	. . .	687.0
Asian and Pacific Islander	404.6	486.0
Hispanic or Latino[1]	587.5	642.7
Health Insurance, 2004		
Percent of all persons without health insurance	11.4	15.7
Percent of children without health insurance	7.5	11.2
Percent of low-income children without health insurance	5.2	7.1

[1]May be of any race.
. . . = Not available.

Table OH-4. Leading Causes of Death, Average 2000–2002

(Number, rate per 100,000 population.)

Cause	Number of deaths	Age-adjusted death rates	
		State	U.S.
ALL CAUSES	108 639	910.9	853.3
Leading Causes			
Major cardiovascular diseases	41 982	350.5	326.5
Cancer	24 988	209.4	196.0
Chronic lower respiratory diseases	5 976	49.8	43.7
Unintentional injuries	3 832	33.1	35.7
Diabetes (underlying cause)	3 762	31.5	25.2
Influenza and pneumonia	2 474	20.6	22.7
Alzheimer's disease	2 420	20.1	19.0
Motor vehicle accidents	1 461	12.8	15.0
Nephritis, nephrotic syndrome, and nephrosis ..	1 923	16.0	13.8
Septicemia	1 535	12.8	11.4
Suicides	1 198	10.4	10.7
Firearm-related	996	8.7	10.3
Cirrhosis	1 023	8.7	9.5
Drug-induced	819	7.2	7.9
Alcohol-induced	590	5.0	6.9
Homicides	512	4.5	6.0
Falls	571	4.8	5.2
HIV	233	2.1	5.0
Viral hepatitis	139	1.2	2.0
Anemias	224	1.9	1.6
Drownings	116	1.0	1.3
Fire deaths	130	1.1	1.2

Note: The rates are age-adjusted to the U.S. 2000 standard population.

Table OH-5. Households and Housing Characteristics, 1990, 2000, and 2004

(Number, percent, and dollars.)

Characteristic	1990	2000	2004	Average annual percent change, 2000–2004
Total Households	4 087 546	4 445 773	4 514 723	0.4
Family households	2 895 223	2 993 023	3 003 551	0.1
Married-couple family	2 294 111	2 285 798	2 253 641	-0.4
Other family	601 112	707 225	749 910	1.5
Male householder, no wife present	123 042	170 347	172 983	0.4
Female householder, no husband present	478 070	536 878	576 927	1.8
Nonfamily households	1 192 323	1 452 750	1 511 172	1.0
Householder living alone	1 020 450	1 215 614	1 291 223	1.5
Householder not living alone	171 873	237 136	219 949	-1.9
Housing Characteristics				
Average size	2.59	2.49	2.47	X
Housing units	4 371 945	4 783 051	4 966 746	0.9
Occupied housing units	4 087 546	4 445 773	4 514 723	0.4
Owner-occupied	2 758 149	3 072 522	3 150 213	0.6
Renter-occupied	1 329 397	1 373 251	1 364 510	-0.2
Median gross rent of renter-occupied housing units (dollars) ...	379	515	587	3.3
Median value of owner-occupied housing units (dollars)	62 900	103 700	122 384	4.2

X = Not applicable.

Median Housing Value and Median Rent, 2004

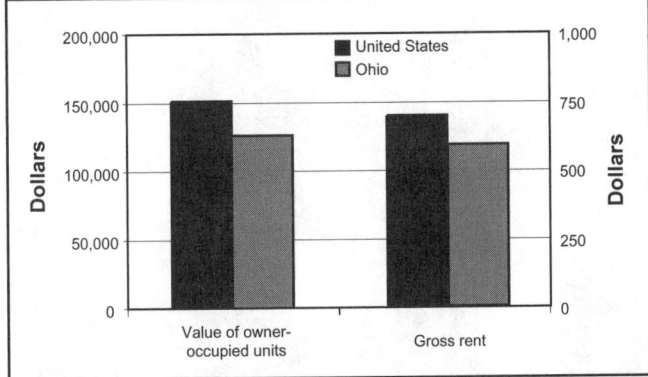

Median Household Income, 1984–2004 (2004 Dollars)

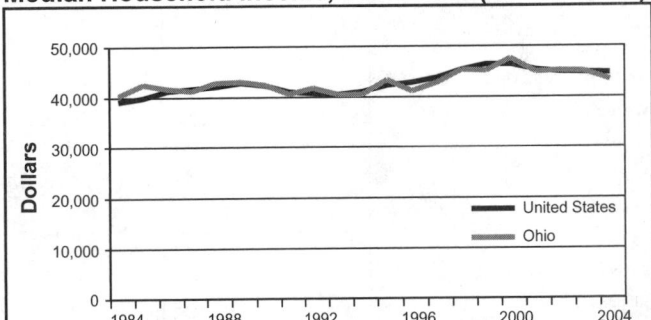

Table OH-6. Household Income and Poverty Status, 1980–2004

(2004 CPI-U-RS adjusted dollars, numbers in thousands, rate.)

Year	State		U.S.	
	Median household income (2004 dollars)	Poverty rate	Median household income (2004 dollars)	Poverty rate
2004	42 954	11.6	44 389	12.7
2003	44 690	10.9	44 482	12.5
2002	44 835	9.8	44 546	12.1
2001	44 589	10.5	45 062	11.7
2000	47 125	10.0	46 058	11.3
1999	44 761	12.0	46 129	11.9
1998	45 050	11.2	45 003	12.7
1997	42 408	11.0	43 430	13.3
1996	40 839	12.7	42 544	13.7
1995	43 008	11.5	41 943	13.8
1994	40 162	14.1	40 677	14.5
1993	40 274	13.0	40 217	15.1
1992	41 435	12.5	40 422	14.8
1991	40 291	13.4	40 746	14.2
1990	42 061	11.5	41 963	13.5
1989	42 693	10.6	42 524	12.8
1988	42 561	12.4	41 771	13.0
1987	40 984	12.7	41 322	13.4
1986	41 298	12.8	40 939	13.6
1985	42 151	12.8	39 545	14.0
1984	40 007	13.5	38 782	14.4
1983	. . .	13.4	. . .	15.2
1982	. . .	12.8	. . .	15.0
1981	. . .	12.7	. . .	14.0
1980	. . .	9.8	. . .	13.0

. . . = Not available.

Table OH-7. Employment Status by Demographic Group, 2004

(Numbers in thousands, rate.)

Characteristic	Civilian noninstitutional population	Civilian labor force		Employed	Unemployment rate
		Number	Participation rate		
SEX AND AGE					
Total	8 828	5 884	66.6	5 514	6.3
16 to 19 years	656	344	52.4	287	16.3
20 to 24 years	774	614	79.3	547	10.8
25 to 34 years	1 446	1 215	84.0	1 129	7.1
35 to 44 years	1 648	1 408	85.4	1 339	4.9
45 to 54 years	1 674	1 351	80.7	1 296	4.1
55 to 64 years	1 195	745	62.3	715	3.9
65 years and over	1 436	207	14.4	199	3.7
Men	4 225	3 105	73.5	2 900	6.6
16 to 19 years	324	161	49.9	136	16.1
20 to 24 years	391	323	82.5	287	11.2
25 to 34 years	704	657	93.3	610	7.2
35 to 44 years	819	765	93.5	723	5.5
45 to 54 years	802	699	87.2	664	4.9
55 to 64 years	564	386	68.5	371	3.8
65 years and over	622	115	18.4	110	4.1
Women	4 603	2 778	60.4	2 613	5.9
16 to 19 years	332	182	54.9	152	16.6
20 to 24 years	382	291	76.2	261	10.4
25 to 34 years	742	558	75.2	520	7.0
35 to 44 years	830	643	77.5	616	4.2
45 to 54 years	872	652	74.8	631	3.2
55 to 64 years	631	359	56.8	344	4.1
65 years and over	814	92	11.4	89	3.2
MARITAL STATUS					
Married men, spouse present	2 378	1 823	76.7	1 757	3.6
Married women, spouse present	2 338	1 423	60.9	1 375	3.4
Women who maintain families	537	380	70.8	347	8.8
RACE, HISPANIC ORIGIN, AND SEX					
White	7 657	5 110	66.7	4 833	5.4
Men	3 694	2 740	74.2	2 583	5.7
Women	3 963	2 370	59.8	2 250	5.1
Black	924	599	64.8	521	13.0
Men	411	269	65.4	228	15.1
Women	513	330	64.3	293	11.3
Asian	130	95	72.8	90	5.1
Men	62	52	83.8	49	5.6
Women	68	43	62.8	41	4.5
Hispanic or Latino[1]	206	156	75.7	147	5.7
Men	119	101	84.7	95	6.1
Women	87	55	63.3	52	4.9
RACE, HISPANIC ORIGIN, AND AGE					
White					
25 to 34 years	1 201	1 020	84.9	961	5.8
35 to 44 years	1 443	1 240	85.9	1 181	4.8
45 to 54 years	1 445	1 181	81.7	1 139	3.5
55 to 64 years	1 071	675	63.0	650	3.7

Note: Data in Table 7 are from the Current Population Survey (CPS) and do not match Bureau of Labor Statistics estimates in Table 8. See notes and definitions for more details.

[1]May be of any race.

Table OH-8. Employment Status, 1990–2004

(Numbers in thousands, rate.)

Year	Civilian labor force	Employed	Unemployed	Unemployment rate
2004	5 884 809	5 523 037	361 772	6.1
2003	5 869 340	5 506 038	363 302	6.2
2002	5 835 503	5 500 016	335 487	5.7
2001	5 829 334	5 570 389	258 945	4.4
2000	5 804 554	5 570 928	233 626	4.0
1999	5 780 725	5 534 376	246 349	4.3
1998	5 736 734	5 488 877	247 857	4.3
1997	5 712 616	5 448 161	264 455	4.6
1996	5 660 805	5 378 491	282 314	5.0
1995	5 604 444	5 330 591	273 853	4.9
1994	5 568 173	5 254 199	313 974	5.6
1993	5 509 715	5 138 818	370 897	6.7
1992	5 475 129	5 072 649	402 480	7.4
1991	5 401 245	5 045 897	355 348	6.6
1990	5 389 113	5 079 472	309 641	5.7

Note: Population age 16 years and over.

Unemployment Rate, 1980–2004

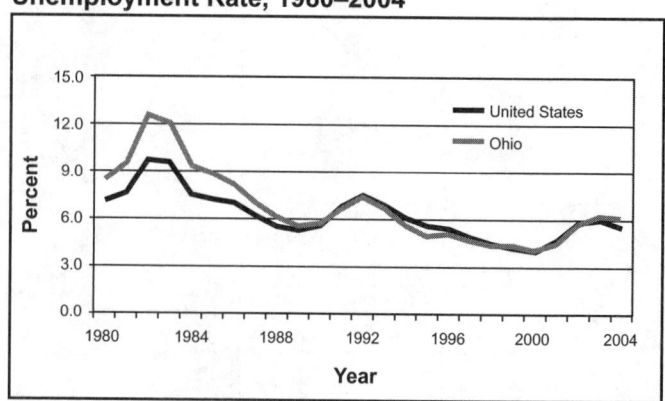

Table OH-9. Employment and Average Wages by Industry, 2001–2004

(Estimates are based on the 2002 North American Industry Classification System [NAICS].)

Industry	2001	2002	2003	2004	Annual average percent change, 2001–2004
	Number of jobs				
TOTAL EMPLOYMENT BY PLACE OF WORK	6 759 196	6 690 747	6 681 398	6 732 896	-0.1
Farm Employment	99 172	96 362	95 797	95 208	-1.4
Nonfarm Employment	6 660 024	6 594 385	6 585 601	6 637 688	-0.1
Private employment	5 825 149	5 747 923	5 736 908	5 787 928	-0.2
Forestry, fishing, hunting, and other[1]	11 427	12 687	11 656	11 785	1.0
Mining	21 786	19 949	21 242	21 808	0.0
Utilities	24 933	22 581	21 987	21 063	-5.5
Construction	359 857	353 240	356 654	362 072	0.2
Manufacturing	975 205	905 038	865 669	847 046	-4.6
Durable goods manufacturing	685 274	623 578	592 202	581 179	-5.3
Nondurable goods manufacturing	289 931	281 460	273 467	265 867	-2.8
Wholesale trade	265 710	256 013	251 872	251 814	-1.8
Retail trade	789 734	774 812	770 079	767 899	-0.9
Transportation and warehousing	215 612	211 198	208 908	213 449	-0.3
Information	119 264	111 851	109 306	105 916	-3.9
Finance and insurance	295 652	299 853	302 980	304 338	1.0
Real estate and rental and leasing	193 938	195 124	201 765	209 502	2.6
Professional and technical services	359 696	350 567	351 541	354 960	-0.4
Management of companies and enterprises	88 770	94 729	96 532	95 659	2.5
Administrative and waste services	380 848	378 605	378 882	398 374	1.5
Educational services	110 320	113 752	117 080	121 494	3.3
Health care and social assistance	699 466	717 793	735 980	751 972	2.4
Arts, entertainment, and recreation	115 471	118 150	117 786	119 213	1.1
Accommodation and food services	436 978	439 227	445 206	454 126	1.3
Other services, except public administration	360 482	372 754	371 783	375 438	1.4
Government and government enterprises	834 875	846 462	848 693	849 760	0.6
	Dollars				
AVERAGE WAGES AND SALARIES BY PLACE OF WORK	32 647	33 548	34 501	35 800	3.1
Farm Earnings	18 127	20 987	21 173	26 454	13.4
Nonfarm Earnings	32 693	33 580	34 539	35 826	3.1
Private earnings	32 595	33 376	34 289	35 603	3.0
Forestry, fishing, hunting, and other[1]	18 236	18 773	19 005	20 227	3.5
Mining	47 139	46 990	48 259	51 285	2.8
Utilities	58 207	61 642	65 187	65 268	3.9
Construction	37 393	38 028	38 349	39 215	1.6
Manufacturing	42 546	43 989	45 727	47 458	3.7
Durable goods manufacturing	43 764	45 257	47 243	49 058	3.9
Nondurable goods manufacturing	39 652	41 165	42 433	43 951	3.5
Wholesale trade	45 265	46 182	47 384	49 936	3.3
Retail trade	21 164	21 878	22 458	22 759	2.5
Transportation and warehousing	35 039	36 040	36 940	38 283	3.0
Information	46 460	45 777	46 675	48 972	1.8
Finance and insurance	45 914	46 957	49 559	52 379	4.5
Real estate and rental and leasing	27 641	28 765	29 417	31 258	4.2
Professional and technical services	47 565	48 196	49 272	51 629	2.8
Management of companies and enterprises	63 994	69 736	69 828	80 103	7.8
Administrative and waste services	21 403	22 358	23 214	24 031	3.9
Educational services	22 589	23 206	24 040	24 679	3.0
Health care and social assistance	31 277	32 249	33 129	34 455	3.3
Arts, entertainment, and recreation	22 729	23 030	23 431	23 392	1.0
Accommodation and food services	11 829	12 078	12 207	12 445	1.7
Other services, except public administration	20 653	21 236	21 886	22 738	3.3
Government and government enterprises	33 264	34 733	35 939	37 077	3.7

Note: Average wages and salaries are a calculation by the editors of wage and salary disbursements divided by full- and part-time wage and salary employment. Data may not add to total or may appear as zero due to rounding.

[1] "Other" consists of the number of jobs held by U.S. residents employed by international organizations and foreign embassies and consulates in the United States.

LABOR MARKET

Ohio's unemployment rate has been higher than the national average for several years, as the state's industrial base has declined. In 2004, the unemployment rate was 6.1 percent, which was higher than that of neighboring Indiana but lower than that of Michigan, which had a similar employment profile. Ohio was one of four states with a net loss in employment from 2001 to 2004. This was largely caused by a sharp decline in the number of manufacturing jobs. Government overtook manufacturing to become the state's largest employer. Educational services, management, and health care had high rates of employment growth from 2001 to 2004. Ohio's average wages and salaries were below the national average.

Employment by Industry, 2004

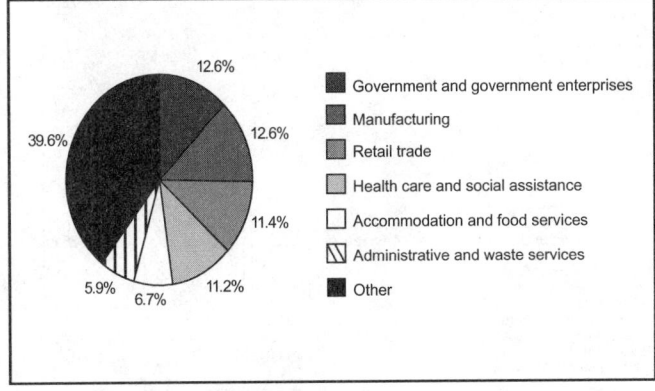

- 39.6% / 12.6% / 12.6% / 11.4% / 11.2% / 6.7% / 5.9%

- Government and government enterprises
- Manufacturing
- Retail trade
- Health care and social assistance
- Accommodation and food services
- Administrative and waste services
- Other

Table OH-10. Personal Income by Major Source, Selected Years 1980–2004

(Millions of dollars, except where noted.)

Item	1980	1990	2000	2001	2002	2003	2004	Average annual percent change, 2000–2004
Earnings by Place of Work	85 750	152 807	244 121	247 277	254 049	263 305	274 040	2.9
Wage and salary disbursements	66 589	115 689	186 214	187 826	189 858	193 629	201 274	2.0
Supplements to wages and salaries	12 799	24 263	36 302	38 098	42 983	47 448	48 888	7.7
Proprietors' income[1]	6 362	12 855	21 604	21 353	21 208	22 228	23 878	2.5
Farm proprietors' income	375	882	593	304	-77	305	271	-17.8
Nonfarm proprietors' income	5 987	11 973	21 011	21 049	21 284	21 923	23 608	3.0
(-) Contributions for government social insurance[2]	7 615	16 872	25 426	26 189	26 363	27 026	28 248	2.7
(+) Adjustment for residence[3]	-153	-1 079	-1 526	-1 405	-1 436	-1 441	-1 463	X
(=) **Net Earnings by Place of Residence**	77 983	134 856	217 168	219 684	226 250	234 838	244 329	3.0
(+) Dividends, interest, and rent[4]	16 735	40 065	57 209	55 602	53 187	51 246	53 133	-1.8
(+) Personal current transfer receipts	13 783	28 709	46 161	50 337	53 682	56 340	59 312	6.5
Personal income	108 500	203 630	320 538	325 623	333 120	342 424	356 774	2.7
Farm income	107 952	202 492	319 630	324 970	332 882	341 766	356 073	2.7
Nonfarm income	549	1 138	908	653	238	658	701	-6.3
Per Capita Personal Income (Dollars)[5]	10 046	18 743	28 207	28 594	29 194	29 938	31 135	2.5

Note: Data may not add to total or may appear as zero due to rounding.

[1]Proprietors' income includes the inventory valuation adjustment and the capital consumption adjustment.
[2]Contributions for government social insurance are included in earnings by type and industry, but they are excluded from personal income.
[3]The adjustment for residence is the net inflow of the earnings of interarea commuters.
[4]Rental income of persons includes the capital consumption adjustment.
[5]Per capita personal income is total personal income divided by total midyear population.
X = Not applicable.

Per Capita Personal Income, 1980–2004 (Current Dollars)

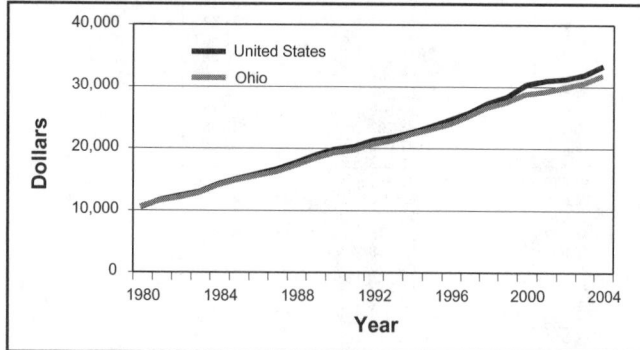

ECONOMIC ACTIVITY

Economic activity in Ohio was severely impacted by the 2001 recession. Real gross state product (GSP) grew by just 5.4 percent from 2001 to 2004, the 6th lowest growth rate in the nation. The GSP growth was modest due to small gains in the industrial and service-providing sectors. Mining, construction, educational services, accommodation and food services, and agriculture all suffered significant losses from 2001 to 2004. Housing price appreciation occurred at a rate below the national average. In 2004, the median value of owner-occupied housing in Ohio ranked 28th in the nation.

Table OH-11. Real Gross State Product, 1997–2004

(Millions of chained 2000 dollars, percent.)

Industry	1997	1998	1999	2000	2001	2002	2003	2004	Average annual percent change, 2001–2004
GROSS STATE PRODUCT	350 603	362 461	367 895	371 228	365 791	369 354	375 740	385 373	1.8
As a percent of U.S. gross product	4.1	4.0	3.9	3.8	3.7	3.7	3.7	3.6	X
Private Industries	312 343	323 880	329 351	331 986	326 309	330 187	336 358	345 286	1.9
Agriculture, forestry, fishing, and hunting	2 081	1 789	1 410	1 815	1 601	1 566	1 869	1 550	-1.1
Mining	1 236	1 437	1 403	1 366	1 331	1 184	1 015	985	-9.5
Utilities	7 319	7 258	7 367	7 484	7 403	7 708	8 156	7 953	2.4
Construction	15 763	16 006	16 046	15 453	14 557	14 017	13 647	13 583	-2.3
Manufacturing	80 537	84 646	83 019	83 986	76 052	78 107	80 791	82 161	2.6
As a percent of gross state product	23.0	23.4	22.6	22.6	20.8	21.1	21.5	21.3	X
Wholesale trade	20 886	22 870	23 525	22 675	23 988	24 258	23 423	23 945	-0.1
Retail trade	23 364	24 584	25 511	26 417	27 924	28 898	30 258	30 831	3.4
Transportation and warehousing	10 256	10 693	11 047	11 342	10 672	10 769	11 095	11 491	2.5
Information	9 109	9 569	10 546	10 260	10 759	10 989	11 567	12 511	5.2
Finance and insurance	23 336	24 018	25 186	26 299	26 133	26 244	27 978	29 543	4.2
Real estate and rental and leasing	35 786	36 418	38 479	39 252	40 613	39 967	38 645	39 810	-0.7
Services	82 810	84 553	85 889	85 635	85 343	86 697	88 362	91 492	2.3
As a percent of gross state product	23.6	23.3	23.3	23.1	23.3	23.5	23.5	23.7	X
Professional and technical services	16 982	18 107	18 954	19 183	19 477	19 584	20 087	20 629	1.9
Management of companies and enterprises	9 036	8 701	8 948	8 470	8 320	8 864	9 150	9 816	5.7
Administrative and waste services	10 653	10 961	11 065	10 101	9 473	9 865	10 246	10 780	4.4
Educational services	2 361	2 391	2 332	2 475	2 382	2 350	2 289	2 256	-1.8
Health care and social assistance	24 754	24 787	25 085	25 695	26 365	26 957	27 581	28 290	2.4
Arts, entertainment, and recreation	2 406	2 405	2 622	2 623	2 725	2 710	2 651	2 589	-1.7
Accommodation and food services	7 734	8 073	7 932	8 176	7 968	7 904	7 988	8 225	1.1
Other services, except public administration	8 884	9 128	8 951	8 912	8 633	8 463	8 370	8 907	1.0
Government	38 308	38 592	38 541	39 243	39 477	39 179	39 416	40 118	0.5
As a percent of gross state product	10.9	10.6	10.5	10.6	10.8	10.6	10.5	10.4	X

X = Not applicable.

Table OH-12. Government Transfer Payments, Selected Years 1980–2004

(Millions of dollars, percent.)

Item	1980	1990	2000	2001	2002	2003	2004	Average annual percent change, 2000–2004
CURRENT TRANSFER PAYMENTS TO INDIVIDUALS	13 034	27 334	43 149	46 991	50 646	53 463	56 357	6.9
Retirement and Disability Insurance Benefits	6 720	13 689	20 067	21 067	21 953	22 724	23 700	4.2
Old-age, survivors, and disability insurance (OASDI) benefits	5 770	11 622	17 733	18 607	19 366	19 872	20 722	4.0
Railroad retirement and disability benefits	272	412	455	459	471	475	483	1.5
Workers' compensation	570	1 484	1 717	1 840	1 913	2 028	2 122	5.4
Other government retirement and disability insurance benefits	109	171	162	160	204	349	373	23.3
Medical Benefits	2 540	8 980	17 077	19 100	20 793	22 311	24 313	9.2
Medicare benefits	1 632	5 350	9 102	10 035	10 695	11 263	12 317	7.9
Public assistance medical care benefits	896	3 582	7 929	8 998	10 002	10 963	11 891	10.7
Military medical insurance benefits	11	48	46	67	96	85	105	23.2
Income Maintenance Benefits	1 414	2 877	4 046	4 212	4 600	5 099	5 384	7.4
Supplemental Security Income (SSI) benefits	201	482	1 114	1 162	1 190	1 204	1 259	3.1
Family assistance	585	893	716	741	642	714	642	-2.7
Food stamps	405	888	528	602	750	913	1 052	18.8
Other income maintenance benefits	223	614	1 688	1 708	2 018	2 268	2 432	9.6
Unemployment Insurance Compensation	1 615	753	714	1 224	1 819	1 790	1 332	16.9
Veterans' Benefits	576	696	836	867	936	1 003	1 058	6.1
Federal Education and Training Assistance	163	322	379	457	514	509	541	9.3
Other Payments to Individuals	6	17	30	64	31	28	29	-1.2

Note: See notes and definitions for more details. Data may not add to total or may appear as zero due to rounding.

EXPORTS

Ohio was the sixth largest exporter of goods in 2004, with a total value of exports amounting to $31.2 billion. Exports grew slowly after the 2001 recession, but increased by over 12 percent from 2002 to 2004. The state's leading exports were transportation equipment and machinery manufactures, which together made up half of all the state's exports. Canada was by far the largest export market, accounting for almost half of Ohio's foreign sales. Transportation equipment made up nearly half of all exports to Canada. Exports to China more than doubled from 2001 to 2004, making the country the sixth leading market for Ohio's goods.

Leading Exports, 2004

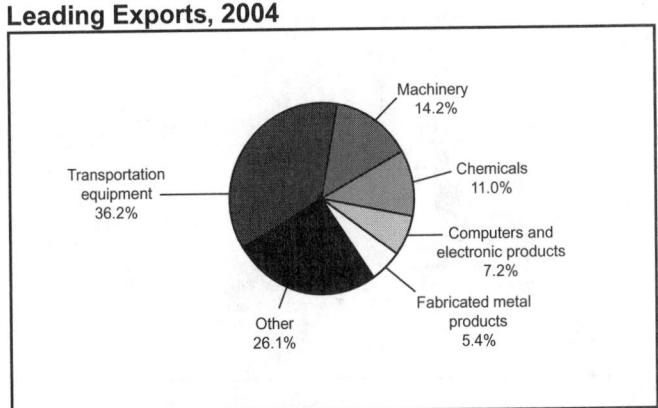

Table OH-13. Exports of Goods by Leading Products and Destinations, 2001–2004

(Millions of dollars, percent, rank based on 2004 dollar values.)

Product and market	2001	2002	2003	2004	Percent share of total, 2004	Average annual percent change, 2001–2004
Total Goods						
Total	27 095	27 723	29 764	31 208	100.0	4.8
Manufactures	26 236	26 841	28 643	30 005	96.1	4.6
Agriculture and livestock	378	458	660	744	2.4	25.3
Other commodities	481	424	461	460	1.5	-1.5
Five Leading Exports (NAICS Code)						
Transportation equipment (336)	10 353	11 220	12 502	11 295	36.2	2.9
Machinery manufactures (333)	4 050	3 702	3 596	4 419	14.2	3.0
Chemical manufactures (325)	2 588	2 532	2 834	3 418	11.0	9.7
Computers and electronic products (334)	1 677	1 837	1 783	2 233	7.2	10.0
Fabricated metal products (332)	1 613	1 737	1 728	1 693	5.4	1.6
Five Leading Markets	25 351	26 085	27 881	28 825	92.4	4.4
Canada	13 843	15 420	16 894	15 537	49.8	3.9
Mexico	2 109	2 109	2 102	2 410	7.7	4.6
Japan	1 389	1 190	1 101	1 359	4.4	-0.7
United Kingdom	1 284	1 229	1 242	1 185	3.8	-2.6
Germany	759	631	727	1 024	3.3	10.5

Table OH-14. Agriculture, 1997 and 2002

(Number, acres, and dollars.)

Item	1997	2002
Number of farms	78 737	77 797
Land in farms (acres)	14 738 028	14 583 435
Farm Size		
Average size of farm (acres)	187	187
Farms by size (percent distribution)		
Fewer than 50 acres	34.4	39.5
50 to 499 acres	56.9	51.5
500 acres or more	8.7	9.0
Market Value of Land and Equipment (Dollars)		
Land and buildings average value per farm	384 631	509 307
Average value per acre	2 068	2 732
Machinery and equipment average value per farm	53 070	68 119
Value of Sales (Thousands of Dollars)		
Agricultural products sold	4 744 521	4 263 549
Crops	2 871 092	2 304 895
Livestock, poultry, and their products	1 873 429	1 958 654
Average per farm (dollars)	60 258	54 804
Value of sales (percent distribution)		
Less than $10,000	53.1	60.0
$10,000 to $99,999	33.3	28.6
$100,000 or more	13.6	11.4
Government Payments		
Payments (thousands of dollars)	146 279	197 425
Percent of farms receiving government payments	45.2	37.1
Farm operators whose principal occupation is farming (percent)	42.2	55.9

AGRICULTURE

Cash receipts from farming in Ohio totaled $4.3 million in 2002, according to the Department of Agriculture's Census of Agriculture. This represented a decline of over 8 percent from the previous census in 1997. The state's major farm products were soybeans, corn, and dairy products. Nearly 40 percent of farms spanned fewer than 50 acres, and 60 percent of farms had total sales of less than $10,000. The proportion of farm operators reporting farming as their principal occupation grew from 42.2 percent in 1997 to 55.9 percent in 2002.

ENERGY

Energy expenditures per person were $2,553 in 2001, the 19th highest in the country. Energy prices were slightly above average. Per capita consumption dropped significantly from 2000 to 2001, but remained above the national average. The industrial sector accounted for nearly 36 percent of the state's energy consumption. The chief energy sources were coal, petroleum, and natural gas.

Energy Consumption by Source, 2001

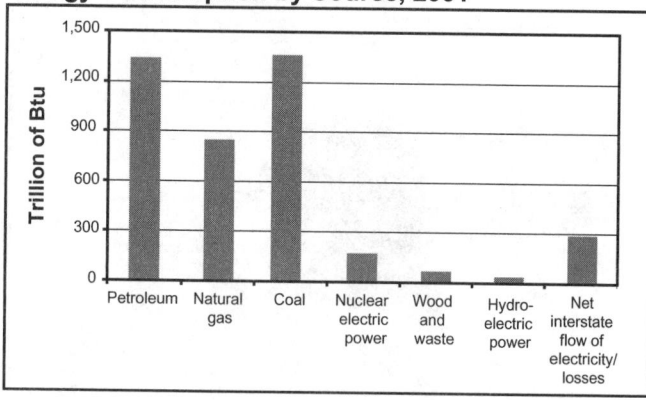

Energy Consumption by Sector, 2001

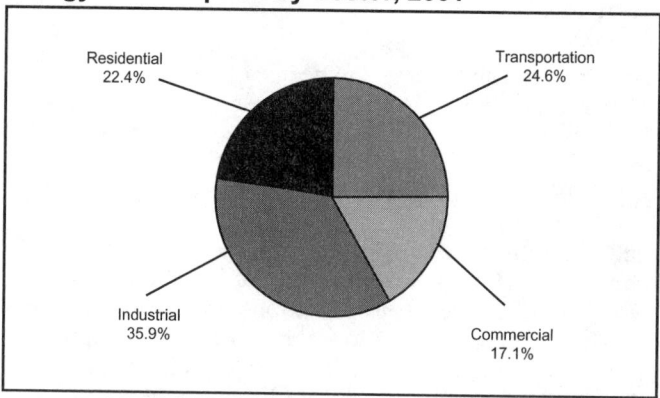

Table OH-15. Energy Consumption, Expenditures, and Prices, Selected Years 1960–2001

(Dollars, Btu [British Thermal Unit], percent distribution.)

Item	1960	1965	1970	1975	1980	1985	1990	1995	2000	2001
Total Consumption (Billion Btu)	2 995 462	3 374 884	3 944 072	3 993 933	4 066 740	3 666 707	3 828 066	4 089 982	4 263 714	3 982 276
Consumption per capita (million Btu)	308.6	330.8	370.1	370.8	376.6	341.6	352.9	366.6	375.6	349.8
Consumption by Sector (Percent Distribution)										
Residential	21.0	21.2	21.7	22.1	22.0	22.3	21.7	22.7	21.9	22.4
Commercial	8.7	8.9	10.8	11.4	11.9	14.1	15.1	16.0	16.6	17.1
Industrial	54.0	53.7	50.4	47.5	46.8	43.0	42.5	40.4	38.4	35.9
Transportation	16.2	16.2	17.1	19.1	19.4	20.6	20.8	20.9	23.1	24.6
Consumption by Source (Billion Btu)										
Coal	1 269 205	1 324 406	1 571 427	1 619 050	1 528 107	1 389 464	1 425 329	1 379 813	1 428 480	1 343 002
Natural gas	724 824	909 391	1 077 151	978 885	911 335	765 373	776 589	923 946	928 427	835 709
Petroleum	797 425	923 173	1 082 499	1 212 200	1 347 199	1 105 382	1 122 247	1 167 815	1 315 471	1 305 171
Nuclear electric power	0	255	0	0	23 115	20 638	112 845	176 182	175 013	161 565
Hydroelectric power[1]	210	111	78	77	63	1 827	1 887	2 395	5 948	5 197
Wood and waste	36 755	38 609	44 071	46 222	103 913	116 280	64 686	67 541	75 696	43 414
Other	0	0	0	0	0	0	366	570	882	946
Net interstate flow of electricity/losses[2]	167 043	178 939	168 846	137 499	153 010	267 743	324 117	371 720	333 798	287 272
Total Expenditures (Thousands of Dollars)	. . .	. . .	4 655 900	9 166 600	18 377 000	20 680 700	21 038 500	23 149 900	29 549 600	29 070 500
Expenditures per capita (dollars)	. . .	. . .	437	851	1 702	1 926	1 940	2 075	2 603	2 553
Prices by Sector (Dollars Per Million Btu)										
Total	. . .	. . .	1.50	3.05	6.23	8.23	8.19	8.49	10.36	10.92
Residential	. . .	. . .	1.68	3.11	6.33	9.70	10.10	10.64	12.72	14.16
Commercial	. . .	. . .	1.91	3.53	7.03	10.68	11.17	11.59	13.17	14.91
Industrial	. . .	. . .	0.84	2.17	4.43	6.18	5.63	5.93	6.93	7.48
Transportation	. . .	. . .	2.66	4.39	8.87	8.92	8.97	8.73	11.33	10.68

[1]A negative number in this row results from pumped storage for which, overall, more electricity is expended than created to provide electricity during peak demand periods.
[2]Net interstate flow of electricity is the difference between the amount of energy in the electricity sold within a state (including associated losses) and the energy input at the electric utilities within the state. A positive number indicates that more electricity (including associated losses) came into the state than went out of the state during the year; conversely, a negative number indicates that more electricity (including associated losses) went out of the state than came into the state.
. . . = Not available.

Table OH-16. State Taxes, Fiscal 2004

(Dollars, percent distribution.)

Item	Thousands of dollars	Percent distribution	Dollars per capita	
			State	U.S.
TOTAL TAXES	22 475 528	100.0	1 961.4	2 024.8
Property Taxes	40 636	0.2	3.6	38.9
Sales and Gross Receipts	10 783 304	48.0	941.0	1 003.4
General sales and gross receipts	7 881 510	35.1	687.8	677.0
Selective sales taxes	2 901 794	12.9	253.2	326.4
Insurance premiums	423 078	1.9	36.9	47.0
Motor fuels	1 541 151	6.9	134.5	114.6
Public utilities	275 811	1.2	24.1	39.2
Tobacco products	557 569	2.5	48.7	42.0
Licenses	1 813 479	8.1	158.3	134.9
Corporation	297 031	1.3	25.9	21.6
Motor vehicle	713 149	3.2	62.2	59.4
Occupation and business, not elsewhere classified	666 510	3.0	58.2	37.1
Other Taxes	9 838 109	43.8	858.6	847.6
Individual income	8 705 161	38.7	759.7	673.6
Corporation net income	1 060 594	4.7	92.6	105.1

GOVERNMENT FINANCE

Per capita revenues and expenditures were slightly below the national average in 2003. Ohio's per capita spending on education, health, correctional facilities, and government administration was slightly higher than average, while outlays for health and police protection were below average. Taxes per person were also lower than the average in 2004. The major source of revenue was individual income taxes, followed by general sales taxes and motor fuel taxes. Ohio's per capita individual income tax of $760 was the 17th highest among the 46 states with such taxes. The state's per capita debt was below the national average.

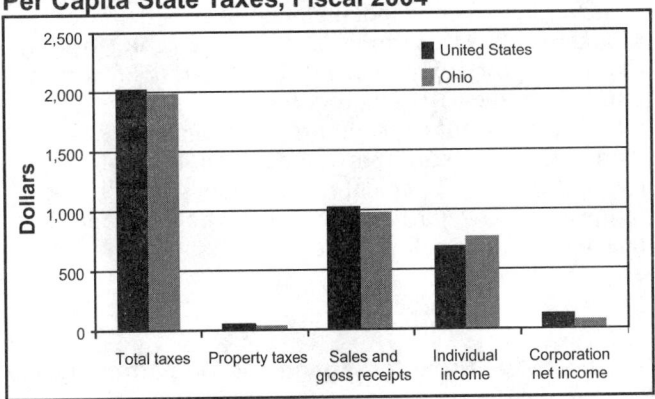

Per Capita State Taxes, Fiscal 2004

Table OH-17. State Government Finances, 2003

(Dollars, percent distribution.)

Item	Millions of dollars	Percent distribution	Dollars per capita	
			State	U.S.
GENERAL REVENUE	42 422 137	100.0	3 708.9	3 832.6
Intergovernmental revenue	14 058 065	33.1	1 229.1	1 246.0
Taxes	20 651 597	48.7	1 805.5	1 891.6
General sales	6 761 515	15.9	591.1	636.0
Selective sales	3 329 634	7.8	291.1	307.4
License taxes	1 701 782	4.0	148.8	123.6
Individual income tax	7 916 410	18.7	692.1	626.8
Corporate income tax	794 645	1.9	69.5	97.8
Other taxes	147 611	0.3	12.9	99.9
Current charges	4 538 357	10.7	396.8	366.5
Miscellaneous general revenue	3 174 118	7.5	277.5	328.6
GENERAL EXPENDITURE	44 613 676	100.0	3 900.5	4 010.5
Intergovernmental expenditure	15 249 395	34.2	1 333.2	1 316.9
Direct expenditure	29 364 281	65.8	2 567.3	2 693.6
Expenditure by Function				
Education	16 327 787	36.6	1 427.5	1 416.4
Public welfare	12 527 978	28.1	1 095.3	1 083.3
Hospitals	1 367 067	3.1	119.5	132.3
Health	2 022 067	4.5	176.8	173.0
Highways	3 183 792	7.1	278.4	295.4
Police protection	278 653	0.6	24.4	38.4
Correction	1 686 179	3.8	147.4	135.0
Natural resources	383 998	0.9	33.6	64.0
Parks and recreation	94 534	0.2	8.3	20.1
Government administration	1 851 955	4.2	161.9	151.3
Interest on general debt	1 146 890	2.6	100.3	107.8
Other and unallocable	3 742 776	8.4	327.2	393.4
DEBT AT END OF FISCAL YEAR	21 054 220	X	1 840.7	2 404.7
CASH AND SECURITY HOLDINGS	143 620 156	X	12 556.4	8 938.4

X = Not applicable.

Table OH-18. Education Indicators, 2000–2004

(Percent, number.)

Item	State	U.S.
Total Population 25 Years and Over (Thousands), 2004	7 362	186 877
Educational Attainment, 2004		
Percent high school graduate or more	88.1	85.2
Percent college graduate or more	24.6	27.7
Elementary and Secondary Schools, 2002–2003		
Total students	1 838 285	48 202 324
Percent of students eligible for free or reduced-price lunch ..	33.2	40.6
Percent of students who were English language learners	1.3	7.8
Total schools	3 815	92 330
Student/teacher ratio	15.2	15.9
Per student expenditures	8 632	8 041
Dropouts, Grades 9–12, 2000–2001 (Percent)	3.1	. . .
Higher Education, 2002–2003		
Total enrollment	612 008	17 035 027
Bachelor's degrees awarded	54 852	1 348 503
Percent women	57.2	57.5

. . . = Not available.

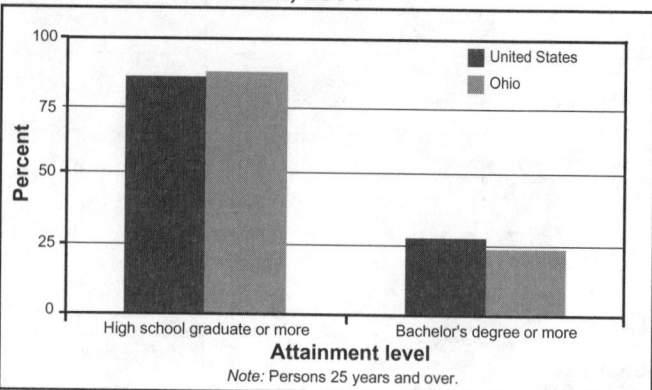

Educational Attainment, 2004

Legend: United States, Ohio

Attainment level: High school graduate or more, Bachelor's degree or more

Note: Persons 25 years and over.

EDUCATION

More than 88 percent of Ohio's residents age 25 years and over held high school diplomas in 2004. This was well above the U.S. proportion of 85.2 percent. However, the state's proportion of college graduates (24.6 percent) fell short of the national proportion of 27.7 percent. Ohio's per student expenditures were significantly higher than average, ranking 16th in the nation. The state's dropout rate of 3.1 percent ranked among the 10 lowest of the 46 states reporting such data. Ohio's student/teacher ratio was below average.

VOTER PARTICIPATION

In 2000, Ohio's participation rate was just above the national average; however, the state's rate increased in 2004, ranking 14th in the country. This increase likely reflected the state's position as a "swing" state, in which either major candidate could have won. Persons 65 to 74 years old had the highest participation rate, with 73 percent of eligible voters in this age group casting ballots. According to the official tally by the Clerk of the U.S. House of Representatives, 50 percent of eligible voters cast ballots for the Republican presidential candidate in 2000; this proportion increased slightly to 50.8 percent in 2004.

Table OH-19. Reported Voting and Registration, November 2000 and November 2004

(Numbers in thousands, percent.)

Characteristic	Total population 18 years and over	Total citizen		Total registered		Total voted	
		Number	Percent	Number	Percent	Number	Percent
NOVEMBER 2000							
Total	8 301	8 143	98.1	5 561	67.0	4 823	58.1
Male	3 916	3 836	98.0	2 559	65.4	2 201	56.2
Female	4 385	4 307	98.2	3 002	68.5	2 622	59.8
NOVEMBER 2004							
Total	8 469	8 305	98.1	6 003	70.9	5 485	64.8
Male	4 037	3 953	97.9	2 813	69.7	2 581	63.9
Female	4 432	4 352	98.2	3 190	72.0	2 905	65.5
Race and Hispanic Origin							
White alone	7 381	7 263	98.4	5 268	71.4	4 802	65.1
Non-Hispanic White alone	7 188	7 149	99.4	5 179	72.0	4 723	65.7
Black alone	895	876	97.9	630	70.3	586	65.5
Asian alone	73	45	B	20	B	20	B
Hispanic or Latino[1]	209	130	62.5	100	47.7	90	43.1
White alone or in combination	7 460	7 342	98.4	5 318	71.3	4 844	64.9
Non-Hispanic White alone or in combination	7 257	7 218	99.5	5 222	72.0	4 757	65.5
Black alone or in combination	923	904	97.9	648	70.3	603	65.3
Asian alone or in combination	80	52	B	25	B	25	B
Age							
18 to 24 years	1 099	1 082	98.4	686	62.4	599	54.5
25 to 44 years	3 052	2 935	96.2	2 062	67.6	1 861	61.0
45 to 64 years	2 840	2 824	99.5	2 161	76.1	2 018	71.1
65 to 74 years	787	777	98.7	609	77.3	575	73.0
75 years and over	691	686	99.3	485	70.3	432	62.6

[1]May be of any race.
B = Base is too small to show derived measure.

At a Glance:

- Oklahoma's population exceeded 3.5 million in 2004, ranking it as the 28th most populous state in the nation.

- Nearly 73 percent of the state's population was non-Hispanic White. Oklahoma had the fourth highest proportion of American Indian residents in the nation in 2004.

- The state's median household income was well below the national average, ranking 40th in the country. However, Oklahoma's poverty rate of 10.8 percent was also well below the national average.

- Economic activity slowed over the 2001–2002 period, and subsequent growth was modest. In 2004, Oklahoma's real gross state product ranked 30th in the nation. The state's unemployment rate was 4.8 percent, which was below the national average.

- Nearly 20 percent of the state's residents lacked health insurance, which was the third highest proportion in the nation.

- Oklahoma's per student expenditures for grades K–12 were the third lowest in the country.

Table OK-1. Population by Sex and Age, 1990, 2000, and 2004

(Number, percent.)

Sex and age	1990	2000	2004	Percent distribution, 2004	Average annual percent change, 2000–2004
Total Population	3 145 585	3 450 654	3 523 553	X	0.5
Percent of total U.S. population	1.3	1.2	1.2	X	X
Sex					
Male	1 530 819	1 695 895	1 740 265	49.4	0.6
Female	1 614 766	1 754 759	1 783 288	50.6	0.4
Age					
Under 5 years	226 523	236 353	242 240	6.9	0.3
5 to 17 years	610 484	656 007	617 630	17.5	0.1
18 years and over	601 416	2 558 294	2 663 683	75.6	1.0
18 to 24 years	2 308 578	357 085	385 439	10.9	1.3
25 to 44 years	321 389	975 169	958 067	27.2	0.0
45 to 64 years	961 560	770 090	855 737	24.3	2.6
65 years and over	424 213	455 950	464 440	13.2	0.7
85 years and over	45 848	57 175	54 305	1.5	1.3
Median age (years)	33.1	35.5	36.0	X	X

X = Not applicable.

Average Annual Rate of Population Growth, 1980–2004

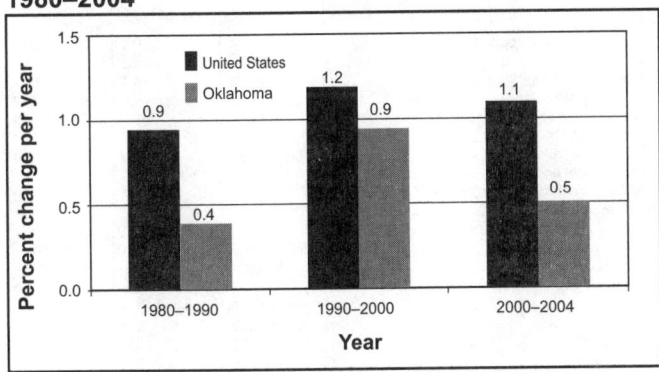

POPULATION

Oklahoma's population growth has been slow in recent years. From 2000 to 2004, the state's population increased just 2.1 percent, a rate well below the national growth rate of 4.3 percent. In 2001, Oregon overtook Oklahoma to become the 27th most populous state in the nation. The state lost over 18,000 residents to other locations during the 2000–2004 period; however, this was offset by an influx of over 30,000 new residents from abroad. Oklahoma had the largest number and the fourth highest proportion of American Indian residents in the nation. The state's population was somewhat older than the nation as a whole, with 13.2 percent of its residents age 65 years and over.

Table OK-2. Population by Race and Hispanic Origin, 1990, 2000, and 2004

(Number, percent.)

Race and Hispanic origin	1990	2000	2004
Total Population	3 145 585	3 450 654	3 523 553
Non-Hispanic (Percent)			
One race[1]			
White	81.0	74.3	72.9
Black	7.4	7.5	7.5
American Indian, Alaska Native[2]	8.0	7.7	7.8
Asian and Pacific Islander[2]	1.1	1.4	1.6
Other race[2]	1.3	. . .	. . .
Two or more races	. . .	3.9	3.8
Hispanic or Latino[3] (Percent)	2.7	5.2	6.3

[1]Individuals could report only one race in the 1990 census and could report one or more races on the 2000 census. Data on race in 2000 and 2004 are not comparable to 1990.
[2]Data for 1990 include people of Hispanic or Latino origin.
[3]May be of any race.
. . . = Not available.

Minority Population as a Percent of Total Population, 2004

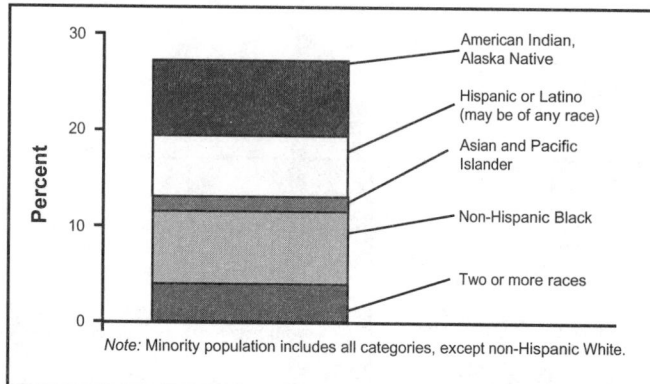

Note: Minority population includes all categories, except non-Hispanic White.

Age-Adjusted Death Rates, Average 2000–2002

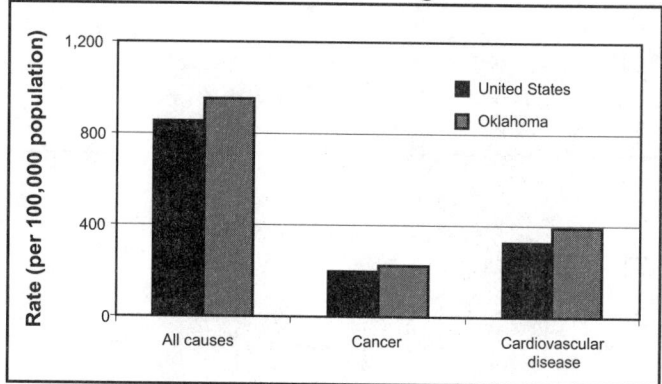

HEALTH

Nearly 20 percent of Oklahoma's population lacked health insurance coverage in 2004. This high rate of uninsured residents was exceeded only by the rates in Texas and New Mexico. The state's infant mortality rate and age-adjusted death rates were among the highest in the nation.

Table OK-3. Health Characteristics, 2000–2004

(Number, rate, percent.)

Item	State	U.S.
Births, 2003–2004		
Number of births	50 981	4 089 950
Birth rate (per 1,000 population)	14.5	14.1
Teenage birth rate (per 1,000 women age 15–19 years)	55.9	41.6
Mortality Rates, Average 2000–2002		
Infant mortality rate (per 1,000 live births)	8.0	6.9
Age-adjusted mortality rate (per 100,000 population)		
All races	970.8	853.3
Non-Hispanic White	972.9	843.1
Black	1 165.7	1 097.7
American Indian, Alaska Native	. . .	687.0
Asian and Pacific Islander	455.9	486.0
Hispanic or Latino[1]	731.0	642.7
Health Insurance, 2004		
Percent of all persons without health insurance	19.9	15.7
Percent of children without health insurance	16.9	11.2
Percent of low-income children without health insurance	9.7	7.1

[1]May be of any race.
. . . = Not available.

Table OK-4. Leading Causes of Death, Average 2000–2002

(Number, rate per 100,000 population.)

Cause	Number of deaths	Age-adjusted death rates	
		State	U.S.
ALL CAUSES	35 088	970.8	853.3
Leading Causes			
Major cardiovascular diseases	14 494	398.6	326.5
Cancer	7 429	205.5	196.0
Chronic lower respiratory diseases	1 963	54.1	43.7
Unintentional injuries	1 615	45.9	35.7
Diabetes (underlying cause)	1 036	28.7	25.2
Influenza and pneumonia	904	24.8	22.7
Alzheimer's disease	691	18.9	19.0
Motor vehicle accidents	708	20.1	15.0
Nephritis, nephrotic syndrome, and nephrosis ..	534	14.7	13.8
Septicemia	427	11.8	11.4
Suicides	504	14.6	10.7
Firearm-related	465	13.3	10.3
Cirrhosis	380	10.7	9.5
Drug-induced	262	7.7	7.9
Alcohol-induced	245	7.0	6.9
Homicides	202	5.8	6.0
Falls	175	4.8	5.2
HIV	100	3.0	5.0
Viral hepatitis	85	2.4	2.0
Anemias	60	1.7	1.6
Drownings	57	1.6	1.3
Fire deaths	58	1.7	1.2

Note: The rates are age-adjusted to the U.S. 2000 standard population.

Table OK-5. Households and Housing Characteristics, 1990, 2000, and 2004

(Number, percent, and dollars.)

Characteristic	1990	2000	2004	Average annual percent change, 2000–2004
Total Households	1 206 135	1 342 293	1 360 032	0.3
Family households	855 321	921 750	912 709	-0.2
Married-couple family	695 961	717 611	683 810	-1.2
Other family	159 360	204 139	228 899	2.9
Male householder, no wife present	33 891	51 564	61 765	4.6
Female householder, no husband present	125 469	152 575	167 134	2.3
Nonfamily households	350 814	420 543	447 323	1.6
Householder living alone	309 369	358 560	374 114	1.1
Householder not living alone	41 445	61 983	73 209	4.2
Housing Characteristics				
Average size	2.53	2.49	2.51	X
Housing units	1 406 499	1 514 400	1 572 756	0.9
Occupied housing units	1 206 135	1 342 293	1 360 032	0.3
Owner-occupied	821 188	918 259	927 641	0.3
Renter-occupied	384 947	424 034	432 391	0.5
Median gross rent of renter-occupied housing units (dollars)	340	456	525	3.6
Median value of owner-occupied housing units (dollars)	47 600	70 700	85 060	4.7

X = Not applicable.

Median Housing Value and Median Rent, 2004

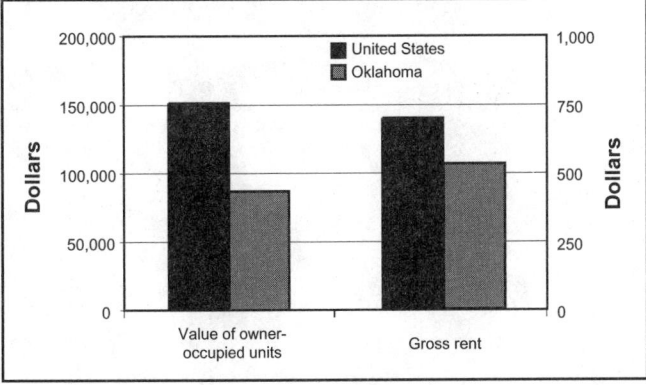

Median Household Income, 1984–2004 (2004 Dollars)

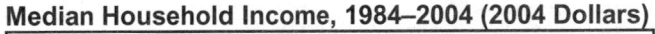
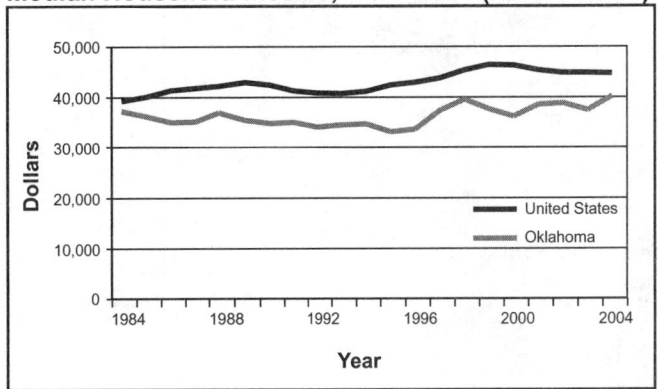

Table OK-6. Household Income and Poverty Status, 1980–2004

(2004 CPI-U-RS adjusted dollars, rate.)

Year	State		U.S.	
	Median household income (2004 dollars)	Poverty rate	Median household income (2004 dollars)	Poverty rate
2004	39 681	10.8	44 389	12.7
2003	36 867	12.8	44 482	12.5
2002	38 296	14.1	44 546	12.1
2001	37 999	15.1	45 062	11.7
2000	35 574	14.9	46 058	11.3
1999	37 046	12.8	46 129	11.9
1998	39 034	14.1	45 003	12.7
1997	36 795	13.7	43 430	13.3
1996	32 889	16.6	42 544	13.7
1995	32 385	17.1	41 943	13.8
1994	34 029	16.7	40 677	14.5
1993	33 805	19.9	40 217	15.1
1992	33 360	18.6	40 422	14.8
1991	34 438	17.0	40 746	14.2
1990	34 172	15.6	41 963	13.5
1989	34 817	14.7	42 524	12.8
1988	36 312	17.3	41 771	13.0
1987	34 492	17.0	41 322	13.4
1986	34 446	14.7	40 939	13.6
1985	35 505	16.0	39 545	14.0
1984	36 590	13.3	38 782	14.4
1983	. . .	17.0	. . .	15.2
1982	. . .	15.4	. . .	15.0
1981	. . .	13.8	. . .	14.0
1980	. . .	13.9	. . .	13.0

. . . = Not available.

Table OK-7. Employment Status by Demographic Group, 2004

(Numbers in thousands, rate.)

Characteristic	Civilian noninstitutional population	Civilian labor force		Employed	Unemployment rate
		Number	Participation rate		
SEX AND AGE					
Total	2 671	1 714	64.2	1 630	4.9
16 to 19 years	189	89	47.3	79	12.2
20 to 24 years	281	210	74.8	190	9.7
25 to 34 years	450	361	80.2	345	4.4
35 to 44 years	466	373	80.1	357	4.3
45 to 54 years	460	374	81.3	360	3.7
55 to 64 years	374	232	62.0	226	2.2
65 years and over	451	74	16.5	73	1.8
Men	1 284	915	71.3	874	4.5
16 to 19 years	103	52	50.8	45	13.1
20 to 24 years	131	107	81.6	98	8.2
25 to 34 years	218	199	91.1	192	3.6
35 to 44 years	234	206	88.1	197	4.4
45 to 54 years	215	186	86.5	181	3.1
55 to 64 years	184	122	66.4	119	2.7
65 years and over	198	42	21.3	42	1.1
Women	1 387	798	57.6	756	5.3
20 to 24 years	149	103	68.8	91	11.2
25 to 34 years	232	162	70.0	154	5.4
35 to 44 years	231	166	71.9	159	4.3
45 to 54 years	245	188	76.7	179	4.4
55 to 64 years	190	110	57.7	108	1.7
MARITAL STATUS					
Married men, spouse present	757	563	74.4	549	2.5
Married women, spouse present	767	460	60.0	445	3.2
Women who maintain families	143	89	62.2	82	7.6
RACE, HISPANIC ORIGIN, AND SEX					
White	2 111	1 358	64.4	1 302	4.1
Men	1 024	734	71.6	707	3.7
Women	1 087	625	57.5	596	4.6
Black	198	125	63.2	116	7.2
Men	86	55	63.7	50	9.3
Women	112	70	62.8	66	5.5
Hispanic or Latino[1]	97	70	72.5	67	4.6
Men	50	45	89.5	43	3.3
RACE, HISPANIC ORIGIN, AND AGE					
White					
16 to 19 years	136	67	49.3	60	10.2
20 to 24 years	213	161	75.4	145	9.5
25 to 34 years	337	277	82.2	268	3.5
35 to 44 years	352	284	80.7	273	4.0
45 to 54 years	377	309	81.9	301	2.6
55 to 64 years	309	196	63.5	192	2.1
65 years and over	386	64	16.5	63	1.4

Note: Data in Table 7 are from the Current Population Survey (CPS) and do not match Bureau of Labor Statistics estimates in Table 8. See notes and definitions for more details.

[1]May be of any race.

Table OK-8. Employment Status, 1990–2004

(Numbers in thousands, rate.)

Year	Civilian labor force	Employed	Unemployed	Unemployment rate
2004	1 710 412	1 627 828	82 584	4.8
2003	1 709 750	1 614 418	95 332	5.6
2002	1 693 278	1 612 228	81 050	4.8
2001	1 676 529	1 615 033	61 496	3.7
2000	1 659 119	1 607 541	51 578	3.1
1999	1 650 302	1 590 838	59 464	3.6
1998	1 640 979	1 569 498	71 481	4.4
1997	1 610 541	1 543 105	67 436	4.2
1996	1 580 815	1 514 880	65 935	4.2
1995	1 562 793	1 490 602	72 191	4.6
1994	1 556 432	1 469 487	86 945	5.6
1993	1 542 973	1 450 076	92 897	6.0
1992	1 526 930	1 432 081	94 849	6.2
1991	1 520 524	1 426 240	94 284	6.2
1990	1 520 852	1 434 566	86 286	5.7

Note: Population age 16 years and over.

Unemployment Rate, 1980–2004

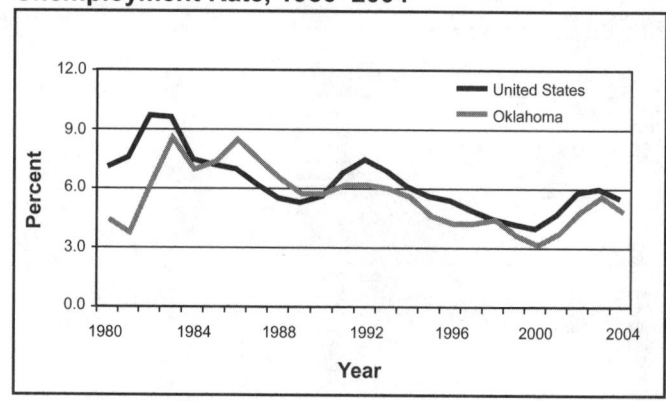

Table OK-9. Employment and Average Wages by Industry, 2001–2004

(Estimates are based on the 2002 North American Industry Classification System [NAICS].)

Industry	2001	2002	2003	2004	Annual average percent change, 2001–2004
	Number of jobs				
TOTAL EMPLOYMENT BY PLACE OF WORK	2 024 718	2 007 210	1 993 802	2 027 356	0.0
Farm Employment	99 574	98 243	93 496	94 583	-1.7
Nonfarm Employment	1 925 144	1 908 967	1 900 306	1 932 773	0.1
Private employment	1 590 084	1 571 221	1 567 483	1 594 678	0.1
Forestry, fishing, hunting, and other[1]	8 838	9 602	8 921	8 547	-1.1
Mining	57 404	53 709	60 394	64 494	4.0
Utilities	11 326	11 119	11 156	10 963	-1.1
Construction	112 007	108 329	110 736	110 965	-0.3
Manufacturing	176 517	158 817	149 639	149 276	-5.4
Durable goods manufacturing	117 680	103 603	97 157	97 748	-6.0
Nondurable goods manufacturing	58 837	55 214	52 482	51 528	-4.3
Wholesale trade	61 653	61 681	60 479	60 492	-0.6
Retail trade	225 663	224 807	223 217	224 532	-0.2
Transportation and warehousing	61 431	59 111	57 157	57 064	-2.4
Information	40 890	38 577	36 449	36 005	-4.2
Finance and insurance	77 589	79 460	80 167	81 399	1.6
Real estate and rental and leasing	59 016	60 002	61 591	64 631	3.1
Professional and technical services	92 592	93 690	94 708	96 225	1.3
Management of companies and enterprises	13 217	13 294	13 079	13 295	0.2
Administrative and waste services	123 037	119 653	116 353	123 859	0.2
Educational services	22 646	24 047	24 281	25 840	4.5
Health care and social assistance	178 687	182 994	186 306	189 128	1.9
Arts, entertainment, and recreation	25 313	26 022	25 812	26 814	1.9
Accommodation and food services	123 677	124 173	125 132	127 714	1.1
Other services, except public administration	118 581	122 134	121 906	123 435	1.3
Government and government enterprises	335 060	337 746	332 823	338 095	0.3
	Dollars				
AVERAGE WAGES AND SALARIES BY PLACE OF WORK	27 520	28 207	29 370	30 425	3.4
Farm Earnings	14 433	12 000	17 555	19 969	11.4
Nonfarm Earnings	27 636	28 331	29 441	30 494	3.3
Private earnings	27 304	27 801	28 874	30 042	3.2
Forestry, fishing, hunting, and other[1]	16 376	17 290	18 622	19 862	6.6
Mining	53 626	53 515	57 211	60 458	4.1
Utilities	51 867	53 754	56 971	59 218	4.5
Construction	30 403	29 919	30 563	30 992	0.6
Manufacturing	34 141	35 756	37 618	38 592	4.2
Durable goods manufacturing	35 144	36 871	38 782	39 760	4.2
Nondurable goods manufacturing	32 124	33 656	35 459	36 370	4.2
Wholesale trade	37 955	38 989	38 785	41 111	2.7
Retail trade	19 061	19 533	20 222	20 793	2.9
Transportation and warehousing	36 470	36 355	37 592	40 380	3.5
Information	36 680	37 445	38 604	40 438	3.3
Finance and insurance	34 562	35 152	37 239	39 310	4.4
Real estate and rental and leasing	26 223	26 585	28 020	29 057	3.5
Professional and technical services	39 787	39 760	41 299	42 363	2.1
Management of companies and enterprises	48 568	47 401	52 415	57 696	5.9
Administrative and waste services	19 467	20 632	21 542	22 544	5.0
Educational services	19 888	20 155	21 837	22 576	4.3
Health care and social assistance	27 016	27 906	28 756	30 198	3.8
Arts, entertainment, and recreation	15 095	15 581	16 214	16 851	3.7
Accommodation and food services	11 076	11 336	11 394	11 582	1.5
Other services, except public administration	18 825	19 332	20 138	20 887	3.5
Government and government enterprises	28 869	30 240	31 477	32 108	3.6

Note: Average wages and salaries are a calculation by the editors of wage and salary disbursements divided by full- and part-time wage and salary employment. Data may not add to total or may appear as zero due to rounding.

1 "Other" consists of the number of jobs held by U.S. residents employed by international organizations and foreign embassies and consulates in the United States.

LABOR MARKET

Oklahoma's unemployment rate rose significantly as a result of the 2001 recession, despite having been below the national average since the mid-1990s. The state also had a relatively low labor force participation rate. There was little growth in jobs during the 2001–2004 period. Employment in the state's largest industries of government and retail trade showed small increases, while manufacturing jobs declined throughout the period. Health care and other smaller service industries helped provide a modest net increase in jobs. Average wages and salaries in Oklahoma were below the national averages across all major industries.

Employment by Industry, 2004

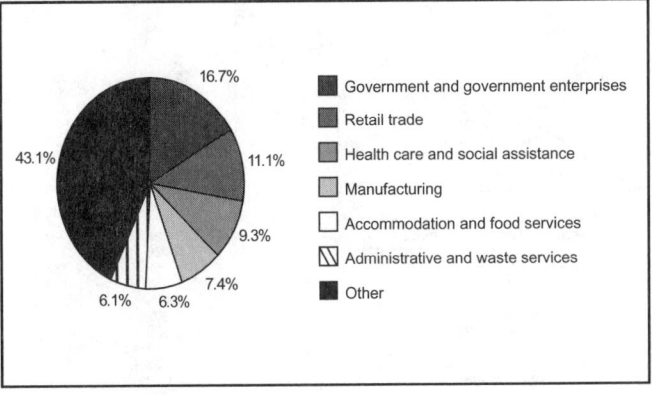

■	Government and government enterprises
■	Retail trade
■	Health care and social assistance
▨	Manufacturing
□	Accommodation and food services
◩	Administrative and waste services
■	Other

Table OK-10. Personal Income by Major Source, Selected Years 1980–2004

(Millions of dollars, except where noted.)

Item	1980	1990	2000	2001	2002	2003	2004	Average annual percent change, 2000–2004
Earnings by Place of Work	22 905	37 490	61 598	66 341	66 126	68 790	73 080	4.4
Wage and salary disbursements	16 671	26 039	41 905	43 783	44 206	45 159	47 309	3.1
Supplements to wages and salaries	3 297	5 841	9 375	9 980	11 007	11 901	12 949	8.4
Proprietors' income[1]	2 937	5 610	10 318	12 577	10 913	11 729	12 822	5.6
Farm proprietors' income	150	695	513	398	635	593	648	6.0
Nonfarm proprietors' income	2 786	4 915	9 804	12 179	10 278	11 136	12 174	5.6
(-) Contributions for government social insurance[2]	1 964	3 966	6 355	6 798	7 032	7 305	7 807	5.3
(+) Adjustment for residence[3]	171	560	1 008	1 010	1 035	1 064	1 125	2.8
(=) **Net Earnings by Place of Residence**	21 113	34 084	56 251	60 553	60 129	62 548	66 399	4.2
(+) Dividends, interest, and rent[4]	4 383	9 765	15 290	15 478	14 914	14 764	15 039	-0.4
(+) Personal current transfer receipts	3 410	7 121	12 770	14 130	15 121	15 806	16 583	6.7
Personal income	28 906	50 971	84 310	90 161	90 164	93 118	98 020	3.8
Farm income	28 654	50 133	83 605	89 544	89 373	92 353	97 155	3.8
Nonfarm income	252	838	705	617	791	765	865	5.2
Per Capita Personal Income (Dollars)[5]	9 506	16 187	24 407	26 009	25 848	26 556	27 819	3.3

Note: Data may not add to total or may appear as zero due to rounding.

[1]Proprietors' income includes the inventory valuation adjustment and the capital consumption adjustment.
[2]Contributions for government social insurance are included in earnings by type and industry, but they are excluded from personal income.
[3]The adjustment for residence is the net inflow of the earnings of interarea commuters.
[4]Rental income of persons includes the capital consumption adjustment.
[5]Per capita personal income is total personal income divided by total midyear population.

Per Capita Personal Income, 1980–2004 (Current Dollars)

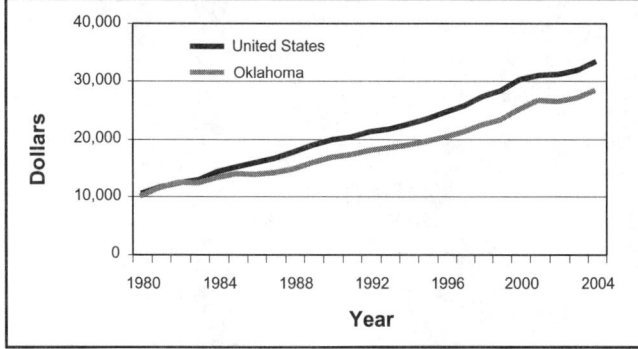

ECONOMIC ACTIVITY

Real gross state product growth (GSP) was slow over 2001–2004 period. Economic activity diminished significantly as a result of the 2001 recession, and its recovery rate was below the national average in subsequent years. Contributing to this slow growth was a decline in the agricultural sector, which was only partly offset by stronger performances in retail trade and many service-providing industries. Housing price appreciation has occurred at half of the national average rate in recent years; in 2004, the median value of owner-occupied housing in the state ranked among the five lowest in the nation.

Table OK-11. Real Gross State Product, 1997–2004

(Millions of chained 2000 dollars, percent.)

Industry	1997	1998	1999	2000	2001	2002	2003	2004	Average annual percent change, 2001–2004
GROSS STATE PRODUCT	82 858	84 664	87 198	89 851	90 267	91 793	93 750	96 876	2.4
As a percent of U.S. gross product	1.0	0.9	0.9	0.9	0.9	0.9	0.9	0.9	X
Private Industries	68 632	70 358	72 679	74 965	75 117	76 533	78 489	81 116	2.6
Agriculture, forestry, fishing, and hunting	1 176	1 084	1 326	1 618	1 353	1 660	2 013	1 445	2.2
Mining	5 634	4 725	4 574	4 515	4 391	4 564	4 576	4 800	3.0
Utilities	1 972	1 943	1 931	2 040	2 071	2 119	2 299	2 392	4.9
Construction	3 289	3 437	3 611	3 581	3 824	3 593	3 590	3 545	-2.5
Manufacturing	11 658	11 956	12 726	13 374	11 079	10 772	11 210	11 642	1.7
As a percent of gross state product	14.1	14.1	14.6	14.9	12.3	11.7	12.0	12.0	X
Wholesale trade	4 180	4 607	4 739	4 692	5 235	5 475	5 123	5 289	0.3
Retail trade	6 360	6 581	6 831	7 046	7 536	7 902	8 367	8 743	5.1
Transportation and warehousing	2 942	2 996	2 991	3 148	3 170	3 182	3 203	3 381	2.2
Information	2 709	2 985	3 172	3 512	3 910	4 029	4 189	4 563	5.3
Finance and insurance	3 755	3 912	3 957	4 125	4 274	4 568	4 854	5 198	6.7
Real estate and rental and leasing	7 814	7 996	8 387	8 601	9 142	9 163	9 125	9 472	1.2
Services	17 794	18 402	18 498	18 711	19 148	19 549	20 018	20 848	2.9
As a percent of gross state product	21.5	21.7	21.2	20.8	21.2	21.3	21.4	21.5	X
Professional and technical services	3 398	3 599	3 733	3 959	4 043	4 131	4 361	4 437	3.1
Management of companies and enterprises	920	920	834	863	1 114	1 142	1 265	1 346	6.5
Administrative and waste services	2 752	2 937	3 005	2 780	2 712	2 801	2 815	3 042	3.9
Educational services	431	418	436	428	432	432	424	435	0.2
Health care and social assistance	5 459	5 539	5 549	5 679	5 890	6 099	6 250	6 457	3.1
Arts, entertainment, and recreation	392	410	437	434	438	463	448	469	2.3
Accommodation and food services	2 025	2 077	2 130	2 223	2 200	2 187	2 177	2 240	0.6
Other services, except public administration	2 417	2 502	2 374	2 345	2 319	2 294	2 278	2 422	1.5
Government	14 233	14 307	14 518	14 886	15 149	15 263	15 280	15 772	1.4
As a percent of gross state product	17.2	16.9	16.6	16.6	16.8	16.6	16.3	16.3	X

X = Not applicable.

Table OK-12. Government Transfer Payments, Selected Years 1980–2004

(Millions of dollars, percent.)

Item	1980	1990	2000	2001	2002	2003	2004	Average annual percent change, 2000–2004
CURRENT TRANSFER PAYMENTS TO INDIVIDUALS	3 189	6 709	11 999	13 282	14 361	15 104	15 880	7.3
Retirement and Disability Insurance Benefits	1 647	3 336	5 400	5 692	5 940	6 114	6 381	4.3
Old-age, survivors, and disability insurance (OASDI) benefits	1 532	3 166	5 145	5 432	5 717	5 949	6 212	4.8
Railroad retirement and disability benefits	44	61	74	76	79	80	82	2.7
Workers' compensation	61	100	174	176	134	72	75	-19.1
Other government retirement and disability insurance benefits	10	9	8	9	10	12	12	10.4
Medical Benefits	743	2 079	4 550	5 302	5 735	5 970	6 444	9.1
Medicare benefits	451	1 269	2 741	3 028	3 236	3 420	3 747	8.1
Public assistance medical care benefits	283	755	1 732	2 165	2 348	2 421	2 547	10.1
Military medical insurance benefits	8	55	77	109	152	130	150	18.2
Income Maintenance Benefits	358	652	1 146	1 225	1 398	1 616	1 728	10.8
Supplemental Security Income (SSI) benefits	142	192	340	354	366	377	394	3.7
Family assistance	94	139	103	115	139	181	173	13.7
Food stamps	76	195	209	243	305	374	411	18.5
Other income maintenance benefits	47	126	494	512	587	684	750	11.0
Unemployment Insurance Compensation	87	120	124	197	335	397	246	18.7
Veterans' Benefits	290	382	605	641	712	771	831	8.2
Federal Education and Training Assistance	54	126	157	198	224	217	229	9.9
Other Payments to Individuals	10	15	17	27	17	20	22	7.1

Note: See notes and definitions for more details. Data may not add to total or may appear as zero due to rounding.

EXPORTS

Oklahoma was among the smallest exporting states, with the value of its exports ranking 36th overall in 2004. The state's exports totaled about $3.2 billion, which represented a sizable increase since the 2001 recession. Machinery manufactures and transportation equipment were the dominant exports, together accounting for more than 47 percent of total exports. Machinery manufactures and fabricated metal products were the fastest-growing among the state's major export products. Oklahoma's leading export market was Canada, followed by Mexico. Russia and China have been the fastest-growing overseas customers. Exports to the United Kingdom and Japan fell considerably from 2001 to 2004.

Leading Exports, 2004

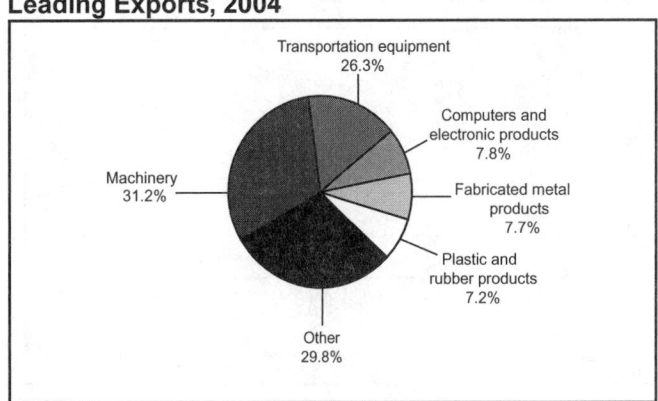

Table OK-13. Exports of Goods by Leading Products and Destinations, 2001–2004

(Millions of dollars, percent, rank based on 2004 dollar values.)

Product and market	2001	2002	2003	2004	Percent share of total, 2004	Average annual percent change, 2001–2004
Total Goods						
Total	2 661	2 444	2 660	3 178	100.0	6.1
Manufactures	2 544	2 323	2 543	3 002	94.5	5.7
Agriculture and livestock	60	52	65	113	3.6	23.6
Other commodities	57	68	52	62	2.0	3.0
Five Leading Exports (NAICS Code)						
Machinery manufactures (333)	775	656	846	990	31.2	8.5
Transportation equipment (336)	495	499	467	518	16.3	1.6
Computers and electronic products (334)	219	202	202	249	7.8	4.3
Fabricated metal products (332)	186	150	172	244	7.7	9.5
Plastic and rubber products (326)	197	224	240	229	7.2	5.1
Five Leading Markets	2 266	2 084	2 321	2 798	88.0	7.3
Canada	917	926	1 054	1 154	36.3	8.0
Mexico	196	200	221	330	10.4	18.9
Japan	206	150	146	172	5.4	-5.8
Russia	72	51	85	140	4.4	25.0
United Kingdom	143	107	79	95	3.0	-12.7

Table OK-14. Agriculture, 1997 and 2002

(Number, acres, and dollars.)

Item	1997	2002
Number of farms	84 028	83 300
Land in farms (acres)	34 069 201	33 661 826
Farm Size		
Average size of farm (acres)	405	404
Farms by size (percent distribution)		
Fewer than 50 acres	23.2	24.2
50 to 499 acres	57.8	57.8
500 acres or more	19.0	18.0
Market Value of Land and Equipment (Dollars)		
Land and buildings average value per farm	257 665	285 730
Average value per acre	628	699
Machinery and equipment average value per farm	35 893	42 155
Value of Sales (Thousands of Dollars)		
Agricultural products sold	4 253 753	4 456 404
Crops	951 705	819 078
Livestock, poultry, and their products	3 302 048	3 637 326
Average per farm (dollars)	50 623	53 498
Value of sales (percent distribution)		
Less than $10,000	63.5	62.8
$10,000 to $99,999	28.8	29.5
$100,000 or more	7.6	7.7
Government Payments		
Payments (thousands of dollars)	135 546	149 942
Percent of farms receiving government payments	29.5	29.2
Farm operators whose principal occupation is farming (percent)	42.4	55.3

AGRICULTURE

Cash receipts from farming totaled over $4.4 billion in 2002, according to the Department of Agriculture's Census of Agriculture. This was a 7.5 percent increase from the previous farm census in 1997. Cattle were the dominant farm product. More than 92 percent of farms had sales of less than $100,000, with nearly 63 percent of all farms having receipts under $10,000. About 55 percent of all farm operators reported farming as their principal occupation. Less than one-fourth of all the state's farms spanned fewer than 50 acres.

ENERGY

Although energy prices in Oklahoma were slightly below the national average, expenditures per person were the sixth highest in the nation in 2001. The state's per capita consumption of 444 Btu was the eighth highest in the country. The industrial and transportation sectors combined accounted for over 65 percent of the state's energy consumption. The chief energy sources were petroleum, natural gas, and coal.

Energy Consumption by Source, 2001

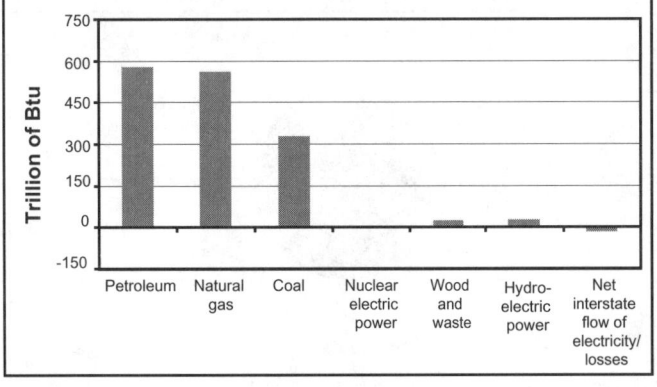

Energy Consumption by Sector, 2001

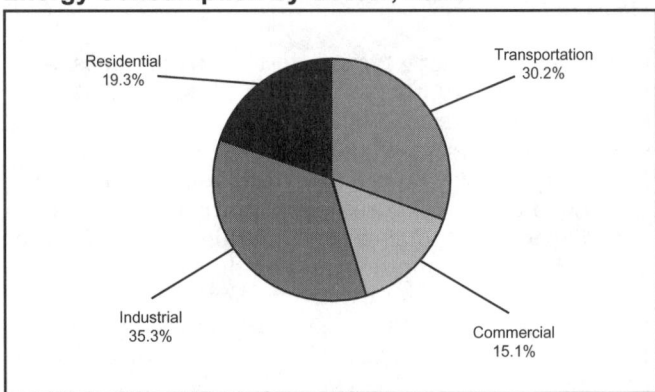

Table OK-15. Energy Consumption, Expenditures, and Prices, Selected Years 1960–2001

(Dollars, Btu [British Thermal Unit], percent distribution.)

Item	1960	1965	1970	1975	1980	1985	1990	1995	2000	2001
Total Consumption (Billion Btu)	582 091	776 169	939 598	1 070 091	1 221 669	1 299 151	1 392 647	1 377 576	1 468 580	1 539 471
Consumption per capita (million Btu)	250.0	318.1	367.1	385.7	403.8	397.1	442.7	421.9	425.6	444.0
Consumption by Sector (Percent Distribution)										
Residential	19.9	18.0	20.6	20.1	19.3	19.5	19.5	19.1	20.4	19.3
Commercial	10.3	9.1	11.2	12.2	12.9	14.0	14.3	14.0	15.4	15.1
Industrial	43.9	49.5	42.5	41.8	42.6	40.4	41.7	40.7	35.2	35.3
Transportation	25.9	23.4	25.7	26.0	25.2	26.2	24.4	26.2	29.0	30.2
Consumption by Source (Billion Btu)										
Coal	1 826	697	154	537	106 346	237 168	278 813	369 887	381 081	376 764
Natural gas	319 270	480 079	616 279	678 851	738 931	603 855	628 223	586 433	546 705	548 395
Petroleum	255 861	296 184	365 468	421 235	443 156	458 652	432 045	438 024	518 364	588 433
Nuclear electric power	0	0	0	0	0	0	0	0	0	0
Hydroelectric power[1]	7 582	8 622	14 751	30 646	13 655	41 579	28 609	28 000	21 929	22 548
Wood and waste	10 185	7 607	6 979	11 997	17 333	14 868	23 837	25 223	17 499	17 204
Other	0	0	0	0	0	0	92	90	69	63
Net interstate flow of electricity/losses[2]	-12 632	-17 020	-64 032	-73 175	-97 752	-56 972	1 028	-70 081	-17 067	-13 936
Total Expenditures (Thousands of Dollars)	...	...	1 051 400	2 030 000	5 016 600	6 546 100	6 196 900	6 291 600	9 269 500	10 180 700
Expenditures per capita (dollars)	...	...	411	732	1 658	2 001	1 970	1 927	2 686	2 936
Prices by Sector (Dollars Per Million Btu)										
Total	...	...	1.85	3.08	6.47	7.74	7.31	7.14	9.90	10.24
Residential	...	...	2.22	3.16	6.33	10.01	11.22	11.60	13.71	15.23
Commercial	...	...	1.68	2.96	6.11	10.68	10.53	10.65	12.53	13.67
Industrial	...	...	0.77	1.72	3.92	5.31	3.54	3.77	6.59	7.75
Transportation	...	...	2.44	4.11	9.12	8.27	8.45	7.78	10.19	9.51

[1]A negative number in this row results from pumped storage for which, overall, more electricity is expended than created to provide electricity during peak demand periods.
[2]Net interstate flow of electricity is the difference between the amount of energy in the electricity sold within a state (including associated losses) and the energy input at the electric utilities within the state. A positive number indicates that more electricity (including associated losses) came into the state than went out of the state during the year; conversely, a negative number indicates that more electricity (including associated losses) went out of the state than came into the state.
... = Not available.

Table OK-16. State Taxes, Fiscal 2004

(Dollars, percent distribution.)

Item	Thousands of dollars	Percent distribution	Dollars per capita	
			State	U.S.
TOTAL TAXES	6 426 713	100.0	1 823.7	2 024.8
Property Taxes	X	X	X	38.9
Sales and Gross Receipts	2 339 028	36.4	663.7	1 003.4
General sales and gross receipts	1 594 246	24.8	452.4	677.0
Selective sales taxes	744 782	11.6	211.4	326.4
Alcoholic beverages	68 420	1.1	19.4	15.7
Insurance premiums	144 186	2.2	40.9	47.0
Motor fuels	415 318	6.5	117.8	114.6
Tobacco products	63 398	1.0	18.0	42.0
Licenses	840 421	13.1	238.5	134.9
Corporation	41 960	0.7	11.9	21.6
Motor vehicle	552 799	8.6	156.9	59.4
Occupation and business, not elsewhere classified	199 713	3.1	56.7	37.1
Other Taxes	3 247 264	50.5	921.5	847.6
Individual income	2 319 123	36.1	658.1	673.6
Corporation net income	133 309	2.1	37.8	105.1
Death and gift	111 143	1.7	31.5	19.6
Severance	655 051	10.2	185.9	21.5

X = Not applicable.

GOVERNMENT FINANCE

State revenue and expenditures per person were below the national average in 2003, ranking 33rd and 31st, respectively. Outlays per capita for education and highways were above average, while spending on public welfare, health, and hospitals was below average. Oklahoma's per capita taxes were also below the U.S. average in fiscal year 2004, ranking 33rd in the nation. The largest sources of revenue were general sales taxes, individual income taxes, severance (taxes on the removal of natural resources such as oil and minerals), and motor fuel taxes. The state's individual income taxes were slightly below average, ranking 25th among the 43 states with such taxes.

Per Capita State Taxes, Fiscal 2004

Table OK-17. State Government Finances, 2003

(Dollars, percent distribution.)

Item	Millions of dollars	Percent distribution	Dollars per capita	
			State	U.S.
GENERAL REVENUE	12 903 184	100.0	3 680.3	3 832.6
Intergovernmental revenue	4 255 172	33.0	1 213.7	1 246.0
Taxes	5 905 884	45.8	1 684.5	1 891.6
General sales	1 480 137	11.5	422.2	636.0
Selective sales	758 680	5.9	216.4	307.4
License taxes	785 044	6.1	223.9	123.6
Individual income tax	2 113 947	16.4	603.0	626.8
Corporate income tax	104 448	0.8	29.8	97.8
Other taxes	663 628	5.1	189.3	99.9
Current charges	1 747 861	13.5	498.5	366.5
Miscellaneous general revenue	994 267	7.7	283.6	328.6
GENERAL EXPENDITURE	13 305 832	100.0	3 795.2	4 010.5
Intergovernmental expenditure	3 395 494	25.5	968.5	1 316.9
Direct expenditure	9 910 338	74.5	2 826.7	2 693.6
Expenditure by Function				
Education	5 564 983	41.8	1 587.3	1 416.4
Public welfare	3 177 322	23.9	906.2	1 083.3
Hospitals	181 208	1.4	51.7	132.3
Health	460 187	3.5	131.3	173.0
Highways	1 283 363	9.6	366.0	295.4
Police protection	92 508	0.7	26.4	38.4
Correction	486 313	3.7	138.7	135.0
Natural resources	212 083	1.6	60.5	64.0
Parks and recreation	78 259	0.6	22.3	20.1
Government administration	572 182	4.3	163.2	151.3
Interest on general debt	286 842	2.2	81.8	107.8
Other and unallocable	910 582	6.8	259.7	393.4
DEBT AT END OF FISCAL YEAR	6 747 020	X	1 924.4	2 404.7
CASH AND SECURITY HOLDINGS	24 653 738	X	7 031.9	8 938.4

X = Not applicable.

Table OK-18. Education Indicators, 2000–2004

(Percent, number.)

Item	State	U.S.
Total Population 25 Years and Over (Thousands), 2004	2 164	186 877
Educational Attainment, 2004		
Percent high school graduate or more	85.2	85.2
Percent college graduate or more	22.9	27.7
Elementary and Secondary Schools, 2002–2003		
Total students	624 548	48 202 324
Percent of students eligible for free or reduced-price lunch ..	53.0	40.6
Percent of students who were English language learners	6.4	7.8
Total schools	1 806	92 330
Student/teacher ratio	16.0	15.9
Per student expenditures	6 092	8 041
Dropouts, Grades 9–12, 2000–2001 (Percent)	4.4	. . .
Higher Education, 2002–2003		
Total enrollment	210 375	17 035 027
Bachelor's degrees awarded	16 348	1 348 503
Percent women	56.1	57.5

. . . = Not available.

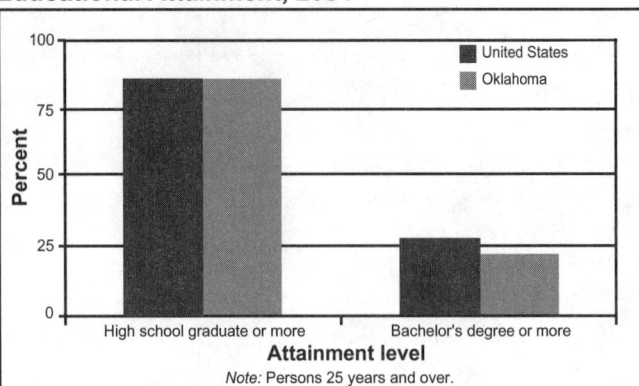

Educational Attainment, 2004

Note: Persons 25 years and over.

EDUCATION

The proportion of Oklahoma residents age 25 years and over holding high school diplomas was identical to the national average in 2004; however, the state's proportion of college graduates—just 22.9 percent—was well below the national average. Despite having a below average proportion of school-age population, Oklahoma's student/teacher ratio was just above the national average. Expenditures per student of $6,092 ranked 48th in the nation. Oklahoma's dropout rate of 4.4 percent ranked 16th among the 46 states reporting such data. More than half of all students in the state were eligible for free or reduced-price lunch.

VOTER PARTICIPATION

Voter turnout rose less than 1 percentage point from 2000 to 2004, compared to the national increase of close to 4 percentage points. However, Oklahoma's voter participation rate remained above the national average. Less than 19 percent of eligible Hispanics in Oklahoma voted in 2004. More than 77 percent of eligible residents age 65 to 74 years cast ballots. Voter turnout was well above average in 2000 and slightly above average in 2004. According to the official tally by the Clerk of the U.S. House of Representatives, Oklahoma's residents overwhelmingly favored the Republican presidential candi-

Table OK-19. Reported Voting and Registration, November 2000 and November 2004

(Numbers in thousands, percent.)

Characteristic	Total population 18 years and over	Total citizen		Total registered		Total voted	
		Number	Percent	Number	Percent	Number	Percent
NOVEMBER 2000							
Total	2 457	2 400	97.7	1 679	68.3	1 431	58.3
Male	1 155	1 124	97.3	761	65.9	653	56.5
Female	1 302	1 276	98.0	918	70.5	778	59.8
NOVEMBER 2004							
Total	2 602	2 476	95.2	1 781	68.4	1 541	59.2
Male	1 247	1 184	94.9	844	67.7	724	58.0
Female	1 355	1 292	95.4	937	69.2	818	60.3
Race and Hispanic Origin							
White alone	2 031	1 946	95.8	1 450	71.4	1 271	62.6
Non-Hispanic White alone	1 925	1 902	98.8	1 423	73.9	1 248	64.8
Black alone	190	183	96.0	118	61.8	104	54.7
Asian alone	34	17	B	10	B	5	B
Hispanic or Latino[1]	135	57	42.6	29	21.7	25	18.9
White alone or in combination	2 232	2 131	95.5	1 573	70.4	1 366	61.2
Non-Hispanic White alone or in combination	2 102	2 078	98.9	1 543	73.4	1 341	63.8
Black alone or in combination	204	196	96.2	123	60.3	110	53.7
Asian alone or in combination	36	19	B	10	B	5	B
Age							
18 to 24 years	376	344	91.4	173	46.1	149	39.5
25 to 44 years	932	853	91.5	554	59.4	439	47.1
45 to 64 years	879	875	99.6	703	79.9	650	74.0
65 to 74 years	205	200	97.5	177	86.5	158	77.2
75 years and over	209	204	97.6	174	83.0	145	69.5

[1]May be of any race.
B = Base is too small to show derived measure.

At a Glance:

- Oregon's population was close to 3.6 million in 2004, ranking it as the 27th most populous state in the nation.

- Non-Hispanic Whites accounted for 82 percent of the population, followed by Hispanics (of any race), who made up 9.5 percent of the population.

- More than 16 percent of the state's residents lacked health insurance, which was the 14th highest proportion of uninsured population in the country.

- The state's median household income of $41,484 was below the national average. However, Oregon's poverty rate of 11.7 percent was also below average.

- Oregon's unemployment rate of 7.4 percent was the third highest in the country. Only the District of Columbia and Alaska had higher unemployment rates.

- Average wages and salaries grew just 7.6 percent from 2001 to 2004, which was among the 5 lowest growth rates in the nation.

- More than 70 percent of the state's eligible residents voted in the 2004 election, the fifth highest participation rate in the nation.

Table OR-1. Population by Sex and Age, 1990, 2000, and 2004

(Number, percent.)

Sex and age	1990	2000	2004	Percent distribution, 2004	Average annual percent change, 2000–2004
Total Population	2 842 321	3 421 399	3 594 586	X	1.2
Percent of total U.S. population	1.1	1.2	1.2	X	X
Sex					
Male	1 397 073	1 696 550	1 786 769	49.7	1.3
Female	1 445 248	1 724 849	1 807 817	50.3	1.2
Age					
Under 5 years	201 421	223 005	226 069	6.3	0.7
5 to 17 years	522 709	623 521	626 288	17.4	1.3
18 years and over	532 944	2 574 873	2 742 229	76.3	1.9
18 to 24 years	2 118 191	327 884	350 458	9.7	1.9
25 to 44 years	267 528	997 269	1 016 650	28.3	0.7
45 to 64 years	926 395	811 543	915 300	25.5	4.0
65 years and over	391 324	438 177	459 821	12.8	1.2
85 years and over	38 815	57 431	69 898	1.9	4.4
Median age (years)	34.5	36.3	36.8	X	X

X = Not applicable.

Average Annual Rate of Population Growth, 1980–2004

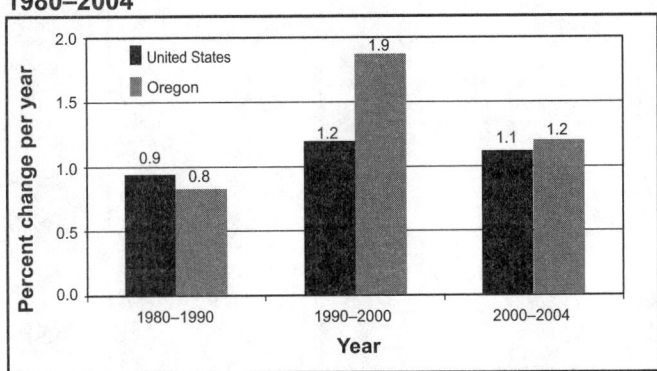

POPULATION

Oregon's population grew 5.1 percent from 2000 to 2004, which was the 15th highest rate of growth in the nation. The state benefited from substantial immigration during this period. From 2001 to 2004, Oregon gained more than 61,000 new residents from abroad and nearly 53,000 people from other states. This influx of new residents accounted for two-thirds of the state's population increase, as Oregon's birth rate was well below the national average. Just 23.7 percent of the state's population was 18 years old and under, which was well below the national proportion of 25 percent.

Table OR-2. Population by Race and Hispanic Origin, 1990, 2000, and 2004

(Number, percent.)

Race and Hispanic origin	1990	2000	2004
Total Population	2 842 321	3 421 399	3 594 586
Non-Hispanic (Percent)			
One race[1]			
White	90.8	83.9	82.0
Black	1.6	1.6	1.6
American Indian, Alaska Native[2]	1.4	1.2	1.1
Asian and Pacific Islander[2]	2.4	3.2	3.6
Other race[2]	1.8	. . .	. . .
Two or more races	. . .	2.0	2.1
Hispanic or Latino[3] (Percent)	4.0	8.0	9.5

[1]Individuals could report only one race in the 1990 census and could report one or more races on the 2000 census. Data on race in 2000 and 2004 are not comparable to 1990.
[2]Data for 1990 include people of Hispanic or Latino origin.
[3]May be of any race.
. . . = Not available.

Minority Population as a Percent of Total Population, 2004

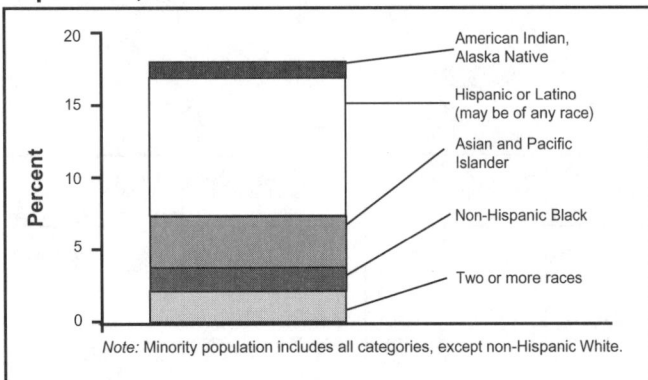

Note: Minority population includes all categories, except non-Hispanic White.

Age-Adjusted Death Rates, Average 2000–2002

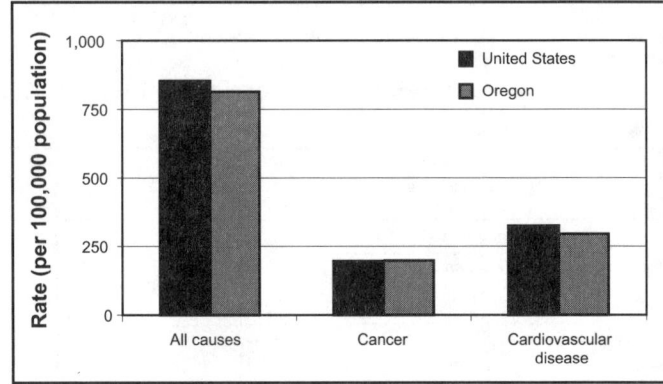

HEALTH

Oregon's infant mortality rate was below average, ranking among the 10 lowest in the country. The age-adjusted death rates for most causes were slightly lower than the national averages. The state's overall birth rate and birth rate for teenage mothers were both well below average.

Table OR-3. Health Characteristics, 2000–2004

(Number, rate, percent.)

Item	State	U.S.
Births, 2003–2004		
Number of births	45 953	4 089 950
Birth rate (per 1,000 population)	12.9	14.1
Teenage birth rate (per 1,000 women age 15–19 years)	34.4	41.6
Mortality Rates, Average 2000–2002		
Infant mortality rate (per 1,000 live births)	5.5	6.9
Age-adjusted mortality rate (per 100,000 population)		
All races	828.8	853.3
Non-Hispanic White	837.8	843.1
Black	1 038.2	1 097.7
American Indian, Alaska Native	. . .	687.0
Asian and Pacific Islander	504.3	486.0
Hispanic or Latino[1]	496.0	642.7
Health Insurance, 2004		
Percent of all persons without health insurance	16.5	15.7
Percent of children without health insurance	10.0	11.2
Percent of low-income children without health insurance	6.1	7.1

[1]May be of any race.
. . . = Not available.

Table OR-4. Leading Causes of Death, Average 2000–2002

(Number, rate per 100,000 population.)

Cause	Number of deaths	Age-adjusted death rates State	Age-adjusted death rates U.S.
ALL CAUSES	30 276	828.8	853.3
Leading Causes			
Major cardiovascular diseases	10 623	287.2	326.5
Cancer	7 086	196.9	196.0
Chronic lower respiratory diseases	1 749	48.4	43.7
Unintentional injuries	1 319	36.9	35.7
Diabetes (underlying cause)	965	26.6	25.2
Influenza and pneumonia	628	16.7	22.7
Alzheimer's disease	1 021	27.0	19.0
Motor vehicle accidents	459	13.1	15.0
Nephritis, nephrotic syndrome, and nephrosis ..	297	8.1	13.8
Septicemia	184	5.0	11.4
Suicides	505	14.3	10.7
Firearm-related	370	10.5	10.3
Cirrhosis	334	9.3	9.5
Drug-induced	345	9.8	7.9
Alcohol-induced	370	10.3	6.9
Homicides	99	2.9	6.0
Falls	245	6.6	5.2
HIV	71	2.1	5.0
Viral hepatitis	98	2.7	2.0
Anemias	52	1.4	1.6
Drownings	68	2.0	1.3
Fire deaths	36	1.0	1.2

Note: The rates are age-adjusted to the U.S. 2000 standard population.

Table OR-5. Households and Housing Characteristics, 1990, 2000, and 2004

(Number, percent, and dollars.)

Characteristic	1990	2000	2004	Average annual percent change, 2000–2004
Total Households	1 103 313	1 333 723	1 427 711	1.7
Family households	750 844	877 671	919 188	1.2
Married-couple family	613 297	692 532	709 458	0.6
Other family	137 547	185 139	209 730	3.2
Male householder, no wife present	35 785	54 357	62 871	3.7
Female householder, no husband present	101 762	130 782	146 859	2.9
Nonfamily households	352 469	456 052	508 523	2.8
Householder living alone	278 716	347 624	393 655	3.2
Householder not living alone	73 753	108 428	114 868	1.5
Housing Characteristics				
Average size	2.52	2.51	2.46	X
Housing units	1 193 567	1 452 709	1 535 381	1.4
Occupied housing units	1 103 313	1 333 723	1 427 711	1.7
Owner-occupied	695 957	856 951	899 196	1.2
Renter-occupied	407 356	476 772	528 515	2.6
Median gross rent of renter-occupied housing units (dollars) ...	408	620	681	2.4
Median value of owner-occupied housing units (dollars)	66 800	152 100	181 544	4.5

X = Not applicable.

Median Housing Value and Median Rent, 2004

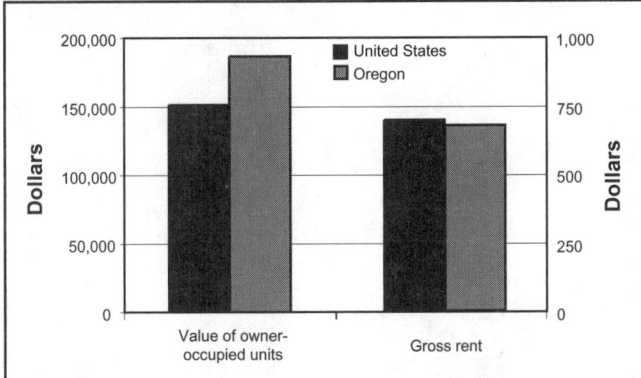

Median Household Income, 1984–2004 (2004 Dollars)

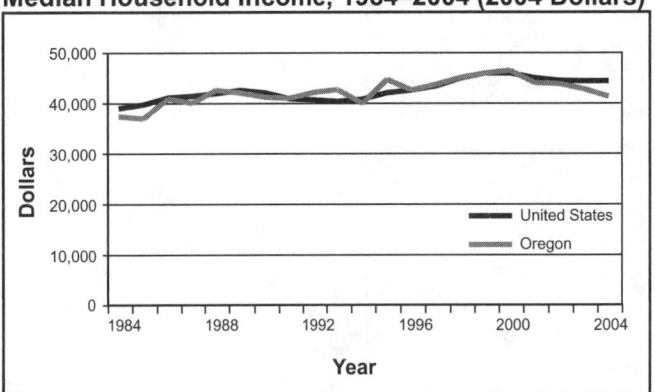

Table OR-6. Household Income and Poverty Status, 1980–2004

(2004 CPI-U-RS adjusted dollars, rate.)

Year	State		U.S.	
	Median household income (2004 dollars)	Poverty rate	Median household income (2004 dollars)	Poverty rate
2004	41 184	11.7	44 389	12.7
2003	42 757	12.5	44 482	12.5
2002	43 909	10.9	44 546	12.1
2001	44 043	11.8	45 062	11.7
2000	46 617	10.9	46 058	11.3
1999	46 042	12.6	46 129	11.9
1998	45 214	15.0	45 003	12.7
1997	43 714	11.6	43 430	13.3
1996	42 544	11.8	42 544	13.7
1995	44 772	11.2	41 943	13.8
1994	39 659	11.8	40 677	14.5
1993	42 659	11.8	40 217	15.1
1992	42 125	11.4	40 422	14.8
1991	40 832	13.5	40 746	14.2
1990	41 035	9.2	41 963	13.5
1989	41 970	11.2	42 524	12.8
1988	42 574	10.4	41 771	13.0
1987	39 815	14.2	41 322	13.4
1986	40 736	12.3	40 939	13.6
1985	36 659	11.9	39 545	14.0
1984	37 024	12.8	38 782	14.4
1983	. . .	16.1	. . .	15.2
1982	. . .	13.9	. . .	15.0
1981	. . .	12.3	. . .	14.0
1980	. . .	11.5	. . .	13.0

. . . = Not available.

Table OR-7. Employment Status by Demographic Group, 2004

(Numbers in thousands, rate.)

Characteristic	Civilian noninstitutional population	Civilian labor force		Employed	Unemployment rate
		Number	Participation rate		
SEX AND AGE					
Total	2 800	1 850	66.1	1 710	7.6
16 to 19 years	176	78	44.1	60	22.3
20 to 24 years	216	163	75.3	139	14.8
25 to 34 years	520	441	84.8	410	7.0
35 to 44 years	534	444	83.2	417	6.2
45 to 54 years	498	406	81.6	385	5.3
55 to 64 years	415	261	62.8	245	5.9
65 years and over	440	57	12.9	54	5.7
Men	1 375	1 010	73.5	930	8.0
16 to 19 years	90	39	43.7	31	21.8
20 to 24 years	116	94	81.1	79	15.9
25 to 34 years	259	239	92.5	223	6.8
35 to 44 years	269	249	92.7	232	6.8
45 to 54 years	248	217	87.3	204	5.8
55 to 64 years	202	141	69.9	132	6.5
65 years and over	191	30	15.6	28	6.1
Women	1 425	840	59.0	780	7.1
16 to 19 years	86	38	44.4	29	23.0
20 to 24 years	100	68	68.7	59	13.2
25 to 34 years	261	202	77.3	187	7.3
35 to 44 years	266	195	73.5	184	5.5
45 to 54 years	250	190	76.0	181	4.8
55 to 64 years	213	120	56.1	113	5.1
65 years and over	250	27	10.9	26	5.3
MARITAL STATUS					
Married men, spouse present	774	588	76.0	561	4.6
Married women, spouse present	770	466	60.4	449	3.7
Women who maintain families	149	100	67.3	85	14.7
RACE, HISPANIC ORIGIN, AND SEX					
White	2 545	1 678	65.9	1 554	7.4
Men	1 242	910	73.3	841	7.6
Women	1 303	768	58.9	713	7.1
Black	46	32	69.1	28	11.6
Asian	92	65	70.2	60	7.4
Men	46	37	79.5	33	9.7
Women	46	28	61.0	27	4.4
Hispanic or Latino[1]	224	176	78.6	158	9.8
Men	125	113	90.1	103	8.4
Women	98	63	63.9	55	12.2
RACE, HISPANIC ORIGIN, AND AGE					
White					
16 to 19 years	154	70	45.5	55	21.7
20 to 24 years	198	150	76.0	129	14.3
25 to 34 years	455	387	85.0	361	6.8
35 to 44 years	474	396	83.6	372	6.2
45 to 54 years	463	378	81.7	358	5.3
55 to 64 years	386	243	62.9	229	5.8
65 years and over	416	54	12.9	51	4.2

Note: Data in Table 7 are from the Current Population Survey (CPS) and do not match Bureau of Labor Statistics estimates in Table 8. See notes and definitions for more details.

[1]May be of any race.

Table OR-8. Employment Status, 1990–2004

(Numbers in thousands, rate.)

Year	Civilian labor force	Employed	Unemployed	Unemployment rate
2004	1 856 237	1 718 504	137 733	7.4
2003	1 852 147	1 701 577	150 570	8.1
2002	1 839 129	1 699 742	139 387	7.6
2001	1 826 472	1 708 957	117 515	6.4
2000	1 815 065	1 721 365	93 700	5.2
1999	1 795 724	1 697 288	98 436	5.5
1998	1 779 423	1 678 407	101 016	5.7
1997	1 750 818	1 652 997	97 821	5.6
1996	1 715 236	1 618 571	96 665	5.6
1995	1 664 941	1 583 153	81 788	4.9
1994	1 636 048	1 546 552	89 496	5.5
1993	1 600 756	1 489 808	110 948	6.9
1992	1 562 363	1 448 017	114 346	7.3
1991	1 522 025	1 425 231	96 794	6.4
1990	1 506 240	1 424 864	81 376	5.4

Note: Population age 16 years and over.

Unemployment Rate, 1980–2004

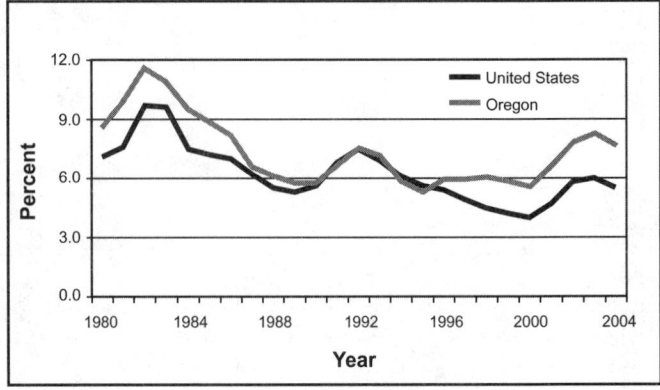

Table OR-9. Employment and Average Wages by Industry, 2001–2004

(Estimates are based on the 2002 North American Industry Classification System [NAICS].)

Industry	2001	2002	2003	2004	Annual average percent change, 2001–2004
	Number of jobs				
TOTAL EMPLOYMENT BY PLACE OF WORK	2 103 668	2 092 319	2 095 882	2 136 952	0.5
Farm Employment	66 948	67 531	66 519	63 050	-2.0
Nonfarm Employment	2 036 720	2 024 788	2 029 363	2 073 902	0.6
Private employment	1 758 538	1 745 528	1 751 500	1 795 070	0.7
Forestry, fishing, hunting, and other[1]	36 095	38 618	37 585	35 279	-0.8
Mining	3 484	3 134	3 438	3 628	1.4
Utilities	5 587	5 386	5 403	5 491	-0.6
Construction	120 021	116 357	115 963	122 093	0.6
Manufacturing	227 751	213 710	206 809	211 986	-2.4
Durable goods manufacturing	169 436	156 887	150 966	155 804	-2.8
Nondurable goods manufacturing	58 315	56 823	55 843	56 182	-1.2
Wholesale trade	81 667	80 747	81 644	82 859	0.5
Retail trade	238 102	235 369	234 949	240 648	0.4
Transportation and warehousing	63 040	62 747	62 016	63 099	0.0
Information	45 714	41 384	39 793	38 939	-5.2
Finance and insurance	80 932	81 430	82 876	82 004	0.4
Real estate and rental and leasing	79 614	78 147	81 422	84 690	2.1
Professional and technical services	116 567	114 620	114 861	117 983	0.4
Management of companies and enterprises	27 600	26 426	26 061	26 990	-0.7
Administrative and waste services	107 423	109 504	110 331	116 751	2.8
Educational services	35 094	37 169	38 841	40 514	4.9
Health care and social assistance	197 938	204 108	208 254	213 159	2.5
Arts, entertainment, and recreation	42 080	43 485	44 445	45 831	2.9
Accommodation and food services	140 640	141 053	143 443	147 228	1.5
Other services, except public administration	109 189	112 134	113 366	115 898	2.0
Government and government enterprises	278 182	279 260	277 863	278 832	0.1
	Dollars				
AVERAGE WAGES AND SALARIES BY PLACE OF WORK	32 590	32 988	33 743	35 000	2.4
Farm Earnings	22 650	20 891	21 226	23 504	1.2
Nonfarm Earnings	32 755	33 191	33 953	35 166	2.4
Private earnings	32 660	32 937	33 697	34 934	2.3
Forestry, fishing, hunting, and other[1]	25 755	27 754	27 214	27 551	2.3
Mining	36 376	38 467	40 097	40 733	3.8
Utilities	60 118	64 271	64 155	67 375	3.9
Construction	39 509	39 488	38 398	38 632	-0.7
Manufacturing	43 959	43 509	44 969	46 818	2.1
Durable goods manufacturing	47 186	46 530	48 241	50 402	2.2
Nondurable goods manufacturing	34 414	34 996	35 967	36 691	2.2
Wholesale trade	47 017	48 374	50 026	53 799	4.6
Retail trade	22 393	23 039	23 331	24 044	2.4
Transportation and warehousing	34 041	34 407	34 904	36 468	2.3
Information	47 454	47 020	50 346	54 155	4.5
Finance and insurance	46 337	48 112	51 265	52 018	3.9
Real estate and rental and leasing	25 499	25 831	26 663	27 872	3.0
Professional and technical services	47 325	47 045	47 951	49 627	1.6
Management of companies and enterprises	59 506	59 695	61 660	64 851	2.9
Administrative and waste services	22 352	23 570	23 817	23 702	2.0
Educational services	19 259	19 567	20 350	21 304	3.4
Health care and social assistance	31 802	33 033	34 245	35 923	4.1
Arts, entertainment, and recreation	21 749	22 777	21 361	21 221	-0.8
Accommodation and food services	13 315	13 697	14 121	14 577	3.1
Other services, except public administration	21 025	21 080	21 734	22 575	2.4
Government and government enterprises	33 230	34 439	35 215	36 327	3.0

Note: Average wages and salaries are a calculation by the editors of wage and salary disbursements divided by full- and part-time wage and salary employment. Data may not add to total or may appear as zero due to rounding.

[1] "Other" consists of the number of jobs held by U.S. residents employed by international organizations and foreign embassies and consulates in the United States.

LABOR MARKET

Oregon's unemployment rate has been significantly higher than average since the mid-1990s, and was the third highest in the nation in 2004. Employment fell between 2001 and 2002, and its recovery was slow in subsequent years. Manufacturing employment declined significantly throughout the period; in 2004, it was still below its 2001 level. Job gains in health care, educational services, and administrative and waste services helped give the state a net employment increase during this period. Average wages and salaries were below the U.S. average and had one of the lowest rates of growth in the nation from 2001 to 2004.

Employment by Industry, 2004

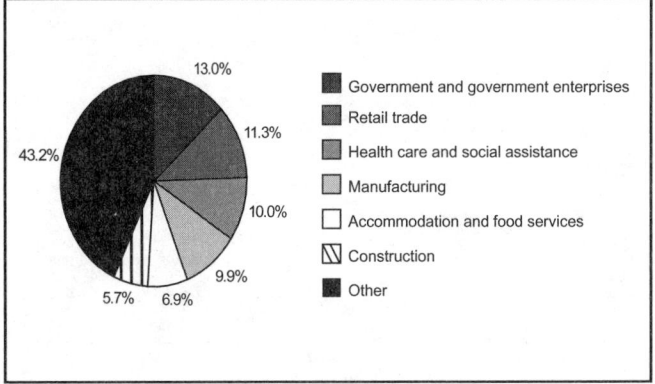

- 13.0%
- 11.3%
- 43.2%
- 10.0%
- 9.9%
- 5.7%
- 6.9%

- Government and government enterprises
- Retail trade
- Health care and social assistance
- Manufacturing
- Accommodation and food services
- Construction
- Other

Table OR-10. Personal Income by Major Source, Selected Years 1980–2004

(Millions of dollars, except where noted.)

Item	1980	1990	2000	2001	2002	2003	2004	Average annual percent change, 2000–2004
Earnings by Place of Work	20 919	38 501	74 105	75 572	77 913	80 111	85 555	3.7
Wage and salary disbursements	15 407	27 694	54 803	55 239	55 320	56 362	59 334	2.0
Supplements to wages and salaries	3 060	6 221	11 671	12 147	14 586	15 533	17 050	9.9
Proprietors' income[1]	2 453	4 586	7 631	8 186	8 006	8 215	9 171	4.7
Farm proprietors' income	277	335	119	24	99	268	505	43.5
Nonfarm proprietors' income	2 176	4 251	7 512	8 162	7 908	7 947	8 665	3.6
(-) Contributions for government social insurance[2]	2 125	4 615	9 090	9 158	9 321	9 642	10 272	3.1
(+) Adjustment for residence[3]	-253	-608	-1 904	-1 891	-1 913	-1 904	-2 039	X
(=) **Net Earnings by Place of Residence**	18 541	33 278	63 111	64 523	66 679	68 565	73 244	3.8
(+) Dividends, interest, and rent[4]	4 920	11 646	20 303	19 999	19 502	19 343	20 101	-0.3
(+) Personal current transfer receipts	3 248	6 591	12 988	14 498	15 721	16 080	16 591	6.3
Personal income	26 710	51 515	96 402	99 020	101 902	103 988	109 935	3.3
Farm income	26 245	50 849	95 618	98 322	101 181	103 091	108 825	3.3
Nonfarm income	465	666	783	698	721	897	1 110	9.1
Per Capita Personal Income (Dollars)[5]	10 113	18 010	28 097	28 502	28 922	29 175	30 584	2.1

Note: Data may not add to total or may appear as zero due to rounding.

[1]Proprietors' income includes the inventory valuation adjustment and the capital consumption adjustment.
[2]Contributions for government social insurance are included in earnings by type and industry, but they are excluded from personal income.
[3]The adjustment for residence is the net inflow of the earnings of interarea commuters.
[4]Rental income of persons includes the capital consumption adjustment.
[5]Per capita personal income is total personal income divided by total midyear population.
X = Not applicable.

Per Capita Personal Income, 1980–2004 (Current Dollars)

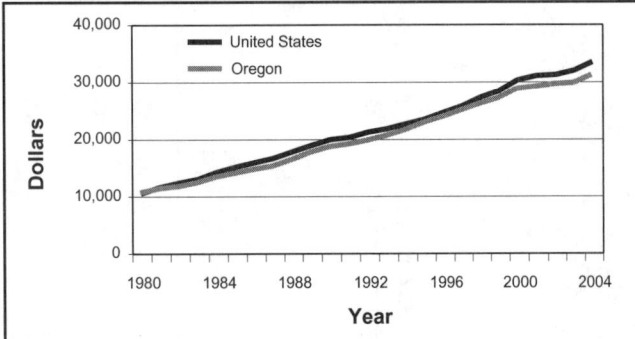

ECONOMIC ACTIVITY

Oregon's economy experienced a sharp decline during the 2001 recession, although the subsequent growth of its real gross state product (GSP) was slightly higher than the national average. From 2003 to 2004, the GSP grew by 4.5 percent, the 20th fastest rate in the country. Contributors to this increase were manufacturing, wholesale and retail trade, government, and real estate and related activities. Housing prices have increased at a rate close to the national average in recent years. In 2004, the median value of owner-occupied housing in Oregon was well above the national average, ranking 14th in the country.

Table OR-11. Real Gross State Product, 1997–2004

(Millions of chained 2000 dollars, percent.)

Industry	1997	1998	1999	2000	2001	2002	2003	2004	Average annual percent change, 2001–2004
GROSS STATE PRODUCT	95 568	101 072	104 715	112 964	110 925	112 943	116 113	121 385	3.0
As a percent of U.S. gross product	1.1	1.1	1.1	1.2	1.1	1.1	1.1	1.1	X
Private Industries	82 474	87 802	90 698	99 265	96 816	98 789	102 326	107 288	3.5
Agriculture, forestry, fishing, and hunting	2 620	2 556	2 811	3 098	2 824	3 202	3 253	3 074	2.9
Mining	89	105	120	122	112	113	115	110	-0.6
Utilities	1 433	1 434	1 452	1 711	1 682	1 764	1 859	1 977	5.5
Construction	6 470	6 143	5 874	5 744	5 282	5 007	4 798	4 943	-2.2
Manufacturing	12 693	15 407	15 783	21 848	18 702	18 924	21 433	23 828	8.4
As a percent of gross state product	13.3	15.2	15.1	19.3	16.9	16.8	18.5	19.6	X
Wholesale trade	7 014	7 590	7 680	7 610	7 949	8 148	8 073	8 553	2.5
Retail trade	6 110	6 350	6 700	6 787	7 153	7 554	7 853	8 388	5.5
Transportation and warehousing	3 176	3 217	3 315	3 367	3 127	3 250	3 355	3 480	3.6
Information	2 704	2 812	3 404	3 830	3 847	3 760	4 017	4 495	5.3
Finance and insurance	4 432	5 151	5 041	5 240	5 588	6 129	6 473	6 418	4.7
Real estate and rental and leasing	13 771	14 061	14 714	15 249	15 680	15 595	15 632	15 961	0.6
Services	23 234	23 412	24 205	24 658	24 725	25 218	25 756	26 757	2.7
As a percent of gross state product	24.3	23.2	23.1	21.8	22.3	22.3	22.2	22.0	X
Professional and technical services	4 795	4 982	5 268	5 696	5 702	5 561	5 683	5 900	1.1
Management of companies and enterprises	2 723	2 483	2 500	2 439	2 282	2 270	2 336	2 404	1.8
Administrative and waste services	2 983	2 968	2 995	2 873	2 738	2 981	3 060	3 140	4.7
Educational services	631	654	674	673	640	634	623	628	-0.6
Health care and social assistance	6 442	6 550	6 845	7 131	7 479	7 866	8 102	8 397	3.9
Arts, entertainment, and recreation	672	656	707	749	778	821	780	781	0.1
Accommodation and food services	2 486	2 584	2 702	2 753	2 680	2 719	2 795	2 935	3.1
Other services, except public administration	2 502	2 535	2 514	2 344	2 426	2 366	2 377	2 572	2.0
Government	13 170	13 287	14 050	13 700	14 097	14 152	13 841	14 177	0.2
As a percent of gross state product	13.8	13.1	13.4	12.1	12.7	12.5	11.9	11.7	X

X = Not applicable.

Table OR-12. Government Transfer Payments, Selected Years 1980–2004

(Millions of dollars, percent.)

Item	1980	1990	2000	2001	2002	2003	2004	Average annual percent change, 2000–2004
CURRENT TRANSFER PAYMENTS TO INDIVIDUALS	3 062	6 213	12 243	13 664	14 975	15 429	15 942	6.8
Retirement and Disability Insurance Benefits	1 654	3 376	5 926	6 151	6 436	6 765	7 115	4.7
Old-age, survivors, and disability insurance (OASDI) benefits	1 463	3 172	5 203	5 539	5 851	6 097	6 420	5.4
Railroad retirement and disability benefits	68	109	127	129	134	137	139	2.4
Workers' compensation	122	92	592	476	445	524	548	-1.9
Other government retirement and disability insurance benefits	1	3	4	5	6	7	8	21.1
Medical Benefits	591	1 681	4 412	5 159	5 423	5 315	5 904	7.6
Medicare benefits	392	1 083	2 189	2 433	2 616	2 777	3 067	8.8
Public assistance medical care benefits	194	577	2 194	2 683	2 750	2 492	2 787	6.2
Military medical insurance benefits	5	21	29	42	57	46	51	14.7
Income Maintenance Benefits	338	528	944	1 086	1 219	1 343	1 443	11.2
Supplemental Security Income (SSI) benefits	41	114	249	267	283	292	305	5.2
Family assistance	149	154	135	187	167	165	169	5.8
Food stamps	92	173	206	257	329	391	429	20.1
Other income maintenance benefits	56	87	354	375	439	495	540	11.2
Unemployment Insurance Compensation	247	280	409	667	1 242	1 305	723	15.3
Veterans' Benefits	179	236	392	419	464	503	551	8.9
Federal Education and Training Assistance	50	91	141	158	175	177	187	7.3
Other Payments to Individuals	3	20	19	25	17	20	19	-0.3

Note: See notes and definitions for more details. Data may not add to total or may appear as zero due to rounding.

EXPORTS

The value of Oregon's exports amounted to nearly $11.2 billion in 2004, ranking 23rd in the country. Exports increased by over 25 percent from 2001 to 2004. The leading export was computers and electronic products, followed by crops and transportation equipment. Exports of transportation equipment more than doubled from 2001 to 2004. The leading market for transportation equipment was Canada, which was also the top overall importer of Oregon's products. Exports to China increased by nearly 75 percent from 2001 to 2004, and Mexico was also a rapidly growing market for Oregon's products. Exports to Japan have fallen in recent years.

Leading Exports, 2004

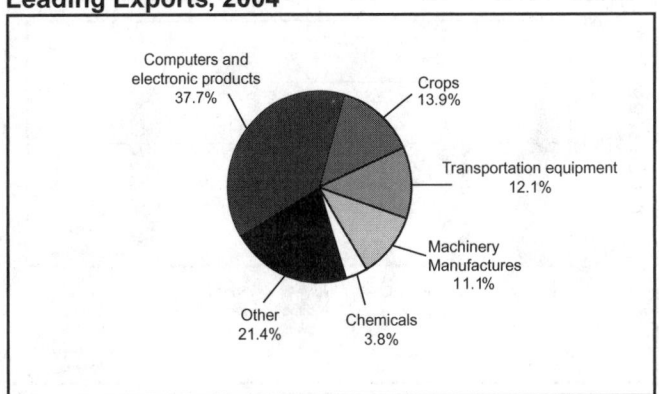

Table OR-13. Exports of Goods by Leading Products and Destinations, 2001–2004

(Millions of dollars, percent, rank based on 2004 dollar values.)

Product and market	2001	2002	2003	2004	Percent share of total, 2004	Average annual percent change, 2001–2004
Total Goods						
Total	8 900	10 086	10 357	11 172	100.0	7.9
Manufactures	7 502	8 656	8 785	9 292	83.2	7.4
Agriculture and livestock	1 209	1 285	1 365	1 654	14.8	11.0
Other commodities	190	145	208	225	2.0	5.9
Five Leading Exports (NAICS Code)						
Computers and electronic products (334)	3 842	4 682	4 602	4 212	37.7	3.1
Crop production (111)	1 132	1 214	1 288	1 551	13.9	11.1
Transportation equipment (336)	617	966	1 116	1 353	12.1	29.9
Machinery manufactures (333)	933	946	871	1 238	11.1	9.9
Chemical manufactures (325)	334	357	410	424	3.8	8.3
Five Leading Markets	8 208	9 440	9 665	10 431	93.4	8.3
Canada	1 269	1 440	1 567	1 889	16.9	14.2
Japan	1 587	1 382	1 276	1 213	10.9	-8.6
South Korea	829	1 170	1 363	1 122	10.0	10.6
China	453	682	575	791	7.1	20.5
Philippines	528	829	767	676	6.0	8.6

Table OR-14. Agriculture, 1997 and 2002

(Number, acres, and dollars.)

Item	1997	2002
Number of farms	39 975	40 033
Land in farms (acres)	17 658 213	17 080 422
Farm Size		
Average size of farm (acres)	442	427
Farms by size (percent distribution)		
Fewer than 50 acres	59.5	62.5
50 to 499 acres	29.4	27.3
500 acres or more	11.1	10.2
Market Value of Land and Equipment (Dollars)		
Land and buildings average value per farm	444 005	508 882
Average value per acre	1 025	1 202
Machinery and equipment average value per farm	51 358	63 462
Value of Sales (Thousands of Dollars)		
Agricultural products sold	3 036 767	3 195 497
Crops	2 180 412	2 194 911
Livestock, poultry, and their products	856 355	1 000 586
Average per farm (dollars)	75 967	79 822
Value of sales (percent distribution)		
Less than $10,000	65.8	69.1
$10,000 to $99,999	22.6	20.5
$100,000 or more	11.7	10.5
Government Payments		
Payments (thousands of dollars)	49 813	52 085
Percent of farms receiving government payments	14.6	11.1
Farm operators whose principal occupation is farming (percent)	43.4	53.9

AGRICULTURE

Cash receipts from farming totaled nearly $3.2 billion in 2002, according to the Department of Agriculture's Census of Agriculture, an increase of 7.6 percent from the previous agriculture census in 1997. The state's chief agricultural products were greenhouse/nursery products (Washington, Oregon, and northern California nurseries were major suppliers of plants to the nation) and dairy products. Much of the farming was small-scale, with 69.1 percent of farms reporting sales of less than $10,000. More than 62 percent of farms spanned fewer than 50 acres, which was the fourth highest proportion of farms of this size in the nation.

ENERGY

Energy expenditures per person were $2,154 in 2001. This was the eighth lowest amount in the country, despite the state's above average energy prices. The chief energy sources were petroleum, hydroelectric power, and natural gas. The state's per capita consumption was below the national average.

Energy Consumption by Source, 2001

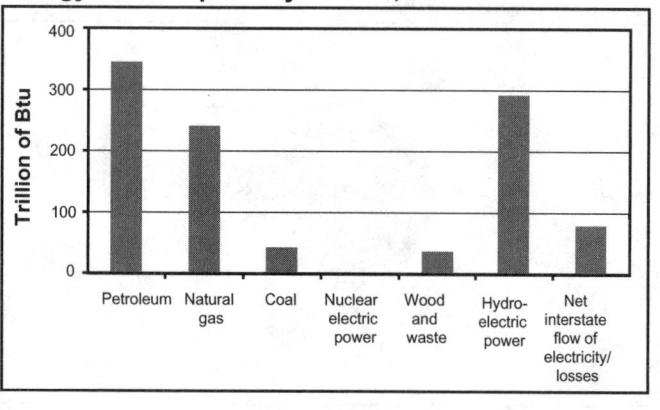

Energy Consumption by Sector, 2001

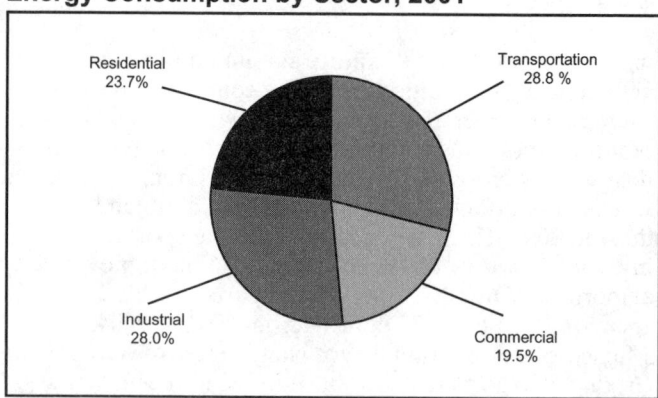

Table OR-15. Energy Consumption, Expenditures, and Prices, Selected Years 1960–2001

(Dollars, Btu [British Thermal Unit], percent distribution.)

Item	1960	1965	1970	1975	1980	1985	1990	1995	2000	2001
Total Consumption (Billion Btu)	470 817	592 574	754 292	868 331	948 292	914 309	991 196	1 050 555	1 140 992	1 064 263
Consumption per capita (million Btu)	266.1	305.9	360.6	372.7	360.1	342.1	348.7	334.4	333.5	306.5
Consumption by Sector (Percent Distribution)										
Residential	23.1	22.3	22.1	22.6	21.0	23.1	22.2	22.1	23.0	23.7
Commercial	12.3	13.3	14.6	15.4	16.5	16.1	17.1	17.4	18.7	19.5
Industrial	41.0	41.8	39.1	37.4	37.2	34.5	32.4	32.1	30.3	28.0
Transportation	23.6	22.5	24.2	24.6	25.3	26.4	28.3	28.3	28.1	28.8
Consumption by Source (Billion Btu)										
Coal	8 943	7 110	3 047	2 673	12 102	10 045	15 659	20 173	38 701	43 364
Natural gas	31 941	59 990	99 572	114 184	82 324	85 492	111 727	152 113	230 965	235 522
Petroleum	212 677	248 987	295 739	306 612	334 299	317 791	346 178	364 536	384 856	368 221
Nuclear electric power	0	0	0	23	58 844	73 406	64 273	0	0	0
Hydroelectric power[1]	134 134	172 561	313 901	359 650	313 951	426 032	428 982	420 363	388 818	291 430
Wood and waste	56 355	57 849	57 448	57 737	89 334	102 449	60 912	47 081	39 600	41 378
Other	0	0	0	-1	0	17 388	3 626	3 758	2 638	2 946
Net interstate flow of electricity/losses[2]	26 767	46 078	-15 415	27 452	57 439	-118 294	-40 161	42 531	55 414	81 402
Total Expenditures (Thousands of Dollars)	...	...	883 200	1 668 000	3 906 400	4 517 700	4 969 900	5 694 600	7 613 900	7 411 100
Expenditures per capita (dollars)	...	...	422	716	1 484	1 690	1 748	1 813	2 225	2 134
Prices by Sector (Dollars Per Million Btu)										
Total	...	...	1.85	3.16	7.07	8.27	8.03	8.50	10.52	10.81
Residential	...	...	2.41	3.70	7.91	10.60	10.68	11.81	13.12	14.34
Commercial	...	...	2.30	3.66	7.28	10.83	10.03	10.89	11.57	12.62
Industrial	...	...	0.84	1.70	4.12	5.60	5.10	5.37	6.34	6.90
Transportation	...	...	2.41	3.98	8.81	8.40	8.56	8.93	12.10	11.43

[1]A negative number in this row results from pumped storage for which, overall, more electricity is expended than created to provide electricity during peak demand periods.
[2]Net interstate flow of electricity is the difference between the amount of energy in the electricity sold within a state (including associated losses) and the energy input at the electric utilities within the state. A positive number indicates that more electricity (including associated losses) came into the state than went out of the state during the year; conversely, a negative number indicates that more electricity (including associated losses) went out of the state than came into the state.
. . . = Not available.

Table OR-16. State Taxes, Fiscal 2004

(Dollars, percent distribution.)

Item	Thousands of dollars	Percent distribution	Dollars per capita	
			State	U.S.
TOTAL TAXES	6 103 071	100.0	1 697.7	2 024.8
Property Taxes	15 865	0.3	4.4	38.9
Sales and Gross Receipts	748 882	12.3	208.3	1 003.4
Selective sales taxes	748 882	12.3	208.3	326.4
Insurance premiums	52 167	0.9	14.5	47.0
Motor fuels	404 547	6.6	112.5	114.6
Tobacco products	265 348	4.3	73.8	42.0
Licenses	651 016	10.7	181.1	134.9
Hunting and fishing	39 882	0.7	11.1	4.2
Motor vehicle	418 903	6.9	116.5	59.4
Motor vehicle operators	31 752	0.5	8.8	6.4
Occupation and business, not elsewhere classified	131 592	2.2	36.6	37.1
Other Taxes	4 687 308	76.8	1 303.8	847.6
Individual income	4 270 740	70.0	1 188.0	673.6
Corporation net income	320 065	5.2	89.0	105.1
Death and gift	73 608	1.2	20.5	19.6

GOVERNMENT FINANCE

Oregon's per capita revenues and expenditures were slightly below the national average in 2003. Spending per capita on natural resources, hospitals, highways, government administration, and correctional facilities was above average, while expenditures on health were below average. The state's taxes per person were significantly below average, ranking 40th in the nation. The state did not have a general sales tax, making individual income taxes the largest source of revenue. Oregon's individual income taxes of $1,188 in fiscal year 2004 were the fourth highest in the nation. Debt per capita was below average, amounting to $2,094.

Per Capita State Taxes, Fiscal 2004

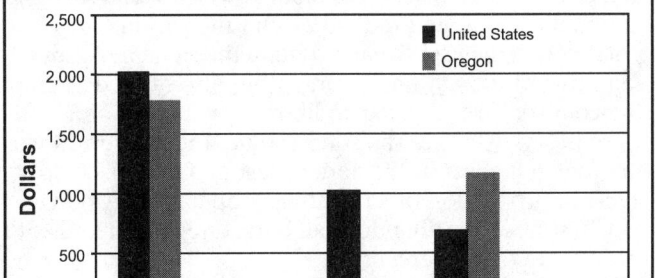

Table OR-17. State Government Finances, 2003

(Dollars, percent distribution.)

Item	Millions of dollars	Percent distribution	Dollars per capita	
			State	U.S.
GENERAL REVENUE	13 282 526	100.0	3 726.9	3 832.6
Intergovernmental revenue	4 215 696	31.7	1 182.9	1 246.0
Taxes	5 701 691	42.9	1 599.8	1 891.6
General sales	0	0.0	0.0	636.0
Selective sales	746 272	5.6	209.4	307.4
License taxes	576 207	4.3	161.7	123.6
Individual income tax	4 023 579	30.3	1 129.0	626.8
Corporate income tax	225 501	1.7	63.3	97.8
Other taxes	130 132	1.0	36.5	99.9
Current charges	1 959 153	14.7	549.7	366.5
Miscellaneous general revenue	1 405 986	10.6	394.5	328.6
GENERAL EXPENDITURE	14 130 154	100.0	3 964.7	4 010.5
Intergovernmental expenditure	4 071 501	28.8	1 142.4	1 316.9
Direct expenditure	10 058 653	71.2	2 822.3	2 693.6
Expenditure by Function				
Education	4 815 553	34.1	1 351.2	1 416.4
Public welfare	3 818 049	27.0	1 071.3	1 083.3
Hospitals	741 215	5.2	208.0	132.3
Health	256 379	1.8	71.9	173.0
Highways	1 126 861	8.0	316.2	295.4
Police protection	180 957	1.3	50.8	38.4
Correction	533 090	3.8	149.6	135.0
Natural resources	426 280	3.0	119.6	64.0
Parks and recreation	64 010	0.5	18.0	20.1
Government administration	909 024	6.4	255.1	151.3
Interest on general debt	285 327	2.0	80.1	107.8
Other and unallocable	973 409	6.9	273.1	393.4
DEBT AT END OF FISCAL YEAR	7 463 722	X	2 094.2	2 404.7
CASH AND SECURITY HOLDINGS	50 892 797	X	14 279.7	8 938.4

X = Not applicable.

Table OR-18. Education Indicators, 2000–2004

(Percent, number.)

Item	State	U.S.
Total Population 25 Years and Over (Thousands), 2004	2 428	186 877
Educational Attainment, 2004		
Percent high school graduate or more	87.4	85.2
Percent college graduate or more	25.9	27.7
Elementary and Secondary Schools, 2002–2003		
Total students	554 071	48 202 324
Percent of students eligible for free or reduced-price lunch ..	40.2	40.6
Percent of students who were English language learners	. . .	7.8
Total schools	1 262	92 330
Student/teacher ratio	20.6	15.9
Per student expenditures	7 491	8 041
Dropouts, Grades 9–12, 2000–2001 (Percent)	4.9	. . .
Higher Education, 2002–2003		
Total enrollment	207 579	17 035 027
Bachelor's degrees awarded	15 601	1 348 503
Percent women	57.0	57.5

. . . = Not available.

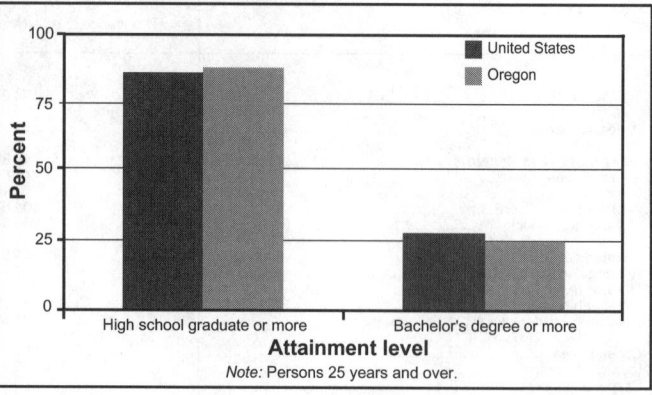

Educational Attainment, 2004

Note: Persons 25 years and over.

EDUCATION

More than 87 percent of Oregon's residents age 25 years and over held high school diplomas, which was above the national average and ranked 24th in the nation. The proportion of college graduates among the same age group fell short of the national average, but also ranked 24th in the country. Oregon's expenditures per student of $7,491 were below average. The state's student/teacher ratio was the fourth highest in the nation, despite Oregon's below average proportion of student-age population. Among the 46 states reporting dropout data, Oregon ranked 15th with a rate of 4.9 percent.

VOTER PARTICIPATION

Voter turnout was above the national average for both the 2000 and 2004 elections, but was particularly strong in 2004, when Oregon had the fifth highest participation rate in the nation. More than 80 percent of eligible voters over 45 years old voted in 2004. However, less than 38 percent of eligible Asian voters and 21.7 percent of eligible Hispanic voters turned out in 2004. According to the official tally by the Clerk of the U.S. House of Representatives, Oregon's voters cast 47 percent of their votes for the Democratic presidential candidate in 2000; this proportion increased to 51.3 percent in 2004.

Table OR-19. Reported Voting and Registration, November 2000 and November 2004

(Numbers in thousands, percent.)

Characteristic	Total population 18 years and over	Total citizen		Total registered		Total voted	
		Number	Percent	Number	Percent	Number	Percent
NOVEMBER 2000							
Total	2 515	2 295	91.3	1 714	68.2	1 529	60.8
Male	1 219	1 106	90.7	806	66.1	712	58.4
Female	1 296	1 189	91.7	908	70.1	817	63.0
NOVEMBER 2004							
Total	2 727	2 600	95.3	2 049	75.2	1 924	70.6
Male	1 340	1 266	94.5	972	72.5	911	68.0
Female	1 387	1 333	96.1	1 078	77.7	1 013	73.0
Race and Hispanic Origin							
White alone	2 498	2 405	96.3	1 941	77.7	1 824	73.0
Non-Hispanic White alone	2 348	2 334	99.4	1 902	81.0	1 791	76.2
Black alone	48	48	B	21	B	21	B
Asian alone	103	81	78.7	41	39.4	39	37.6
Hispanic or Latino[1]	165	79	47.9	41	25.0	36	21.7
White alone or in combination	2 540	2 446	96.3	1 970	77.6	1 853	72.9
Non-Hispanic White alone or in combination	2 386	2 372	99.4	1 929	80.8	1 817	76.1
Black alone or in combination	52	52	B	26	B	26	B
Asian alone or in combination	111	90	80.3	47	41.9	44	39.4
Age							
18 to 24 years	297	280	94.1	167	56.1	140	47.2
25 to 44 years	1 056	974	92.3	722	68.4	669	63.4
45 to 64 years	899	876	97.4	750	83.4	723	80.4
65 to 74 years	254	250	98.1	214	84.0	209	82.2
75 years and over	221	221	100.0	196	89.0	183	83.0

[1]May be of any race.
B = Base is too small to show derived measure.

At a Glance:

- Pennsylvania's population was 12.4 million in 2004, making it the sixth most populous state in the country. Its population increase of just 1.0 percent from 2000 to 2004 was among the lowest in the nation.

- Non-Hispanic Whites accounted for nearly 83 percent of the population. Pennsylvania had the third highest proportion of population age 65 years and over.

- Median household income was below the national average in 2004, as was the state's poverty rate of 11.3 percent.

- Pennsylvania's unemployment rate was 5.5 percent, identical to the national average. Real gross state product growth slowed as result of the 2001 recession, and its subsequent recovery ccurred at a below average rate.

- Less than 12 percent of the state's population lacked health insurance in 2004, which was well below the national average rate of 15.7 percent.

- The educational attainment levels of the state's population age 25 years and over were close to the national averages, ranking 30th for proportion with a high school diploma and 29th for proportion with a bachelor's degrees or more.

Table PA-1. Population by Sex and Age, 1990, 2000, and 2004

(Number, percent.)

Sex and age	1990	2000	2004	Percent distribution, 2004	Average annual percent change, 2000–2004
Total Population	11 881 643	12 281 054	12 406 292	X	0.3
Percent of total U.S. population	4.8	4.4	4.2	X	X
Sex					
Male	5 694 265	5 929 663	6 013 662	48.5	0.4
Female	6 187 378	6 351 391	6 392 630	51.5	0.2
Age					
Under 5 years	797 058	727 804	719 125	5.8	-0.9
5 to 17 years	1 997 752	2 194 417	2 117 884	17.1	0.4
18 years and over	2 373 629	9 358 833	9 569 283	77.1	0.4
18 to 24 years	9 086 833	1 094 449	1 185 180	9.6	-0.3
25 to 44 years	1 226 775	3 508 562	3 294 379	26.6	-0.7
45 to 64 years	3 657 323	2 836 657	3 193 221	25.7	2.2
65 years and over	1 829 106	1 919 165	1 896 503	15.3	0.3
85 years and over	171 836	237 567	290 886	2.3	4.0
Median age (years)	34.9	38.0	39.2	X	X

X = Not applicable.

Average Annual Rate of Population Growth, 1980–2004

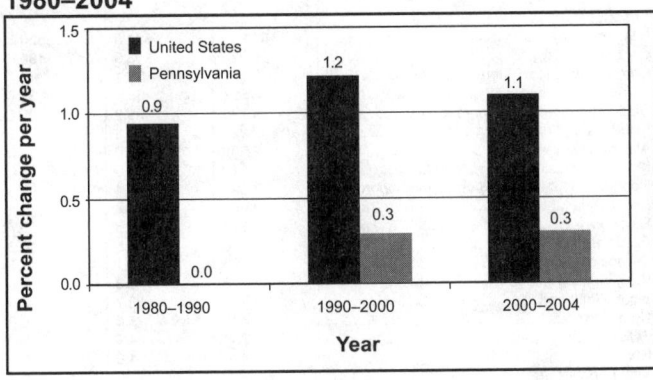

POPULATION

Pennsylvania's population growth rate from 2000 to 2004 was the sixth lowest rate in the nation. However, its growth rate was higher than those of neighboring West Virginia and Ohio. Although the eastern part of the state experienced a population expansion, western Pennsylvania saw a sizable number of its residents leave the state, due to a decline in industrial employment. The state experienced a net loss of over 19,00 residents to other locations. However, over 86,000 new residents arrived from abroad. Less than 23 percent of Pennsylvania's population was under 18 years old, which was among the smallest proportions of this age group in the nation.

Table PA-2. Population by Race and Hispanic Origin, 1990, 2000, and 2004

(Number, percent.)

Race and Hispanic origin	1990	2000	2004
Total Population	11 881 643	12 281 054	12 406 292
Non-Hispanic (Percent)			
One race[1]			
White	87.7	84.2	82.9
Black	9.0	9.9	10.1
American Indian, Alaska Native[2]	0.1	0.1	0.1
Asian and Pacific Islander[2]	1.2	1.8	2.2
Other race[2]	1.0	. . .	. . .
Two or more races	. . .	0.7	0.8
Hispanic or Latino[3] (Percent)	2.0	3.2	3.8

[1]Individuals could report only one race in the 1990 census and could report one or more races on the 2000 census. Data on race in 2000 and 2004 are not comparable to 1990.
[2]Data for 1990 include people of Hispanic or Latino origin.
[3]May be of any race.
. . . = Not available.

Minority Population as a Percent of Total Population, 2004

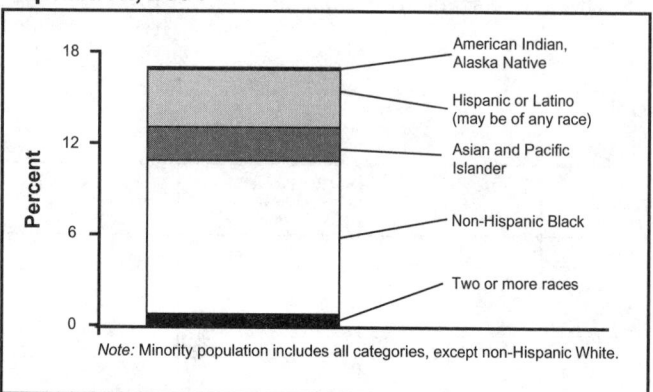

Note: Minority population includes all categories, except non-Hispanic White.

Age-Adjusted Death Rates, Average 2000–2002

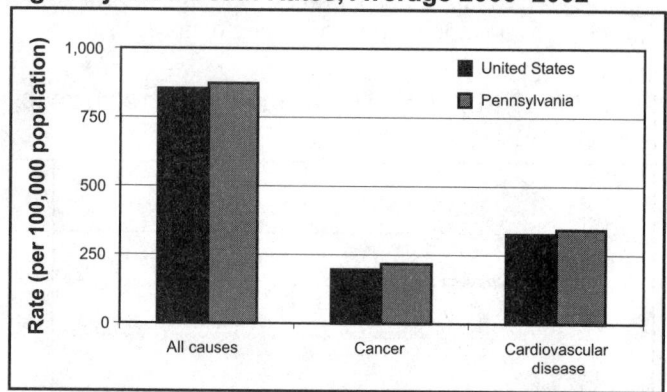

HEALTH

The proportion of Pennsylvanians lacking health insurance was low. Pennsylvania's infant mortality rate was above average, ranking 20th in the nation. The state's age-adjusted death rate for all causes was also higher than average. The overall birth rate and birth rate for teenage mothers were among the lowest in the nation.

Table PA-3. Health Characteristics, 2000–2004

(Number, rate, percent.)

Item	State	U.S.
Births, 2003–2004		
Number of births	145 959	4 089 950
Birth rate (per 1,000 population)	11.8	14.1
Teenage birth rate (per 1,000 women age 15–19 years)	31.2	41.6
Mortality Rates, Average 2000–2002		
Infant mortality rate (per 1,000 live births)	7.3	6.9
Age-adjusted mortality rate (per 100,000 population)		
All races	873.3	853.3
Non-Hispanic White	850.0	843.1
Black	1 157.9	1 097.1
American Indian, Alaska Native	. . .	687.0
Asian and Pacific Islander	393.9	486.0
Hispanic or Latino[1]	734.0	642.7
Health Insurance, 2004		
Percent of all persons without health insurance	11.9	15.7
Percent of children without health insurance	10.7	11.2
Percent of low-income children without health insurance	6.6	7.1

[1]May be of any race.
. . . = Not available.

Table PA-4. Leading Causes of Death, Average 2000–2002

(Number, rate per 100,000 population.)

Cause	Number of deaths	Age-adjusted death rates	
		State	U.S.
ALL CAUSES	130 255	873.3	853.3
Leading Causes			
Major cardiovascular diseases	51 290	334.5	326.5
Cancer	29 975	203.6	196.0
Chronic lower respiratory diseases	5 980	39.1	43.7
Unintentional injuries	4 621	35.1	35.7
Diabetes (underlying cause)	3 776	25.3	25.2
Influenza and pneumonia	2 920	18.8	22.7
Alzheimer's disease	2 706	17.0	19.0
Motor vehicle accidents	1 549	12.3	15.0
Nephritis, nephrotic syndrome, and nephrosis ..	2 820	18.4	13.8
Septicemia	2 601	17.2	11.4
Suicides	1 323	10.5	10.7
Firearm-related	1 216	9.8	10.3
Cirrhosis	1 126	8.1	9.5
Drug-induced	1 129	9.3	7.9
Alcohol-induced	483	3.7	6.9
Homicides	644	5.4	6.0
Falls	730	4.9	5.2
HIV	498	4.0	5.0
Viral hepatitis	211	1.6	2.0
Anemias	278	1.8	1.6
Drownings	94	0.8	1.3
Fire deaths	148	1.1	1.2

Note: The rates are age-adjusted to the U.S. 2000 standard population.

Table PA-5. Households and Housing Characteristics, 1990, 2000, and 2004

(Number, percent, and dollars.)

Characteristic	1990	2000	2004	Average annual percent change, 2000–2004
Total Households	4 495 966	4 777 003	4 817 757	0.2
Family households	3 155 989	3 208 388	3 216 764	0.1
Married-couple family	2 502 072	2 467 673	2 448 014	-0.2
Other family	653 917	740 715	768 750	0.9
Male householder, no wife present	146 909	186 022	200 241	1.9
Female householder, no husband present	507 008	554 693	568 509	0.6
Nonfamily households	1 339 977	1 568 615	1 600 993	0.5
Householder living alone	1 150 694	1 320 941	1 359 425	0.7
Householder not living alone	189 283	247 674	241 568	-0.6
Housing Characteristics				
Average size	2.57	2.48	2.48	X
Housing units	4 938 140	5 249 750	5 385 729	0.6
Occupied housing units	4 495 966	4 777 003	4 817 757	0.2
Owner-occupied	3 176 121	3 406 337	3 506 411	0.7
Renter-occupied	1 319 845	1 370 666	1 311 346	-1.1
Median gross rent of renter-occupied housing units (dollars)	404	531	611	3.6
Median value of owner-occupied housing units (dollars)	69 100	97 000	116 520	4.7

X = Not applicable.

Median Housing Value and Median Rent, 2004

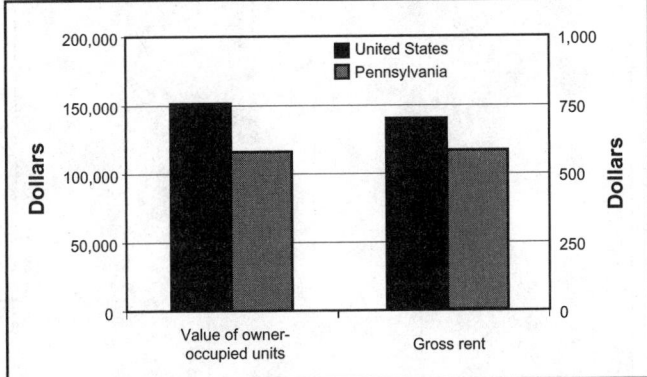

Median Household Income, 1984–2004 (2004 Dollars)

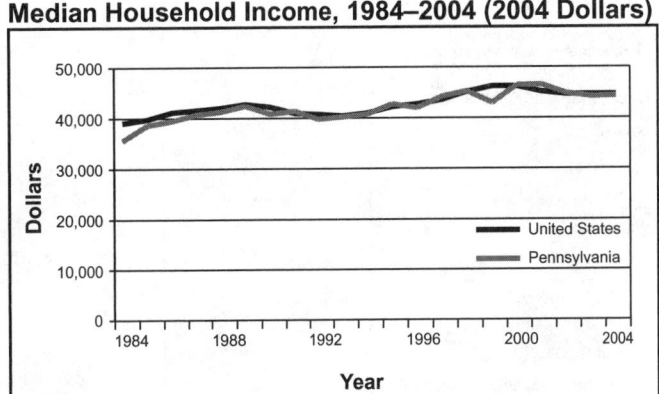

Table PA-6. Household Income and Poverty Status, 1980–2004

(2004 CPI-U-RS adjusted dollars, rate.)

Year	State Median household income (2004 dollars)	State Poverty rate	U.S. Median household income (2004 dollars)	U.S. Poverty rate
2004	44 131	11.3	44 389	12.7
2003	44 087	10.5	44 482	12.5
2002	44 640	9.5	44 546	12.1
2001	46 418	9.6	45 062	11.7
2000	46 262	8.6	46 058	11.3
1999	42 799	9.3	46 129	11.9
1998	45 154	11.3	45 003	12.7
1997	44 031	11.2	43 430	13.3
1996	41 833	11.6	42 544	13.7
1995	42 495	12.2	41 943	13.8
1994	40 428	12.5	40 677	14.5
1993	39 900	13.2	40 217	15.1
1992	39 427	11.9	40 422	14.8
1991	41 072	11.0	40 746	14.2
1990	40 648	11.0	41 963	13.5
1989	42 207	10.4	42 524	12.8
1988	41 030	10.3	41 771	13.0
1987	40 429	10.6	41 322	13.4
1986	39 147	10.1	40 939	13.6
1985	38 305	10.5	39 545	14.0
1984	35 202	15.6	38 782	14.4
1983	. . .	15.4	. . .	15.2
1982	. . .	13.5	. . .	15.0
1981	. . .	11.6	. . .	14.0
1980	. . .	9.8	. . .	13.0

. . . = Not available.

Table PA-7. Employment Status by Demographic Group, 2004

(Numbers in thousands, rate.)

Characteristic	Civilian noninstitutional population	Civilian labor force		Employed	Unemployment rate
		Number	Participation rate		
SEX AND AGE					
Total	9 702	6 260	64.5	5 911	5.6
16 to 19 years	692	337	48.8	275	18.4
20 to 24 years	779	576	73.9	523	9.2
25 to 34 years	1 439	1 215	84.4	1 151	5.2
35 to 44 years	1 835	1 545	84.2	1 472	4.7
45 to 54 years	1 867	1 544	82.7	1 484	3.9
55 to 64 years	1 275	808	63.3	779	3.5
65 years and over	1 815	236	13.0	226	4.0
Men	4 621	3 310	71.6	3 103	6.3
16 to 19 years	359	169	47.1	129	23.7
20 to 24 years	376	296	78.8	265	10.6
25 to 34 years	707	647	91.6	610	5.8
35 to 44 years	902	828	91.8	789	4.7
45 to 54 years	910	806	88.6	770	4.4
55 to 64 years	630	440	69.8	421	4.2
65 years and over	738	124	16.8	118	4.6
Women	5 082	2 950	58.1	2 808	4.8
16 to 19 years	332	168	50.6	146	13.0
20 to 24 years	403	280	69.4	258	7.7
25 to 34 years	733	567	77.4	541	4.6
35 to 44 years	934	717	76.8	683	4.8
45 to 54 years	957	738	77.1	714	3.3
55 to 64 years	645	368	57.0	358	2.7
65 years and over	1 077	112	10.4	108	3.4
MARITAL STATUS					
Married men, spouse present	2 639	1 978	75.0	1 911	3.4
Married women, spouse present	2 597	1 600	61.6	1 549	3.2
Women who maintain families	566	362	64.0	336	7.3
RACE, HISPANIC ORIGIN, AND SEX					
White	8 561	5 552	64.9	5 279	4.9
Men	4 106	2 961	72.1	2 803	5.3
Women	4 455	2 592	58.2	2 476	4.5
Black	893	540	60.5	476	11.8
Men	391	255	65.2	213	16.3
Women	502	285	56.8	263	7.7
Asian	170	119	69.7	110	7.1
Men	84	68	80.7	64	6.4
Women	86	51	58.9	47	8.1
Hispanic or Latino[1]	320	216	67.5	199	8.0
Men	159	118	74.2	107	9.4
Women	160	98	60.9	92	6.3
RACE, HISPANIC ORIGIN, AND AGE					
White					
25 to 34 years	1 203	1 028	85.4	986	4.1
35 to 44 years	1 623	1 377	84.8	1 318	4.3
45 to 54 years	1 669	1 398	83.8	1 348	3.6
55 to 64 years	1 157	735	63.6	709	3.6

Note: Data in Table 7 are from the Current Population Survey (CPS) and do not match Bureau of Labor Statistics estimates in Table 8. See notes and definitions for more details.

[1]May be of any race.

Table PA-8. Employment Status, 1990–2004

(Numbers in thousands, rate.)

Year	Civilian labor force	Employed	Unemployed	Unemployment rate
2004	6 274 731	5 926 978	347 753	5.5
2003	6 185 885	5 835 076	350 809	5.7
2002	6 247 254	5 897 438	349 816	5.6
2001	6 163 146	5 870 495	292 651	4.7
2000	6 085 795	5 831 634	254 161	4.2
1999	6 077 826	5 809 824	268 002	4.4
1998	6 068 343	5 787 593	280 750	4.6
1997	6 085 770	5 775 178	310 592	5.1
1996	5 987 872	5 662 126	325 746	5.4
1995	5 900 042	5 554 303	345 739	5.9
1994	5 902 687	5 529 551	373 136	6.3
1993	5 923 245	5 504 269	418 976	7.1
1992	5 909 823	5 455 450	454 373	7.7
1991	5 841 971	5 437 439	404 532	6.9
1990	5 826 666	5 510 009	316 657	5.4

Note: Population age 16 years and over.

Unemployment Rate, 1980–2004

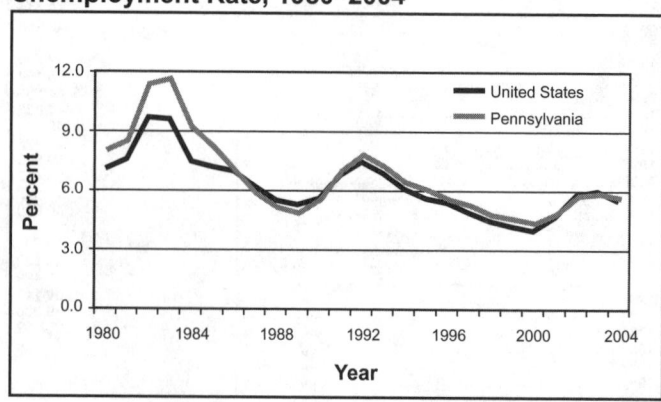

Table PA-9. Employment and Average Wages by Industry, 2001–2004

(Estimates are based on the 2002 North American Industry Classification System [NAICS].)

Industry	2001	2002	2003	2004	Annual average percent change, 2001–2004
	Number of jobs				
TOTAL EMPLOYMENT BY PLACE OF WORK	6 979 434	6 956 046	6 959 905	7 026 724	0.2
Farm Employment	83 279	83 977	79 405	79 251	-1.6
Nonfarm Employment	6 896 155	6 872 069	6 880 500	6 947 473	0.2
Private employment	6 103 485	6 066 218	6 066 223	6 136 941	0.2
Forestry, fishing, hunting, and other[1]	19 404	20 313	18 256	17 545	-3.3
Mining	27 556	25 675	26 709	28 226	0.8
Utilities	33 563	32 181	30 656	29 722	-4.0
Construction	379 792	371 864	378 407	383 772	0.3
Manufacturing	845 445	781 983	738 849	718 946	-5.3
Durable goods manufacturing	508 195	466 242	437 623	429 719	-5.4
Nondurable goods manufacturing	337 250	315 741	301 226	289 227	-5.0
Wholesale trade	248 711	245 230	247 023	250 196	0.2
Retail trade	821 482	815 759	819 635	827 977	0.3
Transportation and warehousing	241 751	243 387	239 928	242 100	0.0
Information	147 610	135 862	132 277	126 309	-5.1
Finance and insurance	346 845	348 566	349 631	347 794	0.1
Real estate and rental and leasing	176 223	179 221	185 429	192 486	3.0
Professional and technical services	431 869	430 511	433 314	441 308	0.7
Management of companies and enterprises	63 328	69 282	70 557	75 944	6.2
Administrative and waste services	336 233	334 121	333 078	354 241	1.8
Educational services	225 110	227 694	232 102	235 702	1.5
Health care and social assistance	835 389	856 065	871 104	888 136	2.1
Arts, entertainment, and recreation	122 904	127 999	129 303	133 178	2.7
Accommodation and food services	412 092	419 981	424 277	430 561	1.5
Other services, except public administration	388 178	400 524	405 688	412 798	2.1
Government and government enterprises	792 670	805 851	814 277	810 532	0.7
	Dollars				
AVERAGE WAGES AND SALARIES BY PLACE OF WORK	34 193	35 047	36 240	37 770	3.4
Farm Earnings	18 640	23 735	23 627	26 010	11.7
Nonfarm Earnings	34 252	35 090	36 282	37 809	3.3
Private earnings	34 134	34 894	36 098	37 644	3.3
Forestry, fishing, hunting, and other[1]	21 873	22 408	23 142	24 679	4.1
Mining	46 738	47 116	48 082	50 314	2.5
Utilities	68 029	71 443	75 932	77 848	4.6
Construction	40 219	41 038	41 853	42 836	2.1
Manufacturing	41 089	42 503	44 058	45 905	3.8
Durable goods manufacturing	41 243	42 563	44 030	45 937	3.7
Nondurable goods manufacturing	40 858	42 416	44 098	45 858	3.9
Wholesale trade	46 676	47 845	49 994	53 470	4.6
Retail trade	21 081	21 581	22 438	22 814	2.7
Transportation and warehousing	35 135	35 514	35 987	37 196	1.9
Information	48 521	47 797	49 798	51 933	2.3
Finance and insurance	52 895	54 182	56 723	60 562	4.6
Real estate and rental and leasing	32 041	33 051	35 557	37 930	5.8
Professional and technical services	56 708	57 301	58 768	62 218	3.1
Management of companies and enterprises	64 568	64 590	67 438	73 421	4.4
Administrative and waste services	24 819	25 842	26 958	27 735	3.8
Educational services	28 781	30 580	32 359	33 714	5.4
Health care and social assistance	31 793	32 925	34 156	35 816	4.1
Arts, entertainment, and recreation	22 322	23 069	23 897	23 969	2.4
Accommodation and food services	13 104	13 366	13 582	14 006	2.2
Other services, except public administration	21 007	22 085	22 958	23 788	4.2
Government and government enterprises	35 014	36 323	37 420	38 833	3.5

Note: Average wages and salaries are a calculation by the editors of wage and salary disbursements divided by full- and part-time wage and salary employment. Data may not add to total or may appear as zero due to rounding.

[1] "Other" consists of the number of jobs held by U.S. residents employed by international organizations and foreign embassies and consulates in the United States.

LABOR MARKET

Pennsylvania's unemployment rate rose sharply in response to the 2001 recession. However, in 2004, it remained below the rates of Ohio and New York. This reflected a low labor force participation rate rather than a strong labor market. Employment increased in 2004, as the number of jobs rose in service-providing industries, particularly health care and management. Health care and government were Pennsylvania's largest employers. Manufacturing jobs declined throughout the 2001–2004 period, and remained well below their 2001 level in 2004. Average wages and salaries were below the national average, but grew at a faster than average rate from 2001 to 2004.

Employment by Industry, 2004

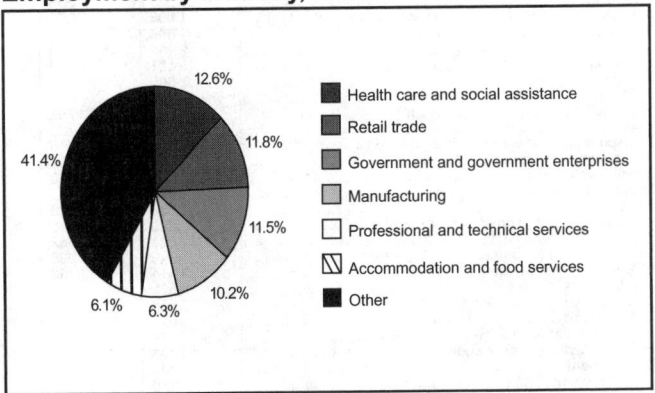

Table PA-10. Personal Income by Major Source, Selected Years 1980–2004

(Millions of dollars, except where noted.)

Item	1980	1990	2000	2001	2002	2003	2004	Average annual percent change, 2000–2004
Earnings by Place of Work	93 600	171 659	268 169	273 398	281 598	291 856	307 924	3.5
Wage and salary disbursements	69 959	124 244	197 702	202 875	206 476	212 394	222 267	3.0
Supplements to wages and salaries	14 950	27 485	39 089	40 884	45 384	48 403	52 051	7.4
Proprietors' income[1]	8 691	19 931	31 378	29 639	29 738	31 060	33 605	1.7
Farm proprietors' income	175	594	652	447	-108	439	441	-9.3
Nonfarm proprietors' income	8 516	19 337	30 725	29 192	29 846	30 621	33 164	1.9
(-) Contributions for government social insurance[2]	9 194	19 763	30 697	31 880	32 769	33 808	35 462	3.7
(+) Adjustment for residence[3]	-431	959	3 355	3 389	3 471	3 588	3 750	2.8
(=) Net Earnings by Place of Residence	83 975	152 855	240 827	244 907	252 301	261 636	276 212	3.5
(+) Dividends, interest, and rent[4]	18 022	47 166	66 085	65 227	63 611	61 620	63 731	-0.9
(+) Personal current transfer receipts	17 695	34 314	57 926	62 205	66 331	69 272	72 648	5.8
Personal income	119 692	234 334	364 838	372 339	382 243	392 528	412 591	3.1
Farm income	119 289	233 385	363 716	371 429	381 767	391 589	411 610	3.1
Nonfarm income	402	949	1 122	910	475	938	981	-3.3
Per Capita Personal Income (Dollars)[5]	10 085	19 687	29 695	30 275	31 005	31 730	33 257	2.9

Note: Data may not add to total or may appear as zero due to rounding.

[1]Proprietors' income includes the inventory valuation adjustment and the capital consumption adjustment.
[2]Contributions for government social insurance are included in earnings by type and industry, but they are excluded from personal income.
[3]The adjustment for residence is the net inflow of the earnings of interarea commuters.
[4]Rental income of persons includes the capital consumption adjustment.
[5]Per capita personal income is total personal income divided by total midyear population.

Per Capita Personal Income, 1980–2004 (Current Dollars)

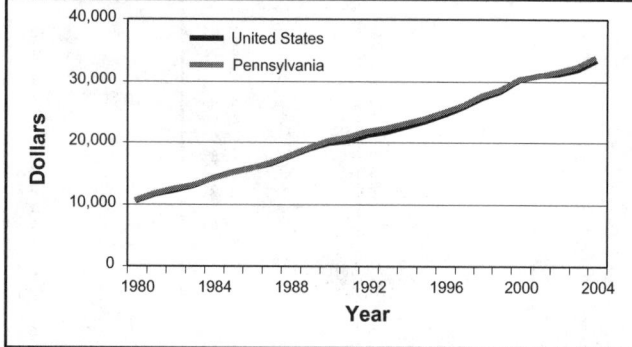

ECONOMIC ACTIVITY

Economic growth slowed as a result of the 2001 recession. While many states' real gross state products (GSP) rebounded in 2003 and 2004, Pennsylvania's did not. The state's GSP growth rate during the 2003–2004 period was well below the national average, ranking 43rd in the nation. Contributing to this performance was sluggish growth in manufacturing, retail trade, and wholesale trade, which offset gains in several service-providing industries. Housing price appreciation in the state was close to the national average; in 2004, the median value of owner-occupied housing ranked 34th in the country.

Table PA-11. Real Gross State Product, 1997–2004

(Millions of chained 2000 dollars, percent.)

Industry	1997	1998	1999	2000	2001	2002	2003	2004	Average annual percent change, 2001–2004
GROSS STATE PRODUCT	362 900	377 112	385 332	391 501	396 814	404 630	415 281	427 883	2.5
As a percent of U.S. gross product	4.2	4.2	4.1	4.0	4.0	4.0	4.0	4.0	X
Private Industries	324 330	337 583	346 803	353 120	358 720	366 509	376 972	389 075	2.7
Agriculture, forestry, fishing, and hunting	1 665	1 908	2 065	2 547	2 241	2 111	2 334	2 035	-3.2
Mining	1 888	2 281	2 392	2 344	2 237	2 321	2 106	2 087	-2.3
Utilities	9 440	9 440	9 779	10 237	9 760	10 071	10 745	10 881	3.7
Construction	16 131	16 312	16 688	16 613	16 786	16 393	16 348	16 327	-0.9
Manufacturing	63 805	66 943	67 301	69 806	68 436	70 532	72 215	72 873	2.1
As a percent of gross state product	17.6	17.8	17.5	17.8	17.2	17.4	17.4	17.0	X
Wholesale trade	18 697	20 752	21 582	21 340	22 746	24 175	24 219	25 391	3.7
Retail trade	23 948	24 736	25 760	26 378	28 272	29 642	31 698	32 880	5.2
Transportation and warehousing	11 693	11 990	12 160	12 338	12 530	13 074	13 733	13 978	3.7
Information	11 727	12 709	14 213	14 412	15 374	15 845	17 188	18 279	5.9
Finance and insurance	26 296	27 970	28 026	28 358	29 300	29 273	31 045	32 800	3.8
Real estate and rental and leasing	41 899	42 805	44 428	45 704	47 798	48 392	48 213	50 023	1.5
Services	97 682	99 920	102 517	103 041	103 346	104 983	107 685	112 244	2.8
As a percent of gross state product	26.9	26.5	26.6	26.3	26.0	25.9	25.9	26.2	X
Professional and technical services	22 023	23 362	25 097	26 369	26 958	27 084	27 904	29 155	2.6
Management of companies and enterprises	7 443	6 998	6 966	6 319	6 017	6 042	6 467	7 159	6.0
Administrative and waste services	9 414	9 759	10 617	10 243	9 890	10 239	10 621	11 267	4.4
Educational services	6 591	6 724	6 606	6 648	6 547	6 563	6 540	6 423	-0.6
Health care and social assistance	31 525	31 467	31 978	31 977	32 850	33 805	34 674	35 737	2.8
Arts, entertainment, and recreation	2 640	2 982	2 787	2 840	2 818	2 962	2 996	3 022	2.4
Accommodation and food services	7 942	8 342	8 349	8 652	8 497	8 596	8 659	8 951	1.8
Other services, except public administration	10 104	10 286	10 117	9 993	9 769	9 692	9 824	10 530	2.5
Government	38 642	39 582	38 536	38 381	38 098	38 140	38 360	38 878	0.7
As a percent of gross state product	10.6	10.5	10.0	9.8	9.6	9.4	9.2	9.1	X

X = Not applicable.

Table PA-12. Government Transfer Payments, Selected Years 1980–2004

(Millions of dollars, percent.)

Item	1980	1990	2000	2001	2002	2003	2004	Average annual percent change, 2000–2004
CURRENT TRANSFER PAYMENTS TO INDIVIDUALS	16 616	32 349	54 928	58 877	63 402	66 462	69 725	6.1
Retirement and Disability Insurance Benefits	8 535	15 983	23 371	24 509	25 750	26 438	27 424	4.1
Old-age, survivors, and disability insurance (OASDI) benefits	7 518	14 684	22 131	23 281	24 255	24 941	25 885	4.0
Railroad retirement and disability benefits	415	623	634	634	644	645	656	0.9
Workers' compensation	74	199	249	243	232	241	251	0.2
Other government retirement and disability insurance benefits	527	477	357	351	619	610	632	15.3
Medical Benefits	3 731	11 059	24 160	26 226	27 793	29 604	32 409	7.6
Medicare benefits	2 266	7 207	12 756	14 038	14 939	15 689	17 051	7.5
Public assistance medical care benefits	1 452	3 786	11 348	12 111	12 748	13 821	15 241	7.7
Military medical insurance benefits	13	66	57	78	107	94	116	19.6
Income Maintenance Benefits	2 015	2 926	4 424	4 315	4 684	5 052	5 517	5.7
Supplemental Security Income (SSI) benefits	312	637	1 371	1 468	1 554	1 601	1 673	5.1
Family assistance	771	826	756	455	487	499	544	-7.9
Food stamps	384	692	649	651	705	823	977	10.8
Other income maintenance benefits	547	771	1 648	1 742	1 938	2 130	2 323	9.0
Unemployment Insurance Compensation	1 404	1 251	1 535	2 237	3 468	3 613	2 482	12.8
Veterans' Benefits	710	787	986	1 028	1 122	1 198	1 250	6.1
Federal Education and Training Assistance	219	335	423	509	561	523	556	7.1
Other Payments to Individuals	2	8	29	52	25	35	87	31.5

Note: See notes and definitions for more details. Data may not add to total or may appear as zero due to rounding.

EXPORTS

Pennsylvania was the 14th largest exporter in 2004, with the value of its exports totaling nearly $18.5 billion. Exports were severely impacted by the 2001 recession, falling sharply in 2002, but their subsequent recovery was significant—they had grown over 17 percent by 2004. The leading export products were chemical manufactures and machinery manufactures, which together accounted for over 30 percent of the state's exports. Exports of computers and electronic products, the state's third leading export, fell by 25 percent from 2001 to 2004. Canada was the largest export market, followed distantly by Mexico and Japan. Exports to China more than doubled from 2001 to 2004.

Leading Exports, 2004

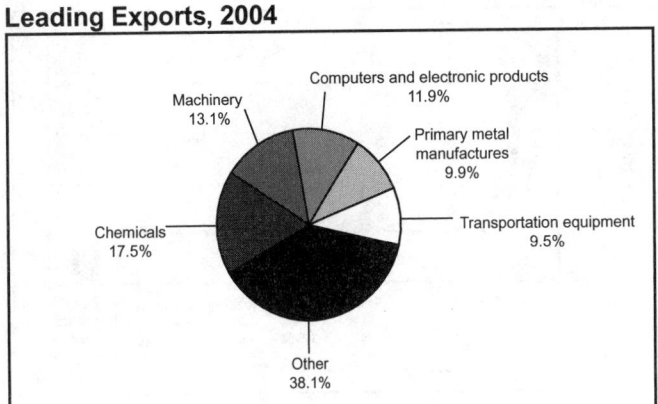

Table PA-13. Exports of Goods by Leading Products and Destinations, 2001–2004

(Millions of dollars, percent, rank based on 2004 dollar values.)

Product and market	2001	2002	2003	2004	Percent share of total, 2004	Average annual percent change, 2001–2004
Total Goods						
Total	17 433	15 768	16 299	18 487	100.0	2.0
Manufactures	16 442	14 983	15 410	17 390	94.1	1.9
Agriculture and livestock	445	408	355	425	2.3	-1.5
Other commodities	546	377	534	673	3.6	7.2
Five Leading Exports (NAICS Code)						
Chemical manufactures (325)	2 424	2 555	2 612	3 228	17.5	10.0
Machinery manufactures (333)	2 677	2 172	2 131	2 417	13.1	-3.4
Computers and electronic products (334)	2 951	2 174	2 058	2 203	11.9	-9.3
Primary metal manufactures (331)	1 419	1 307	1 439	1 831	9.9	8.9
Transportation equipment (336)	1 532	1 565	1 783	1 758	9.5	4.7
Five Leading Markets						
Canada	15 424	14 105	14 501	16 309	88.2	1.9
Mexico	5 668	5 558	5 849	6 395	34.6	4.1
Japan	1 427	1 236	1 112	1 199	6.5	-5.6
United Kingdom	993	861	819	924	5.0	-2.4
China	1 205	887	846	903	4.9	-9.2
	320	425	565	781	4.2	34.7

Table PA-14. Agriculture, 1997 and 2002
(Number, acres, and dollars.)

Item	1997	2002
Number of farms	60 222	58 105
Land in farms (acres)	7 819 648	7 745 336
Farm Size		
Average size of farm (acres)	130	133
Farms by size (percent distribution)		
Fewer than 50 acres	36.3	37.8
50 to 499 acres	59.8	58.0
500 acres or more	3.9	4.2
Market Value of Land and Equipment (Dollars)		
Land and buildings average value per farm	331 252	452 874
Average value per acre	2 524	3 419
Machinery and equipment average value per farm	47 657	59 995
Value of Sales (Thousands of Dollars)		
Agricultural products sold	4 247 568	4 256 959
Crops	1 452 843	1 320 914
Livestock, poultry, and their products	2 794 725	2 936 045
Average per farm (dollars)	70 532	73 263
Value of sales (percent distribution)		
Less than $10,000	54.7	60.9
$10,000 to $99,999	28.3	22.5
$100,000 or more	16.9	16.5
Government Payments		
Payments (thousands of dollars)	32 382	85 794
Percent of farms receiving government payments	25.2	20.6
Farm operators whose principal occupation is farming (percent)	50.3	56.7

AGRICULTURE

Cash receipts from farming totaled close to $4.3 billion in 2002, according to the Department of Agriculture's Census of Agriculture. This was a 6.5 percent increase from the 1997 farm census. Pennsylvania was among the largest providers of dairy products, which were the state's predominant agricultural product. Sales of crops accounted for 31 percent of agricultural sales, a drop from 1997. More than 60 percent of the farms had sales of less than $10,000. Close to 39 percent of farms spanned fewer than 50 acres, and nearly 57 percent of all farm operators reported that farming was their principal occupation.

ENERGY

Pennsylvania's energy prices were the 16th highest in the nation. However, energy expenditures per person totaled $2,430 in 2001, an amount very close to the national average. The state's per capita energy consumption was below average. The chief energy sources were petroleum, coal, and nuclear power.

Energy Consumption by Source, 2001

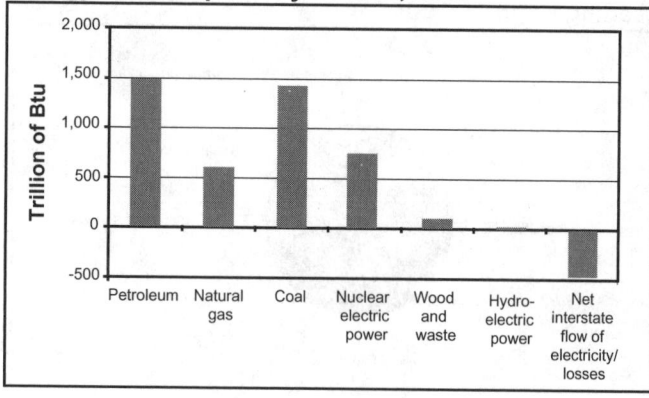

Energy Consumption by Sector, 2001

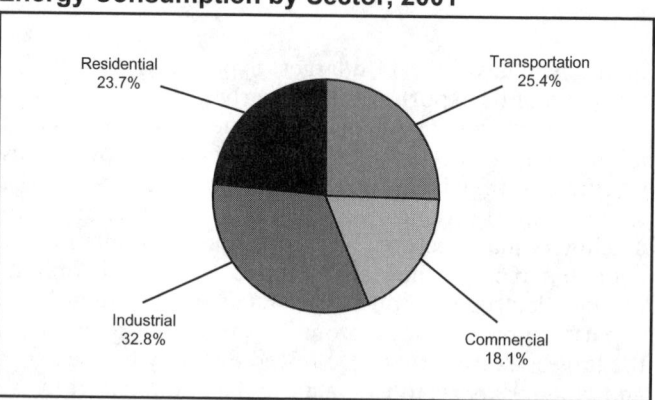

Table PA-15. Energy Consumption, Expenditures, and Prices, Selected Years 1960–2001
(Dollars, Btu [British Thermal Unit], percent distribution.)

Item	1960	1965	1970	1975	1980	1985	1990	1995	2000	2001
Total Consumption (Billion Btu)	3 253 691	3 735 144	4 111 239	3 919 939	4 039 844	3 455 730	3 696 086	3 912 484	3 954 205	3 922 516
Consumption per capita (million Btu)	287.5	321.4	348.4	329.2	340.5	293.6	311.1	324.8	322.0	318.9
Consumption by Sector (Percent Distribution)										
Residential	21.3	19.3	20.7	21.4	22.7	24.2	22.8	23.6	23.9	23.7
Commercial	9.4	8.6	9.2	10.5	11.2	13.5	14.8	16.0	17.6	18.1
Industrial	52.8	56.8	52.6	48.5	45.8	40.1	39.5	37.4	33.2	32.8
Transportation	16.5	15.3	17.5	19.6	20.2	22.1	22.8	23.1	25.3	25.4
Consumption by Source (Billion Btu)										
Coal	1 530 508	1 751 318	1 698 980	1 646 695	1 636 051	1 409 068	1 469 696	1 484 085	1 508 093	1 378 522
Natural gas	540 094	652 906	797 877	670 085	792 780	646 939	680 696	761 505	727 483	669 071
Petroleum	1 121 324	1 248 954	1 532 945	1 473 547	1 461 951	1 245 646	1 332 560	1 341 167	1 433 350	1 454 352
Nuclear electric power	2 674	3 691	5 102	174 766	131 893	278 637	611 503	698 311	769 361	770 339
Hydroelectric power[1]	19 646	13 888	14 336	16 402	7 628	10 149	20 699	8 147	19 174	10 526
Wood and waste	46 454	47 374	53 189	57 464	140 985	132 459	54 627	93 924	99 351	95 251
Other	0	0	0	0	0	0	657	900	1 076	1 100
Net interstate flow of electricity/losses[2]	-7 008	17 013	8 810	-119 019	-131 443	-267 170	-474 352	-475 555	-603 685	-456 644
Total Expenditures (Thousands of Dollars)	. . .	. . .	4 796 000	9 716 300	18 739 700	20 536 800	22 287 700	24 074 000	29 107 700	29 887 600
Expenditures per capita (dollars)	. . .	. . .	406	816	1 580	1 745	1 876	1 999	2 370	2 430
Prices by Sector (Dollars Per Million Btu)										
Total	. . .	. . .	1.47	3.25	6.37	8.39	8.50	8.74	10.66	11.20
Residential	. . .	. . .	1.97	3.96	7.09	10.60	11.74	12.18	13.77	15.29
Commercial	. . .	. . .	1.90	4.35	7.30	10.99	11.50	11.97	13.38	14.89
Industrial	. . .	. . .	0.79	2.25	4.29	6.02	5.57	5.47	6.41	7.25
Transportation	. . .	. . .	2.48	4.16	8.86	8.67	8.74	8.78	11.39	10.58

[1]A negative number in this row results from pumped storage for which, overall, more electricity is expended than created to provide electricity during peak demand periods.
[2]Net interstate flow of electricity is the difference between the amount of energy in the electricity sold within a state (including associated losses) and the energy input at the electric utilities within the state. A positive number indicates that more electricity (including associated losses) came into the state than went out of the state during the year; conversely, a negative number indicates that more electricity (including associated losses) went out of the state than came into the state.
. . . = Not available.

Table PA-16. State Taxes, Fiscal 2004

(Dollars, percent distribution.)

Item	Thousands of dollars	Percent distribution	Dollars per capita	
			State	U.S.
TOTAL TAXES	25 346 869	100.0	2 043.1	2 024.8
Property Taxes	68 389	0.3	5.5	38.9
Sales and Gross Receipts	12 529 644	49.4	1 010.0	1 003.4
General sales and gross receipts	7 773 131	30.7	626.6	677.0
Selective sales taxes	4 756 513	18.8	383.4	326.4
Alcoholic beverages	221 408	0.9	17.8	15.7
Insurance premiums	639 578	2.5	51.6	47.0
Motor fuels	1 785 200	7.0	143.9	114.6
Public utilities	1 016 641	4.0	82.0	39.2
Tobacco products	981 253	3.9	79.1	42.0
Licenses	2 547 849	10.1	205.4	134.9
Corporation	787 502	3.1	63.5	21.6
Motor vehicle	792 430	3.1	63.9	59.4
Occupation and business, not elsewhere classified	763 240	3.0	61.5	37.1
Other Taxes	10 200 987	40.2	822.3	847.6
Individual income	7 323 364	28.9	590.3	673.6
Corporation net income	1 677 998	6.6	135.3	105.1
Death and gift	708 587	2.8	57.1	19.6
Documentary and stock transfer	470 789	1.9	38.0	27.1

GOVERNMENT FINANCE

State revenues and expenditures per person were below the national averages in 2003. Spending per capita was below average on education and health, but outlays were well above average for public welfare, highways, and police protection. Pennsylvania's per capita taxes were slightly above average, ranking 20th in the nation. The chief sources of tax revenues were general sales taxes, individual income taxes, and motor fuel taxes. The state's individual income taxes ranked 33rd among the 43 states with such taxes. The debt per person amounted to $1,967, which was below average and ranked 29th in the nation.

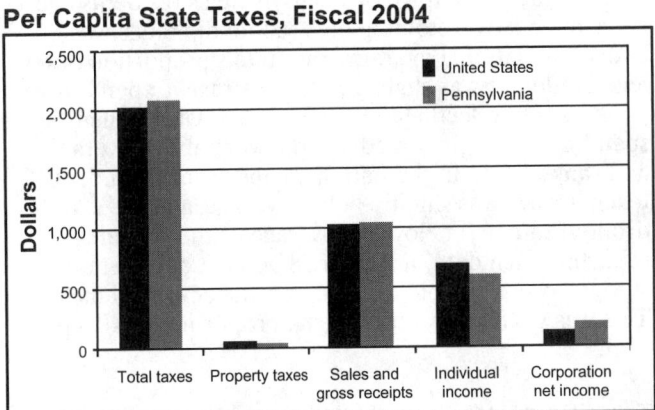

Per Capita State Taxes, Fiscal 2004

Table PA-17. State Government Finances, 2003

(Dollars, percent distribution.)

Item	Millions of dollars	Percent distribution	Dollars per capita	
			State	U.S.
GENERAL REVENUE	46 904 770	100.0	3 791.5	3 832.6
Intergovernmental revenue	14 466 919	30.8	1 169.4	1 246.0
Taxes	23 187 302	49.4	1 874.3	1 891.6
General sales	7 561 149	16.1	611.2	636.0
Selective sales	4 410 858	9.4	356.6	307.4
License taxes	2 213 875	4.7	179.0	123.6
Individual income tax	6 661 780	14.2	538.5	626.8
Corporate income tax	1 189 314	2.5	96.1	97.8
Other taxes	1 150 326	2.5	93.0	99.9
Current charges	5 642 131	12.0	456.1	366.5
Miscellaneous general revenue	3 608 418	7.7	291.7	328.6
GENERAL EXPENDITURE	48 252 480	100.0	3 900.4	4 010.5
Intergovernmental expenditure	11 943 470	24.8	965.4	1 316.9
Direct expenditure	36 309 010	75.2	2 935.0	2 693.6
Expenditure by Function				
Education	14 838 088	30.8	1 199.4	1 416.4
Public welfare	16 085 269	33.3	1 300.2	1 083.3
Hospitals	1 945 368	4.0	157.2	132.3
Health	1 495 004	3.1	120.8	173.0
Highways	5 032 532	10.4	406.8	295.4
Police protection	1 026 678	2.1	83.0	38.4
Correction	1 359 531	2.8	109.9	135.0
Natural resources	579 003	1.2	46.8	64.0
Parks and recreation	171 050	0.4	13.8	20.1
Government administration	2 208 949	4.6	178.6	151.3
Interest on general debt	1 087 130	2.3	87.9	107.8
Other and unallocable	2 423 878	5.0	195.9	393.4
DEBT AT END OF FISCAL YEAR	24 330 327	X	1 966.7	2 404.7
CASH AND SECURITY HOLDINGS	93 430 245	X	7 552.4	8 938.4

X = Not applicable.

Table PA-18. Education Indicators, 2000–2004

(Percent, number.)

Item	State	U.S.
Total Population 25 Years and Over (Thousands), 2004	8 272	186 877
Educational Attainment, 2004		
Percent high school graduate or more	86.5	85.2
Percent college graduate or more	25.3	27.7
Elementary and Secondary Schools, 2002–2003		
Total students	1 816 747	48 202 324
Percent of students eligible for free or reduced-price lunch ..	28.3	40.6
Percent of students who were English language learners	. . .	7.8
Total schools	3 186	92 330
Student/teacher ratio	15.2	15.9
Per student expenditures	8 997	8 041
Dropouts, Grades 9–12, 2000–2001 (Percent)	3.3	. . .
Higher Education, 2002–2003		
Total enrollment	676 408	17 035 027
Bachelor's degrees awarded	72 351	1 348 503
Percent women	56.9	57.5

. . . = Not available.

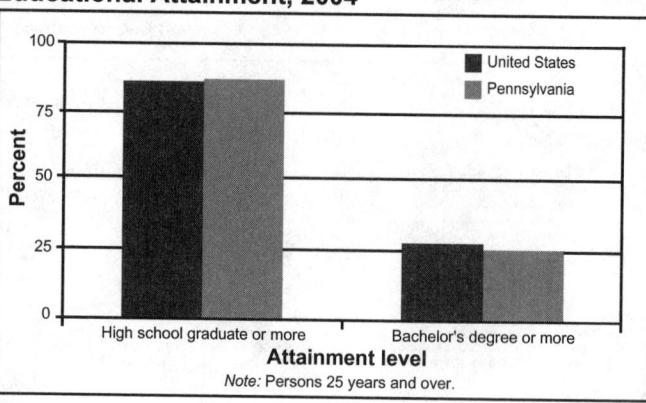

Educational Attainment, 2004

Legend: United States, Pennsylvania

Note: Persons 25 years and over.

EDUCATION

In 2004, the percentage of Pennsylvania's residents age 25 years and over holding high school diplomas was above the national average. The state's proportion of college graduates was slightly below average. Expenditures per student, reflecting Pennsylvania's relatively high spending per capita on education, were above average and ranked 13th in the nation. Pennsylvania's student/teacher ratio was slightly below average, and the state's dropout rate was below the average of the 46 states reporting such data. Just over 28 percent of the state's students were eligible for free or reduced-price lunch. This was well below the national proportion of 40.6 percent.

VOTER PARTICIPATION

The state's voter turnout in the 2000 elections was close to average. In 2004, more than 62 percent of eligible voters cast ballots, which was well above the national average. According to the official tally by the Clerk of the U.S. House of Representatives, 50.6 percent of voters cast ballots for the Democratic presidential candidate in 2000, and 50.9 percent voted similarly in 2004. Asians and Hispanics (of any race) had the lowest voter participation rates in 2004. Close to 71 percent of eligible persons age 65 to 74 years turned out to vote in 2004.

Table PA-19. Reported Voting and Registration, November 2000 and November 2004

(Numbers in thousands, percent.)

Characteristic	Total population 18 years and over	Total citizen		Total registered		Total voted	
		Number	Percent	Number	Percent	Number	Percent
NOVEMBER 2000							
Total	8 950	8 687	97.1	5 847	65.3	4 988	55.7
Male	4 287	4 154	96.9	2 836	66.1	2 373	55.4
Female	4 663	4 533	97.2	3 011	64.6	2 615	56.1
NOVEMBER 2004							
Total	9 356	9 055	96.8	6 481	69.3	5 845	62.5
Male	4 467	4 311	96.5	3 052	68.3	2 740	61.3
Female	4 889	4 743	97.0	3 429	70.1	3 105	63.5
Race and Hispanic Origin							
White alone	8 218	8 036	97.8	5 853	71.2	5 291	64.4
Non-Hispanic White alone	7 998	7 886	98.6	5 769	72.1	5 209	65.1
Black alone	853	816	95.6	523	61.3	474	55.6
Asian alone[1]	210	135	64.3	60	28.7	43	20.5
Hispanic or Latino[1]	255	179	70.3	95	37.5	88	34.5
White alone or in combination	8 259	8 077	97.8	5 884	71.2	5 316	64.4
Non-Hispanic White alone or in combination	8 038	7 927	98.6	5 800	72.2	5 234	65.1
Black alone or in combination	889	851	95.8	549	61.8	500	56.3
Asian alone or in combination	210	135	64.3	60	28.7	43	20.5
Age							
18 to 24 years	1 101	1 048	95.2	547	49.7	448	40.7
25 to 44 years	3 257	3 101	95.2	2 214	68.0	1 958	60.1
45 to 64 years	3 275	3 199	97.7	2 429	74.2	2 280	69.6
65 to 74 years	874	863	98.7	658	75.3	619	70.8
75 years and over	849	844	99.5	632	74.5	540	63.7

[1]May be of any race.

At a Glance:

- Rhode Island was the smallest state in the nation in terms of land area. (However, the District of Columbia was smaller in size.) With a population of 1.1 million, the state ranked 43rd in the country for population size.

- Residents were largely non-Hispanic White; this racial group accounted for over 80 percent of the population. In 2004, Hispanics (of any race) made up 10.3 percent of Rhode Island's population, which was the 13th highest proportion of this ethnic group in the nation.

- Just 11.4 percent of the state's residents lacked health insurance, compared to 15.7 percent for the nation as a whole.

- Median household income was well above the national average, ranking 14th in the country. Rhode Island's poverty rate of 11.5 percent was below average.

- The state's unemployment rate was 5.2 percent in 2004, compared to the national average of 5.5 percent.

- Real gross state product was the seventh smallest in the country, and it rose moderately throughout the 2001–2004 period.

Table RI-1. Population by Sex and Age, 1990, 2000, and 2004

(Number, percent.)

Sex and age	1990	2000	2004	Percent distribution, 2004	Average annual percent change, 2000–2004
Total Population	1 003 464	1 048 319	1 080 632	X	0.8
Percent of total U.S. population	0.4	0.4	0.4	X	X
Sex					
Male	481 496	503 635	521 215	48.2	0.9
Female	521 968	544 684	559 417	51.8	0.7
Age					
Under 5 years	66 969	63 896	61 538	5.7	-0.8
5 to 17 years	158 721	183 926	182 275	16.9	1.0
18 years and over	185 628	800 497	836 819	77.4	0.5
18 to 24 years	777 774	106 607	112 484	10.4	-0.5
25 to 44 years	120 358	310 636	305 401	28.3	-0.3
45 to 64 years	321 241	230 852	268 347	24.8	2.7
65 years and over	150 547	152 402	150 587	13.9	0.0
85 years and over	16 016	20 897	26 290	2.4	3.8
Median age (years)	33.8	36.7	38.0	X	X

X = Not applicable.

Average Annual Rate of Population Growth, 1980–2004

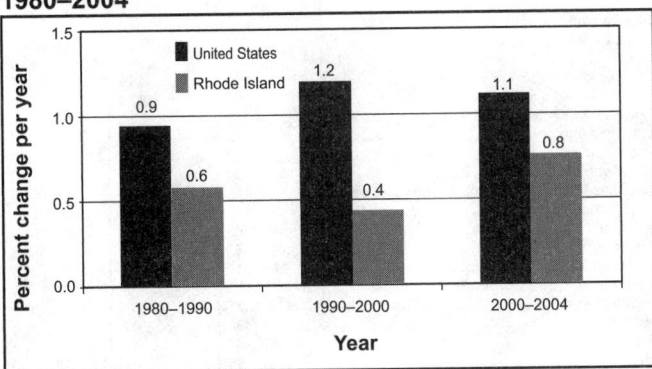

POPULATION

Rhode Island's population increased by 3.1 percent from 2000 to 2004. This was below both the national average growth rate and the rate of its fast-growing neighbor, Connecticut, but above the growth rate of its northern neighbor, Massachusetts. The state's birth rate was the sixth lowest in the nation. However, Rhode Island was able to add to its population through migration. The state benefited from 15,990 new residents from abroad and nearly 6,000 new residents from other states; when combined, these new residents accounted for more than two-thirds of Rhode Island's population growth. In 2004, persons age 65 years and over accounted for 13.9 percent of the population, the 8th highest proportion of this age group in the nation.

Table RI-2. Population by Race and Hispanic Origin, 1990, 2000, and 2004

(Number, percent.)

Race and Hispanic origin	1990	2000	2004
Total Population	1 003 464	1 048 319	1 080 632
Non-Hispanic (Percent)			
One race[1]			
White	89.3	82.9	80.5
Black	3.4	4.5	4.8
American Indian, Alaska Native[2]	0.4	0.4	0.4
Asian and Pacific Islander[2]	1.8	2.4	2.7
Other race[2]	2.5	. . .	. . .
Two or more races	. . .	1.1	1.2
Hispanic or Latino[3] (Percent)	4.6	8.7	10.3

[1]Individuals could report only one race in the 1990 census and could report one or more races on the 2000 census. Data on race in 2000 and 2004 are not comparable to 1990.
[2]Data for 1990 include people of Hispanic or Latino origin.
[3]May be of any race.
. . . = Not available.

Minority Population as a Percent of Total Population, 2004

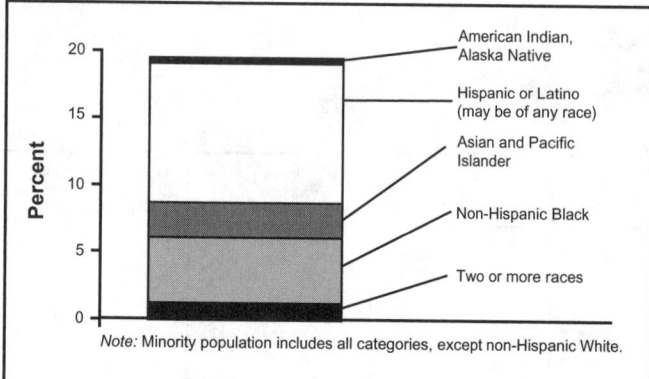

Note: Minority population includes all categories, except non-Hispanic White.

Age-Adjusted Death Rates, Average 2000–2002

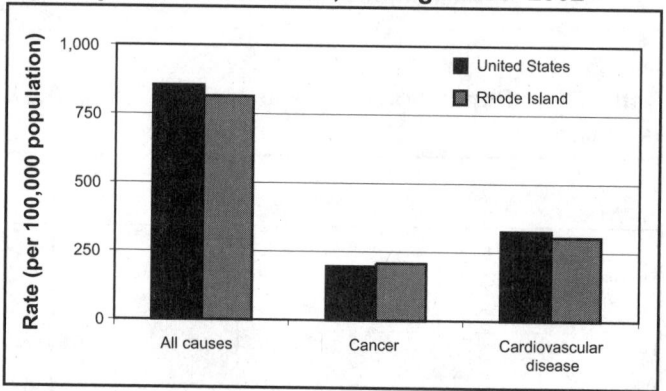

HEALTH

Rhode Island's infant mortality rate was below the national average. Its age-adjusted death rates were below average for most causes of death. The state's birth rate was among the six lowest in the nation, and the birth rate for teenage mothers was also below average.

Table RI-3. Health Characteristics, 2000–2004

(Number, rate, percent.)

Item	State	U.S.
Births, 2003–2004		
Number of births	13 209	4 089 950
Birth rate (per 1,000 population)	12.3	14.1
Teenage birth rate (per 1,000 women age 15–19 years)	31.3	41.6
Mortality Rates, Average 2000–2002		
Infant mortality rate (per 1,000 live births)	6.7	6.9
Age-adjusted mortality rate (per 100,000 population)		
All races	811.7	853.3
Non-Hispanic White	810.0	843.1
Black	926.3	1 097.7
American Indian, Alaska Native	. . .	687.0
Asian and Pacific Islander	456.6	486.0
Hispanic or Latino[1]	460.8	642.7
Health Insurance, 2004		
Percent of all persons without health insurance	11.4	15.7
Percent of children without health insurance	7.4	11.2
Percent of low-income children without health insurance	4.3	7.1

[1]May be of any race.
. . . = Not available.

Table RI-4. Leading Causes of Death, Average 2000–2002

(Number, rate per 100,000 population.)

Cause	Number of deaths	Age-adjusted death rates	
		State	U.S.
ALL CAUSES	10 098	811.7	853.3
Leading Causes			
Major cardiovascular diseases	3 930	306.3	326.5
Cancer	2 412	201.1	196.0
Chronic lower respiratory diseases	511	40.6	43.7
Unintentional injuries	268	22.9	35.7
Diabetes (underlying cause)	273	22.3	25.2
Influenza and pneumonia	319	24.2	22.7
Alzheimer's disease	252	18.5	19.0
Motor vehicle accidents	89	8.1	15.0
Nephritis, nephrotic syndrome, and nephrosis ..	128	10.0	13.8
Septicemia	137	10.9	11.4
Suicides	83	7.6	10.7
Firearm-related	52	4.8	10.3
Cirrhosis	117	10.3	9.5
Drug-induced	101	9.4	7.9
Alcohol-induced	71	6.4	6.9
Homicides	38	3.6	6.0
Falls	81	6.3	5.2
HIV	30	2.8	5.0
Viral hepatitis	18	1.6	2.0
Anemias	16	1.2	1.6
Drownings	7	0.6	1.3
Fire deaths	12	1.1	1.2

Note: The rates are age-adjusted to the U.S. 2000 standard population.

Table RI-5. Households and Housing Characteristics, 1990, 2000, and 2004

(Number, percent, and dollars.)

Characteristic	1990	2000	2004	Average annual percent change, 2000–2004
Total Households	377 977	408 424	409 767	0.1
Family households	258 886	265 398	267 908	0.2
Married-couple family	202 283	196 757	191 449	-0.7
Other family	56 603	68 641	76 459	2.7
Male householder, no wife present	12 261	16 032	18 837	4.1
Female householder, no husband present	44 342	52 609	57 622	2.3
Nonfamily households	119 091	143 026	141 859	-0.2
Householder living alone	99 111	116 678	113 819	-0.6
Householder not living alone	19 980	26 348	28 040	1.6
Housing Characteristics				
Average size	2.55	2.47	2.53	X
Housing units	414 572	439 837	446 305	0.4
Occupied housing units	377 977	408 424	409 767	0.1
Owner-occupied	224 792	245 156	253 102	0.8
Renter-occupied	153 185	163 268	156 665	-1.0
Median gross rent of renter-occupied housing units (dollars) ...	489	553	740	7.6
Median value of owner-occupied housing units (dollars)	132 700	133 000	240 150	15.9

X = Not applicable.

Median Housing Value and Median Rent, 2004

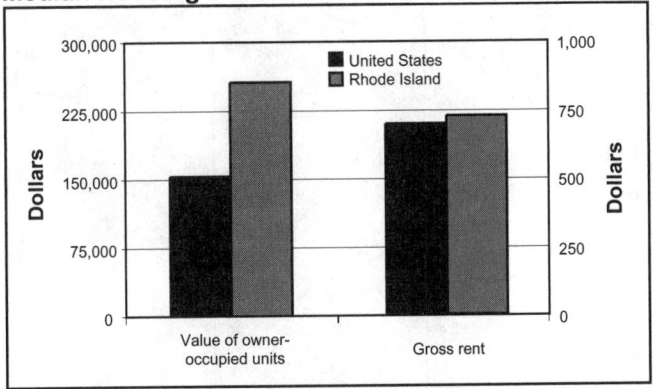

Median Household Income, 1984–2004 (2004 Dollars)

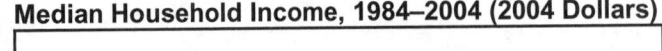
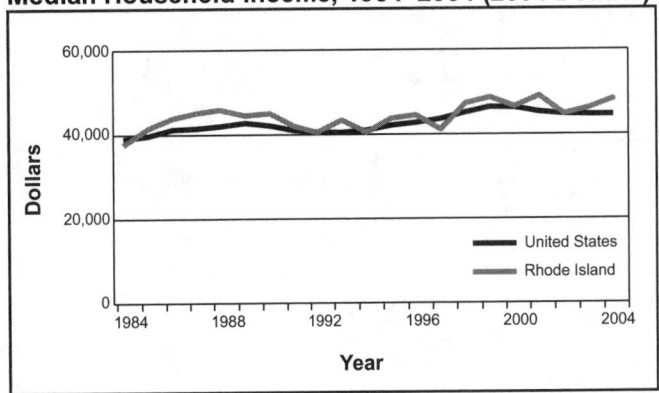

Table RI-6. Household Income and Poverty Status, 1980–2004

(2004 CPI-U-RS adjusted dollars, rate.)

Year	State		U.S.	
	Median household income (2004 dollars)	Poverty rate	Median household income (2004 dollars)	Poverty rate
2004	48 129	11.5	44 389	12.7
2003	45 913	11.5	44 482	12.5
2002	44 555	11.0	44 546	12.1
2001	48 791	9.6	45 062	11.7
2000	46 285	10.2	46 058	11.3
1999	48 422	10.0	46 129	11.9
1998	47 088	11.6	45 003	12.7
1997	40 839	12.7	43 430	13.3
1996	44 335	11.0	42 544	13.7
1995	43 522	10.6	41 943	13.8
1994	40 254	10.3	40 677	14.5
1993	43 137	11.2	40 217	15.1
1992	40 153	12.4	40 422	14.8
1991	41 706	10.4	40 746	14.2
1990	44 801	7.5	41 963	13.5
1989	44 316	6.7	42 524	12.8
1988	45 787	9.8	41 771	13.0
1987	44 989	8.1	41 322	13.4
1986	43 641	9.1	40 939	13.6
1985	41 232	9.0	39 545	14.0
1984	37 393	12.8	38 782	14.4
1983	. . .	14.5	. . .	15.2
1982	. . .	13.3	. . .	15.0
1981	. . .	11.7	. . .	14.0
1980	. . .	10.7	. . .	13.0

. . . = Not available.

Table RI-7. Employment Status by Demographic Group, 2004

(Numbers in thousands, rate.)

Characteristic	Civilian noninstitutional population	Civilian labor force		Employed	Unemployment rate
		Number	Participation rate		
SEX AND AGE					
Total	848	562	66.4	532	5.4
16 to 19 years	67	35	51.7	30	14.5
20 to 24 years	72	57	78.9	51	9.2
25 to 34 years	133	109	82.6	103	6.2
35 to 44 years	169	142	83.6	136	3.9
45 to 54 years	152	125	82.6	121	3.4
55 to 64 years	111	79	71.4	76	4.0
65 years and over	145	16	11.1	16	2.1
Men	402	288	71.5	272	5.5
16 to 19 years	34	18	51.2	15	16.0
20 to 24 years	37	29	79.2	26	9.6
25 to 34 years	63	57	91.3	53	7.0
35 to 44 years	82	73	89.4	71	2.7
45 to 54 years	73	62	85.5	60	3.9
55 to 64 years	52	39	75.3	37	4.5
65 years and over	62	9	14.5	9	1.5
Women	445	275	61.7	261	5.2
16 to 19 years	32	17	52.2	15	13.0
20 to 24 years	35	27	78.7	25	8.9
25 to 34 years	70	52	74.7	50	5.2
35 to 44 years	87	68	78.2	65	5.2
45 to 54 years	79	63	80.0	61	2.8
55 to 64 years	59	40	67.9	39	3.5
65 years and over	83	7	8.6	7	2.8
MARITAL STATUS					
Married men, spouse present	212	159	75.1	154	3.1
Married women, spouse present	211	138	65.5	133	3.9
Women who maintain families	58	41	70.4	38	7.0
RACE, HISPANIC ORIGIN, AND SEX					
White	765	506	66.2	481	4.9
Men	361	259	71.6	245	5.2
Women	403	247	61.3	236	4.6
Black	47	32	68.7	29	11.0
Men	23	15	66.1	14	10.2
Women	24	17	71.3	15	11.7
Asian	23	16	69.0	14	8.6
Men	12	9	76.8	8	7.1
Women	11	7	60.6	6	10.7
Hispanic or Latino[1]	71	47	66.6	44	7.7
Men	35	25	73.2	24	7.3
Women	36	22	60.4	20	8.1
RACE, HISPANIC ORIGIN, AND AGE					
White					
25 to 34 years	116	96	83.3	91	5.7
35 to 44 years	153	128	83.7	124	3.3
45 to 54 years	137	114	83.4	110	3.4
55 to 64 years	103	74	71.8	71	3.6

Note: Data in Table 7 are from the Current Population Survey (CPS) and do not match Bureau of Labor Statistics estimates in Table 8. See notes and definitions for more details.

[1]May be of any race.

Table RI-8. Employment Status, 1990–2004

(Numbers in thousands, rate.)

Year	Civilian labor force	Employed	Unemployed	Unemployment rate
2004	562 289	533 313	28 976	5.2
2003	568 712	537 873	30 839	5.4
2002	556 196	527 991	28 205	5.1
2001	544 814	520 008	24 806	4.6
2000	542 952	520 922	22 030	4.1
1999	541 407	518 848	22 559	4.2
1998	534 011	509 551	24 460	4.6
1997	531 882	504 147	27 735	5.2
1996	517 429	489 929	27 500	5.3
1995	508 872	477 409	31 463	6.2
1994	515 881	480 669	35 212	6.8
1993	526 673	484 965	41 708	7.9
1992	530 139	483 329	46 810	8.8
1991	523 070	480 591	42 479	8.1
1990	525 851	493 674	32 177	6.1

Note: Population age 16 years and over.

Unemployment Rate, 1980–2004

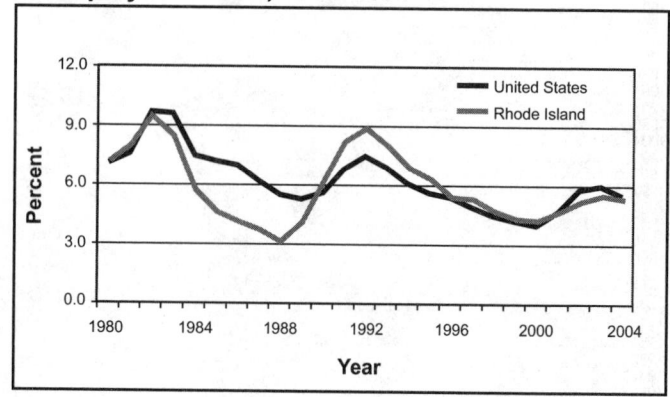

Table RI-9. Employment and Average Wages by Industry, 2001–2004

(Estimates are based on the 2002 North American Industry Classification System [NAICS].)

Industry	2001	2002	2003	2004	Annual average percent change, 2001–2004
	Number of jobs				
TOTAL EMPLOYMENT BY PLACE OF WORK	586 774	588 988	597 005	604 079	1.0
Farm Employment	1 440	1 464	1 472	1 361	-1.9
Nonfarm Employment	585 334	587 524	595 533	602 718	1.0
Private employment	508 406	510 247	517 908	525 972	1.1
Forestry, fishing, hunting, and other[1]	D	D	2 349	2 286	. . .
Mining	D	D	623	651	. . .
Utilities	D	D	1 234	1 156	. . .
Construction	28 874	D	31 278	31 656	3.1
Manufacturing	70 169	64 772	60 793	59 069	-5.6
Durable goods manufacturing	46 901	42 787	39 758	D	. . .
Nondurable goods manufacturing	23 268	21 985	21 035	D	. . .
Wholesale trade	17 950	18 162	18 225	18 095	0.3
Retail trade	61 027	62 445	63 166	63 231	1.2
Transportation and warehousing	D	D	12 357	12 213	. . .
Information	12 352	12 341	12 315	12 184	-0.5
Finance and insurance	30 824	31 188	31 668	31 901	1.2
Real estate and rental and leasing	16 535	16 848	18 006	19 094	4.9
Professional and technical services	33 279	33 619	34 393	35 469	2.1
Management of companies and enterprises	6 804	6 778	7 843	8 606	8.1
Administrative and waste services	29 831	29 263	29 193	31 937	2.3
Educational services	23 254	23 788	24 582	25 506	3.1
Health care and social assistance	76 675	78 435	80 650	82 086	2.3
Arts, entertainment, and recreation	12 772	13 224	13 462	13 719	2.4
Accommodation and food services	42 059	43 136	44 450	45 228	2.5
Other services, except public administration	29 433	30 741	31 321	31 885	2.7
Government and government enterprises	76 928	77 277	77 625	76 746	-0.1
	Dollars				
AVERAGE WAGES AND SALARIES BY PLACE OF WORK	32 898	34 153	35 727	36 925	3.9
Farm Earnings	18 557	24 390	20 196	26 140	12.1
Nonfarm Earnings	32 917	34 166	35 749	36 938	3.9
Private earnings	31 813	32 902	34 497	35 588	3.8
Forestry, fishing, hunting, and other[1]	D	D	33 530	34 788	. . .
Mining	D	D	45 314	44 618	. . .
Utilities	D	D	70 346	66 130	. . .
Construction	40 426	D	43 533	43 648	2.6
Manufacturing	36 701	38 047	39 146	40 852	3.6
Durable goods manufacturing	37 772	38 740	39 457	D	. . .
Nondurable goods manufacturing	34 543	36 700	38 560	D	. . .
Wholesale trade	47 185	47 877	49 701	51 602	3.0
Retail trade	21 985	23 017	23 885	24 508	3.7
Transportation and warehousing	D	D	31 835	32 635	. . .
Information	52 121	48 489	52 896	59 160	4.3
Finance and insurance	48 672	51 304	53 988	56 599	5.2
Real estate and rental and leasing	30 116	31 299	33 420	34 078	4.2
Professional and technical services	48 386	49 915	52 387	53 653	3.5
Management of companies and enterprises	62 443	63 891	83 977	78 409	7.9
Administrative and waste services	22 072	22 158	23 080	24 195	3.1
Educational services	27 971	29 397	30 887	31 623	4.2
Health care and social assistance	30 546	32 738	33 511	34 974	4.6
Arts, entertainment, and recreation	19 786	20 933	22 216	21 815	3.3
Accommodation and food services	14 221	14 775	15 014	15 394	2.7
Other services, except public administration	21 007	22 175	22 723	23 477	3.8
Government and government enterprises	39 039	41 131	42 681	44 574	4.5

Note: Average wages and salaries are a calculation by the editors of wage and salary disbursements divided by full- and part-time wage and salary employment. Data may not add to total or may appear as zero due to rounding.

[1] "Other" consists of the number of jobs held by U.S. residents employed by international organizations and foreign embassies and consulates in the United States.
D = Suppressed to avoid disclosure of data of individual companies.
. . . = Not available.

LABOR MARKET

Rhode Island's unemployment rate has been below the national average for many years. However, the state's unemployment rate of 5.2 percent in 2004 was higher than any of its New England neighbors. Employment rose slowly over the 2001–2004 period, as a sharp decline in manufacturing jobs was offset by increases in retail trade and in several service-providing industries, particularly health care. In 2004, health care, government, and retail trade were Rhode Island's largest employers. Average wages and salaries ranked 21st in the nation; however, their rate of growth from 2001 to 2004 was the 4th highest in the country.

Employment by Industry, 2004

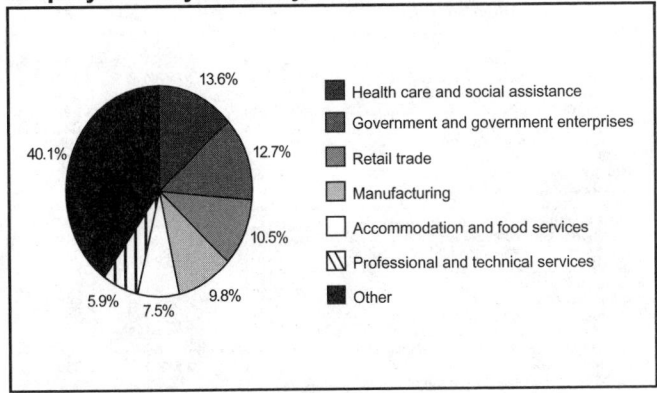

- Health care and social assistance
- Government and government enterprises
- Retail trade
- Manufacturing
- Accommodation and food services
- Professional and technical services
- Other

13.6% 12.7% 40.1% 10.5% 9.8% 7.5% 5.9%

Table RI-10. Personal Income by Major Source, Selected Years 1980–2004

(Millions of dollars, except where noted.)

Item	1980	1990	2000	2001	2002	2003	2004	Average annual percent change, 2000–2004
Earnings by Place of Work	6 890	14 167	21 271	22 376	23 249	24 586	25 885	5.0
Wage and salary disbursements	5 273	10 634	16 062	16 576	17 202	18 157	18 892	4.1
Supplements to wages and salaries	1 080	2 403	3 344	3 496	3 879	4 204	4 558	8.1
Proprietors' income[1]	536	1 130	1 866	2 303	2 168	2 225	2 435	6.9
Farm proprietors' income	2	20	1	. . .	-2	1	2	9.8
Nonfarm proprietors' income	535	1 110	1 864	2 303	2 170	2 224	2 433	6.9
(-) Contributions for government social insurance[2]	746	1 716	2 619	2 748	2 867	3 025	3 160	4.8
(+) Adjustment for residence[3]	124	665	1 344	1 341	1 306	1 288	1 366	0.4
(=) **Net Earnings by Place of Residence**	6 268	13 117	19 996	20 969	21 688	22 849	24 091	4.8
(+) Dividends, interest, and rent[4]	1 484	4 123	5 713	5 951	6 057	5 982	6 275	2.4
(+) Personal current transfer receipts	1 428	2 887	4 988	5 559	5 899	6 090	6 570	7.1
Personal income	9 181	20 126	30 697	32 478	33 644	34 921	36 936	4.7
Farm income	9 174	20 096	30 682	32 465	33 629	34 904	36 917	4.7
Nonfarm income	7	30	15	14	15	16	18	5.5
Per Capita Personal Income (Dollars)[5]	9 677	20 006	29 214	30 680	31 475	32 452	34 180	4.0

Note: Data may not add to total or may appear as zero due to rounding.

[1]Proprietors' income includes the inventory valuation adjustment and the capital consumption adjustment.
[2]Contributions for government social insurance are included in earnings by type and industry, but they are excluded from personal income.
[3]The adjustment for residence is the net inflow of the earnings of interarea commuters.
[4]Rental income of persons includes the capital consumption adjustment.
[5]Per capita personal income is total personal income divided by total midyear population.
. . . = Not available.

Per Capita Personal Income, 1980–2004 (Current Dollars)

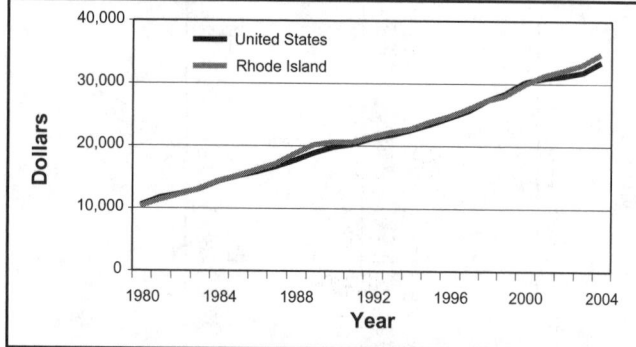

ECONOMIC ACTIVITY

Real gross state product (GSP) rose moderately throughout the 2001–2004 period, but did not experience the rebound in economic activity felt by many other states from 2003 to 2004. Consequently, Rhode Island's growth rate of 3.5 percent from 2003 to 2004 was well below the national average and ranked 36th in the country. Slow growth in the industrial sector and in retail trade offset the more substantial growth rates in many of the service-providing industries. Real estate and related activity contributed substantially to the GSP growth in 2004. The median value of owner-occupied housing in Rhode Island was the sixth highest in the nation in 2004.

Table RI-11. Real Gross State Product, 1997–2004

(Millions of chained 2000 dollars, percent.)

Industry	1997	1998	1999	2000	2001	2002	2003	2004	Average annual percent change, 2001–2004
GROSS STATE PRODUCT	30 438	30 958	31 794	33 835	34 493	35 025	36 547	37 809	3.1
As a percent of U.S. gross product	0.4	0.3	0.3	0.3	0.4	0.3	0.4	0.4	X
Private Industries	26 542	27 056	27 833	29 695	30 328	30 815	32 361	33 541	3.4
Agriculture, forestry, fishing, and hunting	42	41	40	40	83	87	91	92	3.5
Mining	9	10	10	10	10	12	11	10	0.0
Utilities	677	589	631	760	650	619	654	649	-0.1
Construction	1 591	1 701	1 879	1 808	1 839	1 863	2 010	1 968	2.3
Manufacturing	3 848	3 813	3 766	4 042	3 879	3 833	3 879	3 949	0.6
As a percent of gross state product	12.6	12.3	11.8	11.9	11.2	10.9	10.6	10.4	X
Wholesale trade	1 456	1 597	1 686	1 713	1 817	1 927	1 946	1 952	2.4
Retail trade	1 743	1 821	1 966	2 157	2 307	2 567	2 750	2 857	7.4
Transportation and warehousing	477	522	542	569	520	550	605	598	4.8
Information	1 130	1 052	1 085	1 100	1 259	1 306	1 488	1 745	11.5
Finance and insurance	3 203	3 360	3 455	4 480	4 732	4 564	4 907	5 256	3.6
Real estate and rental and leasing	4 064	4 075	4 206	4 338	4 632	4 631	4 646	4 821	1.3
Services	8 286	8 482	8 577	8 678	8 608	8 880	9 425	9 730	4.2
As a percent of gross state product	27.2	27.4	27.0	25.6	25.0	25.4	25.8	25.7	X
Professional and technical services	1 577	1 644	1 712	1 750	1 769	1 805	1 949	2 039	4.8
Management of companies and enterprises	645	634	624	644	530	540	799	774	13.5
Administrative and waste services	793	805	802	807	783	781	810	904	4.9
Educational services	646	661	662	680	664	665	667	659	-0.3
Health care and social assistance	2 865	2 951	2 918	2 852	2 897	3 072	3 142	3 222	3.6
Arts, entertainment, and recreation	254	237	251	267	286	303	314	305	2.2
Accommodation and food services	789	814	890	953	957	991	1 018	1 048	3.1
Other services, except public administration	717	736	718	725	722	723	726	779	2.6
Government	3 899	3 903	3 962	4 140	4 165	4 211	4 194	4 278	0.9
As a percent of gross state product	12.8	12.6	12.5	12.2	12.1	12.0	11.5	11.3	X

X = Not applicable.

Table RI-12. Government Transfer Payments, Selected Years 1980–2004

(Millions of dollars, percent.)

Item	1980	1990	2000	2001	2002	2003	2004	Average annual percent change, 2000–2004
CURRENT TRANSFER PAYMENTS TO INDIVIDUALS	1 354	2 744	4 748	5 295	5 665	5 873	6 352	7.5
Retirement and Disability Insurance Benefits	641	1 233	1 888	1 995	2 125	2 195	2 317	5.3
Old-age, survivors, and disability insurance (OASDI) benefits	601	1 150	1 740	1 822	1 893	1 946	2 023	3.8
Railroad retirement and disability benefits	8	9	9	9	9	9	9	1.1
Workers' compensation	9	9	11	11	11	11	12	1.6
Other government retirement and disability insurance benefits	24	66	129	154	212	230	273	20.7
Medical Benefits	357	955	2 096	2 472	2 604	2 714	3 082	10.1
Medicare benefits	193	477	991	1 091	1 160	1 217	1 327	7.6
Public assistance medical care benefits	162	466	1 097	1 370	1 430	1 485	1 742	12.2
Military medical insurance benefits	2	11	8	11	13	12	14	14.7
Income Maintenance Benefits	158	260	449	459	487	505	522	3.8
Supplemental Security Income (SSI) benefits	25	53	131	142	147	150	157	4.6
Family assistance	72	103	142	135	138	130	127	-2.7
Food stamps	32	46	59	60	64	70	75	6.5
Other income maintenance benefits	30	58	118	122	138	154	162	8.3
Unemployment Insurance Compensation	98	178	148	187	258	261	214	9.5
Veterans' Benefits	74	85	109	113	124	132	137	6.1
Federal Education and Training Assistance	25	30	51	59	64	61	65	6.4
Other Payments to Individuals	*	3	8	10	4	5	16	17.5

Note: See notes and definitions for more details. Data may not add to total or may appear as zero due to rounding.

* = Less than $500,000.

EXPORTS

Rhode Island was not a large exporter, which was unsurprising given its small economy. In 2004, the value of its exports ranked fifth smallest in the nation. The state's exports amounted to about $1.9 billion, and grew by only about 0.5 percent per year between 2001 and 2004. The chief exports were computers and electronic products, miscellaneous manufactures, and waste and scrap materials. Machinery manufactures exports fell considerably from 2001 to 2004. The state's leading export markets were Canada and Singapore, with Canada accounting for 34 percent of Rhode Island's exports. From 2001 to 2004, exports to the United Kingdom and Mexico declined.

Leading Exports, 2004

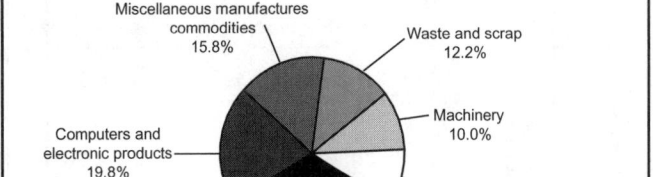

Miscellaneous manufactures commodities 15.8%
Waste and scrap 12.2%
Machinery 10.0%
Chemicals 9.5%
Computers and electronic products 19.8%
Other 32.7%

Table RI-13. Exports of Goods by Leading Products and Destinations, 2001–2004

(Millions of dollars, percent, rank based on 2004 dollar values.)

Product and market	2001	2002	2003	2004	Percent share of total, 2004	Average annual percent change, 2001–2004
Total Goods						
Total	1 269	1 121	1 177	1 286	100.0	0.5
Manufactures	1 098	944	1 020	1 098	85.4	0.0
Agriculture and livestock	18	23	29	25	2.0	11.8
Other commodities	156	158	137	168	13.1	2.5
Five Leading Exports (NAICS Code)						
Computers and electronic products (334)	265	206	259	254	19.8	-1.4
Miscellaneous manufactures (339)	164	142	154	203	15.8	7.5
Waste and scrap (910)	141	145	127	157	12.2	3.7
Machinery manufactures (333)	236	108	122	128	10.0	-18.4
Chemical manufactures (325)	89	126	123	123	9.5	11.4
Five Leading Markets	1 134	1 022	1 087	1 167	90.8	1.0
Canada	352	375	408	439	34.1	7.6
Singapore	60	79	99	85	6.6	12.3
United Kingdom	125	55	51	67	5.2	-18.8
Mexico	69	75	67	65	5.1	-2.1
Germany	47	43	41	49	3.8	1.0

Table RI-14. Agriculture, 1997 and 2002

(Number, acres, and dollars.)

Item	1997	2002
Number of farms	994	858
Land in farms (acres)	65 083	61 223
Farm Size		
Average size of farm (acres)	65	71
Farms by size (percent distribution)		
Fewer than 50 acres	63.1	59.8
50 to 499 acres	35.4	38.9
500 acres or more	1.5	1.3
Market Value of Land and Equipment (Dollars)		
Land and buildings average value per farm	401 259	658 290
Average value per acre	6 128	9 225
Machinery and equipment average value per farm	34 490	57 882
Value of Sales (Thousands of Dollars)		
Agricultural products sold	51 133	55 546
Crops	41 472	47 138
Livestock, poultry, and their products	9 661	8 408
Average per farm (dollars)	51 442	64 740
Value of sales (percent distribution)		
Less than $10,000	60.1	57.7
$10,000 to $99,999	29.5	29.3
$100,000 or more	10.5	13.1
Government Payments		
Payments (thousands of dollars)	123	528
Percent of farms receiving government payments	6.8	6.1
Farm operators whose principal occupation is farming (percent)	47.0	51.5

AGRICULTURE

Cash receipts from farming totaled $55.6 million in 2002, according to the Department of Agriculture's Census of Agriculture. This represented a 15 percent increase from the previous farm census in 1997. Rhode Island was one of smallest agricultural states, with its value of sales ranking 49th in the country. Close to 58 percent of all farms had sales of less than $10,000. Just over half of the state's farm operators reported farming as their principal occupation. Nearly 60 percent of the state's farms spanned fewer than 50 acres.

ENERGY

Rhode Island's energy prices were the fifth highest in the nation. However, energy expenditures per person were $2,184 in 2001, among the 10 lowest in the country, largely reflecting the state's low usage of energy for industrial activities. Per capita consumption was the lowest in the nation. Rhode Island's chief sources of energy were natural gas and petroleum.

Energy Consumption by Source, 2001

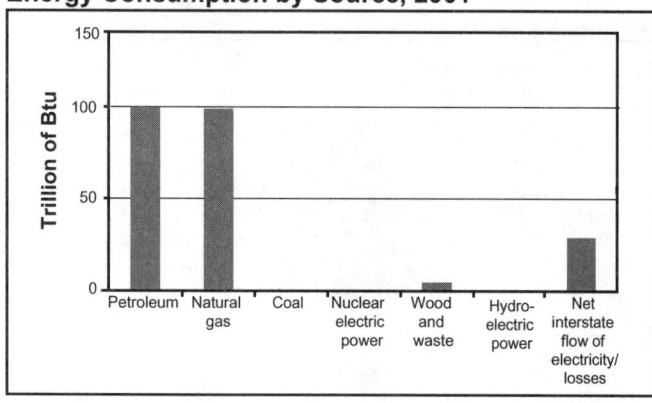

Energy Consumption by Sector, 2001

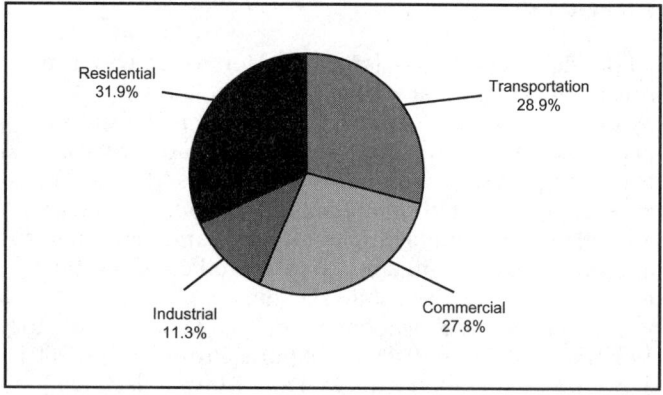

Table RI-15. Energy Consumption, Expenditures, and Prices, Selected Years 1960–2001

(Dollars, Btu [British Thermal Unit], percent distribution.)

Item	1960	1965	1970	1975	1980	1985	1990	1995	2000	2001
Total Consumption (Billion Btu)	187 120	173 784	223 033	206 594	186 286	204 689	209 207	243 450	223 191	227 338
Consumption per capita (million Btu)	217.8	194.6	234.8	219.1	196.7	211.2	208.5	246.1	212.9	214.7
Consumption by Sector (Percent Distribution)										
Residential	28.2	30.0	29.7	32.2	32.7	32.3	32.0	29.0	32.3	31.9
Commercial	12.1	11.8	15.8	16.8	18.3	19.1	22.8	21.2	25.4	27.8
Industrial	27.0	27.2	26.1	23.4	21.0	23.8	17.5	25.9	13.0	11.3
Transportation	32.8	31.0	28.4	27.6	28.0	24.8	27.6	23.8	29.2	28.9
Consumption by Source (Billion Btu)										
Coal	16 754	11 461	228	147	165	213	129	74	52	54
Natural gas	12 253	17 036	25 620	23 453	28 210	30 860	40 452	103 527	91 787	98 578
Petroleum	153 661	127 752	167 612	137 125	104 942	115 013	104 468	98 860	97 231	99 812
Nuclear electric power	0	0	0	0	0	0	0	0	0	0
Hydroelectric power[1]	93	18	35	36	13	0	103	95	50	32
Wood and waste	2 858	3 543	5 234	4 015	5 404	4 581	4 219	5 081	4 182	3 685
Other	0	0	0	0	0	1 435	164	4 397	5 381	1 433
Net interstate flow of electricity/losses[2]	1 500	13 973	24 305	41 819	47 553	52 588	59 673	31 416	24 509	23 742
Total Expenditures (Thousands of Dollars)	...	...	357 700	695 000	1 258 100	1 519 700	1 643 500	1 874 500	2 177 000	2 312 600
Expenditures per capita (dollars)	...	...	377	737	1 328	1 568	1 638	1 895	2 077	2 184
Prices by Sector (Dollars Per Million Btu)										
Total	...	...	1.92	4.14	8.96	9.56	10.45	9.88	13.18	13.95
Residential	...	...	2.18	4.30	8.78	10.48	11.27	11.64	13.83	15.12
Commercial	...	...	2.08	5.23	10.66	12.38	12.85	13.25	15.21	17.13
Industrial	...	...	1.16	3.19	7.27	7.49	8.16	6.12	11.22	13.41
Transportation	...	...	2.17	4.19	9.40	9.03	9.72	10.02	12.23	11.53

[1]A negative number in this row results from pumped storage for which, overall, more electricity is expended than created to provide electricity during peak demand periods.
[2]Net interstate flow of electricity is the difference between the amount of energy in the electricity sold within a state (including associated losses) and the energy input at the electric utilities within the state. A positive number indicates that more electricity (including associated losses) came into the state than went out of the state during the year; conversely, a negative number indicates that more electricity (including associated losses) went out of the state than came into the state.
... = Not available.

Table RI-16. State Taxes, Fiscal 2004

(Dollars, percent distribution.)

Item	Thousands of dollars	Percent distribution	Dollars per capita	
			State	U.S.
TOTAL TAXES	2 408 861	100.0	2 228.4	2 024.8
Property Taxes	1 532	0.1	1.4	38.9
Sales and Gross Receipts	1 305 374	54.2	1 207.6	1 003.4
General sales and gross receipts	804 647	33.4	744.4	677.0
Selective sales taxes	500 727	20.8	463.2	326.4
Insurance premiums	43 350	1.8	40.1	47.0
Motor fuels	133 415	5.5	123.4	114.6
Public utilities	88 640	3.7	82.0	39.2
Tobacco products	115 503	4.8	106.8	42.0
Other selective sales	104 561	4.3	96.7	49.8
Licenses	94 481	3.9	87.4	134.9
Motor vehicle	56 986	2.4	52.7	59.4
Occupation and business, not elsewhere classified	30 031	1.2	27.8	37.1
Other Taxes	1 007 474	41.8	932.0	847.6
Individual income	899 939	37.4	832.5	673.6
Corporation net income	69 479	2.9	64.3	105.1
Death and gift	25 313	1.1	23.4	19.6
Documentary and stock transfer	12 645	0.5	11.7	27.1

GOVERNMENT FINANCE

In 2003, state revenues and expenditures per person were much higher than the national averages, ranking 7th and 11th, respectively. Per capita expenditures were especially high for public welfare and government administration. Spending per person was lower for education and hospitals. In fiscal year 2004, taxes amounted to $2,228, which ranked 14th in the nation. General sales taxes, motor fuels taxes, and tobacco taxes were the state's main source of revenue. Rhode Island ranked 15th in the nation for individual income taxes among the 46 states with such taxes.

Per Capita State Taxes, Fiscal 2004

Table RI-17. State Government Finances, 2003

(Dollars, percent distribution.)

Item	Millions of dollars	Percent distribution	Dollars per capita	
			State	U.S.
GENERAL REVENUE	5 171 932	100.0	4 806.6	3 832.6
Intergovernmental revenue	1 855 350	35.9	1 724.3	1 246.0
Taxes	2 256 654	43.6	2 097.3	1 891.6
General sales	764 217	14.8	710.2	636.0
Selective sales	469 660	9.1	436.5	307.4
License taxes	93 032	1.8	86.5	123.6
Individual income tax	824 870	15.9	766.6	626.8
Corporate income tax	67 118	1.3	62.4	97.8
Other taxes	37 757	0.7	35.1	99.9
Current charges	437 741	8.5	406.8	366.5
Miscellaneous general revenue	622 187	12.0	578.2	328.6
GENERAL EXPENDITURE	5 026 490	100.0	4 671.5	4 010.5
Intergovernmental expenditure	828 198	16.5	769.7	1 316.9
Direct expenditure	4 198 292	83.5	3 901.8	2 693.6
Expenditure by Function				
Education	1 385 449	27.6	1 287.6	1 416.4
Public welfare	1 803 847	35.9	1 676.4	1 083.3
Hospitals	108 890	2.2	101.2	132.3
Health	190 225	3.8	176.8	173.0
Highways	228 646	4.5	212.5	295.4
Police protection	50 475	1.0	46.9	38.4
Correction	159 095	3.2	147.9	135.0
Natural resources	42 396	0.8	39.4	64.0
Parks and recreation	24 051	0.5	22.4	20.1
Government administration	271 097	5.4	252.0	151.3
Interest on general debt	251 321	5.0	233.6	107.8
Other and unallocable	510 998	10.2	474.9	393.4
DEBT AT END OF FISCAL YEAR	6 189 389	X	5 752.2	2 404.7
CASH AND SECURITY HOLDINGS	10 761 870	X	10 001.7	8 938.4

X = Not applicable.

Table RI-18. Education Indicators, 2000–2004

(Percent, number.)

Item	State	U.S.
Total Population 25 Years and Over (Thousands), 2004	709	186 877
Educational Attainment, 2004		
Percent high school graduate or more	81.1	85.2
Percent college graduate or more	27.2	27.7
Elementary and Secondary Schools, 2002–2003		
Total students	159 205	48 202 324
Percent of students eligible for free or reduced-price lunch ..	35.7	40.6
Percent of students who were English language learners	6.1	7.8
Total schools	326	92 330
Student/teacher ratio	13.4	15.9
Per student expenditures	10 349	8 041
Dropouts, Grades 9–12, 2000–2001 (Percent)	4.3	. . .
Higher Education, 2002–2003		
Total enrollment	79 489	17 035 027
Bachelor's degrees awarded	9 108	1 348 503
Percent women	57.2	57.5

. . . = Not available.

Educational Attainment, 2004

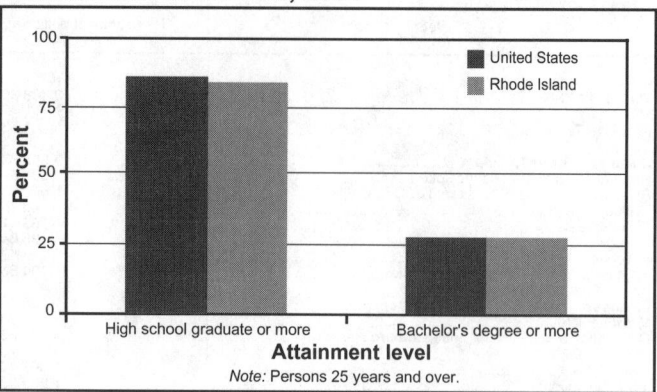

Note: Persons 25 years and over.

EDUCATION

Rhode Island ranked 46th in the nation for its proportion of residents age 25 years and over with high school diplomas. In 2004, 27.2 percent of the population age 25 years and over held bachelor's degrees or more, which ranked 20th in the nation. The state's student/teacher ratio was among the 10 lowest in the country. Rhode Island was among seven states with per student expenditures exceeding $10,000. Of the 46 states reporting dropout data, Rhode Island ranked 17th with 4.3 percent. The state had a lower than average proportion of students eligible for free or reduced-price lunch.

VOTER PARTICIPATION

Rhode Island was among five states and the District of Columbia with a drop in voter participation from 2000 to 2004. In 2000, more than 60 percent of eligible voters cast ballots, but this proportion fell to 57.4 percent in 2004. The proportion of female voters dropped by 3 percentage points; however, the female participation rate remained above that of males. According to the official tally by the Clerk of the U.S. House of Representatives, 61 percent of voters cast ballots for the Democratic presidential candidate in 2000, and 59.4 percent voted similarly in 2004.

Table RI-19. Reported Voting and Registration, November 2000 and November 2004

(Numbers in thousands, percent.)

Characteristic	Total population 18 years and over	Total citizen		Total registered		Total voted	
		Number	Percent	Number	Percent	Number	Percent
NOVEMBER 2000							
Total	729	690	94.6	508	69.7	438	60.1
Male	339	322	95.0	230	67.7	193	56.8
Female	390	368	94.4	279	71.5	245	62.9
NOVEMBER 2004							
Total	813	732	90.0	522	64.2	467	57.4
Male	385	342	88.9	236	61.3	213	55.4
Female	428	390	91.1	286	66.7	253	59.2
Race and Hispanic Origin							
White alone	732	681	93.1	494	67.4	442	60.4
Non-Hispanic White alone	680	655	96.4	478	70.3	431	63.3
Black alone	46	34	B	19	B	17	B
Asian alone	27	11	B	5	B	5	B
Hispanic or Latino[1]	58	28	B	17	B	13	B
White alone or in combination	735	684	93.1	496	67.4	444	60.4
Non-Hispanic White alone or in combination	683	658	96.3	480	70.3	432	63.3
Black alone or in combination	48	36	B	21	B	18	B
Asian alone or in combination	28	11	B	5	B	5	B
Age							
18 to 24 years	93	78	B	38	B	34	B
25 to 44 years	307	267	87.1	179	58.2	155	50.6
45 to 64 years	259	239	92.2	188	72.3	173	66.6
65 to 74 years	77	74	B	61	B	56	B
75 years and over	78	74	B	57	B	50	B

[1]May be of any race.
B = Base is too small to show derived measure.

At a Glance:

- South Carolina's population was close to 4.2 million in 2004, ranking the state as 25th most populous in the nation. South Carolina was one of the leading destinations for people migrating from other states.

- More than 29 percent of the state's population was Black, which was the fifth highest proportion of this racial group in the country.

- The infant mortality rate in South Carolina was the sixth highest in the nation.

- Median household income was well below the national average, ranking among the 10 lowest in the nation. South Carolina's poverty rate of 14.9 percent was well above average.

- In 2004, the state's unemployment rate was 6.8 percent, the fifth highest in the country.

- South Carolina's economy grew at about the same pace as the national economy after the 2001 recession. In 2004, the state's real gross state product ranked 27th in the nation.

- South Carolina had below average educational attainment levels.

Table SC-1. Population by Sex and Age, 1990, 2000, and 2004

(Number, percent.)

Sex and age	1990	2000	2004	Percent distribution, 2004	Average annual percent change, 2000–2004
Total Population	3 486 703	4 012 012	4 198 068	X	1.1
Percent of total U.S. population	1.4	1.4	1.4	X	X
Sex					
Male	1 688 510	1 948 929	2 045 177	48.7	1.2
Female	1 798 193	2 063 083	2 152 891	51.3	1.1
Age					
Under 5 years	256 337	264 679	280 272	6.7	0.5
5 to 17 years	663 870	744 962	744 428	17.7	0.8
18 years and over	648 392	3 002 371	3 173 368	75.6	1.5
18 to 24 years	2 566 496	407 851	428 864	10.2	0.3
25 to 44 years	406 526	1 185 955	1 179 222	28.1	0.4
45 to 64 years	1 114 643	923 232	1 044 890	24.9	3.5
65 years and over	396 935	485 333	520 392	12.4	2.0
85 years and over	30 749	50 269	59 451	1.4	5.0
Median age (years)	31.9	35.4	36.4	X	X

X = Not applicable.

Average Annual Rate of Population Growth, 1980–2004

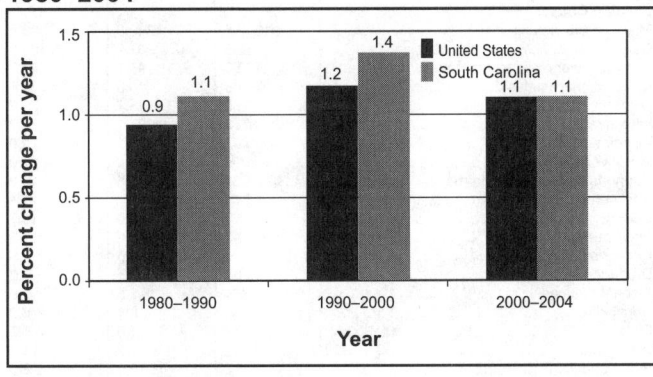

POPULATION

South Carolina's population grew at an above average rate from 2000 to 2004. The state's birth rate was below average, but South Carolina's population was augmented by immigration from both domestic and international sources, which together accounted for almost 60 percent of the state's population growth. About 30,000 new residents moved in from abroad and more than 79,000 new residents arrived from other states during this period. The state's median age was slightly older than the national average, as South Carolina had a slightly below average proportion of population under 18 years old.

Table SC-2. Population by Race and Hispanic Origin, 1990, 2000, and 2004

(Number, percent.)

Race and Hispanic origin	1990	2000	2004
Total Population	3 486 703	4 012 012	4 198 068
Non-Hispanic (Percent)			
One race[1]			
White	68.5	66.2	65.6
Black	29.7	29.4	29.1
American Indian, Alaska Native[2]	0.2	0.3	0.3
Asian and Pacific Islander[2]	0.6	0.9	1.1
Other race[2]	0.3	. . .	. . .
Two or more races	. . .	0.7	0.8
Hispanic or Latino[3] (Percent)	0.9	2.4	3.1

[1]Individuals could report only one race in the 1990 census and could report one or more races on the 2000 census. Data on race in 2000 and 2004 are not comparable to 1990.
[2]Data for 1990 include people of Hispanic or Latino origin.
[3]May be of any race.
. . . = Not available.

Minority Population as a Percent of Total Population, 2004

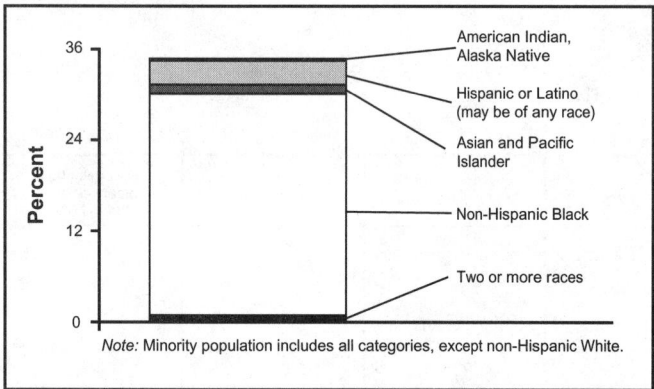

Note: Minority population includes all categories, except non-Hispanic White.

Age-Adjusted Death Rates, Average 2000–2002

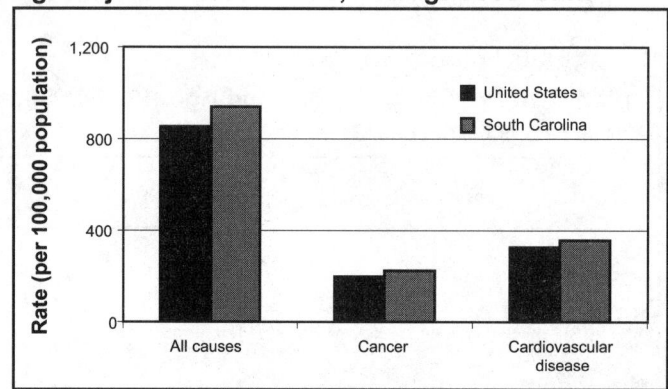

HEALTH

South Carolina had an above average proportion of its population covered by health insurance. The state's infant mortality rate was among the highest in the nation, as were its age-adjusted death rates. The state's birth rate for teenage mothers was the 13th highest in the nation.

Table SC-3. Health Characteristics, 2000–2004

(Number, rate, percent.)

Item	State	U.S.
Births, 2003–2004		
Number of births	55 649	4 089 950
Birth rate (per 1,000 population)	13.4	14.1
Teenage birth rate (per 1,000 women age 15–19 years)	51.5	41.6
Mortality Rates, Average 2000–2002		
Infant mortality rate (per 1,000 live births)	9.0	6.9
Age-adjusted mortality rate (per 100,000 population)		
All races	952.5	853.3
Non-Hispanic White	899.2	843.1
Black	1 136.8	1 097.7
American Indian, Alaska Native	. . .	687.0
Asian and Pacific Islander	407.0	486.0
Hispanic or Latino[1]	332.8	642.7
Health Insurance, 2004		
Percent of all persons without health insurance	14.7	15.7
Percent of children without health insurance	7.7	11.2
Percent of low-income children without health insurance	5.8	7.1

[1]May be of any race.
. . . = Not available.

Table SC-4. Leading Causes of Death, Average 2000–2002

(Number, rate per 100,000 population.)

Cause	Number of deaths	Age-adjusted death rates	
		State	U.S.
ALL CAUSES	37 099	952.5	853.3
Leading Causes			
Major cardiovascular diseases	13 386	348.9	326.5
Cancer	8 285	207.2	196.0
Chronic lower respiratory diseases	1 783	45.8	43.7
Unintentional injuries	1 969	48.8	35.7
Diabetes (underlying cause)	1 135	28.7	25.2
Influenza and pneumonia	788	21.1	22.7
Alzheimer's disease	907	25.1	19.0
Motor vehicle accidents	996	24.2	15.0
Nephritis, nephrotic syndrome, and nephrosis ..	651	16.8	13.8
Septicemia	570	14.7	11.4
Suicides	450	11.0	10.7
Firearm-related	543	13.2	10.3
Cirrhosis	436	10.5	9.5
Drug-induced	264	6.5	7.9
Alcohol-induced	354	8.5	6.9
Homicides	334	8.1	6.0
Falls	177	4.6	5.2
HIV	291	7.2	5.0
Viral hepatitis	87	2.1	2.0
Anemias	84	2.2	1.6
Drownings	72	1.8	1.3
Fire deaths	84	2.1	1.2

Note: The rates are age-adjusted to the U.S. 2000 standard population.

Table SC-5. Households and Housing Characteristics, 1990, 2000, and 2004

(Number, percent, and dollars.)

Characteristic	1990	2000	2004	Average annual percent change, 2000–2004
Total Households	1 258 044	1 533 854	1 611 401	1.2
Family households	928 206	1 072 822	1 101 678	0.7
Married-couple family	710 089	783 142	804 775	0.7
Other family	218 117	289 680	296 903	0.6
Male householder, no wife present	41 913	62 722	72 629	3.7
Female householder, no husband present	176 204	226 958	224 274	-0.3
Nonfamily households	329 838	461 032	509 723	2.5
Householder living alone	281 347	383 142	429 494	2.9
Householder not living alone	48 491	77 890	80 229	0.7
Housing Characteristics				
Average size	2.68	2.53	2.52	X
Housing units	1 424 155	1 753 670	1 890 682	1.9
Occupied housing units	1 258 044	1 533 854	1 611 401	1.2
Owner-occupied	878 704	1 107 617	1 123 764	0.4
Renter-occupied	379 340	426 237	487 637	3.4
Median gross rent of renter-occupied housing units (dollars)	376	510	610	4.6
Median value of owner-occupied housing units (dollars)	60 700	94 900	113 910	4.7

X = Not applicable.

Median Housing Value and Median Rent, 2004

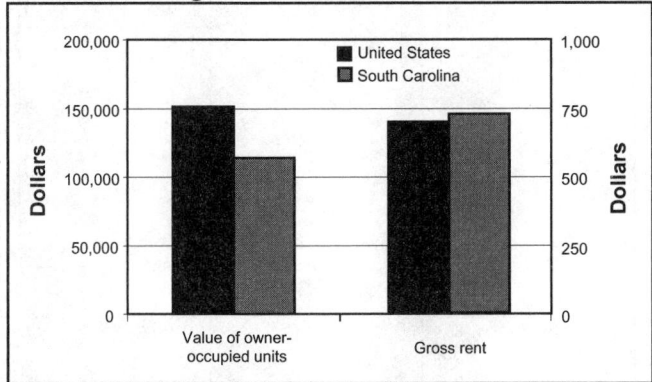

Median Household Income, 1984–2004 (2004 Dollars)

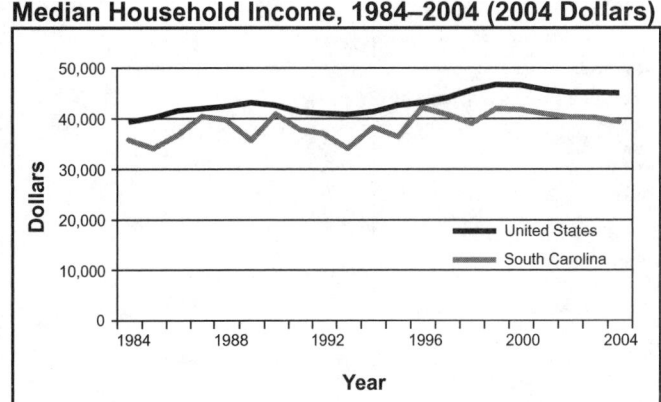

Table SC-6. Household Income and Poverty Status, 1980–2004

(2004 CPI-U-RS adjusted dollars, rate.)

Year	State		U.S.	
	Median household income (2004 dollars)	Poverty rate	Median household income (2004 dollars)	Poverty rate
2004	38 747	14.9	44 389	12.7
2003	39 513	12.7	44 482	12.5
2002	39 718	14.3	44 546	12.1
2001	40 268	15.1	45 062	11.7
2000	41 210	11.1	46 058	11.3
1999	41 330	11.7	46 129	11.9
1998	38 501	13.7	45 003	12.7
1997	40 211	13.1	43 430	13.3
1996	41 553	13.0	42 544	13.7
1995	35 783	19.9	41 943	13.8
1994	37 629	13.8	40 677	14.5
1993	33 539	18.7	40 217	15.1
1992	36 387	19.0	40 422	14.8
1991	37 144	16.4	40 746	14.2
1990	40 270	16.2	41 963	13.5
1989	35 010	17.0	42 524	12.8
1988	39 175	15.5	41 771	13.0
1987	39 832	15.6	41 322	13.4
1986	36 123	17.3	40 939	13.6
1985	33 548	15.2	39 545	14.0
1984	35 138	17.2	38 782	14.4
1983	. . .	20.8	. . .	15.2
1982	. . .	21.2	. . .	15.0
1981	. . .	18.4	. . .	14.0
1980	. . .	16.8	. . .	13.0

. . . = Not available.

Table SC-7. Employment Status by Demographic Group, 2004

(Numbers in thousands, rate.)

Characteristic	Civilian noninstitutional population	Civilian labor force		Employed	Unemployment rate
		Number	Participation rate		
SEX AND AGE					
Total	3 193	2 077	65.1	1 935	6.9
16 to 19 years	247	92	37.3	77	16.8
20 to 24 years	311	231	74.3	199	13.8
25 to 34 years	527	448	84.9	414	7.4
35 to 44 years	570	481	84.3	458	4.8
45 to 54 years	594	477	80.3	454	4.8
55 to 64 years	449	273	60.8	261	4.4
65 years and over	495	76	15.4	72	5.1
Men	1 510	1 075	71.2	1 004	6.7
16 to 19 years	123	47	38.3	40	15.2
20 to 24 years	154	120	77.7	101	15.4
25 to 34 years	247	225	91.1	208	7.7
35 to 44 years	282	258	91.7	247	4.6
45 to 54 years	271	231	85.5	222	4.0
55 to 64 years	227	150	66.1	143	4.3
65 years and over	206	44	21.1	42	2.5
Women	1 683	1 002	59.5	931	7.1
16 to 19 years	124	45	36.3	37	18.5
20 to 24 years	157	111	70.9	98	12.1
25 to 34 years	280	222	79.3	207	7.1
35 to 44 years	288	222	77.1	211	5.0
45 to 54 years	323	246	76.0	232	5.5
55 to 64 years	222	123	55.4	117	4.6
65 years and over	289	33	11.3	30	8.6
MARITAL STATUS					
Married men, spouse present	842	628	74.6	608	3.2
Married women, spouse present	832	529	63.5	510	3.6
Women who maintain families	225	159	70.6	141	11.1
RACE, HISPANIC ORIGIN, AND SEX					
White	2 254	1 469	65.2	1 387	5.6
Men	1 092	785	71.9	744	5.2
Women	1 162	684	58.9	642	6.0
Black	892	573	64.2	514	10.2
Men	395	272	69.0	242	11.0
Women	498	301	60.4	272	9.4
Hispanic or Latino[1]	59	46	77.8	44	4.6
Men	37	32	86.6	30	5.3
RACE, HISPANIC ORIGIN, AND AGE					
White					
25 to 34 years	358	307	85.9	285	7.3
35 to 44 years	404	341	84.4	326	4.5
45 to 54 years	397	329	82.9	320	2.9
55 to 64 years	352	216	61.2	206	4.6
Black					
20 to 24 years	112	79	70.8	62	22.5
25 to 34 years	159	131	82.1	120	8.3
35 to 44 years	158	132	83.7	125	5.5
45 to 54 years	189	141	74.7	128	9.0
55 to 64 years	91	54	59.0	52	3.7

Note: Data in Table 7 are from the Current Population Survey (CPS) and do not match Bureau of Labor Statistics estimates in Table 8. See notes and definitions for more details.

[1]May be of any race.

Table SC-8. Employment Status, 1990–2004

(Numbers in thousands, rate.)

Year	Civilian labor force	Employed	Unemployed	Unemployment rate
2004	2 046 179	1 906 572	139 607	6.8
2003	2 013 061	1 878 397	134 664	6.7
2002	1 966 724	1 849 036	117 688	6.0
2001	1 955 527	1 850 436	105 091	5.4
2000	1 965 089	1 895 902	69 187	3.5
1999	1 956 674	1 876 895	79 779	4.1
1998	1 918 305	1 849 075	69 230	3.6
1997	1 903 857	1 819 508	84 349	4.4
1996	1 892 377	1 785 646	106 731	5.6
1995	1 849 866	1 754 633	95 233	5.1
1994	1 840 416	1 729 363	111 053	6.0
1993	1 827 755	1 696 068	131 687	7.2
1992	1 792 544	1 673 620	118 924	6.6
1991	1 760 801	1 653 770	107 031	6.1
1990	1 722 150	1 638 580	83 570	4.9

Note: Population age 16 years and over.

Unemployment Rate, 1980–2004

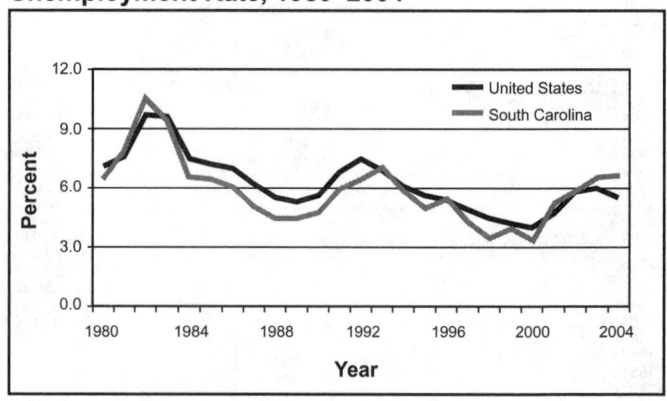

Table SC-9. Employment and Average Wages by Industry, 2001–2004

(Estimates are based on the 2002 North American Industry Classification System [NAICS].)

Industry	2001	2002	2003	2004	Annual average percent change, 2001–2004
	Number of jobs				
TOTAL EMPLOYMENT BY PLACE OF WORK	2 265 724	2 259 264	2 275 330	2 313 823	0.7
Farm Employment	32 003	33 028	31 822	32 652	0.7
Nonfarm Employment	2 233 721	2 226 236	2 243 508	2 281 171	0.7
Private employment	1 854 932	1 847 730	1 864 768	1 901 951	0.8
Forestry, fishing, hunting, and other[1]	13 533	13 491	12 899	12 915	-1.5
Mining	2 462	2 341	2 514	2 511	0.7
Utilities	12 560	12 316	12 168	12 013	-1.5
Construction	158 670	156 271	159 044	162 592	0.8
Manufacturing	320 491	297 073	283 373	275 220	-4.9
Durable goods manufacturing	153 063	143 353	138 246	137 179	-3.6
Nondurable goods manufacturing	167 428	153 720	145 127	138 041	-6.2
Wholesale trade	69 714	69 494	69 405	72 267	1.2
Retail trade	273 725	271 537	272 944	279 668	0.7
Transportation and warehousing	61 738	61 230	60 770	61 588	-0.1
Information	33 409	32 076	31 484	30 692	-2.8
Finance and insurance	79 646	82 963	85 474	86 419	2.8
Real estate and rental and leasing	69 159	71 115	74 630	78 093	4.1
Professional and technical services	95 193	96 354	98 443	100 965	2.0
Management of companies and enterprises	11 274	10 861	10 547	10 310	-2.9
Administrative and waste services	140 917	140 733	146 458	156 868	3.6
Educational services	26 772	28 144	29 480	30 397	4.3
Health care and social assistance	153 544	159 242	164 670	168 813	3.2
Arts, entertainment, and recreation	37 349	38 121	39 118	39 938	2.3
Accommodation and food services	170 425	174 539	179 631	186 594	3.1
Other services, except public administration	124 351	129 829	131 716	134 088	2.5
Government and government enterprises	378 789	378 506	378 740	379 220	0.0
	Dollars				
AVERAGE WAGES AND SALARIES BY PLACE OF WORK	28 722	29 525	30 334	31 444	3.1
Farm Earnings	18 176	17 732	14 669	17 752	-0.8
Nonfarm Earnings	28 762	29 574	30 395	31 502	3.1
Private earnings	28 560	29 221	29 969	31 022	2.8
Forestry, fishing, hunting, and other[1]	23 583	23 240	24 183	24 662	1.5
Mining	38 700	39 534	39 815	42 632	3.3
Utilities	55 050	55 390	58 925	63 307	4.8
Construction	31 045	31 356	32 450	33 591	2.7
Manufacturing	35 847	37 583	38 994	40 753	4.4
Durable goods manufacturing	36 430	37 983	39 551	41 421	4.4
Nondurable goods manufacturing	35 318	37 213	38 467	40 092	4.3
Wholesale trade	39 973	41 499	42 733	44 893	3.9
Retail trade	20 772	21 213	21 711	22 311	2.4
Transportation and warehousing	31 584	32 264	33 502	34 589	3.1
Information	38 660	38 327	39 741	42 698	3.4
Finance and insurance	39 362	40 775	42 212	43 827	3.6
Real estate and rental and leasing	27 458	27 982	28 072	29 775	2.7
Professional and technical services	45 445	45 522	45 772	47 250	1.3
Management of companies and enterprises	44 811	48 024	54 057	61 064	10.9
Administrative and waste services	22 790	23 976	24 635	25 434	3.7
Educational services	20 177	20 911	21 509	22 297	3.4
Health care and social assistance	31 337	31 881	32 554	33 822	2.6
Arts, entertainment, and recreation	16 592	16 794	16 953	17 621	2.0
Accommodation and food services	12 741	12 974	13 230	13 521	2.0
Other services, except public administration	19 765	20 246	20 836	21 612	3.0
Government and government enterprises	29 595	31 006	32 126	33 481	4.2

Note: Average wages and salaries are a calculation by the editors of wage and salary disbursements divided by full- and part-time wage and salary employment. Data may not add to total or may appear as zero due to rounding.

[1] "Other" consists of the number of jobs held by U.S. residents employed by international organizations and foreign embassies and consulates in the United States.

LABOR MARKET

South Carolina's unemployment rate has been well above the national average and higher than those of neighboring Georgia and North Carolina since the 2001 recession. Employment declined in 2002, following the 2001 recession, but began to recover thereafter (and was particularly strong in 2004). Total employment grew at an above average rate from 2003 to 2004. The service-providing sector added jobs steadily and retail trade experienced moderate job growth. However, employment in manufacturing fell throughout the 2001–2004 period. Average wages and salaries were among the lowest in the nation, but grew at an above average rate from 2001 to 2004.

Employment by Industry, 2004

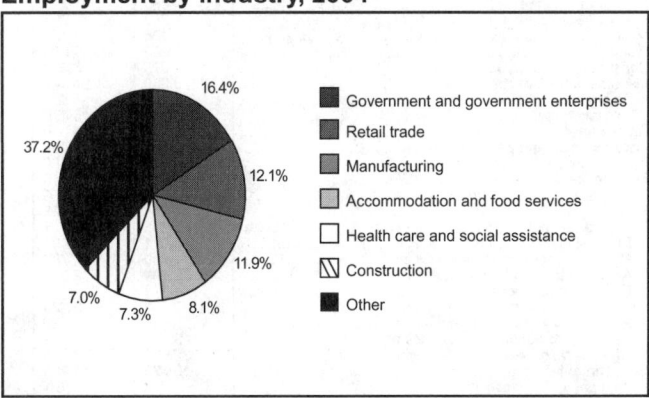

Table SC-10. Personal Income by Major Source, Selected Years 1980–2004

(Millions of dollars, except where noted.)

Item	1980	1990	2000	2001	2002	2003	2004	Average annual percent change, 2000–2004
Earnings by Place of Work	19 699	43 049	72 441	74 323	76 302	79 551	84 005	3.8
Wage and salary disbursements	15 393	32 784	54 757	55 826	56 816	58 424	61 311	2.9
Supplements to wages and salaries	2 950	7 157	11 424	11 916	13 356	14 643	15 664	8.2
Proprietors' income[1]	1 356	3 108	6 260	6 581	6 130	6 484	7 030	2.9
Farm proprietors' income	-60	189	358	433	42	414	416	3.9
Nonfarm proprietors' income	1 417	2 919	5 902	6 149	6 088	6 070	6 613	2.9
(-) Contributions for government social insurance[2]	1 777	4 817	8 132	8 425	8 736	9 070	9 523	4.0
(+) Adjustment for residence[3]	320	505	1 398	1 371	1 391	1 408	1 499	1.8
(=) Net Earnings by Place of Residence	18 242	38 737	65 707	67 270	68 957	71 889	75 982	3.7
(+) Dividends, interest, and rent[4]	2 939	9 845	17 289	17 216	16 654	16 291	16 919	-0.5
(+) Personal current transfer receipts	3 088	7 064	15 274	16 982	18 443	19 480	21 088	8.4
Personal income	24 270	55 647	98 270	101 468	104 054	107 660	113 988	3.8
Farm income	24 242	55 359	97 789	100 891	103 862	107 129	113 415	3.8
Nonfarm income	27	288	481	577	192	532	574	4.5
Per Capita Personal Income (Dollars)[5]	7 743	15 894	24 424	24 985	25 343	25 950	27 153	2.7

Note: Data may not add to total or may appear as zero due to rounding.

[1]Proprietors' income includes the inventory valuation adjustment and the capital consumption adjustment.
[2]Contributions for government social insurance are included in earnings by type and industry, but they are excluded from personal income.
[3]The adjustment for residence is the net inflow of the earnings of interarea commuters.
[4]Rental income of persons includes the capital consumption adjustment.
[5]Per capita personal income is total personal income divided by total midyear population.

Per Capita Personal Income, 1980–2004 (Current Dollars)

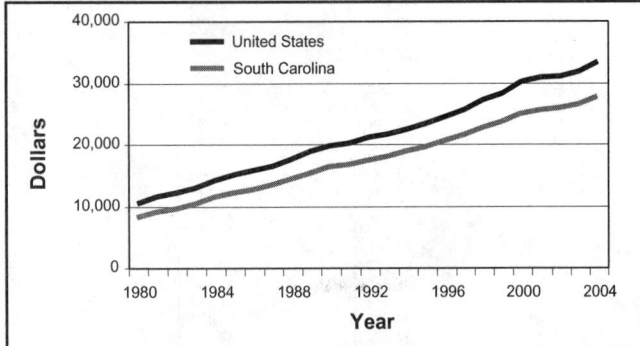

ECONOMIC ACTIVITY

South Carolina's real gross state product (GSP) grew at about the national average rate from 2001 to 2004; however, this growth slowed somewhat during the 2003–2004 period. The leading contributors to growth were manufacturing, wholesale trade, retail trade, information services, real estate and related activities, and government. By 2004, construction had risen back to its 2001 level, but remained below its 2000 level. Housing values in South Carolina have risen at a below average rate in recent years. The median value of owner-occupied housing in the state was $113,910 in 2004, ranking 35th in the country.

Table SC-11. Real Gross State Product, 1997–2004

(Millions of chained 2000 dollars, percent.)

Industry	1997	1998	1999	2000	2001	2002	2003	2004	Average annual percent change, 2001–2004
GROSS STATE PRODUCT	103 331	107 537	111 486	112 831	114 539	116 437	119 973	124 836	2.9
As a percent of U.S. gross product	1.2	1.2	1.2	1.2	1.2	1.2	1.2	1.2	X
Private Industries	87 560	91 298	94 620	95 381	97 201	98 940	102 396	106 612	3.1
Agriculture, forestry, fishing, and hunting	868	795	872	1 080	1 101	847	1 123	1 037	-2.0
Mining	138	154	173	175	142	137	142	131	-2.7
Utilities	2 905	2 808	3 039	2 935	3 019	2 920	3 251	3 482	4.9
Construction	6 375	6 631	6 614	6 303	6 151	6 006	6 077	6 139	-0.1
Manufacturing	23 830	24 142	23 296	23 487	23 503	23 942	24 816	25 642	2.9
As a percent of gross state product	23.1	22.4	20.9	20.8	20.5	20.6	20.7	20.5	X
Wholesale trade	5 156	5 876	6 212	6 133	6 655	6 907	6 824	7 237	2.8
Retail trade	8 143	8 610	9 169	9 245	9 633	9 970	10 658	11 342	5.6
Transportation and warehousing	2 412	2 486	2 604	2 812	2 707	2 741	2 809	2 851	1.7
Information	2 316	2 466	2 579	2 863	3 061	3 167	3 400	3 714	6.7
Finance and insurance	4 348	4 715	4 899	4 933	4 940	5 468	5 773	6 020	6.8
Real estate and rental and leasing	10 823	11 375	12 097	12 411	13 148	13 149	13 045	13 534	1.0
Services	20 214	21 225	23 085	23 004	23 168	23 756	24 609	25 691	3.5
As a percent of gross state product	19.6	19.7	20.7	20.4	20.2	20.4	20.5	20.6	X
Professional and technical services	4 021	4 494	4 648	4 550	4 899	4 996	5 145	5 302	2.7
Management of companies and enterprises	865	797	767	706	646	657	730	761	5.6
Administrative and waste services	2 799	2 928	4 204	4 159	3 914	4 100	4 386	4 692	6.2
Educational services	473	485	518	519	518	523	512	505	-0.8
Health care and social assistance	5 102	5 224	5 400	5 616	6 039	6 254	6 450	6 649	3.3
Arts, entertainment, and recreation	946	1 020	1 156	974	878	900	911	925	1.8
Accommodation and food services	3 329	3 479	3 663	3 723	3 625	3 683	3 818	4 010	3.4
Other services, except public administration	2 679	2 798	2 729	2 757	2 649	2 643	2 657	2 847	2.4
Government	15 773	16 235	16 862	17 451	17 340	17 502	17 606	18 250	1.7
As a percent of gross state product	15.3	15.1	15.1	15.5	15.1	15.0	14.7	14.6	X

X = Not applicable.

Table SC-12. Government Transfer Payments, Selected Years 1980–2004

(Millions of dollars, percent.)

Item	1980	1990	2000	2001	2002	2003	2004	Average annual percent change, 2000–2004
CURRENT TRANSFER PAYMENTS TO INDIVIDUALS	2 872	6 610	14 340	15 930	17 429	18 338	19 898	8.5
Retirement and Disability Insurance Benefits	1 406	3 261	6 151	6 652	7 068	7 413	7 807	6.1
Old-age, survivors, and disability insurance (OASDI) benefits	1 354	3 119	5 910	6 358	6 769	7 096	7 478	6.1
Railroad retirement and disability benefits	37	66	88	91	96	99	101	3.6
Workers' compensation	13	72	140	163	189	200	209	10.5
Other government retirement and disability insurance benefits	2	5	13	41	14	18	20	10.1
Medical Benefits	584	2 062	5 734	6 535	7 066	7 342	8 450	10.2
Medicare benefits	308	995	2 895	3 235	3 492	3 722	4 125	9.3
Public assistance medical care benefits	263	988	2 756	3 182	3 407	3 471	4 143	10.7
Military medical insurance benefits	13	78	83	118	168	149	182	21.6
Income Maintenance Benefits	445	673	1 608	1 629	1 928	2 166	2 335	9.8
Supplemental Security Income (SSI) benefits	126	245	443	459	466	484	506	3.4
Family assistance	72	96	112	55	62	63	32	-26.9
Food stamps	190	195	240	284	368	459	519	21.3
Other income maintenance benefits	57	137	813	830	1 032	1 160	1 278	12.0
Unemployment Insurance Compensation	150	145	207	398	573	570	404	18.1
Veterans' Benefits	228	275	469	507	568	612	655	8.7
Federal Education and Training Assistance	59	86	153	184	211	218	231	10.9
Other Payments to Individuals	*	107	18	25	15	17	16	-3.8

Note: See notes and definitions for more details. Data may not add to total or may appear as zero due to rounding.

* = Less than $500,000.

EXPORTS

In 2004, South Carolina was the 18th largest exporter in the nation, with goods amounting to $13.4 billion. This was an increase of more than 34 percent from 2001. The largest exports were transportation equipment and chemical manufactures, which together accounted for nearly half of the state's exports. Computers and electronic products were the fastest-growing export, increasing from $429 million in 2001 to $1.4 billion in 2004. The leading overseas markets were Canada and Germany. Exports to Germany, the second leading market, nearly doubled from 2001 to 2004. The Netherlands and China were also among the state's fastest-growing export markets.

Leading Exports, 2004

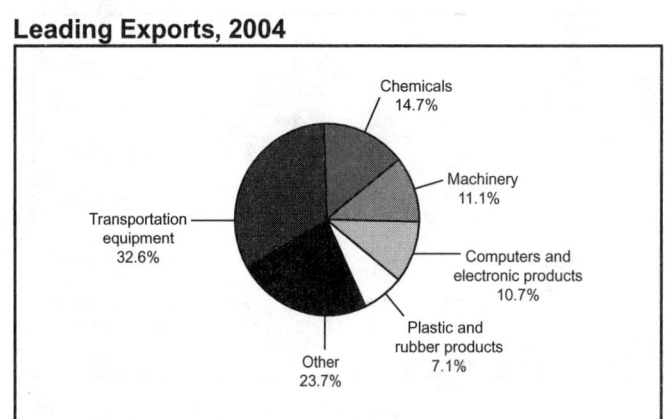

Table SC-13. Exports of Goods by Leading Products and Destinations, 2001–2004

(Millions of dollars, percent, rank based on 2004 dollar values.)

Product and market	2001	2002	2003	2004	Percent share of total, 2004	Average annual percent change, 2001–2004
Total Goods						
Total	9 956	9 656	11 773	13 376	100.0	10.3
Manufactures	9 762	9 445	11 540	13 007	97.2	10.0
Agriculture and livestock	78	87	111	237	1.8	45.1
Other commodities	117	125	122	132	1.0	4.0
Five Leading Exports (NAICS Code)						
Transportation equipment (336)	3 099	2 761	4 333	4 367	32.6	12.1
Chemical manufactures (325)	1 573	1 665	1 691	1 970	14.7	7.8
Machinery manufactures (333)	1 355	1 298	1 271	1 486	11.1	3.1
Computers and electronic products (334)	429	573	915	1 427	10.7	49.2
Plastic and rubber products (326)	758	805	843	954	7.1	8.0
Five Leading Markets	8 891	8 612	10 569	11 919	89.1	10.3
Canada	2 352	2 411	2 598	2 819	21.1	6.2
Germany	1 454	1 685	2 703	2 816	21.1	24.6
Mexico	731	782	752	869	6.5	5.9
United Kingdom	1 203	556	817	825	6.2	-11.8
Netherlands	203	213	299	556	4.2	39.9

Table SC-14. Agriculture, 1997 and 2002

(Number, acres, and dollars.)

Item	1997	2002
Number of farms	25 807	24 541
Land in farms (acres)	4 974 138	4 845 923
Farm Size		
Average size of farm (acres)	193	197
Farms by size (percent distribution)		
Fewer than 50 acres	38.6	41.7
50 to 499 acres	53.0	49.9
500 acres or more	8.4	8.3
Market Value of Land and Equipment (Dollars)		
Land and buildings average value per farm	293 342	410 897
Average value per acre	1 552	2 067
Machinery and equipment average value per farm	40 896	53 108
Value of Sales (Thousands of Dollars)		
Agricultural products sold	1 679 193	1 489 750
Crops	821 107	593 245
Livestock, poultry, and their products	858 086	896 505
Average per farm (dollars)	65 067	60 705
Value of sales (percent distribution)		
Less than $10,000	73.1	78.4
$10,000 to $99,999	17.5	14.8
$100,000 or more	9.4	6.8
Government Payments		
Payments (thousands of dollars)	30 931	38 384
Percent of farms receiving government payments	34.0	24.9
Farm operators whose principal occupation is farming (percent) ...	36.7	46.4

AGRICULTURE

Cash receipts from farming amounted to nearly $1.5 billion in 2002, according to the Department of Agriculture's Census of Agriculture. This amount ranked 35th in the nation and was a moderate decline from the amount recorded on the 1997 agriculture census. South Carolina's leading product was poultry, followed by tobacco and cotton. Farming in the state was small-scale—over 78 percent of farms reported sales of less than $10,000, and only 46.4 percent of all farm operators indicated that farming was their principal occupation. Nearly 42 percent of farms spanned fewer than 50 acres.

ENERGY

In 2001, energy expenditures per person in South Carolina totaled $2,430, an amount slightly above the national average. Average energy prices were slightly below average. The state ranked 18th in the nation for per capita energy consumption. South Carolina's chief energy sources were nuclear power, petroleum, and coal.

Energy Consumption by Source, 2001

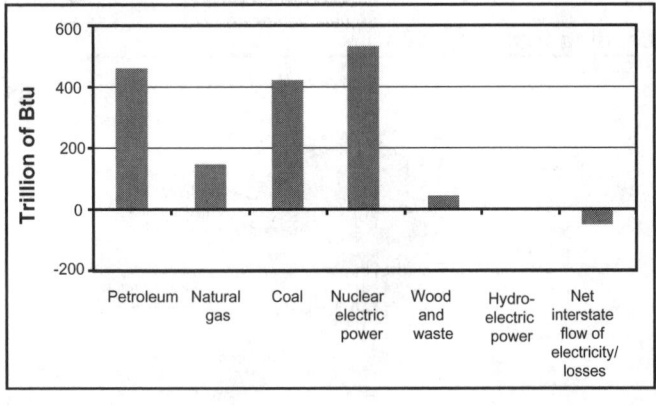

Energy Consumption by Sector, 2001

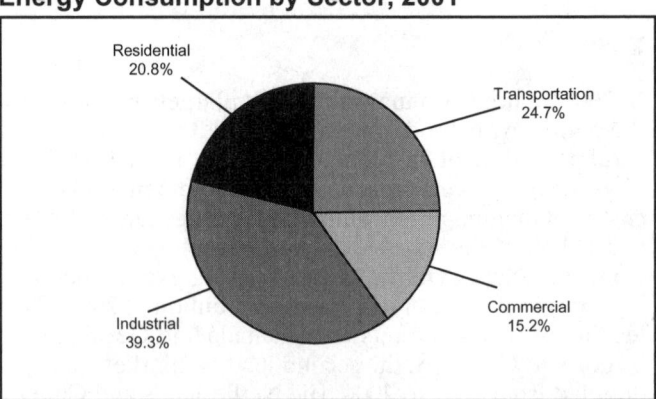

Table SC-15. Energy Consumption, Expenditures, and Prices, Selected Years 1960–2001

(Dollars, Btu [British Thermal Unit], percent distribution.)

Item	1960	1965	1970	1975	1980	1985	1990	1995	2000	2001
Total Consumption (Billion Btu)	489 472	555 673	747 585	844 618	1 009 962	1 088 356	1 290 691	1 443 754	1 609 554	1 548 839
Consumption per capita (million Btu)	205.4	222.8	288.6	291.0	323.5	329.5	370.2	390.2	401.2	381.5
Consumption by Sector (Percent Distribution)										
Residential	22.2	19.9	20.1	19.6	19.5	19.9	19.3	20.0	20.7	20.8
Commercial	7.8	8.1	9.8	13.1	13.3	12.5	13.1	13.6	14.8	15.2
Industrial	44.1	45.5	43.5	40.1	42.6	43.2	43.8	44.3	40.9	39.3
Transportation	25.8	26.5	26.6	27.2	24.6	24.4	23.9	22.1	23.6	24.7
Consumption by Source (Billion Btu)										
Coal	96 414	121 474	140 118	140 171	245 769	262 653	289 222	314 510	432 198	414 424
Natural gas	60 581	90 513	164 305	125 900	146 922	100 198	134 107	156 021	165 090	147 173
Petroleum	219 450	225 789	302 186	340 499	365 755	357 487	404 329	426 505	471 456	469 514
Nuclear electric power	0	880	76	214 291	189 846	338 056	453 763	516 666	530 708	521 042
Hydroelectric power[1]	38 849	36 758	24 064	45 926	31 421	19 169	29 039	28 866	4 606	1 930
Wood and waste	43 120	40 588	41 000	41 879	36 179	45 774	73 443	88 088	76 684	62 804
Other	0	0	0	0	0	0	97	117	159	174
Net interstate flow of electricity/losses[2]	31 059	39 670	75 837	-64 049	-5 931	-34 981	-93 309	-87 019	-71 344	-68 222
Total Expenditures (Thousands of Dollars)	. . .	. . .	972 600	2 120 500	4 816 300	5 985 600	6 935 300	7 610 200	10 152 000	9 867 100
Expenditures per capita (dollars)	. . .	. . .	375	731	1 543	1 812	1 989	2 057	2 530	2 430
Prices by Sector (Dollars Per Million Btu)										
Total	. . .	. . .	1.82	3.74	7.18	8.74	8.51	8.36	10.31	10.41
Residential	. . .	. . .	2.73	5.63	9.62	14.40	15.84	16.66	17.96	18.94
Commercial	. . .	. . .	2.41	4.82	7.58	12.75	13.72	13.84	14.96	15.63
Industrial	. . .	. . .	0.90	2.43	4.33	6.28	5.35	5.03	6.09	6.39
Transportation	. . .	. . .	2.34	4.04	9.42	8.39	8.50	8.10	10.74	10.00

[1]A negative number in this row results from pumped storage for which, overall, more electricity is expended than created to provide electricity during peak demand periods.
[2]Net interstate flow of electricity is the difference between the amount of energy in the electricity sold within a state (including associated losses) and the energy input at the electric utilities within the state. A positive number indicates that more electricity (including associated losses) came into the state than went out of the state during the year; conversely, a negative number indicates that more electricity (including associated losses) went out of the state than came into the state.
. . . = Not available.

Table SC-16. State Taxes, Fiscal 2004

(Dollars, percent distribution.)

Item	Thousands of dollars	Percent distribution	Dollars per capita	
			State	U.S.
TOTAL TAXES	6 803 568	100.0	1 620.7	2 024.8
Property Taxes	11 597	0.2	2.8	38.9
Sales and Gross Receipts	3 689 986	54.2	879.0	1 003.4
General sales and gross receipts	2 726 657	40.1	649.5	677.0
Selective sales taxes	963 329	14.2	229.5	326.4
Alcoholic beverages	146 658	2.2	34.9	15.7
Amusements	39 627	0.6	9.4	17.0
Insurance premiums	106 643	1.6	25.4	47.0
Motor fuels	489 322	7.2	116.6	114.6
Public utilities	45 071	0.7	10.7	39.2
Other selective sales	106 266	1.6	25.3	49.8
Licenses	383 505	5.6	91.4	134.9
Corporation	72 898	1.1	17.4	21.6
Motor vehicle	122 056	1.8	29.1	59.4
Motor vehicle operators	36 094	0.5	8.6	6.4
Occupation and business, not elsewhere classified	113 236	1.7	27.0	37.1
Other Taxes	2 718 480	40.0	647.6	847.6
Individual income	2 438 712	35.8	580.9	673.6
Corporation net income	196 510	2.9	46.8	105.1
Documentary and stock transfer	50 493	0.7	12.0	27.1

GOVERNMENT FINANCE

In 2003, South Carolina's revenues per person of $3,714 were slightly below the national average. The state's expenditures per capita amounted to $4,262. The difference between per capita expenditures and revenues was among the highest in the nation. Spending per capita was above average for education, public welfare, hospitals, and government administration, but below average for health. South Carolina's per capita taxes of $1,621 were among the 10 lowest in the nation. The largest tax sources were general sales taxes and individual income taxes. The state's individual income taxes of $581 were well below the U.S. average of $674.

Per Capita State Taxes, Fiscal 2004

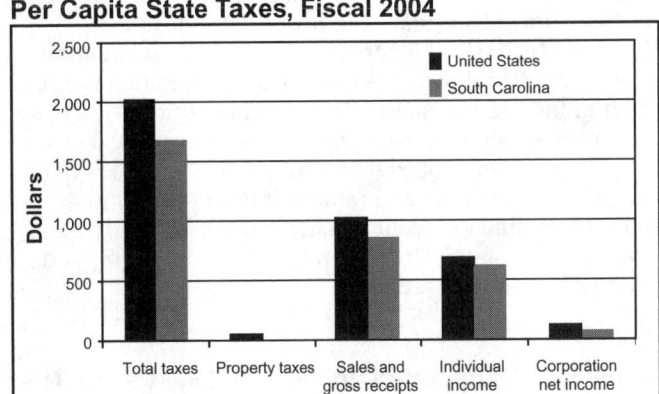

Table SC-17. State Government Finances, 2003

(Dollars, percent distribution.)

Item	Millions of dollars	Percent distribution	Dollars per capita	
			State	U.S.
GENERAL REVENUE	15 408 525	100.0	3 713.8	3 832.6
Intergovernmental revenue	5 738 966	37.2	1 383.2	1 246.0
Taxes	6 353 115	41.2	1 531.2	1 891.6
General sales	2 555 851	16.6	616.0	636.0
Selective sales	875 158	5.7	210.9	307.4
License taxes	325 511	2.1	78.5	123.6
Individual income tax	2 334 066	15.1	562.6	626.8
Corporate income tax	173 886	1.1	41.9	97.8
Other taxes	88 643	0.6	21.4	99.9
Current charges	2 376 569	15.4	572.8	366.5
Miscellaneous general revenue	939 875	6.1	226.5	328.6
GENERAL EXPENDITURE	17 684 894	100.0	4 262.4	4 010.5
Intergovernmental expenditure	4 155 920	23.5	1 001.7	1 316.9
Direct expenditure	13 528 974	76.5	3 260.8	2 693.6
Expenditure by Function				
Education	6 037 317	34.1	1 455.1	1 416.4
Public welfare	4 775 314	27.0	1 151.0	1 083.3
Hospitals	1 112 095	6.3	268.0	132.3
Health	698 202	3.9	168.3	173.0
Highways	1 341 643	7.6	323.4	295.4
Police protection	243 452	1.4	58.7	38.4
Correction	426 300	2.4	102.8	135.0
Natural resources	190 004	1.1	45.8	64.0
Parks and recreation	71 732	0.4	17.3	20.1
Government administration	682 434	3.9	164.5	151.3
Interest on general debt	333 213	1.9	80.3	107.8
Other and unallocable	1 773 188	10.0	427.4	393.4
DEBT AT END OF FISCAL YEAR	10 990 201	X	2 648.9	2 404.7
CASH AND SECURITY HOLDINGS	28 498 350	X	6 868.7	8 938.4

X = Not applicable.

Table SC-18. Education Indicators, 2000–2004

(Percent, number.)

Item	State	U.S.
Total Population 25 Years and Over (Thousands), 2004	2 636	186 877
Educational Attainment, 2004		
Percent high school graduate or more	83.6	85.2
Percent college graduate or more	24.9	27.7
Elementary and Secondary Schools, 2002–2003		
Total students	694 584	48 202 324
Percent of students eligible for free or reduced-price lunch ..	51.0	40.6
Percent of students who were English language learners	1.5	7.8
Total schools	1 081	92 330
Student/teacher ratio	15.3	15.9
Per student expenditures	7 040	8 041
Dropouts, Grades 9–12, 2000–2001 (Percent)	3.3	. . .
Higher Education, 2002–2003		
Total enrollment	203 288	17 035 027
Bachelor's degrees awarded	17 817	1 348 503
Percent women	58.8	57.5

. . . = Not available.

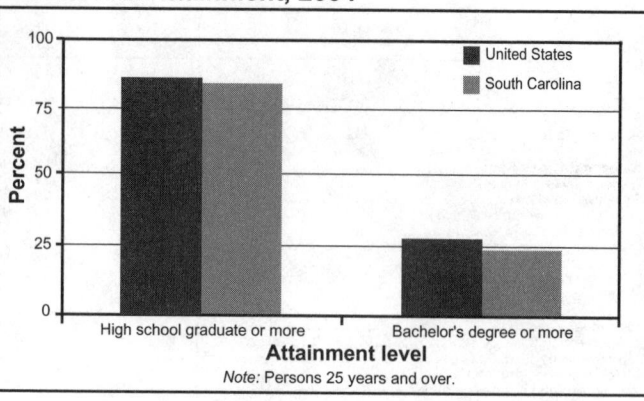

Educational Attainment, 2004

Note: Persons 25 years and over.

EDUCATION

South Carolina's educational attainment rates were higher than North Carolina's but lower than those of Georgia. In 2004, 83.6 percent of the state's population age 25 years and over held high school diplomas, ranking 39th in the nation. Nearly 25 percent of residents in the same age group held bachelor's degrees or more. Per student expenditures of $7,040 were about $1,000 less than the national average and ranked 36th in the country. South Carolina's student/teacher ratio was slightly below average. The state's dropout rate of 3.3 percent ranked 36th of the 46 states reporting such data.

VOTER PARTICIPATION

In 2000, 58.9 percent of eligible residents voted. This proportion increased to 62 percent in 2004. For both elections, South Carolina's participation rate was above the national average. Between elections, the proportion of eligible residents who registered to vote increased from 68 percent to 73.1 percent. In 2004, South Carolina had the 14th highest voter registration rate in the country. According to the official tally by the Clerk of the U.S. House of Representatives, large majorities of the state's residents voted for the Republican presidential candidate in 2000 (56.9 percent) and 2004 (58 percent).

Table SC-19. Reported Voting and Registration, November 2000 and November 2004

(Numbers in thousands, percent.)

Characteristic	Total population 18 years and over	Total citizen		Total registered		Total voted	
		Number	Percent	Number	Percent	Number	Percent
NOVEMBER 2000							
Total	2 929	2 897	98.9	1 993	68.0	1 725	58.9
Male	1 355	1 336	98.7	869	64.2	752	55.5
Female	1 575	1 561	99.1	1 124	71.4	973	61.8
NOVEMBER 2004							
Total	3 061	3 002	98.1	2 238	73.1	1 899	62.0
Male	1 441	1 408	97.7	1 009	70.0	862	59.8
Female	1 620	1 594	98.4	1 230	75.9	1 037	64.0
Race and Hispanic Origin							
White alone	2 188	2 132	97.5	1 627	74.4	1 387	63.4
Non-Hispanic White alone	2 142	2 120	98.9	1 617	75.5	1 377	64.3
Black alone	837	834	99.6	595	71.1	498	59.5
Asian alone	4	4	B	-	B	-	B
Hispanic or Latino[1]	52	16	B	13	B	13	B
White alone or in combination	2 208	2 153	97.5	1 636	74.1	1 394	63.1
Non-Hispanic White alone or in combination	2 163	2 140	99.0	1 626	75.2	1 384	64.0
Black alone or in combination	843	840	99.6	599	71.1	500	59.3
Asian alone or in combination	4	4	B	-	B	-	B
Age							
18 to 24 years	357	350	98.0	199	55.8	153	42.8
25 to 44 years	1 158	1 116	96.4	794	68.6	664	57.3
45 to 64 years	1 029	1 021	99.2	810	78.7	731	71.0
65 to 74 years	276	273	99.2	232	84.2	200	72.6
75 years and over	241	241	100.0	202	83.9	151	62.6

[1]May be of any race.
- = Represents zero or rounds to zero.
B = Base is too small to show derived measure.

At a Glance:

- South Dakota's population reached nearly 771,000 in 2004, placing it among just 7 states and the District of Columbia with fewer than one million residents.

- More than 87 percent of the state's population was non-Hispanic White, which was the 11th highest proportion of this racial group in the nation. Over 8 percent of South Dakota's residents were American Indian, which was the third highest proportion of this racial group in the nation.

- In 2004, just 12 percent of the state's population lacked health insurance, compared to the national rate of 15.7 percent.

- The state's median household income of $41,189 was well below the national average. South Dakota's poverty rate of 13.4 percent was above average, ranking among the 15 highest in the country.

- Economic activity was not dampened by the 2001 recession, as real gross state product (GSP) grew at an above average rate from 2001 to 2004. South Dakota's economy was small in relation to the rest of the states, and its GSP ranked 47th in the country. The state's unemployment rate was the third lowest in the country.

- Over 87 percent of South Dakota's population age 25 years and over held high school diplomas, which was above the national average of 85.2 percent.

Table SD-1. Population by Sex and Age, 1990, 2000, and 2004

(Number, percent.)

Sex and age	1990	2000	2004	Percent distribution, 2004	Average annual percent change, 2000–2004
Total Population	696 004	754 844	770 883	X	0.5
Percent of total U.S. population	0.3	0.3	0.3	X	X
Sex					
Male	342 498	374 558	383 249	49.7	0.6
Female	353 506	380 286	387 634	50.3	0.5
Age					
Under 5 years	54 504	51 069	51 720	6.7	-0.5
5 to 17 years	143 958	151 580	139 154	18.1	-0.2
18 years and over	122 469	552 195	580 009	75.2	1.1
18 to 24 years	497 542	77 634	86 646	11.2	1.7
25 to 44 years	68 113	206 399	198 636	25.8	-0.2
45 to 64 years	204 629	160 031	185 234	24.0	3.0
65 years and over	102 331	108 131	109 493	14.2	0.5
85 years and over	13 343	16 086	17 658	2.3	2.1
Median age (years)	32.4	35.6	36.7	X	X

X = Not applicable.

Average Annual Rate of Population Growth, 1980–2004

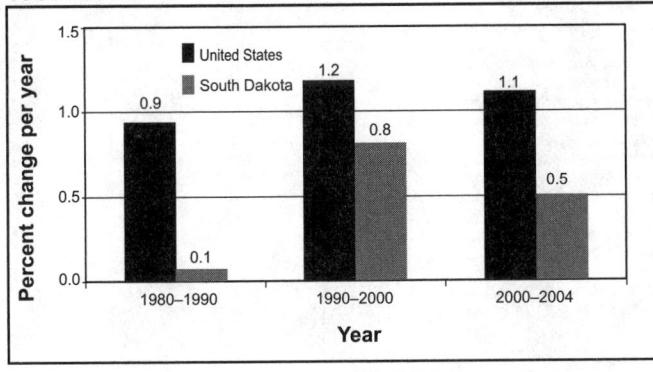

POPULATION

South Dakota's population increased by 2.1 percent between 2000 and 2004, which was well below the national average rate of growth, but similar to the rates of Nebraska and Wyoming. Its neighbor to the north, North Dakota, lost population over the period. South Dakota lost nearly 2,000 residents to other locations; however, this was offset by the addition of 3,259 new residents from abroad. More than 14 percent of South Dakota's residents were 65 years old and over, which was the 7th largest proportion of this age group in the nation. The state's birth rate was above the national average, ranking 16th in the country. Sioux Falls was South Dakota's largest city.

Table SD-2. Population by Race and Hispanic Origin, 1990, 2000, and 2004

(Number, percent.)

Race and Hispanic origin	1990	2000	2004
Total Population	696 004	754 844	770 883
Non-Hispanic (Percent)			
One race[1]			
White	91.2	88.1	87.1
Black	0.5	0.6	0.7
American Indian, Alaska Native[2]	7.3	8.1	8.5
Asian and Pacific Islander[2]	0.4	0.6	0.7
Other race[2]	0.2	. . .	. . .
Two or more races	. . .	1.1	1.1
Hispanic or Latino[3] (Percent)	0.8	1.4	2.0

[1]Individuals could report only one race in the 1990 census and could report one or more races on the 2000 census. Data on race in 2000 and 2004 are not comparable to 1990.
[2]Data for 1990 include people of Hispanic or Latino origin.
[3]May be of any race.
. . . = Not available.

Minority Population as a Percent of Total Population, 2004

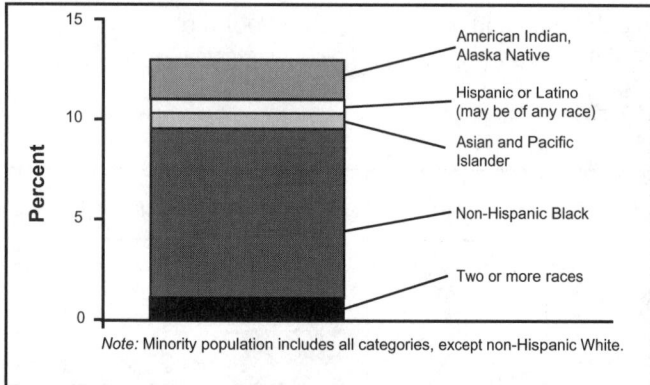

Note: Minority population includes all categories, except non-Hispanic White.

Age-Adjusted Death Rates, Average 2000–2002

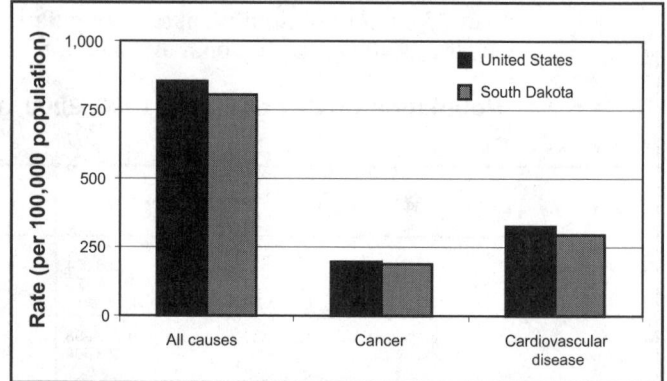

HEALTH

South Dakota ranked 17th in the nation for its proportion of residents with health insurance coverage, partly reflecting a low unemployment rate and a high proportion of elderly residents (who were covered by Medicare). The state's infant mortality rate and age-adjusted death rates were well below the national averages.

Table SD-3. Health Characteristics, 2000–2004

(Number, rate, percent.)

Item	State	U.S.
Births, 2003–2004		
Number of births	11 027	4 089 950
Birth rate (per 1,000 population)	14.4	14.1
Teenage birth rate (per 1,000 women age 15–19 years)	34.7	41.6
Mortality Rates, Average 2000–2002		
Infant mortality rate (per 1,000 live births)	6.4	6.9
Age-adjusted mortality rate (per 100,000 population)		
All races	786.0	853.3
Non-Hispanic White	751.6	843.1
Black	. . .	1 097.7
American Indian, Alaska Native	1 471.0	687.0
Asian and Pacific Islander	. . .	486.0
Hispanic or Latino[1]	. . .	642.7
Health Insurance, 2004		
Percent of all persons without health insurance	12.0	15.7
Percent of children without health insurance	8.3	11.2
Percent of low-income children without health insurance	3.9	7.1

[1]May be of any race.
. . . = Not available.

Table SD-4. Leading Causes of Death, Average 2000–2002

(Number, rate per 100,000 population.)

Cause	Number of deaths	Age-adjusted death rates	
		State	U.S.
ALL CAUSES	6 947	786.0	853.3
Leading Causes			
Major cardiovascular diseases	2 688	293.0	326.5
Cancer	1 583	186.9	196.0
Chronic lower respiratory diseases	376	42.7	43.7
Unintentional injuries	350	43.8	35.7
Diabetes (underlying cause)	196	22.5	25.2
Influenza and pneumonia	213	22.4	22.7
Alzheimer's disease	167	16.9	19.0
Motor vehicle accidents	168	21.8	15.0
Nephritis, nephrotic syndrome, and nephrosis ..	120	13.1	13.8
Septicemia	64	7.2	11.4
Suicides	98	12.9	10.7
Firearm-related	57	7.5	10.3
Cirrhosis	78	10.2	9.5
Drug-induced	25	3.3	7.9
Alcohol-induced	66	8.9	6.9
Homicides	18	2.4	6.0
Falls	74	7.9	5.2
HIV	*	*	5.0
Viral hepatitis	8	1.1	2.0
Anemias	13	1.4	1.6
Drownings	10	1.4	1.3
Fire deaths	9	1.2	1.2

Note: The rates are age-adjusted to the U.S. 2000 standard population.

* = Unreliable data.

Table SD-5. Households and Housing Characteristics, 1990, 2000, and 2004

(Number, percent, and dollars.)

Characteristic	1990	2000	2004	Average annual percent change, 2000–2004
Total Households	259 034	290 245	300 629	0.9
Family households	180 306	194 330	196 481	0.3
Married-couple family	152 519	157 391	159 251	0.3
Other family	27 787	36 939	37 230	0.2
Male householder, no wife present	7 076	10 734	11 835	2.5
Female householder, no husband present	20 711	26 205	25 395	-0.8
Nonfamily households	78 728	95 915	104 148	2.1
Householder living alone	68 308	80 040	87 595	2.3
Householder not living alone	10 420	15 875	16 553	1.1
Housing Characteristics				
Average size	2.59	2.50	2.47	X
Housing units	292 436	323 208	342 620	1.5
Occupied housing units	259 034	290 245	300 629	0.9
Owner-occupied	171 161	197 940	207 737	1.2
Renter-occupied	87 873	92 305	92 892	0.2
Median gross rent of renter-occupied housing units (dollars) ...	306	426	493	3.7
Median value of owner-occupied housing units (dollars)	45 000	79 600	95 523	4.7

X = Not applicable.

Median Housing Value and Median Rent, 2004

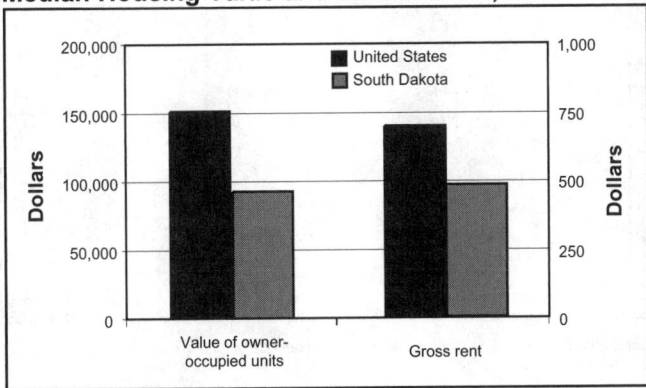

Median Household Income, 1984–2004 (2004 Dollars)

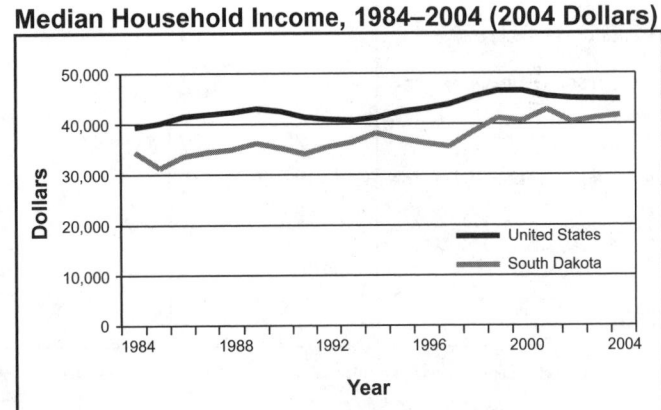

Table SD-6. Household Income and Poverty Status, 1980–2004

(2004 CPI-U-RS adjusted dollars, rate.)

Year	State		U.S.	
	Median household income (2004 dollars)	Poverty rate	Median household income (2004 dollars)	Poverty rate
2004	41 189	13.4	44 389	12.7
2003	40 584	12.7	44 482	12.5
2002	39 782	11.5	44 546	12.1
2001	42 333	8.4	45 062	11.7
2000	40 009	10.7	46 058	11.3
1999	40 611	7.7	46 129	11.9
1998	37 945	10.8	45 003	12.7
1997	34 850	16.5	43 430	13.3
1996	35 393	11.8	42 544	13.7
1995	36 407	14.5	41 943	13.8
1994	37 486	14.5	40 677	14.5
1993	35 706	14.2	40 217	15.1
1992	34 647	15.1	40 422	14.8
1991	33 324	14.0	40 746	14.2
1990	34 434	13.3	41 963	13.5
1989	35 466	13.2	42 524	12.8
1988	34 206	14.2	41 771	13.0
1987	33 634	15.2	41 322	13.4
1986	32 719	17.0	40 939	13.6
1985	30 377	17.3	39 545	14.0
1984	33 581	14.5	38 782	14.4
1983	. . .	18.4	. . .	15.2
1982	. . .	16.8	. . .	15.0
1981	. . .	19.5	. . .	14.0
1980	. . .	18.8	. . .	13.0

. . . = Not available.

Table SD-7. Employment Status by Demographic Group, 2004
(Numbers in thousands, rate.)

Characteristic	Civilian noninstitutional population	Civilian labor force		Employed	Unemployment rate
		Number	Participation rate		
SEX AND AGE					
Total	586	431	73.7	416	3.7
16 to 19 years	46	30	64.7	27	10.3
20 to 24 years	68	58	84.9	54	6.2
25 to 34 years	91	81	88.8	78	3.7
35 to 44 years	95	86	91.0	84	3.3
45 to 54 years	112	100	89.2	98	2.0
55 to 64 years	75	57	75.7	56	1.7
65 years and over	98	19	19.8	19	1.7
Men	287	224	78.1	216	3.5
16 to 19 years	24	15	64.2	14	10.9
20 to 24 years	33	29	87.1	27	6.3
25 to 34 years	45	42	93.2	41	3.6
35 to 44 years	48	46	96.0	45	2.9
45 to 54 years	55	51	92.7	50	2.0
55 to 64 years	36	29	80.2	29	1.4
65 years and over	45	11	24.8	11	1.5
Women	299	207	69.4	200	3.8
16 to 19 years	22	14	65.2	13	9.6
20 to 24 years	35	29	82.8	27	6.0
25 to 34 years	46	39	84.5	37	3.9
35 to 44 years	47	40	85.8	39	3.7
45 to 54 years	57	49	85.8	48	2.1
55 to 64 years	39	28	71.4	27	2.1
MARITAL STATUS					
Married men, spouse present	162	129	79.6	127	1.6
Married women, spouse present	164	118	72.0	116	1.6
Women who maintain families	28	20	71.8	19	7.9
RACE, HISPANIC ORIGIN, AND SEX					
White	540	403	74.6	391	2.9
Men	264	209	79.0	203	2.8
Women	276	194	70.3	188	3.0
RACE, HISPANIC ORIGIN, AND AGE					
White					
16 to 19 years	41	28	68.3	25	9.5
20 to 24 years	61	54	88.0	51	4.9
25 to 34 years	81	73	90.3	71	2.4
35 to 44 years	87	80	92.1	78	2.6
45 to 54 years	105	95	90.7	93	1.7
55 to 64 years	72	55	76.4	54	1.6
65 years and over	95	19	19.7	18	1.4

Note: Data in Table 7 are from the Current Population Survey (CPS) and do not match Bureau of Labor Statistics estimates in Table 8. See notes and definitions for more details.

Table SD-8. Employment Status, 1990–2004
(Numbers in thousands, rate.)

Year	Civilian labor force	Employed	Unemployed	Unemployment rate
2004	428 169	413 121	15 048	3.5
2003	423 660	408 805	14 855	3.5
2002	417 931	404 090	13 841	3.3
2001	413 402	400 574	12 828	3.1
2000	409 106	398 208	10 898	2.7
1999	406 328	394 898	11 430	2.8
1998	401 677	389 748	11 929	3.0
1997	395 276	383 216	12 060	3.1
1996	392 554	379 222	13 332	3.4
1995	386 088	373 515	12 573	3.3
1994	377 093	364 452	12 641	3.4
1993	365 745	352 666	13 079	3.6
1992	358 701	345 996	12 705	3.5
1991	353 780	341 025	12 755	3.6
1990	350 642	337 503	13 139	3.7

Note: Population age 16 years and over.

Unemployment Rate, 1980–2004

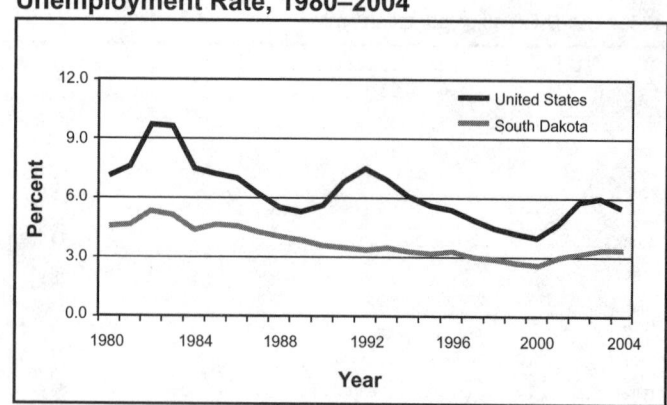

Table SD-9. Employment and Average Wages by Industry, 2001–2004

(Estimates are based on the 2002 North American Industry Classification System [NAICS].)

Industry	2001	2002	2003	2004	Annual average percent change, 2001–2004
	Number of jobs				
TOTAL EMPLOYMENT BY PLACE OF WORK	517 285	519 377	521 838	531 211	0.9
Farm Employment	37 337	37 301	35 079	35 569	-1.6
Nonfarm Employment	479 948	482 076	486 759	495 642	1.1
Private employment	400 847	402 765	406 802	415 120	1.2
Forestry, fishing, hunting, and other[1]	4 158	4 436	4 050	3 990	-1.4
Mining	1 556	1 260	1 305	1 272	-6.5
Utilities	2 086	2 111	2 094	2 098	0.2
Construction	29 174	29 058	30 491	31 365	2.4
Manufacturing	42 674	40 191	39 446	40 672	-1.6
Durable goods manufacturing	28 841	26 928	26 325	27 347	-1.8
Nondurable goods manufacturing	13 833	13 263	13 121	13 325	-1.2
Wholesale trade	18 099	18 060	17 944	18 432	0.6
Retail trade	62 554	62 688	63 261	64 070	0.8
Transportation and warehousing	14 630	14 649	14 416	14 378	-0.6
Information	7 813	7 635	7 663	7 661	-0.7
Finance and insurance	31 234	31 377	30 762	30 854	-0.4
Real estate and rental and leasing	10 979	11 066	11 489	12 184	3.5
Professional and technical services	15 590	15 486	15 670	16 233	1.4
Management of companies and enterprises	3 998	4 061	3 402	2 838	-10.8
Administrative and waste services	18 027	17 493	17 790	18 194	0.3
Educational services	8 059	8 490	8 972	9 300	4.9
Health care and social assistance	55 626	56 494	58 231	59 390	2.2
Arts, entertainment, and recreation	10 166	10 321	10 511	10 850	2.2
Accommodation and food services	36 011	36 961	37 338	38 388	2.2
Other services, except public administration	28 413	30 928	31 967	32 951	5.1
Government and government enterprises	79 101	79 311	79 957	80 522	0.6
	Dollars				
AVERAGE WAGES AND SALARIES BY PLACE OF WORK	25 151	26 043	26 944	28 035	3.7
Farm Earnings	27 629	26 940	27 311	30 335	3.2
Nonfarm Earnings	25 120	26 033	26 941	28 014	3.7
Private earnings	24 922	25 751	26 599	27 642	3.5
Forestry, fishing, hunting, and other[1]	14 596	16 275	17 106	18 525	8.3
Mining	40 234	40 989	39 285	40 262	0.0
Utilities	45 211	49 383	51 573	52 906	5.4
Construction	28 985	29 879	30 172	30 626	1.9
Manufacturing	29 818	30 793	32 074	33 515	4.0
Durable goods manufacturing	30 550	31 538	32 844	34 456	4.1
Nondurable goods manufacturing	28 280	29 267	30 523	31 575	3.7
Wholesale trade	33 651	34 603	35 649	38 008	4.1
Retail trade	18 118	18 765	19 412	19 875	3.1
Transportation and warehousing	29 611	30 314	31 220	32 796	3.5
Information	31 720	32 293	33 050	34 570	2.9
Finance and insurance	33 252	34 232	35 806	37 782	4.3
Real estate and rental and leasing	19 295	19 784	20 017	21 101	3.0
Professional and technical services	32 767	33 627	35 459	35 738	2.9
Management of companies and enterprises	60 775	57 369	59 682	68 796	4.2
Administrative and waste services	22 034	21 695	22 357	22 846	1.2
Educational services	18 805	20 084	21 052	22 076	5.5
Health care and social assistance	28 005	29 762	31 174	32 612	5.2
Arts, entertainment, and recreation	13 657	13 799	14 370	14 615	2.3
Accommodation and food services	10 087	10 616	10 828	11 081	3.2
Other services, except public administration	18 059	19 775	20 250	21 129	5.4
Government and government enterprises	25 910	27 149	28 293	29 493	4.4

Note: Average wages and salaries are a calculation by the editors of wage and salary disbursements divided by full- and part-time wage and salary employment. Data may not add to total or may appear as zero due to rounding.

[1] "Other" consists of the number of jobs held by U.S. residents employed by international organizations and foreign embassies and consulates in the United States.

LABOR MARKET

The unemployment rate has been well below average in South Dakota for some years. This has been accompanied by a high labor force participation rate, indicating that job seekers have been successful in finding employment. Jobs grew moderately during the 2001–2004 period, with increases in utilities, wholesale trade, health care, and tourism-related industries. The government sector, retail trade, and health care services were the state's largest employers. Average wages and salaries grew by 11.5 percent from 2001 to 2004, which was the 10th highest growth rate in the nation. However, the state's average wages and salaries were the second lowest in the country, above only those of Montana.

Employment by Industry, 2004

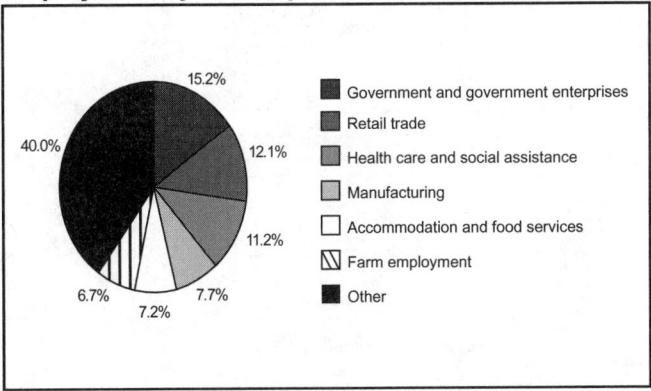

- Government and government enterprises
- Retail trade
- Health care and social assistance
- Manufacturing
- Accommodation and food services
- Farm employment
- Other

Table SD-10. Personal Income by Major Source, Selected Years 1980–2004

(Millions of dollars, except where noted.)

Item	1980	1990	2000	2001	2002	2003	2004	Average annual percent change, 2000–2004
Earnings by Place of Work	3 966	8 120	14 215	14 696	14 588	16 314	17 527	5.4
Wage and salary disbursements	2 819	5 061	9 697	10 049	10 380	10 756	11 357	4.0
Supplements to wages and salaries	510	1 122	2 023	2 125	2 392	2 580	2 817	8.6
Proprietors' income[1]	637	1 938	2 495	2 522	1 816	2 978	3 354	7.7
Farm proprietors' income	47	912	987	715	-8	1 106	1 311	7.4
Nonfarm proprietors' income	590	1 026	1 509	1 807	1 824	1 872	2 043	7.9
(-) Contributions for government social insurance[2]	344	821	1 535	1 593	1 664	1 730	1 819	4.3
(+) Adjustment for residence[3]	18	-56	-280	-235	-220	-213	-227	X
(=) Net Earnings by Place of Residence	3 640	7 243	12 400	12 867	12 704	14 371	15 482	5.7
(+) Dividends, interest, and rent[4]	1 180	2 505	4 393	4 703	4 655	4 712	4 790	2.2
(+) Personal current transfer receipts	758	1 525	2 645	2 859	3 070	3 148	3 331	5.9
Personal income	5 577	11 273	19 438	20 429	20 429	22 231	23 602	5.0
Farm income	5 453	10 273	18 329	19 574	20 309	21 030	22 171	4.9
Nonfarm income	124	1 000	1 109	856	120	1 200	1 431	6.6
Per Capita Personal Income (Dollars)[5]	8 073	16 172	25 720	26 944	26 864	29 063	30 617	4.5

Note: Data may not add to total or may appear as zero due to rounding.

[1]Proprietors' income includes the inventory valuation adjustment and the capital consumption adjustment.
[2]Contributions for government social insurance are included in earnings by type and industry, but they are excluded from personal income.
[3]The adjustment for residence is the net inflow of the earnings of interarea commuters.
[4]Rental income of persons includes the capital consumption adjustment.
[5]Per capita personal income is total personal income divided by total midyear population.
X = Not applicable.

Per Capita Personal Income, 1980–2004 (Current Dollars)

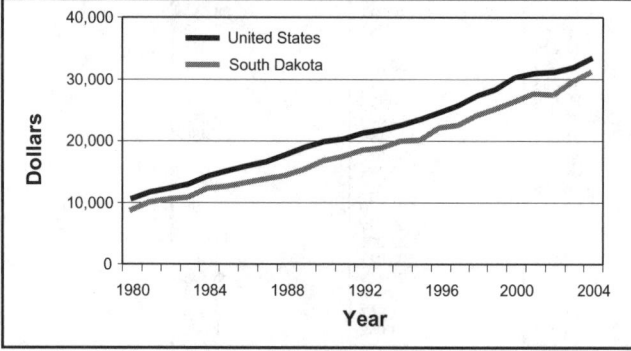

ECONOMIC ACTIVITY

From 2001 to 2004, real gross state product increased at the third fastest rate in the country. Contributing to this increase were manufacturing, wholesale trade, retail trade, finance and insurance services, real estate and related activities, and government. Utilities, management, and education services all experienced declines during this period. In recent years, housing prices in South Dakota have increased at a rate significantly lower than the national average. In 2004, the median value of owner-occupied housing was $95,923, ranking South Dakota among the 10 states with median values of owner-occupied housing of less than $100,000.

Table SD-11. Real Gross State Product, 1997–2004

(Millions of chained 2000 dollars, percent.)

Industry	1997	1998	1999	2000	2001	2002	2003	2004	Average annual percent change, 2001–2004
GROSS STATE PRODUCT	20 155	21 106	21 941	23 230	23 544	24 691	25 609	26 771	4.4
As a percent of U.S. gross product	0.2	0.2	0.2	0.2	0.2	0.2	0.2	0.2	X
Private Industries	17 142	18 071	18 920	20 103	20 428	21 679	22 524	23 569	4.9
Agriculture, forestry, fishing, and hunting	1 341	1 404	1 284	1 519	1 308	1 133	1 520	1 491	4.5
Mining	108	96	101	89	88	74	70	60	-12.0
Utilities	390	369	397	411	374	403	433	442	5.7
Construction	883	902	921	939	928	932	961	976	1.7
Manufacturing	1 916	2 363	2 514	3 115	2 882	2 908	3 197	3 500	6.7
As a percent of gross state product	9.5	11.2	11.5	13.4	12.2	11.8	12.5	13.1	X
Wholesale trade	1 177	1 289	1 334	1 316	1 451	1 481	1 440	1 500	1.1
Retail trade	1 680	1 706	1 789	1 851	1 979	2 151	2 302	2 408	6.8
Transportation and warehousing	632	607	626	646	643	653	652	662	1.0
Information	478	517	592	597	644	677	740	809	7.9
Finance and insurance	2 365	2 402	2 688	2 914	3 453	4 460	4 385	4 638	10.3
Real estate and rental and leasing	1 676	1 729	1 814	1 844	1 945	1 915	1 838	1 994	0.8
Services	4 581	4 689	4 894	4 862	4 737	4 876	5 001	5 147	2.8
As a percent of gross state product	22.7	22.2	22.3	20.9	20.1	19.7	19.5	19.2	X
Professional and technical services	497	511	559	579	584	593	627	645	3.4
Management of companies and enterprises	426	427	428	400	286	271	232	208	-10.1
Administrative and waste services	475	527	563	489	461	444	465	467	0.4
Educational services	137	140	145	150	145	145	143	144	-0.2
Health care and social assistance	1 668	1 681	1 768	1 820	1 851	1 962	2 063	2 129	4.8
Arts, entertainment, and recreation	238	254	258	229	229	245	248	254	3.5
Accommodation and food services	586	600	625	645	631	671	682	709	4.0
Other services, except public administration	554	549	548	550	550	546	541	591	2.4
Government	3 029	3 042	3 022	3 126	3 116	3 020	3 095	3 212	1.0
As a percent of gross state product	15.0	14.4	13.8	13.5	13.2	12.2	12.1	12.0	X

X = Not applicable.

Table SD-12. Government Transfer Payments, Selected Years 1980–2004

(Millions of dollars, percent.)

Item	1980	1990	2000	2001	2002	2003	2004	Average annual percent change, 2000–2004
CURRENT TRANSFER PAYMENTS TO INDIVIDUALS	709	1 437	2 490	2 688	2 922	3 013	3 197	6.4
Retirement and Disability Insurance Benefits	386	760	1 149	1 212	1 271	1 312	1 369	4.5
Old-age, survivors, and disability insurance (OASDI) benefits	373	739	1 125	1 187	1 243	1 283	1 340	4.5
Railroad retirement and disability benefits	12	15	17	18	19	19	19	2.3
Workers' compensation	1	5	7	7	9	9	9	7.0
Other government retirement and disability insurance benefits	*	*	*	*	1	1	1	23.9
Medical Benefits	156	442	959	1 059	1 190	1 196	1 312	8.2
Medicare benefits	97	254	507	561	598	631	690	8.0
Public assistance medical care benefits	57	180	439	481	571	548	600	8.1
Military medical insurance benefits	2	8	12	17	21	18	22	14.9
Income Maintenance Benefits	66	105	188	198	219	244	263	8.8
Supplemental Security Income (SSI) benefits	11	27	51	53	55	54	57	2.9
Family assistance	19	22	17	15	17	20	22	7.8
Food stamps	19	36	37	40	46	51	56	10.6
Other income maintenance benefits	18	20	84	90	101	118	129	11.2
Unemployment Insurance Compensation	21	12	16	23	36	39	33	19.3
Veterans' Benefits	51	61	98	104	115	124	131	7.6
Federal Education and Training Assistance	18	30	39	46	52	49	52	7.0
Other Payments to Individuals	10	28	40	45	38	49	36	-2.1

Note: See notes and definitions for more details. Data may not add to total or may appear as zero due to rounding.

* = Less than $500,000.

EXPORTS

South Dakota's exports totaled just $826 million in 2004, ranking among the five lowest values in the nation. However, total exports grew by nearly 39 percent from 2001 to 2004. The two leading exports were computers and electronic products and processed foods, which together accounted for about 60 percent of the state's exports. Crop exports, which were the fourth leading export in 2000, fell almost 79 percent by 2004 and were no longer among the state's 10 leading exports. The leading export markets were Canada and Mexico, with Canada importing nearly 35 percent of South Dakota's goods. Exports to Hong Kong, the state's third leading market, doubled from 2003 to 2004.

Leading Exports, 2004

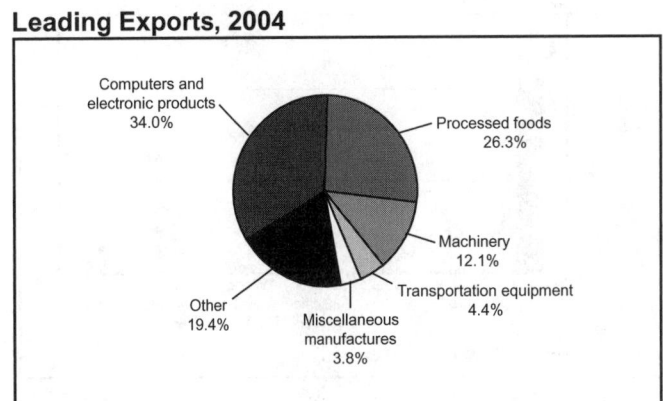

Table SD-13. Exports of Goods by Leading Products and Destinations, 2001–2004

(Millions of dollars, percent, rank based on 2004 dollar values.)

Product and market	2001	2002	2003	2004	Percent share of total, 2004	Average annual percent change, 2001–2004
Total Goods						
Total	595	597	672	826	100.0	11.5
Manufactures	553	534	608	764	92.6	11.4
Agriculture and livestock	28	30	33	26	3.2	-2.4
Other commodities	14	33	31	35	4.3	36.5
Five Leading Exports (NAICS Code)						
Computers and electronic products (334)	192	168	218	281	34.0	13.5
Processed foods (311)	154	179	179	217	26.3	12.2
Machinery manufactures (333)	63	65	77	100	12.1	16.4
Transportation equipment (336)	22	23	26	36	4.4	17.5
Miscellaneous manufactures (339)	22	27	29	31	3.8	12.7
Five Leading Markets	547	573	646	796	96.4	13.3
Canada	269	290	289	287	34.8	2.2
Mexico	58	75	124	159	19.2	39.9
Hong Kong	16	36	42	90	10.9	77.5
Japan	41	37	51	41	5.0	-0.3
China	6	10	10	30	3.6	71.4

Table SD-14. Agriculture, 1997 and 2002

(Number, acres, and dollars.)

Item	1997	2002
Number of farms	33 191	31 736
Land in farms (acres)	44 141 892	43 785 079
Farm Size		
Average size of farm (acres)	1 330	1 380
Farms by size (percent distribution)		
Fewer than 50 acres	13.4	13.6
50 to 499 acres	37.9	37.3
500 acres or more	48.8	49.0
Market Value of Land and Equipment (Dollars)		
Land and buildings average value per farm	473 015	618 651
Average value per acre	358	442
Machinery and equipment average value per farm	89 285	107 376
Value of Sales (Thousands of Dollars)		
Agricultural products sold	3 664 129	3 834 625
Crops	1 744 438	1 575 910
Livestock, poultry, and their products	1 919 692	2 258 715
Average per farm (dollars)	110 395	120 829
Value of sales (percent distribution)		
Less than $10,000	25.3	31.9
$10,000 to $99,999	45.8	37.6
$100,000 or more	29.0	30.5
Government Payments		
Payments (thousands of dollars)	183 645	215 084
Percent of farms receiving government payments	73.4	63.8
Farm operators whose principal occupation is farming (percent)	70.8	72.6

AGRICULTURE

Cash receipts from farming amounted to $3.8 billion in 2002, according to the Department of Agriculture's Census of Agriculture. This was the 21st highest value of sales in the nation, and an increase of 7.4 percent from the previous agriculture census in 1997. Cattle and soybeans were the state's main farm products. Farming was relatively large-scale: more than two-thirds of farms had sales of $10,000 or more, and 30 percent recorded sales of over $100,000. More than 70 percent of all farm operators responded that farming was their chief occupation. In 2002, 86.4 percent of farms in South Dakota spanned 50 acres or more, which was the second highest proportion of farms of this size in the nation.

ENERGY

Energy expenditures per person totaled $2,481 in 2001, an amount just above the national average. South Dakota's energy prices were slightly above average, while per capita consumption was below average.

Energy Consumption by Source, 2001

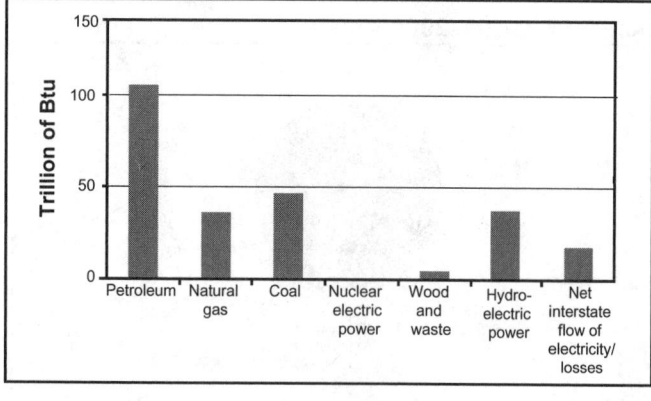

Energy Consumption by Sector, 2001

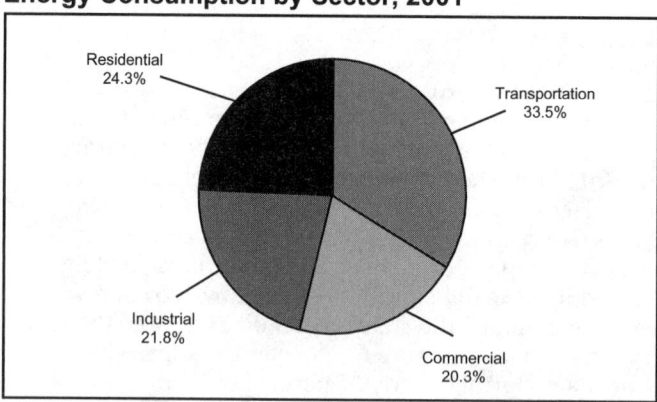

Table SD-15. Energy Consumption, Expenditures, and Prices, Selected Years 1960–2001

(Dollars, Btu [British Thermal Unit], percent distribution.)

Item	1960	1965	1970	1975	1980	1985	1990	1995	2000	2001
Total Consumption (Billion Btu)	129 074	140 338	168 693	181 825	191 288	194 263	210 994	237 364	258 691	247 994
Consumption per capita (million Btu)	189.5	202.8	253.2	267.0	276.9	278.2	303.2	325.9	342.7	327.1
Consumption by Sector (Percent Distribution)										
Residential	25.8	26.4	26.9	26.2	27.7	27.2	26.7	24.9	23.3	24.3
Commercial	12.1	13.9	15.5	14.5	13.3	17.6	15.4	17.3	17.5	20.3
Industrial	30.2	27.5	25.8	25.2	26.0	21.6	26.9	24.2	26.4	21.8
Transportation	31.8	32.2	31.8	34.1	33.0	33.6	31.0	33.7	32.8	33.5
Consumption by Source (Billion Btu)										
Coal	6 707	5 652	5 674	24 282	36 564	34 530	34 882	37 428	50 603	44 273
Natural gas	25 392	26 884	36 464	32 534	24 029	25 454	25 456	34 776	38 131	37 041
Petroleum	86 416	90 257	103 676	103 321	101 795	96 104	108 236	111 734	117 691	111 851
Nuclear electric power	0	0	0	0	0	0	0	0	0	0
Hydroelectric power[1]	12 437	40 479	69 037	82 484	60 436	55 711	40 926	61 974	58 304	34 916
Wood and waste	1 537	1 117	1 147	1 475	3 857	3 795	2 137	2 229	1 884	1 655
Other	0	0	0	0	0	0	0	154	487	488
Net interstate flow of electricity/losses[2]	-3 415	-24 050	-47 306	-62 272	-35 393	-21 329	-798	-11 026	-8 407	17 771
Total Expenditures (Thousands of Dollars)	...	...	307 000	534 100	1 130 200	1 250 200	1 375 700	1 448 600	1 934 600	1 881 000
Expenditures per capita (dollars)	...	...	461	784	1 636	1 790	1 976	1 989	2 563	2 481
Prices by Sector (Dollars Per Million Btu)										
Total	...	...	2.13	3.63	7.74	8.55	8.64	8.27	10.42	10.82
Residential	...	...	2.40	3.81	7.81	10.56	10.14	10.72	13.07	14.03
Commercial	...	...	1.95	2.71	5.97	9.11	9.46	9.57	11.63	12.58
Industrial	...	...	1.42	2.93	5.98	6.29	6.60	5.42	6.35	6.95
Transportation	...	...	2.56	4.23	9.21	8.64	9.02	8.49	11.65	10.97

[1]A negative number in this row results from pumped storage for which, overall, more electricity is expended than created to provide electricity during peak demand periods.
[2]Net interstate flow of electricity is the difference between the amount of energy in the electricity sold within a state (including associated losses) and the energy input at the electric utilities within the state. A positive number indicates that more electricity (including associated losses) came into the state than went out of the state during the year; conversely, a negative number indicates that more electricity (including associated losses) went out of the state than came into the state.
... = Not available.

Table SD-16. State Taxes, Fiscal 2004

(Dollars, percent distribution.)

Item	Thousands of dollars	Percent distribution	Dollars per capita	
			State	U.S.
TOTAL TAXES	1 062 722	100.0	1 378.4	2 024.8
Property Taxes	X	X	X	38.9
Sales and Gross Receipts	865 262	81.4	1 122.3	1 003.4
General sales and gross receipts	586 389	55.2	760.6	677.0
Selective sales taxes	278 873	26.2	361.7	326.4
Alcoholic beverages	12 435	1.2	16.1	15.7
Insurance premiums	55 339	5.2	71.8	47.0
Motor fuels	126 017	11.9	163.4	114.6
Tobacco products	27 644	2.6	35.8	42.0
Other selective sales	54 583	5.1	70.8	49.8
Licenses	138 877	13.1	180.1	134.9
Hunting and fishing	22 129	2.1	28.7	4.2
Motor vehicle	42 167	4.0	54.7	59.4
Occupation and business, not elsewhere classified	57 993	5.5	75.2	37.1
Other licenses	10 673	1.0	13.8	2.6
Other Taxes	58 583	5.5	76.0	847.6
Corporation net income	47 108	4.4	61.1	105.1
Death and gift	9 322	0.9	12.1	19.6

X = Not applicable.

GOVERNMENT FINANCE

State revenues and expenditures per person were about 10 percent below the national average in 2003. South Dakota was among the 12 states with per capita revenues that exceeded per capita expenditures. Spending per capita was below the norm for most categories, except for highways and natural resources. As the state had no property or individual income taxes and only a small tax rate for corporations, the largest tax collections were in the form of general sales taxes, motor fuels taxes, and licenses. In fiscal year 2004, South Dakota had the second smallest per capita taxes in the nation. The state's per capita debt amounted to $3,355 in 2003, which was the 13th highest amount in the country.

Per Capita State Taxes, Fiscal 2004

Table SD-17. State Government Finances, 2003

(Dollars, percent distribution.)

Item	Millions of dollars	Percent distribution	Dollars per capita	
			State	U.S.
GENERAL REVENUE	2 682 852	100.0	3 507.0	3 832.6
Intergovernmental revenue	1 111 450	41.4	1 452.9	1 246.0
Taxes	1 012 955	37.8	1 324.1	1 891.6
General sales	539 396	20.1	705.1	636.0
Selective sales	271 780	10.1	355.3	307.4
License taxes	127 683	4.8	166.9	123.6
Individual income tax	0	0.0	0.0	626.8
Corporate income tax	43 976	1.6	57.5	97.8
Other taxes	30 120	1.1	39.4	99.9
Current charges	194 380	7.2	254.1	366.5
Miscellaneous general revenue	364 067	13.6	475.9	328.6
GENERAL EXPENDITURE	2 663 081	100.0	3 481.2	4 010.5
Intergovernmental expenditure	514 949	19.3	673.1	1 316.9
Direct expenditure	2 148 132	80.7	2 808.0	2 693.6
Expenditure by Function				
Education	838 579	31.5	1 096.2	1 416.4
Public welfare	621 617	23.3	812.6	1 083.3
Hospitals	44 658	1.7	58.4	132.3
Health	90 008	3.4	117.7	173.0
Highways	420 985	15.8	550.3	295.4
Police protection	26 076	1.0	34.1	38.4
Correction	79 858	3.0	104.4	135.0
Natural resources	114 037	4.3	149.1	64.0
Parks and recreation	27 218	1.0	35.6	20.1
Government administration	115 547	4.3	151.0	151.3
Interest on general debt	113 155	4.2	147.9	107.8
Other and unallocable	171 343	6.4	224.0	393.4
DEBT AT END OF FISCAL YEAR	2 566 542	X	3 355.0	2 404.7
CASH AND SECURITY HOLDINGS	8 593 070	X	11 232.8	8 938.4

X = Not applicable.

Table SD-18. Education Indicators, 2000–2004

(Percent, number.)

Item	State	U.S.
Total Population 25 Years and Over (Thousands), 2004	459	186 877
Educational Attainment, 2004		
Percent high school graduate or more	87.5	85.2
Percent college graduate or more	25.5	27.7
Elementary and Secondary Schools, 2002–2003		
Total students	128 039	48 202 324
Percent of students eligible for free or reduced-price lunch ..	31.4	40.6
Percent of students who were English language learners	3.6	7.8
Total schools	738	92 330
Student/teacher ratio	13.6	15.9
Per student expenditures	6 547	8 041
Dropouts, Grades 9–12, 2000–2001 (Percent)	2.8	. . .
Higher Education, 2002–2003		
Total enrollment	47 919	17 035 027
Bachelor's degrees awarded	4 344	1 348 503
Percent women	55.2	57.5

. . . = Not available.

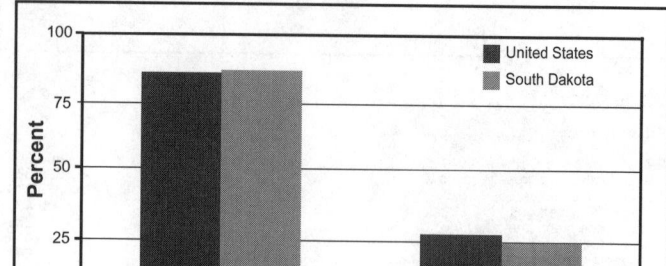

Educational Attainment, 2004

Note: Persons 25 years and over.

EDUCATION

In 2004, 87.5 percent of South Dakota residents age 25 years and over held high school diplomas, ranking 23rd in the nation. Just over 25 percent of residents in this age group were college graduates, a proportion that ranked 26th in the country but was lower than the national average. The state's student/teacher ratio of 13.6 was among the 10 lowest in the nation. Expenditures per student of $6,547 were well below the national average of $8,041. South Dakota's dropout rate of 2.8 percent ranked 39th among the 46 states reporting such data. About 31 percent of students were eligible for free or reduced-price lunch, which was less than the national average.

VOTER PARTICIPATION

South Dakota's voter turnout was above average at 58.7 percent in 2000, ranking 24th in the nation. In 2004, voter participation increased to 67.1 percent, the 9th highest proportion in the country. This was partly caused by a heated Senate race that brought eligible voters out to the polls. More than 76 percent of eligible voters age 45 to 64 years cast ballots in 2004. According to the official tally by the Clerk of the U.S. House of Representatives, the Republican presidential candidate received 60.7 percent of South Dakota's votes in 2000 and 59.9 percent in 2004. The comparable percentage totals for the Democratic candidate were 37.6 and 40.9 percent, respectively.

Table SD-19. Reported Voting and Registration, November 2000 and November 2004

(Numbers in thousands, percent.)

Characteristic	Total population 18 years and over	Total citizen		Total registered		Total voted	
		Number	Percent	Number	Percent	Number	Percent
NOVEMBER 2000							
Total	530	525	99.1	376	70.9	311	58.7
Male	263	260	98.8	184	69.8	149	56.6
Female	266	264	99.3	192	72.1	162	60.7
NOVEMBER 2004							
Total	564	554	98.2	425	75.5	378	67.1
Male	275	269	98.0	196	71.4	174	63.3
Female	289	284	98.4	229	79.3	204	70.6
Race and Hispanic Origin							
White alone	530	524	98.9	408	77.0	366	69.0
Non-Hispanic White alone	521	519	99.6	405	77.8	363	69.6
Black alone	2	1	B	-	B	-	B
Asian alone	7	4	B	1	B	1	B
Hispanic or Latino[1]	10	6	B	4	B	4	B
White alone or in combination	535	530	98.9	412	76.9	368	68.6
Non-Hispanic White alone or in combination	527	525	99.6	409	77.6	365	69.2
Black alone or in combination	3	2	B	1	B	1	B
Asian alone or in combination	7	4	B	1	B	1	B
Age							
18 to 24 years	82	80	B	51	B	39	B
25 to 44 years	196	191	97.5	136	69.2	114	58.2
45 to 64 years	195	192	98.7	158	81.2	148	76.2
65 to 74 years	47	46	B	42	B	41	B
75 years and over	45	45	B	38	B	35	B

[1]May be of any race.
- = Represents zero or rounds to zero.
B = Base is too small to show derived measure.

At a Glance:

- Tennessee's population was 5.9 million in 2004, making it the 16th most populous state in the nation.

- Blacks made up 16.7 percent of Tennessee's population in 2004, which was the 11th largest proportion of this racial group in the nation. Non-Hispanic Whites were the predominate racial group, accounting for 78.1 percent of the state's population.

- Tennessee had the sixth highest infant mortality rate and the seventh highest age-adjusted death rate for all causes in the country.

- The state's median household income of $38,223 ranked 44th in the nation. Tennessee's poverty rate of 15.9 percent was the eighth highest in the country.

- Economic activity rebounded strongly from the 2001 recession. Tennessee's real gross state product (GSP) grew 13.7 percent from 2001 to 2004, which was the third fastest rate in the nation. The state's unemployment rate was 5.4 percent, just below the national average.

- Tennessee ranked 41st in the nation for high school attainment, with less than 83 percent of its population age 25 years and over holding high school diplomas. The state ranked 38th in the nation for college attainment, with 24.3 percent of this age group holding bachelor's degrees or more.

Table TN-1. Population by Sex and Age, 1990, 2000, and 2004

(Number, percent.)

Sex and age	1990	2000	2004	Percent distribution, 2004	Average annual percent change, 2000–2004
Total Population	4 877 185	5 689 283	5 900 962	X	0.9
Percent of total U.S. population	2.0	2.0	2.0	X	X
Sex					
Male	2 348 928	2 770 275	2 886 284	48.9	1.0
Female	2 528 257	2 919 008	3 014 678	51.1	0.8
Age					
Under 5 years	333 415	374 880	384 704	6.5	0.9
5 to 17 years	883 189	1 023 641	1 006 585	17.1	0.9
18 years and over	960 799	4 290 762	4 509 673	76.4	1.5
18 to 24 years	3 660 581	548 856	575 689	9.8	0.6
25 to 44 years	527 655	1 718 428	1 714 986	29.1	0.7
45 to 64 years	1 553 309	1 320 167	1 480 945	25.1	3.2
65 years and over	618 818	703 311	738 053	12.5	1.3
85 years and over	58 794	81 465	83 725	1.4	2.7
Median age (years)	33.5	35.9	36.9	X	X

X = Not applicable.

Average Annual Rate of Population Growth, 1980–2004

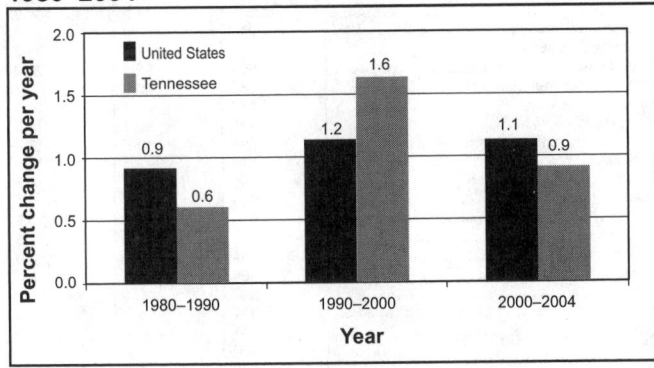

POPULATION

Tennessee's population has been growing strongly in recent years, as the state has drawn in both domestic and international immigrants. Between 2000 and 2004, the population growth slowed from previous periods and increased at a rate of just 3.7 percent, which was below the national average. Net immigration accounted for over half of the population growth during this period. Tennessee gained over 71,000 new residents from other states, the 7th highest number in the nation, and over 42,000 immigrants from abroad. The state had a smaller proportion of school-age population and an average proportion of residents over 65 years old. Nashville and Memphis were the state's largest metropolitan areas.

Table TN-2. Population by Race and Hispanic Origin, 1990, 2000, and 2004

(Number, percent.)

Race and Hispanic origin	1990	2000	2004
Total Population	4 877 185	5 689 283	5 900 962
Non-Hispanic (Percent)			
One race[1]			
White	82.6	79.4	78.1
Black	15.9	16.4	16.7
American Indian, Alaska Native[2]	0.2	0.2	0.2
Asian and Pacific Islander[2]	0.7	1.0	1.2
Other race[2]	0.2	. . .	. . .
Two or more races	. . .	0.8	0.9
Hispanic or Latino[3] (Percent)	0.7	2.2	2.8

[1]Individuals could report only one race in the 1990 census and could report one or more races on the 2000 census. Data on race in 2000 and 2004 are not comparable to 1990.
[2]Data for 1990 include people of Hispanic or Latino origin.
[3]May be of any race.
. . . = Not available.

Minority Population as a Percent of Total Population, 2004

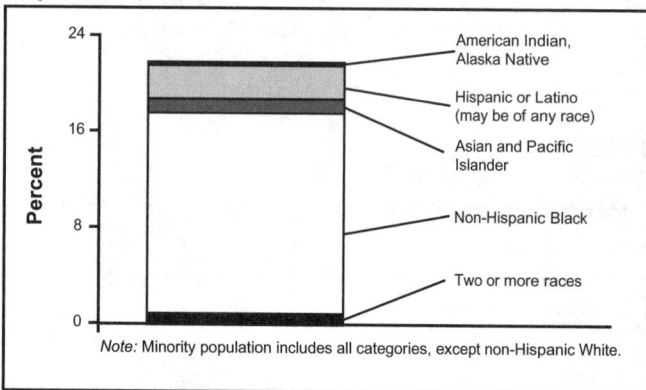

Note: Minority population includes all categories, except non-Hispanic White.

Age-Adjusted Death Rates, Average 2000–2002

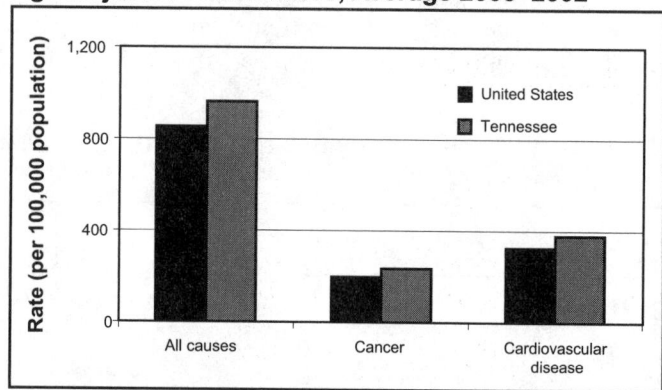

HEALTH

Tennessee's rate of health insurance coverage was above average. About 14.1 percent of residents lacked health insurance in 2004, compared with the national rate of 15.7 percent. The state's birth rate was below average, but its birth rate for teenage mothers was the ninth highest in the country.

Table TN-3. Health Characteristics, 2000–2004

(Number, rate, percent.)

Item	State	U.S.
Births, 2003–2004		
Number of births	78 890	4 089 950
Birth rate (per 1,000 population)	13.5	14.1
Teenage birth rate (per 1,000 women age 15–19 years)	53.5	41.6
Mortality Rates, Average 2000–2002		
Infant mortality rate (per 1,000 live births)	9.0	6.9
Age-adjusted mortality rate (per 100,000 population)		
All races	982.0	853.3
Non-Hispanic White	952.2	843.1
Black	1 236.8	1 097.7
American Indian, Alaska Native	. . .	687.0
Asian and Pacific Islander	443.5	486.0
Hispanic or Latino[1]	331.7	642.7
Health Insurance, 2004		
Percent of all persons without health insurance	14.1	15.7
Percent of children without health insurance	10.1	11.2
Percent of low-income children without health insurance	6.5	7.1

[1]May be of any race.
. . . = Not available.

Table TN-4. Leading Causes of Death, Average 2000–2002

(Number, rate per 100,000 population.)

Cause	Number of deaths	Age-adjusted death rates	
		State	U.S.
ALL CAUSES	55 668	982.0	853.3
Leading Causes			
Major cardiovascular diseases	21 497	382.1	326.5
Cancer	12 362	214.8	196.0
Chronic lower respiratory diseases	2 946	52.0	43.7
Unintentional injuries	2 732	47.6	35.7
Diabetes (underlying cause)	1 695	29.7	25.2
Influenza and pneumonia	1 666	30.0	22.7
Alzheimer's disease	1 157	21.1	19.0
Motor vehicle accidents	1 280	22.2	15.0
Nephritis, nephrotic syndrome, and nephrosis ..	592	10.5	13.8
Septicemia	536	9.5	11.4
Suicides	740	12.7	10.7
Firearm-related	883	15.2	10.3
Cirrhosis	606	10.3	9.5
Drug-induced	473	8.1	7.9
Alcohol-induced	389	6.5	6.9
Homicides	464	8.0	6.0
Falls	302	5.4	5.2
HIV	304	5.2	5.0
Viral hepatitis	141	2.4	2.0
Anemias	106	1.9	1.6
Drownings	90	1.6	1.3
Fire deaths	110	1.9	1.2

Note: The rates are age-adjusted to the U.S. 2000 standard population.

Table TN-5. Households and Housing Characteristics, 1990, 2000, and 2004

(Number, percent, and dollars.)

Characteristic	1990	2000	2004	Average annual percent change, 2000–2004
Total Households	1 853 725	2 232 905	2 314 688	0.9
Family households	1 348 019	1 547 835	1 556 090	0.1
Married-couple family	1 059 569	1 173 960	1 152 881	-0.5
Other family	288 450	373 875	403 209	1.9
Male householder, no wife present	55 751	85 976	93 163	2.0
Female householder, no husband present ...	232 699	287 899	310 046	1.9
Nonfamily households	505 706	685 070	758 598	2.6
Householder living alone	442 129	576 401	629 866	2.2
Householder not living alone	63 577	108 669	128 732	4.3
Housing Characteristics				
Average size	2.56	2.48	2.48	X
Housing units	2 026 067	2 439 443	2 595 060	1.6
Occupied housing units	1 853 725	2 232 905	2 314 688	0.9
Owner-occupied	1 261 118	1 561 363	1 619 882	0.9
Renter-occupied	592 607	671 542	694 806	0.9
Median gross rent of renter-occupied housing units (dollars) ...	357	505	564	2.8
Median value of owner-occupied housing units (dollars)	58 000	93 000	110 198	4.3

X = Not applicable.

Median Housing Value and Median Rent, 2004

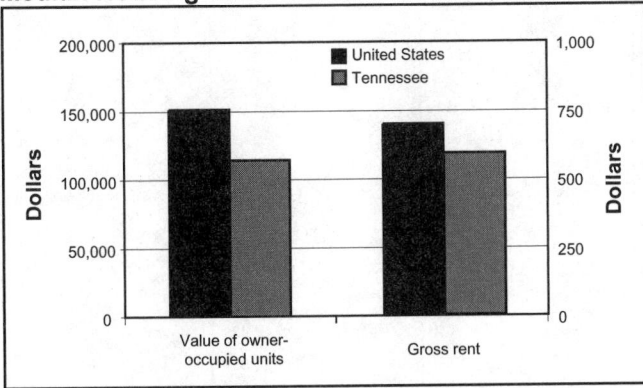

Median Household Income, 1984–2004 (2004 Dollars)

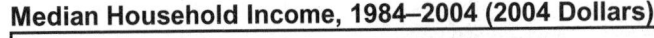
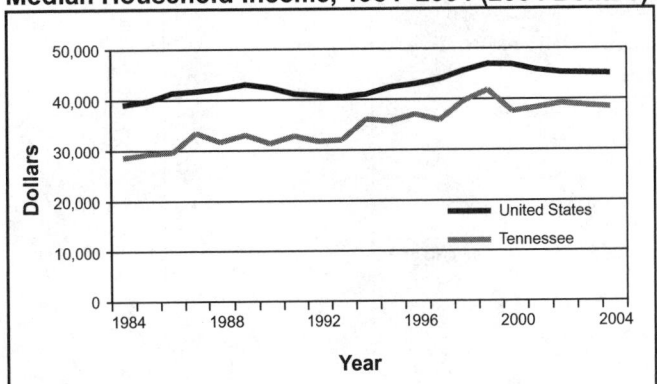

Table TN-6. Household Income and Poverty Status, 1980–2004

(2004 CPI-U-RS adjusted dollars, rate.)

Year	State		U.S.	
	Median household income (2004 dollars)	Poverty rate	Median household income (2004 dollars)	Poverty rate
2004	38 223	15.9	44 389	12.7
2003	38 531	14.0	44 482	12.5
2002	38 896	14.8	44 546	12.1
2001	38 184	14.1	45 062	11.7
2000	37 400	13.5	46 058	11.3
1999	41 398	11.9	46 129	11.9
1998	39 455	13.4	45 003	12.7
1997	35 955	14.3	43 430	13.3
1996	36 908	15.9	42 544	13.7
1995	35 714	15.5	41 943	13.8
1994	36 107	14.6	40 677	14.5
1993	32 314	19.6	40 217	15.1
1992	32 086	17.0	40 422	14.8
1991	33 073	15.5	40 746	14.2
1990	31 661	16.9	41 963	13.5
1989	33 264	18.4	42 524	12.8
1988	31 999	18.0	41 771	13.0
1987	33 678	16.9	41 322	13.4
1986	30 019	18.3	40 939	13.6
1985	29 767	18.1	39 545	14.0
1984	29 036	17.4	38 782	14.4
1983	. . .	20.0	. . .	15.2
1982	. . .	23.6	. . .	15.0
1981	. . .	20.9	. . .	14.0
1980	. . .	19.6	. . .	13.0

. . . = Not available.

Table TN-7. Employment Status by Demographic Group, 2004

(Numbers in thousands, rate.)

Characteristic	Civilian noninstitutional population	Civilian labor force		Employed	Unemployment rate
		Number	Participation rate		
SEX AND AGE					
Total	4 564	2 894	63.4	2 747	5.1
16 to 19 years	319	144	45.0	123	14.4
20 to 24 years	455	332	73.1	298	10.4
25 to 34 years	817	661	80.9	629	4.8
35 to 44 years	808	655	81.1	629	4.1
45 to 54 years	855	662	77.4	643	2.9
55 to 64 years	667	353	52.8	340	3.5
65 years and over	644	87	13.6	85	2.3
Men	2 187	1 529	69.9	1 452	5.1
16 to 19 years	161	74	46.3	63	15.3
20 to 24 years	233	171	73.6	155	9.7
25 to 34 years	401	359	89.5	338	5.7
35 to 44 years	392	344	87.7	329	4.3
45 to 54 years	397	336	84.8	327	2.8
55 to 64 years	326	200	61.4	197	1.7
Women	2 378	1 365	57.4	1 295	5.1
16 to 19 years	158	69	43.7	60	13.5
20 to 24 years	222	161	72.6	143	11.1
25 to 34 years	416	302	72.6	291	3.7
35 to 44 years	416	312	75.0	300	3.8
45 to 54 years	459	326	71.1	316	3.0
55 to 64 years	341	152	44.7	143	6.0
MARITAL STATUS					
Married men, spouse present	1 259	924	73.3	900	2.6
Married women, spouse present	1 289	733	56.9	708	3.4
Women who maintain families	294	197	67.0	183	7.0
RACE, HISPANIC ORIGIN, AND SEX					
White	3 759	2 361	62.8	2 263	4.1
Men	1 826	1 285	70.4	1 233	4.0
Women	1 933	1 076	55.7	1 030	4.3
Black	693	458	66.1	411	10.2
Men	310	202	65.2	178	12.2
Women	382	256	66.9	233	8.7
Hispanic or Latino[1]	112	83	74.3	80	4.3
Men	73	67	91.7	64	4.1
RACE, HISPANIC ORIGIN, AND AGE					
White					
16 to 19 years	257	130	50.6	115	11.5
20 to 24 years	353	259	73.4	240	7.5
25 to 34 years	632	509	80.4	489	3.8
35 to 44 years	662	530	80.1	512	3.3
45 to 54 years	702	547	78.0	531	2.9
55 to 64 years	581	305	52.5	296	3.0
65 years and over	571	81	14.1	79	1.7
Black					
20 to 24 years	85	63	73.8	48	23.2
25 to 34 years	157	131	83.4	119	8.6
35 to 44 years	125	105	84.4	97	8.1
45 to 54 years	133	101	75.9	98	2.9

Note: Data in Table 7 are from the Current Population Survey (CPS) and do not match Bureau of Labor Statistics estimates in Table 8. See notes and definitions for more details.

[1]May be of any race.

Table TN-8. Employment Status, 1990–2004

(Numbers in thousands, rate.)

Year	Civilian labor force	Employed	Unemployed	Unemployment rate
2004	2 907 804	2 751 755	156 049	5.4
2003	2 902 990	2 742 225	160 765	5.5
2002	2 883 414	2 733 702	149 712	5.2
2001	2 859 661	2 728 496	131 165	4.6
2000	2 864 005	2 749 702	114 303	4.0
1999	2 838 738	2 722 124	116 614	4.1
1998	2 811 700	2 685 151	126 549	4.5
1997	2 788 348	2 640 005	148 343	5.3
1996	2 758 346	2 610 975	147 371	5.3
1995	2 718 047	2 574 000	144 047	5.3
1994	2 645 733	2 511 085	134 648	5.1
1993	2 543 274	2 391 568	151 706	6.0
1992	2 479 459	2 316 661	162 798	6.6
1991	2 425 381	2 265 985	159 396	6.6
1990	2 401 093	2 269 015	132 078	5.5

Note: Population age 16 years and over.

Unemployment Rate, 1980–2004

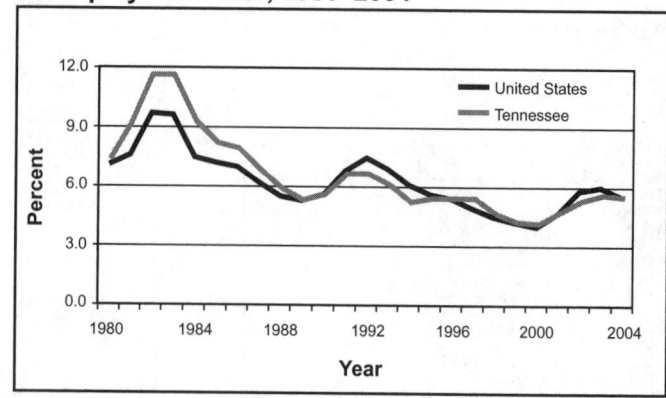

Table TN-9. Employment and Average Wages by Industry, 2001–2004

(Estimates are based on the 2002 North American Industry Classification System [NAICS].)

Industry	2001	2002	2003	2004	Annual average percent change, 2001–2004
	Number of jobs				
TOTAL EMPLOYMENT BY PLACE OF WORK	3 458 846	3 451 613	3 473 834	3 543 256	0.8
Farm Employment	104 033	103 775	103 675	101 292	-0.9
Nonfarm Employment	3 354 813	3 347 838	3 370 159	3 441 964	0.9
Private employment	2 930 866	2 917 238	2 937 723	3 006 515	0.9
Forestry, fishing, hunting, and other[1]	12 401	12 634	11 302	10 659	-4.9
Mining	6 458	5 692	5 934	5 953	-2.7
Utilities	3 867	3 779	3 869	3 819	-0.4
Construction	211 885	201 866	209 091	212 717	0.1
Manufacturing	466 445	442 748	426 693	424 890	-3.1
Durable goods manufacturing	285 052	269 749	260 599	263 110	-2.6
Nondurable goods manufacturing	181 393	172 999	166 094	161 780	-3.7
Wholesale trade	138 507	136 414	137 391	139 298	0.2
Retail trade	399 620	395 769	398 801	408 539	0.7
Transportation and warehousing	167 694	161 892	163 194	165 313	-0.5
Information	62 213	59 001	58 930	57 311	-2.7
Finance and insurance	138 917	138 734	140 109	142 809	0.9
Real estate and rental and leasing	103 827	105 122	110 289	115 509	3.6
Professional and technical services	159 581	159 478	163 237	167 354	1.6
Management of companies and enterprises	25 889	24 155	23 144	23 923	-2.6
Administrative and waste services	220 956	229 419	218 108	237 024	2.4
Educational services	50 375	52 143	54 518	57 379	4.4
Health care and social assistance	287 265	298 733	311 070	319 743	3.6
Arts, entertainment, and recreation	55 811	58 237	59 730	61 619	3.4
Accommodation and food services	225 820	229 042	237 184	244 347	2.7
Other services, except public administration	193 335	202 380	205 129	208 309	2.5
Government and government enterprises	423 947	430 600	432 436	435 449	0.9
	Dollars				
AVERAGE WAGES AND SALARIES BY PLACE OF WORK ...	30 885	31 919	32 949	34 308	3.6
Farm Earnings	13 320	17 024	14 215	15 878	6.0
Nonfarm Earnings	30 959	31 976	33 038	34 392	3.6
Private earnings	31 141	32 121	33 126	34 489	3.5
Forestry, fishing, hunting, and other[1]	17 400	17 362	17 933	19 898	4.6
Mining	45 093	44 907	44 790	48 015	2.1
Utilities	45 230	46 880	47 480	49 834	3.3
Construction	34 196	34 585	35 236	35 976	1.7
Manufacturing	36 852	38 584	40 062	41 992	4.4
Durable goods manufacturing	36 455	38 144	39 452	41 156	4.1
Nondurable goods manufacturing	37 474	39 268	41 016	43 348	5.0
Wholesale trade	41 913	43 296	44 823	47 720	4.4
Retail trade	21 883	22 626	23 107	23 589	2.5
Transportation and warehousing	37 361	39 093	39 867	41 371	3.5
Information	39 862	40 714	41 396	43 637	3.1
Finance and insurance	47 563	49 422	53 133	55 738	5.4
Real estate and rental and leasing	29 062	30 092	31 577	33 033	4.4
Professional and technical services	45 684	47 001	47 559	50 011	3.1
Management of companies and enterprises	45 452	48 319	53 255	57 060	7.9
Administrative and waste services	22 877	23 371	24 208	25 076	3.1
Educational services	27 802	29 862	31 343	33 083	6.0
Health care and social assistance	33 357	34 408	35 083	37 096	3.6
Arts, entertainment, and recreation	26 023	28 594	30 509	31 709	6.8
Accommodation and food services	13 886	14 277	14 389	14 672	1.9
Other services, except public administration	21 080	21 825	22 426	23 044	3.0
Government and government enterprises	29 942	31 186	32 563	33 861	4.2

Note: Average wages and salaries are a calculation by the editors of wage and salary disbursements divided by full- and part-time wage and salary employment. Data may not add to total or may appear as zero due to rounding.

[1] "Other" consists of the number of jobs held by U.S. residents employed by international organizations and foreign embassies and consulates in the United States.

LABOR MARKET

Tennessee's unemployment rate was slightly below the national average during the 2001 recession and the subsequent recovery period; it was similar to those of Kentucky and other neighboring states. Employment declined in 2002, following the previous year's recession, but rebounded significantly in the 2003–2004 period. The number of jobs increased 2.4 percent from 2001 to 2004, which was above the national growth rate. While the number of manufacturing jobs declined throughout the period, jobs in retail trade and in several service-providing industries increased steadily. Average wages and salaries were below the national average, but their growth rate was above average.

Employment by Industry, 2004

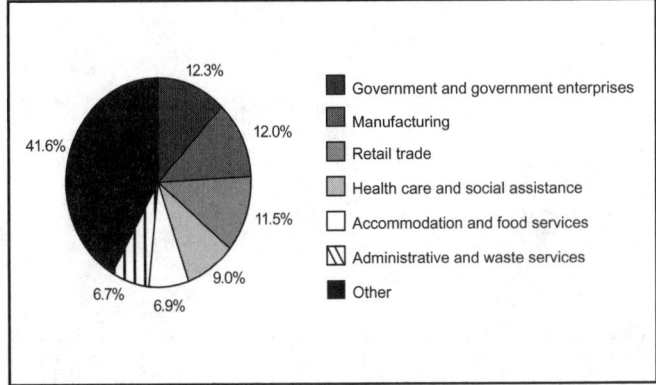

Table TN-10. Personal Income by Major Source, Selected Years 1980–2004

(Millions of dollars, except where noted.)

Item	1980	1990	2000	2001	2002	2003	2004	Average annual percent change, 2000–2004
Earnings by Place of Work	30 815	63 737	117 216	121 237	126 371	132 957	141 436	4.8
Wage and salary disbursements	23 264	47 365	85 279	86 617	88 791	91 744	97 109	3.3
Supplements to wages and salaries	4 410	9 747	16 734	17 491	19 991	22 113	23 463	8.8
Proprietors' income[1]	3 140	6 625	15 202	17 130	17 589	19 101	20 864	8.2
Farm proprietors' income	79	283	231	120	-304	-141	-178	X
Nonfarm proprietors' income	3 061	6 342	14 972	17 009	17 893	19 242	21 043	8.9
(-) Contributions for government social insurance[2]	2 675	6 916	12 650	13 069	13 638	14 232	15 006	4.4
(+) Adjustment for residence[3]	-425	-595	-1 456	-1 517	-1 511	-1 441	-1 507	X
(=) Net Earnings by Place of Residence	27 714	56 226	103 110	106 651	111 222	117 285	124 923	4.9
(+) Dividends, interest, and rent[4]	5 143	14 157	22 659	22 614	20 939	20 220	20 555	-2.4
(+) Personal current transfer receipts	5 136	11 317	23 065	25 150	26 942	28 570	30 407	7.2
Personal income	37 994	81 700	148 833	154 416	159 102	166 075	175 885	4.3
Farm income	37 811	81 284	148 458	154 125	159 214	166 013	175 843	4.3
Nonfarm income	183	416	375	291	-112	62	42	-42.2
Per Capita Personal Income (Dollars)[5]	8 259	16 692	26 097	26 864	27 468	28 412	29 806	3.4

Note: Data may not add to total or may appear as zero due to rounding.

[1]Proprietors' income includes the inventory valuation adjustment and the capital consumption adjustment.
[2]Contributions for government social insurance are included in earnings by type and industry, but they are excluded from personal income.
[3]The adjustment for residence is the net inflow of the earnings of interarea commuters.
[4]Rental income of persons includes the capital consumption adjustment.
[5]Per capita personal income is total personal income divided by total midyear population.
X = Not applicable.

Per Capita Personal Income, 1980–2004 (Current Dollars)

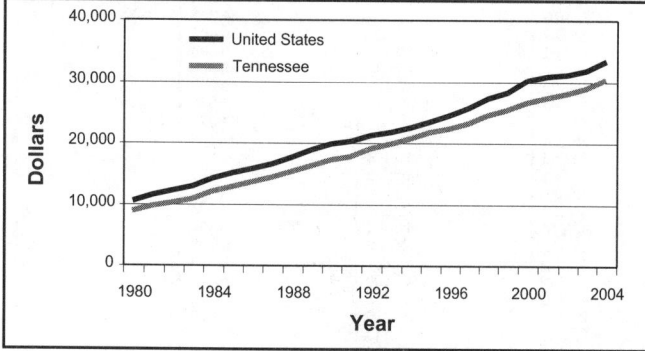

ECONOMIC ACTIVITY

Economic activity in Tennessee rebounded robustly from the 2001 recession and grew at an above average rate. From 2001 to 2004, real gross state product grew 13.7 percent, the third highest growth rate in the nation. Contributing to this growth were manufacturing, wholesale trade, retail trade, finance and insurance, real estate and related activities, and government. Housing prices remained subdued, despite the increases in economic activity and the state's population growth. Home values have appreciated at only half of the national average rate in recent years. In 2004, the median value of owner-occupied housing in Tennessee was $110,198, ranking 37th in the country.

Table TN-11. Real Gross State Product, 1997–2004

(Millions of chained 2000 dollars, percent.)

Industry	1997	1998	1999	2000	2001	2002	2003	2004	Average annual percent change, 2001–2004
GROSS STATE PRODUCT	163 038	168 048	173 276	174 349	175 936	183 168	191 186	200 107	4.4
As a percent of U.S. gross product	1.9	1.9	1.8	1.8	1.8	1.8	1.9	1.9	X
Private Industries	143 835	148 289	153 201	154 830	156 881	162 442	169 042	177 344	4.2
Agriculture, forestry, fishing, and hunting	1 060	930	860	1 182	1 131	1 069	1 178	981	-4.6
Mining	359	396	448	441	406	380	355	320	-7.6
Utilities	669	658	670	697	668	730	768	782	5.4
Construction	7 607	7 667	7 605	7 368	6 721	6 574	6 744	6 818	0.5
Manufacturing	32 634	32 970	33 618	33 136	32 357	33 663	35 138	37 000	4.6
As a percent of gross state product	20.0	19.6	19.4	19.0	18.4	18.4	18.4	18.5	X
Wholesale trade	10 645	11 724	12 440	11 982	12 696	13 202	13 158	13 782	2.8
Retail trade	13 413	13 938	14 747	14 938	15 681	16 755	18 125	19 148	6.9
Transportation and warehousing	7 854	8 250	8 873	9 103	8 653	8 920	9 384	9 598	3.5
Information	4 017	4 327	4 646	5 140	5 573	5 885	6 280	6 714	6.4
Finance and insurance	8 564	8 978	9 264	9 985	10 650	10 827	11 776	12 695	6.0
Real estate and rental and leasing	16 279	16 851	17 760	18 081	19 073	19 313	19 663	20 761	2.9
Services	40 812	41 651	42 297	42 776	43 331	45 245	46 661	49 041	4.2
As a percent of gross state product	25.0	24.8	24.4	24.5	24.6	24.7	24.4	24.5	X
Professional and technical services	7 339	7 674	7 852	8 254	8 419	8 631	9 027	9 395	3.7
Management of companies and enterprises	1 873	1 802	1 883	1 910	2 119	2 139	2 263	2 371	3.8
Administrative and waste services	5 802	6 167	6 565	6 395	6 363	6 951	6 887	7 492	5.6
Educational services	1 194	1 250	1 307	1 352	1 363	1 390	1 405	1 449	2.1
Health care and social assistance	12 876	12 650	12 621	12 919	13 444	14 193	14 798	15 494	4.8
Arts, entertainment, and recreation	1 523	1 617	1 571	1 560	1 548	1 661	1 768	1 838	5.9
Accommodation and food services	5 317	5 466	5 611	5 607	5 432	5 585	5 783	5 998	3.4
Other services, except public administration	4 888	5 025	4 887	4 779	4 643	4 695	4 730	5 004	2.5
Government	19 215	19 771	20 081	19 519	19 058	20 707	22 100	22 727	6.0
As a percent of gross state product	11.8	11.8	11.6	11.2	10.8	11.3	11.6	11.4	X

X = Not applicable.

Table TN-12. Government Transfer Payments, Selected Years 1980–2004

(Millions of dollars, percent.)

Item	1980	1990	2000	2001	2002	2003	2004	Average annual percent change, 2000–2004
CURRENT TRANSFER PAYMENTS TO INDIVIDUALS	4 822	10 710	21 864	23 805	25 734	27 454	29 290	7.6
Retirement and Disability Insurance Benefits	2 407	5 012	8 810	9 394	9 964	10 417	10 925	5.5
Old-age, survivors, and disability insurance (OASDI) benefits	2 233	4 765	8 540	9 114	9 660	10 106	10 608	5.6
Railroad retirement and disability benefits	97	142	164	169	178	184	187	3.3
Workers' compensation	19	52	61	66	77	75	77	5.8
Other government retirement and disability insurance benefits	58	53	45	45	49	53	53	4.3
Medical Benefits	1 009	3 682	9 567	10 539	11 250	12 174	13 410	8.8
Medicare benefits	604	2 087	4 359	4 855	5 216	5 539	6 111	8.8
Public assistance medical care benefits	385	1 541	5 148	5 598	5 913	6 528	7 169	8.6
Military medical insurance benefits	20	54	60	87	121	106	130	21.4
Income Maintenance Benefits	667	1 191	2 295	2 352	2 720	3 054	3 301	9.5
Supplemental Security Income (SSI) benefits	199	385	664	689	705	719	752	3.1
Family assistance	85	174	207	200	218	196	168	-5.1
Food stamps	295	390	422	471	576	748	849	19.1
Other income maintenance benefits	88	242	1 001	992	1 221	1 391	1 532	11.2
Unemployment Insurance Compensation	318	275	383	606	812	775	546	9.2
Veterans' Benefits	334	407	602	634	694	749	805	7.6
Federal Education and Training Assistance	87	130	188	243	275	269	285	10.9
Other Payments to Individuals	1	13	20	38	19	16	19	-1.5

Note: See notes and definitions for more details. Data may not add to total or may appear as zero due to rounding.

EXPORTS

In 2004, Tennessee's exports amounted to $16.1 billion, making the state the 16th largest exporter in the country. Exports abroad have grown substantially in recent years, increasing 42.4 percent from 2001 to 2004. Transportation equipment, computers and electronic products, and chemical manufactures were the leading export products. Crops were the fastest growing of Tennessee's major exports, increasing in value from $469 million in 2001 to close to $1.8 billion in 2004. Canada accounted for about a third of the state's exports, followed by Mexico. China was Tennessee's most rapidly growing overseas market, with exports to this country increasing from $184 million in 2001 to $1.2 billion in 2004. About two-thirds of these exports were crops.

Leading Exports, 2004

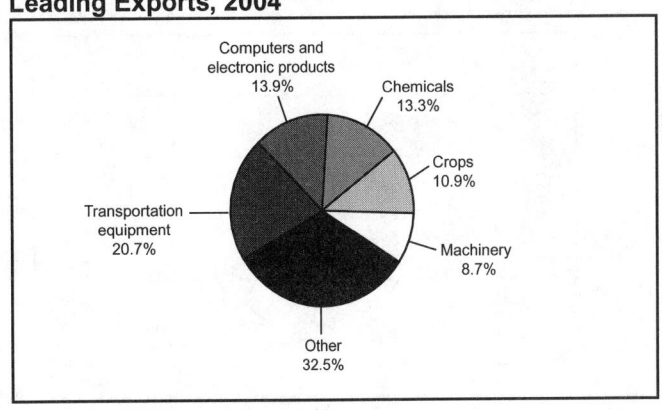

Table TN-13. Exports of Goods by Leading Products and Destinations, 2001–2004

(Millions of dollars, percent, rank based on 2004 dollar values.)

Product and market	2001	2002	2003	2004	Percent share of total, 2004	Average annual percent change, 2001–2004
Total Goods						
Total	11 320	11 621	12 612	16 123	100.0	12.5
Manufactures	10 440	10 670	11 027	13 869	86.0	9.9
Agriculture and livestock	533	717	1 199	1 827	11.3	50.8
Other commodities	348	234	386	427	2.6	7.1
Five Leading Exports (NAICS Code)						
Transportation equipment (336)	2 431	2 766	2 391	3 338	20.7	11.2
Computers and electronic products (334)	1 584	1 361	1 773	2 237	13.9	12.2
Chemical manufactures (325)	1 397	1 584	1 723	2 139	13.3	15.3
Crop production (111)	469	671	1 149	1 763	10.9	55.4
Machinery manufactures (333)	1 252	1 221	1 265	1 408	8.7	4.0
Five Leading Markets	10 225	10 400	11 297	14 548	90.2	12.5
Canada	4 128	3 947	4 214	5 197	32.2	8.0
Mexico	1 370	1 420	1 476	1 791	11.1	9.3
China	184	339	636	1 214	7.5	87.5
United Kingdom	656	633	646	719	4.5	3.1
Japan	614	600	529	620	3.8	0.3

Table TN-14. Agriculture, 1997 and 2002

(Number, acres, and dollars.)

Item	1997	2002
Number of farms	91 536	87 595
Land in farms (acres)	11 986 258	11 681 533
Farm Size		
Average size of farm (acres)	131	133
Farms by size (percent distribution)		
Fewer than 50 acres	42.8	43.6
50 to 499 acres	53.0	52.1
500 acres or more	4.2	4.3
Market Value of Land and Equipment (Dollars)		
Land and buildings average value per farm	245 186	325 783
Average value per acre	1 859	2 405
Machinery and equipment average value per farm	31 425	45 263
Value of Sales (Thousands of Dollars)		
Agricultural products sold	2 263 035	2 199 814
Crops	1 173 774	1 072 548
Livestock, poultry, and their products	1 089 261	1 127 266
Average per farm (dollars)	24 723	25 113
Value of sales (percent distribution)		
Less than $10,000	75.6	77.5
$10,000 to $99,999	20.0	18.1
$100,000 or more	4.4	4.4
Government Payments		
Payments (thousands of dollars)	50 801	59 231
Percent of farms receiving government payments	19.1	18.3
Farm operators whose principal occupation is farming (percent)	33.5	50.3

AGRICULTURE

Cash receipts from farming totaled about $2.2 billion in 2002, according to the Department of Agriculture's Census of Agriculture. This represented a nearly 3 percent decline from the previous agriculture census in 1997. Between censuses, the value of crop sales declined, while sales of livestock, poultry, and their products increased. Tennessee's chief products were cattle, poultry, and tobacco. More than three-quarters of farms had sales of less than $10,000, and only about half of farm operators considered farming to be their chief occupation. More than 43 percent of farms spanned fewer than 50 acres.

ENERGY

Tennessee's per capita consumption was the 16th highest in the nation. Energy prices were well below average, ranking as the 13th lowest in the country. Energy expenditures per person amounted to $2,403 in 2001, an amount below the national average. Petroleum, coal, nuclear power, and natural gas were the state's chief energy sources.

Energy Consumption by Source, 2001

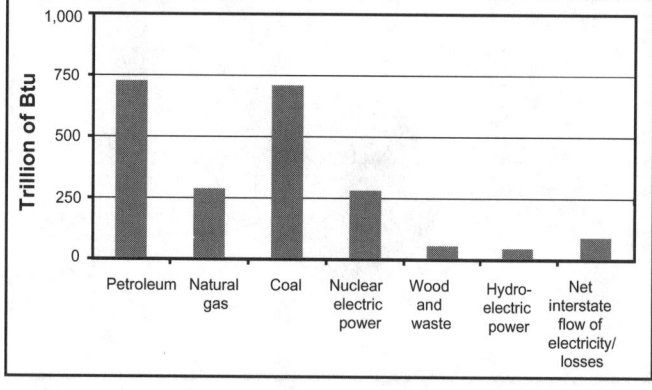

Energy Consumption by Sector, 2001

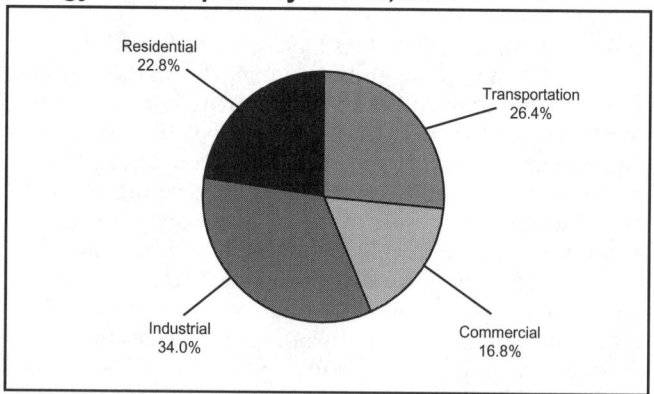

Table TN-15. Energy Consumption, Expenditures, and Prices, Selected Years 1960–2001

(Dollars, Btu [British Thermal Unit], percent distribution.)

Item	1960	1965	1970	1975	1980	1985	1990	1995	2000	2001
Total Consumption (Billion Btu)	962 879	1 147 043	1 383 270	1 626 470	1 748 591	1 723 680	1 844 926	2 004 992	2 201 248	2 195 375
Consumption per capita (million Btu)	269.9	302.0	352.3	380.4	380.9	365.6	378.3	382.5	386.9	382.1
Consumption by Sector (Percent Distribution)										
Residential	19.3	19.0	21.8	21.6	21.4	21.5	21.8	21.8	22.9	22.8
Commercial	7.5	7.9	9.6	8.9	12.9	10.6	11.4	6.8	16.8	16.8
Industrial	55.2	53.0	46.4	45.5	42.3	42.8	41.7	45.3	33.8	34.0
Transportation	18.1	20.1	22.3	24.0	23.4	25.0	25.2	26.2	26.5	26.4
Consumption by Source (Billion Btu)										
Coal	374 478	338 853	403 742	471 919	576 894	599 665	600 527	669 033	705 056	688 021
Natural gas	151 740	211 142	261 784	224 065	233 335	196 735	227 526	264 889	280 679	265 395
Petroleum	228 478	300 921	406 674	503 621	529 669	554 313	590 362	661 104	710 207	708 198
Nuclear electric power	0	0	0	0	5 660	102 737	148 175	165 048	269 327	298 567
Hydroelectric power[1]	93 352	91 464	84 656	122 852	91 045	68 316	99 206	92 943	57 786	63 209
Wood and waste	45 355	46 541	53 761	54 447	62 111	89 594	55 660	61 848	58 492	72 128
Other	0	0	0	0	0	0	87	94	98	102
Net interstate flow of electricity/losses[2]	69 475	158 121	172 653	249 565	249 877	112 321	123 382	90 033	119 603	99 754
Total Expenditures (Thousands of Dollars)	...	...	1 496 000	3 483 400	7 697 300	8 705 800	9 762 500	10 332 600	13 762 700	13 808 400
Expenditures per capita (dollars)	...	...	381	815	1 677	1 846	2 002	1 971	2 419	2 403
Prices by Sector (Dollars Per Million Btu)										
Total	...	...	1.71	3.52	7.26	8.07	8.41	8.04	9.91	9.92
Residential	...	...	2.09	4.41	7.77	10.76	12.19	12.42	14.24	15.18
Commercial	...	...	1.92	3.47	7.92	8.97	10.46	8.59	13.48	14.39
Industrial	...	...	0.94	2.55	5.04	6.66	6.00	6.05	5.91	6.18
Transportation	...	...	2.49	4.19	9.20	8.29	8.97	8.33	10.38	9.69

[1]A negative number in this row results from pumped storage for which, overall, more electricity is expended than created to provide electricity during peak demand periods.
[2]Net interstate flow of electricity is the difference between the amount of energy in the electricity sold within a state (including associated losses) and the energy input at the electric utilities within the state. A positive number indicates that more electricity (including associated losses) came into the state than went out of the state during the year; conversely, a negative number indicates that more electricity (including associated losses) went out of the state than came into the state.
... = Not available.

Table TN-16. State Taxes, Fiscal 2004

(Dollars, percent distribution.)

Item	Thousands of dollars	Percent distribution	Dollars per capita	
			State	U.S.
TOTAL TAXES	9 536 031	100.0	1 616.0	2 024.8
Property Taxes	X	X	X	38.9
Sales and Gross Receipts	7 344 662	77.0	1 244.6	1 003.4
General sales and gross receipts	5 845 206	61.3	990.5	677.0
Selective sales taxes	1 499 456	15.7	254.1	326.4
Alcoholic beverages	92 062	1.0	15.6	15.7
Insurance premiums	351 111	3.7	59.5	47.0
Motor fuels	832 168	8.7	141.0	114.6
Tobacco products	119 482	1.3	20.2	42.0
Other selective sales	99 872	1.0	16.9	49.8
Licenses	1 045 665	11.0	177.2	134.9
Corporation	506 776	5.3	85.9	21.6
Motor vehicle	255 137	2.7	43.2	59.4
Occupation and business, not elsewhere classified	203 248	2.1	34.4	37.1
Other Taxes	1 145 704	12.0	194.2	847.6
Individual income	146 851	1.5	24.9	673.6
Corporation net income	694 798	7.3	117.7	105.1
Death and gift	96 534	1.0	16.4	19.6
Documentary and stock transfer	174 206	1.8	29.5	27.1

X = Not applicable.

GOVERNMENT FINANCE

Tennessee's revenue per person amounted to $3,298 in 2003. The state's per capita expenditures of $3,317 were the sixth lowest in the country. Public welfare was the only category in which per capita spending exceeded the national average. Per capita taxes were among the lowest in the nation, amounting to $1,616. The bulk of the state's revenues came from general sales taxes, motor fuels taxes, and licenses. Tennessee's individual income tax collections were the lowest among the 43 states with such taxes. Debt per person, at less than $600, was the lowest in the country.

Per Capita State Taxes, Fiscal 2004

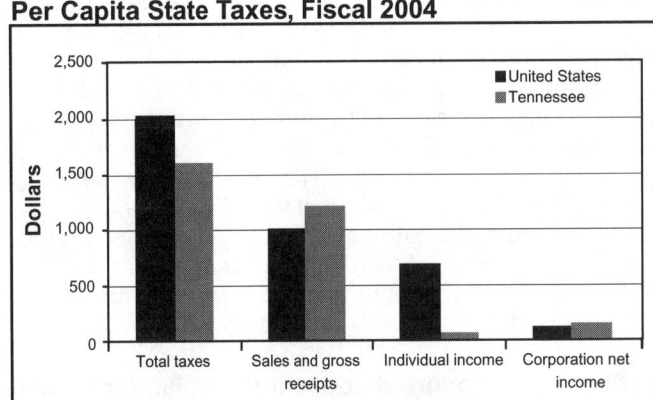

Table TN-17. State Government Finances, 2003

(Dollars, percent distribution.)

Item	Millions of dollars	Percent distribution	Dollars per capita	
			State	U.S.
GENERAL REVENUE	19 278 302	100.0	3 298.3	3 832.6
Intergovernmental revenue	8 292 209	43.0	1 418.7	1 246.0
Taxes	8 811 612	45.7	1 507.6	1 891.6
General sales	5 414 674	28.1	926.4	636.0
Selective sales	1 446 075	7.5	247.4	307.4
License taxes	953 999	4.9	163.2	123.6
Individual income tax	115 593	0.6	19.8	626.8
Corporate income tax	612 943	3.2	104.9	97.8
Other taxes	268 328	1.4	45.9	99.9
Current charges	1 449 396	7.5	248.0	366.5
Miscellaneous general revenue	725 085	3.8	124.0	328.6
GENERAL EXPENDITURE	19 386 815	100.0	3 316.8	4 010.5
Intergovernmental expenditure	4 952 923	25.5	847.4	1 316.9
Direct expenditure	14 433 892	74.5	2 469.4	2 693.6
Expenditure by Function				
Education	6 169 486	31.8	1 055.5	1 416.4
Public welfare	7 634 185	39.4	1 306.1	1 083.3
Hospitals	348 111	1.8	59.6	132.3
Health	881 367	4.5	150.8	173.0
Highways	1 576 290	8.1	269.7	295.4
Police protection	144 177	0.7	24.7	38.4
Correction	558 669	2.9	95.6	135.0
Natural resources	211 306	1.1	36.2	64.0
Parks and recreation	102 721	0.5	17.6	20.1
Government administration	474 505	2.4	81.2	151.3
Interest on general debt	187 328	1.0	32.0	107.8
Other and unallocable	1 098 670	5.7	188.0	393.4
DEBT AT END OF FISCAL YEAR	3 496 139	X	598.1	2 404.7
CASH AND SECURITY HOLDINGS	28 065 993	X	4 801.7	8 938.4

X = Not applicable.

Table TN-18. Education Indicators, 2000–2004

(Percent, number.)

Item	State	U.S.
Total Population 25 Years and Over (Thousands), 2004	3 972	186 877
Educational Attainment, 2004		
Percent high school graduate or more	82.9	85.2
Percent college graduate or more	24.3	27.7
Elementary and Secondary Schools, 2002–2003		
Total students	928 000	48 202 324
Percent of students eligible for free or reduced-price lunch ..	. . .	40.6
Percent of students who were English language learners	. . .	7.8
Total schools	1 628	92 330
Student/teacher ratio	15.7	15.9
Per student expenditures	6 118	8 041
Dropouts, Grades 9–12, 2000–2001 (Percent)	3.8	. . .
Higher Education, 2002–2003		
Total enrollment	274 833	17 035 027
Bachelor's degrees awarded	24 369	1 348 503
Percent women	58.5	57.5

. . . = Not available.

Educational Attainment, 2004

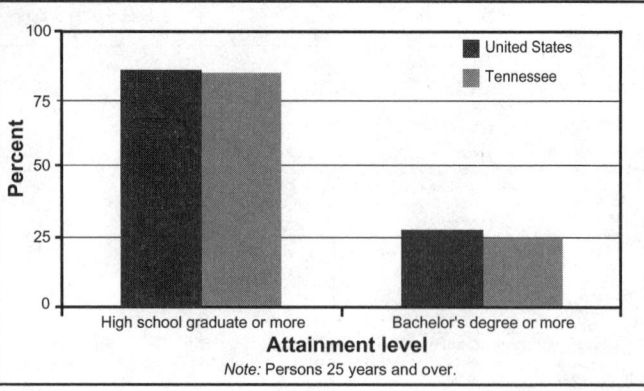

Note: Persons 25 years and over.

EDUCATION

Tennessee's educational attainment rates have improved significantly since the 1990s, but remained well below the national averages in 2004. The state ranked 41st in the nation for high school attainment, with 82.9 percent of its residents age 25 years and over holding high school diplomas. Just over 24 percent of its population age 25 years and over held bachelor's degrees or more. Tennessee's expenditures per student were $6,118, nearly $2,000 less than the national average and ranking 46th in the country. The state's student/teacher ratio was slightly below average. Its dropout rate of 3.8 percent ranked 26th out of the 46 states reporting such data.

VOTER PARTICIPATION

Voter turnout in both the 2000 and 2004 elections was below the national average. In 2004, 52.7 percent of eligible voters cast ballots, which was the sixth lowest proportion in the country. Just 7.2 percent of eligible Hispanics voted in 2004, while participation rates for Blacks and Whites were over 50 percent. According to the official tally by the Clerk of the U.S. House of Representatives, 51.1 percent of eligible voters cast their ballots for the Republican presidential candidate in 2000, a proportion that rose to 56.8 percent in 2004. The comparable percentages for the Democrats were 47.3 and 42.5 percent, respectively.

Table TN-19. Reported Voting and Registration, November 2000 and November 2004

(Numbers in thousands, percent.)

Characteristic	Total population 18 years and over	Total citizen		Total registered		Total voted	
		Number	Percent	Number	Percent	Number	Percent
NOVEMBER 2000							
Total	4 173	4 067	97.4	2 590	62.1	2 183	52.3
Male	2 036	1 960	96.3	1 239	60.8	1 042	51.2
Female	2 137	2 107	98.6	1 351	63.2	1 142	53.4
NOVEMBER 2004							
Total	4 402	4 250	96.5	2 739	62.2	2 319	52.7
Male	2 118	2 035	96.1	1 262	59.6	1 075	50.8
Female	2 283	2 215	97.0	1 477	64.7	1 243	54.5
Race and Hispanic Origin							
White alone	3 655	3 550	97.1	2 288	62.6	1 954	53.5
Non-Hispanic White alone	3 548	3 510	99.0	2 273	64.1	1 945	54.8
Black alone	651	638	98.0	416	63.9	334	51.3
Asian alone	29	6	B	6	B	6	B
Hispanic or Latino[1]	128	48	37.3	16	12.3	9	7.2
White alone or in combination	3 695	3 585	97.0	2 309	62.5	1 971	53.3
Non-Hispanic White alone or in combination	3 582	3 545	99.0	2 294	64.0	1 962	54.8
Black alone or in combination	651	638	98.0	416	63.9	334	51.3
Asian alone or in combination	29	6	B	6	B	6	B
Age							
18 to 24 years	687	636	92.6	304	44.3	243	35.4
25 to 44 years	1 529	1 447	94.6	847	55.4	693	45.4
45 to 64 years	1 478	1 459	98.7	1 073	72.6	957	64.8
65 to 74 years	449	449	100.0	335	74.7	291	64.8
75 years and over	259	259	100.0	179	69.4	134	51.9

[1]May be of any race.
B = Base is too small to show derived measure.

At a Glance:

- The population of Texas was almost 22.5 million in 2004, making it the second most populous state in the country after California. It was the second largest state in land area behind Alaska.

- Non-Hispanic Whites made up 49.8 percent of the state's population. Along with Hawaii, the District of Columbia, New Mexico, and California, Texas had a majority of its population composed of minorities.

- Hispanics (of any race) made up 34.6 percent of Texas's population in 2004, which was the third largest proportion of this ethnic group in the country.

- Texas's rate of health insurance coverage was the lowest in the nation, with 25 percent of residents lacking insurance.

- Texas's median household income of $41,326 was about $3,000 less than the national average. The state's poverty rate of 16.5 percent was the sixth highest in the country.

- The state's real gross product was the third highest in the country in 2004. Its rate of growth was slightly above average from 2001 to 2004. Texas's unemployment rate was substantially higher than average at 6.1 percent, ranking 10th in the nation.

Table TX-1. Population by Sex and Age, 1990, 2000, and 2004

(Number, percent.)

Sex and age	1990	2000	2004	Percent distribution, 2004	Average annual percent change, 2000–2004
Total Population	16 986 510	20 851 820	22 490 022	X	1.9
Percent of total U.S. population	6.8	7.4	7.7	X	X
Sex					
Male	8 365 963	10 352 910	11 201 268	49.8	2.0
Female	8 620 547	10 498 910	11 288 754	50.2	1.8
Age					
Under 5 years	1 390 054	1 624 628	1 842 808	8.2	1.9
5 to 17 years	3 445 785	4 262 131	4 423 971	19.7	1.8
18 years and over	2 918 055	14 965 061	16 223 243	72.1	2.1
18 to 24 years	12 150 671	2 198 881	2 400 474	10.7	1.7
25 to 44 years	1 890 844	6 484 321	6 673 546	29.7	1.2
45 to 64 years	5 625 196	4 209 327	4 932 613	21.9	3.9
65 years and over	1 716 576	2 072 532	2 216 610	9.9	1.9
85 years and over	166 605	237 940	245 992	1.1	3.0
Median age (years)	30.6	32.3	32.8	X	X

X = Not applicable.

Average Annual Rate of Population Growth, 1980–2004

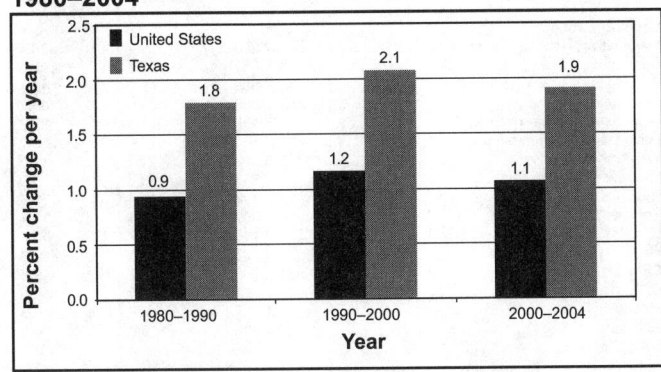

POPULATION

The population of Texas has been growing rapidly for many years. It increased over 7.9 percent from 2000 to 2004, the fourth highest growth rate in the country. During this period, the state gained over 1.6 million new residents. About 558,000 were immigrants from abroad, while nearly 158,000 arrived from other states. Texas's birth rate, the second highest in the country, also contributed to the state's high population growth. Nearly 28 percent of the population was under 18 years old, which was the third highest proportion of this age group in the nation. Just 9.9 percent of Texas's population was 65 years old and over, ranking among the lowest 5 proportions of elderly residents in the country.

Table TX-2. Population by Race and Hispanic Origin, 1990, 2000, and 2004

(Number, percent.)

Race and Hispanic origin	1990	2000	2004
Total Population	16 986 510	20 851 820	22 490 022
Non-Hispanic (Percent)			
One race[1]			
White	60.6	52.7	49.8
Black	11.6	11.4	11.3
American Indian, Alaska Native[2]	0.4	0.3	0.3
Asian and Pacific Islander[2]	1.9	2.8	3.2
Other race[2]	10.6	. . .	. . .
Two or more races	. . .	0.8	0.9
Hispanic or Latino[3] (Percent)	25.5	32.0	34.6

[1]Individuals could report only one race in the 1990 census and could report one or more races on the 2000 census. Data on race in 2000 and 2004 are not comparable to 1990.
[2]Data for 1990 include people of Hispanic or Latino origin.
[3]May be of any race.
. . . = Not available.

Minority Population as a Percent of Total Population, 2004

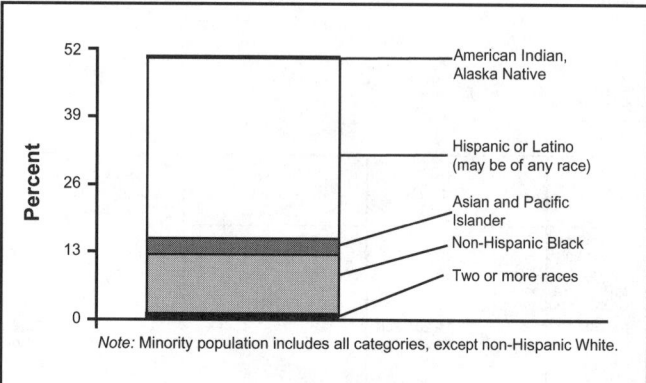

Note: Minority population includes all categories, except non-Hispanic White.

Age-Adjusted Death Rates, Average 2000–2002

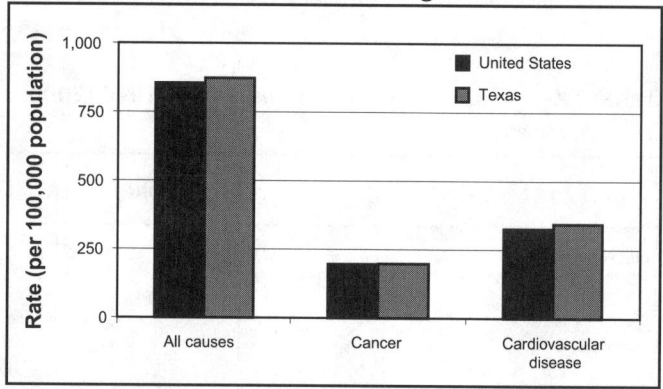

HEALTH

Texas had the lowest proportion of residents covered by health insurance in the country. Along with a high overall birth rate, the state had the highest birth rate for teenage mothers. The infant mortality rate was below the national average. However, the age-adjusted death rates were above average.

Table TX-3. Health Characteristics, 2000–2004

(Number, rate, percent.)

Item	State	U.S.
Births, 2003–2004		
Number of births	377 476	4 089 950
Birth rate (per 1,000 population)	17.1	14.1
Teenage birth rate (per 1,000 women age 15–19 years)	62.9	41.6
Mortality Rates, Average 2000–2002		
Infant mortality rate (per 1,000 live births)	5.9	6.9
Age-adjusted mortality rate (per 100,000 population)		
All races	877.4	853.3
Non-Hispanic White	884.4	843.1
Black	1 140.2	1 097.7
American Indian, Alaska Native	. . .	687.0
Asian and Pacific Islander	418.3	486.0
Hispanic or Latino[1]	744.5	642.7
Health Insurance, 2004		
Percent of all persons without health insurance	25.0	15.7
Percent of children without health insurance	21.4	11.2
Percent of low-income children without health insurance	14.4	7.1

[1]May be of any race.
. . . = Not available.

Table TX-4. Leading Causes of Death, Average 2000–2002

(Number, rate per 100,000 population.)

Cause	Number of deaths	Age-adjusted death rates	
		State	U.S.
ALL CAUSES	152 747	877.4	853.3
Leading Causes			
Major cardiovascular diseases	57 268	339.7	326.5
Cancer	33 651	192.0	196.0
Chronic lower respiratory diseases	7 582	45.2	43.7
Unintentional injuries	7 853	39.0	35.7
Diabetes (underlying cause)	5 435	31.4	25.2
Influenza and pneumonia	3 662	22.0	22.7
Alzheimer's disease	3 472	21.5	19.0
Motor vehicle accidents	3 853	18.3	15.0
Nephritis, nephrotic syndrome, and nephrosis ..	2 102	12.4	13.8
Septicemia	2 080	12.1	11.4
Suicides	2 196	10.7	10.7
Firearm-related	2 273	10.9	10.3
Cirrhosis	2 196	11.7	9.5
Drug-induced	1 503	7.2	7.9
Alcohol-induced	1 205	6.2	6.9
Homicides	1 384	6.3	6.0
Falls	797	4.6	5.2
HIV	1 071	5.1	5.0
Viral hepatitis	510	2.7	2.0
Anemias	292	1.7	1.6
Drownings	334	1.5	1.3
Fire deaths	234	1.2	1.2

Note: The rates are age-adjusted to the U.S. 2000 standard population.

Table TX-5. Households and Housing Characteristics, 1990, 2000, and 2004

(Number, percent, and dollars.)

Characteristic	1990	2000	2004	Average annual percent change, 2000–2004
Total Households	6 070 937	7 393 354	7 790 853	1.3
Family households	4 343 878	5 247 794	5 482 591	1.1
Married-couple family	3 435 540	3 989 741	4 044 993	0.3
Other family	908 338	1 258 053	1 437 598	3.4
Male householder, no wife present	206 512	320 464	355 535	2.6
Female householder, no husband present	701 826	937 589	1 082 063	3.6
Nonfamily households	1 727 059	2 145 560	2 308 262	1.8
Householder living alone	1 452 936	1 752 141	1 926 971	2.4
Householder not living alone	274 123	393 419	381 291	-0.8
Housing Characteristics				
Average size	2.73	2.74	2.81	X
Housing units	7 008 999	8 157 575	8 846 728	2.0
Occupied housing units	6 070 937	7 393 354	7 790 853	1.3
Owner-occupied	3 695 115	4 716 959	5 074 719	1.8
Renter-occupied	2 375 822	2 676 395	2 716 134	0.4
Median gross rent of renter-occupied housing units (dollars) ...	395	574	648	3.1
Median value of owner-occupied housing units (dollars)	58 900	82 500	99 858	4.9

X = Not applicable.

Median Housing Value and Median Rent, 2004

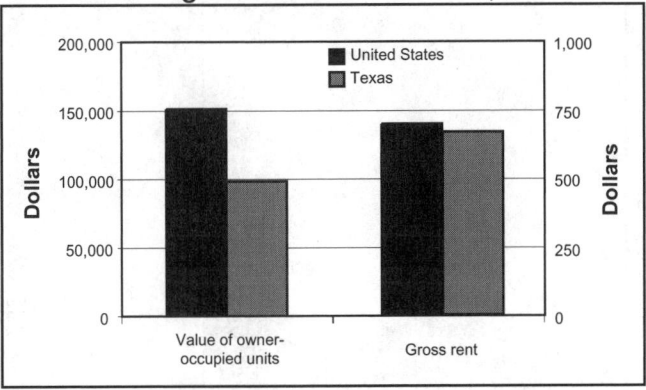

Median Household Income, 1984–2004 (2004 Dollars)

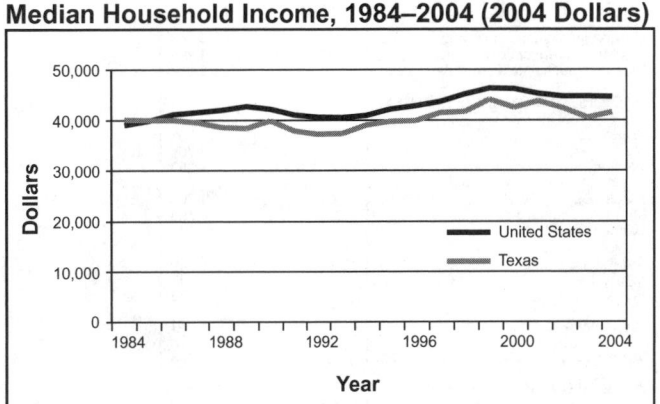

Table TX-6. Household Income and Poverty Status, 1980–2004

(2004 CPI-U-RS adjusted dollars, rate.)

Year	State		U.S.	
	Median household income (2004 dollars)	Poverty rate	Median household income (2004 dollars)	Poverty rate
2004	41 326	16.5	44 389	12.7
2003	40 326	17.0	44 482	12.5
2002	42 173	15.6	44 546	12.1
2001	43 602	14.9	45 062	11.7
2000	42 350	15.5	46 058	11.3
1999	43 853	15.2	46 129	11.9
1998	41 413	15.1	45 003	12.7
1997	41 165	16.7	43 430	13.3
1996	39 643	16.6	42 544	13.7
1995	39 436	17.4	41 943	13.8
1994	38 775	19.1	40 677	14.5
1993	36 981	17.4	40 217	15.1
1992	36 882	18.3	40 422	14.8
1991	37 509	17.5	40 746	14.2
1990	39 559	15.9	41 963	13.5
1989	38 081	17.1	42 524	12.8
1988	38 301	18.0	41 771	13.0
1987	39 311	17.6	41 322	13.4
1986	39 731	17.3	40 939	13.6
1985	39 755	15.9	39 545	14.0
1984	39 836	15.7	38 782	14.4
1983	. . .	16.0	. . .	15.2
1982	. . .	16.2	. . .	15.0
1981	. . .	15.4	. . .	14.0
1980	. . .	15.7	. . .	13.0

. . . = Not available.

Table TX-7. Employment Status by Demographic Group, 2004

(Numbers in thousands, rate.)

Characteristic	Civilian noninstitutional population	Civilian labor force		Employed	Unemployment rate
		Number	Participation rate		
SEX AND AGE					
Total	16 388	10 989	67.1	10 332	6.0
16 to 19 years	1 274	477	37.4	389	18.5
20 to 24 years	1 594	1 180	74.0	1 060	10.2
25 to 34 years	3 292	2 674	81.2	2 501	6.5
35 to 44 years	3 244	2 716	83.7	2 583	4.9
45 to 54 years	2 884	2 344	81.3	2 255	3.8
55 to 64 years	1 982	1 231	62.1	1 188	3.5
65 years and over	2 119	367	17.3	356	3.0
Men	7 971	6 087	76.4	5 718	6.1
16 to 19 years	621	244	39.3	193	21.0
20 to 24 years	788	647	82.1	577	10.8
25 to 34 years	1 678	1 568	93.5	1 467	6.4
35 to 44 years	1 598	1 491	93.3	1 419	4.8
45 to 54 years	1 426	1 252	87.8	1 208	3.5
55 to 64 years	945	655	69.3	630	3.7
65 years and over	916	231	25.2	223	3.6
Women	8 417	4 901	58.2	4 614	5.9
16 to 19 years	653	233	35.7	196	15.9
20 to 24 years	806	533	66.1	483	9.4
25 to 34 years	1 615	1 106	68.5	1 034	6.5
35 to 44 years	1 646	1 225	74.4	1 164	5.0
45 to 54 years	1 458	1 092	75.0	1 046	4.2
55 to 64 years	1 037	577	55.6	558	3.3
65 years and over	1 203	136	11.3	133	1.9
MARITAL STATUS					
Married men, spouse present	4 648	3 762	80.9	3 630	3.5
Married women, spouse present	4 468	2 585	57.9	2 479	4.1
Women who maintain families	1 077	775	71.9	708	8.6
RACE, HISPANIC ORIGIN, AND SEX					
White	13 752	9 211	67.0	8 728	5.2
Men	6 769	5 216	77.1	4 938	5.3
Women	6 983	3 995	57.2	3 790	5.1
Black	1 764	1 172	66.4	1 034	11.7
Men	793	542	68.3	470	13.3
Women	971	630	64.9	564	10.4
Asian	520	356	68.5	342	3.9
Men	245	193	78.5	183	5.1
Women	275	164	59.6	159	2.5
Hispanic or Latino[1]	5 591	3 715	66.4	3 474	6.5
Men	2 788	2 214	79.4	2 075	6.3
Women	2 803	1 501	53.5	1 399	6.8
RACE, HISPANIC ORIGIN, AND AGE					
White					
25 to 34 years	2 747	2 231	81.2	2 105	5.6
35 to 44 years	2 665	2 220	83.3	2 123	4.4
45 to 54 years	2 404	1 958	81.4	1 891	3.4
55 to 64 years	1 705	1 091	64.0	1 057	3.1

Note: Data in Table 7 are from the Current Population Survey (CPS) and do not match Bureau of Labor Statistics estimates in Table 8. See notes and definitions for more details.

[1]May be of any race.

Table TX-8. Employment Status, 1990–2004

(Numbers in thousands, rate.)

Year	Civilian labor force	Employed	Unemployed	Unemployment rate
2004	11 035 379	10 362 982	672 397	6.1
2003	10 927 433	10 195 950	731 483	6.7
2002	10 746 387	10 065 924	680 463	6.3
2001	10 530 577	10 003 723	526 854	5.0
2000	10 364 854	9 913 119	451 735	4.4
1999	10 250 025	9 766 299	483 726	4.7
1998	10 097 882	9 600 982	496 900	4.9
1997	9 926 594	9 395 279	531 315	5.4
1996	9 736 646	9 175 983	560 663	5.8
1995	9 572 436	8 985 635	586 801	6.1
1994	9 395 679	8 778 660	617 019	6.6
1993	9 203 082	8 543 207	659 875	7.2
1992	8 991 315	8 307 176	684 139	7.6
1991	8 752 200	8 139 722	612 478	7.0
1990	8 593 724	8 041 859	551 865	6.4

Unemployment Rate, 1980–2004

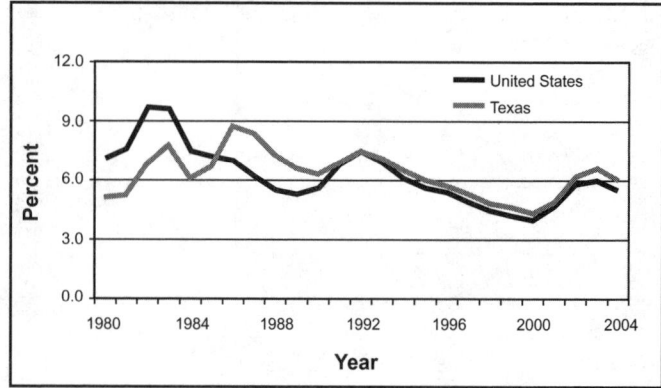

Note: Population age 16 years and over.

Table TX-9. Employment and Average Wages by Industry, 2001–2004

(Estimates are based on the 2002 North American Industry Classification System [NAICS].)

Industry	2001	2002	2003	2004	Annual average percent change, 2001–2004
	Number of jobs				
TOTAL EMPLOYMENT BY PLACE OF WORK	12 356 260	12 371 219	12 443 683	12 651 828	0.8
Farm Employment	295 167	290 229	281 756	279 282	-1.8
Nonfarm Employment	12 061 093	12 080 990	12 161 927	12 372 546	0.9
Private employment	10 323 448	10 304 201	10 363 193	10 570 318	0.8
Forestry, fishing, hunting, and other[1]	67 196	72 212	66 398	65 092	-1.1
Mining	234 238	218 786	238 042	250 299	2.2
Utilities	52 681	53 173	50 335	49 264	-2.2
Construction	851 666	835 644	844 846	843 862	-0.3
Manufacturing	1 072 125	994 726	945 955	935 512	-4.4
Durable goods manufacturing	673 952	617 479	587 021	586 989	-4.5
Nondurable goods manufacturing	398 173	377 247	358 934	348 523	-4.3
Wholesale trade	515 176	501 681	499 646	506 672	-0.6
Retail trade	1 383 611	1 388 621	1 372 303	1 389 935	0.2
Transportation and warehousing	454 816	444 028	438 933	453 436	-0.1
Information	299 177	275 347	266 346	256 294	-5.0
Finance and insurance	577 529	590 808	600 856	611 269	1.9
Real estate and rental and leasing	431 780	441 341	462 134	481 467	3.7
Professional and technical services	746 250	738 427	742 098	766 138	0.9
Management of companies and enterprises	46 616	56 469	51 926	57 541	7.3
Administrative and waste services	741 791	740 194	753 359	795 106	2.3
Educational services	153 132	163 258	168 889	176 206	4.8
Health care and social assistance	1 018 154	1 061 316	1 104 793	1 133 793	3.7
Arts, entertainment, and recreation	178 283	187 428	188 399	195 289	3.1
Accommodation and food services	799 266	810 229	829 700	854 078	2.2
Other services, except public administration	699 961	730 513	738 235	749 065	2.3
Government and government enterprises	1 737 645	1 776 789	1 798 734	1 802 228	1.2
	Dollars				
AVERAGE WAGES AND SALARIES BY PLACE OF WORK	35 376	35 615	36 415	37 963	2.4
Farm Earnings	14 433	12 008	16 257	19 610	10.8
Nonfarm Earnings	35 501	35 735	36 512	38 046	2.3
Private earnings	36 291	36 230	36 913	38 541	2.0
Forestry, fishing, hunting, and other[1]	18 525	19 015	19 441	20 575	3.6
Mining	77 808	79 457	81 327	87 473	4.0
Utilities	76 220	72 559	68 586	72 927	-1.5
Construction	36 130	36 585	37 278	38 347	2.0
Manufacturing	46 103	46 762	48 629	51 196	3.6
Durable goods manufacturing	48 028	48 241	49 898	52 447	3.0
Nondurable goods manufacturing	42 822	44 323	46 540	49 073	4.6
Wholesale trade	53 136	51 818	53 107	55 876	1.7
Retail trade	23 482	23 899	24 461	24 866	1.9
Transportation and warehousing	44 499	42 759	43 206	44 329	-0.1
Information	54 463	53 213	53 356	56 546	1.3
Finance and insurance	52 894	52 529	54 582	57 062	2.6
Real estate and rental and leasing	34 001	35 121	35 499	38 102	3.9
Professional and technical services	60 240	60 001	60 548	62 547	1.3
Management of companies and enterprises	61 371	60 293	64 144	74 985	6.9
Administrative and waste services	25 374	26 304	26 665	28 593	4.1
Educational services	26 313	26 800	27 675	28 977	3.3
Health care and social assistance	30 993	32 175	32 754	34 158	3.3
Arts, entertainment, and recreation	23 293	24 688	25 390	25 250	2.7
Accommodation and food services	14 492	14 601	14 749	15 196	1.6
Other services, except public administration	20 621	20 899	21 506	22 313	2.7
Government and government enterprises	31 758	33 469	34 718	35 798	4.1

Note: Average wages and salaries are a calculation by the editors of wage and salary disbursements divided by full- and part-time wage and salary employment. Data may not add to total or may appear as zero due to rounding.

[1] "Other" consists of the number of jobs held by U.S. residents employed by international organizations and foreign embassies and consulates in the United States.

LABOR MARKET

Texas's unemployment rate rose to an above average level following the 2001 recession. In 2004, the state's unemployment rate was well above those of its neighbors, Oklahoma, Arkansas, Louisiana, and New Mexico. While employment grew by an above average rate of 2.4 percent from 2001 to 2004, it could not keep up with the state's expanding population and growing number of job seekers. Employment gains were especially evident in mining, educational services, and health care. Texas's largest employers were government, retail trade, and health care. Average wages and salaries were only slightly below the national average. However, their rate of growth was one of the five lowest growth rates in the nation.

Employment by Industry, 2004

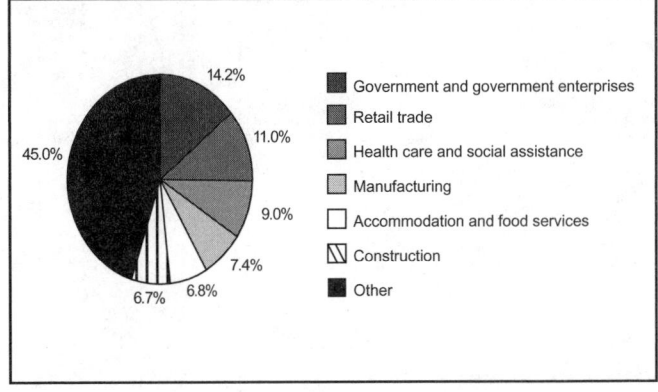

- Government and government enterprises
- Retail trade
- Health care and social assistance
- Manufacturing
- Accommodation and food services
- Construction
- Other

Table TX-10. Personal Income by Major Source, Selected Years 1980–2004

(Millions of dollars, except where noted.)

Item	1980	1990	2000	2001	2002	2003	2004	Average annual percent change, 2000–2004
Earnings by Place of Work	119 509	235 873	489 607	512 355	517 744	536 542	571 411	3.9
Wage and salary disbursements	89 996	169 302	341 572	354 780	354 576	360 822	380 354	2.7
Supplements to wages and salaries	16 928	35 497	64 714	69 415	76 943	83 112	90 203	8.7
Proprietors' income[1]	12 584	31 074	83 320	88 161	86 225	92 609	100 855	4.9
Farm proprietors' income	67	2 247	1 904	2 099	2 521	3 248	3 074	12.7
Nonfarm proprietors' income	12 517	28 827	81 416	86 061	83 703	89 361	97 780	4.7
(-) Contributions for government social insurance[2]	10 479	23 633	47 231	49 836	50 518	52 306	55 064	3.9
(+) Adjustment for residence[3]	-544	-504	-1 254	-1 442	-1 459	-1 465	-1 560	X
(=) Net Earnings by Place of Residence	108 486	211 737	441 122	461 077	465 767	482 772	514 787	3.9
(+) Dividends, interest, and rent[4]	20 452	53 929	87 612	87 505	83 046	85 546	88 472	0.2
(+) Personal current transfer receipts	12 721	31 480	64 405	71 060	77 970	82 690	87 117	7.8
Personal income	141 658	297 146	593 139	619 642	626 784	651 009	690 376	3.9
Farm income	141 099	294 181	590 413	616 616	623 601	646 931	686 362	3.8
Nonfarm income	559	2 966	2 726	3 026	3 183	4 078	4 014	10.2
Per Capita Personal Income (Dollars)[5]	9 880	17 421	28 313	29 044	28 853	29 453	30 697	2.0

Note: Data may not add to total or may appear as zero due to rounding.

[1]Proprietors' income includes the inventory valuation adjustment and the capital consumption adjustment.
[2]Contributions for government social insurance are included in earnings by type and industry, but they are excluded from personal income.
[3]The adjustment for residence is the net inflow of the earnings of interarea commuters.
[4]Rental income of persons includes the capital consumption adjustment.
[5]Per capita personal income is total personal income divided by total midyear population.
X = Not applicable.

Per Capita Personal Income, 1980–2004 (Current Dollars)

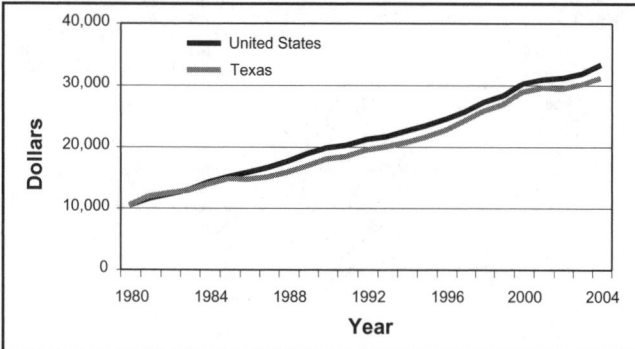

ECONOMIC ACTIVITY

Texas had the third largest real gross state product (GSP) in the country in 2004. Its economic activity grew at slightly above average rates during the 2001–2004 period. From 2003 to 2004, the GSP grew by 4.6 percent, which was the 17th highest growth rate in the nation. Contributing to this growth were manufacturing, retail trade, transportation and warehousing, and most service-providing industries. Management services increased by 46 percent from 2001 to 2004. Housing prices increased at the lowest rate of all the states. In 2004, the median value of owner-occupied housing in Texas was $99,858, ranking 41st in the nation.

Table TX-11. Real Gross State Product, 1997–2004

(Millions of chained 2000 dollars, percent.)

Industry	1997	1998	1999	2000	2001	2002	2003	2004	Average annual percent change, 2001–2004
GROSS STATE PRODUCT	627 501	664 153	696 383	722 832	734 864	755 448	769 410	804 598	3.1
As a percent of U.S. gross product	7.3	7.4	7.4	7.4	7.5	7.5	7.5	7.5	X
Private Industries	551 904	588 107	618 387	642 236	653 449	671 524	683 263	716 486	3.1
Agriculture, forestry, fishing, and hunting	5 174	4 950	6 269	6 470	5 960	7 467	7 188	6 468	2.8
Mining	54 412	46 997	45 242	42 211	40 430	41 000	38 243	39 755	-0.6
Utilities	17 046	17 175	18 174	21 681	21 545	21 676	22 203	23 380	2.8
Construction	30 511	32 599	33 290	34 232	33 893	32 621	32 060	31 776	-2.1
Manufacturing	81 120	91 082	90 624	94 117	94 191	97 677	101 342	106 723	4.3
As a percent of gross state product	12.9	13.7	13.0	13.0	12.8	12.9	13.2	13.3	X
Wholesale trade	41 118	47 732	52 877	53 409	56 251	55 859	54 340	56 363	0.1
Retail trade	43 592	46 050	49 419	51 786	56 091	59 091	61 272	63 771	4.4
Transportation and warehousing	22 953	24 697	26 141	28 653	27 280	27 692	29 302	31 079	4.4
Information	26 421	29 932	33 239	36 584	38 066	37 294	38 509	41 441	2.9
Finance and insurance	34 519	36 811	40 037	42 670	43 954	45 773	50 625	54 285	7.3
Real estate and rental and leasing	64 562	67 063	71 540	74 276	72 261	78 926	78 123	81 544	4.1
Services	138 550	145 839	152 617	156 145	163 833	166 706	170 960	181 495	3.5
As a percent of gross state product	22.1	22.0	21.9	21.6	22.3	22.1	22.2	22.6	X
Professional and technical services	37 078	41 259	44 111	47 320	49 189	48 750	49 442	51 588	1.6
Management of companies and enterprises	3 109	3 056	3 847	3 635	8 707	8 584	10 017	12 705	13.4
Administrative and waste services	21 689	22 775	23 864	22 126	21 646	22 433	22 936	24 939	4.8
Educational services	2 916	3 048	3 461	3 611	3 637	3 589	3 443	3 459	-1.7
Health care and social assistance	36 665	36 845	37 373	38 734	40 701	43 204	44 749	46 295	4.4
Arts, entertainment, and recreation	4 020	4 020	4 352	4 196	4 313	4 642	4 628	4 683	2.8
Accommodation and food services	16 162	17 232	18 123	18 908	18 738	18 813	19 109	20 054	2.3
Other services, except public administration	16 911	17 604	17 486	17 615	16 902	16 691	16 636	17 772	1.7
Government	75 735	76 052	77 995	80 596	81 418	83 917	86 102	88 131	2.7
As a percent of gross state product	12.1	11.5	11.2	11.2	11.1	11.1	11.2	11.0	X

X = Not applicable.

Table TX-12. Government Transfer Payments, Selected Years 1980–2004

(Millions of dollars, percent.)

Item	1980	1990	2000	2001	2002	2003	2004	Average annual percent change, 2000–2004
CURRENT TRANSFER PAYMENTS TO INDIVIDUALS	11 747	29 310	59 911	65 655	73 434	78 473	82 867	8.4
Retirement and Disability Insurance Benefits	6 030	13 557	23 582	25 092	26 616	27 909	29 457	5.7
Old-age, survivors, and disability insurance (OASDI) benefits	5 704	13 036	22 895	24 380	25 827	27 094	28 621	5.7
Railroad retirement and disability benefits	251	390	469	480	499	513	521	2.7
Workers' compensation	72	109	185	200	250	249	256	8.4
Other government retirement and disability insurance benefits	4	22	31	32	40	54	58	16.8
Medical Benefits	2 835	9 497	25 290	28 386	31 839	33 923	36 625	9.7
Medicare benefits	1 772	5 812	13 890	15 459	16 630	17 696	19 605	9.0
Public assistance medical care benefits	1 000	3 390	11 113	12 510	14 645	15 750	16 451	10.3
Military medical insurance benefits	63	295	287	417	564	477	569	18.6
Income Maintenance Benefits	1 229	3 580	7 016	7 211	8 401	9 733	10 649	11.0
Supplemental Security Income (SSI) benefits	366	756	1 575	1 683	1 799	1 903	1 990	6.0
Family assistance	134	428	475	487	498	584	476	0.1
Food stamps	535	1 514	1 217	1 316	1 568	1 986	2 416	18.7
Other income maintenance benefits	194	882	3 749	3 726	4 535	5 260	5 767	11.4
Unemployment Insurance Compensation	348	825	1 088	1 648	2 935	3 005	1 919	15.2
Veterans' Benefits	1 097	1 318	2 047	2 209	2 472	2 689	2 949	9.5
Federal Education and Training Assistance	205	503	797	978	1 087	1 083	1 149	9.6
Other Payments to Individuals	2	31	91	130	84	130	120	7.0

Note: See notes and definitions for more details. Data may not add to total or may appear as zero due to rounding.

EXPORTS

Texas was the largest exporting state in 2004, with exports valued at $117.2 billion in 2004. The leading exports were computers and electronic products, chemical manufactures, and machinery manufactures, which together accounted for almost 60 percent of the state's exports. Chemical manufactures exports grew 54.5 percent from 2001 to 2004. Petroleum and coal products, Texas's fifth leading export, grew 66.7 percent during this period. Mexico was the state's largest export market, accounting for 39 percent of exports. South Korea and China have been the fastest growing of Texas's leading markets. Exports to both countries increased by over 180 percent from 2001 to 2004.

Leading Exports, 2004

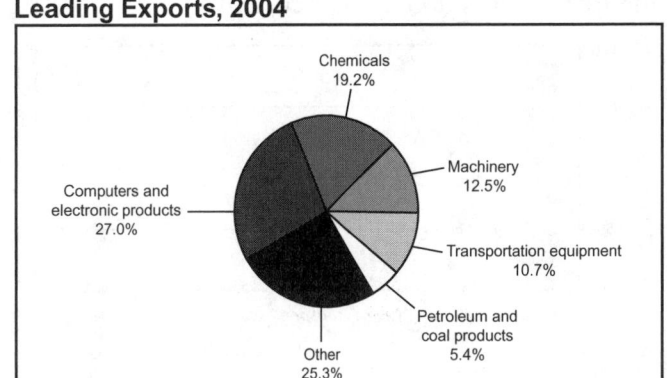

Table TX-13. Exports of Goods by Leading Products and Destinations, 2001–2004

(Millions of dollars, percent, rank based on 2004 dollar values.)

Product and market	2001	2002	2003	2004	Percent share of total, 2004	Average annual percent change, 2001–2004
Total Goods						
Total	94 995	95 396	98 846	117 245	100.0	7.3
Manufactures	90 574	90 302	93 677	111 489	95.1	7.2
Agriculture and livestock	2 884	3 449	3 565	4 193	3.6	13.3
Other commodities	1 537	1 645	1 605	1 563	1.3	0.6
Five Leading Exports (NAICS Code)						
Computers and electronic products (334)	25 688	26 707	28 378	31 656	27.0	7.2
Chemical manufactures (325)	14 600	15 002	17 125	22 564	19.2	15.6
Machinery manufactures (333)	12 821	12 602	11 408	14 610	12.5	4.4
Transportation equipment (336)	11 258	10 508	9 903	12 577	10.7	3.8
Petroleum and coal products (324)	3 705	3 595	4 701	6 177	5.3	18.6
Five Leading Markets	83 933	84 473	86 696	102 260	87.2	6.8
Mexico	41 648	41 647	41 561	45 707	39.0	3.1
Canada	10 555	9 916	10 809	12 399	10.6	5.5
South Korea	1 766	2 032	2 777	5 022	4.3	41.7
China	1 578	2 064	3 060	4 456	3.8	41.3
Taiwan	2 642	3 665	2 766	4 002	3.4	14.9

Table TX-14. Agriculture, 1997 and 2002

(Number, acres, and dollars.)

Item	1997	2002
Number of farms	228 173	228 926
Land in farms (acres)	133 956 359	129 877 666
Farm Size		
Average size of farm (acres)	587	567
Farms by size (percent distribution)		
Fewer than 50 acres	30.9	32.6
50 to 499 acres	50.4	49.4
500 acres or more	18.6	18.0
Market Value of Land and Equipment (Dollars)		
Land and buildings average value per farm	361 821	439 066
Average value per acre	616	768
Machinery and equipment average value per farm	37 795	40 553
Value of Sales (Thousands of Dollars)		
Agricultural products sold	14 016 017	14 134 744
Crops	4 475 682	3 731 751
Livestock, poultry, and their products	9 540 334	10 402 993
Average per farm (dollars)	61 427	61 744
Value of sales (percent distribution)		
Less than $10,000	70.2	71.5
$10,000 to $99,999	22.2	22.1
$100,000 or more	7.6	6.4
Government Payments		
Payments (thousands of dollars)	426 566	528 979
Percent of farms receiving government payments	23.3	18.4
Farm operators whose principal occupation is farming (percent)	40.4	53.6

AGRICULTURE

Cash receipts from farming totaled $14.1 billion in 2002, according to the Department of Agriculture's Census of Agriculture. Texas was the second largest agricultural state after California. Its farm production grew slowly after the previous agriculture census in 1997, experiencing an increase of only 2.7 percent. Despite the size of the farming sector, most farms were relatively small-scale enterprises—some 71 percent had sales of less than $10,000, and less than 54 percent of all farm operators considered farming to be their principal occupation. Almost one-third of farms spanned fewer than 50 acres.

ENERGY

Energy prices in Texas were among the lowest in the nation in 2001. Energy expenditures per person amounted to $3,404, which was the fifth highest amount in the country. The state's per capita energy consumption was the fifth highest in the nation, due to heavy industrial use. The industrial sector accounted for over 53 percent of energy consumption in Texas. Petroleum and natural gas were the state's chief energy sources.

Energy Consumption by Source, 2001

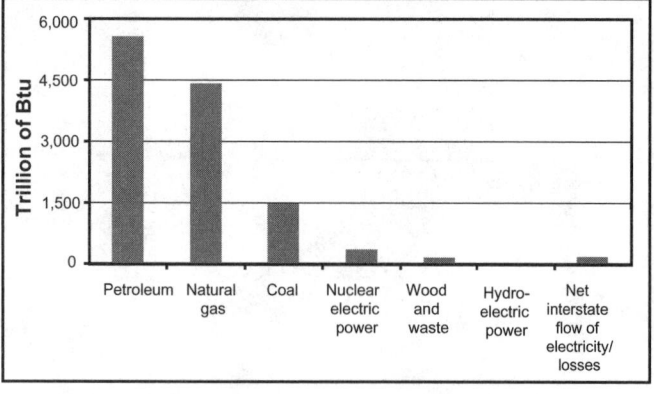

Energy Consumption by Sector, 2001

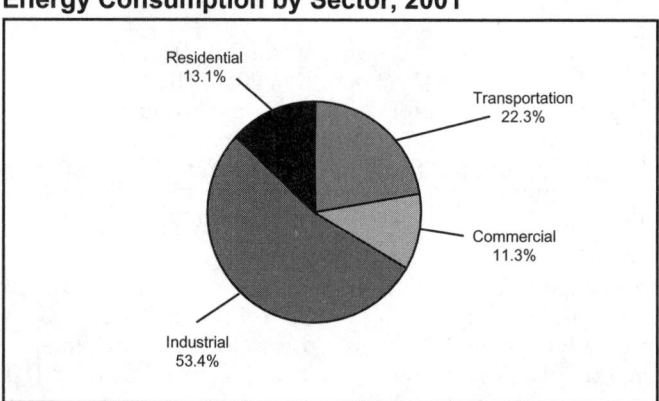

Table TX-15. Energy Consumption, Expenditures, and Prices, Selected Years 1960–2001

(Dollars, Btu [British Thermal Unit], percent distribution.)

Item	1960	1965	1970	1975	1980	1985	1990	1995	2000	2001
Total Consumption (Billion Btu)	4 432 134	5 158 058	6 780 950	7 367 848	9 059 061	8 823 421	9 932 711	10 650 079	12 073 470	12 028 830
Consumption per capita (million Btu)	462.6	497.0	605.5	586.2	636.7	542.2	584.7	570.1	579.0	563.7
Consumption by Sector (Percent Distribution)										
Residential	8.3	9.1	10.1	10.4	10.6	12.2	12.0	12.0	12.9	13.1
Commercial	4.5	5.3	6.7	7.6	8.4	10.1	10.2	10.7	11.2	11.3
Industrial	69.3	67.7	65.3	60.8	61.1	54.7	56.2	57.0	54.7	53.4
Transportation	18.0	17.8	17.9	21.2	19.9	22.9	21.7	20.4	21.3	22.3
Consumption by Source (Billion Btu)										
Coal	24 974	29 182	30 767	196 172	734 145	1 148 998	1 333 651	1 364 829	1 548 171	1 493 398
Natural gas	2 815 483	3 181 456	4 203 877	4 046 930	4 226 105	3 514 373	3 877 833	4 037 540	4 550 105	4 434 592
Petroleum	1 551 954	1 908 986	2 469 058	3 074 390	4 092 186	3 998 789	4 407 508	4 766 664	5 453 025	5 521 036
Nuclear electric power	0	0	0	0	0	0	167 823	379 842	391 670	398 726
Hydroelectric power[1]	11 859	7 771	10 550	20 052	10 171	14 636	18 657	17 565	8 456	12 212
Wood and waste	38 296	41 196	52 207	55 820	83 522	76 230	87 280	101 081	88 378	74 469
Other	-598	-280	-416	-1 169	-1 982	-14	400	-2 296	6 104	13 304
Net interstate flow of electricity/losses[2]	-9 832	-10 253	14 907	-24 345	-85 085	70 411	39 559	-15 145	27 561	81 093
Total Expenditures (Thousands of Dollars)	. . .	. . .	5 328 100	12 506 200	35 449 000	42 828 700	43 234 000	46 866 500	73 258 900	72 652 500
Expenditures per capita (dollars)	. . .	. . .	476	995	2 491	2 632	2 545	2 509	3 513	3 404
Prices by Sector (Dollars Per Million Btu)										
Total	. . .	. . .	1.29	2.82	6.05	7.07	6.47	6.44	8.82	8.80
Residential	. . .	. . .	2.47	4.06	8.39	13.70	14.01	15.49	17.69	19.64
Commercial	. . .	. . .	1.91	3.92	7.76	12.42	11.73	12.24	14.26	16.50
Industrial	. . .	. . .	0.64	1.97	4.81	5.10	4.11	4.05	6.45	6.09
Transportation	. . .	. . .	2.07	3.54	7.42	7.45	7.57	7.37	9.63	8.96

[1]A negative number in this row results from pumped storage for which, overall, more electricity is expended than created to provide electricity during peak demand periods.
[2]Net interstate flow of electricity is the difference between the amount of energy in the electricity sold within a state (including associated losses) and the energy input at the electric utilities within the state. A positive number indicates that more electricity (including associated losses) came into the state than went out of the state during the year; conversely, a negative number indicates that more electricity (including associated losses) went out of the state than came into the state.
. . . = Not available.

Table TX-16. State Taxes, Fiscal 2004

(Dollars, percent distribution.)

Item	Thousands of dollars	Percent distribution	Dollars per capita	
			State	U.S.
TOTAL TAXES	30 751 860	100.0	1 367.4	2 024.8
Property Taxes	X	X	X	38.9
Sales and Gross Receipts	24 620 778	80.1	1 094.7	1 003.4
General sales and gross receipts	15 460 221	50.3	687.4	677.0
Selective sales taxes	9 160 557	29.8	407.3	326.4
Alcoholic beverages	601 841	2.0	26.8	15.7
Insurance premiums	1 130 499	3.7	50.3	47.0
Motor fuels	2 918 842	9.5	129.8	114.6
Public utilities	793 107	2.6	35.3	39.2
Tobacco products	534 577	1.7	23.8	42.0
Other selective sales	3 146 812	10.2	139.9	49.8
Licenses	4 083 148	13.3	181.6	134.9
Corporation	1 896 287	6.2	84.3	21.6
Motor vehicle	1 232 494	4.0	54.8	59.4
Occupation and business, not elsewhere classified	681 645	2.2	30.3	37.1
Other Taxes	2 047 934	6.7	91.1	847.6
Severance	1 896 803	6.2	84.3	21.5

X = Not applicable.

GOVERNMENT FINANCE

State revenues and expenditures per person were lower than average. Texas ranked 48th for both measures in 2003. The state had no individual income, corporate income, or property taxes. Spending per capita was lower than average for all major categories, except for correctional facilities. The chief sources of tax revenue in fiscal year 2004 were general sales taxes, public utility taxes, and, to a lesser extent, severance (a tax on the removal of natural resources that is prevalent in western states). Per capita taxes were the lowest in the nation. Texas's per capita debt of $661 was the second lowest in the country.

Per Capita State Taxes, Fiscal 2004

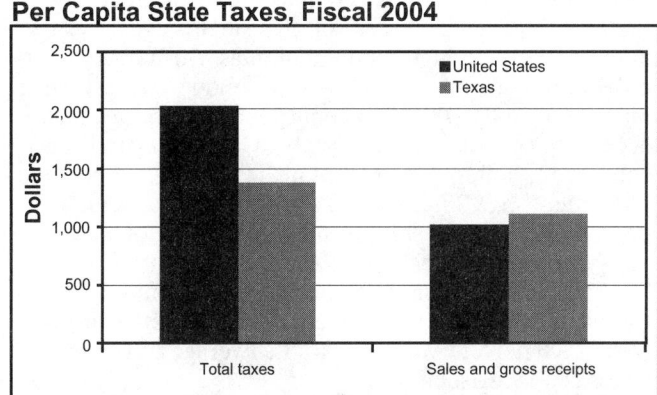

Table TX-17. State Government Finances, 2003

(Dollars, percent distribution.)

Item	Millions of dollars	Percent distribution	Dollars per capita	
			State	U.S.
GENERAL REVENUE	66 457 732	100.0	3 006.7	3 832.6
Intergovernmental revenue	24 349 595	36.6	1 101.6	1 246.0
Taxes	29 098 584	43.8	1 316.5	1 891.6
General sales	14 347 144	21.6	649.1	636.0
Selective sales	9 013 791	13.6	407.8	307.4
License taxes	3 980 083	6.0	180.1	123.6
Individual income tax	0	0.0	0.0	626.8
Corporate income tax	0	0.0	0.0	97.8
Other taxes	1 757 566	2.6	79.5	99.9
Current charges	6 321 818	9.5	286.0	366.5
Miscellaneous general revenue	6 687 735	10.1	302.6	328.6
GENERAL EXPENDITURE	66 803 548	100.0	3 022.4	4 010.5
Intergovernmental expenditure	17 332 957	25.9	784.2	1 316.9
Direct expenditure	49 470 591	74.1	2 238.2	2 693.6
Expenditure by Function				
Education	26 995 012	40.4	1 221.3	1 416.4
Public welfare	18 498 427	27.7	836.9	1 083.3
Hospitals	2 833 200	4.2	128.2	132.3
Health	1 401 878	2.1	63.4	173.0
Highways	5 265 805	7.9	238.2	295.4
Police protection	430 531	0.6	19.5	38.4
Correction	3 201 068	4.8	144.8	135.0
Natural resources	789 999	1.2	35.7	64.0
Parks and recreation	114 090	0.2	5.2	20.1
Government administration	1 570 287	2.4	71.0	151.3
Interest on general debt	951 418	1.4	43.0	107.8
Other and unallocable	4 751 833	7.1	215.0	393.4
DEBT AT END OF FISCAL YEAR	14 616 237	X	661.3	2 404.7
CASH AND SECURITY HOLDINGS	181 581 079	X	8 215.2	8 938.4

X = Not applicable.

Table TX-18. Education Indicators, 2000–2004

(Percent, number.)

Item	State	U.S.
Total Population 25 Years and Over (Thousands), 2004	13 356	186 877
Educational Attainment, 2004		
Percent high school graduate or more	78.3	85.2
Percent college graduate or more	24.5	27.7
Elementary and Secondary Schools, 2002–2003		
Total students	4 259 823	48 202 324
Percent of students eligible for free or reduced-price lunch ..	46.7	40.6
Percent of students who were English language learners	15.3	7.8
Total schools	7 757	92 330
Student/teacher ratio	15.0	15.9
Per student expenditures	7 136	8 041
Dropouts, Grades 9–12, 2000–2001 (Percent)	3.8	...
Higher Education, 2002–2003		
Total enrollment	1 184 082	17 035 027
Bachelor's degrees awarded	82 649	1 348 503
Percent women	57.9	57.5

... = Not available.

Educational Attainment, 2004

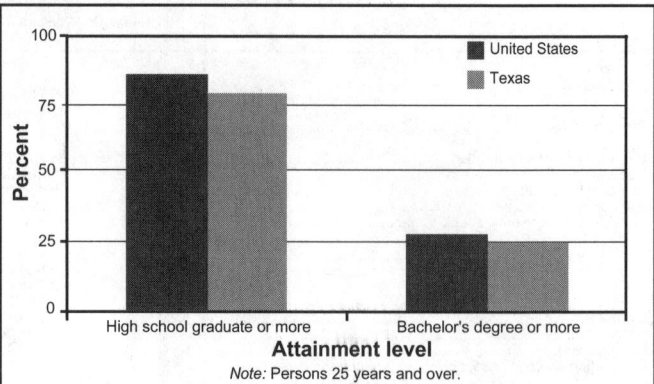

Note: Persons 25 years and over.

EDUCATION

Texas ranked 51st in the nation for high school attainment, with just 78.3 percent of its residents age 25 years and over holding high school diplomas. This largely reflected the state's high number of immigrant residents, many of whom came from countries in which they lacked access to secondary education. Texas ranked 35th in the country for college attainment in 2004, with 24.5 percent of residents age 25 years and over holding bachelor's degrees or more. Despite its high proportion of student-age population, Texas's per student expenditures of $7,136 ranked 35th in the country. The student/teacher ratio was below the national average. The state's dropout rate of 3.8 percent was close to the average of the 46 states reporting such data.

VOTER PARTICIPATION

Texas's voter turnout was among the lowest in the country for both the 2000 and 2004 elections, despite the fact that the Republican presidential candidate in both elections was a Texan. About 30 percent of eligible Asians and Hispanics cast ballots in 2004. About 63 percent of non-Hispanic Whites and 55 percent of Blacks participated in the 2004 election. According to the official tally by the Clerk of the U.S. House of Representatives, 59.3 percent of voters cast their ballots for the Republican presidential candidate in 2000; this proportion rose to 61.1 percent in 2004. The comparable percentages for the Democratic candidate were 47.3 and 42.5 percent, respectively.

Table TX-19. Reported Voting and Registration, November 2000 and November 2004

(Numbers in thousands, percent.)

Characteristic	Total population 18 years and over	Total citizen		Total registered		Total voted	
		Number	Percent	Number	Percent	Number	Percent
NOVEMBER 2000							
Total	14 533	12 937	89.0	8 929	61.4	7 005	48.2
Male	7 079	6 222	87.9	4 189	59.2	3 305	46.7
Female	7 454	6 715	90.1	4 740	63.6	3 700	49.6
NOVEMBER 2004							
Total	15 813	13 925	88.1	9 681	61.2	7 950	50.3
Male	7 667	6 689	87.2	4 548	59.3	3 684	48.1
Female	8 146	7 237	88.8	5 133	63.0	4 266	52.4
Race and Hispanic Origin							
White alone	13 246	11 639	87.9	8 148	61.5	6 706	50.6
Non-Hispanic White alone	8 246	8 107	98.3	6 065	73.6	5 232	63.4
Black alone	1 669	1 613	96.7	1 141	68.4	931	55.8
Asian alone	508	356	70.0	190	37.5	152	29.9
Hispanic or Latino[1]	5 232	3 688	70.5	2 170	41.5	1 533	29.3
White alone or in combination	13 490	11 826	87.7	8 282	61.4	6 808	50.5
Non-Hispanic White alone or in combination	8 370	8 225	98.3	6 144	73.4	5 292	63.2
Black alone or in combination	1 721	1 662	96.6	1 173	68.2	955	55.5
Asian alone or in combination	535	376	70.3	199	37.2	160	30.0
Age							
18 to 24 years	2 119	1 841	86.9	990	46.7	709	33.5
25 to 44 years	6 638	5 482	82.6	3 680	55.4	2 897	43.6
45 to 64 years	4 944	4 587	92.8	3 430	69.4	3 002	60.7
65 to 74 years	1 126	1 074	95.4	853	75.7	739	65.6
75 years and over	986	941	95.5	728	73.8	602	61.1

[1]May be of any race.

At a Glance:

- In 2004, Utah's population was close to 2.4 million; this represented a 7 percent increase from 2001.

- Nearly 84 percent of the state's residents were non-Hispanic White. Hispanics (of any race) made up 10.6 percent of the population, which was the 12th highest proportion of this ethnic group in the country.

- In 2004, 31 percent of Utah's population was under 18 years old, which was the highest proportion of this age group in the nation. The state had the lowest median age in the country.

- Utah had the highest birth rate in the nation, which accounted for most of its population growth in recent years.

- The state's median household income was almost $51,000, ranking as the 11th highest in the nation. Utah's poverty rate of 9.9 percent was well below the national average of 12.7 percent.

- Utah's real gross state product (GSP) ranked 33rd in the nation in 2004. From 2003 to 2004, the state's GSP grew 5.2 percent, which was the 12th highest growth rate in the country. The state's unemployment rate of 5.2 percent was slightly below the national average.

Table UT-1. Population by Sex and Age, 1990, 2000, and 2004

(Number, percent.)

Sex and age	1990	2000	2004	Percent distribution, 2004	Average annual percent change, 2000–2004
Total Population	1 722 850	2 233 169	2 389 039	X	1.7
Percent of total U.S. population	0.7	0.8	0.8	X	X
Sex					
Male	855 759	1 119 031	1 199 315	50.2	1.7
Female	867 091	1 114 138	1 189 724	49.8	1.7
Age					
Under 5 years	169 633	209 378	232 793	9.7	2.2
5 to 17 years	457 811	509 320	507 321	21.2	0.8
18 years and over	245 892	1 514 471	1 648 925	69.0	3.0
18 to 24 years	1 095 406	317 431	312 896	13.1	3.2
25 to 44 years	199 986	626 600	690 645	28.9	2.4
45 to 64 years	499 570	380 218	437 673	18.3	4.2
65 years and over	149 958	190 222	207 711	8.7	2.4
85 years and over	13 611	21 751	25 700	1.1	4.7
Median age (years)	26.2	27.1	27.9	X	X

X = Not applicable.

Average Annual Rate of Population Growth, 1980–2004

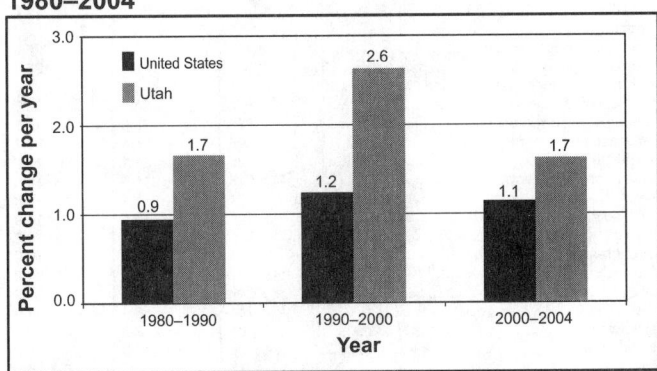

POPULATION

Utah has experienced relatively fast population growth in recent years. This was due to its younger population, which had a high birth rate, and a relatively low number of deaths. Between 2000 and 2004, the population increased by 7 percent, the 7th fastest growth rate in the nation, despite an out-migration of nearly 39,000 people to other states. Due to its high birth rate and larger family size, Utah had the highest proportion of population under 18 years old in the country. Just 8.7 percent of its population was over 65 years old, which was the second lowest proportion of this age group in the country, behind only Alaska. Utah had the highest average household size in the nation, exceeding 3 persons per household.

Table UT-2. Population by Race and Hispanic Origin, 1990, 2000, and 2004

(Number, percent.)

Race and Hispanic origin	1990	2000	2004
Total Population	1 722 850	2 233 169	2 389 039
Non-Hispanic (Percent)			
One race[1]			
White	91.2	85.6	83.8
Black	0.6	0.7	0.8
American Indian, Alaska Native[2]	1.4	1.2	1.2
Asian and Pacific Islander[2]	1.9	2.4	2.5
Other race[2]	2.2	. . .	. . .
Two or more races	. . .	1.1	1.2
Hispanic or Latino[3] (Percent)	4.9	9.0	10.6

[1]Individuals could report only one race in the 1990 census and could report one or more races on the 2000 census. Data on race in 2000 and 2004 are not comparable to 1990.
[2]Data for 1990 include people of Hispanic or Latino origin.
[3]May be of any race.
. . . = Not available.

Minority Population as a Percent of Total Population, 2004

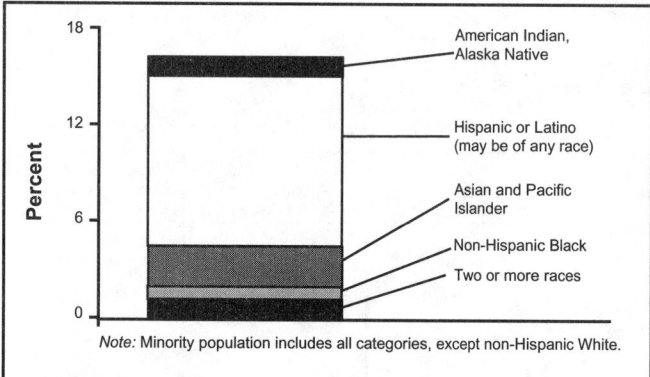

Note: Minority population includes all categories, except non-Hispanic White.

Age-Adjusted Death Rates, Average 2000–2002

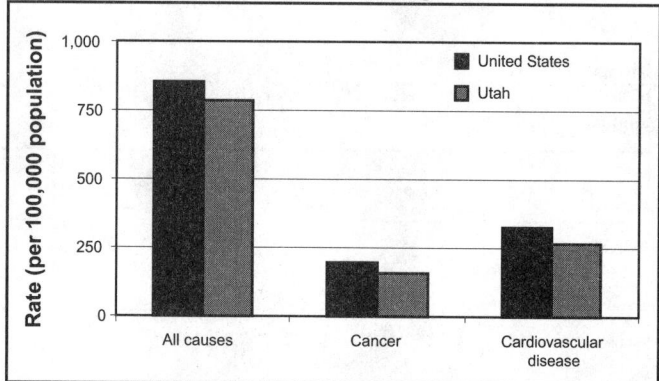

HEALTH

In 2004, the proportion of Utah residents without health insurance was substantially below the national average; however, this proportion has risen slightly since 1999. The infant mortality rate was among the five lowest in the country. Age-adjusted death rates also ranked among the lowest in the nation.

Table UT-3. Health Characteristics, 2000–2004

(Number, rate, percent.)

Item	State	U.S.
Births, 2003–2004		
Number of births	49 860	4 089 950
Birth rate (per 1,000 population)	21.2	14.1
Teenage birth rate (per 1,000 women age 15–19 years)	34.6	41.6
Mortality Rates, Average 2000–2002		
Infant mortality rate (per 1,000 live births)	5.3	6.9
Age-adjusted mortality rate (per 100,000 population)		
All races	780.2	853.3
Non-Hispanic White	781.8	843.1
Black	1 020.8	1 097.7
American Indian, Alaska Native	804.8	687.0
Asian and Pacific Islander	673.4	486.0
Hispanic or Latino[1]	642.5	642.7
Health Insurance, 2004		
Percent of all persons without health insurance	14.1	15.7
Percent of children without health insurance	10.4	11.2
Percent of low-income children without health insurance	6.1	7.1

[1]May be of any race.

Table UT-4. Leading Causes of Death, Average 2000–2002

(Number, rate per 100,000 population.)

Cause	Number of deaths	Age-adjusted death rates	
		State	U.S.
ALL CAUSES	12 714	780.2	853.3
Leading Causes			
Major cardiovascular diseases	4 131	265.4	326.5
Cancer	2 349	145.6	196.0
Chronic lower respiratory diseases	551	35.3	43.7
Unintentional injuries	674	34.0	35.7
Diabetes (underlying cause)	518	32.6	25.2
Influenza and pneumonia	408	26.4	22.7
Alzheimer's disease	320	21.1	19.0
Motor vehicle accidents	316	14.5	15.0
Nephritis, nephrotic syndrome, and nephrosis ..	177	11.4	13.8
Septicemia	104	6.5	11.4
Suicides	320	15.4	10.7
Firearm-related	210	10.1	10.3
Cirrhosis	132	7.8	9.5
Drug-induced	247	12.2	7.9
Alcohol-induced	114	6.4	6.9
Homicides	61	2.6	6.0
Falls	96	5.8	5.2
HIV	18	0.9	5.0
Viral hepatitis	30	1.7	2.0
Anemias	26	1.7	1.6
Drownings	29	1.2	1.3
Fire deaths	8	0.4	1.2

Note: The rates are age-adjusted to the U.S. 2000 standard population.

Table UT-5. Households and Housing Characteristics, 1990, 2000, and 2004

(Number, percent, and dollars.)

Characteristic	1990	2000	2004	Average annual percent change, 2000–2004
Total Households	537 273	701 281	780 029	2.7
Family households	410 862	535 294	595 432	2.7
Married-couple family	348 029	442 931	491 520	2.6
Other family	62 833	92 363	103 912	3.0
Male householder, no wife present	13 756	26 422	32 058	5.0
Female householder, no husband present	49 077	65 941	71 854	2.2
Nonfamily households	126 411	165 987	184 597	2.7
Householder living alone	101 640	124 756	143 654	3.6
Householder not living alone	24 771	41 231	40 943	-0.2
Housing Characteristics				
Average size	3.15	3.13	3.01	X
Housing units	598 388	768 594	848 737	2.5
Occupied housing units	537 273	701 281	780 029	2.7
Owner-occupied	365 979	501 547	543 666	2.0
Renter-occupied	171 294	199 734	236 363	4.3
Median gross rent of renter-occupied housing units (dollars)	369	597	662	2.6
Median value of owner-occupied housing units (dollars)	68 700	146 100	157 275	1.9

X = Not applicable.

Median Housing Value and Median Rent, 2004

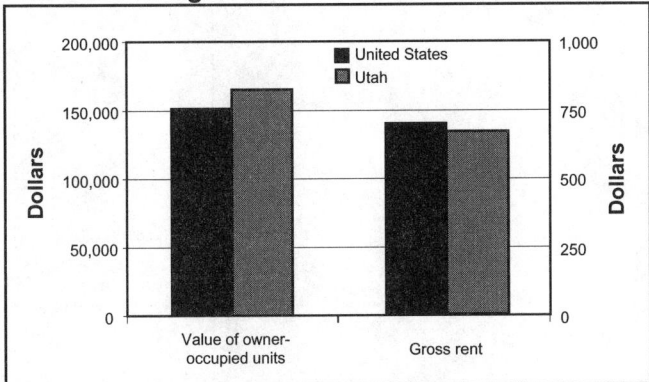

Median Household Income, 1984–2004 (2004 Dollars)

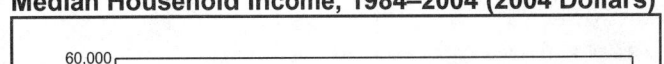
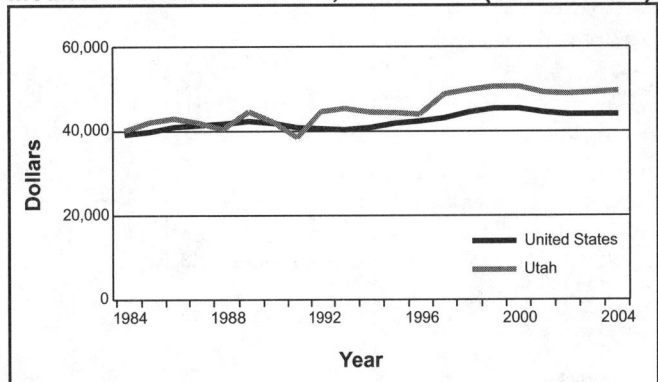

Table UT-6. Household Income and Poverty Status, 1980–2004

(2004 CPI-U-RS adjusted dollars, rate.)

Year	State Median household income (2004 dollars)	State Poverty rate	U.S. Median household income (2004 dollars)	U.S. Poverty rate
2004	50 970	9.9	44 389	12.7
2003	50 599	9.1	44 482	12.5
2002	50 273	9.9	44 546	12.1
2001	50 519	10.5	45 062	11.7
2000	52 157	7.6	46 058	11.3
1999	52 198	5.7	46 129	11.9
1998	51 269	9.0	45 003	12.7
1997	50 202	8.9	43 430	13.3
1996	44 397	7.7	42 544	13.7
1995	44 902	8.4	41 943	13.8
1994	45 030	8.0	40 677	14.5
1993	46 068	10.7	40 217	15.1
1992	45 192	9.4	40 422	14.8
1991	37 892	12.9	40 746	14.2
1990	42 242	8.2	41 963	13.5
1989	45 188	8.2	42 524	12.8
1988	40 372	9.8	41 771	13.0
1987	42 186	10.2	41 322	13.4
1986	43 215	12.6	40 939	13.6
1985	42 258	10.9	39 545	14.0
1984	39 893	11.1	38 782	14.4
1983	. . .	13.5	. . .	15.2
1982	. . .	14.5	. . .	15.0
1981	. . .	12.2	. . .	14.0
1980	. . .	10.0	. . .	13.0

. . . = Not available.

Table UT-7. Employment Status by Demographic Group, 2004

(Numbers in thousands, rate.)

Characteristic	Civilian noninstitutional population	Civilian labor force		Employed	Unemployment rate
		Number	Participation rate		
SEX AND AGE					
Total	1 697	1 206	71.0	1 142	5.3
16 to 19 years	167	99	59.4	82	17.0
20 to 24 years	226	186	82.1	173	7.0
25 to 34 years	378	308	81.5	293	5.0
35 to 44 years	289	249	86.3	241	3.4
45 to 54 years	265	225	84.7	218	3.1
55 to 64 years	173	110	63.8	107	2.4
65 years and over	199	28	14.3	28	2.4
Men	839	668	79.5	633	5.2
16 to 19 years	83	50	60.2	42	16.5
20 to 24 years	118	99	84.4	93	6.6
25 to 34 years	189	177	93.9	169	4.6
35 to 44 years	145	138	95.1	132	3.9
45 to 54 years	131	123	93.9	118	4.0
55 to 64 years	84	65	77.3	64	2.2
Women	858	538	62.7	509	5.4
16 to 19 years	84	49	58.6	41	17.6
20 to 24 years	109	87	79.6	80	7.4
25 to 34 years	190	131	69.2	124	5.5
35 to 44 years	144	111	77.4	108	2.7
45 to 54 years	135	102	75.7	100	2.0
55 to 64 years	89	45	50.9	44	2.7
MARITAL STATUS					
Married men, spouse present	519	429	82.7	417	2.8
Married women, spouse present	507	306	60.3	297	2.8
Women who maintain families	76	56	73.6	52	7.6
RACE, HISPANIC ORIGIN, AND SEX					
White	1 615	1 147	71.0	1 088	5.1
Men	798	635	79.6	604	5.0
Women	817	511	62.6	484	5.3
Hispanic or Latino[1]	149	111	74.8	100	10.0
Men	82	68	83.7	63	7.9
Women	67	43	63.9	37	13.2
RACE, HISPANIC ORIGIN, AND AGE					
White					
16 to 19 years	154	94	60.7	78	16.7
20 to 24 years	213	174	81.9	163	6.7
25 to 34 years	359	292	81.3	277	4.9
35 to 44 years	272	234	86.3	227	3.1
45 to 54 years	256	218	85.2	211	2.9
55 to 64 years	167	106	63.7	104	2.5
65 years and over	195	28	14.6	28	2.5
Hispanic or Latino[1]					
25 to 34 years	43	34	81.0	31	10.6
35 to 44 years	34	30	89.6	29	5.0

Note: Data in Table 7 are from the Current Population Survey (CPS) and do not match Bureau of Labor Statistics estimates in Table 8. See notes and definitions for more details.

[1]May be of any race.

Table UT-8. Employment Status, 1990–2004

(Numbers in thousands, rate.)

Year	Civilian labor force	Employed	Unemployed	Unemployment rate
2004	1 203 459	1 140 498	62 961	5.2
2003	1 188 279	1 121 088	67 191	5.7
2002	1 174 582	1 107 379	67 203	5.7
2001	1 153 387	1 103 028	50 359	4.4
2000	1 133 870	1 095 657	38 213	3.4
1999	1 120 591	1 080 441	40 150	3.6
1998	1 101 973	1 061 282	40 691	3.7
1997	1 068 279	1 034 429	33 850	3.2
1996	1 040 493	1 004 347	36 146	3.5
1995	1 014 959	979 367	35 592	3.5
1994	983 265	945 389	37 876	3.9
1993	931 787	892 956	38 831	4.2
1992	889 272	845 398	43 874	4.9
1991	851 100	810 806	40 294	4.7
1990	820 436	784 050	36 386	4.4

Note: Population age 16 years and over.

Unemployment Rate, 1980–2004

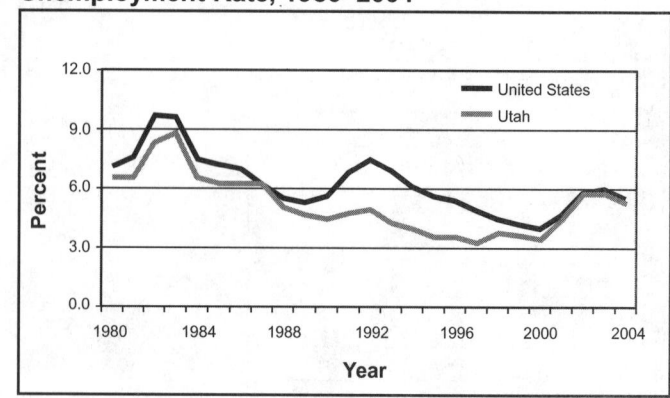

Table UT-9. Employment and Average Wages by Industry, 2001–2004

(Estimates are based on the 2002 North American Industry Classification System [NAICS].)

Industry	2001	2002	2003	2004	Annual average percent change, 2001–2004
	Number of jobs				
TOTAL EMPLOYMENT BY PLACE OF WORK	1 393 316	1 394 356	1 405 443	1 445 498	1.2
Farm Employment	20 418	19 678	20 114	19 835	-1.0
Nonfarm Employment	1 372 898	1 374 678	1 385 329	1 425 663	1.3
Private employment	1 165 611	1 162 965	1 171 704	1 210 434	1.3
Forestry, fishing, hunting, and other[1]	3 006	3 302	3 030	2 949	-0.6
Mining	8 859	8 345	8 513	9 097	0.9
Utilities	4 357	4 152	4 023	4 047	-2.4
Construction	95 865	91 122	92 173	97 836	0.7
Manufacturing	127 588	119 891	118 224	120 790	-1.8
Durable goods manufacturing	87 952	80 789	78 611	79 984	-3.1
Nondurable goods manufacturing	39 636	39 102	39 613	40 806	1.0
Wholesale trade	45 973	45 044	44 813	46 031	0.0
Retail trade	161 781	163 472	164 035	168 648	1.4
Transportation and warehousing	47 873	46 523	45 657	46 695	-0.8
Information	36 548	33 526	33 211	33 467	-2.9
Finance and insurance	77 876	80 112	81 953	82 860	2.1
Real estate and rental and leasing	52 635	52 976	54 254	56 912	2.6
Professional and technical services	80 872	80 947	83 329	85 454	1.9
Management of companies and enterprises	21 814	21 657	20 299	20 509	-2.0
Administrative and waste services	78 362	76 672	77 374	83 887	2.3
Educational services	31 517	33 523	34 636	35 867	4.4
Health care and social assistance	102 721	105 976	110 575	114 876	3.8
Arts, entertainment, and recreation	28 156	29 464	28 335	29 015	1.0
Accommodation and food services	87 333	89 403	89 911	92 501	1.9
Other services, except public administration	72 475	76 858	77 359	78 993	2.9
Government and government enterprises	207 287	211 713	213 625	215 229	1.3
	Dollars				
AVERAGE WAGES AND SALARIES BY PLACE OF WORK ...	29 677	30 301	30 866	31 971	2.5
Farm Earnings	21 511	30 818	22 329	22 945	2.2
Nonfarm Earnings	29 711	30 299	30 902	32 005	2.5
Private earnings	29 758	30 113	30 669	31 768	2.2
Forestry, fishing, hunting, and other[1]	20 145	17 615	18 088	18 638	-2.6
Mining	50 962	49 285	50 742	55 094	2.6
Utilities	73 675	83 344	64 123	66 179	-3.5
Construction	30 441	30 764	30 533	31 087	0.7
Manufacturing	36 250	36 847	37 950	38 647	2.2
Durable goods manufacturing	38 396	38 952	40 275	40 901	2.1
Nondurable goods manufacturing	31 448	32 472	33 326	34 226	2.9
Wholesale trade	41 744	42 156	42 745	44 971	2.5
Retail trade	20 215	20 607	21 385	22 441	3.5
Transportation and warehousing	35 689	36 884	37 773	39 089	3.1
Information	41 023	40 616	40 810	42 613	1.3
Finance and insurance	39 928	41 248	43 279	45 093	4.1
Real estate and rental and leasing	25 259	26 136	26 362	28 239	3.8
Professional and technical services	46 361	45 649	47 218	49 267	2.0
Management of companies and enterprises	48 914	46 072	47 747	50 484	1.1
Administrative and waste services	19 917	20 612	20 589	21 795	3.1
Educational services	20 840	21 160	21 865	22 441	2.5
Health care and social assistance	28 537	29 286	30 061	31 100	2.9
Arts, entertainment, and recreation	18 605	23 406	19 172	19 455	1.5
Accommodation and food services	11 897	12 240	12 311	12 621	2.0
Other services, except public administration	28 855	30 047	31 169	32 593	4.1
Government and government enterprises	29 500	31 108	31 903	33 049	3.9

Note: Average wages and salaries are a calculation by the editors of wage and salary disbursements divided by full- and part-time wage and salary employment. Data may not add to total or may appear as zero due to rounding.

[1] "Other" consists of the number of jobs held by U.S. residents employed by international organizations and foreign embassies and consulates in the United States.

LABOR MARKET

Utah's unemployment rate has been below the national average for many years. However, in 2004, its unemployment rate of 5.2 percent was above the rates of its neighbors, Colorado, Wyoming, and Nevada. Employment in Utah increased by 3.7 percent from 2001 to 2004, which was the 10th highest rate of growth in the nation. Manufacturing jobs declined after the 2001 recession, but rebounded in 2004; however, employment remained below its 2001 level. The decline in employment in manufacturing, information, and management services was offset by job growth in retail trade, government, health care, and tourist-related industries (accommodation and food services). The state's average wages and salaries were considerably below the national average.

Employment by Industry, 2004

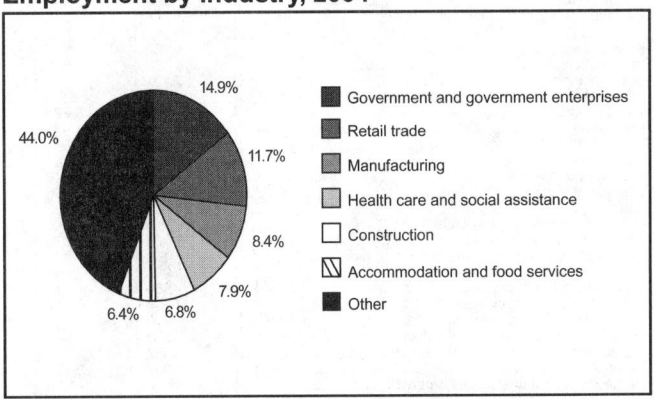

Table UT-10. Personal Income by Major Source, Selected Years 1980–2004

(Millions of dollars, except where noted.)

Item	1980	1990	2000	2001	2002	2003	2004	Average annual percent change, 2000–2004
Earnings by Place of Work	10 071	20 473	43 760	46 273	47 545	49 578	53 235	5.0
Wage and salary disbursements	7 652	15 279	32 707	33 827	34 356	35 078	37 268	3.3
Supplements to wages and salaries	1 481	3 332	6 770	7 210	7 925	8 443	9 277	8.2
Proprietors' income[1]	938	1 862	4 283	5 237	5 263	6 058	6 690	11.8
Farm proprietors' income	8	181	85	160	51	102	129	11.0
Nonfarm proprietors' income	930	1 681	4 198	5 077	5 212	5 956	6 561	11.8
(-) Contributions for government social insurance[2]	897	2 293	4 797	5 030	5 189	5 351	5 748	4.6
(+) Adjustment for residence[3]	52	17	4	18	10	19	30	66.9
(=) Net Earnings by Place of Residence	9 226	18 197	38 967	41 261	42 365	44 246	47 517	5.1
(+) Dividends, interest, and rent[4]	2 118	4 795	9 148	9 372	9 302	9 214	9 604	1.2
(+) Personal current transfer receipts	1 175	2 825	5 447	5 961	6 495	6 860	7 255	7.4
Personal income	12 519	25 817	53 561	56 594	58 163	60 320	64 376	4.7
Farm income	12 463	25 576	53 369	56 325	57 983	60 105	64 138	4.7
Nonfarm income	56	242	193	268	179	215	238	5.4
Per Capita Personal Income (Dollars)[5]	8 501	14 913	23 878	24 809	25 073	25 645	26 946	3.1

Note: Data may not add to total or may appear as zero due to rounding.

[1]Proprietors' income includes the inventory valuation adjustment and the capital consumption adjustment.
[2]Contributions for government social insurance are included in earnings by type and industry, but they are excluded from personal income.
[3]The adjustment for residence is the net inflow of the earnings of interarea commuters.
[4]Rental income of persons includes the capital consumption adjustment.
[5]Per capita personal income is total personal income divided by total midyear population.

Per Capita Personal Income, 1980–2004 (Current Dollars)

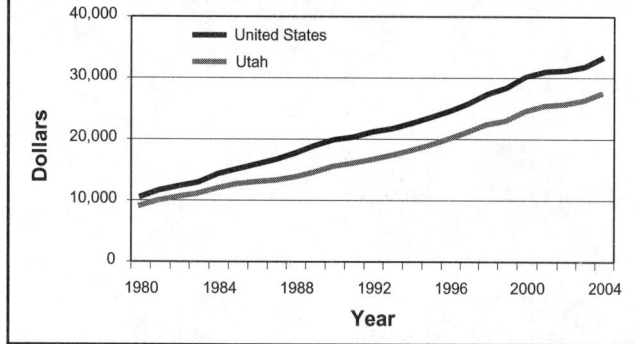

ECONOMIC ACTIVITY

In recent years, economic growth was relatively subdued in Utah. The state's real gross state product (GSP) ranked 33rd in the nation. From 2003 to 2004, the GSP grew by 5.2 percent, the 12th fastest rate in the country. Contributing to this growth were construction, manufacturing, retail trade, information, real estate and related activities, and government. Agriculture, mining, and educational services showed the largest declines, but these industries represented only a small part of the state's economy. Housing prices have risen sharply in recent years. In 2004, the median value of owner-occupied housing in Utah above average and ranked 20th in the nation.

Table UT-11. Real Gross State Product, 1997–2004

(Millions of chained 2000 dollars, percent.)

Industry	1997	1998	1999	2000	2001	2002	2003	2004	Average annual percent change, 2001–2004
GROSS STATE PRODUCT	60 081	63 063	65 877	67 889	68 666	70 086	71 605	75 327	3.1
As a percent of U.S. gross product	0.7	0.7	0.7	0.7	0.7	0.7	0.7	0.7	X
Private Industries	51 059	53 893	56 536	58 280	58 920	60 219	61 719	65 152	3.4
Agriculture, forestry, fishing, and hunting	343	378	435	461	497	478	495	389	-7.8
Mining	963	918	935	969	892	815	815	810	-3.2
Utilities	968	985	1 045	1 013	1 015	1 095	1 023	1 065	1.6
Construction	4 000	4 086	4 164	4 025	3 825	3 686	3 628	3 819	-0.1
Manufacturing	7 101	7 542	7 720	8 426	7 513	7 544	7 954	8 354	3.6
As a percent of gross state product	11.8	12.0	11.7	12.4	10.9	10.8	11.1	11.1	X
Wholesale trade	2 933	3 477	3 629	3 651	3 910	3 983	3 854	4 040	1.1
Retail trade	4 687	4 977	5 269	5 148	5 507	5 878	6 274	6 827	7.4
Transportation and warehousing	2 595	2 664	2 719	2 853	2 662	2 780	2 861	3 002	4.1
Information	2 005	2 186	2 731	2 858	2 759	2 801	2 938	3 348	6.7
Finance and insurance	4 428	4 670	4 909	5 149	6 028	6 181	6 596	6 831	4.3
Real estate and rental and leasing	6 943	7 246	7 747	7 890	8 168	8 414	8 465	9 031	3.4
Services	14 198	14 801	15 249	15 837	16 145	16 576	16 882	17 773	3.3
As a percent of gross state product	23.6	23.5	23.1	23.3	23.5	23.7	23.6	23.6	X
Professional and technical services	3 069	3 375	3 563	3 958	4 106	4 147	4 383	4 595	3.8
Management of companies and enterprises	1 402	1 349	1 390	1 482	1 552	1 490	1 538	1 561	0.2
Administrative and waste services	1 926	2 001	2 123	1 878	1 827	1 874	1 900	2 120	5.1
Educational services	569	573	605	655	651	639	612	603	-2.5
Health care and social assistance	3 206	3 262	3 250	3 397	3 490	3 658	3 835	4 002	4.7
Arts, entertainment, and recreation	456	471	494	508	618	732	591	594	-1.3
Accommodation and food services	1 533	1 627	1 670	1 747	1 747	1 819	1 809	1 892	2.7
Other services, except public administration	2 037	2 143	2 154	2 212	2 154	2 217	2 214	2 406	3.8
Government	9 037	9 175	9 340	9 609	9 745	9 869	9 896	10 193	1.5
As a percent of gross state product	15.0	14.5	14.2	14.2	14.2	14.1	13.8	13.5	X

X = Not applicable.

Table UT-12. Government Transfer Payments, Selected Years 1980–2004

(Millions of dollars, percent.)

Item	1980	1990	2000	2001	2002	2003	2004	Average annual percent change, 2000–2004
CURRENT TRANSFER PAYMENTS TO INDIVIDUALS	1 074	2 602	4 962	5 419	6 009	6 414	6 806	8.2
Retirement and Disability Insurance Benefits	598	1 404	2 375	2 562	2 736	2 884	3 052	6.5
Old-age, survivors, and disability insurance (OASDI) benefits	510	1 176	2 153	2 300	2 441	2 564	2 721	6.0
Railroad retirement and disability benefits	49	75	86	86	88	90	91	1.6
Workers' compensation	31	145	130	168	199	222	232	15.6
Other government retirement and disability insurance benefits	9	9	8	8	8	9	9	4.2
Medical Benefits	194	698	1 717	1 904	2 114	2 313	2 580	10.7
Medicare benefits	112	379	864	966	1 042	1 112	1 236	9.4
Public assistance medical care benefits	77	302	830	903	1 021	1 156	1 291	11.7
Military medical insurance benefits	5	17	23	35	51	45	53	23.6
Income Maintenance Benefits	108	248	489	435	464	547	598	5.1
Supplemental Security Income (SSI) benefits	12	38	87	93	98	99	104	4.5
Family assistance	48	65	51	41	55	59	59	3.6
Food stamps	24	74	68	68	83	107	128	17.2
Other income maintenance benefits	24	71	283	233	228	282	306	2.0
Unemployment Insurance Compensation	74	65	117	182	316	289	176	10.7
Veterans' Benefits	68	88	131	141	155	167	178	8.0
Federal Education and Training Assistance	31	87	118	152	172	178	188	12.4
Other Payments to Individuals	2	12	14	42	50	36	34	24.0

Note: See notes and definitions for more details. Data may not add to total or may appear as zero due to rounding.

EXPORTS

From 2001 to 2004, Utah's exports increased quite rapidly, growing by 34.6 percent. In 2004, the state was the nation's 31st largest exporter, with total exports valued at $4.7 billion. The chief exports were primary metal manufactures (primarily gold), computers and electronic products, and transportation equipment. Chemical manufactures were the fastest-growing export. Transportation equipment exports dropped about 20 percent from 2001 to 2004. Canada was the state's largest export market, followed by Switzerland (which was the primary purchaser of Utah's gold), the United Kingdom, and Japan. China was the state's fastest-growing overseas market, as exports to this country tripled from 2001 to 2004.

Leading Exports, 2004

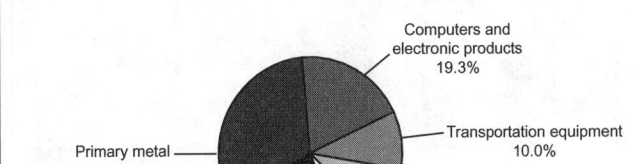

Computers and electronic products 19.3%
Transportation equipment 10.0%
Chemicals 9.1%
Processed foods 6.5%
Other 23.1%
Primary metal manufactures 32.0%

Table UT-13. Exports of Goods by Leading Products and Destinations, 2001–2004

(Millions of dollars, percent, rank based on 2004 dollar values.)

Product and market	2001	2002	2003	2004	Percent share of total, 2004	Average annual percent change, 2001–2004
Total Goods						
Total	3 506	4 543	4 115	4 718	100.0	10.4
Manufactures	3 306	4 377	3 961	4 472	94.8	10.6
Agriculture and livestock	118	69	53	113	2.4	-1.5
Other commodities	82	96	101	133	2.8	17.6
Five Leading Exports (NAICS Code)						
Primary metal manufactures (331)	1 008	1 913	1 466	1 508	32.0	14.3
Computers and electronic products (334)	511	758	624	911	19.3	21.2
Transportation equipment (336)	589	489	467	470	10.0	-7.3
Chemical manufactures (325)	230	265	340	430	9.1	23.2
Processed foods (311)	231	255	283	309	6.5	10.1
Five Leading Markets	3 204	4 314	3 832	4 424	93.8	11.4
Canada	543	513	544	866	18.3	16.8
Switzerland	696	1 341	1 105	773	16.4	3.5
United Kingdom	421	710	487	560	11.9	9.9
Japan	396	427	476	542	11.5	11.0
Germany	94	69	119	170	3.6	22.1

Table UT-14. Agriculture, 1997 and 2002

(Number, acres, and dollars.)

Item	1997	2002
Number of farms	15 810	15 282
Land in farms (acres)	12 008 137	11 731 228
Farm Size		
Average size of farm (acres)	760	768
Farms by size (percent distribution)		
Fewer than 50 acres	49.6	54.8
50 to 499 acres	35.9	31.2
500 acres or more	14.5	14.0
Market Value of Land and Equipment (Dollars)		
Land and buildings average value per farm	456 494	586 310
Average value per acre	600	756
Machinery and equipment average value per farm	48 784	62 600
Value of Sales (Thousands of Dollars)		
Agricultural products sold	888 579	1 115 898
Crops	255 336	257 797
Livestock, poultry, and their products	633 243	858 101
Average per farm (dollars)	56 204	73 020
Value of sales (percent distribution)		
Less than $10,000	59.9	66.4
$10,000 to $99,999	29.6	23.2
$100,000 or more	10.5	10.4
Government Payments		
Payments (thousands of dollars)	15 958	26 669
Percent of farms receiving government payments	17.1	19.5
Farm operators whose principal occupation is farming (percent)	39.7	48.7

AGRICULTURE

Cash receipts from farming totaled $11.1 billion in 2002, according to the Department of Agriculture's Census of Agriculture. This was a 27 percent increase from the previous agriculture census in 1997. Cattle was the state's chief product. About two-thirds of farms had sales of less than $10,000, a significant increase from 1997. Only 49 percent of all farm operators considered farming to be their principal occupation. Nearly 55 percent of farms in Utah spanned fewer than 50 acres, which was the 11th largest proportion of farms of this size in the country.

ENERGY

Energy consumption in Utah was below average, ranking 32nd in the nation. The state's energy prices were well below average. Utah's energy expenditures per person were about $1,989, the second lowest in the country. The chief sources of energy were coal, petroleum, and natural gas. The industrial sector was the largest consumer of energy in the state.

Energy Consumption by Source, 2001

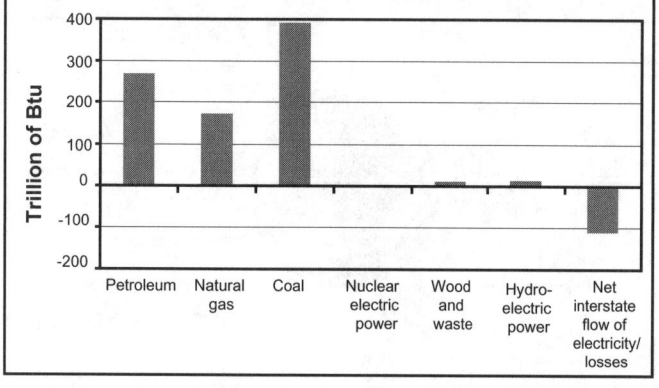

Energy Consumption by Sector, 2001

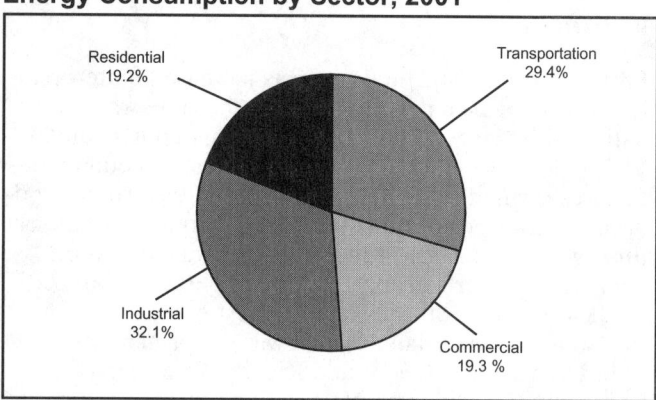

Table UT-15. Energy Consumption, Expenditures, and Prices, Selected Years 1960–2001

(Dollars, Btu [British Thermal Unit], percent distribution.)

Item	1960	1965	1970	1975	1980	1985	1990	1995	2000	2001
Total Consumption (Billion Btu)	303 315	339 632	397 006	480 927	504 960	500 272	551 223	645 294	749 835	725 378
Consumption per capita (million Btu)	340.4	342.7	374.8	389.1	345.6	304.5	319.9	326.4	335.8	318.2
Consumption by Sector (Percent Distribution)										
Residential	14.0	14.6	17.2	19.3	21.0	23.5	18.5	17.6	18.4	19.2
Commercial	9.4	12.0	10.7	11.0	10.8	14.0	15.8	16.3	18.0	19.3
Industrial	55.2	52.6	49.0	46.0	43.0	36.2	38.7	38.0	34.2	32.1
Transportation	21.3	20.8	23.1	23.7	25.1	26.4	27.0	28.1	29.5	29.4
Consumption by Source (Billion Btu)										
Coal	90 967	75 449	78 777	115 740	168 254	199 366	366 836	361 428	403 075	389 584
Natural gas	72 441	99 810	114 377	117 952	124 990	123 750	126 913	166 860	173 438	168 112
Petroleum	127 635	142 350	165 790	203 894	200 384	173 979	193 200	228 303	269 011	261 372
Nuclear electric power	0	0	0	0	0	0	0	0	0	0
Hydroelectric power[1]	3 275	9 545	7 776	11 181	8 533	10 646	5 289	9 990	7 657	5 173
Wood and waste	2 219	1 956	2 303	2 893	4 497	6 250	3 306	3 858	5 652	4 962
Other	0	0	0	0	0	2 329	3 668	3 454	3 777	3 841
Net interstate flow of electricity/losses[2]	6 779	10 521	27 982	29 267	-1 697	-16 047	-147 989	-128 599	-112 775	-107 665
Total Expenditures (Thousands of Dollars)	...	...	429 800	989 500	2 202 700	2 629 400	2 736 700	3 121 700	4 504 200	4 533 000
Expenditures per capita (dollars)	...	...	406	801	1 508	1 600	1 588	1 579	2 017	1 988
Prices by Sector (Dollars Per Million Btu)										
Total	...	...	1.31	2.60	5.80	7.25	7.15	7.00	8.70	9.16
Residential	...	...	1.61	2.37	4.65	7.70	8.44	8.29	9.39	11.11
Commercial	...	...	1.81	3.29	7.53	11.61	9.35	8.81	9.36	10.72
Industrial	...	...	0.57	1.61	3.48	4.52	4.20	3.99	4.51	5.06
Transportation	...	...	2.28	3.97	8.82	8.29	8.39	8.29	11.06	10.39

[1]A negative number in this row results from pumped storage for which, overall, more electricity is expended than created to provide electricity during peak demand periods.
[2]Net interstate flow of electricity is the difference between the amount of energy in the electricity sold within a state (including associated losses) and the energy input at the electric utilities within the state. A positive number indicates that more electricity (including associated losses) came into the state than went out of the state during the year; conversely, a negative number indicates that more electricity (including associated losses) went out of the state than came into the state.
... = Not available.

Table UT-16. State Taxes, Fiscal 2004

(Dollars, percent distribution.)

Item	Thousands of dollars	Percent distribution	Dollars per capita	
			State	U.S.
TOTAL TAXES	4 189 172	100.0	1 753.5	2 024.8
Property Taxes	X	X	X	38.9
Sales and Gross Receipts	2 138 897	51.1	895.3	1 003.4
General sales and gross receipts	1 556 332	37.2	651.5	677.0
Selective sales taxes	582 565	13.9	243.8	326.4
Alcoholic beverages	28 174	0.7	11.8	15.7
Insurance premiums	105 965	2.5	44.4	47.0
Motor fuels	344 121	8.2	144.0	114.6
Tobacco products	61 663	1.5	25.8	42.0
Other selective sales	28 797	0.7	12.0	49.8
Licenses	155 547	3.7	65.1	134.9
Motor vehicle	91 372	2.2	38.2	59.4
Occupation and business, not elsewhere classified	27 232	0.7	11.4	37.1
Other Taxes	1 894 728	45.2	793.1	847.6
Individual income	1 692 277	40.4	708.4	673.6
Corporation net income	145 005	3.5	60.7	105.1
Severance	47 772	1.1	20.0	21.5

X = Not applicable.

GOVERNMENT FINANCE

Utah's per capita revenue amounted to $3,724 in 2003. The state's per capita expenditures of $3,902 ranked 28th in the nation. Spending per person was above average on education, hospitals, highways, and natural resources, but below average on public welfare and health. Utah's per capita taxes in fiscal year 2004 were $1,754, which ranked 38th in the nation. The largest sources of tax revenue were individual income taxes, general sales taxes, and motor fuels taxes. Unlike many other western states, severance (taxes on the removal of natural resources) made only a small contribution to state revenues. Utah had no property taxes.

Per Capita State Taxes, Fiscal 2004

Table UT-17. State Government Finances, 2003

(Dollars, percent distribution.)

Item	Millions of dollars	Percent distribution	Dollars per capita	
			State	U.S.
GENERAL REVENUE	8 758 929	100.0	3 724.0	3 832.6
Intergovernmental revenue	2 493 503	28.5	1 060.2	1 246.0
Taxes	3 954 815	45.2	1 681.5	1 891.6
General sales	1 485 977	17.0	631.8	636.0
Selective sales	528 507	6.0	224.7	307.4
License taxes	148 835	1.7	63.3	123.6
Individual income tax	1 572 512	18.0	668.6	626.8
Corporate income tax	148 218	1.7	63.0	97.8
Other taxes	70 766	0.8	30.1	99.9
Current charges	1 763 397	20.1	749.7	366.5
Miscellaneous general revenue	547 214	6.2	232.7	328.6
GENERAL EXPENDITURE	9 176 425	100.0	3 901.5	4 010.5
Intergovernmental expenditure	2 165 151	23.6	920.6	1 316.9
Direct expenditure	7 011 274	76.4	2 981.0	2 693.6
Expenditure by Function				
Education	4 189 768	45.7	1 781.4	1 416.4
Public welfare	1 758 344	19.2	747.6	1 083.3
Hospitals	532 586	5.8	226.4	132.3
Health	247 222	2.7	105.1	173.0
Highways	771 231	8.4	327.9	295.4
Police protection	82 771	0.9	35.2	38.4
Correction	261 283	2.8	111.1	135.0
Natural resources	189 195	2.1	80.4	64.0
Parks and recreation	36 732	0.4	15.6	20.1
Government administration	558 195	6.1	237.3	151.3
Interest on general debt	190 363	2.1	80.9	107.8
Other and unallocable	358 735	3.9	152.5	393.4
DEBT AT END OF FISCAL YEAR	5 064 112	X	2 153.1	2 404.7
CASH AND SECURITY HOLDINGS	16 919 090	X	7 193.5	8 938.4

X = Not applicable.

Table UT-18. Education Indicators, 2000–2004

(Percent, number.)

Item	State	U.S.
Total Population 25 Years and Over (Thousands), 2004	1 291	186 877
Educational Attainment, 2004		
Percent high school graduate or more	91.0	85.2
Percent college graduate or more	30.8	27.7
Elementary and Secondary Schools, 2002–2003		
Total students	489 072	48 202 324
Percent of students eligible for free or reduced-price lunch ..	33.1	40.6
Percent of students who were English language learners	10.0	7.8
Total schools	803	92 330
Student/teacher ratio	22.4	15.9
Per student expenditures	4 838	8 041
Dropouts, Grades 9–12, 2000–2001 (Percent)	3.7	. . .
Higher Education, 2002–2003		
Total enrollment	186 079	17 035 027
Bachelor's degrees awarded	19 086	1 348 503
Percent women	49.8	57.5

. . . = Not available.

Educational Attainment, 2004

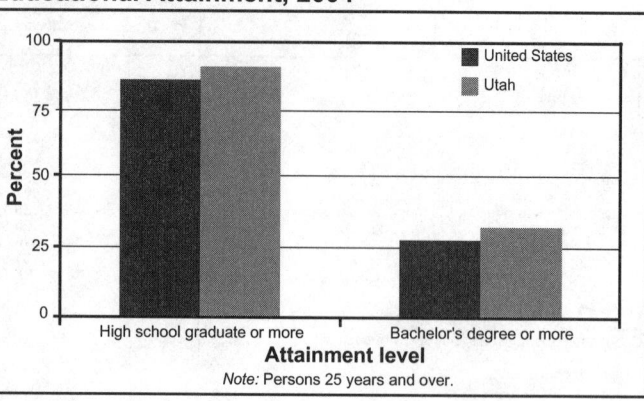

Note: Persons 25 years and over.

EDUCATION

In 2004, 91 percent of Utah's residents age 25 years and over held high school diplomas, which was the fifth highest proportion in the nation. Nearly 31 percent of the population in this age group held bachelor's degrees or more; this proportion ranked eighth in the country. Expenditures per student of $4,838 were the lowest in the nation, while the student/teacher ratio was the highest in the country. Both of these measures reflected the state's large student-age population. Utah's dropout rate of 3.7 percent ranked 37th of the 46 states reporting such data. Within the state, 10 percent of students were English language learners, compared with 7.8 percent nationally

VOTER PARTICIPATION

Voter turnout was only just above the national average for both the 2000 and 2004 elections. The participation rate increased from 56.3 percent in 2000 to 62.8 percent in 2004. About 67 percent of non-Hispanic Whites voted in 2004, while just 25.8 percent of Hispanics (of any race) cast ballots. According to the official tally by the Clerk of the U.S. House of Representatives, 66.8 percent of Utah's voters cast ballots for the Republican presidential candidate in 2000, and this proportion increased to 71.3 percent in 2004. The comparable percentages for the Democratic candidate were 26.3 percent and 26 percent, respectively.

Table UT-19. Reported Voting and Registration, November 2000 and November 2004

(Numbers in thousands, percent.)

Characteristic	Total population 18 years and over	Total citizen		Total registered		Total voted	
		Number	Percent	Number	Percent	Number	Percent
NOVEMBER 2000							
Total	1 472	1 378	93.6	953	64.7	829	56.3
Male	724	677	93.5	453	62.5	386	53.3
Female	748	701	93.7	500	66.9	443	59.3
NOVEMBER 2004							
Total	1 629	1 508	92.5	1 141	70.1	1 022	62.8
Male	811	745	91.9	547	67.5	494	60.9
Female	818	763	93.2	594	72.6	529	64.6
Race and Hispanic Origin							
White alone	1 561	1 469	94.1	1 120	71.7	1 003	64.3
Non-Hispanic White alone	1 461	1 404	96.1	1 094	74.9	979	67.0
Black alone	10	6	B	5	B	5	B
Asian alone	32	15	B	8	B	8	B
Hispanic or Latino[1]	104	67	64.3	28	27.0	27	25.8
White alone or in combination	1 569	1 476	94.0	1 125	71.7	1 007	64.2
Non-Hispanic White alone or in combination	1 466	1 409	96.1	1 097	74.8	981	66.9
Black alone or in combination	11	7	B	6	B	5	B
Asian alone or in combination	33	16	B	8	B	8	B
Age							
18 to 24 years	305	286	93.7	178	58.3	145	47.4
25 to 44 years	685	610	89.0	448	65.4	404	59.0
45 to 64 years	417	396	94.9	321	77.0	289	69.3
65 to 74 years	123	118	96.1	110	89.4	106	86.5
75 years and over	98	97	B	84	B	78	B

[1]May be of any race.
B = Base is too small to show derived measure.

At a Glance:

- Vermont's population was just over 621,000, making it the 49th most populous state in the country. Only the District of Columbia and Wyoming had fewer residents.

- Non-Hispanic Whites made up 96 percent of Vermont's population, giving the state the second highest proportion of this racial group in the nation.

- Just over 11 percent of Vermont's residents lacked health insurance, which was among the 10 lowest proportions of uninsured population in the nation.

- The state's median household income of $47,487 was well above average in 2004, ranking 16th in the country. Vermont's poverty rate of 7.9 percent was the third lowest in the nation.

- Economic activity grew steadily from 2001 to 2004, despite the recession in 2001. In 2004, Vermont's real gross state product was the second smallest in the nation, larger only than that of North Dakota. The state's unemployment rate of 3.7 percent was among the lowest in the country.

- The educational attainment rates of Vermont's population age 25 years and over were above average for both high school and college.

Table VT-1. Population by Sex and Age, 1990, 2000, and 2004

(Number, percent.)

Sex and age	1990	2000	2004	Percent distribution, 2004	Average annual percent change, 2000–2004
Total Population	562 758	608 827	621 394	X	0.5
Percent of total U.S. population	0.2	0.2	0.2	X	X
Sex					
Male	275 492	298 337	305 802	49.2	0.6
Female	287 266	310 490	315 592	50.8	0.4
Age					
Under 5 years	41 261	33 989	31 181	5.0	-2.1
5 to 17 years	101 822	113 534	103 713	16.7	0.1
18 years and over	102 657	461 304	486 500	78.3	1.1
18 to 24 years	419 675	56 586	62 080	10.0	-0.2
25 to 44 years	63 166	176 456	164 655	26.5	-0.9
45 to 64 years	187 689	150 752	179 003	28.8	4.1
65 years and over	66 163	77 510	80 762	13.0	1.5
85 years and over	7 523	9 996	11 478	1.8	3.2
Median age (years)	32.9	37.7	40.2	X	X

X = Not applicable.

Average Annual Rate of Population Growth, 1980–2004

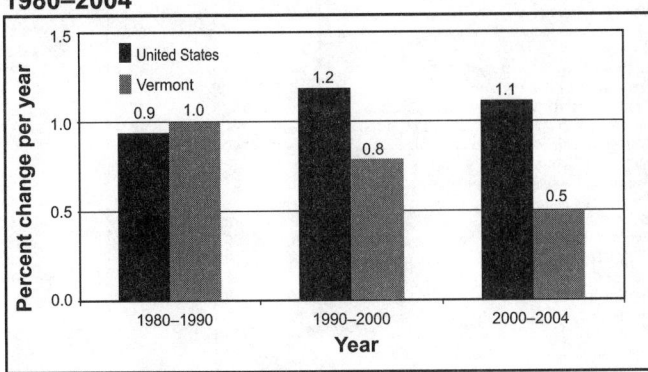

POPULATION

Vermont's population has grown slowly in recent years. From 2000 to 2004, the number of residents increased by 2.1 percent, a growth rate lower than the rates of its New England neighbors, New Hampshire and Maine, but faster than the rates of New York and Massachusetts. Just over 60 percent of the state's population increase from 2000 to 2004 was due to the in-migration of new residents from other states and other countries. Just 21.7 percent of Vermont's population was 18 years old and under, which was among the lowest proportions of this age group in the nation. Vermont had the third highest median age in the country in 2004. Burlington was the state's largest city.

Table VT-2. Population by Race and Hispanic Origin, 1990, 2000, and 2004

(Number, percent.)

Race and Hispanic origin	1990	2000	2004
Total Population	562 758	608 827	621 394
Non-Hispanic (Percent)			
One race[1]			
White	98.1	96.3	96.0
Black	0.3	0.5	0.6
American Indian, Alaska Native[2]	0.3	0.4	0.4
Asian and Pacific Islander[2]	0.6	0.9	1.0
Other race[2]	0.1	. . .	. . .
Two or more races	. . .	1.0	1.0
Hispanic or Latino[3] (Percent)	0.7	0.9	1.0

[1]Individuals could report only one race in the 1990 census and could report one or more races on the 2000 census. Data on race in 2000 and 2004 are not comparable to 1990.
[2]Data for 1990 include people of Hispanic or Latino origin.
[3]May be of any race.
. . . = Not available.

Minority Population as a Percent of Total Population, 2004

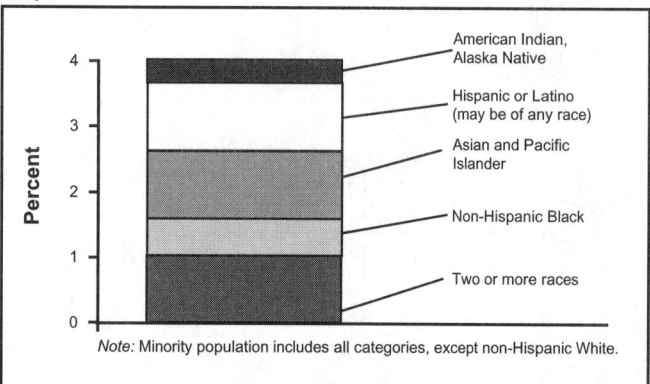

Note: Minority population includes all categories, except non-Hispanic White.

Age-Adjusted Death Rates, Average 2000–2002

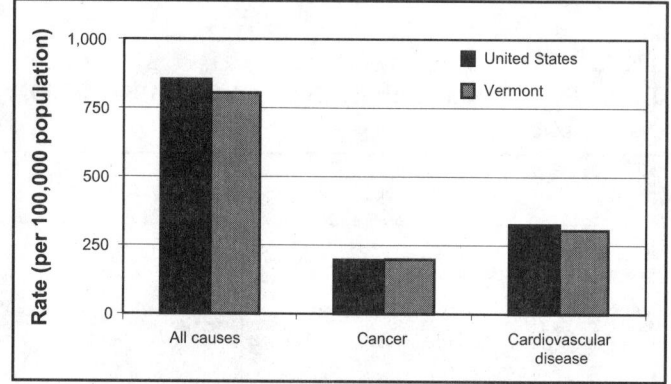

HEALTH

Vermont's infant mortality rate was among the 10 lowest in the nation. The state's age-adjusted death rate for all causes was also below the national average. Vermont, which had the second lowest birth rate for teenage mothers, tied with Maine for the lowest overall birth rate in the country.

Table VT-3. Health Characteristics, 2000–2004

(Number, rate, percent.)

Item	State	U.S.
Births, 2003–2004		
Number of births	6 589	4 089 950
Birth rate (per 1,000 population)	10.6	14.1
Teenage birth rate (per 1,000 women age 15–19 years)	18.9	41.6
Mortality Rates, Average 2000–2002		
Infant mortality rate (per 1,000 live births)	5.5	6.9
Age-adjusted mortality rate (per 100,000 population)		
All races	800.5	853.3
Non-Hispanic White	805.2	843.1
Black	. . .	1 097.9
American Indian, Alaska Native	. . .	687.0
Asian and Pacific Islander	. . .	486.0
Hispanic or Latino[1]	. . .	642.7
Health Insurance, 2004		
Percent of all persons without health insurance	11.2	15.7
Percent of children without health insurance	4.8	11.2
Percent of low-income children without health insurance	1.4	7.1

[1]May be of any race.
. . . = Not available.

Table VT-4. Leading Causes of Death, Average 2000–2002

(Number, rate per 100,000 population.)

Cause	Number of deaths	Age-adjusted death rates	
		State	U.S.
ALL CAUSES	5 134	800.5	853.3
Leading Causes			
Major cardiovascular diseases	1 877	291.3	326.5
Cancer	1 238	192.7	196.0
Chronic lower respiratory diseases	298	46.9	43.7
Unintentional injuries	235	37.2	35.7
Diabetes (underlying cause)	164	25.6	25.2
Influenza and pneumonia	121	18.6	22.7
Alzheimer's disease	149	22.9	19.0
Motor vehicle accidents	79	12.6	15.0
Nephritis, nephrotic syndrome, and nephrosis ..	67	10.5	13.8
Septicemia	44	6.8	11.4
Suicides	80	12.6	10.7
Firearm-related	56	8.8	10.3
Cirrhosis	48	7.3	9.5
Drug-induced	48	7.7	7.9
Alcohol-induced	48	7.2	6.9
Homicides	11	1.8	6.0
Falls	44	6.7	5.2
HIV	*	*	5.0
Viral hepatitis	*	*	2.0
Anemias	7	1.1	1.6
Drownings	7	1.2	1.3
Fire deaths	8	1.4	1.2

Note: The rates are age-adjusted to the U.S. 2000 standard population.

* = Unreliable data.

Table VT-5. Households and Housing Characteristics, 1990, 2000, and 2004

(Number, percent, and dollars.)

Characteristic	1990	2000	2004	Average annual percent change, 2000–2004
Total Households	210 650	240 634	249 590	0.9
Family households	144 895	157 763	162 020	0.7
Married-couple family	118 905	126 413	129 304	0.6
Other family	25 990	31 350	32 716	1.1
Male householder, no wife present	6 630	9 078	10 405	3.5
Female householder, no husband present	19 360	22 272	22 311	0.0
Nonfamily households	65 755	82 871	87 570	1.4
Householder living alone	49 366	63 112	66 729	1.4
Householder not living alone	16 389	19 759	20 841	1.3
Housing Characteristics				
Average size	2.57	2.44	2.41	X
Housing units	271 214	294 382	304 291	0.8
Occupied housing units	210 650	240 634	249 590	0.9
Owner-occupied	145 368	169 784	182 863	1.9
Renter-occupied	65 282	70 850	66 727	-1.5
Median gross rent of renter-occupied housing units (dollars)	446	553	674	5.1
Median value of owner-occupied housing units (dollars)	95 600	111 500	154 318	8.5

X = Not applicable.

Median Housing Value and Median Rent, 2004

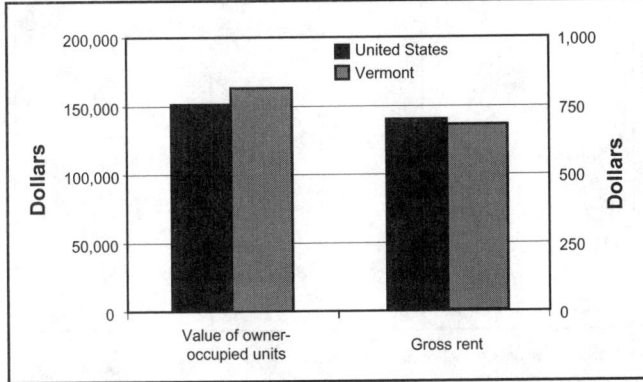

Median Household Income, 1984–2004 (2004 Dollars)

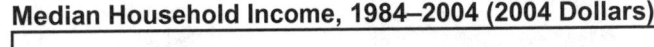
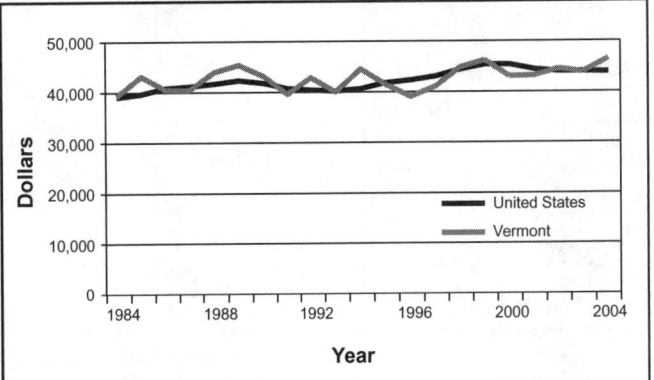

Table VT-6. Household Income and Poverty Status, 1980–2004

(2004 CPI-U-RS adjusted dollars, rate.)

Year	State		U.S.	
	Median household income (2004 dollars)	Poverty rate	Median household income (2004 dollars)	Poverty rate
2004	47 487	7.9	44 389	12.7
2003	44 424	8.5	44 482	12.5
2002	45 166	9.9	44 546	12.1
2001	43 532	9.7	45 062	11.7
2000	43 430	10.0	46 058	11.3
1999	47 135	9.6	46 129	11.9
1998	45 567	9.9	45 003	12.7
1997	41 139	9.3	43 430	13.3
1996	38 787	12.6	42 544	13.7
1995	41 633	10.3	41 943	13.8
1994	45 138	7.6	40 677	14.5
1993	39 991	10.0	40 217	15.1
1992	43 218	10.5	40 422	14.8
1991	39 432	12.6	40 746	14.2
1990	43 582	10.9	41 963	13.5
1989	46 039	8.0	42 524	12.8
1988	44 476	8.1	41 771	13.0
1987	40 414	9.3	41 322	13.4
1986	40 449	11.0	40 939	13.6
1985	43 534	9.2	39 545	14.0
1984	39 064	12.6	38 782	14.4
1983	. . .	15.6	. . .	15.2
1982	. . .	12.9	. . .	15.0
1981	. . .	12.3	. . .	14.0
1980	. . .	12.0	. . .	13.0

. . . = Not available.

Table VT-7. Employment Status by Demographic Group, 2004

(Numbers in thousands, rate.)

Characteristic	Civilian noninstitutional population	Civilian labor force		Employed	Unemployment rate
		Number	Participation rate		
SEX AND AGE					
Total	499	353	70.8	340	3.7
16 to 19 years	36	21	57.8	19	11.8
20 to 24 years	44	35	80.4	34	5.3
25 to 34 years	74	64	87.0	61	4.9
35 to 44 years	93	81	86.9	79	2.7
45 to 54 years	100	88	87.2	86	2.3
55 to 64 years	67	49	72.7	48	1.8
65 years and over	85	15	18.2	15	3.2
Men	243	185	75.9	177	4.0
16 to 19 years	19	11	56.7	9	14.2
20 to 24 years	21	17	82.1	16	5.5
25 to 34 years	37	34	92.8	33	4.3
35 to 44 years	47	44	93.9	42	3.2
45 to 54 years	49	44	90.4	43	2.6
55 to 64 years	34	26	76.4	25	2.1
65 years and over	37	9	23.5	8	2.9
Women	256	169	65.8	163	3.4
16 to 19 years	17	10	59.0	9	9.2
20 to 24 years	23	18	78.9	17	5.2
25 to 34 years	37	30	81.1	28	5.6
35 to 44 years	47	37	80.0	36	2.2
45 to 54 years	52	44	84.2	43	1.9
55 to 64 years	33	23	68.9	22	1.6
65 years and over	48	7	14.1	6	3.6
MARITAL STATUS					
Married men, spouse present	135	105	77.7	103	2.4
Married women, spouse present	133	91	68.3	89	2.0
Women who maintain families	24	17	73.5	16	5.4
RACE, HISPANIC ORIGIN, AND SEX					
White	484	343	70.8	330	3.7
Men	236	179	76.0	172	3.9
Women	248	163	65.9	158	3.4
RACE, HISPANIC ORIGIN, AND AGE					
White					
16 to 19 years	35	20	58.6	18	11.2
20 to 24 years	43	34	80.6	33	5.5
25 to 34 years	70	61	87.0	58	5.0
35 to 44 years	90	79	87.5	76	2.6
45 to 54 years	98	86	87.5	84	2.3
55 to 64 years	65	48	73.1	47	1.8
65 years and over	84	15	18.3	15	3.2

Note: Data in Table 7 are from the Current Population Survey (CPS) and do not match Bureau of Labor Statistics estimates in Table 8. See notes and definitions for more details.

Table VT-8. Employment Status, 1990–2004

(Numbers in thousands, rate.)

Year	Civilian labor force	Employed	Unemployed	Unemployment rate
2004	353 435	340 374	13 061	3.7
2003	351 533	335 823	15 710	4.5
2002	347 504	333 703	13 801	4.0
2001	340 663	329 460	11 203	3.3
2000	335 411	326 560	8 851	2.6
1999	335 415	325 581	9 834	2.9
1998	331 859	321 608	10 251	3.1
1997	328 820	315 806	13 014	4.0
1996	323 924	309 653	14 271	4.4
1995	318 986	305 279	13 707	4.3
1994	316 225	301 836	14 389	4.6
1993	314 881	298 277	16 604	5.3
1992	312 421	292 288	20 133	6.4
1991	308 636	288 280	20 356	6.6
1990	309 280	294 074	15 206	4.9

Note: Population age 16 years and over.

Unemployment Rate, 1980–2004

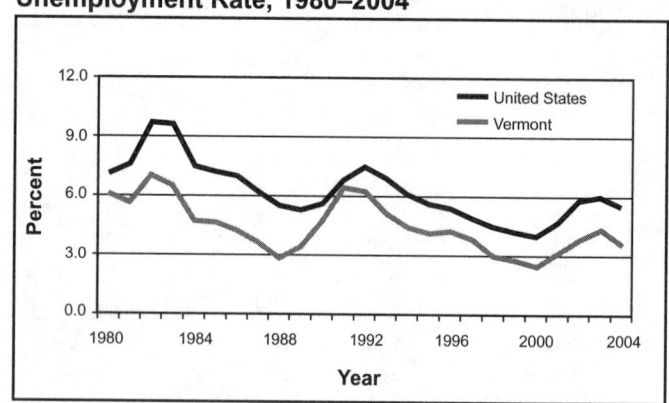

Table VT-9. Employment and Average Wages by Industry, 2001–2004

(Estimates are based on the 2002 North American Industry Classification System [NAICS].)

Industry	2001	2002	2003	2004	Annual average percent change, 2001–2004
	Number of jobs				
TOTAL EMPLOYMENT BY PLACE OF WORK	407 733	409 692	411 500	418 438	0.9
Farm Employment	9 489	9 714	9 541	8 976	-1.8
Nonfarm Employment	398 244	399 978	401 959	409 462	0.9
Private employment	345 146	346 125	347 533	354 556	0.9
Forestry, fishing, hunting, and other[1]	3 667	3 878	3 387	3 284	-3.6
Mining	1 349	1 153	1 171	1 186	-4.2
Utilities	1 734	1 769	1 802	1 787	1.0
Construction	27 978	27 568	29 148	30 754	3.2
Manufacturing	48 315	43 663	40 304	39 869	-6.2
Durable goods manufacturing	35 143	31 090	28 423	28 139	-7.1
Nondurable goods manufacturing	13 172	12 573	11 881	11 730	-3.8
Wholesale trade	11 403	11 399	11 629	11 627	0.7
Retail trade	49 467	49 875	49 477	50 382	0.6
Transportation and warehousing	9 124	9 168	8 924	9 095	-0.1
Information	8 080	D	7 848	7 730	-1.5
Finance and insurance	13 361	13 271	13 259	13 152	-0.5
Real estate and rental and leasing	11 200	11 258	11 504	12 160	2.8
Professional and technical services	23 521	23 476	23 699	24 374	1.2
Management of companies and enterprises	405	427	369	388	-1.4
Administrative and waste services	13 438	13 733	14 483	15 587	5.1
Educational services	15 595	16 846	17 206	17 488	3.9
Health care and social assistance	44 653	47 547	49 794	51 097	4.6
Arts, entertainment, and recreation	9 131	9 718	9 807	10 032	3.2
Accommodation and food services	31 757	31 830	31 643	32 104	0.4
Other services, except public administration	20 968	D	22 079	22 460	2.3
Government and government enterprises	53 098	53 853	54 426	54 906	1.1
	Dollars				
AVERAGE WAGES AND SALARIES BY PLACE OF WORK	29 428	30 143	31 221	32 443	3.3
Farm Earnings	18 603	24 401	20 196	26 112	12.0
Nonfarm Earnings	29 524	30 197	31 327	32 494	3.2
Private earnings	29 451	29 951	30 912	32 026	2.8
Forestry, fishing, hunting, and other[1]	23 706	24 293	25 708	26 280	3.5
Mining	34 997	38 975	41 116	39 739	4.3
Utilities	64 584	70 326	68 638	78 700	6.8
Construction	32 761	32 809	33 403	34 786	2.0
Manufacturing	41 378	42 775	44 178	45 281	3.1
Durable goods manufacturing	44 373	46 226	47 677	48 890	3.3
Nondurable goods manufacturing	33 094	33 832	35 496	36 286	3.1
Wholesale trade	41 071	42 499	44 212	44 649	2.8
Retail trade	20 899	21 616	22 442	23 351	3.8
Transportation and warehousing	30 772	31 183	31 901	33 134	2.5
Information	35 176	D	37 237	38 859	3.4
Finance and insurance	44 538	46 262	50 018	52 073	5.3
Real estate and rental and leasing	25 745	26 978	27 640	29 270	4.4
Professional and technical services	43 017	43 635	47 041	48 673	4.2
Management of companies and enterprises	47 003	56 266	59 461	57 847	7.2
Administrative and waste services	23 040	23 830	23 618	26 338	4.6
Educational services	21 774	21 869	22 850	24 340	3.8
Health care and social assistance	28 577	29 232	29 768	30 737	2.5
Arts, entertainment, and recreation	16 907	16 605	17 511	19 469	4.8
Accommodation and food services	15 040	15 638	16 181	16 815	3.8
Other services, except public administration	19 715	D	20 897	21 608	3.1
Government and government enterprises	29 888	31 396	33 322	34 753	5.2

Note: Average wages and salaries are a calculation by the editors of wage and salary disbursements divided by full- and part-time wage and salary employment. Data may not add to total or may appear as zero due to rounding.

[1] "Other" consists of the number of jobs held by U.S. residents employed by international organizations and foreign embassies and consulates in the United States.
D = Suppressed to avoid disclosure of data of individual companies.

LABOR MARKET

Vermont's unemployment rate has been well below average since the mid-1990s, and remained lower than the rates of neighboring Maine and New Hampshire. The state's unemployment rate rose following the 2001 recession, but declined in subsequent years, reaching 3.7 percent in 2004. Employment grew steadily over the 2001–2004 period, as job gains in construction and most service-providing industries offset declines in manufacturing. The state's major employers were government, health care, and retail trade. Average wages and salaries were below the national average for most major industry groups, but rose at an above average rate from 2001 and 2004.

Employment by Industry, 2004

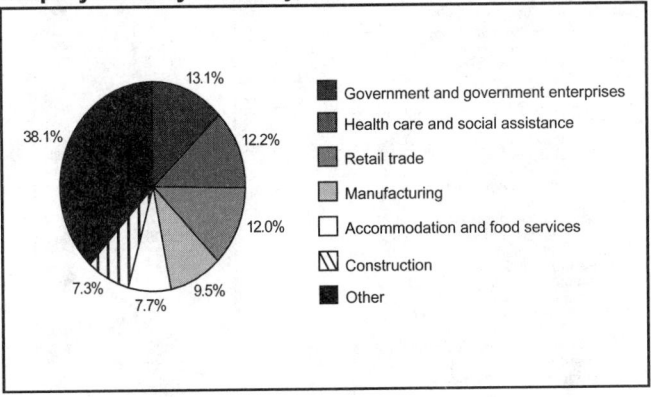

- 38.1% Government and government enterprises
- 13.1% Health care and social assistance
- 12.2% Retail trade
- 12.0% Manufacturing
- 9.5% Accommodation and food services
- 7.7% Construction
- 7.3% Other

Table VT-10. Personal Income by Major Source, Selected Years 1980–2004

(Millions of dollars, except where noted.)

Item	1980	1990	2000	2001	2002	2003	2004	Average annual percent change, 2000–2004
Earnings by Place of Work	3 327	7 473	12 234	12 836	13 150	13 743	14 608	4.5
Wage and salary disbursements	2 435	5 434	8 965	9 405	9 628	9 950	10 459	3.9
Supplements to wages and salaries	451	1 108	1 791	1 927	2 153	2 330	2 534	9.1
Proprietors' income[1]	440	930	1 478	1 504	1 369	1 462	1 615	2.2
Farm proprietors' income	74	70	104	82	-2	35	45	-19.1
Nonfarm proprietors' income	367	861	1 373	1 422	1 371	1 427	1 570	3.4
(-) Contributions for government social insurance[2]	310	845	1 392	1 486	1 533	1 587	1 661	4.5
(+) Adjustment for residence[3]	14	49	219	232	236	267	292	7.5
(=) Net Earnings by Place of Residence	3 031	6 677	11 060	11 582	11 853	12 423	13 240	4.6
(+) Dividends, interest, and rent[4]	756	2 163	3 407	3 513	3 329	3 226	3 337	-0.5
(+) Personal current transfer receipts	627	1 256	2 416	2 647	2 847	2 994	3 144	6.8
Personal income	4 414	10 096	16 883	17 742	18 030	18 644	19 721	4.0
Farm income	4 309	9 988	16 723	17 601	17 953	18 541	19 604	4.1
Nonfarm income	106	108	160	140	77	102	117	-7.6
Per Capita Personal Income (Dollars)[5]	8 613	17 876	27 680	28 944	29 245	30 103	31 737	3.5

Note: Data may not add to total or may appear as zero due to rounding.

[1]Proprietors' income includes the inventory valuation adjustment and the capital consumption adjustment.
[2]Contributions for government social insurance are included in earnings by type and industry, but they are excluded from personal income.
[3]The adjustment for residence is the net inflow of the earnings of interarea commuters.
[4]Rental income of persons includes the capital consumption adjustment.
[5]Per capita personal income is total personal income divided by total midyear population.

Per Capita Personal Income, 1980–2004 (Current Dollars)

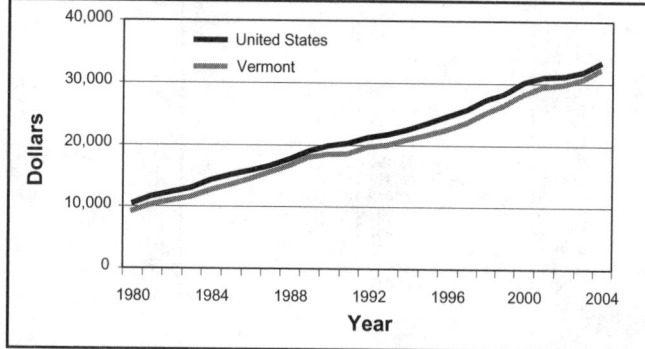

ECONOMIC ACTIVITY

The economy was largely immune to the national slow-down in 2001, showing steady growth throughout the 2001–2004 period. Vermont's real gross state product grew 11.5 percent during this period, giving the state the 16th highest rate of growth in the country. Contributing to this growth were utilities, construction, durable goods manufacturing, retail trade, real estate and related activi-ties, and government. Manufacturing, government, and health care were the leading sectors of the state's econo-my. In recent years, housing prices have risen at a rate above the national average. The median value of owner-occupied housing in 2004 was above average at $154,318; this value represented an increase of 38.4 percent from 2000.

Table VT-11. Real Gross State Product, 1997–2004

(Millions of chained 2000 dollars, percent.)

Industry	1997	1998	1999	2000	2001	2002	2003	2004	Average annual percent change, 2001–2004
GROSS STATE PRODUCT	15 501	16 155	16 896	17 661	18 350	18 748	19 562	20 454	3.7
As a percent of U.S. gross product	0.2	0.2	0.2	0.2	0.2	0.2	0.2	0.2	X
Private Industries	13 449	14 061	14 767	15 426	16 030	16 391	17 145	17 957	3.9
Agriculture, forestry, fishing, and hunting	220	253	285	321	290	267	274	243	-5.7
Mining	21	24	26	27	28	27	27	23	-6.3
Utilities	455	437	459	477	411	433	496	562	11.0
Construction	732	782	787	742	787	758	787	844	2.4
Manufacturing	2 031	2 251	2 482	2 823	2 971	2 990	3 188	3 340	4.0
As a percent of gross state product	13.1	13.9	14.7	16.0	16.2	15.9	16.3	16.3	X
Wholesale trade	772	815	833	807	964	1 030	1 064	1 050	2.9
Retail trade	1 256	1 292	1 366	1 420	1 576	1 705	1 806	1 930	7.0
Transportation and warehousing	379	385	391	423	389	398	408	420	2.6
Information	576	618	617	651	702	721	790	850	6.6
Finance and insurance	923	936	953	1 004	1 062	1 075	1 158	1 178	3.5
Real estate and rental and leasing	1 988	2 017	2 086	2 112	2 304	2 284	2 291	2 455	2.1
Services	4 171	4 290	4 499	4 620	4 557	4 723	4 894	5 106	3.9
As a percent of gross state product	26.9	26.6	26.6	26.2	24.8	25.2	25.0	25.0	X
Professional and technical services	808	864	937	980	947	965	1 036	1 082	4.5
Management of companies and enterprises	121	120	143	132	37	42	44	44	5.9
Administrative and waste services	316	337	338	313	325	339	354	404	7.5
Educational services	325	334	344	348	333	325	316	315	-1.8
Health care and social assistance	1 268	1 277	1 357	1 422	1 520	1 621	1 693	1 739	4.6
Arts, entertainment, and recreation	147	156	160	150	143	155	157	166	5.1
Accommodation and food services	750	760	781	813	805	850	858	891	3.4
Other services, except public administration	436	442	439	462	447	426	436	465	1.3
Government	2 058	2 097	2 129	2 235	2 320	2 358	2 420	2 502	2.5
As a percent of gross state product	13.3	13.0	12.6	12.7	12.6	12.6	12.4	12.2	X

X = Not applicable.

Table VT-12. Government Transfer Payments, Selected Years 1980–2004

(Millions of dollars, percent.)

Item	1980	1990	2000	2001	2002	2003	2004	Average annual percent change, 2000–2004
CURRENT TRANSFER PAYMENTS TO INDIVIDUALS	584	1 161	2 245	2 458	2 677	2 843	2 991	7.4
Retirement and Disability Insurance Benefits	284	559	938	994	1 044	1 090	1 142	5.0
Old-age, survivors, and disability insurance (OASDI) benefits	273	542	918	973	1 023	1 068	1 119	5.1
Railroad retirement and disability benefits	11	15	14	14	14	14	14	0.1
Workers' compensation	*	2	3	4	4	4	4	5.6
Other government retirement and disability insurance benefits	*	*	3	3	3	4	4	12.9
Medical Benefits	130	345	950	1 070	1 165	1 257	1 374	9.7
Medicare benefits	69	178	405	449	482	511	562	8.5
Public assistance medical care benefits	59	164	541	616	675	740	806	10.4
Military medical insurance benefits	1	3	3	5	7	6	7	17.4
Income Maintenance Benefits	88	145	230	234	247	267	281	5.1
Supplemental Security Income (SSI) benefits	16	31	52	54	56	58	60	3.8
Family assistance	32	52	54	54	58	59	60	2.6
Food stamps	19	24	31	32	34	38	42	7.3
Other income maintenance benefits	21	39	92	94	99	113	119	6.5
Unemployment Insurance Compensation	35	53	44	65	112	121	84	17.4
Veterans' Benefits	35	43	58	65	77	82	82	9.2
Federal Education and Training Assistance	13	15	24	27	30	26	27	3.1
Other Payments to Individuals	*	*	2	3	1	1	1	-4.5

Note: See notes and definitions for more details. Data may not add to total or may appear as zero due to rounding.

* = Less than $500,000.

EXPORTS

Vermont was a relatively small exporter of goods, ranking 33rd in nation for the value of its exports. In 2004, exports amounted to $3.3 billion, which represented a 16 percent increase from 2001. The state's primary exports were computers and electronic products, which accounted for 78.5 percent of total exports. Machinery manufactures and transportation equipment followed distantly as the second and third leading exports. Exports of transportation equipment and fabricated metal products fell significantly from 2001 to 2004. Canada was by far the state's largest export market, followed by Taiwan and South Korea. Vermont's fastest-growing overseas markets were located in Southeast Asia.

Leading Exports, 2004

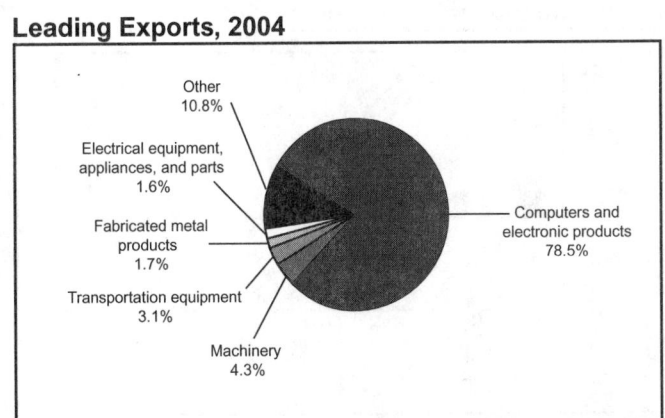

Table VT-13. Exports of Goods by Leading Products and Destinations, 2001–2004

(Millions of dollars, percent, rank based on 2004 dollar values.)

Product and market	2001	2002	2003	2004	Percent share of total, 2004	Average annual percent change, 2001–2004
Total Goods						
Total	2 830	2 521	2 627	3 283	100.0	5.1
Manufactures	2 701	2 422	2 541	3 194	97.3	5.7
Agriculture and livestock	56	55	56	58	1.8	0.9
Other commodities	73	44	29	32	1.0	-24.4
Five Leading Exports (NAICS Code)						
Computers and electronic products (334)	2 037	1 864	1 976	2 578	78.5	8.2
Machinery manufactures (333)	110	103	127	140	4.3	8.4
Transportation equipment (336)	122	91	79	101	3.1	-6.1
Fabricated metal products (332)	80	58	49	57	1.7	-10.9
Electrical equipment, appliances, and parts (335)	34	36	45	53	1.6	15.7
Five Leading Markets	2 713	2 463	2 555	3 233	98.5	6.0
Canada	1 390	1 054	1 079	1 516	46.2	2.9
Taiwan	191	326	416	512	15.6	38.9
South Korea	187	332	243	260	7.9	11.5
Hong Kong	51	37	49	139	4.2	39.8
Singapore	21	41	141	133	4.0	86.4

Table VT-14. Agriculture, 1997 and 2002

(Number, acres, and dollars.)

Item	1997	2002
Number of farms	7 063	6 571
Land in farms (acres)	1 315 315	1 244 909
Farm Size		
Average size of farm (acres)	186	189
Farms by size (percent distribution)		
Fewer than 50 acres	30.8	33.7
50 to 499 acres	61.2	57.9
500 acres or more	8.0	8.4
Market Value of Land and Equipment (Dollars)		
Land and buildings average value per farm	303 211	386 695
Average value per acre	1 618	2 051
Machinery and equipment average value per farm	44 275	66 094
Value of Sales (Thousands of Dollars)		
Agricultural products sold	478 781	473 065
Crops	63 775	71 583
Livestock, poultry, and their products	415 007	401 482
Average per farm (dollars)	67 787	71 993
Value of sales (percent distribution)		
Less than $10,000	56.8	60.6
$10,000 to $99,999	24.7	21.6
$100,000 or more	18.5	17.8
Government Payments		
Payments (thousands of dollars)	2 972	24 377
Percent of farms receiving government payments	16.3	19.7
Farm operators whose principal occupation is farming (percent)	51.2	53.1

AGRICULTURE

Cash receipts from farming amounted to $473 million in 2002, according to the Department of Agriculture's Census of Agriculture. This reflected a slight decline from the previous agriculture census in 1997. Dairy products, particularly butter, cheese, and milk, were predominant. Over 60 percent of farms reported sales of less than $10,000, and 17.8 percent had sales of $100,000 or more. Just over half of farm operators reported farming as their principal occupation. Less than 34 percent of farms spanned fewer than 50 acres, which was close to the national average for farms of this size.

ENERGY

Energy expenditures per person were the 13th highest in the nation in 2001. This reflected Vermont's high cost of energy, which was the fourth highest in the country. The state's per capita consumption was well below average, ranking 44th in the nation. Like its New England neighbors, Vermont's chief energy source was petroleum, with nuclear power ranking second.

Energy Consumption by Source, 2001

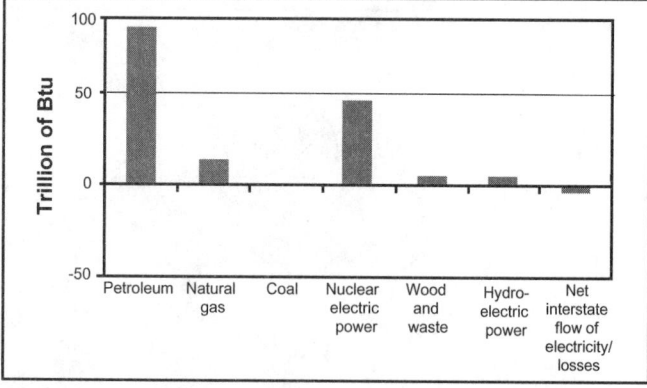

Energy Consumption by Sector, 2001

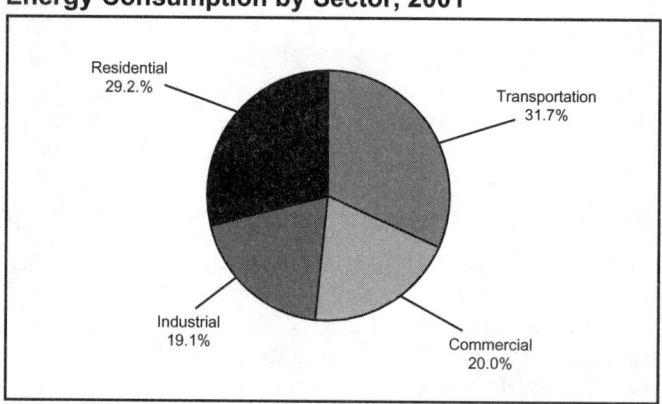

Table VT-15. Energy Consumption, Expenditures, and Prices, Selected Years 1960–2001

(Dollars, Btu [British Thermal Unit], percent distribution.)

Item	1960	1965	1970	1975	1980	1985	1990	1995	2000	2001
Total Consumption (Billion Btu)	68 629	83 174	113 222	114 368	124 746	134 250	135 524	150 312	165 074	163 614
Consumption per capita (million Btu)	176.0	205.9	254.6	238.4	243.9	253.3	240.8	257.9	271.1	266.9
Consumption by Sector (Percent Distribution)										
Residential	39.1	41.2	39.0	36.5	32.5	30.8	31.8	30.5	29.2	29.2
Commercial	12.4	13.2	13.9	13.9	14.1	13.2	18.6	17.7	19.6	20.0
Industrial	20.4	20.1	21.3	20.4	26.2	28.5	18.6	18.7	19.8	19.1
Transportation	28.1	25.4	25.8	29.2	27.2	27.5	31.0	33.1	31.4	31.7
Consumption by Source (Billion Btu)										
Coal	3 507	2 707	2 129	744	537	1 982	201	74	26	54
Natural gas	0	0	2 679	4 005	3 951	4 958	6 679	7 263	10 551	8 015
Petroleum	46 697	58 990	73 883	68 927	61 597	68 310	71 750	80 259	87 854	88 891
Nuclear electric power	0	0	0	39 220	32 497	31 860	38 267	40 541	47 432	43 580
Hydroelectric power[1]	9 396	7 464	8 244	9 761	8 449	9 635	14 199	10 030	12 456	8 996
Wood and waste	7 943	6 932	6 472	6 600	13 300	16 942	5 187	9 392	9 368	8 697
Other	220	139	170	257	637	1 094	5 841	13 509	9 753	9 178
Net interstate flow of electricity/losses[2]	867	6 942	19 646	-15 146	3 778	-532	-6 601	-10 756	-12 367	-3 796
Total Expenditures (Thousands of Dollars)	...	...	204 200	365 200	737 900	922 700	1 078 400	1 212 200	1 634 100	1 660 300
Expenditures per capita (dollars)	...	...	459	761	1 443	1 741	1 916	2 080	2 684	2 709
Prices by Sector (Dollars Per Million Btu)										
Total	...	...	2.37	4.33	9.01	10.11	11.24	11.23	13.77	14.08
Residential	...	...	2.20	4.41	9.31	10.56	12.62	12.87	16.01	16.88
Commercial	...	...	2.17	4.49	8.91	12.18	13.91	15.14	16.84	17.91
Industrial	...	...	1.69	3.59	6.89	9.56	10.83	10.37	10.27	11.79
Transportation	...	...	2.94	4.49	9.72	9.46	9.62	9.43	12.59	11.84

[1]A negative number in this row results from pumped storage for which, overall, more electricity is expended than created to provide electricity during peak demand periods.
[2]Net interstate flow of electricity is the difference between the amount of energy in the electricity sold within a state (including associated losses) and the energy input at the electric utilities within the state. A positive number indicates that more electricity (including associated losses) came into the state than went out of the state during the year; conversely, a negative number indicates that more electricity (including associated losses) went out of the state than came into the state.
... = Not available.

Table VT-16. State Taxes, Fiscal 2004

(Dollars, percent distribution.)

Item	Thousands of dollars	Percent distribution	Dollars per capita	
			State	U.S.
TOTAL TAXES	1 766 719	100.0	2 845.0	2 024.8
Property Taxes	448 203	25.4	721.7	38.9
Sales and Gross Receipts	687 595	38.9	1 107.2	1 003.4
General sales and gross receipts	256 958	14.5	413.8	677.0
Selective sales taxes	430 637	24.4	693.5	326.4
Alcoholic beverages	16 894	1.0	27.2	15.7
Insurance premiums	49 018	2.8	78.9	47.0
Motor fuels	85 994	4.9	138.5	114.6
Public utilities	10 769	0.6	17.3	39.2
Tobacco products	51 182	2.9	82.4	42.0
Other selective sales	216 780	12.3	349.1	49.8
Licenses	98 758	5.6	159.0	134.9
Motor vehicle	62 566	3.5	100.8	59.4
Occupation and business, not elsewhere classified	18 873	1.1	30.4	37.1
Other Taxes	532 163	30.1	857.0	847.6
Individual income	429 817	24.3	692.1	673.6
Corporation net income	62 228	3.5	100.2	105.1
Death and gift	14 712	0.8	23.7	19.6
Documentary and stock transfer	20 762	1.2	33.4	27.1

GOVERNMENT FINANCE

With per capita revenues of $5,416 in 2003, Vermont ranked 4th in the country. The state's expenditures per person were the second highest in the country. Revenues per capita were 40 percent above the U.S. average, and spending was more than 60 percent higher than average. Outlays per person were above average for all categories, except for health and hospitals. Tax collections also exceeded the national average, with the largest shares derived from property taxes, selective sales taxes, and individual income taxes. Vermont's per capita individual income taxes were slightly above average, but its property taxes were the highest in the country.

Per Capita State Taxes, Fiscal 2004

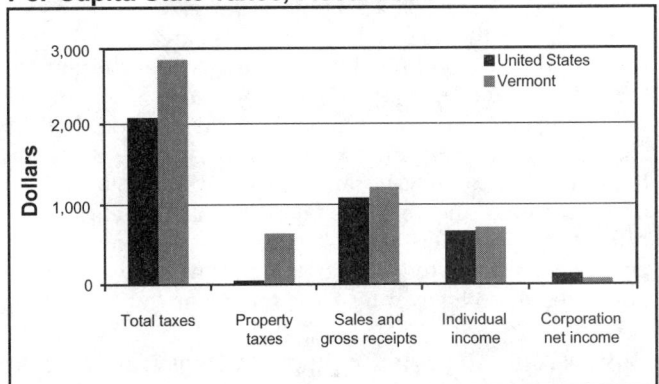

Table VT-17. State Government Finances, 2003

(Dollars, percent distribution.)

Item	Millions of dollars	Percent distribution	Dollars per capita	
			State	U.S.
GENERAL REVENUE	3 352 248	100.0	5 415.6	3 832.6
Intergovernmental revenue	1 152 305	34.4	1 861.6	1 246.0
Taxes	1 558 712	46.5	2 518.1	1 891.6
General sales	220 827	6.6	356.8	636.0
Selective sales	326 635	9.7	527.7	307.4
License taxes	102 721	3.1	166.0	123.6
Individual income tax	411 343	12.3	664.5	626.8
Corporate income tax	41 641	1.2	67.3	97.8
Other taxes	455 545	13.6	735.9	99.9
Current charges	345 241	10.3	557.7	366.5
Miscellaneous general revenue	295 990	8.8	478.2	328.6
GENERAL EXPENDITURE	3 593 817	100.0	5 805.8	4 010.5
Intergovernmental expenditure	938 085	26.1	1 515.5	1 316.9
Direct expenditure	2 655 732	73.9	4 290.4	2 693.6
Expenditure by Function				
Education	1 442 926	40.2	2 331.1	1 416.4
Public welfare	913 772	25.4	1 476.2	1 083.3
Hospitals	13 024	0.4	21.0	132.3
Health	78 710	2.2	127.2	173.0
Highways	300 353	8.4	485.2	295.4
Police protection	59 903	1.7	96.8	38.4
Correction	81 767	2.3	132.1	135.0
Natural resources	92 995	2.6	150.2	64.0
Parks and recreation	11 860	0.3	19.2	20.1
Government administration	195 330	5.4	315.6	151.3
Interest on general debt	141 884	3.9	229.2	107.8
Other and unallocable	261 293	7.3	422.1	393.4
DEBT AT END OF FISCAL YEAR	2 532 071	X	4 090.6	2 404.7
CASH AND SECURITY HOLDINGS	4 916 965	X	7 943.4	8 938.4

X = Not applicable.

Table VT-18. Education Indicators, 2000–2004

(Percent, number.)

Item	State	U.S.
Total Population 25 Years and Over (Thousands), 2004	416	186 877
Educational Attainment, 2004		
Percent high school graduate or more	90.8	85.2
Percent college graduate or more	34.2	27.7
Elementary and Secondary Schools, 2002–2003		
Total students	99 978	48 202 324
Percent of students eligible for free or reduced-price lunch ..	27.4	40.6
Percent of students who were English language learners	2.0	7.8
Total schools	359	92 330
Student/teacher ratio	11.3	15.9
Per student expenditures	10 454	8 041
Dropouts, Grades 9–12, 2000–2001 (Percent)	4.0	. . .
Higher Education, 2002–2003		
Total enrollment	36 630	17 035 027
Bachelor's degrees awarded	4 545	1 348 503
Percent women	55.3	57.5

. . . = Not available.

Educational Attainment, 2004

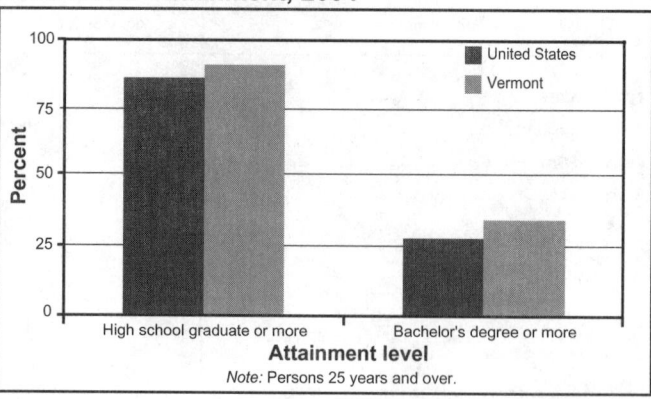

Note: Persons 25 years and over.

EDUCATION

Nearly 90 percent of Vermont's residents age 25 years and over held high school diplomas, the sixth highest proportion in the nation. More than 34 percent of residents in this age group held bachelor's degrees or more, the eighth highest proportion in the country. Vermont's student/teacher ratio was the lowest in the nation. The state's expenditures per student of $10,454 were the sixth highest in the country. Vermont had the 19th highest dropout rate of the 46 states reporting such data, with a rate of 4 percent. Less than 28 percent of students were eligible for free or reduced-price lunch, which was well below the national average of 40.6 percent.

VOTER PARTICIPATION

Voter turnout for both the 2000 and 2004 elections was far above the national average. In 2000, 63.3 percent of eligible voters cast ballots; this proportion increased to 65.4 percent in 2004. Nearly 75 percent of eligible voters age 45 to 64 years participated in the 2004 election. According to the official tally by the Clerk of the U.S. House of Representatives, 50.6 percent of voters cast ballots for the Democratic presidential candidate in 2000, and 58.9 percent voted similarly in 2004. The comparable percentages for the Republican candidate were 40.7 percent and 38.8 percent, respectively.

Table VT-19. Reported Voting and Registration, November 2000 and November 2004

(Numbers in thousands, percent.)

Characteristic	Total population 18 years and over	Total citizen		Total registered		Total voted	
		Number	Percent	Number	Percent	Number	Percent
NOVEMBER 2000							
Total	458	451	98.5	330	72.0	290	63.3
Male	221	216	98.1	152	68.8	131	59.1
Female	238	235	98.8	178	74.9	159	67.1
NOVEMBER 2004							
Total	482	469	97.2	354	73.5	316	65.4
Male	233	228	97.5	168	72.1	147	63.2
Female	249	241	96.9	186	74.7	168	67.6
Race and Hispanic Origin							
White alone	463	454	98.0	344	74.4	308	66.5
Non-Hispanic White alone	460	450	98.0	342	74.4	306	66.5
Black alone	2	1	B	-	B	-	B
Asian alone	7	3	B	2	B	1	B
Hispanic or Latino[1]	3	3	B	2	B	2	B
White alone or in combination	471	461	98.1	350	74.4	312	66.3
Non-Hispanic White alone or in combination	467	458	98.0	348	74.4	310	66.3
Black alone or in combination	2	1	B	-	B	-	B
Asian alone or in combination	8	4	B	2	B	2	B
Age							
18 to 24 years	59	58	B	32	B	25	B
25 to 44 years	168	159	94.3	115	68.1	101	59.8
45 to 64 years	167	165	99.0	136	81.8	127	76.2
65 to 74 years	46	45	B	36	B	33	B
75 years and over	42	42	B	36	B	30	B

[1]May be of any race.
- = Represents zero or rounds to zero.
B = Base is too small to show derived measure.

At a Glance:

- Virginia's population was almost 7.5 million in 2004, making it the 12th most populous state in the country.

- More than 19 percent of the state's residents were Black, which was the 10th highest proportion of this racial group in the nation. With Asians and Pacific Islanders representing 4.4 percent of the population, Virginia also had the 10th highest proportion of that racial group in the country.

- The state's median household income of $51,438 was above average and ranked ninth in the nation. Virginia's poverty rate of 9.3 percent was among the lowest in the country.

- Although Virginia's economy was notably impacted by the 2001 recession, the subsequent growth of its real gross state product (GSP) has been substantial. From 2003 to 2004, the GSP grew 6.3 percent, the third highest rate of growth in the nation. The state's unemployment rate of 3.7 percent was among the five lowest in the country.

- An above average proportion of Virginia's population age 25 years and over held high school diplomas. Among the same age group, the state ranked ninth in the nation for proportion of college graduates.

Table VA-1. Population by Sex and Age, 1990, 2000, and 2004

(Number, percent.)

Sex and age	1990	2000	2004	Percent distribution, 2004	Average annual percent change, 2000–2004
Total Population	6 187 358	7 078 515	7 459 827	X	1.3
Percent of total U.S. population	2.5	2.5	2.5	X	X
Sex					
Male	3 033 974	3 471 895	3 671 433	49.2	1.4
Female	3 153 384	3 606 620	3 788 394	50.8	1.2
Age					
Under 5 years	443 155	461 982	498 386	6.7	0.7
5 to 17 years	1 061 583	1 276 280	1 306 514	17.5	1.5
18 years and over	1 165 975	5 340 253	5 654 927	75.8	1.4
18 to 24 years	4 682 620	679 398	748 049	10.0	0.2
25 to 44 years	719 731	2 237 655	2 188 434	29.3	0.2
45 to 64 years	2 132 444	1 630 867	1 871 523	25.1	3.5
65 years and over	664 470	792 333	846 921	11.4	1.8
85 years and over	59 709	87 266	102 561	1.4	4.1
Median age (years)	32.5	35.7	36.5	X	X

X = Not applicable.

Average Annual Rate of Population Growth, 1980–2004

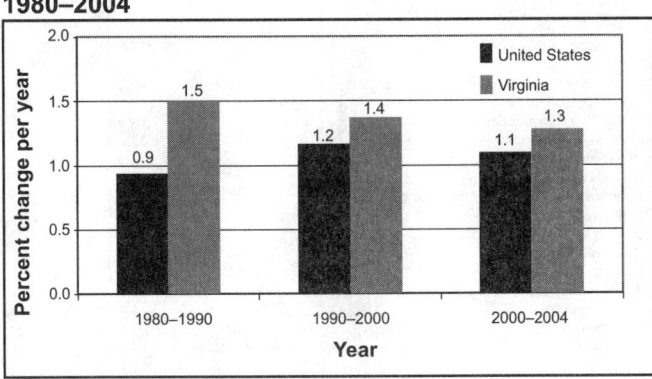

POPULATION

Virginia's population has grown quite quickly during recent years, primarily in the northern area of the state, which is near the District of Columbia. From 2000 to 2004, the state's population increased by 5.4 percent, a rate well above the national average. Virginia was also home to Loudoun County, the fastest-growing county in the nation (among counties with populations exceeding 10,000 people). This county experienced a population increase of 41 percent from 2000 to 2004. Over the 2000–2004 period, Virginia was the recipient of significant domestic and international immigration, which together accounted for about two-thirds of the state's population growth. Virginia had the seventh highest number of new residents from other states.

Table VA-2. Population by Race and Hispanic Origin, 1990, 2000, and 2004

(Number, percent.)

Race and Hispanic origin	1990	2000	2004
Total Population	6 187 358	7 078 515	7 459 827
Non-Hispanic (Percent)			
One race[1]			
White	76.0	70.5	68.7
Black	18.6	19.6	19.5
American Indian, Alaska Native[2]	0.2	0.3	0.3
Asian and Pacific Islander[2]	2.6	3.8	4.4
Other race[2]	0.9	. . .	. . .
Two or more races	. . .	1.3	1.4
Hispanic or Latino[3] (Percent)	2.6	4.7	5.7

[1]Individuals could report only one race in the 1990 census and could report one or more races on the 2000 census. Data on race in 2000 and 2004 are not comparable to 1990.
[2]Data for 1990 include people of Hispanic or Latino origin.
[3]May be of any race.
. . . = Not available.

Minority Population as a Percent of Total Population, 2004

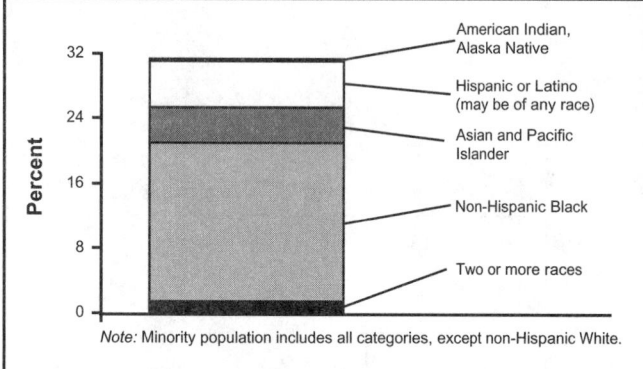

Note: Minority population includes all categories, except non-Hispanic White.

Age-Adjusted Death Rates, Average 2000–2002

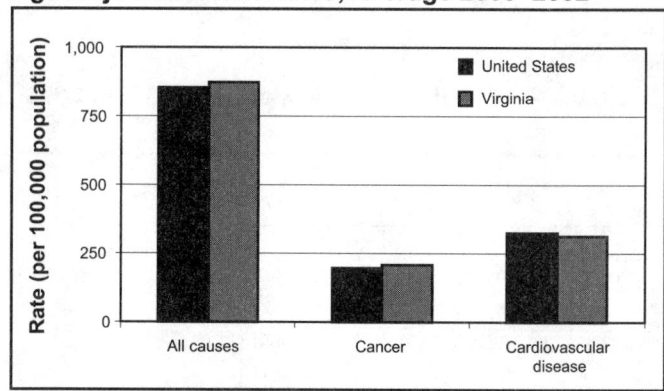

HEALTH

Virginia's rate of health insurance coverage was below the national average, with 14.4 percent of the state's residents lacking coverage. Its infant mortality rate was above average, as were its age-adjusted death rates for leading causes. Virginia's birth rate was slightly below the national average.

Table VA-3. Health Characteristics, 2000–2004

(Number, rate, percent.)

Item	State	U.S.
Births, 2003–2004		
Number of births	101 254	4 089 950
Birth rate (per 1,000 population)	13.7	14.1
Teenage birth rate (per 1,000 women age 15–19 years)	36.1	41.6
Mortality Rates, Average 2000–2002		
Infant mortality rate (per 1,000 live births)	7.2	6.9
Age-adjusted mortality rate (per 100,000 population)		
All races	867.0	853.3
Non-Hispanic White	836.4	843.1
Black	1 085.6	1 097.7
American Indian, Alaska Native	. . .	687.0
Asian and Pacific Islander	441.2	486.0
Hispanic or Latino[1]	490.4	642.7
Health Insurance, 2004		
Percent of all persons without health insurance	14.4	15.7
Percent of children without health insurance	8.1	11.2
Percent of low-income children without health insurance	4.5	7.1

[1]May be of any race.
. . . = Not available.

Table VA-4. Leading Causes of Death, Average 2000–2002

(Number, rate per 100,000 population.)

Cause	Number of deaths	Age-adjusted death rates	
		State	U.S.
ALL CAUSES	56 586	867.0	853.3
Leading Causes			
Major cardiovascular diseases	20 349	317.9	326.5
Cancer	13 492	202.3	196.0
Chronic lower respiratory diseases	2 772	43.2	43.7
Unintentional injuries	2 436	35.1	35.7
Diabetes (underlying cause)	1 578	23.9	25.2
Influenza and pneumonia	1 490	23.9	22.7
Alzheimer's disease	1 215	19.9	19.0
Motor vehicle accidents	943	13.2	15.0
Nephritis, nephrotic syndrome, and nephrosis ..	1 161	18.1	13.8
Septicemia	1 117	17.3	11.4
Suicides	788	10.9	10.7
Firearm-related	790	10.9	10.3
Cirrhosis	567	8.1	9.5
Drug-induced	490	6.6	7.9
Alcohol-induced	342	4.7	6.9
Homicides	412	5.6	6.0
Falls	311	4.8	5.2
HIV	275	3.7	5.0
Viral hepatitis	96	1.3	2.0
Anemias	113	1.7	1.6
Drownings	94	1.3	1.3
Fire deaths	85	1.2	1.2

Note: The rates are age-adjusted to the U.S. 2000 standard population.

Table VA-5. Households and Housing Characteristics, 1990, 2000, and 2004

(Number, percent, and dollars.)

Characteristic	1990	2000	2004	Average annual percent change, 2000–2004
Total Households	2 291 830	2 699 173	2 846 417	1.3
Family households	1 629 490	1 847 796	1 952 639	1.4
Married-couple family	1 302 219	1 426 044	1 484 627	1.0
Other family	327 271	421 752	468 012	2.6
Male householder, no wife present	72 165	101 462	109 279	1.9
Female householder, no husband present	255 106	320 290	358 733	2.9
Nonfamily households	662 340	851 377	893 778	1.2
Householder living alone	523 770	676 907	728 672	1.9
Householder not living alone	138 570	174 470	165 106	-1.4
Housing Characteristics				
Average size	2.61	2.54	2.54	X
Housing units	2 496 334	2 904 192	3 116 827	1.8
Occupied housing units	2 291 830	2 699 173	2 846 417	1.3
Owner-occupied	1 519 521	1 837 939	1 968 555	1.7
Renter-occupied	772 309	861 234	877 862	0.5
Median gross rent of renter-occupied housing units (dollars)	495	650	757	3.9
Median value of owner-occupied housing units (dollars)	90 400	125 400	179 191	9.3

X = Not applicable.

Median Housing Value and Median Rent, 2004

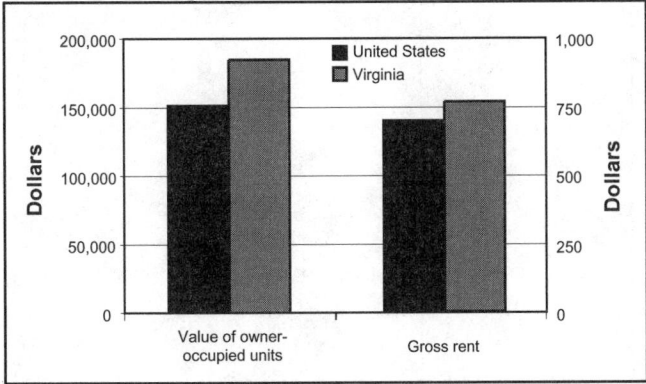

Median Household Income, 1984–2004 (2004 Dollars)

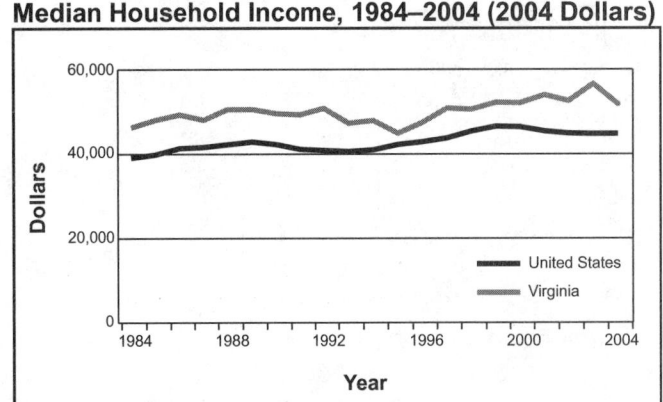

Table VA-6. Household Income and Poverty Status, 1980–2004

(2004 CPI-U-RS adjusted dollars, rate.)

Year	State		U.S.	
	Median household income (2004 dollars)	Poverty rate	Median household income (2004 dollars)	Poverty rate
2004	51 438	9.3	44 389	12.7
2003	56 255	10.0	44 482	12.5
2002	52 132	9.9	44 546	12.1
2001	53 612	8.0	45 062	11.7
2000	51 733	8.3	46 058	11.3
1999	51 793	7.9	46 129	11.9
1998	50 175	8.8	45 003	12.7
1997	50 416	12.7	43 430	13.3
1996	47 002	12.3	42 544	13.7
1995	44 585	10.2	41 943	13.8
1994	47 464	10.7	40 677	14.5
1993	46 901	9.7	40 217	15.1
1992	50 399	9.5	40 422	14.8
1991	48 876	9.9	40 746	14.2
1990	49 152	11.1	41 963	13.5
1989	50 192	10.9	42 524	12.8
1988	50 092	10.8	41 771	13.0
1987	47 699	9.9	41 322	13.4
1986	48 862	9.7	40 939	13.6
1985	47 601	10.0	39 545	14.0
1984	45 893	10.0	38 782	14.4
1983	. . .	11.3	. . .	15.2
1982	. . .	12.5	. . .	15.0
1981	. . .	12.6	. . .	14.0
1980	. . .	12.4	. . .	13.0

. . . = Not available.

Table VA-7. Employment Status by Demographic Group, 2004

(Numbers in thousands, rate.)

Characteristic	Civilian noninstitutional population	Civilian labor force		Employed	Unemployment rate
		Number	Participation rate		
SEX AND AGE					
Total	5 605	3 766	67.2	3 619	3.9
16 to 19 years	414	182	43.9	162	10.9
20 to 24 years	466	354	76.0	327	7.7
25 to 34 years	904	753	83.3	721	4.3
35 to 44 years	1 164	988	84.9	958	3.0
45 to 54 years	1 064	865	81.3	838	3.1
55 to 64 years	763	500	65.5	493	1.3
65 years and over	830	124	15.0	120	3.3
Men	2 660	1 975	74.3	1 901	3.8
16 to 19 years	215	97	45.0	86	11.3
20 to 24 years	236	190	80.5	175	7.7
25 to 34 years	430	401	93.1	384	4.3
35 to 44 years	542	497	91.5	483	2.7
45 to 54 years	521	452	86.8	441	2.5
55 to 64 years	360	266	73.8	261	1.6
Women	2 945	1 791	60.8	1 718	4.0
16 to 19 years	198	85	42.7	76	10.4
20 to 24 years	230	164	71.5	152	7.6
25 to 34 years	474	352	74.3	337	4.3
35 to 44 years	622	491	79.0	475	3.4
45 to 54 years	543	412	75.9	397	3.8
55 to 64 years	403	234	58.1	232	1.0
MARITAL STATUS					
Married men, spouse present	1 533	1 207	78.7	1 185	1.8
Married women, spouse present	1 566	982	62.7	956	2.7
Women who maintain families	335	239	71.4	226	5.3
RACE, HISPANIC ORIGIN, AND SEX					
White	4 237	2 849	67.2	2 764	3.0
Men	2 052	1 540	75.0	1 494	3.0
Women	2 185	1 309	59.9	1 271	2.9
Black	1 036	681	65.7	629	7.7
Men	460	314	68.4	291	7.6
Women	576	367	63.6	338	7.7
Asian	270	192	71.0	184	4.2
Men	122	99	81.0	95	3.7
Women	148	93	62.8	89	4.8
Hispanic or Latino[1]	276	223	80.8	213	4.7
Men	159	146	91.8	139	4.9
RACE, HISPANIC ORIGIN, AND AGE					
White					
16 to 19 years	286	130	45.5	116	11.0
20 to 24 years	322	250	77.6	239	4.5
25 to 34 years	660	554	83.9	531	4.2
35 to 44 years	864	736	85.2	721	2.0
45 to 54 years	820	673	82.0	659	2.0
55 to 64 years	608	405	66.7	401	1.1
65 years and over	677	101	15.0	98	3.2

Note: Data in Table 7 are from the Current Population Survey (CPS) and do not match Bureau of Labor Statistics estimates in Table 8. See notes and definitions for more details.

[1]May be of any race.

Table VA-8. Employment Status, 1990–2004

(Numbers in thousands, rate.)

Year	Civilian labor force	Employed	Unemployed	Unemployment rate
2004	3 814 793	3 674 434	140 359	3.7
2003	3 766 801	3 612 229	154 572	4.1
2002	3 716 127	3 560 462	155 665	4.2
2001	3 641 231	3 524 335	116 896	3.2
2000	3 572 790	3 491 294	81 496	2.3
1999	3 536 409	3 441 589	94 820	2.7
1998	3 483 900	3 384 653	99 247	2.8
1997	3 450 181	3 323 266	126 915	3.7
1996	3 400 416	3 252 499	147 917	4.3
1995	3 472 328	3 317 434	154 894	4.5
1994	3 426 621	3 265 139	161 482	4.7
1993	3 369 606	3 195 680	173 926	5.2
1992	3 353 338	3 146 997	206 341	6.2
1991	3 296 942	3 103 294	193 648	5.9
1990	3 220 117	3 076 925	143 192	4.4

Note: Population age 16 years and over.

Unemployment Rate, 1980–2004

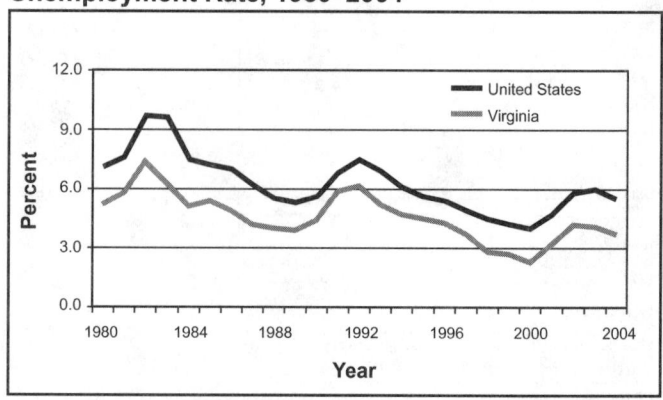

Table VA-9. Employment and Average Wages by Industry, 2001–2004

(Estimates are based on the 2002 North American Industry Classification System [NAICS].)

Industry	2001	2002	2003	2004	Annual average percent change, 2001–2004
	Number of jobs				
TOTAL EMPLOYMENT BY PLACE OF WORK	4 439 053	4 439 914	4 482 439	4 593 698	1.1
Farm Employment	59 796	61 498	61 637	60 126	0.2
Nonfarm Employment	4 379 257	4 378 416	4 420 802	4 533 572	1.2
Private employment	3 567 488	3 555 159	3 594 610	3 695 847	1.2
Forestry, fishing, hunting, and other[1]	14 037	14 480	13 115	12 854	-2.9
Mining	11 927	11 119	11 213	11 518	-1.2
Utilities	12 283	12 226	12 334	12 201	-0.2
Construction	292 562	289 451	300 436	316 304	2.6
Manufacturing	352 759	330 962	314 403	308 369	-4.4
Durable goods manufacturing	196 934	182 919	172 801	172 935	-4.2
Nondurable goods manufacturing	155 825	148 043	141 602	135 434	-4.6
Wholesale trade	124 978	122 733	122 846	125 341	0.1
Retail trade	483 600	485 937	489 631	502 925	1.3
Transportation and warehousing	138 005	133 134	133 502	134 659	-0.8
Information	131 428	117 200	113 794	111 926	-5.2
Finance and insurance	165 340	169 569	172 152	172 510	1.4
Real estate and rental and leasing	140 780	144 288	154 556	162 636	4.9
Professional and technical services	387 684	387 084	395 949	417 870	2.5
Management of companies and enterprises	73 603	70 029	69 326	71 411	-1.0
Administrative and waste services	242 521	242 907	243 803	255 651	1.8
Educational services	67 269	69 310	72 422	75 053	3.7
Health care and social assistance	334 822	345 318	354 318	364 060	2.8
Arts, entertainment, and recreation	76 754	80 439	79 648	81 855	2.2
Accommodation and food services	273 556	275 052	282 375	293 815	2.4
Other services, except public administration	243 580	253 921	258 787	264 889	2.8
Government and government enterprises	811 769	823 257	826 192	837 725	1.1
	Dollars				
AVERAGE WAGES AND SALARIES BY PLACE OF WORK	36 245	36 907	38 328	40 332	3.6
Farm Earnings	17 944	19 205	18 051	22 197	7.3
Nonfarm Earnings	36 298	36 965	38 402	40 389	3.6
Private earnings	36 164	36 401	37 773	39 722	3.2
Forestry, fishing, hunting, and other[1]	20 174	21 041	21 827	23 020	4.5
Mining	44 670	44 732	45 861	49 666	3.6
Utilities	63 819	66 101	72 740	75 159	5.6
Construction	34 826	35 632	36 271	38 359	3.3
Manufacturing	37 950	38 917	40 466	41 938	3.4
Durable goods manufacturing	39 408	39 805	41 553	42 990	2.9
Nondurable goods manufacturing	36 115	37 823	39 146	40 600	4.0
Wholesale trade	51 394	51 144	52 904	56 229	3.0
Retail trade	21 262	21 978	22 631	23 382	3.2
Transportation and warehousing	36 013	37 284	37 218	38 728	2.5
Information	76 649	64 984	67 377	71 779	-2.2
Finance and insurance	54 956	56 142	61 204	65 117	5.8
Real estate and rental and leasing	32 970	33 740	35 062	37 789	4.7
Professional and technical services	62 094	63 520	66 275	69 534	3.8
Management of companies and enterprises	64 663	69 442	72 373	79 851	7.3
Administrative and waste services	23 356	24 086	25 455	27 393	5.5
Educational services	25 411	27 055	27 983	29 830	5.5
Health care and social assistance	32 203	33 662	34 555	35 938	3.7
Arts, entertainment, and recreation	18 328	19 235	20 528	20 682	4.1
Accommodation and food services	13 720	14 047	14 482	15 048	3.1
Other services, except public administration	25 152	25 595	26 475	27 578	3.1
Government and government enterprises	36 788	38 974	40 639	42 789	5.2

Note: Average wages and salaries are a calculation by the editors of wage and salary disbursements divided by full- and part-time wage and salary employment. Data may not add to total or may appear as zero due to rounding.

[1] "Other" consists of the number of jobs held by U.S. residents employed by international organizations and foreign embassies and consulates in the United States.

LABOR MARKET

Since the early 1990s, Virginia's unemployment rate has been below the national average and similar to that of Maryland. Neighboring West Virginia and the District of Columbia experienced much higher unemployment rates. Employment grew steadily throughout the 2001–2004 period, as declines in manufacturing and information were more than offset by substantial gains in retail trade, real estate and related activities, health care, construction, and accommodation and food services. Average wages and salaries were above the national average, ranking 10th in the country. Over the 2001–2004 period, average wages and salaries increased by 11.3 percent, which was an above average rate of growth.

Employment by Industry, 2004

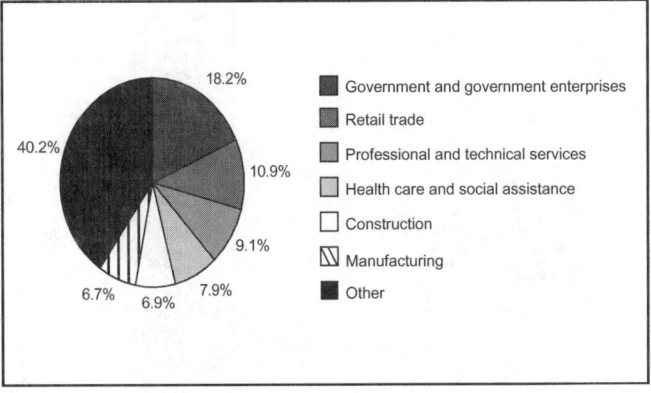

- Government and government enterprises
- Retail trade
- Professional and technical services
- Health care and social assistance
- Construction
- Manufacturing
- Other

40.2% · 18.2% · 10.9% · 9.1% · 7.9% · 6.9% · 6.7%

Table VA-10. Personal Income by Major Source, Selected Years 1980–2004

(Millions of dollars, except where noted.)

Item	1980	1990	2000	2001	2002	2003	2004	Average annual percent change, 2000–2004
Earnings by Place of Work	41 421	96 819	172 507	183 052	187 922	196 456	213 279	5.4
Wage and salary disbursements	31 788	73 462	131 678	137 501	139 200	144 952	155 881	4.3
Supplements to wages and salaries	6 688	16 903	28 161	29 889	32 945	35 407	39 610	8.9
Proprietors' income[1]	2 944	6 455	12 669	15 662	15 777	16 097	17 788	8.9
Farm proprietors' income	-81	490	340	229	-9	66	126	-22.0
Nonfarm proprietors' income	3 025	5 965	12 329	15 433	15 786	16 031	17 662	9.4
(-) Contributions for government social insurance[2]	3 388	10 329	18 568	19 642	20 297	21 290	23 035	5.5
(+) Adjustment for residence[3]	3 164	5 419	6 275	6 037	7 327	7 443	7 846	5.7
(=) Net Earnings by Place of Residence	41 198	91 909	160 214	169 448	174 952	182 609	198 090	5.4
(+) Dividends, interest, and rent[4]	8 052	23 997	39 100	40 332	39 648	41 059	43 425	2.7
(+) Personal current transfer receipts	5 208	11 223	21 531	23 991	25 558	26 696	28 346	7.1
Personal income	54 457	127 129	220 845	233 770	240 158	250 365	269 862	5.1
Farm income	54 400	126 469	220 334	233 331	239 917	250 036	269 451	5.2
Nonfarm income	57	661	512	440	240	329	411	-5.4
Per Capita Personal Income (Dollars)[5]	10 144	20 449	31 087	32 534	33 018	33 993	36 175	3.9

Note: Data may not add to total or may appear as zero due to rounding.

[1]Proprietors' income includes the inventory valuation adjustment and the capital consumption adjustment.
[2]Contributions for government social insurance are included in earnings by type and industry, but they are excluded from personal income.
[3]The adjustment for residence is the net inflow of the earnings of interarea commuters.
[4]Rental income of persons includes the capital consumption adjustment.
[5]Per capita personal income is total personal income divided by total midyear population.

Per Capita Personal Income, 1980–2004 (Current Dollars)

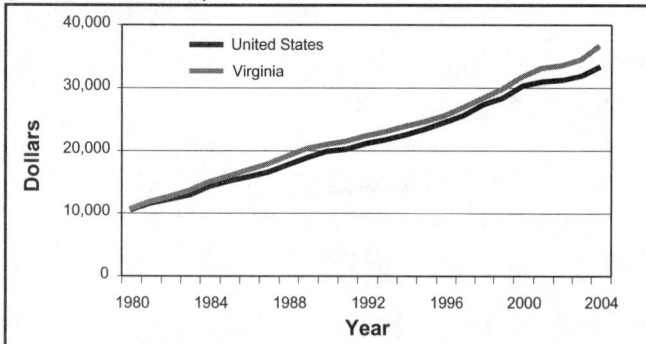

ECONOMIC ACTIVITY

After a slowdown in growth following the 2001 recession, Virginia's economy rebounded strongly. Over the 2003–2004 period, the state's real gross state product grew 6.3 percent, the third fastest growth rate in the nation. Contributing to this increase were gains in construction, durable goods manufacturing, retail trade, professional and technical services, and real estate and related activities. Housing prices have appreciated quite rapidly in the northern part of the state, which was one of the fastest-growing and most expensive regions in the country. The median value of owner-occupied housing in Virginia was the 17th highest in the nation.

Table VA-11. Real Gross State Product, 1997–2004

(Millions of chained 2000 dollars, percent.)

Industry	1997	1998	1999	2000	2001	2002	2003	2004	Average annual percent change, 2001–2004
GROSS STATE PRODUCT	226 029	237 274	247 815	260 257	270 072	274 458	283 922	301 738	3.8
As a percent of U.S. gross product	2.6	2.6	2.6	2.7	2.7	2.7	2.8	2.8	X
Private Industries	183 130	194 169	204 232	215 600	224 985	228 536	238 109	252 592	3.9
Agriculture, forestry, fishing, and hunting	965	1 031	1 068	1 348	1 197	1 026	1 185	1 154	-1.2
Mining	823	905	967	980	992	990	1 046	1 038	1.5
Utilities	4 253	4 181	4 124	4 533	4 240	4 332	4 575	4 752	3.9
Construction	11 129	10 992	11 262	11 535	11 909	11 790	11 958	12 763	2.3
Manufacturing	27 676	29 221	30 644	33 601	35 024	35 459	36 375	36 744	1.6
As a percent of gross state product	12.2	12.3	12.4	12.9	13.0	12.9	12.8	12.2	X
Wholesale trade	10 160	11 271	12 265	12 094	12 864	12 896	12 825	13 481	1.6
Retail trade	13 979	14 762	15 692	16 170	17 548	18 641	19 797	21 267	6.6
Transportation and warehousing	6 331	6 707	6 931	7 119	7 357	7 330	7 741	8 017	2.9
Information	11 100	14 350	15 233	16 912	17 568	15 441	16 566	18 611	1.9
Finance and insurance	11 985	12 769	13 498	14 541	15 797	17 260	18 888	20 088	8.3
Real estate and rental and leasing	27 586	28 348	30 015	30 868	33 156	33 171	33 990	35 918	2.7
Services	57 651	59 748	62 608	65 899	67 372	70 178	73 235	78 935	5.4
As a percent of gross state product	25.5	25.2	25.3	25.3	24.9	25.6	25.8	26.2	X
Professional and technical services	18 798	20 400	22 189	24 470	25 871	27 516	29 333	32 322	7.7
Management of companies and enterprises	6 580	6 420	6 480	6 662	5 967	6 103	6 293	6 743	4.2
Administrative and waste services	6 447	6 645	6 778	6 710	6 680	6 934	7 331	7 998	6.2
Educational services	1 542	1 514	1 611	1 644	1 663	1 639	1 578	1 607	-1.1
Health care and social assistance	11 310	11 403	11 818	12 293	13 059	13 760	14 138	14 644	3.9
Arts, entertainment, and recreation	1 292	1 310	1 308	1 304	1 398	1 496	1 500	1 512	2.6
Accommodation and food services	5 489	5 674	5 927	6 175	6 125	6 175	6 416	6 882	4.0
Other services, except public administration	6 193	6 382	6 497	6 641	6 609	6 555	6 646	7 227	3.0
Government	43 000	43 148	43 593	44 657	45 093	45 925	45 912	49 196	2.9
As a percent of gross state product	19.0	18.2	17.6	17.2	16.7	16.7	16.2	16.3	X

X = Not applicable.

Table VA-12. Government Transfer Payments, Selected Years 1980–2004

(Millions of dollars, percent.)

Item	1980	1990	2000	2001	2002	2003	2004	Average annual percent change, 2000–2004
CURRENT TRANSFER PAYMENTS TO INDIVIDUALS	4 837	10 405	19 916	22 200	23 950	25 222	26 858	7.8
Retirement and Disability Insurance Benefits	2 545	5 321	9 504	10 159	10 767	11 247	11 839	5.6
Old-age, survivors, and disability insurance (OASDI) benefits	2 282	4 930	9 064	9 712	10 293	10 768	11 356	5.8
Railroad retirement and disability benefits	139	222	264	270	280	287	292	2.6
Workers' compensation	25	61	89	92	104	104	106	4.7
Other government retirement and disability insurance benefits	99	108	88	85	90	88	85	-0.9
Medical Benefits	1 061	3 302	7 259	8 673	8 937	9 506	10 499	9.7
Medicare benefits	626	1 984	4 259	4 752	5 120	5 445	6 028	9.1
Public assistance medical care benefits	380	1 116	2 809	3 648	3 449	3 744	4 097	9.9
Military medical insurance benefits	55	202	191	273	369	317	375	18.4
Income Maintenance Benefits	548	902	1 899	1 829	2 059	2 337	2 513	7.3
Supplemental Security Income (SSI) benefits	126	273	556	576	594	606	634	3.3
Family assistance	160	179	244	147	161	176	163	-9.6
Food stamps	166	261	261	270	312	424	450	14.6
Other income maintenance benefits	95	189	838	835	992	1 130	1 266	10.9
Unemployment Insurance Compensation	188	189	195	376	922	793	448	23.2
Veterans' Benefits	410	533	811	859	943	1 017	1 086	7.6
Federal Education and Training Assistance	85	153	232	276	305	279	298	6.5
Other Payments to Individuals	1	5	16	27	17	44	174	81.9

Note: See notes and definitions for more details. Data may not add to total or may appear as zero due to rounding.

EXPORTS

Virginia's exports amounted to $11.6 billion in 2004, ranking 22nd in the nation. The state's sales abroad slipped noticeably as a result of the 2001 recession, and only increased back to their 2001 levels in 2004. The chief exports were transportation equipment and chemical manufactures, which together accounted for about one-third of total exports. Despite the strong technology presence in Virginia, computers and electronic products accounted for just 11.6 percent of exports in 2004. Canada, Germany, and Japan were Virginia's leading export markets. China, the state's fifth leading export market, was the fastest-growing overseas destination, as exports to this country more than doubled from 2001 to 2004.

Leading Exports, 2004

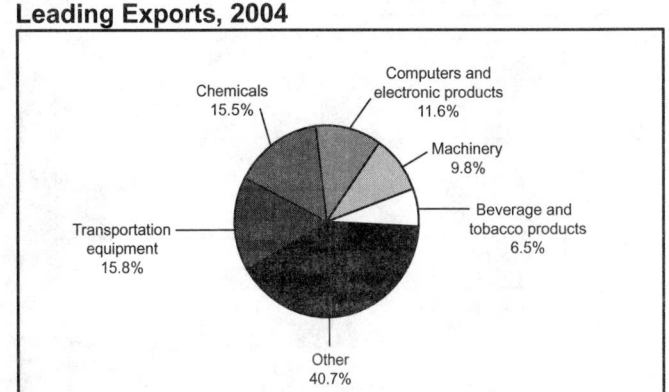

Table VA-13. Exports of Goods by Leading Products and Destinations, 2001–2004

(Millions of dollars, percent, rank based on 2004 dollar values.)

Product and market	2001	2002	2003	2004	Percent share of total, 2004	Average annual percent change, 2001–2004
Total Goods						
Total	11 631	10 796	10 853	11 631	100.0	0.0
Manufactures	9 876	9 252	9 206	9 980	85.8	0.3
Agriculture and livestock	1 259	1 027	1 139	1 292	11.1	0.9
Other commodities	496	516	508	359	3.1	-10.2
Five Leading Exports (NAICS Code)						
Transportation equipment (336)	1 064	1 126	1 464	1 843	15.8	20.1
Chemical manufactures (325)	1 191	1 348	1 444	1 804	15.5	14.9
Computers and electronic products (334)	2 088	1 569	1 378	1 354	11.6	-13.4
Machinery manufactures (333)	1 105	1 389	1 131	1 134	9.8	0.9
Beverage and tobacco products (312)	1 507	979	951	756	6.5	-20.6
Five Leading Markets	9 567	9 212	9 179	9 979	85.8	1.4
Canada	1 781	1 839	2 106	2 515	21.6	12.2
Germany	1 080	1 158	990	1 125	9.7	1.4
Japan	1 318	1 322	908	940	8.1	-10.7
United Kingdom	733	654	724	663	5.7	-3.3
China	263	369	521	608	5.2	32.3

Table VA-14. Agriculture, 1997 and 2002
(Number, acres, and dollars.)

Item	1997	2002
Number of farms	49 366	47 606
Land in farms (acres)	8 753 625	8 624 829
Farm Size		
Average size of farm (acres)	177	181
Farms by size (percent distribution)		
Fewer than 50 acres	36.0	35.9
50 to 499 acres	56.5	56.6
500 acres or more	7.6	7.5
Market Value of Land and Equipment (Dollars)		
Land and buildings average value per farm	356 425	490 064
Average value per acre	1 975	2 675
Machinery and equipment average value per farm	39 063	43 303
Value of Sales (Thousands of Dollars)		
Agricultural products sold	2 394 779	2 360 911
Crops	794 010	718 219
Livestock, poultry, and their products	1 600 769	1 642 692
Average per farm (dollars)	48 511	49 593
Value of sales (percent distribution)		
Less than $10,000	65.9	67.3
$10,000 to $99,999	25.6	24.5
$100,000 or more	8.4	8.2
Government Payments		
Payments (thousands of dollars)	24 428	54 677
Percent of farms receiving government payments	21.0	19.3
Farm operators whose principal occupation is farming (percent)	41.5	53.6

AGRICULTURE

Cash receipts from farming amounted to almost $2.4 billion in 2002, according to the Department of Agriculture's Census of Agriculture. This was slightly less than the value reported on the previous agriculture census in 1997. Chickens, cattle, and dairy products were Virginia's chief agricultural outputs. More than 67 percent of Virginia's farms had sales of less than $10,000, and almost 54 percent of all farm operators considered farming to be their principal occupation. Nearly 36 percent of farms spanned fewer than 50 acres.

ENERGY

Energy expenditures per person totaled $2,265 in 2001, which was among the lowest amounts in the country. Virginia's average energy prices matched the national average, and the state's per capita consumption was below average. The chief energy sources were petroleum, coal, and nuclear power. In 2001, the transportation sector was the largest consumer of energy in Virginia, as the industrial sector's energy use had declined from previous years.

Energy Consumption by Source, 2001

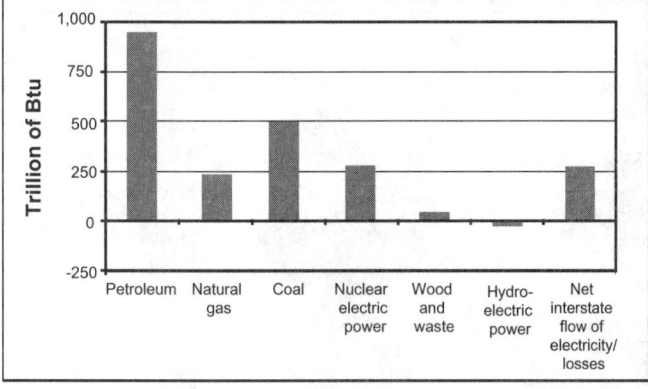

Energy Consumption by Sector, 2001

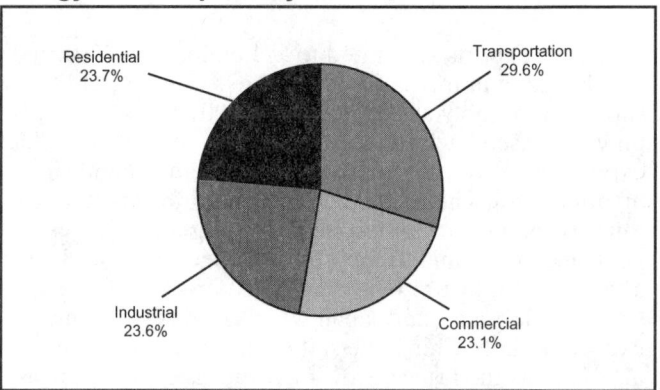

Table VA-15. Energy Consumption, Expenditures, and Prices, Selected Years 1960–2001
(Dollars, Btu [British Thermal Unit], percent distribution.)

Item	1960	1965	1970	1975	1980	1985	1990	1995	2000	2001
Total Consumption (Billion Btu)	851 515	1 050 815	1 285 608	1 364 243	1 567 620	1 682 705	1 964 654	2 144 963	2 386 322	2 314 640
Consumption per capita (million Btu)	214.6	238.2	276.4	270.3	293.2	294.4	317.5	324.9	337.1	321.8
Consumption by Sector (Percent Distribution)										
Residential	22.6	21.1	23.1	23.8	22.8	23.1	22.2	23.8	23.9	23.7
Commercial	9.4	10.4	13.8	15.9	16.3	18.2	20.1	21.4	22.4	23.1
Industrial	33.8	36.9	28.4	26.0	30.1	28.9	28.1	26.9	25.0	23.6
Transportation	34.1	31.6	34.7	34.3	30.7	29.8	29.6	27.8	28.6	29.6
Consumption by Source (Billion Btu)										
Coal	316 395	386 296	275 311	169 188	231 849	297 127	355 063	385 108	506 969	482 443
Natural gas	68 431	98 615	140 072	123 625	161 015	144 897	192 084	284 331	278 197	246 653
Petroleum	442 465	518 239	752 165	828 797	779 398	697 929	763 032	769 439	896 240	911 168
Nuclear electric power	0	0	0	98 782	125 071	236 905	252 065	264 092	295 361	269 131
Hydroelectric power[1]	13 634	9 234	7 254	13 637	9 264	8 833	4 950	2 337	-6 417	-12 472
Wood and waste	56 072	54 205	55 458	53 223	70 041	87 683	93 496	116 197	108 974	93 192
Other	0	0	0	0	0	0	255	378	529	600
Net interstate flow of electricity/losses[2]	-45 482	-15 775	55 349	76 990	190 982	209 332	303 710	323 081	306 469	323 923
Total Expenditures (Thousands of Dollars)	. . .	. . .	1 756 900	3 886 200	8 645 000	9 872 600	11 374 300	12 422 600	16 505 900	16 290 200
Expenditures per capita (dollars)	. . .	. . .	378	770	1 617	1 727	1 838	1 882	2 332	2 265
Prices by Sector (Dollars Per Million Btu)										
Total	. . .	. . .	1.80	3.94	7.94	8.65	8.57	8.70	10.47	10.72
Residential	. . .	. . .	2.39	5.08	10.10	12.02	13.85	14.59	15.70	16.90
Commercial	. . .	. . .	2.58	5.48	10.01	11.90	11.91	11.66	12.16	13.01
Industrial	. . .	. . .	0.84	2.47	4.73	5.26	4.37	4.33	5.29	5.63
Transportation	. . .	. . .	1.95	3.91	8.73	8.55	8.47	8.23	10.86	10.32

[1]A negative number in this row results from pumped storage for which, overall, more electricity is expended than created to provide electricity during peak demand periods.
[2]Net interstate flow of electricity is the difference between the amount of energy in the electricity sold within a state (including associated losses) and the energy input at the electric utilities within the state. A positive number indicates that more electricity (including associated losses) came into the state than went out of the state during the year; conversely, a negative number indicates that more electricity (including associated losses) went out of the state than came into the state.
. . . = Not available.

Table VA-16. State Taxes, Fiscal 2004

(Dollars, percent distribution.)

Item	Thousands of dollars	Percent distribution	Dollars per capita	
			State	U.S.
TOTAL TAXES	14 233 065	100.0	1 907.9	2 024.8
Property Taxes	20 778	0.1	2.8	38.9
Sales and Gross Receipts	5 212 063	36.6	698.7	1 003.4
General sales and gross receipts	2 977 401	20.9	399.1	677.0
Selective sales taxes	2 234 662	15.7	299.6	326.4
Alcoholic beverages	146 019	1.0	19.6	15.7
Insurance premiums	351 278	2.5	47.1	47.0
Motor fuels	909 468	6.4	121.9	114.6
Public utilities	128 815	0.9	17.3	39.2
Other selective sales	682 833	4.8	91.5	49.8
Licenses	613 910	4.3	82.3	134.9
Motor vehicle	340 085	2.4	45.6	59.4
Occupation and business, not elsewhere classified	147 815	1.0	19.8	37.1
Other Taxes	8 386 314	58.9	1 124.2	847.6
Individual income	7 422 071	52.1	994.9	673.6
Corporation net income	422 119	3.0	56.6	105.1
Death and gift	149 647	1.1	20.1	19.6
Documentary and stock transfer	340 591	2.4	45.7	27.1

GOVERNMENT FINANCE

State revenues and expenditures per person were well below the national average in 2003; Virginia ranked among the 15 lowest in the country for both amounts. The state spent more per person on hospitals, highways, police protection, and correctional facilities, but less on education, public welfare, and health. In fiscal year 2004, per capita taxes amounted to $1,907, a below average amount that ranked 31st in the nation. The main source of revenue was individual income taxes, followed by general sales taxes and motor fuels taxes. Virginia's individual income taxes were the 7th highest among the 46 states with such taxes.

Per Capita State Taxes, Fiscal, 2004

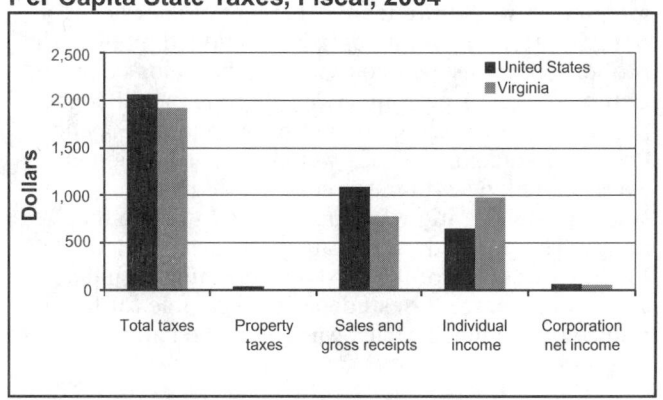

Table VA-17. State Government Finances, 2003

(Dollars, percent distribution.)

Item	Millions of dollars	Percent distribution	Dollars per capita	
			State	U.S.
GENERAL REVENUE	25 528 061	100.0	3 466.1	3 832.6
Intergovernmental revenue	5 679 471	22.2	771.1	1 246.0
Taxes	12 969 177	50.8	1 760.9	1 891.6
General sales	2 692 151	10.5	365.5	636.0
Selective sales	2 070 831	8.1	281.2	307.4
License taxes	588 665	2.3	79.9	123.6
Individual income tax	6 775 746	26.5	920.0	626.8
Corporate income tax	328 444	1.3	44.6	97.8
Other taxes	513 340	2.0	69.7	99.9
Current charges	4 076 034	16.0	553.4	366.5
Miscellaneous general revenue	2 803 379	11.0	380.6	328.6
GENERAL EXPENDITURE	26 289 267	100.0	3 569.5	4 010.5
Intergovernmental expenditure	8 352 635	31.8	1 134.1	1 316.9
Direct expenditure	17 936 632	68.2	2 435.4	2 693.6
Expenditure by Function				
Education	9 776 565	37.2	1 327.4	1 416.4
Public welfare	5 234 986	19.9	710.8	1 083.3
Hospitals	1 886 966	7.2	256.2	132.3
Health	682 070	2.6	92.6	173.0
Highways	2 588 474	9.8	351.5	295.4
Police protection	552 064	2.1	75.0	38.4
Correction	1 194 241	4.5	162.2	135.0
Natural resources	175 851	0.7	23.9	64.0
Parks and recreation	76 086	0.3	10.3	20.1
Government administration	1 060 990	4.0	144.1	151.3
Interest on general debt	647 384	2.5	87.9	107.8
Other and unallocable	2 413 590	9.2	327.7	393.4
DEBT AT END OF FISCAL YEAR	13 530 190	X	1 837.1	2 404.7
CASH AND SECURITY HOLDINGS	50 836 361	X	6 902.4	8 938.4

X = Not applicable.

Table VA-18. Education Indicators, 2000–2004

(Percent, number.)

Item	State	U.S.
Total Population 25 Years and Over (Thousands), 2004	4 865	186 877
Educational Attainment, 2004		
Percent high school graduate or more	88.4	85.2
Percent college graduate or more	33.1	27.7
Elementary and Secondary Schools, 2002–2003		
Total students	1 177 229	48 202 324
Percent of students eligible for free or reduced-price lunch ..	31.3	40.6
Percent of students who were English language learners	5.1	7.8
Total schools	1 846	92 330
Student/teacher ratio	13.2	15.9
Per student expenditures	7 822	8 041
Dropouts, Grades 9–12, 2000–2001 (Percent)	2.9	...
Higher Education, 2002–2003		
Total enrollment	414 639	17 035 027
Bachelor's degrees awarded	34 657	1 348 503
Percent women	58.5	57.5

. . . = Not available.

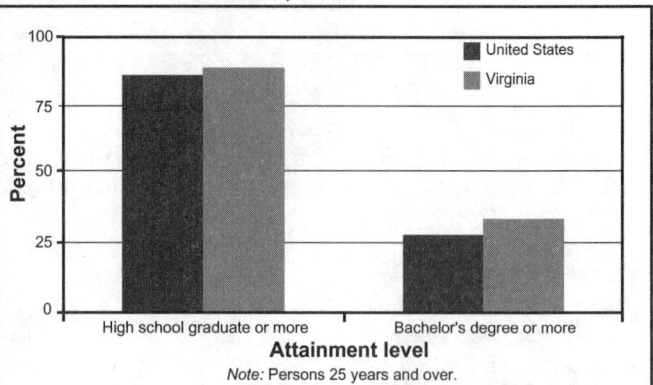

Educational Attainment, 2004

Note: Persons 25 years and over.

EDUCATION

Virginia ranked 15th in the country for high school attainment, with more than 88 percent of its residents age 25 years and over holding high school diplomas. The proportion of this age group holding bachelor's degrees or more was 33.1 percent, giving Virginia the 9th highest proportion of college graduates in the nation. Expenditures per student of $7,822 were below the national average, ranking 24th in the country. Virginia's student/teacher ratio was among the 6 lowest in the nation. The state's dropout rate of 2.9 percent ranked as the 9th lowest out of the 46 states reporting such data. Just over 31 percent of students were eligible for free or reduced-price lunch, which was below the national average.

VOTER PARTICIPATION

Voter turnout was just above the national average for both the 2000 and 2004 elections. Asians and Hispanics had the lowest participation rates in 2004, with less than 25 percent of eligible voters in each group casting ballots. About 50 percent of eligible Blacks and 66 percent of eligible non-Hispanic Whites voted in 2004. According to the official tally by the Clerk of the U.S. House of Representatives, 52.5 percent of eligible voters in Virginia cast ballots for the Republican presidential candidate in 2000, and 53.7 percent voted similarly in 2004. The comparable percentages for the Democratic presidential candidate were 44.4 percent and 45.5 percent, respectively.

Table VA-19. Reported Voting and Registration, November 2000 and November 2004

(Numbers in thousands, percent.)

Characteristic	Total population 18 years and over	Total citizen		Total registered		Total voted	
		Number	Percent	Number	Percent	Number	Percent
NOVEMBER 2000							
Total	5 177	4 912	94.9	3 317	64.1	2 962	57.2
Male	2 431	2 305	94.8	1 512	62.2	1 344	55.3
Female	2 745	2 608	95.0	1 805	65.8	1 619	59.0
NOVEMBER 2004							
Total	5 364	4 971	92.7	3 441	64.1	3 134	58.4
Male	2 538	2 325	91.6	1 584	62.4	1 444	56.9
Female	2 826	2 646	93.7	1 856	65.7	1 690	59.8
Race and Hispanic Origin							
White alone	4 101	3 863	94.2	2 798	68.2	2 586	63.0
Non-Hispanic White alone	3 814	3 741	98.1	2 731	71.6	2 525	66.2
Black alone	961	915	95.2	551	57.4	477	49.6
Asian alone	251	149	59.5	58	23.0	43	17.3
Hispanic or Latino[1]	301	135	45.0	78	26.0	70	23.1
White alone or in combination	4 129	3 890	94.2	2 819	68.3	2 604	63.1
Non-Hispanic White alone or in combination	3 836	3 764	98.1	2 749	71.7	2 543	66.3
Black alone or in combination	972	926	95.2	560	57.6	481	49.5
Asian alone or in combination	255	153	60.0	61	24.1	45	17.6
Age							
18 to 24 years	578	536	92.7	260	45.0	215	37.2
25 to 44 years	2 088	1 835	87.9	1 213	58.1	1 091	52.2
45 to 64 years	1 823	1 735	95.2	1 305	71.6	1 243	68.2
65 to 74 years	546	544	99.6	404	73.9	368	67.4
75 years and over	329	320	97.4	259	78.7	217	66.1

[1]May be of any race.

At a Glance:

- Washington's population was over 6.2 million in 2004, making it the 15th most populous state in the nation.

- Over 77 percent of Washington's residents were non-Hispanic White; 6.6 percent were Asian and Pacific Islander (the fourth highest proportion of this racial group in the nation) and 1.5 percent were American Indian (the ninth highest proportion of this racial group in the country).

- In 2004, 13 percent of the population lacked health insurance coverage, which was well below the national average.

- Washington's median household income of $49,820 was well above the national average, ranking 12th in the country. The state's poverty rate of 11.5 percent was below the national average.

- Economic activity was adversely impacted by the 2001 recession, and its subsequent recovery was about average. Real gross state product was the 14th largest in the country. The state's unemployment rate was 6.2 percent, the 6th highest rate in the nation.

- Washington had high educational attainment levels, ranking among the top 15 for its proportions of high school and college graduates among residents age 25 years and over.

Table WA-1. Population by Sex and Age, 1990, 2000, and 2004

(Number, percent.)

Sex and age	1990	2000	2004	Percent distribution, 2004	Average annual percent change, 2000–2004
Total Population	4 866 692	5 894 121	6 203 788	X	1.3
Percent of total U.S. population	2.0	2.1	2.1	X	X
Sex					
Male	2 413 747	2 934 300	3 094 471	49.9	1.3
Female	2 452 945	2 959 821	3 109 317	50.1	1.2
Age					
Under 5 years	366 780	394 306	387 403	6.2	0.3
5 to 17 years	894 607	1 119 537	1 098 617	17.7	1.5
18 years and over	882 527	4 380 278	4 717 768	76.0	2.0
18 to 24 years	3 605 305	559 361	634 717	10.2	1.8
25 to 44 years	488 539	1 816 217	1 815 067	29.3	0.7
45 to 64 years	1 658 951	1 342 552	1 564 839	25.2	4.2
65 years and over	575 288	662 148	703 145	11.3	1.5
85 years and over	56 301	84 085	103 259	1.7	4.5
Median age (years)	33.0	35.3	36.3	X	X

X = Not applicable.

Average Annual Rate of Population Growth, 1980–2004

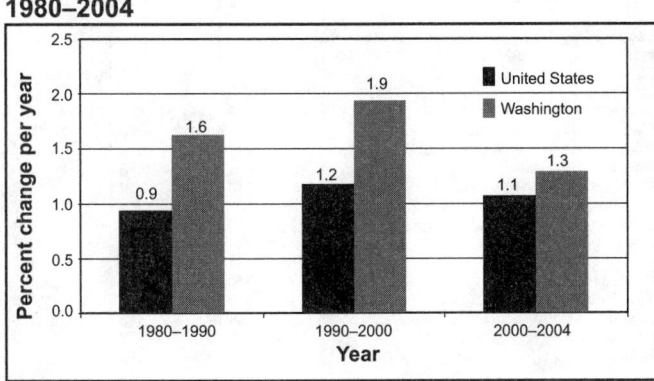

POPULATION

Like neighboring Oregon, Washington has experienced substantial population growth in recent years. Between 2000 and 2004, its number of residents increased by 5.3 percent, the 13th highest growth rate in the nation. Over half of this growth was attributable to an influx of international and domestic immigrants. Washington gained over 112,000 new residents from other countries and nearly 53,000 from other states during this period. Although Washington's population is projected to exceed that of Indiana (the 14th largest state) by 2010, Arizona's population, due to its rapid rate of growth, is projected to overtake Washington's by that time.

Table WA-2. Population by Race and Hispanic Origin, 1990, 2000, and 2004

(Number, percent.)

Race and Hispanic origin	1990	2000	2004
Total Population	4 866 692	5 894 121	6 203 788
Non-Hispanic (Percent)			
One race[1]			
White	86.7	79.4	77.5
Black	3.0	3.2	3.3
American Indian, Alaska Native[2]	1.7	1.5	1.5
Asian and Pacific Islander[2]	4.3	5.9	6.6
Other race[2]	2.4	. . .	. . .
Two or more races	. . .	2.5	2.7
Hispanic or Latino[3] (Percent)	4.4	7.5	8.5

[1]Individuals could report only one race in the 1990 census and could report one or more races on the 2000 census. Data on race in 2000 and 2004 are not comparable to 1990.
[2]Data for 1990 include people of Hispanic or Latino origin.
[3]May be of any race.
. . . = Not available.

Minority Population as a Percent of Total Population, 2004

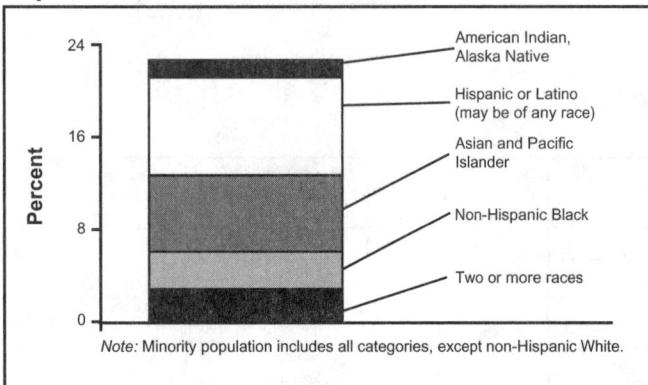

Note: Minority population includes all categories, except non-Hispanic White.

Age-Adjusted Death Rates, Average 2000–2002

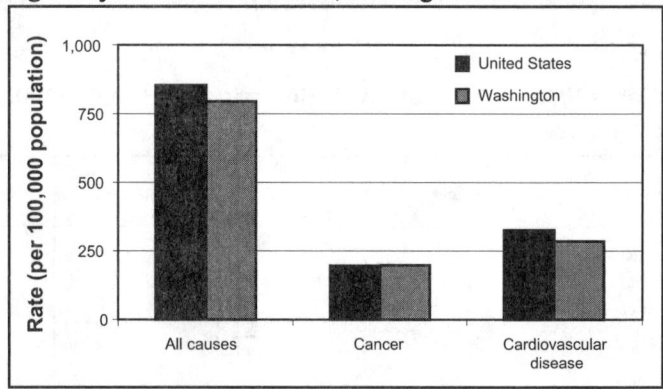

HEALTH

Washington's infant mortality rate was among the 10 lowest in the nation, as was its age-adjusted death rate for all causes. Washington's overall birth rate and its birth rate for teenage mothers were well below the national averages. The state's rate of health insurance coverage was above average.

Table WA-3. Health Characteristics, 2000–2004

(Number, rate, percent.)

Item	State	U.S.
Births, 2003–2004		
Number of births	80 489	4 089 950
Birth rate (per 1,000 population)	13.1	14.1
Teenage birth rate (per 1,000 women age 15–19 years)	31.5	41.6
Mortality Rates, Average 2000–2002		
Infant mortality rate (per 1,000 live births)	5.5	6.9
Age-adjusted mortality rate (per 100,000 population)		
All races	792.3	853.3
Non-Hispanic White	799.9	843.1
Black	982.5	1 097.1
American Indian, Alaska Native	943.4	687.0
Asian and Pacific Islander	534.1	486.0
Hispanic or Latino[1]	535.4	642.7
Health Insurance, 2004		
Percent of all persons without health insurance	13.0	15.7
Percent of children without health insurance	7.0	11.2
Percent of low-income children without health insurance	3.6	7.1

[1]May be of any race.

Table WA-4. Leading Causes of Death, Average 2000–2002

(Number, rate per 100,000 population.)

Cause	Number of deaths	Age-adjusted death rates	
		State	U.S.
ALL CAUSES	44 640	792.3	853.3
Leading Causes			
Major cardiovascular diseases	16 155	288.1	326.5
Cancer	10 776	192.6	196.0
Chronic lower respiratory diseases	2 666	48.4	43.7
Unintentional injuries	2 108	35.6	35.7
Diabetes (underlying cause)	1 409	25.2	25.2
Influenza and pneumonia	961	17.0	22.7
Alzheimer's disease	2 015	35.8	19.0
Motor vehicle accidents	714	11.9	15.0
Nephritis, nephrotic syndrome, and nephrosis ..	293	5.2	13.8
Septicemia	346	6.2	11.4
Suicides	750	12.5	10.7
Firearm-related	534	8.9	10.3
Cirrhosis	530	9.1	9.5
Drug-induced	613	10.0	7.9
Alcohol-induced	564	9.5	6.9
Homicides	203	3.3	6.0
Falls	471	8.3	5.2
HIV	120	1.9	5.0
Viral hepatitis	173	2.9	2.0
Anemias	57	1.0	1.6
Drownings	108	1.8	1.3
Fire deaths	59	1.0	1.2

Note: The rates are age-adjusted to the U.S. 2000 standard population.

Table WA-5. Households and Housing Characteristics, 1990, 2000, and 2004

(Number, percent, and dollars.)

Characteristic	1990	2000	2004	Average annual percent change, 2000–2004
Total Households	1 872 431	2 271 398	2 416 301	1.6
Family households	1 264 934	1 499 127	1 566 251	1.1
Married-couple family	1 029 267	1 181 995	1 208 680	0.6
Other family	235 667	317 132	357 571	3.0
Male householder, no wife present	60 145	92 514	110 178	4.5
Female householder, no husband present	175 522	224 618	247 393	2.4
Nonfamily households	607 497	772 271	850 050	2.4
Householder living alone	476 320	594 325	667 739	3.0
Householder not living alone	131 177	177 946	182 311	0.6
Housing Characteristics				
Average size	2.53	2.53	2.51	X
Housing units	2 032 378	2 451 075	2 606 623	1.6
Occupied housing units	1 872 431	2 271 398	2 416 301	1.6
Owner-occupied	1 171 580	1 467 009	1 548 022	1.4
Renter-occupied	700 851	804 389	868 279	1.9
Median gross rent of renter-occupied housing units (dollars)	445	663	727	2.3
Median value of owner-occupied housing units (dollars)	93 200	168 300	204 719	5.0

X = Not applicable.

Median Housing Value and Median Rent, 2004

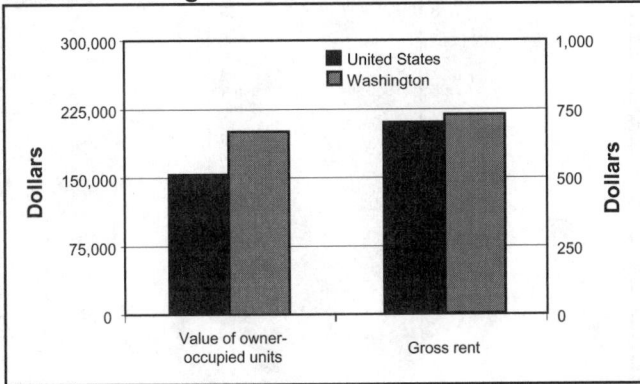

Median Household Income, 1984–2004 (2004 Dollars)

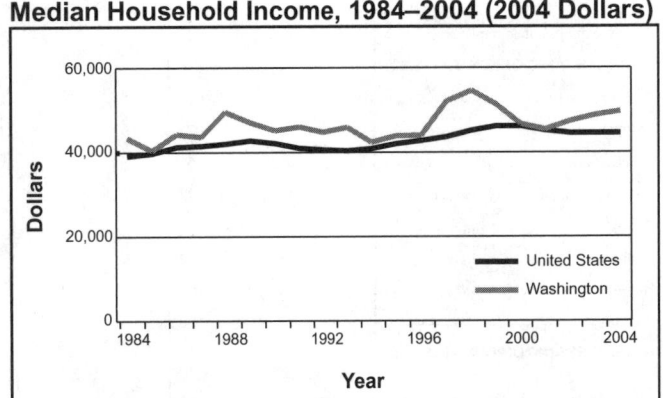

Table WA-6. Household Income and Poverty Status, 1980–2004

(2004 CPI-U-RS adjusted dollars, rate.)

Year	State		U.S.	
	Median household income (2004 dollars)	Poverty rate	Median household income (2004 dollars)	Poverty rate
2004	49 820	11.5	44 389	12.7
2003	48 785	12.6	44 482	12.5
2002	47 460	11.0	44 546	12.1
2001	45 341	10.7	45 062	11.7
2000	46 645	10.8	46 058	11.3
1999	51 544	9.6	46 129	11.9
1998	54 882	8.9	45 003	12.7
1997	52 300	9.2	43 430	13.3
1996	43 963	11.9	42 544	13.7
1995	43 780	12.5	41 943	13.8
1994	42 277	11.7	40 677	14.5
1993	45 899	12.1	40 217	15.1
1992	44 728	11.2	40 422	14.8
1991	45 945	9.5	40 746	14.2
1990	45 003	8.9	41 963	13.5
1989	47 019	9.6	42 524	12.8
1988	49 599	8.7	41 771	13.0
1987	43 442	10.0	41 322	13.4
1986	44 202	12.9	40 939	13.6
1985	40 185	12.0	39 545	14.0
1984	43 284	11.3	38 782	14.4
1983	. . .	10.8	. . .	15.2
1982	. . .	12.9	. . .	15.0
1981	. . .	11.3	. . .	14.0
1980	. . .	12.7	. . .	13.0

. . . = Not available.

Table WA-7. Employment Status by Demographic Group, 2004

(Numbers in thousands, rate.)

Characteristic	Civilian noninstitutional population	Civilian labor force		Employed	Unemployment rate
		Number	Participation rate		
SEX AND AGE					
Total	4 777	3 240	67.8	3 037	6.2
16 to 19 years	340	148	43.6	116	21.9
20 to 24 years	416	326	78.3	298	8.5
25 to 34 years	843	696	82.6	654	6.1
35 to 44 years	946	788	83.3	739	6.3
45 to 54 years	965	822	85.2	788	4.1
55 to 64 years	614	388	63.1	375	3.3
65 years and over	653	71	10.9	67	5.8
Men	2 338	1 746	74.7	1 637	6.2
16 to 19 years	184	80	43.3	63	21.5
20 to 24 years	193	164	84.9	149	8.9
25 to 34 years	435	400	92.1	374	6.5
35 to 44 years	462	425	92.1	401	5.7
45 to 54 years	485	436	89.9	418	4.1
55 to 64 years	303	205	67.6	198	3.4
Women	2 440	1 494	61.2	1 400	6.3
16 to 19 years	156	69	44.0	53	22.4
20 to 24 years	223	162	72.7	149	8.1
25 to 34 years	408	296	72.5	280	5.5
35 to 44 years	484	363	75.0	338	6.9
45 to 54 years	480	386	80.4	370	4.1
55 to 64 years	312	183	58.8	177	3.2
MARITAL STATUS					
Married men, spouse present	1 330	1 034	77.7	995	3.7
Married women, spouse present	1 313	821	62.5	785	4.3
Women who maintain families	253	183	72.3	169	7.7
RACE, HISPANIC ORIGIN, AND SEX					
White	4 074	2 757	67.7	2 589	6.1
Men	2 004	1 499	74.8	1 409	6.0
Women	2 071	1 258	60.7	1 180	6.2
Black	139	98	70.6	90	8.7
Men	67	48	71.3	42	11.8
Women	72	50	70.0	48	5.8
Asian	307	206	67.1	195	5.0
Men	134	99	73.6	95	4.5
Women	172	107	61.9	101	5.5
Hispanic or Latino[1]	299	216	72.3	201	6.9
Men	161	137	84.9	128	6.4
Women	138	79	57.4	73	7.7
RACE, HISPANIC ORIGIN, AND AGE					
White					
16 to 19 years	281	123	43.6	96	21.7
20 to 24 years	345	276	80.0	253	8.4
25 to 34 years	667	555	83.3	521	6.1
35 to 44 years	804	673	83.8	632	6.1
45 to 54 years	846	727	86.0	699	3.9
55 to 64 years	540	338	62.5	327	3.1
65 years and over	592	65	11.0	61	6.4

Note: Data in Table 7 are from the Current Population Survey (CPS) and do not match Bureau of Labor Statistics estimates in Table 8. See notes and definitions for more details.

[1]May be of any race.

Table WA-8. Employment Status, 1990–2004

(Numbers in thousands, rate.)

Year	Civilian labor force	Employed	Unemployed	Unemployment rate
2004	3 233 648	3 032 299	201 349	6.2
2003	3 160 332	2 926 836	233 496	7.4
2002	3 109 445	2 881 443	228 002	7.3
2001	3 050 497	2 861 417	189 080	6.2
2000	3 051 143	2 899 189	151 954	5.0
1999	3 066 165	2 917 577	148 588	4.8
1998	3 032 019	2 886 871	145 148	4.8
1997	2 966 651	2 822 223	144 428	4.9
1996	2 882 432	2 711 963	170 469	5.9
1995	2 812 611	2 636 011	176 600	6.3
1994	2 744 838	2 566 663	178 175	6.5
1993	2 691 873	2 500 782	191 091	7.1
1992	2 634 582	2 445 866	188 716	7.2
1991	2 543 895	2 383 588	160 307	6.3
1990	2 537 038	2 406 444	130 594	5.1

Note: Population age 16 years and over.

Unemployment Rate, 1980–2004

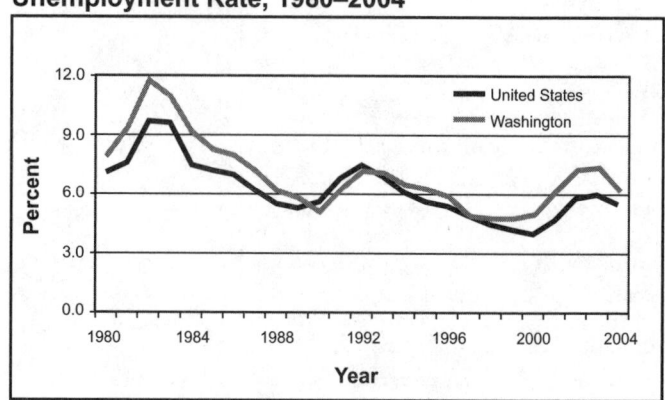

Table WA-9. Employment and Average Wages by Industry, 2001–2004

(Estimates are based on the 2002 North American Industry Classification System [NAICS].)

Industry	2001	2002	2003	2004	Annual average percent change, 2001–2004
	Number of jobs				
TOTAL EMPLOYMENT BY PLACE OF WORK	3 557 145	3 526 609	3 550 008	3 620 382	0.6
Farm Employment	79 721	79 486	82 208	81 581	0.8
Nonfarm Employment	3 477 424	3 447 123	3 467 800	3 538 801	0.6
Private employment	2 905 685	2 862 372	2 877 505	2 944 659	0.4
Forestry, fishing, hunting, and other[1]	50 941	52 534	50 157	50 289	-0.4
Mining	5 766	5 031	5 451	5 898	0.8
Utilities	5 155	4 780	4 724	4 727	-2.8
Construction	216 143	208 838	212 456	221 682	0.8
Manufacturing	332 319	301 372	282 228	279 527	-5.6
Durable goods manufacturing	235 499	209 769	193 822	192 289	-6.5
Nondurable goods manufacturing	96 820	91 603	88 406	87 238	-3.4
Wholesale trade	132 365	127 633	127 807	132 035	-0.1
Retail trade	392 062	387 409	391 083	397 329	0.4
Transportation and warehousing	105 386	102 011	100 912	103 348	-0.6
Information	108 349	101 589	100 637	101 702	-2.1
Finance and insurance	140 186	140 436	143 948	144 739	1.1
Real estate and rental and leasing	131 046	132 361	139 859	145 920	3.6
Professional and technical services	233 234	230 366	231 144	234 843	0.2
Management of companies and enterprises	30 835	31 940	33 341	34 076	3.4
Administrative and waste services	161 095	161 852	167 531	180 458	3.9
Educational services	53 563	54 558	56 929	59 358	3.5
Health care and social assistance	319 763	327 872	334 274	342 351	2.3
Arts, entertainment, and recreation	75 744	79 333	80 351	83 985	3.5
Accommodation and food services	222 567	220 092	224 152	229 430	1.0
Other services, except public administration	189 166	192 365	190 521	192 962	0.7
Government and government enterprises	571 739	584 751	590 295	594 142	1.3
	Dollars				
AVERAGE WAGES AND SALARIES BY PLACE OF WORK	37 590	38 382	39 164	40 320	2.4
Farm Earnings	22 652	20 892	19 629	22 703	0.1
Nonfarm Earnings	37 819	38 653	39 493	40 611	2.4
Private earnings	38 369	38 971	39 647	40 731	2.0
Forestry, fishing, hunting, and other[1]	26 576	27 751	28 842	29 379	3.4
Mining	47 034	48 222	49 700	51 687	3.2
Utilities	58 606	58 224	58 862	62 975	2.4
Construction	39 285	40 319	40 294	41 426	1.8
Manufacturing	47 802	51 029	50 639	52 417	3.1
Durable goods manufacturing	51 252	53 682	54 645	56 694	3.4
Nondurable goods manufacturing	39 325	44 883	41 784	42 911	3.0
Wholesale trade	47 774	48 790	50 031	53 819	4.1
Retail trade	25 176	26 127	26 654	27 600	3.1
Transportation and warehousing	39 360	40 620	41 653	43 426	3.3
Information	110 617	102 039	102 152	92 770	-5.7
Finance and insurance	52 184	54 550	59 015	62 999	6.5
Real estate and rental and leasing	29 323	30 005	30 784	32 098	3.1
Professional and technical services	55 130	56 284	58 354	60 154	3.0
Management of companies and enterprises	65 408	67 775	69 933	76 250	5.2
Administrative and waste services	29 173	31 041	32 609	33 798	5.0
Educational services	21 368	22 292	22 768	23 851	3.7
Health care and social assistance	32 637	33 867	35 035	36 541	3.8
Arts, entertainment, and recreation	23 819	23 090	23 903	25 740	2.6
Accommodation and food services	14 574	15 090	15 487	16 030	3.2
Other services, except public administration	22 404	22 919	23 543	24 464	3.0
Government and government enterprises	35 582	37 413	38 899	40 142	4.1

Note: Average wages and salaries are a calculation by the editors of wage and salary disbursements divided by full- and part-time wage and salary employment. Data may not add to total or may appear as zero due to rounding.

[1] "Other" consists of the number of jobs held by U.S. residents employed by international organizations and foreign embassies and consulates in the United States.

LABOR MARKET

Washington's unemployment rate, which had been above average for many years, rose sharply following the 2001 recession. During the 2001–2003 period, employment growth was relatively flat, due to declines in manufacturing and sluggish rates of growth in construction and retail trade. In 2004, job growth rebounded in most industries, with the notable exception of manufacturing. Washington's largest employers were government, health care, and manufacturing. In 2004, average wages and salaries were above average, ranking 11th in the country; however, their growth rate of 7.3 percent from 2001 to 2004 was among the 5 lowest rates in the nation.

Employment by Industry, 2004

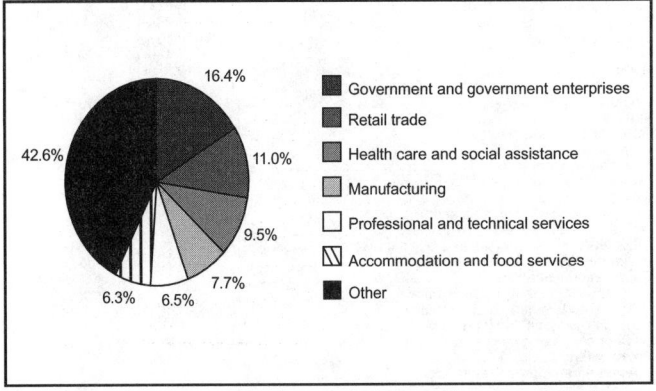

- Government and government enterprises
- Retail trade
- Health care and social assistance
- Manufacturing
- Professional and technical services
- Accommodation and food services
- Other

Table WA-10. Personal Income by Major Source, Selected Years 1980–2004

(Millions of dollars, except where noted.)

Item	1980	1990	2000	2001	2002	2003	2004	Average annual percent change, 2000–2004
Earnings by Place of Work	36 386	75 218	147 026	150 023	152 987	157 752	167 417	3.3
Wage and salary disbursements	27 019	54 125	110 001	110 616	111 411	114 090	119 265	2.0
Supplements to wages and salaries	5 638	12 436	22 875	23 245	25 493	27 227	29 772	6.8
Proprietors' income[1]	3 729	8 656	14 149	16 163	16 083	16 435	18 379	6.8
Farm proprietors' income	551	612	444	214	370	655	847	17.5
Nonfarm proprietors' income	3 178	8 045	13 705	15 948	15 712	15 779	17 532	6.4
(-) Contributions for government social insurance[2]	3 862	9 615	18 189	17 821	18 235	18 997	20 213	2.7
(+) Adjustment for residence[3]	389	926	2 182	2 312	2 348	2 336	2 509	3.6
(=) Net Earnings by Place of Residence	32 913	66 528	131 019	134 515	137 100	141 090	149 713	3.4
(+) Dividends, interest, and rent[4]	7 185	19 251	34 521	33 906	33 594	32 335	39 035	3.1
(+) Personal current transfer receipts	4 907	11 620	22 314	25 078	26 629	27 917	28 493	6.3
Personal income	45 004	97 399	187 853	193 498	197 324	201 342	217 240	3.7
Farm income	44 164	96 255	186 359	192 222	195 977	199 682	215 240	3.7
Nonfarm income	840	1 145	1 494	1 276	1 347	1 661	2 000	7.6
Per Capita Personal Income (Dollars)[5]	10 832	19 865	31 779	32 289	32 523	32 838	35 017	2.5

Note: Data may not add to total or may appear as zero due to rounding.

[1]Proprietors' income includes the inventory valuation adjustment and the capital consumption adjustment.
[2]Contributions for government social insurance are included in earnings by type and industry, but they are excluded from personal income.
[3]The adjustment for residence is the net inflow of the earnings of interarea commuters.
[4]Rental income of persons includes the capital consumption adjustment.
[5]Per capita personal income is total personal income divided by total midyear population.

Per Capita Personal Income, 1980–2004 (Current Dollars)

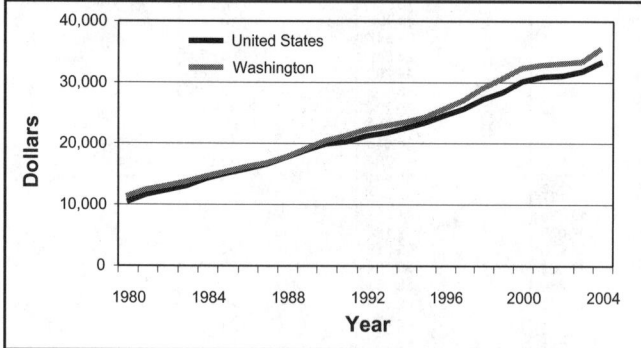

ECONOMIC ACTIVITY

In 2004, Washington's real gross state product (GSP) was the 14th largest in the country. The GSP declined as a result of the 2001 recession, and its subsequent recovery was at a slightly below average rate. During the 2003–2004 period, retail trade and durable goods manufacturing, particularly aircraft manufacturing, had stronger rates of growth. Several service-providing industries also expanded. Washington's largest industries were government, retail trade, and health care. Overall housing prices increased moderately; however, the areas around Seattle that experienced higher rates of population growth saw sharper housing price appreciation. In 2004, the median value of owner-occupied housing in Washington was the 12th highest in the county.

Table WA-11. Real Gross State Product, 1997–2004

(Millions of chained 2000 dollars, percent.)

Industry	1997	1998	1999	2000	2001	2002	2003	2004	Average annual percent change, 2001–2004
GROSS STATE PRODUCT	188 481	203 413	219 394	221 314	220 096	223 456	229 680	239 833	2.9
As a percent of U.S. gross product	2.2	2.3	2.3	2.3	2.2	2.2	2.2	2.2	X
Private Industries	159 940	174 149	190 088	192 049	190 418	192 921	198 490	207 735	2.9
Agriculture, forestry, fishing, and hunting	3 621	3 702	3 988	4 637	4 011	4 618	4 579	4 579	4.5
Mining	254	287	335	334	281	284	286	289	0.9
Utilities	2 187	2 139	2 222	2 316	2 132	2 095	2 143	2 306	2.6
Construction	9 486	10 292	10 771	10 611	10 075	9 702	9 671	10 015	-0.2
Manufacturing	19 792	21 896	22 123	23 270	21 975	22 050	21 035	21 774	-0.3
As a percent of gross state product	10.5	10.8	10.1	10.5	10.0	9.9	9.2	9.1	X
Wholesale trade	11 825	13 315	13 810	13 717	14 378	14 291	14 137	15 257	2.0
Retail trade	13 357	14 189	15 412	16 207	16 618	17 416	18 467	19 630	5.7
Transportation and warehousing	5 989	6 021	6 125	6 404	6 177	6 370	6 618	6 968	4.1
Information	13 987	18 426	26 998	22 050	20 570	20 193	21 376	22 055	2.4
Finance and insurance	10 161	10 358	10 445	11 526	11 941	12 492	13 842	14 688	7.1
Real estate and rental and leasing	27 569	29 013	30 871	31 583	32 392	32 413	33 231	34 529	2.2
Services	42 048	44 653	47 014	49 391	49 904	51 088	53 254	55 843	3.8
As a percent of gross state product	22.3	22.0	21.4	22.3	22.7	22.9	23.2	23.3	X
Professional and technical services	9 823	11 290	12 542	14 483	14 287	14 537	15 402	15 891	3.6
Management of companies and enterprises	3 179	2 905	3 235	2 972	3 157	3 318	3 634	3 825	6.6
Administrative and waste services	5 735	5 701	5 932	5 988	5 788	6 145	6 612	7 193	7.5
Educational services	1 012	1 027	1 062	1 113	1 085	1 051	999	1 005	-2.5
Health care and social assistance	10 997	12 098	12 536	12 723	13 337	13 890	14 308	14 830	3.6
Arts, entertainment, and recreation	1 483	1 458	1 542	1 720	1 753	1 749	1 783	1 948	3.6
Accommodation and food services	4 906	5 215	5 174	5 503	5 444	5 422	5 569	5 849	2.4
Other services, except public administration	4 913	4 959	4 991	4 889	5 053	4 976	4 947	5 302	1.6
Government	28 642	29 314	29 309	29 265	29 674	30 520	31 185	32 106	2.7
As a percent of gross state product	15.2	14.4	13.4	13.2	13.5	13.7	13.6	13.4	X

X = Not applicable.

Table WA-12. Government Transfer Payments, Selected Years 1980–2004

(Millions of dollars, percent.)

Item	1980	1990	2000	2001	2002	2003	2004	Average annual percent change, 2000–2004
CURRENT TRANSFER PAYMENTS TO INDIVIDUALS	4 606	10 995	20 817	23 397	25 152	26 512	27 061	6.8
Retirement and Disability Insurance Benefits	2 383	5 826	9 380	9 985	10 522	11 028	11 621	5.5
Old-age, survivors, and disability insurance (OASDI) benefits	2 085	4 635	7 901	8 431	8 914	9 313	9 831	5.6
Railroad retirement and disability benefits	81	134	167	171	177	181	184	2.4
Workers' compensation	214	1 051	1 304	1 374	1 416	1 507	1 577	4.9
Other government retirement and disability insurance benefits	4	5	8	10	16	28	30	40.1
Medical Benefits	955	3 118	7 658	9 032	9 037	9 788	10 527	8.3
Medicare benefits	517	1 681	3 465	3 853	4 147	4 411	4 882	9.0
Public assistance medical care benefits	425	1 373	4 116	5 066	4 735	5 245	5 492	7.5
Military medical insurance benefits	12	64	78	114	155	133	153	18.3
Income Maintenance Benefits	524	1 011	1 822	1 879	1 970	2 149	2 331	6.4
Supplemental Security Income (SSI) benefits	85	210	485	522	540	546	571	4.1
Family assistance	257	446	361	434	412	394	415	3.6
Food stamps	95	196	244	272	330	409	477	18.2
Other income maintenance benefits	86	160	731	651	689	800	868	4.4
Unemployment Insurance Compensation	370	455	953	1 405	2 427	2 290	1 243	6.9
Veterans' Benefits	295	400	746	805	895	965	1 032	8.5
Federal Education and Training Assistance	72	134	219	241	267	255	271	5.5
Other Payments to Individuals	8	50	39	49	34	36	36	-1.6

Note: See notes and definitions for more details. Data may not add to total or may appear as zero due to rounding.

EXPORTS

In 2004, Washington was the fifth largest exporter in the country, with exports valued at $33.8 billion. Total exports declined over the 2001–2004 period; however, this was largely due to the volatility of the aircraft manufacturing industry, which made up a substantial share of the state's manufacturing exports. Outside of manufacturing, Washington's exports of agricultural products (soybeans, corn, wheat, and apples) and computers and electronic products increased substantially. (Software and computer services were not counted as "goods" and thus were not included in export figures.) Japan and Canada were Washington's largest export markets.

Leading Exports, 2004

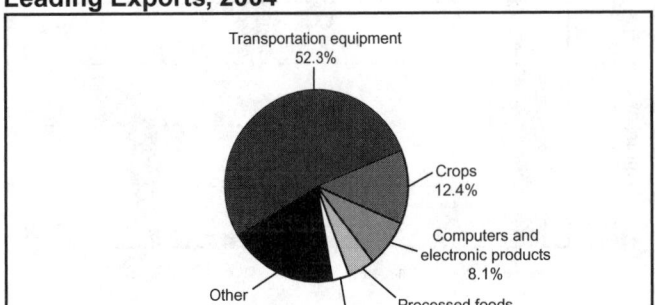

Table WA-13. Exports of Goods by Leading Products and Destinations, 2001–2004

(Millions of dollars, percent, rank based on 2004 dollar values.)

Product and market	2001	2002	2003	2004	Percent share of total, 2004	Average annual percent change, 2001–2004
Total Goods						
Total	34 929	34 627	34 173	33 793	100.0	-1.1
Manufactures	31 046	31 127	29 374	27 908	82.6	-3.5
Agriculture and livestock	3 540	3 116	4 357	5 374	15.9	14.9
Other commodities	342	384	441	510	1.5	14.2
Five Leading Exports (NAICS Code)						
Transportation equipment (336)	22 740	23 377	20 438	17 686	52.3	-8.0
Crop production (111)	2 312	2 094	3 333	4 181	12.4	21.8
Computers and electronic products (334)	2 229	1 958	2 354	2 746	8.1	7.2
Processed foods (311)	1 276	1 278	1 602	1 585	4.7	7.5
Machinery manufactures (333)	980	800	839	1 031	3.1	1.7
Five Leading Markets	28 066	28 884	29 826	30 945	91.6	3.3
Japan	3 384	4 349	5 429	6 312	18.7	23.1
Canada	2 737	2 944	3 314	4 041	12.0	13.9
China	2 929	3 831	3 211	3 094	9.2	1.9
Taiwan	1 594	1 047	1 958	2 138	6.3	10.3
South Korea	2 131	2 056	1 673	2 061	6.1	-1.1

Table WA-14. Agriculture, 1997 and 2002

(Number, acres, and dollars.)

Item	1997	2002
Number of farms	40 113	35 939
Land in farms (acres)	15 778 606	15 318 008
Farm Size		
Average size of farm (acres)	393	426
Farms by size (percent distribution)		
Fewer than 50 acres	59.8	57.5
50 to 499 acres	27.9	29.7
500 acres or more	12.3	12.8
Market Value of Land and Equipment (Dollars)		
Land and buildings average value per farm	520 306	623 333
Average value per acre	1 292	1 486
Machinery and equipment average value per farm	57 987	80 212
Value of Sales (Thousands of Dollars)		
Agricultural products sold	4 947 886	5 330 740
Crops	3 403 524	3 582 818
Livestock, poultry, and their products	1 544 362	1 747 922
Average per farm (dollars)	123 349	148 327
Value of sales (percent distribution)		
Less than $10,000	61.3	59.4
$10,000 to $99,999	21.0	22.2
$100,000 or more	17.7	18.4
Government Payments		
Payments (thousands of dollars)	101 318	133 763
Percent of farms receiving government payments	23.2	20.4
Farm operators whose principal occupation is farming (percent)	46.5	58.5

AGRICULTURE

According to the Department of Agriculture's 2002 Census of Agriculture, cash receipts from farming in Washington totaled $5.3 billion, which was the 11th highest amount in the country. Washington's leading products were dairy products, apples, and cattle. The state produced about half of the nation's apple crop. Over 80 percent of farms had sales of less than $100,000, and 58.5 percent of farm operators considered farming to be their principal occupation. In 2002, 57.5 percent of farms spanned fewer than 50 acres, which was the 10th highest proportion of farms of this size in the nation.

ENERGY

Washington's energy expenditures per person amounted to $2,154 in 2001, ranking among the lowest in the country and similarly to those of Oregon. This was partly due to the relatively low price of energy in Washington, as per capita consumption was average. The state's chief energy sources were petroleum, hydroelectric power, and natural gas.

Energy Consumption by Source, 2001

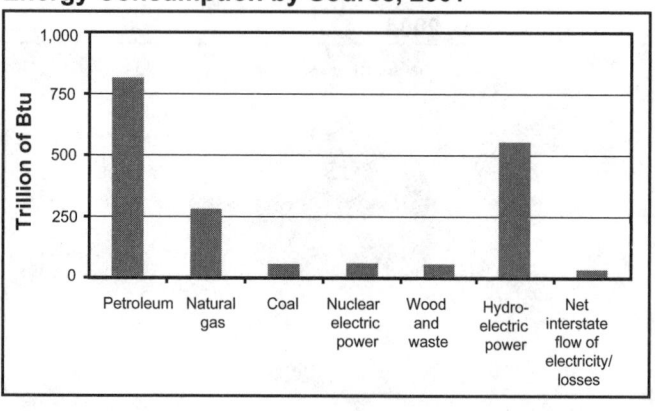

Energy Consumption by Sector, 2001

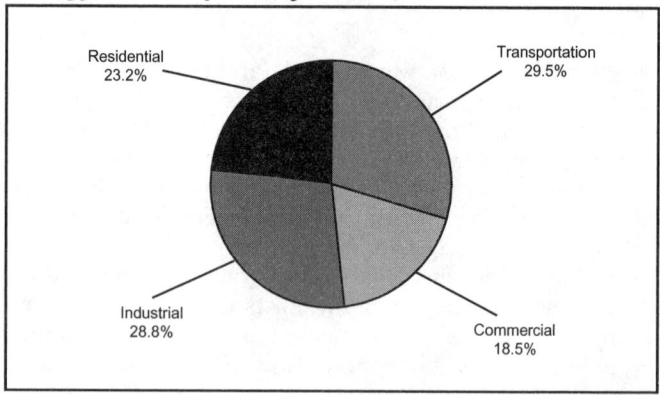

Table WA-15. Energy Consumption, Expenditures, and Prices, Selected Years 1960–2001

(Dollars, Btu [British Thermal Unit], percent distribution.)

Item	1960	1965	1970	1975	1980	1985	1990	1995	2000	2001
Total Consumption (Billion Btu)	807 393	996 751	1 294 295	1 459 339	1 642 278	1 725 996	2 063 514	2 128 956	2 222 171	2 033 894
Consumption per capita (million Btu)	283.0	335.9	379.2	403.0	397.4	392.3	424.0	392.0	377.0	339.4
Consumption by Sector (Percent Distribution)										
Residential	21.8	20.2	20.8	20.6	21.4	22.3	19.6	20.1	21.5	23.2
Commercial	8.0	8.0	9.0	11.5	12.7	16.6	14.5	15.2	17.0	18.5
Industrial	47.9	51.0	47.7	43.8	40.5	37.0	38.2	34.9	33.3	28.8
Transportation	22.3	20.7	22.5	24.1	25.3	24.0	27.6	29.8	28.2	29.5
Consumption by Source (Billion Btu)										
Coal	15 231	12 134	5 860	76 241	90 956	93 669	85 575	69 790	106 237	99 506
Natural gas	67 207	116 216	158 242	171 236	135 466	139 983	167 617	264 474	297 569	323 067
Petroleum	356 908	406 010	506 663	548 859	594 726	607 476	763 158	825 704	844 558	842 521
Nuclear electric power	0	0	28 693	36 432	22 269	85 377	60 762	72 938	89 744	86 200
Hydroelectric power[1]	369 596	515 280	729 600	871 063	863 361	804 970	909 829	850 742	818 762	556 863
Wood and waste	58 533	66 250	66 521	64 299	91 656	110 216	98 872	92 618	88 792	80 022
Other	-172	-1 641	2 105	5 902	2 932	3 083	1 279	-2 053	-3 215	-16 626
Net interstate flow of electricity/losses[2]	-59 910	-117 499	-203 388	-314 693	-159 089	-118 777	-23 577	-45 257	-20 275	62 341
Total Expenditures (Thousands of Dollars)	...	...	1 250 100	2 427 300	5 477 400	7 326 300	8 572 400	9 682 600	12 945 800	12 906 000
Expenditures per capita (dollars)	...	...	366	670	1 326	1 665	1 761	1 783	2 196	2 154
Prices by Sector (Dollars Per Million Btu)										
Total	...	...	1.58	2.79	5.89	7.36	7.00	7.31	9.46	9.89
Residential	...	...	2.09	3.20	5.69	9.42	9.99	10.81	11.68	13.24
Commercial	...	...	1.90	2.94	5.33	7.85	8.57	10.08	10.78	12.52
Industrial	...	...	0.70	1.51	3.29	4.80	4.30	4.51	5.51	5.82
Transportation	...	...	2.23	3.73	7.86	8.24	7.52	7.38	10.76	10.18

[1]A negative number in this row results from pumped storage for which, overall, more electricity is expended than created to provide electricity during peak demand periods.
[2]Net interstate flow of electricity is the difference between the amount of energy in the electricity sold within a state (including associated losses) and the energy input at the electric utilities within the state. A positive number indicates that more electricity (including associated losses) came into the state than went out of the state during the year; conversely, a negative number indicates that more electricity (including associated losses) went out of the state than came into the state.
. . . = Not available.

Table WA-16. State Taxes, Fiscal 2004

(Dollars, percent distribution.)

Item	Thousands of dollars	Percent distribution	Dollars per capita	
			State	U.S.
TOTAL TAXES	13 895 346	100.0	2 239.7	2 024.8
Property Taxes	1 526 617	11.0	246.1	38.9
Sales and Gross Receipts	10 864 600	78.2	1 751.2	1 003.4
General sales and gross receipts	8 423 160	60.6	1 357.7	677.0
Selective sales taxes	2 441 440	17.6	393.5	326.4
Alcoholic beverages	192 618	1.4	31.0	15.7
Insurance premiums	345 614	2.5	55.7	47.0
Motor fuels	925 723	6.7	149.2	114.6
Public utilities	353 136	2.5	56.9	39.2
Tobacco products	352 527	2.5	56.8	42.0
Other selective sales	269 992	1.9	43.5	49.8
Licenses	686 564	4.9	110.7	134.9
Motor vehicle	334 244	2.4	53.9	59.4
Occupation and business, not elsewhere classified	190 476	1.4	30.7	37.1
Other Taxes	817 565	5.9	131.8	847.6
Death and gift	139 855	1.0	22.5	19.6
Documentary and stock transfer	640 086	4.6	103.2	27.1

GOVERNMENT FINANCE

In 2003, Washington's revenues and expenditures per person were well above the national averages. The state's spending per capita on natural resources, education, hospitals, and health were all above average. Outlays for government administration were well below average. Tax collections per person in fiscal year 2004 were above the national average, ranking 13th in the nation. The state primarily relied on its high general sales taxes and property taxes. Washington had no individual income or corporate income taxes. The state's property taxes were the fifth highest of the 37 states with such taxes.

Per Capita State Taxes, Fiscal 2004

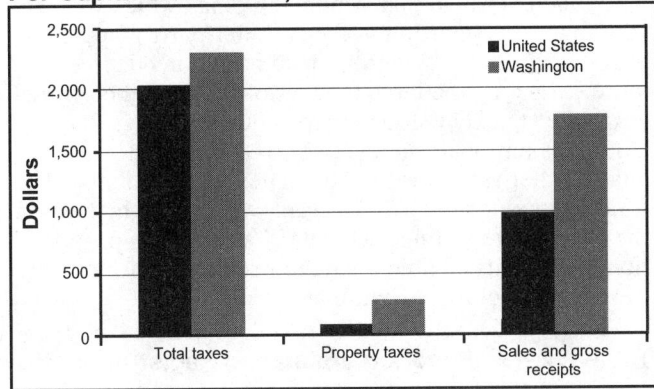

Table WA-17. State Government Finances, 2003

(Dollars, percent distribution.)

Item	Millions of dollars	Percent distribution	Dollars per capita	
			State	U.S.
GENERAL REVENUE	24 133 548	100.0	3 936.3	3 832.6
Intergovernmental revenue	7 012 389	29.1	1 143.8	1 246.0
Taxes	12 960 220	53.7	2 113.9	1 891.6
General sales	8 007 337	33.2	1 306.0	636.0
Selective sales	2 096 067	8.7	341.9	307.4
License taxes	671 917	2.8	109.6	123.6
Individual income tax	0	0.0	0.0	626.8
Corporate income tax	0	0.0	0.0	97.8
Other taxes	2 184 899	9.1	356.4	99.9
Current charges	2 678 313	11.1	436.8	366.5
Miscellaneous general revenue	1 482 626	6.1	241.8	328.6
GENERAL EXPENDITURE	26 020 778	100.0	4 244.1	4 010.5
Intergovernmental expenditure	6 785 341	26.1	1 106.7	1 316.9
Direct expenditure	19 235 437	73.9	3 137.4	2 693.6
Expenditure by Function				
Education	10 696 522	41.1	1 744.7	1 416.4
Public welfare	6 250 197	24.0	1 019.4	1 083.3
Hospitals	1 073 482	4.1	175.1	132.3
Health	1 374 328	5.3	224.2	173.0
Highways	1 906 430	7.3	311.0	295.4
Police protection	245 281	0.9	40.0	38.4
Correction	786 781	3.0	128.3	135.0
Natural resources	696 612	2.7	113.6	64.0
Parks and recreation	121 566	0.5	19.8	20.1
Government administration	588 709	2.3	96.0	151.3
Interest on general debt	727 208	2.8	118.6	107.8
Other and unallocable	1 553 662	6.0	253.4	393.4
DEBT AT END OF FISCAL YEAR	14 620 855	X	2 384.7	2 404.7
CASH AND SECURITY HOLDINGS	59 772 274	X	9 749.2	8 938.4

X = Not applicable.

Table WA-18. Education Indicators, 2000–2004

(Percent, number.)

Item	State	U.S.
Total Population 25 Years and Over (Thousands), 2004	4 029	186 877
Educational Attainment, 2004		
Percent high school graduate or more	89.7	85.2
Percent college graduate or more	29.9	27.7
Elementary and Secondary Schools, 2002–2003		
Total students	1 014 798	48 202 324
Percent of students eligible for free or reduced-price lunch ..	36.7	40.6
Percent of students who were English language learners	5.7	7.8
Total schools	2 207	92 330
Student/teacher ratio	19.3	15.9
Per student expenditures	7 252	8 041
Dropouts, Grades 9–12, 2000–2001 (Percent)	7.1	. . .
Higher Education, 2002–2003		
Total enrollment	346 078	17 035 027
Bachelor's degrees awarded	25 908	1 348 503
Percent women	57.1	57.5

. . . = Not available.

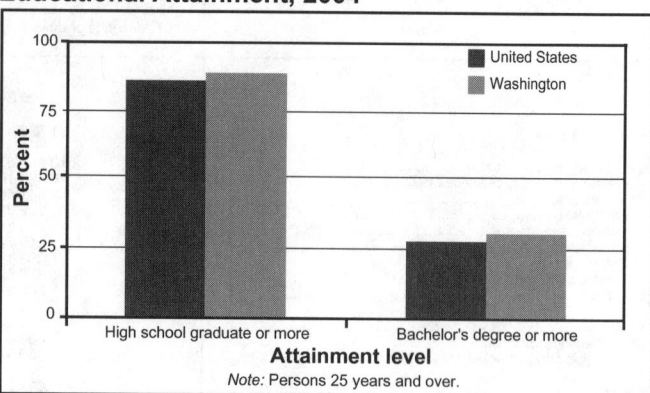

Educational Attainment, 2004

Note: Persons 25 years and over.

EDUCATION

In 2004, 89.7 percent of Washington's residents age 25 years and over held high school diplomas, which was the 10th highest proportion in the nation. Nearly 30 percent of residents in this age group held bachelor's degrees or more, reflecting the large number of highly-skilled workers in the state. Per student expenditures of $7,252 were below the national average of $8,041. Washington's student/teacher ratio was the 5th highest in the country. The state's dropout rate of 7.1 percent was the 3rd highest of the 46 states reporting such data. Washington's proportion of students eligible for free or reduced-price lunch was slightly below the national average.

VOTER PARTICIPATION

Voter turnout was above average for both the 2000 and 2004 elections. Asians and Hispanics had the lowest voter participation rates in 2004. More than 77 percent of eligible voters age 65 to 74 years turned out, while just 48.2 percent of eligible voters age 18 to 24 years cast ballots. According to the official tally by the Clerk of the U.S. House of Representatives, 50.2 percent of Washington's voters cast their ballots for the Democratic presidential candidate in 2000; this proportion increased to 52.8 percent in 2004. The comparable percentages for the Republican candidate were 44.6 and 45.6 percent, respectively.

Table WA-19. Reported Voting and Registration, November 2000 and November 2004

(Numbers in thousands, percent.)

Characteristic	Total population 18 years and over	Total citizen		Total registered		Total voted	
		Number	Percent	Number	Percent	Number	Percent
NOVEMBER 2000							
Total	4 314	4 078	94.5	2 852	66.1	2 527	58.6
Male	2 053	1 936	94.3	1 361	66.3	1 196	58.3
Female	2 261	2 142	94.8	1 491	66.0	1 331	58.9
NOVEMBER 2004							
Total	4 596	4 220	91.8	3 133	68.2	2 851	62.0
Male	2 214	2 031	91.7	1 488	67.2	1 343	60.7
Female	2 382	2 190	91.9	1 645	69.0	1 508	63.3
Race and Hispanic Origin							
White alone	3 792	3 584	94.5	2 722	71.8	2 497	65.9
Non-Hispanic White alone	3 584	3 483	97.2	2 674	74.6	2 461	68.7
Black alone	141	141	100.0	80	56.7	67	47.6
Asian alone	404	257	63.7	159	39.4	147	36.3
Hispanic or Latino[1]	248	120	48.4	56	22.4	44	17.6
White alone or in combination	3 941	3 728	94.6	2 842	72.1	2 592	65.8
Non-Hispanic White alone or in combination	3 720	3 619	97.3	2 791	75.0	2 553	68.6
Black alone or in combination	175	167	95.3	99	56.8	83	47.5
Asian alone or in combination	443	297	66.9	191	43.2	169	38.1
Age							
18 to 24 years	544	482	88.5	318	58.5	262	48.2
25 to 44 years	1 795	1 568	87.4	1 084	60.4	948	52.8
45 to 64 years	1 671	1 603	95.9	1 274	76.2	1 198	71.7
65 to 74 years	309	298	96.3	242	78.3	239	77.5
75 years and over	277	269	97.3	215	77.6	202	73.1

[1]May be of any race.

At a Glance:

- West Virginia's population was over 1.8 million in 2004, making it the 37th most populous state in the nation.

- Non-Hispanic Whites made up 94.4 percent of the state's population, which was the third largest proportion of this racial group in the nation. The state had among the smallest proportions of Hispanic and Asian and Pacific Islander residents in the country.

- West Virginia's age-adjusted death rate for all causes was the fourth highest in the nation.

- The state's median household income of $33,286 was the lowest in the country. West Virginia's poverty rate of 14.2 percent was the 14th highest in the nation.

- Economic activity grew slowly between 2001 and 2004. The state's real gross state product was among the country's smallest, ranking 42nd in the nation in 2004. However, West Virginia's unemployment rate of 5.3 percent was below the national average.

- The state had the lowest proportion of college graduates in the country. Among its residents age 25 years and over, just 15.3 percent held bachelor's degrees or more in 2004.

Table WV-1. Population by Sex and Age, 1990, 2000, and 2004

(Number, percent.)

Sex and age	1990	2000	2004	Percent distribution, 2004	Average annual percent change, 2000–2004
Total Population	1 793 477	1 808 344	1 815 354	X	0.1
Percent of total U.S. population	0.7	0.6	0.6	X	X
Sex					
Male	861 536	879 170	887 302	48.9	0.2
Female	931 941	929 174	928 052	51.1	0.0
Age					
Under 5 years	106 659	101 805	101 109	5.6	-0.5
5 to 17 years	336 918	300 588	283 532	15.6	-1.2
18 years and over	368 205	1 405 951	1 430 713	78.8	0.4
18 to 24 years	1 349 900	172 431	172 806	9.5	-0.3
25 to 44 years	179 991	501 343	478 437	26.4	-0.8
45 to 64 years	532 807	455 282	501 116	27.6	2.2
65 years and over	268 897	276 895	278 354	15.3	0.3
85 years and over	25 451	31 779	32 535	1.8	1.9
Median age (years)	35.3	38.9	40.2	X	X

X = Not applicable.

Average Annual Rate of Population Growth, 1980–2004

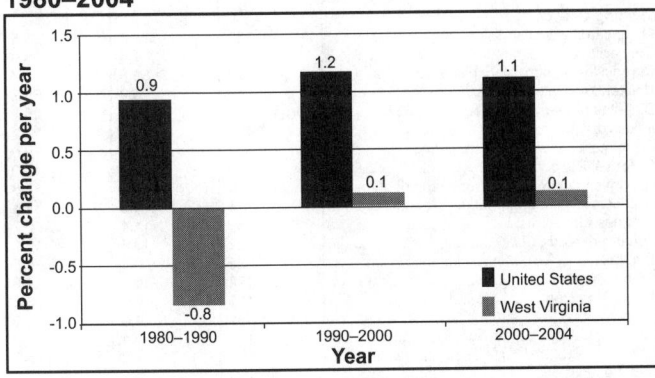

POPULATION

West Virginia's population continued to be one of the slowest growing in the country. Over the 2000–2004 period, the state's population grew just 0.4 percent, ranking 19th in the country and well below the rates of its neighborings. An influx of people from other states and from abroad prevented a potential population loss due to the state's low birth rate (which ranked 48th in the country). In 2004, West Virginia's population age 65 years and over was the second highest in the country, below only the proportion in Florida. The state's population age 18 years and under was the second lowest in the country, above only that of the District of Columbia.

Table WV-2. Population by Race and Hispanic Origin, 1990, 2000, and 2004

(Number, percent.)

Race and Hispanic origin	1990	2000	2004
Total Population	1 793 477	1 808 344	1 815 354
Non-Hispanic (Percent)			
One race[1]			
White	95.8	94.7	94.4
Black	3.1	3.2	3.2
American Indian, Alaska Native[2]	0.1	0.2	0.2
Asian and Pacific Islander[2]	0.4	0.5	0.6
Other race[2]	0.1	. . .	. . .
Two or more races	. . .	0.7	0.8
Hispanic or Latino[3] (Percent)	0.5	0.7	0.8

[1]Individuals could report only one race in the 1990 census and could report one or more races on the 2000 census. Data on race in 2000 and 2004 are not comparable to 1990.
[2]Data for 1990 include people of Hispanic or Latino origin.
[3]May be of any race.
. . . = Not available.

Minority Population as a Percent of Total Population, 2004

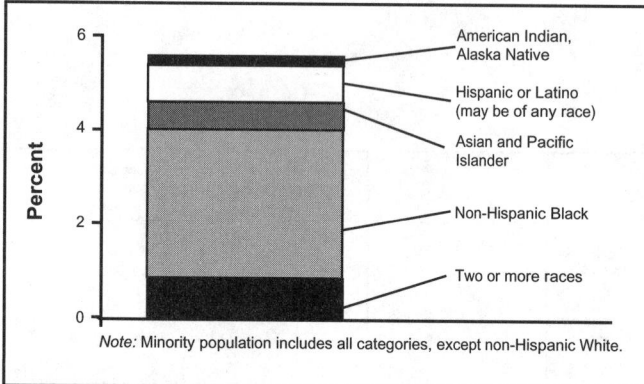

Note: Minority population includes all categories, except non-Hispanic White.

Age-Adjusted Death Rates, Average 2000–2002

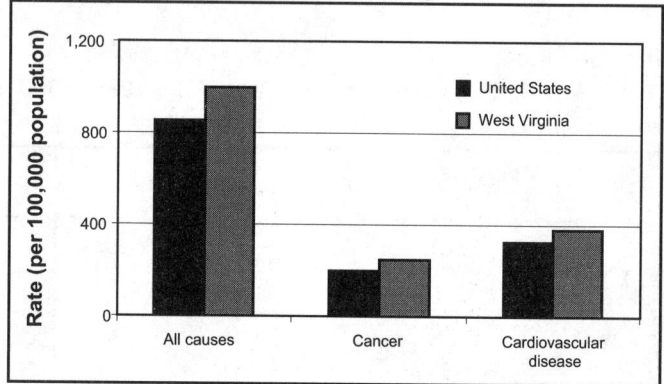

HEALTH

In 2004, 16.4 percent of West Virginians lacked health insurance coverage, compared with 15.7 percent of people nationally. The state's infant mortality rate was the 13th highest in the country. Despite West Virginia's very low birth rate, its birth rate for teenage mothers was above the national average.

Table WV-3. Health Characteristics, 2000–2004

(Number, rate, percent.)

Item	State	U.S.
Births, 2003–2004		
Number of births	20 935	4 089 950
Birth rate (per 1,000 population)	11.6	14.1
Teenage birth rate (per 1,000 women age 15–19 years)	44.8	41.6
Mortality Rates, Average 2000–2002		
Infant mortality rate (per 1,000 live births)	7.9	6.9
Age-adjusted mortality rate (per 100,000 population)		
All races	998.8	853.3
Non-Hispanic White	1 002.2	843.1
Black	1 119.6	1 097.7
American Indian, Alaska Native	. . .	687.0
Asian and Pacific Islander	. . .	486.0
Hispanic or Latino[1]	342.7	642.7
Health Insurance, 2004		
Percent of all persons without health insurance	16.4	15.7
Percent of children without health insurance	8.8	11.2
Percent of low-income children without health insurance	6.6	7.1

[1]May be of any race.
. . . = Not available.

Table WV-4. Leading Causes of Death, Average 2000–2002

(Number, rate per 100,000 population.)

Cause	Number of deaths	Age-adjusted death rates	
		State	U.S.
ALL CAUSES	21 032	998.8	853.3
Leading Causes			
Major cardiovascular diseases	8 159	381.9	326.5
Cancer	4 697	219.4	196.0
Chronic lower respiratory diseases	1 282	59.3	43.7
Unintentional injuries	869	46.2	35.7
Diabetes (underlying cause)	802	37.6	25.2
Influenza and pneumonia	455	21.4	22.7
Alzheimer's disease	388	18.1	19.0
Motor vehicle accidents	374	20.5	15.0
Nephritis, nephrotic syndrome, and nephrosis ..	410	19.1	13.8
Septicemia	314	14.8	11.4
Suicides	269	14.4	10.7
Firearm-related	255	13.6	10.3
Cirrhosis	223	10.8	9.5
Drug-induced	192	10.7	7.9
Alcohol-induced	133	6.7	6.9
Homicides	81	4.6	6.0
Falls	114	5.4	5.2
HIV	22	1.2	5.0
Viral hepatitis	23	1.1	2.0
Anemias	48	2.3	1.6
Drownings	30	1.7	1.3
Fire deaths	28	1.4	1.2

Note: The rates are age-adjusted to the U.S. 2000 standard population.

Table WV-5. Households and Housing Characteristics, 1990, 2000, and 2004

(Number, percent, and dollars.)

Characteristic	1990	2000	2004	Average annual percent change, 2000–2004
Total Households	688 557	736 481	736 954	0.0
Family households	500 259	504 055	493 917	-0.5
Married-couple family	406 105	397 499	387 215	-0.7
Other family	94 154	106 556	106 702	0.0
Male householder, no wife present	20 627	27 436	26 981	-0.4
Female householder, no husband present	73 527	79 120	79 721	0.2
Nonfamily households	188 298	232 426	243 037	1.1
Householder living alone	168 735	199 587	208 640	1.1
Householder not living alone	19 563	32 839	34 397	1.2
Housing Characteristics				
Average size	2.55	2.40	2.40	X
Housing units	781 295	844 623	866 944	0.7
Occupied housing units	688 557	736 481	736 954	0.0
Owner-occupied	510 058	553 699	545 274	-0.4
Renter-occupied	178 499	182 782	191 680	1.2
Median gross rent of renter-occupied housing units (dollars) ...	303	401	461	3.5
Median value of owner-occupied housing units (dollars)	47 600	72 800	81 826	3.0

X = Not applicable.

Median Housing Value and Median Rent, 2004

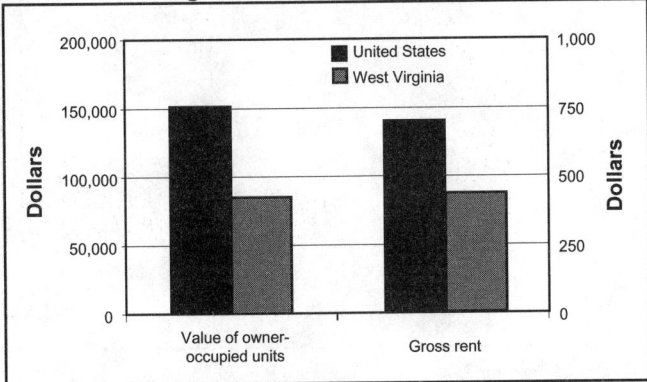

Median Household Income, 1984–2004 (2004 Dollars)

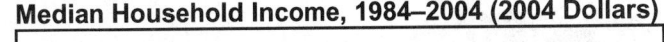
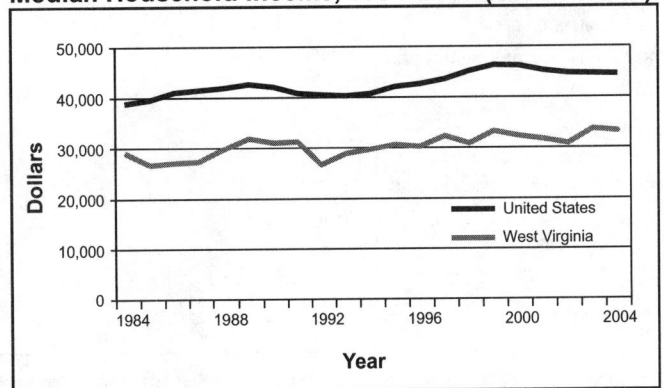

Table WV-6. Household Income and Poverty Status, 1980–2004

(2004 CPI-U-RS adjusted dollars, rate.)

Year	State		U.S.	
	Median household income (2004 dollars)	Poverty rate	Median household income (2004 dollars)	Poverty rate
2004	33 286	14.2	44 389	12.7
2003	33 644	17.4	44 482	12.5
2002	30 839	16.8	44 546	12.1
2001	31 664	16.4	45 062	11.7
2000	32 261	14.7	46 058	11.3
1999	33 208	15.7	46 129	11.9
1998	30 906	17.8	45 003	12.7
1997	32 261	16.4	43 430	13.3
1996	30 263	18.5	42 544	13.7
1995	30 624	16.7	41 943	13.8
1994	29 709	18.6	40 677	14.5
1993	28 863	22.2	40 217	15.1
1992	26 746	22.3	40 422	14.8
1991	31 306	17.9	40 746	14.2
1990	31 023	18.1	41 963	13.5
1989	31 890	15.7	42 524	12.8
1988	29 693	17.9	41 771	13.0
1987	27 362	21.6	41 322	13.4
1986	27 073	22.4	40 939	13.6
1985	26 762	22.3	39 545	14.0
1984	29 142	20.4	38 782	14.4
1983	. . .	22.1	. . .	15.2
1982	. . .	24.8	. . .	15.0
1981	. . .	19.9	. . .	14.0
1980	. . .	15.2	. . .	13.0

. . . = Not available.

Table WV-7. Employment Status by Demographic Group, 2004

(Numbers in thousands, rate.)

Characteristic	Civilian noninstitutional population	Civilian labor force		Employed	Unemployment rate
		Number	Participation rate		
SEX AND AGE					
Total	1 452	795	54.7	753	5.3
16 to 19 years	104	38	36.3	32	16.0
20 to 24 years	110	77	70.1	70	9.2
25 to 34 years	224	167	74.6	157	6.2
35 to 44 years	251	197	78.5	187	5.1
45 to 54 years	266	187	70.1	181	2.9
55 to 64 years	227	104	46.1	102	2.8
65 years and over	270	25	9.2	24	1.6
Men	700	425	60.8	401	5.8
16 to 19 years	45	14	32.4	11	21.8
20 to 24 years	56	41	72.9	37	8.7
25 to 34 years	111	90	80.9	84	6.7
35 to 44 years	131	111	84.5	104	5.8
45 to 54 years	129	99	76.8	96	3.4
55 to 64 years	113	57	50.1	55	3.2
65 years and over	115	14	11.9	13	2.1
Women	752	369	49.1	352	4.7
16 to 19 years	59	23	39.1	20	12.3
20 to 24 years	54	36	67.1	32	9.8
25 to 34 years	113	77	68.3	73	5.6
35 to 44 years	120	86	72.0	83	4.1
45 to 54 years	137	88	63.9	86	2.3
55 to 64 years	114	48	42.1	47	2.3
MARITAL STATUS					
Married men, spouse present	412	267	64.8	256	3.9
Married women, spouse present	391	204	52.3	198	3.1
Women who maintain families	83	47	56.4	43	8.2
RACE, HISPANIC ORIGIN, AND SEX					
White	1 390	760	54.7	723	4.9
Men	672	408	60.7	386	5.3
Women	718	352	49.1	337	4.4
Black	37	21	55.6	17	15.5
RACE, HISPANIC ORIGIN, AND AGE					
White					
16 to 19 years	98	36	36.6	31	14.6
20 to 24 years	103	72	69.4	66	8.1
25 to 34 years	210	158	75.1	149	5.3
35 to 44 years	243	191	78.7	182	4.9
45 to 54 years	253	178	70.1	172	2.9
55 to 64 years	221	102	46.3	99	2.7
65 years and over	262	24	9.3	24	1.7

Note: Data in Table 7 are from the Current Population Survey (CPS) and do not match Bureau of Labor Statistics estimates in Table 8. See notes and definitions for more details.

Table WV-8. Employment Status, 1990–2004

(Numbers in thousands, rate.)

Year	Civilian labor force	Employed	Unemployed	Unemployment rate
2004	788 403	746 542	41 861	5.3
2003	795 556	747 637	47 919	6.0
2002	800 400	753 108	47 292	5.9
2001	803 656	762 107	41 549	5.2
2000	809 344	765 068	44 276	5.5
1999	813 380	762 395	50 985	6.3
1998	807 092	754 629	52 463	6.5
1997	800 715	746 442	54 273	6.8
1996	794 589	735 710	58 879	7.4
1995	785 582	723 904	61 678	7.9
1994	780 764	712 664	68 100	8.7
1993	778 015	696 784	81 231	10.4
1992	777 421	689 628	87 793	11.3
1991	769 291	688 512	80 779	10.5
1990	756 306	691 184	65 122	8.6

Note: Population age 16 years and over.

Unemployment Rate, 1980–2004

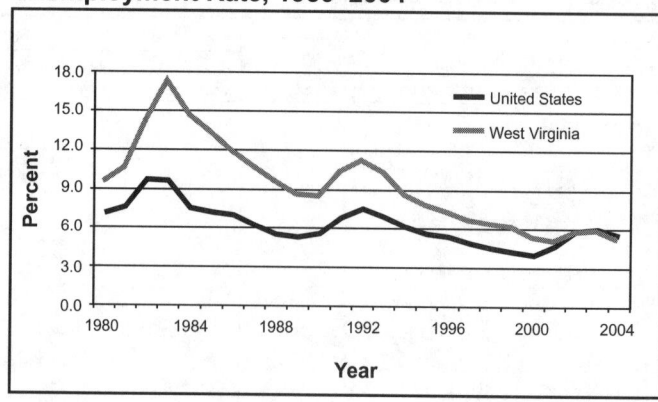

Table WV-9. Employment and Average Wages by Industry, 2001–2004

(Estimates are based on the 2002 North American Industry Classification System [NAICS].)

Industry	2001	2002	2003	2004	Annual average percent change, 2001–2004
	Number of jobs				
TOTAL EMPLOYMENT BY PLACE OF WORK	883 128	883 499	883 228	898 192	0.6
Farm Employment	22 861	23 098	23 046	23 007	0.2
Nonfarm Employment	860 267	860 401	860 182	875 185	0.6
Private employment	711 622	709 980	709 872	723 980	0.6
Forestry, fishing, hunting, and other[1]	4 254	4 352	3 860	3 770	-3.9
Mining..	28 210	27 270	27 754	30 038	2.1
Utilities..	7 003	6 795	6 410	6 319	-3.4
Construction..	51 149	49 056	48 803	51 229	0.1
Manufacturing	74 820	71 332	67 167	65 661	-4.3
Durable goods manufacturing	46 293	43 973	41 421	41 040	-3.9
Nondurable goods manufacturing	28 527	27 359	25 746	24 621	-4.8
Wholesale trade	26 363	25 482	24 933	25 547	-1.0
Retail trade...	111 678	110 716	110 735	112 719	0.3
Transportation and warehousing	25 678	25 064	24 600	25 123	-0.7
Information	15 256	14 083	14 150	13 278	-4.5
Finance and insurance	27 988	28 868	28 362	27 785	-0.2
Real estate and rental and leasing	19 941	20 326	21 260	22 176	3.6
Professional and technical services	35 870	36 581	36 964	37 810	1.8
Management of companies and enterprises	2 968	2 968	2 932	3 127	1.8
Administrative and waste services	39 463	38 662	38 649	40 323	0.7
Educational services	11 882	12 182	12 520	12 789	2.5
Health care and social assistance	106 641	110 244	112 122	114 225	2.3
Arts, entertainment, and recreation	13 428	14 677	15 041	16 217	6.5
Accommodation and food services	58 422	59 121	61 118	62 259	2.1
Other services, except public administration	50 608	52 201	52 492	53 585	1.9
Government and government enterprises	148 645	150 421	150 310	151 205	0.6
	Dollars				
AVERAGE WAGES AND SALARIES BY PLACE OF WORK ...	27 407	28 046	28 764	29 870	2.9
Farm Earnings	13 305	16 924	14 175	15 814	5.9
Nonfarm Earnings	27 443	28 074	28 809	29 912	2.9
Private earnings	27 046	27 520	28 069	29 278	2.7
Forestry, fishing, hunting, and other[1]	18 657	18 727	19 193	19 995	2.3
Mining..	49 670	50 330	51 463	54 385	3.1
Utilities..	59 252	59 147	61 621	62 825	2.0
Construction..	32 404	31 631	30 887	32 424	0.0
Manufacturing	38 992	39 633	40 831	42 680	3.1
Durable goods manufacturing	34 614	35 635	36 574	38 720	3.8
Nondurable goods manufacturing	46 046	46 027	47 627	49 238	2.3
Wholesale trade	36 423	37 960	38 845	40 860	3.9
Retail trade...	17 736	18 434	18 926	19 504	3.2
Transportation and warehousing	35 989	36 218	37 308	38 677	2.4
Information	33 427	35 751	36 855	37 844	4.2
Finance and insurance	31 458	31 687	32 952	34 630	3.3
Real estate and rental and leasing	21 168	22 465	22 998	23 671	3.8
Professional and technical services	32 864	34 641	36 168	37 711	4.7
Management of companies and enterprises	45 921	45 157	44 944	49 988	2.9
Administrative and waste services	17 109	17 533	18 269	19 564	4.6
Educational services	16 396	16 266	17 008	17 857	2.9
Health care and social assistance	27 742	28 463	29 320	30 492	3.2
Arts, entertainment, and recreation	15 545	16 794	18 073	18 991	6.9
Accommodation and food services	11 519	11 859	12 095	12 360	2.4
Other services, except public administration	17 519	18 019	18 621	19 805	4.2
Government and government enterprises	29 001	30 207	31 643	32 360	3.7

Note: Average wages and salaries are a calculation by the editors of wage and salary disbursements divided by full- and part-time wage and salary employment. Data may not add to total or may appear as zero due to rounding.

[1] "Other" consists of the number of jobs held by U.S. residents employed by international organizations and foreign embassies and consulates in the United States.

LABOR MARKET

West Virginia's unemployment rate was slightly below average over the 2001–2004 period. This was caused by a low labor force participation rate, rather than a dynamic labor market. Employment was static over the 2001–2003 period and only showed some growth in 2004. Over the period as a whole, jobs in service-providing industries, particularly health care, rose steadily, and mining employment also increased. Employment in manufacturing industries declined, while construction and retail trade showed little change. The government sector was the state's largest employer, followed by health care and retail trade. Average wages and salaries were well below the national averages across all industries.

Employment by Industry, 2004

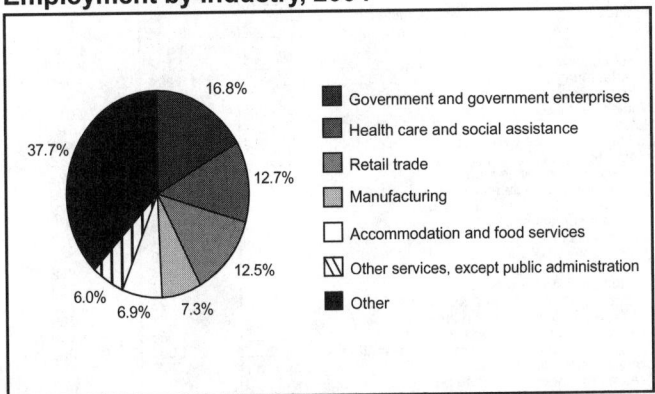

- 16.8%
- 37.7%
- 12.7%
- 6.0%
- 6.9%
- 7.3%
- 12.5%

- Government and government enterprises
- Health care and social assistance
- Retail trade
- Manufacturing
- Accommodation and food services
- Other services, except public administration
- Other

Table WV-10. Personal Income by Major Source, Selected Years 1980–2004

(Millions of dollars, except where noted.)

Item	1980	1990	2000	2001	2002	2003	2004	Average annual percent change, 2000–2004
Earnings by Place of Work	12 575	18 177	26 951	28 192	28 835	29 721	31 588	4.0
Wage and salary disbursements	9 531	13 315	19 387	20 106	20 543	20 942	22 027	3.2
Supplements to wages and salaries	2 038	3 133	5 156	5 290	5 721	6 075	6 603	6.4
Proprietors' income[1]	1 007	1 729	2 409	2 796	2 572	2 704	2 958	5.3
Farm proprietors' income	-14	14	-7	-47	-88	-83	-81	X
Nonfarm proprietors' income	1 021	1 715	2 415	2 843	2 660	2 787	3 038	5.9
(-) Contributions for government social insurance[2]	1 297	2 420	3 905	3 952	3 990	4 135	4 356	2.8
(+) Adjustment for residence[3]	-301	70	568	663	718	754	806	9.1
(=) Net Earnings by Place of Residence	10 978	15 827	23 615	24 902	25 563	26 340	28 038	4.4
(+) Dividends, interest, and rent[4]	2 034	4 759	6 676	6 689	6 413	6 025	6 075	-2.3
(+) Personal current transfer receipts	2 829	5 394	9 292	10 312	11 294	11 925	12 507	7.7
Personal income	15 841	25 980	39 582	41 902	43 270	44 290	46 619	4.2
Farm income	15 834	25 940	39 567	41 922	43 325	44 338	46 662	4.2
Nonfarm income	7	40	15	-19	-56	-48	-43	X
Per Capita Personal Income (Dollars)[5]	8 118	14 493	21 900	23 256	23 969	24 450	25 681	4.1

Note: Data may not add to total or may appear as zero due to rounding.

[1]Proprietors' income includes the inventory valuation adjustment and the capital consumption adjustment.
[2]Contributions for government social insurance are included in earnings by type and industry, but they are excluded from personal income.
[3]The adjustment for residence is the net inflow of the earnings of interarea commuters.
[4]Rental income of persons includes the capital consumption adjustment.
[5]Per capita personal income is total personal income divided by total midyear population.
X = Not applicable.

Per Capita Personal Income, 1980–2004 (Current Dollars)

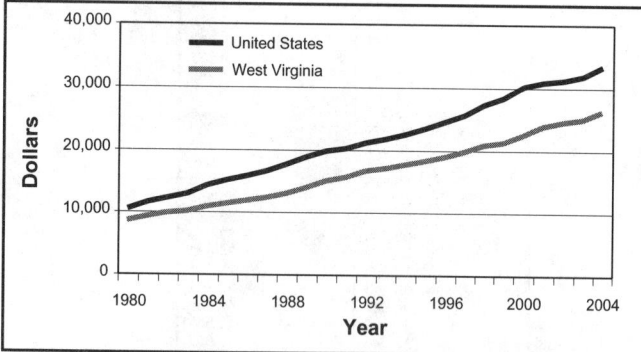

ECONOMIC ACTIVITY

Economic activity grew at rates below the national average throughout the 2001–2004 period. In 2004, the growth rate of West Virginia's gross state product was among the lowest in the country, ranking 43rd in the nation. Contributing to this performance was the relatively slow growth across a broad range of industries in both the service-providing and goods-producing sectors, with the notable exceptions of retail trade and government (West Virginia's two largest sectors). Housing price increases have occurred at a rate about one-third below the national average . In 2004, the median value of owner-occupied housing in West Virginia was the third lowest in the country.

Table WV-11. Real Gross State Product, 1997–2004

(Millions of chained 2000 dollars, percent.)

Industry	1997	1998	1999	2000	2001	2002	2003	2004	Average annual percent change, 2001–2004
GROSS STATE PRODUCT	40 605	41 020	42 234	41 690	42 065	42 703	43 158	44 299	1.7
As a percent of U.S. gross product	0.5	0.5	0.4	0.4	0.4	0.4	0.4	0.4	X
Private Industries	34 229	34 525	35 503	34 801	35 104	35 629	36 027	37 046	1.8
Agriculture, forestry, fishing, and hunting	188	201	201	265	238	220	253	251	1.8
Mining	2 645	2 915	2 870	2 911	2 951	2 922	2 807	2 814	-1.6
Utilities	1 981	1 939	1 904	1 999	1 929	1 945	2 127	2 154	3.7
Construction	2 133	2 009	1 859	1 803	1 913	1 722	1 627	1 721	-3.5
Manufacturing	6 204	5 921	6 492	5 704	5 053	5 130	5 080	5 055	-3.5
As a percent of gross state product	15.3	14.4	15.4	13.7	12.0	12.0	11.8	11.4	X
Wholesale trade	1 862	2 015	2 053	1 983	2 145	2 247	2 147	2 245	1.5
Retail trade	3 109	3 195	3 366	3 392	3 620	3 771	3 962	4 194	5.0
Transportation and warehousing	1 544	1 475	1 490	1 459	1 361	1 365	1 401	1 455	2.3
Information	953	1 015	1 068	1 079	1 186	1 234	1 356	1 363	4.7
Finance and insurance	1 460	1 483	1 508	1 558	1 686	1 756	1 722	1 760	1.4
Real estate and rental and leasing	3 483	3 499	3 664	3 705	3 962	4 049	4 053	4 102	1.2
Services	8 730	8 879	9 028	8 941	9 071	9 308	9 557	10 005	3.3
As a percent of gross state product	21.5	21.6	21.4	21.4	21.6	21.8	22.1	22.6	X
Professional and technical services	1 351	1 416	1 479	1 426	1 527	1 616	1 697	1 756	4.8
Management of companies and enterprises	229	207	213	201	265	271	291	329	7.5
Administrative and waste services	829	862	895	816	812	819	851	914	4.0
Educational services	227	223	218	212	208	193	185	182	-4.4
Health care and social assistance	3 696	3 723	3 754	3 789	3 788	3 888	3 961	4 055	2.3
Arts, entertainment, and recreation	253	268	278	315	336	386	400	467	11.6
Accommodation and food services	1 058	1 100	1 153	1 172	1 157	1 169	1 204	1 237	2.3
Other services, except public administration	1 087	1 080	1 038	1 010	978	966	968	1 065	2.9
Government	6 370	6 492	6 729	6 889	6 961	7 073	7 131	7 253	1.4
As a percent of gross state product	15.7	15.8	15.9	16.5	16.5	16.6	16.5	16.4	X

X = Not applicable.

Table WV-12. Government Transfer Payments, Selected Years 1980–2004

(Millions of dollars, percent.)

Item	1980	1990	2000	2001	2002	2003	2004	Average annual percent change, 2000–2004
CURRENT TRANSFER PAYMENTS TO INDIVIDUALS	2 694	5 164	8 894	9 874	10 900	11 575	12 130	8.1
Retirement and Disability Insurance Benefits	1 675	2 981	4 367	4 877	5 422	5 639	5 845	7.6
Old-age, survivors, and disability insurance (OASDI) benefits	1 175	2 247	3 491	3 692	3 878	4 016	4 168	4.5
Railroad retirement and disability benefits	83	135	153	154	158	160	163	1.6
Workers' compensation	115	330	541	860	1 222	1 307	1 368	26.1
Other government retirement and disability insurance benefits	301	269	181	170	165	156	147	-5.2
Medical Benefits	380	1 301	3 212	3 520	3 783	4 156	4 492	8.7
Medicare benefits	264	856	1 760	1 945	2 082	2 199	2 403	8.1
Public assistance medical care benefits	112	432	1 435	1 553	1 669	1 928	2 056	9.4
Military medical insurance benefits	4	13	17	23	32	28	33	18.9
Income Maintenance Benefits	262	525	842	920	992	1 031	1 099	6.9
Supplemental Security Income (SSI) benefits	73	146	318	335	349	357	374	4.1
Family assistance	61	112	96	137	135	116	111	3.7
Food stamps	91	198	182	182	200	220	240	7.2
Other income maintenance benefits	37	69	246	265	308	338	374	11.0
Unemployment Insurance Compensation	197	117	118	145	230	257	187	12.2
Veterans' Benefits	151	182	269	299	352	377	386	9.5
Federal Education and Training Assistance	29	56	81	104	115	108	114	9.0
Other Payments to Individuals	*	1	5	10	5	6	6	2.8

Note: See notes and definitions for more details. Data may not add to total or may appear as zero due to rounding.

* = Less than $500,000.

EXPORTS

In 2004, West Virginia's exports ranked 34th in the country, amounting to $3.3 billion. However, a proportion of the state's coal products were shipped to Virginia and exported from there. Consequently, these exports were attributed to that state, rather than to West Virginia. Chemical manufactures were the largest reported export product, followed by transportation equipment and mining products. Computers and electronic products were the fastest growing of West Virginia's leading exports. The state's chief export markets were Canada, Mexico, and Japan, which was a rapidly expanding market for West Virginia's goods.

Leading Exports, 2004

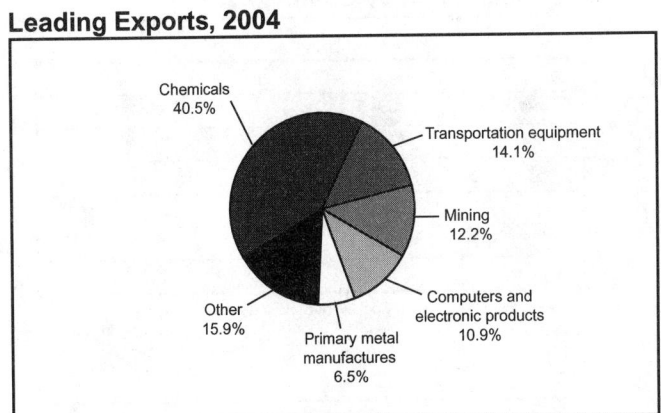

Table WV-13. Exports of Goods by Leading Products and Destinations, 2001–2004

(Millions of dollars, percent, rank based on 2004 dollar values.)

Product and market	2001	2002	2003	2004	Percent share of total, 2004	Average annual percent change, 2001–2004
Total Goods						
Total	2 241	2 237	2 380	3 262	100.0	13.3
Manufactures	1 804	2 006	2 097	2 816	86.3	16.0
Agriculture and livestock	427	219	262	411	12.6	-1.2
Other commodities	10	12	21	35	1.1	51.9
Five Leading Exports (NAICS Code)						
Chemical manufactures (325)	934	1 051	1 116	1 321	40.5	12.2
Transportation equipment (336)	178	230	239	459	14.1	37.0
Mining (212)	408	200	246	397	12.2	-0.9
Computers and electronic products (334)	34	46	59	357	10.9	119.8
Primary metal manufactures (331)	229	217	200	210	6.5	-2.8
Five Leading Markets	2 113	2 121	2 243	3 137	96.2	14.1
Canada	776	739	760	980	30.0	8.1
Mexico	44	76	81	436	13.4	114.1
Japan	214	242	234	362	11.1	19.2
Belgium	227	205	236	283	8.7	7.5
Netherlands	68	70	80	136	4.2	26.0

Table WV-14. Agriculture, 1997 and 2002

(Number, acres, and dollars.)

Item	1997	2002
Number of farms	21 531	20 812
Land in farms (acres)	3 698 204	3 584 668
Farm Size		
Average size of farm (acres)	172	172
Farms by size (percent distribution)		
Fewer than 50 acres	24.8	27.3
50 to 499 acres	69.2	66.4
500 acres or more	6.0	6.3
Market Value of Land and Equipment (Dollars)		
Land and buildings average value per farm	195 213	231 999
Average value per acre	1 123	1 315
Machinery and equipment average value per farm	22 962	26 188
Value of Sales (Thousands of Dollars)		
Agricultural products sold	459 387	482 814
Crops	68 964	69 693
Livestock, poultry, and their products	390 423	413 121
Average per farm (dollars)	21 336	23 199
Value of sales (percent distribution)		
Less than $10,000	82.5	82.5
$10,000 to $99,999	14.5	14.2
$100,000 or more	3.0	3.3
Government Payments		
Payments (thousands of dollars)	3 983	5 180
Percent of farms receiving government payments	11.6	8.0
Farm operators whose principal occupation is farming (percent) ...	37.7	50.5

AGRICULTURE

Cash receipts from farming amounted to nearly $483 million in 2002, according to the Department of Agriculture's Census of Agriculture. This represented an 8 percent increase from the previous agriculture census in 1997. The state's chief products were chickens and cattle. A very large proportion of farms (82.5 percent) had sales of less than $10,000, and 50.5 percent of all farm operators considered farming to be their principal occupation. Just over 27 percent of West Virginia's farms spanned fewer than 50 acres, which was lower than the national average proportion of farms of this size.

ENERGY

West Virginia ranked 10th in the nation for energy consumption, but state's the low price of energy (the fifth lowest in the country) kept per capita expenditures lower. As a result, energy expenditures per person were just below the national average, totaling $2,385 in 2001. The state's chief energy sources were coal, natural gas, and petroleum. The industrial sector accounted for more than 40 percent of total energy use in West Virginia.

Energy Consumption by Source, 2001

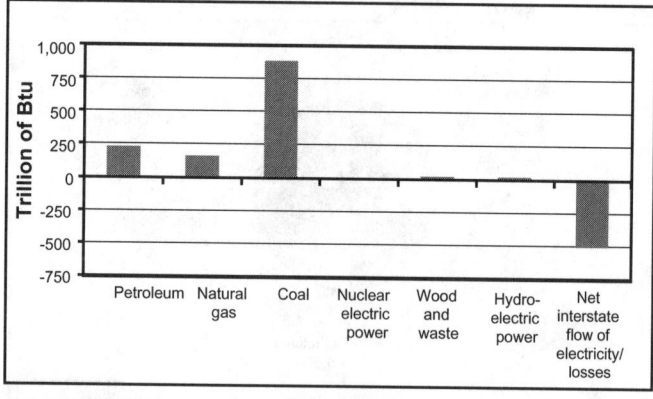

Energy Consumption by Sector, 2001

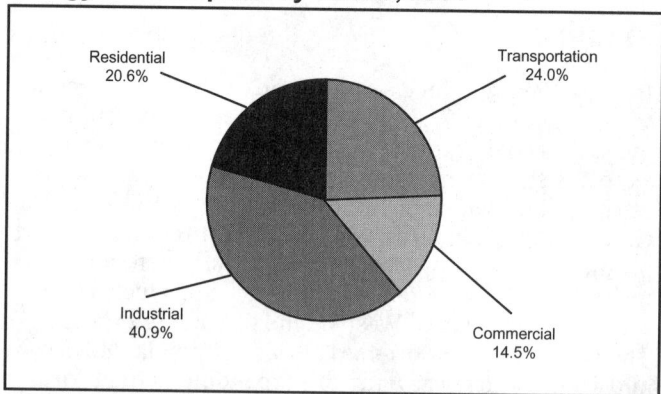

Table WV-15. Energy Consumption, Expenditures, and Prices, Selected Years 1960–2001

(Dollars, Btu [British Thermal Unit], percent distribution.)

Item	1960	1965	1970	1975	1980	1985	1990	1995	2000	2001
Total Consumption (Billion Btu)	618 094	797 980	859 065	856 459	880 393	726 924	824 469	823 938	774 048	761 657
Consumption per capita (million Btu)	332.3	446.8	492.5	464.9	451.6	381.2	459.7	452.6	428.0	422.8
Consumption by Sector (Percent Distribution)										
Residential	14.0	11.8	13.1	14.5	16.3	17.8	16.0	18.4	19.9	20.6
Commercial	5.4	4.8	6.0	7.6	8.1	10.6	10.9	11.9	14.6	14.5
Industrial	66.9	71.1	68.3	61.6	59.0	50.2	55.2	48.1	41.4	40.9
Transportation	13.7	12.3	12.6	16.3	16.6	21.4	17.8	21.6	24.0	24.0
Consumption by Source (Billion Btu)										
Coal	354 418	477 365	612 375	817 441	857 779	871 750	873 486	871 343	977 811	872 307
Natural gas	155 554	176 111	186 535	164 297	147 624	125 018	129 005	157 816	157 926	152 165
Petroleum	126 839	180 966	217 723	263 952	311 510	255 985	295 479	266 837	213 044	215 015
Nuclear electric power	0	0	0	0	0	0	0	0	0	0
Hydroelectric power[1]	10 097	8 657	10 449	11 058	11 571	11 052	13 471	12 299	11 740	9 685
Wood and waste	13 367	11 903	10 703	11 740	9 558	12 989	5 965	7 539	6 062	5 556
Other	0	0	0	0	0	0	0	32	47	46
Net interstate flow of electricity/losses[2]	-42 182	-57 022	-178 720	-412 028	-457 650	-549 870	-492 969	-491 936	-592 583	-493 115
Total Expenditures (Thousands of Dollars)	...	...	798 400	1 885 300	3 808 700	3 651 100	3 922 200	4 032 000	4 394 500	4 297 200
Expenditures per capita (dollars)	...	...	458	1 023	1 954	1 915	2 187	2 215	2 430	2 385
Prices by Sector (Dollars Per Million Btu)										
Total	...	...	1.13	2.78	5.76	7.27	6.64	7.25	8.82	8.74
Residential	...	...	1.72	3.47	6.37	9.74	10.32	11.65	12.36	12.61
Commercial	...	...	1.88	3.34	6.21	9.74	8.98	10.12	9.80	10.45
Industrial	...	...	0.67	2.10	4.31	5.16	4.25	4.15	4.92	4.84
Transportation	...	...	2.67	4.50	9.61	9.13	9.72	9.71	12.09	11.34

[1]A negative number in this row results from pumped storage for which, overall, more electricity is expended than created to provide electricity during peak demand periods.
[2]Net interstate flow of electricity is the difference between the amount of energy in the electricity sold within a state (including associated losses) and the energy input at the electric utilities within the state. A positive number indicates that more electricity (including associated losses) came into the state than went out of the state during the year; conversely, a negative number indicates that more electricity (including associated losses) went out of the state than came into the state.
... = Not available.

Table WV-16. State Taxes, Fiscal 2004

(Dollars, percent distribution.)

Item	Thousands of dollars	Percent distribution	Dollars per capita	
			State	U.S.
TOTAL TAXES	3 749 013	100.0	2 065.6	2 024.8
Property Taxes	3 370	0.1	1.9	38.9
Sales and Gross Receipts	2 093 253	55.8	1 153.3	1 003.4
General sales and gross receipts	1 021 365	27.2	562.7	677.0
Selective sales taxes	1 071 888	28.6	590.6	326.4
Insurance premiums	102 181	2.7	56.3	47.0
Motor fuels	309 274	8.2	170.4	114.6
Public utilities	188 412	5.0	103.8	39.2
Tobacco products	107 609	2.9	59.3	42.0
Other selective sales	346 251	9.2	190.8	49.8
Licenses	179 107	4.8	98.7	134.9
Motor vehicle	83 663	2.2	46.1	59.4
Occupation and business, not elsewhere classified	39 790	1.1	21.9	37.1
Other Taxes	1 473 283	39.3	811.7	847.6
Individual income	1 068 212	28.5	588.6	673.6
Corporation net income	181 515	4.8	100.0	105.1
Severance	204 126	5.4	112.5	21.5

GOVERNMENT FINANCE

West Virginia's revenues and expenditures per person were well above the national averages. The state ranked 12th in the nation for per capita revenue. Spending per capita was above average on education, public welfare, government administration, and highways, but below average on hospitals and health. Tax collections were slightly higher than average in fiscal year 2004, as the state's selective sales taxes on utilities, tobacco, and motor fuels were above average. West Virginia ranked 19th in the nation for per capita taxes. Individual income and severance (taxes imposed on the removal of natural resources) were other major sources of revenue.

Per Capita State Taxes, Fiscal 2004

Table WV-17. State Government Finances, 2003

(Dollars, percent distribution.)

Item	Millions of dollars	Percent distribution	Dollars per capita	
			State	U.S.
GENERAL REVENUE	8 316 567	100.0	4 592.2	3 832.6
Intergovernmental revenue	2 975 382	35.8	1 643.0	1 246.0
Taxes	3 593 993	43.2	1 984.5	1 891.6
General sales	978 022	11.8	540.0	636.0
Selective sales	975 291	11.7	538.5	307.4
License taxes	186 386	2.2	102.9	123.6
Individual income tax	1 055 523	12.7	582.8	626.8
Corporate income tax	182 364	2.2	100.7	97.8
Other taxes	216 407	2.6	119.5	99.9
Current charges	832 027	10.0	459.4	366.5
Miscellaneous general revenue	915 165	11.0	505.3	328.6
GENERAL EXPENDITURE	7 997 646	100.0	4 416.2	4 010.5
Intergovernmental expenditure	1 544 758	19.3	853.0	1 316.9
Direct expenditure	6 452 888	80.7	3 563.2	2 693.6
Expenditure by Function				
Education	2 759 464	34.5	1 523.7	1 416.4
Public welfare	2 230 629	27.9	1 231.7	1 083.3
Hospitals	105 211	1.3	58.1	132.3
Health	232 084	2.9	128.2	173.0
Highways	961 586	12.0	531.0	295.4
Police protection	53 903	0.7	29.8	38.4
Correction	182 064	2.3	100.5	135.0
Natural resources	184 606	2.3	101.9	64.0
Parks and recreation	68 499	0.9	37.8	20.1
Government administration	482 981	6.0	266.7	151.3
Interest on general debt	207 095	2.6	114.4	107.8
Other and unallocable	529 524	6.6	292.4	393.4
DEBT AT END OF FISCAL YEAR	4 260 461	X	2 352.6	2 404.7
CASH AND SECURITY HOLDINGS	10 380 874	X	5 732.1	8 938.4

X = Not applicable.

Table WV-18. Education Indicators, 2000–2004

(Percent, number.)

Item	State	U.S.
Total Population 25 Years and Over (Thousands), 2004	1 237	186 877
Educational Attainment, 2004		
Percent high school graduate or more	80.9	85.2
Percent college graduate or more	15.3	27.7
Elementary and Secondary Schools, 2002–2003		
Total students	282 455	48 202 324
Percent of students eligible for free or reduced-price lunch ..	49.3	40.6
Percent of students who were English language learners	0.5	7.8
Total schools	768	92 330
Student/teacher ratio	14.0	15.9
Per student expenditures	8 319	8 041
Dropouts, Grades 9–12, 2000–2001 (Percent)	3.7	...
Higher Education, 2002–2003		
Total enrollment	97 221	17 035 027
Bachelor's degrees awarded	9 335	1 348 503
Percent women	55.3	57.5

. . . = Not available.

Educational Attainment, 2004

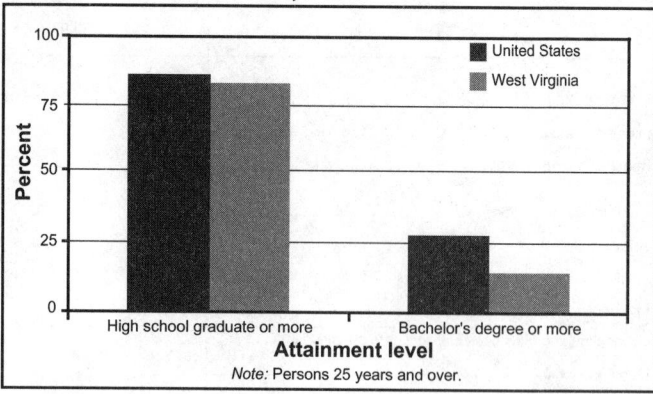

Note: Persons 25 years and over.

EDUCATION

West Virginia's spending on education was above the U.S. average, but the educational attainment of its population remained quite low in 2004. The state's expenditures per student were the 18th highest in the country. Just 80.9 percent of residents age 25 years and over held high school diplomas, and just 15.3 percent held bachelor's degrees or more. The state had the lowest proportion of college graduates in the nation. This partly reflected the higher proportion of older residents, who may have had fewer educational opportunities than their younger counterparts. It also reflected the relatively low skill level required by many of the state's largest employers.

VOTER PARTICIPATION

Voter turnout was below the national average for both the 2000 and 2004 elections. In 2000, the male and female participation rates were about equal. In 2004, the female voter participation rate increased nearly 8 percentage points, while the male participation rate increased just 2 percentage points. According to the official tally by the Clerk of the U.S. House of Representatives, 51.9 percent of eligible West Virginians voted for the Republican presidential candidate in 2000, and this proportion increased to 56.1 percent in 2004. The comparable percentages for the Democratic candidate were 45.6 and 43.2 percent, respectively.

Table WV-19. Reported Voting and Registration, November 2000 and November 2004

(Numbers in thousands, percent.)

Characteristic	Total population 18 years and over	Total citizen		Total registered		Total voted	
		Number	Percent	Number	Percent	Number	Percent
NOVEMBER 2000							
Total	1 405	1 397	99.4	886	63.1	732	52.1
Male	654	651	99.5	412	62.9	341	52.2
Female	750	746	99.4	475	63.2	390	52.0
NOVEMBER 2004							
Total	1 395	1 394	99.9	935	67.0	798	57.2
Male	676	676	100.0	434	64.2	367	54.3
Female	720	718	99.8	502	69.7	431	59.8
Race and Hispanic Origin							
White alone	1 331	1 330	99.9	897	67.4	765	57.5
Non-Hispanic White alone	1 326	1 325	99.9	896	67.5	764	57.6
Black alone	42	42	B	23	B	20	B
Asian alone	5	5	B	3	B	2	B
Hispanic or Latino[1]	5	5	B	1	B	1	B
White alone or in combination	1 345	1 344	99.9	907	67.5	775	57.6
Non-Hispanic White alone or in combination	1 340	1 339	99.9	906	67.6	774	57.7
Black alone or in combination	46	46	B	26	B	22	B
Asian alone or in combination	5	5	B	3	B	2	B
Age							
18 to 24 years	157	157	100.0	89	56.4	72	45.9
25 to 44 years	468	468	100.0	294	62.7	244	52.1
45 to 64 years	502	501	99.8	347	69.2	311	61.9
65 to 74 years	134	134	100.0	99	73.9	92	68.6
75 years and over	133	133	100.0	107	80.0	78	58.8

[1]May be of any race.
B = Base is too small to show derived measure.

At a Glance:

- Wisconsin's population was over 5.5 million in 2004. Its slow rate of population growth from 2000 to 2004 contributed to its fall from the 18th most populous state in 2000 to the 20th most populous state in 2004.

- The state's residents were largely non-Hispanic White; this racial group made up 86.2 percent of the population.

- Just 10.4 percent of Wisconsin's residents lacked health insurance, giving the state one of the five lowest proportions of uninsured population in the nation.

- Wisconsin's median household income was just above the national average, ranking 19th in the country. The state's poverty rate was below the national average.

- Economic growth was average over the 2001–2004 period. In 2004, Wisconsin's real gross state product was the 19th largest in the country. Its unemployment rate of 4.9 percent was well below the national average.

- The educational attainment levels of Wisconsin's population were above average. The state had the 13th highest proportion of residents age 25 years and over with high school diplomas.

Table WI-1. Population by Sex and Age, 1990, 2000, and 2004

(Number, percent.)

Sex and age	1990	2000	2004	Percent distribution, 2004	Average annual percent change, 2000–2004
Total Population	4 891 769	5 363 675	5 509 026	X	0.7
Percent of total U.S. population	2.0	1.9	1.9	X	X
Sex					
Male	2 392 935	2 649 041	2 726 992	49.5	0.7
Female	2 498 834	2 714 634	2 782 034	50.5	0.6
Age					
Under 5 years	360 730	342 340	338 310	6.1	-0.6
5 to 17 years	928 252	1 026 416	969 676	17.6	0.3
18 years and over	892 408	3 994 919	4 201 040	76.3	1.1
18 to 24 years	3 602 787	520 629	574 901	10.4	0.8
25 to 44 years	512 326	1 581 690	1 535 043	27.9	0.0
45 to 64 years	1 546 832	1 190 047	1 375 528	25.0	3.2
65 years and over	651 221	702 553	715 568	13.0	0.7
85 years and over	74 293	95 625	111 027	2.0	3.0
Median age (years)	32.8	36.0	37.4	X	X

X = Not applicable.

Average Annual Rate of Population Growth, 1980–2004

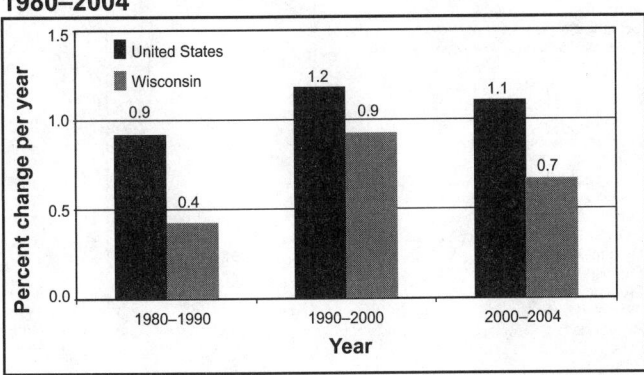

POPULATION

Wisconsin's population grew 2.7 percent between 2000 and 2004, which was below the national average and the rate of neighboring Minnesota, but above the rates of Michigan and Illinois. The state benefited from both international and domestic immigration, which together added 54,000 new residents and accounted for over one-third of the state's population growth during this period. Wisconsin's birth rate was below average, which contributed to the slow population growth. The state had a below average proportion of its population under 18 years old and an above average proportion of elderly residents. Milwaukee was the state's largest city.

Table WI-2. Population by Race and Hispanic Origin, 1990, 2000, and 2004

(Number, percent.)

Race and Hispanic origin	1990	2000	2004
Total Population	4 891 769	5 363 675	5 509 026
Non-Hispanic (Percent)			
One race[1]			
White	91.3	87.4	86.2
Black	4.9	5.6	5.8
American Indian, Alaska Native[2]	0.8	0.8	0.9
Asian and Pacific Islander[2]	1.1	1.7	1.9
Other race[2]	0.9	. . .	. . .
Two or more races	. . .	0.8	0.9
Hispanic or Latino[3] (Percent)	1.9	3.6	4.3

[1]Individuals could report only one race in the 1990 census and could report one or more races on the 2000 census. Data on race in 2000 and 2004 are not comparable to 1990.
[2]Data for 1990 include people of Hispanic or Latino origin.
[3]May be of any race.
. . . = Not available.

Minority Population as a Percent of Total Population, 2004

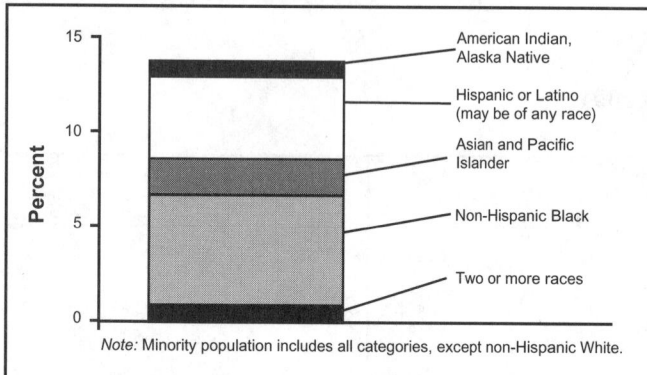

Note: Minority population includes all categories, except non-Hispanic White.

Age-Adjusted Death Rates, Average 2000–2002

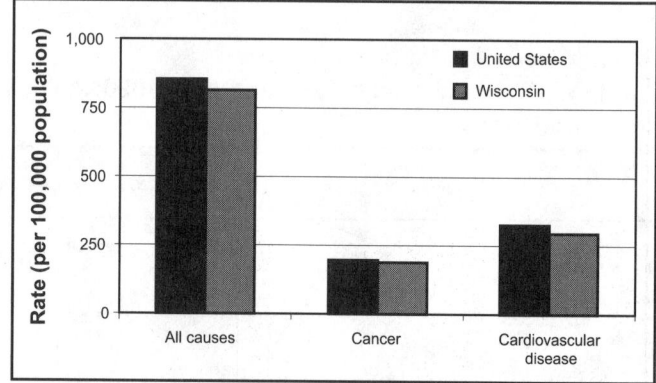

HEALTH

Wisconsin's infant mortality rate was identical to the national average. The state's age-adjusted death rate for all causes was below average, ranking 33rd in the nation. The overall birth rate and the birth rate for teenage mothers were below average.

Table WI-3. Health Characteristics, 2000–2004

(Number, rate, percent.)

Item	State	U.S.
Births, 2003–2004		
Number of births	70 040	4 089 950
Birth rate (per 1,000 population)	12.8	14.1
Teenage birth rate (per 1,000 women age 15–19 years)	31.3	41.6
Mortality Rates, Average 2000–2002		
Infant mortality rate (per 1,000 live births)	6.9	6.9
Age-adjusted mortality rate (per 100,000 population)		
All races	807.6	853.3
Non-Hispanic White	798.9	843.1
Black	1 098.9	1 097.7
American Indian, Alaska Native	. . .	687.0
Asian and Pacific Islander	478.7	486.0
Hispanic or Latino[1]	350.3	642.7
Health Insurance, 2004		
Percent of all persons without health insurance	10.4	15.7
Percent of children without health insurance	5.1	11.2
Percent of low-income children without health insurance	3.8	7.1

[1]May be of any race.
. . . = Not available.

Table WI-4. Leading Causes of Death, Average 2000–2002

(Number, rate per 100,000 population.)

Cause	Number of deaths	Age-adjusted death rates	
		State	U.S.
ALL CAUSES	46 690	807.6	853.3
Leading Causes			
Major cardiovascular diseases	17 932	305.1	326.5
Cancer	10 748	190.6	196.0
Chronic lower respiratory diseases	2 342	40.8	43.7
Unintentional injuries	2 178	38.6	35.7
Diabetes (underlying cause)	1 333	23.3	25.2
Influenza and pneumonia	1 262	21.0	22.7
Alzheimer's disease	1 263	20.7	19.0
Motor vehicle accidents	819	14.9	15.0
Nephritis, nephrotic syndrome, and nephrosis ..	798	13.6	13.8
Septicemia	418	7.2	11.4
Suicides	619	11.3	10.7
Firearm-related	451	8.2	10.3
Cirrhosis	437	7.9	9.5
Drug-induced	312	5.7	7.9
Alcohol-induced	384	7.0	6.9
Homicides	193	3.6	6.0
Falls	674	11.3	5.2
HIV	75	1.4	5.0
Viral hepatitis	39	0.7	2.0
Anemias	78	1.3	1.6
Drownings	66	1.2	1.3
Fire deaths	46	0.9	1.2

Note: The rates are age-adjusted to the U.S. 2000 standard population.

Table WI-5. Households and Housing Characteristics, 1990, 2000, and 2004

(Number, percent, and dollars.)

Characteristic	1990	2000	2004	Average annual percent change, 2000–2004
Total Households	1 822 118	2 084 544	2 172 924	1.0
Family households	1 275 172	1 386 815	1 417 606	0.6
Married-couple family	1 048 010	1 108 597	1 121 982	0.3
Other family	227 162	278 218	295 624	1.5
Male householder, no wife present	52 632	77 918	80 295	0.8
Female householder, no husband present	174 530	200 300	215 329	1.8
Nonfamily households	546 946	697 729	755 318	2.0
Householder living alone	443 673	557 875	604 765	2.0
Householder not living alone	103 273	139 854	150 553	1.9
Housing Characteristics				
Average size	2.61	2.50	2.46	X
Housing units	2 055 774	2 321 144	2 463 802	1.5
Occupied housing units	1 822 118	2 084 544	2 172 924	1.0
Owner-occupied	1 215 350	1 426 361	1 519 124	1.6
Renter-occupied	606 768	658 183	653 800	-0.2
Median gross rent of renter-occupied housing units (dollars)	399	540	609	3.1
Median value of owner-occupied housing units (dollars)	62 100	112 200	137 727	5.3

X = Not applicable.

Median Housing Value and Median Rent, 2004

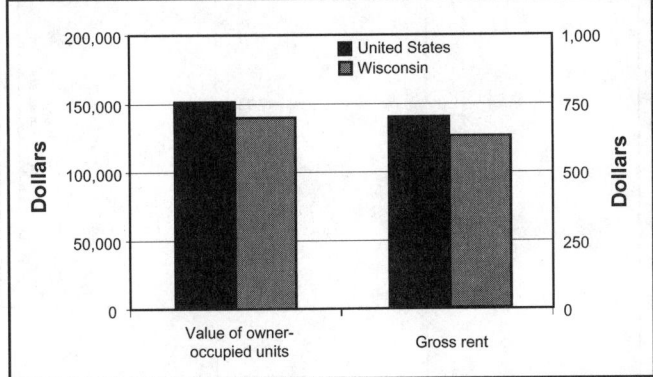

Median Household Income, 1984–2004 (2004 Dollars)

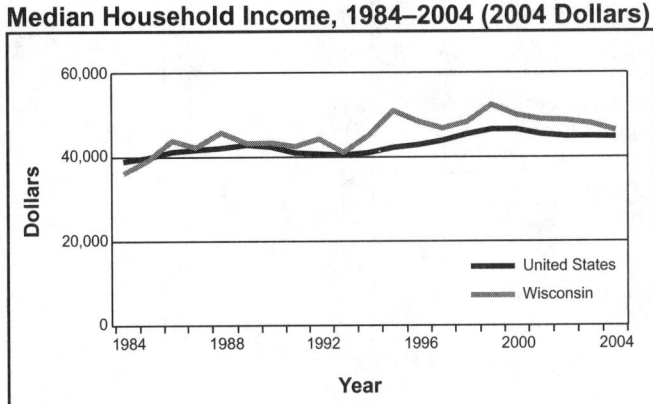

Table WI-6. Household Income and Poverty Status, 1980–2004

(2004 CPI-U-RS adjusted dollars, rate.)

Year	State Median household income (2004 dollars)	State Poverty rate	U.S. Median household income (2004 dollars)	U.S. Poverty rate
2004	45 931	12.3	44 389	12.7
2003	47 513	9.8	44 482	12.5
2002	48 217	8.6	44 546	12.1
2001	48 389	7.9	45 062	11.7
2000	49 457	9.3	46 058	11.3
1999	51 763	8.6	46 129	11.9
1998	47 829	8.8	45 003	12.7
1997	46 470	8.2	43 430	13.3
1996	47 949	8.8	42 544	13.7
1995	50 410	8.5	41 943	13.8
1994	44 616	9.0	40 677	14.5
1993	40 893	12.6	40 217	15.1
1992	43 947	10.9	40 422	14.8
1991	42 108	9.9	40 746	14.2
1990	43 039	9.3	41 963	13.5
1989	42 844	8.4	42 524	12.8
1988	45 377	7.8	41 771	13.0
1987	41 931	9.0	41 322	13.4
1986	43 460	10.7	40 939	13.6
1985	38 923	11.6	39 545	14.0
1984	35 889	15.5	38 782	14.4
1983	. . .	10.7	. . .	15.2
1982	. . .	9.5	. . .	15.0
1981	. . .	8.1	. . .	14.0
1980	. . .	8.5	. . .	13.0

. . . = Not available.

Table WI-7. Employment Status by Demographic Group, 2004
(Numbers in thousands, rate.)

Characteristic	Civilian noninstitutional population	Civilian labor force		Employed	Unemployment rate
		Number	Participation rate		
SEX AND AGE					
Total	4 280	3 071	71.8	2 917	5.0
16 to 19 years	304	186	61.1	164	11.9
20 to 24 years	381	328	86.1	302	7.8
25 to 34 years	729	638	87.5	600	5.9
35 to 44 years	822	731	88.9	702	3.9
45 to 54 years	805	708	88.0	686	3.2
55 to 64 years	573	378	66.0	362	4.3
65 years and over	666	103	15.4	101	1.7
Men	2 093	1 616	77.2	1 526	5.6
16 to 19 years	151	91	60.7	78	14.8
20 to 24 years	194	169	87.1	153	9.1
25 to 34 years	355	332	93.6	311	6.4
35 to 44 years	425	398	93.6	380	4.4
45 to 54 years	401	367	91.5	357	2.8
55 to 64 years	290	204	70.6	193	5.4
65 years and over	278	54	19.5	53	2.2
Women	2 187	1 456	66.6	1 391	4.4
16 to 19 years	153	94	61.6	86	9.0
20 to 24 years	187	159	85.1	149	6.4
25 to 34 years	374	306	81.7	289	5.4
35 to 44 years	397	333	83.8	322	3.3
45 to 54 years	404	341	84.5	329	3.7
55 to 64 years	283	174	61.3	168	3.1
65 years and over	388	49	12.5	48	1.3
MARITAL STATUS					
Married men, spouse present	1 209	941	77.9	911	3.3
Married women, spouse present	1 186	817	68.9	792	3.1
Women who maintain families	220	159	72.2	145	8.4
RACE, HISPANIC ORIGIN, AND SEX					
White	3 941	2 846	72.2	2 719	4.5
Men	1 945	1 513	77.8	1 437	5.0
Women	1 996	1 333	66.8	1 282	3.8
Black	208	132	63.4	110	16.4
Men	86	57	66.2	47	17.8
Women	122	75	61.5	63	15.3
Asian	72	52	72.7	50	5.1
Hispanic or Latino[1]	197	150	75.8	134	10.3
Men	108	95	88.7	86	9.9
Women	90	54	60.4	48	11.0
RACE, HISPANIC ORIGIN, AND AGE					
White					
16 to 19 years	256	163	63.9	146	10.8
20 to 24 years	335	292	87.1	272	6.8
25 to 34 years	654	579	88.5	552	4.7
35 to 44 years	759	685	90.1	661	3.5
45 to 54 years	749	666	89.0	646	3.1
55 to 64 years	542	362	66.7	346	4.4
65 years and over	646	99	15.4	98	1.6

Note: Data in Table 7 are from the Current Population Survey (CPS) and do not match Bureau of Labor Statistics estimates in Table 8. See notes and definitions for more details.

[1]May be of any race.

Table WI-8. Employment Status, 1990–2004
(Numbers in thousands, rate.)

Year	Civilian labor force	Employed	Unemployed	Unemployment rate
2004	3 071 179	2 919 201	151 978	4.9
2003	3 068 739	2 896 670	172 069	5.6
2002	3 037 928	2 877 047	160 881	5.3
2001	3 032 130	2 898 949	133 181	4.4
2000	2 992 250	2 891 238	101 012	3.4
1999	2 970 026	2 879 024	91 002	3.1
1998	2 967 066	2 869 982	97 084	3.3
1997	2 958 858	2 855 830	103 028	3.5
1996	2 921 029	2 815 599	105 430	3.6
1995	2 881 250	2 773 640	107 610	3.7
1994	2 835 174	2 713 392	121 782	4.3
1993	2 752 773	2 628 814	123 959	4.5
1992	2 695 116	2 556 294	138 822	5.2
1991	2 640 141	2 499 353	140 788	5.3
1990	2 598 898	2 486 129	112 769	4.3

Note: Population age 16 years and over.

Unemployment Rate, 1980–2004

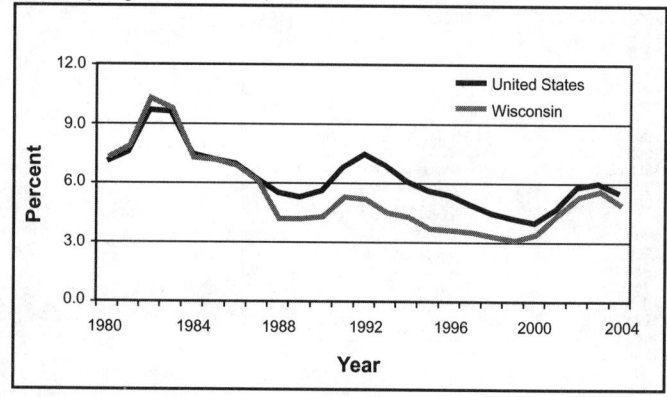

Table WI-9. Employment and Average Wages by Industry, 2001–2004

(Estimates are based on the 2002 North American Industry Classification System [NAICS].)

Industry	2001	2002	2003	2004	Annual average percent change, 2001–2004
	Number of jobs				
TOTAL EMPLOYMENT BY PLACE OF WORK	3 418 677	3 411 073	3 435 056	3 479 948	0.6
Farm Employment	99 421	99 147	102 198	101 675	0.8
Nonfarm Employment	3 319 256	3 311 926	3 332 858	3 378 273	0.6
Private employment	2 896 620	2 884 628	2 903 650	2 950 851	0.6
Forestry, fishing, hunting, and other[1]	15 749	16 955	15 498	15 139	-1.3
Mining	4 052	3 765	4 022	4 233	1.5
Utilities	12 554	12 054	11 871	11 898	-1.8
Construction	180 902	179 325	184 011	187 901	1.3
Manufacturing	573 370	541 802	521 958	520 663	-3.2
Durable goods manufacturing	357 022	333 715	321 240	323 461	-3.2
Nondurable goods manufacturing	216 348	208 087	200 718	197 202	-3.0
Wholesale trade	126 002	124 688	123 056	125 678	-0.1
Retail trade	400 164	397 304	401 409	404 470	0.4
Transportation and warehousing	113 660	113 264	114 248	115 133	0.4
Information	60 119	56 618	56 116	56 664	-2.0
Finance and insurance	158 656	161 662	164 067	166 021	1.5
Real estate and rental and leasing	78 879	80 256	84 061	88 303	3.8
Professional and technical services	141 969	143 496	145 685	147 541	1.3
Management of companies and enterprises	36 652	37 253	39 865	40 917	3.7
Administrative and waste services	143 847	146 136	147 771	156 813	2.9
Educational services	52 398	53 634	55 382	57 499	3.1
Health care and social assistance	343 906	352 757	361 641	368 906	2.4
Arts, entertainment, and recreation	56 980	59 380	61 005	62 030	2.9
Accommodation and food services	225 672	226 867	232 949	239 147	2.0
Other services, except public administration	171 089	177 412	179 035	181 895	2.1
Government and government enterprises	422 636	427 298	429 208	427 422	0.4
	Dollars				
AVERAGE WAGES AND SALARIES BY PLACE OF WORK ...	30 936	31 876	32 760	34 111	3.3
Farm Earnings	29 128	31 696	22 883	28 649	-0.6
Nonfarm Earnings	30 949	31 877	32 846	34 157	3.3
Private earnings	30 911	31 857	32 740	34 123	3.4
Forestry, fishing, hunting, and other[1]	22 964	23 490	24 116	25 459	3.5
Mining	42 727	43 534	43 415	45 727	2.3
Utilities	61 899	63 408	64 324	69 482	3.9
Construction	39 162	39 682	40 232	41 235	1.7
Manufacturing	39 033	40 390	41 969	44 051	4.1
Durable goods manufacturing	39 571	40 928	42 968	45 281	4.6
Nondurable goods manufacturing	38 149	39 530	40 380	42 046	3.3
Wholesale trade	41 731	43 287	44 594	46 485	3.7
Retail trade	19 236	20 151	20 263	20 793	2.6
Transportation and warehousing	32 301	32 867	33 470	34 761	2.5
Information	38 007	38 894	39 638	42 252	3.6
Finance and insurance	42 264	43 806	46 560	48 891	5.0
Real estate and rental and leasing	25 373	25 430	26 862	28 162	3.5
Professional and technical services	45 941	46 373	47 444	49 382	2.4
Management of companies and enterprises	63 254	66 010	68 191	73 460	5.1
Administrative and waste services	19 974	20 669	20 807	21 405	2.3
Educational services	23 127	24 319	25 435	26 330	4.4
Health care and social assistance	31 045	32 626	33 730	35 349	4.4
Arts, entertainment, and recreation	20 632	21 046	20 885	20 982	0.6
Accommodation and food services	10 386	10 652	10 865	11 164	2.4
Other services, except public administration	19 586	20 581	21 142	21 905	3.8
Government and government enterprises	31 168	31 993	33 444	34 351	3.3

Note: Average wages and salaries are a calculation by the editors of wage and salary disbursements divided by full- and part-time wage and salary employment. Data may not add to total or may appear as zero due to rounding.

[1] "Other" consists of the number of jobs held by U.S. residents employed by international organizations and foreign embassies and consulates in the United States.

LABOR MARKET

The state's unemployment rate has been below the national average since the mid-1990s. During the 2001 recession, it rose significantly but still remained below average. Employment growth was moderate over the 2003–2004 period, as Wisconsin recovered from a downturn in 2001–2002. Job losses occurred in the manufacturing sector during the entire 2001–2004 period. The state's large retail trade sector experienced slow employment growth, while service-providing industries, particularly health care, posted moderate gains. Average wages and salaries were below the national average, ranking 30th in the nation. However, their rate of growth from 2001 to 2004 reached 10.3 percent, which was above the national average.

Employment by Industry, 2004

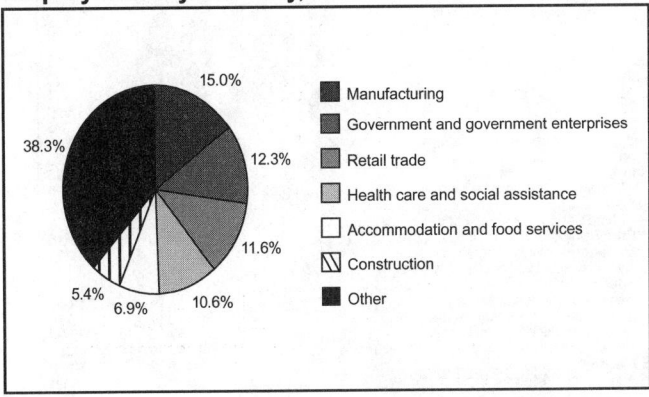

Table WI-10. Personal Income by Major Source, Selected Years 1980–2004

(Millions of dollars, except where noted.)

Item	1980	1990	2000	2001	2002	2003	2004	Average annual percent change, 2000–2004
Earnings by Place of Work	36 288	65 561	114 900	118 830	122 934	127 886	135 494	4.2
Wage and salary disbursements	27 146	49 250	87 848	89 671	91 626	94 363	99 120	3.1
Supplements to wages and salaries	5 270	10 419	17 997	18 864	21 249	23 152	24 985	8.5
Proprietors' income[1]	3 872	5 893	9 055	10 296	10 059	10 371	11 390	5.9
Farm proprietors' income	1 146	882	181	213	188	549	716	41.0
Nonfarm proprietors' income	2 726	5 011	8 874	10 082	9 872	9 823	10 673	4.7
(-) Contributions for government social insurance[2]	3 507	7 464	13 138	13 522	13 953	14 454	15 240	3.8
(+) Adjustment for residence[3]	550	1 356	2 736	2 868	2 919	2 988	3 098	3.2
(=) **Net Earnings by Place of Residence**	33 330	59 453	104 498	108 176	111 900	116 420	123 352	4.2
(+) Dividends, interest, and rent[4]	8 044	17 470	29 870	29 303	28 332	27 624	28 986	-0.7
(+) Personal current transfer receipts	6 249	11 711	19 179	21 409	23 041	23 542	24 297	6.1
Personal income	47 623	88 635	153 548	158 888	163 273	167 586	176 636	3.6
Farm income	46 205	87 318	152 718	158 008	162 415	166 413	175 168	3.5
Nonfarm income	1 419	1 317	830	880	858	1 173	1 468	15.3
Per Capita Personal Income (Dollars)[5]	10 107	18 072	28 570	29 392	30 011	30 613	32 063	2.9

Note: Data may not add to total or may appear as zero due to rounding.

[1]Proprietors' income includes the inventory valuation adjustment and the capital consumption adjustment.
[2]Contributions for government social insurance are included in earnings by type and industry, but they are excluded from personal income.
[3]The adjustment for residence is the net inflow of the earnings of interarea commuters.
[4]Rental income of persons includes the capital consumption adjustment.
[5]Per capita personal income is total personal income divided by total midyear population.

Per Capita Personal Income, 1980–2004 (Current Dollars)

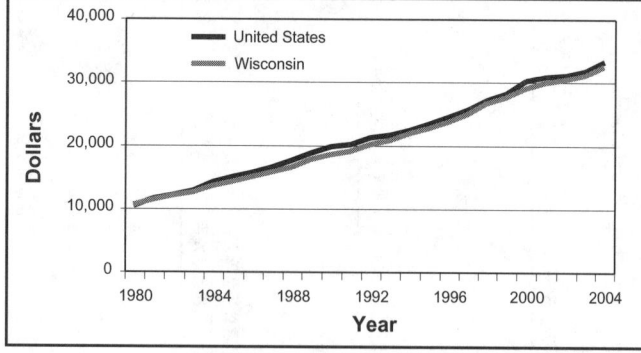

ECONOMIC ACTIVITY

Wisconsin's economy expanded at about the national average rate over the 2001–2004 period. In 2004, the state's real gross state product was the 19th largest in the country. Moderate gains in manufacturing, retail trade, information, finance and insurance, and real estate and related activities contributed to this growth. Agriculture, construction, and educational services were the only industries that experienced declines during this period. Housing price appreciation was not a major factor in Wisconsin's economy. In 2004, the state's median value of owner-occupied housing totaled $137,727, the 26th highest amount in the country.

Table WI-11. Real Gross State Product, 1997–2004

(Millions of chained 2000 dollars, percent.)

Industry	1997	1998	1999	2000	2001	2002	2003	2004	Average annual percent change, 2001–2004
GROSS STATE PRODUCT	160 193	166 511	172 778	176 244	177 842	181 153	186 350	193 900	2.9
As a percent of U.S. gross product	1.9	1.8	1.8	1.8	1.8	1.8	1.8	1.8	X
Private Industries	142 113	148 006	154 147	157 044	158 525	161 869	166 888	174 300	3.2
Agriculture, forestry, fishing, and hunting	2 068	2 385	2 485	2 359	2 581	2 661	2 678	2 489	-1.2
Mining	174	208	241	261	249	250	255	250	0.1
Utilities	2 542	2 560	2 868	2 822	2 915	2 870	3 120	3 399	5.3
Construction	7 462	7 690	8 008	7 792	7 626	7 448	7 457	7 500	-0.6
Manufacturing	38 198	40 048	41 232	43 269	41 241	41 981	43 631	46 151	3.8
As a percent of gross state product	23.8	24.1	24.1	24.6	23.2	23.2	23.4	23.8	X
Wholesale trade	8 500	9 596	10 072	9 940	10 618	11 038	10 622	10 965	1.1
Retail trade	9 753	10 226	10 966	11 790	12 564	13 311	13 865	14 461	4.8
Transportation and warehousing	5 208	5 365	5 540	5 758	5 536	5 628	5 841	5 932	2.3
Information	3 940	4 228	4 714	4 700	5 226	5 542	5 952	6 790	9.1
Finance and insurance	11 063	11 285	11 402	12 115	12 025	12 230	13 634	14 346	6.1
Real estate and rental and leasing	17 915	18 225	19 369	19 650	20 640	20 573	20 290	21 155	0.8
Services	35 625	36 303	37 310	36 589	37 326	38 432	39 715	41 203	3.3
As a percent of gross state product	22.2	21.8	21.6	20.8	21.0	21.2	21.3	21.2	X
Professional and technical services	6 152	6 616	7 108	7 126	7 291	7 442	7 739	7 935	2.9
Management of companies and enterprises	4 436	4 223	4 070	3 268	3 423	3 493	3 877	4 045	5.7
Administrative and waste services	3 626	3 792	4 045	3 680	3 541	3 729	3 818	4 043	4.5
Educational services	1 151	1 166	1 225	1 202	1 197	1 205	1 185	1 179	-0.5
Health care and social assistance	11 476	11 601	11 950	12 394	12 965	13 620	14 063	14 545	3.9
Arts, entertainment, and recreation	1 112	1 110	1 256	1 188	1 252	1 298	1 292	1 275	0.6
Accommodation and food services	3 456	3 504	3 640	3 805	3 775	3 797	3 900	4 069	2.5
Other services, except public administration	4 216	4 291	4 016	3 926	3 882	3 848	3 841	4 112	1.9
Government	18 102	18 518	18 629	19 200	19 318	19 294	19 488	19 656	0.6
As a percent of gross state product	11.3	11.1	10.8	10.9	10.9	10.7	10.5	10.1	X

X = Not applicable.

Table WI-12. Government Transfer Payments, Selected Years 1980–2004

(Millions of dollars, percent.)

Item	1980	1990	2000	2001	2002	2003	2004	Average annual percent change, 2000–2004
CURRENT TRANSFER PAYMENTS TO INDIVIDUALS	5 883	11 005	17 902	19 985	21 890	22 492	23 249	6.8
Retirement and Disability Insurance Benefits	2 817	5 578	8 549	9 026	9 471	9 806	10 260	4.7
Old-age, survivors, and disability insurance (OASDI) benefits	2 721	5 412	8 350	8 822	9 246	9 571	10 017	4.7
Railroad retirement and disability benefits	87	134	153	155	160	162	165	2.0
Workers' compensation	7	13	21	24	28	28	28	7.2
Other government retirement and disability insurance benefits	2	20	24	25	37	45	49	19.5
Medical Benefits	1 484	3 495	6 800	7 907	8 863	8 946	9 341	8.3
Medicare benefits	740	1 887	3 417	3 776	4 036	4 262	4 672	8.1
Public assistance medical care benefits	738	1 593	3 366	4 106	4 790	4 651	4 629	8.3
Military medical insurance benefits	6	15	17	26	37	32	40	23.8
Income Maintenance Benefits	691	1 100	1 438	1 580	1 679	1 835	1 971	8.2
Supplemental Security Income (SSI) benefits	158	290	483	495	511	526	550	3.3
Family assistance	353	440	279	349	352	368	396	9.2
Food stamps	74	186	133	163	202	241	282	20.6
Other income maintenance benefits	106	184	543	573	615	700	743	8.2
Unemployment Insurance Compensation	554	368	519	815	1 179	1 180	899	14.7
Veterans' Benefits	249	310	416	435	474	511	552	7.4
Federal Education and Training Assistance	86	150	162	191	206	195	210	6.8
Other Payments to Individuals	3	5	19	30	17	19	18	-1.9

Note: See notes and definitions for more details. Data may not add to total or may appear as zero due to rounding.

EXPORTS

Wisconsin's exports totaled $12.7 billion in 2004, making the state the 20th largest exporter in the country. The state's chief exports were machinery manufactures, followed distantly by computers and electronic products and transportation equipment. Its largest overseas markets were Canada and Mexico. China was Wisconsin's fastest-growing export market, as exports to this country increased by over 82 percent from 2001 to 2004. Exports to Mexico also increased significantly during this period. Japan, the third leading market, saw a decline in exports from Wisconsin, primarily as a result of a drop in processed food exports.

Leading Exports, 2004

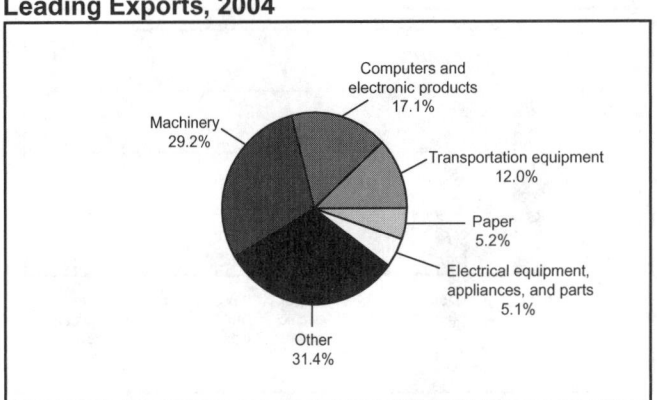

Table WI-13. Exports of Goods by Leading Products and Destinations, 2001–2004

(Millions of dollars, percent, rank based on 2004 dollar values.)

Product and market	2001	2002	2003	2004	Percent share of total, 2004	Average annual percent change, 2001–2004
Total Goods						
Total	10 489	10 684	11 510	12 706	100.0	6.6
Manufactures	9 875	10 018	10 805	11 968	94.2	6.6
Agriculture and livestock	427	499	529	432	3.4	0.4
Other commodities	187	167	176	306	2.4	17.9
Five Leading Exports (NAICS Code)						
Machinery manufactures (333)	2 860	2 979	3 217	3 715	29.2	9.1
Computers and electronic products (334)	1 929	2 000	2 043	2 168	17.1	4.0
Transportation equipment (336)	1 111	1 109	1 374	1 519	12.0	11.0
Paper products (322)	543	528	563	665	5.2	7.0
Electrical equipment, appliances, and parts (335)	533	519	549	653	5.1	7.0
Five Leading Markets	9 166	9 554	10 315	11 328	89.1	7.3
Canada	3 771	3 923	4 349	4 857	38.2	8.8
Mexico	670	717	788	1 064	8.4	16.7
Japan	733	958	817	625	4.9	-5.2
China	320	359	548	583	4.6	22.2
United Kingdom	448	417	494	517	4.1	4.9

Table WI-14.　Agriculture, 1997 and 2002

(Number, acres, and dollars.)

Item	1997	2002
Number of farms	79 541	77 131
Land in farms (acres)	16 232 744	15 741 552
Farm Size		
Average size of farm (acres)	204	204
Farms by size (percent distribution)		
Fewer than 50 acres	23.2	27.6
50 to 499 acres	69.2	64.1
500 acres or more	7.7	8.2
Market Value of Land and Equipment (Dollars)		
Land and buildings average value per farm	258 638	464 127
Average value per acre	1 264	2 272
Machinery and equipment average value per farm	59 899	72 300
Value of Sales (Thousands of Dollars)		
Agricultural products sold	5 794 100	5 623 275
Crops	1 754 487	1 690 071
Livestock, poultry, and their products	4 039 613	3 933 204
Average per farm (dollars)	72 844	72 906
Value of sales (percent distribution)		
Less than $10,000	45.6	54.0
$10,000 to $99,999	33.8	27.9
$100,000 or more	20.6	18.1
Government Payments		
Payments (thousands of dollars)	150 255	247 942
Percent of farms receiving government payments	64.5	48.3
Farm operators whose principal occupation is farming (percent)	54.5	59.4

AGRICULTURE

Cash receipts from farming totaled $5.6 billion in 2002, according to the Department of Agriculture's Census of Agriculture. This represented a modest increase from the previous agriculture census in 1997. Wisconsin ranked 10th in the nation for agricultural sales in 2002. The state's chief products were dairy and soybeans. In 2002, far more farms reported sales of less than $10,000 than in 1997. About 59 percent of all farm operators reported that farming was their principal occupation. Less than 28 percent of farms spanned fewer than 50 acres, which was below the national average proportion of farms of this size.

ENERGY

Energy expenditures per person amounted to $2,471 in 2001, just above the national average. Wisconsin's per capita consumption was slightly above average. Energy prices were slightly below average, ranking 29th in the country. The state's chief energy sources were petroleum, coal, and natural gas. The industrial sector accounted for 39 percent of Wisconsin's energy consumption.

Energy Consumption by Source, 2001

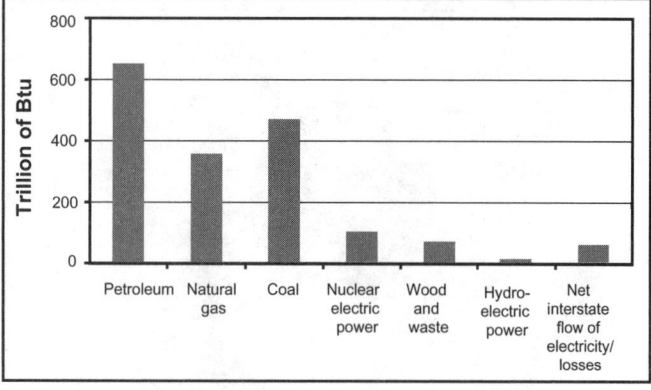

Energy Consumption by Sector, 2001

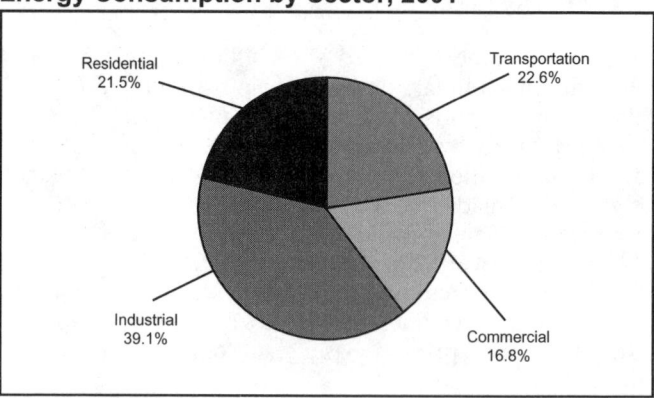

Table WI-15.　Energy Consumption, Expenditures, and Prices, Selected Years 1960–2001

(Dollars, Btu [British Thermal Unit], percent distribution.)

Item	1960	1965	1970	1975	1980	1985	1990	1995	2000	2001
Total Consumption (Billion Btu)	855 102	1 031 849	1 289 507	1 344 057	1 466 596	1 505 602	1 472 625	1 686 712	1 904 307	1 863 373
Consumption per capita (million Btu)	216.4	243.8	291.9	293.5	311.7	317.1	301.0	328.3	355.0	344.7
Consumption by Sector (Percent Distribution)										
Residential	29.2	28.0	27.0	26.9	24.7	24.8	24.5	23.5	21.4	21.5
Commercial	10.6	10.6	12.2	14.1	14.2	15.6	16.1	16.3	16.5	16.8
Industrial	39.1	41.8	39.8	35.3	38.6	39.0	36.2	37.2	40.1	39.1
Transportation	21.0	19.6	21.0	23.7	22.4	20.6	23.1	23.0	22.0	22.6
Consumption by Source (Billion Btu)										
Coal	304 624	347 925	381 558	272 045	327 310	360 704	394 459	441 611	499 242	494 744
Natural gas	93 792	204 093	344 241	372 097	354 672	311 449	311 237	385 342	397 553	363 022
Petroleum	392 961	413 541	510 475	525 827	477 974	442 452	482 088	529 182	665 992	668 450
Nuclear electric power	0	0	1 725	113 356	108 111	116 623	118 793	115 258	120 059	120 226
Hydroelectric power[1]	25 814	22 276	19 980	21 193	21 970	26 594	20 954	24 527	20 308	20 920
Wood and waste	39 155	39 414	38 333	44 874	163 794	188 598	80 657	89 069	96 046	93 427
Other	0	0	0	0	0	1	288	339	364	1 076
Net interstate flow of electricity/losses[2]	-1 243	4 601	-6 805	-5 334	12 765	59 182	64 151	101 385	104 742	101 509
Total Expenditures (Thousands of Dollars)	...	...	1 820 000	3 387 100	6 753 900	8 174 500	8 134 100	9 177 100	13 013 500	13 357 800
Expenditures per capita (dollars)	...	...	412	740	1 435	1 722	1 663	1 786	2 426	2 471
Prices by Sector (Dollars Per Million Btu)										
Total	...	...	1.76	3.27	6.72	8.40	7.96	7.79	9.80	10.30
Residential	...	...	2.04	3.46	6.78	9.90	9.62	9.79	11.94	13.28
Commercial	...	...	2.13	3.54	6.91	9.46	9.23	8.91	10.88	11.99
Industrial	...	...	1.01	2.17	4.36	5.96	5.08	4.77	6.53	7.07
Transportation	...	...	2.49	4.24	8.99	9.18	9.23	9.19	12.01	11.60

[1] A negative number in this row results from pumped storage for which, overall, more electricity is expended than created to provide electricity during peak demand periods.
[2] Net interstate flow of electricity is the difference between the amount of energy in the electricity sold within a state (including associated losses) and the energy input at the electric utilities within the state. A positive number indicates that more electricity (including associated losses) came into the state than went out of the state during the year; conversely, a negative number indicates that more electricity (including associated losses) went out of the state than came into the state.
. . . = Not available.

Table WI-16. State Taxes, Fiscal 2004

(Dollars, percent distribution.)

Item	Thousands of dollars	Percent distribution	Dollars per capita State	Dollars per capita U.S.
TOTAL TAXES	12 531 098	100.0	2 274.7	2 024.8
Property Taxes	104 158	0.8	18.9	38.9
Sales and Gross Receipts	5 795 187	46.2	1 052.0	1 003.4
General sales and gross receipts	3 899 395	31.1	707.8	677.0
Selective sales taxes	1 895 792	15.1	344.1	326.4
Insurance premiums	138 388	1.1	25.1	47.0
Motor fuels	1 028 516	8.2	186.7	114.6
Public utilities	367 650	2.9	66.7	39.2
Tobacco products	307 425	2.5	55.8	42.0
Licenses	729 808	5.8	132.5	134.9
Motor vehicle	330 291	2.6	60.0	59.4
Occupation and business, not elsewhere classified	289 639	2.3	52.6	37.1
Other Taxes	5 901 945	47.1	1 071.3	847.6
Individual income	5 051 612	40.3	917.0	673.6
Corporation net income	681 990	5.4	123.8	105.1
Death and gift	86 357	0.7	15.7	19.6
Documentary and stock transfer	66 325	0.5	12.0	27.1

GOVERNMENT FINANCE

Wisconsin's revenues and expenditures per person were above the national average in 2003. The state ranked 16th in the country for both values. Spending per capita was above average on education, highways, correction, and natural resources, but below average on hospitals and health. The state's per capita taxes of $2,275 in fiscal year 2004 were above average, ranking 12th in the country. The largest proportion of taxes was collected through individual income taxes, followed by general sales taxes and motor fuels taxes. Wisconsin's individual income taxes were the 11th highest in the nation. The state's property taxes were below average.

Per Capita State Taxes, Fiscal 2004

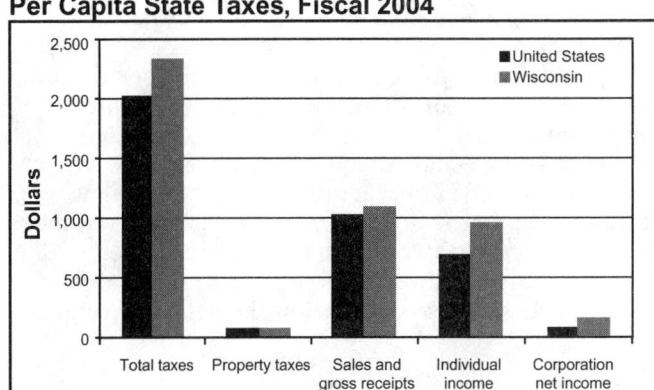

Table WI-17. State Government Finances, 2003

(Dollars, percent distribution.)

Item	Millions of dollars	Percent distribution	Dollars per capita State	Dollars per capita U.S.
GENERAL REVENUE	23 433 155	100.0	4 280.8	3 832.6
Intergovernmental revenue	7 094 092	30.3	1 296.0	1 246.0
Taxes	12 089 770	51.6	2 208.6	1 891.6
General sales	3 738 000	16.0	682.9	636.0
Selective sales	1 712 900	7.3	312.9	307.4
License taxes	645 311	2.8	117.9	123.6
Individual income tax	5 252 500	22.4	959.5	626.8
Corporate income tax	526 500	2.2	96.2	97.8
Other taxes	214 559	0.9	39.2	99.9
Current charges	2 489 539	10.6	454.8	366.5
Miscellaneous general revenue	1 759 754	7.5	321.5	328.6
GENERAL EXPENDITURE	23 813 423	100.0	4 350.3	4 010.5
Intergovernmental expenditure	9 478 166	39.8	1 731.5	1 316.0
Direct expenditure	14 335 257	60.2	2 618.8	2 693.6
Expenditure by Function				
Education	8 664 093	36.4	1 582.8	1 416.4
Public welfare	5 769 188	24.2	1 053.9	1 083.3
Hospitals	697 378	2.9	127.4	132.3
Health	607 032	2.5	110.9	173.0
Highways	1 708 811	7.2	312.2	295.4
Police protection	109 852	0.5	20.1	38.4
Correction	906 725	3.8	165.6	135.0
Natural resources	451 004	1.9	82.4	64.0
Parks and recreation	59 379	0.2	10.8	20.1
Government administration	568 519	2.4	103.9	151.3
Interest on general debt	805 769	3.4	147.2	107.8
Other and unallocable	3 465 673	14.6	633.1	393.4
DEBT AT END OF FISCAL YEAR	14 801 308	X	2 703.9	2 404.7
CASH AND SECURITY HOLDINGS	69 017 013	X	12 608.2	8 938.4

X = Not applicable.

Table WI-18. Education Indicators, 2000–2004

(Percent, number.)

Item	State	U.S.
Total Population 25 Years and Over (Thousands), 2004	3 540	186 877
Educational Attainment, 2004		
Percent high school graduate or more	88.8	85.2
Percent college graduate or more	25.6	27.7
Elementary and Secondary Schools, 2002–2003		
Total students	881 231	48 202 324
Percent of students eligible for free or reduced-price lunch ..	28.4	40.6
Percent of students who were English language learners	3.0	7.8
Total schools	2 232	92 330
Student/teacher ratio	15.1	15.9
Per student expenditures	9 004	8 041
Dropouts, Grades 9–12, 2000–2001 (Percent)	1.9	. . .
Higher Education, 2002–2003		
Total enrollment	330 600	17 035 027
Bachelor's degrees awarded	29 645	1 348 503
Percent women	58.1	57.5

. . . = Not available.

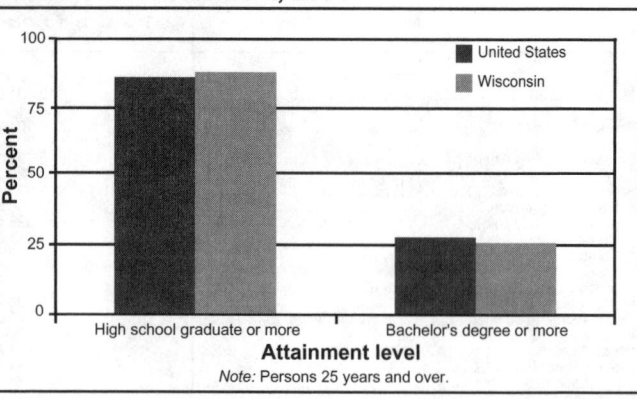

Educational Attainment, 2004

Note: Persons 25 years and over.

EDUCATION

The proportion of Wisconsin residents age 25 years and over holding high school diplomas was 88.8 percent in 2004, ranking 14th in the nation. Just under 26 percent of the population in this age group held bachelor's degrees or more; this proportion ranked 25th in the country. Expenditures per student, at $9,004, were well above the national average and ranked 12th in the country. Wisconsin's student/teacher ratio was slightly below average. The state's dropout rate of 1.9 percent was the lowest of the 46 states reporting such data. Just over 28 percent of students were eligible for free or reduced-price lunch, which was well below the national average.

VOTER PARTICIPATION

Voter turnout rates for both the 2000 and 2004 elections were among the highest in the country. In 2000, Wisconsin had the fourth largest voter participation rate, with 67.8 percent of eligible voters casting ballots. This rate increased to 73 percent in 2004, giving the state the second highest proportion of voters in the nation (behind only its neighbor, Minnesota). According to the official tally by the Clerk of the U.S. House of Representatives, 47.8 percent of Wisconsin's eligible residents voted for the Democratic presidential candidate, and 47.6 percent cast ballots for the Republican presidential candidate in 2000. The proportions were 49.7 percent for the Democratic candidate and 49.3 percent for the Republican candidate in 2004.

Table WI-19. Reported Voting and Registration, November 2000 and November 2004

(Numbers in thousands, percent.)

Characteristic	Total population 18 years and over	Total citizen		Total registered		Total voted	
		Number	Percent	Number	Percent	Number	Percent
NOVEMBER 2000							
Total	3 884	3 755	96.7	2 970	76.5	2 632	67.8
Male	1 912	1 822	95.3	1 420	74.3	1 266	66.2
Female	1 972	1 932	98.0	1 551	78.6	1 367	69.3
NOVEMBER 2004							
Total	4 126	3 928	95.2	3 225	78.2	3 010	73.0
Male	2 017	1 918	95.1	1 551	76.9	1 449	71.9
Female	2 109	2 010	95.3	1 675	79.4	1 561	74.0
Race and Hispanic Origin							
White alone	3 793	3 640	96.0	3 019	79.6	2 816	74.2
Non-Hispanic White alone	3 601	3 546	98.5	2 952	82.0	2 754	76.5
Black alone	195	191	98.3	141	72.6	133	68.1
Asian alone	85	46	B	24	B	24	B
Hispanic or Latino[1]	203	99	48.7	72	35.5	67	33.0
White alone or in combination	3 825	3 669	95.9	3 042	79.5	2 838	74.2
Non-Hispanic White alone or in combination	3 628	3 574	98.5	2 973	81.9	2 774	76.5
Black alone or in combination	204	201	98.4	149	73.0	140	68.7
Asian alone or in combination	86	48	B	26	B	26	B
Age							
18 to 24 years	524	478	91.3	330	63.0	301	57.5
25 to 44 years	1 548	1 427	92.2	1 133	73.2	1 059	68.4
45 to 64 years	1 359	1 341	98.7	1 165	85.7	1 103	81.2
65 to 74 years	363	353	97.2	314	86.3	295	81.2
75 years and over	332	329	99.0	284	85.5	252	75.8

[1]May be of any race.
B = Base is too small to show derived measure.

At a Glance:

- Wyoming was the smallest state in the country in terms of population, but the ninth largest in terms of land area. Its population density was the second smallest in the nation, behind only Alaska.

- Nearly 87 percent of the state's population was non-Hispanic White (the ninth largest proportion of this racial group in the nation) and 2.2 percent was American Indian (the eighth largest proportion of this racial group in the nation).

- Wyoming had a below average proportion of its population under 18 years old and the ninth highest median age in the country.

- Wyoming's median household income of $45,456 was above average, ranking 20th in the nation. The state's poverty rate of 9.9 percent was correspondently low.

- Economic growth in Wyoming was somewhat atypical, as its real gross state product (GSP) expanded strongly in 2001 and 2002, but subsequently slowed. The state's GSP was the third smallest in the country in 2004. Wyoming's unemployment rate in 2004 was 3.9 percent, the eighth lowest in the country

- Nearly 92 percent of Wyoming's residents age 25 years and over held high school diplomas, giving the state the second highest proportion of high school graduates in the nation.

Table WY-1. Population by Sex and Age, 1990, 2000, and 2004

(Number, percent.)

Sex and age	1990	2000	2004	Percent distribution, 2004	Average annual percent change, 2000–2004
Total Population	453 588	493 782	506 529	X	0.6
Percent of total U.S. population	0.2	0.2	0.2	X	X
Sex					
Male	227 007	248 374	255 056	50.4	0.7
Female	226 581	245 408	251 473	49.6	0.6
Age					
Under 5 years	34 780	30 940	30 867	6.1	-1.0
5 to 17 years	100 745	97 933	86 065	17.0	-1.1
18 years and over	80 987	364 909	389 597	76.9	1.5
18 to 24 years	318 063	49 928	57 231	11.3	2.3
25 to 44 years	41 386	138 619	130 452	25.8	-0.9
45 to 64 years	148 495	118 669	140 801	27.8	4.1
65 years and over	47 195	57 693	61 113	12.1	1.9
85 years and over	4 550	6 735	7 374	1.5	3.7
Median age (years)	32.0	36.2	38.0	X	X

X = Not applicable.

Average Annual Rate of Population Growth, 1980–2004

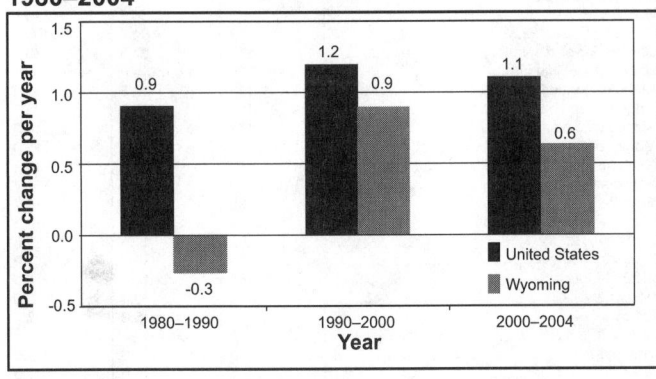

POPULATION

Wyoming had the smallest population and was the most sparsely populated state after Alaska. Its population increased by 2.6 percent between 2000 and 2004. This rate of growth was in line with the rates of Montana and South Dakota, but below the rates of the other Rocky Mountain states, Colorado, Utah, and Idaho. Unlike its neighbors, Wyoming did not benefit substantially from an influx of new residents from other locations. Just 3,220 new residents moved to Wyoming from abroad and from other states. Cheyenne and Casper were Wyoming's largest cities.

Table WY-2. Population by Race and Hispanic Origin, 1990, 2000, and 2004

(Number, percent.)

Race and Hispanic origin	1990	2000	2004
Total Population	453 588	493 782	506 529
Non-Hispanic (Percent)			
One race[1]			
White	91.0	89.1	88.6
Black	0.8	0.7	0.8
American Indian, Alaska Native[2]	2.1	2.1	2.2
Asian and Pacific Islander[2]	0.6	0.6	0.7
Other race[2]	2.3	. . .	. . .
Two or more races	. . .	1.0	1.1
Hispanic or Latino[3] (Percent)	5.7	6.4	6.7

[1]Individuals could report only one race in the 1990 census and could report one or more races on the 2000 census. Data on race in 2000 and 2004 are not comparable to 1990.
[2]Data for 1990 include people of Hispanic or Latino origin.
[3]May be of any race.
. . . = Not available.

Minority Population as a Percent of Total Population, 2004

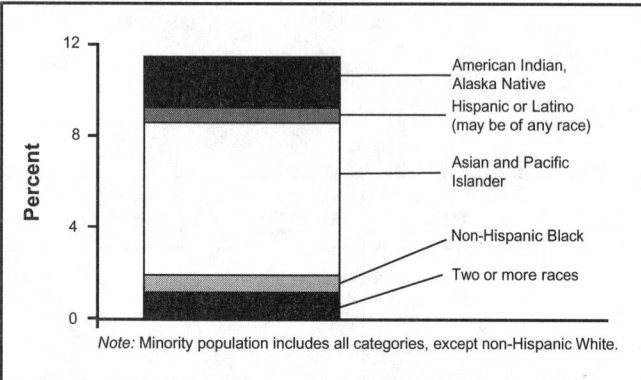

Note: Minority population includes all categories, except non-Hispanic White.

Age-Adjusted Death Rates, Average 2000–2002

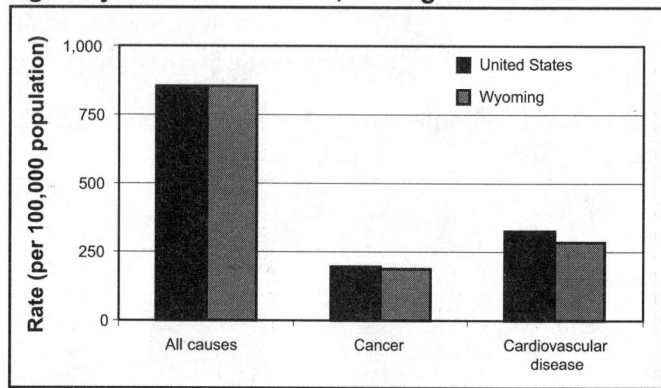

HEALTH

The rate of health insurance coverage for Wyoming's residents was above the national average, with only 14 percent of the population lacking health insurance. The state's infant mortality rate and age-adjusted death rates were also close to the national averages. Wyoming's birth rate was below average.

Table WY-3. Health Characteristics, 2000–2004

(Number, rate, percent.)

Item	State	U.S.
Births, 2003–2004		
Number of births	6 700	4 089 950
Birth rate (per 1,000 population)	13.4	14.1
Teenage birth rate (per 1,000 women age 15–19 years)	40.8	41.6
Mortality Rates, Average 2000–2002		
Infant mortality rate (per 1,000 live births)	6.5	6.9
Age-adjusted mortality rate (per 100,000 population)		
All races	854.9	853.3
Non-Hispanic White	848.8	843.1
Black	822.6	1 097.7
American Indian, Alaska Native	1 266.5	687.0
Asian and Pacific Islander	. . .	486.0
Hispanic or Latino[1]	800.8	642.7
Health Insurance, 2004		
Percent of all persons without health insurance	14.0	15.7
Percent of children without health insurance	9.7	11.2
Percent of low-income children without health insurance ...	4.4	7.1

[1]May be of any race.
. . . = Not available.

Table WY-4. Leading Causes of Death, Average 2000–2002

(Number, rate per 100,000 population.)

Cause	Number of deaths	Age-adjusted death rates	
		State	U.S.
ALL CAUSES	4 041	854.9	853.3
Leading Causes			
Major cardiovascular diseases	1 329	284.3	326.5
Cancer	883	184.4	196.0
Chronic lower respiratory diseases	292	62.5	43.7
Unintentional injuries	269	54.8	35.7
Diabetes (underlying cause)	125	26.5	25.2
Influenza and pneumonia	124	26.9	22.7
Alzheimer's disease	113	24.7	19.0
Motor vehicle accidents	133	26.7	15.0
Nephritis, nephrotic syndrome, and nephrosis ..	47	10.1	13.8
Septicemia	39	8.4	11.4
Suicides	90	18.0	10.7
Firearm-related	74	14.8	10.3
Cirrhosis	56	11.1	9.5
Drug-induced	29	6.1	7.9
Alcohol-induced	64	12.4	6.9
Homicides	16	3.4	6.0
Falls	25	5.3	5.2
HIV	*	*	5.0
Viral hepatitis	8	1.6	2.0
Anemias	7	1.6	1.6
Drownings	13	2.5	1.3
Fire deaths	*	*	1.2

Note: The rates are age-adjusted to the U.S. 2000 standard population.

* = Unreliable data.

Table WY-5. Households and Housing Characteristics, 1990, 2000, and 2004

(Number, percent, and dollars.)

Characteristic	1990	2000	2004	Average annual percent change, 2000–2004
Total Households	168 839	193 608	202 496	1.1
Family households	119 825	130 497	131 438	0.2
Married-couple family	100 800	106 179	107 295	0.3
Other family	19 025	24 318	24 143	-0.2
Male householder, no wife present	5 035	7 481	7 518	0.1
Female householder, no husband present	13 990	16 837	16 625	-0.3
Nonfamily households	49 014	63 111	71 058	3.0
Householder living alone	41 287	50 980	56 807	2.7
Householder not living alone	7 727	12 131	14 251	4.1
Housing Characteristics				
Average size	2.63	2.48	2.43	X
Housing units	203 411	223 854	232 637	1.0
Occupied housing units	168 839	193 608	202 496	1.1
Owner-occupied	114 544	135 514	141 619	1.1
Renter-occupied	54 295	58 094	60 877	1.2
Median gross rent of renter-occupied housing units (dollars) ...	333	437	534	5.1
Median value of owner-occupied housing units (dollars)	61 600	96 600	119 654	5.5

X = Not applicable.

Median Housing Value and Median Rent, 2004

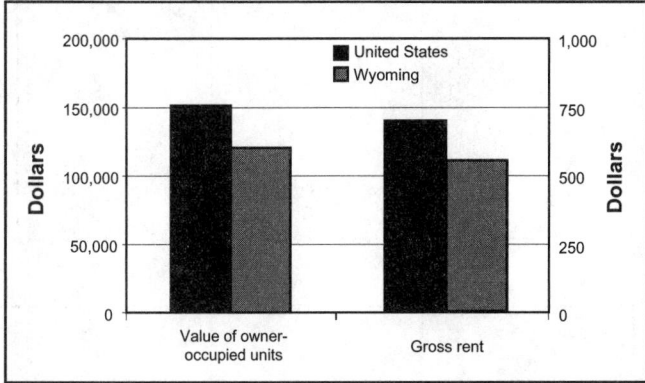

Median Household Income, 1984–2004 (2004 Dollars)

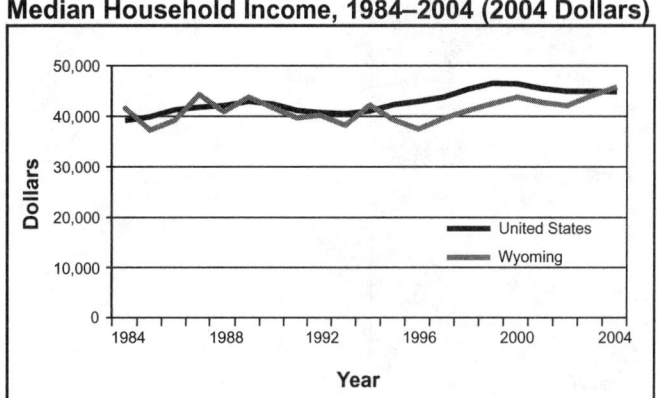

Table WY-6. Household Income and Poverty Status, 1980–2004

(2004 CPI-U-RS adjusted dollars, rate.)

Year	State		U.S.	
	Median household income (2004 dollars)	Poverty rate	Median household income (2004 dollars)	Poverty rate
2004	45 456	9.9	44 389	12.7
2003	43 699	9.8	44 482	12.5
2002	41 767	9.0	44 546	12.1
2001	42 384	8.7	45 062	11.7
2000	43 469	10.8	46 058	11.3
1999	42 221	11.6	46 129	11.9
1998	40 796	10.6	45 003	12.7
1997	39 226	13.5	43 430	13.3
1996	37 103	11.9	42 544	13.7
1995	38 808	12.2	41 943	13.8
1994	41 782	9.3	40 677	14.5
1993	37 901	13.3	40 217	15.1
1992	39 858	10.3	40 422	14.8
1991	39 290	9.9	40 746	14.2
1990	41 286	11.0	41 963	13.5
1989	43 429	10.9	42 524	12.8
1988	40 535	9.6	41 771	13.0
1987	43 873	10.8	41 322	13.4
1986	38 739	14.6	40 939	13.6
1985	36 972	12.0	39 545	14.0
1984	41 206	10.9	38 782	14.4
1983	. . .	12.6	. . .	15.2
1982	. . .	12.0	. . .	15.0
1981	. . .	8.9	. . .	14.0
1980	. . .	10.4	. . .	13.0

. . . = Not available.

Table WY-7. Employment Status by Demographic Group, 2004

(Numbers in thousands, rate.)

Characteristic	Civilian noninstitutional population	Civilian labor force		Employed	Unemployment rate
		Number	Participation rate		
SEX AND AGE					
Total	395	282	71.3	271	3.8
16 to 19 years	34	20	59.7	18	11.2
20 to 24 years	38	30	79.4	28	6.4
25 to 34 years	59	51	85.5	48	4.8
35 to 44 years	66	57	87.5	56	3.0
45 to 54 years	81	71	87.6	70	1.8
55 to 64 years	56	39	69.5	38	2.2
65 years and over	60	12	20.6	12	1.2
Men	196	151	77.3	146	3.4
16 to 19 years	18	11	57.7	9	10.9
20 to 24 years	19	16	85.7	15	6.3
25 to 34 years	29	28	95.8	27	4.1
35 to 44 years	32	30	92.0	29	2.9
45 to 54 years	41	37	91.9	37	1.5
55 to 64 years	29	22	76.2	22	1.5
65 years and over	27	7	26.4	7	1.3
Women	199	130	65.3	125	4.2
16 to 19 years	15	9	62.2	8	11.4
20 to 24 years	20	14	73.4	14	6.5
25 to 34 years	30	23	75.4	21	5.6
35 to 44 years	33	28	83.1	27	3.1
45 to 54 years	41	34	83.2	33	2.2
55 to 64 years	27	17	62.5	17	3.0
MARITAL STATUS					
Married men, spouse present	118	95	80.6	94	1.5
Married women, spouse present	116	78	67.4	76	2.6
Women who maintain families	16	12	75.7	11	7.3
RACE, HISPANIC ORIGIN, AND SEX					
White	379	270	71.3	260	3.5
Men	188	145	77.2	140	3.3
Women	191	125	65.4	120	3.9
Hispanic or Latino[1]	25	18	71.7	17	4.6
Men	13	10	78.1	10	4.1
Women	12	8	64.6	7	5.3
RACE, HISPANIC ORIGIN, AND AGE					
White					
16 to 19 years	32	19	59.9	17	11.3
20 to 24 years	37	29	79.3	27	6.5
25 to 34 years	56	48	85.7	46	4.0
35 to 44 years	62	54	87.5	53	2.8
45 to 54 years	78	69	88.1	68	1.5
55 to 64 years	54	38	70.0	37	2.2
65 years and over	59	12	20.9	12	1.3

Note: Data in Table 7 are from the Current Population Survey (CPS) and do not match Bureau of Labor Statistics estimates in Table 8. See notes and definitions for more details.

[1]May be of any race.

Table WY-8. Employment Status, 1990–2004

(Numbers in thousands, rate.)

Year	Civilian labor force	Employed	Unemployed	Unemployment rate
2004	281 847	270 810	11 037	3.9
2003	277 399	265 200	12 199	4.4
2002	272 518	261 357	11 161	4.1
2001	270 214	259 750	10 464	3.9
2000	266 862	256 616	10 246	3.8
1999	264 676	251 828	12 848	4.9
1998	260 570	247 748	12 822	4.9
1997	256 263	243 944	12 319	4.8
1996	254 717	241 560	13 157	5.2
1995	253 196	240 846	12 350	4.9
1994	249 475	236 885	12 590	5.0
1993	242 599	229 177	13 422	5.5
1992	238 076	224 562	13 514	5.7
1991	235 124	223 192	11 932	5.1
1990	236 043	223 531	12 512	5.3

Note: Population age 16 years and over.

Unemployment Rate, 1980–2004

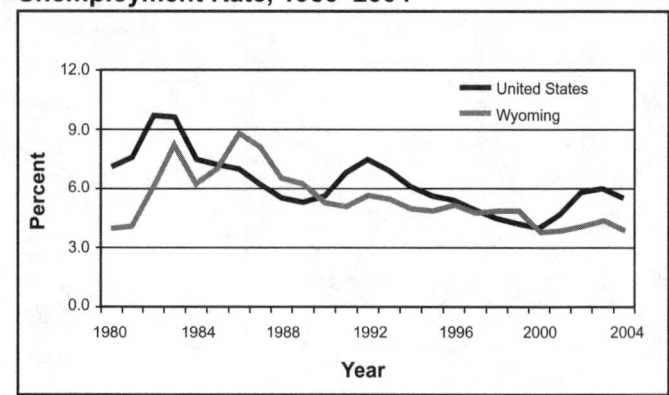

Table WY-9. Employment and Average Wages by Industry, 2001–2004

(Estimates are based on the 2002 North American Industry Classification System [NAICS].)

Industry	2001	2002	2003	2004	Annual average percent change, 2001–2004
	Number of jobs				
TOTAL EMPLOYMENT BY PLACE OF WORK	333 030	337 221	341 801	349 707	1.6
Farm Employment	12 345	12 587	12 167	12 224	-0.3
Nonfarm Employment	320 685	324 634	329 634	337 483	1.7
Private employment	255 324	258 520	262 667	270 010	1.9
Forestry, fishing, hunting, and other[1]	2 821	3 101	2 786	2 746	-0.9
Mining	20 709	20 350	21 582	23 785	4.7
Utilities	D	D	2 205	2 270	...
Construction	27 226	D	27 535	27 388	0.2
Manufacturing	11 468	D	10 714	10 886	-1.7
Durable goods manufacturing	5 967	D	D	D	...
Nondurable goods manufacturing	5 501	D	D	D	...
Wholesale trade	7 814	8 023	7 961	8 357	2.3
Retail trade	39 550	39 618	39 584	40 041	0.4
Transportation and warehousing	D	D	11 746	12 245	...
Information	D	D	4 911	5 043	...
Finance and insurance	10 218	10 777	10 930	11 074	2.7
Real estate and rental and leasing	11 703	11 956	12 433	13 184	4.1
Professional and technical services	14 169	14 270	14 459	14 882	1.6
Management of companies and enterprises	938	894	648	858	-2.9
Administrative and waste services	11 380	11 563	12 171	11 827	1.3
Educational services	2 394	2 578	2 811	3 028	8.1
Health care and social assistance	23 811	24 266	25 284	26 165	3.2
Arts, entertainment, and recreation	6 895	6 242	6 331	6 538	-1.8
Accommodation and food services	28 605	30 139	30 706	31 490	3.3
Other services, except public administration	D	D	17 870	18 203	...
Government and government enterprises	65 361	66 114	66 967	67 473	1.1
	Dollars				
AVERAGE WAGES AND SALARIES BY PLACE OF WORK	27 810	28 838	29 784	31 183	3.9
Farm Earnings	21 550	24 876	23 081	21 982	0.7
Nonfarm Earnings	27 894	28 892	29 870	31 300	3.9
Private earnings	27 892	28 512	29 363	30 855	3.4
Forestry, fishing, hunting, and other[1]	21 256	21 810	20 674	20 594	-1.0
Mining	53 088	54 790	56 196	58 585	3.3
Utilities	D	D	64 126	65 421	...
Construction	31 869	D	32 950	33 247	1.4
Manufacturing	36 505	D	37 317	38 871	2.1
Durable goods manufacturing	30 136	D	D	D	...
Nondurable goods manufacturing	42 870	D	D	D	...
Wholesale trade	36 706	36 934	38 687	41 357	4.1
Retail trade	18 718	19 307	19 902	20 733	3.5
Transportation and warehousing	D	D	41 543	42 549	...
Information	D	D	28 959	30 775	...
Finance and insurance	37 097	35 324	37 370	37 786	0.6
Real estate and rental and leasing	22 002	24 212	24 789	26 714	6.7
Professional and technical services	34 268	36 365	36 140	38 323	3.8
Management of companies and enterprises	41 397	50 946	73 566	80 465	24.8
Administrative and waste services	20 316	19 464	20 553	21 895	2.5
Educational services	17 895	22 079	19 514	20 175	4.1
Health care and social assistance	26 629	27 909	29 081	30 172	4.3
Arts, entertainment, and recreation	15 403	14 594	15 639	16 917	3.2
Accommodation and food services	11 656	12 391	12 792	13 601	5.3
Other services, except public administration	D	D	19 433	19 832	...
Government and government enterprises	27 898	30 001	31 339	32 611	5.3

Note: Average wages and salaries are a calculation by the editors of wage and salary disbursements divided by full- and part-time wage and salary employment. Data may not add to total or may appear as zero due to rounding.

1 "Other" consists of the number of jobs held by U.S. residents employed by international organizations and foreign embassies and consulates in the United States.
D = Suppressed to avoid disclosure of data of individual companies.
. . . = Not available.

LABOR MARKET

Wyoming's unemployment rate has been well below the national average for many years. Together with the state's high labor force participation rate, this indicated a healthy labor market. Employment growth was high relative to the rest of the country throughout the 2001–2004 period. Wyoming experienced job gains in many service-providing industries, particularly in those associated with tourism, recreational activities, educational services, and health care. Growth in government employment also helped offset the sluggish performance of the retail trade sector, which was Wyoming's second largest employer. Average wages and salaries were below the national average, but their rate of growth was the fifth highest in the country.

Employment by Industry, 2004

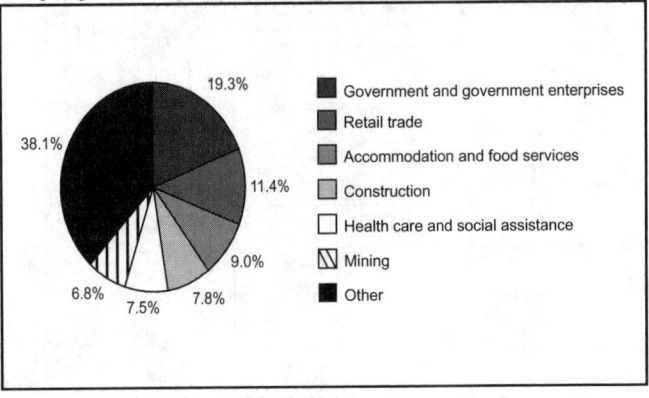

Table WY-10. Personal Income by Major Source, Selected Years 1980–2004

(Millions of dollars, except where noted.)

Item	1980	1990	2000	2001	2002	2003	2004	Average annual percent change, 2000–2004
Earnings by Place of Work	4 761	6 064	9 692	10 520	10 910	11 555	12 427	6.4
Wage and salary disbursements	3 534	4 222	6 763	7 226	7 569	7 881	8 405	5.6
Supplements to wages and salaries	648	924	1 422	1 538	1 718	1 876	2 076	9.9
Proprietors' income[1]	580	917	1 506	1 756	1 622	1 797	1 946	6.6
Farm proprietors' income	24	94	32	65	-1	71	34	1.2
Nonfarm proprietors' income	556	824	1 474	1 691	1 624	1 726	1 912	6.7
(-) Contributions for government social insurance[2]	442	671	1 051	1 132	1 181	1 233	1 321	5.9
(+) Adjustment for residence[3]	-77	-12	13	6	5	3	4	-25.5
(=) Net Earnings by Place of Residence	4 243	5 381	8 653	9 394	9 734	10 325	11 110	6.4
(+) Dividends, interest, and rent[4]	922	1 881	3 706	3 733	3 754	3 770	3 944	1.6
(+) Personal current transfer receipts	392	906	1 704	1 846	1 994	2 131	2 269	7.4
Personal income	5 556	8 167	14 063	14 972	15 481	16 226	17 323	5.3
Farm income	5 475	8 022	13 953	14 828	15 390	16 074	17 210	5.4
Nonfarm income	81	145	110	144	91	153	113	0.6
Per Capita Personal Income (Dollars)[5]	11 718	18 002	28 460	30 301	31 013	32 316	34 199	4.7

Note: Data may not add to total or may appear as zero due to rounding.

[1]Proprietors' income includes the inventory valuation adjustment and the capital consumption adjustment.
[2]Contributions for government social insurance are included in earnings by type and industry, but they are excluded from personal income.
[3]The adjustment for residence is the net inflow of the earnings of interarea commuters.
[4]Rental income of persons includes the capital consumption adjustment.
[5]Per capita personal income is total personal income divided by total midyear population.

Per Capita Personal Income, 1980–2004 (Current Dollars)

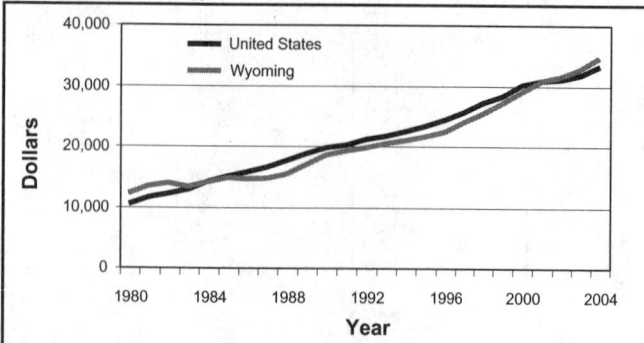

ECONOMIC ACTIVITY

Contrary to the pattern of most other states, Wyoming's real gross state product (GSP) expanded strongly in 2001 and 2002, before slowing down substantially in the following two years. During the 2003–2004 period, the state's GSP growth rate ranked only 40th in the nation. Contributing to this lackluster performance were declines in agricultural and related industries. Gains in mining, construction, retail trade, and real estate and related activities gave the GSP a net increase. Housing prices increased at a below average rate. In 2004, Wyoming's median value of owner-occupied housing of $119,654 ranked 30th in the country.

Table WY-11. Real Gross State Product, 1997–2004

(Millions of chained 2000 dollars, percent.)

Industry	1997	1998	1999	2000	2001	2002	2003	2004	Average annual percent change, 2001–2004
GROSS STATE PRODUCT	16 001	16 261	17 173	17 427	18 417	19 533	19 940	20 589	3.8
As a percent of U.S. gross product	0.2	0.2	0.2	0.2	0.2	0.2	0.2	0.2	X
Private Industries	13 507	13 739	14 620	14 835	15 747	16 777	17 123	17 671	3.9
Agriculture, forestry, fishing, and hunting	326	251	354	373	366	366	426	284	-8.1
Mining	3 316	3 278	3 579	3 667	3 977	4 443	4 387	4 449	3.8
Utilities	867	838	901	852	823	857	936	978	5.9
Construction	928	961	1 016	1 005	1 059	1 063	1 048	1 018	-1.3
Manufacturing	917	967	998	1 144	1 266	1 260	1 259	1 285	0.5
As a percent of gross state product	5.7	5.9	5.8	6.6	6.9	6.5	6.3	6.2	X
Wholesale trade	568	622	630	642	761	794	786	859	4.1
Retail trade	1 014	1 066	1 120	1 130	1 223	1 337	1 410	1 494	6.9
Transportation and warehousing	1 015	1 012	1 049	1 036	1 076	1 142	1 225	1 290	6.2
Information	254	283	353	344	327	339	370	429	9.5
Finance and insurance	562	586	541	527	559	602	589	618	3.4
Real estate and rental and leasing	1 315	1 403	1 470	1 487	1 602	1 706	1 726	1 887	5.6
Services	2 410	2 468	2 606	2 628	2 718	2 886	2 993	3 157	5.1
As a percent of gross state product	15.1	15.2	15.2	15.1	14.8	14.8	15.0	15.3	X
Professional and technical services	425	452	504	501	559	591	604	633	4.2
Management of companies and enterprises	84	65	62	57	47	51	55	80	19.4
Administrative and waste services	218	229	269	245	259	261	285	276	2.1
Educational services	26	28	28	30	34	41	35	36	1.9
Health care and social assistance	647	660	691	742	782	831	883	922	5.6
Arts, entertainment, and recreation	144	156	159	155	157	153	157	166	1.9
Accommodation and food services	530	533	554	563	547	617	635	687	7.9
Other services, except public administration	336	345	339	333	335	341	339	357	2.3
Government	2 492	2 519	2 553	2 592	2 670	2 757	2 818	2 919	3.0
As a percent of gross state product	15.6	15.5	14.9	14.9	14.5	14.1	14.1	14.2	X

X = Not applicable.

Table WY-12. Government Transfer Payments, Selected Years 1980–2004

(Millions of dollars, percent.)

Item	1980	1990	2000	2001	2002	2003	2004	Average annual percent change, 2000–2004
CURRENT TRANSFER PAYMENTS TO INDIVIDUALS	356	838	1 583	1 715	1 879	2 025	2 162	8.1
Retirement and Disability Insurance Benefits	224	485	826	884	933	972	1 022	5.5
Old-age, survivors, and disability insurance (OASDI) benefits	169	388	690	737	778	810	854	5.5
Railroad retirement and disability benefits	25	36	45	47	49	50	51	3.0
Workers' compensation	26	56	87	97	103	108	113	6.8
Other government retirement and disability insurance benefits	5	5	3	3	3	3	3	-2.0
Medical Benefits	62	213	533	604	673	733	827	11.6
Medicare benefits	44	128	293	326	350	372	412	8.8
Public assistance medical care benefits	16	79	225	257	298	342	392	14.9
Military medical insurance benefits	1	5	15	20	25	20	23	12.7
Income Maintenance Benefits	25	68	122	114	131	164	165	7.8
Supplemental Security Income (SSI) benefits	3	10	24	25	25	26	27	2.6
Family assistance	9	21	25	13	22	44	36	9.9
Food stamps	7	21	19	20	22	24	26	8.1
Other income maintenance benefits	6	17	55	56	62	71	76	8.7
Unemployment Insurance Compensation	14	23	28	29	50	62	47	14.4
Veterans' Benefits	25	29	52	55	60	65	70	7.6
Federal Education and Training Assistance	5	18	19	25	27	26	27	9.2
Other Payments to Individuals	1	2	2	4	4	4	3	9.6

Note: See notes and definitions for more details. Data may not add to total or may appear as zero due to rounding.

EXPORTS

Wyoming was the country's third smallest exporter, behind both Montana and Hawaii. In 2004, the state's total exports amounted to just $680 million. Chemical manufactures accounted for over 70 percent, or $480 million, of the state's exports. Mining products and machinery manufactures were also among Wyoming's top five export products. The state's primary export markets were Canada, Mexico, and Japan. Exports to Canada increased by over 72 percent from 2001 to 2004. Indonesia became Wyoming's fourth leading export market in 2004.

Leading Exports, 2004

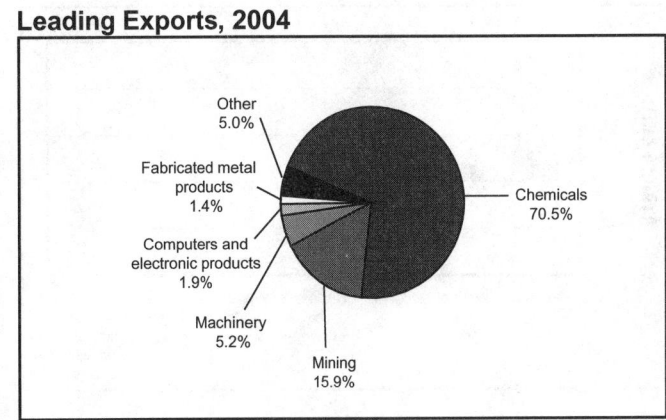

Table WY-13. Exports of Goods by Leading Products and Destinations, 2001–2004

(Millions of dollars, percent, rank based on 2004 dollar values.)

Product and market	2001	2002	2003	2004	Percent share of total, 2004	Average annual percent change, 2001–2004
Total Goods						
Total	503	553	582	680	100.0	10.6
Manufactures	432	463	506	561	82.4	9.1
Agriculture and livestock	63	79	61	111	16.3	21.0
Other commodities	9	11	15	9	1.3	0.8
Five Leading Exports (NAICS Code)						
Chemical manufactures (325)	387	419	438	480	70.5	7.4
Mining (212)	58	76	58	108	15.9	23.0
Machinery manufactures (333)	12	15	20	35	5.2	43.0
Computers and electronic products (334)	8	6	21	13	1.9	16.4
Fabricated metal products (332)	8	8	9	10	1.4	6.6
Five Leading Markets						
Canada	114	141	137	196	28.7	19.9
Mexico	52	57	63	71	10.4	11.0
Japan	49	56	45	51	7.5	0.9
Indonesia	17	28	27	33	4.8	25.1
Chile	25	25	29	26	3.8	1.9

Table WY-14. Agriculture, 1997 and 2002

(Number, acres, and dollars.)

Item	1997	2002
Number of farms	9 443	9 422
Land in farms (acres)	34 302 475	34 402 726
Farm Size		
Average size of farm (acres)	3 633	3 651
Farms by size (percent distribution)		
Fewer than 50 acres	17.2	21.4
50 to 499 acres	33.1	34.1
500 acres or more	49.7	44.5
Market Value of Land and Equipment (Dollars)		
Land and buildings average value per farm	803 958	1 080 945
Average value per acre	224	290
Machinery and equipment average value per farm ...	61 541	74 757
Value of Sales (Thousands of Dollars)		
Agricultural products sold	904 576	863 887
Crops	181 026	137 776
Livestock, poultry, and their products	723 549	726 111
Average per farm (dollars)	95 793	91 688
Value of sales (percent distribution)		
Less than $10,000	38.6	46.8
$10,000 to $99,999	41.3	34.1
$100,000 or more	20.1	19.2
Government Payments		
Payments (thousands of dollars)	17 388	37 913
Percent of farms receiving government payments	25.7	33.6
Farm operators whose principal occupation is farming (percent) ...	59.6	61.1

AGRICULTURE

Cash receipts from farming totaled $863.9 million in 2002, according to the Department of Agriculture's Census of Agriculture. This was the 38th highest total in the country and reflected a modest decline from the previous farm census in 1997. The state's chief agricultural product was cattle. As with many western states, farming was relatively large-scale: over half of all farms had sales of over $10,000, and 61.1 percent of all farm operators regarded farming as their principal occupation. More than 44 percent of farms spanned 500 acres or more.

ENERGY

Wyoming's energy prices were among the five lowest in the country in 2001. However, the state's per capita energy consumption ranked second in the nation, and energy expenditures per person were the highest in the country. The industrial sector accounted for over 54 percent of Wyoming's energy consumption. The chief sources of energy were coal, petroleum, and natural gas.

Energy Consumption by Source, 2001

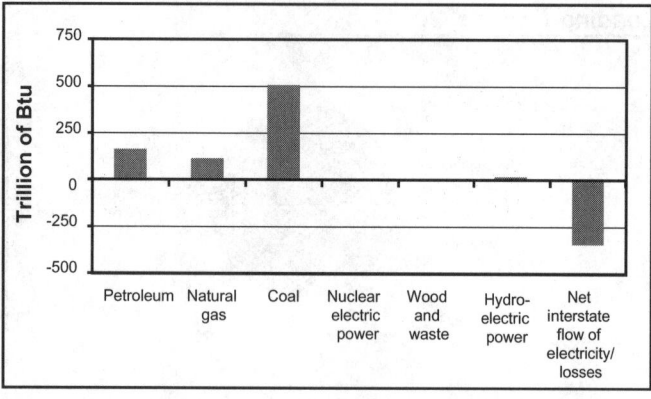

Energy Consumption by Sector, 2001

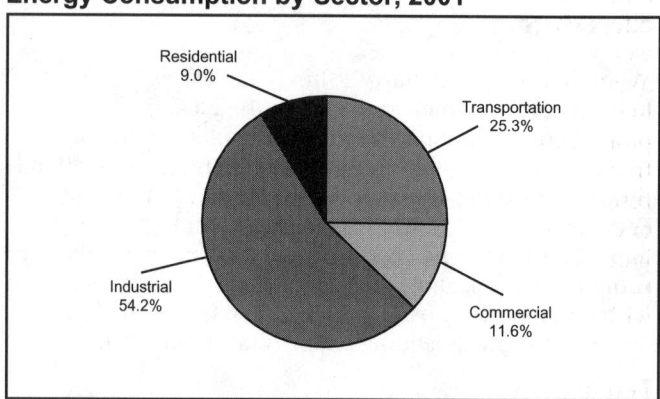

Table WY-15. Energy Consumption, Expenditures, and Prices, Selected Years 1960–2001

(Dollars, Btu [British Thermal Unit], percent distribution.)

Item	1960	1965	1970	1975	1980	1985	1990	1995	2000	2001
Total Consumption (Billion Btu)	141 567	172 930	255 490	277 409	362 640	357 859	402 854	404 938	431 284	439 142
Consumption per capita (million Btu)	429.0	520.9	768.6	726.8	772.3	716.2	888.1	846.4	873.4	889.5
Consumption by Sector (Percent Distribution)										
Residential	11.7	10.9	12.0	9.7	8.6	11.2	8.8	9.5	9.2	9.0
Commercial	6.3	9.5	9.6	7.7	6.6	11.4	10.0	10.5	11.4	11.6
Industrial	52.8	53.9	55.9	58.8	60.5	58.2	61.1	56.3	54.2	54.2
Transportation	29.2	25.6	22.5	23.8	24.4	19.2	20.1	23.7	25.3	25.3
Consumption by Source (Billion Btu)										
Coal	15 763	34 454	63 488	128 034	268 122	405 502	459 772	463 535	506 144	500 212
Natural gas	52 828	54 805	112 526	81 434	73 114	86 363	101 316	103 847	105 974	103 990
Petroleum	75 708	86 690	102 684	129 641	173 563	117 492	122 817	129 699	146 474	156 954
Nuclear electric power	0	0	0	0	0	0	0	0	0	0
Hydroelectric power[1]	6 552	9 243	10 562	11 657	11 511	11 157	6 705	8 234	10 314	8 944
Wood and waste	1 623	1 550	1 566	1 569	2 740	3 566	2 049	1 565	1 195	1 009
Other	0	0	0	0	0	30	651	651	3 182	4 388
Net interstate flow of electricity/losses[2]	-10 907	-13 812	-35 337	-74 925	-166 411	-266 250	-290 457	-302 593	-341 998	-336 355
Total Expenditures (Thousands of Dollars)	. . .	. . .	227 300	470 600	1 401 900	1 447 700	1 515 800	1 659 300	2 162 000	2 321 600
Expenditures per capita (dollars)	. . .	. . .	684	1 233	2 986	2 897	3 342	3 468	4 378	4 702
Prices by Sector (Dollars Per Million Btu)										
Total	. . .	. . .	1.33	2.55	5.86	6.78	6.50	6.16	7.86	8.46
Residential	. . .	. . .	1.44	2.77	5.63	8.13	8.47	8.67	10.44	12.32
Commercial	. . .	. . .	1.10	1.86	5.86	8.58	8.31	7.88	9.06	10.44
Industrial	. . .	. . .	0.76	1.67	3.85	5.18	4.44	4.06	4.86	5.79
Transportation	. . .	. . .	2.19	3.95	8.94	8.26	8.56	8.29	11.14	10.58

[1]A negative number in this row results from pumped storage for which, overall, more electricity is expended than created to provide electricity during peak demand periods.
[2]Net interstate flow of electricity is the difference between the amount of energy in the electricity sold within a state (including associated losses) and the energy input at the electric utilities within the state. A positive number indicates that more electricity (including associated losses) came into the state than went out of the state during the year; conversely, a negative number indicates that more electricity (including associated losses) went out of the state than came into the state.
. . . = Not available.

Table WY-16. State Taxes, Fiscal 2004

(Dollars, percent distribution.)

Item	Thousands of dollars	Percent distribution	Dollars per capita	
			State	U.S.
TOTAL TAXES	1 504 777	100.0	2 968.0	2 024.8
Property Taxes	139 809	9.3	275.8	38.9
Sales and Gross Receipts	574 004	38.1	1 132.2	1 003.4
General sales and gross receipts	462 842	30.8	912.9	677.0
Selective sales taxes	111 162	7.4	219.2	326.4
Insurance premiums	18 034	1.2	35.6	47.0
Motor fuels	69 975	4.7	138.0	114.6
Tobacco products	18 578	1.2	36.6	42.0
Licenses	101 712	6.8	200.6	134.9
Hunting and fishing	27 801	1.8	54.8	4.2
Motor vehicle	50 784	3.4	100.2	59.4
Occupation and business, not elsewhere classified	14 888	1.0	29.4	37.1
Other Taxes	689 252	45.8	1 359.5	847.6
Severance	683 208	45.4	1 347.6	21.5

GOVERNMENT FINANCE

Wyoming's revenues per person of $7,177 were almost twice the national average in 2003 and ranked as the second highest in the country. The state's per capita expenditures of $5,740 were the third highest in the nation, but well below revenues. Spending per capita was above average on education, natural resources, health, and highways, and below average on public welfare and hospitals. Taxes in fiscal year 2004 were primarily derived from severance (taxes on the removal of natural resources, a prominent tax in many western states), general sales taxes, and motor fuels taxes. Wyoming had no individual income or corporate income taxes. The state's property taxes were the fourth highest of the 37 states with such taxes.

Per Capita State Taxes, Fiscal 2004

Table WY-17. State Government Finances, 2003

(Dollars, percent distribution.)

Item	Millions of dollars	Percent distribution	Dollars per capita	
			State	U.S.
GENERAL REVENUE	3 602 966	100.0	7 177.2	3 832.6
Intergovernmental revenue	1 798 192	49.9	3 582.1	1 246.0
Taxes	1 217 154	33.8	2 424.6	1 891.6
General sales	425 244	11.8	847.1	636.0
Selective sales	91 406	2.5	182.1	307.4
License taxes	98 315	2.7	195.8	123.6
Individual income tax	0	0.0	0.0	626.8
Corporate income tax	0	0.0	0.0	97.8
Other taxes	602 189	16.7	1 199.6	99.9
Current charges	121 475	3.4	242.0	366.5
Miscellaneous general revenue	466 145	12.9	928.6	328.6
GENERAL EXPENDITURE	2 881 398	100.0	5 739.8	4 010.5
Intergovernmental expenditure	952 705	33.1	1 897.8	1 316.9
Direct expenditure	1 928 693	66.9	3 842.0	2 693.6
Expenditure by Function				
Education	955 240	33.2	1 902.9	1 416.4
Public welfare	445 458	15.5	887.4	1 083.3
Hospitals	34 498	1.2	68.7	132.3
Health	126 226	4.4	251.4	173.0
Highways	441 804	15.3	880.1	295.4
Police protection	27 714	1.0	55.2	38.4
Correction	89 551	3.1	178.4	135.0
Natural resources	194 431	6.7	387.3	64.0
Parks and recreation	26 021	0.9	51.8	20.1
Government administration	116 315	4.0	231.7	151.3
Interest on general debt	65 303	2.3	130.1	107.8
Other and unallocable	358 837	12.5	714.8	393.4
DEBT AT END OF FISCAL YEAR	1 111 385	X	2 213.9	2 404.7
CASH AND SECURITY HOLDINGS	10 480 143	X	20 876.8	8 938.4

X = Not applicable.

Table WY-18. Education Indicators, 2000–2004

(Percent, number.)

Item	State	U.S.
Total Population 25 Years and Over (Thousands), 2004	317	186 877
Educational Attainment, 2004		
Percent high school graduate or more	91.9	85.2
Percent college graduate or more	22.5	27.7
Elementary and Secondary Schools, 2002–2003		
Total students	88 116	48 202 324
Percent of students eligible for free or reduced-price lunch ..	31.2	40.6
Percent of students who were English language learners	4.0	7.8
Total schools	389	92 330
Student/teacher ratio	13.3	15.9
Per student expenditures	8 985	8 041
Dropouts, Grades 9–12, 2000–2001 (Percent)	5.8	...
Higher Education, 2002–2003		
Total enrollment	32 657	17 035 027
Bachelor's degrees awarded	1 739	1 348 503
Percent women	56.8	57.5

. . . = Not available.

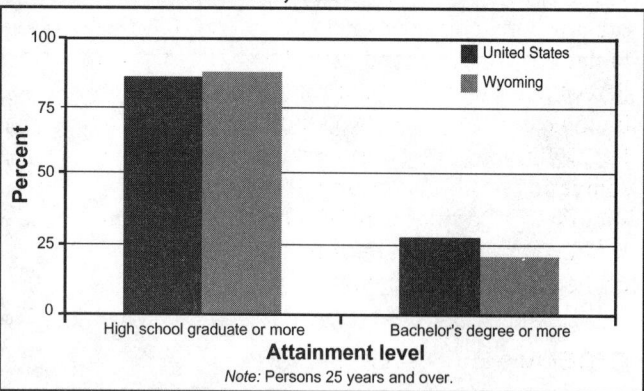

Educational Attainment, 2004

Note: Persons 25 years and over.

EDUCATION

Wyoming ranked second in the country for its proportion of residents age 25 years and over with high school diplomas. The state's per student expenditures of $8,985 were the 14th highest in the nation. The state's student/teacher ratio was well below the national average. Wyoming's dropout rate of 5.8 percent ranked 10th among the 46 states reporting such data. A below average proportion of the state's students were eligible for free or reduced-price lunch. In 2004, just 22.5 percent of Wyoming's population age 25 years and over held bachelor's degrees or more, which was among the 10 lowest proportions of college graduates in the country.

VOTER PARTICIPATION

Wyoming had above average voter turnout rates in 2000 and 2004. Nearly 75 percent of eligible voters age 45 to 64 years participated in the 2004 election. According to the official tally by the Clerk of the U.S. House of Representatives, Wyoming's population voted overwhelmingly for the Republican presidential candidate in both elections. In 2000, 69.2 percent of voters cast ballots for the Republican candidate, and 68.7 percent voted similarly in 2004. The comparable percentages for the Democratic presidential candidates were 28.3 percent and 29 percent, respectively.

Table WY-19. Reported Voting and Registration, November 2000 and November 2004

(Numbers in thousands, percent.)

Characteristic	Total population 18 years and over	Total citizen		Total registered		Total voted	
		Number	Percent	Number	Percent	Number	Percent
NOVEMBER 2000							
Total	350	348	99.3	240	68.6	219	62.5
Male	176	175	99.4	118	67.4	105	59.7
Female	175	173	99.2	122	69.8	114	65.2
NOVEMBER 2004							
Total	373	370	99.1	265	71.0	247	66.3
Male	187	185	98.8	129	69.2	122	65.0
Female	186	185	99.4	135	72.8	126	67.6
Race and Hispanic Origin							
White alone	358	356	99.4	258	72.0	241	67.4
Non-Hispanic White alone	339	339	99.9	247	72.9	231	68.2
Black alone	3	2	B	1	B	1	B
Asian alone	2	2	B	-	B	-	B
Hispanic or Latino[1]	20	17	B	11	B	10	B
White alone or in combination	364	362	99.4	261	71.7	244	67.0
Non-Hispanic White alone or in combination	345	345	99.9	250	72.4	234	67.7
Black alone or in combination	3	2	B	1	B	1	B
Asian alone or in combination	3	3	B	1	B	1	B
Age							
18 to 24 years	50	50	B	28	B	24	B
25 to 44 years	125	123	98.5	83	66.2	76	61.1
45 to 64 years	139	138	99.1	108	77.2	104	74.5
65 to 74 years	32	32	B	25	B	24	B
75 years and over	26	26	B	21	B	19	B

[1]May be of any race.
- = Represents zero or rounds to zero.
B = Base is too small to show derived measure.

NOTES AND DEFINITIONS

The state chapters in this book follow a standard plan of organization, and the same data sources are used for the tables and figures found in each chapter. These notes describe the standard data sources, which are presented by topic in the order in which they appear in each chapter. Definitions, brief descriptions of methodology, and sources of additional information are also provided. For some states, additional information is used in the text. A list of sources for this information follows the discussion of the standard data sources.

GEOGRAPHIC CONCEPTS

REGIONAL DEFINITIONS. The Bureau of Economic Analysis (BEA) groups its state data into eight regions, which are occasionally cited in this publication. The states included in each BEA region are:

- *New England*: Connecticut, Maine, Massachusetts, New Hampshire, Rhode Island, and Vermont.

- *Mid-Atlantic*: Delaware, District of Columbia, Maryland, New Jersey, New York, and Pennsylvania.

- *Great Lakes*: Illinois, Indiana, Michigan, Ohio, and Wisconsin.

- *Plains*: Iowa, Kansas, Minnesota, Missouri, Nebraska, North Dakota, and South Dakota.

- *South Atlantic*: Florida, Georgia, North Carolina, South Carolina, and Virginia.

- *South Central*: Alabama, Arkansas, Kentucky, Louisiana, Mississippi, Tennessee, and West Virginia.

- *Southwest*: Arizona, New Mexico, Oklahoma, and Texas.

- *Rocky Mountain*: Colorado, Idaho, Montana, Utah, and Wyoming.

- *Far West*: Alaska, California, Hawaii, Nevada, Oregon, and Washington.

The Census Bureau defines four broad geographical regions: Northwest, Southeast, South, and West. These regions are sometimes used in the text in this book. The Census Bureau further subdivides the four census regions into nine divisions. The states included in each census region and division are:

- Northeast Region:
  New England Division: Connecticut, Maine, Massachusetts, New Hampshire, Rhode Island, and Vermont.
  Middle Atlantic Division: New Jersey, New York, and Pennsylvania.

- Midwest Region:
  East North Central Division: Illinois, Indiana, Michigan, Ohio, and Wisconsin.

West North Central Division: Iowa, Kansas, Minnesota, Missouri, Nebraska, North Dakota, and South Dakota.

- South Region:
  South Atlantic Division: Delaware, District of Columbia, Florida, Georgia, Maryland, North Carolina, South Carolina, Virginia, and West Virginia.
  East South Central Division: Alabama, Kentucky, Mississippi, and Tennessee.
  West South Central Division: Arkansas, Louisiana, Oklahoma, and Texas.

- West Region:
  Mountain Division: Arizona, Colorado, Idaho, Montana, Nevada, New Mexico, Utah, and Wyoming.
  Pacific Division: Alaska, California, Hawaii, Oregon, and Washington.

POPULATION

Source: U.S. Census Bureau. <http://www.census.gov>. By telephone: (301) 763-3030.
U.S. Census Bureau. Population Estimates Program. (Feb. 2005.) <http://www.census.gov/popest/states/tables/NST-EST2004-01.pdf>. (Accessed Jan. 30, 2006.)
Decennial census data accessed through American FactFinder. U.S. Census Bureau. <http:/factfinder.census.gov/home/saff/main.html?_lang=en>. (Accessed Jan. 12, 2006.)

POPULATION ESTIMATES AND THE DECENNIAL CENSUS. Population data for 2004 are estimates produced by the Census Bureau. The Bureau's Population Estimates Program (PEP) produces estimates of the population as of July 1 for each year following the most recently published decennial census (the actual physical count of the population made every 10 years, which is described below). Existing data on births, deaths, and domestic and international immigration are used to update the decennial census base. PEP estimates are used to set federal funding allocations, update national surveys, and monitor recent demographic changes.

For the 2000 census, people (both civilian and military) were counted at their "usual residence," a principle followed in each census since 1790. Usual residence has been defined as the place in which a person lives and sleeps most frequently, as of April 1 of the census year. A person's usual residence may not be the same as his or her legal or voting residence. The geographic universe for the U.S. resident population is the 50 states and the District of Columbia. Residents of Puerto Rico and outlying areas (American Samoa, Guam, the Northern Mariana Islands, and the U.S. Virgin Islands) under U.S. jurisdiction, U.S. citizens living abroad, and members of the U.S. armed forces serving overseas are excluded. Noncitizens residing in the United States are included, regardless of their immigration status.

Persons temporarily away from their usual residence on Census Day (April 1), for reasons such as vacation or business trips, were counted as being at their usual residence. People who live at more than one residence during the week, month, or year were counted as being at the place in which they lived for the largest part of the year. However, people without a usual residence were counted as being where they were staying on Census Day.

The annual PEP reports build data from the county level up to the state and national levels, starting from the Census 2000 base population or the revised population estimate for the most recent year. (This volume uses the Census Bureau's 2003 estimate for its population base.) The PEP then adds or subtracts the components of population change calculated for the period: births are added; deaths are subtracted; and the result is adjusted for net migration, which is calculated using components such as net internal migration, net foreign-born international migration, net movements to and from Puerto Rico, net movement of federal and civilian population, and net emigration from the United States. Birth and death data are obtained through vital statistics, domestic migration data are estimated through the address matching of federal tax returns, and international migration data are supplied by the Immigration and Naturalization Service.

County population estimates are produced with adjustments for all of the components of population changes. State population estimates are the sum of the county estimates.

With each new annual issue of estimates, PEP revises estimates for the years back to the last decennial census (2000). The new estimates, which take updated data availability, changes in methodology, and/or legal boundary changes into account, supercede previously released reports.

A more detailed explanation of the PEP methodology is provided at <http://quickfacts.census.gov/qfd/meta/long_255027.htm>.

AGE, SEX, RACE, AND ETHNICITY. While estimates of the age and sex of the population are straightforward, estimates of race and ethnicity are not. Decennial census data on race and ethnicity are based on self-identification by the respondent, and the same respondent may answer differently on separate occasions. On the 2000 decennial census, respondents could report more than one race; in previous censuses, respondents had to identify themselves as belonging to only one race. For example, a respondent of partial American Indian descent may have self-identified as American Indian in 1990 and as both White and American Indian in 2000. As a result, race data from the 1990 census are not directly comparable with the 2000

census and subsequent estimates. The Office of Management and Budget (OMB) standards for collecting and presenting data on race, released in 1997, identified five race categories: White; Black or African American; American Indian and Alaska Native; Asian; and Native Hawaiian and Other Pacific Islander. For those not able to identify with these five categories, the classification "some other race" was an option. The OMB standards have been applied to all subsequent July 1 estimates of the population, making the 2000 and 2004 data directly comparable.

The Census Bureau treats Hispanic or Latino origin as a separate and distinct concept from race. Beginning with the 2000 census, a separate self-identification question was asked regarding Hispanic or Latino origin. Persons of Hispanic or Latino origin are those who classified themselves as belonging to one of the specific categories listed on the questionnaire—Mexican, Puerto Rican, Cuban, or Other Spanish/Hispanic origin (including those whose origins are from Spain, the Spanish-speaking countries of Central and South America, or the Dominican Republic). People who are Hispanic may be of any race and people in each race group may be Hispanic. The overlap of race and Hispanic origin is a major comparability issue, because Hispanics may be of any race. For a further discussion of this issue, see: U.S. Census Bureau. *U.S. Census Bureau Guidance on the Presentation and Comparison of Race and Hispanic Origin Data.* (June 12, 2003.) <http://www.census.gov/population/www/socdemo/compraceho.html>. (Accessed Jan. 19, 2006.)

The Census Bureau applied a multi-step process to create the July 1, 2004, state estimates of the resident population by age, sex, race, and Hispanic origin. This consisted of establishing the previous resident state population estimates by age and sex and the previous national resident population estimates by age, sex, race, and Hispanic origin as the base. Next, the Census Bureau estimated the age, sex, race, and Hispanic origin distributions for each state by using a "cohort component" model to estimate the changes in these components since the last decennial census (2000). Finally, these derived distributions were applied to the original state estimates of age, sex, race, and Hispanic origin. A detailed description of the methodology used is available from the Census Bureau at <http://www.census.gov/popest/topics/methodology/2004_st_char_meth.html>.

HEALTH

Source: Centers for Disease Control and Prevention. National Center for Health Statistics. *Vital Statistics Report.* (Jan. 2006.) <http://www.cdc.gov/nchs/products/pubs/pubd/nvsr/54/54-pre.htm>. (Accessed Jan. 19, 2006.) By telephone: (301) 458-4000. *The Vital Statistics Report* provides data on births, deaths, infant mortality rates, and leading causes of death.

For information on health insurance coverage, see: U.S. Census Bureau. *Income, Poverty, and Health Insurance Coverage in the United States: 2004.* (Aug. 2005.) <http://www.census.gov/prod/2005pubs/p60-229.pdf>. (Accessed Jan. 31, 2006.)

The Census Bureau data on health insurance coverage, including private plans (both employment-based and other private plans) and government plans (Medicare, Medicaid, military, etc.), are collected each March in the Annual Social and Economic Supplement (ASEC) to the Current Population Survey (CPS).

With regard to the data collected in the CPS, the Census Bureau notes a caveat: estimates tend to underreport health insurance and Medicare/Medicaid coverage. While underreporting affects most surveys of health insurance coverage, ASEC appears to have a larger problem than other national surveys, as its focus is on income rather than insurance. ASEC's question regarding health insurance coverage refers the respondent back to the previous year, thus increasing the chance of misreported data. Respondent recall may be more accurate for income information (especially since the interview date is close to when people complete their income taxes) than health insurance coverage. However, the ASEC estimate is used in this volume due to its compatibility with income, poverty, and labor force status data. For a comparison with health insurance coverage rates in other federal surveys, see: Congressional Budget Office. *How Many People Lack Insurance and For How Long?* (May 2003.) <http://www.cbo.gov>. (Accessed Jan. 19, 2006.)

HOUSEHOLDS AND HOUSING CHARACTERISTICS

Source: U.S Census Bureau. <http://www.census.gov>. By telephone: (301) 763-3030.
U.S Census Bureau. Population Estimates Program. (Feb. 2005.) <http://www.census.gov/popest/housing/>. (Accessed Feb. 2, 2006.)
Decennial census and *American Community Survey* data accessed through American FactFinder. U.S. Census Bureau. <http://factfinder.census.gov/home/saff/main.html?_lang=en>. (Accessed Jan. 18, 2006.)

HOUSEHOLDS. A household comprises one or more persons occupying a single housing unit, such as a house, apartment, or a room occupied as separate living quarters. A household may consist of a person living alone, a single family, two or more families living together, or any other group of unrelated individuals sharing a housing unit. The Census Bureau counts the number of households as being equal to the number of occupied housing units identified in the decennial census. All persons not living in housing units are classified as living in "group quarters." These individuals may reside in institutions (hospitals, nursing homes, correctional facilities) or in noninstitutional facilities, such as college dormitories, group homes, or military barracks.

HOUSEHOLD OCCUPANCY AND TENURE. Census estimates for 2004 provide data comparable with the 2000 decennial census estimates of the total number of housing units, the proportions of occupied and unoccupied living quarters, and the amount of owner-occupied and rental units.

MEDIAN GROSS RENT OF RENTER-OCCUPIED HOUSING UNITS. Gross rent is the contract rent plus the estimated average monthly cost of utilities (electricity, gas, and water and sewer) and fuels (oil, coal, kerosene, wood, etc.), if these are paid for by the renter (or paid for the renter by someone else). Gross rent is intended to eliminate the differentials that result from the varying practices of inclusion of utilities and fuels as part of the rental payment. The estimated costs of water and sewer and fuels are reported on a 12-month basis, but are converted to monthly figures for the tabulations.

The *American Community Survey* question was the same as the 1990 and 2000 decennial census question. The yearly cost of electricity and gas was collected in the 1990 decennial census, while the *American Community Survey* collected the monthly cost for these two utilities. In the 1990 decennial census, only the yearly cost of water was collected. In the 2000 decennial census, the yearly cost of water and sewer were collected. The *American Community Survey* collected the 12-month cost of water and sewer.

MEDIAN VALUE OF OWNER-OCCUPIED HOUSING UNITS. Data for the median value of owner-occupied housing units are respondents' estimates of how much their property would sell for if it was currently on the market. In 2004, value is shown for all owner-occupied housing units. This is unlike previous years, when the data excluded mobile homes, homes with a business or medical office on the premises, homes on 10 acres or more of land, and housing units in multi-unit buildings.

Other sources of data on housing prices by state and metropolitan area include the Housing Price Index, published by the Office of Federal Housing Enterprise Oversight (OFHEO) on a quarterly basis at <http://www.ofheo.gov>. Proprietary data, which frequently appear in newspaper accounts, are available on a monthly basis from the National Association of Realtors at <http://www.realtor.org>.

INCOME AND POVERTY

Source: U.S. Census Bureau . *Income, Poverty, and Health Insurance Coverage in the United States: 2004.* (Aug. 2005.) <http://www.census.gov/prod/2005pubs/p60-229.pdf>. (Accessed Jan. 19, 2006.)

MEDIAN HOUSEHOLD INCOME. Median household income is defined as money income (the midpoint of all data values) received by households. Money income is the sum of wage or salary income; nonfarm self-employed income; net farm self-employed income; Social Security and railroad retirement income; public assistance; and all other regularly received income such as interest, dividends, veterans' payments, pensions, unemployment compensation, and alimony. The total represents the amount of income received before deductions for personal income taxes, Social Security, Medicare, and other deductions. Money income does not reflect the fact that some families receive noncash benefits, such as health benefits, food stamps, and subsidized housing. The data for 2000 are from the long-form questionnaire used in the decennial census; data for subsequent years are as of March 1 of that year and come from the Annual Social and Economic Supplement (ASEC) to the Current Population Survey (CPS). In order to accurately assess changes in income over time, the data are adjusted for changes in the cost of living using the Consumer Price Index for Urban Consumers (CPI-U-RU), which covers all urban consumers (about 80 percent of the population). The CPI-U-RU removes discontinuities that occurred in the past, due to conceptual changes in the CPI-U index. These disparities cannot be removed from the CPI-U index, because revisions of past years would lead to confusion in indexed contracts.

POVERTY. Poverty rates are also derived from the ASEC. Following OMB standards that have been in use since the late 1960s, the Census Bureau uses a set of money income thresholds that vary by family size and composition to determine the proportion of Americans in poverty. If a household's total income is less than the threshold for the applicable family size, age of householder, and number of children present in the family under 18 years of age, every individual in that household is considered to be living in poverty. The official poverty thresholds do not vary geographically, but they are updated annually using the CPI-U-RU. In 2004, the poverty threshold for a family of four was $19,484.

The Census Bureau also reports data on income and poverty derived from the *American Community Survey* (ACS). The ACS is part of the 2010 Decennial Census Program and will replace the long-form questionnaire. The ACS offers broad, comprehensive information on social, economic, and housing characteristics and is designed to provide this information at detailed geographical levels, including local communities. However, the Census Bureau recommends that researchers use the CPS Annual Social and Economic Supplement for data on income and poverty, as this data source contains the most complete and thorough estimates. More information on the different surveys is provided at <http://www.census.gov/hhes/income/guidance081904.html>.

LABOR FORCE, EMPLOYMENT, AND UNEMPLOYMENT

Source: U.S. Department of Labor. Bureau of Labor Statistics. <http://www.bls.gov>. (Accessed Feb. 1, 2006.) By telephone: (202) 691-6392.

Annual data on the labor force, employment, and unemployment for state and local areas are available from two major sources: the Current Population Survey (CPS) and the Local Area Unemployment Statistics (LAUS) program. The CPS is a sample survey of about 60,000 households, conducted by the Census Bureau for the Bureau of Labor Statistics (BLS). The LAUS program is a federal-state cooperative endeavor in which state employment security agencies (which deal with unemployment insurance) prepare estimates using the concepts, definitions, and estimation procedures prescribed by the BLS. Data from both sources pertain to the civilian noninstitutional population age 16 years and over, and both use the basic labor force, employment, and unemployment concepts of the CPS household survey. These concepts are fully described in the explanatory notes to BLS's monthly employment situation release at <http://www.bls.gov/schedule/archives/empsit_nr.htm>.

Based on responses to a series of questions on work and job search activities, each member of a sample household is classified as employed, unemployed, or not in the labor force during the specified reference period (the calendar week containing the 12th day of the month). The total civilian labor force is the sum of the employed and unemployed, and the unemployment rate is the number of unemployed persons as a percentage of the labor force. The labor force participation rate is the labor force as a percentage of the noninstitutional population, and the employment/population ratio is the number of employed person as a percentage of the population. The survey includes agricultural workers, the self-employed, unpaid family workers, and private household workers.

The LAUS program provides "official" employment and unemployment estimates for about 7,000 state and local areas on a monthly basis. Data are released two weeks after the national data, and are used by a number of U.S.

agencies to allocate over $40 billion of federal funds to states and localities for a variety of socioeconomic programs. These data do not include demographic estimates. In March 2005, the BLS revised all state and local estimates back to 1976 to reflect a redesigned model of estimation and a new monthly benchmarking procedure called "real-time benchmarking," which adjusts local area estimates to the CPS national estimate of employment and unemployment. The estimation methodology is fully described at <http://www.bls.gov/lau/lausredesignqa.htm>. (See also: Brown, Sharon P. 2005. Estimation and benchmarking of state labor force statistics. *Monthly Labor Review* 128(5): 23-31.) With these new estimates, state totals will add up to national estimates of employment and unemployment, thus enhancing statistical comparability across states and over time. Economic changes will be reflected in state estimates on a real-time basis, and year-end revisions will be considerably smaller than those made with previous procedures.

The demographic and economic characteristics of the employed and unemployed are derived from the national CPS sample survey of 60,000 households and are published annually in the *Geographic Profile of Employment and Unemployment*. However, the data do not equal the estimates obtained from the revised LAUS program, because the former are based on the national CPS sample. The data from the CPS sample, which is much smaller than the LAUS sample, contain much more variance. In addition, because Table 8 in the state chapters uses the time series data from the LAUS Program, these figures may differ from Table 7, which is derived from the CPS sample. However, the CPS estimates do provide important and timely information about the characteristics of the states' labor forces, including the employment status of the civilian noninstitutional population by sex, race, Hispanic origin, marital status, and age.

EMPLOYMENT AND EARNINGS, WAGES AND SALARIES, AND PERSONAL INCOME

Source: U.S. Department of Commerce. Bureau of Economic Analysis. (Oct. 2005.) <http://www.bea.gov/bea/regional/data.htm>. (Accessed Feb. 1, 2006.) U.S. Department of Commerce. Bureau of Economic Analysis. 2005. *Survey of Current Business* 85 (10): 1-162. State facts on personal income and its components are also available at <http://www.bea.gov/bea/regional/bearfacts/statebf.cfm>. (Accessed Feb. 1, 2006.)

EMPLOYMENT AND EARNINGS BY SECTOR. The employment data are estimates of total employment in each sector and include employment in the armed forces, civilian wage and salary employment, and self-employment. The estimates represent numbers of jobs, not numbers of individuals. An individual holding two jobs will be counted twice, as will an individual who holds a wage or salary job

and is also self-employed. Estimates of self-employment rely in part on Schedule C filings on individual income tax returns. Thus, a person engaged in two kinds of self-employment and filing two Schedule C forms is counted twice.

This concept of employment differs from that in the Current Population Survey (CPS), which is the source of the employment data in the table on population and labor force. The CPS is a household survey. It counts each individual only once, no matter how many jobs the person holds, and it includes only civilian employment. For these and other reasons, the Bureau of Economic Analysis (BEA) estimates of total employment differ from the estimates obtained from the CPS, and the BEA estimates are typically larger.

LEADING PRIVATE INDUSTRIES. The data by industry reflect the North American Industry Classification System (NAICS), a supply- or production-based system that replaced the Standard Industrial Classification (SIC) system in January 2003. Estimates of state employment and earnings by industry use NAICS from 2001 forward. NAICS was adopted to more fully reflect the current composition of U.S. businesses and to establish a standard measure of industry classification throughout the United States, Canada, and Mexico, in accordance with the North American Free Trade Agreement, to enhance cross-border comparisons among these trading partners.

AVERAGE ANNUAL WAGES AND SALARIES. Average annual wages and salaries were calculated by the editors by dividing total wages and salaries paid during the year in each sector by annual average wage and salary employment in that sector. These statistics were obtained from the Regional Economic Accounts of the BEA, and not from the Bureau of Labor Statistics, which has similar estimates with somewhat different definitions. The data are not adjusted for inflation. They are appropriate for comparing annual average earnings across economic sectors and across states, but do not directly measure changes over time in the purchasing power of these annual earnings.

Wages and salaries not only include the wages of production and nonsupervisory workers, but also the salaries of managerial and professional employees; the compensation of corporate officers; and commissions, tips, and bonuses. Thus, within any particular industry, the annual earnings of production or nonsupervisory workers are typically lower than the average for all types of workers, as shown in this book.

Differences among economic sectors in annual average wages and salaries reflect differences in the length of the work week and of the work year, as well as differences in hourly earnings. For example, work in construction and agriculture is highly seasonal; workers often are employed for less than a full year. Workers in retail trade and in many service industries work fewer hours per week, on average, than workers in manufacturing.

PERSONAL INCOME. Personal income is defined as the income received by all residents of an area from all sources. It consists of the income received by persons from participation in production, government and business transfer payments, and interest payments to individuals. Personal income is the sum of wage and salary disbursements, supplements to wages and salaries, proprietor's income, dividends, interest, rent, and personal current transfer receipts less contributions for government social insurance (mainly Social Security and Medicare).

A comprehensive set of state data on personal income by source is prepared annually by the BEA. Data include earnings and employment by industry, transfer payments, taxes, and farm income. *State Profiles* incorporates the comprehensive revision to the national income and product accounts, released in December 2003, into the data; the volume also uses the annual revision released in October 2005 for data beginning in 2002. These data are designed by BEA to be conceptually and statistically consistent with the national estimates of personal income. County estimates sum to state totals, which in turn sum to national estimates. Data are also consistent with estimates for gross state product (also prepared by the BEA), as detailed below. For a full description of the sources and methodology, see: U.S. Department of Commerce. Bureau of Economic Analysis. Regional Economic Measurement Division. *State Personal Income 1999–2004.* <http://www.bea.gov/bea/regional/articles/spi2004/Complete_Methodology.pdf>. (Accessed Feb. 1, 2006.)

Personal income, as measured in the national income and product accounts, differs conceptually and statistically from the data on household income obtained by the Census Bureau's Annual Social and Economic Supplement (ASEC) to the Current Population Survey. Unlike the latter, which is based on the answers given by respondents from a sample of households, these estimates of state and county personal income are primarily based on administrative records and Census data. Data from administrative records are a byproduct of the administration of various federal and state programs, such as the state unemployment insurance programs of the Bureau of Labor Statistics, the social insurance programs of the Centers for Medicare and Medicaid Services of the Department of Health and Human Resources, the activities of the Social Security Administration, the federal income tax program of the Internal Revenue Service, and the veterans' benefits programs of the Department of Defense. Farm income is derived from the Department of Agriculture's census surveys and administrative records. These data are reported by "place of work" in the state or county in which the establishment is located.

PER CAPITA INCOME. Per capita income is the mean income computed for every man, woman, and child in a particular group. It is derived by dividing the aggregate income of a particular group by the total population in that group. Per capita income is rounded to the nearest whole dollar.

GROSS STATE PRODUCT

Source: U.S. Department of Commerce. Bureau of Economic Analysis. <http://www.bea.gov>. (Accessed Feb. 2, 2006.) By telephone: (202) 606-9234.

Gross state product (GSP) is a comprehensive measure of the goods and services produced within a state. It is the counterpart of the nation's gross domestic product (GDP). GSP is derived as the sum of the gross state product originating in all industries within the state. In concept, an industry's GSP, also called its value added, is equivalent to its gross output (sales, receipts, and other operating income, commodity taxes, and inventory changes) minus intermediate inputs (goods and services imported or purchased from other states). In practice, GSP estimates are measured as the sum of the distributions by industry of the components of gross domestic income—that is, the sum of the costs incurred (compensation of employees, net interest, and indirect business taxes) and the profits earned in the production. Thus, the GSP accounts provide data by industry and state that are consistent with gross domestic product account at the national level. However, for the NAICS-based GSP estimates for 1997 forward, total GSP for the nation differs from the national estimate of GDP for two reasons. First, the GSP excludes compensation of federal civilian and military personnel stationed abroad, as well as expenditures for military structures and equipment located abroad. GSP and GDP also often have different revision schedules.

GOVERNMENT TRANSFER PAYMENTS

Source: U.S. Department of Commerce. Bureau of Economic Analysis. <http://www.bea.gov>. (Accessed Jan. 31, 2006.)

TRANSFER PAYMENTS. Transfer payments are payments to persons for which services have not been rendered during the current period. As a component of personal income, they are payments by government and business to individuals and nonprofit institutions. Although most transfer payments are made in cash, transfer payments also include some important in-kind payments, such as Medicare, Medicaid, and food stamps. Some government transfer payments are entitlements based on a combination of age and work history; examples are retirement payments to government employees and most Social

Security benefits. Medicare is an entitlement based simply on age. Other transfer payments are "needs based," and eligibility for payment is based on low income, as is the case with food stamps, or on a combination of low income and age or disability, as is the case with Supplemental Security Income. *Social Security* in the government transfer payments table is Old Age, Survivors, and Disability Insurance (OASDI) payments. Other *retirement, disability, and insurance* benefits include workers' compensation payments, temporary disability payments, and payments to victims of black lung disease. In the past, pension payments to retired government employees were also included in transfer payments. But now, government retirement is treated like private pensions: employer contributions are classified in *other labor income,* and the ultimate pension pay is treated as a financial transaction rather than an income transaction.

MEDICAL BENEFITS include Medicare and Medicaid and some smaller programs. *Military medical insurance* consists of payments made under the TriCare Management Program (formerly called CHAMPUS) for the medical care of dependents of active duty military personnel and of retired military personnel and their dependents at nonmilitary medical facilities.

FAMILY ASSISTANCE consists of Aid to Families with Dependent Children (AFDC)—generally referred to as welfare–and, beginning with 1996, assistance programs operating under the Personal Responsibility and Work Opportunity Reconciliation Act of 1996 (often referred to as the "welfare reform" legislation). *Other income maintenance* largely consists of the earned income tax credit, a federal payment to qualifying low-income workers who file tax returns. These payments have grown rapidly during the 1990s, due to program expansion, growth of employment, and increased awareness of the availability of this benefit. Other income maintenance also incl-udes general assistance, emergency assistance, refugee assistance, foster home care payments, and energy assistance.

FEDERAL EDUCATION AND TRAINING ASSISTANCE consists largely of federal fellowship payments (National Science Foundation fellowships and traineeships, subsistence payments to state maritime academy cadets, and other federal fellowships), interest subsidy on higher education loans, basic educational opportunity grants, and Job Corps payments.

OTHER PAYMENTS TO INDIVIDUALS consists largely of Bureau of Indian Affairs payments, education exchange payments, Alaska Permanent Fund dividend payments, compensation of survivors of public safety officers, compensation of victims of crime, disaster relief payments, compensation for Japanese internment, and other special payments to individuals.

EXPORTS

Source: U.S. Department of Commerce. The International Trade Administration. Office of Trade and Economic Analysis (OTEA). <http://www.ita.doc.gov/td/industry/otea/> (Accessed Feb. 2, 2006.) Additional information is available from the U.S. Census Bureau at <http://www.census.gov/foreign-trade/statistics/index.html> (Accessed Feb. 2, 2006.)

State export data is reported by the exporter or agent, and denote the state from which the merchandise begins its journey to the port of export. This may not necessarily be the state in which the merchandise is actually grown or manufactured, or the actual location of the exporter. This method of calculating state exports is called "origin of movement." The origin of movement may not be the origin of transportation.

Whenever shipments are consolidated, the state of origin will reflect the consolidation point. This effect is particularly noticeable for non-manufactured goods, which are generally exported by intermediaries. For example, intermediaries located in inland states ship agricultural products down the Mississippi River for export from New Orleans. In these cases, Louisiana would be reported as the state of origin. The most visible result is a tendency to understate exports from some agricultural states and to overstate exports from states like Louisiana, which have ports that handle high-value shipments of farm products.

The use of the state of origin procedure also may affect the tabulation of exported manufactured goods, attributing a sizable amount of manufacturing exports to states known to have little manufacturing capability. For example, commodities produced by out-of-state suppliers can be shipped from in-state distribution centers, and shipments of manufactured commodities from in-state warehouses and other distribution centers can be arranged by out-of-state exporters. In both cases, manufactured exports from non-industrial states are overstated. For a discussion of these issues, see: U.S. Census Bureau . *Description of the Foreign Trade Statistical Program.* (May 2002.) <http://www.census.gov/foreign-trade/guide>. (Accessed Jan. 19, 2006.)

AGRICULTURE

Sources: U.S. Department of Agriculture. National Agricultural Statistics Service. <http/www.usda.gov/nass>. (Accessed Jan. 19, 2006.) By telephone: (800) 727-9540. For farm income: U.S. Department of Commerce. Bureau of Economic Analysis. <http://www.bea.gov>. (Accessed Jan. 19, 2006.)

Data are from the 1997 and 2002 Censuses of Agriculture; farm income data are compiled by the Bureau of Economic Analysis. The Department of Agriculture defines a farm as any place from which $1,000 or more of agricultural goods were produced or sold during the farm census year. This classification includes many farms for which farming generates only a small fraction of household income. In 2002, nearly 60 percent of farms had sales of less than $10,000, and about 42 percent of all farm operators reported a principal occupation other than farming.

The 2002 Census of Agriculture introduced a new methodology to provide more complete coverage of farms and farming in the United States. Subsequent re-estimates have produced more robust data for states and localities. The Census of Agriculture question regarding primary occupation was also reworded. In 2002, the definition of "primary occupation" was not printed on the census form, as it was for the 1997 census. Thus, some respondents may have identified themselves as a farm or ranch operator without understanding that they were reporting farming as their primary occupation. In fact, the number reporting farming as their primary occupation increased substantially between 1997 and 2002. However, the Department of Agriculture estimates that the change in the questionnaire may only partly account for this trend, as the average age of farm operators also increased significantly between 1997 and 2002. Older operators may be retired (with little if any sales), yet still report farming as their primary occupation, since job opportunities may be limited away from the farm.

Farm income data are based on estimates prepared by the Department of Agriculture and then modified by the Bureau of Economic Analysis to maintain consistency with the concepts and definitions used in their state farm and personal income data set. As defined by the BEA, farm income consists of the net income of sole proprietors and hired labor, arising directly from the current production of agricultural commodities. It includes net farm proprietors' income and wages and salaries, payments-in-kind, and supplements to the wages and salaries of hired farm laborers. However, this definition specifically excludes the income of non-family farm corporations.

ENERGY

Source: U.S .Department of Energy. Energy Information Administration. *State Energy Data 2001.* (Jan. 2005.) <http://www.eia.doe.gov/emeu/states/_seds.html>. (Accessed Dec. 16, 2005.) By telephone: (202) 586-8800. The next update will be available in early 2006.

As of late 2005, the latest available data on energy consumption and expenditures by state from the Department of Energy are for 2001. Although the proportion of energy consumed by major source (natural gas, coal, etc.)

and by type of sector (residential, commercial, etc.) are unlikely to show major shifts from 2001 to 2004, data on expenditures should be used with caution, due to the sharp rise in energy prices that have occurred since 2001. National data are much timelier; they are updated monthly and are available at <http://www.eia.doe.gov>.

Small amounts of solar thermal and photovoltaic energy consumed in the commercial sector cannot be separately identified and are included in residential consumption. Natural gas includes supplemental gaseous fuels. "Other" fuel is geothermal, wind, photovoltaic, solar thermal energy, and net imports of electricity.

STATE TAXES AND GOVERNMENT FINANCE

Source: U.S. Census Bureau. Governments Division. *Annual Survey of Government Finance 2003.* (Apr. 2005.) <http://www.census.gov/govs/www/ financegen.html>. (Accessed Dec. 16, 2006.) By telephone: (800) 242-4523.
Source: U.S. Census Bureau. Governments Division. *Annual Survey of Government Tax Collection.* (Apr. 2005.) <http://www.census.gov/govs/www/statetax.html>. (Accessed Dec. 16, 2006.) By telephone: (800) 242-4523.

The Census Bureau conducts an annual survey covering a range of government finance activities carried out by all state and local governments in the United States, including revenue, expenditures, debt, and assets. The data in this volume relate to state revenues and expenditures only, with the exception of the District of Columbia. Data reference state government fiscal years that ended on June 30, 2003. (Exceptions are Alabama and Michigan, whose fiscal years ended on September 30, 2003; New York, whose fiscal year ended on March 31, 2003; and Texas, whose fiscal year ended on August 31, 2003). In addition, 2002 is the latest year of available information for the District of Columbia, whose fiscal year ended September 30, 2002. General revenue comprises all revenue except utilities, liquor store, and insurance trust revenue. Intergovernmental revenue is funds from other governments (mainly the federal government), and includes general support, grants, shared taxes, and loans or advances. Other data on government finance by state, not shown in this volume, include federal government expenditures, obligations, contract awards, and insurance programs. For more information, see: U.S. Census Bureau. *Consolidated Federal Funds Report for Fiscal Year 2003.* (Dec. 2005.) <http://www.census.gov/prod/2005pubs/cffr-04.pdf>. (Accessed Feb. 3, 2006.)

State tax data include all required taxes taken by government for public purposes, except for employer and employee assessments for Social Security and unemployment compensation. These data are available earlier than the finance data and are shown in this volume each state's fiscal year 2004. Per capita data are obtained by dividing taxes by the Census Bureau's annual estimate of the population (as of July 1 for the appropriate year).

EDUCATION

Sources: U.S. Census Bureau. Annual Social and Economic Supplement to the Current Population Survey. (Mar. 2005.) <http://www.census.gov/population/www/socdemo/educ-attn.html>. (Accessed Feb. 2, 2006.) National Center for Education Statistics. U.S. Department of Education. *Common Core of Data*: 2003–2004. <http://nces.ed.gov/ccd/>. (Accessed on Oct. 21, 2005).

The March supplement to the Current Population Survey (CPS) provides data on educational attainment and is largely compatible with information provided by the 2000 census. Data apply to graded public, private, and parochial elementary and secondary schools (both junior and senior high schools), colleges, universities, and professional schools, whether day or night schools. Schooling in other institutions was counted only if the credits obtained were transferable to the regular school system. Data on enrollment and attainment is also available by detailed demographic group from the *American Community Survey* (ACS), which is intended to replace the long form questionnaire on the decennial census. However, as the ACS is still in its testing phase, the data appearing in this volume are from the CPS March survey. More information on these two surveys is available on the Census Web site at <http://www.census.gov/population/www/socdemo/education/FS-educatt.html>.

   The state numbers are from the *Common Core of Data* (CCD) state universe and include approximately 17,000 regular school districts with students in membership. Not included are special districts that typically offer research, administrative, or other support services to client agencies. The CCD data now include charter schools. Since charter schools are managed independently from the local school district, each one is considered a single district. Most of the CCD state data were compiled through the CCD "Build a Table" feature, which can be found on the Internet at <http://nces.ed.gov/ccd/bat>.

VOTER PARTICIPATION

Source: U.S. Census Bureau. November Supplement to the Current Population Survey, 2004. <http://www.census.gov/population/www/socdemo/voting.html>. (Accessed Feb. 2, 2006.)

Voter participation data are obtained from additional questions regarding voting and voter registration, which are added to the CPS each November. Because these data are from a sample of the noninstitutional population, they differ from the "official" tally of voter participation reported by the Clerk of the U.S. House of Representatives. In 2004, the Clerk of the U.S. House of Representatives reported a voter turnout of 122.3 million persons, while the CPS reported 125.7 million persons.

ADDITIONAL SOURCES OF INFORMATION

Most of the statements in this book are based on the data in the accompanying tables or on related data from the federal statistical sources described above. For some states, supplementary sources specific to the individual state have been used. In most cases, this information was taken from Web sites, and the URLs are included in the listings. Each state has its own Web site, with an address of the form <http://www.state.al.us/>. In this example, the "al" stands for Alabama. The Web sites of other states are accessed by substituting in the state's two-letter postal abbreviation. Other data can be found on Web sites maintained by bureaus of business and economic research at state universities, and through the online resources of the regional Federal Reserve Banks.

F

FAMILY ASSISTANCE
FARMS
Agriculture
  see **AGRICULTURE**
FAR WEST REGION
FEDERAL EDUCATION AND TRAINING ASSISTANCE
Government transfer payments
  see **ECONOMIC ACTIVITY**

G

GOVERNMENT FINANCES

GREAT LAKES REGION
GROSS DOMESTIC PRODUCT
GROSS STATE PRODUCT

H

HEALTH AND HEALTH CHARACTERISTICS

HOMELAND SECURITY GRANTS AND PROCUREMENT CONTRACTS

HOUSEHOLDS AND HOUSING CHARACTERISTICS

I

IMMIGRATION

INCOME